**Michael Bull,** Manchester Metropolitan University *(Chapter co-author)*

**Oliver Laasch,** Steinbeis University Berlin *(Chapter editor)*

**Mark Kramer,** FSG, *(Pioneer Interview)*

**Doru Mitrana,** MVV, *(Practitioner Profile)*

**Aurea Christine Tanaka,** United Nations University Institute of Advanced Studies *(Structuring for responsible performance)*

**Jane Best,** Refugees in Japan *(Multi-organization architectures)*

**Jürgen Wittstock,** Keio University *(Multi-organization architectures)*

**Ulpiana Kocollari,** University of Modena *(A future- programming for sustainability)*

**Sharon Dafny,** Management Consultant *(Box contributor Challenges for organizational change)*

**Oliver Laasch,** Center for Responsible Management Education *(Chapter author)*

**Roger Conaway,** Tecnológico de Monterrey *(Chapter co-author)*

**Simon Zadek,** Tsinghua School of Economics and Management *(Pioneer Interview)*

**Anis Ben Brink,** CSR Arabia *(Biking for eco-efficiency, and Setting multiple operational benchmarks)*

**Aranzazu Gomez-Segovia,** Center for Responsible Management Education *(The illusion of waste)*

**Aurea Christine Tanaka,** United Nations University Institute of Advanced Studies *(A question of the right process)*

**Ulpiana Kocollari,** University of Modena *(Box contributor COPIS for health and food safety)*

**Rick Edgeman,** Aarhus University *(Chapter author)*

**Oliver Laasch,** Sustainable Consumption Institute, University of Manchester *(Chapter co-author, editor)*

**Zhaohui Wu,** College of Business, Oregon State University, *(Chapter co-author)*

**Sandra Waddock,** Carroll School of Management, Boston College *(Pioneer Interview)*

**Cecilia del Castillo,** Eaton *(Practitioner Profile)*

**Al Rosenbloom,** Dominican University *(Engaging back to the source – into the Amazon)*

**Anis Ben Brink,** CSR Arabia *(Green logistics and transportation fleet in the middle-East)*

**Rick Edgeman,** Aarhus University *(Chapter co-author)*

**Matthias Wühle,** Policen Direkt *(Unusual recycling)*

**Ulpiana Kocollari,** Universit... *security as an example for social s...*

**Zhaohui Wu,** Oregon State University *(Chapter ...)*

**Oliver Laasch,** Steinbeis University *(Chapter co-author)*

**Michael Braungart,** Erasmus University *(Pioneer Interview)*

**Mariné Rodríguez Azuara,** AES *(Practitioner Profile)*

**Roger N. Conaway,** Monterrey Institute of Technology *(Chapter author)*

**Elaine Cohen,** Beyond Business, *(Chapter co-author)*

**Oliver Laasch,** Center for Responsible Management Education *(Chapter editor)*

**Erika Guzman,** Innovation Packaging & Process S.A. de C.V. *(Practitioner Profile)*

**Shel Horowitz,** GreenAndProfitable.com *(Market differently to green and nongreen Audiences)*

**Pablo Largacha,** The Coca Cola Company *(Coca Cola´s "secret recipe" for effective stakeholder communication)*

**Roger N. Conaway,** Tecnológico de Monterrey *(Chapter author)*

**Oliver Laasch,** Tecnológico de Monterrey *(Chapter co-author)*

**Philip Kotler,** Kellogg School of Management at Northwestern University *(Pioneer Interview)*

**Adela Lustykova,** Chládek & Tintěra, Inc. *(Practitioner Profile)*

**Al Rosenbloom,** Dominican University *(The world´s trash can ..., Sweet business..., and Harnessing ethnic diversity ...)*

**Barbara Coudenhove-Kalergi,** Center for Responsible Management, Vienna *(Critical stakeholder demand in Bulgaria...)*

**Jenik Radon,** School of International and Public Affairs, Columbia University *(A glocal approach against corruption)*

**Shiv K. Tripathi,** Mzumbe University *(Developing a sustainable export business)*

**Mahima Achuthan,** Columbia University *(A glocal approach against corruption)*

**Nick Tolhurst,** Steinbeis University Berlin *(Introductory case, topic adviser)*

**Roger Conaway,** Tecnológico de Monterrey *(Chapter author)*

**Oliver Laasch,** Center for Responsible Management Education *(Chapter co-author)*

**Geert Hofstede,** *(Pioneer Interview)*

**Laura Clise,** AREVA *(Practitioner Profile)*

...**aka,** United Nations ...Advanced Studies *(Indicators ...ip)*

**Kemi Ogunyemi,** Lagos Business School, Pan-African University *(Developing triple-bottom-line indicators...)*

**Loretta O´Donnell,** Australian School of Business, University of New South Wales *(From human capital to...)*

**Martin Perry,** School of Management, Massey University *(Auditing social accounts in New Zealand)*

**Shel Horowitz,** GreenAndProfitable.com *(Did we miss something?)*

**Ulpiana Kocollari,** University of Modena *(Chapter author)*

**Daniel Ette,** Hansgrohe *(Practitioner Profile)*

**Nick Tolhurst,** Steinbeis University, *(Section contributor: Understanding the Basics of Accounting)*

**Ajay Jain,** Aarhus University *(Fiduciary irresponsibility – corruption)*

**Anis Ben Brink,** CSR Arabia *(Leading financial and responsible management practices in the Middle East)*

**Aurea Christine Tanaka,** United Nations University Institute of Advanced Studies *(Maximizing stakeholder return ...)*

**Charles Mc Jilton,** Second Harvest *(Unsellable food finance)*

**Dewi Fitraasari,** School of Accounting and Finance, Bina Nusantara University, Jakarta *(Mandatory CSR budgeting)*

**John Bayles,** Tengu Natural Foods *(Unsellable food finance)*

**Jürgen Wittstock,** Keio University *(Unsellable food finance)*

**Martin Perry,** School of Management, Massey University *(Ethical financing in New Zealand)*

**Reinhard Schmidt,** Goethe University Frankfurt *(Expert Corner Interview: Microfinance)*

**Sharon Dafny,** Management Consultant *(Reducing cost by creating "diverse" jobs in Israel)*

**Oliver Laasch,** Sustainable Consumption Institute, The University of Manchester *(Chapter author)*

**Nick Tolhurst,** Steinbeis University Berlin *(Chapter co-author)*

**Robert Costanza,** Portland State University, Oregon *(Pioneer Interview)*

**Francisco Acuña Mendez,** InTrust *(Practitioner Profile)*

By Oliver Laasch and Roger N. Conaway

Principles of
# RESPONSIBLE
# MANAGEMENT
Glocal Sustainability, Responsibility, and Ethics

# Principles of
# RESPONSIBLE
# MANAGEMENT
## Glocal Sustainability, Responsibility, and Ethics

**Oliver Laasch**
Center for Responsible Management Education (CRME)
and University of Manchester

**Roger N. Conaway**
Tecnológico de Monterrey

A CRME publication in support of PRME

Australia • Brazil • Japan • Korea • Mexico • Singapore • Spain • United Kingdom • United States

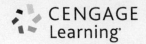

**Principles of Responsible Management: Glocal Sustainability, Responsibility, and Ethics**
**Oliver Laasch and Roger N. Conaway**

Senior Vice President, Global Product Manager, Higher Education: Jack W. Calhoun

Vice President, General Manager, Social Science & Qualitative Business: Erin Joyner

Product Director: Mike Schenk

Senior Product Managers: Michele Rhoades & Mike Roche

Senior Content Developer: Susan Smart

Product Assistant: Tamara Grega

Senior Marketing Manager: Robin LeFevre

Senior Content Project Manager: Colleen A. Farmer

Manufacturing Planner: Ron Montgomery

Production Service: diacriTech

Sr. Art Director: Stacy Jenkins Shirley

Cover and Internal Designer: Red Hangar Design/Joe Devine

Cover Image: © Sapsiwai/Shutterstock

Rights Acquisitions Specialist (Text and Photo): Amber Hosea

For product information and technology assistance, contact us at
**Cengage Learning Customer & Sales Support, 1-800-354-9706**
For permission to use material from this text or product, submit all requests online at **www.cengage.com/permissions**
Further permissions questions can be emailed to
**permissionrequest@cengage.com**

Library of Congress Control Number: 2013946384

ISBN-13: 978-1-285-08026-0

ISBN-10: 1-285-08026-2

**Cengage Learning**
200 First Stamford Place, 4th Floor
Stamford, CT 06902
USA

Cengage Learning is a leading provider of customized learning solutions with office locations around the globe, including Singapore, the United Kingdom, Australia, Mexico, Brazil, and Japan. Locate your local office at: **www.cengage.com/global**

Cengage Learning products are represented in Canada by Nelson Education, Ltd.

To learn more about Cengage Learning Solutions, visit **www.cengage .com**

Purchase any of our products at your local college store or at our preferred online store **www.cengagebrain.com**

Printed in Canada
1 2 3 4 5 6 7 17 16 15 14 13

Welcome to the first comprehensive textbook for responsible management education, *Principles of Responsible Management: Glocal Sustainability, Responsibility, and Ethics*. While the community of practice for responsible management education has grown exponentially, reaching impressive practice results, the development of a shared basic content structure for responsible management courses has been lagging behind. This book aims to close this gap.

Through our work with many educator colleagues in the United Nations Principles for Responsible Management Education (PRME) network, we have seen an increasing shift from the traditional organizational course focus on "What should businesses be and do?" to a focus on the individual level of the single manager as a person, asking "Who should the manager be, what should he or she do, and how should he or she do it?" The shift goes from business sustainability to sustainability management, from business responsibility to responsibility management, and from business ethics to ethics management. Many of the traditional courses in business ethics and business and society are currently experiencing a fundamental shift from the organizational to the individual perspective. Courses sticking to the organizational perspective are enriched by integrating the individual perspective, which explains how employees, especially managers, can act as intrapreneurs, making their organization more responsible. This book aims to be a resource to efficiently and effectively realize this important transition.

**PRME** Principles for Responsible Management Education

The organizational perspective is still an important basis of this book and educators will find many of the established topics traditionally taught. But we also have included information about the logical next evolutionary step of translating the organizational vision into the managerial and operational achievement of this vision by a responsible manager. What we hope to achieve with this book is to provide both experienced educators and those first entering the field of responsible business and management with a resource that helps them to empower thousands of individual students around the world to become responsible managers, to be change agents, and to act as the human foundation for responsible businesses in order to achieve a responsible socioeconomic system and a sustainable world society.

## APPROACH, CONCEPTUAL STRUCTURE, AND TERMINOLOGY

*Principles of Responsible Management* provides business students with the necessary knowledge, tools, skills, and self-perception to become responsible managers. In order to realize these goals, we provide a very profound overview of the conceptual development of the field of responsible business and management. Toward that end, we have pursued several educational and conceptual innovations or realignments that then became the models for shaping the structure, content, and tone of this book.

The first and most visible of these models is the treatment of the three topics of sustainability, responsibility, and ethics—the three domains of responsible business and management—as complementary, mostly mutually reinforcing, but distinct in their core concepts and organizational implementation. We found the ongoing discussion about hierarchical relationships and the dominance of one topic over another—such as the often-discussed relationships of business responsibility as a subtopic of business ethics, or sustainability as a goal of business responsibility—to be overly complicated for students, an impediment to learning, and an inhibitor to the theoretical development of the field. This is why we decided to purposely apply a simplified understanding of the three domains as follows:

- *Sustainability* is centered on the core concept of the triple bottom line and aims to create a neutral or, better, positive triple bottom line.
- *Responsibility* is centered on the core concept of stakeholders and aims to optimize stakeholder value.
- *Ethics* is centered on the core concepts of ethical issues and opportunities, and aims to create moral excellence.

We believe that once this basic understanding has been developed, it will be easier to build a more refined understanding of the three domains. The three domains of sustainability, responsibility, and ethics each have one dedicated chapter (Chapters 3–5), and they are a recurrent theme throughout all other chapters. The following figure further illustrates the underlying conceptual design.

From this three-domain structure emerged the need for an umbrella term that unified and integrated the three domains. The terms *responsible business* and *responsible management*, while being rather new, have been used implicitly to describe topics related to all three domains: sustainability, responsibility, and ethics. We borrowed *responsible business* and *responsible management* as umbrella terms, but we are well aware that they are rather imperfect placeholders until a

**Framing of Responsible Management and Other Central Terms**

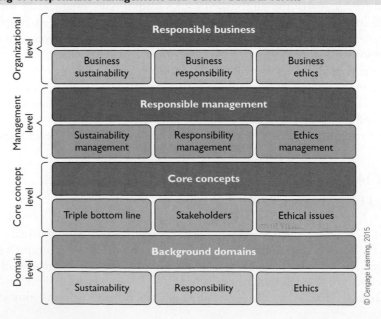

Preface

more accurate terminology emerges. Along the same lines, it is important to not confuse the umbrella terms of *responsible management* and *responsible business* with the subdomain of "business responsibility." As illustrated in the figure, the word *responsible* in "responsible management" and "responsible business" refers to a responsibility for stakeholders (business responsibility), the triple bottom line (business sustainability), and ethical issues (business ethics). The word *responsibility* in the subdomain of "business responsibility" more narrowly refers to the prevalent understanding in the academic literature of the responsibility emerging from a relationship with stakeholders.

The book's main title *Principles of Responsible Management* was chosen to make clear that this is a comprehensive textbook, similar to prominent textbooks with titles such as "Principles of Economics" or "Principles of Marketing Management." The title also addresses the aspiration that responsible management should become a well-established field with broadly accepted concepts and principles. As a welcome side effect, the title closely resembles the name of the Principles for Responsible Management (PRME) initiative, which has been an important network for the development of the book and for whose more than 500 academic member institutions we hope to have created valuable educational material. Toward this end, the book can cover both introductory and advanced courses in business sustainability, responsibility, and ethics and serve as complementary material, "bringing responsibility" to mainstream business courses.

A second consideration regarding the title is the use of the term *glocal*. One might assume that the term was included as a fashionable buzzword for marketing purposes. The opposite is true. After long consideration and a weighing of alternatives, we felt that the focus on globalization assumed by many academics and practitioners is inadequate to describe the thinking in responsible management. "Localization," an adaptation to local circumstances, is as important as global thinking. Readers will find a wide variety of case boxes describing responsible management activities around the world that respond as much to local as to global needs, and that are as relevant globally as they are locally.

## BOOK AND CHAPTER STRUCTURE

The book's first section (Parts A and B: Chapters 1–5) explores the context of responsible management in two chapters and subsequently delves into the theory of sustainability, responsibility, and ethics in the next three chapters. The book's second section (Parts C–F: Chapters 6–15) takes a closer look at primary management functions, including strategic management, entrepreneurship, organization, operations, supply chain management, human resources, marketing and communication, international business, accounting, and financial management. Each topic is addressed in a complete chapter that provides concepts and tools applying sustainability, responsibility, and ethics to the respective management function. Important didactical design features of the chapters include:

- An integrated blend of outstanding "mainstream" management and responsible management concepts
- A "word cloud" summary to introduce chapter content
- An introductory case and In Practice boxes written by international educators and practitioners
- A Pioneer Interview and a Practitioner Profile about the chapter topic
- End-of-chapter review questions

## Text Supplements

- PowerPoint presentations and an Instructor's Manual with Test Bank are available for each chapter. All are created by the text authors and are available online to adopting instructors. Instructors can access the material through a secure website and will need a Single Sign In account (SSO) with Cengage to access these materials. Instructors can access the material at: http://www.cengage.com/login

## USE AND CURRICULA

The book's primary use is as a required textbook for business sustainability, responsibility, and ethics courses, as offered by many business schools. A second use will be for business degree programs, which will find the book's chapters on mainstream business functions—such as strategic management, accounting, and human resources—to provide valuable content for coverage of sustainability, responsibility, and ethics across the curriculum. A third possibility is to use this book as a primary text for first-year courses, such as "Introduction to Management," as each chapter's responsible management content is structured around the logic of mainstream management concepts. We have taught such courses, and the student's experience of learning how to manage responsibly while for the first time learning about management was very valuable. The fourth use of this book is for executive education and corporate training programs, as the book's coverage of management tools and practice examples is well aligned with executive needs. The book has been tried and tested in all four uses by the authors. Educators interested in pedagogy are welcome to get in touch with the authors to discuss educational strategies and designs.

An initial hurdle (for both students and lecturers) might be the usage of the central terms *responsible management* and *responsible business*, and their subdomains of business sustainability, business responsibility, and business ethics. Unfortunately, there are no universally accepted definitions for the respective terms as yet. Many, often contradictory definitions exist in theory and practice. Developing a unifying framework for this book that would follow an internal logic was a challenge and a process that involved much discussion and review with both academics and practitioners. The logic followed here is that the umbrella terms—*responsible management* and *responsible business*—include the responsibility for the triple bottom line (sustainability), for stakeholders (responsibility), and for ethical issues and opportunities (ethics), as illustrated in Figure 1. We recommend that instructors give this framing and structure a try and discover the internal logic together with students in the course. Throughout the dozens of courses we have taught in which we built on this structure, we have come to appreciate its merits and its advantages over different framings of the concepts.

## CONTRIBUTORS, COLLABORATION, AND THE WAY AHEAD

*Principles of Responsible Management: Glocal Sustainability, Responsibility, and Ethics* is a product of the efforts of many individuals. The writing process leading to this publication has been highly collaborative, with more than 50 contributors as chapter authors, case and box contributors, and interviewees. The book includes exclusive interviews with outstanding topic pioneers, such as Edward Freeman,

Philip Kotler, John Elkington, Geert Hofstede, Robert Costanza, Björn Stigson, Simon Zadek, Sandra Waddock, Michael Braungart, Mark Kramer, Linda Treviño, Jonas Härtle, and Liz Maw. While two-thirds of the total chapters have been written by the primary authors, other outstanding specialized educators authored the following chapters:

- Accounting and Controlling: Ulpiana Kocollari (University of Modena)
- Entrepreneurship: Rory Ridley-Duff (Sheffield Hallam University) and Mike Bull (Manchester Metropolitan University)
- Operations: Rick Edgeman (Aarhus University) and Zhaohui Wu (Oregon State University), together with Oliver Laasch
- Supply Chain: Zhaohui Wu (Oregon State University) and Rick Edgeman (Aarhus University), together with Oliver Laasch
- Human Resources: Elaine Cohen (Beyond Business), together with Roger Conaway
- Finance: Nick Tolhurst (Steinbeis University Berlin), together with Oliver Laasch

Nick Tolhurst, author of many landmark publications in corporate social responsibility (CSR), has been a driving force in the conceptual design of the book and in ensuring Pioneer Interviews with outstanding individuals. We hope to enlarge the contributor base for future editions. Responsible management contents are in a dynamic evolution process, and we are building a community to co-develop future versions of this book. Meanwhile we would be very interested in getting in touch with educators adopting the book. Feedback from students is also very welcome. Through the Center for Responsible Management Education (CRME), we have created a community of practice consisting of educators, academics, and practitioners that we hope to enlarge and strengthen with new collaborators.

Also, we are well aware that this book, per design, can only be limited in its representation of different disciplines and contents. Our daring in covering a breadth of contents—touching on disciplines as different as philosophy, environmental studies, sociology, and, of course, management—is prone to come with blind spots and perhaps mistakes given the complexity of representing highly specialized management topics ranging from accounting to strategy. Nevertheless, we are convinced that such broad coverage is necessary to provide students with the necessary background to manage responsibly in a volatile and rapidly changing world, and educators with a broad content basis for adapting their contents to the requirements of each course. Therefore, while we made sure to investigate every topic thoroughly, there must be much room for improvement, and we are looking forward to integrating the input of critical individuals in later editions. Please get in touch with us through olaasch@responsiblemanagement.net.

## ACKNOWLEDGMENTS

Even before its official publication, this book was well received. Positive points our reviewers highlighted included the conceptual rigor, practical application, and strong chapter structure. We thank the following for their valuable input:

- Jacqueline Brassey, Tilburg School of Economics and Management, the Netherlands
- Freek Cronjé, North West University, South Africa

- Robert K. Fleming, National University of Singapore
- Subhasis Ray, Xavier Institute, India
- Paul Sheeran, University of Winchester, United Kingdom
- Gilvan C. Souza, Indiana University, United States
- Helen Tregidga, Auckland University of Technology, New Zealand
- Monika Winn, University of Victoria, British Columbia

The team at the United Nations Principles for Responsible Management Education has to be thanked for its immense support of this publication from its very beginning. Specifically, we would like to thank Manuel Escudero, former head of the PRME Secretariat, for recognizing the book's value for PRME. His successor Jonas Härtle officially accepted the book project as an important project in support of PRME, and provided invaluable help and feedback in the process. We would also like to thank the coordinators in the PRME Secretariat, Lisle Ferreira and Merrill Csuri, for their contributions. In addition, we want to thank our friends and colleagues at the Center for Responsible Management Education for sharing their knowledge and passion to empower educators all around the world, and to help students to become responsible managers.

We would like to thank our team at Cengage Learning South-Western Publishing: Michele Rhoades, our Senior Product Manager who initially took on our book and greatly supported and pushed its development; Michael Roche, our Senior Product Manager who helped wrap up our text in its final stages; Susan Smart, our Senior Content Developer, who worked with us from the beginning to develop and review the book, and directed us with the text supplements; Colleen Farmer, the Senior Content Project Manager who shepherded the book through production to achieve this final product; Robin LeFevre, our Marketing Manager, and Emily Horowitz, our Market Development Manager; and our copyeditors, compositors, media personnel, and the many others involved with the publication of our book.

Finally, and most importantly, we would like to thank our friends and family for their patience, understanding, and support during five years of intense work.

- Oliver Laasch: I would like to thank my wife Aranzazu Gomez Segovia, who has been with me throughout the whole process and whose love and wisdom were there as invaluable "inputs" whenever I needed them; my family—my loved parents, "step-parents," and grandparents, my brother, and my "Mexican Family"; and finally Roger N. Conaway, who once said how impressive it would be if we were able to write a book together and still manage to be friends afterward. I think we made it.

- Roger N. Conaway: Oliver, we indeed made it to the end and we are still friends. You are a great example of how to graciously work as a team, complete deadlines under intense pressure, and demonstrate in-depth intellectual capacity and talent when researching topics. Additionally, without the love and encouragement of my wife, Phyllis, I would not have finished this project. She made the difference. She endured a preoccupied mate who wearily stared during meals, stayed intensely busy during long hours on weekends, and taught full time while writing. She lovingly supported me each moment of the way. Moreover, I wish to thank Isaías Ruiz Solano, Dean, and María del Pilar Castellanos Rueda, Academic Director, in the School of Business for their support and encouragement. Finally, most of all, I thank God for giving me the ability, patience, and endurance to complete this task.

Describing the Process through Procedure
  Documents                                          267
Bundling Processes to Management Systems             271

**Phase 2: Be Efficient through Lean Enterprise
Methods**                                            274

Lean Enterprise Methods                              274
Toyota Production System                             277

**Phase 3: Be Effective through Quality
Management**                                          279

Customer Orientation and Continuous
  Improvement                                        280

**Breakthrough Improvement through Six Sigma
Innovation and Design**                             285

Benchmarking and Breakthrough Improvement           287

**Chapter 10: Supply Chain: Responsible
Supply and Demand**                                  **299**

Responsible Management and the Supply Chain          300

The Goal: Responsible Supply and Demand              301

Phase 1: Understanding the Supply Chain              302

Supply Networks                                      302
Mapping Supply Architectures                         303
The Role of Small and Medium-Sized
  Enterprises (SMEs)                                 304
Social Sustainability                                310

Phase 2: Managing inside the Supply Chain            311

Engagement Practices                                 312
Standardization and Certification inside the
  Supply Chain                                       313
Application of QM Principles in Environmental
  Management in OM and SCM                           315
Ecoefficiency and Ecoeffectiveness                   316
Logistics                                            316

Phase 3: Closing the Loop                            318

Industrial Ecology                                   319
The Circular Economy                                 320
Closed-Loop Supply Chains                            321
End-of-Life (EOL) Design                             322
Further Closed-Loop Tools                            323

**PART E: LEADING**

**Chapter 11: Human Resources: HR-RM
Symbiosis**                                          **330**

Human Resources and Responsible Management           331

The Goal: HR-RM Symbiosis                            332

Phase 0: Understanding the HR-RM
  Interdependent Relationship                        333

The Difference between HRM and Responsible
  HRM                                                334
The Business Case for Responsible HRM                336
The New Skills for Responsible HRM                   336
Responsible HRM Leadership and HRM
  Stakeholders                                       337
The Role of the HR Manager in Advancing
  Responsible Business                               338

Phase 1: Recruitment                                 339

The Traditional Recruitment Process                  339
Developing the Responsible Job Description            340
Obtaining Candidates in a Responsible Way            340
The Selection Process                                341
Hiring in the Responsible Organization               342

Phase 2: Training and Development of
Employees                                            342

New Employee Orientation                             344
A Model for Orientation and Socialization            344
Training                                             346
Employee Development                                 347
Employability                                        348

Phase 3: Performance Management                      349

Performance Evaluation                               349
Core Competencies                                    350
Community Involvement and Environmental
  Stewardship                                        351
Offboarding                                          353

Phase 4: Compensation, Benefits, and Employee
Well-Being                                           354

Driving Principles of a Compensation System          354
Living Wage                                          356
Employee Well-Being                                  356

Phase 5: Employee Relations and
Communications                                       357

Union-Busting                                        357
Employee Communications                              358

**Chapter 12: Marketing and Communication:
Stakeholder Goodwill**                               **366**

Marketing, Communication, and Responsible
Management                                           367

The Goal: Stakeholder Goodwill                       369

Phase 1: Ensuring Effective Integrated
Marketing Communication                              370

Understanding Effective Communication                371
Marketing Responsible Business Performance           377

Phase 2: Applying Responsible Management
Marketing and Communication Tools                    381

Spheres of Application of Responsible
  Management Communication Tools                     381

*Responsible Management Communication Tools* 383

Phase 3: Customizing Stakeholder
Communication 389

*A Stakeholder Communication Model* 389
*Stakeholder Audience Analysis* 391

**Chapter 13: International Business and
Management: Glocally Responsible Business** 402

Responsible Management and International
Business 403

The Goal: Glocally Responsible Business 405

Phase 1: Understanding the Glocal Business
Context 405

*Globalization* 406
*Localizing Responsible Business* 408

Phase 2: Assessing the Responsible International
Business 415

*A Transnational Perspective of Responsible
Management* 415
*Assess the Type of International Firm the
Company Is* 416
*Assessing the Company's Degree of Global
Sustainability, Responsibility, and Ethics* 417

Phase 3: Mapping International Business
Activity 421

*Global Sourcing* 423
*Global Trade* 424
*Foreign Markets* 426
*International Subsidiaries* 428
*Global Strategic Alliances* 430

Phase 4: Responsibly Managing in a Globalized
Business 431

*Cross-National Diversity Management* 432
*Intercultural Management* 432
*Cross-Cultural Ethics* 434

## PART F: CONTROLLING

**Chapter 14: Accounting and Controlling:
Stakeholder Accountability** 446

Accounting and Responsible Management 447

The Goal: Stakeholder Accountability 449

Phase 0: Understand the Basics of Accounting 450

*The Rise of Sustainability Accounting and Its
Role in Responsible Accounting* 453

Phase 1: Identify the Account and Gather Data 454
*Materiality* 457

Phase 2: Evaluation and Elaboration
of the Data 459

*Costing Models* 459
*Responsible Business Performance Metrics* 460
*Indicators* 461
*The Value-Added Model* 464
*Social Return on Investment* 466

Phase 3: Reporting 466

*Global Reporting Initiative* 468
*Integrated Reporting* 470
*Auditing and Assurance* 471
*Ethics of Accounting* 474

Phase 4: Management Control 474
*Responsible Management Dashboard* 476

**Chapter 15: Finance: Responsible Return
on Investment** 485

Responsible Financial Management 486

The Goal: Responsible Return on Investment
(RROI) 488

Phase 0: Understanding Financial
Management 489

*Mechanisms and Structures of Mainstream
Financial Management* 489
*Questioning Paradigms of Financial
Management* 492

Phase 1: Financing Responsible Business 493

*Socially Responsible Investing* 495
*SRI Indices* 497
*Activist Shareholding* 499
*Directed Financing: Private Equity and Impact
Investing* 499
*Alternative Ownership Models* 500
*Cross-Financing and Goodwill Financing* 502
*Debt Financing* 503

Phase 2: Capital Budgeting and Programming
Internal Activities 503

*Calculating the Social Return on Investment* 505
*Subjects of Capital Budgeting* 512

Phase 3: Results and Governance 513

*From Shareholder-Value- to Stakeholder-
Value-Based Management* 513
*Corporate Governance and Fiduciary
Responsibilities* 515
*Fiduciary Responsibilities* 518

**Subject Index** 527

**Name Index** 550

Drivers **Globalization** Poverty **SMES** **Transparency** **NGO**

**Greenwashing**

**Entrepreneurship** Civil Society Sector

**Responsibility** Markets **Issues** **Sustainability**

**CSO** **Context** **Revolution** Economic Crisis **Ethics**

**Megatrend** **Responsibility** Poverty **Sectorial Actors**

# CONTEXT: DRIVERS, ACTORS, SUBJECTS

*You will be able to...*

1  ...understand main sustainability, responsibility, and ethics issues.

2  ...map the main actors and their roles in responsible management.

3  ...adjust to your company's main drivers of responsible management.

4  ...manage barriers, criticisms, and inhibitors of responsible management.

One third of the top fifty MBA programs require all three topics, sustainability, responsibility, *and* ethics, in their core curricula. at least one course is required by 84 percent.[1]

Ninety-seven percent of responsible managers expect their company's responsible business area to expand: through more coverage areas (57%), higher budgets (21%), and more staff (19%).[2]

Most companies (74%) see the potential to reduce costs as the main driver of their responsible business initiatives.[3]

Author: Oliver Laasch; Contributors: Aurea Christine Tanaka, Björn Stigson, Bligh Grant, Dewi Fitraasari, Narine Arustamyan

# Shell in Nigeria: "Have We Got It Right?"

"Have we got it right?" might have been the question leading to the establishment of Royal Dutch Shell's initiative for extensive sustainability, responsibility, and ethics infrastructure and activities. At the end of the 1990s, Shell became one of the most active multinational companies in responsible management. The foundation of this activity was laid in Shell's eight *Business Principles*. The principles define the company's responsibility to primary stakeholder groups (shareholders, employees, business partners, and society), commitment to sustainability by referring to the triple bottom line (environmental, social, and economic performance), commitment to ethics by highlighting the importance of moral principles (nonbribery, respect for the law), and commitment to values (honesty, integrity, and respect). Those business principles were first published in 1976 and have been updated constantly, corresponding to a changing context.

With such a long history of developing high principles, one might guess that Shell has always been a role model in its actions. Nevertheless, this British-Dutch multinational company has a long history of receiving bad press, especially in relationship to its performance in Nigeria. In the African country, the company has encountered a variety of drivers, inhibitors, and issues of different natures. The case, more extensively described by Hennchen and Lozano in 2012, gives an excellent insight into how the context of a company shapes its responsible management activities.

Issues encountered in Nigeria were manifold. The company was found to be highly unsustainable in all three dimensions. Economically, in spite of being one of the most profitable businesses worldwide, the company did not contribute much to poverty reduction and economic development of the country. Socially, there were many health-related issues because of flailing practices (the burning of natural gas). Environmentally, oil spills seriously damaged local ecosystems, not to mention the global impacts of petroleum and related

products. Stakeholder issues, most prominently with the local communities, evolved and Shell found itself involved in accusations of corruption. There were even accusations of a potential involvement in the hanging of the oppositional leader Ken Saro Wiwa. These issues were between Shell and actors from the civil society (the Ogoni people and the Movement for the Emancipation of the Niger Delta, or MEND) and the governmental sector (legislators of the Nigerian government).

A variety of drivers of Shell's new drift toward responsible management emerged. First, there was a profound *business case* for better practices, making sense profitwise. Shell was to decide either to leave the Nigerian location, which was strategically important and profitable, or to appease through a shift toward higher standards of responsible management. Local *stakeholder wants and needs* in the Nigerian community were manifested physically by protests and frequent sabotage, considerably affecting operations. Increasingly, *institutional power* through laws (e.g., the Petroleum Operating Bill), standards (e.g., the Extractives Industry Transparency Initiative), and international organizations (e.g., UNEP, Transparency International) started to target the company.

In opposition to the drivers, inhibitors, criticisms, and challenges emerged. Evidence was found that *lobbying* and *corruption* had allegedly slowed down the implementation of legislation for responsible business in Nigeria. On an international level, the company has been accused of *greenwashing*, or evoking a misleading impression of their responsible business performance. Probably the biggest challenge to responsible management activities for Shell lies in the sustainability dimension. With the core business of petroleum, an unsustainable product in itself, the company's efforts will continue to be hampered as long as there is no change in the very core business.

Sources: Shell. (2010). *Shell general business principles*; Hennchen, E., & Lozano, J. M. (2012). Mind the gap: Royal Dutch Shell's sustainability agenda in Nigeria. *Oikos Global Case Writing Competition*.

## 1-1 THE CONTEXT OF RESPONSIBLE MANAGEMENT

*"It should be noted, however, that specific historical, political, economic, and cultural factors determine ... CSR [corporate social responsibility] of firms. ..."* [4]

How can we compare the management of a cause-related marketing campaign at Walt Disney with the remediation of the environmental consequences of an oil spill by Shell? Both fall under the broad umbrella of responsible management, so obviously there is much diversity among responsible management activities. Responsible management is a completely different animal from organization to organization, from one department to another, and even varies considerably between individual managers. The variations not only stem from different internal approaches, but more importantly are influenced by the different issues addressed and the predominant actors involved. Variation can be further increased by the predominant drivers and strongest inhibitors of responsible management. As illustrated in Figure 1.1, identifying those external factors is crucial for choosing the right answer for each management challenge. They define the general responsible management trend in a given situation.

The first section of this chapter will illustrate the main **issues** encountered in the three aspects of responsible management: sustainability, responsibility, and ethics. It will discuss how responsible management addresses those issues in conjunction with **actors** from nonbusiness sectors, namely, civil society and the public sector.

The second section focuses on the **drivers** of a company's responsible management activities. Depending on the prevalent driver, the specific responsible management approach and activity implemented will vary greatly. For instance, a company that aims to enter new markets through responsible business will have a very distinct focus from one that reacts to the pressure exerted by strong institutions demanding responsible management.

The third section illustrates **inhibitors**, **criticisms**, and **challenges** typically encountered in responsible management. Those negative-influence factors are diverse, ranging from Nobel Prize Laureate Milton Friedman's "The business of business is business" argument to the practical internal challenges encountered by responsible managers.

**Figure 1.1 The Context of Responsible Management**

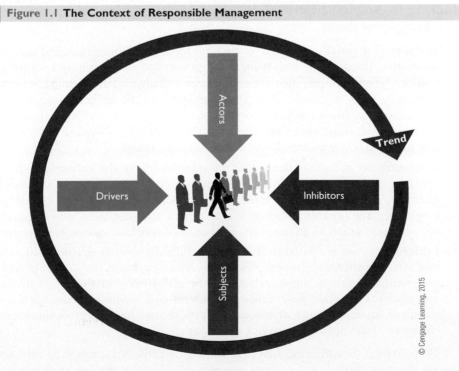

© Cengage Learning. 2015

**Drivers** of responsible management are external and internal factors that foster responsible behavior.

## 1-2 SUBJECTS AND ACTORS OF RESPONSIBLE MANAGEMENT

*"… responsibility in the following seven core subjects: organizational governance; human rights; labour practices; the environment; fair operating practices; consumer issues; and community involvement and development"[5]*

The environment of any responsible management activity is most significantly defined by issues, or subjects, to be addressed by responsible management. Another important element of the responsible management context is actors who co-address or are involved in the same issues in a parallel pattern. A responsible manager must know those contextual elements in order to adjust his/her own actions. In the following sections, we can map those elements only broadly. It is the task of a responsible manager to acquire the necessary expert knowledge for the subset of issues and actors relevant to that manager's sphere of influence.

### 1-2a Subjects and Background Disciplines

Human rights, global warming, corruption, biodiversity, labor rights, fair competition, community well-being—this list of potential **subjects** (also called *issues* or *causes*) to be addressed by responsible management could be extended endlessly. Those subjects, however, can be grouped into three main **background domains** of responsible management: sustainability, responsibility, and ethics. This framework will be the recurrent theme of this book, with practical applications provided in each chapter.

Sustainability, responsibility, and ethics have significant overlap and strongly influence one another; nevertheless, they do describe distinct core concepts of responsible management sufficiently to subsume the different subjects under them. Table 1.1 illustrates how various subjects involved in responsible business management can be categorized within these three subject areas, using the core concepts of each background theory.

- **Sustainability** usually is related to systemic social, environmental, and economic issues that threaten the well-being or even survival of current and future generations.[6] For example, such systemic issues include global warming, which on a business level is translated to $CO_2$ management, the global water crisis, the degradation of life-important ecosystems, and planetary overpopulation. On a business level, those issues are often translated into the so-called *triple bottom line* of social, environmental, and economic performance.[7]

- **Responsibility** at its core deals with the relationship to the various groups that affect or are affected by a business. Those groups are called *stakeholders*.[8] For example, the area of labor standards is concerned with the relationship to employees, the area of consumer rights relates to consumers, and the area of supply chain practices to suppliers. Each is an important stakeholder group.

- **Ethics** at its core is related to making the right decision in dilemma situations[9] and refers to streams of moral philosophy. As an example, the subject of human and natural rights is highly related to the philosophy of the ethics of rights and justice. Corporate governance revolves around *moral dilemmas* such as the principal–agent dilemma of whose interests should be protected, those of the owner or those of the manager of a company.

Of course, a classification like that shown in Table 1.1 cannot be absolutely precise. A good example is corporate governance, which on the one hand fulfills the

**Subjects**, also called **issues or causes,** of responsible management refer to topics to be addressed by responsible management.

The **background domains** of responsible management are sustainability, responsibility, and ethics.

**Table 1.1** Responsible Management Subjects Structured by Background Disciplines

| Sustainability (triple bottom line) | Responsibility (stakeholders) | Ethics (moral dilemma) |
|---|---|---|
| • World water and ocean crisis | • Labor standards | • Human and natural rights |
| • Global warming | • Consumer rights and protection | • Income inequality |
| • Deforestation and soil loss | • Workplace diversity | • Corporate governance |
| • Overpopulation | • Community well-being | • Fair competition |
| • Poverty and hunger | • Supply chain practices | • Corruption |
| • Ecosystem degradation | • Good citizenship | • Marketing ethics |
| • Biodiversity loss | • Respect for the law | • Accounting ethics |

© Cengage Learning, 2015

ethics criterion of the moral dilemma, but at the same time governs the stakeholder relationship between managers and company owners. Another example is the topic of poverty, which has a sustainability characteristic of threatening the well-being of current and future generations, while also having a responsibility dimension of companies' relationships to society and their role of providing social welfare. Next, we will see how those different subjects are related to actors not only from the business world but also from civil society and politics.

## 1-2b Sectorial Actors

Companies can be neither fully responsible for nor solve all the issues mentioned previously. A variety of actors, known as **sectorial actors**, operate in the same subject areas. As illustrated in Figure 1.2, each of the actors belonging to the business, governmental, and civil society sectors have different types of power to contribute to the solution of issues.

**Figure 1.2 Sectorial Actors: Power Resources and Levels**

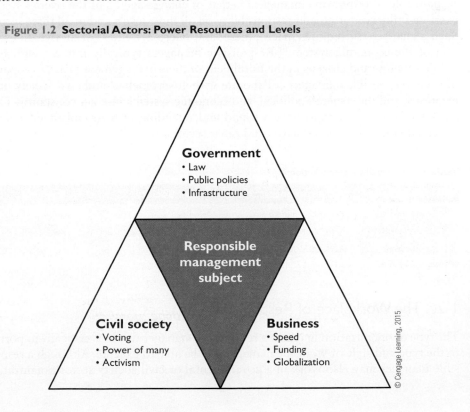

© Cengage Learning, 2015

**Sectorial actors** addressing the subjects of responsible management stem from the governmental, civil society, and business sectors.

- **Governmental actors** have the power of legislation, of forming local public policies, and of creating infrastructure. Governments are often limited to influence in the national or regional areas and lack the necessary speed of decision making required by urgent issues.

- **Civil society actors** have a voting power to influence the other two types of actors. As civil society is "the majority," its power of many exerts a far-reaching influence. Civil society decides which government to appoint. It also decides which company to support by buying or not buying products and can decide whom to work for. In some cases, civil society even becomes an activist for or against responsible business subjects. The effectiveness of civil society power is often mitigated by the lack of organization, professionalization, and a common voice.

- **Business actors** are powerful in that they have broad discretion in terms of their activities, which allows for fast decision making. As long as activities are profitable, business actors have access to a wide range of funding possibilities that can be invested in the mitigating issues. Businesses often act globally and, therefore, are able to provide solutions globally. Business actors, due to the mostly prevailing profit-maximization imperative, may abstain from mitigating an issue because it is not profitable.

Table 1.2 illustrates the *micro* (individual), *meso* (organizational), and *macro* (systemic) **levels** of the three sectors mentioned earlier. Although responsible managers are located in the business sector, on an individual (micro) level, their actions are contextualized by their companies and the economic system in which they work. A main role of responsible managers is that of change agents of the overall system, exerting influence for greater responsibility on all three levels and in all three sectors. Such a change task requires macro, meso, and micro activities for an overall evolution of the economic system.[10] Responsible managers typically interact with both public servants and citizens in the fulfillment of their management tasks. Companies of these responsible managers collaborate with governmental and civil society organizations, and the societal, political, and economic systems interact constantly. Thus, responsible managers must have a sound understanding of their embeddedness and interrelatedness with other actors and other sectors.

**Table 1.2** Sectorial Levels of Action

| Level↓/Sector→ | Government | Civil Society | Business |
|---|---|---|---|
| Micro (individual) | Public servant | Citizen | Employee |
| Meso (organizational) | Governmental organizations | Civil society organizations | Businesses |
| Macro (systemic) | Political system | Social system | Economic system |

© Cengage Learning, 2015

The **levels** on which sectors are influenced by responsible management activities are the micro (individual), meso (organizational), and macro (systemic) levels.

## 1-2c The Workplace of Responsible Managers

The type of organization in which a responsible manager works is critically important to the type and style of work the manager will be able to execute. Although a responsible manager may also work in a governmental or civil society sector organization, the focus of this book is on business sector organizations; but whenever possible we will provide insights into responsible management of the other two sectors. The coverage of entrepreneurship will provide greater insight into the different rationales for responsible management and social entrepreneurship in the three sectors.

Figure 1.3 classifies business organizations by two main questions:

1. Does the **organizational mission** focus primarily on egoistic motives, such as maximum profit or maximum shareholder value, or primarily on philanthropic motives?

2. Does the **value created** by the organization accrue externally (for a broad variety of stakeholders) or internally (for owners)?

Based on those two basic distinctions, we can define the four different types of business-related organizations and different work strategies for responsible managers shown in Figure 1.3:

1. A responsible manager who works in an **irresponsible business**, characterized by a purely egoistic profit mission and creating mostly internal value for the business, is in a hard position. The manager can either decide to leave the workplace or, more desirably, act as a change agent, moving the business toward more responsible ways.

2. The majority of responsible managers probably work in a **responsible business**, with an only slightly egoistic profit mission, creating internal value while also benefiting external stakeholders. Responsible managers in such a business are able to act responsibly when justified by a slight business case, benefiting the business.

3. A **social entrepreneur** typically has a strong philanthropic mission, mostly generating external value, but aiming to be at least profitable enough to survive in the long run. Responsible managers who are social entrepreneurs should aim to maximize external value when their activity creates sufficient internal benefits to cover costs.

**Figure 1.3 Business-Related Organizations, Classified by Value Creation and Mission**

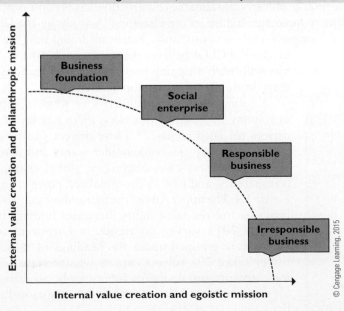

4. A **business foundation** has a purely philanthropic mission to spend a budget stemming from funds of the business on a predefined set of causes. Business foundations are usually stand-alone organizations, run in a parallel pattern to the main business. Responsible managers in business foundations should aim to invest the corporate money and their own activity to create the highest "social return on investment" possible. Such a manager should start to identify alternatives that will generate income for the foundation, beyond the main business's funds, striving to become a social business that is economically self-sustaining.

All four types of organizations add value in different ways and have their right to exist. From a purely practical point of view, it makes sense to move organizations toward the middle area of Figure 1.3 where mission and value creation are balanced. In reality, we can observe such a movement toward the center happening now. Increasingly, foundations and even pure civil society organizations are becoming self-sustaining social enterprises, and irresponsible businesses are becoming responsible. What are the drivers of this movement and the responsible business megatrend that can be observed globally?

## 1-3 THE MEGATREND AND ITS DRIVERS

*"The voices of business establishment have come to identify eight key drivers ... that make responsible corporate behavior an imperative. Not only are they persistent, they are predominant, and they will endure for decades to come."*[1]

Responsible business has become both a business megatrend and a strategic imperative.[12] Whole industries have recently experienced "responsibility waves," times of swift shift toward more sustainable, responsible, and ethical practices. The car industry, in spite of its inherently unsustainable starting position, has made great strides toward increased sustainability in the first decade of the new century. Shifts in key technologies from engines to breaks and shifts from new pricing schemes to business models, have turned the industry upside down.[13] Green IT has become a mainstream topic for information technology.[14] Socially responsible investment is one of the hot topics in the finance industry. Sustainable construction has become a standard for the majority of new buildings. Industries are changing. A study by the United Nations (UN) Global Compact and the consultancy Accenture found that the majority (54 percent) of CEOs believes that, between 2010 and 2020, companies will reach a tipping point where sustainability will be fully embedded into corporate core strategies.[15]

No matter if whole industries or single companies engage in responsible business practices, there is a set of predominant drivers for such change.[16] These **drivers** can be grouped into five broad categories: stakeholder wants and needs, new markets and business case, converging global crises, Internet and transparency, and new institutionalized powers, as illustrated in Figure 1.4. The upper part of the figure shows the five drivers. The lower part of the same figure illustrates findings from Ernst & Young's 2012 survey on trends in corporate sustainability, which were grouped under the headings of those drivers. The survey asked 272 subject experts what drivers were important for corporate sustainability. Interestingly, all drivers mentioned by the survey could be distributed harmoniously through the five categories of drivers.

Figure 1.4 **Drivers of Responsible Management in Theory and Practice**

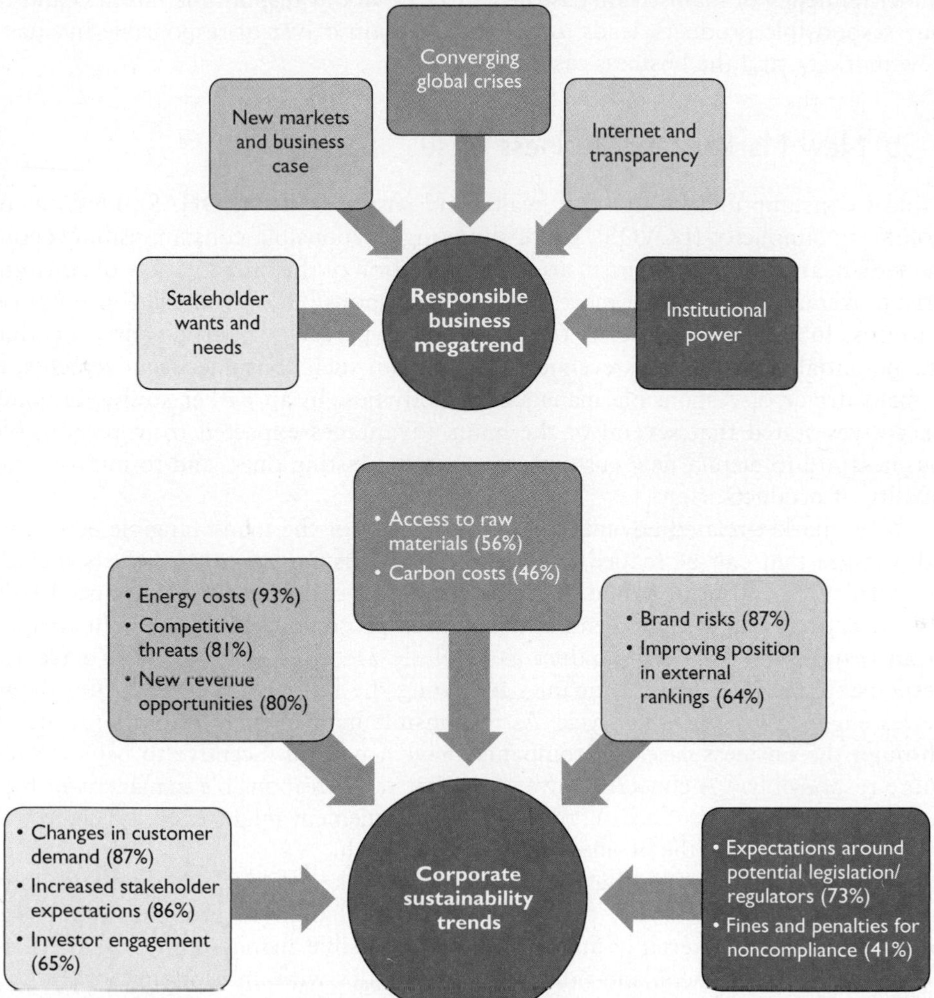

Source: Adapted from Ernst & Young. (2012). *Six growing trends in corporate sustainability.* Ernst & Young.

## 1-3a Stakeholder Wants and Needs

Respondents of the Ernst & Young survey found that 86 percent of corporate sustainability experts mentioned increased stakeholder expectations as a main driver of their activities. The most important stakeholder seems to be the customer, as 87 percent mentioned changes in customer demand and 65 percent investor engagement for topics related to responsible business. A 2011 study conducted by KPMG[17] found that companies are also driven by the motivating power of responsible business over employees (52 percent) and by improving supplier relationships (32 percent).

Responsible managers, if their company is driven by consumer interest in responsible business activities, will primarily base their decisions and behavior on assessing, addressing, and satisfying stakeholder needs. A later chapter on responsibility will provide additional information on stakeholder wants and needs related to sustainability and how companies manage the stakeholder relationship. Repeatedly, customers have been ranked by companies to be the most influential stakeholder driving responsible business conduct.[18] This fact, together with an increasing consumer tendency of mainstream customers to care about responsible business and to buy responsible products, leads to the second main driver of responsible business, new markets, and the business case.

## 1-3b New Markets and Business Case

Ethical consumption, lifestyles of health and sustainability (LOHAS), lifestyles of voluntary simplicity (LOVOS), cause shopping, responsible consumerism, ecoconsumerism, and fair consumerism are only a selection of the broad variety of consumerist movements pushing for more sustainable, responsible, and ethical consumption patterns. In the 2012 Ernst & Young study, 80 percent of participants said that the potential to create new revenues, mostly from such consumerist movements, is a main driver of responsible management activities. In an earlier study, company executives stated that several of the main advantages expected from responsible business are to attract new customers, to retain existing ones, and to improve the quality of products.[19]

New market-related advantages are only some of the many tangible economic advantages that can be reaped from responsible business conduct. Others include the attraction, motivation, and retention of employees; cost savings; reduced risk; the attraction of new investment; and increased profitability. Those benefits reaped from responsible business conduct as a whole are called the **business case** for responsible management. Companies following the business case often find themselves engaged in a virtuous cycle: As responsible management becomes profitable through the business case, the companies have a natural incentive to behave even more responsibly.[20] A concern, however, is that when responsible management topics do not have a business case, responsible management might easily be neglected. Thus, following only the business case is not enough.

For each company, the business case might look different. Building and communicating the business case can be an important handle to promote responsible business practices internally and to "sell" responsible management to superiors, controllers, shareholders, and other involved parties with an economic profit perspective. A responsible manager working in a company driven by the business case for responsible management should try to find the "sweet spot" of responsible management, a win-win situation between companies and stakeholders.[21]

## 1-3c Converging Global Crises

The second millennium has seen not only an increase in the number of global issues and crises but also an increasing interrelatedness and convergence of those crises toward a global megacrisis triggered by multiple causes. Such systemic challenges are increasingly interrelated, which makes solving them more complex.[22]

It naturally follows that businesses also are affected. The before-mentioned Ernst & Young study said 46 percent of respondents stated that increased carbon costs, directly related to the global warming crisis, are a main driver for responsible management activities. A study by the Global Compact and Accenture asked company CEOs which global challenges are most threatening to the future success of their businesses.[23] Interestingly, climate change ranked just second behind the global educational challenge, and before poverty. Other global challenges affecting companies significantly were gender diversity, access to water and clean sanitation, and food security and hunger. Overall, 29 percent of CEOs mentioned

The **business case** for responsible management describes situations where companies are able to reap internal benefits from behaving responsibly.

that those global challenges and development gaps drive their responsible management activities. Environmental challenges seemed to be even more significant. An average of 76 percent of executives in 2012 stated that they expected their core business to be affected significantly by natural resource shortages.

For a responsible manager working in a business driven by external global challenges or crises, the deep familiarization with the respective crisis topic is essential. Many international organizations such as the UN Millennium Development Goals (MDGs) initiative and the World Bank have powerful databases and guidance instruments on the overall "state of the world."[24] More specific organizations to tackle single challenges exist, such as Transparency International for corruption topics,[25] the World Wildlife Fund for biodiversity,[26] and the Global Footprint Network for environmental resource issues.[27] These are but a few of a variety of excellent resources for responsible managers to use to become familiar with global challenges.

## 1-3d Internet, Transparency, and Globalization

Responsible business is good for reputation. Irresponsible practices may lead to immense losses, first in reputation, and then in the value of the brand or even the company. This threat becomes even more pressing when assessing the current business environment in terms of its flow of information. Information on a company's social, environmental, or ethical misconduct may literally travel "around the world" in very little time and destroy company value. Eighty-seven percent of executives state that one of the main drivers for their responsible business activities is the mitigation of such brand risks. Another 64 percent say they aim to increase their company's visibility in external responsible business rankings. A responsible manager working in a company driven by transparency and information-based considerations must pay special attention to avoiding any moral blunder by ensuring congruence between the company's walk and talk and by excelling in stakeholder management and communication.

The International Organization for Standardization (ISO) norm for social responsibility, ISO 26000, states that scrutiny has increased because of globalization, mobile communication technologies, and widespread Internet access.[28] In addition, practices of different companies can be compared more easily, good and bad news can be spread more easily, and stakeholders now have channels to directly communicate with companies all over the world. A variety of institutions, such as the Global Reporting Initiative, the Global Compact, and AccountAbility, provide a new infrastructure and framework for globally available, high-quality information on a company's responsible and irresponsible activities.

## 1-3e Institutionalization of Responsible Management

In 2011, the ISO launched its ISO 26000 standard, the norm for the social responsibility of organizations. Many companies, often with little experience in responsible business, started to investigate the topic only because of this institutional document. In mid-2013, Global Reporting launched its new reporting standards for integrated social, environmental, and economic reporting; these standards have now made responsible business a mainstream consideration in accounting and reporting. Those two institutions stand as excellent examples of a myriad of institutions that are driving responsible business forward.

Governments are increasingly launching formal legislation institutionalizing responsible business topics on a national level. International organizations, such as the UN Global Compact and the World Business Council for Sustainable Development (WBCSD), have established networks of responsible businesses. Norms, such as the before-mentioned ISO 26000 (social responsibility) and ISO 14000 (environmental management), provide guidance for implementation, and often certification, or serve as rankings. Many stock markets also have launched large-scale sustainability indexes; examples are the British FTSE4Good Index Series, the American Dow Jones Sustainability Indexes, and the Chinese Hang Seng Corporate Sustainability Index Series.

Internally, the responsible business infrastructure of a company is created through organizational reference documents (e.g., codes of ethics, sustainability handbooks), job positions (e.g., chief responsibility officers, VPs for sustainability), and organizational structures (e.g., corporate foundations, sustainability departments). This list is only an exemplary representation. It would exceed the scope of this chapter to attempt to provide a complete listing of the many different institutions that are now driving responsible business and management.

A responsible manager whose company's responsible business activities are driven by one or several institutions should primarily aim to comply with the standards set by the institutions. If the company aims at being ranked high in a responsible business rating, this manager must seek to fulfill the various indicators. In the case of upcoming legislation, the responsible manager must ensure compliance and adapt actions to the norms.

## 1-4 BARRIERS, INHIBITORS, AND CRITICISMS

*"What are the barriers to increasing the supply of corporate virtue? And what can companies do to remove those barriers? ... What seems lacking is imagination and intrinsic motivation on the part of corporations and executives."*[29]

No matter how powerful the drivers for responsible business are, there are also barriers, inhibitors, and criticisms related to responsible business and the conduct of responsible management. In order to effectively and efficiently manage responsible business activities, a manager must be familiar with them. A manager who is prepared for critical attitudes of stakeholders that might result in accusations of not walking the talk, or *greenwashing,* will pay special attention to congruence in his/her own actions. A responsible manager who knows about typical operational inhibitors, such as a lack of internal skills and knowledge or the complexity of implementing responsible business across departments, will be able to address those issues before they endanger responsible business conduct. Figure 1.5 summarizes six of the typical barriers, inhibitors, and criticisms encountered in the realm of responsible business.

© Cengage Learning, 2015

## 1-4a Profit Issues

A whole array of inhibitors might occur related to the profitability or nonprofitability of responsible business. The criticisms can be divided into two basic arguments:

1. Companies are focusing on responsible business only to make more profits, to instrumentally and greedily abuse a good topic for profit reasons.

2. The business of business is to generate profit for shareholders, and there is no legitimate responsibility toward any other stakeholder.

The first argument questions the virtue of companies' and managers' motivations to conduct responsible business. The second argument goes in the opposite direction by supposing that responsible business is not the most profitable thing to do and that managers do not fulfill their responsibility to owners if they do anything besides maximize profit at all cost.

Both arguments may be equally harmful to the work of a responsible manager. The first argument might cost valuable stakeholder support, and the second is a thought-terminating cliché, often used by managers with high seniority in organizations to finish discussions about the social responsibility of business before they even get started. What can responsible managers do to deal with those arguments? To provide effective responses to this question, it is crucial to first understand the origins of both types of reasoning.

**Response 1:** Argument number one is related to the field of virtue ethics, where only an action fulfilled out of a virtuous attitude is considered morally correct. A responsible manager could counter such an argument with outcome-based utilitarian ethics. Such an argument would highlight all the good being done if a company engages with responsible business, no matter how virtuous or nonvirtuous is the motivation leading to this activity.

**Response 2:** The second argument, "the only responsibility of business is profit," goes back to Milton Friedman, the late Nobel Prize winner in economics.[30] Friedman argued that managers who spend money on "philanthropic" purposes do not act in the interest of the owners of the company to whom they are primarily responsible. He stated that the only person who can decide to spend money for philanthropic purposes is the owner of the business. Friedman further argued that philanthropic spending increases companies' costs, which must lead to lower wages for employees and higher prices for customers.

Responsible managers could easily invalidate this **Friedman argument** by referring to the completely changed context of responsible business between the 1970s, when Friedman made his point, and today. Responsible business has been shown to be often profitable in the short run and to ensure the survival of the business in the long run, both of which are core interests of shareholders. Friedman could not have known that customers of our present would often pay a voluntary "responsibility premium," a higher price, for products produced responsibly. He could not have known that many employees would give up a significant proportion of their wage in order to work for a responsible company. Friedman made a valid argument in his day, but today it must be adapted to fit drastically changed circumstances.

## 1-4b Economic Crises

There is a hard-to-die prejudice that responsible business activities cannot survive through times of economic hardship. This argument is partly true, at least for activities that are neither profitable nor directly aligned with a company's core business. As with the Friedman argument, however, those two conditions are becoming less and less relevant. Companies have increasingly managed to conduct profitable responsibility through their core business strategies and operations.

Whether a crisis leads to more or less responsible business activity depends primarily on the perspective of a company. Do executives see CSR as a threat or an opportunity in times of crisis?[31] Imagine a company that focuses, for instance, on ecoefficiency in their operations and, by doing so, reduces cost through saving raw materials, electricity, water, and waste. In times of economic crisis, such a company might increase its ecoefficiency activities to reduce costs even more. Compare this company to another one, perhaps from the banking sector, that as part of its responsibility program is involved mainly in sponsoring arts and cultural programs. Cutting back on that spending during times of crisis would be a reasonable approach for this company. Such a cutback would not affect core business, as the activities are largely unrelated to it. Also, terminating such programs would save the company costs in times of crisis, as the sponsoring of arts and cultural programs most likely would not be providing a significant economic return on the money spent for them.

Interestingly, it might seem that most companies have implemented the second approach to responsible business, as a study of 100 randomly sampled Fortune 500 companies showed that responsible business activity during the 2008–2009 global economic crisis was reduced significantly.[32] However, the question remains of how much it had been reduced compared to other activities. Nineteen percent of respondents in a 2010 survey stated that their responsible business budget decreased less than other departments' budgets, and 19 percent said it increased more than the budgets for other departments. The majority of respondents (57 percent) stated the budget was maintained at the same level. Only 4 percent stated that their budget was either eliminated or increased less than other departments' budgets.[33] It looks

The **Friedman argument** against responsible business is the argument that the only responsibility of a business is profit generation.

like responsible business activity actually does better than other mainstream business activities during times of crisis. Therefore, a responsible manager, to make responsible business effective during a time of crisis, must anchor as many activities as possible in core business strategies and operations, and make them as profitable as possible.

## 1-4c Greenwashing

**Greenwashing** is probably the single most dangerous threat to responsible business conduct. Stakeholders might accuse a company of greenwashing when the company creates a misleading impression of its social, environmental, or ethical performance. Many well-intentioned (and also less-well-intentioned) companies have fallen through the "greenwashing trapdoor."[34] Once stakeholder confidence in the company is lost, it is difficult to regain a joint base of trust for collaboration and benevolence. A chapter on marketing and communication will cover the topic of greenwashing at great length.

To avoid greenwashing accusations, a responsible manager will aim to always communicate responsible business activities truthfully and will abstain from exaggeration and misleading communication so that the responsible business talk will match the walk.

## 1-4d Cause Criticism

Stakeholders might criticize the causes a company addresses. For a long time, there was a significant movement of people who were skeptical about the topical flagship cause of responsible businesses: global warming. Denial of environmental or social realities may be a powerful inhibitor of change toward responsible business.[35] Such critical behavior might be brought forward using manifold arguments, justified or not. In the case of unjustified arguments, it is crucial to understand the root motivation of the criticisms. The critics' own interests and lobbying behaviors aimed at protecting outdated irresponsible industries, for example, are common motivations for irrational arguments. Ideologically motivated misinterpretation may be another.

A responsible manager must analyze and resolve such criticisms on a case-by-case basis. Some criticisms might be justified, in which case the manager should have the courage to rethink the company's approach to the topic and actively propose change.

## 1-4e Applicable for Only a "Selected Few"

Another often-uttered argument against the assumption of responsible business is that the topic applies only to big corporations from developed countries involved in producing products for the end consumer. Businesses might excuse themselves from responsible behavior by stating they are too small, they are not involved with the final customer, or they are from a still developing country. As shown in the following, all three arguments are at best only partly applicable.

- **Small and medium enterprises (SMEs) versus big corporations:** Before thinking about the question of whether responsible business makes sense for an SME, one has to ask another question: Would it make sense for society if SMEs were

**Greenwashing** is a situation where stakeholders perceive a business as creating a misleading impression of its social, environmental, and ethics performance.

to evolve into responsible businesses? The answer is yes.[36] SMEs constitute an enormous proportion of businesses worldwide; on average, they contribute to more than 50 percent of countries' gross domestic products.[37] If SMEs are left out, a big part of the responsible business agenda cannot succeed. Fortunately, a majority of SMEs agree on the importance of responsible business activity, and most already have a decent track record of implementing responsible management.[38] Many cases have shown the business advantages for responsible business in SMEs and multiple roads to increased SME competitiveness through responsible business.[39] Responsible managers in SMEs must act differently from those in large companies.[40] Several concrete recommendations for SMEs have been developed. One is to reduce organizational effort and cost of implementation by using a "piggy-back" approach of linking responsible management to already existing management systems.[41] Others are to pay attention to the important role played by values and the influence of business owners, who often in SMEs are at the same time top managers of the organization, and to give consideration to the fact that SMEs tend to apply informal rather than formal responsible business programs.[42] A later chapter on supply chain provides more insight on responsible management in SMEs.

- **Business-to-business (B2B) versus end-consumer companies:** An argument is that responsible business is relevant only for companies directly producing products or services for end consumers, where the reputational benefit can be translated directly into sales and brand value. This argument would be valid if big multinational end-consumer companies did not increasingly ask supply chain partners to be as responsible as they are. Eighty-eight percent of CEOs believe that they should integrate responsible business throughout the supply chain, but only 54 percent believe that they have achieved this goal in their companies.[43] As a result of the increasing pressure from the top of the supply chain, responsible business is becoming an increasingly hot topic in B2B marketing.[44] Responsible managers involved in B2B relationships should consider their management activities as a crucial part of their relationships to clients and as a factor that is highly important for competition.

- **Developing versus developed countries:** The perceived importance of responsible business to mainstream business success is more pronounced in businesses in developing countries than in those in developed countries. When CEOs were asked if responsible business considerations were critical to the future success of their businesses, 98 percent of Asian-Pacific companies and 97 percent of South American and African respondents answered in the affirmative.[45] Responsible business, however, differs economically in developing countries, due to its different context, and has a different focus from that in developed countries.[46] Responsible management in developing countries is often characterized by direct contribution to pressing local causes, and religious or community values, which are often philanthropy or charity-based. Responsible management activities in these countries are often driven by markets, multinational company clients, and business case thinking.[47] Responsible managers from companies located in economically developing countries, therefore, experience a difficult challenge: complying with international standards while lacking a local legal infrastructure and business culture supporting responsible business.

## 1-4f Operational Inhibitors

What do managers do if they have solved all external issues, but there are still the internal problems of implementation? Internal issues, as summarized in Figure 1.6 based on a Global Compact survey of CEOs, may arise from numerous perspectives. One of these is a very simple point: Of the CEOs surveyed, 31 percent were not able to agree on a common definition of *responsible business*. Many of the other differing perspectives were highly related to the drivers and inhibitors of responsible management discussed previously. For example, among those who agreed on a definition of responsible business, 30 percent found it difficult to see how the topic connected to value drivers; it was hard for them to identify the business case. Among companies that had decided to seriously engage in responsible management practices, 49 percent of CEOs found it difficult to accommodate competing strategic priorities with responsible business strategy, and 48 percent encountered high complexity in integrating responsible management practices throughout all business functions. Additional implementation issues were the lack of managers' responsible management skills (24 percent) and difficulties in engaging with external groups (30 percent). Once responsible business activity had been implemented, a number of CEOs believed the financial markets did not sufficiently recognize those efforts as important (34 percent).

Such operational inhibitors may represent powerful obstacles, possibly mitigating responsible managers' output considerably. This book actively aims to provide responsible managers with the necessary skills to tackle such inhibitors in order to contribute to sustainable development, to create value for both the business and a broad set of stakeholders, and to reach moral excellence.

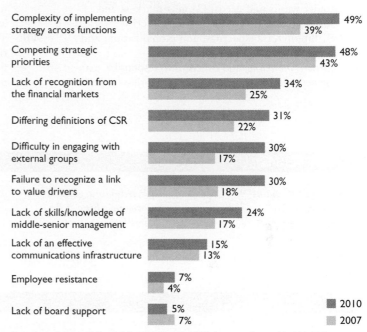

**Figure 1.6 Internal Inhibitors of Responsible Management**

Which barriers keep you, as a CEO, from implementing an integrated and strategic companywide approach to environmental, social, and corporate governance issues?

Respondents identifying each factor in their top three choices

- Complexity of implementing strategy across functions — 49% / 39%
- Competing strategic priorities — 48% / 43%
- Lack of recognition from the financial markets — 34% / 25%
- Differing definitions of CSR — 31% / 22%
- Difficulty in engaging with external groups — 30% / 17%
- Failure to recognize a link to value drivers — 30% / 18%
- Lack of skills/knowledge of middle-senior management — 24% / 17%
- Lack of an effective communications infrastructure — 15% / 13%
- Employee resistance — 7% / 4%
- Lack of board support — 5% / 7%

■ 2010
■ 2007

Source: Lacey, P., Cooper, T., Hayward, R., & Neuberger, L. (2010). *A new era of sustainability: UN global compact-ccenture CEO study 2010.* Accenture Institute for High Performance.

## PRINCIPLES OF CONTEXT: DRIVERS, ACTORS, SUBJECTS

I. Critical factors in the context of responsible management are *issues* encountered and related *actors*, *drivers*, and *barriers* to responsible management.

II. *Subjects*, also called *issues* or *causes*, in responsible management can be categorized into the ones relating primarily to the *triple bottom line (sustainability)*, to *stakeholders (responsibility)*, and to *moral dilemmas (ethics)*.

III. *Sectorial actors* stem from the *governmental*, *civil society*, and *business* sectors. All three sectorial actors typically provide different solution capabilities for the subjects and issues of responsible management.

IV. All responsible business *background domains—sustainability, responsibility, and ethics*—may be applied on a micro (individual), meso (organizational), and macro (systemic) level.

V. Main *drivers* of responsible management efforts can be grouped into five categories: (1) stakeholder wants and needs; (2) new markets and business case; (3) converging global crises; (4) Internet, transparency, and globalization; and (5) institutional power.

VI. *Barriers, inhibitors,* and *criticisms* to responsible management can be grouped into six categories: (1) profit criticism, (2) economic crises, (3) greenwashing, (4) cause criticism, (5) the "selected few" argument, and (6) a set of inhibitors stemming from operational realities.

VI. *Greenwashing* describes a situation where stakeholders perceive a company as creating a misleading impression of it social, environmental, and ethics performance.

VII. The *Friedman argument* is the claim that the only responsibility of a business is profit generation, and thus companies and managers should not spend money on responsible business activities.

## KEY TERMS

background domains  4
business case  10
drivers  3

Friedman argument  14
greenwashing  15
levels  6

sectorial actors  5
subjects (issues, causes)  4

## EXERCISES

### A. Remember and Understand

A.1. List the five main drivers of responsible business management.

A.2. Outline the main types of barriers, inhibitors, and criticisms of responsible business.

A.3. Define the three background domains of responsible management, sustainability, responsibility, and ethics, by elaborating their differences and similarities.

A.4. Define the following terms and explain how they are related: *greenwashing, business case, Friedman criticism.*

### B. Apply and Experience

B.5. Conduct an investigation into one of the global issues or crises in order to deeply understand its roots. Then find two other global issues or crises to which the first one relates. Describe the ways in which they are interdependent.

B.6. Find information about a small- and medium-sized company from a developing country that is involved in B2B marketing. Does the company have responsible business activities?

B.7. Research real examples of each of the four organization types mentioned in Figure 1.3. Look up information on each respective organization and briefly explain why you think the chosen organizations are good examples for each organization type.

### C. Analyze and Evaluate

C.8. What new stakeholder wants and needs can you observe in your personal environment? What do people—in their different roles as employees, consumers, and community members—expect from companies?

C.9. Do you think the Internet has made transparency a reality? Discuss the pros and cons of the type of effects the Internet has on business in the area of transparency.

C.10. Locate a random company's website and use the company's reports to discover one inhibitor of its responsible business conduct and to identify its main responsible business driver.

### D. Change and Create

D.11. Choose a global issue and think about how actors from the three sectors might collaborate to solve the issue. Write a one-page strategy document outlining a plan by which the sectorial actors could jointly solve the issue completely.

Björn Stigson was president of the WBCSD from its foundation in 1995 to 2012. During this time WBCSD coined and promoted important concepts, such as ecoefficiency and the business case for sustainability. The WBCSD *Vision 2050* aims to be a "new agenda for business laying out a pathway to a world in which nine billion people can live well, and within the planet's resources, by mid-century." (Source: WBCSD. [2010]. *Overview*. Retrieved January 29, 2013, from *Vision 2050*: www.wbcsd .org/vision2050.aspx.)

### Do you believe that we will achieve the goals laid out in your *Vision 2050* agenda?

Yes, I believe this is entirely possible, provided the suggestions the report makes are followed. *Vision 2050* is a consensus piece outlining initiatives we hope organizations will consider putting in place. And if the developments it advocates are implemented, then a steady course toward global sustainability in business will be set.

What makes *Vision 2050* unique is that the ambitious pathway it lays out—to a world in which 9 billion people can live well, and within the planet's resources, by midcentury—is both realistic and achievable. The report was compiled by twenty-nine leading global companies from fourteen industries who strongly believe that the world already has the knowledge, science, technologies, skills, and financial resources needed to achieve *Vision 2050*. The next step is to build the foundations at speed and scale during this decade.

### The WBCSD stated that business opportunities in the new fields of sustainability could reach $3-10 trillion in 2050. Do you think companies are stepping up to the challenge to realize these gains?

More and more companies are recognizing the benefits of transitioning to sustainable business models and are starting to see direct revenue gains.

An example is the results companies gained from using the WBCSD's *Guide to Corporate Ecosystem Valuation*—a first-of-its-kind tool that helps companies understand and value the goods and services that ecosystems provide. Using the CEV guide, companies chose restoration options for sand and gravel mines that boosted wildlife habitat, flood control, and recreation—estimated to be worth $1.4 million; monetized the potential return on investment for supporting bee conservation practices on blueberry farms—a $40-per-acre value increase; and compared the costs of replacing a water-treatment plant with a constructed wetland for onsite flood control and water treatment—a saving of $200, 000 at present value but even more over the long term.

### In your opinion, what is the single most important business opportunity a company can gain through its sustainable activities as outlined in *Vision 2050*?

There is a huge opportunity for business to seize competitive advantage as the challenges the world faces become strategic drivers. Population expansion and demographic shifts are resulting in intense competition for resources, which in turn open a window of opportunity for companies to innovate and lead in the production of cleaner technologies and the provision of new and more goods and services.

### Is the "business case" for CSR and sustainability "proven"? In your opinion, roughly what proportion of companies today has made a solid business case for their sustainability activities?

I think that the business case for sustainability has been made: With a global population that will increase 30 percent by midcentury, a very attractive market is emerging. Demand for access to education, health care, energy, communications, and consumer goods will increase significantly, opening up commercial opportunities. Business is an important driver in this space because it creates the innovated technologies that will fuel future growth.

### In your opinion, how will sustainable and CSR issues change the nature of companies in the next twenty years?

In *Vision 2050* we coined the phrase "Turbulent Teens" to describe the period leading up to 2020 and advocate what we call "must haves" or vital developments that need to take place to set business on the path to sustainability. Ultimately, we need to move away from business as usual and adopt a different perspective across the value chain. This includes things like establishing a carbon price and a network of linked emissions trading frameworks, along with policies to avoid deforestation and promote agricultural research. We need better management of ecosystem services and deployment of technologies that improve ecoefficiency and bioproductivity. These are just some examples of changes that, if implemented, will set us on course to achieve the vision we laid out.

---

## PRACTITIONER PROFILE: NARINE ARUSTAMYAN

**Employing organization:** VivaCell-MTS (K-Telecom CJSC) operates under the VivaCell brand in the GSM-900/1800. The company has the widest 2G/3.75G/4G network, spreading a wide range of voice and data services all across Armenia. As of January 2013, it provided services to more than 2 million subscribers and had a 64 percent market share.

**Job title:** CSR Leading Specialist; Chair of the CSR Advisory Committee of K-Telecom CJSC.

**Education:** Currently earning a degree in Master of Arts in Responsible Management, Steinbeis University Berlin, Institute Corporate Responsibility Management.

### In Practice

### What are your responsibilities?

I have been holding a position of CSR Leading Specialist since March 2006, and I lead the CSR Advisory Committee by coordinating the aspects of CSR of the company. I'm responsible for CSR strategy, implementation, and reporting. We report in accordance with the Sustainability Reporting Guidelines of the GRI 3.1 and the Telecommunication Sector Supplement. Being assessed with a mission of integrating the CSR concept into the company's day-to-day operation, we are addressing organizational performance and improvement in socially responsible behavior by applying ten principles of Global Compact, as well as the guidelines of the ISO 26000 standard.

### What are typical activities you carry out during a day at work?

I handle a great deal of communication issues during my day. Calls and meetings with different stakeholders are always part of my routine work. I consolidate the offers and complaints of internal and external stakeholders, evaluate them, and propose ideas of further improvement to management. On the one hand, we closely follow both local and international CSR-related news; on the other hand, our team consolidates data and policies of our company in order to draw comparative analyses. We prepare presentations and develop training courses for the employees and university students. Community development programs are also part of my daily job.

### How do sustainability, responsibility, and ethics topics play a role in your job?

In my opinion, sustainability, responsibility, and ethics are strongly conditioned by personal conscientiousness and start with simple responsibility and respect toward energy saving at the office and at home. Another factor is consideration of the issues of different stakeholders and respect for the company's Code of Ethics.

Concerned with the impact on the environment, our company transferred all company vehicles from petrol to methane gas and equipped them with GPS. This has since had a significant difference in kilometers driven, thus decreasing environmental impact and saving money for the company meantime.

In partnership with the Foundation for the Preservation of Wildlife and Cultural Assets (FPWC) NGO, our company actively participates in community development through nature conservation projects that aim at biodiversity preservation in Armenia. Our country is one of 34 global biodiversity hotspots: Over 50% percent of the world's plant species and 42% of all terrestrial vertebrate species are endemic to the 34 biodiversity hotspots. Thus, the protection of Armenia's nature is of vital importance for us.

Our H&R department implements a benefits plan to employees presented and regulated through our company's Code of Ethics. As a result, the majority of employees remain faithful by working for the company for more than six years. Our Code of Ethics sets forth the principles and ethical standards for the professional conduct and responsibilities of employees. These principles and standards are used as guidelines during our daily professional activities. They constitute normative statements and guidance on issues that we may encounter in our professional day to day work.

### Insights and Challenges

### What recommendation can you give to practitioners in your field?

In my opinion, in order to have better insight in the field of CSR, we need to have combined understanding in the fields of economy, management, leadership, politics, social sciences, communication, diplomacy, environmental management, and finance. I'd recommend always sharing and communicating CSR-related information to your friends, families, and colleagues in order to extend the number of people speaking "CSR language" around you.

### Which are the main challenges of your job?

At first it was difficult to promote the CSR concept throughout the company, and the challenge was to make others speak out for CSR. It took a few years to prove its efficiency and relevance to the organization. Currently, the concept is well-extended and has become the talk of the company and country in general. The other challenges were to differentiate CSR from philanthropy and to define the understanding of resources and environmental management, which is about far more than biophysical manipulation and control. It concerns mutually beneficial management, which begins with a sense of collective vision for the future.

### Is there anything else that you would like to share?

"You join a multitude of caring people. No one knows how many groups and organizations are working on the most salient issues of our day: climate change, poverty, deforestation, peace, water, hunger, conservation, human rights, and more. This is the largest movement the world has ever seen. Rather than control, it seeks connection. Rather than dominance, it strives to disperse concentrations of power. Like Mercy Corps, it works behind the scenes and gets the job done. Large as it is, no one knows the true size of this movement. It provides hope, support, and meaning to billions of people in the world. Its clout resides in idea, not in force" (Paul Hawken). Keep on believing and never give up!

### SOURCES

1. Christensen, L., Peirce, E. H., Christensen, L., Peirce, E., Hartman, P., Hoffman, M., Carrier, J., & Carrier, J. (2007). Ethics, CSR and sustainability education in the *Financial Times* top 50 global business schools: Baseline data and future research directions. *Journal of Business Ethics, 73*(4), 347–368.
2. Corporate Responsibility Magazine. (2010). *Corporate responsibility best practices: Setting the baseline.*
3. Ernst & Young. (2012). *Six growing trends in corporate sustainability.* Ernst & Young.
4. Desta, I. H. (2010). CSR in developing countries. In M. Pohl & N. Tolhurst, *Responsible business: How to manage your CSR strategy successfully* (pp. 265–278). Chichester: Wiley.
5. ISO. (2010). *International Standard ISO 26000: Guidance on Social Responsibility.* Geneva: International Organization for Standardization.
6. Brundtland, G. H. (1987). *Presentation of the report of the World Commission on Environment and Development to UNEP's 14th governing council.* Nairobi.
7. Elkington, J. (1998). *Cannibals with forks: The triple bottom line of 21st century business.* Gabriola Island: New Society Publishers.
8. Freeman, R. E. (1984/2010). *Strategic Management: A Stakeholder Approach.* Cambridge: Cambridge University Press.
9. Crane, A., & Matten, D. (2010). *Business ethics*, 3rd ed. New York: Oxford University Press.
10. Dopfer, K., Foster, J., & Potts, J. (2004). Micro–meso–macro. *Journal of Evolutionary Economics, 14*(3), 263–279.
11. Hollender, E., & Breen, B. (2010). *The responsibility revolution: How the next generation of businesses will win.* San Francisco: Jossey-Bass.
12. Lubin, D. A., & Esty, D. C. (2010). The sustainability imperative. *Harvard Business Review* (May 2010), 1–9; Waddock, S. A., Bodwell, C., & Graves, S. B. (2002). Responsibility : The new business imperative. *Academy of Management Executive, 47*(1), 132–147.

13. Orsato, R., & Wells, P. (2006). The automobile industry and sustainability. *Journal of Cleaner Production, 15* (11–12), 989–993.

14. Murugesan, S. (2008). Harnessing green IT: Principles, practices. *IT Pro* (January/February), 24–33.

15. Lacey, P., Cooper, T., Hayward, R., & Neuberger, L. (2010). *A new era of sustainability: UN global compact-Accenture CEO study 2010.* Accenture Institute for High Performance.

16. Campbell, J. L. (2007). Why would corporations behave in socially responsible ways? An institutional theory of corporate social responsibility. *Academy of Management Review, 32*(3), 946–967; Prätorius, G. (2010). Sustainability management in the automotive sector. In M. Pohl & N. Tolhurst, *Responsible business: How to manage your CSR strategy successfully* (pp. 193–208). Chichester: Wiley.

17. KPMG. (2011). *KPMG international survey of corporate responsibility reporting 2011.*

18. Lacey, P., Cooper, T., Hayward, R., & Neuberger, L. (2010). *A new era of sustainability: UN global compact-Accenture CEO study 2010.* Accenture Institute for High Performance.

19. Economist. (2008). *Doing good: Business and the sustainability challenge.* London: Economist Intelligence Unit.

20. Laasch, O. (2010). Strategic CSR. In W. Visser, D. Matten, M. Pohl, & N. Tolhurst, *The a–z of corporate social responsibility,* 2nd ed. (pp. 378–380). Chichester: Wiley.

21. Savitz, A. W. (2006). *The triple bottom line: How today's best-run companies are achieving economic, social and environmental success—and how you can too.* Chichester: Wiley.

22. Laszlo, C., & Zhexembayeva, N. (2011). *Embedded sustainability: The next big competitive advantage.* Stanford: Stanford University Press.

23. Lacey, P., Cooper, T., Hayward, R., & Neuberger, L. (2010). *A new era of sustainability: UN global compact-Accenture CEO study 2010.* Accenture Institute for High Performance.

24. United Nations. (2012). Retrieved June 8, 2012, from Millennium Development Goals: www.un.org/millenniumgoals/; Worldbank. (2012). *World development indicators.* Retrieved June 8, 2012, from The Worldbank: http://data.worldbank.org/data-catalog/world-development-indicators

25. Transparency International. (2012). Retrieved June 8, 2012, from Transparency International: www.transparency.org/

26. WWF. (2012). *Our living planet.* Retrieved June 8, 2012, from WWF global: http://wwf.panda.org/about_our_earth/all_publications/living_planet_report/

27. Global Footprint Network. (2012). Retrieved June 8, 2012, from Global Footprint Network: Advancing the science of sustainability: www.footprintnetwork.org/en/index.php/GFN/

28. ISO. (2010). *International Standard ISO 26000: Guidance on Social Responsibility.* Geneva: International Organization for Standardization.

29. Martin, R. (2002). The virtue matrix: Calculating the return on corporate responsibility. *Harvard Business Review, 80*(3), 68–75.

30. Friedman, M. (1970, November 14). The only responsibility of business is profit. *New York Times Magazine,* p. 2.

31. Fernández-Feijóo Souto, B. (2009). Crisis and corporate social responsibility: Threat or opportunity? *International Journal of Economic Sciences and Applied Research, 2*(1), 36–50.

32. Karaibrahimoglu, Y. Z. (2010). Corporate social responsibility in times of financial crises. *African Journal of Business Management, 4*(4), 382–389.

33. Corporate Responsibility Magazine. (2010). *Corporate responsibility best practices: Setting the baseline.*

34. Taubken, N., & Leibold, I. (2010). Ten rules for successful CSR communication. In M. Pohl, & N. Tolhurst, *Responsible business: How to manage a CSR strategy successfully.* Chichester: Wiley.

35. Feygina, I., Jost, J. T., & Goldsmith, R. E. (2009). System justification, the denial of global warming, and the possibility of system-sanctioned change. *Personality and Social Psychology Bulletin, 36*(3), 326–338.

36. Morsing, M., & Perrini, F. (2009). CSR in SMEs: Do SMEs matter for the CSR agenda? *Business Ethics: A European Review, 18*(1), 1–6.

37. Ayyagari, M., Beck, T., & Demirguc-Kunt, A. (2007). Small and medium enterprises across the globe. *Small Business Economics, 29,* 415–434.

38. Department of Trade and Industry. (2003). *Engaging SMEs in community and social issues.* London: DTI.

39. Mandl, I. (2005). *CSR and competitiveness: European SMEs good practice.* Vienna: KMU Forschung Austria.

40. Perrini, F. (2006). SMEs and CSR theory: Evidence and implications from an Italian perspective. *Journal of Business Ethics, 67,* 305–316; Perrini, F. (2007). CSR Strategies of SMEs and large firms: Evidence from Italy. *Journal of Business Ethics, 74,* 285–300.

41. Castka, P., Balzarova, M. A., Bamber, C. J., & Sharp, J. M. (2004). How can SMEs effectively implement the CSR agenda? A UK case study perspective. *Corporate Social Responsibility and Environmental Management, 11,* 140–149.

42. Perrini, F. (2007). CSR Strategies of SMEs and large firms: Evidence from Italy. *Journal of Business Ethics, 74,* 285–300.

43. Lacey, P., Cooper, T., Hayward, R., & Neuberger, L. (2010). *A new era of sustainability: UN global compact-Accenture CEO study 2010.* Accenture Institute for High Performance.

44. Kubenka, M., & Myskova, R. (2009). The B2B market: Corporate social responsibility or corporate social responsiveness? *WSEAS Transactions on Business and Economics, 7*(6), 320–330; Vaccaro, V. L. (2009). B2B green marketing and innovation theory for competitive advantage. *Journal of Systems and Information Technology, 11*(4), 315–330.

45. Lacey, P., Cooper, T., Hayward, R., & Neuberger, L. (2010). *A new era of sustainability: UN global compact-Accenture CEO study 2010.* Accenture Institute for High Performance.

46. Visser, W. (2008). Corporate social responsibility in developing countries. In A. Crane, A. McWilliams, D. Matten, J. Moon, & D. Siegel, *The Oxford handbook of corporate social responsibility* (pp. 473–479). Oxford: Oxford University Press.

47. Desta, I. H. (2010). CSR in developing countries. In M. Pohl & N. Tolhurst, *Responsible business: How to manage your CSR strategy successfully* (pp. 265–278). Chichester: Wiley; Raynard, P., & Forstater, M. (2002). *Corporate social responsibility: Implications for small and medium enterprises in developing countries.* Vienna: United Nations Industrial Development Organization.

02

Skills · Controlling · Management · Change Agent · Prime Management · Performance · Competencies · Planning · Efficiency · Sustainability Performance · Ethics · Responsible Business · Effectiveness · Transformation · Goals · Responsible Management · Resources · Leadership · Moral Performance

# MANAGEMENT: BASICS AND PROCESSES

*You will be able to...*

1   ...**understand how traditional management evolves to responsible management.**

2   ...**identify the skills necessary to be a responsible manager.**

3   ...**conduct the traditional management tasks of planning, organizing, leading, and controlling responsibly.**

"Seventy percent of organizations say that sustainability has a permanent place on the management agenda."[1]

The majority of CEOs (88%) consider mind-sets and skills of managers as the most critical condition for creating sustainable companies.[2]

"Forty-nine percent of CEOs cite complexity of implementation across functions as the most significant barrier to implementing an integrated, company-wide approach to sustainability."[3]

Author: Oliver Laasch; Contributors: Aurea Christine Tanaka, Eappen Thiruvattal, Isabel Rimanoczy, Jonas Haertle, Kemi Ogunyemi, Shiv K. Tripathi, Thomas Hügli, Ulpiana Kocollari

# AXA Winterthur in Switzerland: Meet the Responsible Manager

What does a responsible manager do? What are his or her tasks? What skills does the responsible manager need? How does the responsible manager change the company environment? How does the responsible manager plan, organize, lead, and control responsible business performance? Let us ask a responsible manager. Thomas Hügli is the Chief Communication and Corporate Responsibility Officer at AXA Winterthur, the Swiss branch of the multinational insurance company AXA. The Swiss branch earned more than 10 percent of premiums of the AXA Group and is one of the national leaders in AXA in corporate responsibility (CR) topics.

After having been the company's leading communicator for many years, in 2009 Thomas Hügli took on the new responsibility of managing the AXA Winterthur's responsible business performance. He heads the company's CR department, a medium-sized team of responsible management specialists, and implements responsible business topics jointly with the business's assigned managers ("CR network") in departments from operations to procurement to marketing to human resources. Thomas Hügli stresses that his management practice includes all three domains of responsible management: sustainability, responsibility, and ethics. He mentions that majority of his tasks (60%) are related to stakeholder management (responsibility), 30 percent is managing the triple bottom line (sustainability), and approximately 10 percent of his work is related to managing values and moral decision making (ethics). He states that he aims to balance those three domains at a higher level in the future.

Comparing his former job and the new tasks, Thomas realized that the work done by a responsible manager differs greatly from the work in mainstream management. He states that his current job involves much more "selling" of the topic, convincing decision makers of the relevance and crucial importance of the topic. He also engages much more with the topic on the "ground," spending a large amount of time in meetings presenting CR and directing implementation. It is not unusual to find resistance to change. Accordingly, Thomas emphasizes how the competencies needed by a responsible manager must be different from those of a traditional manager. Self-competencies and social competencies, for example, are crucial. For himself and his team, Thomas sees characteristics such as endurance, passion for the topic, assertiveness, leadership, and change competencies as primary assets. Proficiency in specific fields of knowledge, domain competencies and knowledge about how to get things done, and procedural competencies are key to responsible management success. Thomas stresses especially the importance of stakeholder engagement skills in order to challenge senior management and employees constructively, as well as a solid working knowledge of both mainstream business and specialized responsible management topics. In his core team, Thomas works with a diverse crowd, including lawyers, people with responsible management degrees, and people with environmental science degrees. His own academic background is in business and in communication, which he sees as an ideal combination.

AXA Winterthur's responsible management performance is measured primarily through the score of the Dow Jones Sustainability Indexes (DJSI) ranking mechanism. The goal is to achieve a DJSI score of 69 by 2015. The score in 2011 was 59. This indicator is based on forty-six questions, which can be answered on a performance fulfillment level from 1 to 5, with 1 representing the lowest and 5 the highest performance. Planning for responsibility performance at AXA Winterthur means to ensure that the performance in those single questions is increased and to subsequently raise the overall score. Organizing for responsible business performance primarily involves the annual CR week and the coordination between the CR department and mainstream business functions in charge of stakeholder relations. The main leading task for Thomas is his role as chair of the high-level CR steering committee, which meets biannually. The committee involves leaders of many company areas, including the company's CEO. The committee is a powerful leadership tool, as the company's corporate governance structure gives the committee the same importance as, for instance, the risk or pricing committees. In controlling for responsible business peformance, Thomas primarily refers to the yearly self-assessment of how well initiatives have been implemented inside the mainstream business functions and takes corrective actions in case of unsatisfactory results.

The main challenge for the future of Thomas Hügli's job as responsible manager will be to achieve the score of 69 in the DJSI. While first improvements were related mainly to employee engagement, compliance, and policies, his responsible management activity has now reached the stage of maturity "where the going gets tough," as it requires profound and far-reaching changes in the core business activities, including the mainstream business structures and portfolio (products, services), which are the fundamentals of the company.

Source: Hügli, T. (2012, June 6). Responsible management at AXA Winterthur. (O. Laasch, Interviewer).

## 2-1 RESPONSIBLE MANAGEMENT

*"Responsibility for social impacts is a management responsibility—not because it is a social responsibility, but because it is a business responsibility" and "managers must convert society's needs into opportunities for profitable business."*[4]

If we take seriously the above quote of the world's most renowned contemporary management scholar, Peter Drucker, responsible management itself is a pleonasm, an unnecessary accumulation of words not contributing to the overall meaning, such as "black darkness" or "burning fire." Drucker sees responsibility for the social impact of one's management activity as a natural core element of good management which does not need to be specifically mentioned. Paraphrasing Drucker's words, managers must achieve positive social impact as one of their basic responsibilities to their organizations, actively detecting social needs and turning them into business opportunities. Do managers in practice follow this fundamental recommendation? In order to answer this question, we must understand the types of responsibilities potentially fulfilled by managers, and then examine what managers must do to fulfill them. The fundamental questions to be addressed throughout this chapter are: How do traditional management and responsible management differ? and What do managers need to do to rightfully earn the title "responsible manager?"

In this chapter, we first explain the main elements of management theory and illustrate how they need to be interpreted or changed in order to achieve responsible management practice. Central questions are: What does performance, effectiveness, and efficiency mean to a responsible manager? What are the objects to be managed? How does responsible management differ on varying hierarchical levels? Second, we scrutinize the responsible manager on an individual level. What knowledge, skills, and personal attitudes does such a manager need? Third, we revisit the four traditional management functions—planning, organizing, leading, and controlling—and systematically integrate responsible management considerations into each of them. Questions to be answered in this area include: How does one plan and organize one's area of management influence to maximize responsibility performance? How does one integrate responsibility considerations into one's leadership and controlling activities?

## 2-2 MANAGEMENT BASICS AND THE EVOLUTION TO PRIME MANAGEMENT

*"Management like the combustion engine is a mature technology that must now be reinvented for a new age."*[5]

What does **responsible management** for the modern business and society look like? Mainstream management practices have been blamed for many of the world's current ailments, issues, and crises, including the universally important issues of social injustice and environmental destruction. The formalized field of critical management studies has gained considerable momentum, and management has been criticized from a variety of different perspectives.[6] In this chapter, we take a positive

**Responsible management** assumes responsibility for the triple bottom line (sustainability), stakeholder value (responsibility), and moral dilemmas (ethics).

perspective aimed at translating criticism into concrete proposals for change in what management is and does. The underlying belief is that management and its influence on business can move from being a source of problems to being a source of solutions.

Change proposals will be made from the three main domains of sustainability, responsibility, and ethics, which reflect the most powerful streams of thought in current requests for change in management practices. Each of the three domains provides a unique perspective, but the domains also overlap and complement each other in their effects on management. The broad guidance given by those topics is summarized in the following list:

- **Sustainability:** Management activity must lead to a sound, positive triple bottom line that protects, creates, and sustains social, environmental, and economic business value. Management practice must embrace **triple bottom line optimization.**

- **Responsibility:** Management activity must lead to the optimization of overall stakeholder value (SV), instead of the narrow focus on maximizing shareholder value. Management practice must embrace SV **optimization.**

- **Ethics:** Decisions in management must be morally desirable in both process and outcome. Management practice must embrace **ethical decision making** and create **moral excellence.**

Figure 2.1 shows the three elements of business (basics, manager, and process) in which responsible management activities must be incorporated to obtain **prime management.** Figure 2.2 shows how the three domains of responsible management are highly interrelated, complementary, and in some cases overlapping. The numbers 5, 6, and 7 describe the three domains of responsible management: ethics, responsibility, and sustainability. The numbers 2, 3, and 4 illustrate theories representing an overlap between two of the domains. For instance, sustainability ethics, which would fall in number 4, is a hybrid construction between the domains of sustainability and ethics. Number 1 illustrates the perfect situation of responsible

**Figure 2.1  Conceptual Map: Elements of Responsible Management**

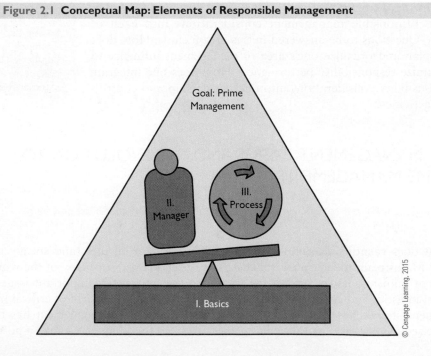

© Cengage Learning, 2015

**Prime management** refers to superior management practice leading to performance that, at the same time, is socially, environmentally, and economically sustainable; optimizes SV; and leads to moral excellence.

Figure 2.2 **Dimensions of Responsible Management**

| Type | # | Exemplary Description |
|---|---|---|
| Responsible | 1 | **Prime:** Sustainable, responsible, ethical |
| Advanced responsible | 2 | **Responsible and ethical:** E.g., following the greatest happiness principle reflected in utilitarian ethics and in stakeholder value |
| | 3 | **Responsible and sustainable:** E.g., stakeholder responsibility as means for the goal of sustainability as indicated by the ISO 26000 |
| | 4 | **Ethical and sustainable:** E.g., following a strict environmental ethics approach that makes environmental sustainability a dominant stakeholder value and part of the broader stakeholder value optimization |
| Emerging responsible | 5 | **Ethics:** Morally excellent |
| | 6 | **Responsibility:** Optimum stakeholder value |
| | 7 | **Sustainability:** Optimum triple bottom line |
| Irresponsible | 8 | **Irresponsible:** Nonsustainable, irresponsible, unethical |

© Cengage Learning, 2015

management where all three domains are satisfied. Responsible management leads to what we might call *prime management*, referring to superior management practice leading to performance that, at the same time, is socially, environmentally, and economically sustainable; optimizes SV; and leads to moral excellence. Number 8 illustrates the opposite situation, irresponsible management, where none of the domains is satisfied.

This integrative model for responsible management can be seen as the highest level in the evolution of responsible business thinking, since it incorporates the three background domains of sustainability, responsibility, and ethics as distinct and equally important bases for **responsible business**. The model is in line with recent developments in theory and practice in which responsible business is seen as being strongly influenced by all three domains. Instead of dividing responsibilities by their economic, legal, ethical, and philanthropic nature,[7] we can divide them into responsibility for the triple bottom line, stakeholder, and moral issues. Only if a business is a responsible business and fulfills all three conditions can it rightfully call itself a **prime business**.

In order to foster an evolution from mainstream management to responsible (prime) management, management practice must integrate sustainability, responsibility, and ethics into its basic elements, processes, and outputs. The next section reexamines the traditional question, What is management? by extending it to ask, What should management be in light of sustainability, responsibility, and ethics?

A **responsible business** assumes responsibility for the triple bottom line, stakeholder value, and moral dilemmas.

**Prime business** refers to a superior type of business that leads to performance that is at the same time socially, environmentally, and economically sustainable; optimizes SV; and displays moral excellence.

## 2-2a What Is Management and How Do We Make It Responsible?

Understanding **management** requires understanding the basic elements of management. Those elements can be grouped in three areas: management inputs, management process, and management output (see Figure 2.3). The main management inputs are the **resources** available for the management process and the **goals** aspired to as outcomes. In the process stage, the two main criteria of evaluation are **effectiveness** (Does management activity contribute to the goals set?) and **efficiency** (Has the contribution been reached with the minimum amount of necessary resources?). Outcomes of the management process are typically called management **performance**. Performance is usually evaluated in the light of the preset goals described in the input stage.

To take the next step toward responsible management, the elements of the management process must be reconfigured to integrate sustainability, responsibility, and ethics. How do they need to change? We will pursue this question in relation to all the elements in the three areas of input, process, and output. The following description provides only a rudimentary and exemplary overview; it will be expanded in the chapters that follow.

**Goals.** Traditionally management goals are centered on the ultimate achievement of increased competitiveness, which leads to above-average profits, which ultimately benefits shareholders. Goals for a sales manager, for instance, might be to increase the number of deals made by his or her team. This rather narrow goal perspective must be broadened in responsible management. **Responsible management goals** have to be aligned with the three dimensions of sustainability, responsibility and ethics. The *responsibility* perspective would apply goals that optimize the value created by management activity for all stakeholders, not just shareholders. For example, the sales manager would need to consider if the product sold is actually good for the customer, the environment, society at large, and all the other stakeholders affected by or affecting the product. From a *sustainability* perspective, a fundamental consideration of corporate goals must be that they are socially, environmentally, and economically sustainable and that

**Management** is the process of working with people and resources to achieve performance effectively, efficiently, and in line with preestablished goals.

**Goals** describe the outcome aspired to in the management process.

**Responsible management goals** should aim at creating value for stakeholders in all three domains of the triple bottom line, and at achieving moral excellence.

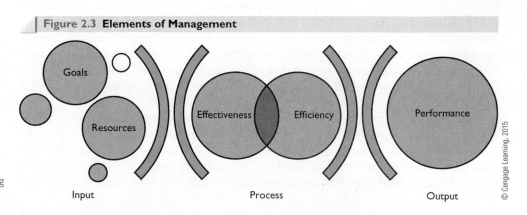

**Figure 2.3 Elements of Management**

Goals · Resources — Input

Effectiveness · Efficiency — Process

Performance — Output

© Cengage Learning, 2015

they are not immoral from an *ethics* perspective. If those points are considered thoroughly and the goals are pursued in a sound management process, an organizational goal becomes a societal goal, and the organization takes its place as an integral contributor to a healthy world community, creating wealth for all stakeholders, and abstaining from morally questionable behaviors.

**Resources.** Mainstream management considers any input for achieving organizational performance a resource. Necessary resources are often classified as technical, social, financial, and human resources. **Responsible management resources** are to be seen through the three perspectives of sustainability, responsibility, and ethics. From a *sustainability* standpoint, resources are understood as the three types of capital—social, environmental, and economic—that need to be sustained or even regenerated in the management process. Responsible management abstains from seeing resources as a mere means for achieving organizational goals. The capital thinking provides them with a broader significance. Capital needs to be sustained and becomes an end in its own right. Responsible managers would withdraw from the excessive use of nonrenewable environmental resources, such as petroleum and other extractive industry product, because using them would mean to reduce, not sustain, this environmental capital. Responsible managers would invest in the education and welfare of the people with whom they work, as this increases the overall social capital. Finally, responsible managers would not engage in financial transactions that put the economic capital of their company at risk to be destroyed rather than sustained. The *responsibility* perspective requires that resources are distributed throughout the management process in a way that optimizes the value created with all stakeholders of the company. A responsible manager of a product development team, for example, would use the human resource creativity of his team to develop the product that yields the highest financial return to owners of the company. He would also consider the value the design creates for customers, how safe and satisfying the production processes will be for employees, and whether the new product will have the potential to include and develop otherwise marginalized suppliers. From an *ethics* standpoint, resource thinking itself is questionable. Consideration of human beings as a mere resource, toiling for the good of an abusive company, has been considered morally questionable. A similar argument applies in regard to the environment, which, from an ethics-of-rights perspective, is often considered to have rights of its own that far exceed the management understanding of it as a mere resource.

**Effectiveness.** Effectiveness must be measured by the achievement of goals set previously. The question is whether the management process contributes to the achievement of the preset goals. If the goals set in the input stage reflect the sustainability, responsibility, and ethics perspectives, then management must merely aim at the highest possible degree of accomplishment of those goals. Nevertheless, management goals are often not cross-checked with responsibility, which means that in many cases, management effectiveness might even be irresponsible. Imagine, for instance, a tobacco company that achieved a successful market entry into an African country where people barely smoked before. No doubt, the effectiveness assessed from the corporate goal-setting perspective is a given. **Responsible management effectiveness** cannot be assessed as positively. The *sustainability* perspective would consider such an outcome of the marketing management process unfavorably, as it destroys the social capital living in the healthy pattern of nonsmoking. From a *responsibility* perspective, this case would be considered by

**Resources** are the input used in the management process to achieve predefined goals.

**Responsible management resources** are social, environmental, and economic capital (triple bottom line), stakeholder inputs, and moral capital.

**Effectiveness** describes the degree to which the management process has contributed to the preestablished managerial goals.

**Responsible management effectiveness** is measured in the amount of triple bottom line value and SV created and the degree of moral excellence achieved.

assessing the overall welfare created by the market access. Responsibility means asking how much welfare is created for company shareholders and the local economy, and how much SV is in turn destroyed through the pulmonary diseases and other detrimental health effects among consumers. From an *ethics* viewpoint—more specifically, an ethics-of-justice perspective—the market entry would be seen as unfair and immoral, based on the fact that the company would be enriching itself at the cost of killing thousands of people through pulmonary diseases.

**Efficiency.** Although effectiveness focuses on the effect of management on the achievement of goals, efficiency scrutinizes the relationship between the resources applied and the achieved output. In mainstream management, a management process is more efficient if it achieves the same or better output with less resource usage. In **responsible management efficiency**, the same basic definition holds true. The *sustainability* perspective aims at sustaining or even renewing social, environmental, and economic capital. Thus, the fewer resources used for a process the better. For instance, the concept of ecoefficiency describes the amount of natural resources, such as water, energy, and raw materials, used to produce a certain product or service. Along the same line, responsible managers might think of social efficiency as an evaluation criterion of their own management processes. How much social welfare is created? Does my team enjoy the work? Are employees growing as human beings in their work, or are they exploited so that they represent lost social capital? From a *responsibility* perspective, efficiency could be defined as SV created (or destroyed) per unit of production. Efficiency from an *ethics* perspective might aim at the lowest amount possible of amoral behavior per unit of product or service. Those alternative interpretations of efficiency provide different options for mainstream management thinking.

**Performance.** The output or performance of a management process may narrowly be interpreted by short-run profit. For a responsible manager, short-run financial performance must be considered only with other criterion to judge the success of the management process. *Sustainability* thinking requires planning in long-run financial performance, including decisions such as selling subprime loans that make short-run money sense, but in the long run may threaten the sustainability of the company or the whole economic system, as demonstrated in the world economic crisis that began in 2007. Performance for a responsible manager is not constrained by economic performance only, but rather is defined as a combination of social, environmental, and economic performances, the triple bottom line. From a *responsibility* perspective, a manager would think in terms of stakeholder performance, the value created for all groups related to the management activities. *Ethics* suggest that the responsible manager would thoroughly scrutinize all facets of the management outcome for potential immoral components. A common prejudice is that **responsible management performance** is harder to measure and evaluate than mainstream management economic performance. Table 2.1 illustrates a basic scheme for the evaluation of performance of responsible management.

## In Practice

### Responsibly Building Capacity for Responsible Performance

In southern Lao PDR, Bolaven Farms is sustainably growing and retailing high-quality coffee while building capacity through a residential training program for local farmers that emphasizes ethical and sustainable production. Resident farmers not only acquire technical training but also receive housing and meals for the whole family, including English classes for the children, a 30 percent contribution to medical bills, and, upon graduation, access to loans that allow them to establish their own farm or become contract farmers. This social enterprise is thus contributing to eradication of poverty, development of sustainable agricultural practices, and biodiversity conservation through organic farming.

Source: ProSPER.Net. (2011). *Integrating sustainability in business school curricula project: Final report.* Bangkok: Asian Institute of Technology.

**Efficiency** describes the proportion between resource input and management output.

**Responsible management efficiency** is measured by the ratios between the triple bottom line capital used and created, the stakeholder input and value created, and the moral issues encountered and moral excellence achieved throughout the management process.

**Performance** is the output of the management process.

**Responsible management performance** is a product of the responsible management effectiveness and efficiency achieved. Responsible management must reassess the criteria applied for evaluating performance as good or bad.

**Table 2.1** Performance Dimensions and Indicators in Responsible Management

| Domain | Performance Domain | Exemplary Indicators |
|---|---|---|
| Sustainability performance | Social, environmental, economic value (performance) (triple bottom line) | Traditional economic performance<br>Social value creation<br>Environmental value creation (e.g., water, $CO_2$, waste, biodiversity) |
| Responsibility performance | SV (performance) | Number of stakeholder complaints<br>Scores in single stakeholder satisfaction surveys (e.g, organizational climate or customer satisfaction surveys) |
| Ethics performance | Moral excellence | Number of ethical failures<br>Percentage of compliance with qualitative indicator lists |

## 2-2b Evolution of Management Thought

In 2009, senior management thinker Gary Hamel brought together a group of thirty-five eminent management specialists, including C-level managers from Google, UBS, and McKinsey, as well as other CEOs and theorists, such as the management gurus Henry Mintzberg and Peter Senge. This eminent team of "renegades," as they called themselves, jointly developed twenty-five recommendations for management of the future. The consensus was that management has to take the next evolutionary step. Interestingly, their first three recommendations all related to ethics, sustainability, and responsibility:

1. Ensure that the work of management serves a **higher purpose.** Management, both in theory and in practice, must orient itself to the achievement of **noble, socially significant goals.**

2. Fully embed the ideas of **community** and **citizenship** in management systems. There is a need for processes and practices that reflect the interdependence of all **stakeholder** groups.

3. Reconstruct management's **philosophical foundations.** To build organizations that are more than merely efficient, we need to draw lessons from such fields as biology, political science, and theology.[8]

If this is the future of management, what is the past? At this point, we will not go into a lengthy discussion of classic management theories. Table 2.2 provides a brief summary that, because of space considerations, is merely a rudimentary overview. Each management school delivers valuable insights for different parts of the management process; interestingly, many ideas of responsible management practices are either rooted in those classic management theories or concerned with rebuking assumptions made by those theories. Therefore, for those who want to be part of the evolution of management, knowing the classics is a must.

As shown in Table 2.2, mainstream management theory can provide many insights for responsible management, both practices to avoid and practices on which to build. Although many of the established management theories include elements of responsible management, in the early twenty-first century, the importance of responsible management has increased exponentially. There is broad consensus among management scholars that responsible management is "here to stay." It is a lasting trend, and time will show whether it is simply a new facet of mainstream management or the next step in an evolution toward a superior management field with superior managers.

**Table 2.2** Mainstream Management Thought and Its Significance for Responsible Management

| Stream of Thought | School | Proponents | Thought | Interpretation and Significance for Responsible Management |
|---|---|---|---|---|
| Science and administration | Administrative learning | Henri Fayol (1841–1925) | The management process consists of the tasks of *planning, organizing, commanding, coordinating,* and *controlling*. Management should be guided by a diverse *set of principles*, from principle 1, the division of work, to principle 14, the team spirit. | Responsible management must explore the integration of sustainability, responsibility, and ethics in each of the management tasks. The fourteen principles of management must be extended to cover responsible management considerations. |
| | Scientific management | Frederick Winslow Taylor (1856–1915) | Management must *analyze* the *efficiency* of workers' tasks through scientific methods and then give workers the right (often monetary) *incentives* to perform more efficiently and increase productivity. | Thinking of employees merely in terms of efficiency and extrinsic functioning may result in abusive management patterns that contradict a SV perspective on employees, which advocates human development through work. |
| | Fordism | Henry Ford (1863–1947) | Management should concentrate on increasing the efficiency of the production through *standardization* of processes and products. | Although standardized and mechanical production processes may lead to ecoefficiency in the usage of natural resources, the value of such work for workers has to be questioned. |
| | Bureaucracy | Max Weber (1864–1920) | The ideal form of organization is the *authority-based bureaucracy*, which is characterized by the subdivision of work into elementary *tasks*, performed by *specialists*, whose positions are organized *hierarchically* and governed through a system of abstract *rules*. Promotion is based on seniority and achievement for the organization. | The rigid structures envisaged by bureaucratic management conflict with the stakeholder view of the firm, where flexibility, multiple perspectives, and a spider-web of relations, responsibilities, and communication channels are imperative. |
| Contingencies and structure | Organizational contingencies | Peter Lawrence; Jay W. Lorsch | Organizations must adapt their structure and management practice to changing environmental conditions, called *contingencies*. | The global issues and crises affecting both general society and organizations are strong contingencies that, according to situational management, require new, responsible forms of organizations. |
| | Contingency model of leadership | Fred E. Fiedler (1922–) | Different situations require different *leadership styles* (measured by leadership perception scores [LPCs]) for outcomes to be effective. Leaders must be matched with the adequate situations, and vice versa. | The organizational transformation in responsible management requires effective leadership, adapted to a varied set of contingencies. |
| | Strategy and structure | Alfred Chandler (1918–2007) | Organizational *structure* must follow the organizational *strategy*. | Responsible management must integrate the triple bottom line, stakeholders, and morality into strategy and, at the same time, develop adequate business structures by which to put those strategies into practice. |

| Stream of Thought | School | Proponents | Thought | Interpretation and Significance for Responsible Management |
|---|---|---|---|---|
| Human relations and behavior | Human relations | Elton Mayo (1880–1949) | Social and psychological processes are more important for employee productivity than monetary incentives. *Human relations* inside groups have to be managed, and an authoritarian leadership style should be replaced with *democratic leadership*. | The human relations approach in work groups can be transferred to broader stakeholder groups related to companies. Stakeholder democracy is the responsible management counterpart to democratic leadership. |
| | Theory X and Theory Y | Douglas McGregor (1906–1964) | The *attitude* managers have toward their employees determines managers' behavior. Managers perceiving employees as inherently lazy (*Theory X*) will use an authoritarian and control-based leadership style. Managers perceiving employees as self-motivated (*Theory Y*) will create a trust-based environment in which employees can fully develop themselves and their tasks. | Theory Y reflects the SV approach of responsible management by focusing on co-creation of employee and organizational value. |
| | Leadership theory | Chester Barnard (1886–1961) | Organizations are *social systems*, and managers inside the system have to balance *employee orientation* with *performance orientation*. | In responsible management, the word *employee* must be replaced with the broader term *stakeholder*, so that a balance is sought between stakeholder orientation and performance orientation thinking. The relationship in responsible management is less antagonistic than in traditional management, as performance is redefined in terms of general stakeholders, rather than only shareholders. |
| | Motivation theory | Frederick Herzberg (1923–2000) | Herzberg explains employee motivation through both *satisfiers* (e.g., professional success, appreciation) and *dissatisfiers* (e.g., work conditions, company reputation). | Responsible management practices must be highly motivating for employees, since those practices reduce dissatisfiers (e.g., bad reputation, poor work conditions) and strengthen satisfiers (e.g., meaningfulness of work, self-fulfillment through work). |
| Mathematics | Management science | Patrick Blackett (1897–1974) | Management science, also called *operations research*, bases managerial decisions on the scientific, mostly statistical analysis and mathematical modeling. | Management science can be a valuable tool for modeling, measuring, and managing the complex social and environmental effects caused by managerial decision making. |
| | Decision theory | Herbert A. Simon (1916–2001) | Right decisions in management are made based on *mathematical models*. | Decision theory requires integration of the triple bottom line, SV, and moral considerations in decision modeling. |

*(Continued)*

**Table 2.2** Mainstream Management Thought and Its Significance for Responsible Management (*Continued*)

| Stream of Thought | School | Proponents | Thought | Interpretation and Significance for Responsible Management |
|---|---|---|---|---|
| Systems, dynamics, and complexity | Evolutionary management and chaos theory | Karl Weick (1936–), Peter Senge (1947–) | Management and organizational structure should be *decentralized* for more *flexibility*, less hierarchy, and less planned, evolutionary development, as this fosters constant learning and the *sense-making* process. | A flexible and evolving management system is likely to adapt more quickly to the changes necessary to implementing responsible management practices. |
| | Systems theory | Norbert Wienter (1894–1964); Hans Ulrich (1919–1997) | Organizations are to be managed as *self-regulating, organizing, complex,* and *interconnected systems* that *interact* with other external systems, such as markets, governments, and society. | Systems-based management is valuable in the implementation of responsible management activities, which aim at a holistic management that interacts with and benefits the various stakeholder systems, as well as the surrounding environment. |
| | Work environments | Kurt Zadek Lewin (1890–1947) | *Environments of work* and managerial action can be classified as authoritarian, democratic, and laissez-faire. | A democratic work environment is likely to deliver the best responsible management results, as it facilitates stakeholder engagement at eye level. |
| | Empirical success research | Peter Drucker (1909–2005) | Good management principles should be derived from *empirical practice* experience. What works in practice should be considered good management. | Responsible management requires the development of good practices, following the principles of sustainability, responsibility, and ethics. |
| Efficiency | Lean management | Taiichi-Ohno (1912–1990) | Lean management aims at the elimination of any resource usage that does not increase *value for customers*. The main goal in the process is to *reduce waste* and *increase quality*, which jointly constitute operational *efficiency*. | Lean management can be applied in responsible management by substituting *stakeholder* for *customer* and focusing on creating SV while saving natural resources in the production process. |
| Strategy | Competitive advantage | Michael Porter (1947–) | Management must find a beneficial *strategic position* that will lead to competitive advantage. This might be based on either unique *resources* (resource-based view) or a unique *market position* (market-based view). | Responsible management can serve to create both unique resources (e.g., loyal and effective employees) and a unique market position (e.g., innovative sustainable products). |

Sources: Barnard, C. I. (1939/1968). *The functions of the executive*. Cambridge: Harvard University Press; Chandler, A. D. (1977). *The visible hand: The managerial revolution in American businesses*. Cambridge: Belknap Press; Fayol, H. (1947). *Administration industrielle et générale: Prévoyance, organisation, commandement, coordination, contrôle*. Paris: Dunod; Fiedler, F. E. (1964). A contingency model of leadership effectiveness. *Advances in Experimental Social Psychology, 1*, 149–190; Herzberg, F. (1987). One more time: How do you motivate employees? *Harvard Business Review, 65*(5), 109–120; Hillier, F. S., & Lieberman, G. J. (1986). *Introduction to operations research*, 4th ed. San Francisco: Holden-Day; Lawrence, P. R., & Lorsch, J. W. (1969). *Organization and environment: Managing differentiation and integration*. Irwin: Homewood; Lewin, K., Lippitt, R., & White, R. (1939). Patterns of aggressive behavior in experimentally created social climates. *Journal of Social Psychology, 10*(2), 271–301; Malik, F., & Probst, G. J. (1982). Evolutionary management. *Cybernetics and Systems: An International Journal, 13*(2), 153–174; March, J. G. (1978). Bounded rationality, ambiguity, and the engineering of choice. *Bell Journal of Economics, 9*(2), 587–608; Mayo, E. (1933). *The human problems of an industrial civilization*. New York: Macmillan Company; McGregor, D. (1960). *The human side of enterprise*. New York: McGraw-Hill; Senge, P. (1990/2010). *The fifth discipline: The art and practice of the learning organization*. New York: Random House; Stürm, J. R. (2005). *The new St. Gallen management model: Basic categories of an approach to integrated management*. New York: Palgrave McMillan; Taylor, F. W. (1911). *Principles of scientific management*. New York: Harper; Weber, M. (1978). *Economy and society*. Berkeley: University of California Press; Weick, K. (1995). *Sensemaking in organizations*. Thousand Oaks: Sage.

## 2-3 THE RESPONSIBLE MANAGER

*"What does it mean to say that 'business' has responsibilities? Only people can have responsibilities."[9]*

Forty-two percent of CEOs mention their personal motivation as the main driver for their company's sustainability initiatives.[10] Powerful high-level managers say they are leading an integral part of their company's activities based on a personal preference to do good. Individuals matter and are critical in responsible management and for the progress toward a better global society.

Those words might sound overly significant. Are we exaggerating the importance and power of management to "do good"? Figure 2.4 illustrates the central role of managers in a broad systemic shift toward sustainability, responsibility, and ethics. As demonstrated by the figure, three broad change mechanisms may well be triggered by a change in a single manager toward truly responsible management. First, managers have the power to change business in their respective spheres of influence, regardless of their hierarchical position. A frontline manager may create a sustainable, responsible, and ethical bubble in managing his or her own team. A top-level manager can do so for the company as a whole. Once the business has shown success in transforming to more responsible ways, its industry peers are likely to follow for competitive reasons, and so might companies from other industries and ultimately the economy as a whole. While the economy is changing, the impact on society of the overall economic system of industries and single companies becomes visible. For instance, consumers are educated through companies and have a broad choice of sustainable and responsible products. Employees who have learned responsible practices in companies might transfer those practices to their individual lives. In developing countries, a waste recycling culture often starts first in companies and is then transferred to civil society. Companies leading in responsible management activities often lobby politicians to foster public policies for sustainability, responsibility, and ethics.

That description of a chain of events is, of course, a highly idealized one. In reality, change is a process that starts at many points. You could also identify consumers or politicians as being the individuals who might trigger a particular change toward a better system. Nevertheless, the chain of beneficial events described here can start with individual managers.

### 2-3a The Role of Managerial Hierarchies

In the last section, we addressed the universal applicability of responsible management on different hierarchical levels inside an organization. Individual managers' areas of influence are typically defined by their hierarchical position. On the lowest hierarchical level, **frontline managers** (operational managers) are directly involved with nonmanagement employees and supervise the company's operations. **Middle managers** (tactical managers) translate the organizational goals and strategy into specific objectives and actions. Middle-level managers usually supervise a team of frontline managers and receive guidance from top-level

Figure 2.4 **A Layered Model of Managerial Influence**

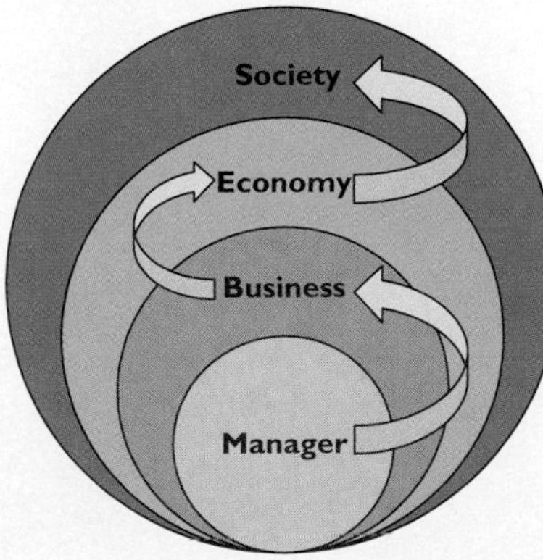

© Cengage Learning, 2015

management. **Top managers** (in the "C-suite") are in charge of defining the organization's normative structure and overall strategy.

On all three levels, two types of responsible managers exist:

- **Mainstream managers** are primarily concerned with the usual economic business operations in the traditional departments, such as marketing, research and development (R&D), and accounting. For mainstream managers to become responsible managers, they need to integrate sustainability, responsibility, and ethics into a long-established job profile.

- **Specialized responsible managers** have an official mandate to focus on sustainability, responsibility, and ethics as their main activity. On the top management level, those jobs might be called chief sustainability officer (CSO), vice president (VP) for responsible business, or chief ethics officer. Specialized middle managers might be called director of sustainable operations or environmental protection officer. Line management positions are titled, for instance, environmental manager or community relation managers.

It is likely that, in the future, those two types of managers will increasingly merge into one amalgam of a management profile that truly integrates responsible management into mainstream management, and vice versa.

As illustrated in Table 2.3, the management tasks typically performed by either type of responsible manager widely differ, depending on each manager's respective hierarchical level. The four main tasks of management—planning, organizing, leading, and controlling—which will be further elaborated in the last section of this chapter, are performed by managers of all levels, but typically take very different forms on different hierarchical levels. For instance, the control task performed

**Table 2.3** Hierarchical Management Levels and Typical Responsible Management Task Descriptions

|  | Top Managers | Middle Managers | Frontline Managers |
|---|---|---|---|
| Plan | Strategically plan a business's transition to becoming a responsible business. (High) | Plan tactical moves to translate the overall responsible business strategy into concrete objectives and actions. (Medium) | Plan how to use the resources available and involve nonmanagement employees in achieving the responsible business objectives provided by middle management. (Low) |
| Organize | Create organizational institutions and responsibilities, and facilitate change processes to become a responsible business. (Medium) | Re-organize frontline management in a way that empowers them to manage responsibly. (High) | Adjust employees' assignments to the necessities of responsible business. (Medium) |
| Lead | Provide the right tone from the top, giving priority to responsible business change. (Medium) | Lead line managers in the implementation of objectives for responsible business. (High) | Lead employees in the day-to-day implementation of responsible business activities. (High) |
| Control | Monitor the responsible business performance of the organization's main areas and decide on corrections in the overall strategy. (Low) | Observe the responsible business performance of frontline managers and decide about tactical moves to improve their performance. (Medium) | Constantly supervise employees' actions and the responsible business output in order to optimize group performance. (High) |

© Cengage Learning, 2015

through a chief sustainability officer (top level) involves monitoring all departments of business based on a bird's eye view. A factory's environment, health, and safety manager (frontline) will fulfill his or her control task by meticulously checking different factory areas and even single employees' contributions to sustainable business performance.

## 2-3b Competencies for Prime Managers

As seen in the previous section, individual responsible managers are influenced externally by conditions governing their activity. Hierarchies are only one example of such conditions; another is organizational culture. Internal competencies are as important as the external conditions of a responsible manager. As responsible management or prime management evolves from traditional management, managers must change internally to a new set of management competencies. A successful prime manager requires a set of attitudes, beliefs, skills, and knowledge that is, in many cases, radically different from the set held by a traditional manager.[11]

**Competencies** can be divided into four main groups (referred to as competence pillars): to *know* (**domain competencies**), to *do* (**methodological competencies**), to *interact* or *live together* (**social competencies**), and to *be* (**self-competencies**).[12] Table 2.4 gives an overview of important competencies in those areas, both those traditionally required for mainstream management and the new competencies to be formed for successful responsible management. Interestingly, those two competence sets are often complementary and contain no major contradictions. For instance, the

**Table 2.4** Examples of Salient Competencies for Prime Managers

| Competence Group | Mainstream Management Competencies | Prime Management Competencies |
|---|---|---|
| Domain (to know) | *Technical* (knowledge of and proficiency in a certain specialized field) | *Responsible management background domains: sustainability* (triple bottom line), *responsibility* (stakeholders), *ethics* (morally right decisions)<br>*Responsible management tools* (for manager's sphere of influence) |
| Procedural (to do) | *Conceptual and diagnostic* (analyzing complex situations and providing an adequate response) | *Systems thinking*<br>*Interdisciplinary work*<br>*Ethical, sustainable, and responsible decision making* |
| Social (to interact) | *Political* (exerting influence)<br>*Communication*<br>*Leadership*<br>*Delegation* | *Stakeholder networking and communication*<br>*Change agency skills* (leadership)<br>*Critical skills* |
| Self (to be) | *Toughness* (endurance of high-workload and high-stress situations)<br>*Efficiency*<br>*Effectiveness*<br>*Loyalty* (to the company) | *Meta-perspective*<br>*Empathy* (for responsibility issues and stakeholders)<br>*Embracing attitude* (toward responsible management practices)<br>*Problem awareness*<br>*Sense of urgency*<br>*Self-perception* (especially about power) |

**Competencies** describe an individual's abilities, which can be subdivided into domain, methodological, social, and self-competencies.

traditionally required domain knowledge that requires proficiency in a certain field, such as marketing or accounting, will be enriched through knowledge of responsible management tools for accounting and marketing. The mainstream management competency of exerting political influence can be translated into change agency skills for more responsible management practices. Only in a few cases do salient mainstream competencies conflict with prime management competencies. For instance, prime management self-competence means to take a meta-perspective—to see oneself, one's job, and one's company from a neutral, external viewpoint. This might easily interfere with the loyalty competence typically required by mainstream management and, in some cases, might cause heightened awareness of the flaws in one's own company.

**Domain competencies.** The primary domain competencies to be acquired to become a responsible manager are related to the three background domains of responsible management: sustainability, ethics, and responsibility. Responsible managers must know about sustainable development and both the global and local social, environmental, and economic issues impeding sustainable development in order to integrate and manage their own triple bottom line. A responsible manager needs to know and understand stakeholders in order to manage for optimization of SV. Only if a responsible manager is able to understand the main streams of moral philosophy will he or she be able to apply those in order to make good ethical decisions and to foster those among employees. Once this background is known, a responsible manager can then translate those three domains for responsible managers into his or her own sphere of influence—to his or her own job, the management function, the company, and the industry.

To apply responsible management in the manager's department, it is necessary to be aware of **responsible management tools** available to each respective function. A marketing manager, for instance, needs to know about social marketing, cause-related marketing, or adapting the traditional marketing mix to the situation of marketing to low-income consumers. A manager working for the accounting department must know about social and environmental accounting methods, sustainability reporting, and sustainability scorecards. Top management must understand the basics of strategic responsibility to use responsible business to differentiate products or to save costs.

**Methodological competencies.** Among the methodological competencies, responsible management requires a stronger focus on systemic and interdisciplinary thinking than does traditional management. Responsible managers must be able to understand the full consequences of their actions in a complex system of interrelations. Systemic thinking enables responsible managers to assess the consequences of their actions through the social, environmental, and economic dimensions and to understand a broad web of stakeholder relationships. Interdisciplinary work is another fundamental competency. Responsible managers are required to merge many disciplines with their management procedures and collaborate with people from many different professions, including philosophers for ethics and biologists and sociologists for sustainability. Often sustainability-related topics require technical know-how and collaboration with engineers.

**Domain competencies** refer to the knowledge that makes one proficient in a certain field.

**Methodological competencies** describe the ability to perform a certain type of task or procedure, either physically or mentally.

## In Practice

### A Need for Awareness and Skill Development in the UAE

A majority of the multinational corporations operating in the United Arab Emirates (UAE) are active in CSR, sustainability, and business ethics. However, this is not the trend among SMEs operating in the country. They tend to limit themselves by practicing whatever is mandatory by law. Awareness of these topics is limited among the SMEs. Government initiatives such as "Dubai Cares" are having great impact on the UAE society. The Center for Responsible Business is a department of the Dubai Chamber that supports businesses in Dubai in practicing CSR, sustainability, and especially employee volunteering. SMEs should cooperate with the business chambers of their emirate and get support and help to implement CSR, sustainability, and business ethics in their organizations.

**Social competencies.** Social skills in responsible management have to be taken to another level. Stakeholder management requires the ability to interrelate, communicate, and co-create with a variety of different stakeholder groups, each of which requires a different type of stakeholder networking strategy. Responsible managers mostly work in companies on the road of development toward becoming a truly responsible business. Therefore, responsible managers often must exert change agency skills, first criticizing nondesirable realities and then actively transforming the organization.

**Self-competencies.** These are as important as social competencies. Especially important for a responsible manager is the ability to take a **meta-perspective**. Assuming a meta-perspective enables a responsible manager to take the stance of an external observer and to neutrally evaluate his or her own behaviors. For a responsible manager to be motivated for bettering social, environmental, and ethical issues, it is crucial to feel **empathy** for those conditions. Responsible managers will want to help a certain stakeholder, to be an ethical person, or to contribute to a specific environmental cause out of a genuine desire to help. Another self-competency is the ability to feel the urgency to make a change and feel powerful enough to contribute.

> **Social competencies** are skills directed at the interaction with others.

## 2-4 THE RESPONSIBLE MANAGEMENT PROCESS

*"The general relevance of **integrating** core managerial **processes and functions** … enabling firms to achieve corporate sustainability and aligning market and non-market forces influencing the firm."*[13]

How does one get the "responsibility" into management? The obvious answer is: Start with what managers do. First, however, the manager must identify the roles, functions, and processes fulfilled by managers. Henry Mintzberg divided **managerial roles** into interpersonal, informational, and decisional ones.[14] Managers interact with others, evaluate and pass on information, and make decisions. To avoid overlaps with coming sections, we will not elaborate on those roles here but instead focus on managerial functions that jointly form the management process.

**Managerial functions** are usually divided into four different types, which as a whole form the **managerial process**. The four functions, as visualized in Figure 2.5, are planning, organizing, controlling, and leading. In former sections, we explained the origin of those functions. Now we will focus on their application in responsible management practices. In order to "responsibilize" the overall management process, each of those four functions must be reinterpreted to evolve around the three domains of responsible management: sustainability, responsibility, and ethics. In the following sections, we will revisit all four functions to illustrate how responsible management transforms each of them.

### 2-4a Planning

What does the **planning** task of a responsible manager look like? Planning is the process of making decisions about goals and activities that will be pursued in the future. Planning tasks can be subdivided into strategic and decisional tasks. Managers need to draft an overall strategy, which is a plan to achieve competitive

> **Self-competencies** are personal characteristics affecting a person's self-perception and management, such as values, attitudes, beliefs, and other psychological conditions.

> The **managerial process** consists of the four functions of management: planning, organizing, leading, and controlling.

> **Planning** is the process of making decisions about goals and activities that will be pursued in the future.

Figure 2.5 **The Responsible Management Process**

advantage. They must also make single decisions and tactical moves in the day-to-day business conduct. The planning process has to consider both the short run and the often-forgotten long-run aspects to become responsible. A later chapter on strategy, Strategy, will extensively cover the strategic aspects of planning, which is why we will focus on the less sophisticated, but highly important, aspect of making single tactical and operational decisions in this chapter.

**Decision making** consists of four main steps: analyzing the situation, generating alternative solutions, evaluating alternative solutions, and selecting the solution to be implemented.[15] Originally, the process also included the final steps of implementation and control, which have been omitted in the following description.

The first step of managerial decision making is the **situational analysis.** A mainstream manager would look mainly at factors that will have potential financial repercussions. How will the decision affect revenue? Are there legal aspects to be considered? How will the decision affect operations? What would my boss want me to do? In **responsible decision making**, while those questions are still important, the responsible manager must make a more complex, multidimensional analysis. From a sustainability point of view, the manager must estimate how the situation affects social, environmental, and economic capital in both the short and long run. The manager must analyze how the complex web of stakeholders relates to the current situation and question the ethical implications of the status quo.

The same considerations are part of the creative process that leads to the **generation of alternative solutions.** Responsible managers must set minimum criteria for eligible solutions. Such minimum criteria may rule out from the beginning any alternative solution that creates an ethically questionable situation, that has the potential to negatively affect a major stakeholder, or that decreases social, environmental, or economic capital. Creativity in the generation of those ideas is crucial. Responsible managers often have to take the role of a change agent. This means that they have to think outside the box of given mainstream business parameters. As a result, alternative solutions might well include potential actions that appear to be unusual or even revolutionary from a traditional business point of view.

The core of the decision-making process is the **evaluation of alternative solutions.** Table 2.5 illustrates a matrix that can be used as a tool for evaluating alternative solutions by considering both the mainstream conditions (solution effectiveness [SE]) and the responsible management conditions that reflect the three background frameworks of responsible management (triple bottom line impact, SV, moral value [MV]). In practice, a responsible manager would use this matrix to assess each alternative solution in terms of how well it fulfills each category on a scale between 0 and 5, with 0 meaning not fulfilled and 5 meaning completely fulfilled (see second column in table). In the SE dimension, an alternative that would solve the problem at hand without any risk of failure would be evaluated as 5, while an alternative that has no potential to solve the problem would be rated 0. The triple bottom line impact (TI) would be evaluated as 0 when environmental, social, and economic capital would be destroyed heavily by the solution, or 5 when all three capitals would be restored. The SV would be evaluated with 0 if main stakeholders would be damaged drastically, or 5 if they would greatly benefit from the solution possibility. The MV of a solution that is completely immoral would be evaluated as 0, while one that has no potential to deliver negative moral consequences would be a 5.

**Decision making** is a process that consists of four steps: analyzing the situation, generating alternative solutions, evaluating alternative solutions, and selecting the solution to be implemented.

**Responsible decision making** bases the judgment on how the decision affects the triple bottom line, stakeholders, and moral value.

The manager would then evaluate how strongly each factor listed in the table should be reflected in the decision to be made (see third column in Table 2.5). The manager defines a weighting factor (wc) between 0 percent and 100 percent for each category. The weighting factors of all categories should add up to 100 percent. If all of them are equally important, each will have an weighting factor of 25 percent. In strict mainstream management, the manager would assign 100 percent to the SE and 0 percent to other categories. The only thing that would count would be solving the organizational problem, no matter what the consequences. Consider a managing director of a nongovernmental organization (NGO), for instance, who has the goal of alleviating AIDS and would orient his or her decision making purely on the SV created for patients with AIDS. This person would probably assign 100 percent of the weighting factor to the indicator for SV. There are many weighting situations, however, that are not so extreme. The concrete scheme depends on organizational goals, culture, personal preferences of the manager, and many other factors

The final stage of the decision-making process is the **final selection of a solution.** In the evaluation process, a manager might follow three main behavior patterns: *maximizing, satisfying,* and *optimizing.* Managers who *maximize* the overall value from the decision would choose the alternative that generates the biggest overall sum. Managers from mainstream management might focus on satisfying by using the first alternative that fulfills a predefined requirement. For example, if the original problem was a manufacturing production method that polluted a nearby river, the manager might pick the first alternative that does not pollute. Responsible managers, however, typically seek decisions to be made in a nexus of competing claims and responsibilities; therefore, the most viable option for a responsible manager probably will be to optimize by choosing the alternative that best satisfies competing claims, even though usually that will involve making compromises and incurring trade-offs between alternatives. It is possible that all alternatives will contradict responsible management, in which case the responsible manager will have to not only make a single decision, but also reexamine the organizational and personal framework under which the decision is to be made. In the most extreme case, a responsible manager might decide to leave the organization or, if having change agent power, to actively effect profound change toward a more responsible infrastructure.

The illustration of the planning process provided in this section is a generalized summary of planning at any level, whether it is personal, departmental, or organizational. Coverage of strategy Strategy, will focus on the organizational level and provide extensive coverage of the tools and cases for planning in responsible business. A chapter on entrepreneurship and the innovation of business models will describe the planning process in the context of seizing an opportunity, envisioning the development of an organization, and conducting the adequate planning to make it work in reality.

**Table 2.5** Responsible Decision-Making Matrix

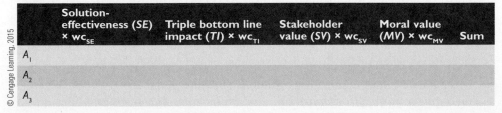

| | Solution-effectiveness (SE) × $wc_{SE}$ | Triple bottom line impact (TI) × $wc_{TI}$ | Stakeholder value (SV) × $wc_{SV}$ | Moral value (MV) × $wc_{MV}$ | Sum |
|---|---|---|---|---|---|
| $A_1$ | | | | | |
| $A_2$ | | | | | |
| $A_3$ | | | | | |

© Cengage Learning, 2015

# On-Site versus Web Meeting: Making Tough Decisions

Imagine you are an assistant to the CEO of a multinational consulting company and you are in charge of organizing the annual budgeting meeting with the local managing directors of the company's four main business regions, USA/Canada, Europe, Latin America, and Australasia. Until this year, those meetings had always been conducted in the corporate headquarters in Paris. With the company's drastically increased revenue from responsible-business consulting, the CEO has decided to also integrate the values of sustainability, responsibility, and ethics into the company's core activities, to make sure the consultancy is "walking the talk." The budget meeting is meant to be a first landmark event for doing so. Your task now is not only to plan a successful meeting, but also to do so under the constraint to optimize triple bottom line, SV, and MV of the meeting decision. The three alternative meeting formats to be considered are:

- $A_1$*"Classic On-Site":* All managing directors travel to the headquarters. *Considerations: Carbon impact of plain travel, advantages of face-to-face meeting experience, not walking the talk of sustainable business (immoral)*

- $A_2$*"On-Site + Carbon Offsetting":* All managing directors travel, but the company pays for carbon offsetting to make the travel carbon neutral. *Considerations: Cost of carbon offsetting*

- $A_3$*"Webmeeting":* The company invests in a sophisticated online-meeting solution and nobody has to travel. *Considerations: Time saved, loss of face-to-face experience, inconvenience for and inexperience of "old-school managers" when using webmeetings, distractions through office environment*

Following your CEO's indications to equally consider all responsible management aspects, you have given the same weighting factor of 0.25 to each of the four condition types. After considering all the above-mentioned aspects, you have come up with Figure 2.6 to describe the situation. Alternative 2, the on-site meeting with carbon offsetting, is your preferred choice, as it combines perfect SE (satisfying the need for an effective meeting) with an improved triple bottom line (much less $CO_2$ emissions, slightly higher cost through offsetting), equal SV, and an increase in MV through "walking the talk" of sustainable business.

**Figure 2.6 Applying the Responsible Decision-Making Matrix**

|  | Solution-effectiveness $(SE) \times wc_{SE}$ | Triple bottom line impact $(TI) \times wc_{TI}$ | Stakeholder value $(SV) \times wc_{SV}$ | Moral value $(MV) \times wc_{MV}$ | Sum |
|---|---|---|---|---|---|
| $A_1$ | $5 \times 0.25$ | $1 \times 0.25$ | $2 \times 0.25$ | $1 \times 0.25$ | 2.25 |
| $A_2$ | $\mathbf{5 \times 0.25}$ | $\mathbf{2 \times 0.25}$ | $\mathbf{2 \times 0.25}$ | $\mathbf{3 \times 0.25}$ | **3.00** |
| $A_3$ | $2 \times 0.25$ | $3 \times 0.25$ | $1 \times 0.25$ | $5 \times 0.25$ | 2.75 |

© Cengage Learning, 2015

## 2-4b Organizing

After planning, the second managerial task is to organize for performance. Later chapters will discuss in depth organization, operations, and supply chain organization. Therefore, the following is a rather brief overview of the managerial organization task that applies to every individual manager.

**Organizing** is the process of building the structure, systems, and culture that are needed to implement a strategy.[16] Managers have the liberty to organize their own area of influence in a manner that best serves performance goals. Such organizational design prominently includes the topics of hierarchies, authority, job positions, and functions. Organizing also includes the task of identifying communication channels, assigning tasks and responsibilities, and establishing accountability. Key considerations when organizing for performance include the following:

**Organizing** is the process of building the structure, systems, and culture needed to implement a strategy.

- **Mechanistic versus organic organization:** *Should I prefer a highly bureaucratic, mechanistic form of organization, with static roles and responsibilities and a* *primary goal of efficiency, or should I organize my area of influence organically, with flexible roles, flat hierarchies, and a high degree of decentralization?* From a responsible management perspective, many arguments speak for an organic organizational form. The single employee's personal and horizontal relationships and responsibilities are at the heart of the organic organizational form. Organic structures enable social interaction necessary for responsible management and also provide an excellent precondition for connection to stakeholders. Also employees in an organic organizational structure experience a higher degree of personal responsibility for making the right sustainable, responsible, and ethical choices. Most importantly, mechanistic organizational structures have too little flexibility in times of change, and responsible management, with its central change agency characteristics, would be hard to implement in a mechanistic organization.[17]

- **Differentiation and integration:** *How can I create enough specialization to get the job done and at the same time reintegrate all the varying contributions into a coherent output?* Management requires identification of functional areas inside a manager's area of influence. Differentiation, similar to Frederick Taylor's division of labor, means everybody takes the part of the work that corresponds best to that person's capabilities. Differentiation leads to specialization of single employees or whole functions. Responsible management, due to its novel character and interdisciplinary nature, often requires expert competencies in a manager's team. Integration then helps to reassemble the specialized contribution into a coherent whole, usually a product, service, or process. A responsible manager's integration task often is very complex, since responsible managers must integrate not only the contributions of a diverse set of employees (or organizational departments) with varying attitudes and skills, but also external stakeholders' contributions, which leads us to the next key consideration.

- **Delegation, collaboration, and decentralization:** *To what degree should I pass responsibilities on to others, and how should collaboration be organized?* Responsible managers, more than mainstream managers, may not always be able to perform tasks themselves. In responsible management delegation, however, unlike mainstream management delegation, the restraining factor is expertise rather than time. Responsible managers must learn not only to delegate to employees, but also to build collaborative, automatically decentralized networks of stakeholder collaborators in order to acquire the necessary expertise.

## 2-4c Leading

A common understanding of **leadership** is the ability to influence others to attain goals. Goals may be understood as the goals of the leader's organization, the goals of the leader's followers, or both.[18] The crucial question here is: Who are the followers? In mainstream leadership thinking, followers are usually understood as subordinate employees. For **responsible leadership**, such thinking has to be broadened to a stakeholder perspective.

Responsible managers must be leaders of a varied group of individuals with different backgrounds. For example, followers of responsible managers may include, to mention only a few: consumers, who must be led to more responsible consumption patterns; politicians, who must be led and lobbied to create public policies for sustainability, responsibility, and morality; and suppliers, who must be lead to transform

**Leadership** is the process of influencing others to attain goals.

**Responsible leadership** is the process of building stakeholder relationships to lead toward the fulfillment of a shared vision and goals.

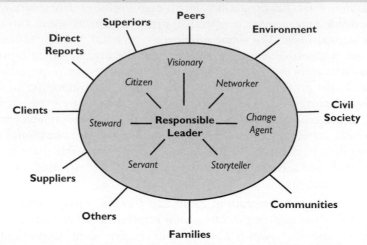

**Figure 2.7 Role Model of Responsible Leadership**

Source: Maak, T., & Pless, N. M. (2006). Responsible leadership in a stakeholder society: A relational perspective. *Journal of Business Ethics*, 66, 99–115; Pless, N. M. (2007). Understanding responsible leadership: Role identity and motivational drivers. *Journal of Business Ethics*, 74, 437–456.

**Power** is the ability to influence others.

their companies to be responsible businesses. Responsible leadership is a multistakeholder process that requires social skills and mental flexibility different from those needed by mainstream managers. Figure 2.7 sums up the various roles of responsible leaders. Those roles range from being a visionary and storyteller to being a servant and steward to stakeholders.[19]

A crucial question for managers who aim at being responsible leaders is: How do I build legitimacy and become accepted as a leader? This question becomes even more important when one considers that in contrast to manager–employee relationships, there is no legal or contractual obligation of subordination between a responsible leader and most stakeholders. Responsible leaders are not assigned but become such leaders through an organic process of authority and relationship building, through the creation of credibility, and through the acquisition of leader legitimacy.[20] A central question is: From where does the responsible leader obtain power to lead such a varied set of stakeholders?

French and Raven[21] divide the sources of **power** into categories that each have significance for responsible leadership:

1. **Legitimate** power (legal or contractual relationship): Responsible leaders may have contractual relationships with employees, suppliers, and even clients that enable them to exert a legal influence favoring the implementation of responsible business activities among followers.

2. **Coercive** power (controlling punishment): Responsible leaders have the possibility to, directly or indirectly, punish followers for irresponsible behavior even in the absence of a contractual basis. A typical example is the withdrawal from collaborations; for instance, a weapons producer might abstain from delivering supplies to a party that is under suspicion of human rights abuses.

3. **Reward** power (controlling rewards): Responsible leaders might be able to reward stakeholders for responsible behavior. For instance, a company lobbying for tighter environmental legislations might support a political party's election campaign with such legislation on the agenda.

4. **Referent** power (appealing personal characteristics): Managers might be considered responsible leaders on the basis of their personal characteristics. For instance, charismatic responsible business pioneers, such as Ann Roderick from The Bodyshop or Dean Anderson from InterfaceFlor, have inspired industry peers to adopt responsible practices.

5. **Expert** power (expertise and knowledge): In a field as novel and complex as responsible business, power through expertise is an important phenomenon. There are few experts yet, and stakeholders may be very inclined to follow those rare managers with extensive knowledge.

Once leadership power has been established, it is time to begin the leadership process as described in Figure 2.8. Responsible leadership is a transformative process of achieving the shared vision of both stakeholder (followers) and the responsible manager (leader). The first step of the leadership process must be to challenge the status quo. Such a challenge could be to critically question and attack existing irresponsible products, structures, and behaviors. Second, the challenge has to be translated into concrete proposals for improvement, eventually summarized in a concrete vision and a single goal. Third, followers must be empowered to act upon that vision and goal. Stakeholders must be given the means, such as basic knowledge, financial resources, and platforms, by which to follow the responsibility vision. Fourth, leaders must model the way by establishing milestones and proposing activities and processes needed to achieve the vision of the stakeholder community. Finally, leaders must ensure, on an operational level, that stakeholders are doing the right things to make the shared vision a reality.

Later chapters will discuss how leadership is seen from a broader, more inclusive perspective than it has been in traditional management and will illustrate how to lead employees and how to exert leadership through effective marketing communication.

**Figure 2.8 The Leadership Process**

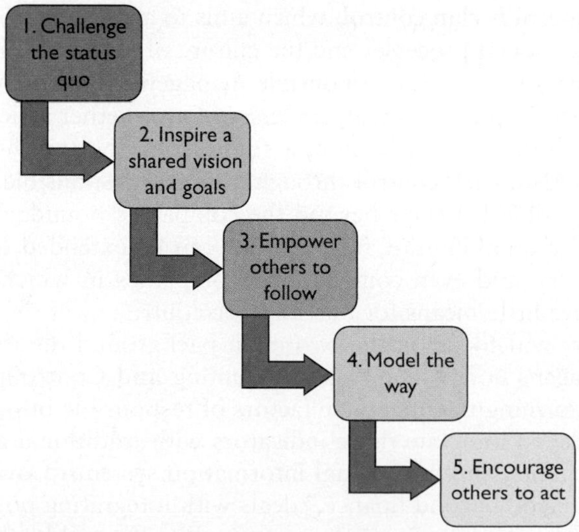

Source: Kouzes, J. M., & Posner, B. Z. (2002). *The Leadership Challenge*. Chichester: Wiley.

**Figure 2.9 The Controlling Process**

Take corrective actions

Define performance standards

Measure performance

Assess performance fulfillment

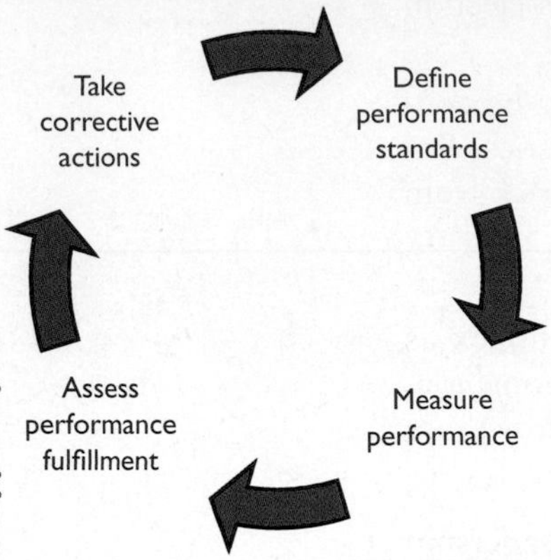

© Cengage Learning, 2015

Leading multistakeholders is an important prerequisite to achieving responsible management goals.

## 2-4d Controlling

The last part of the management process is concerned with ensuring that aspired performance is achieved. When excellent responsible business programs have been terminated, the reason often given has been: "The controller could not see the value." Responsible management and business that cannot be evaluated against a set of predefined performance standards is likely to be unstable, as all business activities are under a constant demand for legitimization.

**Controlling** is more complex in a responsible business than it is in mainstream business, since often responsible managers must translate intangible social, environmental, and ethical performance goals into measurable performance indicators. Figure 2.9 illustrates the controlling process, which begins with the *definition of performance standards*. Those standards are the output of the planning process presented earlier. The *measurement of those performance indicators* is the second step, which directly leads to the third step of *assessing performance* by comparing set performance standards with achieved performance. The final step involves *taking corrective actions* to strengthen the fulfillment of performance indicators, or to begin fulfilling the indicators in the case of complete nonfulfillment. In both cases, performance standards have to be reviewed and redefined. Controlling is an ongoing dynamic process in responsible business and must become a driver for responsible business and management through the incorporation of periodically tightened performance standards, including the use of more sophisticated measurement instruments that will lead to a positive overall development of responsible business performance.

Most companies use **bureaucratic control** systems, which are characterized by strict rules, hierarchies, and policies. There are, however, well-established alternative control mechanisms that can provide viable alternatives for control in a responsible business. One alternative mechanism is **market control,** which involves the creation of internal markets within companies. Business departments may, for instance, function as an internal company and sell their services to other departments. Another alternative mechanism is **clan control,** which aims to achieve performance standard fulfillment through social processes and the culture of an organization.[22] Clan control is a promising approach for responsible management, as managers are dependent on multiple stakeholders for truly understanding whether actions and outcomes are really in line with SV optimization, a sound triple bottom line, and desirable ethical decisions. Also, such control through a shared responsible culture can help to establish responsible behavior beyond the company's boundaries and sphere of influence. Organizational culture, for example, can be extended to, among others, suppliers, customers, and even competitors—companies in which an organization usually would have little means for bureaucratic control.

Later chapters will focus on the two main background disciplines used in the responsible manager's controlling task. Accounting and Controlling will illustrate methods of transforming the intangible factors of responsible business into tangible indicators, in order to integrate those indicators with traditional accounting topics such as reports, audits, and managerial information systems. Coverage of Finance, which could be called "beyond finance," deals with integrating nonfinancial factors into traditional finance tools. Examples are socially responsible investment and the social return on investment.

**Controlling** is the process of assessing and steering business activities and outcomes within a set of predefined goals.

I.   *Responsible management* (i.e., *prime management*) is management that embraces sustainability (triple bottom line), responsibility (SV), and ethics (morally favorable decisions).

II.  The *three domains of responsible management* are: sustainability, responsibility, and ethics.

III. Responsible managers can be at the center of a *virtuous circle of change* in moving toward the achievement of more responsible companies, economies, and societies.

IV.  A responsible manager requires a set of *competencies* (domain, procedural, social, and self-competencies) that is different from the set required in mainstream management.

V.   The responsible or prime management process is based on the traditional four management tasks of *planning, organizing, leading,* and *controlling,* which evolve around sustainability, responsibility, and ethics.

VI.  *Responsible decision making* must assess SV, triple bottom line impact, and the MV created by alternative choices.

VII. Responsible leadership is the process of building stakeholder relationships to lead toward the fulfillment of a shared vision and goals.

## KEY TERMS

*competencies* 37
*controlling* 46
*decision making* 40
*domain competencies* 38
*effectiveness* 29
*efficiency* 30
*goals* 28
*leadership* 43
*management* 28
*managerial process* 39
*methodological
    competencies* 38

*organizing* 42
*performance* 30
*planning* 39
*power* 44
*prime business* 27
*prime management* 26
*resources* 29
*responsible business* 27
*responsible decision
    making* 40
*responsible leadership* 43
*responsible management* 25

*responsible management
    effectiveness* 29
*responsible management
    efficiency* 30
*responsible management
    goals* 28
*responsible management
    performance* 30
*responsible management
    resources* 29
*self-competencies* 39
*social competencies* 39

## EXERCISES

### A. Remember and Understand

A.1. Describe the three domains of responsible management, mention each domain's core concept, and define *prime management*.

A.2. Describe the different layers of managerial influence that can lead toward a more responsible society.

A.3. Explain each type of competency required by a responsible manager: domain, procedural, social, and self-competencies. Provide an example for each type of competency.

A.4. Briefly describe the four main tasks of the management process.

### B. Apply and Experience

B.5. Use the competencies list in Table 2.4 to check whether you are equipped to become a responsible manager. Can you think of helpful competencies for a responsible manager that are not been mentioned in that list?

B.6. Talk to a manager of your choice and ask whether—and if so, how—the topics of SV, triple bottom line, and morally desirable decisions affect that person's work.

B.7. Look up the Global Business Oath for Managers at www.globalbusinessoath.org/businessoath.php. How does this oath relate to the contents of this chapter?

### C. Analyze and Evaluate

C.8. Analyze the answers of the manager you interviewed in Exercise B.6 and evaluate whether you would consider the person a responsible manager.

C.9. Search online for a management decision for which a manager has been publicly criticized. Corporate scandals are interesting for this purpose. Use the responsible decision-making matrix in Table 2.5 to score decision alternatives in that management situation. Then decide what you would have done had you been in that manager's situation.

C.10. Imagine you could rewrite management theory to make it responsible management theory. Which of the classic mainstream management theories summarized in Table 2.2 would you integrate, and which ones would you completely exclude?

### D. Change and Create

D.11. Propose concrete changes that the manager discussed in Exercises B.6 and C.8 could make in order to become a more responsible manager. Refer to the three domains: responsibility, sustainability, and ethics.

D.12. Imagine you want to hire a responsible manager for your organization. Write a one-page job profile, describing the exact tasks to be performed on the job and the skills and experience you would want that person to possess. Imagine you will post this job letter in order to attract interested applicants.

---

Courtesy of Jonas Haertle

Jonas Haertle is Head of the Principles for Responsible Management Education (PRME) Secretariat. The PRME initiative has gathered more than 500 business schools around the world in a joint quest to educate managers for a globally inclusive and sustainable economic system.

**Why does the PRME network focus on management education, and what makes the managerial role special in achieving sustainability, responsibility, and good ethics?**

One of the primary reasons why PRME is focusing on management education is because it has remained quite aloof from transformation of practices. Education is at the crossroads of connecting society, business, and world at large; and therefore, it is one of the most important means by which to create future leaders. Through transformation in curriculum, teaching practices, and research based on the PRME, we envisage a way to create managers who are more sensitive and aware about issues pertaining to sustainability. Unlike in previous times, the role of the manager today is no longer limited to "getting the job done"; rather, the question has become, How can we get the job done in a responsible way?

**What competencies must a responsible manager have?**

Apart from good functional knowledge, responsible managers should:

- Be creative and innovative
- Demonstrate openness to continuous learning
- Be sensitive to all stakeholders of the organization and the organization's environmental impact
- Be well-equipped in cross-cultural understanding

**If we succeed in the education of responsible managers, "change agents for a sustainable and inclusive economic system," how do you think the manager of the future will be different from today's typical manager?**

Henry Mintzberg said that management is a practice that blends a great deal of craft (experience) with a certain amount of art (insight) and some science (analysis). The present industry has always emphasized capabilities of managers that are built through experience. With the emergence of new knowledge, however, today's managers are not only being well trained but are learning to think more creatively as well as more scientifically. These managers are no longer limited to one domain; they blend the knowledge from different streams to create a unique solution. Moreover, these managers will not limit themselves to monotonous work; rather, they participate in dialogues, discussions, and debates. They contribute in more than one standard way; for example, while some may seek to be part-time entrepreneurs, others may collaborate with think thanks and other forms of association. The essence behind all this is to pursue change that is systemic and well aligned with the thoughts and actions of managers.

**If you had one wish for business education, what would it be?**

It would be radical transformation. The PRME signatories have proven that we can deliver cutting-edge research, curriculum innovations, and new pedagogies, so now we have to move into the mode of "action." I would say that management education has to go through a phase of "disruptive innovation" to produce a new paradigm of management education based on the PRME.

## What else would you like to communicate?

We at the PRME initiative and the UN Global Compact believe in collaboration and dialogue and are always open to new ideas. From our side, we will always encourage and appreciate the efforts of management institutions to take the lead in responsible management.

---

## SPECIAL PERSPECTIVE: HOW TO BECOME A BIG BANG BEING?

*Music in the soul can be heard by the Universe.*

*LaoTzu*

The shift from an unsustainable way of living on this planet to a sustainability-focused civilization requires more than changing a few habits or adopting a couple of new business practices. It requires nothing less than the development of a far-reaching sustainability mind-set. Although this mind-set represents a dramatic change from what we have become used to, it also represents the path to a deeper set of values that we all carry but may have lost sight of during the past five or six decades. The challenge contains within it the opportunity of a major leap for humanity: Think of it as the move toward becoming the *Big Bang Being*.

The cosmic Big Bang started the Universe, as singular energy was converted into particles and rapidly expanded. The Big Bang of humanity follows the same pattern and structure. It starts with a personal experience, something that deeply touches our hearts and makes us review our purpose—a fleeting moment of wisdom that whispers into our ears that "something is wrong." Suddenly, we have an opportunity to make a difference. We radiate something that we are not controlling, and it is noticed by others. It spreads and touches others even when we are not in physical proximity to them, just as a single Twitter message can cause a revolution. This connection is a viral spread of "light-ness": It is the collective impulse toward wholeness.

---

## TEN STEPS IN THE JOURNEY TOWARD BECOMING A BIG BANG BEING

### Step One: Get Prepared for the Journey

Are you curious to find out what that journey is about, why it is important, what you need to do, and what impact it promises? Good. The first step, then, is to let go of past expectations, and open your heart to the unexpected. While you are hearing about all that is going wrong on this planet, pay attention to your feelings. Explore the dimension of empathy. Go from your head to your heart. Just be with the feeling.

### Step Two: Know It Is "Against all Odds"

Fine, you really want to *do* something about the problems, and not just witness them. The impulse behind business leaders who champion sustainability initiatives frequently comes from a deep-felt urge to act. Connect with your inner pioneer, your warrior, your strategist, or the child who goes fearlessly through the world. Find that place of courage and creativity, because our task is to go against the mainstream. Are you ready? If so, remember that you

are not alone. Many are now going against the mainstream with you.

### Step Three: Explore Your Thinking

As Einstein put it, the thinking that created the problem in the first place cannot help us find the solution to it. We need to reinvent and redesign what we produce, what resources we use, and how we do it. Let "what if" become your mantra. We start to create a different world when we begin to imagine it. Smile at your negative "self-talk" and shelve it for a while. Explore what is beyond the short term, where there are cycles, patterns, and interconnections. You are on the right path; the signs will confirm it, so stay tuned.

### Step Four: Revisit Your Dimension of Being

Begin to ask yourself: Who am I? What is my purpose? "I wish someone would have asked me those questions before," said Dean Cycon, founder of DeansBeans, an organic, fair trade and kosher coffee bean roaster. We can get so distracted by the hassle of doing that we forget the foundation of what we do: Why am I here? What gives meaning to my life? How fulfilling is my life today?

## Step Five: Speed up the Sustainability Shift

It is not lack of interest that is holding us back; it is the values we cling to that keep us anchored in unsustainability. And we are not even aware that this is happening! Take a moment to reflect on the meaning of economic growth, wealth, comfort, independence, competition, and speed. Can you see their unsustainable side?

## Step Six: Detect the Enablers

The values holding us back and keeping us stuck are not just personal: They are promoted and enabled by features of our contemporary world, such as the power and role of the media, the reliance on "objective" science and almighty technology, and the blanket of globalization that covers our planet. All these modern things can be good, but wait: What if we have been living in a bubble by believing that this is all there is? Does a collective belief in it make an interpretation right?

## Step Seven: Redefine and Reshape

What alternatives to prosperity and growth could you consider incorporating into your life? What unsustainable comfort have you become used to? Our habits become difficult to change when they are symbols of our identity. Now is the time to revisit Step Four.

## Step Eight: Develop Your Whole Brain

Our culture has come to place the highest priority on rational analysis, logic, objectivity, measurable facts, science, and math. These are good left-brain features. Many of our social, economic, and environmental problems, however, seem to originate in the lack of a systemic understanding of right-brain features: the big picture, empathy, compassion, complexity, and ancestral wisdom—not to mention intuition, creativity, and the power of an image or a poem to convey a message. Why do you think we have two brain hemispheres? Try to give equal power to both voices in making decisions. If you were to do so, how would that work, and how would it feel?

## Step Nine: Seize the Opportunity to Evolve

There is a Buddhist saying that difficulties and pain are our teachers. Seize the opportunity to slow down, to ponder what matters most, to sense the interconnectedness of all that is, and how we are a part of Nature, not above or beyond it. If you could be known for a difference you made, what would that be?

## Step Ten: Make Ripples

You have journeyed across your being: noticing feelings; identifying thinking patterns, values, and habits; redefining and seizing the opportunity to evolve. Now what? Interestingly, before you have done anything, you have already begun to make ripples. You are beginning to be a walking statement: a role model of a Big Bang Being. Whatever you decide to do, it will be a move toward the right horizon. Now, just do it.

Source: Rimanoczy, I. (2013). *Big bang being: Developing the sustainability mindset*. Sheffield: Greenleaf Publishing.

## SOURCES

1. BCG. (2012). *Sustainability nears a tipping point*. North Hollywood: MIT Sloan Management Review.
2. Lacey, P., Cooper, T., Hayward, R., & Neuberger, L. (2010). *A new era of sustainability: UN global compact-Acccenture CEO study 2010*. Accenture Institute for High Performance.
3. Lacey, P., Cooper, T., Hayward, R., & Neuberger, L. (2010). *A new era of sustainability: UN global compact-Acccenture CEO study 2010*. Accenture Institute for High Performance.
4. Drucker, P. (2001). *The essential Drucker* (p. 55). New York: Harper Collins.
5. Hamel, G. (2009). Moon shots for management. *Harvard Business Review, 87*(2), 91–98, p. 91.
6. Adler, P. S., Forbes, L. C., & Willmott, H. (2007). Critical management studies. *The Academy of Management Annals, 1*(1), 119–179.
7. Carroll, A. B. (1991, July–August). The pyramid of corporate social responsibility: Toward the moral management of organizational stakeholders. *Business Horizons*, 225–235.
8. Hamel, G. (2009). Moon shots for management. *Harvard Business Review, 87*(2), 91–98.
9. Friedman, M. (1970, November 14). The only responsibility of business is profit. *New York Times Magazine*, p. 2.
10. Lacey, P., Cooper, T., Hayward, R., & Neuberger, L. (2010). *A new era of sustainability: UN global compact-Acccenture CEO study 2010*. Accenture Institute for High Performance.
11. Kakabadse, N. K., Kakabadse, A. P., & Lee-Davies, L. (2009). CSR leaders road-map. *Corporate Governance, 9*(1), 50–57;Lindgreen, A., Swaen, V., Harness, D., & Hoffman, M. (2011). The role of "high potentials" in integrating and implementing corporate social responsibility. *Journal of Business Ethics, 99*(1), 73–91.
12. Delors, J., Mufti, I. A., Amagi, I., Carneiro, R., Chung, F., et al. (1996). Highlights: Learning: The treasure within. *Report to UNESCO of the International Commission on Education for the Twenty-First Century*. Paris: UNESCO Publishing;Erpenbeck, J., & Heyse, V. (2007). *Die Kompetenzbiographie: Wege der Kompetenzentwicklung*. Muenster: Waxmann.

13. Upton, D. M., & Fuller, V. (2003). ITC e-Choupal Initiative. *HBS Premier Case Collection.*
14. Mintzberg, H. (1973). *The nature of managerial work.* New York: Harper & Row.
15. Bateman, T. S., & Snell, S. A. (2011). *Management.* New York: McGraw-Hill.
16. Daniels, J. D., Radebaugh, L. H., & Sullivan, D. P. (2013). *International business: Environments and operations,* 14th ed. (p. 563). Upper Saddle River, NJ: Pearson Education.
17. Lawrence, P. R., & Lorsch, J. W. (1969). *Organization and environment: Managing differentiation and integration.* Irwin: Homewood.
18. Bateman, T. S., & Snell, S. A. (2011). *Management.* New York: McGraw-Hill.
19. Maak, T., & Pless, N. M. (2006). Responsible leadership in a stakeholder society: A relational perspective. *Journal of Business Ethics,* 66, 99–115; Pless, N. M. (2007). Understanding responsible leadership: Role identity and motivational drivers. *Journal of Business Ethics,* 74, 437–456.
20. Maak, T., & Pless, N. M. (2006). Responsible leadership in a stakeholder society: A relational perspective. *Journal of Business Ethics,* 66, 99–115.
21. French, J. R., & Raven, B. H. (1959). The bases of social power. In D. Cartwright, *Studies in social power* (pp. 150–167). Ann Arbor: University of Michigan Press.
22. Ouchi, W. G. (1979). A conceptual framework for the design of organizational control mechanisms. *Management Science,* 25(9), 833–848.

# 03

Impact Footprint
Triple Bottom Line
Population
Social Capital
Overshoot
Sustainability Operating System
Kuznets
WBCSD
Sustainable Living
Rio Summit
Intergenerational Equity
Economic Capital
Poverty
People Planet Profit
Life-Cycle Assessment
Brundtland Report
Environmental Capital

# SUSTAINABILITY: MANAGING FOR THE TRIPLE BOTTOM LINE

*You will be able to...*

1  **...know and understand the history of sustainable development.**

2  **...know the central tools you need to manage business sustainability.**

3  **...manage your business for the triple bottom line.**

4  **...understand the ideal goal of a sustainable business.**

Each of the 7 billion global citizens in 2010 used an average of 1.7 earths.[1]

Global population is excepted to increase to 9 billion people by 2050.[2]

Ninety-three percent of CEOs believe that sustainability issues will be critical to the future success of their business.[3]

Over half of high-level managers (53%) believe that their companies' investment into sustainability will increase between 2012 and 2015; thirty-nine percent expect it to stay at least on the same level.[4]

Author: Oliver Laasch; Contributors: John Elkington, Judith Ruppert

## "Climbing Mount Sustainability": Mission Zero at InterfaceFLOR

InterfaceFLOR manufactures and sells carpet tiles. One might guess that a carpet business is not exactly the easiest possible point of departure for going on the journey to becoming a truly sustainable business. Plastics used in carpet production are usually petroleum based, and the glue often toxic. The production process involves heat, is energy intensive, and creates a high amount of $CO_2$. Nevertheless, in 1994, InterfaceFLOR declared its "Mission Zero," the goal of becoming a truly sustainable business, one that has no negative social, environmental, or economic impact by the year 2020. A sustainable business is one that contributes to sustainable development. The final goal of the company is to become not only a business that does no harm, but also one that has a net positive impact, that is, a restorative business. InterfaceFLOR's late founder Ray Anderson called the mission "climbing mount sustainability"—difficult, but not impossible.

Let's start from the beginning. InterfaceFLOR began to produce carpet tiles in 1973, and in 1994, the company declared that it would follow a "Less Is More" philosophy. The company showed tangible actions from the beginning, reducing average consumption of fiber by 10 percent in just twelve months. In this initial stage, the company implemented the innovative ReEntry® program to recover used carpet tiles from customers and recycle them into new products. Until today, InterfaceFLOR has shown leadership through innovative measures to become a responsible business. Through the "Cool Carpet" program, customers participate in a carbon-offsetting scheme, through which a part of the price paid for carpet is invested into activities such as renewable-energy programs and carbon-neutral initiatives. In production, the company uses smart conveyor belts, the "Intelliveyor," which always stop when there is no product to be moved, something that saves considerable amounts of energy.

However impressive those programs sound, the most important tool that is applied while climbing mount sustainability is the product life-cycle assessment (LCA).

All products of InterfaceFLOR are accompanied by a report stating the complete environmental impact made by the product throughout the three life-cycle stages: production, use, and consumption. The report from InterfaceFLOR, called the Environmental Product Declaration (EPD), reveals detailed information on the environmental impacts made through the product in clear categories such as global warming, ozone, and abiotic depletion (depletion of nonrenewable resources). The assessment includes other details such as the product's water footprint and the degree of impact in the specific life-cycle stage. Such an assessment informs customers and allows the company to track and improve progress.

The results are impressive. The company has reduced waste by 78 percent since 1994, reduced energy usage by 44 percent, diverted 100,000 tons of raw material from landfills, and saved $433 million in waste costs. Those are sound positive environmental and economic indicators, but one uncertainty may keep the company from climbing mount sustainability. There is no information on the social impact of the business. To be a truly sustainable business, the complete triple bottom line of environmental, economic, and social impacts needs to be a neutral or even positive one.

Sources: Bradford Metropolitan District Council. (2012). *Case study: InterfaceFLOR*. Retrieved March 13, 2012, from Bradford Metropolitan District Council: www.bradford.gov.uk/bmdc/the_environment/climate_change/for_businesses/case_study_interfaceFLOR; Ethical performance. (2010). *InterfaceFLOR's new era in sustainability reporting: Full product transparency*. Retrieved March 13, 2012 from Ethical Performance: www.ethicalperformance.com/reports/reportdetail.php?reportid=511; InterfaceFLOR. (2007). *Squarely focused on cool programs for a warm planet*. LaGrange: InterfaceFLOR; InterfaceFLOR. (2011). *Carpet tile: GlasBac, type 6 nylon*. LaGrange: InterfaceFLOR; InterfaceFLOR. (2012a). *Environmental*. Retrieved March 13, 2012, from InterfaceFLOR: www.interfaceflor.com/default.aspx?section=3&sub=4; InterfaceFLOR. (2012b). *History*. Retrieved March 13, 2012, from InterfaceFLOR: www.interfaceflor.com/default.aspx?Section=3&Sub=2; InterfaceFLOR. (2012c). *Giving you the complete picture—InterfaceFLOR's EPDs*. Retrieved March 13, 2012, from InterfaceFLOR: www.interfaceflor.com/default.aspx?Section=2&Sub=3&Ter=3; InterfaceFLOR. (2012d). *Mount sustainability*. LaGrange: InterfaceFLOR.

## 3-1 BUSINESS SUSTAINABILITY: MANAGING FOR THE TRIPLE BOTTOM LINE

*"The triple bottom line (TBL) captures the essence of sustainability by measuring the impact of a business on the world."[5]*

Should a business have as its highest goal to ensure humanity's survival on earth? However philosophical that might sound, this is the exact purpose of managing a company's sustainability performance. As illustrated in Figure 3.1, a business's

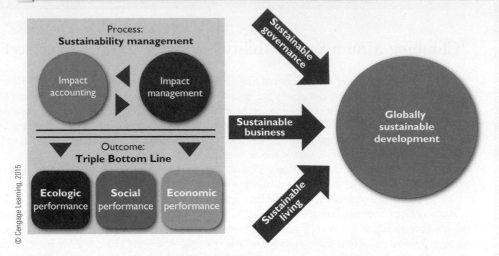

social, environmental, and economic performance, its triple bottom line, is the central element of sustainability management. If such management succeeds, businesses might become sustainable or even restorative, reinforcing the social, environmental, and economic systems of which our planet is made. Sustainable business is the necessary contribution to the sustainable development of the world as a whole and to the survival of humanity on this planet.

This first section of this chapter will provide a systematic overview of factors that have led to today's global unsustainability, describe the status quo, and provide an outlook on future scenarios of sustainable and unsustainable development. The section also presents the historic events that have led to the development of the central theoretical concepts and global institutions involved in setting the stage for sustainable development.

The second section will introduce the most important theoretical concepts needed for analyzing sustainability. This section also will introduce the Brundtland definition of sustainable development and illustrate different approaches to interpreting sustainability. Central topics include the systemic, holistic approach taken by sustainability, the degree of change that is needed to reach sustainability, and whether sustainability can be reached through economic growth. The section will address whether de-growth should be the new paradigm. Finally, the section describes three kinds of capital—social, environmental, and economic—and illustrates how sustainable development can be reached only if societal, governmental, business, and civil sectors reach sectorial sustainability.

The third section of the chapter focuses attention on business sector sustainability and sustainability management as the central instruments to reach such sectorial sustainability. This section places the triple bottom line concept of social, environmental, and economic performance at the center of sustainability management activities. This approach helps us to achieve the goal of a neutral or even positive overall business performance in the three dimensions by applying the meta-tools of footprinting, which provides a sum of a specific impact, such as water usage or jobs creation, and product LCA, which adds up those impacts throughout all stages of a product's production, use, and end-of-useful life. Each tool can be used to calculate elements of the triple bottom line.

## 3-2 ORIGINS OF BUSINESS SUSTAINABILITY

*"In the final analysis I decided to accept the challenge. The challenge of facing the future, and of safeguarding the interest of coming generations. For it was abundantly clear: We need a mandate for change."*[6]

The challenge referred to in the preceding quote is the challenge of sustainable world development, a challenge that seems ever more difficult to reach in the face of the current social, environmental, and economic crises shaking our earth. The person stating the concern about safeguarding the world for coming generations was Gro Harlem Brundtland, chair of the World Commission on Environment and Development (WCED). In 1987, a United Nations (UN) report named after Ms. Brundtland coined the term *sustainable development* and put it on the agenda of politics, business, and private individuals. This historic moment was crucial in triggering a new wave of discussion and sustainable activity, but the Brundtland Report was by no means the beginning of sustainable development. As shown in Table 3.1, even ancient cultures showed interest in sustainability; the table gives a quick overview of the history of the issue from ancient times until now.

### 3-2a Roots: Indigenous Sustainability

Although global unsustainability is a problem that started in the twentieth century, sustainable and unsustainable behaviors have been an issue from the dawn of human civilization. Ancient practices may be a valuable source of inspiration for humanity today as we move toward sustainable global development. The Australian Nhunggabarra aboriginal tribe managed to practice sustainably for thousands of years in an environmentally constrained and fragile ecosystem, a record that is truly sustainable. The sustainability of their society has been attributed to an extensive set of "law stories" that defined their sustainable behaviors through social, economic, and ecological rules.[7] The Polynesian Maori people in New Zealand also had an integrated system of penalties and rewards, called Kaitiakitanga, that ensured social

**Table 3.1** Historic Milestones in the Development of Sustainability

| Milestone | Facts |
|---|---|
| Roots | *Ancient examples:* aboriginal laws for sustainability; Easter Islands and Tikopia<br>*Historic causes:* colonialism, industrial revolutions, green revolution<br>*Ancient warning:* Cree Indian prophecy |
| Theory | *Foreboders:* Malthus's limited growth; Carson's *Silent Spring*; limits of growth by the Club of Rome<br>*Analysis:* ecology; external effects and Coase theorem; Barbier's Venn diagram of sustainable development; pillar model of sustainable development<br>*Solutions:* sustainable development through the Brundtland Report, life-cycle assessment, footprinting |
| Institutionalization | *Pioneering:* Club of Rome<br>*Political:* United Nations conferences; Millennium Development Goals (MDGs); Kyoto Protocol<br>*Business:* World Business Council for Sustainable Development (WBCSD) |
| Status quo and future | *Globe:* humanity's footprint<br>*Issues:* social and environmental challenges<br>*Theory:* four scenarios<br>*Practice:* WBCSD's *Vision 2050* |

© Cengage Learning, 2015

## DIG DEEPER

**Dig for Stories!**

Look up additional information on the ancient stories of sustainable and unsustainable behavior online, and try to find detailed information about **indigenous practices**. Then make a list of the five most important things, demonstrated through the stories, that humanity can do to achieve sustainable world development.

and environmental sustainability. The Kaitiakitanga framework followed the ideal of "guardianship" over a certain territory and social group, which was based on a system of social and environmental resource management, not unlike today's sustainability management activities. The importance of protecting ecosystems and the sustainability of communities progressed to the point where certain endangered species were declared "rahui," or untouchable, and those who violated "rahui" were placed under a death sentence.[8]

Society can also learn about sustainability from the comparison between the two histories of the Easter Islands and the small island of Tikopia. Much like planet earth today, both islands, around 1500 A.D., faced resource depletion and overpopulation, but they took significantly different courses. The inhabitants of the Easter Islands overharvested trees for transport and for building the huge head-shaped statues for which the islands are famous. The consequences included soil and sweet water loss, which resulted in resource wars and an ultimate reduction of the island's population by two thirds. By contrast, when the population of Tikopia Island hit its resource limits, the people reacted in a fundamentally different manner. They substituted "slash-and-burn" practices for sustainable agriculture, and even took such drastic measures as allowing only first-borns to have children and practicing abortion and infanticide. They also killed all the pigs on the island, in spite of the high value those animals had for them, because the pigs had a considerable negative impact on the island's resources.[9] These stories represent just two of many postcolonial sustainability scenarios, all of which may have valuable lessons for us regarding the actual achievement of sustainable development on a global scale.[10]

## 3-2b Historical Beginnings of Unsustainability

In the last section, we saw how sustainable development worked on a local scale in extreme environmental situations on isolated islands with scare resources and, therefore, limited carrying capacity. Before the current global resource scarcity and unsustainability, however, no one really questioned human survival on earth or the fragility of society's existence. Had it not been for a couple of primary developments in human history, human population and lifestyles may never have exceeded the earth's carrying capacity.

The first important development was the age of discovery and colonialism between the fifteenth and eighteenth centuries. This age fueled a general conviction of endless abundance of natural resources and wealth and endless growth. Whenever the resources in a European home country became scarce, other resources from one of the colonies were substituted. Such behavior is still visible today. Multinational corporations "outsource pollution" to developing countries with less environmental legislation and may even outsource complete high-pollution industries.[11]

The second important development was a series of large-scale changes in production methods, which began with the first industrial revolution in the mid-1700s. Manual labor was substituted by machine-based factories that offered new employment opportunities, increased average wages, and improved living conditions. Those changes resulted in an explosion of population in industrialized countries, which positioned population growth on the unsustainable path we see today. As will be illustrated later, the planet cannot sustain the number of people living on it in the long run.

The second industrial revolution began in the mid-1800s, initiated by the usage of petroleum-based, nonrenewable fuels. This revolution was the beginning of today's fossil fuel dependency. Fossil fuel usage is a problem not only because of the pollution caused through burning it, but also because of its nonrenewability. Petroleum, which was formed over many years under high geologic pressures and heat, is now being used up at an alarming speed. As a result, society is using energy beyond what can be harvested on the earth. We are living on "ancient sunlight." This nonrenewable energy source, which is the basis of our economies and the goods used to grow the population even more, cannot be sustained by earth's carrying capacity.[12]

The green revolution may be called the industrial revolution of the agricultural sector. During the 1940s to 1960s, agricultural production experienced geometric increases in productivity through the use of chemical herbicides and pesticides, monoculture, and technology in cultivation. This development had a double impact on world sustainability. First, it reduced food costs, which furthered overconsumption and additional population increase, and second, it caused environmental degradation, most notably water pollution from chemical products and biodiversity loss from both pesticides and extended monoculture.

## 3-2c Theoretical Advances

Theoretical advances in sustainability can be subdivided into predictions pointing to the necessity for sustainable development, analytical frameworks for understanding the characteristics of sustainable development, and frameworks for the development of solutions for sustainable development, which have been summarized in Figure 3.2.

When the English scholar and reverend Thomas Malthus in 1798 published his *Essay on the Principle of Population*, he warned about the dangers of overpopulation. He based his warning on the fact that at this time population was growing at a geometrical rate, while food production grew arithmetically. Malthus predicted famines and suffering for the future point in time, where food supplies could not keep up with growing world population.[13] Malthus's views on society's sustainability can be contrasted with those of two of his contemporaries. The Marquis de Condorcet proposed that population growth will automatically stop through the free will of enlightened individuals and families, who consciously abstain from having many children.[14] This position is close to William Golding's ideal of a self-perfecting individual who would finally counteract unsustainable population growth.[15]

One of the first predictors of the unsustainability of Western lifestyles was the Native American Cree prophecy dated in the 1850s. The prophecy reads as follows: "When the earth is being ravaged and polluted, the forests being destroyed, the birds would fall from the air, the waters would be blackened, the fish being poisoned in the streams, and the trees would no longer be, mankind as we would know it would all but cease to exist."[16] This warning was enforced by more scientifically grounded sources.

## DIG DEEPER

### Forests and Sustainability
Probably one of the earliest theoretical texts on sustainability was published in 1713 by Hans Carl von Carlowitz, who was concerned about the state of German forests. In his book, *Sylvicultura Oeconomica*, he developed a strategy for socially, environmentally, and economically sustainable forestry.

Source: Carlowitz, 1713/2000, as cited in Kloepffer, W. (2008). Life cycle sustainability assessment of products. *International Journal of Life Cycle Assessment, 13*(2), 89–95.

Figure 3.2 **Figureheads and Central Ideas of Sustainability**

**Thomas Malthus (1789)**
World population will "outgrow" the natural resources (food) needed for survival.

**Rachel Carson (1962)**
The "green revolution" will lead to a loss in biodiversity and destruction of ecosystems.

**Marquis De Condorcet (1794)**
Population growth will automatically stop through the free will of enlightened individuals and families.

**Edward Barbier (1987)**
Sustainable development can be subdivided into social, environmental, and economic development.

**Chief Seattle (Aprox. 1850)**
Mankind will cause itself to become extinct through pollution and abuse of natural resources.

**Gro Harlem Brundtland (1987)**
Sustainable development must meet the needs of current generations without compromising future generations needs.

**Ernst Haeckel (1866)**
Ecology is the science of the interdependencies of environmental and social systems.

**John Elkington (1999)**
Businesses must pay attention to a triple bottom line of social, environmental, and economic performance.

**Alfred C. Pigou (1920)**
Economic activity has internal and external costs, so-called social costs.

**William Mc Donough & Michael Braungarth (2002)**
Economic activity must become a closed loop, which elminates waste "from cradle to cradle."

A modern counterpart of the classic warnings about unsustainability is the book *The Limits to Growth* published in 1972 by the Club of Rome, a pioneering sustainability organization founded by a mixed group of diplomats, business-people, and scientists. *The Limits to Growth* warned of an "overshoot," a situation of economic and societal collapse from unsustainable usage of natural resources.[17] The book *Silent Spring* published in 1962 by Rachel Carson has become a classic publication in the field of ecological sustainability. Carson warned of the environmental consequences of the Green Revolution and illustrated the probable loss of biodiversity by the picture of a "silent spring" without any birdsongs or insect sounds.[18]

We will describe in-depth theoretical advances to analyze sustainability and the development of solutions in the second section of this chapter. An early important concept for the analysis of sustainability is *ecology*, a term coined by the biologist Ernst Haeckel in 1866. The field of ecology analyzes the interdependence between the social and environmental spheres.[19] For the analysis of a company's impact on society and environment, the concept of external effects is crucial.

External effects, first conceptualized by Alfred C. Pigou[20] as social costs, describe the social and environmental impacts of economic activities. As mentioned earlier, the term *sustainable development* was coined in 1987 by the Brundtland Commission[21] and triggered a vision of sustainable development resulting from the interaction of social, environmental, and economic factors. Edward Barbier in the same year provided the graphical representation through a Venn diagram of intersecting circles that is the most commonly used visualization of sustainable development.[22] In 2005, the UN World Summit introduced the pillar model of sustainable development with the pillars of "economic development, social development and environmental protection," which were described as interdependent and mutually reinforcing in their contributions to global sustainability.[23]

Several business frameworks for developing solutions toward sustainable development were developed at the end of the twentieth century. An important tool is life-cycle assessment, developed in 1969, which helps to describe social, environmental, and economic impacts of a product along all stages of its life cycle, from production to usage to disposal.[24] The cradle-to-cradle framework calls for a circular economy, without any waste. Leftovers at the end of a product's life cycle become an input for a new production process.[25] The triple bottom line approach is an approach of summing up all social, environmental, and economic (triple) impacts of a business through a triple bottom line, instead of a purely financial single bottom line.[26]

## 3-2d Institutionalization of Sustainability

Global and local institutions related to sustainability have been created in an overwhelming variety, discussion of which exceeds the scope of this chapter. The following institutional developments reflect some of the most influential entities.

Most of the important global sustainability institutions are related to the UN. A starting point of sustainable development was the Conference on the Human Environment (UNCHE) that took place in 1972 in Stockholm, where the UN declared the need for a "common outlook and for common principles to inspire and guide the peoples of the world in the preservation and enhancement of the human environment."[27] This goal led, in 1987, to definition of sustainable development through various smaller steps,[28] which was then translated into concrete action plans at the Rio Earth Summit in 1992. Concrete outcomes were, among others, the *Rio Declaration on Environment and Development*, the global sustainability action plan *Agenda 21*, and the *Convention on Biological Diversity*.[29] Another outcome was the foundation of the Framework Convention on Climate Change (UNFCCC), which was the basis for the climate change action plan of the Kyoto Protocol in 1997.[30] In 2005, the Millennium Development Goals (MDG) were established, which are eight international social and environmental goals for sustainable development centered on combating poverty.[31]

Two other institutional developments not directly related to the UN are important. The foundation of the World Business Council for Sustainable Development (WBCSD) in 1990 marked the beginning of companies' embedded implementation of sustainable management goals and practices into strategy and process. The WBCSD is a CEO-led initiative that aims at scalable and tangible contributions to sustainable development from the business sector.[32] The Global Reporting Initiative (GRI), initiated by the CERES network in 1999, has developed reporting guidelines for sustainability reports. The GRI guidelines are now the world's primary framework for reporting on companies' triple bottom line and have been applied by thousands of businesses.[33]

## 3-2e The Status Quo and the Future

Many social, environmental, and economic issues impede true sustainable world development. But where do societies as a whole stand? Is the situation really that critical?

The status quo is anything but reassuring. The last time we could have stated that humanity is living a sustainable existence on planet earth was in 1975, when we had an overall environmental footprint of one, which meant we were using up exactly as many natural resources as the planet could replenish.[34] In 2010, the human footprint had reached 1.5 times the earth's long-run carrying capacity, which means we are slowly moving toward disaster. As environmental resources, such as water and food, become scarcer, the world population keeps growing. In 2011, when the world population reached 7 billion, common estimates suggested that there will be 9 billion people on the planet in 2050.[35]

What is the outlook for the future? Many scenarios exist. For instance, the famous independent scientist James Lovelock is of the opinion that efforts to reach sustainable development, especially to stop climate change, are in vain. He believes society should prepare to survive the inevitable catastrophe, rather than try to stop it.[36] The WBCSD, with its *Vision 2050*, represents the other extreme view, in which 9 billion people will be able to live sustainably within the planet's resource limits from 2050 on.[37] The WBCSD suggests that the time from 2010 to 2020 could be called the "turbulent teens," a time in which the way to sustainable development becomes clear through much energy, dynamism, and activity in many levels of society. From 2020 to 2050, there will be, according to WBCSD, a transition phase in which a constant change in all parts of society will happen and sustainable development will be reached. Between these two extremes are other future scenarios. The various scenarios can be conceptualized as representing four main possibilities:[38]

- *Scenario 1:* **Society and environment win**—we are in the perfect scenario of sustainable development, in which humanity lives inside the resource limits of a healthy planet.

- *Scenario 2:* **Society wins and environment loses**—developing countries will have reached economic welfare at the cost of the global ecosystem, finally making the situation unsustainable.

- *Scenario 3:* **Society loses and environment wins**—the industrial elite will have reached a stable situation, while poorer countries will have remained economically underdeveloped, will live in poverty, and will have little in the way of an environmental footprint, which will allow richer countries to afford a higher environmental impact without needing to cut back too much on consumption. This situation might be environmentally sustainable, but it is not socially sustainable.

- *Scenario 4:* **Society and environment lose**—development is unsustainable due to a downward spiral of mutually reinforcing social and environmental crises, which finally will lead to the destruction of both society and environment as we know them today.

# 3-3 CONCEPTS OF SUSTAINABILITY

*"Sustainable development is fundamentally about recognizing, understanding and acting on interconnections—above all those between the economy, society and the natural environment. Sustainable development is about seeing the whole picture."*[39]

## 3-3a Defining Sustainability

The term *sustainability* has become a fashionable buzzword in the early 2000s. Unfortunately, the proliferation of a term does not necessarily imply an increase in understanding the meaning of it. Without a doubt, this is the case for terms such as *sustainability* and *sustainable development*. Nevertheless, we must start somewhere; and defining the central terms is a first step.

Fortunately, there is strong agreement on the definition of the term **sustainable development**, thanks to the UN report entitled "Our Common Future," also known as the Bruntland Report, published by the UN WCED. The report states that sustainable development "meets the needs of the present, without compromising the needs of future generations."[40] This simple definition, which has become commonly accepted, implies much more meaning than first meets the eye. It implies what is meant by another central term: intergenerational justice, which means that what we do today must both meet our needs and not interfere with the needs of coming generations. Although this seems to imply that future generations' needs might keep today's generations from living a decent life, the word *needs* is an elusive term. We do not actually know what the needs of future generations will be, so the only thing we can do is to abstain from destroying basic prerequisites for needs fulfillment, which serve as a basis for our offspring. *Needs* also should not be confused with superficial **wants**. We can safely assume that many of the amenities of "modern" society serve superficial wants, instead of profound needs such as food, shelter, and belonging.

A situation is sustainable when it is able to maintain itself, as in the case of sustainable development, where present generations' needs fulfillment should be able to maintain the possibility of needs fulfillment for future generations. **Sustainability** is the degree to which a situation will maintain the three types of capital (social, environmental, and economic). We may also refer to social sustainability, following the question if social capital will be maintained, or to environmental and economic sustainability. It is important to note that sustainability does not refer to conserving an exact situation, but rather the capital necessary to create this situation.

## 3-3b The Three Dimensions of Sustainability

The Brundtland Report on sustainability outlined necessary social, environmental, and economic conditions that are necessary for needs satisfaction of future generations. Central topics included ecosystems, population growth, and industry development.[41] In 1987, Edward Barbier formalized those three dimensions through his famous Venn circle diagram, which describes how social, environmental, and economic dimensions interact to create truly sustainable development (see the first illustration in Figure 3.3).[42]

---

### THINK ETHICS

The social dimension of sustainability is often neglected. Although how well we work and live might not necessarily be crucial for the survival of humanity on earth, it is at the heart of how current and future generations satisfy their needs.

---

**Sustainable development** is a development that meets the needs of the present, without compromising the needs of future generations.

**Sustainability** is the degree to which a situation will maintain the three types of capital (social, environmental, and economic).

Figure 3.3 **Models of the Three Dimensions of Sustainable Development**

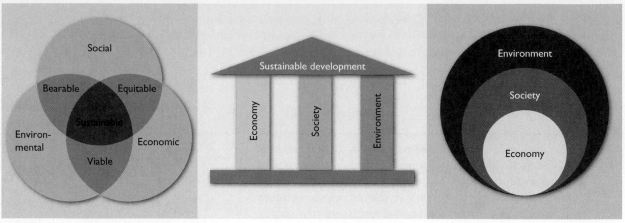

Sources: Barbier, E. (1987). The concept of sustainable economic development. *Environmental Conservation, 14*(2), 101–110; United Nations. (2005). *2005 World Summit outcome* (p. 12). New York: United Nations.

As shown in Figure 3.3, Barbier emphasized that true sustainable development can be reached only if it is based on social, environmental, and economic co-development. If a country focuses mainly on economic and social development (e.g., as China has done), the results might be equitable (i.e., fair between the social and private sectors), but they will be neither bearable nor viable. The missing environmental development and quality, for instance, leads to consequences such as unbearable smog in major cities and the fueling of the economy with nonrenewable resources. In this situation, even economic growth can become not viable anymore if those resources need to be bought at horrendous prices through external trade because internal, nonrenewable resources have been used up completely.

The circle model has been translated into a less complex model of mutually interdependent pillars, all of which are necessary to carry "the roof" of sustainable development (see the second illustration in Figure 3.3). In this model, which was developed at the UN World Summit in 2005,[43] it is crucial to understand exactly how the three pillars interrelate to reach sustainability in any form, whether on a global, business, or even personal level.

The third illustration in Figure 3.3 provides a clue to how economic activity is limited by society's potential to consume and how society's growth is limited by the planet's environmental resource limitations. A deeper analysis of this model can be reached by translating the three dimensions to a capital level. In simple terms, economic development is the increase in quality and quantity of financial capital. Social development implies an increase in the quality and quantity of social capital, and environmental development an increase in environmental capital. Accordingly, sustainable development must be development that increases all three types of capital simultaneously, or at least does not decrease any of them.[44]

It will be helpful to examine more closely what is meant by the term *capital*. The three types of capital, in more detail, are as follows.

→**Social capital** is any qualitative value directly embodied in human beings. Social capital, on the one hand, comprises individual, human capital, including knowledge, skills, values, physical health, and personal well-being. On the other hand, social capital also comprises capital that is collectively created by interaction inside groups of human beings, such as joint values, culture, and collective welfare. Qualitatively, a measure of social capital could be population growth, or the number of people.

→**Environmental capital** (often called natural capital) quantitatively comprises the amount of both renewable and nonrenewable natural resources. Resources here should not be narrowly construed as only material production inputs, but should also encompass nonmaterial services provided by the natural environment, such as recreational value that is realized while enjoying nature, and flower pollination by bees. A qualitative measure of environmental capital avoids the narrow, instrumental output focus and includes the internally valuable characteristics of the biosphere, such as the resilience of ecosystems and the richness of interconnections represented by high biodiversity.

→**Economic capital** is expressed in monetary terms. From a quantitative point of view, it comprises tangible assets (often called human-made capital) such as machines and production facilities, intangible assets such as customer loyalty and brand value, and financial resources, such as cash flows and a certain revenue margin. Economic capital can be attributed to an individual company or to the economic system as a whole. Economic capital, however, might also include qualitative aspects, such as the stability of a company or of the whole economic system.

Those three types of capital form the foundation of the triple bottom line business application of sustainability,[45] which will be illustrated extensively later in this chapter. First, however, the following section interpreting sustainability will focus on different understandings of the three types of capital and of sustainability as a whole.

## 3-3c Interpreting Sustainability

The Brundtland definition of sustainable development, a development that meets the needs of the present without compromising the needs of future generations, and the three types of capital in sustainability have become merged into mainstream business and society. Most companies and institutions accept these concepts. Nevertheless, there is still much discussion on how to interpret sustainability and how to reach sustainable development, and several discussion points are central to understanding sustainability and being able to manage a business sustainably.

The following points represent typical opposing views, or polarized interpretations, that are encountered in discussions of sustainability and sustainable development.[46]

1. The **fragmentation versus holism** polarization[47] asks whether sustainable development can be reached by solving sustainability problems in isolated systems: Economists make the economy sustainable, while sociologists make the society

sustainable and ecologists deal with the natural environment. Such a fragmented (silo) approach contrasts with a holistic approach in which all three dimensions of sustainable development are considered as one joint "mother" system that can be made sustainable only if analyzed and changed holistically.

2. The **substitution versus complementation** polarization asks whether we can actually substitute one type of capital for another. Can environmental capital destroyed through pollution, for example, be replaced with economic capital investment in a new technology that repairs the damage? A good example for substitutionary thinking are the statements by the famous macroeconomist Robert Solow that "goods and services can be substituted one for another" and "sustainability doesn't require that any particular species of owl or any particular species of fish or any particular tract of forest be preserved."[48] The complementary perspective considers social, environmental, and economic systems as a mutually reinforcing network in which all elements are important.

3. The **status quo versus change** polarization asks whether sustainable development is achievable within the existing economic and social structures. Proponents of the status quo sustainability paradigm aim to reach sustainable development through incremental changes in organization and simple increases in efficiency of the existing systems and structures. Change-based sustainability considers the existing systems inept and advocates drastic systemic changes to reach a truly sustainable world development.

4. The **masters versus equals** polarization asks whether human beings should be owners and masters of nature or just an equal in the global ecosystem. The masters perspective is reflected well by the statement, "The world is made for man, not man for the world," attributed to the father of modern science, Francis Bacon. The perspective of humans as an equal in the ecosystem can be best described by the question, Should natural objects, such as animals, forests, and ecosystems, have rights of their own and be treated with responsibility and respect, similar to the way we treat other human beings?[49]

Those opposing views reflect the discourse between a weak and a strong sustainability paradigm (see Figure 3.4).[50] **Weak sustainability** aims at reaching sustainable development "where business controls both the language and practice of sustainable development with its own, usually economic, interests, firmly to the fore."[51] In other words, business strategies and activities meet the needs of the enterprise first. Weak sustainability is reflected by the first term in each of the polarized, opposing views listed above. Thus, weak sustainability in its most extreme form perceives business as mastering nature, aims to achieve sustainability without changing existing systems and structures, considers social and environmental capital as substitutable, and believes that the pursuit of isolated economic, social, and environmental sustainability will result in globally sustainable development.

**Strong sustainability,** by contrast, takes unconventional stances and approaches to criticize, challenge, and change existing beliefs and structures. This approach "advocates that society cannot simply let economic activity result in a continual decline in the quality and functions of the environment and of life in general."[52] Strong sustainability is reflected by the second term in each opposing view listed earlier. Thus, strong sustainability in its most extreme form views humanity as equal

Figure 3.4 **Weak and Strong Sustainability Approaches**

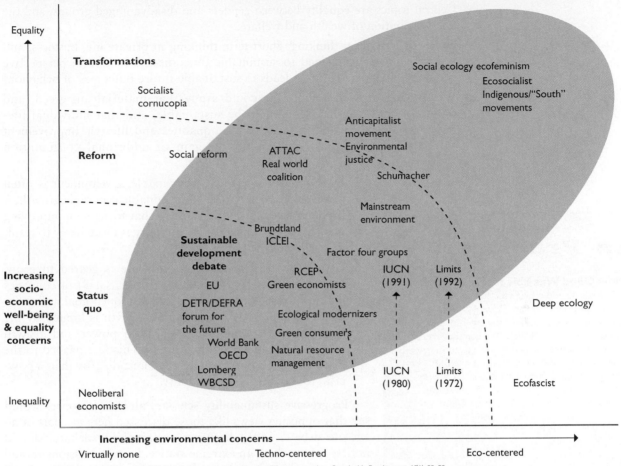

Source: Hopwood, B., Mellor, M., & O'Brien, G. (2005). Sustainable development: Mapping different approaches. *Sustainable Development, 13*(1), 38–52.

living beings in the global ecosystem, promotes disruptive systemic change, considers social and environmental capital as nonsubstitutable, and achieves sustainable development holistically.

The four polarizations (or opposing views) listed previously serve to help us understand basic attitudes (weak or strong) toward sustainability. In addition to those polarizations, it is important to understand the practical considerations central to achieving sustainability. The following six considerations are summaries of important lines of thought in this regard.

1. **Process or outcome:** Sustainability in common usage can be considered both the process of becoming sustainable and the aspired end-state of being sustainable. Likewise, sustainable development can describe a development that leads to a sustainable situation or the final outcome itself.[53]

2. **Intergenerational or intragenerational justice:** Intergenerational justice is best described by the Brundtland definition of sustainable development: a fair situation where both current and future generations live a decent life. Critics have said for a development process to be truly sustainable, there must be intragenerational (i.e., among the people of the same generation) justice or fairness. The term

*equitable development* picks up on this social development component of sustainable development, which aims at fair development inside the same generation. Central topics are equality between genders and disadvantaged groups, and the fair distribution of wealth and welfare.[54]

3. **Short- or long-term thinking:** Short-term thinking in private life, business, and political life may not lead to sustainable outcomes. A long-term perspective should be adapted, as it best leads to sustainable future outcomes of behavior.

4. **Well-having or well-being:** One could argue that materialism, greed, and the quest for "well-having" cannot be sustainable, and that individual lifestyles should be driven by their intrinsic qualities and lifestyle improvement rather than by a quest for quantitative gain of additional consumption opportunities.[55]

5. **Development or growth:** Sustainable development is often misunderstood narrowly as sustainable economic growth. A broader development perspective that focuses on improving quality of life instead of just quantity is more likely to result in sustainable development.[56]

6. **Growth or de-growth:** Economic life is geared to grow. Growth in the gross domestic product (GDP) of countries and in business revenue is an unquestioned goal and paradigm. Clearly, however, economic growth is limited by the boundaries of society's consumption power and growth and by the planet's resource limits. This fact has led to the discussion on how to achieve economic de-growth as a powerful tool to reach sustainability.[57]

Progressive sustainability scholars and practitioners would say that opposing views like those discussed here are part of an age-old debate. Today, however, sustainability debates should not be about taking an extreme stance. Such discussions should be about finding a synthesis that benefits society and environment while guaranteeing economic sustainability of business, industry, and the global economy.

## 3-4 ECONOMIC DEVELOPMENT VERSUS SUSTAINABLE DEVELOPMENT

An important factor that prevents reaching global sustainability is the constant growth of world population and the effect of economic development on the environmental footprint of underdeveloped countries. Most developed countries have a fertility rate close to or below the rate of 2.0 (two children per woman) (e.g., Germany, 1.41; United States, 2.06; Singapore, 0.78), which means that the population of those countries is decreasing. Most of the economically least-developed countries have a fertility rate far beyond the replacement rate of 2.0 (e.g., Cambodia, 2.78; Afghanistan, 5.64; Niger, 7.52; Honduras, 3.01).[58] If we take the fertility-reducing effects of socioeconomic development as a given, we can assume that to reduce stress on global resources, we would "only" need to bring social and economic development to all developing countries: Their fertility rates would drop, humanity's environmental impact would drop, and the world population would shrink itself to a sustainable level. There are, however, several problems with this assumption, which will be illustrated in the following text.

The Kuznets curve is named after the economist Simon Kuznets, who revolutionized the understanding of relationship between economic development and wealth inequalities. The Kuznets curve helps us to understand the effect of an aspired future economic development of poor countries and sustainability. The curve evaluates the impact economic development has on the two crucial components of sustainable development, environmental degradation[59] and the degree to which wealth is equally distributed between the rich and the poor.[60] Figure 3.5 suggests that economic development affects wealth inequality and environmental degradation in an inverted U-shaped pattern. Economic development in economically underdeveloped countries creates an increase in income inequality, increased differences between rich and poor people, and additional environmental degradation through the pollution created by the increased economic activity. The sustainability threshold marks the level of inequality and pollution that is unsustainable in the long run. Thus, the parts of the Kuznets curve ($K_1$) that are located above this sustainability threshold are unsustainable: Pollution exceeds the earth's carrying capacity, and inequality increases above the socially bearable level.

Let us assume that typical countries first focus on economic development before focusing on social and environmental development. Thus, at the peak of economic development efforts, we assume that such countries would begin to focus on reducing environmental impact and increasing social equality. Countries in different stages of this development path can be divided into five categories.

1. **Economically underdeveloped countries** have little inequality, as most people are homogenously poor. Because of low levels of consumption and economic activity, the country's environmental impact is within the planetary resource limits. Countries such as Afghanistan and Niger represent countries at this stage.

2. **Economically developing countries** increase inequality, as lucrative entrepreneurial opportunities of economic development initially increase the wealth of only a minority of society. The environmental impact of the country begins to

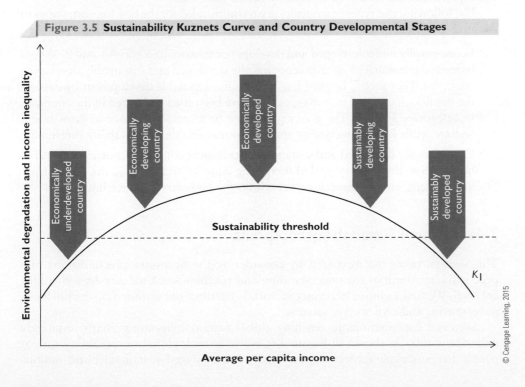

**Figure 3.5 Sustainability Kuznets Curve and Country Developmental Stages**

© Cengage Learning, 2015

exceed the planetary resource limits because of the higher exploitation of the country's natural capital and lower ecoefficient production methods. Prominent examples of this type of country are Thailand, Mexico, and Brazil.

3. **Economically developed countries** decrease income inequality but start to create a major middle-class society. This group shares the social benefits of economic development through equitable wages and employment schemes. Negative environmental impact, however, decreases because of more ecoefficient production schemes. Good examples of countries at this stage are South Korea and, on a more advanced level, the United States.

4. **Sustainably developing countries** have reached high equality through developing a solid middle class and reducing the country's footprint by mainstreaming sustainable production and consumption patterns. Good examples here are Japan, Germany, and the United Kingdom.

5. **Sustainably developed countries** are characterized by an almost equal distribution of wealth at a socially acceptable level and a global environmental footprint that is within the planetary resource threshold, along with an advanced standard of living. Such countries exist only in the future.

There are two main hurdles in reaching sustainable development. First, the vast majority of the world population lives in countries that are either underdeveloped or developing. If we believe in the Kuznets curve, those countries will become much more unsustainable before they start to reduce their negative social and environmental impact. The crucial question is: Can the planetary system resist this increase in environmental and social stress? If not, we are moving toward a global showdown of crises. Second, none of the developed countries has reached the level of a sustainably developed country, which would be necessary for globally sustainable development. Will developed countries be able to make the transition toward a truly sustainable situation? Fortunately, a large group of specialists agree that the social and environmental Kuznets curves can be altered by public policies.[61]

The following two types of strategies are recommended for the first four categories of countries in order for them to move toward becoming a sustainably developed country.

1. **Economically underdeveloped and developing countries** (categories 1 and 2) should harness the learning of already economically developed and sustainably developing countries. They should become fast learners in sustainable development by deploying methodologies and technologies that have been tried and tested in the countries in categories 3 and 4. The policy goal must be to achieve economic growth and welfare while keeping inequality and pollution inside the sustainability threshold.

2. **Economically developed and sustainably developing countries** (categories 3 and 4) must follow the primary goal of increasing equality and bringing their industries' and citizens' environmental impact within the planetary resource limits.

## 3-4a Sectorial Sustainability Footprints

This section takes the next step by considering the necessary preconditions and practical contributions for understanding and reaching sustainability on a theoretical level. We first examine necessary sectorial contributions required by the business, government, and civil society sectors.

Sectorial contributions to reaching global sustainability are perhaps intuitively understandable. As shown in Figure 3.6, we will reach global sustainability only if people live sustainable lifestyles, businesses are managed sustainably, and nations

## Figure 3.6 Sectorial Contributions to Sustainability

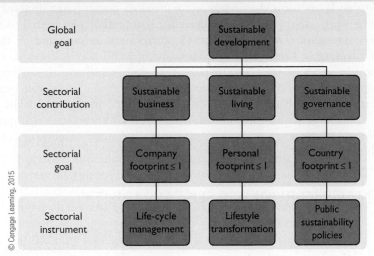

© Cengage Learning, 2015

| Global goal | Sustainable development |
| Sectorial contribution | Sustainable business / Sustainable living / Sustainable governance |
| Sectorial goal | Company footprint ≤ 1 / Personal footprint ≤ 1 / Country footprint ≤ 1 |
| Sectorial instrument | Life-cycle management / Lifestyle transformation / Public sustainability policies |

are governed sustainably. If only one level does not make a commitment to sustainable development, global sustainability will be impossible.[62]

But what commitment is needed to become sustainable? The **footprinting** methodology provides a clear answer: Every "entity," including people, organizations, and states, should not use up more environmental resources than the planet can reproduce. The footprinting methodology can establish single footprints for specific environmental impacts, such as a water footprint (e.g., water usage per product) or a $CO_2$ footprint (e.g., $CO_2$ emissions per employee). This methodology can be used to evaluate social and economic, as well as environmental, dimensions. A company can use footprinting, for instance, to measure community impact (e.g., volunteering hours per employee) and economic return (e.g., revenue per dollar spent).

A specific type of footprint measures the relationship between the entity's resource usage and planetary resource availability. If an individual's or a company's footprint corresponds to the planet's resource replenishing capacity, also called biocapacity, it is expressed with the number 1, meaning that exactly "one planet is used,"[63] and the situation is **neutrally sustainable**. If the footprint is smaller than 1, fewer resources are being used up than are being replenished; hence, the situation is **restoratively sustainable**, or just restorative. If more natural capital is used up than that which the biosphere can replenish, the footprint is greater than 1, and the situation is **unsustainable**. Accordingly, each entity must achieve a footprint of 1 or lower to reach a sustainable situation in any of the three sectors (i.e., business, government, or civil society).

Such a sustainable situation is far from reality. An average global citizen in 2007 had an average footprint of 1.5, which is highly unsustainable.[64] This tendency is mirrored by national footprints. Most developed countries by far exceed the biocapacity of their national territories, and many are even worsening the situation by further lowering their biocapacities through environmental depletion and the increasing impacts of growing consumption.[65] The footprint of the business sector is less well documented, but the general consensus is that truly sustainable businesses still exist only in utopia.

A **footprint** sums up one or several types of environmental, social, or economic impacts for one predefined entity.

A situation in which resource usage exceeds the global resource reproduction rate is **unsustainable**. When both correspond exactly, the situation is **neutrally sustainable**. When fewer resources are used up than are reproduced, the situation is termed **restorative** or **restoratively sustainable**.

## In Practice

### Modeling Sustainable Systems

Lynedoch EcoVillage in South Africa is a small-scale role model for the integration of sustainable living, governance, and business. The village comprises twenty-five families, a primary school, organic gardening and waste treatment facilities, and the Sustainability Institute. It is almost self-sufficient in food, waste, and energy usage. As a concrete example, the village's "swop shop" combines social and environmental sustainability, as children from low-income families can swap recyclable waste they have collected for points, which they can in turn exchange for necessary goods such as school books, shoes, and toothpaste.

Source: Cain, J. (2010). *Lynedoch EcoVillage: A journey towards sustainable living*. Retrieved April 1, 2012, from YouTube: www.youtube.com/watch?v=OFrZXe_MTT4; Day, M. (2009). *The Swop Shop kids*, 3-minute cut. Retrieved April 1, 2012, from Vimeo: http://vimeo.com/7859730; Sustainability Institute. (2005). *Lynedoch EcoVillage development*. Retrieved April 1, 2012, from The Sustainability Institute: www.sustainabilityinstitute.net/lynedoch-ecovillage/detailed-story

The crucial question that needs to be answered in order to change this unsatisfying situation is: What tools does each sector need to become sustainable? For the governmental sector, shaping public policies for sustainability is crucial to reaching sustainable governance. The private sector's efforts must be centered on the development of sustainable lifestyles (sustainable living); and the business sector must manage the life cycles of their products so that the overall social, environmental, and economic impact becomes either neutral or restorative (sustainable business).

The first two sections of this chapter have provided profound insight into the background, theory, and analysis of sustainability. This knowledge is important as we move into a closer examination of managing for sustainability in companies, which is the topic of the last two sections of this chapter.

## 3-5 MANAGING BUSINESS SUSTAINABILITY

*"We strive to do business in a more enlightened way, where we take responsibility for the impact of our business on society and the environment, aiming to move these impacts from negative to neutral or (better still) positive. It's part of our quest to become a truly sustainable business where we have a net positive effect on the wonderful world around us."*[66]

The sustainability mission of the British fruit smoothie company, Innocent, displays the very essence of what **sustainability management** in a business means. The company gives the perfect definition of a **sustainable business**, one that that has a *"net positive impact."* Innocent also defines the necessary measurement tool, the **triple bottom line**, as *"business, society and environment."* In order to measure the triple bottom line, sustainability management has to consider all three **impacts** made or, as Innocent puts it, to *"take responsibility for the impact of our business."*

Figure 3.7 illustrates the necessary steps to become a sustainable business. Companies must measure and manage all impacts to create a neutral to positive triple bottom line of social, environmental, and economic business impacts.

### 3-5a The Goal: A Neutral to Positive Triple Bottom Line

The triple bottom line (often abbreviated as TBL or 3BL[67]) of social, environmental, and economic performance is also paraphrased through the three Ps of sustainability: *people, planet,* and *profit*. The triple bottom line is the keystone for any sustainability management activity.[68] When companies measure the triple impact, how exactly will they know if their business has become sustainable? The following list links the five types of unsustainable, sustainable, and restorative businesses with three different triple bottom line results—negative, neutral, and positive triple bottom line impacts.[69]

1. A **below-average unsustainable business** exerts a net *negative triple bottom line* impact on economy, society, and environment that is below the impacts of peer businesses.

2. An **average unsustainable business** exerts a net *negative triple bottom line* impact on economy, society, and environment that corresponds to the impact of a majority of its industry peers.

---

**Sustainability management** is the process of managing a business and every single one of its activities in a way that makes it reach a neutral or positive triple bottom line.

A **sustainable business** is one that has reached a neutral or even positive triple bottom line and sustains social, environmental, and economic capital in the long run.

The **triple bottom line** is the social, environmental, and economic performance of an organizationor single activities. It is calculated by summing up all impacts.

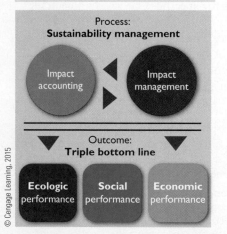

**Figure 3.7 Process and Outcome of Sustainability Management**

Process:
**Sustainability management**

Impact accounting

Impact management

Outcome:
**Triple bottom line**

**Ecologic** performance

**Social** performance

**Economic** performance

© Cengage Learning, 2015

---

3. A **sustainable business** exerts a small net *negative triple bottom line* impact that does not exceed the planetary system's restorative capacity.

4. A **neutral impact business** exerts a net *neutral triple bottom line* impact on economy, society, and environment.

5. A **restorative business** exerts a net *positive triple bottom line* impact, which means it replenishes at least one type of capital while not depleting any of the others.

Does this mean that, for instance, a business that is economically highly profitable, socially neutral, and only "a little bad" for the environment is a restorative business? We say it is not restorative. To be truly sustainable or even restorative, the business must be sustainable in each of the three dimensions. As an example, imagine a business that is good to all its stakeholders and has reached a situation where its environmental impact is neutral. This business is socially restorative and environmentally sustainable. Further imagine that, unfortunately, this business's extensive philanthropic activities affected its economic bottom line negatively and it went bankrupt. That means the business was not economically sustainable—making it overall an unsustainable business. This same analysis holds in many scenarios and leads us to the main meta-task of sustainability: managing the business to balance and sustain all three types of capital.[70]

When a business does not sustain one type of capital, this failure threatens the overall sustainability of management activities as well as the overall business. Not sustaining social capital, for example, may cause a situation in which social groups start to actively oppose the business. This would be the case when labor union protests are triggered by exploitative (i.e., not socially sustaining) company behavior. The lack of balance among the three capitals also causes problems because of mutual interdependence. *Balancing* here refers to creating a mutually reinforcing co-development of social, environmental, and economic capital. The final goal is to create what John Elkington[71] calls a triple win, or win-win-win, situation for business, society, and the environment.

In this section, we examine closely how to manage a business and each one of its activities to create a positive or even restorative triple bottom line. To do so, the sustainability manager needs to work with the elementary unit of triple bottom line management: the impact. Sustainability management in practice is about accounting and managing single positive or negative social, environmental, and economic impacts of a business. In sum, each should add up to a neutral or positive triple bottom line. The next two sections, Process 1 and Process 2, propose tools for impact accounting and provide guidance on impact management for the good of society, environment, and the economy.

An **impact** is a negative or positive value created through business activity. Impacts may be categorized as social, environmental, or economic.

### In Practice

**Sustainability Progress or Regress at Apple?**

In 2011, Apple began to provide a detailed life-cycle report, accounting for the environmental impacts caused by its products in sales. This was an important step toward impact transparency. The Spanish edition of *The Economist* compared the impacts of the iPad2 and its new version, the iPad3, and presented the results: "The new iPad3 increases its environmental impact by 38 percent." Social sustainability also may be challenged. Over time, Apple was forced to admit to problems, including suicides, at the factories of its main production subcontractor, Foxconn. In the economic dimension, however, the iPad3 is expected to be a commercial success.

Sources: Apple. (2011). *iPad 2: Environmental report*; Apple. (2012). *Product Environmental reports*. Retrieved April 1, 2012, from Apple and the Environment: www.apple.com/environment/reports/; Economista España. (2012). *El nuevo ipad3 incrementa en un 38 por ciento su impacto medioambiental*. Retrieved April 1, 2012, from El Economista España: http://ecodiario.eleconomista.es/empresas-finanzas/noticias/3806203/03/12/rsc el nuevo ipad3 incrementa-en-un-38-por-ciento-su-impacto-medioambiental.html; Vascellaro, J. E. (2012). *Audit faults Apple supplier: Outside audit finds health, safety violations at Foxconn*. Retrieved April 1, 2012, from Wall Street Journal Technology: http://online.wsj.com/article/SB10001424052702303404704577311943943416560.html

## 3-5b Process 1: Impact Accounting

The triple bottom line has been criticized as a mere "article of faith" and accused of being "vague, confused and often contradictory."[72] Even accounting for the single, economic bottom line can be difficult and has led to a fair amount of business scandals. Accounting for the three interconnected bottom lines is a highly complex task.

### DIG DEEPER

**The Life Cycle of the Global Economy**

The movie clip "The Story of Stuff," which is available online at www.storyofstuff.com, illustrates a high-speed, LCA of the global economy in 21 minutes.

Source: The story of stuff project. (2007). *The story of stuff*. Retrieved April 1, 2012 from The Story of Stuff Project: www.storyofstuff.org/movies-all/

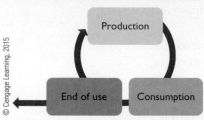

**Figure 3.8 The Product Life-Cycle Model**

© Cengage Learning, 2015

## DIG DEEPER

### Go Life-Cycling!

Think about one product that you use frequently and try to identify one social, environmental, and economic impact per life-cycle stage. If you cannot do this without resources, do an online search to determine the product's production process, consumption, and the end-of-life impacts.

In the following text, we examine appropriate tools that can be used to assess the triple bottom line. These tools make social and environmental impacts manageable. We also provide an overview of social and environmental indicators and describe methods for "making sustainable development operational."[73] Before impacts can be managed, it is necessary to map them. The product life-cycle model illustrated in Figure 3.8 can be used to provide a complete overview of impacts along all stages, from the extraction of the first raw material to the end of the product's useful life.

Companies must map and measure social, environmental, and economic impacts through all product life-cycle stages. The final goal of this mapping process is to establish a complete life-cycle impact inventory, summing up all impacts for all products of the company. Table 3.2 provides an example of an inventory of the three types of impact throughout the three life-cycle stages by Samsung Electronics.[74] The table is a snapshot of selected aspects of the company's triple bottom line for 2011.

The company's overall LCA is an accumulative measure of the life cycles of the company's products and services. (Although LCA can be conducted for both products and services, here, for the sake of simplicity, we will use the word *product* to refer to both products and services.) Traditionally product LCA was

**Table 3.2** Samsung Electronics: Company Life-Cycle Impact Portfolio

| | Social | Environmental | Economic |
|---|---|---|---|
| Production | Employee education in 2010 of 29,300 people, with an average of 87 hours per person and an education cost of $977 per person | Reduction in GHG emission (relative to sales) by 31 percent from the level in 2008, resulting 5.11 tons of $CO_2$ per $88,800 (100,000 KRW) revenue | Direct economic value creation of $130 billion out of which $99 billion have been redistributed to suppliers, $12 billion to employees, and the remainder reinvested or distributed to other stakeholders |
| Use | Total customer inquiries and complaints: 57 million | Ratio of ecoproducts: 91 percent of company products were classified as ecoproducts, with above-average performance in material reduction, energy usage, and toxicity | Economic savings for clients: Energy savings—between 17 and 88 percent Reduced repairs and longer product usage—price ceiling on repairs of products provides incentives and savings |
| End-of-useful lifetime | Laptop models from 2011 on 100% free of PVC/BFR (chemical substances that cause toxic waste and harm human health) | Recovery of 1.06 million cell phones in Korea through end-of-life, take-back scheme; company has collected more than 2,000 collection points in 61 countries | In-kind donations of used electronic products for low-income communities |

Note: Many of the impacts mentioned in this table are relative impacts expressed in percentages. For the purpose of establishing a company's triple bottom line, total impacts expressed through sums are preferable.

Source: Greenpeace. (2010). *Why BFRs and PVC should be phased out of electronic devices.* Retrieved March 28, 2012, from Greenpeace International: www.greenpeace.org/international/en/campaigns/toxics/electronics/the-e-waste-problem/what-s-in-electronic-devices/bfr-pvc-toxic/; Samsung. (2012). *Global harmony with people, society & environment: 2011 sustainability report.* Suwon: Samsung Electronics.

A **life-cycle impact portfolio** is an extensive list of a company's impacts. This list results from a cumulative LCA, summing up all impacts of a business along with all products in its portfolio.

applied to determin only environmental impact, but for purposes of sustainable management (understanding environmental, social, and economic impact), it has been broadened to account for social and economic factors.[75]

Typical impacts that are summarized in an environmental life-cycle assessment (ELCA) are impacts on water, air quality, and biodiversity. The assessment of economic factors, often called life-cycle costing (LCC), might include the amount of wages paid, economic value added, and profit made per life-cycle stage. Assessing social life-cycle impacts through a social life-cycle assessment (SLCA) may require more complex measurable indicators than the first two categories. Valuable support in identifying these indicators can be found through the GRI and the Dow Jones Sustainability Indexes.[76] SLCA is an emerging tool that is crucially important for including the social dimension in the management of business sustainability.[77]

The **life-cycle assessment (LCA)** process can be subdivided into four stages, as illustrated in Figure 3.9. These stages are broadly accepted by groups that are setting international standards, for example, the International Organization for Standardization (ISO), which provides a detailed description of LCA standards.[78] The following text describes the four stages in detail.[79]

**Goal and scope (G&S).** The G&S of the LCA first serves to develop a deep understanding of why the LCA is conducted. In the context of sustainability management, the primary goal should be a complete description of all social, environmental, and economic impacts as a basis for subsequent responsibility management activities. A secondary goal might be to create comparability to other products or alternative actions. For example, a company that is considering substituting petroleum-based diesel with biodiesel in its processes would need to compare the triple bottom line of both products before making a decision to improve sustainability performance. Another secondary goal might be external communication purposes and the creation of transparency about the company's impacts.

Defining the scope of the assessment involves defining the product system to be analyzed and setting the boundaries of the LCA, which means deciding which parts of the system will be included in the assessment. Figure 3.10 illustrates how the three life-cycle stages can be divided into functional units, which together form the product system. The overall production process runs through the functional units of extraction, supply, manufacturing, distribution, and retailing. The use stage can be divided into first use and following secondary uses. At the product's end of life, the functional units are either disposal or the revalorization of the product, which reintegrates the product into previous life-cycle stages. The scope of a LCA defines which of those stages will be included and with what detail.

> The **life-cycle assessment** is the process of mapping social, environmental, and economic impacts along the stages of production, use, and end-of-useful life of a product.

**Figure 3.9  Stages of the Life-Cycle Assessment Process**

| Goal and scope | Life-cycle inventory | Life-cycle impact assessment | Life-cycle interpretation |
|:---:|:---:|:---:|:---:|
| 1 | 2 | 3 | 4 |
| G&S | LCI | LCIA | LCI |

© Cengage Learning, 2015

**Figure 3.10  Interconnectedness of Supply Chain and a Life Cycle's Product System**

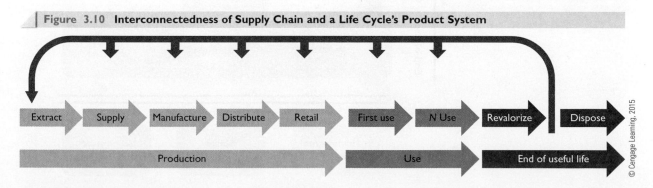

Extract → Supply → Manufacture → Distribute → Retail → First use → N Use → Revalorize → Dispose

Production — Use — End of useful life

© Cengage Learning, 2015

The ideal scope for maximum-quality sustainability management would be a complete inclusion of all functions at the largest depth possible.

**Life-cycle inventory (LCI).** A product LCI serves to quantify all inputs and outputs of the product's life cycle. This inventory consists of the three stages of data collection, data calculation, and the allocation of flows and releases. Central to the stage of data collection is the development and measurement of quantifiable indicators for inputs and outputs in all three dimensions. Inputs are, for instance, the number of employees (social), the amount of water used (environmental), and the capital invested (economic). Related examples for output are employee well-being (social), the water quality after the production process (environmental), and the profit made (economic). At the stage of data calculation, the measurements made are related to specific process and functional units. Few processes result in only one product output. Therefore, the allocation of flows and releases to respective products in processes helps to reach a clear picture of the impact of a single product.

**Life-cycle impact assessment (LCIA).** The stage of conducting an LCIA serves to evaluate the significance of impacts listed in the inventory and organizes them for analysis and management purposes. Impacts at this stage refer to real-life outcomes caused by the life cycle. Figure 3.11 illustrates different types of data organization. For instance, sustainability management might need to specify the product's "water footprint." A company could plan to use the economic savings generated from a

**Figure 3.11 Application of Impact Assessment, Life-Cycle Management, and Footprints**

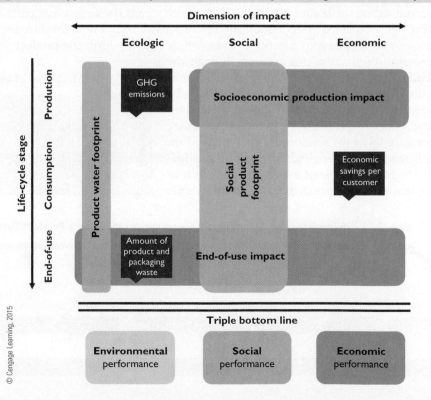

© Cengage Learning, 2015

new energy-efficient product as a sales argument, and therefore it would need to know the single impact of "economic savings per customer." The company could plan to fundamentally redesign the product's end of life and require understanding of the "end-of-use impact" in all three dimensions. The LCIA pursues the final goal of categorizing life-cycle inventory data by their importance, which can depend on the size of the impact, the negative or positive external consequences of the impact, and its instrumental value for the business.

**Life-cycle interpretation (LCI).** The interpretation is the connecting element between LCA and impact management. In the interpretation stage, the task is to plan actions based on the outcomes of the life-cycle process.

## 3-5c Process 2: Impact Management

The management of social, environmental, and economic impacts is based on a sound LCA. It constitutes the core task of sustainability management. In order to lead to sustainable management outcomes, the basic goal of impact management must be based on the goal of achieving neutral to restorative sustainable outcome in any management activity. To become a sustainable business, sustainability management must be part of the tasks of any employee or department on any hierarchical level. Similar to financial performance, the cumulative triple bottom line of all activities in a business result in the company's sustainability performance. Thus, each person in the company should base his or her actions on the following simple set of principles:

- **Optimize triple bottom line impacts** to move toward sustainability. Optimizing impacts does not always mean reducing negative and increasing positive impacts. A company that is highly profitable (positive economic impact) might become so at the cost of its social and environmental bottom lines. In this case, the company should actually reinvest the positive economic bottom line into boosting the social and environmental bottom lines.

- **Eliminate waste** in whatever form. Wasting resources will result in an unnecessary loss of social, environmental, and economic capital and automatically reduce the business's triple bottom line performance.

- **Scale** your sustainability management practices to have a larger impact. Grow your own activities, and inspire others to share your good practices inside and outside your business.

Whenever sustainability management practices are based on a sound life-cycle analysis and a systemic understanding of the social, environmental, and economic factors of sustainable development, they enable the manager to make a lasting impact for the best of people, planet, and profit.

### PRINCIPLES OF SUSTAINABILITY: MANAGING FOR THE TRIPLE BOTTOM LINE

I. *Sustainable development* is a development that meets the needs of present generations without compromising the needs of future generations.

II. *Sectorial sustainability* is a necessary precondition to reaching sustainable development. The three sectorial sustainability goals are *sustainable business, sustainable living*, and *sustainable governance*.

III. Three types of *capital* have to be sustained and balanced in order to reach sustainable development: *social, environmental*, and *economic* capital. Those three capitals comprise the elements measured by the triple bottom line.

IV. The *triple bottom line* sums up all social, environmental, and economic impacts of an activity.

V. An *unsustainable business* is one with a negative triple bottom line; a *sustainable business* is one with a neutral one; and a *restorative business* has a positive triple bottom line.

VI. *Sustainability management* is the process of managing a business and every one of its activities in a way that reaches a neutral or positive triple bottom line.

VII. The *sustainability management process* is based on the tool of product life-cycle impact management and can be subdivided into two main activities: *impact accounting* and *impact management*.

VIII. Product *life-cycle impact management* administers all social, environmental, and economic impacts of a product through the stages of production, use, and end-of-useful product life.

IX. The *stages of life-cycle impact management* are (1) G&S definition, (2) LCI, (3) LCIA, and (4) life-cycle interpretation.

## KEY TERMS

footprinting  69
impacts  71
life-cycle assessment (LCA)  73
life-cycle impact portfolio  72
neutrally sustainable  69

restoratively sustainable  69
strong sustainability  64
sustainable business  70
sustainable development  61
sustainability  61

sustainability management  70
triple bottom line  70
unsustainable  69
weak sustainability  64

## EXERCISES

### A. Remember and Understand

A.1. Note the Brundtland definition of sustainable development and explain its main components.

A.2. Describe the two main processes of sustainability management.

A.3. Define the following terms: *triple bottom line, sectorial sustainability*, and *sustainability management*.

A.4. Define and differentiate the following three terms: *unsustainable, sustainable*, and *restorative*.

### B. Apply and Experience

B.5. Look up a sustainability report of a business on its corporate website and make a list of the social, environmental, and economic performance indicators (three for each) used in the report.

B.6. Map the typical social, environmental, and economic life-cycle impacts through the three stages of the life cycle of a product type (e.g., a T-shirt, a kilo of coffee, a car) of your choice.

### C. Analyze and Evaluate

C.7. Compare two concrete products of two different brands by conducting in-depth research that deepens the initial assessment conducted in Exercise B.6. Decide which of the two products is the more sustainable one by ranking both products on a scale between 0 (highly unsustainable) and 10 (highly restorative).

C.8. Analyze and broadly categorize all product groups of a corporation of your choice into unsustainable, sustainable, and restorative products. Then summarize your finding in a sustainability product portfolio that provides an overview of the main impacts of the company's products.

### D. Change and Create

D.9. Use the sustainability product portfolio of the company that you established in Exercise C.8 to describe concrete impact improvement proposals for the three most unsustainable products. Provide a strategy to make one product in the portfolio a restorative product.

D.10. Imagine and describe a restorative business with a focus on how this business will restore social, environmental, and economic capital through its products and processes.

D.11. Get in touch with a real company of your choice to explain your sustainability improvement ideas developed through the former exercises. You can do so through hotlines, online contact forms, or the contact provided in the company's sustainability report. Document the company's reaction.

Courtesy of John Elkington

John Elkington is probably the single most influential writer and thought leader in sustainable business. His triple bottom line concept of people, planet, and profit has become sustainability professionals' mantra.

**In an interview you talked about how the environmental and sustainability movement comes in waves. When do you think will the last wave arrive that truly brings us sustainable development? What does the wave have to bring with it to reach this goal?**

In some parts of the world, that last wave will never come; elsewhere it may be achieved for short periods of time, then lost. Sustainability is a dynamic state, a resolution of forces in tension, so it depends on the quality of leadership (and followership/implementation) over time. Fundamentally, it is a cultural (and civilizational) challenge. Changing mind-sets does not guarantee the necessary changes in behavior, and the cultures that lock in unsustainable behaviors may require a paradigm shift to change sufficiently.

We think a fifth breakthrough wave will begin to build within two to three years and peak around 2020–2022. It will likely be driven by growing frustrations with the failures and weaknesses of current CSR, SRI, and similar agendas.

**In your book *The Zeronauts*, you talked about how outstanding individuals "break the sustainability barrier" by achieving zero-goals. Is zero emissions, zero waste, or zero ethical misconduct possible for any kind of business, or does this rather work for a chosen few? What does a business have to do to make it work?**

Zeroing is possible for any company, any industry, in the sense that "the impossible takes a little longer," as the U.S. Army Corps of Engineers used to say. But it depends on a timely alignment of drivers and on leadership. At a time when most leaders are defensive or incremental in this space, and elsewhere, the chances are that breakthrough change will come in fits and starts. Zero-based targets help jolt leaders and C-suites

out of complacency—and need well-designed financial incentives and recognition-based rewards (and penalties) to sustain the necessary levels of change.

**The Power of Unreasonable People was one of your book titles. What is the advantage of being unreasonable? Do we have to rely on unreasonable people to achieve sustainable development?**

The point is, as the playwright George Bernard Shaw put it, reasonable people adapt themselves to the world as they find it, whereas unreasonable people can imagine a different world, different realities. So, in the early stages, anyone who aims to change the system in which people currently operate is going to be seen as unreasonable. And our future depends on the success of the more positive among them.

**How do you see operations and supply chain management contributing to translation of triple top line (equity, economy, ecology) strategy into triple bottom line (people, planet, profit) actions and results?**

I am answering this set of questions on a Eurostar train to Paris, for a session organized by the supply chain management firm EcoVadis for a growing group of major corporate customers. Such organizations are helping to drive triple bottom line considerations through supply chains, as are market gatekeepers like Walmart with its "Sustainability Index" and Marks & Spencer with its "Plan A." One of the most interesting recent initiatives has been the Zero Discharge of Hazardous Chemicals platform, catalyzed by Greenpeace's "Detox" campaign, and now involving a growing range of manufacturers, retailers, and others in driving a major detoxification process through their supply chains into China.

**How do you see product, system, and service innovation and design contributing to triple bottom line performance? What kind of innovation do we need to create sustainable businesses?**

We need all sorts of innovation for sustainable business. Clayton Christensen talks in terms of enabling, sustaining, and efficiency forms of innovation, all of which have a role to play here. But we are at a point in all of this where incremental innovation must increasingly give way (or lead) to innovation that drives the necessary system change. Which is where unreasonable leaders come in again.

**What else would you like to communicate?**

This is an agenda we tackle in our latest report, "Breakthrough: Business Leaders, Market Revolutions," to be published early in March, and in a new book I am writing, with former PUMA CEO Jochen Zeitz, called *Tomorrow's Bottom Line*, due out late in 2013.

---

## PRACTITIONER PROFILE: JUDITH RUPPERT

Courtesy of Judith Ruppert

**Employer organization:** 360 Environmental is a Western Australian environmental management consultancy, providing a wide range of environmental services, including carbon and energy management; impact, site, and contamination assessments; flora and fauna surveys; compliance reporting; and environmental monitoring and training.

**Job title:** Environmental Consultant

**Education:** Bachelor of Business, Goethe University, Frankfurt, Germany; Master of Environmental Policy and Management, Lincoln University, Christchurch, New Zealand

### In Practice

**What are your responsibilities?** I am responsible for undertaking environmental impact assessments (EIAs), developing and implementing environmental management plans, conducting audits, and managing and reducing our clients' carbon footprints. I also ensure our clients comply with relevant environmental legislation and help them prepare compliance documents for submission to the Environmental Protection Agency. In addition, I develop, organize, and present environmental training workshops to enhance environmental awareness throughout a company. Apart from the typical office work, I also go out into the field and do fauna surveys to assess the impact of projects on conservation significant species.

**What are typical activities you carry out during a day at work?**

For an EIA, for example, I do background research about the site I am assessing, which includes finding out about, for instance, the biological, hydrological, geological, and social/cultural situation onsite. I then do a risk assessment, analyzing the probability and potential consequences of the project. After that, I would give recommendations on how to mitigate potential adverse effects. For more business-related topics, I would do research on different ways of improving energy efficiency and reducing carbon or water footprints. I'd then put together a management plan and a presentation and liaise with the client on how to best convey the message to employees. There are, of course, also more mundane tasks to do such as data entry, reviewing energy or carbon data, and making sure everything is on track and compliant. When I'm out in the field, I walk through environmentally sensitive areas, counting animal scat or finding tracks and nests to be able to assess the likely occurrence of a species.

**How do sustainability, responsibility, and ethics topics play a role in your job?**

Our business is based on the triple bottom line; in fact, our slogan is: people, planet, profit. Every day we have to juggle the economic interests of our clients with the environmental and social impacts of a big infrastructure, mining or oil and gas projects. Especially in Australia, where the resource sector is a major part of the economy, environmental and social impacts are often significant. Also, given the fact that many projects in Western Australia affect indigenous communities, a whole different level of social impacts occurs than the usual neighboring-properties issue. As environmental practitioners, we have the responsibility to protect the environment as well as possible while not stifling the national resource industry, which in some situations is a big challenge. Barrow Island, for example, is a class A nature reserve off the coast of northern Western Australia that now has LNG and oil being extracted from it—probably one of the most controversial projects in Australia, which requires a balancing act between economic and environmental interests.

**Out of the topics covered in this chapter, which concepts, tools, and topics are most relevant to your work?**

When working with clients on increasing their energy efficiency and reducing their carbon footprint, decisions are based on environmental and moreover financial factors. With one client, who had numerous car yards around Australia and also owned a refrigerated truck/logistics company, I had to work viable energy-efficiency opportunities. In this specific case, we had seven different opportunities identified: from staging compressor loads so the big compressor was only used during peak hours, to upgrading to more energy-efficient equipment, to changing their entire lighting system. I first calculated their energy cost savings over the life of the project and then subtracted the sum of the initial investment cost, the ongoing maintenance cost over the life of the project, the cost of assessment, and other compliance costs. I then divided that number by the number of project years, which enabled me to compare the seven net annual savings.

The initial investment cost included, for example, the cost of buying a new compressor or more fuel-efficient trucks, while maintenance cost covered all costs arising when, for example, servicing the new equipment. Costs of assessment typically include consultant fees, energy consumption metering cost, or time spent by staff members to collect data or communicate outcomes. Compliance costs cover all fees occurring through hiring consultants to write compliance reports or internal staff time when liaising with the external consultant.

Although this approach does not take into account the depreciation over time, it gives us an indication of which project was the most financially viable. For companies that have to report under the Australian Clean Energy Mechanism (Carbon Tax), factoring in carbon liabilities with $23 per ton $CO_2$ would be an addition to the above-mentioned calculation. However, for this approach, energy consumption has to be converted into $CO_2$ emissions before financial burdens can be calculated.

## Insights and Challenges

### What recommendation can you give to practitioners in your field?

When talking to decision makers, you rarely encounter people with an environmental or CSR background—you are more likely to talk to business-minded people. In this case, it is crucial to use an approach that uses business-speak when trying to convince your client why they should spend a lot of money for something that is not part of their core business. Good indicators to use are figures around return on investment (ROI), cost savings, decreased legal liabilities, enhanced reputation amongst the public, increase in sales, and so on. However, it always depends on who you are talking to—don't play the hard businessperson when talking to very environmentally and socially aware people—motivate them with passion. In contrast to that, don't talk about hugging trees when talking to the CFO of a business. Appealing to people's emotions is great, but backing it up with numbers often helps projects getting realized.

### Which are the main challenges of your job?

The main challenge of being an environmental consultant is the balancing act between the triple bottom line factors: ideally, you want to achieve the best environmental and social outcomes possible, but this is often being stifled by economic and especially financial interests. As the market is very competitive in Western Australia, the project budgets are usually very tight, which often leads to decisions based on "best information available" and "the best solution for the resource industry" rather than the best outcomes for the environment and indigenous communities.

## SOURCES

1. WWF. (2010). *Living planet report 2010: Biodiversity, biocapacity and development*. Gland: WWF International.
2. WBCSD. (2010). *Vision 2050: The new agenda for business in brief*. Geneva: World Business Council for Sustainable Development.
3. Lacey, P., Cooper, T., Hayward, R., & Neuberger, L. (2010). *A new era of sustainability: UN global compact-acccenture CEO study 2010*. Accenture Institute for High Performance.
4. Ernst & Young. (2012). *Six growing trends in corporate sustainability*. Ernst & Young.
5. Savitz, A. W., & Weber, K. (2006). *The triple bottom line: How today's best-run companies are achieving economic, social, and environmental success—and how you can too*. San Francisco: Jossey-Bass.
6. United Nations. (1987). *Our common future*. United Nations, World Commission on the Environment and Development. New York: United Nations.
7. Sveiby, K.-E. (2009). Aboriginal principles for sustainable development as told in traditional law stories. *Sustainable Development, 17*(6), 341–356.
8. Kamira, R. (2003). Kaitiakitanga: Introducing useful indigenous concepts of governance. In E. Coiera, S. Chu, & C. Simpson, *HIC 2003 RACGP12CC : Proceedings* (pp. 499–507). Brunswick East:

Health Informatics Society of Australia;Kawharu, M. (2000). Kaitiakitanga: A Maori anthropological perspective of the Maori socio-environmental ethic of resource management. *Journal of the Polynesian Society, 109*(4), 349–370; Morad, M., & Jay, G. M. (2000). Kaitiakitanga: Protecting New Zealand's native biodiversity. *Biologist, 47*(4), 197–201; New Zealand in History. (2008). *The Māori*. Retrieved March 13, 2012, from New Zealand in History: http://history-nz.org/maori6.html

9.  Cairns, J. (2004). Sustainability ethics: Tales of two cultures. *Ethics in Science and Environmental Politics, 4*, 39–43.

10. Maragia, B. (2006). The indigenous sustainability paradox and the quest for sustainability in post-colonial societies: Is indigenous knowledge all that is needed? *Georgetown International Environmental Law Review, 18*(2), 198–234.

11. Cole, M. A., Elliott, R., & Okubo, T. (2011). *Environmental outsourcing*. Discussion Paper Series RIEB Kobe University, *DP2011*(12), 1–39.

12. Hartmann, T. (1999). *The last hours of ancient sunlight: Waking up to personal and global transformation*. New York: Harmony Books.

13. Malthus, T. R. (1798/2011). *An essay on the principle of population: A view of its past and present effects on human hapiness*. Forgotten Books.

14. Cohen, J. E. (1995). Population growth and earth's human carrying capacity. *Science, 269*(5222), 341–346; Condorcet, J.-A.N. (1794/1979). *Sketch for a historical picture of the progress of the human mind*. Westport: Greenwood Press; Issar, A. S. (2007). Whose forecast will be verified in 2025: Malthus' or Condorcet's? *Hydrogeology Journal, 15*(2), 419–422.

15. Philp, M. (2009). William Godwin. In E. N. Zalta, *The Stanford encyclopedia of philosophy*, Summer 2009 ed. Palo Alto: Stanford University.

16. Cree indian prophecy. (2004). *Cree indian prophecy: Warriors of the rainbow*. Retrieved August 30, 2008, from Bird Clan of East Central Alabama: www.birdclan.org/rainbow.htm

17. Meadows, D. H., Meadows, D. L., Randers, J., & Behrens, W. W. (1972). *The limits to growth*. New York: Universe Books; Meadows, D. H., Randers, J., & Meadows, D. L. (2005). *Limits to growth: The 30-year update*. London: Earthscan.

18. Carson, R. (1962/2002). *Silent spring*. New York: Houghton Mifflin.

19. Haeckel, E. (1866/1988). *Generelle morphologie der organismen [General morphology of organisms]*. Berlin: Gruyter.

20. Pigou, A. C. (1920/2005). *The economics of welfare: Volume 1*. New York: Cosimo.

21. United Nations. (1987). *Our common future*. United Nations, World Commission on the Environment and Development. New York: United Nations.

22. Barbier, E. (1987). The concept of sustainable economic development. *Environmental Conservation, 14*(2), 101–110.

23. United Nations. (2005). *2005 World Summit outcome*. New York: United Nations.

24. U.S. Environmental Protection Agency. (2006). *Life cycle assessment: Principles and practice*. Ohio: U.S. Environmental Protection Agency.

25. McDonough, W., & Braungart, M. (2002). *Cradle to cradle: Remaking the way we make things*. San Francisco: North Point Press.

26. Elkington, J. (1998). *Cannibals with forks: The triple bottom line of 21st century business*. Gabriola Island: New Society Publishers.

27. UNEP. (1972). *Declaration of the United Nations Conference on the Human Environment*. Retrieved March 15, 2012, from United Nations Environment Programme: www.unep.org/Documents.Multilingual/Default.asp?documentid=97&articleid=1503

28. United Nations. (1987). *Our common future*. United Nations, World Commission on the Environment and Development. New York: United Nations.

29. United Nations. (1997). *UN Conference on Environment and Development* (1992). Retrieved March 15, 2012, from Earth Summit: www.un.org/geninfo/bp/enviro.html

30. UNFCCC. (2012). *Kyoto Protocol*. Retrieved March 15, 2012, from United Nations Framework Convention on Climate Change: http://unfccc.int/kyoto_protocol/items/2830.php

31. United Nations. (2012). Millennium development goals. Retrieved March 20, 2012, from www.un.org/millenniumgoals/

32. Timberlake, L. (2006). *Catalyzing change: A short history of the WBCSD*. Retrieved August 30, 2011, from World Business Council for Sustainable Development: www.wbcsd.org/DocRoot/acZUEFxTAKIvTs0KOtii/catalyzing-change.pdf; WBCSD. (2011). *About WBCSD*. Retrieved November 6, 2011, from WBCSD: Business Solutions for a Sustainable World: www.wbcsd.org/about.aspx

33. Global Reporting Initiative. (2011). *Global Reporting Initiative*. Retrieved August 30, 2011, from www.globalreporting.org/Home

34. WWF. (2010). *Living planet report 2010: Biodiversity, biocapacity and development*. Gland: WWF International.

35. WBCSD. (2010). *Vision 2050: The new agenda for business in brief*. Geneva: World Business Council for Sustainable Development.

36. Lovelock, J. (2010). *The vanishing face of Gaia*. New York: Basic Books.

37. WBCSD. (2010). *Vision 2050: The new agenda for business in brief*. Geneva: World Business Council for Sustainable Development.

38. SustainAbility. (2007). *Raising our game: Can we sustain globalization?* London: Pensord Press.

39. United Nations. (2012). *Resilient people, resilient planet: A future worth choosing* (p. 16). New York: United Nations Publications.

40. United Nations. (1987). *Our common future*. United Nations, World Commission on the Environment and Development. New York: United Nations.

41. United Nations. (1987). *Our common future*. United Nations, World Commission on the Environment and Development. New York: United Nations.

42. Barbier, E. (1987). The concept of sustainable economic development. *Environmental Conservation, 14*(2), 101–110.

43. United Nations. (2005). *2005 World Summit outcome*. New York: United Nations.

44. Laasch, O., & Conaway, R. (2013). *Responsible business: Managing for sustainability, ethics, and citizenship*. Monterrey: Editorial Digital ITESM.

45. Elkington, J. (1998). *Cannibals with forks: The triple bottom line of 21st century business*. Gabriola Island: New Society Publishers; Elkington, J. (2011). *What is the tripple bottom line?* Retrieved October 14, 2011, from Big Picture TV: www.bigpicture .tv/?id=3456

46. Goodland, R. (1995). The concept of environmental sustainability. *Annual Review of Ecology and Systematics, 26*, 1–24; Sveiby, K.-E. (2009). Aboriginal principles for sustainable development as told in traditional law stories. *Sustainable Development, 17*(6), 341–356.

47. Jones, A. (1987). From fragmentation to wholeness: A green approach to science and society (Part I). *Ecologist, 17*(6), 236–240.

48. Solow, R. M. (1993). Sustainability: An economist's perspective. In R. Dorfman, & N. S. Dorfman, *Economics of the environment: Selected readings* (pp. 179–187). New York: Norton.

49. Stone, C. D. (1972). Should trees have standing? *Southern California Law Review, 45*.

50. Naess, A. (1973). The shallow and the deep, long-range ecology movement: A summary. *Interdisciplinary Journal of Philosophy, 16*(1–4), 95–100; Neumayer, E. (2003). *Weak versus strong sustainability: Exploring the limits of two opposing paradigms.* CheltenHam: Edward Elgar.

51. Kearins, K., & Springett, D. (2003). Educating for sustainability: Developing critical skills. *Journal of Management Education, 27*(2), 188–204, p. 190.

52. Kearins, K., & Springett, D. (2003). Educating for sustainability: Developing critical skills. *Journal of Management Education, 27*(2), 188–204, p. 193.

53. Strange, T., & Bayley, A. (2008). *Sustainable development*. Paris: OECD.

54. Blackwell, A. G. (2001). Promoting equitable development. *Indiana Law Review, 34*(4), 1273–1291; Goodland, R. (1995). The concept of environmental sustainability. *Annual Review of Ecology and Systematics, 26*, 1–24.

55. Fromm, E. (2005). *To have or to be?* London: Continuum; Goodland, R. (1995). The concept of environmental sustainability. *Annual Review of Ecology and Systematics, 26*, 1–24.

56. Schneider, F., Kallis, G., & Martinez-Alier, J. (2010). Crisis or opportunity? Economic degrowth for social equity and ecological sustainability: Introduction to this special issue. *Journal of Cleaner Production, 18*(6), 511–518.

57. Schneider, F., Kallis, G., & Martinez-Alier, J. (2010). Crisis or opportunity? Economic degrowth for social equity and ecological sustainability: Introduction to this special issue. *Journal of Cleaner Production, 18*(6), 511–518.

58. Adserà, A. (2004). Changing fertility rates in developed countries. The impact of labor market institutions. *Journal of Population Economic, 17*(1), 17–43; CIA. (2012). Central Intelligence Agency. Retrieved March 22, 2012, from *The world factbook:* www.cia.gov/library/publications/the-world-factbook/rankorder/2127rank. html; Janowitz, B. S. (1971). An empirical study of the effects of socio-economic development on fertility rates. *Demography, 8*(3), 319–330.

59. Grossman, G. M., & Krueger, A. B. (1995). Economic growth and the environment. *Quarterly Journal of Economics, 110*(2), 353–378.

60. Kuznets, S. (1955). Economic growth and income inequality. *American Economic Review, 45*(1), 1–28.

61. Panayotou, T. (2002). Demystifying the environmental Kuznets curve: Turning a black box into a policy tool. *Review of Economics and Statistics, 84*(3), 541–551; Stern, D. I., Common, M. S., & Barbier, E. B. (1996). Economic growth and environmental degradation: The environmental Kuznets curve and sustainable development. *World Development, 24*(7), 1151–1160; Yandle, B., Bhattarai, M., & Vijayaraghavan, M. (2004). Environmental Kuznets curves: A review of findings, methods, and policy implications. *Research Study, 2*(1), 1–16.

62. Laasch, O., & Conaway, R. (2013). *Responsible business: Managing for sustainability, ethics, and citizenship*. Monterrey: Editorial Digital ITESM.

63. GFN. (2011). *Global Footprint Network.* Retrieved March 22, 2010, from Footprint Basics: www .footprintnetwork.org/en/index.php /GFN/page/footprint_basics_ overview/; Wackernagel, M., & Rees, W. (1996). *Our ecological footprint*. Canada: New Society.

64. WWF. (2010). *Living planet report 2010: Biodiversity, biocapacity and development.* Gland: WWF International.

65. Moore, E. B., Goldfinger, S., Oursler, A., Reed, A., & Wackernagel, M. (2010). *The ecological footprint atlas 2010*. Oakland: Global Footprint Network.

66. Innocent. (2012). *Being sustainable*. Retrieved March 3, 2012, from Innocent: www.innocentdrinks.co.uk /us/being-sustainable

67. Blackburn, W. R. (2007). *The sustainability handbook: The complete management guide to achieving social, economic and environmental responsibility.* Washington: Earthscan; Norman, W., & MacDonald, C. (2003). Getting to the bottom of "triple bottom line." *Business Ethics Quarterly, 14*(2), 243–262.

68. Elkington, J. (1998). *Cannibals with forks: The triple bottom line of 21st century business.* Gabriola Island: New Society Publishers; Elkington, J. (2011). *What is the tripple bottom line?* Retrieved October 14, 2011, from Big Picture TV: www .bigpicture.tv/?id=3456; Savitz, A. W., & Weber, K. (2006). *The triple bottom line: How today's best-run companies are achieving economic, social, and environmental success—and how you can too.* San Francisco: Jossey-Bass.

69. Laasch, O., & Conaway, R. (2013). *Responsible business: Managing for sustainability, ethics, and citizenship.* Monterrey: Editorial Digital ITESM.

70. Laasch, O., & Conaway, R. (2013). *Responsible business: Managing for sustainability, ethics, and citizen ship.* Monterrey: Editorial Digital ITESM.

71. Elkington, J. (1994). Towards the sustainable corporation: Win-win-win business strategies for sustainable development. *California Management Review, 36*(2), 90–101.

72. Norman, W., & MacDonald, C. (2003). Getting to the bottom of "triple bottom line." *Business Ethics Quarterly, 14*(2), 243–262, p. 1.

73. Hunkeler, D., & Rebitzer, G. (2005). The future of life cycle assessment. *International Journal of Life Cycle Assessment, 10*(5), 305–308.

74. Samsung. (2012). *Global harmony with people, society & environment: 2011 sustainability report.* Suwon: Samsung Electronics.

75. Kloepffer, W. (2008). Life cycle sustainability assessment of products. *International Journal of Life Cycle Assessment, 13*(2), 89–95; LCI. (2010). *Starting life cycling.* Retrieved March 28, 2012, from Life Cycle Initiative: http://www.lifecycleinitiative.org; Zamagni, A. (2012). Life cycle sustainability assessment. *International Journal of Life Cycle Assessment, 1–4.*

76. Dow Jones Indexes. (2011). *Dow Jones Sustainability World Indexes guide book.* Zurich: SAM Indexes.

77. Dreyer, L. C., Hauschild, M. Z., & Schierbeck, J. (2006). A framework for social life cycle impact assessment. *Journal of Life Cycle Assessment, 11*(2), 88–97; Jørgensen, A., Finkbeiner, M., Jørgensen, M. S., & Hauschild, M. Z. (2010). Defining the baseline in social life cycle assessment. *International Journal of Life-Cycle Assessment, 15*(4), 376–384; Swarr, T. E. (2009). Societal life-cycle assessment—could you repeat the question? *International Journal of Life-Cycle Assessment, 14*(4), 285–289.

78. ISO. (2006). *ISO/FDIS 14040 Environmental management: Life cycle assessment, principles and framework.* Geneva: International Standardization Organization;ISO. (2006). *ISO standards for life cycle assessment to promote sustainable development.* Retrieved March 28, 2012, from International Standardization Organization: www.iso.org/iso/pressrelease?refid=Ref1019

79. ISO. (2006). *ISO standards for life cycle assessment to promote sustainable development.* Retrieved March 28, 2012, from International Standardization Organization: www.iso.org/iso/pressrelease?refid=Ref1019; Rebitzer, G., Ekvall, T., Frischknecht, R., Hunkeler, D., Norris, G., Rydberg, T., et al. (2004). Life-cycle assessment part 1: Framework, goal and scope definition, inventory analysis, and applications. *Environment International, 30*(5), 701–720; SAIC. (2006). *Life cycle assessment: Principles and practice.* Reston: Scientific Applications International Corporation.

## 04

Friedman
Issue
Responsiveness
Materiality
CSR
Philanthropy Corporate Social Entrepreneurship
Engagement Cause Corporate Responsibility
CSP vs CFP Stakeholder Corporate Social Performance Issues License to Operate Carroll
Freeman
Corporate Citizenship

# RESPONSIBILITY: MANAGING FOR STAKEHOLDER VALUE

*You will be able to...*

1 **...know and understand the history of business responsibility.**

2 **...get to know the central tools you need to manage business responsibility.**

3 **...manage your business for the creation of stakeholder value.**

4 **...conduct a stakeholder assessment and excel in stakeholder management.**

Out of the biggest companies, 96 percent have a formal corporate responsibility department.[1]

There are three stakeholder groups that most influence a company's business responsibility initiatives. Thirty-seven percent of managers mention customers as being most influential, followed by employees (22%) and shareholders (15%).[2]

In 2011, 95 percent of the world's largest 250 companies formally reported on their corporate responsibility activities. In 1999, merely 35 percent did so.[3]

Author: Oliver Laasch; Contributors: Barbara Coudenhove-Kalergi, Dewi Fitraasari, Edward Freeman, Sudhir Kumar Sinha

# LEGO: A Stakeholder-Driven Brand?

The Danish LEGO company, best known for its colorful interlocking plastic bricks, calls itself a stakeholder-driven brand and a successful business that earns money "the responsible way." What does a business have to do to become a stakeholder-driven brand?

LEGO gives four brand promises. The "play promise" is directly related to the company's product. The "planet promise" commits to creating a positive social and environmental impact. The "partner promise" involves teaming up with stakeholders in order to mutually create value, and the "people promise" specifically refers to the purpose of being jointly successful with the employee stakeholder. Interestingly, each of the three promises corresponds to one of the primary stakeholders identified by the company. LEGO defines customers (play promise), employees (people promise), partners (partner promise), and the environment (planet promise) as primary stakeholders. Each promise fulfills another value proposition for those important stakeholders. LEGO has created an explicit strategy to create stakeholder value.

How does LEGO work with those stakeholders to create shared value for them and the business? The first step was a materiality assessment, in which LEGO identified the important issues to be addressed jointly. Materiality combines the importance of issues to the company and the stakeholders in a joint evaluation. Out of fifty-eight potential issues, LEGO identified thirty-six relevant (material) topics, fifteen top topics, and eight topics categorized as most important. LEGO then assessed the needs of stakeholders through "respectful stakeholder dialogue" in order to develop an active stakeholder engagement characterized by strong collaboration.

So how does LEGO interact with its stakeholders?

- **Customers:** LEGO aims to satisfy and educate its customers at the same time. The company engages with children ("LEGO builders") and parents, mainly through the issues of product safety, education ("learning manifesto"), and an extensive collaboration with parents.

- **Employees:** LEGO engages with employees about the main issues of gender diversity, motivation and satisfaction, work–life balance, and health and safety.

- **Partners/suppliers:** Topics addressed with partners are the sustainability of materials (polymers), anticorruption policies, auditing, and supplier responsibilities toward their own stakeholders.

- **Environment:** Issues related to the environment at LEGO are energy efficiency, waste reduction, recycling, and the end of life of the product.

Apart from interaction with the company's four primary stakeholders, the company also interacts with secondary stakeholders, such as the broader society, through the LEGO Foundation, with the government through lobbying, and with local communities through community development programs. In its annual progress report, LEGO provides performance data for all stakeholders. Joining in 2003, LEGO was one of the early companies to participate in the world's biggest business responsibility initiative, the United Nations Global Compact (GC).

Source: LEGO, Progress Report (2011), pp. 6, 8, 9.

## 4-1 BUSINESS RESPONSIBILITY: MANAGING FOR STAKEHOLDER VALUE

*"It is again time to ask ourselves the most fundamental of questions: What's a business for?"*[4]

What is the responsibility of a business and its managers? What is a business good for? For whom should it create value? Whom should it make "happy"? Should the answer to these questions include only owners—or should they also include customers, employees, the government, or nongovernmental organizations (NGOs)? There are, of course, many different opinions about the appropriate answers. In this chapter, we will draw a picture of a business that operates for the good of a broad set of stakeholders with the goal of maximizing long-run stakeholder value. We call it business responsibility when a business assumes its responsibilities to its various stakeholders. To succeed in business responsibility, a company must apply

Figure 4.1 **Responsibility Management and Stakeholder Value**

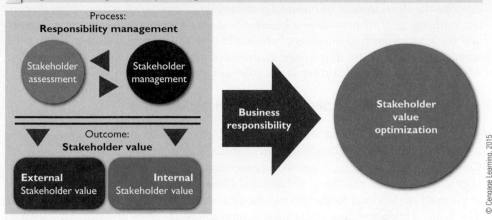

responsibility management practices that are based on the two fundamental practices of stakeholder assessment and stakeholder management (see Figure 4.1).

In the first section, this chapter will provide a quick overview of the development of the field of business responsibility. You will learn about the historic development of different understandings and frameworks such as philanthropy, corporate citizenship, and corporate social responsibility (CSR). Central concepts and scientific discussions, such as Milton Friedman's argument against business responsibility and Archie B. Carroll's responsibility pyramid will be introduced. The actual state of business responsibility will highlight the current state of implementation and understanding and provide a forecast about the future development of the field.

The second section will focus on the in-depth explanation of central concepts for the understanding of business responsibilities. We will distinguish between CSR, accountability, responsiveness, and performance and provide a first insight into the field of stakeholder theory.

The third section illustrates the field of responsibility management, which has the assessment and subsequent management of stakeholder relations at its core. The aspired outcome of responsibility management is to create maximum stakeholder value.

Note that the term *business responsibility* will be used throughout this chapter as a neutral meta-term for the description for business practices related to stakeholders. The goal is to avoid ambiguous connotations as well as disturbing biases and attitudes that might be attributed to the more established terms, such as *corporate social responsibility* and *corporate citizenship*, used to describe business responsibility.

## 4-2 ORIGINS OF BUSINESS RESPONSIBILITY

*"The development, strengthening, and multiplication of socially minded business men is the central problem of business."*[5]

The preceding quote illustrates that the responsibility of business and businesspeople has been an important topic for a long time. In 1927, Wallace Donham prophetically warned that "civilization may well head for one of its periods of decline" if business leaders do not "learn to exercise their powers and responsibilities with … responsibility towards other groups in the community."[6] The Great Depression came only two years afterward. History repeats itself. CSR was a buzzword and peak topic right before the economic crisis triggered by the irresponsible use of subprime loans in 2009. Has business really not learned anything about taking responsibility throughout the last century? To answer this question, the following paragraphs will describe the development of business responsibility between those two historic periods with the goal of providing a baseline understanding of business responsibility, and the management of business to create the best value for stakeholders. Table 4.1 summarizes important milestones in the development of business responsibility, which will be explained further in the following paragraphs.

## 4-2a Religious Roots of An Evolving Discipline

Religious morality defined the baseline for business responsibility conduct, long before there was an acknowledged field studying the responsibilities of business. Confucianism, for instance, is based on a pronounced community thinking, which translates to management practices.[7] Judaism and Christianity both favor donations, such as in the story of the Good Samaritan and the idea of donating one-tenth of one's income.[8] The Islamic understanding of business responsibility revolves around terms such as *justice, balance, trust,* and *benevolence,* which are highly related to the modern understanding of stakeholder theory.[9] Religions until today influence the attitudes of many different groups (e.g., managers, consumers) toward business responsibility practices.[10]

It was not until the early 1900s that repercussions of religious business morality appeared in theory and business science. Since then, the concepts used to frame business responsibility have gone through various stages. In the early years, between 1925 and 1955, business responsibilities referred to businessman responsibility. In both the article by Wallace Donham[11] mentioned before and the book *Social Responsibilities of the Businessman* published in 1951 by Howard Bowen,[12] which is often referred to as the first formal appearance of business responsibility,[13] the businessperson is the one to assume the responsibility.

From the early 1960s on, this individual responsibility increasingly developed toward CSR, a term highlighting the role of big businesses and corporations. The term CSR remained prominent in discussions of business responsibility until the early 2000s, although there were many variations in terminology. Corporate philanthropy, for example, made reference primarily to donations and charity-related business contributions to society. In the 1990s, increasing globalization and community thinking led to use of the term *corporate citizenship*, which highlights the political role of a company in society.

**Table 4.1** Historic Milestones in the Development of Business Responsibility

| Milestone | Facts |
| --- | --- |
| Historic roots | Religious business morality<br>Philanthropy<br>Responsibility of the businessman<br>Corporate social responsibility<br>Corporate citizenship<br>Corporate responsibility<br>Corporate social entrepreneurship |
| Scientific concepts and institutions | Friedman criticism: "The only responsibility of business is business"<br>Carroll's CSR pyramid<br>Stakeholder theory<br>European Union CSR policy<br>Global Compact |
| Status quo and the future | Facts and figures<br>Responsibility imperative<br>CSR 2.0 |

In the 2010s, there was a move toward an entrepreneurial understanding (corporate social entrepreneurship [CSE]), in which businesses develop entrepreneurial solutions to pressing stakeholder issues. The term *corporate responsibility* (CR) also appeared, a term that disconnects the topic from merely social topics and serves to include environmental responsibilities. Many of the terminologies mentioned are still in use today in varying degrees and in different regions and applications.

## 4-2b Theoretical Advances and Institutionalization

Interestingly, an article by the economist Milton Friedman, which is the most cited article on CSR,[14] strongly argues against the assumption of social responsibilities by business. In 1970 Milton Friedman stated in a *New York Times* article that "there is one and only one social responsibility of business—to use its resources and engage in activities designed to increase its profits."[15] Friedman was a Nobel Prize laureate in economics in 1976 and was called "the most influential economist of the second half of the 20th century."[16] With such a renowned supporter, it is no wonder that the criticism of business responsibility concepts, begun by Donham in the 1920s and continued by others through the 1950s,[17] held sway for much longer than it might have otherwise.[18]

**DIG DEEPER**

**Still Up-to-Date?**
The original text of Milton Friedman's article is available at many sources online. Look it up and make list of the arguments that he poses against CSR. Do you think his rejection of CSR is justified in today's world?

Nevertheless, a theoretical milestone for business responsibility was laid in the 1980s. Interestingly, the development came not from the business responsibility field, but from the field of strategic management. In 1984, Edward Freeman published the book *Strategic Management: A Stakeholder Approach*, which formalized the field of **stakeholder theory**. He defined a **stakeholder** as any "groups and individuals that can affect or are affected" by business activity.[19] In other words, business responsibility means responsibility toward various groups and types of stakeholders. Only seven years later, Archie B. Carroll created his pyramid of CSR,[20] which has served until the present as a framework for categorizing business responsibilities into economic, legal, ethical, and philanthropic responsibilities. These important individuals, who shaped the theory of business responsibility, are shown in Figure 4.2.

With the creation of theoretical concepts and increasing maturity of the scientific framework for the development of business responsibility, many kinds of institutions in various spheres also became involved in business responsibility development. Here we will highlight two major ones. The first is the Commission of the European Communities, which drafted a European Union CSR strategy for the

**Stakeholders** are any groups, individuals, or entities that can affect or are affected by an activity.

---

**Figure 4.2 Figureheads and Central Ideas of Business Responsibility**

**Howard Bowen (1951)**
First formally illustrates the social responsibility of the businessman.

**Edward Freeman (1984)**
Stakeholders are all groups and individuals that influence or are influenced by a business.

**Milton Friedman (1970)**
The only responsibility of business is profit. Businesses should not pursue any other responsibility.

**Archie B. Carroll (1991)**
Corporate responsibility consists of economic, legal, ethical, and discretionary responsibilities.

Travis manley/Shutterstock.com; Chris Kleponis/Bloomberg/Getty images; Mark Richards/ZUMAPRESS/Newscom; Courtesy of Archie B. Carroll

whole economic region.[21] This action triggered an avalanche of important developments.[22] The definition of CSR given by the European Union is frequently used because of its inclusive understanding of business responsibility. The European Multi-Stakeholder Forum provides European businesses with a unique institutionalized societal feedback mechanism.[23] The organization CSR Europe is the region's business responsibility network, and the European Academy of Business in Society (EABIS) connects academic and business fields in joint efforts to further develop business responsibility.[24]

A second crucial institutional development was the foundation of the United Nations GC in 2000, which quickly became the world's biggest global network for business responsibility involving many big multinational corporations. The GC members commit to a decalogue of business responsibility principles and to participating in a regularly published report of progress in implementing those principles.[25] The GC Principles of Responsible Management Education (PRME) initiative is a similar network of business schools, committed to educating responsible managers.[26] In addition, in 2010, the International Organization for Standardization launched the ISO 26000 standard for social responsibility, also called the ISO SR, which is expected to have a far-reaching influence and to unify many different existing approaches to business responsibility.[27]

## 4-2c Status Quo and the Future

During the early 2000s, assuming stakeholder responsibilities became a true business imperative.[28] For instance, the number of worldwide GC subscribers had well exceeded the 6,000-member mark by 2010. CSR Europe was working with more than 3,000 companies, only in Europe.[29] Although quantitative growth of implementing companies now seems a given, shortcomings in increasing qualitative aspects have become revealed. Two areas of sluggish growth have been the implementation of business responsibility activities in developing countries and the adoption of these activities by small- and medium-sized enterprises (SMEs).[30]

What will the business responsibility of the future look like? Scholars and practitioners forecast that a new version of business responsibility, called *CSR 2.0*, will emerge.[31] This new type of CSR is characterized by a number of dominant features, some of which are described in the following list:

- **Integration:** Stakeholder responsibilities are increasingly seen as a part of the core business and considered when crafting core-business strategies. Disconnected philanthropic activities will become a less frequent phenomenon. Integration of stake holder business responsibility leads to an amalgam of mainstream and business responsibility that will make it hard to distinguish between the two.

- **Transformation:** While traditional responsibilities were added on to the existing business activities, the new business responsibility often causes transformative changes to structure, processes, and products in order to be able to better fulfill stakeholder responsibilities.

- **Scale:** The more integrated and transformative stakeholder responsibilities become, the more effective become the solutions developed for stakeholders, and the bigger becomes the scale of such solutions.

## In Practice

### Going 2.0 with Small-Scale Distribution

An example showcasing the three characteristics of CSR 2.0 is Unilever's small-scale distribution program. Unilever, which traditionally is sold in large established supermarkets and shops, trains members of local communities to be distributors of the company's products and thus creates employment, opportunity, and wealth. The example is integrated into the business, as it attaches to the mainstream business function of sales and distribution. It is transformative, as the activity is profoundly different from the processes established for the traditional distribution systems. In India alone, 45,000 small-scale distributors, called "Shakti Ammas," in 2011 sold to more than 3 million households—an extraordinary scale. This approach is also highly entrepreneurial. Each distributor represents an independent microbusiness.

Source: Unilever. (2012). *Unilever sustainable living plan: Progress report 2011*. Rotterdam: Unilever.

- **Entrepreneurship:** Increasingly stakeholder issues are solved through entrepreneurial tactics, which systematically target their solution. Such entrepreneurship can be conducted either through CSE in established companies or through new ventures, often called *social businesses*.

# 4-3 CONCEPTS OF BUSINESS RESPONSIBILITY

*"Corporate social responsibility (CSR) is a concept whereby companies* **integrate** *social and environmental concerns in their business operations and in their interaction with their* **stakeholders** *on a* **voluntary** *basis."*[32]

## 4-3a Defining Business Responsibility

Defining business responsibility cannot be an easy task. Currently, the most common terms[33] used to describe business responsibility are CSR and CR, the latter of which more broadly includes environmental and economic business responsibilities, not just social ones. A recent survey summarizing common definitions of CSR found that no fewer than thirty-seven distinct definitions had been established in theory and practice sources between 1980 and 2003 internationally. The survey, however, found five common elements in a majority of those definitions. In the list of those five elements below, the percentages in parentheses denote how frequently the term was contained in the surveyed definitions.[34]

1. Stakeholder thinking (88%)
2. Social dimension (88%)
3. Economic dimension (86%)
4. Voluntary character of assuming responsibility (80%)
5. Environmental dimension (59%)

Using those five main elements, we can "reverse-engineer" a meta-definition of CSR. The following definition actively aims at defining business responsibility independently from the size of a business and therefore avoids the word *corporation*, which is associated primarily with big businesses. The definition also adds the idealistic goal of the maximization of value creation for all of its stakeholders. Using this process, we can say that **business responsibility** *means voluntarily assuming accountability for social, environmental and economic stakeholder issues in order to optimize stakeholder value.* This definition describes an ideal outcome of business responsibility conduct, after a business has found perfection in its responsibility management activity. Such a business exists only in a utopia. There is large continuum between an irresponsible business and the ideal state of a business responsibility as defined here, which will be illustrated in the next section.

## 4-3b Related Terms

Individuals first diving into the field of business responsibility are confronted with a bewildering variety of terms.[35] Unfortunately, a unanimous understanding of what business responsibility is and what it should be called has not yet been developed. In

**Business responsibility** means voluntarily assuming accountability for social, environmental, and economic stakeholder issues in order to optimize stakeholder value.

**THINK | ETHICS**

**Irresponsible Products— Not Even for Free!**

The biggest German daily newspaper, *Bild-Zeitung*, had been accused by various groups of poor journalistic standards that caused its content to confuse readers. The newspaper's impact on society was questioned. The criticism reached a climax in April 2012 when more than 170,000 German citizens decided to sign an online pledge against *Bild-Zeitung*. The pledgees refused to become recipients of a mail campaign that aimed to send a free sample of the newspaper to every German household. Based on the description of those events, where on the continuum between irresponsible and business responsibility should we place a company behaving like *Bild-Zeitung*?

Source: Halberschmidt, T. (2012). Netz-Kampagne macht gegen Bild-Zeitung mobil [Net campaign mobilizes against Bild-Zeitung]. *Handelsblatt*. Retrieved April 22, 2012, from www.handelsblatt.com/technologie/it-tk/it-internet/web-2-0-netz-kampagne-macht-gegen-bild-zeitung-mobil/6502346.html; Schuttenberg, S. (2012). 170,000 "Menschen meinen: BILD? Nein, danke!" [More than 170,000 people say: "No, thank you, BILD"], *Blog.Compact.de: Demokratie in Aktion*. Retrieved April 22, 2012, from www.handelsblatt.com/technologie/it-tk/it-internet/web-2-0-netz-kampagne-macht-gegen-bild-zeitung-mobil/6502346.html

this section, we aim to relate business responsibility to the terms typically mentioned in its context, as illustrated in Figure 4.3.

The three main synonyms used to describe the concept are *business responsibility, CR,* and *CSR.* CSR is the term that has been long-established in both academic and practice vocabulary. Using the word *social* refers to the social characteristics of stakeholders. The term CR has been introduced, mainly through practitioners, in order to avoid the purely social bias and to include also responsibilities toward environmental stakeholders. business responsibility is probably the least-used term, but the most generally and pragmatically applicable. It includes responsibilities to both social and environmental stakeholders and applies to all types of business equally, independent of size, maturity, or organizational structure. In spite of the slight differences in connotation, all three terms are often used interchangeably.

Another term often used as a synonym for business responsibility is business sustainability. In the context of this book, however, we would like to clearly differentiate *business responsibility* from *business sustainability* because of the latter term's significant distinctness in managerial implementation. As described in the preceding chapter, business sustainability is based on the management of the triple bottom line, while business responsibility is centered on the management of stakeholder relations. Both, if implemented well, will contribute to the overarching goal of sustainable development. Business sustainability will do so directly through a sound triple bottom line, and business responsibility indirectly through assuming responsibility for future generations as a central stakeholder, as described in the Brundtland definition of sustainable development.[36] Business responsibility, as defined by the ISO 26000 norm for organizational responsibility, is an important tool for reaching sustainable development.[37] It must be highlighted, therefore, that sustainable development is just one of many goals, as it refers to only one stakeholder group and a

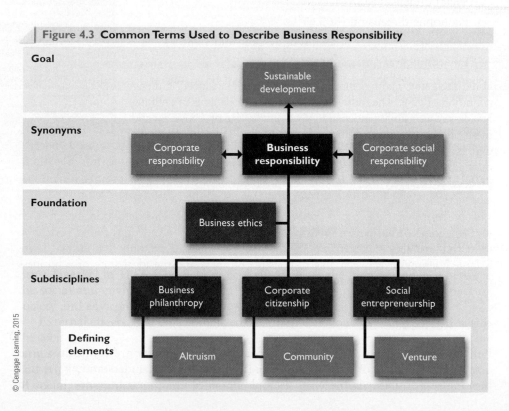

**Figure 4.3  Common Terms Used to Describe Business Responsibility**

Goal — Sustainable development

Synonyms — Corporate responsibility ⟷ **Business responsibility** ⟷ Corporate social responsibility

Foundation — Business ethics

Subdisciplines — Business philanthropy · Corporate citizenship · Social entrepreneurship

Defining elements — Altruism · Community · Venture

future responsibility. As will be illustrated in the following text, fulfilling responsibilities toward present stakeholders is an equally important goal.

A similar relationship exists with the term *business ethics*. Making morally right decisions in business, which is the central element of business ethics, is the foundation of any good stakeholder relationship, and stakeholder management must be informed by ethical principles.[38] Nevertheless, *business ethics* should not be understood as synonymous or even superior to *business responsibility*. The business implementation of both terms is too distinct and significant for each to not differentiate them clearly.

Business responsibilities can be subdivided into many subdisciplines, all covering different aspects of stakeholder responsibilities. The terms used for the subdisciplines are organized around different defining elements. **Business philanthropy** is probably the longest-established term. *Philanthropy* is best understood through its Greek roots, from which it translates as "love for mankind." The defining element of business philanthropy is altruism. So business philanthropic activities would be the ones motivated by love for mankind and the desire to help human beings and society. Business responsibility conduct that is truly philanthropic would consist of selfless, altruistic actions, which means that concepts such as strategic philanthropy or strategic giving[39] would hold implicit contradictions. Business philanthropy generally describes corporate giving, without anticipation of receiving a positive return. A study of British companies found that only one out of sixty companies surveyed had a truly altruistic motivation in their "philanthropic" activities. This result led the authors to question whether corporate philanthropy exists at all.[40] In practice, business responsibility activities typically subsumed under the philanthropy umbrella are donations, corporate foundations, and volunteer programs.

**Corporate citizenship (CC)** describes an understanding of the company as a political actor, assuming its responsibility as a good citizen of the local community, the state, or, in the broadest sense, the world community. Thus, the defining element of CC is community thinking. CC has been described as a further development of business philanthropy that exceeds pure altruistic activities as it involves a reciprocal relationship of a citizen's rights and responsibilities. In this point of view, CC is the right term to describe the implicitly contradictory "strategic philanthropy" mentioned earlier.[41] Three main understandings of CC have been suggested. A *limited view* of CC equates it with strategic philanthropy in local communities. The *equivalent view* equates CC with CSR and embraces all stakeholder relationships of the company. In this view, citizenship is a mere rebranding, a mask behind which lies the established concept of CSR. In the *extended view,* CC is attributed with a strong political role. The company becomes an enabler and protector of individuals in their role as citizens. Companies in the extended view help citizens to realize their civil, social, and political rights fully.[42]

The subcategory of **social entrepreneurship** has gained crucial importance at the beginning of the twenty-first century. The central element of social entrepreneurship is to use a venture-based approach to solve or mitigate stakeholder issues, such as poverty or education. The organizational vehicles for social entrepreneurship might be either established or newly founded businesses. There are many different classifications of such ventures, depending on the issues they aim at solving (social or environmental); on the types of organizations doing the venturing (NGOs, SMEs, corporations); and on the novelty of business. The most relevant type in the context

---

## In Practice

### Crisis-Resilient Responsibility

An often-made assumption is that business responsibility is costly and that business responsibility activities stand and fall with the money being spent on them. A survey studying the effects of the global financial crisis in 2007–2008 showed that, as a matter of fact, business responsibility projects dropped by approximately 55 percent. It can be assumed that peripheral philanthropy-based activities, which represent a pure cost, are more vulnerable to crisis-related cuts in spending than deeply integrated CSR programs, which represent an investment (with a potential return) into key stakeholder relationships. Also, entrepreneurial approaches that represent a profit and long-run perspective on social performance are less likely to suffer strong effects during crises.

Source: Karaibrahimoğlu, Y. Z. (2010). Corporate social responsibility in times of financial crises. *African Journal of Business Management*, 4(4), 382–389.

---

**Business philanthropy** describes business responsibility activities conducted with an altruistic mind-set.

**Corporate citizenship (CC)** describes business responsibility activities focusing on businesses' role in and contribution to community.

**Social entrepreneurship** describes business responsibility activities with an entrepreneurial venture approach to addressing social and environmental issues.

of this chapter is the CSE, which refers to a big established business that aims at solving social stakeholder problems.[43] CSE proactively levers company resources for the good of stakeholders and business, while most other business responsibility approaches aim rather passively at responding to stakeholder claims.[44]

## 4-3c Classification and Interpretation

Business responsibility is understood differently by various groups of people. The most commonly accepted approach to categorize and map those different understandings has been made through a four-domain model of business responsibility.[45] Those domains are

1. an **instrumental** understanding, where business responsibility is considered a tool for profit generation
2. **political** theories, which highlight the role of business as value generator for society
3. an **integrative** understanding, arguing that business can only survive, prosper, and grow if it integrates stakeholder demands into its activities
4. **ethical** theories that interpret the business–society relationship as embedded into an ethical framework

These categories are important for understanding the varying perspectives of business responsibility academics and practitioners. A company that takes an *instrumental* stance, for example, will highlight the strategic importance of its business responsibility activities. A business with a *political* stance will assume the role of generating value for local communities and society. Groups like NGOs that campaign against social or environmental corporate misconduct will take an *integrative* stance and stress that society will oppose a company that is not assuming its stakeholder responsibilities.

Although this categorization framework is the most accepted, it is not the only one. The following list summarizes different salient interpretations of business responsibility and the key questions leading to the orientation of each.

- **Explicit versus implicit:** Should corporations follow an individual pathway, voluntarily adapting to single stakeholder group claims (explicit), or should their business responsibility implementation follow a generalized pathway given by the social and institutional consensus on what business responsibility should be and do?[46]

- **Convergent versus divergent:** Should companies "follow the flock" and adopt common, tried and tested stakeholder practices (convergent), or should they aim at differentiating themselves by innovating new stakeholder practices (divergent)?[47]

- **Immediate versus future responsibilities:** To what degree should businesses focus on responsibilities corresponding to stakeholders' current situation (immediate), and to what degree should they take responsibility for later generations of stakeholders into account (future)?

- **Social versus nonsocial stakeholders:** Should business responsibility respond only to the claims of stakeholders such as customers, NGOs, and governments (social stakeholders), or should they also consider stakeholders such as animals, the natural environment, and future generations (nonsocial stakeholders)?[48]

- **Responsibility and accountability:** Should responsible companies voluntarily assume responsibilities (responsibility), or should there be strong mechanisms by which stakeholders can hold companies accountable if they do not voluntarily do so (accountability)?[49]

- **Soft versus hard or radical:** In becoming responsible, should businesses act within the rules of the game (soft), or should they act in a way that requires fundamental shifts in the rules of the economic system (hard), or even aim at creating a whole new economic system (radical)?[50]

This section has illustrated different forms of interpreting and naming business responsibility. The next section will explain the corporate social performance framework, an assessment that can be used to evaluate the degree of business responsibility achieved on a case-to-case basis.

## 4-3d Assessing Corporate Social Performance

A wide variety of methods and concepts have been applied to analyze the degree of responsibility assumed by a business, which is referred to as a business's **corporate social performance (CSP)**. This section summarizes central frameworks for the assessment of CSP. The frameworks can be applied on many levels, from evaluating a single business responsibility activity to evaluating the business as a whole. Assessing CSP also can involve using either qualitative or quantitative methods.[51]

### Qualitative Assessment

The qualitative methods and concepts illustrated here are (1) responsibility categories, following Archie B. Carroll's CSR pyramid; (2) the corporate social responsiveness framework, which assesses how companies react to stakeholder claims; (3) issues maturity, which explains how advanced a company is in the issues it covers; and (4) organizational implementation stages, which show the degree to which stakeholder responsibilities are embedded into a company's organizational processes. As illustrated in Figure 4.4, using those four concepts jointly will produce a multidimensional picture of how advanced a business is in terms of CSP; however, be aware that those four qualitative assessment methodologies are just a few of the many different ones that have been applied to assess CSP.

The first dimension of CSP is the **responsibility category**, which is determined by answering the question, *Which category of responsibilities does the company fulfill?* Archie B. Carroll illustrated the sequence of four categories of economic, legal, ethical, and discretionary responsibilities with the CSR pyramid illustrated in Figure 4.5.[52] The concept of the pyramid views the progress of companies toward responsibility as moving through four stages. First, a company must ensure its survival by fulfilling economic responsibilities (e.g., making a profit, paying employees). Second, the company aims to fulfill legal responsibilities (e.g., complying with laws, such as labor or environmental regulations). At the third stage, the company takes on ethical responsibilities, that is, those required by moral standards but not formalized through laws (e.g., increasing workplace safety beyond the legally required level). The final stage comprises discretionary responsibilities, which are those not required by any of the preceding levels; they are the nice things to do that are not economically, legally, or morally required (e.g., philanthropic giving of donations for disaster relief).

The second dimension of CSP is **stakeholder responsiveness**, which answers the question, *How does the company respond to stakeholder claims?* The lowest level of responsiveness is reactive behavior, where a company tries to deny the validity of

**Corporate social performance (CSP)** is an umbrella term referring to the assessment made by both qualitative and quantitative methods used to evaluate the degree of responsibility assumed by a company.

The **responsibility category** describes the type of responsibility assumed by a company and is based on Carroll's four categories of economic, legal, ethical, and discretionary responsibilities.

**Stakeholder responsiveness** describes the manner in which companies answer to stakeholder claims and is typically divided into reactive, defensive, accommodative, and proactive responsiveness categories.

## Figure 4.4 Dimensions of Corporate Social Performance

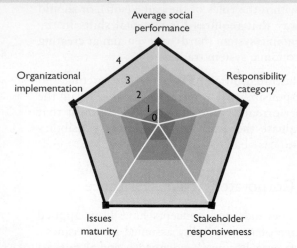

© Cengage Learning, 2015

| Application level | Responsibility category | Stakeholder responsiveness | Issues maturity | Organizational implementation |
|---|---|---|---|---|
| 1 | Economic | Reactive | Institutionalized | Isolated |
| 2 | Legal | Defensive | Consolidating | Managerial |
| 3 | Ethical | Accommodative | Emerging | Strategic |
| 4 | Discretionary | Proactive | Latent | Civic |

## Figure 4.5 Carroll's Corporate Social Responsibility Pyramid

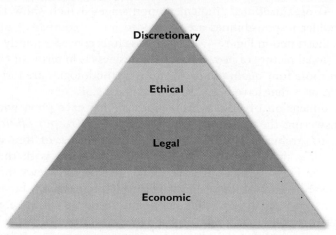

Source: Carroll, A. B. (1979). A three-dimensional conceptual model of corporate performance. *Academy of Management Review*, 4(4), 497–505; Carroll, A. B. (1991, July–August). The pyramid of corporate social responsibility: Toward the moral management of organizational stakeholders. *Business Horizons*, 225–235; Schwartz, M. S., & Carroll, A. B. (2003). Corporate social responsibility: A three-domain approach. *Business Ethics Quarterly*, 13(4), 503–530.

stakeholders' claims and the resulting responsibilities. At the next defensive level, a company accepts its responsibilities but tries to avoid them. The accommodative level is where a company accepts stakeholder claims and acts on the resulting responsibilities. Companies at the final level are proactive; they anticipate stakeholder claims and act on them even before the claims are explicitly uttered. Those four levels of responsiveness are referred to as the RDAP scale (with the acronym RDAP formed from the first letters of each level).[53]

While the second dimension evaluates how companies react to stakeholder claims, the third dimension focuses on how advanced companies are in responding to social, environmental, and economic issues. The dimension of **issues maturity** answers the question, *How well established are the issues to which the company is responding?* The goal is to find out whether company activity addresses only the very baseline of issues or rather approaches an innovative frontier.[54] A company is at the lowest level of issues maturity when its engagement with issues is completely institutionalized (e.g., focus on avoiding human rights issues, which is common to the norms of many international organizations). At the next level is the company that engages with consolidated issues, that is, issues that have not yet reached a high level of institutionalization but that are well accepted as common business practice (e.g., disclosure of carbon emissions, which is not yet completely institutionalized but nevertheless has become a consolidated practice among many businesses). A company at the next level is a pioneer through its engagement with emerging issues of which there is only a very basic awareness among businesses; and at the fourth level, the company is going even further by opening up new ground through addressing latent issues that have not yet reached public awareness.[55]

The fourth and final dimension of CSP, which describes the stage of companies in their **organizational implementation** of stakeholder responsibilities, is based on the underlying question, *How deeply embedded are the company's stakeholder responsibilities in organizational processes and structures?* On a rudimentary level, a company applies isolated policies, which are weakly integrated add-ons to processes (e.g., manufacturing plants often comply both with local legislation and with norms like the ISO 14000 for environmental management that are required by clients or the mother company).[56] The second level is managerial implementation, in which the company considers stakeholder responsibilities in its core processes. At the strategic implementation level, the company considers stakeholder responsibilities as an integral element of its strategic planning process (e.g., a soft drink producer that assumes its responsibility toward customers for providing a healthy product, and thus changes from products based on industrial sugar to organically produced fruit juices, and strategically positions these products). At the civic implementation level, a company not only has succeeded in meeting its stakeholder responsibilities internally but also has acted as a change agent for business responsibility practices externally and has inspired business partners, suppliers, and even clients to do the same.

## Quantitative Assessment

While the qualitative dimensions provide indicators of good practices in business responsibility, they also have been translated into a wide variety of quantitative indicators that have been applied in evaluating companies' CSP. Examples range from reputation scores, responsibility indices, content analyses of corporate documents, and social audits to spending and investment into stakeholder programs. Quantification of stakeholder responsibility indicators, however, remains a difficult task.[57]

Quantified CSP indicators are often used to analyze whether there is a link between company financial performance (CFP) and CSP. Researchers into this CSP–CFP linkage have said that it appears, in the majority of cases, that social performance and financial performance are correlated. In the most favorable interpretation, it actually pays off to take care of stakeholders, especially the ones closest to the company, the so-called primary stakeholders. In the least favorable interpretation, it

**Issues maturity** describes the degree of acceptance of a specific issue among stakeholders and is typically divided into institutionalized, consolidated, emerging, and latent issues.

**Organizational implementation** describes the degree of integration of business responsibility into organizational processes and structures using the four levels of isolated, managerial, strategic, and civic implementation.

# Intercontinental Hotel Group versus Starbucks: A CSP Challenge

How does one compare the world's largest hotel chain with the world's largest coffeehouse brand? The CSP model provides a reliable framework with which to compare businesses from very different industries. Both companies have become involved in responsible sourcing programs, which will be the subject of our analysis.

Starbucks (SB) has pioneered its responsibility toward community stakeholders in the supply chain through its Coffee and Farmer Equity (C.A.F.E.) Practices program, which supports small local farmers in their community development and integrates them into Starbucks's fair trade network to provide communities with a decent income. Starbucks procured 367 million pounds of coffee (86% of their global purchase) through the C.A.F.E. Practices program in 2011. The signature program of the Intercontinental Hotel Group (IHG) for involvement with community stakeholders in the supply chain is the IHG Academy, a training program that prepares individuals from local communities to work in the hotel sector. The IHG Academy annually trains 5,000 students, mostly in China, but also in the United Kingdom (UK), the United States, and Russia. Students are offered permanent jobs with IHG after graduating from the program.

In the CSP analysis, which is summarized in Figure 4.6, we find widely varying results for the two companies. For the responsibility category, SB can be placed on level 4, discretionary responsibilities, as the program is far exceeding the scope of what would be morally required

from the company. IHG's activity, on the other hand, would be categorized as economic responsibility (level 1), as the company mentions, as the reason for creating and implementing its academy program, that they "have found it difficult to attract and retain talented employees in the region [referring to China]."

SB's stakeholder responsiveness can be assessed as proactive (level 4). When Starbucks instituted C.A.F.E., there was little fair trade activity in the agricultural sector and no for-profit company that showed a comparable degree of involvement. SB proactively anticipated the needs of small communities (the stakeholder). The IHG Academy follows good practice examples of other companies with similar programs (e.g., Cisco's Networking Academy and the often-made claim for the necessity of hotels becoming more closely involved with their communities). Those features suggest accommodative stakeholder responsiveness (level 3).

The issues maturity for SB can be categorized as consolidating (level 2). The issue of community development through fair trade in the coffee industry is a mature topic, which has been well consolidated among stakeholders. IHG's topic of economic community development in the hotel industry, however, is a rather new, emerging issue (level 3).

The organizational implementation of SB's program has exceeded the strategic level (strategic positioning of SB through its deeply implemented responsibility practices) and can be placed on a civic stage (level 4), where SB has long been a role model inspiring other actors inside and outside its industry to improve their practices. IHG's implementation level is managerial (level 2), as the program is embedded into central management processes (e.g., human resources management and hotel operations) but has not yet found application on a corporate strategy level.

Those findings result in an average CSP score of 2 out of 4 for Intercontinental and 3.5 out of 4 for SB.

Sources: Baer, E. (2012). Lessons from Starbucks: Building a sustainable supply chain. *GreenBiz.* Retrieved March 30, 2012, from www .greenbiz.com/blog/2012/03/21/lessons-starbucks-learned-building-sustainable-supply-chain?utm_source=GreenBuzz&utm_campaign=ac0abb9d73-GreenBuzz-2012-03-21&utm_medium=email; IHG. (2012). *Corporate responsibility report.* Intercontinental Hotels Group. Retrieved March 30, 2012, from www.ihgplc.com/index.asp?pageid=722; Ashley, C., et al. (2007). The role of the tourism sector in expanding economic opportunity. *Corporate Social Responsibility Initiative Report, 23;* CISCO. (2012). Cisco Networking Academy. *CISCO.* Retrieved March 29, 2012, from www.cisco.com/web/learning/netacad/index.html

**Figure 4.6** **CSP of Intercontinental's and Starbucks's Responsible Sourcing Programs**

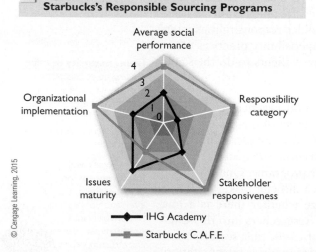

© Cengage Learning. 2015

at least does not hurt financial performance to care for stakeholders.[58] As demonstrated in the example provided in the box entitled "Intercontinental Hotel Group versus Starbucks," the qualitative CSP framework introduced in the last section can be translated into a quantitative assessment that is useful in planning and evaluating companies' business responsibility initiatives.

In the next section, we illustrate the use of the tool of stakeholder management in the creation of stakeholder value and in the central management of business responsibility.

## 4-4 RESPONSIBILITY MANAGEMENT AS STAKEHOLDER MANAGEMENT

*"The purpose of stakeholder management was to devise methods to manage the myriad groups and relationships that resulted in a strategic fashion."[59]*

Management for business responsibility, or **responsibility management**, has the management of stakeholders at its core. It is how the company administers this "myriad of groups and relationships"[60] that finally results in the CSP discussed in the preceding section. The ultimate goal of **stakeholder management** as defined for this book is the creation of value for all those different groups that "affect or are affected" by the business, that is, the creation of value for stakeholders.[61] Stakeholder management practice as illustrated in Figure 4.7 is subdivided into stakeholder assessment and stakeholder interaction with the joint goal of creating stakeholder value.

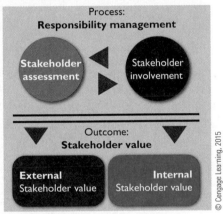

Figure 4.7 **The Responsibility Management Process**

Process:
**Responsibility management**

Stakeholder assessment

Stakeholder involvement

Outcome:
**Stakeholder value**

**External** Stakeholder value

**Internal** Stakeholder value

© Cengage Learning, 2015

### 4-4a The Goal: Stakeholder Value Optimization

What does **stakeholder value** actually mean? This abstract term can be translated into concrete indicators for each individual stakeholder group, such as customer satisfaction for customers, employee welfare for workers, and return on investment for shareholders. For other stakeholders, such as NGOs, governments, or the media, developing indicators to measure the value created for them through the business might be somewhat more complex. The crucial question to answer is: *What is their stake in the company?* Once the mutual relationship between a particular stakeholder and the company is understood, it becomes easier to define how the company could create value for the stakeholder, and vice versa. One thing is clear: Stakeholder value means something different from one stakeholder to another, and therefore stakeholder management is a highly complex, multidimensional task. The contemporary understanding of stakeholder management is that "the question of *who* and *what* really counts should be replaced by the question of *how* value is created in stakeholder relationships."[62]

Does stakeholder value mean the ones who win are all those external stakeholders, while the company does not benefit from the process? There is sound evidence that excellence in stakeholder management also increases financial business performance.[63] Good stakeholder management benefits both internal and external stakeholders of a business, creating a shared value for both.[64]

The idea of managing in a way that benefits both business and society, both internal and external stakeholders, sounds nice, but what fundamental guidelines can management follow to create such shared value? First, the primary goal of any management activity must be the optimization of stakeholder value in the long

**Responsibility management** is an administrative practice centered on stakeholders and aimed at the maximization of stakeholder value, which is a necessary condition for business responsibility.

**Stakeholder management** is the process of managing relationships with the various groups, individuals, and entities that affect or are affected by an activity.

**Stakeholder value** is the degree of satisfaction of either single stakeholders or all stakeholders of a specific activity.

CHRIS KLEPONIS/BLOOMBERG/
GETTY IMAGES

## Edward Freeman

**Q:** Since, ultimately, keeping the shareholders and customers happy is the bottom line for managers, do other stakeholders really matter that much?

**A:** Yes, others matter, because their interests are joint. You can't create value for shareholders or customers without creating value for suppliers, employees, and communities. All five are critical to most businesses. In some, it may be best to start value creation thinking with customers, but in other businesses, it may be best to start with employees, or suppliers, or the financiers.

run.[65] Second, such a value optimization must consider the whole "extended enterprise," consisting of the complex net of stakeholder relations throughout the company's sphere of influence.[66] Third, managers must understand that the connectedness and synergies among stakeholders require a holistic understanding and management of those relationships. This third guideline, which could be stated as "no stakeholder stands alone,"[67] illustrates the complexity involved in creating stakeholder value. Therefore, while the broader rules are helpful, a more concise decision-making framework is needed for translating stakeholder value creation into actual practice. Figure 4.8 provides such a framework.

Figure 4.8 illustrate the relationships between internal (e.g., owners, employees) and external (e.g., government, community) stakeholders and value creation for each. The left image describes a corridor of shared value, where both stakeholder groups have a close-to-equal share of the value creation. The right image compares the stakeholder value created by three alternative management choices through distribution on a numeric scale. The numbers represent the cumulative amount of stakeholder value created internally and externally.

As a concrete example, let's imagine that the Head of Corporate Responsibility at an information technology (IT) company such as Google, SAP, or Microsoft has received proposals to spend the department's budget on either (choice 1) a philanthropic community volunteering campaign, (choice 2) developing a new application for mobile devices that helps private customers to lead a more environmental friendly life, or (choice 3) an energy-efficiency program for the company's server infrastructure. How should the manager decide? We propose two basic optimization criteria, a maximization maxim and a fairness maxim.

**Figure 4.8 Shared Value and Stakeholder Value Optimization**

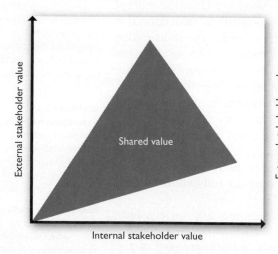
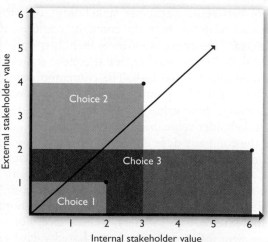

Source: (left) Adapted from Porter, M., & Kramer, M. (2002). The competitive advantage of corporate philanthropy. *Harvard Business Review*, 80(12), 56–68; (right) author elaboration.

1. **Maximization of stakeholder value** suggests that choice 1 is not attractive, as the overall value created of 2 (the boxed area on the right side of Figure 4.8) is topped by choices 2 and 3, both of which would create a value of 12. How then should the manager decide between those two remaining options?

2. **Fairness in distribution** of the value created suggests that the manager, in the case of two equal options, should decide for the choice that provides a fairer distribution of value. Proponents of equality in the fairness criterion would opt for choice 2, which is closer to the 45-degree line of equal distribution between internal and external stakeholders. (Note that with traditional neoclassical economics, choice 3 would be the right one, as the company's internal stakeholders are considered the creators and subsequently owners of value, which should then benefit them most.)

The decision pattern just illustrated is only one of many proposed mechanisms for the creation of stakeholder value. Other prominent proposals include, for instance, the idea of stakeholder democracy,[68] where stakeholders should have a say in decisions regarding company value creation, and stakeholder governance, which tunes corporate governance mechanisms to the creation of stakeholder value as the main criterion for governance. Traditional corporate governance tunes the company in on shareholder value.[69]

Regardless of how one defines maximization of stakeholder value, in practice, the first step toward stakeholder value creation is a thorough stakeholder assessment. This process will be illustrated in the following section.

# Expert Corner

## Freeman about Friedman

Are you interested in stakeholder thinking? Edward Freeman answers "tricky" questions on stakeholder management in an interview series that is available free online. Highlights of the interview are Edward Freeman refuses to be seen as the creator of stakeholder theory; and his guess is that the biggest opponent of business responsibility, the late Milton Friedman, if he were still alive, would be a stakeholder theorist.

Source: Freeman, E. (2008). Interview transcript: R. Edward Freeman on stakeholder theory. *Masters Seminars in Business Ethics Video Series.* Retrieved April 22, 2012, from www.darden.virginia.edu/corporate-ethics/Video_Stakeholder_Theory/transcript_freeman_stakeholders.html

## 4-4b Management Process 1: Stakeholder Assessment

The crucial basis for involving stakeholders is to understand them. This is easier said than done. Stakeholders may differ greatly both in their internal characteristics and in their relationship to the company. One can easily imagine that a loyal customer requires a very different stakeholder management strategy than, for instance, an aggressive customer group or a governmental representative. **Stakeholder assessment**, which is the process of understanding stakeholders and their relationship to the company, can be subdivided into two steps, stakeholder identification and stakeholder prioritization.

Stakeholder identification typically involves the mapping of stakeholders and relationships. Figure 4.9 illustrates a generalized exemplary stakeholder map, which is the main tool for stakeholder identification. The AA1000 stakeholder engagement standard recommends for stakeholder identification to ask the following questions:[70]

1. *Dependency:* What groups or individuals are directly or indirectly dependent on the organization's activities, products, or services and associated performance, and on whom is the organization dependent in order to operate?

2. *Responsibility:* To what groups or individuals does the organization have—or in the future might have—legal, commercial, operational, or ethical/moral responsibilities?

3. *Tension:* What groups or individuals need immediate attention from the organization with regard to financial, wider economic, social, or environmental issues?

4. *Influence:* What groups or individuals can have impact on the organization's or a stakeholder's strategic or operational decision making?

**Stakeholder assessment** is the process of understanding stakeholders and their relationship to a specific activity; it can be subdivided into two steps, stakeholder identification and stakeholder prioritization.

Figure 4.9 Categorized Stakeholder Map

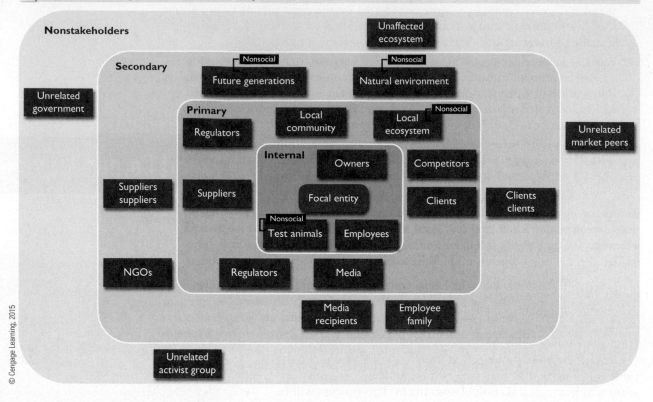

On a stakeholder map such as that shown in Figure 4.9, we can typically find several main groups of stakeholders. Internal stakeholders are the ones forming part of the company's internal organizational structure, such as employees and owners. External stakeholders are the opposite category.[71] Primary stakeholders are the ones that have a direct connection with the company. Such connections may be of many different natures, such as legal connections (e.g., governments), involvement in exchanges (e.g., direct suppliers), or a physical proximity (e.g., local community). Secondary stakeholders are the opposite category and might be of equal or even greater importance than the primary ones. For instance, a third-tier supplier who triggers a scandal due to inhumane working conditions might be more critical than a well-controlled direct supplier.[72] Social stakeholders are individuals or groups of human beings currently alive, as opposed to nonsocial stakeholders, such as animals, the natural environment, and future generations. Social stakeholders, unlike nonsocial stakeholders, can voice their concerns, which has profound implications for the management of their relationship.[73] The stakeholder status of the natural environment, especially, has been discussed extensively; the main question is whether nature should be seen as a stakeholder in its own right and which therefore qualifies for protection, or whether nature is only an instrument for the satisfaction of human needs.[74] The last and broadest differentiation exists between stakeholders and nonstakeholders, that is, those who do not have any relationship with the company.[75]

## DIG DEEPER

### Gods, Mountains, Avatars?

If you think those three words are unrelated to business responsibility, you are mistaken. The Eastern Indian Dongria Kondh tribe appealed to the director James Cameron, who created the science fiction movie *Avatar* in which the existence of an alien tribe living on a floating mountain is endangered by the activities of an unscrupulous mining corporation. The Dongria Kondh say the fictional story is reality for them. Their existence on their holy mountain, considered a god, is threatened by the mining company Vedanta Resources and its plan to convert the site into a mine. The mountain is estimated to hold the metal bauxite, which is used to produce aluminum, worth $2 billion. Can mountains, gods, and local tribes be considered stakeholders?

Sources: Hopkins, K. (2010). Indian tribe appeals for *Avatar* director's help to stop Vedanta. *The Guardian.* Retrieved April 22, 2012, from www.guardian.co.uk; Cernansky, R. (2012). Foreign companies eye sacred mountains in Montana and India for new mines. *Treehugger.* Retrieved April 22, 2012, from www.treehugger.com/corporate-responsibility/foreign-companies-pursue-mine-sacred-mountains.html

To build a stakeholder map, the following three logical steps are recommended:

1. **Identify the focal entity** of the stakeholder map. A focal entity defines the perspective from which the stakeholder analysis is conducted; it could be everything from a single decision, to a company or policy, a product, or even the company as a whole.

2. **List stakeholders** independently from the type or strength of relationship to the focal entity.

3. **Group** the stakeholders into the categories defined above, and organize the map based on those categories.

Once the stakeholder identification process is completed, stakeholders need to be understood and ranked in priority. Applying **stakeholder prioritization** models provides a way to look into the "black box" of stakeholder thinking.[76] Many frameworks have been developed for analyzing and prioritizing stakeholder groups in order to decide with whom to become involved. Table 4.2 illustrates the priorities given to stakeholder groups by companies as reported through six large-scale surveys conducted from 2007 to 2012.

Three interesting facts about the results in Table 4.2 need to be highlighted. First, there are prominent stakeholder groups that are repeatedly ranked to be of high priority: customers, employees, investors, and governments. Second, the importance of stakeholder groups differs depending on the time and situation (e.g., stable versus a turbulent economic macroclimate) and on whom you ask (e.g., middle management versus CEO). Third, nonsocial stakeholder groups and aggressive NGOs, which in the past have exerted critical influence on companies' success or failure, are not represented as priority stakeholders in company perception. Those three observations provide an important argument in support of not trusting generalized acceptance

**Table 4.2** Stakeholder Influence in Practice*

| Survey/Year | Economist/2008 | IBM/2008 | Accenture/2010 | Corporate Responsibility Magazine/2010 | Ernst & Young/2012 |
|---|---|---|---|---|---|
| **Rank 1** | Governments | Employees | Customers | Customers | Customers |
| **Rank 2** | Competitors | Business partners | Employees | Employees | Employees |
| **Rank 3** | Customers | Investors | Governments | Investors | Investors |
| **Rank 4** | Regulators | Community | Communities | Governments | Government |
| **Content focus** | Which of the following will have the greatest influence over your sustainability strategy during the next five years? | Stakeholders that companies collaborate with in their corporate social responsibility initiatives. | Over the next five years, which stakeholder groups do you believe will have the greatest impact on the way you manage societal expectations? | My company's five *top* corporate responsibility audiences are … | Rank the top three stakeholder groups in order of importance in driving your sustainability initiatives. |
| **Respondents** | More than 1,200 executives, half of them from the C-suite and 26% of them CEOs worldwide | 250 worldwide business leaders | 766 CEOs of Global Compact member companies world wide | Corporate responsibility officers from 650 companies worldwide | 272 executives and thought leaders, 85% of whom were based in the United States |

* Stakeholder denominations have been standardized to ensure comparability.

Sources: Economist. (2008). *Doing good: Business and the sustainability challenge.* London: Economist Intelligence Unit; Pohle, G., & Hittner, J. (2008). *Attaining sustainable growth through corporate social responsibility.* Somers: IBM Institute for Business Value; Lacey, P., et al. (2010). *A new era of sustainability: UN Global Compact-Acccenture CEO study 2010.* New York: Accenture Institute for High Performance; Corporate Responsibility Magazine. (2010). The state of corporate responsibility: Setting the baseline. *Corporate Responsibility Magazine.* Retrieved September 4, 2011, from www.thecro .com; Ernst & Young. (2012). *Six growing trends in corporate sustainability: An Ernst & Young survey in cooperation with GreenBiz group.* London: Ernst & Young.

of stakeholder priorities but instead applying stakeholder prioritization tools on a case-by-case basis and frequently updating the results.

Figure 4.10 summarizes three of the most commonly applied approaches for assessing stakeholder prioritization. Mitchel, Agle, and Wood[77] used a Venn diagram (see left side of Figure 4.10) to explain the stakeholder salience of a stakeholder in three dimensions: *power* (how strong the stakeholder's potential influence over the company is), *legitimacy* (how "rightful" the stakeholder's claim is), and *urgency* (how bad the consequences would be if there was not quick reaction to the claim). According to this well-accepted theory, the most important stakeholder is the one that combines all three categories, a so-called definite stakeholder.

Savage et al. use a collaboration-harm grid (see middle of Figure 4.10) that combines the power of the stakeholder to pose a threat to the company (yes/no) with the power of that stakeholder to cooperate with the company (yes/no). For the resulting four types of stakeholders, recommendations for engagement are given. Stakeholder Type 4, a "mixed blessing" stakeholder, should be involved in collaboration, as this stakeholder, on the one hand, has a high potential to collaborate and because collaboration, in this case, will also serve to "keep an eye" on the stakeholder and make sure that the stakeholder does not exert his or her power to harm the company.[78]

The simplest, but very powerful, form of stakeholder prioritization is the core-strategic-environmental framework (see right side of Figure 4.10). Core stakeholders are the most important ones, as they are crucial for the existence of the company. The second-most important category is strategic stakeholders, which if unattended do not threaten the survival of the company, but which do affect its success. The third group of environmental stakeholders should not be confused with the natural environment as a stakeholder. Environmental stakeholders are all stakeholders that exist in the company's surroundings, but which are important for neither the survival nor the success of the company.

All those stakeholder prioritization approaches fulfill different functions and provide the best results when applied in combination. It is important to remember that stakeholder prioritization is an ongoing process. The importance of stakeholders changes over time, with the company's life cycle, and stakeholders

**Figure 4.10 Main Stakeholder Prioritization Approaches**

Sources: (left) Mitchel, R. K., Agle, B. R., & Wood, Donna J. (1997). Toward a theory of stakeholder salience: Defining the principles of who and what really counts. *Academy of Management Review*, 22(4), 853–886; (middle) Savage, G. T., Nix, Timothy W., Whitehead, Carlton J., & Blair, John D. (1991). Strategies for assessing and managing organizational stakeholders. *Academy of Management Executive*, 2(5), 61–75; (right) Clarkson. (1994). In A. B. Carroll & A. K. Buchholtz (2008), *Business and society*, 7th ed. Scarborough, Canada: Cengage.

are even able to actively influence their importance for the business.[79] After stakeholders have been mapped and prioritized, it is time to start engaging with relevant stakeholders.

## 4-4c Management Process 2: Stakeholder Engagement

**Stakeholder engagement** is subdivided into two phases, which often happen in a parallel pattern: stakeholder communication and joint co-creation of activities. Stakeholder communication, which aims to create a deeper understanding of the prioritized stakeholders and facilitate co-creation of joint activities, should happen in a dialectic pattern. Companies should both talk and listen to the prioritized set of stakeholders.[80] Stakeholder communication will be described more extensively in Chapter 12, Communication and Marketing.

An important communication task is to ask stakeholders which issues they consider to be important, and *how* important. This dialogue is part of the **materiality assessment,** by which companies identify the importance of certain issues for stakeholders and contrast it with their importance to the company. This process is a central point of understanding how to create value for stakeholders. The underlying logic is that the more material or important a certain topic or issue is for a stakeholder, the more value will be created if that topic or issue is addressed by the company. In order to create maximum stakeholder value, the most material issues should be translated into indicators, measuring the degree of stakeholder satisfaction reached by the company in addressing those issues.[81] A typical analysis tool for materiality assessment is a materiality graph, as shown in Figure 4.11. Business responsibility topics, also called issues, are analyzed by deriving an overall priority from the importance of an issue to the company (horizontal axis) and to stakeholders (vertical axis). Such an assessment is the basis for an informed decision about which issues should be addressed first by a company.

**Figure 4.11 Materiality Assessment for Typical Generic Issues**

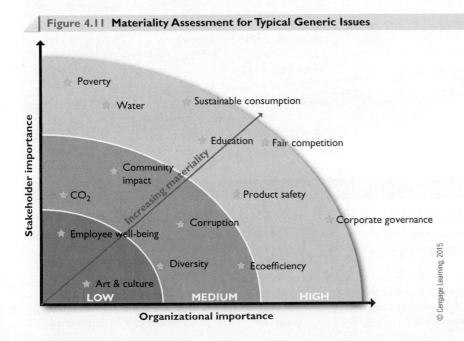

© Cengage Learning, 2015

**Stakeholder engagement** is the process of interaction with stakeholders and can be subdivided into stakeholder communication and the co-creation of joint activities.

**Materiality assessment** describes the shared importance of a specific issue to both company and stakeholders.

The ultimate step in stakeholder management is the co-creation of activities to address issues jointly between company and stakeholders. It is recommended that the company establish a portfolio of issues and related stakeholders to keep track of the value created for stakeholders and the mitigation of issues. In this chapter, we will not dive into the myriad of potential activities that could be created, as the third section of this book extensively illustrates exemplary stakeholder management practices throughout the main business functions.

Table 4.3 outlines the levels of stakeholder engagement. In the first line, you can find the different degrees of stakeholder engagement ranging from a pure one-way transmission of information to a close supporting relationship. For each degree of engagement listed, the table provides typical methods that are available. The framework also includes basic resources needed to start, a recommended attitude, and issues and benefits for initiators.[82]

**Table 4.3** Understanding the Levels of Stakeholder Engagement

| Level/stance | Information | Consultation | Deciding together | Acting together | Supporting |
|---|---|---|---|---|---|
| Typical process | Presentation and promotion | Communication and feedback | Consensus building | Partnership building | Community development |
| Typical methods | Leaflets Media Video | Surveys Meetings | Workshops Planning for real strategic choice | Partnership bodies | Advice Support Funding |
| Initiator stance | "Here's what we are going to do." | "Here's our options—what do you think?" | "We want to develop options and decide actions together." | "We want to carry out joint decisions together." | "We can help you achieve what you want within these guidelines." |
| Initiator benefits | Apparently least effort | Improves chances of getting it right | New ideas and commitment from others | Brings in additional resources | Develops capacity in the community and may reduce calls for service |
| Issues for initiator | Will people be willing to consult? | Are the options realistic? Are there others? | Do we have similar ways of deciding? Do we know and trust each other? | Where will the balance of control lie? Can we work together? | Will our aims be met as well as those of other interests? |
| Needed to start ... | Clear vision Identified audience Common language | Realistic options Ability to deal with responses | Readiness to accept new ideas and follow them through | Willingness to learn new ways of working | Commitment to continue support |

Source: Wilcox, D. (1994). *The guide to effective participation*. London: Partnership.org.

## PRINCIPLES OF RESPONSIBILITY: MANAGING FOR STAKEHOLDER VALUE

I.  Business responsibility means voluntarily assuming accountability for social, economic, and environmental issues related to stakeholders in order to optimize stakeholder value.

II. *Responsibility management* is an administrative practice centered on stakeholders and aimed at the maximization of stakeholder value, which is a necessary condition for business responsibility.

III. *Stakeholder value* is created in many different ways and differs from stakeholder to stakeholder. The goal of business responsibility is to create *shared value* between external and internal stakeholders.

IV. *CSP* is a theoretical construct that aims at defining the degree of responsibility achieved by a company. Corporate social performance can be determined quantitatively and qualitatively. CSP provides an estimate for the amount of stakeholder value created.

V. The process of *stakeholder management* consists of the two tasks: stakeholder assessment (understanding stakeholders) and stakeholder engagement (interacting with stakeholders).

VI. *Stakeholder assessment* consists of the two steps of *stakeholder identification,* through which stakeholders are mapped, and *stakeholder prioritization,* through which stakeholders' characteristics are understood and categorized by their priority for engagement.

VII. *Stakeholder engagement* consists of the two steps: *stakeholder communication,* through which direct contact with stakeholders is established, and the *co-creation of activities,* through which stakeholders and the company start to collaborate for a joint objective.

## KEY TERMS

business responsibility  89
business philanthropy  91
corporate citizenship (CC)  91
corporate social performance
    (CSP)  93
issues maturity  95

materiality assessment  103
organizational implementation  95
responsibility category  93
responsibility management  97
social entrepreneurship  91
stakeholder  87

stakeholder assessment  99
stakeholder engagement  103
stakeholder management  97
stakeholder responsiveness  93
stakeholder value  97

## EXERCISES

### A. Remember and Understand

A.1. Define the following terms and explain how they are interrelated: (a) *business responsibility,* (b) *stakeholder,* and (c) *shared value.*

A.2. Identify the four responsibility categories as they are displayed in Carroll's responsibility pyramid.

A.3. Explain the relationship, including similarities and differences, between business responsibility and (a) sustainability and (b) business ethics.

A.4. List the four levels of stakeholder responsiveness, and give a practice example for each.

### B. Apply and Experience

B.5. To which subdiscipline of business responsibility—philanthropy, citizenship, or social entrepreneurship—does each of the following examples most apply?

(a) Cisco Systems created the Networking Academy program, through which individuals of local communities can learn the skills needed to work in the network industry.

(b) Microsoft founder Bill Gates transferred a large proportion of his personal money to the Bill and Melinda Gates Foundation.

(c) With its foundation, The Body Shop tapped into the lucrative and responsible market opportunity represented by organic cosmetic products, developed without animal testing.

B.6. Look up a CSR report of a company of your choice and identify how the company prioritizes stakeholders.

B.7. Use the same report you analyzed in Exercise B.6 to classify the company stakeholders using one of the stakeholder prioritization frameworks illustrated in Figure 4.10.

### C. Analyze and Evaluate

C.8. Pick one specific business responsibility activity by a company of your choice, and analyze its CSP in the four categories used in Figure 4.4 and Figure 4.6.

C.9. Prepare a materiality graph for a business with which you are familiar. First, identify typical issues encountered in the business. Second, assess the importance of those issues to the business and main stakeholders in a materiality graph similar to the one illustrated in Figure 4.11.

C.10. Look up a leading institution in business responsibility in your region. (e.g., "CSR Europe" or "China CSR"), and analyze how it interprets business responsibility by applying the considerations discussed in the section of this chapter entitled "Classification and Interpretation."

### D. Change and Create

D.11. Imagine you are the owner of a small grocery store in the suburb of one of the world's capitals. Conduct a complete stakeholder assessment, including a stakeholder map, a stakeholder prioritization, and a materiality assessment. Based on this analysis, create three concrete lines of action that such a business could implement in order to create more stakeholder value. You could do the same exercise for an alternative business of your choice.

D.12. Approach a real business's responsibility department (most CSR reports have a contact e-mail) and propose a concrete idea for the creation of additional stakeholder value. Be clear and concise, and follow up on the topic until you receive feedback from the business. Document the exchange.

Chris Kleponis/Bloomberg/Getty images

Edward Freeman has been called the "godfather" of stakeholder theory. He changed business thinking for good, and created the basis for business responsibility theory and practice as we know it today, when he published his book *Strategic Management: A Stakeholder Perspective* in 1981.

**Since, ultimately, keeping the shareholders and customers happy is the bottom line for managers, do other stakeholders really matter that much?**

Yes, others matter, because their interests are joint. You can't create value for shareholders or customers without creating value for suppliers, employees, and communities. All five are critical to most businesses. In some, it may be best to start value creation thinking with customers, but in other businesses, it may be best to start with employees, or suppliers, or the financiers.

**How much is stakeholder management innovative value creating strategic management as opposed to merely risk management?**

Managing for stakeholders asks you to think about how a business creates value for stakeholders. How any business model evolves will entail some idea of risk. But it is important not to see "stakeholder management" as something separate from the business model.

**What are the most important issues a company should consider in managing its stakeholder relations to maximize strategic competitive advantage?**

What's important here is the purpose of the company. Managing for stakeholders assumes that there is some purpose (usually not just profits) and that "realizing purpose" is a better way to frame a business than "strategic competitive advantage."

**Can a company measure a financial return on its stakeholder policies?**

A company's financial return is an outcome of how it creates value for stakeholders. A better question is whether or not "profit" captures all the nuances that managers need to know to create as much value as possible for stakeholders. I am skeptical, though it is a place to start.

**What place does stakeholder management have in the strategic management process today?**

What else could a strategic management process be, other than how to improve the business model, which is nothing more than how the company creates value for its customers, employees, suppliers, communities, and financiers. Any strategic management process that is not oriented around such value creation could probably be improved.

**Should it, in your opinion, be given a higher priority in business schools?**

There are a lot of myths in business schools. One of them is that shareholder value and stakeholder value are opposed to each other. A number of scholars have dispelled that myth, and business schools need to take note. In a recent book, *Stakeholder Theory: The State of the Art,* my co-authors and I try to show how managing for stakeholders could be more influential in the disciplines of business. There is much work to be done.

Courtesy of Sudhir Kumar Sinha

**Employer organization:** Cipla Ltd., established in 1935, is one of the world's largest generic pharmaceutical companies with a presence in more than 170 countries. Cipla is renowned for making affordable, world-class medicines that meet the needs of patients across therapies.

**Job title:** Corporate Head—CSR
**Education:** LEAD Fellow; PGD in Rural Development

### In Practice

### What are your responsibilities?

*   Managing and heading the CR/CSR operations, devising CR policies and procedures, advising the management on issues associated with CR/sustainability standards, streamlining the CR/

CSR process, and ensuring adherence to the CR/CSR standards

- Conceptualizing and implementing community development initiatives
- Managing the entire gamut of operations including financial/statutory compliances/administrative functions
- Building and managing positive perception, and maintaining close coordination with the top management and employees
- Carrying out assessment studies, and being responsible for disclosure and CR/sustainability reporting

## What typical activities do you carry out during a day at work?

- Evaluate and assess the company's business decisions and activities on the sustainability parameters, and accordingly communicate with the top management/ board
- Intensely engage with the team, management, and employees to identify the sustainability strengths and gaps; plan and evolve policies, strategies, action plans, and measurement processes in consultation
- Engage with external stakeholders on material issues and plan strategies to address them
- Monitor and manage the MIS routinely, draw inferences from the analyses, and send in recommendations to the management
- Be responsible for all communications; be accountable to all stakeholders in addressing their expectations/concerns
- Design and implement financial systems, policies, and procedures in line with the corporate objectives to facilitate internal financial control
- Screen new projects; evaluate project reports to assess the viability of projects, predictable cash flow, and growth opportunities
- Build relationships with external stakeholders
- Integrate and push employee volunteering into the culture of the organization
- Interface with the CR teams horizontally, with the teams working in the plants of the company, in order to supplement and reinforce the company's overall CR and social commitments
- Represent the company as well as the sector at various international and national CR forums, academic discussions, and through ensuring space in various national and international committees

## How do sustainability, responsibility, and ethics topics play a role in your job?

Sustainability, responsibility, and ethics are "core values" for doing business responsibility. They are complementary to each other. To me, they are three essential pillars for any business that provide strengths to the sustainable business.

Sustainability has emerged as a result of significant concerns about the unintended social, environmental, and economic consequences of rapid population growth, economic growth, and consumption of our natural resources. A right balance is sought to be maintained while strategizing the business's economic objectives that leaves no negative impact on people and planet. Therefore, the role of a CR leader in an organization is to engage at every level with the management, managers, and employees in order to make sustainability an internal driver for everyone in the organization.

The concept of CR is associated with the negative impacts that businesses make on a wide range of stakeholders. From this perspective, the responsibility of a business is to mitigate all its negative impacts and externalities. Therefore, the role of CR leader is to study the "life cycle" of the business (products/ services) and do assessments of the impact in order to get them integrated into business strategies/plans.

"Doing right things" always can be ensured through demonstrating the highest standards of ethics in the workplace, marketplace, and in communities. While the CR leader has to work in partnerships with the different stakeholder groups in establishing the codes of ethics for employees and suppliers, the CR leader also has a role toward facilitating the board and management on the company's righteous conduct toward communities, employees, and customers.

## Insights and Challenges

### What recommendations can you give to practitioners in your field?

**Positioning of CSR:** Work hard for the CR/CSR function to be strategically positioned in the organization under the board or CEO.

**CSR versus CR:** Don't endorse the charity-led philanthropy model of CSR. Even the philanthropy has to be replaced with strategic philanthropy. Broaden the horizon of CSR; go for strategizing multistakeholder models of CR.

**Raising the bar:** Keep updating the knowledge on evolving universal consensus on understanding and great practices of CR, and accordingly set new targets by raising the bar of CR standards each time for your company.

**Stand-up firm:** Function as "whistleblowers" rather than merely as CSR managers, and stand firm and show perseverance until the issues/concerns are understood in the organization.

**Join networking:** Join local as well as international professional networks and actively participate in debates/discussions. Contribute and simultaneously learn from the network. Also encourage your CEO and senior management to attend and join CR/sustainability forums/public discourse. Facilitate their understanding of CR from the viewpoint of the overarching responsibilities of the business.

### What are the main challenges of your job?

There is always a clear conflict in the global and local understanding of CSR. While the global understanding of corporate responsibility has evolved to encompass ethics, governance, human rights, supply chain, environment, community, and employees into its fold, the local understanding of CSR in India, to large extent, remains tilted to businesses' philanthropic response to society. In general in India, the major challenge for a CSR leader lies in shifting the mind-set within the management from philanthropy-led CSR to accepting to mitigate the impact as a first and foremost "mandatory responsibility" and then to creating shared value for all as the expected and desired responsibility.

## SOURCES

1. Corporate Responsibility Magazine. (2010). The state of corporate responsibility: Setting the baseline. *Corporate Responsibility Magazine.* Retrieved September 4, 2011, from www.thecro.com
2. Ernst & Young. (2012). *Six growing trends in corporate sustainability: An Ernst & Young survey in cooperation with GreenBiz group.* London: Ernst & Young.
3. KPMG. (2011). *KPMG international survey of corporate responsibility reporting 2011.*
4. Handy, C. (2002). What's a business for? *Harvard Business Review, 80*(4), 49-54.
5. Donham, W. B. (1927). The social significance of business. *Harvard Business Review, 5*(4), 406–419.
6. Donham, W. B. (1927). The social significance of business. *Harvard Business Review, 5*(4), 406–419, p. 406.
7. Sprunger, M. (2011). An introduction to Confucianism. *VI. Confucianism: The religion of social propriety.* Retrieved August 29, 2011, from http://urantiabook.org/archive/readers/601_confucianism.htm
8. Melzer, U. (2011). *50 biblische Erfolgsgrundlagen im Geschäftsleben—23. Kapitel—Gib den Zehnten!* Retrieved April 10, 2012, from Word Press: http://50-erfolgsgrundlagen.de/blog/?p=274
9. Beekun, R. I., & Badawi, J. A. (2005). Balancing ethical responsibility among multiple organizational stakeholders: The Islamic perspective. *Journal of Business Ethics, 60*(2), 131–145; Siwar, C., & Hossain, M. T. (2009). An analysis of Islamic CSR concept and the opinions of Malaysian managers. *Management of Environmental Quality: An International Journal, 20*(3), 290–298.
10. O'Brien, T., & Paeth, S. (2007). *Religious perspectives on business ethics: An anthology.* Lanham, MD: Rowman & Littlefield; Hemingway, C. A., & Maclagan, P. W. (2004). Managers' personal values as drivers of corporate social responsibility. *Journal of Business Ethics, 50*(1), 33–44; Ramasamy, B., Yeung, M. C. H., & Au, A. K. M. (2010). Consumer support for corporate social responsibility (CSR): The role of religion and values. *Journal of Business Ethics, 91*(1), 61–72; Brammer, S., Williams, G., & Zinkin, J. (2007). Religion and attitudes to corporate social responsibility in a large cross-country sample. *Journal of Business Ethics, 71,* 229–243.
11. Donham, W. B. (1927). The social significance of business. *Harvard Business Review, 5*(4), 406–419.
12. Bowen, H. R. (1953). *Social responsibilities of the businessman.* New York: Harper. Retrieved from http://books.google.com/books?id=4y0vAAAAMAAJ&q=The+Social+Responsibility+of+the+Business+Man&dq=The+Social+Responsibility+of+the+Business+Man&hl=es&ei=m2hdTpKSN8LlsQKWgZkj&sa=X&oi=book_result&ct=result&resnum=1&ved=0CDAQ6AEwAA
13. Carroll, A. B. (1999). Corporate social responsibility: A definitional construct. *Business & Society, 38*(3), 268–295.
14. In a Google scholar search conducted on March 18, 2012, the *New York Times Magazine* article by Friedman (see note 15) was cited 5,216 times, while the second-most frequently cited paper, Carroll's article on the responsibility pyramid (see note 20), was cited merely 1,830 times. The third most-cited (1,764 times) article was Porter and Kramer's article on strategy and society: Porter, M., & Kramer, M. (2006). Strategy and society: The link between competitive advantage and corporate social responsibility. *Harvard Business Review, 84*(12), 78–92.
15. Friedman, M. (1970, November 14). The only responsibility of business is profit. *New York Times Magazine,* p. 2.
16. Economist. (2006). A heavyweight champ, at five foot two: The legacy of Milton Friedman, a giant among economists. *The Economist.* Retrieved April 10, 2012, from www.economist.com/node/8313925?story_id=8313925
17. Levitt, T. (1958). The dangers of social responsibility. *Harvard Business Review, 36*(5), 41–50.
18. Husted, B. W., & Salazar, J. D. J. (2006). Taking Friedman seriously: Maximizing profits and social performance. *Journal of Management Studies, 43*(1), 75–91.

19. Freeman, R. E. (1984/2010). *Strategic management: A stakeholder approach* (p. 25). Cambridge: Cambridge University Press. First published in 1984.

20. Carroll, A. B. (1991, July–August). The pyramid of corporate social responsibility: Toward the moral management of organizational stakeholders. *Business Horizons*, 225–235.

21. Commission of the European Communities. (2006). *Implementing the partnership for growth and jobs: Making Europe a pole of excellence of CSR*. Brussels: European Union.

22. Habisch, A., et al. (2005). *Corporate social responsibility across Europe*. New York: Springer.

23. Commission of the European Communities. (2012). Sustainable and responsible business: Multi-stakeholder forum on corporate social responsibility (CSR). *Enterprise and Industry*. Retrieved April 9, 2012, from http://ec.europa.eu/enterprise/policies/sustainable-business/corporate-social-responsibility/multi-stakeholder-forum/index_en.htm

24. EABIS. (2012). *Academy of Business in Society*. Retrieved April 9, 2012, from www.eabis.org/; CSR Europe. (2012). CSR Europe: The European business network for CSR. *CSR Europe*. Retrieved April 9, 2012, from www.csreurope.org/

25. Global Compact. (2011). The United Nations Global Compact. Retrieved August 30, 2011, from www.unglobalcompact.org/

26. PRME. (2011). Principles of responsible management education. Retrieved August 30, 2011, from www.unprme.org/

27. ISO. (2010). *International standard ISO 26000: Guidance on social responsibility*. Geneva: International Organization for Standardization.

28. Waddock, S. A., Bodwell, C., & Graves, S. B. (2002). Responsibility: The new business imperative. *Academy of Management Executive*, 47(1), 132–147.

29. CSR Europe. (2012). National partner network. *CSR Europe: The European business network for CSR*. Retrieved April 9, 2012, from www.csreurope.org/nationalpartnernetwork.php

30. Spence, L. J. (2007). CSR and small business in a European policy context: The five "C"s of CSR and small business research agenda 2007. *Business and Society Review*, 112(4), 533–552; Jenkins, H. M. (2004). A critique of conventional CSR theory: An SME perspective (2004). *Journal of General Management*, 29(4), 37–57; Visser, W. (2006). Corporate social responsibility in developing countries. *Millennium Development Goals*, 11(1), 473–499; Raynard, P., & Forstater, M. (2002). *Corporate social responsibility: Implications for small and medium enterprises in developing countries*. Vienna: UNIDO.

31. Visser, W. (2010). *The age of responsibility: CSR 2.0 and the new DNA of business*. Chichester: Wiley; Laasch, O., & Flores, U. (2010). Implementing profitable CSR: The CSR 2.0 business compass. In M. Pohl & N. Tolhurst, *Responsible business: How to manage a CSR strategy successfully* (pp. 289–309). Chichester: Wiley; Visser, W. (2008). CSR 2.0: The new era of corporate sustainability and responsibility. *CSR Inspiration Series, 1*.

32. Commission of the European Communities. (2006). *Implementing the partnership for growth and jobs: Making Europe a pole of excellence of CSR*. Brussels: European Union.

33. Additional terms, such as *corporate citizenship (CC)*, *philanthropy*, and *social entrepreneurship*, will be dealt with in the next section, entitled "Interpreting Responsible Business."

34. Dahlsrud, A. (2006). How corporate social responsibility is defined: An analysis of 37 definitions. *Corporate Social Responsibility and Environmental Management*, 15(1), 1–13.

35. Valor, C. (2005). Corporate social responsibility and corporate citizenship: Towards corporate accountability. *Business and Society Review*, 110(2), 191–212.

36. United Nations. (1987). *Our common future*. World Commission on the Environment and Development. New York: United Nations.

37. ISO. (2010). *International standard ISO 26000: Guidance on social responsibility*. Geneva: International Organization for Standardization.

38. ISO. (2010). *International standard ISO 26000: Guidance on social responsibility*. Geneva: International Organization for Standardization.

39. Fioravante, P. L. (2010). Corporate philanthropy: A strategic marketing consideration. *Journal of Applied Business and Economics*, 11(3), 91–96; Bruch, H., & Walter, F. (2005). The keys to rethinking corporate philanthropy. *MIT Sloan Management Review*, 47(1), 49–55; Porter, M., & Kramer, M. (2002). The competitive advantage of corporate philanthropy. *Harvard Business Review*, 80(12), 56–68; Godfrey, P. C. (2005). The relationship between corporate philanthropy and shareholder wealth: A risk management perspective. *Academy of Management Review*, 30(4), 777–798.

40. Moir, L., & Taffler, R. (2004). Does corporate philanthropy exist? Business giving to the arts in the U.K. *Journal of Business Ethics*, 54(2), 149–161.

41. Matten, D., & Crane, A. (2005). Corporate citizenship: Toward an extended theoretical conceptualization. *Academy of Management Review*, 30(1), 166–179; Altman, B. W., & Vidaver-Cohen, D. (2002). A framework for understanding corporate citizenship: Introduction to the special edition of *Business and Society Review* "corporate citizenship for the new millennium." *Business and Society Review*, 105(1), 1–7.

42. Matten, D., Crane, A., & Chapple, W. (2003). Behind the mask: Revealing the true face of corporate citizenship. *Journal of Business Ethics*, 45(1–2), 109–120; Matten, D., & Crane, A. (2005). Corporate citizenship: Toward an extended theoretical conceptualization. *Academy of Management Review*, 30(1), 166–179.

43. Austin, J., & Reficco, E. (2009). *Corporate Social Entrepreneurship*. HBS Working Paper Series, Vol. 101, No. 9.

44. Matten, D., & Moon, J. (2008). "Implicit" and "explicit" CSR: A conceptual framework for a comparative understanding of corporate social responsibility. *Academy of Management Review*, 33(2), 404–424.

45. Garriga, E., & Melé, D. (2004). Corporate social responsibility theories: Mapping the territory. *Journal of Business Ethics, 53*, 51–71.

46. Matten, D., & Moon, J. (2008). "Implicit" and "explicit" CSR: A conceptual framework for a comparative understanding of corporate social responsibility. *Academy of Management Review*, 33(2), 404–424.

47. Misani, N. (2010). The convergence of corporate social responsibility practices. *Management Research Review*, 33(7), 734–748.

48. See an extensive illustration of the difference between social and nonsocial stakeholders in the section later in this chapter entitled "Management Process 1: Stakeholder Assessment (Planning)."

49. FOE. (2005). *Briefing: Corporate accountability*. London: Friends of Earth; Valor, C. (2005). Corporate social responsibility and corporate citizenship: Towards corporate accountability. *Business and Society Review*, 110(2), 191–212; AccountAbility. (2008). *AA1000 accountability principles standard 2008*. London: AccountAbility.

50. Vanberg, V. J. (2007). Corporate social responsibility and the "game of catallaxy": The perspective of constitutional economics. *Constitutional Political Economy*, 18(3), 199–222.

51. Wood, D. J. (1991). Corporate social performance revisited. *Academy of Management Review*, 16(4), 691–718; Wartick, S. L., & Cochran, P. L. (1985). The evolution of the corporate social performance model. *Academy of Management Review*, 10(4), 758–769.

52. Carroll, A. B. (1979). A three-dimensional conceptual model of corporate performance. *Academy of Management Review*, 4(4), 497–505; Carroll, A. B. (1991, July–August). The pyramid of corporate social responsibility: Toward the moral management of organizational stakeholders. *Business Horizons*, 225–235; Schwartz, M. S., & Carroll, A. B. (2003). Corporate social responsibility: A three-domain approach. *Business Ethics Quarterly*, 13(4), 503–530.

53. Clarkson, M. B. E. (1995). A stakeholder framework for analyzing and evaluating corporate social performance. *Academy of Management Review*, 20(1), 82–117.

54. Martin, R. (2002). The virtue matrix: Calculating the return on corporate. *Harvard Business Review*, 80(3), 68–75.

55. Zadeck, S. (2004). The path to corporate social responsibility. *Harvard Business Review*, 82, 125–132.

56. Zadeck, S. (2004). The path to corporate social responsibility. *Harvard Business Review*, 82, 125–132. Note that Zadeck divides the first level into two levels, called *compliant* and *defensive*, but we have altered those features in order to integrate the model into the overall CSP framework provided here.

57. Waddock, S. A., Bodwell, C., & Graves, S. B. (2002). Responsibility: The new business imperative. *Academy of Management Executive*, 47(1), 132–147.

58. Orlitzky, M., Schmidt, F. L., & Rynes, S. L. (2003). Corporate social and financial performance: A meta-analysis. *Organization Studies*, 24(3), 403–441; Waddock, S. A., Bodwell, C., & Graves, S. B. (2002). Responsibility: The new business imperative. *Academy of Management Executive*, 47(1), 132–147.

59. Freeman, R. E., & McVea, J. (2001). *A stakeholder approach to strategic management*. Darden Business School Working Paper, Vol. 1, No. 2, p. 4.

60. Freeman, R. E., & McVea, J. (2001). *A stakeholder approach to strategic management*. Darden Business School Working Paper, Vol. 1, No. 2, p. 4.

61. Freeman, R. E. (1984/2010). *Strategic management: A stakeholder approach* (p. 25). Cambridge: Cambridge University Press. First published in 1984.

62. Myllykangas, P., Kujala, J., & Lehtimäki, H. (2010). Analyzing the essence of stakeholder relationships: What do we need in addition to power, legitimacy, and urgency? *Journal of Business Ethics*, 96(1), 65–72, p. 65.

63. Hillman, A. J., & Keim, G. D. (2001). Shareholder value, stakeholder management, and social issues: What's the bottom line? *Strategic Management Journal*, 22(2), 125–139; Berman, S. L., et al. (1999). Does stakeholder orientation matter? The relationship between stakeholder management models and firm financial performance. *Academy of Management Journal*, 42(5), 488–506; Preston, L. E., & Donaldson, T. (1999). Stakeholder management and organizational wealth. *Academy of Management Review*, 24(4), 619–620.

64. Porter, M., & Kramer, M. (2002). The competitive advantage of corporate philanthropy. *Harvard Business Review*, 80(12), 56–68; European Commission. (2011). *A renewed EU strategy 2011–14 for corporate social responsibility*. Brussels: European Union.

65. Jensen, M. C. (2002). Value maximization, stakeholder theory, and the corporate objective function. *Business Ethics Quarterly*, 12(2), 235–256; Freeman, R. E. (2010). Managing for stakeholders: Trade-offs or value creation. *Journal of Business Ethics*, 96(1), 7–9.

66. ISO. (2010). *International standard ISO 26000: Guidance on social responsibility*. Geneva: International Organization for Standardization; Sachs, S., Post, J. E., & Preston, L. E. (2002). Managing the extended enterprise: The new stakeholder view. *California Management Review*, 45(1), 6–28.

67. Berman, S. L., et al. (1999). Does stakeholder orientation matter? The relationship between stakeholder management models and firm financial performance. *Academy of Management Journal*, 42(5), 488–506.

68. Crane, A., Matten, D., & Moon, J. (2004). Stakeholders as citizens? Rethinking rights, participation, and democracy. *Journal of Business Ethics*, 53(1–2), 107–122; Matten, D., & Crane, A. (2005). What is stakeholder democracy? Perspectives and issues. *Business Ethics: A European Review*, 14(1), 6–13.

69. Freeman, E., & Reed, D. L. (1983). Stockholders and stakeholders: A new perspective on corporate governance. *California Management Review*, 25(3), 88–106; Freeman, E., & Evan, W. M. (1990). Corporate governance: A stakeholder interpretation. *Journal of Behavioral Economics*, 19(4), 337–359.

70. AccountAbility. (2008). *AA1000 accountability principles standard 2008*. London: AccountAbility.

71. Freeman, R. E. (1984/2010). *Strategic management: A stakeholder approach*. Cambridge: Cambridge University Press. First published in 1984; ISO. (2010). *International standard ISO 26000: Guidance on social responsibility*. Geneva: International Organization for Standardization; Carroll, A. B., & Buchholtz, A. K. (2008). *Business and society*, 7th ed. Scarborough, Canada: Cengage.

72. Clarkson, M. B. E. (1995). A stakeholder framework for analyzing and evaluating corporate social performance. *Academy of Management Review*, 20(1), 82–117.

73. Carroll, A. B., & Buchholtz, A. K. (2008). *Business and society*, 7th ed. Scarborough, Canada: Cengage. Fitch, H. G. (1976). Achieving corporate social responsibility. *Academy of Management Review*, 1(1), 38–46.

74. Starik, M. (1995). Should trees have managerial standing? Toward stakeholder status for non-human nature. *Journal of Business Ethics*, *14*(3), 207–217; Fitch, H. G. (1976). Achieving corporate social responsibility. *Academy of Management Review*, *1*(1), 38–46; Driscoll, C., & Starik, M. (2004). The primordial stakeholder: Advancing the conceptual consideration of stakeholder status for the natural environment. *Journal of Business Ethics*, *49*(1), 55–73.

75. Mitchel, R. K., Agle, B. R., & Wood, Donna J. (1997). Toward a theory of stakeholder salience: Defining the principles of who and what really counts. *Academy of Management Review*, *22*(4), 853–886.

76. Pajunen, K. (2010). A "black box" of stakeholder thinking. *Journal of Business Ethics*, *96*(1), 27–32.

77. Mitchel, R. K., Agle, B. R., & Wood, Donna J. (1997). Toward a theory of stakeholder salience: Defining the principles of who and what really counts. *Academy of Management Review*, *22*(4), 853–886.

78. Savage, G. T., Nix, T. W., Whitehead, C. J., & Blair, J. D. (1991). Strategies for assessing and managing organizational stakeholders. *Academy of Management Executive*, *2*(5), 61–75.

79. Myllykangas, P., Kujala, J., & Lehtimäki, H. (2010). Analyzing the essence of stakeholder relationships: What do we need in addition to power, legitimacy, and urgency? *Journal of Business Ethics*, *96*(1), 65–72.

80. Conaway, R. N., & Laasch, O. (2012). *Communicating business responsibility: Strategies, concepts and cases for integrated marketing communication*. New York: Business Expert Press; Morsing, M., & Schultz, M. (2006). Corporate social responsibility communication: Stakeholder information, response and involvement strategies. *Business Ethics: A European Review*, *15*(4), 323–338; Hemmati, M. (2010). *Multi-stakeholder processes for governance and sustainability: Beyond deadlock and conflict*. London: Earthscan.

81. Jensen, M. C. (2002). Value maximization, stakeholder theory, and the corporate objective function. *Business Ethics Quarterly*, *12*(2), 235–256.

82. Wilcox, D. (1994). *The guide to effective participation*. London: Partnership.org.

## 05

Rights Fairness
Whistleblowing Behavioral Ethics Values
Consequentialism Greates Happiness Principle
Dilemma Discourse Compliance Absolutism vs Relativism Justice Categorical Imperative Ethics Management
Deontology Integrity
Ethical Decision
Descriptive Ethics

# ETHICS: MANAGING FOR MORAL EXCELLENCE

*You will be able to...*

1  **...solve moral dilemma situations by applying the three main theories of moral philosophy.**

2  **...analyze why people do right or wrong things.**

3  **...apply ethics management instruments to help people make the right decisions and take the right actions when facing moral issues and opportunities.**

Ninety-eight percent of employees with a weak ethics management program observe ethical misconduct. Only 43 percent of employees in companies with a strong ethics program do so.[1]

Ninety-five percent of companies either steadily maintained their budget for ethics and compliance (E&C) or increased it. Ninety-eight percent maintained or even increased their staffing for E&C.[2]

Fortune 500 companies deploy a wide variety of ethics management tools. Written standards exist in 96 percent. Other tools are disciplining of employees' ethical misconduct (92%), ethics training (91%), anonymous whistleblowing mechanisms (91%), ethics advising (90%), and ethical employee performance evaluation (81%).[3]

Author: Oliver Laasch; Contributors: Bligh Grant, John C. Lenzi, Josie Fisher, Linda K. Treviño, Matthias Wühle, Sharon Dafny

# "We Are Innocent!" Are You Really?

"Hello, we're innocent" is the ambiguous main heading of the British company Innocent's "us" section. Comments like "A sad day for independent and ethical business," "You just killed your business," "Your business is tainted" are but a few of those made by customers after the once-hailed, all-natural smoothie business Innocent accepted major funding from The Coca-Cola Company (TCCC) in 2009. Did the founders of Innocent make the right ethical decision? Did they manage the moral dilemma of either accepting or not accepting the TCCC offer? Let's start at the beginning.

Innocent was founded by three friends who jointly graduated from Cambridge University. The idea came during a snowboarding holiday in 1998, which led to the foundation of the company less than a year later. One crucial point involved pilot-testing their smoothies at a London music festival, having people try their smoothies and vote on the question, "Should we quit our jobs to make these smoothies?" The "yes" voting bin was full, while there were only three votes in the "no" bin.

After twelve years, Innocent had become the number-one smoothie brand in the United Kingdom. The company sold more than 2 million pure fruit smoothies per week through 11,000 outlets. A team of 250 people worked across Europe and in the London headquarters, called the "fruit tower." Products were sold in thirteen different countries. The annual revenue was in excess of £100 million.

What issue upset customers so much in the Coca-Cola deal? Innocent implicitly had developed an ethical corporate identity of high values and literally had "innocence" in anything the company did. Innocent claimed to be all natural and organic, to use green electricity, and to apply fair sourcing practices. The company's claim of doing everything out of its virtuous character is, in moral philosophy, called virtue ethics. Customers expected the company to be virtuous and literally innocent in every respect. When Innocent first accepted a percentage of ownership by TCCC in 2009, which was raised to 58 percent stock ownership, Innocent customers perceived this move as contraditory to the virtuous image of the company. TCCC,

having been often criticized for the adverse health effects of many of its flagship products, was perceived as the exact opposite of what Innocent should be, and therefore as the enemy.

One of the three company founders, Richard Reed, disagreed, basing his argument on a different moral philosophy than virtue. He said that the involvement of TCCC would enable Innocent to bring the advantages of the smoothies to customers that otherwise could not be reached and, in this way, would create even more good. This argument goes in line with the ethical stream of argumentation called consequentialism, judging how good a decision is by its outcome. In consequentialism, the end of creating "the greatest happiness possible" may justify many means. In retrospect, Reed did a very good job of combining both contradictory paradigms by assuring customers that TCCC would, in spite of having the majority stake, not be granted any control in the company's operations. So, Reed assured customers that although the money might not be virtuous, the company's operations would be. This clever "walk on the tightrope" is probably the reason for the company's ongoing success.

What can the company learn from this episode? To remain successful, it will need to create a culture of ethics that pays its dues to both ethics theories mentioned. First, the company will have to assess the situational and individual factors that play a role in employees' decision making. This is called descriptive ethics. Once those factors are understood, there is a need to apply ethics management tools such as a code of ethics, ethics training, and counseling to make sure that everybody in the company is able to make the morally right decisions and act upon them at any time. If the company succeeds in this endeavor, it will be able to assure customers not only that "We are innocent," but also that they will remain so.

Sources: Innocent. (2012). *Hello, we're innocent.* Retrieved August 20, 2012, from Innocent: www.innocentdrinks.co.uk/us/our-story; The Independent. (2009, April 12). Slaughter of the innocent? Or is Coke the real deal? *The Independent;* Innocent. (2012). *About innocent.* Retrieved August 20, 2012, from Innocent: www.innocentdrinks.co.uk/us/press/about-innocent

# 5-1 ETHICAL BUSINESS AND ETHICS MANAGEMENT

*"Managers engage in discretionary decision-making behavior affecting the lives and well-being of others. Thus, they are involved in ethical decision making."*[4]

Does business have issues? The answer is yes. As with any other type of organization, business and the managers working in organizations face a wide variety of ethical

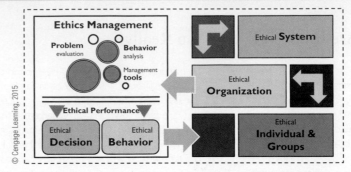

problems, dilemmas, and issues for which there is not one clear answer. Should I fire an older employee as he or she is performing less consistently, or should I keep that person as a reward for all the years served to the company? Should I close the deal with that cigarette company in spite of knowing that their products kill millions of people? Should I recommend that marketing campaign of unhealthy food products to children for its profit potential? Business ethics is about doing the right thing in such ethical problem situations and about realizing ethical opportunities to do good. In these situations, managers first have to understand that there is an issue, then decide what is the right alternative, and finally, act accordingly. The more managers and employees do the right thing and separate the acceptable from the unacceptable, the higher will be the whole organization's ethical performance. The management tool for achieving such performance is ethics management, the management of ethical issues. Figure 5.1 describes the processes and outcomes of ethics management with greater detail.

In the first section of this chapter, we provide an overview of the development of ethics from its philosophical roots, to the formation of the field of business ethics, to its current practice in business, such as the use of ethical business rankings and the topic of compliance.

The second section provides the basic concepts of business ethics. Moral dilemmas are introduced and illustrated as the core piece of business ethics. The three main topic areas of business ethics—normative ethics, descriptive ethics, and ethics management—are introduced and illustrated extensively. Normative ethics is illustrated by the three main streams of moral theories: consequentialism, deontology, and virtue ethics. Descriptive ethics explains peoples' moral behavior by individual and situational factors. Ethics management tools are listed and discussed, including codes of ethics, whistleblowing hotlines, and ethics audits.

The third section sketches the ethics management process in its three phases of issue assessment and discusses ethical behavior analysis and the application of ethics management tools with greater detail, while drawing from insights of the first two sections.

## 5-2 ORIGINS OF BUSINESS ETHICS

*"We start here tonight a new foundation to deal with one of the greatest of topics—a subdivision of ethics; for business ethics with its own peculiar characteristics is, after all, a subdivision of general ethics."*[5]

While ethics in the form of moral philosophy has a long history, dating back to the ancient Greek philosopher Plato, business ethics is a rather young discipline that has exceeded its purely philosophical roots. As illustrated in Table 5.1, business ethics

**Table 5.1** Milestones in the Development of Business Ethics

| Milestone | Facts |
|-----------|-------|
| Roots | Prephilosophical versus philosophical roots |
| Concepts and the disciplines | Business ethics, ethics management, normative ethics, descriptive ethics, ethical decision making, applied ethics |
| Institutionalization, status quo, and future | Ethics & Compliance Officer Association (ECOA)<br>Annual evaluation of most ethical corporations<br>Use of ethics management tools |

© Cengage Learning, 2015

is a fascinating multidisciplinary mix of concepts that have long been institutionalized. The following subsections will provide a brief overview of the development of business ethics.

## 5-2a Roots of Business Ethics

In order to understand business ethics fully, it is helpful to appreciate its origins. Three main stages of development can be characterized: first, the prephilosophical phase; second, the philosophical phase; and third, the transition from philosophy to business ethics. During the prephilosophical phase, moral order and what is right and good was defined through the customs, values, and norms of a society. The question arose of what higher principles such norms should be based upon. The search for such higher principles led to the beginning of the long philosophical phase, which provided a varied set of different reasoning mechanisms and higher principles by which to find out what good and right should mean in different contexts. Those philosophies included, among others, decision principles, such as the virtue of the person; responsibilities to others and oneself; and arguments related to human rights, justice, and the creation of greatest happiness for oneself or others.[6] When those general moral principles of right and wrong began to be applied to special areas of decision making, such as ethics in medicine and ethics of the businessperson and business, they were called **applied ethics**.

Another root of what we today know as business ethics are the social sciences. Business ethics is a multidisciplinary field in which major thinkers from many fields have played an important role. Topics such as moral development, behavioral psychology, organizational theory, and, of course, business and economics have contributed much to business ethics. Figure 5.2 introduces some of the most influential thinkers and thoughts that have played a role in the development of business ethics. Some of the personalities mentioned, like Immanuel Kant and Lawrence Kohlberg, are godfathers of established groundbreaking theories, while others, like Linda Klebe Treviño, are outstanding pioneers in new fields.

## 5-2b The Discipline of Business Ethics

Business ethics as the applied ethics of the business field started developing in the early twentieth century in isolated situations. As early as 1929, Wallace B. Donham claimed to "start business ethics as a subdivision of general ethics" in the management journal *Harvard Business Review*. The development of business ethics as a field has been divided into five main phases. As illustrated in Figure 5.3, those phases have jointly resulted in today's understanding of business ethics.[7]

In the first phase before 1960, entitled "Ethics in business" in Figure 5.3, there was no accepted field of business ethics. General ethical principles, derived from

**Applied ethics** are disciplines where ethical theories have been applied to a specific type or area of decision making.

## Figure 5.2 Figureheads and Central Ideas of Business Ethics

**Plato & Aristotle (422–322 B.C.)**
Virtue ethics and good life

**Lawrence Kohlberg (1958)**
Stages of Moral Development

**Immanuel Kant (1785)**
Ethics of duty

**John Bordley Rawls (1971)**
Theory of justice

**Jeremy Bentham (1789)**
Greatest happiness principle

**Jürgen Habermas (1981)**
Discourse ethics

**John Stewart Mill (1863)**
Utilitarianism

**Linda K. Treviño (1986)**
Behavioral ethics: Situational & individual

The Art Archive/Alamy; Lee Lockwood/Time & Life Pictures/Getty Images; Lebrecht Music and Arts Photo Library/Alamy; Steve Pyke/Getty Images; Stock Montage/Archive Photos/Getty Images; Arne Dedert/picture-alliance/dpa/Newscom; Library of Congress Prints and Photographs Division; Courtesy of Linda K. Treviño

## Figure 5.3 The Development of Business Ethics

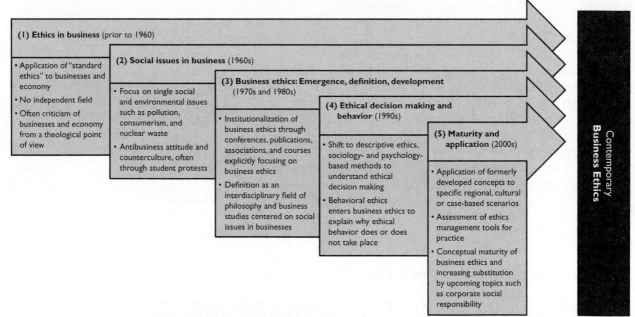

Sources: Based on DeGeorge, R. T. (1987). The status of business ethics: Past and future. *Journal of Business Ethics*, 6(3), 201; Ma, Z. (2009). The status of contemporary business ethics research: Present and future. *Journal of Business Ethics*, 90(3), 255–265; Liedekerke, L., & Dubbink, W. (2008). Twenty years of European business ethics—Past developments and future concerns. *Journal of Business Ethics*, 82(2), 273–280.

**Moral philosophy** is the discipline that uses philosophy to evaluate moral dilemma situations.

classic **moral philosophy,** were applied to the field of business. Criticism was often theologically and religiously motivated. Theological scholars such as Messner and Niebuhr criticized the morality of business focusing on issues such as just wages, the morality of capitalism, and materialistic values. In the second phase, "Social issues in business," the criticism moved from a theological basis to a broader societal movement of countercultures, such as the hippie culture. The issues in business, criticized often in a spontaneous and not very profoundly reasoned manner, were broadened to include topics such as pollution and toxic and nuclear waste. In the third phase from the 1970s on, business ethics began to emerge as a field. First conferences, publications, and business school courses allowed for a discourse that led to the development of business ethics as an academic discipline, and then increasingly the ideas were picked up by companies and translated into practice. This process led to the still valid understanding of business ethics as the interdisciplinary study of ethical problems in business. From this basic understanding, the discipline of business ethics was developed to great relevance in both theory and practice.[8]

From the early 1990s on, business ethics began to add to the moral considerations about right and wrong by studying the ethical decision-making process of individuals and groups in organizations. The field moved from merely defining what is right or wrong, so-called normative ethics, to describing why right or wrong decisions are made. This approach is called descriptive ethics.[9] In the early years of the new century, it became clear that the biggest conceptual advances in business ethics had been made and the focus shifted to applying those concepts to varying contexts and environments. A good example is the search for a truly international framework of business ethics, exceeding the two main regions, North America and Europe.[10] Also, practical applications became a prominent research topic; how to use ethical management tools, such as codes of ethics, training, counseling, and whistleblowing mechanisms (tools for reporting legal or ethical misconduct in a company), especially, received heightened attention.

Contemporary business ethics is now a mature field, based on rich and useful concepts that are continually being refined for valuable practice application. With the maturity of the field has come a point where former subtopics of the field have spun off to form their own fields. Most notably, the topics centered on stakeholder responsibilities, corporate responsibility, and corporate citizenship described in Chapter 4 have now detached to a degree that makes them form an independent field.

## 5-2c Institutionalization, Status Quo, and Future

While the academic field of business ethics seems to have entered into a maturity stage, the topic itself has led to flourishing activity by business practitioners. Ninety-six percent of Fortune 500 companies, for instance, have a code of ethics. Many other ethics management tools have become a standard feature of modern businesses.[11] Budgets and staffing for the E&C functions are expected to remain stable and even slightly increase.[12] The job position of ethics and compliance officer has become a given for many companies. It has been institutionalized, as an example, through the Ethics & Compliance Officer Association (ECOA), which is a professional network of ethics management practitioners.[13] Annual rankings, such as the "World's Most Ethical" (WME) Companies, have established pragmatic methodologies for benchmarking the ethical performance of companies. WME helps companies to self-assess their "Ethics Quotient" through a series of questions addressing, among other topics, ethics management practices, external rankings, and potential involvement in ethical or legal issues or scandals.[14] Other salient organizations dealing with business ethics in practice are, for instance, the Better Business Bureau (BBB), the Business Roundtable (BRT), and the Ethics Resource Center (ERC). More specifically, many international organizations treating single ethical issues such as human rights, corruption, and fair trade and labor practices are in place.

Unfortunately, this business sector activity has not always led to the aspired outcomes. Ethics activities also have had little effect on the overall economic system. Corporate scandals of unethical behavior from slavery to corruption are uncovered frequently. Also, the 2007 financial crisis was caused by ethical misconduct on individual, organizational, and systemic levels. The ethical dilemma of either forfeiting short-run profits or accepting subprime loans that were not viable in the long run was the trigger of the global economic crisis, which has caused great suffering. Business ethics theory has been found to have little effect on the real-life ethical performance of businesses. Thus, the main challenge for business ethics in the future will be to translate theory to real-life impact and relevance for the business sector.[15] If there will ever be a fundamental redesign process of the economic system, the normative component of economic ethics will play a crucial role in questioning existing paradigms and developing alternative approaches.

## 5-3 BASIC CONCEPTS OF BUSINESS ETHICS

*"In our conventional understanding of the economy as a totality, that is, in the academic field of economics, any ethical precondition is absent; there is no room for it in the logic of economics."*[16]

As seen in the preceding quote, pairing economics and business with ethics can, in itself, seem like an inherent contradiction. In the following conceptual part of this chapter, we provide the most important concepts needed for a basic understanding of how business and ethics can be combined.

### 5-3a Defining Business Ethics

An early article on defining business ethics states that practicing business ethics is as difficult as "nailing Jello to a wall." The authors surveyed 254 texts on business ethics and found 308 different concepts in the definitions given.[17] In order to reduce complexity, we will provide a very narrow, but clear, working definition of business ethics. Readers will also be exposed to diverging understandings of business ethics, which will then be condensed to frame the working definition used in this book.

Our working definition is that **business ethics** is the interdisciplinary study of ethical issues and opportunities in business. This very basic definition has two core elements, *interdisciplinary* and *moral issues*. The latter, the ethical issue, is the main subject of business ethics in theory and practice. Business ethics in practice aims at achieving the right decision and behavior in a certain ethical issue, or dilemma, situation. Business ethics in theory aims at studying how people in business should act and why they do or do not act that way. Business ethics needs to draw from many disciplines. Most notably, the discipline of philosophy helps to define what the right thing to do is, psychology helps us understand why people do or do not act in a ethically correct way, and the discipline of business and economics is necessary to understand ethical issues in the context of business. Although this simplistic definition of business ethics neglects the complexity of the overall topic, it establishes a good entry point to the topic. In the following, you will find discussion of the central conceptual areas of business ethics that are important for framing the topic and reaching a deeper understanding of business ethics.

**Business ethics** is the interdisciplinary study of ethical issues and opportunities in business.

## 5-3b Levels of Application

The field of business ethics, in its common understanding, is applied on three different levels, as shown in Figure 5.4. On the most elementary level, business ethics scrutinizes single individuals and small groups together. Typical questions might be: Why does this accountant become involved in fraudulent accounting practices? Why did that superior make discriminatory remarks to a female colleague? This level of analysis has also been called **individual ethics** or, when applied to the behavior of individuals in a certain vocational function, professional ethics.

Organizations are the object to be studied on the next broader level of analysis. Intuitively, this level is the one that should rightfully be called business ethics, as businesses are a specific type of an organization. Examples of an analysis on the level of **organizational ethics** could ask: Why did this company venture into a sin industry? (A sin industry is an industry that is perceived as having an imminent negative impact in the social, environmental, or ethical sense, such as arms, tobacco or alcohol.) Another question might be: Should this company outsource operations to developing countries?

The broadest level of analysis in business ethics is the whole economic system. An analysis on this whole-system level is called **economic ethics**. An analysis of economic ethics might ask questions such as: Is the globalization of the world economy good or bad? Should profit maximization be the ultimate goal of business, or should it be social welfare? From a management perspective, the individual and group perspectives are the most immediately relevant ones. Therefore, this chapter will focus mainly on individual and professional ethics.

### THINK | ETHICS

**Developing a Professional Ethics for the Secondary Market for Life Insurances**

The German secondary life insurance market faced a fraud problem, which led to disservice. Policen Direkt, the market leader, therefore not only cooperated with the federal association for the secondary market, but also actively helped to develop general ethical guidelines for policy sales, and distributes those guidelines throughout press and consumer associations.

## 5-3c Moral Dilemmas and the Relationship to Law and Compliance

Often in practice the borders between the law, compliance, and ethics are blurred. As illustrated in Figure 5.5, those three topics often overlap and will therefore play a role in this chapter. Business ethics deals with **moral dilemmas**, in situations of right or wrong in a business context. One may apply a simple scheme to find out what a

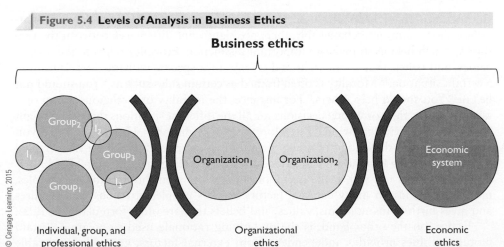

**Figure 5.4 Levels of Analysis in Business Ethics**

Business ethics

Individual, group, and professional ethics — Organizational ethics — Economic ethics

© Cengage Learning, 2015

**Individual ethics** is the study of ethical issues as encountered by single individuals.

**Organizational ethics** is the study of ethical issues on an organizational level.

**Economic ethics** is the study of systemic ethical issues of the economy.

A **moral dilemma** is a situation that requires an ethically relevant decision where right or wrong is questioned through a set of alternative actions that are likely to have significant effects on others.

**Figure 5.5 The Relationship between Ethics, Law, and Compliance**

**Ethics**
• What moral dilemmas are faced?

**Law**
• What behavior is legally required?

**Compliance**
• What norms are to be obeyed?

© Cengage Learning, 2015

moral dilemma is. According to Crane and Matten,[18] the "moral status" of a situation may be decided by the following three key considerations:

1. Is the decision to be made likely to have significant effects on others?

2. Does the decision to be made provide choices and alternative actions?

3. Is the decision perceived as ethically relevant, about moral right or wrong?

In the last section of this chapter on ethics management, we will go much deeper into the identification and assessment of moral dilemmas, which is a main part of the ethics management process. We will also illustrate the difference between a moral dilemma and other types of ethical issues. As you will see in the next paragraph, determining whether a moral dilemma, issue, or conflict exists is very important in delineating the boundary among ethics, law, compliance, and governance topics, all of which play a great role in the practice and theory of business ethics. As will be illustrated in the last section of this chapter, managing business ethics problems in practice may involve both dilemma-related issues and compliance-related ones.

Ethics is always based on defining right or wrong in a moral dilemma situation. The law often regulates topics for businesses that do not necessarily involve moral dilemmas and other ethical issues. For instance, the legislation defining different company types such as "limited" in Great Britain or the German GmbH hardly has any moral implications. Although not ethically relevant, choosing the right legal term for a company is relevant. **Compliance** is a term commonly used in management practice that often subsumes behavior in ethical dilemma situations as well as legal considerations. Strictly speaking, compliance is the field that answers the question: What norms are to be obeyed? While many norms are of legal nature, there is also a variety of norms that stem from other sources. Business customs, voluntary standards, and values might be nonlegal norms. This chapter will deal exclusively with ethical issues and moral dilemmas and will only touch on legal and compliance topics, if they involve such.

## 5-3d Morality and Values

Another term that is often confused with ethics is *morality*. Although many dictionaries use those terms interchangeably, there are significant differences between the two topics, which help us to make an important distinction. **Morality** refers to the norms, values, and beliefs that define right and wrong for a specific individual or a group in a certain situation.[19] Morality is often framed as certain rules such as "You should not lie" or "You should help others." For instance, the morality of a religious group or a family dictates right or wrong decisions for all the different situations this group might encounter. Likewise, individuals develop their own morality. How often have you heard "I don't do those kind of things" from someone referring to her or his personal morality? There is also morality in situations, such as riding in a full metro and knowing "You should not yell, make noise, or smoke." As seen through these examples, morality depends on many external factors such as people, situations, and cultures and gives birth to many norms, values, and beliefs that are often formulated as rules.

Ethics, on the other hand, is the underlying rationale used to create a certain morality. Ethics provides, independent from external factors, generally applicable

**Compliance** describes efforts related to complying with generally accepted norms of behavior.

**Morality** describes norms, values, and beliefs that define right and wrong for a specific individual or a group in a certain situation.

methods to assess what is right or wrong. In a simplified way, such general methods might, for example, involve questions such as: What is best for all? How can I respect the rights of all people involved? and How can I act in a way that I would want to be a role model for everybody else? As you will experience in the next section that deals with ethical theories, all of these questions represent one of the traditions of ethical decision making.

To sum up the difference between ethics and morality, one can say, "Ethics is making rules. Morality is applying rules." Ethics is generally applicable, whereas morality applies to narrowly defined circumstances. Ethics is intercultural, as it can be applied in any cultural setting, whereas morality is subcultural, as it always applies to a specific group and its culture.[20] In this chapter, the words *ethics* and *ethical* will always be used when referring to general principles of defining right or wrong, such as the ethics of justice, the ethical decision-making process, and ethical principles. The words *morality* and *moral* will be used when referring to right or wrong in a specific setting, such as the morality of a certain company, religious moral obligations, or the morality of a colleague.

In business ethics people often talk about values. Examples of values are fairness, trustworthiness, honesty, and caring for others. **Values** are aspired goals, beliefs, and concepts that shape thinking and actions.[21] Right or wrong behavior can be evaluated by comparing it to the aspired values. Values are located in between ethics and morality. On one hand, values are a central element of ethical theory. As an example, the theory of ethics of justice aims at fairness as the main value. Virtue ethics aims at a set of values defining a "good life" and good behavior. On the other hand, the morality of a certain group almost inevitably involves a set of values, defining right or wrong behavior. This could be the values of truthfulness and reliability for an accounting department or the Bible's ten commandments for Christian people.[22]

Four main "families of values"—the ones related to persons, virtue, happiness, and relationship—must, in the context of values in business, be extended by values related to the goals of the business.[23] The resulting five categories of values central to business ethics are listed below:

1. Values focusing on persons are based on the perception that persons are special and must be protected. Examples are justice, fairness, and equality.

2. Values focusing on virtue are attached to a "good" character. Examples are honesty, self-discipline, and responsibility.

3. Values focusing on happiness are based on the search for happiness and the avoidance of suffering. Examples are security, personal gain, and contentment.

4. Values focusing on relationship center on the social nature of human beings. Examples are caring, participation, and community.

5. Values focusing on the goals of the organization refer to the importance of achieving the business's purpose. Examples are productivity, efficiency, and growth.

In business practice, values are most prevalent in corporate codes of ethics, which are most often based on the six values of (1) trustworthiness, (2) respect, (3) responsibility, (4) fairness,(5) caring, and (6) citizenship.[24] These values can all be found in the aforementioned five values categories. Codes of ethics and other institutional documents are one way in which values can be fostered in and through organizations.

Once a value results in constant actions, it becomes "operationalized," and a natural habit of individuals of the organization, and the organization can be said to stand for this value and to have a culture based on this value. Such a value-based organization can be achieved through both changing the values of existing

**Values** are aspired ideal goals, beliefs, and concepts that shape thinking and actions.

employees and hiring new employees with the right personal value set.[25] The values held by employees may either help them in making the right decisions or obstruct them from doing so. A study found that altruistic values are likely to increase the amount of ethical decisions being made, while so-called self-enhancement, egoistic values decrease the likelihood of good ethical decisions.[26] To create responsible, sustainable, and ethical organizations, values have to reflect those topics. A negative indicator for this to happen might be that studies suggest that values in business tend to change very little over time.[27]

## 5-3e Interpreting Business Ethics

Business ethics is a highly interdisciplinary field and almost inevitably must consist of largely different perspectives. Thinking about the status of business ethics as a whole is the subject of so-called meta-ethics. Meta-ethics is not concerned with concrete ethical dilemmas or theories but scrutinizes ethics itself.[28] To understand from what standpoint people argue is a valuable asset for any ethical discussion and helps as much in theory as it does in the business practice of ethics management. The following list sums up some of the most important antagonistic views:

- *Umbrella versus lens:* Opinions vary largely among business ethics specialists in terms of the role and position of business ethics. Some specialists see business ethics as a superordinate umbrella field. Business sustainability and responsibility are to be subsumed under business ethics. "All is ethics" is the credo. The opposite perspective is to use ethics as a "lens," a tool that can be used to better understand the topics of business responsibility and sustainability. The credo is "All can be interpreted through ethics." This book takes an intermediate perspective, where ethics responsibility and sustainability are seen as background theories that are complementary and mutually reinforcing.

- *Absolutism versus relativism:* The position of philosophical absolutism is based on the belief that there are universally applicable moral principles, and therefore, right and wrong are objective truths that can always be defined clearly through philosophical reasoning. In other words, there are absolute truths. Relativism takes the opposite stance by stating that right and wrong are a matter of perspective and, thus, cannot be defined objectively. Right or wrong depends on the context and, therefore, is different throughout different cultures, times, and other contingencies.[29] This book takes an intermediate stance of pluralism, in which differing moral norms and contexts are accepted, but which emphasizes that consensus should be reached.[30]

- *Philosophy versus social science:* Normative ethics, as will be illustrated in the following section, is based on the moral philosophy throughout millennia beginning from ancient Greek philosophers like Plato, Aristotle, and Socrates. Proponents of business ethics as a social science stress that we need the social sciences like psychology and business studies for changing ethical behavior in practice.[31] This chapter takes an integrative perspective, accepting the crucial importance of both the normative rigor that philosophy brings and of the pragmatic implementation facilitated through the social sciences.

- *Against versus pro-business:* Business ethics often serves to establish a critical "against" perspective, seeing business as inherently bad, almost as an enemy. The opposite extreme is a pro-business perspective in which business is seen as inherently good and as trying, out of its own motivation, to do everything possible to choose the best thing morally.[32] The perspective assumed in this book might be called a pragmatic one. It accepts that in order to change business, we first need to acknowledge business as principally "okay." Then we need to create a basis for helping businesses, through constructive criticism, to become morally excellent.

- *Western versus international:* Business ethics today is dominated by Western thinking, mainly from Europe and North America. Philosophers, values, and cultural determinants of morality are primarily viewed from a Western perspective, although even the European and the North American perspectives display very distinct differences.[33] In order to create truly global businesses, the ethics of those businesses must become truly global.[34] This book focuses on the U.S.-European understanding, but acknowledges the necessity to transform this long-established perspective through a truly international influence.

Figure 5.6 illustrates how those opposing views on business ethics establish a nexus of different positions. In this nexus, the preceding positions can be described as traditional and narrow perspectives, while the positions mentioned second can be subsumed under a more progressive, broad perspective.

**Figure 5.6 A Nexus of Opposing Views on Business Ethics**

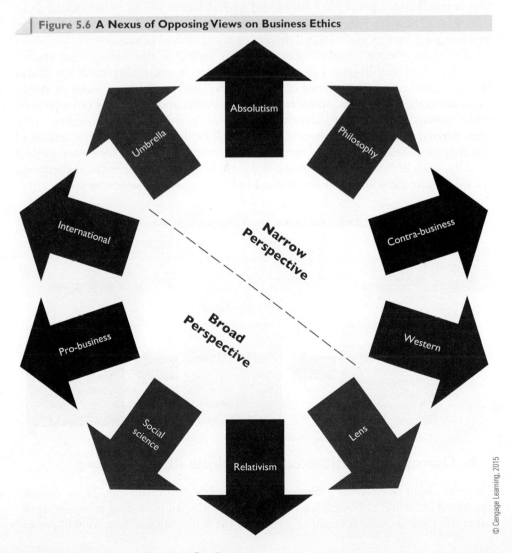

© Cengage Learning, 2015

# 5-4 DOMAINS OF BUSINESS ETHICS

*"I argue for a reconciliation of normative and descriptive approaches and methods of research in business ethics ... we must recognize the limitations that these approaches reciprocally place on each other."[35]*

Business ethics, in its interdisciplinary nature, consists of three main domains, as illustrated in Figure 5.7. The first domain, *normative ethics*, is largely related to the field of moral philosophy and is often used as a synonym for ethics. Normative ethics provides universally applicable rules of right and wrong that fulfill the function of evaluating what should be considered right or wrong in a business context. Is it morally right to outsource jobs, to accept arms dealers as clients, or to take office material home? Normative ethics helps to evaluate the right and wrong in those and other situations.

The function of the second domain, *descriptive ethics*, explains why people do or do not act morally correct in practice, and explains how all of us make ethical decisions and how we act upon them. Descriptive ethics is mostly based on behavioral and organizational psychology as a background discipline. A typical series of questions might be: Why did Mr. Jones steal those office supplies from his company? Was it retaliation against his boss, or did he feel like it would be fair to do so to compensate him for what he perceives to be lousy pay? What were the internal psychological factors and external drivers of his unethical behavior?

The third domain of *ethics management* is rooted in the management studies discipline and fulfills the function of applying management tools to foster morally excellent behavior. Some of the tools typically applied are codes of ethics, ethics councils and officers, ethics training, and audits and screenings of employees. Ethics management in the application of ethics management tools largely relies on the clues derived from domains one and two. As will be illustrated in the last section of this chapter, in practice, all three domains are absolutely necessary for business ethics practice. They are mutually reinforcing and complementary. In the following sections, we will briefly introduce each domain and how it applies to business ethics.

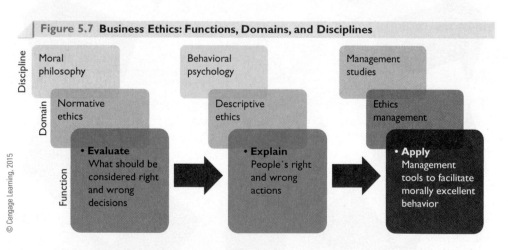

**Figure 5.7 Business Ethics: Functions, Domains, and Disciplines**

© Cengage Learning, 2015

## 5-4a Domain 1: Normative Ethics—Evaluate Right or Wrong

**Normative ethics** is centered on ethical theories of right and wrong to solve ethical dilemmas.

Theories about **normative ethics** are the core piece of domain one. Those theories are based on moral philosophy, which is concerned with providing generally applicable rules for deciding on right or wrong. In the following sections, we will present

Figure 5.8 Major Theories of Moral Philosophy

| Virtue Ethics "Be virtuous!" | Deontology "Follow higher principles and duties!" | Consequentialism "Judge by the outcome!" |
| --- | --- | --- |
| **Concepts:** Good life, values in action | **Concepts:** Moral principles, duties, rights, justice | **Concepts:** Greatest happiness principle, utility, hedonism |
| **Philosophers:** Aristotle, Saint Thomas Aquinas, Confucius | **Philosophers:** Immanuel Kant, John Locke, John Rawls | **Philosophers:** Jeremy Bentham, John Stuart Mill |
| **Criticism:** Limited applicability to concrete dilemmas and situational ambiguity; value conservatism and need to define virtues in a quickly changing world | **Criticism:** Conflicting duties and principles; practicability versus moral rigorism; neglect of consequences of actions | **Criticism:** Feasibility and complexity of assessment; inferiority of single individuals' and minorities' interest; fair distribution |

Sources: Adapted from Bleisch, B., & Huppenbauer, M. (2011). *Ethische Entscheidungsfindung [Ethical decision making]*. Zurich: Versus; Hursthouse, R. (2012). Virtue ethics. In *The Stanford Encyclopedia of Philosophy*. Retrieved September 5, 2012, from http://plato.stanford.edu/entries/ethics-virtue/

three main theoretical streams of thought typically considered in business ethics, as illustrated in Figure 5.8. The first, virtue ethics, highlights that the one who lives a virtuous life, based on a virtuous character and virtuous habits, will make right decisions. The stream of thinking called deontology (derived from the Greek word for duty) is based on the importance of duties and rules and higher moral principles to be applied among human beings. The third stream of normative ethical theories is consequentialism, which judges by the consequences of one's actions and aims at creating the biggest value possible for all involved actors.[36] We will propose a "tripartite" approach to ethical theories that acknowledges both advantages and disadvantages of all three theories, but stresses their complementary character.[37]

While the three main ethical theories mentioned constitute the basis of moral philosophy and ethical reasoning, more recently, major alternatives have been developed that complement the traditional theories. Good examples are discourse ethics, which aims at ethical decisions through good communication, and feminist ethics, which bases good decisions on empathy.[38] To keep complexity low and to stay within the scope and scale of this introductory ethics chapter, we will not elaborate on those theories in detail.

## Virtue Ethics: "Be Virtuous!"

**Virtue ethics** considers an ethical decision and behavior right when it is conducted by a person with a virtuous character out of a virtuous motivation. A virtue is a combination of good traits of character, such as honesty, prudence, and wisdom. There is a strong connection between virtues and values. One could say that a virtue is a series of lived values, which would then lead to a good or virtuous life.[39] Interestingly, such a virtuous life is not only interpreted as good morally, but is also thought to lead to personal happiness, or *Eudaimonia* in ancient Greek. Happiness in the sense of virtue ethics means activities that involve virtues and make appropriate use of our capacities. Happiness is generated through a way of life in which one functions optimally according to his or her purpose as a human being.[40] This idea of a good, virtuous life is also prevalent in many other philosophers' writings. Examples are Thomas Aquinas's new lifestyle or *modus vivendi* and the Confucian virtuous life, which is based on the virtue foundation of benevolence, propriety, and piety.[41] Christian morality is founded on a virtue ethics approach based in the Old Testament scriptures.[42] Virtuousness is the fundamental criterion for deciding if a decision or action is good. Thus, an action conducted by a nonvirtuous actor or out of a nonvirtuous motivation is always bad, however good the outcome might be.

**Virtue ethics** judges decisions as right that are taken based on a virtuous mind-set and congruent with a good, "virtuous" life.

Virtue ethics has much to contribute to business ethics. Through its motivational aspect and lasting perspective, it can provide distinct insights complementary to consequentialist and deontological ethics.[43] Modern virtue ethics has been applied in many ways to business ethics, from an entire corporation with a virtuous character to the virtuousness of a single manager.[44] Aristotle's virtues are still applicable to business today.[45] In practice, one can assess if an action is morally good or bad, from a virtue ethics standpoint, by assessing the virtues displayed in the actions of an individual. Bragues[46] distills seven main virtues from Aristotle's original catalog of thirteen virtues that are especially important to actions in businesses. The virtues identified are courage, self-control, generosity, magnificence, magnanimity, sociability, and justice.

The following short checklist groups those seven virtues into three main groups. It may help to assess ethical situations in the sense of "What would a virtuous person do?"—a pragmatic application of virtue ethics. It is important to consider that each virtue is to be seen as an intermediate point, a "golden mean," in between two nonvirtuous (vicious) conducts. For instance, courage is located between cowardice and rashness, self-control between self-indulgence and prudishness.

1. *To the inside (courage and self-control):* A *courageous* person is able to overcome fear and risk when necessary for a higher goal. In a business context, courage might lead to ethically favorable outcomes when the person needs to fight for the right outcomes against animosity, or overcome the fear of risk in an entrepreneurial venture for a higher good as, for instance, in social entrepreneurship. *Self-control* regulates our attraction to pleasure. The virtue of self-control can be understood as being a role model to others. Business personnel would, as an example, abstain from seducing others and losing their self-restraint. Furthermore, a company would abstain from excessive marketing and from selling products that promise overabundant pleasures, such as the newest fashion fad, high-fat meals, or pornography.

2. *To the outside (generosity, magnificence, magnanimity, and sociability):* Generosity is the virtue that regulates our desire for wealth. A person who does not pursue wealth at all costs is more likely to abstain from engaging in ethically questionable business practices. *Magnificence* strongly relates to generosity, but refers to the capability to spend large sums for a worthy purpose. A large-scale example is Bill Gates, who through his foundation has donated $4.2 billion to improving health in developing countries. *Magnanimity* refers to a humble, but articulated attitude toward honors and success. A manager with the virtue of magnanimity would neither brag about success nor shyly refrain from mentioning it, would neither rush for success nor endanger it by behavior that is too risk-adverse. *Sociability* is the virtue that results in a good-natured attitude toward others. Good nature may lead to morally favorable outcomes through the consideration of others in decisions and behavior.

3. *Toward fairness (justice):* The virtue of *justice* can be seen in obedience to law, or in more general fairness thinking. Acting just and fair includes both fairness in decisions and activities, and fairness in the outcomes of such activities. An example of lacking the virtue of justice is when a CEO passes up a hardworking and competent brand manager for promotion to Vice President of Marketing in favor of the CEO's patently less qualified cousin. Or a company might apply

inhumane labor conditions to thousands of workers in order to facilitate a little cheaper product for consumers in searching for the ultimate low price.

There is much criticism on the capability of virtue ethics to solve ethical dilemmas and to be a guiding light for businesses. The most extreme criticism is the one of incompatibility between virtue ethics and businesses as we know them. A business that would thoroughly apply a virtue ethical philosophy would quickly put itself out of business.[47] A less drastic, but equally powerful, criticism of virtue ethics addresses its limited applicability to concrete dilemmas and situational ambiguity. We would need to know the entire personal history, thoughts, and motivation of the actor in order to authoritatively assess his or her virtuousness. Another difficulty in applying virtue ethics is the need to constantly reassess the adequateness of virtues in a quickly changing and international world.[48]

In spite of all those criticisms, virtue ethics displays one main favorable characteristic that sets it apart from the other two main ethical theories. Virtue ethics evaluates virtuous actions and, unlike most other ethical theories, the theoretical decision. Thus, virtue ethics is a natural bridge to the field of descriptive ethics that will be illustrated later in the section "Domain 2: Descriptive Ethics—Explain right and Wrong Actions".[49]

## Deontology: "Follow Higher Rules and Duties!"

**Deontology** is an umbrella term for ethical theories that refer to higher duties that must be derived from universal rules.[50] Deon means rule or duty in Greek. Human beings should be able to derive those rules themselves. Deontological ethics and the related moral principles have largely been applied to business ethics. The philosopher who has been most predominantly interpreted for application in business ethics is Immanuel Kant.[51] In his work *Groundwork of the Metaphysics of Morals,* Kant proposed the "categorical imperative" as the ultimate decision-making instrument for defining moral behavior based on one's duties.[52] The categorical imperative is only the first of three maxims Kant offered by which to derive higher duties. According to Kant, every action to be considered right and good has to comply with the following three rules:[53]

1. *Universal law and the golden rule:* Would you want your action to become universally lawgiving? Would you wish everybody else to act the same way? Those questions address what is summarized by "the golden rule." Act as if, by your action, what you do would automatically become a natural law. For instance, a manager who considers lying to a subordinate who is also a personal friend about the reasons for the friend's layoff would be intrinsically proposing the rule of "lie if convenient." By applying the golden rule to morally check his self-made rule, the manager would realize that if everybody always lied when convenient (once the rule had become a universal law), ultimately his organization, and probably the whole society, would face severe problems.

2. *Noninstrumentalization, or end in itself:* Do you treat rational (human) beings as *means* or as an *end?* It is desired not to use human beings for a certain purpose, but instead to align your action for the good of humanity. Some authors have gone so far as to assume that if this maxim were taken seriously, businesses would not be able to operate. For instance, most businesses "use" employees to fulfill a purpose that is different from the employees' ends. They are not ends in themselves.[54]

3. *The kingdom of ends:* Make sure that the maxims you base your actions on are acceptable for every other rational being. Would other rational beings who are part of the society, or the "kingdom of ends," and who applied rules one and two, judge as you did? To test whether you are acting in the interest of every

**Deontology** judges right or wrong by referring to higher duties that must be derived from universal rules.

citizen in this "kingdom of ends," a disclosure, also called the *New York Times* test, has been proposed. If you published your rule for behavior on the front page of the *New York Times,* would rational beings agree with it?[55] In the business realm, the respective question would be: Do I want our rules of behavior to be published on the front page of all our company's communication channels, from annual report to website?

There are other prominent examples of such higher rules. One important deontological philosopher was John Locke, who initiated the notion of natural, given rights of human beings, which ultimately resulted in today's powerful human rights movement.[56] Another important example is John Rawls, who proposed justice as another universal, natural principle from which to derive duties.[57]

As with any other ethical theory, there is criticism of deontology. One typical criticism is that moral principles might often be conflicting. If, as an example, the moral principle of fairness opposed the principle of natural human rights, which one should be considered more important and which should be overridden in favor of the other? Imagine you are a manager at a medium-sized factory. There have been repeated thefts of employees' personal items in your facility. You know those items must be hidden in one of the employees' lockers. The fair thing to the ones who have been stolen from would be to search everybody's lockers. The human rights principle of privacy would contradict this search. What should you do? Another criticism is that moral principles, if applied rigorously, often lack practicability, and that deontological ethics only focuses on the actions, but neglects the outcomes of those actions.[58]

In spite of extensive criticisms, deontological arguments are influential for both of the other main ethical theories. In virtue ethics, as an example, the virtue of justice can at the same time be used to derive deontological rules. Deontology and moral principles also play roles in consequentialist ethics. Interestingly, Kant's golden rule can also be interpreted for classical consequentialist, often economic thinking, which will be illustrated further in the following section.[59]

### Consequentialism: Judge by the Outcome!

Deontology's foil is **consequentialism**, which is also called a teleological approach to ethics, derived from the ancient Greek word *telos* for "end." Both theories start from completely opposing assumptions. While deontology aims at applying ethical principles to actions, consequentialists are merely interested in the outcomes (ends) of those actions.[60] Consequentialism bases its assessment of right or wrong on the idea of hedonism that the only good is human happiness, which can be measured in terms of pleasure and pain. Thus, no matter the moral quality of the action, the good decision is always that one that maximizes pleasure and minimizes pain.

The most prominently applied consequentialist theory is utilitarianism. **Utilitarianism** aims at creating maximum utility or welfare for all groups and individuals affected by a decision. The fathers of utilitarian thinking are Jeremy Bentham and John Stewart Mill. Bentham described utilitarianism and the greatest overall happiness caused by a behavior as the main end of ethical decision making. Mill based his arguments on the central idea of welfare and the "greatest happiness principle" proposed by Jeremy Bentham.[61] In contrast to egoism, which also has

**Consequentialism** is the moral theory judging right or wrong based on outcomes.

**Utilitarianism** bases judgments of right and wrong on the principle of creating the greatest happiness possible for all affected by a decision.

been subsumed under consequentialist thinking, the right decision is not the one making the decision maker "maximum happy," but the one creating the greatest happiness for all involved—or, in a common slogan, "the greatest happiness for the greatest number."[62]

Mainstream economic thinking has often been related to utilitarian theory. Microeconomics, for instance, commonly analyzes the utility of economic actors in order to find out what the rational economic decision should be. Welfare economics aims at maximizing the overall utility, called, in this context, the *welfare of all involved*. Profit maximization, which has often been criticized as one of the main reasons for unethical decisions and business, is the maximization of utility for single individuals, the owners of the business. Much of stakeholder management as described in the preceding chapter is based on utilitarian thinking, as it facilitates a consideration of all effects that a certain business activity has on the various groups that "can affect or are affected by" the business activity.[63] The main tenants of classic utilitarianism are summarized in Table 5.2.[64]

Let us assume the example of outsourcing labor from the developed country France to a developing country such as India. For a well-rounded consequentialist analysis of a decision, we propose to approach moral dilemmas such as the outsourcing decision through three consequentialist decision criteria:

**Table 5.2** Aspects of Classic Utilitarianism

| Term | Explanation | Delineation |
|---|---|---|
| Consequentialism = | Whether an act is morally right depends only on consequences… | …as opposed to the circumstances or the intrinsic nature of the act or anything that happens before the act. |
| Actual Consequentialism = | Whether an act is morally right depends only on the actual consequences… | …as opposed to foreseen, foreseeable, intended, or likely consequences. |
| Direct Consequentialism = | Whether an act is morally right depends only on the consequences of that act itself… | …as opposed to the consequences of the agent's motive, of a rule or practice that covers other acts of the same kind, and so on. |
| Evaluative Consequentialism = | Moral rightness depends only on the value of the consequences… | …as opposed to nonevaluative features of the consequences. |
| Hedonism = | The value of the consequences depends only on the pleasures and pains in the consequences… | …as opposed to other goods, such as freedom, knowledge, life, and so on. |
| Maximizing Consequentialism = | Moral rightness depends only on which consequences are best… | …as opposed to merely satisfactory or an improvement over the status quo. |
| Aggregative Consequentialism = | Which consequences are best is some function of the values of parts of those consequences… | …as opposed to rankings of whole worlds or sets of consequences. |
| Total Consequentialism = | Moral rightness depends only on the total net good in the consequences… | …as opposed to the average net good per person. |
| Universal Consequentialism = | Moral rightness depends on the consequences for all people or sentient beings… | …as opposed to only the individual agent, members of the individual's society, present people, or any other limited group. |
| Equal Consideration = | In determining moral rightness, benefits to one person matter just as much as similar benefits to any other person… | …meaning that all who count, count equally. |
| Agent-Neutrality = | Whether some consequences are better than others does not depend on whether the consequences are evaluated from the perspective of the agent… | …as opposed to an observer. |

Source: Sinnott-Armstrong, W. (2011). Consequentialism. In E. N. Zalta (ed.), *The Stanford Encyclopedia of Philosophy (Winter 2011 Edition)*.

1. *Act utilitarianism:* "Does the single act I am conducting create more pleasure or pain?" To find out if the outsourcing should take place, a consequentialist would try to compare the outcomes for the main involved groups and individuals, such as the employees of the company. A simple consideration might be: How much employment would be created in India compared to the amount of employment lost in France? Another group might be customers. Is the value provided to customers bigger or smaller with or without outsourcing? The same arguments can and must be created for all other involved parties.

2. *Rule utilitarianism:* "Does the type of behavior in general create more pleasure or pain?" The question here shifts from the single action to the type of action. Does outsourcing in general create more pleasure or pain? Is the socioeconomic development in host countries bigger than the loss in home countries? Do companies win or lose through outsourcing?

3. *Distribution fairness:* "Are costs and benefits created and distributed fairly?" Although fairness is not a classic consequentialist argument, it has been increasingly integrated into utilitarian thinking in order to counter the common argument of utilitarianism, purely maximizing value without paying attention to how fairly this value is distributed. Questions asked are, for instance: Do workers in developing countries benefit sufficiently from the benefits created for the company and customers? Does the company and benefiting consumers share the pain inflicted upon the workers through often inhumane working conditions?

Many philosophers have completely rejected utilitarian thinking. The normative dialogue about deontology or teleology as the better theory for making ethical decisions seems to have come to a stalemate.[65] Typical criticism about consequentialist and more specifically utilitarian thinking is about the feasibility and complexity of assessing all pleasure and pain for all involved parties, the danger of neglecting single individuals' and minorities' interests, and a fair distribution of the benefits of utilitarian value maximization.[66]

### Integrating and Operationalizing Traditional Theories

All of the preceding ethical theories have been criticized from many different angles. Nevertheless, each also has specific strengths. In practice, mitigating the weaknesses of one theory by the strength of another can make ethical theory accessible and transform it into a powerful management tool.[67] Research suggests that management decisions are mixtures between outcome orientation (consequentialist), moral rules (deontology), and values in action (virtue).[68] A practice example might be office theft. An employee might not do big damage (no big negative outcome) by stealing an envelope for a letter to a friend. From a virtue ethics perspective, this act is highly unethical. It displays a lack of self-control, greed (the opposite of generosity), and unfairness toward the company and other employees who do not share the same benefit. One example of a deontological argument would be that the stealing employee acts against the golden rule. She would probably not want her action to become a general and natural law, since if everybody stole from the company, it would probably go bankrupt and everybody, including the employee, would lose their jobs.

Making decision makers in business understand how those moral theories interact and can be used to make better decisions is crucial for business ethics. Thus, integrating those different ethical theories is a practical imperative. In this chapter, we integrate the three main ethical theories—virtue ethics, deontology, and consequentialism—through the perspective of ethical pluralism. In ethical pluralism, the use of moral theories as a "prism" helps us see an ethical dilemma in "different colors," depending on which ethical theory is applied as a lens.[69]

In Figure 5.9, we illustrate a mixed quantitative-qualitative assessment tool integrating all the three theories mentioned. It is called a 360-degree ethics assessment because it views ethical dilemmas from all angles. Imagine you are the person facing the dilemma and thinking through different alternatives of decision and action. Conduct a 360-degree ethics assessment for each alternative by following the next three steps:

- *Step 1: Evaluate* the degree of fulfillment of each of the nine questions from A1 to C3 on a continuum from $-5$ = completely amoral to $+5$ = morally excellent, and write your evaluation grade in the boxes to the left of the respective question. Use the background information provided in the earlier chapters to ensure the quality and depth of your assessment.

- *Step 2: Calculate* the average evaluation grade per ethical theory (A, B, and C) by adding up the grades of all three questions and dividing them by three. Write the result down in the gray field under each respective theory. Also calculate the average grade for all three theories by summing the three theory grades and dividing them by three. Note your result in the dark gray field under the text "overall assessment grade."

- *Step 3: Compare* the assessment for your different alternatives of decision and action. In the comparison process, you can and should also decide how to weight the different moral theories and questions. For instance, the utilitarian focus of the greatest happiness might be almost neglected in situations where the outcomes are not significant but the virtue implications are drastic.

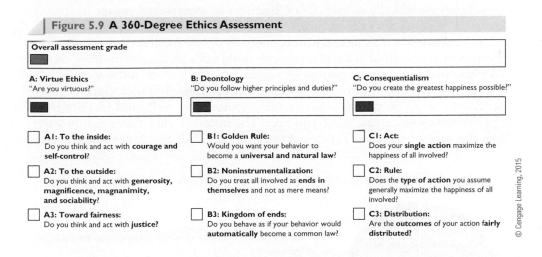

**Figure 5.9 A 360-Degree Ethics Assessment**

**Overall assessment grade**

| **A: Virtue Ethics** | **B: Deontology** | **C: Consequentialism** |
|---|---|---|
| "Are you virtuous?" | "Do you follow higher principles and duties?" | "Do you create the greatest happiness possible?" |

- **A1: To the inside:** Do you think and act with **courage and self-control**?
- **A2: To the outside:** Do you think and act with **generosity, magnificence, magnanimity, and sociability**?
- **A3: Toward fairness:** Do you think and act with **justice**?

- **B1: Golden Rule:** Would you want your behavior to become a **universal and natural law**?
- **B2: Noninstrumentalization:** Do you treat all involved as **ends in themselves** and not as mere means?
- **B3: Kingdom of ends:** Do you behave as if your behavior would **automatically** become a common law?

- **C1: Act:** Does your **single action** maximize the happiness of all involved?
- **C2: Rule:** Does the **type of action** you assume generally maximize the happiness of all involved?
- **C3: Distribution:** Are the **outcomes** of your action **fairly distributed**?

© Cengage Learning, 2015

## 5-4b Domain 2: Descriptive Ethics—Explain Right and Wrong Actions

If we look at corporate scandals caused by ethical dilemma situations, it often seems very clear from the outside what the actors should have done if they had acted in an ethically correct way. Of course, they should not have falsified the books. Of course, pressuring employees into suicide is bad. Of course, you should not make a tobacco company your main customer. Unfortunately, for individuals facing those decisions in practice, it usually is not as easy to make the right decision, even if they know what should be done. A variety of personal and external factors influence people in deciding whether to do the right thing in real life. The domain of business ethics that analyzes why people do or do not do the right thing in practice is called *descriptive ethics*. Descriptive ethics is largely based on behavioral psychology, which is why it is often also called behavioral ethics or moral psychology.[70] **Descriptive ethics** fulfills the important function for business ethics of describing, understanding, influencing, and predicting ethical behavior of individuals and groups.

Translating a good ethical decision into good ethical behavior is crucial and complex. What counts in practice and constitutes the moral performance of a company depends strongly on the actual actions taken. Making the ethical decision is, as you will see in the following paragraphs, just one factor leading to this moral performance in action. The fundamental factors of how ethical decisions are made and translated into actions can be described as an ethical decision-making and action model, which is illustrated in the next section.

### The Ethical Decision-Making and Action Model

Do people just do the right thing, once they know what the right thing is in a specific situation? The answer is no. In order for a person to behave ethically, he or she needs to fulfill four components of ethical behavior, which are illustrated in Figure 5.10. Only if all four components are fulfilled will ethical behavior take place. If an individual coincidentally acts (behavior) ethically correct, but without knowing why he or she does so (judgment), and without recognizing (awareness) that there is actually an ethical issue or opportunity we can call this neither an ethical decision nor ethical behavior. Another person might be aware of an ethically relevant situation and motivated to do the right thing, but might not able to make the ethical judgment necessary to know what the right behavior is. Such a person might either abstain from behaving ethically correct out of insecurity or, even worse, engage in ethically incorrect behavior out of ignorance.

Ethical decision making and action, and how people fulfill the four components mentioned, is embedded in a process that we could call a person situation interaction. As illustrated in the upper portion of Figure 5.11, the person–influences the ethical decision and action through individual factors. Those factors include cognitive processes (how you think), affective factors (how you feel), and identity-based characteristics (who you think you are). The influence that the situation exerts (see the lower portion of Figure 5.11) can be divided into issue-related factors

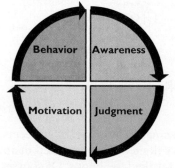

| Figure 5.10 **Components of Ethical Decisions and Actions**

1. **Awareness:** The individual or group recognizes an ethical issue or opportunity.
2. **Judgment:** The individual has made a moral judgment upon what right means in this situation.
3. **Motivation:** The individual or group wants (has established a moral intent) to behave right.
4. **Behavior:** The individual or group engages in the morally right behavior.

**Descriptive ethics** serves to describe, understand, influence, and predict moral behavior of individuals and groups.

Source: Rest, J. R. (1986). *Moral development: Advances in research and theory.* New York: Praeger; Jones, T. M. (1991). Ethical decision making by individuals in organizations: An issue-contingent model. *Academy Management Review, 16*(2), 366–395.

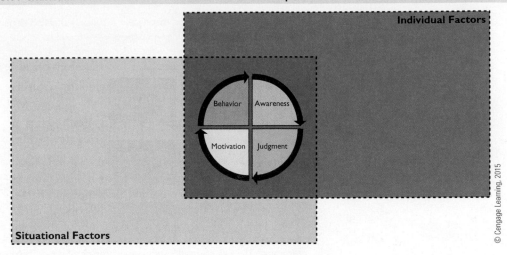

© Cengage Learning, 2015

(regarding the ethical dilemma), and situational factors (regarding the surrounding circumstances). The following two sections will provide extensive insight into how individual and situational factors influence ethical decisions and behavior.[71]

## Individual Factors in Ethical Decisions and Behaviors

**Individual factors** are all factors "that are uniquely associated with the individual decision maker."[72] Such individual factors can be approached from many different angles. Research suggests that your ethical decision making and action depend on whether you are a man or a woman, what region you come from, what religion you adhere to, what your educational background is, and what job you do. Another group of individual factors includes topics such as your personal integrity, your cognitive moral development, and how much "moral imagination" you have.[73] The first group contains examples of what we can call *demographic factors*—socioeconomic factors that are typically considered in a census or population statistics. The second group can be called *psychological factors*—based on the individual's mental functions. Understanding individual factors of ethical decision making may lead to valuable insights that can then be a toehold for ethics management actions.

The individual factors of ethical wrongdoing, for example, resemble a doctor's assessment of the causes of a patient's disease. Interestingly, some authors have taken the perspective that bad ethics is a "cognitive pathology," a disease that can be cured.[74] As an example, let's compare two common individual drivers of unethical behavior of two different managers. A situation in which an individual's specific misbehavior stems from the individual perceiving work and private life as two different worlds, one with high and another one with low ethical standards,[75] will require a different remedy from a situation in which an individual acts unethically for hedonistic or egoistic reasons.[76] Figure 5.12 summarizes main demographic and psychological factors and their importance for moral decision making.

**Individual factors** are all factors uniquely associated with the individual decision maker that can be divided into demographic and psychological factors.

## Situational Factors in Ethical Decisions and Behaviors

A study by the Ethics Resource Center summarized the pressures to behave unethically as perceived by employees of Fortune 500 companies. The number-one source of pressure was to keep

### In Practice

**Tough Decision: CEO Grounds Airline**

In October of 2011, in the face of ongoing industrial disputes, Qantas CEO Alan Joyce made the tough decision to immediately ground the airline. In his statement, Joyce emphasized that despite the short-term detrimental effect upon the company's customers, the unique nature of the situation required decisive action.

Source: Brisbane Times. (2011). *Alan Joyce grounds Quantas.* Retrieved February 2, 2013, from *Brisbane Times:* http://media.brisbanetimes.com.au/business/businessday/in-full-alan-joyce-grounds-qantas-2739891.html

## Figure 5.12 Individual Influences on Ethical Decision Making and Behavior

| | | |
|---|---|---|
| Demographic factors | Age | Age influences ethical decision making, but in a highly situation-dependent pattern. In some situations, older employees were found to adhere to higher ethical standards; the same is true for older students. On the other hand, studies in different environments showed that younger managers had more ethical viewpoints than their older counterparts. |
| | Gender | Women seem to be more critical about ethical issues, behave at higher ethical standards, and are less likely to conceal their unethical behavior. Interestingly, women tend to stronger unethical behavior patterns in unethical environments. |
| | National and cultural characteristics | The studies conducted in this factor often have a U.S.-centric approach, which needs to be questioned in a global world. Non-U.S. citizens were found to behave more unethically from a U.S. point of view. Other surveys, for instance, comparing Australian and South African employees, found that managers behaved equally ethically. |
| | Religion | Strong religiousness matters in the perception of importance of ethical misconduct. There is no relationship in the strength of ethical behavior between different denominations. |
| | Education | The general education level has been found to have little influence on ethical decision making and action, although the type of education has been found to play a role. Business majors have repeatedly been found to display weaker ethics than other majors. Specific ethics education, both in business school and on the job, showed an increase in the ethical reasoning of attendees. |
| | Employment | It has been found that, on one hand, the greater the work experience, the more ethical do people respond, while, on the other hand, unethical behavior increases with job ascension. For instance, CEO tenure was found to increase unethical behavior. In most studies, executives are found to display higher ethics than students. |
| Psychological factors | Moral philosophy and ethical judgment | Individuals with more highly developed ethical judgment skills have been found to display higher ethical intentions and actions. Deontologically oriented individuals are ranked with higher ethical scores than consequentialists. Individuals display differing levels of moral development in private and professional life and use different reasoning mechanisms in varying situations. |
| | Intelligence and need for cognition | Individuals of high intelligence have been found to be less ethically oriented than individuals of low intelligence. High need for cognition (the inclination to enjoy effortful cognitive activities) showed stronger contextual biases, but also investigated more about ethical issues. |
| | Locus of control | Individuals with an internal locus of control (who believe they can influence their environment) were more likely to act ethically than individuals with an external locus of control (who believe they are not able to influence their environment). |
| | Values and attitudes | Idealist individuals (ones pursuing strong values) act more ethically than relativist individuals (ones who change values depending on situations). Individuals with Machiavellian attitudes (characterized by manipulative cunningness and deceit), which are often found among managers, and individuals with a high personal gain and money orientation are more likely to apply ethically questionable practices. |
| | Awareness and moral imagination | Individuals with higher sensitivity for ethical issues (awareness) and the ability to creatively perceive many facets of issues and potential consequences (moral imagination) are more likely to make highly ethical decisions and act upon them. |

Sources: Based on Crane, A., & Matten, D. (2004). *Business ethics.* New York: Oxford University Press; Ford, R. C., & Richardson, W. D. (1994). Ethical decision making: A review of the empirical literature. *Journal of Business Ethics, 13*(3), 206; Treviño, L. K., Weaver, G. R., & Reynolds, S. J. (2006). Behavioral ethics in organizations: A review. *Journal of Management, 32*(6), 951–990; O'Fallon, M. J., & Butterfield, K. D. (2005). A review of the empirical ethical decision-making literature: 1996–2003. *Journal of Business Ethics, 59*(4), 375–413.

their own job, followed by meeting personal financial obligations, and the pressure to meet quarterly earnings targets. Exemplary other items on the top ten list of pressures to behave unethically were to ensure the financial success of the company, to expand globally, to advance the individual's career, and, ironically, the pressure to uphold the company's brands and reputation.[77] As illustrated in Figure 5.13, descriptive ethics proposes an extensive list of **situational factors,** or all external

**Situational factors** are all external factors that influence a decision and can be divided into issue-related and context-related components.

| Figure 5.13 | Situational Influences on Ethical Decision Making and Behavior | |
|---|---|---|
| Issue-related factors | Moral intensity | The relative importance of an ethical issue (moral intensity) strongly influences individuals' ethical decision-making process. Especially how big the potential harm to be done is (magnitude of consequences), and how likely it is to be deemed acting unethically by others (moral social consensus) influence how individuals make decisions and act. The higher the moral intensity, the more sophisticated becomes the ethical judgment, which increases individuals' intentions to act ethically correct. |
| | Moral framing | In different contexts, individuals might perceive the same issue as differing in importance. The moral intensity mentioned before differs from situation to situation. Ethical decisions and actions have been found to differ for the same individual, depending on which environment the person was in, private or professional. Also, personal situations, such as peer pressure, might move individuals to attribute different moral intensities to the same moral issue. |
| | Moral complexity | Issues and subsequently the capacity to correctly interpret and act upon them vary in complexity. Examples are the interrelatedness with other issues, the complexity of assessing potential consequences, the lack of quality information, and conflicting moral principles applying to the same issue. |
| Context-related factors | Significant others | Individuals and groups with the potential to influence a person's ethics have been called "significant others." Both peer groups and top management have been found to be especially influential in individuals' ethical decisions and actions. Especially powerful are peers' reporting behavior in terms of ethical misconduct, direct superiors' influence, and the tone from the top provided by high-level executives. |
| | Rewards and sanctions | The higher the potential gain and the lower the potential sanction from an unethical behavior are, the more likely are individuals to engage in such behavior. An important role is played by incentive schemes, which can be used to both discourage and encourage correct ethical behavior. |
| | Organization size, structure, and bureaucracy | Increasing size of an organization has been found to favor ethical misconduct. Bureaucratic structures are assumed to have negative effects on the ethics of individuals working in those structures. |
| | Ethics management tools | Ethics management tools have been found to potentially increase ethical behavior, when applied diligently. The best-researched tool is codes of ethics. Codes of ethics and subsequent actions for enforcement were found to further ethical awareness and behavior, and to reduce employees' perceived pressure to behave unethically. |
| | Culture and climate | Ethical climate and culture in organizations have been found to consistently be conducive to good ethics. Some studies have found evidence that an ethical culture might also lead to too trusting situations and negative influences on whistleblowing mechanisms. |
| | National and cultural context | Although there is little empirical research on the effects of the extent to which an ethical action is embedded into a certain national culture (not the one of the individual), the differing norms, customs, and regulations are very likely to have an impact on ethical decisions and actions. |
| | Industry type | The estimation that ethical behavior varies from industry to industry is supported by strong research evidence. Research could not derive a ranking of industries' ethical performance, but there are significant differences between the ethical reasoning, based on the comparison of two or a few industries. |
| | Competitiveness | Practices increasing competitive behavior have been found to increase the perception of moral issues, and are likely to create ethical misconduct through higher pressure to perform. |

Source: Adapted from Crane, A., & Matten, D. (2004). *Business ethics.* New York: Oxford University Press.

factors influencing ethical behavior of employees. External factors that influence your ethical behavior might be, for instance, how relevant, drastic, and severe you perceive an ethical issue to be. Another group of external factors includes the company's rewards systems, topics related to authorities and hierarchies, work roles, and national and cultural contexts.[78] The first group of factors is called *issue-related factors*; the second describes broader *context-related factors*.

## 5-4c Domain 3: Ethics Management—Apply Management Tools for Right Actions

In the preceding two domains of business ethics, we first learned how to apply normative ethical theories to analyze what is right or wrong in a specific situation. Then descriptive ethics, also called behavioral ethics, was introduced as an instrument to understand the various factors of why people make or do not make ethical decisions. In this last domain, we will now extend those first two domains by introducing a set of ethics management tools that are aimed at helping people in business make the right decisions and to assume the right behaviors. These tools aim to influence situational and individual factors to maximize the number of right decisions. The subject to be managed by ethics management is *ethics performance*, which, if managed well, can be called *moral excellence*. Moral excellence is the goal of **ethics management**.

### The Goal: Moral Excellence through Ethics Performance

In order to understand how good a company's ethics are and how important it is to manage effectively, we must rely on a solid understanding of what **ethics performance** means. It is rather uncomplicated to keep track of infringements of ethical standards. A company can, for example, conduct an anonymous survey among its employees to find out how many infringements of the business's code of ethics they have observed. This value, let's say an average of two infringements per employee per year, could then be used as a benchmark and the focus of the company's ethics management system. The goal might, for instance, be to reduce the observed ethical misconduct to one per employee per year within a time frame of six months. But is this enough? The company might realize that this one measurement does not provide concise data. Employees might simply become better at hiding unethical behavior, or they might comply with the standards without any awareness of why, or without making a judgment of their own. One measurement tool cannot provide the complete picture. Both theory and practice have provided a varied set of methods. In order to obtain a concise picture of ethics performance, it is important to apply a mix of measurement methods.

As explained in the preceding section, ethical decisions and actions depend on the four main components of ethical awareness, judgment, motivation, and behavior. Theoretically, in order to assess ethics performance, each component of ethical decision making and behavior would require checking to assess ethics performance. Figure 5.14 illustrates how a set of typically applied performance assessment tools can be combined to produce a performance assessment system for all four components with the capacity to holistically explain the ethical performance of a single individual, a group, or the entire company. In practice, performance assessments are usually less comprehensive. In the following, we will introduce three main approaches/methods for assessing ethical performance in practice (see Figure 5.15).

**Ethics management** is the process of managing ethical problems through management tools.

**Ethics performance** is the sum of right and wrong decisions and behaviors in a specific entity and for a determined time period.

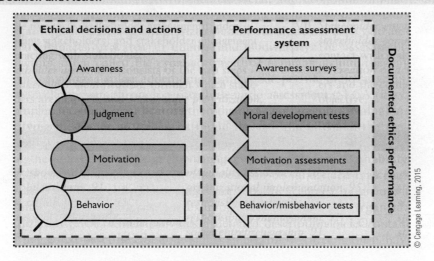

Figure 5.15 **Ethics Performance Assessment Approaches**

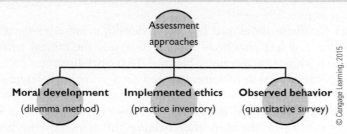

The first approach to measuring ethical performance aims at assessing the **moral development** of the ethical decision makers and is based on the work of Laurence Kohlberg. The assumption is that the more capable moral actors are, the more ethical are the decisions made by them. As illustrated in Figure 5.16 (left), Kohlberg divided moral development into six stages on three levels.

The intermediate level of reasoning is called conventional. According to Kohlberg, most adult people reason on this level, based on either stage three of conformity with society and mutual expectations ("I do what is expected by my social group") or stage four of focusing on what is good for society and the overall system ("I do what is right to maintain order").[79] The lower level is called preconventional. Individuals with a moral development on the preconventional level either base their decision on stage one, obedience and punishment ("I do anything that is not punished"), or on stage two, an interpersonal exchange ("if you do this, I do that"). The highest level of moral development is called principled. At this level, individuals are in stage five, where they orient their decisions on a greater social contract that is based on individual rights, values, and in which some cases might stand above the law and general customs ("I do what is right to hold up the social contract"), or in stage six, where people orient their decisions on self-chosen ethical principles as ultimate decision criteria ("I do what I know is right").

Based on Kohlberg's stages, schemes that are mostly questionnaire-based have been developed to assess an individual's moral development and ethics performance.[80] Most of those questionnaires work by exposing decision makers to hypothetical dilemma situations and asking them for their recommendation of action.

**Moral development** is an approach to assessing ethics performance, based on the level of ethical reasoning of decision makers in dilemma scenarios.

| Figure 5.16 **Ethics Performance Models Based on Moral Development**

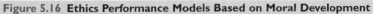

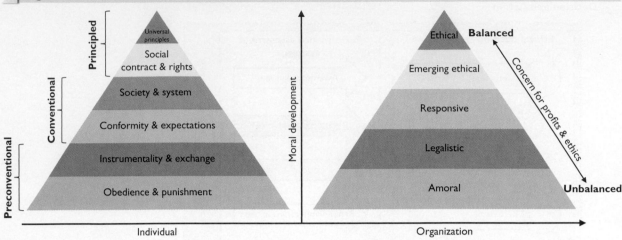

Sources: (Left) Kohlberg & Turiel (1973), as cited in Treviño, L. K. (1986). Ethical decision making in organizations: A person-situation interactionist model. *Academy of Management Review, 11*(3), 601–617; (right) Reidenbach, R. E., & Robin, D. P. (1991). A conceptual model of corporate moral development. *Journal of Business Ethics, 10*(4), 273–284.

Those answers are then evaluated to find out on which level of ethical reasoning the individual argues.[81]

Although Kohlberg developed his moral development assessment scheme for single individuals, it has also been applied to assess the ethical performance of groups and even whole organizations. Figure 5.16 (right) illustrates a framework for assessing corporate moral development, based on a company's internal structures, processes, and typical behaviors.[82] The model assumes the conflict between ethics and profit as the main ethical dilemma of a business. Companies are considered more morally developed, the more they balance the profit-seeking principle with ethical principles. Reidenbach's model applies stages of moral development that are different from Kohlberg's, but the underlying mechanism is still the same: Moral development is used as an indicator for ethical performance.

A recurrent criticism of moral development as proxy for ethical performance is that it assesses cognitive ability to potentially act ethically, which does not necessarily lead to ethical actions in practice. This criticism is theoretically valid because not everybody who knows what is right will automatically do the right thing. Nevertheless, many studies have shown that individuals with an advanced moral development are significantly more likely to do the right thing in practice.[83]

While the moral development approach can only assess the capacity of making good decisions, the next approach focuses on the ethics management practice inside the organization. We title it the **implemented ethics** approach. The implementation of ethics management practices and tools, assuming their effect on ethics performance, can be used as another proxy for ethics performance. The idea is that organizations that have ethics management tools such as codes of ethics, ethics training, or ethics policies are more likely to reach high ethics performance. An inventory of ethics practices and tools is the main methodology used to assess "implemented ethics." Often this inventory is established using a checklist approach, where standard items of ethics practice are checked to establish the implemented ethics inventory. The decision based on an item in the inventory or checklist is usually substantiated by so-called artifacts or evidences. For example, the inventory item of human rights in the issues checklist (see Figure 5.17) would be substantiated by artifacts such as a company's human rights policy, a section on human rights in the code of ethics, or commitment to the Global Compact principles, which includes

**Implemented ethics** is an approach to assessing ethics performance based on the quantitative and qualitative levels of ethics management practices implemented.

## Figure 5.17 Implemented Ethics Checklist: Types and Exemplary Items

**Issues**

- ☐ Human rights
- ☐ Corruption
- ☐ Nondiscrimination
- ☐ Principal-agent conflicts
- ☐ Labor issues
- ☐ Marketing practices
- ☐ Etc.

**Tools**

- ☐ Code of Ethics
- ☐ Ethics Council
- ☐ Ethics adviser
- ☐ Ethics officer
- ☐ Ethics department
- ☐ Values statement
- ☐ Etc.

© Cengage Learning, 2015

a central section on human rights. Companies may establish such a portfolio internally or use it to report their implemented ethics to external rankings, labels, and certifications such as the Ethisphere ranking, the Ethos label, or the ethics section of the Latin American ESR distinction.[84]

We identify the performance assessment approach as **observed behavior**, and usually it is based on quantitative surveys describing observed ethical behavior. One easy way of observing ethical misconduct is, for instance, the number of ethics scandals or public incidents observed on a company level. On an individual level, which is the typical degree of analysis, quantitative surveys serve to obtain data describing (usually) ethical misconduct. Observed behavior approaches generally focus on ethical misconduct, as it is easier to identify than ethically correct actions. If the morally right decisions are taken, one might not even realize that a moral dilemma or conflict was looming. Companies might use internal survey mechanisms, for instance, through the information obtained at a whistleblowing hotline, the gathering of quantitative data, or by conducting anonymous surveys.

An impressive overview of figures on observed (un)ethical behavior is established by the macro-surveys conducted that ask questions such as "How often do you observe ethical misconduct in your team?" "What are the biggest pressures for you to behave unethically?" or "In how many incidents annually do you feel you do not comply with ethical standards?"[85] In favor of the observed ethics is their power to describe the actual outcomes. The first two assessment methods mentioned are mere "surrogate indicators."[86] The disadvantage of the observed behavior approach lies in the lack of information on why individuals show a certain behavior.

As illustrated before, all three assessment methods have different strengths in both methodology and the assessed outcomes. To concisely evaluate a company's ethics performance, a combination of the three approaches is recommended. Assessments can be conducted on three different levels, characterized by the different scopes of individual, group, and whole organization assessment. Table 5.3 exemplifies different assessment methods for the three scopes and all three ethics performance assessment types explained before.

The goal of the ethics management process is **moral excellence**. Achieving moral excellence requires both mitigating ethical issues, and realizing ethical opportunities. Moral excellence can

**Observed behavior** is an approach to assessing ethics performance based on the quantitative surveys of observed ethical behavior or misbehavior.

**Moral excellence** is an above-average ethics performance.

### THINK ETHICS

**Imposing Ethical Auditing?**

Ethics auditing can be viewed as an imposition upon business. In 2010, Australian supermarket chain Woolworths refused to alter its requirement that suppliers undertake ethics audits. Richard Mulcahy, CEO of the Australian Vegetable Growers' Association (AUSVEG), claimed: "the company seems to be stepping further and further into the business activities of their suppliers."

Source: Hall, A. (2010). Woolworths rejects changes to ethics audits. Retrieved February 2, 2013, from *The World Today*: www.abc.net.au/worldtoday/content/2010/s2833058.htm

**Table 5.3** Ethics Performance Assessment Methods: Different Assessment Types and Scopes

| Assessment Type → Assessment Scope ↓ | Moral Development | Implemented Ethics | Observed Ethics |
|---|---|---|---|
| **Individual** | Individual dilemma analysis | Inventory of ethical practices taken by the single individual | Quantitative assessment of individual behaviors |
| **Group** | Group moral reasoning assessed through joint solution development for given dilemma situations (real or hypothetical) | Inventory of ethical practices applied in the group | Quantitative assessment of (un)ethical behaviors observed in a group |
| **Organization** | Organizational moral reasoning as observed in the behaviors shown in moral dilemma situations concerning the organization as a whole | Inventory of organization-wide ethical practices | Quantitative assessment of (un)ethical behaviors observed on an organizational level |

be defined as an above-average ethics performance. Above-average moral performance can be reflected through above-average results in all three assessment methods. A critical consideration is whether we should define above average in relationship to other actors, or in relationship to a normative "on average, actors should do this or that." In this chapter, we endorse the application of the second version, a normative average. The opposite of moral excellence can be called "moral bankruptcy," a situation in which a business is so deeply involved in unethical practices that it has lost its moral license to operate; it has lost its "ethical profitability."[87]

### Ethics Management Tools

Ethics management deploys a varied set of tools stemming from both origins, mainstream business and specific business ethics background. Mainstream **ethics management tools** are the use of a new payment scheme that rewards ethically correct behavior (human resources), the introduction of ethical key performance indicators (accounting), or the inclusion of ethics in the company's mission statement (strategy). All of those are powerful tools influencing employees' ethical decision-making factors, but they must be complemented by specialized ethics management tools, such as codes of ethics, ethics councils, and ethics training, to mention a few. In the following sections, we will provide greater insight into both types of tools.

The third type of ethics management tools is to ensure that every single manager does the right thing in his or her immediate sphere of influence. Figure 5.18 illustrates the overall ethics performance and how an organization depends on all three types of ethics management instruments, which in their complementary character create what we could call the organization's ethics performance margin. This can be called an ethics value chain, leading to an ethics margin. Such a margin may describe the difference between ethical misbehavior and ethically correct behavior. While a mainstream business value chain and its margin describe the difference between the financial costs of doing business and the total value added by its activity, an ethics value chain describes the difference between ethical misbehaviors and good deeds of a business.

The basis of good ethics performance is the individual manager's **ethical management** behavior. Not only does such good ethical behavior add up to the organization's overall ethics performance, but it also serves a role-model function of ethical leadership. In a survey by the Ethics Resource Center,[88] this fact was confirmed by impressive numbers. The study observed how central factors of ethics performance changed when leaders were observed to behave ethically in comparison to the situation when they did not. When direct supervisors were observed to

**Ethics management tools** are managerial means by which to improve ethics performance.

**Ethical management** describes individual managers' ethical behavior in their immediate sphere of managerial influence.

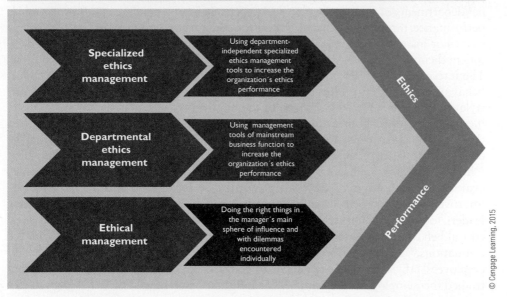

© Cengage Learning, 2015

behave unethically, 42 percent of employees felt the pressure to do so too, 89 percent observed ethical misconduct, and 40 percent did not report misconduct. Those negative behaviors were more than halved when supervisors were perceived as behaving ethically themselves. The pressure to compromise standards was reduced by 25 percent, the observed misconduct by 45 percent, and the number of unreported incidents was reduced by 37 percent to only 3 percent of unreported incidents of ethical misconduct. When employees report misconduct, the large majority do so to their supervisors (86%). The perceived behavior of companies' top management had a similarly significant impact.

**Departmental ethics management tools** harness the standard instruments of management of old-established business departments to manage ethical performance. Thus, strictly speaking, mainstream ethics management tools are not ethics management tools, but the use of "normal business" to influence ethical behavior. Chapters 6 through 15 will provide a deeper insight into all of the main business functions and how sustainability, responsibility, and ethics are managed throughout them.

Mainstream business departments are crucial in ethics management in two ways. First, some departments seem to be more vulnerable for ethical misconduct. A survey among 175 company leaders revealed that they are most concerned about ethical issues occurring in the sales department. Fifty-three percent of the officials stated sales as the area of greatest concern, 51 percent identified operations, especially in emerging markets, and 20 percent found accounting and finance a reason to worry.[89] This first type of importance of mainstream ethics management tools is inside the department, referring to the internal ethics performance. A first and powerful step to ensuring good ethics inside single departments is to create formal ethics policies, such as an ethical sourcing policy for procurement, ethical marketing for customer relationship management, and an accounting ethics policy for the accounting and controlling departments.

**Departmental ethics management tools** are standard management instruments used throughout mainstream business departments and functions to improve ethics performance.

# Expert Corner

## The Challenge of Ethical Leadership

According to the Centre for Ethical Leadership at Melbourne Business School, "the greatest barrier to ethical leadership is not a lack of individual character, but rather the lack of a framework for understanding what it means to act as an ethical leader and how to provide this leadership in complex and dynamic situations."

Source: MBS. (2012). *Vincent Fairfax Fellowship*. Retrieved February 2, 2013, from Melbourne Business School: www.mbs.edu/index.cfm?objectid=4908AD95-ED7E-6096-6725D9BACBECF5F5

The second type of significance of mainstream ethics management tools lies in mainstream management's support of the creation of ethics performance in other external departments of the organization and in actively improving the organization's ethics performance through shaping of structures and practices that make people behave right. For instance, the controlling function might implement dilemma-related indicators in their work, such as the average ethical misconduct reported to an ethics hotline. The internal communication department can send messages about the desired ethical behavior internally or conduct a monthly internal dilemma solution competition in the style of "What would you do?" One of the most powerful functions for the management of ethics through mainstream management instruments is the human resources (HR) management department. HR management has many ways of increasing the ethics performance of the company, such as rewarding ethical behaviors in payment schemes, conducting ethics training, and considering ethical behavior in performance evaluations. Those tools have been proven to be remarkable in their potential to improve ethics performance and are already applied widely. A survey among company leaders found that almost half of the participating companies (49%) considered good ethical behavior at least as important as business outcomes in employees' performance evaluations.[90] Eighty-one percent of Fortune 500 companies had an assessment of employees' ethical conduct as one part of performance evaluation. Ninety-one percent trained their employees on ethics.[91] More information on how HR can foster good ethics will be provided in Chapter 11 on human resources management.

**Specialized ethics management tools** comprise a set of instruments that in its origins has been developed to manage the ethics performance of organizations. This set of tools is typically administered by the ethics and compliance department that specializes in the management of the organization's overall ethics performance. The following list provides an overview of the most commonly applied specialized ethics management tools.

- *Normative leadership:* Codes of conduct are probably the most often applied instrument in ethics management. As a matter of fact, codes of conduct can rightfully be called codes of ethics. A survey about ethics and leadership in corporations found that 90 percent of codes of conduct are meant as guidance for ethical decision making. Codes of ethics aim at giving guidance about what to do or not to do. Mostly this goal is achieved by a combination of ethical rules and values. Fifty-nine percent of employees in the same survey applied the code on their job most of the time and another 35 percent applied the code sometimes.[92] It has been found that companies that have a better code of conduct are usually ranked higher for their ethics, responsibility, and sustainability performance.[93] Those facts show that codes of conduct with high ethical content are a central element of companies' ethics management activities. The code of conduct is often the basis and a first step for subsequent ethics instruments deployed by organizations. That is all the more reason that it is important to get the code right. Figure 5.19 lists central considerations for establishing high-quality codes.

- *Organizational structure:* Ethics departments and officers are usually the roles assigned in the organizational infrastructure to manage companies' sets of ethics management instruments. Usually, ethics departments and officers fulfill a double role, as they also cover the function of compliance with laws and regulations. The resulting ethics and compliance function can often be of considerable size, which is best measured by the number of full-time employees of such departments. Fifty-five percent of companies with an ethics and compliance officer have been found to employ two to nine full-time employees, 18 percent zero to one, 12 percent more than fifty, and 11 percent twenty to forty-nine employees, dedicated full-time

**Specialized ethics management tools** are tools with the purpose of managing ethics throughout the whole organization.

**Figure 5.19 Quality Criteria for Codes of Conduct according to Ethisphere**

| Analysis component | Component description | Weight (%) |
|---|---|---|
| Public Availability | A Code should be made readily available to all stakeholders. What is the availability and ease of access to the Code? | 5 |
| Tone from the Top | Level at which the leadership of the organization is visibly committed to the values and topics covered in the Code | 15 |
| Readability and Tone | What is the style and tone of the language used in the document? Is it easy to read and reflective of its target audience? | 20 |
| Nonretaliation and Reporting | Is there a stated and explicit nonretaliation commitment and dedicated resources available for making reports of code violation? If so, is it presented clearly? | 10 |
| Commitment and Values | Does the Code embed corporate values or mission language? Does it identify the ethical commitments held to its stakeholders (e.g., customers, vendors, communities)? | 10 |
| Risk Topics | Does the Code address all of the appropriate and key risk areas for the company's given industry? | 20 |
| Comprehension Aids | Does the Code provide any comprehension aids (Q&As, FAQs, checklists, examples, case studies) to help employees and other stakeholders understand key concepts? | 5 |
| Presentation and Style | How compelling (or difficult) is the Code to read? This depends on layout, fonts, pictures, taxonomy, and structure | 15 |

Source: Ethisphere, as cited in Erwin, P. M. (2011). Corporate codes of conduct: The effects of code content and quality on ethical performance. *Journal of Business Ethics, 99*(4), 535–548.

to the management of ethics and compliance.[94] The job of the ethics officer has been described as crucial for ethics performance, but as highly complex in reality. Ethics officers are often seen as "troublemakers" who have little power and unclear job descriptions. To ensure ethics officers' positive impact on ethics performance, it has been recommended to position them directly under the board of external directors (for greater independence from the managers they are to observe), to clearly define and communicate their job descriptions, and to pay extra attention to the moral profile and preparation of the person who will do the job.[95]

- *Feedback mechanisms:* Whistleblowing, councils, ombudsmen, and audits are ethics management tools that fulfill a double function of, on the one hand, obtaining information about ethical conduct and misconduct and, on the other hand, providing feedback and advice. Whistleblowing (blowing the whistle is a symbol for making public others' misconduct) can be achieved through many different anonymous or personalized mechanisms. Ethics hotlines where employees can report misconduct to an independent person are widely applied. Ethics councils, often called ombudsmen, are persons that employees can contact for advice in a dilemma situation or who may even become active as mediators. Ethics audits are a third mechanism to detect misconduct where the ethics performance of an organization is checked systematically.

How can such feedback mechanisms as those mentioned above be managed to highest effectiveness? In a survey among Fortune 500 companies, of the people who did not report an ethical misbehavior, 61 percent stated they did not report it because they believed that no corrective action would be taken anyway. In most cases, this is not true; in one survey, 71 percent of people who had reported misconduct stated that their reports were substantiated by their company. The second biggest inhibitor for employee reporting (42%) was that reporting channels were not

## In Practice

### Corporate Whistleblowers: Who Is Protected?

Many countries have legislation that protects whistleblowers. In Australia, to be protected by the Corporations Act as a whistleblower, you must identify yourself (you cannot remain anonymous) and be an officer (usually a director or secretary) of the company, an employee, or a contractor, or contractor's employee, who has a current contract to supply goods or services to the company.

Source: ASIC. (2010). *Protection for whistleblowers.* Retrieved February 2, 2013, from Australian Securities and Investments Commission: www.asic.gov.au/asic/asic.nsf/byheadline/Protection+for+whistleblowers?openDocument

confidential, which led directly to the fear of retaliation. A large number of survey respondents did not report misconduct because they feared retaliation, 29 percent from coworkers, 28 percent from top management, and 25 percent from their direct supervisor. Unfortunately, this fear is rooted in a real risk. Fifteen percent of respondents did not report because they experienced retaliation when they reported before. Retaliation ranged from other employees giving them the cold shoulder, to abuse and exclusion from decisions.[96] When designing the before-mentioned feedback channels, it is important to keep in mind and avoid what keeps people from reporting.

## 5-4d Ethics Programs and Culture

Ethics management instruments, based on the three groups of tools mentioned in the last section, are typically bundled to jointly form an **ethics program**, which aims at the maximization of ethics performance through a set of mutually reinforcing management instruments. Sixty percent of Fortune 500 companies have an ethics program consisting of at least six distinct ethics management instruments. Programs may be a powerful start toward ethics performance, but good ethics only become truly institutionalized and lasting when a "socialization of ethics" takes place, when doing the right thing has become part of the organizational identity and is its natural character.[97]

The consistent application of an ethics program should lead to an ethical organizational culture, which in turn helps to stabilize the ethics performance of the company in the long run and make it crisis-proof, even if one or another ethics management tool fails in the future. An ethical organizational culture creates an organizational environment in which it is easy and natural to do the right thing in every decision and action. The paradox of **ethics culture** is that, on one hand, once such a culture has been achieved and ethics has become the "character of the company,"[98] all previously mentioned ethics management tools virtually render themselves irrelevant, since people are doing the right thing; on the other hand, ethics management instruments are the main means of achieving an ethical culture.

Achieving an ethical culture is a worthwhile endeavor from both an ethics performance perspective and a mainstream management perspective. Employees working in organizations with strong ethical cultures feel a decreased pressure to compromise ethical standards. The observed ethical misconduct is more than halved, and an average of 97 percent of employees reported misconduct when they saw it.[99] Ethical culture may also bring manifold advantages for mainstream management, most notably an increase in the long-term value of the business, compliance with rules and regulations, and a heightened employee commitment to organizational mission and values.[100]

So what is the secret to creating an ethics culture? Why does it work in some cases and does not work in others? What are the drivers and inhibitors of ethical organizational culture? Creating an ethics culture is a primary task of the ethics and compliance (E&C) department, but it is in need of allies. The main allies from which active support for the E&C department is needed are the C-suite (the highest managers of the company), the human resources department, operations management, and the internal corporate communication department. Interestingly, the role of C-suite management is almost as important as that of the E&C department. The strongest three hurdles to achieving ethical culture are organizational complexity, lack of support by middle managers, and the lack of appreciation of ethical culture as a business driver.[101]

### The Process of Ethics Management

How do you manage the ethics of a whole organization? The answer is, you cannot. Ethics management as a process must rely on the management of one ethical issue or opportunity at a time. This **ethics management process** is independent from

An **ethics program** is a set of ethics management instruments chosen by a specific organization to create ethics performance.

An **ethics culture** describes a situation where ethical behavior has become part of the natural character of the company.

The **ethics management process** is the management of ethical issues with the goal of achieving maximum ethics performance. The process consists of the three phases of issue evaluation, behavior explanation, and tool application.

the level and subject of management. The top manager who manages the corruption issue for the whole company will apply the same ethics management process as a sales manager who needs to decide whether to sell to a tobacco company or not.

Figure 5.20 illustrates the process of ethics management in its three main stages. At every stage, one of the three domains of business ethics is predominantly important. At stage one in the issue or opportunity evaluation, the focus lies on understanding the situation and finding out what the right behavior should be. The normative ethics stage delivers the answers to those questions by applying the theories of moral philosophy to the situation at hand. In this stage the main task is to understand why people do or do not act according to what has been defined as ethically correct. Descriptive ethics provides the answers by evaluating individual and situational factors that may be inhibitors and drivers of making the right decisions. At stage three, ethics management is the domain that delivers the right tools to manage ethics performance.

At stage one of the ethics management process, the evaluation of the **ethical issue** or **ethical opportunity** means deeply understanding the situation at hand. The first question to be answered before the dilemma evaluation is to determine if the management challenge at hand is actually an ethical issue or not. Many problems that are commonly subsumed under the ethics topic are not strictly ethical issues, but rather mainstream business challenges or legal compliance issues. Business ethics textbooks typically exemplify ethical core issues as discrimination, sexual harassment, bribery,

**Figure 5.20 The Ethics Management Process**

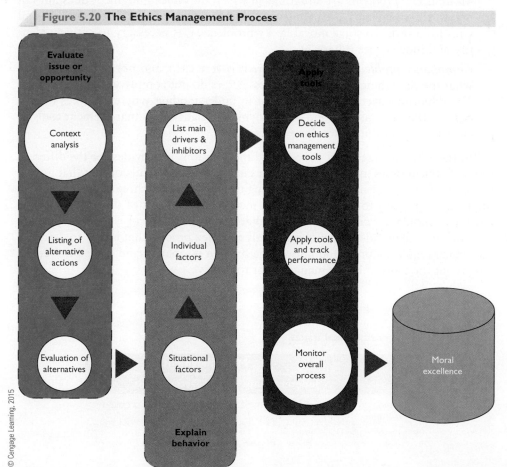

An **ethical opportunity** is a possibility to do good and to achieve positive ethics performance.

An **ethical issue** is a critical situation caused by a realized or potential, right or wrong decision or behavior.

© Cengage Learning, 2015

## In Practice

**Expensive Advice—A Genuine Ethical Problem?**

In March 2006, the Doyles owned a house worth $450,000 and had superannuation (a retirement fund) of $640,000. Following advice provided by Storm Financial in Townsville, two and one-half years later their super had gone, their share portfolio had been sold, and they owed $456,000. In return for this disastrous investment advice, they paid Storm $152,000 in fees.

Source: Barry, P. (2011). *In the eye of the storm: The collapse of Storm Financial.* Retrieved February 2, 2013, from *The Monthly*: www.themonthly.com.au/collapse-storm-financial-eye-storm-paul-barry-2980

equal treatment of employees, advertisement, occupational health and safety, unjust dismissal, financial issues, and pollution.[102] Ethical issues also do not always have to be dilemmas. Ethical issues can be divided into four broad types, based on the two dimensions of clarity of the *moral judgment* and the *motivation* of decision makers to do the right thing (see Figure 5.21). The four types of ethical issues are genuine dilemmas, compliance problems, moral laxity, and no-problem problems.

The different types of ethical issues mentioned, due to their different characteristics, each require a different focus at different phases of the ethics management process.

- *Genuine ethical dilemmas* are characterized by a high motivation to do the right thing and a dilemma situation highly difficult to judge morally. Actors want to do the right thing but have difficulties understanding what the right thing is. The required action is to assist in the ethical decision-making process to create clarity (Phase 1).
- *No-problem problems* exist when the moral judgment is clear and actors are highly motivated to act upon it. In this case, it remains for ethics management to create an organizational environment in which motivation and judgment can easily be translated into ethical action (Phase 3).
- *Moral laxity problems* are situations in which the ethical judgment does not fail due to the complexity of the dilemma, but due to a lack of motivation to deal with it. In order to solve moral laxity problems, it is necessary to actively identify and judge issues (Phase 1).
- *Compliance problems* are issues where it is very clear, and normatively defined, what the right thing is, but nevertheless actors do not comply with those norms. The ethics management task lies first in understanding why employees do not comply (Phase 2) and second in deploying the right ethics management tools to ensure the right things are done (Phase 3).

In the ethics management process and the solutions it provides for the different types of ethical issues in organizations, we encounter a powerful concept that unifies the long history of business ethics, allowing us to capture the three main domains of the field in one easy-to-understand road map. The simplicity of description in this road map should not create the illusion that ethics management is simple. Creating organizations of moral excellence is a highly complex process that is easy to describe, but which requires a profound knowledge basis in normative and descriptive ethics and about the tools of ethics management to achieve.

**Figure 5.21 Types of Ethical Issues**

| | | Moral judgment | |
|---|---|---|---|
| | | **Indeterminate** | **Determinate** |
| Motivation | High | Genuine dilemma | No-problem problem |
| | Low | Moral laxity | Compliance problem |

Source: Geva, A. (2006). A typology of moral problems in business: A framework for ethical management. *Journal of Business Ethics, 69*(2), 133–147.

I. *Business ethics* is the interdisciplinary study of ethical issues and opportunities in business. It can be applied on the levels of individual, organizational, and economic ethics.

II. Business ethics overlaps with the fields of *law* and *compliance.* It is related to *morality,* as ethics provides the rules for deciding what is right or wrong, while morality explicitly describes right or wrong for a specific group and situation.

III. *Interpretations* of business ethics vary greatly and can be subdivided into a narrow and a broad perspective.

IV. The three *domains of business ethics* are *normative ethics,* based on moral philosophy; *descriptive ethics,* based on behavioral psychology; and *ethics management,* based on management studies.

V. The three major theories of moral philosophy, inside the domain of *normative ethics,* are *virtue ethics,* based on a virtuous life; *deontology,* based on rules; and *consequentialism,* based on achieving the best-possible outcome.

VI. *Descriptive ethics* aims to describe, understand, influence, and predict ethical behavior of individuals and groups. It is based on the *ethical decision-making process,* which revolves around the four stages of ethical *awareness, judgment, motivation,* and *behavior* and takes both *individual* and *situational factors* into account.

VII. *Ethics management* is the process of managing ethical issues and opportunities through management tools with the goal of improving ethics performance.

VIII. *Ethics performance* can be assessed through the three approaches of moral development, implemented ethics, and observed behavior.

IX. *Ethics management tools* to achieve ethics performance fall into the categories of ethical management, departmental ethics management, and specialized ethics management. If applied well, those tools serve to create a self-reinforcing *ethical organizational culture.*

## KEY TERMS

applied ethics 115
business ethics 118
compliance 120
consequentialism 128
deontology 127
departmental ethics management
    tools 141
descriptive ethics 132
economic ethics 119
ethical issues 145
ethical management 140
ethical opportunity 145

ethics culture 144
ethics management 136
ethics management process 144
ethics management tools 140
ethics performance 136
ethics program 144
implemented ethics 138
individual ethics 119
individual factors 133
moral development 137
moral dilemma 119
moral excellence 139

moral philosophy 116
morality 120
normative ethics 124
observed behavior 139
organizational ethics 119
situational factors 135
specialized ethics management
    tools 142
utilitarianism 128
values 121
virtue ethics 125

## EXERCISES

### A. Remember and Understand

A.1. Define the following terms, and interrelate them: (a) *normative theories,* (b) *descriptive ethics,* and (c) *ethics management.*

A.2. Define the following terms, and interrelate them: (a) *business ethics,* (b) *law,* and (c) *compliance.*

A.3. Explain the relationship, similarities and differences, between ethics and morality. Use your own examples.

A.4. Mention the four types of ethical issues and describe how to approach each in one sentence.

### B. Apply and Experience

B.5. Enter the *Stanford Encyclopedia of Ethics* through http://plato.stanford.edu/. Compare the ethical theories of virtue ethics, deontology, and consequentialism and their variants. Which of the theories reflects most how you personally judge in moral decision situations?

B.6. Talk to a company employee you know well and ask her or him about one specific moral dilemma on his or her job. Then use the concepts of descriptive ethics to find out how people behave in this dilemma situation and why they do so.

B.7. Think of one situation for each individual and situational factor mentioned in Figure 5.12 and Figure 5.13. In the situations constructed, the individual or situational factor scrutinized should be of significant help to assess the ethical decision making and behavior.

## C. Analyze and Evaluate

C.8. Use Figure 5.6 to analyze in which part of the nexus of opposing views on business ethics you are. Do the same thing for your professor and compare the results. What areas of conflict might occur between you and your professor based on your respective understandings of business ethics?

C.9. Look up an ethical dilemma that has been covered extensively in the news. Prepare a 360-degree ethics assessment for three different alternative decisions and actions that could have been taken in the dilemma situation.

C.10. Look up a company's website, examine the company reports, and prepare an "implemented ethics assessment" in which you list the ethical issues explicitly addressed by the company and the ethics management tools deployed.

## D. Change and Create

D.11. Imagine you are the newly assigned ethics officer of Siemens. Write an ethics management plan for the company, describing a set of ethics management tools to be applied. Explain how this ethics management system will create ethical excellence and avoid ethically wrong decisions and actions.

D.12. Engage a representative of a specific profession, company, or industry in a discussion on a typical ethical issue encountered in his/her professional sphere. Try to jointly analyze the person's behavior and develop strategies to increase his/her ethical performance. The exchange will probably be easier if you have a personal connection to this person.

## PIONEER INTERVIEW WITH LINDA K. TREVIÑO

Courtesy of Linda K. Treviño

Linda K. Treviño is a pioneer in the topics of behavioral and descriptive ethics—the ethics domain that deals with the question of why people do or do not behave ethically.

**You have written extensively about behavioral ethics and why people do the things they do in companies. Many ethics books, especially in the European area, focus rather on the normative aspect of business ethics. Which one do you think is the more important question for ethical practice in businesses—"What should people do?" or "How do we get people to do the right thing?"**

I think that both are extremely important. We need the normative ethics tools to help us decide what's right in a particular situation. But, we all know that people don't always follow those prescriptions. So, we also need to understand the psychology of human decision making and behavior. Psychology can help us to figure out why people think and behave as they do, and that knowledge can inform how we structure organizations and lead people in an ethical direction.

**An article that you wrote about how ethics is perceived at different levels of the organizational hierarchy was titled "It's Lovely at the Top." How do top managers perceive their companies' ethics performance differently from employees lower in the organizational hierarchy? Is this a problem in practice?**

That study demonstrated what many of us know intuitively—that top executives are often out of touch with what's happening at lower levels in their organizations because information gets filtered and bad news often stops at lower levels. That doesn't just apply to ethics, but when it does, it has huge implications. If everything looks rosy and fine at the top, executives won't commit resources that are necessary to develop ethical cultures and ethical leadership in their organizations. I encourage organizations to do serious ethical culture assessments at least every few years to find out what employees are saying and doing. They then need to take the results of such assessments seriously and make necessary changes.

**You have published a very successful book on *Managing Business Ethics*, subtitled "Straight Talk about How to Do It Right." What would be your top three recommendations for students to get business ethics right?**

First, I believe that it's so important to know yourself. Figuring out who you are, what your values are, and what you stand for before you enter the workplace can go a long way toward ensuring ethical behavior because there will be challenges along the way. If you know what your values are, and work toward standing up for them, you are more likely to resist pressure to behave in ways that are inconsistent with those values.

Second, I encourage students to do their best to figure out what an organization's values are before joining it. This is because good values fit makes for happier employees generally. But, it also helps to avoid the serious ethical challenges that employees sometimes face. If they've made a good match, they are more likely to agree with how their employer does business.

Third, it's important for students to understand their own responsibility for ethical leadership. They are in business school in part because they expect to be leaders. And, as leaders, they have a responsibility to design workplaces in ways that support ethical conduct and discourage unethical conduct. That applies to all sorts of things managers do from setting goals to designing reward and punishment systems to conducting performance evaluations.

**Nowadays *business ethics, sustainability,* and *responsibility* are often used interchangeably by business practitioners. How would you differentiate and interconnect those three terms? Can all three be managed together, for instance, by the same department, or are they too different?**

I think responsibility is broader than but connects the other two. Business ethics focuses on responsible behavior of individuals and organizations—being responsible toward multiple stakeholders and acting in a way that reduces harm and creates greater societal good. Sustainability is also about being responsible, but it reminds us that we are responsible to future generations as well as the current stakeholders who have a louder voice in the moment.

---

## PRACTITIONER PROFILE: JOHN C. LENZI

Courtesy of John C. Lenzi

**Employer organization:** ITT is a diversified leading manufacturer of highly engineered critical components and customized technology solutions for the energy, transportation, and industrial markets. Building on its heritage of innovation, ITT partners with its customers to deliver enduring solutions to the key industries that underpin our modern way of life. Founded in 1920, ITT is headquartered in White Plains, New York, with employees in more than 35 countries and sales in a total of approximately 125 countries. The company generated 2011 revenues of $2.1 billion.

**Job title:** Vice President, Corporate Responsibility and Chief Ethics Officer, ITT Corporation
**Education:** Bachelor of Arts, University of Minnesota; Juris Doctor, Rutgers University School of Law

### In Practice

**What are your responsibilities?** I manage a team of more than 150 professionals worldwide developing and implementing global strategies that deliver proactive, measurable, and sustainable value to the business across diverse corporate governance disciplines including Ethics; Environment, Safety, Health and Security (ESH&S); Global Trade Programs; and Environmental Affairs. Our functions target critical success factors directly aligned with business strategies and on meeting internal and external stakeholder expectations. Strict legal and regulatory compliance is of course the minimum deliverable, but we are also focused on value creation within our functions. Corporate Responsibility (CR) also helps manage ITT's Sustainability initiatives and obviously is a key partner in further enhancing our corporate culture.

### What are typical activities you carry out during a day at work?

One of my top responsibilities—beyond supporting our various teams and their efforts to deliver against a given years' goals/plans—is to also proactively think about future trends and emerging best practices for each of the disciplines in the Corporate Responsibility department. The world continues to evolve at an incredible pace, including expectations on corporate performance, and a large part of my job is to think about the function three to five years from now and begin shaping that strategy and journey now.

While ITT has a 90-plus year history, in its current iteration, the company is little more than a year old at the time of this interview. Because our global footprint and product portfolio is so different than the recent past, we have an incredible opportunity to rethink the programs, processes, and strategies of the past, LEAN out that which no longer applies or adds value, and focus on essential strategies and tactics that elevate functional performance and thus contribute to ITT's drive for business results.

Another large part of my focus is on the professional development of our staff and exposing them to company issues somewhat outside of their functional accountabilities and their comfort zones. These experiences, along with discipline-specific continuing education/development, help shape the most well-rounded and thoughtful professionals.

## How do sustainability, responsibility, and ethics topics play a role in your job?

These subjects are critical to everything the CR function does and are obviously important elements contributing to a healthy corporate culture. Research has shown that high ethical cultures and managers who act with integrity not only enhance individual contributor performance, but also impact the company's overall business performance. This is true regardless of global geography.

An open, transparent workplace, one where employees are empowered to speak up, raise a concern, or make a suggestion related to specific *business matters*—and managers who indicate a willingness to listen—is also the kind of workplace that if and when necessary, those same employees will raise a concern related to *potential misconduct*. Such a workplace is also self-policing; over time the large majority of employees who feel and act as they are empowered will not tolerate individuals who deviate from that standard.

At ITT, we know that sustainability, responsibility, and ethics, while overlapping in scope and definition, are nonetheless understood and expected by our employees and, critically, our customers. Our efforts to reduce injury frequency and severity metrics, for example, are tied to employee well-being (and doing the right thing), overall insurance costs, as well as being a key metric for our customers. Much the same is true for managing/reducing our carbon footprint and water usage or waste creation; it's expected that we'll constantly seek self-improvement via internal and external audits on ESH&S.

The same holds for a host of metrics on Ethics and Trade, including self-disclosures, improved free trade agreement or duty initiatives, ethics investigations and outcomes, anticorruption due diligence, and certainly employee perceptions of potential retaliation or their belief in organizational justice—the belief that the company will not tolerate inappropriate behaviors.

## Out of the topics covered in the chapter into which your interview will be included, which concepts, tools, and topics are most relevant to your work?

I was most struck by the simplicity and visual imagery surrounding the Ethics Performance models in Figure 5.16. While individual and organizational development is different in every organization, the value of the journey is indisputable. The pyramids provide a beautiful imagery and show the path to optimum alignment, Universal Principles (individual) and Ethical (organizations). In a very real sense, these images, reflecting a sophisticated theory and analysis, support and validate the ongoing effort here at ITT, and hopefully other companies as well.

Every organization needs a set of guiding principles and values that serve as the foundation for all other activity; resulting policies and procedures, a Code of Conduct, organizational structures and reporting lines, and other "checks and balances" simply support (or not) business conduct within and under those principles and values. The degree to which a company communicates about—and trains its employees on—these matters also reflects that principle-based commitment. At ITT, we continue to communicate and train on our values of Respect, Responsibility, and Integrity, as they must be nurtured continuously.

As I said above, we do these things to develop a healthy culture and to unleash business creativity and intellectual capital; the fact that empowered employees will not tolerate—and will report—potential wrongdoing is a dividend from those efforts. But it all starts at the top and commitment to a set of guiding principles and/or values.

### Insights and Challenges

### What recommendation can you give to practitioners in your field?

Don't ever settle for simply being good. Don't simply "check the box" for your ethics, responsibility, or sustainability programs; don't settle by delivering just the "basics." Whatever your resources, strive to be great. Fight for resources; make the argument tied to enhanced performance—and make the argument stick. Seek the experience of other, larger more experienced companies and learn from their successes and failures. Join global professional organizations like the Ethics & Compliance Officer Association (ECOA) or the Ethics Resource Center (ERC) to not only learn from colleagues, but give back to the community as well.

I've engaged the corporate ethics network since 2003 and cannot overstate the value of learning from other practitioners; the same is true of Trade Compliance and ESH&S related organizations. These fields are remarkable for their emerging role in corporate governance, and the willingness to share experiences, even among "competitors" in the marketplace.

A critical component in all you do is of course senior management; develop a relationship with your CEO and all of his/her direct reports. Provide them with everything they need to know, *not* everything you know. Don't expect buy-in and support if you've not fully vetted strategy in advance. Be honest and direct when delivering success stories, as well as issues or challenge areas. At ITT, I have direct access to our CEO when needed, and regularly scheduled checkpoints throughout the year. More importantly, we've developed a very good relationship, and her support and engagement are outstanding. Strive for that same understanding with your Board of Directors.

Finally, don't avoid tough metrics. Most of us would agree with the old adage, "What gets measured, gets done," and we should hope it gets rewarded too. Partnering with sister corporate functions like Human Resources to define the attributes your company seeks to assess and reward is clearly an important component in individual and functional performance management.

**Which are the main challenges of your job?**
Time. There's really never enough time to get done what we hope to accomplish (in life and in business). In corporations, that necessitates a premium on prioritization and delegation; change to sustainable, responsible, ethical cultures comes slowly. Building multiyear strategies and measurement criteria are keys to managing the never-ending pressures of time. And it's important to move the debate from strictly providing legal and regulatory compliance via Ethics, Trade, and Environmental matters.

Delivering only "compliance" is not enough; compliance is the minimum expected deliverable. The dialogue ought to focus on how these corporate governance functions can also bring financial savings to the company through LEAN program management, functional optimization, a healthier culture, and technology improvements. In fact, it's quite possible that one can improve and expand a company's risk mitigation efforts and save costs at the same time.

### Is there anything else that you would like to share?

The absolute key to success in this or any other field is to find good people and empower them to perform at their best. It is only a cliché if you don't take it seriously. Seek out and utilize best practice when and where you can—right-sizing it for your company when necessary. Micro-managers who rarely delegate responsibilities not only tend to burn out, but also adversely impact performance. As leaders, help set strategies, listen to your staff, and fight for resources—then let your teams execute. As individual contributors, take that responsibility and use it judiciously; be courageous and seek creative solutions, raise problems or issues along with potential solutions too, and never be afraid to ask for help. Communication and coordination are essential to effective teams and corporate initiatives; ensure that it is a two-way dialogue.

---

## SOURCES

1. ERC. (2012). *National business ethics survey of Fortune 500 employees.* Virginia: Ethics Resource Center.
2. LRN Corporation. (2012). *Ethics and compliance leadership survey report.* New York: LRN Corporation.
3. ERC. (2012). *National business ethics survey of Fortune 500 employees.* Virginia: Ethics Resource Center.
4. Treviño, L. K. (1986). Ethical decision making in organizations: A person-situation interactionist model. *Academy of Management Review, 11*(3), 601–617.
5. Donham, W. B. (1929). Business ethics: A general survey. *Harvard Business Review, 7*(4), 385–394.

6. MacIntyre, A. (1998). *A short history of ethics: A history of moral philosophy from the Homeric age to the twentieth century*. Great Britain: Routledge.

7. DeGeorge, R. T. (1987). The status of business ethics: Past and future. *Journal of Business Ethics, 6*(3), 201; Ma, Z. (2009). The status of contemporary business ethics research: Present and future. *Journal of Business Ethics, 90*(3), 255–265; Liedekerke, L., & Dubbink, W. (2008). Twenty years of European business ethics—Past developments and future concerns. *Journal of Business Ethics, 82*(2), 273–280.

8. DeGeorge, R. T. (1987). The status of business ethics: Past and future. *Journal of Business Ethics, 6*(3), 201.

9. Werhane, P. H. (1994). The normative/descriptive distinction in methodologies of business. *Business Ethics Quarterly, 4*(2), 175–180.

10. Ma, Z. (2009). The status of contemporary business ethics research: Present and future. *Journal of Business Ethics, 90*(3), 255–265; Liedekerke, L., & Dubbink, W. (2008). Twenty years of European business ethics—Past developments and future concerns. *Journal of Business Ethics, 82*(2), 273–280.

11. ERC. (2012). *National business ethics survey of Fortune 500 employees*. Virginia: Ethics Resource Center.

12. LRN Corporation. (2012). *Ethics and compliance leadership survey report*. New York: LRN Corporation.

13. ECOA. (2012). *Welcome to the Ethics & Compliance Officer Association*. Retrieved August 20, 2012, from the Ethics & Compliance Officer Association: www.theecoa.org/imis15/ECOAPublic/Home/ECOAPublic/Default.aspx?hkey=bce1bd2e-a2a4-4984-8fa1-7943ca8a50f7; Chavez, G. A., Wiggins, R. A., & Yolas, M. (2001). The impact of membership in the Ethics Officer Association. *Journal of Business Ethics, 34*(1), 39–56.

14. Ethisphere. (2012). *World's most ethical companies methodology*. Retrieved August 20, 2012, from Ethisphere: http://ethisphere.com/wme/methodology.html; Ethisphere. (2012). *Ethics quotient survey 2012*. Retrieved August 20, 2012, from Ethisphere: http://ethisphere.com/wme/methodology.html

15. Cragg, W. (2012). The state and future directions of business ethics research and practice. *Business Ethics Quarterly, 20*(4), 720–721; Jones, T. M. (2010). The future of business ethics research: Reflections on the twentieth anniversay of *Business Ethics Quarterly*. *Business Ethics Quarterly, 20*(4), 746–747.

16. Aasland, D. G. (2004). On the ethics behind "business ethics." *Journal of Business Ethics, 53*, 3–8, p. 7.

17. Lewis, P. V. (1985). Defining "business ethics": Like nailing Jello to a wall. *Journal of Business Ethics, 4*(5), 377–385.

18. Crane, A., & Matten, D. (2004). *Business ethics*. New York: Oxford University Press.

19. Crane, A., & Matten, D. (2004). *Business ethics*. New York: Oxford University Press; Weston, A. (2008). *A 21st century ethical toolbox*, 2nd ed. New York: Oxford University Press.

20. Brinkmann, J. & Ims, K. J. (2004). A conflict case approach to business ethics. *Journal of Business Ethics, 53*(1–2), 123–136.

21. Weston, A. (2008). *A 21st century ethical toolbox*, 2nd ed. New York: Oxford University Press; Argandoña, A. (2003). Fostering values in organizations. *Journal of Business Ethics,45*(1–2), 15–28.

22. Weston, A. (2008). *A 21st century ethical toolbox*, 2nd ed. New York: Oxford University Press.

23. England, G. W. (1967). Personal value system of American managers. *Academy of Management Journal,10*(1), 53.

24. Schwartz, M. S. (2005). Universal moral values for corporate code of ethics. *Journal of Business Ethics, 59*(1–2), 27–44.

25. Argandoña, A. (2003). Fostering values in organizations. *Journal of Business Ethics,45*(1–2), 15–28; Alas, R., Ennulo, J., & Türnpuu, L. (2006). Managerial values in the institutional context. *Journal of Business Ethics, 65*(3), 269–278.

26. Fritzsche, D. J., & Oz, E. (2007). Personal values' influence on the ethical dimension of decision making. *Journal of Business Ethics, 75*(4), 335–343.

27. Oliver, B. L. (1999). Comparing corporate managers' personal values over three decades 1967–1995. *Journal of Business Ethics, 20*(2), 147–161.

28. Greene, J. (2003). From neural "is" to moral "ought": What are the moral implications of neuroscientific moral psychology? *Nature Reviews Neuroscience, 4*(10), 846–850.

29. Crane, A., & Matten, D. (2004). *Business ethics*. New York: Oxford University Press.

30. Buchholz, R. A., & Rosenthal, S. B. (1996). Toward a new understanding of moral pluralism. *Business Ethics Quarterly, 6*(3), 263–275.

31. Werhane, P. H. (1994). The normative/descriptive distinction in methodologies of business. *Business Ethics Quarterly, 4*(2), 175–180; Bowie, N. E. (2000). Business ethics, philosophy and the next 25 years. *Business Ethics Quarterly, 10*(1), 7–20.

32. Donaldson, L. (2007). Ethics problems and problems with ethics: Toward a pro-management theory. *Journal of Business Ethics, 78*(3), 299–311.

33. Crane, A., & Matten, D. (2004). *Business ethics*. New York: Oxford University Press; Liedekerke, L., & Dubbink, W. (2008). Twenty years of European business ethics—Past developments and future concerns. *Journal of Business Ethics, 82*(2), 273–280.

34. Hartman, E. M. (2000). Socratic ethics and the challenge of globalziation. *Business Ethics Quarterly, 10*(1), 211–220.

35. Alzola, M. (2011). The reconciliation project: Separation and integration in business ethics research. *Journal of Business Ethics, 99*(1), 19–36, p. 19.

36. Hursthouse, R. (2012). Virtue ethics. In *The Stanford Encyclopedia of Philosophy*. Retrieved September 5, 2012, from http://plato.stanford.edu/entries/ethics-virtue/; Bleisch, B., & Huppenbauer, M. (2011). *Ethische Entscheidungsfindung [Ethical decision making]*. Zurich: Versus.

37. Whetstone, J. T. (2001). How virtue fits within business ethics. *Journal of Business Ethics, 33*(2), 101.

38. Crane, A., & Matten, D. (2004). *Business ethics*. New York: Oxford University Press.

39. Hursthouse, R. (2012). Virtue ethics. In *The Stanford Encyclopedia of Philosophy*. Retrieved September 5, 2012, from http://plato.stanford.edu/entries/ethics-virtue/

40. Bragues, G. (2006). Seek the good life, not money: The Aristotelian approach to business ethics. *Journal of Business Ethics, 67*(4), 341–357.

41. Weston, A. (2008). *A 21st century ethical toolbox,* 2nd ed. New York: Oxford University Press; McInerny, R., & O'Callaghan, J. (2010). Saint Thomas Aquinas. In *The Stanford Encyclopedia of Philosophy.* Retrieved from http://plato.stanford.edu/entries/aquinas/

42. Velasquez, M., & Brady, F. N. (1997). Natural law and business ethics. *Business Ethics Quarterly, 7*(2), 83–107.

43. Koehn, D. (1995). A role for virtue ethics in the analysis of business practice. *Business Ethics Quarterly, 5*(3), 533–539; Audi, R. (2012). Virtue ethics as a resource in business. *Business Ethics Quarterly, 22*(2), 273–291; Whetstone, J. T. (2001). How virtue fits within business ethics. *Journal of Business Ethics, 33*(2), 101.

44. Moore, G. (2008). Re-imagining the morality of management: A modern virtue ethics approach. *Business Ethics Quarterly, 18*(4), 483–511; Moore, G. (2005). Corporate character: Modern virtue ethics and the virtuous corporation. *Business Ethics Quarterly, 15*(4), 659–685.

45. Solomon, R. C. (1992). Corporate roles, personal virtues: An Aristotelean approach to business ethics. *Business Ethics Quarterly, 2*(3), 317–339.

46. Bragues, G. (2006). Seek the good life, not money: The Aristotelian approach to business ethics. *Journal of Business Ethics, 67*(4), 341–357.

47. MacIntyre (1985, 2007), as cited in Bragues, G. (2006). Seek the good life, not money: The Aristotelian approach to business ethics. *Journal of Business Ethics, 67*(4), 341–357.

48. Bleisch, B., & Huppenbauer, M. (2011). *Ethische Entscheidungsfindung [Ethical decision making].* Zurich: Versus.

49. Solomon, R. C. (2003). Victim of circumstances? A defense of virtue ethics in business. *Business Ethics Quarterly, 13*(1), 43–62.

50. Alexander, L., & Moore, M. (2008). Deontological ethics. In E. N. Zalta (ed.), *The Stanford Encyclopedia of Philosophy (Fall 2008 Edition).*

51. Smith, J., & Dubbink, W. (2011). Understanding the role of moral principles in business ethics: A Kantian perspective. *Business Ethics Quarterly, 21*(2), 205–231; Micewski, E. R., & Troy, C. (2007). Business ethics—deontologically revisited. *Journal of Business Ethics,* 72(1), 17–25; Bowie, N. E. (1998). A Kantian theory of capitalism. *Business Ethics Quarterly, 1,* 37–60.

52. Kant, I., & Patton, H. J. (1785/2005). *Moral law: Groundwork of the metaphysic of morals.* New York: Routledge.

53. Kant, I., & Patton, H. J. (1785/2005). *Moral law: Groundwork of the metaphysic of morals.* New York: Routledge.

54. Bowie, N. E. (1999) *Business ethics: A Kantian perspective.* Malden, Mass.: Blackwell Publishers. As cited by Joann B. Ciulla (2001).

55. Treviño, L. K., & Nelson, K. A. (2011). *Managing business ethics,* 5th ed. New Jersey: John Wiley & Sons.

56. Chappel, V. (1994). *The Cambridge companion to Locke.* Cambridge: Cambridge University Press; Sheridan, P. (2011). Locke's moral philosophy. In E. N. Zalta (ed.), *The Stanford Encyclopedia of Philosophy (Winter 2011 Edition).*

57. Rawls, J. (1999). *A theory of justice,* rev. ed. Cambridge: Harvard University Press.

58. Bleisch, B., & Huppenbauer, M. (2011). *Ethische Entscheidungsfindung [Ethical decision making].* Zurich: Versus.

59. Roemer, J. E. (2010). Kantian equilibrium. *Scandinavian Journal of Economics, 112*(1), 1–24.

60. Alexander, L., & Moore, M. (2008). Deontological ethics. In E. N. Zalta (ed.), *The Stanford Encyclopedia of Philosophy (Fall 2008 Edition).*

61. Mill, J. S. (1863/2008). *Utilitarianism.* Forgotten Books: www.forgottenbooks.org/

62. Mill, J. S. (1863/2008). *Utilitarianism.* Forgotten Books: www.forgottenbooks.org/

63. Freeman, R. E. (1984/2010). *Strategic management: A stakeholder approach.* Cambridge: Cambridge University Press, p. 25.

64. Sinnott-Armstrong, W. (2011). Consequentialism. In E. N. Zalta (ed.), *The Stanford Encyclopedia of Philosophy (Winter 2011 Edition).*

65. Scheffler, S. (1994). *The rejection of consequentialism: A philosophical investigation of the considerations underlying rival moral conceptions.* New York: Oxford University Press.

66. Bleisch, B., & Huppenbauer, M. (2011). *Ethische Entscheidungsfindung [Ethical decision making].* Zurich: Versus.

67. Derry, R., & Green, R. M. (1989). Ethical theory in business ethics: A critical assessment. *Journal of Business Ethics, 8*(7), 521.

68. Bazerman, M. H., & Messick, D. M. (1998). On the power of a clear definition of rationality. *Business Ethics Quarterly, 8*(3), 477–480; Curlo, E., & Strudler, A. (1997). Cognitive pathology and moral judgment in managers. *Business Ethics Quarterly, 7*(4), 27–30.

69. Crane, A., & Matten, D. (2004). *Business ethics.* New York: Oxford University Press.

70. Treviño, L. K., Weaver, G. R., & Reynolds, S. J. (2006). Behavioral ethics in organizations: A review. *Journal of Management, 32*(6), 951–990; Haidt, J. (2007). The new synthesis in moral psychology. *Science, 316*(5827), 998–1002; Greene, J. (2003). From neural "is" to moral "ought": What are the moral implications of neuroscientific moral psychology? *Nature Reviews Neuroscience, 4*(10), 846–850.

71. Treviño, L. K., Weaver, G. R., & Reynolds, S. J. (2006). Behavioral ethics in organizations: A review. *Journal of Management, 32*(6), 951–990; Treviño, L. K. (1986). Ethical decision making in organizations: A person-situation interactionist model. *Academy of Management Review, 11*(3), 601–617.

72. Ford, R. C., & Richardson, W. D. (1994). Ethical decision making: A review of the empirical literature. *Journal of Business Ethics, 13*(3), 206.

73. Ford, R. C., & Richardson, W. D. (1994). Ethical decision making: A review of the empirical literature. *Journal of Business Ethics, 13*(3), 206; Treviño, L. K., Weaver, G. R., & Reynolds, S. J. (2006). Behavioral ethics in organizations: A review. *Journal of Management, 32*(6), 951–990; Crane, A., & Matten, D. (2004). *Business ethics.* New York: Oxford University Press.

74. Curlo, E., & Strudler, A. (1997). Cognitive pathology and moral judgment in managers. *Business Ethics Quarterly, 7*(4), 27–30.

75. Carr, A. Z. (1968). Is bluffing ethical? *Harvard Business Review,* 143–153.

76. Blickle, G., et al. (2006). Some personality correlates of business white-collar crime. *Applied Psychology, 55*(2), 220–233; Ralson, D. A., et al. (2011). A twenty-first

century assessment of values across the global workforce. *Journal of Business Ethics, 104*(1), 1–31.

77. ERC. (2012). *National business ethics survey of Fortune 500 employees.* Virginia: Ethics Resource Center.

78. Crane, A., & Matten, D. (2004). *Business ethics.* New York: Oxford University Press; Treviño, L. K., Weaver, G. R., & Reynolds, S. J. (2006). Behavioral ethics in organizations: A review. *Journal of Management, 32*(6), 951–990; Ford, R. C., & Richardson, W. D. (1994). Ethical decision making: A review of the empirical literature. *Journal of Business Ethics, 13*(3), 206.

79. Kohlberg & Turiel (1973), as cited in Treviño, L. K. (1986). Ethical decision making in organizations: A person-situation interactionist model. *Academy of Management Review, 11*(3), 601–617.

80. Gibbs, J. C., Basinger, K. S., & Fuller, D. (1992). *Moral maturity: Measuring the development of sociomoral reflection.* Hillsdale, NJ: Lawrence Erlbaum.

81. Kohlberg & Turiel (1973), as cited in Treviño, L. K. (1986). Ethical decision making in organizations: A person-situation interactionist model. *Academy of Management Review, 11*(3), 601–617.

82. Reidenbach, R. E., & Robin, D. P. (1991). A conceptual model of corporate moral development. *Journal of Business Ethics, 10*(4), 273–284.

83. Treviño, L. K. (1986). Ethical decision making in organizations: A person-situation interactionist model. *Academy of Management Review, 11*(3), 601–617.

84. CEMEFI. (2012). *Empresa socialmente responsable.* Retrieved November 1, 2012, from Centro Mexicano para la Filantropia [Mexican Center for Philanthropy]: www.cemefi.org/esr/; Ethisphere. (2012). Retrieved November 1, 2012, from Ethisphere Institute: http://ethisphere.com/

85. LRN Corporation. (2012). *Ethics and compliance leadership survey report.* New York: LRN Corporation;

ERC. (2012). *National business ethics survey of Fortune 500 employees.* Virginia: Ethics Resource Center.

86. Gatewood, R. D., & Carroll, A. B. (1991). Assessment of ethical performance of organization members: A conceptual framework. *Academy of Management Review, 16*(4), 667–690, p. 674.

87. Swamy, M. R. K. (2000). Focus on moral bankruptcy through money laundering case studies of Nigeria and Russia—Proposal for a new approach to financial statements analysis. *Journal of Financial Management & Analysis, 13*(1), 59–68; Swamy, M. R. K. (2009). Financial management call for a new approach to ethical-based financial statements analysis. *Journal of Financial Management & Analysis, 22*(2), 70.

88. ERC. (2012). *National business ethics survey of Fortune 500 employees.* Virginia: Ethics Resource Center.

89. LRN Corporation. (2012). *Ethics and compliance leadership survey report.* New York: LRN Corporation.

90. LRN Corporation. (2012). *Ethics and compliance leadership survey report.* New York: LRN Corporation.

91. ERC. (2012). *National business ethics survey of Fortune 500 employees.* Virginia: Ethics Resource Center.

92. LRN Corporation. (2012). *Ethics and compliance leadership survey report.* New York: LRN Corporation.

93. Erwin, P. M. (2011). Corporate codes of conduct: The effects of code content and quality on ethical performance. *Journal of Business Ethics, 99*(4), 535–548.

94. LRN Corporation. (2012). *Ethics and compliance leadership survey report.* New York: LRN Corporation.

95. Adobor, H. (2006). Exploring the role performance of corporate ethics officers. *Journal of Business Ethics, 69*(1), 57–75; Hoffman, W. M. (2010). Repositioning the corporate ethics officer. *Business Ethics Quarterly, 20*(4), 744–745.

96. ERC. (2012). *National business ethics survey of Fortune 500 employees.* Virginia: Ethics Resource Center.

97. Balmer, J. M. T., Fukukawa, K., & Gray, E. R. (2007). The nature and management of ethical corporate identity: A commentary on corporate identity, corporate social responsibility and ethics. *Journal of Business Ethics, 76*(1), 7–15; Duh, M., Belak, J., & Milfelner, B. (2010). Core values, culture and ethical climate as constitutional elements of ethical behaviour: Exploring differences between family and non-family enterprises. *Journal of Business Ethics, 97*(3), 473–489; Gatewood, R. D., & Carroll, A. B. (1991). Assessment of ethical performance of organization members: A conceptual framework. *Academy of Management Review, 16*(4), 667–690, p. 684.

98. Moore, G. (2005). Corporate character: Modern virtue ethics and the virtuous corporation. *Business Ethics Quarterly, 15*(4), 659–685, p. 659.

99. ERC. (2012). *National business ethics survey of Fortune 500 employees.* Virginia: Ethics Resource Center.

100. LRN Corporation. (2012). *Ethics and compliance leadership survey report.* New York: LRN Corporation; ERC. (2012). *National business ethics survey of Fortune 500 employees.* Virginia: Ethics Resource Center.

101. LRN Corporation. (2012). *Ethics and compliance leadership survey report.* New York: LRN Corporation.

102. Liedekerke, L., & Dubbink, W. (2008). Twenty years of European business ethics—Past developments and future concerns. *Journal of Business Ethics, 82*(2), 273–280.

## 06

Synergy 5 Forces
Competitiveness Stakeholder SWOT
Diversification Responsible Competitiveness
Strategy Objectives Key Indicator Balanced Scorecard
Competitive Advantage Value Chain Vision Strategic Environment Tactics
BCG Matrix Monopoly

# STRATEGY: RESPONSIBLE COMPETITIVENESS

**You will be able to...**

1   **...integrate responsible management into your organization's strategy.**

2   **...analyze your organization's responsible business strengths, weaknesses, threats, and opportunities.**

3   **...achieve responsible competitiveness.**

Ninety-six percent of CEOs believe that environmental, social, and corporate governance issues should be fully integrated into the strategy of a company.[1]

Over half of executives (54%) believe that their companies'"CSR activities are already giving them an advantage over their top competitors."[2]

Executives assume that the most commonly achieved business advantages from sustainable practices are attraction of customers (37%) improved shareholder value (34%), and increased profitability (31%).[3]

# Changing the Rules of the Game at Betapharm

Since 1993, a small pharmaceutical company of little more than 300 workers in the south German town of Augsburg has created waves way beyond its size and its Bavarian homeland. Indeed, the small generic drug firm has become renowned for increasingly challenging the ways one views firms' business strategies. Betapharm has made a point of not just following accepted industry standards in responsible practices but also pursuing a complete responsible management based strategy even when this goes against immediate profit calculations.

The rationale behind this seemingly counterintuitive strategy is that as a producer of generic nonpatented drugs, the company has no real product or dominant market power to leverage market share or profits. Instead, the founding fathers of Betapharm, Peter Walter and Horst Erhardt, realized that the way to stay ahead of the competition was to place the firm's reputational and cultural value before immediate cost/profit calculations.

The basic strategy of the company has been to dispense almost completely with all forms of traditional advertising and marketing and instead to invest massively in care initiatives such as the *Beta Institut*. The company developed, at its own expense, medical and social literature that has become one of the main information sources for pharmacies and medical practices throughout Germany. Further, it has helped trained nurses and care assistants and has set up organizations to help people in such diverse areas as post-stroke treatment, women with breast cancer, and teenage addiction and violence. The strategy can best be described as a combination of extreme stakeholder outreach and a core responsible management brand positioning. The result of this strategy has been to enshrine the Betapharm brand so positively within the medical stakeholder community (doctors, pharmacies, government, regulators, patients, and researchers) that the Betapharm brand is able to trump other considerations—even cost.

The long-term result has been that Betapharm has rapidly grown to become one of the biggest generic drug companies in Germany despite a complete lack of pricing power, which traditionally had been the basis of competition in the generic drug industry. Interestingly, the company grew so rapidly that when it was taken over by the Indian pharmaceutical giant Dr. Reddy's, not only did that corporation pay a substantial premium in recognition of the company's "reputational capital," but, post-takeover, the new owners also declined to make significant changes to the "Betapharm model." The reputational advantage of Betapharm was deemed too valuable to the business to put it at risk by cutting back on the company's long-term responsible management strategy—or, as Horst Erhardt put it, "our rise from the 28th biggest generic drug company to the 4th is due more or less completely to our CSR strategy not because we have different products."

A considerable part of Betapharm's economic competitiveness is based on its above-average social performance. Betapharm has reached responsible competitiveness, the ultimate goal of responsible strategic management.

Source: www.betapharm.de/

# 6-1 STRATEGY AND RESPONSIBLE MANAGEMENT

*"We have come to recognize that best-run businesses do not simply embrace a sustainability strategy. Instead, they make their corporate strategy sustainable."*[4]

Business strategy should be the starting point for any business activity. Whatever management function of the business we scrutinize, it will, if managed well, always be aligned with the overall business strategy or strategies. This is why this very first chapter on the business tools for responsible management deals with strategic management. Before understanding how other business functions are managed responsibly, we have to craft the overarching responsible business strategy.

In practice, we see a parallel pattern. A survey among CEOs worldwide has shown that the integration of responsible and strategic management is taken seriously. Fifty-nine percent stated that they need to implement environmental social and governance issues much more into strategy. Thirty-four percent said those topics have to be integrated more. Merely seven percent aimed at the same or less integration for their companies.[5] Three years later, companies were already much further down the road. In the second round of the survey, CEOs stated that they had largely integrated responsible management into their strategy and that the new task then would be to deeply embed responsible management throughout the companies' main operational functions.[6]

The intersection between **strategic management** and responsible management has been discussed, criticized, and glorified. Interest in strategic corporate social responsibility and philanthropy has peaked ever since strategic management guru Michael Porter teamed up with the NGO specialist Mark Kramer and jointly started to formally explore how strategy relates to society and vice versa.[7] The topic of strategic management and responsible business performance goes back even to the very roots of the field of strategic management. Igor Ansoff, who is often cited as creator of the term *strategic management* and the field itself, highlighted the importance of strategic management issues as a cornerstone of the strategic management process.[8] Nowadays, when the world has witnessed a wide variety of cases where social, environmental, and ethical risks have forced companies to completely cease to exist, this topic is more than ever an important factor to be considered throughout the strategic management process.

As impressively shown by Porter and Kramer,[9] there is an immense potential for the co-creation of business value complementing value for society and environment. This concept, termed *shared value,* is the center base of the field that was first called *strategic philanthropy* and then *strategic corporate social responsibility*. This intersection between responsible management and strategy is commonly understood from two distinct perspectives. The **broad perspective**, or *business case perspective,* refers to any advantage that business could potentially reap from activities related to society and the natural environment. Into this category falls a wide variety of "recipes" for profitable CSR, such as the book *Corporate Social Opportunity* and the whole field of instrumental stakeholder management.[10] Such advantages can be achieved in a manner largely unrelated to the field of strategic management. The **narrow perspective** on responsible management and strategy explicitly refers to the field of strategic management.[11] In this chapter, the primary focus will originate from the narrow perspective and from how responsible business performance can support the strategic management process and serve to create level-two responsible competitiveness. The business case for responsible business has been illustrated extensively elsewhere.

The overall goal of strategic management is the achievement of a sustained competitive advantage: a situation where an organization is able to outperform its peers or competitors in the long run. Throughout this chapter, the recurrent question will be: *How can a business achieve a sustained competitive advantage and at the same time create value for society and the environment through the strategic management process?*

**DIG DEEPER**

**A Match Made in (Business) Heaven**
The intersection between strategy and responsible management gained broad attention when the godfather of strategic management, Michael Porter, and the NGO specialist Mark Kramer teamed up to explore the intersection between business and society. Look up their joint papers published in the *Harvard Business Review,* and follow the development of the concept of strategic corporate social responsibility.

**Strategic management** is the process of crafting and implementing organizational strategies with the goal of achieving sustained competitive advantage.

The **broad perspective** on the intersection between strategy and responsible management describes any advantage business can reap from responsible business behavior, while the **narrow perspective** specifically refers to the integration of responsible management factors into the traditional strategic management process.

### Edward Freeman

*Edward Freeman, who coined the term stakeholder management, has stated: "What else could a strategic management process be, other than how to improve the business model, which is nothing more than how the company creates value for its customers, employees, suppliers, communities and financiers? Any strategic management process that is not oriented around such value creation, could probably be improved."*

Source: Interview with R. Edward Freeman, 2012. See page 106 in Chapter 4, Responsibility.

CHRIS KLEPONIS/BLOOMBERG/ GETTY IMAGES

The **strategic management process** consists of four phases: the definition of vision, mission, and strategic objectives; analysis of the internal and external environments; strategy formulation; and implementation for the intended outcome of a sustained competitive advantage.

The **strategic management process** can be subdivided into four phases. In phase 1, the task is to define the business's broad strategic direction by crafting the *vision and mission statements* and *strategic objectives*. The environmental analysis conducted throughout phase 2 serves to identify strategically relevant internal and external parameters, often summarized in a *strengths-weaknesses-opportunities-threats(SWOT) analysis*. Phase 3, the *strategy formulation* process, consists of the development of strategies for manifold management situations. Strategies can be developed for single functional areas, a specific business unit, or the whole corporation. *Strategy implementation* (phase 4) translates these strategies into organizational realities such as governance and organizational architecture structures, change management activities, leadership, and entrepreneurial processes. The strategic management process is valid for any kind of organization from business to governmental and civil society organizations.

As illustrated in Figure 6.1, responsible business factors play a crucial role in the strategic management process. The process of strategic management is a circular process and does not necessarily begin with vision and mission statements. Its phases should constantly be connected by feedback links in order to ensure an alignment of all its phases for maximum effectiveness in achieving responsible competitiveness.

---

| Figure 6.1 **The Strategic Responsible Management Process** |

**Phase 1: Vision, Mission, Objectives**
"Shape a vision, mission, and strategic objectives aiming at the creation of a well-balanced triple bottom line of stakeholder, value, and moral excellence."

**Phase 4: Implementation & Control**
"Execute the chosen strategies effectively, leading to responsible competitiveness and the achievement of organizational vision, mission, and objectives."

**Goal: Responsible Competitiveness**

**Phase 2: Environmental Analysis**
"Analyze the social, environmental, and economic factors inside and outside your organization as a basis for strategy development."

**Phase 3: Strategy Formulation**
"Develop corporate, business unit, and functional strategies that lead your organization to responsible competitiveness."

© Cengage Learning, 2015

## 6-2 THE GOAL: RESPONSIBLE COMPETITIVENESS

*"Are, then, the Global Compact signatories better at strategy? I think so, at least insofar as they continue to be better than many others. The goals of sustainability, the challenges of social responsibility and the leadership's inspiration from principles higher than the sole profit motivation all foster business excellence. I like to call this responsible excellence, in the broadest sense of each word."*[12]

What is competitiveness? The answer given by the field of strategic management is that competitiveness is defined by the strength of the **strategic competitive advantage** an organization has established over its peers. Such a strong position can take different forms for distinct organization types. For businesses, strategic competitive advantage is believed to be reflected in the performance and value of companies' stocks. Hence, a company achieving a strategic competitive advantage is supposed to render above-average returns to shareholders and other owner groups.[13] Porter and Kramer[14] highlight strategies for social value creation by philanthropic organizations in order to deliver an above-average social return for donors. Broadening this example, in a responsible management context, above-average returns do not necessarily have to be financial returns, nor do they have to be returns for the owners of an organization. Depending on the interest a specific stakeholder has in the organization, an above-average social or environmental value creation can define the competitiveness of a given organization in the eyes of virtually any stakeholder group. This broader understanding of competitiveness will be associated with responsible competitiveness in a later section of this chapter.

The strategic management process aims at reaching such a competitive position by the planning and execution of **strategies**. How exactly do strategies lead to competitive advantage? While the environmental view explains competitive advantages by an advantageous external environment, the resource-based view contributes competitive advantage to internal strengths and resources of an organization. In this chapter, the two schools on the origin of competitive advantage are merged in practice for the sake of achieving a tool set for strategy development that will apply to the broadest possible number of situations. An important quality of a competitive advantage, once achieved, is its durability in time. A sustained competitive advantage is hard to imitate by competitors and does not easily lose its value due to changes in external circumstances.

**Responsible competitiveness** is a situation in which an organization achieves a coexistence of an economic competitive advantage and above-average social and environmental value creation. Accordingly, irresponsible competitiveness, or "level-zero responsible competitiveness," occurs when an organization is competitive at the cost of society and the environment. Level-one responsible competitiveness is achieved by pure coexistence of socio-environmental competitiveness and economic competitiveness, while level-two responsible competitiveness occurs when an organization is able to leverage its responsible business excellence to increase its economic competitiveness. Although the creator of the concept, Simon Zadeck,[15] framed responsible competitiveness with a strong focus on how responsible business practices enhance competitiveness of regions and clusters, the understanding used here applies it to single organizations.

Responsible competitiveness might sound like a rather theoretical concept, but a study conducted in 2008 revealed that

A **strategic competitive advantage** is an overall position advantageous in comparison with peers' positions, which commonly leads to above-average returns on investment for the owners of an organization.

A **strategy** is an integrated and coordinated set of commitments and actions designed to gain a competitive advantage.

**Responsible competitiveness** is the achievement of a competitive advantage for an organization through the strategic management process while also creating above average responsible business performance.

## Expert Corner

### Edward Freeman

*"What's important here is the purpose of the company. Managing for stakeholders assumes that there is some purpose (usually not just profits) and that 'realizing purpose' is a better way to frame a business than 'strategic competitive advantage.'"*

Source: Interview with R. Edward Freeman, 2012. See page 106 in Chapter 4, Responsibility.

over half (54%) of companies believed that responsible management activities were creating a competitive advantage over their most significant competitors.[16] Another study found that of the companies adopting sustainable business practices, 75 percent had done so in order to achieve a competitive advantage. It was the second most important reason after an enhanced reputation (90%).[17]

## 6-3 PHASE 1: FORMULATING THE MISSION, VISION, AND STRATEGIC OBJECTIVES

*"In our research, we found that the visionary companies displayed a remarkable ability to achieve even their most audacious goals."*[18]

One of the best-known statements of a vision started with the words "I have a dream. . . ." These words were spoken by Martin Luther King Jr. when he addressed a crowd of thousands of people on August 28, 1963, at the Lincoln Memorial in Washington, DC.[19] Those words have been a guiding light for immense social progress in many areas, including common responsible management jargon: They evoke the vision of social value creation. While traditional organizational vision and mission statements ultimately aim at the creation of economic internal gain for a business, King's words show how big the positive social impact of a well-crafted vision can be. In this text, we will focus on providing you with tools to strategically harness vision and mission statements, and subsequent strategic objectives, to the good of company, society, and environment.

The first step toward achieving the goal of a well-balanced triple bottom line has to be the alignment of organizational activity with a three-dimensional organizational goal serving as a "lighthouse" for truly sustainable business performance.[20] For instance, Ben & Jerry's ice cream business has split its mission statement into a social, an economic, and a product mission, and therefore it covers at least two of the three dimensions. One of the longest established fair trade social businesses, OXFAM, has made its single mission the goal of ending poverty. Furthermore, the shoe company Timberland's mission statement aims at supporting people in being change agents.

Edward Freeman, in his book *Strategic Management: A Stakeholder Approach*, has impressively made the case for considering stakeholders from the very beginning of the strategic management process. In order to be successful, businesses have to create value for their stakeholders. Freeman impressively shows how not living up to stakeholders' expectations will inevitably force any business into decline. He therefore claims that companies have to readjust their priorities based on a stakeholder audit and, as a result, review and readjust their mission statement in order to fulfill stakeholders' wants and needs.[21] This standpoint has been widely accepted among mainstream strategic management scholars and practitioners. Freeman finds the repercussions of his argument in most of the popular strategic management textbooks. For instance, Hill and Jones[22] describe the mission statement as a "formal commitment" and "key indicator" in terms of companies' incorporation of the various stakes into business strategy. David[23] evaluates as a good mission statement the one that "indicates the relative attention that an organization will devote to meeting the claims of various stakeholders." Hitt and colleagues[24] conclude that the ultimate responsibility of strategy is to serve the needs of stakeholders. This is why Werther and Chandler[25] highlight that responsible management and stakeholder assessment have to serve as a filter for strategy in general and specifically for the development of strategic vision, mission, and objectives.

Defining what an organization wants to achieve and be is usually done in the natural flow from a long-run vision to an actual mission statement, to short- and medium-run objectives, and finally to concrete short-run activities. These strategic management tools have achieved general relevance not only for classic for-profit businesses, but also for a variety of other organizational forms from foundations to NGOs and social entrepreneurs. Vision, mission, and objectives are commonly used concepts for giving direction to both whole organizations and to single business units, business functions, and even specific business activities such as a project. In the following paragraphs, we will mostly refer to the application in a business context. This business focus, however, should not understate the importance of vision, mission, and strategic objectives for other forms of organization. For instance, for social and environmental entrepreneurs, it is of crucial importance to diligently define a position integrating cause and business. The topic of marketing and communication provides further insight into the communication aspects of shaping vision, mission, and value statements.

A **vision statement** delineates what an organization—be it a for-profit business, an NGO, or even a governmental institution—aims to become and achieve. In order to craft a vision that is powerful enough to move a whole organization toward a higher future goal, a necessary condition is to make it strong enough to "fuel an obsessive will to win at every level of the organization, and to sustain this will."[26] This concept is called "strategic intent" and involves the usage of overarching stretch goals, which require innovative measures to be reached. Strategic intent leads to a relentless pursuit of this ambitious strategic vision and to concentrating full resources and strategic actions on its achievement.[27] On the one hand, responsible business components of a strategic vision might not come naturally to a typical profit-maximizing business. On the other hand, those topics often have a high motivational value that facilitates employees' involvement in their pursuit. It is of utmost importance to search for a mutually reinforcing relationship between a vision's social, environmental, and economic components. For instance, a costly vision of becoming the world's biggest donor company would not be in accordance with the vision of being the market's cost leader.

An excellent example of an organization showcasing both strategic intent and a mutually reinforcing relationship between the three dimensions of a responsible management vision is Procter & Gamble. The company's sustainability vision combines highly ambitious environmental visions such as "having zero manufacturing waste going to landfills" and a $50 billion income from sustainable innovation products with an excellent alignment of those goals with the company's economic objectives.[28]

The mission statement is frequently called the "statement of purpose," creed statement, statement of beliefs, or statement of business principles. It can be described as a statement "defining our business."[29] While the vision statement gives future direction, the **mission statement** defines what the business is and does right now. Mission statements answer the question "What is your business?"[30] by describing what the organization exists for and what it should be doing.[31] The answer to this question covers typical markets, customers, main products, and processes as well as

A **vision statement** delineates what an organization ultimately should become and achieve.

A **mission statement** defines what the business is and does at a certain point in time, typically including the business's market, customers, products, processes, and values.

the values to which the business adheres. The process of establishing a well-crafted mission statement can grow extensively when taken seriously. In order to include stakeholders' perspectives on what the company is and how it should conduct its business, a detailed, dialogue-based stakeholder assessment process is needed. Some strategic management classics recommend a management-exclusive mission development approach;[32] however, focusing exclusively on the core stakeholder group managers, while likely to ensure full support from this group, bears the eminent danger of losing other stakeholders' support for subsequent strategic and tactic moves following such a highly imbalanced mission statement.

**Strategic objectives and goals** translate the often lofty directions given by vision and mission statements into concrete medium- and long-run "to-dos." Often, *objectives* refers to specific quantitative targets, such as "sustain a 40% debt/equity ratio" or "source 100% of our agricultural raw materials sustainably."[33] *Goals,* on the other hand, refer to qualitative intentions in the same time frame, such as "design products to delight customers while maximizing the conservation of natural resources."[34] In 2010, the British consumer packaged goods corporation Unilever announced its sustainable living plan, a conglomerate of more than fifty social, environmental, and economic targets.[35] Objectives and goals constitute the necessary milestones to achieve vision and mission and the starting point for their achievement. In phase 4 of the strategic management process, strategy implementation, we will get back to the necessary translation of medium- and long-run objectives and goals into short-run tactical indicators, as typically encountered in the balanced scorecard. The next section deals with phase 2, the environmental analysis, which is necessary to setting effective objectives and goals.

It is important to understand that while the direction-setting process constituted by vision, mission, and objectives is typically considered phase 1 of the strategic management process, there has to be a constant readjustment of this starting point based on the work done in the subsequent phases. For instance, it is very difficult to set effective (challenging, but reachable) goals before having conducted phase 3, the strategy definition, and even more difficult without phase 2, the environmental assessment. It is very likely that the objectives, having been drafted based on the vision and mission statements, will have to be adjusted to the status quo as encountered during the environmental analysis.

## 6-4 PHASE 2: ANALYZING THE STRATEGIC ENVIRONMENT

*"The strategic management process does not begin or end with your vision. Strategy is a circular progression in which the starting and finish line should be redrawn continually by a consistent, comprehensive examination of the various environments surrounding the company."*[36]

**Strategic objectives and goals** translate vision and mission statements to medium- and long-run operational goals.

As depicted in Figure 6.2, organizations exist in an external and an internal strategic environment, defining the basic conditions for all strategic decision making. The internal environment can be represented by the company's value chain. The value chain describes all the different functions establishing the internal processes such as

**Figure 6.2 Strategic Organizational Environments**

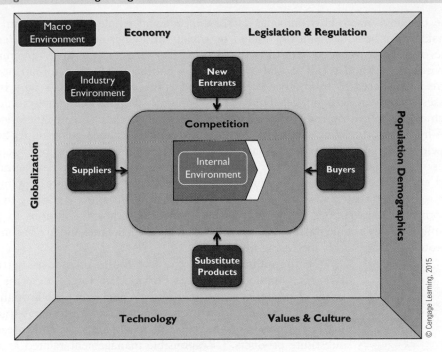

© Cengage Learning, 2015

marketing, human resources management, and accounting and, therefore, provides a complete picture of the company internally.[37] The external environment can be subdivided into two layers. The first layer is the industry environment, also called the meta-environment, including competitors, suppliers, customers, industry entrants, and substitute products.[38] The second layer is the general macro-environment surrounding industries. The macro-environment is characterized by, among other factors, technology and political and cultural influences.[39] At this point, a connection between stakeholders and environments must be made. The internal and external stakeholder environment as described throughout a stakeholder assessment is a crucial part of the analysis.

As illustrated in Figure 6.2, strategic management knows two different views on the origin of competitive advantages. The environmental view focuses on a company's external environment as a source of competitive advantage. In a simplified statement: The company that chooses the right industry and operates in the right macro-environment will be competitive. The resource-based view attributes competitiveness to internal factors, or the internal environment. In practice, both environments and their roles in achieving competitive advantage can hardly be separated.[40] There is a strong mutually influencing relationship between responsible management activity and the company environments. Porter and Kramer[41] specify this mutual strategic relationship. **Inside-out linkages** describe situations in which the company's internal environment positively or negatively influences social, environmental, and economic factors of its external environnment. **Outside-in linkages** describe how the external social and natural-environment-related factors influence the company's ability to compete. The essence of strategic responsible management, according to Porter and Kramer, is to harness those linkages in order to support strategy development and execution and to ultimately achieve strategic competitive advantage.

**Inside-out linkages**
describe how the business's internal environment influences the external environment, while **outside-in linkages** describe the influence of external factors on internal productivity and strategy execution.

### 6-4a External Environment Analysis

The business macro-environment's factors influencing whole industries from the outside have been dramatically altered by society and environment-related trends. The overall economic system of many regions has seen an extensive "greening." Environmental and social legislation as well as national and international norms have been increased in number, coverage, and enforcement, which is why businesses encounter increasing legal and societal pressure. Population demographics—such as the poor or so-called base-of-pyramid customers, the so-called generation Y ("Why"), and the aging society—have fostered industry change adapting to those developments. The contemporary culture in many developed and developing countries increasingly embraces values such as social justice, sustainable development, and ethical decision making. In contrast to former decades, people are very much aware of the threatening social and environmental problems and are starting to feel responsible for solutions. Increasingly, well-engineered technical solutions to predominantly environmental, but also social, problems are available and are becoming adapted at a constantly increasing rate.

On the industry level, the five forces of industry attractiveness, commonly know as Porter's five forces, describe the basic characteristics of an industry environment throughout the categories of competition, supplier and customer bargaining power, threat of new entrants to the industry, and threat of substitute products.[42] Responsible management related factors have considerably shaken up many industries. Customers extensively request more sustainable products and services. Substitute products with improved social or environmental characteristics have become increasingly attractive. The task of reinforcing the upstream value chain's responsible business performance is forcing companies to turn their supplier relations upside down. Old industry incumbents are increasingly competing on the best sustainable business performance. Although those developments constitute challenges, and in some cases even threats, to be taken seriously by businesses of all sizes and shapes, the business opportunities are at least equally significant. Social entrepreneurs and green technology companies have successfully broken down long-established industry entry barriers. An excellent example is Nobel Peace Prize winner Muhammad Yunus, who was able to enter the banking business with his group-lending and microcredit-based Grameen Bank. Figure 6.3 illustrates a wide variety of responsible management related factors changing the basic parameters of industries.

External factors are likely to cause turbulent changes, which require extensive observation in order to be aware of external threats and opportunities. The following three common techniques for an ongoing environmental analysis are presented.[43] *Environment scanning* helps to identify early signals of changes. For instance, automakers might have scanned the first alternative engine technologies in the 1980s. Monitoring provides an ongoing observation of environmental trends. Any company producing end-consumer products is well advised to monitor the constantly increasing LOHAS (lifestyles of health and sustainability) consumer trends in order to identify the moment when a critical mass is reached for attacking this highly attractive new market segment. Effective *forecasting* provides

## In Practice

**Environmental Woes**

Ramin Talaie/Corbis

The Grameen Bank founded by Muhammad Yunus has become an example of how an organization's macro-environment can make or break an organization. The demographic condition of extreme poverty in the bank's home base, Bangladesh, is a necessary environmental condition for the successful microfinance business model. Grameen has a customer base of more than 7 million and employs 25 000 people. In 2011, turbulences in the political environment forced Yunus to step back from the leadership of the bank he had founded.

Source: Grameen Bank. (2007). Key information of Grameen Bank in USD. Retrieved June 12, 2011, from Grameen bank: Bank for the poor: www.grameen.com/index.php?option=com_content&task=view&id=37&Itemid=426; Alam, S. (2011, January 20). Bangladesh's Nobel winner Yunus in trouble at home. Retrieved June 8, 2011, from Yunus Centre: http://www.grameen.com/

**Threat of New Entrants**

- Government incentives lowering entry barriers
- Sustainability-competence-based start-ups
- Social and environmental entrepreneurs

**Suppliers' Bargaining Power**

- Specialized, new suppliers providing hard-to-substitute inputs
- Supply chain cost reduction through ecoefficiency
- Supplier bonding by supply chain sustainability initiatives

**Competitors**

- Competitors' moves toward sustainable business practices and products
- Competition in effecting market shifts toward sustainability

**Buyers' Bargaining Power**

- Higher willingness to pay for sustainable product features
- Lower acceptance of unsustainable products
- Increasing choice among sustainable innovation product alternatives

**Threat of Substitutes**

- Attractiveness and availability of environmentally friendly alternatives
- Servicization as a substitute for consumption
- Product redundancy due to changing consumption patterns

Source: Adapted from from Porter, M. (1980). Competitive strategy: Techniques for analizing industries and competitors. New York: The Free Press.

a future projection of anticipated outcomes as detected throughout the monitoring process. As early as 1993, a forecasting of Toyota's anticipated environmental constraints due to future increased fuel prices and the environmental consequences was the birth point of Toyota's groundbreaking Prius, the first mass-produced and competitively priced alternative to traditional combustion engines.[44] *Assessing* is the final step of external environment analysis that evaluates the environmental observations in terms of their importance and necessary timing of a strategic answer. It seems an increasing number of companies have assessed the importance of the overall sustainability trend as requiring an institutionalized strategically aligned answer. Among many other corporations, for instance, the Coca Cola Company and SAP have recently created the high-level job position of the Chief Sustainability Officer as the strategic answer.[45] Some companies have even created the job position of Sustainable Strategy Director.[46]

## 6-4b Internal Environment Analysis

Typically applied internal environment analysis instruments include the value chain model, reflecting a company's functional areas,[47] and an analysis of the resources with which a company is endowed. Both analyses are profoundly influenced by responsible business factors.

The basic purpose of the **value chain** model is to describe the complete company and all its activities as they are bundled into business functions such as human

The **value chain** is a generic description of a company's activities as they are bundled into functions.

resources, procurement, and marketing. In the original value chain model, the intended outcome was a maximum financial margin resulting from the difference between the cost caused and the nonprice buyer value created by all the business functions as a whole. The purpose of the value chain model is to map every single function's contribution to this financial margin, either by cost reduction or value creation for customers.

For responsible business, we propose a three-dimensional (social, environmental, economic) value chain model, as illustrated in Figure 6.4, that results in a triple bottom line[48] depicted by a social, environmental, and financial economic margin. Every business function not only produces a certain economic cost and value, but it does so in both social and environmental dimensions. A simplified social margin of a tobacco company, for instance, might be the difference between the social cost of health problems caused and the social value created by employing thousands of people. The environmental margin of an ecotourist business might be the difference between the environmental value of the ecosystems protected for tourist activity and the environmental cost of $CO_2$ emissions caused by the tourists while traveling to their destination. Each and every business function and every business exhibits a different social-environmental-economic cost and value structure, contributing to the overall three-dimensional (3D) margin in different ways. After analyzing the actual 3D performance or margin of a single business function, the overarching goal should be not only to reach at least a positive overall 3D margin but, even better, to also deliver positive results throughout all three value dimensions—a positive triple bottom line. A business that achieves such a situation may call itself a regenerative business, one that has reached the highest level of business sustainability. In addition to the traditional management tools, every business function in the value chain can be matched with responsible

## Figure 6.4 The Responsible Management Value Chain

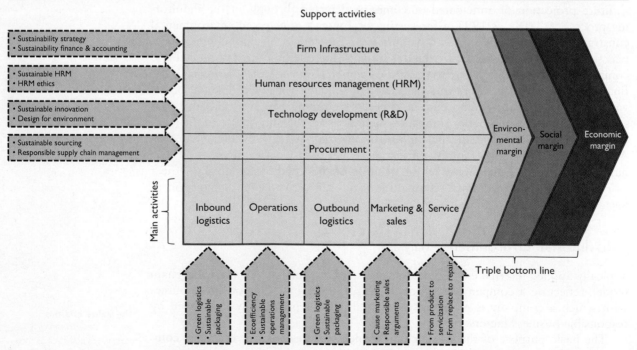

Source: Adapted from Porter, M., & Kramer, M. (2006). Strategy and society: The link between competitive advantage and corporate social responsibility. *Harvard Business Review, 84*(12), 78–92.

management tools tuned in to three-dimensional value creation. Examples include sustainable innovation for the research and development function and sustainable packaging for outbound logistics. The marketing function has the specialized cause-related marketing tool, and socioenvironmental accounting falls into the accounting function.

The **resource-based view** of the business, unlike the value chain model, does not scrutinize single business functions, but a company's resources and how they contribute to the achievement of competitive advantage—in the best case, a sustainable and lasting competitive advantage. A resource can be physical (e.g., buildings, technology), human (e.g., knowledge and skills), or organizational (e.g., organizational rules and controls, management systems).[49] Resources need a management capability to harness them in a way that puts them to best use and unfurls them completely.[50]

Once put to good use, resources can lead to different types of competencies. A **competence** is something a company is good at, while a **core competence** is central to a company's strategy and competitiveness. The most valuable type of competence is a **distinctive competence**, being a competitively valuable activity that a company performs better than competitors and which therefore leads to a competitive advantage.[51] A company's resource portfolio usually offers manifold competencies and might offer one or several core competencies. Distinctive competencies, on the other hand, are rare; not every company has one. Still, that does not mean that resources and the resulting competencies are a given and cannot be created. Companies have the potential to actively foster resources and resulting competencies up to the point where they can even become distinctive competencies.

There is a strong interdependence between companies' resources and the different kinds of competitive positions being created from those resources. As illustrated in Figure 6.5, three questions lead to a classification of four different qualities of competencies and the four different competitive outcomes associated with them.[52] If question 1, "Is the resource valuable?," is answered with no, it leads to a competitive disadvantage. If a resource is not valuable, in most cases it will still create a certain cost and effort to maintain it, which is a disadvantageous situation in comparison with competitors. For instance, an organizational culture resource of regularly conducting anonymous donations without any tax or reputational advantage directly from departments' budgets might be valuable and

The **resource-based view** of the company aims at explaining how company resources and their management contribute to the achievement of competitive advantage.

A **competence** is merely something a company is good at, while a **core competence** is central to a company's strategy and competitiveness. The most valuable type of competence is a **distinctive competence,** being a competitively valuable activity that a company performs better than competitors and which therefore leads to a competitive advantage.

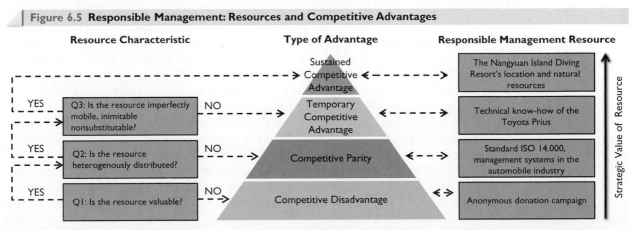

**Figure 6.5 Responsible Management: Resources and Competitive Advantages**

Source: Adapted from Mata, F. J., Fuerst, W. L., & Barney, J. B. (1995). Information technology and sustained competitive advantage: A resource-based perspective. *MIS Quarterly, 19*(4), 494–505.

personally satisfactory for the manager directing those funds to a good social cause, but for certain it is not advantageous to the company as a whole. The costs caused, if reaching a high scope, might lead to a competitive disadvantage in comparison with competitors that do not have this organizational donation culture. If a resource is valuable, but the answer to question 2, "Is the resource heterogenously distributed?," is negative, it will encounter a competitive parity. As competitors have the same valuable resource at their disposal, the company draws even. On the other hand, if the question is answered in the affirmative, the company is able to reach an at least temporary competitive advantage. Toyota's early effort and success in developing the Prius as the first mass-produced hybrid vehicle resulted in a temporary competitive advantage based on technological learning, increased brand image, and free publicity from celebrities' public appeareances with their hybrid Toyotas. Still, if Toyota is not able to protect the resource that has led to this advantage, it will have only a temporary competitive advantage that will soon disappear. If question 3, "Is the resource hard to imitate?," is answered in the affirmative, it leads to a genuine sustainable competitive advantage. For instance, the ecotourism resort on Nangyuan Island in the gulf of Thailand has such a unique and hard-to-copy resource. The island, with its unusual romantic setting and ecosystem, can hardly be copied and is therefore most likely to lead to a truly sustained competitive advantage. In spite of being hard to imitate, the resort has recently encountered a growing threat to its main core competence by increased diving traffic in the surrounding coral reefs, overfishing, and residual waste by its customers and island visitors.[53]

## 6-4c Strengths-Weaknesses-Opportunities-Threats (SWOT) Analysis

The most frequently used and probably easiest-to-understand tool for analyzing an organization's environment is the **SWOT** (**s**trengths-**w**eaknesses-**o**pportunities-**t**hreats) **analysis**, which summarizes the external and internal analysis in the same management tool. The SWOT analysis often is a rather shallow summary of a more detailed and extensive analysis process throughout businesses' external and internal environments. It is also used to achieve a quick first glance at environmental factors. In the context of this chapter, we propose the SWOT analysis as an instrument summarizing the results obtained from a deeper analysis. Strengths and weaknesses are the outcomes of the internal company environment analysis as described before, while threats and opportunities are the outcomes of the external company environment analysis. Figure 6.6 summarizes important factors related to responsible management that may influence the SWOT analysis.

The overarching message for responsible management practice is that the business environment externally and internally is changing significantly and swiftly throughout all its social and environmental factors. Business strategies have to follow! Responsible management is the new business imperative and has to lead to the formulation of new strategies responding to those changes.[54]

The **SWOT analysis** is an environmental assessment tool that sums up helpful and harmful internal factors (**s**trengths and **w**eaknesses) and helpful and harmful external factors (**o**pportunities and **t**hreats).

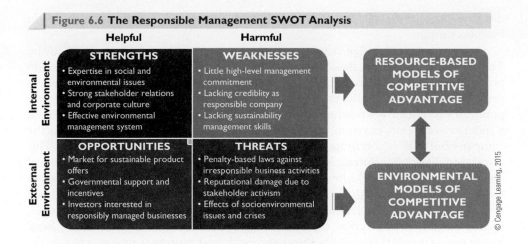

Figure 6.6 The Responsible Management SWOT Analysis

|  | Helpful | Harmful |
|---|---|---|
| **Internal Environment** | **STRENGTHS**<br>• Expertise in social and environmental issues<br>• Strong stakeholder relations and corporate culture<br>• Effective environmental management system | **WEAKNESSES**<br>• Little high-level management commitment<br>• Lacking crediblity as responsible company<br>• Lacking sustainability management skills |
| **External Environment** | **OPPORTUNITIES**<br>• Market for sustainable product offers<br>• Governmental support and incentives<br>• Investors interested in responsibly managed businesses | **THREATS**<br>• Penalty-based laws against irresponsible business activities<br>• Reputational damage due to stakeholder activism<br>• Effects of socioenvironmental issues and crises |

RESOURCE-BASED MODELS OF COMPETITIVE ADVANTAGE

ENVIRONMENTAL MODELS OF COMPETITIVE ADVANTAGE

© Cengage Learning, 2015

# 6-5 PHASE 3: CRAFTING THE STRATEGY

*"Almost every strategic management theory and nearly every corporate planning system is premised on a strategy hierarchy in which corporate goals guide business unit strategies and business unit strategies guide functional tactics."*[55]

On the basis of sound external and internal environment analysis, organizations formulate strategies. The overall strategic structure of an organization is a construct of several strategies for the different situations and environments of strategic decision making. The three main hierarchical types of organizational strategies are also called strategy levels. The *corporate level strategy* answers the question "In how many markets do I want to compete and how many stages of my value chain activities do I perform myself?" The *business level strategy* gives guidance on "How do I manage a strategic business unit competing on a certain product market?" The *functional level strategy* answers the question "How do single business functions support the overarching strategic objectives?" Together those three strategy levels constitute the strategic backbone of a company to which various other strategies covering additional situations can be attached. Those additional strategies might, for instance, be an internationalization strategy for global expansion, a cooperative strategy for alliance arrangements, and a competitive rivalry strategy for the direct confrontation with competitors.

## 6-5a Corporate Level Strategy

The **corporate level strategy** defines how to manage a company that is competing in more than one market, each being covered by another business unit. The process of increasing the number of business units and markets in which the company is competing is called **diversification**, while the process of decreasing the number of business units is called **divestment**. This process of managing the number of parallel businesses competing in unconnected markets is called **horizontal integration**, while the process of managing businesses on a number of different levels of the value chain in the same industry is called **vertical integration**. Vertical integration can be forward, with owning businesses engaged in the main business's

The **corporate level strategy** defines in how many markets a company competes (**horizontal integration**) and to what degree the business performs activities throughout its upstream and downstream supply chain (**vertical integration**).

The process of increasing the number of business units and markets in which a company is competing is called **diversification**, while the process of decreasing the number of business units is called **divestment**.

distribution activities, or backward, with owning businesses producing the main business's input.[56]

An excellent example of corporate level strategy making is the company Clorox. The Oakland, California, based corporation shows highly interesting diversification practices, as illustrated in Figure 6.7. While the flagship product Clorox bleach is perceived as harmful to the environment and potentially to users' health, the corporation's recent diversification activities have focused strongly on businesses with a superior social and environmental impact. In November 2007, Clorox bought the company Burt's Bees, a business that focuses on organic personal care products. This **unrelated diversification** activity is mirrored by a highly **related diversification** of launching the Green Works brand in 2008, which competes in Clorox's main market for cleaning products with a strong design for an environmental approach as Green Works's main distinctive feature. Through those two strategic diversification moves, Clorox has aimed at greening the overall corporation by learning from Burt's Bees' highly environmental friendly business approach and putting it into practice at the Green Works business unit. The motivation of Clorox for the Green Works move may have been manifold. The similar features of Green Works and Clorox products make a strategic cannibalization plan of the low-environmental-performance Clorox products by the Green Works's sustainable innovation products a feasible rationale. Due to customers' increased willingness to pay for Green Works because of its environmental features, this might be not only a clever way of transitioning the Clorox business to a better overall environmental performance, but also an attractive profit margin–increasing tactic.

Such strategic diversification moves involving highly responsible companies are not uncommon. Colgate Palmolive also has tried to hedge the environmentally questionable product structure of its main business by buying the long-hailed role-model environmental entrepreneurship company The Body Shop.[57]

A frequently used tool for analyzing and crafting diversification strategies is the Boston Consulting Groups' matrix. The *BCG matrix,* also called *share/growth matrix,* has served as a starting point for many subsequent instruments aimed at evaluating the portfolio of the diversified business units of a corporation and giving

> A **related diversification** is diversification into a new business activity that has an obvious link to a company's actual business activity, while an **unrelated diversification** misses such a relationship.

---

**Figure 6.7  Corporate Level Strategies at the Clorox Company**

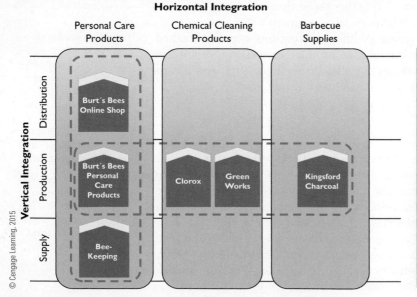

© Cengage Learning, 2015

recommendations for strategic diversification moves. Figure 6.7 Illustrates how the BCG matrix applies to the Clorox case described before. Actual further developments of the matrix include the broadening of the market growth rate (as one consideration for the assessment of market attractiveness) to the category of overall market attractiveness. It must be remarked that the category of relative market share, albeit a significant factor, is just one characteristic for the evaluation of the overall competitive strength of the business unit.[58]

Because of the global sustainable consumption megatrend, many business units focusing on responsible business topics are to be found in the upper half of the BCG matrix, which represents high market growth; sustainability-related industries are often highly attractive industries. As illustrated in Figure 6.7, each quadrant of the BCG matrix reflects another strategic classification of business units. A business unit classified as star not only operates in an attractive market, but also holds an attractive industry position. General Electric's wind energy sector business unit falls into the star category. Its 1.5 MW series has been the most widely deployed wind turbine installed globally and is involved in a neck-to-neck race for market leadership with the Danish company Vestas.[59] This is a highly attractive market position. In terms of market growth, wind power is an attractive market, with the global wind power volume estimated to grow an average 15.5 percent annually from 2011 to 2015.[60] Another example at GE is the Ecoimagination campaign. The growth rate in sales from environmentally friendly consumer products resulting from Ecoimagination are estimated to outrun the company's remaining products' growth rate by 100 percent for at least five years from 2011 to 2015, and therefore the company has a highly attractive growth position inside the market segment for green home appliances.[61] Digging deeper into the attractiveness of this market, using the five forces model presented in the section on external environment analysis helps with the decision of classifying the market for environmentally friendly home appliances. If the market is found to be highly attractive, Ecomagination will be evaluated as a star business unit, while in the opposite case it is a question mark, meaning additional assessment is needed in order to define its strategic value. Cash cows are well-positioned products in markets with a limited growth rate and should be "milked" while showing strong performance. Dogs are business units with a weak market position in an unattractive market. The strategic recommendation for a business unit in this situation is "dogs must be killed." They weaken the overall position of the company.

## 6-5b Business Unit Level Strategy

The **business unit level strategy**, which is "an integrated and coordinated set of commitments and actions the firm uses to gain a competitive advantage by exploiting core competencies in specific product markets,"[62] delivers answers to the question of how to manage a strategy for attacking a specific product market from the perspective of the strategic business unit operating in this market. The central questions to be answered are: Who are my customers? What product do I offer? How do I reach those customers?[63] Michael Porter[64] has done the groundwork to define four generic market strategies in a two-by-two matrix, as illustrated in Figure 6.8. Companies can either compete on a low cost and resulting price or the differentiation of their product. Differentiation here means any product feature (excluding a low price) that makes consumers buy a product, the so-called nonprice buyer's value.[65] Companies can pursue such strategies based on different market scopes. A broad market scope means attacking a significant part of the overall market, while a narrow scope is characterized by attacking a smaller niche market.

The **business unit level strategy** is an integrated and coordinated set of commitments and actions a firm uses to gain a competitive advantage by exploiting core competencies in specific product markets.

## Figure 6.8  Effects of Responsible Management on Strategic Positioning

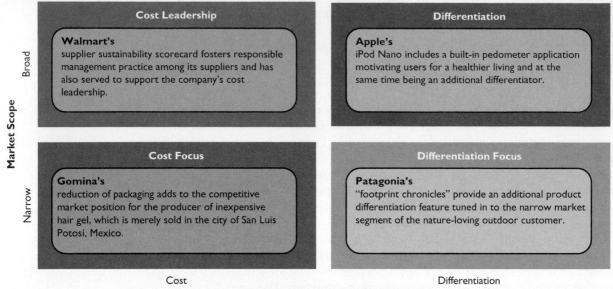

Source: Adapted from Porter, M. (1985). *Competitive advantage: Creating and sustaining superior performance.* New York: Free Press.

Porter[66] warned about being "stuck in the middle," where companies aim at achieving low price while simultaneously pursuing high product differentiation. Porter argued that this strategy cannot lead to competitive advantage. Recent developments toward more effective production methods, highly effective information systems, and flexible manufacturing, though, have given rise to successful integrated cost leadership/differentiation strategies.[67] Also, Kim and Mauborgne[68] have successfully shown the attractiveness of a simultaneous achievement of low price and high differentiation, which even creates new market space. This "blue ocean strategy" has become a world best-seller and has been applied in practice on a worldwide scale.

Responsible management can have a strong influence on the two crucial factors of price and differentiation, leading to or supporting a beneficial strategic market position. It can lead to major cost savings from increased efficiency in natural resource usage[69] and, at the same time, achieve a "sustainability premium" due to customers' higher willingness to pay for products with improved responsible business performance, so-called sustainable innovation products.[70] In the past, such products often were perceived as niche products (narrow scope) for the green idealists. Even for those niches, they were frequently perceived as being overpriced and of low quality and convenience of usage (low differentiation). In short, according to Porter, those products did not display any potential for a beneficial strategic market position. This picture is quickly changing. As can be seen in Figure 6.8, many businesses have achieved clear strategic positioning supported by their responsible management activities.

Often crafting a strategy on the business unit level involves a thorough internal value chain analysis and an analysis of the five forces of industry attractiveness, as described in phase 2.

Based on the internal value chain analysis, companies are able to understand how each and every functional unit contributes to the current strategic positioning, whether cost or differentiation. Walmart, for instance, found out that sustainability in the procurement and inbound logistics function might strongly support its low-price or, using Porter's wording, price-leadership position. The introduction of its sustainable packaging scorecard in 2006 was a logical consequence and brought not only significant reductions in energy usage and packaging waste (improving the environmental margin), but also additional cost reduction in logistics and purchase prices.[71] Walmart's human resources function—which in the past was characterized as extremely low-cost, in this specific case meaning low-wage—was supposed to contribute to its cost-leadership position too. Nevertheless, cheap human resources finally resulted in a rather costly strategy due to the immense reputational damage the company sustained when it caught broad public attention and resistance to its exploitative characteristics.[72] An internal value chain assessment can then be used to craft a change strategy apt to move the company toward the desired strategic positioning. The five forces of industry attractiveness serve to assess the industry environment's conditions for such a strategic shift.

Another tool frequently used to shape business level strategy is Michael Porter's activity map.[73] The *activity map*, also called *synergy map,* serves to analyze how the company's activities interrelate and create synergies, which finally add to the strategic market position pursued by a company. Porter calls those synergies strategic fit help to align the companies' activities with the aspired strategic positioning goal, be it differentiation or price leadership. Figure 6.9 shows how

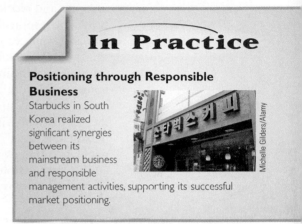

## In Practice

**Positioning through Responsible Business**

Starbucks in South Korea realized significant synergies between its mainstream business and responsible management activities, supporting its successful market positioning.

Michelle Gilders/Alamy

**Figure 6.9  Synergy Map of the Strategic Alignment of Responsible Management Activities at Starbucks Korea**

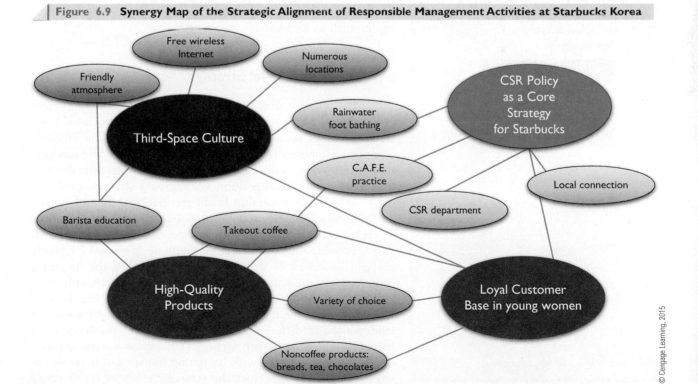

© Cengage Learning, 2015

Starbucks South Korea's differentiation strategy is based on a mutually reinforcing activity network adding to the overall differentiation of Starbuck's value proposition.[74] Starbucks, which ventured into South Korea in the year 2000, quickly experienced aggressive imitation by local competitors. Nevertheless, Starbucks's set of unique buyers' value-creating activities helped the company to transfer the competitive advantage achieved in other countries to this new location. For instance, Starbucks's often-hailed C.A.F.E. (Coffee and Farmer Equity) program is an important factor leading to its high-quality products, which are in turn one of the main reasons why the company can charge a price premium for its products.[75] Another salient point of Starbucks is its "third-place" value proposition to customers. Starbucks's activity systems are aimed at creating a third place, where people will spend their time after the first and second places of home and work. The comfort and acceptance of that third place depends on a subset of responsible management related activities, one of them being the high human resources standards of Starbucks as represented, for instance, in its constantly high ranking as a great place to work. A result is Starbucks's "barista" training, which aims at translating employees' good work experience to an "at home away from home" feeling for customers. The job description reads as follows: "Baristas are the face of Starbucks. They create uplifting experience for the people who visit our stores and make perfect beverages—one drink and one person at a time."[76] As a result of the activity analysis of Starbucks in Korea, one might become aware of a missing link between Starbucks's "third-place" culture and its responsible business policy. A group of researchers from Seoul National University proposed an additional activity to fill this gap: creating synergies and capitalizing on the outstanding CSR activity to strengthen the third-space culture. A rainwater harvesting–based foot bathing shop feature was proposed. The proposal was to at the same time deliver an additional relaxing spa experience and cast light on Starbucks's leadership in responsible business topics such as rainwater harvesting.[77]

The **functional level strategy** aims at the development of strategies of single business functions that support the company's overall strategy.

## 6-5c Functional Level Strategy

While the business unit level strategy aims at the achievement of a strategic position in a specific market, the **functional level strategy** seeks to develop strategies supporting the business unit strategic positioning from the inside of a specific function such as marketing and sales or accounting. As mentioned previously, the basis of competition leading to a strategic positioning is either price leadership or differentiation. Hill and Jones[78] describe how single functions or departments can contribute to create either of the bases of competition. In order to reach cost leadership, functions have to facilitate low costs by highly efficient processes. To reach high differentiation, the functions of innovation capability and quality management are crucial.

For instance, responsible management in the human resources department has immense potential to create both cost leadership and differentiation. The computer producer Dell, for example, aims at supporting Dell's mass customization-differentiation strategy with its strong human resources diversity strategy. Dell describes the strategic effect of its diversity

# In Practice

### Differentiation Strategy in the Toy Business

Richard Levine/Alamy

Wonderworld, a toy manufacturer from Thailand, achieved a 50 percent personnel rotation reduction by a series of responsible management human resources programs for staff. Wonderworld's basis of competition is the product-variety based differentiation of being able to offer a broad spectrum of kids' toys. Each toy is produced in a distinct process that makes time- and cost-intensive personnel training necessary. Thus, a reduction in rotation in the human resources function directly supported Wonderworld's differentiation strategy.

Source: Mavro, A. P. (2010). Thailand. In W. Visser & N. Tolhurst, *The World Guide to CSR: A Country by Country Analysis of Corporate Sustainability and Responsibility* (pp. 404–409). Sheffield: Greenleaf; Porter, M. (1996). What is strategy? *Harvard Business Review*, 74(6), 61–78; Wonderworld. (2011). Wonderworld products. Retrieved May 31, 2011, from Wonderworld: www.wonderworldtoy.com/product.php

activities with the following words: "[W]e are committed to being a place where our team members can combine their varied experiences and creativity to achieve innovative solutions for a diverse customer marketplace."[79] Responsible management, especially ecoefficiency activities in the inbound logistics and procurement functions, often has immense potential to drive down supply chain costs and support a cost-leadership strategy. Sustainable product innovation in the research and development function can facilitate product innovation delivering additional nonprice buyer value and, thereby, diversification by creating new socially and environmentally friendly product features. These are just a few of many mechanisms through which responsible management, as part of a functional strategy, can support a business's strategic positioning activities.

## 6-6 PHASE 4: EXECUTING AND EVALUATING STRATEGY

*"We have learned that a dual approach of hardwiring business processes and softwiring, developing competencies and reaching the hearts and minds of people, is the key combination necessary to create meaning around sustainable development and create lasting change."[80]*

The rather theoretical exercise of strategic planning finds its practical counterpart in *strategy execution,* also called *implementation.* The "on-road" test of a strategy that looked magnificent on the drawing board can reveal significant practical complications. As a matter of fact, when asked about what has kept them from implementing a fully integrated strategic approach to responsible management, 43 percent of CEOs stated that they had competing strategic priorities and 39 percent mentioned the difficulty of implementing strategy throughout the various business functions.[81] This difficulty is even more meaningful when we consider the evidence that the more a responsible management strategy is integrated into core business and mainstream functions, the greater are the returns to be realized.[82] The task of aligning business on all levels and in all spheres with the crafted strategy, to bring the strategy into every instance of the business, is the main task of strategy implementation. After strategy has been implemented, companies should enter into a process of scrutinizing the effects—the success or failure—of the strategy and use this observation to readjust parts of strategy to achieve the ultimate goal of a responsible competitive advantage.

### DIG DEEPER

**Learning from the Sustainable Strategy Specialist**
Listen to InterfaceFLOR's Melissa Vernon, Director of Sustainable Strategy, explaining the company's strategy implementation from the CEO's epiphany to concrete implementation.

Source: Vernon, M. (2011, June 9). From supply chain to business development: Sustainability as business advantage at InterfaceFLOR. Retrieved June 12, 2011, from Net Impact: www.netimpact.org/displaycommon.cfm?an=1&subarticlenbr=3720

### 6-6a Strategy Implementation

Strategy implementation, especially when it is related to responsible management, needs to be based on two fundamental activities. First, **hardwiring** of a responsible management strategy achieves the alignment of business infrastructure, corporate governance, and organizational structure with the chosen strategy. The field of organization studies illustrates how to hardwire responsible business in the organization structure. Second, **softwiring** refers to the social-human and knowledge components of implementation.[83] Softwiring is mostly achieved through the work of the human resources and through internal communication measures. Companies often make the mistake of overemphasizing the hardwiring activities while neglecting softwiring. A five-year survey among more than 1,000 companies

**Hardwiring** of a responsible management strategy refers to its implementation in the organizational infrastructure, while **softwiring** implements responsible management throughout the organization's social fabric.

from fifty countries, completed in 2008, revealed that the drivers of effectively executed strategy are not the structural components. The number-one reason for failure in strategy implementation was missing information (54%), followed by not clearly defining decision rights (50%) and human motivators (26%). Structural considerations were only a reason for failure in strategy execution in 25 percent of the cases.[84]

Strategy implementation always requires a certain change process. The more powerful the strategy, the more drastic is the change. The bigger the change, the higher is usually the social resistance to change. John P. Kotter[85] developed a seven-step recipe describing the human, formerly called softwiring, dimension of change. His publication has given birth to the field of change management. In 2007, Procter & Gamble introduced its $50 billion strategy to achieve a major part of its projected revenues from sustainable innovation products until 2012. In order to implement this market strategy throughout the different business units (P&G has twenty business units worth more than a billion dollars), a major part of the company had to be changed considerably toward an improved responsible business performance.[86] The implementation task was immense and had a striking human implementation component. P&G's strategic innovation program substituted traditional research and development (R&D) with the new C&D (connect and develop) approach. The C&D innovation process is being conducted involving a broad set of external and internal stakeholders. Aligning this stakeholder-based innovation model is a crucial part of the softwiring necessary for implementing the $50 billion strategy.[87] Other softwiring tools are the strategic leadership necessary to provide strategic direction and empower others to act on it, and strategic entrepreneurship (also called intrapreneurship), which involves taking an entrepreneurial approach in order to realize business opportunities from the inside of the company.[88] Corporate culture management provides the tool to deeply root a responsible management strategy into the "character of the company's internal work climate and personality."[89] Once a strategy has reached the cultural implementation level, it is very likely to become a self-fulfilling prophecy that does not need much more external push to succeed.

Hardwiring is commonly achieved by using two main tools. First, organizational governance mechanisms ensure the congruence between the strategic goals and performance and the owners' expectations. Recent definitions increasingly broaden this definition toward congruence with not only owners, but also general stakeholder expectations. The three main corporate governance mechanisms are executive pay, concentration of ownership, and the board of directors.[90] For instance, the South Korean Steel Producer Posco's board of directors consists of fifteen members, nine of whom are outside directors, independent from the company.[91] A board of directors consciously chosen from a broad and balanced set of stakeholders can greatly contribute to a sound stakeholder performance of the overall business. Second, ensuring the alignment of organizational structure ensures that "the firm's formal reporting relationships, procedures, controls, and authority and decision-making processes" are contributing to the successful implementation of the chosen strategy. Thus, "the correct organizational structure is a design that best supports the execution of strategy."[92] The trend toward the introduction of high-level, high-impact executive job positions for responsible management is a salient development toward an organizational structure that is more apt to roll out a responsible business strategy successfully.[93] Also, it is important that the organizational structure include the information management mechanisms necessary for establishing a facts-and-figures-based strategy control system, which will be described with more detail in the following section.

## 6-6b Strategy Control, Review, and Evaluation

It is in strategy control, review, and evaluation where the strategic management process cycle closes. Measuring and evaluating the outcomes of the crafted and executed strategy against the company objectives, the mission statement, and the ultimate vision directly connects to phase 1 of the strategic management process. The chosen strategy's effectiveness has to be checked not only against the company's aspirational goal structure as preset in phase 1, but also against the overarching goal of the achievement of a responsible competitive advantage. A failure to reach responsible competitive advantage can be rooted in any part of the strategic management process. Following the chosen vision and mission statements and strategic objectives just might not lead to competitive advantage. There might be mistakes in the environmental analysis or significant changes in the environment itself. The strategy crafted might not be adequate for competitive advantage or it might have been poorly executed. **Organizational controls** are aimed at tracking the implemented strategy's performance and providing the basis for corrective actions. They "guide the use of strategy, indicate how to compare actual results with expected results, and suggest corrective actions to take when the difference between actual and expected results is unacceptable."[94]

The point of departure for an effective control of strategic outcomes is the definition of quantitative and qualitative goals, metrics, and milestones leading to the achievement of the strategic objectives set. If an adequate strategy has been chosen, the achievement of these goals ultimately will lead to responsible competitiveness. An effective accounting of responsible business performance is the necessary condition to make the evaluation of an implemented strategy work. Management information systems such as enterprise resource planning systems (ERPs) are increasingly being adapted to also deliver information of responsible business performance.

The balanced scorecard, a strategy execution and control tool first developed by Kaplan and Norton,[95] is increasingly being adjusted to explicitly plan and track how a responsible business strategy translates into concise facts and figures. Already the originally developed balanced scorecard has triggered a revolutionary development from a purely financial goal structure to the integration of goals and metrics related to learning and growth, internal business processes, and customers. Now those categories are experiencing a renewed review, integrating responsible management related indicators.[96] A scorecard translates strategic company objectives to business units, departments, single employees, and even suppliers. Prominent examples include Walmart's and Procter & Gamble's sustainability scorecards.[97] As shown in Figure 6.10, Cinépolis, the world's third-largest cinema theater chain, has extensively integrated responsible business performance indicators into their company-wide-applied balanced scorecard.[98] The balanced scorecard is the tool closing the cycle of the strategic management process. It ensures that an organization does the right things to follow its vision and mission statements, based on accurate internal and external environmental analyses. The balanced scorecard supports the chosen strategy and ultimately helps to achieve a responsible competitive advantage, based on a well-balanced triple-bottom-line performance.

**Organizational controls** guide the use of strategy, indicate how to compare actual with expected results, and suggest corrective actions when the difference between actual and expected results is unacceptable.

Figure 6.10 **Responsible Management Balanced Scorecard at Cinépolis**

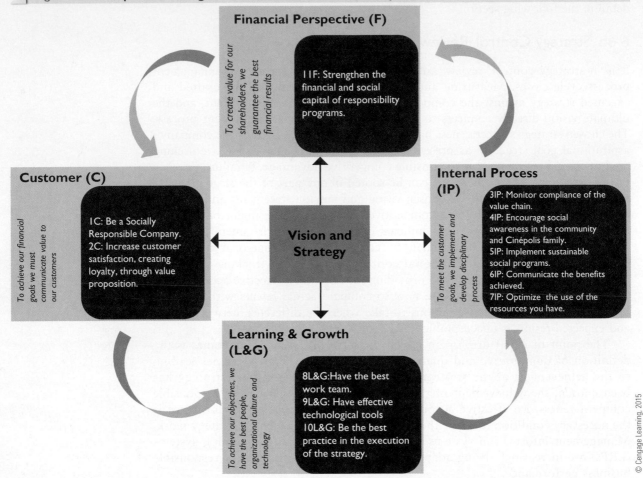

**Financial Perspective (F)**

*To create value for our shareholders, we guarantee the best financial results*

11F: Strengthen the financial and social capital of responsibility programs.

**Customer (C)**

*To achieve our financial goals we must communicate value to our customers*

1C: Be a Socially Responsible Company.
2C: Increase customer satisfaction, creating loyalty, through value proposition.

**Vision and Strategy**

**Internal Process (IP)**

*To meet the customer goals, we implement and develop disciplinary process*

3IP: Monitor compliance of the value chain.
4IP: Encourage social awareness in the community and Cinépolis family.
5IP: Implement sustainable social programs.
6IP: Communicate the benefits achieved.
7IP: Optimize the use of the resources you have.

**Learning & Growth (L&G)**

*To achieve our objectives, we have the best people, organizational culture and technology*

8L&G: Have the best work team.
9L&G: Have effective technological tools
10L&G: Be the best practice in the execution of the strategy.

© Cengage Learning, 2015

## PRINCIPLES OF STRATEGY: RESPONSIBLE COMPETITIVENESS

I. The goal of strategic responsible management is the achievement of level-two *responsible competitiveness,* a situation in which the organization's economic competitiveness is based on and enhanced by responsible business competitiveness.

II. The *strategic management process* consists of four phases: (1) shaping vision and mission, (2) analyzing the internal and external strategic environments, (3) shaping strategies, and (4) implementing and evaluating strategies.

III. *Mission and vision statements* are a "lighthouse" for any subsequent organizational activity and therefore should integrate responsible business considerations in addition to economic aspirations.

IV. The three *strategic environments* are the company's internal environment, the industry, and the macro-environment. In each environment, responsible management factors play a crucial role.

V. The *strategy hierarchy* consists of corporate strategies for a company with several strategic business units, the business unit strategy, and the functional strategy.

VI. Responsible management can create valuable diversification advantages on the corporate level, support strategic positioning for business units, and support functions' contributions to the *overall organizational strategy*.

VII. The *implementation* of responsible management strategies is based on "hardwiring" them into organizational structure, and "softwiring" them throughout the human factors.

VIII. The *balanced scorecard* is an excellent tool for controlling the social, environmental, and economic indicators leading to responsible competitiveness.

| Process Phase | | Sustainability | Responsibility | Ethics |
|---|---|---|---|---|
| **Phase 1: Vision, mission, objectives (normative strategy)** | Does our normative strategy ... | ... centrally refer to the triple bottom line and aim at ultimately becoming a sustainable business with zero or positive impact? | ... aim at the long-run maximization of stakeholder value? | ... build on the ethical principles for the achievement of moral excellence? |
| **Phase 2: Environmental analysis** | Have we ... | ... assessed the social, environmental, and ethical impacts of the whole life cycle of all our products? | ... assessed and prioritized all stakeholders influencing or influenced by our business conduct along the whole life cycle of all our products? | ... mapped and understood all ethical dilemmas along the whole life cycle of all our products? |
| **Phase 3: Strategy formulation** | Will the strategy formulated ... | ... lead to a neutral to positive triple bottom line for our organization and products? | ... maximize long-run stakeholder value generated by our organization and products? | ... minimize the ethical dilemmas caused by the business and create moral excellence? |
| **Phase 4: Implementation and control** | Will our implementation practices and control mechanisms ... | ... ensure that we become a sustainable business? | ... enable stakeholders to monitor and influence? | ... ensure moral excellence in the process? |

## KEY TERMS

broad perspective 157
business unit level strategy 171
competence 167
core competence 167
corporate level strategy 169
distinctive competence 167
diversification 169
divestment 169
functional level strategy 174
hardwiring 175

horizontal integration 169
inside-out linkages 163
mission statement 161
narrow perspective 157
organizational controls 177
outside-in linkages 163
related diversification 170
resource-based view 167
responsible competitiveness 159
softwiring 175

strategic competitive advantage 159
strategic management 157
strategic management process 158
strategic objectives and goals 162
strategy 159
SWOT analysis 168
unrelated diversification 170
value chain 165
vertical integration 169
vision statement 161

## EXERCISES

### A. Remember and Understand

A.1. Mention the three levels of responsible competitiveness and describe the main differences and commonalities.

A.2. Describe the four phases of the strategic management process and give an example of a typical management task for each phase.

A.3. Mention the three levels of the strategy hierarchy and describe one strategic choice to be made for each level.

A.4. Describe the difference between the following:
- Broad versus narrow perspectives
- Inside-out versus outside-in linkages
- Hardwiring versus softwiring

### B. Apply and Experience

B.5. Look up the mission statement of a company of your choice and rewrite it by integrating responsible business considerations. Then rewrite the strategic objectives based on the new statement.

B.6. Design a balanced scorecard for a company of your choice, integrating at least two responsible business indicators per scorecard category (financial, customer, process, learning, and growth).

## C. Analyze and Evaluate

C.7. Look up information on the strategic move of L'Oreal buying up The Body Shop. Use the BCG matrix to categorize both brands and evaluate the strategic value of the move for both brands.

C.8. Look up the most recent sustainability report of the United Parcel Services (UPS) and analyze if the company's responsible business activities support the strategic market position chosen.

## D. Change and Create

D.9. Design the strategic management approach of the future. What should strategic management be in fifteen years to make a maximum contribution to sustainable development?

---

## PIONEER INTERVIEW WITH MARK KRAMER

Courtesy of Mark Kramer

Mark Kramer has pioneered the topic of strategy and society together with the strategic management guru Michael Porter. They developed concepts such as strategic corporate social responsibility (CSR) and shared value.

**Do you think "strategic CSR" as you defined it is a thing of the past, now that responsibility, sustainability, and ethics are moving increasingly into the mainstream? Are strategy and society again "just strategy," as the societal dimension has become a natural component of strategic management? Are we there yet?**

Well, I certainly do not think we are there yet. I would say that Michael and I have both been pleased and surprised by the resonance that the shared value idea has had all over the world, and by the number of companies that have managed to make this thinking part of their strategies. So there is certainly a movement.

Shared value becomes the strategy, but as we talked about before, it is not just strategy. We also need new tools around measurement and decision making. Because of the social dimension that we are adding, the strategy is not well measured or evaluated by the existing corporate strategy tools.

I certainly think that shared value does not replace sustainability or corporate responsibility. There are things that companies should and must do to be responsible citizens of the world. Those things are not necessarily going to contribute to their profit or to their competitive advantage. Those are the true areas of corporate responsibility. And

they remain even if they do not create shared value. There is also a much broader sustainability agenda that top leaders like John Elkington have proposed that really looks at the global system and the sustainability of that system in all of its dimensions—in terms of the welfare of people, in terms of the impact on the planet, in terms of the pricing of resources, and so on. And there are certainly dimensions to that larger vision that go beyond just shared value activities by corporations. They have implications for governments, and they have implications for nonprofit organizations and citizens; again, it goes beyond shared value.

So we think shared value represents a new and important opportunity for business and a new and tremendously important opportunity for society by bringing global corporations to the table to help address social problems, not just by writing checks to nonprofits or NGOs, but by actually using their capabilities in a profit-seeking way to solve social issues. We're able to generate a level of scale and impact that very, very few NGOs are able to generate.

One quick example: We cited GE a number of times as an example of shared value through their "Ecomagination" and "healthy imagination" initiatives. Well, GE has committed $10 billion to research and development of new, more energy-efficient devices and new health care devices, medical devices that can be used by lower-income populations around the world. I cannot think of any NGO that is in a position to commit $10 billion to this kind of resources. And the examples go on and on. Dow Chemical has developed this new heart-healthy cooking oil for fast food and commercial restaurants that has taken literally billions of pounds of trans fats out of the diet in America. The scale of impact the companies can have when

180

Part C  Planning

they decide that they want to solve a social issue, not just to be nice or to look good but because it is in the company's economic interest to do so, is tremendously powerful, and this is why Michael and I are so hopeful about the positive impact that shared value can have in the world.

## What else would you like to communicate?

One quick thought, as we have worked with companies, we have seen that moving toward a shared value strategy is a journey that takes quite a few years. It is really a different way of thinking at every level. It is not just the CEO thinking differently about strategy. It has to influence the behavior of people in the operating level and people within the operations of each division.

And so what we have seen is that for this really to influence the thinking and really become embedded in the company takes not just one project or two projects or a shared value department that is off to the side like CSR often is. It is rather an executive education process that goes throughout the company—a lot of internal communication. We have to begin to look at the social dimension of people's performance and how we compensate and reward and promote them if we are serious about this. It really requires every operation within the company from procurement to HR, from marketing to research and development, to be undertaken with a different lens, and it takes years however. Maybe it takes years for a company really to embed this approach in all aspects of its operations.

## PRACTITIONER PROFILE: CANSU GEDIK

Courtesy of Cansu Gedik

**Employing organization:** Mikado Consulting is a social enterprise based in Turkey that crafts innovative solutions for sustainable development. Mikado's raison d'etre is to serve sustainable development through establishment of a responsible private sector, a sustainable and transparent civil society, and social innovation.

**Job title:** Project Coordinator

**Education:** Steinbeis University, Germany, MA Responsible Management (2012–2013); Blekinge Institute of Technology, Sweden, Introduction to Strategic Sustainable Development (2010); Boğaziçi University, Turkey, BA Translation and Interpreting Studies (2004–2008).

### In Practice

**What are your responsibilities?** My responsibilities include building and executing the corporate responsibility and sustainability strategy, planning and preparing the sustainability reports, development and coordination of community investment projects of the companies we work with.

I have been coordinating the "Business and Human Rights Capacity Development Program," a one-year project consisting of trainings and mentoring for participant companies funded by the Consulate General of the Netherlands in Turkey.

My colleagues and I are also responsible for the management of our blog and social media accounts.

### What are typical activities you carry out during a day at work?

As a sustainable development consulting company, we are engaged in a wide range of tasks and the activities we carry out during a day vary considerably according to the projects we work on. I feel lucky that my job does not have a lot of repetitive work and that it allows me to be creative.

Strategic planning for sustainability takes a significant amount of my time, especially when we have new clients, when we revise our yearly plans with our existing clients, and when we embark on new projects. I assist and coordinate the processes and activities that serve the corporate responsibility strategies of the companies we work with. Planning and content management for sustainability reports of our clients take a considerable amount of time and effort, especially in the first six months of the year.

I prepare training content for our corporate trainings. I carry out research on various subjects related to responsible management and sustainability. I follow the global corporate responsibility and sustainability agenda and share relevant information with our stakeholders on our blog and social media accounts.

### How do sustainability, responsibility, and ethics topics play a role in your job?

Sustainability, responsibility, and ethics are at the core of my job. Mikado assists private sector companies in developing and implementing their corporate responsibility and sustainability strategies in order for them to meet their responsibilities toward their internal and external stakeholders in an ethical, transparent, and accountable manner. We help companies to have ethically driven and responsible corporate governance and a well-balanced triple bottom line.

Mikado, well aware of NGOs' crucial role in fostering democratization and active citizenship, assists them to strengthen their organizational capacities and expand their social impact.

We embed stakeholder engagement processes into the governance of every organization we work with. We also guide them in developing monitoring and evaluation mechanisms and encourage them to report their performance and impact so that they can be more transparent toward their stakeholders.

As a social enterprise, Mikado itself is an ethically driven company. We are proud to be a Certified B Corporation™.

**Out of the topics covered in the chapter into which your interview will be included, which concepts, tools, or topics are most relevant to your work?**

While consulting with companies in responsible management, we carry out a very similar process to the "strategic responsible management process" introduced in the chapter. With the Sustainability Committees of our clients, we revise the vision and mission statements and prepare a sustainability policy statement. We realize SWOT analysis, taking both internal and external environments into account, and decide on the strategy and a set of actions. We guide them in implementing the strategy. This involves both "hardwiring" and "softwiring." Softwiring is especially important,

since it enables a change in corporate culture. In order to achieve this transformation, we provide trainings, introduce sustainability approach to leadership mechanisms, encourage employee volunteering, etc. We constantly review, evaluate, and improve the strategy.

### Insights and Challenges

### What recommendation can you give to practitioners in your field?

I would recommend that they be inquisitive and never lose their enthusiasm for research on responsible management and sustainability, since new approaches and tools emerge each day. I would also suggest that they track best practices in the field; it is both informative and motivating to learn what has been achieved.

Top management's support is crucial for corporate responsibility. Hence, they have to make sure that top management understands and communicates (both verbally and nonverbally) the value of being a responsible company.

Finally, I would recommend consultants in the field to make sure that they establish lasting and self-sustaining structures and processes that will continue to exist even after they cease assisting the company.

### Which are the main challenges of your job?

Since responsible management and sustainability are highly dynamic fields, one has to spend a significant amount of time and effort in order to keep track of the progress.

In addition, although there may be some low-hanging fruits, many of the sustainability initiatives have long-term and intangible returns. Moreover, in many cases, it is rather difficult to measure the impact those initiatives create.

## SOURCES

1. Lacey, P., et al. (2010). *A new era of sustainability: UN Global Compact-Accenture CEO study 2010.* New York: Accenture Institute for High Performance.

2. Pohle, G., & Hittner, J. (2008). *Attaining sustainable growth through corporate social responsibility.* Somers: IBM Institute for Business Value.

3. Economist. (2008). *Doing good: Business and the sustainability challenge.* London: Economist Intelligence Unit.

4. McDermott, B., & Hagemann, J. (2010). Letter from our CEOs. Retrieved May 28, 2011, from *SAP*: www .sapsustainabilityreport.com/co-ceo-letter

5. Oppenheim, J., et al. (2007). *Shaping the new rules of competition: UN global compact participant mirror.* Chicago: McKinsey & Company.

6. Lacey, P., et al. (2010). *A new era of sustainability: UN Global Compact-Accenture CEO study 2010.* New York: Accenture Institute for High Performance.

7. Porter, M., & Kramer, M. (1999). Philanthropy's new agenda: Creating value. *Harvard Business Review, 77*(6), 121–130; Porter, M., & Kramer, M. (2006). Strategy and society: The link between competitive advantage and corporate social responsibility. *Harvard Business*

*Review, 84*(12), 78–92; Porter, M., & Kramer, M. (2002). The competitive advantage of corporate philanthropy. *Harvard Business Review, 80*(12), 56–68.

8. Ansoff, I. H. (1980). Strategic issue management. *Strategic Management Journal, 1*(2), 131–148.

9. Porter, M., & Kramer, M. (2002). The competitive advantage of corporate philanthropy. *Harvard Business Review, 80*(12), 56–68.

10. Grayson, D., & Hodges, A. (2004). *Corporate social opportunity!: Seven steps to make corporate social responsibility work for your business.* Sheffield: Greenleaf.

11. Laasch, O. (2010). Strategic CSR. In W. Visser, et al., *The A–Z of Corporate Social Responsibility* (pp. 378–380). Chichester: Wiley, 2010.

12. Fussler, C. (2004). Responsible excellence pays! *Journal of Corporate Citizenship, 16,* 33–44, p. 41.

13. Hitt, M. A., Ireland, R. D., & Hoskisson, R. E. (2007). *Strategic management: Competitiveness and globalization* (pp. 4–5). Mason, OH: Thomson South-Western.

14. Porter, M., & Kramer, M. (1999). Philanthropy's new agenda: Creating value. *Harvard Business Review, 77*(6), 121–130.

15. Zadeck, S. (2006). Responsible competitiveness: Reshaping global markets through responsible business practices. *Corporate Governance, 6*(4), 334–348.

16. Pohle, G., & Hittner, J. (2008). *Attaining sustainable growth through corporate social responsibility.* Somers: IBM Institute for Business Value.

17. PriceWaterhouseCoopers. (2002). *2002 Sustainability survey report.* London: PriceWaterhouseCoopers.

18. Collins, J. C., & Porras, J. I. (1996). Building your company's vision. *Harvard Business Review, 74*(5), 65–77, p. 75.

19. King Jr., M. L. (1963, August 18). I have a dream. Retrieved June 8, 2011, from American Rhetoric: www.americanrhetoric.com/speeches/mlkihaveadream.htm

20. Elkington, J. (1998). *Cannibals with forks: The triple bottom line of 21st century business.* Gabriola Island: New Society Publishers.

21. Freeman, R. E. (2010). *Strategic management: A stakeholder approach.* Cambridge: Cambridge University Press. First published in 1984; Freeman, R. E. (2009, September 15). Stakeholder theory [interview]. Darden Business School. Business Roundtable: Institute for Corporate Ethics.

22. Hill, C. W. L., & Jones, G. R. (2001). *Strategic management: An integrated approach.* Boston: Houghton Mifflin.

23. David, F. R. (2007). *Strategic management: Concepts* (p. 64). Upper Saddle River, NJ: Pearson.

24. Hitt, M. A., Ireland, R. D., & Hoskisson, R. E. (2007). *Strategic management: Competitiveness and globalization.* Mason, OH: Thomson South-Western.

25. Werther, W. B., & Chandler, D. (2010). *Strategic corporate social responsibility: Stakeholders in a global environment* (p. 86). Thousand Oaks, CA: Sage.

26. Hamel, G., & Prahalad, C. K. (1989). Strategic intent. *Harvard Business Review, 67*(3), 63–76.

27. Hill, C. W. L., & Jones, G. R. (2001). *Strategic management: An integrated approach.* Boston: Houghton Mifflin.

28. The Guardian. (2010, November 5). The guardian sustainable business. Retrieved May 18, 2011, from *Signed, sealed and to be delivered: Procter & Gamble's new sustainability vision:*www.guardian.co.uk/sustainable-business/procter-gamble-sustainability-vision; Procter & Gamble. (2010). *Sustainability overview.* Retrieved May 18, 2011, from Procter & Gamble: www.pg.com/en_US/sustainability/environmental_sustainability/index.shtml

29. David, F. R. (2007). *Strategic management: Concepts.* Upper Saddle River, NJ: Pearson.

30. David, F. R. (2007). *Strategic management: Concepts* (p. 60). Upper Saddle River, NJ: Pearson.

31. Hill, C. W. L., & Jones, G. R. (2001). *Strategic management: An integrated approach.* Boston: Houghton Mifflin.

32. David, F. R. (2007). *Strategic management: Concepts* (p. 21). Upper Saddle River, NJ: Pearson.

33. Unilever. (2010, November). The plan: Small actions, big differences. Retrieved June 6, 2011, from *Unilever sustainable living plan:*www.sustainable-living.unilever.com/the-plan/

34. Collis, D. J., & Montgomery, C. A. (1997). *Corporate strategy: Resources and the scope of the firm* (p. 8). New York: Irwin/McGraw-Hill.

35. Unilever. (2010, November). The plan: Small actions, big differences. Retrieved June 6, 2011, from *Unilever sustainable living plan:* http://www.unilever.co.uk/sustainable-living/

36. Humphreys, J. (2004). The vision thing. *Sloan Management Review, 45*(4), 96.

37. Porter, M. (1980). *Competitive strategy: Techniques for analyzing industries and competitors.* New York: Free Press. Available at: http://books.google.com/books?id=QN0kyeHXtJMC&pg=PR10&dq=porter+1980+competitive+strategy&hl=es&ei=OD_iTdW0IOXq0gHh4aCjBw&sa=X&oi=book_result&ct=result&resnum=1&ved=0CCkQ6AEwAA#v=onepage&q=porter%201980%20competitive%20strategy&f=false

38. Porter, M. (1980). *Competitive strategy: Techniques for analyzing industries and competitors.* New York: Free Press. Available at: http://books.google.com/books?id=QN0kyeHXtJMC&pg=PR10&dq=porter+1980+competitive+strategy&hl=es&ei=OD_iTdW0IOXq0gHh4aCjBw&sa=X&oi=book_result&ct=result&resnum=1&ved=0CCkQ6AEwAA#v=onepage&q=porter%201980%20competitive%20strategy&f=false

39. Lenssen, G., et al. (2006). Corporate responsibility and competitiveness. *Corporate Governance, 6*(4), 323–333.

40. Barney, J. (1991). Firm resources and sustained competitive advantage. *Journal of Management, 17*(1), 99–120.

41. Porter, M., & Kramer, M. (2006). Strategy and society: The link between competitive advantage and corporate social responsibility. *Harvard Business Review, 84*(12), 78–92.

42. Porter, M. (1980). *Competitive strategy: Techniques for analyzing industries and competitors.* New York: Free Press. Available at: http://books.google.com/books?id=QN0kyeHXtJMC&pg=PR10&dq=porter+1980+competitive+strategy&hl=es&ei=OD_iTdW0IOXq0gHh4aCjBw&sa=X&oi=book_result&ct=result&resnum=1&ved=0CCkQ6AEwAA#v=onepage&q=porter%201980%20competitive%20strategy&f=false

43. Hitt, M. A., Ireland, R. D., & Hoskisson, R. E. (2007). *Strategic management: Competitiveness and globalization.* Mason, OH: Thomson South-Western.

44. Taylor, A. (2006). Toyota: The birth of the Prius. Retrieved June 12, 2011, from *CNN Money:*http://money.cnn.com/2006/02/17/news/companies/mostadmired_fortune_toyota/index.htm

45. Galbraith, K. (2009, March 2). Companies add chief sustainability officers. Retrieved June 8, 2011, from *The New York Times:*http://green.blogs.nytimes.com/2009/03/02/companies-add-chief-sustainability-officers/

46. Vernon, M. (2011, June 9). From supply chain to business development: Sustainability as business advantage at InterfaceFLOR. Retrieved June 12, 2011, from Net Impact: www.netimpact.org/displaycommon.cfm?an=1&subarticlenbr=3720

47. Porter, M. (1980). *Competitive strategy: Techniques for analyzing industries and competitors.* New York: Free Press. Available at: http://books.google.com/books?id=QN0kyeHXtJMC&pg=PR10&dq=porter+

1980+competitive+strategy&hl=es&
ei=OD_iTdW0IOXq0gHh4aCjBw&
sa=X&oi=book_result&ct=result&
resnum=1&ved=0CCkQ6AEwAA#
v=onepage&q=porter%201980%20
competitive%20strategy&f=false

48. Elkington, J. (1998). *Cannibals with forks: The triple bottom line of 21st century business*. Gabriola Island: New Society Publishers.

49. Barney, J. (1991). Firm resources and sustained competitive advantage. *Journal of Management, 17*(1), 99–120; Wernerfelt, B. (1995). A resource-based view of the firm: Ten years after. *Strategic Management Journal, 16*, 171–174; Wernerfelt, B. (1984). A resource based view of the firm. *Strategic Management Review, 5*, 171–180.

50. Hill, C. W. L., & Jones, G. R. (2001). *Strategic management: An integrated approach*. Boston: Houghton Mifflin.

51. Thompson, A. A., Strickland, A. J., & Gamble, J. E. (2005). *Crafting and executing strategy: The quest for competitive advantage*. New York: McGraw-Hill.

52. Barney, J. (1991). Firm resources and sustained competitive advantage. *Journal of Management, 17*(1), 99–120; Mata, F. J., Fuerst, W. L., & Barney, J. B. (1995). Information technology and sustained competitive advantage: A resource-based perspective. *MIS Quarterly, 19*(4), 494–505.

53. Nangyuan Island Dive Resort. (2010). Nangyuan Island. Retrieved June 6, 2011, from Nangyuan Island Dive Resort: www.nangyuan.com /en/nangyuan.html

54. Lubin, D. A., & Esty, D. C. (2010, May). The sustainability imperative. *Harvard Business Review*, 1–9; Waddock, S. A., Bodwell, C., & Graves, S. B. (2002). Responsibility: The new business imperative. *Academy of Management Executive, 47*(1), 132–147.

55. Hamel, G., & Prahalad, C. K. (1989). Strategic intent. *Harvard Business Review, 67*(3), 63–76, p. 75.

56. Hitt, M. A., Ireland, R. D., & Hoskisson, R. E. (2007). *Strategic management: Competitiveness and globalization* (p. 179). Mason, OH: Thomson South-Western.

57. Story, L. (2008, January 6). Can Burt's Bees turn Clorox green? Retrieved May 28, 2011, from *The New York Times*: www.nytimes.com/2008/01/06 /business/06bees.html?pagewanted=1; Green Works. (2011). Home.

Retrieved May 28, 2011, from Green Works: www.greenworkscleaners .com/; Burt's Bees. (2011). The environmental friendly natural personal care for the greater good. Retrieved May 28, 2011, from Burt's Bees: www.burtsbees.com/; Cate, S. N., et al. (2009). The story of Clorox Green Works™—In designing a winning green product experience Clorox cracks the code. Retrieved May 28, 2011, from Product Development Consulting, Inc.: www.pdcinc.com /files/Visions_March09.pdf

58. Thompson, A. A., Strickland, A. J., & Gamble, J. E. (2005). *Crafting and executing strategy: The quest for competitive advantage* (pp. 258–262). New York: McGraw-Hill; Morrison, A., & Wensley, R. (1991). Boxing up or boxed in?: A short history of the Boston consulting group share/ growth matrix. *Journal of Marketing Management, 7*(2), 105–129.

59. The Wall Street Journal. (2008). Wind shear: GE wins, Vestas loses in wind-power market race. Retrieved May 29, 2011, from *Environmental capital*: http://blogs.wsj.com /environmentalcapital/2009/03/25 /wind-shear-ge-wins-vestas-loses -in-wind-power-market-race/; GE. (2011). Wind turbines. Retrieved May 29, 2011, from GE Energy: www .ge-energy.com/products_and_services /products/wind_turbines/index.jsp

60. BTM Consult. (2010). International wind power market update 2010. Retrieved May 29, 2011, from BTM Consult: www.btm.dk/public /Selected_PPT-WMU2010.pdf

61. Ricketts, C. (2010, June 24). GE pumps $10B more into green technology R&D. Retrieved May 29, 2011, from *Green Beat*: http://venturebeat .com/2010/06/24/ge-pumps-10b-more -into-green-technology-rd/

62. Hitt, M. A., Ireland, R. D., & Hoskisson, R. E. (2007). *Strategic management: Competitiveness and globalization* (p. 134). Mason, OH: Thomson South-Western.

63. Hill, C. W. L., & Jones, G. R. (2001). *Strategic management: An integrated approach* (p. 203). Boston: Houghton Mifflin; Hitt, M. A., Ireland, R. D., & Hoskisson, R. E. (2007). *Strategic management: Competitiveness and globalization* (p. 104). Mason, OH: Thomson South-Western.

64. Porter, M. (1980). *Competitive strategy: Techniques for analyzing*

*industries and competitors*. New York: Free Press. Available at: http:// books.google.com/books?id=QN0ky eHXtJMC&pg=PR10&dq=porter+1 980+competitive+strategy&hl=es&ei =OD_iTdW0IOXq0gHh4aCjBw&sa= X&oi=book_result&ct=result& resnum=1&ved=0CCkQ6AEwAA# v=onepage&q=porter%201980%20 competitive%20strategy&f=false

65. Porter, M. (1985). *Competitive advantage: Creating and sustaining superior performance*. New York: Free Press.

66. Porter, M. (1980). *Competitive strategy: Techniques for analyzing industries and competitors*. New York: Free Press. Available at: http://books. google.com/books?id=QN0kyeHXtJM C&pg=PR10&dq=porter+1980+com petitive+strategy&hl=es&ei=OD_iTd W0IOXq0gHh4aCjBw&sa=X&oi=b ook_result&ct=result&resnum=1&v ed=0CCkQ6AEwAA#v=onepage&q= porter%201980%20competitive%20 strategy&f=false; Porter, M. (1996). What is strategy? *Harvard Business Review, 74*(6), 61–78.

67. Hitt, M. A., Ireland, R. D., & Hoskisson, R. E. (2007). *Strategic management: Competitiveness and globalization* (pp. 127–130). Mason, OH: Thomson South-Western; Hill, C. W. L., & Jones, G. R. (2001). *Strategic management: An integrated approach* (pp. 210–213). Boston: Houghton Mifflin.

68. Kim, W. C., & Mauborgne, R. (1999). Creating new market space. *Harvard Business Review, 77*(1), 83–93; Kim, W. C., & Mauborgne, R. (2004). Blue ocean strategy. *Harvard Business Review, 82*(10), 76–84.

69. WBCSD. (2000). *Eco-efficiency: Creating more value with less impact*. Geneva: World Business Council for Sustainable Development.

70. Barbier, E. B., Markandya, A., & Pearce, D. W. (1990). Environmental sustainability and cost-benefit analysis. *Environment and Planning, 22*(9), 1259–1266. http://scholar.google.com /scholar?q=%22sustainability+premium %22&hl=es&btnG=Buscar&lr=

71. Walmart. (2006, November 1). Wal-Mart unveils "packaging scorecard" to suppliers. Retrieved May 31, 2011, from Walmart corporate: http:// walmartstores.com/pressroom /news/6039.aspx; Walmart. (2010). Packaging progress. Retrieved May 31, 2011, from Walmart corporate: http://walmartstores.com

/Sustainability/10601.aspx?p=9125; Arzoumanian, M. (2008, November 15). Walmart updates scorecard status. Retrieved May 31, 2011, from Packaging-online.com: www.packaging-online.com /paperboard-packaging-content /walmart-updates-scorecard-status

72. Maclay, K. (2004, August 2). UC berkeley study estimates Wal-Mart employment policies cost California taxpayers $86 million a year. Retrieved May 31, 2011, from *UC Berkeley News:*http://berkeley.edu /news/media/releases/2004/08/02 _walmart.shtml; Dube, A., & Jacobs, K. (2004). *The hidden cost of Wal-Mart jobs.* Berkeley: UK Berkeley Labor Center.

73. Porter, M. (1996). What is strategy? *Harvard Business Review, 74*(6), 61–78.

74. Cha, S., et al. (2008). *Proposal: Rainwater harvesting at Starbucks.* Seoul: Seoul National University, Graduate School of Civil and Environmental Engineering.

75. Starbucks. (1997). C.A.F.E. practices generic evaluation guidelines 2.0. Retrieved May 31, 2011, from Starbucks corporate: www.scscertified .com/retail/docs/CAFE_GUI_Evaluation Guidelines_V2.0_093009.pdf

76. Starbucks. (2011). Retail careers. Retrieved May 31, 2011, from Starbucks corporate: www.starbucks .com/career-center/retail-positions

77. Cha, S., et al. (2008). *Proposal: Rainwater harvesting at Starbucks.* Seoul: Seoul National University, Graduate School of Civil and Environmental Engineering.

78. Hill, C. W. L., & Jones, G. R. (2001). *Strategic management: An integrated approach* (p. 160). Boston: Houghton Mifflin.

79. Dell. (2011). Diversity and inclusion. Retrieved May 31, 2011, from Dell: About us: http://content.dell.com/us/en /corp/diversity.aspx; Forsythe, J. (2004). Leading with diversity. Retrieved May 31, 2011, from *The New York Times:*www.nytimes.com/marketing /jobmarket/diversity/dell.html

80. Wit, M., Wade, M., & Schouten, E. (2006). Hardwiring and softwiring corporte responsibility: A vital combination. *Corporate Governance, 5*(4), 491–505, p. 503.

81. Oppenheim, J., et al. (2007). *Shaping the new rules of competition: UN global compact participant mirror.* Chicago: McKinsey & Company.

82. Pohle, G., & Hittner, J. (2008). *Attaining sustainable growth through corporate social responsibility.* Somers: IBM Institute for Business Value.

83. Wit, M., Wade, M., & Schouten, E. (2006). Hardwiring and softwiring corporte responsibility: A vital combination. *Corporate Governance, 5*(4), 491–505.

84. Neilson, G. L., Martin, K. L., & Powers, E. (2008). The secrets to successfull strategy execution. *Harvard Business Review, 86*(6), 61–70, p. 62.

85. Kotter, J. P. (1995). Leading change: Why transformation efforts fail. *Harvard Business Review, 73*(2), 59–67.

86. Laasch, O., & Flores, U. (2010). Implementing profitable CSR: The CSR 2.0 business compass. In M. Pohl & N. Tolhurst, *Responsible Business: How to Manage a CSR Strategy Successfully* (pp. 289–309). Chichester: Wiley; King, H. (2010, June 28). The view from the C-Suite: P&G's Len Sauers. Retrieved June 3, 2011, from GreenBiz.com: www .greenbiz.com/blog/2010/06/28 /view-c-suite-pgs-len-sauers

87. Huston, L., & Sakkab, N. (2006). Connect and develop: Inside Procter & Gamble's new model for innovation. *Harvard Business Review, 84*(3), 58–66; Ma, M. (2009, March 2). How "open" should innovation be? Retrieved June 3, 2011, from *Psychology Today:*www.psychology-today.com/blog/the-tao-innovation /200903/how-open-should -innovation-be

88. Hitt, M. A., Ireland, R. D., & Hoskisson, R. E. (2007). *Strategic management: Competitiveness and globalization.* Mason, OH: Thomson South-Western.

89. Thompson, A. A., Strickland, A. J., & Gamble, J. E. (2005). *Crafting and executing strategy: The quest for competitive advantage* (p. 369). New York: McGraw-Hill.

90. Hitt, M. A., Ireland, R. D., & Hoskisson, R. E. (2007). *Strategic management: Competitiveness and globalization.* Mason, OH: Thomson South-Western.

91. Moad, J. (2011, November). ERP tackles the environment. Retrieved June 6, 2011, from *Manufacturing Executive:* www .manufacturing-executive.com /community/leadership_dialogues

/sustainability/blog/2011/02/24 /erp-tackles-the-environment

92. Werther, W. B., & Chandler, D. (2010). *Strategic corporate social responsibility: Stakeholders in a global environment* (p. 187). Thousand Oaks, CA: Sage.

93. Luijkenaar, A., & Spinley, K. (2007). *The emergence of the chief sustainability officer: From compliance manager to business partner.* Amsterdam: Heidrick & Struggles. www .heidrick.com/PublicationsReports /PublicationsReports/HS _ChiefSustainabilityOfficer.pdf

94. Hitt, M. A., Ireland, R. D., & Hoskisson, R. E. (2007). *Strategic management: Competitiveness and globalization* (p. 337). Mason, OH: Thomson South-Western.

95. Kaplan, R. S., & Norton, D. P. (1996). Using the balanced scorecard as strategic management system. *Harvard Business Review, 74*(1), 75–85.

96. Kaplan, R. S., & Norton, D. P. (1996). Using the balanced scorecard as strategic management system. *Harvard Business Review, 74*(1), 75–85; Figge, F., et al. (2002). The sustainability balanced scorecard: Linking sustainability management to business strategy. *Business Strategy and the Environment, 11,* 269–284.

97. Walmart. (2006, November 1). Wal-Mart unveils "packaging scorecard" to suppliers. Retrieved June 6, 2011, from Walmart corporate: http://walmartstores. com/pressroom/news/6039.aspx; 2 Sustain. (2011, May 11). P&G first year supplier sustainability scorecard results. Retrieved June 6, 2011, from 2 Sustain: http://2sustain. com/2011/05/pg-first-year-supplier -sustainability-scorecard-results.html; Baier, P. (2010, July 12). Comparing the Walmart and P&G supplier sustainability scorecards. Retrieved June 6, 2011, from Greenbiz.com: www.greenbiz.com/blog/2010/07/13 /comparing-walmart-and-pg-supplier -sustainability-scorecards

98. Kaplan, R. S., & Norton, D. P. (2004). *Strategy maps.* Boston: Harvard Business School Press; Cinépolis Foundation. (2010). *Presentación de caso "Del amor nace la vista" [Presentation of the case "Love gives birth to eyesight"]* [PowerPoint]. Mexico City: Cinépolis Foundation.

## 07

Ecopreneurship

Social Demand

Intapreneurship

Market Logic

NPM

Reciprocity

Corporate Social Entrepreneurship

Opportunity

Hybridization

Business Plan

Mutuality

Social Innovation

Change Agents

Ashoka

Grameen

Third Sector

Social Entrepreneurship

Socialized Ownership

# ENTREPRENEURSHIP: VALUE-ADDED VENTURES

*You will be able to...*

1  ...**analyze your organization's relationship to the social economy.**

2  ...**select social entrepreneurial strategies.**

3  ...**create value-added ventures.**

An average of 2.8 percent of world's working-age adult population during 2009 was involved in social activities, measured as explicit social enterprise.[1]

The social economy in the EU covered 10 percent of the European GDP and 6 percent of total employment, with more than 11 millions of workers.[2]

Of social enterprises in the UK, 14 percent were start-ups, 74 percent involved their communities in decision making, 82 percent invested back into communities to further social and environmental goals, and 88 percent minimized the environmental impact of their own operations.[3]

Author: Rory Ridley-Duff and Michael Bull; Contributors: Doru Mitrana, Mark Kramer, Martin Perry, Oliver Laasch

## Participatory Democracy in the Mondragon Corporation

In 1941, a Catholic priest arrived in the civil war–torn town of Mondragon, in the Basque region of Spain. When Union Cerrajera, the largest local employer, refused to open its schools to all children in the community, Father Arizmendi chartered a parents' association and organized door-to-door collections to fund a new technical school.

In 1955, five of Arizmendi's graduates began an industrial enterprise that adopted a cooperative model of democratic ownership and member-control. Each worker-member was given a capital account into which trading profits were paid each year. The accounts were held in a credit union arranged by Arizmendi. This approach spread both ownership and wealth rapidly throughout the community and funded the creation of new enterprises. By the year 2000, roughly half of the population of the town of Mondragon were co-owners of the cooperative that employed them, and the Mondragon Corporation operated internationally through hundreds of member cooperatives and overseas partnerships.

A comparison with U.S. companies is striking. In the United States, wage differentials between CEOs and workforce members have grown to 450:1. Comparable Mondragon cooperatives have chosen to limit wage differentials to a maximum of 9:1. How have they stopped executive wage inflation? To widen the starting differential of 3:1, all capital account holders have to approve the change on a one-member, one-vote basis. In the last fifty-seven years, no workforce has approved a differential of more than 9:1. The average is 5:1.

This system of wage solidarity led researchers from the London School of Economics to conclude that Mondragon has a huge "cooperative advantage" that comes from lower-wage bills and extraordinarily high levels of trust between managers and workforce members. And it works. In each decade there has been rapid growth. There are now 83,000 employees (85% of which are member-owners). There are 9,000 students studying in Mondragon's cooperative schools, colleges, and university. At the height of the 2008–2009 recession, membership still grew by 6.1 percent. New growth is supported by expansion of Eroski, a chain of retail outlets that extends ownership and profit sharing to both staff and customers.

Mondragon is the outcome of both visionary social entrepreneurship and collective social action. Father Arizmendi, who died in 1976, has been lauded for the democratic design of Mondragon's banking and governance systems. His individual vision has been supplemented by a collective commitment to economic solidarity and cooperative principles. The result is responsible management: the by-product of organizational structures that require managers to serve the interests of the workforce and customers, rather than capital markets. The result? Mondragon is now the seventh-largest corporation in Spain, with a track record of high productivity, profitability, and corporate social responsibility.

Source: www.mondragon-corporation.com/

# 7-1 SOCIAL ENTREPRENEURSHIP AND RESPONSIBLE MANAGEMENT

*"Those who opt to make history and change the course of events themselves have an advantage over those who decide to wait passively for the results of the change."*[4]

The Mondragon Co-operative Corporation is an excellent starting point for a discussion of innovation in social entrepreneurship, because it represents an exemplar case that integrates different perspectives. Social entrepreneurship, and its connection to social enterprise creation, is still the subject of definitional debates.[5] In this chapter, we clarify issues by problematizing three dominant "schools" of social entrepreneurial thought. We will argue that a more useful perspective is to examine the socioeconomic origins of different schools to identify the challenges that arise when responsible managers pursue socioentrepreneurial goals from different starting points.

The topic of strategy scrutinizes how to plan and strategically align an organization. This chapter goes even deeper and scrutinizes the very nature of an organization. Organizations might be private, public, or civil society sector organizations. This chapter describes how those types of organizations can evolve through social innovation by including characteristics and strengths of the other sectors, with the goal of creating even more value for society. Although this chapter on social entrepreneurship and innovation has a strong planning component of planning the pathway of development of an organization, it also has a strong organizing component. Social entrepreneurship business models often include unique organizational structures, such as stakeholder ownership and complex democratic co-decision mechanisms. While those topics are touched upon in this chapter, the focus on such elements of organizational architecture can be understood with more depth through the field of organizational studies.

It must be highlighted that this chapter also fulfills one additional important function for responsible managers. It helps to map the territory. Responsible managers often find themselves working in hybrid structures between the three sectors. For instance, a manager working in a corporate foundation shares characteristics of both the private for-profit sector and the social society not-for-profit sector. A manager working in a public commodity company has a public sector purpose, but functions in many ways with a private sector market system. This chapter helps such responsible managers to understand the distinct characteristics of such different sectors and how they shape their day-to-day activities. For managers who do not work in a hybrid organization, understanding those sectorial differences is key to successfully collaborating with hybrid organizations or the organizations from different sectors.

We will develop this chapter in two steps, which represent the phases of the social entrepreneurship process as illustrated in Figure 7.1. Phase 1 involves understanding social entrepreneurship in its three main perspectives—understanding the nature of economic exchanges, as well as the basic paradigms of the three sectors. Phase 2 helps to understand the potential pathways for social entrepreneurship ventures, depending on the sector in which the organization is placed. Both phases serve to help in achieving the goal of creating a "value-added venture," which includes the aims to "socialize" the organization and to create social value both externally and internally.

| **Figure 7.1 The Social Entrepreneurship Process**

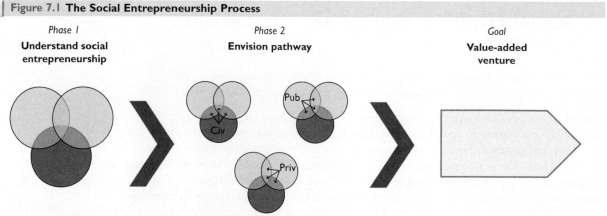

Phase 1
**Understand social entrepreneurship**

Phase 2
**Envision pathway**

Goal
**Value-added venture**

© Cengage Learning, 2015

## 7-2 GOAL: THE VALUE-ADDED VENTURE

*"[S]ocial ventures pursue economic, social, or environmental aims, generating at least part of their income from trading. They fill market gaps between private enterprise and public sector provision, and, increasingly, policy makers consider them to be valuable agents in social, economic, and environmental regeneration and renewal."[6]*

The goal of social entrepreneurship as we describe it in this chapter is a **value-added venture**. What is this? A venture is an undertaking that involves uncertainty and the pursuit of reward or opportunity. The term *value-added* here refers to social-value added, often through the solution or mitigation of a social issue. In the case of social entrepreneurship, such social value can be added in two ways.

- First, the socialization of the organization will lead to more democratic structures in which main stakeholders are integrated into the ownership, governance, and management of the enterprise. This is social-value added for all stakeholders involved in the decision process.

- Second, social entrepreneurship usually involves a "social mission" that, when fulfilled, benefits society, often transforming the society and its systems. This is value added for society as a whole.

We could call the first type of value-added *internal* and the second *external* or *systemic value creation*. Thus, the value-added venture is one that at the same time "socializes" the organization to the inside and creates social value systemically to the outside.

> ## In Practice
>
> **Inside and Outside Value Added for Mäori**
>
> Te Whanau o Waipareira Trust works to advance the position of the Mäori living in the western suburbs of New Zealand's largest city, Auckland, through health, social, justice, and education services provided to the Mäori irrespective of their situation. Working for the Mäori, the workplace is guided by the Mäori *kaupapa* and *tikanga* (values and ethics).
>
> Source: Te Whanau Waipareira Trust. (2013). Retrieved February 2, 2013, from Te Whanau Waipareira: www.waipareira.com/index

## 7-3 PHASE 1: UNDERSTANDING SOCIAL ENTREPRENEURSHIP AND SOCIAL INNOVATION

*"Social entrepreneurship describes the discovery and sustainable exploitation of opportunities to create social and environmental benefits."[7]*

To understand **social entrepreneurship** and the related social innovation process, we will illustrate the three elementary perspectives of social entrepreneurship, examine the market as just one form of exchange in economic systems, and finally identify the starting point of social entrepreneurship, based on the organization's initial position inside the sector.

### 7-3a Elementary Perspectives of Social Entrepreneurship

The first school presents social entrepreneurship as action that leads to **social innovation**.[8] At Mondragon, the systems of entrepreneurship and governance have been advanced as "inventions" that improve community well-being. As Turnbull states:

> *None of the existing theories of the firm were used to provide the criteria for designing the structure of the Mondragon co-operatives in the mid-1950s. These co-operatives introduced a number of "social inventions"[9] which*

The **value-added venture** at the same time "socializes" the organization to the inside and creates social value systemically to the outside.

**Social entrepreneurship** describes the discovery and sustainable exploitation of opportunities to create social and environmental benefits.

**Social innovation** is innovation of structures, processes, or products that leads to social value creation.

*have proved to be outstandingly successful.*[10] *One of the design criteria for developing the Mondragon inventions was based on Catholic social doctrine, which believed in the "priority of labor over capital."*[11] *People, rather than money, became the fundamental unit of concern. This approach ... is at variance with the Coasian/Williamson theory of the firm, which is based on transactions. ...*[12]

In the social innovation school, entrepreneurs are presented as heroes. In the case of Mondragon, Father Arizmendi, the priest deemed responsible for the "social inventions" linked to Mondragon's success, is revered as a teacher and founder even though he never held a formal position in any of the Mondragon cooperatives.[13] A museum has been created to tell the story of his role, and a statue has been erected at Mondragon University to honor his teaching.

The second school of social entrepreneurship is linked to the first in its emphasis on understanding and developing the social entrepreneur. However, here the emphasis is on **value proposition** and **social mission**.[14] Value propositions are translated into social objects that make the entrepreneurs' (and their enterprises') social impact measurable. In Mondragon's management model, the social mission is defined in terms of achieving *social transformation* (one of ten core principles). It places the education of members (both political and technical) at the heart of the model so that managers can subordinate the interests of capital to those of labor. Other principles that make up the corporate management model include: open membership; democratic organization; participatory management; wage solidarity; cooperation between cooperatives; and support for social movements committed to economic democracy.[15]

The third school of social entrepreneurship emphasizes the creation of social enterprises that have **socialized ownership and control** using democratic principles.[16] In the case of Mondragon, this is achieved through the deployment of a cooperative model that ensures that executive decision making is a shared process involving managers, elected representatives, and a general assembly of members. In contrast to unitary boards in multinational corporations with appointed directors, Mondragon is controlled by more than 1,000 local boards made up of elected audit committees and governing and social councils that interact with each other to coordinate and make decisions about activities.[17]

This school, strongly influenced by the concept of a European *social economy*, makes a clear distinction between the "reciprocal interdependence" that underpins mutual care and "charity" based on philanthropy. *Mutuality* implies a bidirectional or network relationship to promote *reciprocity* in which parties accept a social obligation to help, support, and supervise each other. This is qualitatively different from both the unidirectional power relationship between managers and subordinates, and the paternalistic relationship between philanthropists and beneficiaries. Although it may be present in mutual relations, charity is legally framed in both law and practice as a one-way relationship in which one party gives/directs while the other receives/obeys. This asymmetry in obligations (i.e., the lack of "reciprocal interdependence") distinguishes mutuality from charity.[18]

For the purposes of our argument, the authors recognize a distinction between a socialization perspective, which emphasizes collective action and mutual principles to develop a social economy, and a social purpose perspective, which focuses on the social innovations and missions of the social entrepreneur within a market economy.[19] The *socialization perspective* has a relationship orientation that regards tasks as components in relationship building rather than ends in

The **social mission** is a **value proposition** guiding strategy and actions of a social enterprise.

**Socialized ownership and control** refers to democratic decision-making models based on a membership model for stakeholders.

their own right. Organizational design and governance arrangements promote the education of members, with tasks as the building blocks of relationships designed to facilitate sharing of wealth and power. The *social purpose perspective* has a task orientation that studies the philanthropic impulse of social entrepreneurs and the social goals of their enterprises.[20] As the Mondragon Co-operative example demonstrates, these goals are not necessarily in opposition to each other, as there is evidence of:

- Social innovation
- Social purposes (leading to social impact and transformation)
- Socialized ownership and control

However, many purported examples of social entrepreneurship do not show evidence of the integration of all three schools. For example, the pharmaceutical company Betapharm in Germany, which excelled in its social activities, provides an example of social innovation, purpose, and impact, but it retains a private sector model of ownership and control. Worker cooperatives and employee-owned businesses may deploy highly innovative approaches to governance without being explicit about their social mission.[21] Charities and nonprofit corporations can develop trading strategies and subsidiaries to support social missions without necessarily innovating or democratizing ownership and control.[22]

It is, therefore, worth linking schools of social entrepreneurial thought to different change agendas. Although each is useful for highlighting single strands of responsible management thinking, combining them to create the exemplar system at Mondragon may be subject to cognitive constraints (internally imposed) and sociological constraints (externally imposed). In the final part of our introduction, therefore, we identify socioeconomic contexts in which social entrepreneurs operate, and the systems of exchange that influence their approach.

## 7-3b Economic Systems

Insights into schools of social entrepreneurial thought can be developed by studying the work of Karl Polanyi.[23] Polanyi offered a critique of economic exchange systems. First, he outlined a *communal system* that operates on a large scale, based on principles of mutuality and reciprocity. In this system, there is a limited need for financial transactions, written records, and markets. There is a stronger focus on production for use than for exchange, with the outputs of production held within an extended community, sometimes based on pairing by families in different communities, and paired communities. In this system, the allocation of shared resources is subject to debate by community elders.

Next, Polanyi identified *systems of redistribution,* rooted in the practice of pooling produce both for reciprocal exchange with other communities and to ensure provision for public events and economic uncertainty. Where there is a system of redistribution, written records are needed to track who has contributed to, and drawn from, the common pool of resources.

Last, Polanyi identifies the idea of *production for markets,* in which the notions of gain, profit, and loss become more important. Production for markets, not unsurprisingly, needs written financial records of all transactions to calculate market prices. Within this system, obligations to record price changes and to calculate gains replace alternative obligations to reciprocate and to contribute to collective wealth. Social entrepreneurship research, and social entrepreneurs themselves, are divided on the question of whether to accept the dominance of market logic. Authors vary in their attitude to market thinking and the assumption that humans act from rational self-interest.[24]

Polanyi goes to great lengths to emphasize that societies dominated by market logic are a recent, not a historical, phenomenon. The notions of "gain" and "profit" apply only where there is production for markets, and not where people are involved in production for household consumption or the community. The marginalization of reciprocity and redistribution started with the works of Adam Smith.[25] His followers—even after empirical evidence established that market exchange was peripheral rather than central to early human societies—continued to propagate a view that market exchanges are a natural human state and historical norm.[26] The centrality of this issue—whether markets are imposed unnatural structures or the natural product of human behavior—explains divergences in schools of social entrepreneurial thought. It also has profound implications for the conceptualization and practice of responsible management.

An acceptance of market logic as "natural" will lead to responsible management that devalues reciprocity and redistribution as valid forms of economic exchange, and leads to a reductionist view that only market logic should inform decision making. The resistance (or lack of attention) to mutuality, reciprocity, and democracy in the social innovation and social purpose schools of thought provides evidence of this.[27] Instead of valuing reciprocity and redistribution, arguments focus on reform of market institutions together with calls for new market institutions that enable investors to back the "right" social entrepreneur.[28] In contrast, skepticism toward market logic leads responsible management toward action that balances market exchange, reciprocity, and redistribution. Polanyi himself argued for a rebalancing to ensure that people, money, and land are not treated as market commodities. Such arguments surface most readily in calls for economic pluralism and workplace democracy.[29]

In the remainder of this chapter, therefore, we cannot assume there is a single pathway or planning system that leads to responsible management. The pathway chosen will depend both on the socioeconomic context of a manager as well as his or her own assumptions of the relative importance of reciprocity, redistribution, and market exchange in economics. In the sections that follow, we review the self-analysis, challenges, and actions based on the assumption that social entrepreneurship is a contextual variable shaped by the path chosen. While we keep in mind the exemplar of social economy at the Mondragon Corporation, we draw attention to alternative pathways that arise, when cognitive (internal) and sociological (external) barriers are encountered. A main goal of the following description is to map the territory for planning a social entrepreneurship venture through an understanding of alternative pathways.

## 7-3c Identifying the Starting Point for Social Innovation

Before we examine the challenges encountered during the pursuit of social entrepreneurship, it is worth setting out a theoretical framework to guide discussion. We start by linking Polanyi's concept of reciprocity to Pearce's model of a third system[30] (see Figure 7.2). There is a narrow, perhaps misleading, definition that the

**Figure 7.2 The First, Second, and Third Systems of Economy**

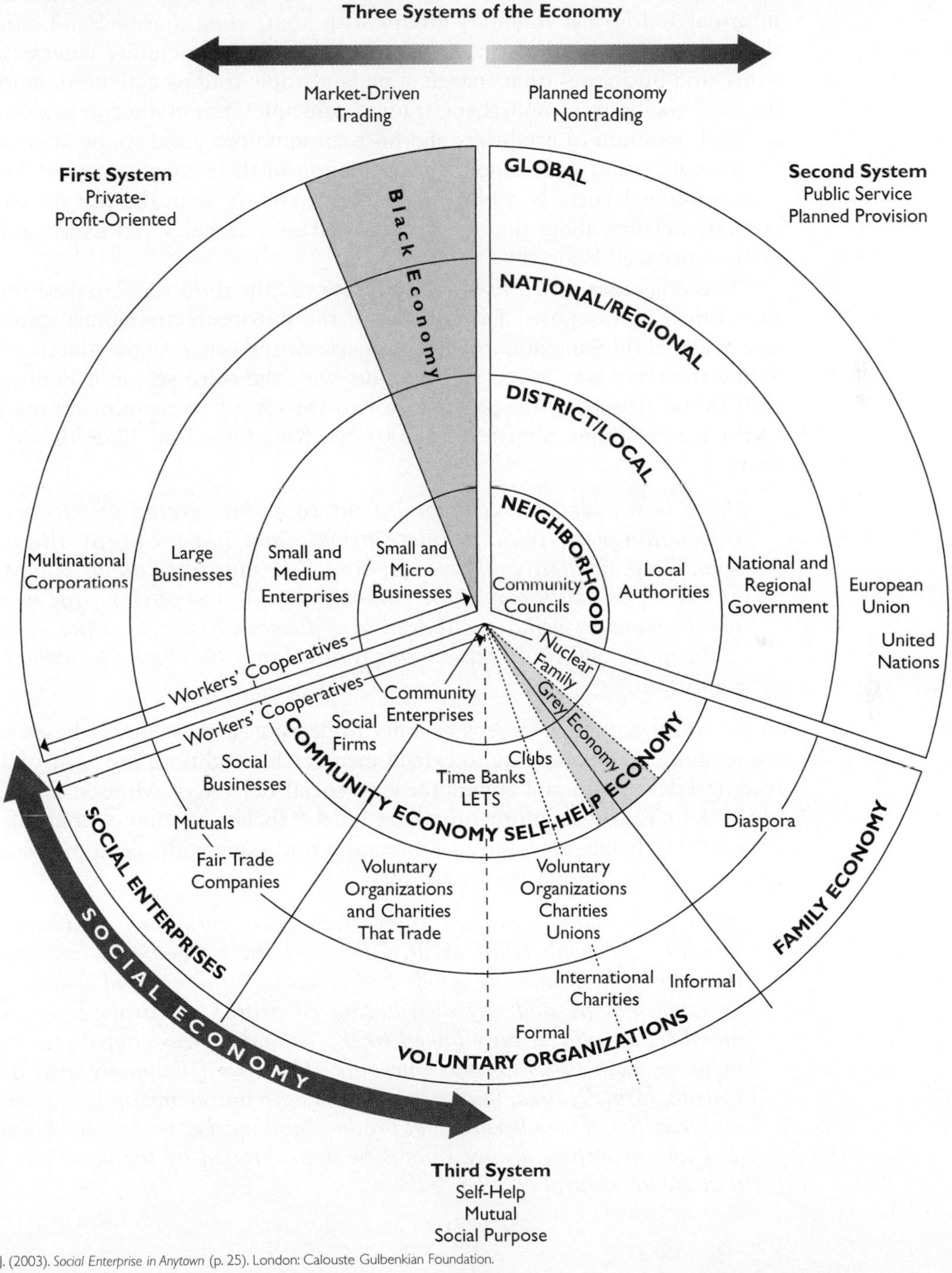

Three Systems of the Economy

Market-Driven Trading

Planned Economy Nontrading

**First System** Private-Profit-Oriented

**Second System** Public Service Planned Provision

GLOBAL

NATIONAL/REGIONAL

DISTRICT/LOCAL

NEIGHBORHOOD

Black Economy

Multinational Corporations

Large Businesses

Small and Medium Enterprises

Small and Micro Businesses

Community Councils

Local Authorities

National and Regional Government

European Union

United Nations

Workers' Cooperatives

Workers' Cooperatives

Community Enterprises

Social Firms

Nuclear Family

Grey Economy

Social Businesses

Time Banks LETS

Clubs

Diaspora

Mutuals

COMMUNITY ECONOMY

SELF-HELP ECONOMY

FAMILY ECONOMY

Fair Trade Companies

Voluntary Organizations and Charities That Trade

Voluntary Organizations Charities Unions

SOCIAL ENTERPRISES

International Charities

Informal

SOCIAL ECONOMY

Formal

VOLUNTARY ORGANIZATIONS

**Third System** Self-Help Mutual Social Purpose

Source: Pearce, J. (2003). *Social Enterprise in Anytown* (p. 25). London: Calouste Gulbenkian Foundation.

third system is "nonprofit" in outlook. This obscures both the notion of not-for-private-profit[31] and a century of history and knowledge about the effectiveness of cooperatives and mutual societies.[32]

The appeal of Pearce's diagram lies in its attempt to provide a comprehensive description of the organizations that engage in the types of exchange described by Polanyi.[33] First, it recognizes entities at neighborhood, district, regional, national, and international levels. Interestingly, Pearce defines the third system as "social purpose." Within that system, he differentiates a formally organized community economy and a self-help economy grounded in family life. Pearce's model clusters informal and formal voluntary groups with nontrading charities, and differentiates these from organizations that trade. He identifies community enterprises, social firms, and businesses (that engage in philanthropic trading activities), mutuals (that use reciprocity as an underlying trading principle), fair trade companies (that pay a social premium to producers and host communities), and cooperatives (designed to promote social and economic participation of their members in production and consumption). There is a blurring at the boundary with the private sector, with contested claims about the best way to address external social issues and improve community well-being.[34]

This coincides with a rise in the concept of "the third way" to describe changes in political philosophy.[35] The collapse of the European communist states led to a new wave of thinking in Europe, the Americas, and other Anglo-American cultures. While the third way is not synonymous with the third sector, it implies a major shift in the attitude of the public sector toward it.[36] Commenting on the approach of the former Prime Minister of the United Kingdom, Tony Blair, the BBC argued that:

> there is no ideological commitment to public sector provision—there is a willingness to contemplate private and not-for-profit alternatives, something manifestly different from more traditional Labour policy which at times was indifferent to the voluntary sector and often hostile to private involvement in welfare.... Indeed it is the social services white paper that is the most explicit on this, stating quite clearly that "who provides" is not important.[37]

In the social economy, there is hostility to decision-making power based on capital ownership and a preference to extend membership rights on the basis of a person's trading relationship and commitment to social objectives. Monson and Claves set out a definition that informs thinking on the social economy within the Eurpean Union (EU). It integrates social democratic traditions with social purpose goals to create a social economy comprised of:

> private, formally organized enterprises, with autonomy of decision and freedom of membership, created to meet their members' needs through the market by producing goods and services, insurance and finance, where decision-making and any distribution of profits or surpluses among the members are not directly linked to the capital or fees contributed by each member, each of whom has one vote. The Social Economy also includes private, formally organized organisations with autonomy of decision-making and freedom of membership that produce non-market services for households and whose surplus, if any, cannot be appropriated by the economic agents that create, control or finance them.[38]

## 7-3d Implications for Social Entrepreneurship

This leads to two perspectives on social enterprise in relation to the third sector. First, there is the argument of Defourny[39] that social enterprises are embedded *within* the third system between cooperatives (that promote reciprocity and market exchange) and nonprofits (that promote reciprocity and redistribution). This perspective is illustrated in Figure 7.3.

A similar argument is implicit in Pearce's[40] model. Social enterprise is depicted as a subsector sitting between voluntary and charity organizations (that engage in redistribution and reciprocal relationships) and the private sector (that promotes market exchange).

Building on acceptance that **hybridization** of economic systems can occur, it follows that social entrepreneurship can occur both inside and outside the third sector.[41] We argue that the areas between the third and public sectors, between the public and private sectors, and between the third and private sector catalyze social entrepreneurship. Westall[42] goes even further by articulating the social economy as a distinct fourth sector (see Figure 7.4). The distinctiveness of this view, of a social economy comprised primarily of social enterprises, rests on two competences: the ability to hybridize systems of economic exchange (markets, reciprocity, and redistribution), and the ability to manage multiple owners and/or a multistakeholder system of governance.

This view places social enterprise at a unique locus in the wider economy, able to engage with and understand the logics of third, public and private sector partners, but developing its own constellation of management practices that combine entrepreneurial action with the integration of different stakeholders. Nyssens[43] concurs with this analysis when she cites Polanyi in her own definition: "we argue that social enterprises mix the economic principles of market, redistribution and reciprocity, and hybridize their three types of economic exchange so that they work together rather than in isolation from each other."[44]

**Hybridization** refers to the creation of structures that share characteristics of more than one sector.

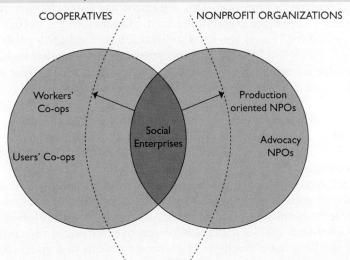

**Figure 7.3 Social Enterprise at the Crossroads of Economic Systems**

COOPERATIVES          NONPROFIT ORGANIZATIONS

Workers' Co-ops

Users' Co-ops

Social Enterprises

Production oriented NPOs

Advocacy NPOs

Source: Defourny, J. (2001). From third sector to social enterprise. In C. Borzaga & J. Defourny, *The emergence of social enterprise* (pp. 1–28, p. 22). London: Routledge.

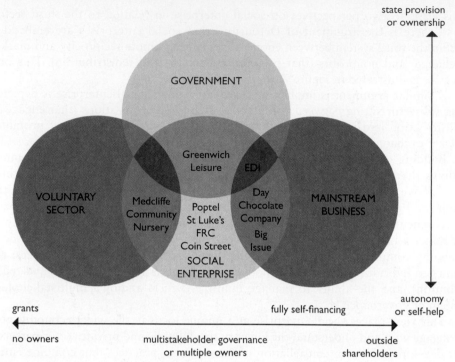

**Figure 7.4 Social Enterprise as Multistakeholder Enterprise Development**

state provision or ownership

GOVERNMENT

Greenwich Leisure

EDI

VOLUNTARY SECTOR

Medcliffe Community Nursery

Poptel St Luke's FRC Coin Street SOCIAL ENTERPRISE

Day Chocolate Company Big Issue

MAINSTREAM BUSINESS

autonomy or self-help

grants                    fully self-financing

no owners        multistakeholder governance          outside
                 or multiple owners                  shareholders

Source: Westall, A. (2001). *Value-Led, Market-Driven: Social Enterprise Solutions to Public Policy Goals* (p. 9). London: IPPR.

## 7-3e Money, Labor, and Land

Importantly, Polanyi[45] does not argue against market logic in its entirety, only against the commoditization of "fictitious goods." Money, labor, and land, he asserts, cannot be treated as commodities. If they are, each will be degraded and their value destroyed or distorted. This argument has contemporary relevance as persuasive texts connect the commoditization of money to the destructive effects of "casino capitalism,"[46] and the commoditization of land to degradation of the environment.[47] Prompted by popular perceptions that private banks are trying to restore the value of capital by forcing down wages and taking over state assets, there has also been a resurgence of interest in Marx's writings on the commoditization of labor.[48]

In Ridley-Duff,[49] a multistakeholder model based on social economy principles is put forward as a "socially rational" approach to integrating economic systems. In this model, there are a number of variants where integration is partial rather than complete (see Figure 7.5).

While each type of social entrepreneurship expresses itself in a variety of forms, the substance of each is underpinned by the capacity of entrepreneur-owners to develop viable relationships between actors who depend on different systems of exchange. Ridley-Duff takes a dialectical perspective that social entrepreneurship is a process of working out a synthesis of exchange systems in a given social context and instituting forms of social enterprise. This gives rise to four types of social entrepreneurship that are influenced by the hybridization that occurs when exchange systems are mixed (see Table 7.1).

Figure 7.5 **Four Types of Socioentrepreneurial Development**

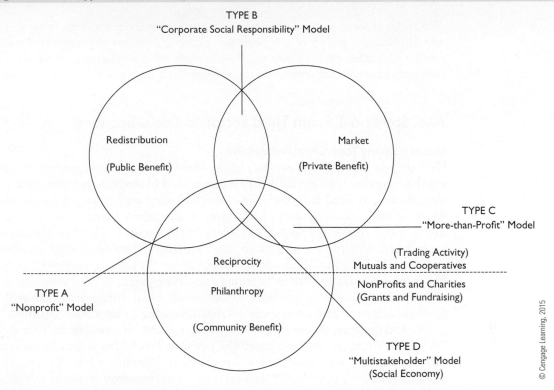

**Table 7.1** Overview: Types of Hybridization

| Type | Approach | Synthesis of Exchange Systems |
|------|----------|-------------------------------|
| A | Nonprofit | Redistribution and Reciprocity |
| B | Corporate Social Responsibility | Redistribution and Market |
| C | More-than-Profit | Reciprocity and Market |
| D | Multistakeholder (Social Economy) | Reciprocity, Redistribution, and Market |

Source: Based on Ridley-Duff, R. J., & Bull, M. (2011). *Understanding social enterprise: Theory and practice* (p. 75). London: Sage.

There are advantages to theorizing social entrepreneurship this way. First, it provides a robust framework for exploring the ambiguity, origins, and ethos of the different schools of social entrepreneurship.[50] Second, it provides a base from which to theorize the development of alliances, organizational forms, and management practices needed to integrate systems of exchange. As each trajectory requires a different course of action, our discussions in the next three sections of the chapter will be framed by this model.

In each section, we break the discussion down in three phases: understanding one's own perspective and trajectory for change; reviewing challenges and opportunities; and actions that can lead to socioentrepreneurial outcomes. For responsible managers reading this chapter, it makes sense both to focus on the implications for the owner/employer organization and to gain understanding of how actors from the other sectors manage social entrepreneurship. This second perspective is especially significant in assessing and managing cross-sectorial partnerships for a common purpose.

# 7-4 PHASE 2: ENVISION YOUR PATHWAY

*"The origins of social enterprises are significant because the social enterprise sector is in a state of emergence and social enterprises are developing from very different roots. These different roots affect the transitions they have to make and can influence both the way governance structures are constructed and developed, and the types of issues that emerge."*[51]

## 7-4a Scenario 1: From Third Sector to Social Economy

### Understanding Your Own Perspective

How do you know if you are part of the **third sector**? One approach to answering this question is to examine the language used to describe organizational activities. Bull[52] gathered information on the language and concepts in use in third sector organizations as part of a project to adapt the balanced scorecard.[53] He found more references to "stakeholders" than "shareholders" or "customers," more references to "multi-bottom line" measures than "financial accounting," and a preference for "internal activities" over "business processes" and for a "learning organization" over "learning and development."[54] The language reflects differences in thinking, attempts to design of social enterprises that will serve multiple interests, and an orientation that limits the influence of "business" talk.

We can illustrate this further by examining accounting terms. In the United States, "nonprofit" organizations use Form 990, or Form 990-EZ, to declare "total receipts" (income from trading, investments, donations, and grants), while "for-profit" companies report their income as "sales revenue" (total turnover from the sale of goods and services). In the UK, smaller charities use cash-accounting based on "receipts" and "expenses," while larger ones (incorporated as companies) have to produce a "profit-and-loss" statement. Grant income is subject to trust law, not company law, because money is "granted" by a donor to form a "trust" with the recipient on how the money can be used.[55]

Organizations with a closer affiliation to social economy (mutuals, associations and cooperatives, and social enterprises) use terms in a different way than private businesses. For example, cooperatives use the term *patronage* to describe trading and working in a cooperative. Worker cooperatives differentiate *surplus* (created by worker-members) from *profits* (created by employees) and use the term *patronage refund* to describe the distribution of surpluses to "patrons."[56] If the term *dividend* is used, it refers to the patronage refund issued to members based on their trading activities, not a dividend on their shareholding.[57] In mutuals and associations, no shares are issued. In bona fide cooperatives, however, shares are issued. Unlike private sector shares that can be traded and vary in value, cooperative shares are frequently nontransferable amounts of capital with a "par value." This prevents them from being commoditized through trading activity.[58]

Before deciding on a social entrepreneurial strategy in third sector organizations, an evaluation of Type A (Nonprofit), Type C (More-than-Profit), and Type D (Social Economy) takes place (see Figure 7.6). In making this choice, a consideration of the organization's governance model, sources of income, and supply chain can be important.

The **third sector**, or third system, consists of organizations that undertake social activity without profit purpose, which is typically based on reciprocity.

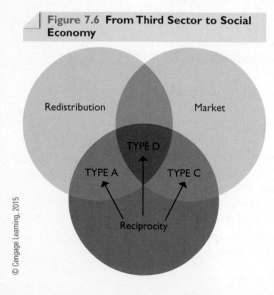

**Figure 7.6 From Third Sector to Social Economy**

Redistribution

Market

TYPE D

TYPE A

TYPE C

Reciprocity

## Challenges and Opportunities in Transforming the Third Sector

The context for social entrepreneurship in a third sector organization might be either contextually determined or a product of aspirations to develop and change.

Where a third sector organization operates a philanthropic model based primarily on grant bidding, a strategy orientated toward contracting to deliver public services will probably involve less organizational change than trading in markets or growing a membership base. A philanthropic model, particularly one where funds are acquired from corporate sources, is already premised on principles of redistribution rather than reciprocity. However, where a philanthropic model is based on strong relations with large numbers of small donors (particularly if there is regular information exchange with them), that orientation lends itself to developing reciprocity as a social entrepreneurial strategy. In this case, the move to trading with donors (perhaps through paid events or the creation of new member services) may involve less effort than acquiring the skills to secure public sector contracts. Where a third sector organization is a mutual with a large number of members, switching to a cooperative model makes it possible to raise capital by issuing cooperative shares.

The choices, however, may not be straightforward. For example, association members may resist the introduction of paid-for services and prefer executives to secure public or private money to fund free services for members. The culture among organization members (and their willingness to trade) will need testing before a business model is developed.

Similarly, the governance practices of an organization will influence thinking on taking public or private funds. If taking government money results in a loss of autonomy, will there be sufficient alignment between the goals of members and government funders? If taking a corporate donation, will giving access to members (beneficiaries) be against their long-term interests? In Bull and Crompton's research,[59] unpublished data of representatives from social enterprise organizations suggested differing views on income sources, with some against the notion of spending someone else's money (i.e., grant) and others viewing public sector contracting as (1) highly resource intensive, (2) risky for cash flow as an income strategy due to poor payment terms, and (3) having onerous reporting requirements.

Multiple income streams are, however, commonplace in the third sector (unlike the public sector that relies overwhelming on taxation for redistribution, and the private sector that relies overwhelmingly on market transformations for profit). Wei-Skillern and colleagues[60] used *The John Hopkins Comparative Non-profit Sector Project* to demonstrate the mixed income arrangements of third sector organizations (see Table 7.2). They vary widely by region. Overall, 53 percent represents fee income, with 35 percent coming from governments (mostly through contracts) and 12 percent coming from philanthropic giving. Trading income is particularly high in some countries (e.g., Kenya, 81%; Mexico, 85%; Philippines, 92%). In other cases, government contracts offer more opportunities (compare Europe, 56%, to Latin America, 15%). Hence, the balance of income streams available influences the social entrepreneurial paths that are open.

---

# In Practice

### A Quest for the Community

In 1977, the Coin Street Action Group started campaigning to prevent the development of a luxury hotel and office complex on the South Side of the River Thames (London). In its place, they drew up plans for mixed use of local land, including housing, a river park, shops, leisure facilities, and a walkway. After seven years and two public inquiries, the developers decided to sell the land to the Greater London Council (GLC), which in turn sold the land to a newly formed Company Limited by Guarantee called Coin Street Community Builders (CSCB). The case provides an example of a voluntary group making the transition from voluntary action to social entrepreneurship, evolving into an incorporated company and diversifying its income-generating activities through social purpose commercial activities using a variety of social enterprise forms.

"The ethos of CSCB is to create affordable housing, recreational space, workspaces, and shopping and leisure facilities, for use by the whole community. Revenue streams are varied. Commercial lets, for example, to Harvey Nichols help to subsidise rents to artists and designers in Oxo Tower Wharf, and for social housing provision. The Wharf itself was refurbished through a mix of bank loans, Housing Corporation and English Partnership grants and CSCB equity. CSCB also established Coin Street Secondary Housing Co-operative as a registered housing association which is creating six housing developments that are being set up as primary tenant-owned housing co-operatives."

Source: Westall, A. (2001). *Value-led, market-driven: Social enterprise solutions to public policy goals* (p. 5). London: IPPR. Additional source material from www.coinstreet.org/aboutus/historybackground.html

**Table 7.2** Streams of Income by Source (%)

|  | Fees (Trading) | Government | Philanthropy |
|---|---|---|---|
| Latin America | 75 | 15 | 10 |
| Scandinavia | 59 | 33 | 7 |
| USA | 57 | 31 | 13 |
| Asia | 56 | 22 | 12 |
| Africa | 55 | 25 | 19 |
| Eastern Europe | 49 | 31 | 19 |
| Europe | 38 | 56 | 6 |

Source: Wei-Skillern, J., Austin, J., Leonard, H., & Stevenson, H. (2007). *Enterpreneurship in the social sector* (p. 136). Thousand Oaks, CA: Sage.

### Figure 7.7  Classifying Activities

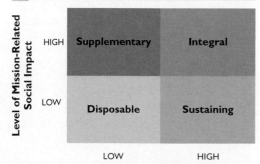

Source: Wei-Skillern, J., Austin, J., Leonard, H., & Stevenson, H. (2007). *Enterpreneurship in the social sector* (p. 140). Thousand Oaks, CA: Sage.

### Figure 7.8  From Private to Social Economy

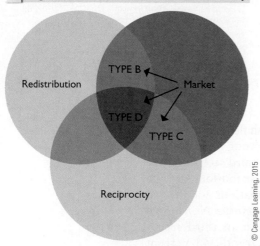

© Cengage Learning, 2015

Wei-Skillern and colleagues[61] provide another model that can be helpful in deciding project priorities, but which depends on information from accounting systems. Figure 7.7 shows *disposable* activities as those that inhibit the achievement of both social impacts and trading surpluses. *Supplementary* activities may achieve social impact, but do not generate surpluses. Nevertheless, supplementary activities may be desirable so an enterprise may choose to engage in *sustaining* activities to fund them, even if those do not contribute to social impact.

Too many sustaining activities can trigger mission drift that demotivates staff[62] and damages the reputation of the enterprise.[63] A strategic goal, therefore, is to find trading opportunities that are *integral* because they contribute to both social impact and surpluses. Emerson[64] describes this approach as one based on "blended value" (the generation of both social and economic value simultaneously).

Wei-Skillern and colleagues[65] warn that all activities "are initially, and on an on-going basis, capital absorbing." For example, selling goods and services to service users requires investments in marketing, not just in terms of devising and implementing strategies, but also in terms of the staff time to make them happen. Similarly, bidding for contracts takes time and commitment. If successful, the contract also needs servicing (monitoring outputs, outcomes, and impacts) and reporting back to commissioning bodies. Consequently, experience and know-how are needed to identify ancillary and project management costs (including rents, building maintenance, office services, and management time) so that bids are based on the principle of *full-cost recovery*. The life cycle of contract bidding includes a further challenge: the *renegotiation* skills needed to avoid negotiating away full-cost recovery during competitive tendering.[66]

Third sector organizations typically mix all three types of economic exchange, with a particular emphasis on reciprocity within mutuals, associations, and cooperatives, and on redistribution within nonprofits and charities. Developing socioentrepreneurial results, therefore, involves a review of the balance between different forms of exchange, and the cost-benefit of establishing a social enterprise (see Figure 7.8). The guide to action in Table 7.3 examines the changes needed at each step on each path.

**Table 7.3** Steps to Achieve Socioentrepreneurial Outcomes in the Third Sector

| Trajectory | Skills Developments | Legal Form Awareness |
|---|---|---|
| TYPE A ("Nonprofit") | • Develop public bid/tender writing, and (re)negotiation skills<br>• Acquire social and financial accounting skills (e.g., Social Auditing/SROI) to demonstrate social impact and public sector cost savings<br>• Plan an investment readiness strategy aimed at building the capacity to manage statutory requirements and public sector expectations | • Community Benefit Society<br>• Social Cooperative<br>• UK Charity / U.S. Nonprofit/NGO<br>• Voluntary Association |
| TYPE C ("More-than-Profit") | • Develop an understanding of private sector business planning/tender writing norms<br>• Improve financial accounting skills to show value for money and the impact of investment activities on profitability<br>• Plan an investment readiness program to manage private/social investor expectations | • Social Firm (Private Membership)<br>• Community Enterprise (Private Membership)<br>• Company (Private Membership) |
| TYPE D ("Social Economy") | • Establish open membership systems and build a membership base<br>• Survey members to assess their willingness to trade and contribute capital<br>• Develop participatory governance systems<br>• Develop social auditing skills and systems<br>• Develop member and/or employment relations skills | • Social Firm (Open Membership)<br>• Credit Union/Mutual Society<br>• Employee-Owned Business/Employee Mutual<br>• Cooperative Society<br>• Community Enterprise (Open Membership)<br>• Company (Open Membership) |

© Cengage Learning, 2015

## 7-4b Scenario 2: From Private to Social Economy

### Understanding Your Own Perspective

What language and mode of thinking dominates a private market perspective, and how would this change if responsible management practice aimed at further development of a social market economy? The **private sector** (and capitalist economies more generally) is dominated by a view that goods and services are commodities that can be traded for profit.[67] The concept of profit and loss from commodity trading is the bedrock on which private sector accounting is based. It extends beyond commoditization of the products of labor to the company itself—the money system, the environment, and labor.[68]

For example, in both management and economic theory, labor is regarded as a cost to be minimized by paying a fixed wage at market rates so that profits from labor activity can be converted into "shareholder value."[69] The commoditization of labor in this trading system leaves many people in a precarious situation. This thinking applies not only in private companies (to maximize investor returns) but also in charities (to maximize funds available for social projects). As Kalmi[70] argues, the same logic can also apply in consumer cooperatives (to maximize dividends for consumer-members). Theories about how to treat "labor" may vary, but in all these cases labor is treated as a commodity within the paradigm of market logic, leading either to the exclusion of labor from membership (and governance) or their acceptance on condition they abandon institutions designed to protect labor interests (e.g., trade unions, employment rights). The UK government recently made this explicit by announcing a plan to create companies in which employees may be forced to swap employment rights for ownership rights if they want the status of "employee-owner."[71]

The **private sector** is composed of privately owned organizations and businesses that act based on market principles.

Nor is it just the products of companies and labor that are subject to the logic of the market; it is also the elements that make them up. The income-generating capacity of companies is traded (as share capital). Customer lists, market intelligence, intellectual property, and even whole companies are bought and sold, with people transferred en masse between them, perhaps to be "broken up" so their market value can be "realized" in another round of market exchanges. The money in company banks accounts is bought and sold for gain on "money markets." Entrepreneurs, management teams, sporting heroes, and celebrities of all types cash in on the "market value" of their reputations and trade them for private or charitable gains.

Polanyi, citing Aristotle as his source, identifies a key boundary between market and nonmarket transactions. He distinguishes *householding* and *production for market,* and sees no obvious argument why "production for market" should replace "householding" in a market economy. Householding involves production for both self and market, with market logic applied only to production that is surplus to requirements. The rise of neoliberal consumerism has created a world in which needs are satisfied through markets, attaching a price to more and more things, and gradually replacing householding, reciprocity, and redistribution as systems of exchange.[72] This change could not have taken place without a weakening of householding principles. Miller and Rice[73] detail how arguments for equal opportunity legislation in the United States gained the support of big business not because business was concerned to advance "equal opportunity" at work, but because such legislation would enable big business to break up family businesses and acquire the wealth created by them.

However, in the social economy, the principle of householding remains strong. If we return to the example of Mondragon, the goal of its member organizations is to empower people in the community to produce for themselves *concurrently* with developing market relations. Unlike corporations that focus on core competences, Mondragon has diverse operations in banking, insurance, retail goods and services, industrial tools, construction (including housing), education, and research.[74] Similarly, the UK's Co-operative Group recently updated its strapline "from cradle to grave" to "here for you for life" to communicate the breadth of goods and services it provides, up to and including funeral care.[75]

If commercial activity is guided by production for members and markets (rather than only markets), prices change. The inclination to maximize profits is countered by a pressure from members (i.e., business owners) to keep prices affordable. This explains why Barcelona FC's most expensive season ticket is cheaper than Arsenal FC's least expensive season ticket (see Table 7.4). Barcelona FC, as a supporter-owned club, has hundreds of thousands of owners (not just consumers of football) who want football to remain affordable.

Beyond member benefit, however, is the wider question of community and public benefit. While organizations in the social economy operate for member and community benefit, their commitment to wider public benefit has been questioned.[76] Where public benefits are desired, the creation of charitable companies, foundations, and trusts might be preferred.[77] For example, the ASHOKA foundation in the USA and the UnLtd Charitable Company in the UK both make major investments

**Table 7.4** Comparing the Systems of Barcelona FC and Arsenal FC*

|  | Barcelona FC | Arsenal FC |
|---|---|---|
| Shareholders | In 2006, 142,000 members; one member, one vote. By 2011, it had grown to 170,000 members | In 2006, four major shareholders owned 87 percent of voting shares; one share, one vote. By 2011, two shareholders owned 96 percent of shares |
| Leadership | President elected by members for four-year term (maximum two terms) | Chair of the Board decided by the majority shareholder |
| Cheapest adult season ticket | £69 | £885 |
| Most expensive adult season ticket | £579 | £1,825 |

* Prices based on 2006 prices published in UK national newspapers

Source: Ridley-Duff, R. J. (2012, November 10). The UN International Year of Co-operative [Key Note]. Sheffield: Sheffield Hallam University, ESRC Festival of Social Science, Regather Trading Co-operative.

in the development of social entrepreneurship on a charitable (philanthropic) basis. In Italy, "social co-operative" legal status is available only when operating for community and public benefit, and tax reliefs on profits are granted only if capital is reinvested in the social economy. Similarly, in the UK, the Social Enterprise Mark company requires proof of a community benefit before being awarded the "mark," and Community Benefit Societies enjoy tax benefits afforded to charities only if they can demonstrate their charitable objects.

Managers based in the private sector, therefore, are faced with a choice of Type B (Corporate Social Responsibility, or CSR), Type C (More-than-Profit), or Type D (Social Economy) social entrepreneurship. The organization's approach to governance and the socioeconomic benefits of spreading ownership and membership rights to employees and customers become key aspects in evaluating the choices. Where ownership and democratic governance is possible, a transformation based on conversion to social economy is possible (Type D). If not possible (or not desired), the pathways open are CSR projects using charitable trusts and foundations (Type B) or more-than-profit enterprises that focus more on external beneficiaries than primary stakeholders (Type C).

## Expert Corner

### David P. Ellerman

"A capitalist economy within a political democracy can evolve to an economy of economic democracy by extending the principle of democratic self-determination to the workplace. It would be viewed by many as the perfection of capitalism since it replaces the demeaning employer-employee relationship with ownership and co-entrepreneurship for all the workers.

*A state socialist economy can evolve into an economic democracy by restructuring itself along the lines of the self-management socialist tradition. It would be viewed by many as the perfection of socialism since the workers would finally become masters of their own destiny in firms organized as free associations of producers."*

Source: Ellerman, D. (1997). The democratic corporation (p. 108). Beijing: Xinhua.

## Challenges and Opportunities in Transforming the Private Sector

Let us dwell on the question of transformation to a social economy, as this is the most far-reaching and challenging option for a manager in the private sector. Resistance to the idea by governments and capital markets (at both institutional and ideological levels) is one reason that CSR and "more-than-profit" companies might become favored approaches. They do not require a transfer of power from powerful elites to a wider population. Indeed, it can be argued that the reverse occurs: Elites extend their power into new areas of economic life.

Among Anglo-American thinkers, democratization of the workplace and wider economy has attracted support as a coherent strategy for balancing (and reducing) the influence of institutional shareholders and private banks to improve societal well-being.[78] Gates[79] describes a period during the 1920s and 1930s when U.S. conceptions of business ownership came under sustained attack from state

## In Practice

### Making the Transition

During a field trip to Mondragon, Mikel Lezamiz, the director of Mondragon's Management School, described how staff acquire a new private company and transform it into a cooperative. He discussed this as a gradual transition from:

1. Private to employee ownership
2. Employee ownership to participative management (collaborative working practices)
3. The introduction of cooperative management (elected councils)
4. The introduction of cooperative ownership

At Mondragon, employee ownership is the first step in a much longer process. The main goal is the socialization of management and governance (which can take many years to achieve). As an example, Lezamiz talked about eDesa, a company the local council asked MCC to buy (to save 1,000 jobs). It took from 1989 to 1994 to educate and prepare the workforce to take a vote to convert to a cooperative. In 1994, the workforce voted by 87 percent to 13 percent to convert (following a vote in its General Assembly). At eDesa, the reaction of trade unions was interesting. Two were supportive, and two were skeptical but eventually came around. With the backing of all four unions, eDesa eventually converted to a cooperative. Now, although the unions still have an "ambiguous" attitude to the MCC, many union members (about 100 people) are active disseminating information on the values and principles of the cooperative.

Source: Based on a transcript of a meeting, March 6, 2003, Mondragon Co-operative Corporation.

governor Huey Long. Long was elected to the Senate and gave radio speeches that proposed a redistribution of wealth and ownership. With the United States in the grip of depression, Long received the mass support required to organize a presidential challenge to Roosevelt. When Long was assassinated (in 1935), his legacy continued through his son Russell, who entered the Senate and worked on influential finance committees with Louis Kelso. Together they established employee share ownership plans (ESOPs), and by the late 1980s, enabling legislative environments started to propagate rapidly around the world. By the year 2000, 80 percent of the top 100 FTSE companies had established an ESOP, and tens of millions of employees in the UK and United States held shares in their own company.[80]

However, as Melman[81] discusses, despite "new right" rhetoric that share ownership would increase individuals' control over their own destiny, these changes made little impact on the lives of workers in the majority of cases. If shareholdings did not confer any control rights, they made little change in the pattern of worker layoffs, profitability, or manager-subordinate relations. The exception came from cases where majority employee ownership was established. In the United States today, a growing number of companies are majority-owned by employees, and the size of these companies is growing. The National Center for Employee Ownership lists the top 100 employee-owned companies, and even the company that is 100th on this list has more than 1,000 employee-owners.[82]

In Europe, worker cooperatives and employee-owned businesses have also been networking successfully to outperform their private sector counterparts.[83] In the Basque region of Spain and the Emilia Romagna region of Italy, local economies have strong cooperative networks of industrial companies, retailers, and welfare and educational organizations.[84] The density of employee-owned and cooperative companies has been linked to positive health outcomes and increased life expectancy across the community.[85] Notable innovations include the rejection of employer-employee relationships in favor of member-ownership principles[86] and the distribution of power to governing bodies representing worker, manager, and owner interests.[87]

The significance of these developments is twofold. First, U.S. ESOPs have established pluralist models of ownership where the legitimacy of worker ownership (either individually, collectively, or a mix) is accepted alongside third-party investments. Second, the cooperative movement has begun a shift toward ownership models that recognize suppliers, consumers, and workers as "strategic stakeholders," coordinated through pluralist forms of corporate control that contribute to member solidarity.[88] All these examples fit Westall's[89] characterization of social enterprise as multiple owner/multistakeholder businesses operating without the philanthropic funding (or labor) of voluntary organizations or funding by private capital markets.

Major[90] has researched the problems faced by co-ops and ESOPs in the USA and contends that most suffer from "equity degeneration"—a situation in which one or more stakeholder is unable to realize the full value of their past efforts, risk-taking, investments, and decisions. To overcome this, organizations typically have to sell equity on the open market to obtain full value for employee-shareholders. Baxi Investments, however, deploys an approach based on a using a profitable track record to secure loans that purchase the shares of the largest shareholders and place them in an employee benefit trust.[91] Subsequent annual surpluses initially service the loan, but once paid they are used to buy shares and allocate them to individual worker accounts.

In some cases (notably, Scott Bader), a charitable rather than employee benefit trust owns the trading company. Staff bonuses match payments into the charitable trust to fund social projects.[92] By providing 50 percent (+1) of shares with control rights remaining in trust, and having an embedded mechanism for issuing new shares to individual member accounts, a profitable company can create an internal share market that enables employees to access their wealth if needed, while also preventing reliance on outside investors. Important to this approach is education on social ownership and the introduction of Mondragon-type democratic controls to prevent a management takeover.[93] Mikel Lezamiz (see the "In Practice" box in the previous section) contends that it can take between five and ten years for a workforce to develop readiness to take over ownership and control of their enterprise (i.e., embed cooperative management into an organization, and then convert to a cooperative legal form). Interestingly, he distinguishes four steps:

1. Employee ownership (financial participation)

2. Participative management (the introduction of soft HRM practices)

3. Cooperative management (putting in place elected governing and social councils to oversee executive management proposals)

4. Cooperative ownership (establishing a cooperative legal entity)

It is not only the workforce, however, that can take years to make adjustments in their mode of thought. The educational implications for business support staff, academics, accountants, trade unionists, bankers, funders, and lawyers are equally substantive. Current course curricula and assessment strategies for professions reinforce dominant approaches to accounting, management, learning, and decision making.[94] To support worker (and community) ownership, business education needs its own paradigm shift to provide effective support for social economy development.[95]

Figure 7.9 shows the laws passed in Europe between 1991 and 2006. In some countries, there is a choice between cooperative (social economy) and company (more-than-profit) enterprise forms, while in others the legislative framework is less well developed. As Galera and Borzaga[96] argue, there has been a temporary trend between 2006 and 2009 to advance "social purpose" company legislation rather than "social economy" mutuals. This is mirrored in the United States where legislation for "low-profit" limited liability companies (L3Cs) has been introduced. This trend, however, is not stemming the rising interest in employee ownership and mutual ownership.[97] Responsible managers, therefore, first need to be able to distinguish between mutual, charitable, and nonprofit organizations. If seeking to develop the social economy, there is a choice between social enterprise forms based on company law (primarily designed for Type C "more-than-profit" entrepreneurship) and cooperative and mutual legislation (for Type D "social economy" entrepreneurship). The guide to action in Table 7.5 examines the changes needed at each step on each path.

## Figure 7.9 Laws Passed in Europe to Support Social Enterprise Development

1991 – Italy   November 8 – Social Co-operative Law
1993 – Spain   Social Initiative Co-operative (regional laws started to be introduced in twelve regions)
1995 – Belgium   April 13 – Social Finality Enterprise Law
1996 – Portugal   September 7 – Social Solidarity Co-operative Code
1998 – Portugal   January 15 – Social Solidarity Co-operative – Legislative Decree
1999 – Spain   Social Initiative Co-operative – National Law
2001 – France   July 17 – Collective Interest Cooperative Society (SCIC)
2004 – Finland   Social Enterprise Law
2004 – United Kingdom   Community Interest Company (CIC)
2005 – Italy   June 13 – Social Enterprise Law
2006 – Italy   March 24 – Social Enterprise Law Decree
2006 – Poland   June 5 – Social Cooperative Law

Source: CECOP. (2006, November 9). Social enterprises and worker cooperatives: Comparing models of corporate governance and social inclusion. Paper to CECOP European Seminar, Manchester.

**Table 7.5** Steps to Achieve Socioentrepreneurial Outcomes in the Private Sector

| Trajectory | Skills Developments | Legal Form Awareness |
|---|---|---|
| TYPE B ("Corporate Social Responsibility") | • Lobby for an enabling legislative environment for corporate social responsibility and philanthropy<br>• Develop knowledge of the legislative framework for creating and operating foundations, charities, trusts, and public-private partnerships<br>• Upgrade knowledge base to develop social accounting skills (particularly, SROI)<br>• Ensure executive education including nonprofit/low-profit management | • Charitable Foundation<br>• Nonprofit/Low-Profit Corporation<br>• Charitable/Nonprofit Company |
| TYPE C ("More-than-Profit") | • Lobby for an enabling environment conducive to social enterprise development<br>• Acquire country-specific knowledge of social enterprise and social cooperative laws affecting joint/new venture creation<br>• Identify differences in the performance criteria of financial and social investors<br>• Develop an investment readiness program to manage social investor expectations | • Community Enterprise (with Private Membership)<br>• Social Purpose Company (with Private Membership)<br>• Social Enterprise Law (varies from country to country)<br>• Social Firms (with Private Membership) |
| TYPE D ("Social Economy") | • Lobby for an enabling environment conducive to social economy principles<br>• Design communications to raise awareness of the possible exit route into the social economy for small business owners<br>• Design communications to raise awareness of social economy principles among employees, customers, and service users<br>• Develop the debating forums and voting systems needed to build workplace democracy<br>• Develop a transition strategy based on employee ownership, participatory management, cooperative governance, and ownership<br>• Develop social accounting skills (particularly social audit) to support multistakeholder governance | • Credit Union/Mutual Society<br>• Employee-Owned Business/Employee Mutuals<br>• Cooperative Society<br>• Community Enterprise (with Open Membership)<br>• Social Purpose Company (with Open Membership)<br>• Social Firm (with Open Membership) |

## 7-4c Scenario 3: From Public Service to Social Entrepreneurship

### Understanding Your Own Perspective

This section examines the development of social entrepreneurial thinking in the **public sector**. Chandler[98] maintains that this represents an ideological shift toward new-right thinking in the management of social services and the marketization of public goods. This initially manifested itself in programs to privatize state-owned utility companies but, more recently, has been theorized as a number of "doctrines" associated with **new public management (NPM)**. These marketization doctrines replace collaborative approaches based on professional judgment with target-driven approaches based on managerial control. Hood[99] set out the operational and accounting implications (see Table 7.6).

The "right to request" and "right to provide" legislation in the UK health sector and local authorities illustrates how the practices associated with NPM continue to influence public sector reform, and are also linked to public sector social entrepreneurship that relies less on reciprocity among professional groups, and more on market relations between managers and employees. The National Health Service in the UK has been divided into commissioning and provider bodies to create a quasi-market system, with clinical commissioning groups controlling spending and an array of new organizations providing services. This has been encouraged through a "right to request" policy that allows staff to externalize existing services into discrete social enterprises.[100] However, this policy has two faces: marketization occurs through *privatizations* based on a market ideology and *localization* fostered through community ownership or community benefit regulations. Interestingly, Hood spots this divergence between private and social-democratic reactions to change in NPM itself, in that social enterprise might be deployed to *limit* the influence of private enterprise:

> *it might be argued that NPM has been adopted in some contexts to ward off the New Right agenda for privatisation … and in other countries as the first step towards realizing that agenda. Much of NPM is built on the idea (or ideology) of homeostatic control; that is, the clarification of goals and missions in advance, and then building the accountability systems in relation to those pre-set goals….*[101]

This being the case, social entrepreneurship in the public sector is affected by both manager and professional inclinations to privatize or socialize the services they contribute, and also whether such provisions should be on a nonprofit or profit-making basis (see Figure 7.10). Where the shift is toward nonprofit provision under private control, NHS practitioners will opt for charitable/nonprofit corporations, or voluntary associations that maintain management control over provision (Type A, Nonprofit). However, if there is a preference for socialized (rather than management) control, the shift will be toward member-ownership models that promote reciprocity and collaboration between consumer and producer members (Type D, Social Economy). Lastly, where managers and clinicians are persuaded by the logic of market relations, the shift is likely to be toward public-private partnerships, or tendering processes to select providers (Type B, CSR). Whatever the future holds, it will be influenced by the conditions under which the externalization of

The **public sector** consists of organizations providing goods and services for governments or their citizens, based on the redistribution principle.

**New public management (NPM)** aims to modernize public administration to make it more efficient.

| Figure 7.10 **From Public Service to Social Entrepreneurship** |

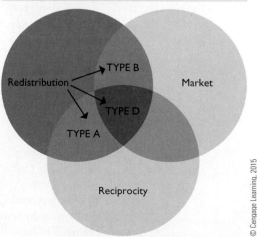

© Cengage Learning, 2015

**Table 7.6** The Seven Doctrines of "New Public Management"

| No. | Doctrine | Justification | Replaces | Operational Implications | Accounting Implications |
|---|---|---|---|---|---|
| **Public Sector Distinctiveness** | | | | | |
| 1. | Transformation of public sector bodies into corporatized units organized to deliver discrete products and services | Makes units manageable; focuses blame for failure; splits commissioning and production to reduce waste | Belief in uniform, inclusive public sector; belief in collaborative approaches to public service provision | Erosion of single service employment; arms-length management to separate commissioning and provision of services; devolved budgeting | More cost centers; move to activity-based costing (ABC) |
| 2. | More contract-based, competitive tendering; internal markets and fixed-term contracts | Competition lowers costs and improves standards; contracts enable setting of performance standards | Unspecified employment contracts, open-ended provision agreements; linking purchase, provision, and production to achieve efficiencies throughout the supply chain | Distinction of primary and secondary public sector labor force (through separation of commissioners and providers) | Stress on identification of costs and cost structures; providers treat cost data as commercially confidential; cooperative behavior discouraged |
| 3. | Emphasis on private sector styles of management | Private sector management tools are "proven" to be efficient and need application in the public sector | Stress on public service ethics, fixed pay and hiring rules, acting as a model employer, and centrally determined personnel structure; job for life | Move away from public sector pay, career service, nonmonetary rewards, and "due process" in employee entitlements | Private sector accounting norms |
| 4. | More stress on discipline and frugality in use of resources | Need to cut direct costs, raise labor discipline, do more with less | Stable base budgets and financial norms; minimum standards; union voice/veto | Less primary employment; less job security; less producer-friendly working practices | More stress on bottom line and on cost benefits |
| **Rules versus Discretion** | | | | | |
| 5. | More emphasis on visible, hands-on top management | Accountability requires clear assignment of responsibility, not diffusion of power | Paramount stress on policy skills and rules, not active management | More freedom to manage by discretionary power | Fewer constraints on handling cash, contracts, and staff; more financial data for management accountability |
| 6. | Formal standards and measures of performance and success | Accountability to include clearly stated aims; efficiency based on "hard" outcome goals | Qualitative standards and implicit norms | Erosion of self-management by professionals | Performance indicators and audit culture |
| 7. | Emphasis on output controls | Greater stress on results | Collaborative procedures and control processes | Resources and pay based on performance | Move to broad cost center accounting and blurring of staff and activity costs |

Source: Adapted from: Hood, C. (1995). The new public management in the 1980s: Variations of a theme. *Accounting, Organisation and Society, 20*, 93–109, p. 96.

services takes place, and the power of clinicians and health managers to determine the criteria that influence the commissioning process.

## Challenges and Opportunities in Transforming Public Service
Concern that nonprofits and social enterprises are being sucked into a "contracting culture" is based on analyses of a deep shift in management thought.[102] Contracts typically embed new forms of management control and governance that are

considerably less "empowering" than the rhetoric accompanying them.[103] The increased formalization (visioning, mission statements, audit), and the outcome-driven character of measurement (targets, service level agreements, competition), represent a cultural shift in the direction of a legal-rational society based on market logic. Hebson and colleagues[104] found that introducing contracting as a replacement for bureaucracy decreases the opportunity for collaborative decision making and undermines systems of reciprocity and redistribution that guided the creation of welfare services. Transparency decreases and the use of legal remedies increases as service commissioners adjust to their monitoring function and use their power to adjust rewards (i.e., pay) in line with service level agreements.

The practices of NPM, therefore, tend to advance the interests of entrepreneurial and management classes, and erode the influence of professionals seeking to maintain collective management practices guided by social need. NPM invites a new breed of entrepreneurial professional or, failing this, a new layer of managers to supervise professional practice, equipped with a range of hard and soft HRM techniques to instill "discipline" that "drives up standards." Its advocates portray it as progressive because:

> the state is recast in the role of enabler rather than provider [where] government is moving away from those standardized, mass production, models of service delivery which arose in the 1900–1940 period towards a new form of entrepreneurial government which is more concerned to use public resources in new ways to maximize productivity and effectiveness. This echoes many of the arguments for greater organizational flexibility, adaptability, and customer orientation to be found in the private sector "excellence" literature.[105]

## In Practice

### Ventures for Public Benefit

The contemporary expression of NPM in the form of social enterprise can be found in the National Health Service (NHS) of the UK. The "right to request" allows any health professional to put forward a business case for a social enterprise. The presentation of social enterprise to health professionals states that it is "fundamentally about business approaches to achieving public benefit." The focus on innovation and reorganization into business units providing discrete services with outcome-driven management are evident in the Chief Health Professions Officer's statement:

> Social enterprise will not be the answer for everyone, but allied health professionals have a long history of providing innovative services in a variety of sectors, settings and throughout care pathways and patient journeys. Consequently, allied health professionals are in an excellent position to take advantage of the "right to request." This may be for a particular profession, such as podiatry or physiotherapy, a specialism such as musculoskeletal physiotherapy, a particular care group, or a combination of these. What is most important though is that this is about developing a service that will meet local need and maximise your potential to innovate and ultimately improve outcomes for patients, clients and families, whilst remaining part of the NHS family.

Source: National Health Service. (2008). *Social enterprise—Making a difference: A guide to the right to request* (pp. 3, 6). London: Department of Health.

In contrast to the situation at Eaga PLC where socialized ownership and control reverted to private control after capture by an executive group, Restakis[106] writes extensively about collaborative arrangements in the north of Italy based on the principles of mutuality and reciprocity. In his analysis of the public sector, he states that:

> Social care is being commoditized. The desocializing dynamics of the industrial revolution that were, at least in theory, contained within the market economy have now reached deep into the public systems that were once the preserve of the state. The colonization of the public domain by commercial interests in the late 20th century is in some ways analogous to the enclosure of the commons in the 18th century.[107]

In this context, Restakis discusses how members of the social economy have reacted to this situation in Emilia Romagna. He puts forward a thesis that in situations where public authorities are knowledgeable about the social economy, the values of civil society (and Pearce's third system) can drive the process of public sector reform. Following political campaigns toward the end of the 1970s, the municipality of Bologna granted a contract to a worker cooperative to provide social care. The system grew throughout the 1980s, and by 1991 the model had become sufficiently well established to trigger legislation for social cooperatives.[108] Restakis details the longer-term impacts:

> The model spread, transmitted by the innumerable networks of the region's co-operative organizations, professional associations and parent groups, finding ready ground in the continuing dysfunction of state programmes and government cutbacks.... Today, social co-ops are a central aspect of Italy's social services system. In the city of Bologna, 87 percent of the city's social services are provided through municipal contracts with social co-ops.[109]

Restakis states that careers and patients acquire a stronger voice in social cooperatives, and can influence investment in new services through their own capital contributions. The operation by social cooperatives of a "solidarity model" with both worker and consumer owners is part of a broader movement to embed multi-stakeholder principles in social enterprise design.[110] As Hertz notes, Anglo-American economies are lagging behind the rest of the world in this respect. In fast-growing BRIC countries (Brazil, Russia, India, China), nearly four times more people are buying shares in cooperatives compared to private companies.[111]

Responsible managers in the public sector, therefore, can choose between non-profit social entrepreneurship (Type A) through partnerships with charities and voluntary organizations, CSR initiatives through private-public sector partnerships and endowed foundations (Type B), or social economy development by associations, mutual, and social cooperatives that deliver public services (Type D). See Table 7.7 for a summary of the steps to socioentrepreneurial outcomes in the public sector.

**Table 7.7** Steps to Achieve Socioentrepreneurial Outcomes in the Public Sector

| Trajectory | Skills Developments | Legal Form Awareness |
|---|---|---|
| TYPE A ("Nonprofit") | • Lobby politicians to ensure that public procurement guidelines recognize the value created by nonprofit social enterprises<br>• Organize government contracting to ensure there is no discrimination against charitable companies, foundations, and trusts<br>• Endow charitable foundations to advance areas of public policy<br>• Develop and deploy social accounting skills to assess social returns on investment (e.g., Social Auditing/SROI)<br>• Fund joint ventures with third sector/nonprofit providers<br>• Support executive education in nonprofit/low-profit management | • Charitable Foundations<br>• UK Charities / U.S. Nonprofits/NGOs<br>• Voluntary Associations<br>• Companies Limited by Guarantee (Private Membership) |
| TYPE B ("Corporate Social Responsibility") | • Create a legal framework for the operation of joint ventures with foundations, charities, and public-private partnerships<br>• Allow charitable companies and foundations to manage public funds where public policy and charitable objects are aligned<br>• Develop and support a social accounting/social auditing profession (e.g., SROI)<br>• Support executive education through secondments to CSR projects | • Charitable Foundations<br>• Nonprofit/Low-Profit Corporations<br>• Social Purpose Companies (Private Membership)<br>• Social Businesses/Firms (Private Membership) |
| TYPE D ("Social Economy") | • Design communications to raise awareness of social economy principles amongst council officers and politicians<br>• Design communications to raise awareness of social economy principles among users of public services<br>• Develop debating forums and voting system to facilitate participatory democracy and social economy development<br>• Adapt management practices to emphasize trust and reciprocity when working with mutuals and/or cooperatives<br>• Develop social auditing and accounting skills that facilitate participation by local people in service developments | • Credit Unions/Mutual Societies<br>• Community Benefit Societies/Social Cooperatives<br>• Cooperative Societies<br>• Employee-Owned Companies/ Employee Benefit Trusts/Employee Share Plans<br>• Community/Social Businesses (with Open Membership)<br>• Social Purpose Companies (with Open Membership)<br>• Social Firms (with Open Membership) |

© Cengage Learning, 2015

## PRINCIPLES OF ENTREPRENEURSHIP: VALUE-ADDED VENTURES

I. *Social entrepreneurship* describes the discovery and sustainable exploitation of opportunities to create social and environmental benefits.

II. The *goal* of the social entrepreneurship process is to create a value-added venture that at the same time "socializes" the organization to the inside and creates social value systemically to the outside.

III. The *market* is only one type of economic system. There are alternatives.

IV. The *nonprofit model* of social entrepreneurship emphasizes reciprocity and redistribution facilitated by voluntary and political action.

V. The *corporate social responsibility model* of social entrepreneurship emphasizes redistribution through new types of market exchange.

VI. The *more-than-profit model* of social entrepreneurship emphasizes market exchanges that encourage reciprocity.

VII. The *social economy model* of social entrepreneurship emphasizes the hybridization of reciprocity, redistribution, and market exchange to maximize human well-being.

| | Social Entrepreneurial Assumptions | Responsible Management |
|---|---|---|
| Type A | *Nonprofit Model—emphasis on reciprocity and redistribution facilitated by voluntary and political action;* in the boundary areas of the public and third sectors; shares a "public interest" outlook and hostility to market logic based on private ownership and equity finance | Social entrepreneurship as the creation of nonprofit organizations that pursue social objectives using grants, donations, and contracts with public sector bodies; structured to prevent profit and asset transfers to the private sector |
| Type B | *Corporate Social Responsibility Model—emphasis on redistribution through new types of market exchange;* in the overlap between public and private sectors; often dismissive of voluntary sector approaches to economic development | Social entrepreneurship as corporate social responsibility; support for fair trade; social firms and social businesses in private ownership; public-private partnerships |
| Type C | *More-than-Profit Model—emphasis on market exchanges that encourage reciprocity;* in the boundary areas of private and third sectors; skeptical of government interventions that prevent reciprocity and market exchange; conscious of state's role in oppressing minorities and opposition interests | Social entrepreneurship as the creation of "more-than-profit" social firms and businesses, private third sector partnerships; philanthropy through primary purpose trading; societies and associations that reinvest profits in social objectives and share benefits with members |
| Type D (ideal) | *Social Economy Model—emphasis on the hybridization of reciprocity, redistribution, and market exchange to maximize human well-being;* replaces a competitive public, private, and third sector model with multistakeholder cooperatives and mutuals; democratic governance; social auditing to support participative management; solidarity among primary stakeholders | Social entrepreneurship as the creation of multistakeholder enterprises: solidarity cooperatives, associations of charities, networks of voluntary associations, clusters of co-owned businesses, and fair trade networks; democratic control over the distribution of social and economic benefits |

| | | Sustainability | Responsibility | Ethics |
|---|---|---|---|---|
| **Goal: The Value-Added Venture** | Will the venture... | ...improve the triple bottom line? | ...lead to an optimized stakeholder value creation? | ...lead to moral excellence? |
| **Phase 1: Understanding Social Entrepreneurship and Social Innovation** | Does your understanding of social entrepreneurship and social innovation... | ...consider the role of the triple bottom line? | ...consider the role of stakeholder value? | ...consider the role of moral dilemmas? |
| **Phase 2: Envision Your Pathway** | Does the envisioned pathway of your venture... | ...create a positive triple bottom line in the process? | ...create optimum stakeholder value in the process? | ...involve means to best solve potential moral dilemmas and create moral excellence? |

## KEY TERMS

*hybridization 195*
*new public management (NPM) 207*
*private sector 201*
*public sector 207*

*social entrepreneurship 189*
*social innovation 189*
*socialized ownership and control 190*
*social mission 190*

*third sector 198*
*value-added venture 189*
*value proposition 190*

## A. Remember and Understand

A.1. Define social entrepreneurship. What is the difference between social and mainstream entrepreneurship?

A.2. Mention the three perspectives of social entrepreneurship and explain each briefly. Must a social enterprise always have elements of all three perspectives?

A.3. Which three economic models were mentioned in the chapter? Give one example of each.

A.4. Explain each of the following terms in writing or by developing an illustration of it.
- Nonprofit model
- Corporate social responsibility
- More-than-profit model
- Social economy

## B. Apply and Experience

B.5. Conduct Internet research to find examples in your country of the following organization types: nonprofit model, corporate social responsibility, more-than-profit model, social economy. Explain for each example why you think the respective model applies to it.

B.6. Conduct Internet research on quantifiable data about social entrepreneurship in your country ("Social Entrepreneurship in …"). Write a one-page research report, citing the most important facts and figures.

## C. Analyze and Evaluate

C.7. Look up the GRI (sustainability or responsibility) reports of several multinational companies. Based on that information, determine where the company is located in the model represented by Figure 7.5.

C.8. Look up information on the business model of the organization OXFAM. Analyze the organization using the three perspectives on social entrepreneurship.

C.9. Polanyi states that market economies are a recent phenomenon. Discuss what type of economic system and coordination might be prevalent in the future.

## D. Change and Create

D.10. Conduct research about a real organization and classify it as a third sector, private, or public sector organization. Develop a social entrepreneurship plan for the organization, based on the recommendations of this chapter. Summarize your plan and send it to the organization.

## PIONEER INTERVIEW WITH MARK KRAMER

Courtesy of Mark Kramer

Mark Kramer is founder and managing director of FSG, a consultancy that works with foundations, corporations, and nonprofits alike. He has been a driver of social innovation and the sector-integrating perspective of organizations.

**Your background is in the not-for-profit and philanthropic sector. You largely collaborated with Michael Porter who has been called the most influential (mainstream) business thinker. How similar are for-profit and not-for-profit organizations in their management activities? What can for-profits learn from not-for-profits, and vice versa?**

First, my background actually does include work with foundations and nonprofits, but I also spend about fifteen years doing investment capital. I think of myself as having a combination of business and nonprofit background. But I think there are key differences between for-profit and not-for-profit organizations, and I identify two of them in particular.

The first is around *the way that social change happens versus the success of a business.* For me to profit from the success of a business, I have to focus on the financial dimension.

In the case of the social sector, ideas can influence change whether or not I can fund them. Muhammad Yunus might have created the idea behind microfinance, but there are now literally billions of dollars of microfinance operating around the world that Muhammad Yunus has had nothing to do with. And the impact? In terms of the social impact, it is just as great. So, the first difference is, you have an organization and think about how to spread the idea and influence others.

The second dimension is about *control*. I would say we used to have a strong degree of control in business over the people who matter to our performance. So, we control our employees; we control our suppliers; we control the relationship with our distributors.

The people we want to influence around social issues are often people over whom we have no control. They are maybe other business enterprises; they are maybe government officials; they are maybe citizens who want to exercise, or to eat in a more healthy way. But whatever the issue we are trying to address, we do not actually have control over the people who make the difference on the issue. And therefore what we have to do to succeed in our mission is significantly different from what we have to do as a for-profit company.

There is one other difference that I will point to, which is the difference around *goals and measuring progress*. In the for-profit sector, the goal, pretty clearly, is to make money. It becomes very easy to make choices and decisions, because you can look back to which one is more likely to make more money and make that choice. But in the nonprofit sector, setting your goal is a real challenge. Do you care about nuclear proliferation? Do you care about child obesity? Do you care about the symphony orchestra, or do you care about undernourished children in China or India? The choice, our goal, is really influenced by personal preferences. We come up with different goals and those different goals are often not tangible.

I can look at different investments, and as long as they have the same investment return, I am pretty neutral between them. But when I look at different social investments, one of them may reduce carbon emissions while the other provides micronutrients to undernourished children and a third one improves the quality of my local symphony. There is no way to compare these results. Measurements tend to be unique to each social issue. And the goal depends on the personal values of the participants rather than some objective measure.

These are the key differences between operating a for-profit and a nonprofit sector organization. On the other hand, basic issues—such as strategy, understanding the context in which you are operating, building on strengths, and finding a positioning where your particular combination of skills and resources and expertise is going to be most impactful; building on that particular positioning, trying to be the best in the world at what you do, and really drawing on data and research and facts to make your decisions rather than just going with your gut—*t*hese things are critical for both profits and not-for-profits.

---

Courtesy of Doru Mitrana

**Employment:** Environmental and social activist running Mai-MultVerde (MuchMoreGreen), the NGO he co-founded in 2008 to achieve environmental and social impact by developing educational, advocacy, entrepreneurship, and volunteering projects, programs, and campaigns in Romania.

**Job title:** Managing Director

**Education:** M.A. in Responsible Management, Steinbeis University Berlin, 2012; Dipl.ecc, Diploma in Marketing and Economics, Academy of Economic Studies, Bucharest, 1998

**In Practice**

**What are your responsibilities?** I am in charge of:
—Coordinating the overall activity of the organization in line with the status, values, aim, and objectives
—Working with the management team to set the yearly strategy and objectives and working over the year to accomplish them
—Representing the organization in relation to public authorities, companies, board members, or fellow organizations
—The fundraising function of the organization

**What are typical activities you carry out during a day at work?**

The daily routine includes tasks in the areas of:
—Financial management: approving payments, checking financial and fiscal reports, forecasts, etc.
—HR management: status meeting with all staff or specific departments or projects team but also counseling and discussions, planning and evaluating, and interviewing when necessary
—Fundraising: setting up meetings, and exchanging e-mails or telephone calls with representatives of active and potential funding organizations, private or public

—Project management: keeping a close relationship with the project managers, for a close eye on the project status

—Communication: articles, interviews, press conferences, online/social media reactions; keeping permanent contact to all relevant stakeholders and continuously acting as liaison between the inner and outer part of the organization

## How do sustainability, responsibility, and ethics topics play a role in your job?

MaiMultVerde promotes corporate but also general responsibility toward the society and the environment. The success of the organization, or even its very existence, depends on the way we walk our talk. Being credible for companies, environmental activists, public authorities, and general public at the same time is only possible when the organization is the first to adopt and apply the changes it promotes.

MaiMultVerde promotes sustainability by proposing sustainable projects and advocates for responsibility and ethics in corporations and politics by being the first to act responsibly. Being continuously in the public eye is a great asset for the organization but can also be lethal if the credibility would be challenged.

The values of the association are continuously and strongly pressed by the financial, fiscal, political, and social environment, but at the same time are well defended by the "participatory democracy" adopted for decision making. Having all members of the core team and extended team active in the decisional process makes it easier for the organization and for me to keep on the right track.

## Out of the topics covered in the chapter into which your interview will be included, which concepts, tools, or topics are most relevant to your work?

The explanation and graphics on the four types of socioentrepreneurial development, as MaiMultVerde's projects are placed exactly between public, private, and nonprofit sectors, "borrowing" characteristics from all three. Having a rigorous explanation for this position is useful for any argumentation of where we are and what we stand for.

### Insights and Challenges

## What recommendation can you give to practitioners in your field?

Social entrepreneurship has a very strong personal motivation. Starting a social-value-adding venture must be preceded by an introspective analysis of the entrepreneurs and their true motives, aspirations, and beliefs. Walking the talk, staying in the public eye with the head up high, and allowing public scrutiny and input in the decisional process are key elements for success in this sector.

## Which are the main challenges of your job?

—Resisting the "temptations" of other sectors, like a nine-to-five, cosy, well-paid job with no extra worries in the public or private sector

—Having a lot of patience in waiting for the true social and environmental results to show up

—Having to convince everyone, every day, that the way you are promoting is the right way, that you are not just an extravagant, exotic being but you actually understand the world around you and choose to be different because different is what we need to be

## SPECIAL PERSPECTIVE: SUSTAINABLE INNOVATION PRIMER

Innovation involves turning an idea or invention into a good or service that improves on existing alternatives. It can be evolutionary or revolutionary in its impact, depending on the extent to which it brings incremental improvements or provides something novel that greatly modifies some aspect of how people live and work. Innovation is generally perceived as something to be encouraged, but it can bring unforeseen impacts, some of which may be recognized only when the consequences become significant. Simply improving on existing alternatives may not resolve all the negative outcomes of what existed before.

Sustainable innovation is driven by the search for products and services that eradicate or at least minimize the defects associated with existing offerings and solutions and that enable society to function with improved outcomes for the physical, social, and economic environment.[112] The environmental dimension of sustainable innovation is associated with minimizing materials extraction and processing in manufacture and then, most importantly, in consumption and patterns of use of goods and services, including the elimination of waste. The social dimension is associated with the elimination of degrading and exploitative work and the spreading of opportunity for people to participate in society. Another measure of sustainable innovation is its impact in reducing the discrepancy between the environmental footprint of wealthy and poor nations. Sustainable innovation should bring the footprint of rich countries closer to a level that all of the world's population could share.

Understanding the life cycle impacts of goods and services is a tool that helps to identify opportunities for sustainable innovation. Life-cycle analysis seeks to identify the total impact of the activity associated with products and services. Focusing on the entire life cycle gives more scope for identifying opportunities for sustainable innovation, as securing substantial gains can compromise the position of organizations attached to one part of the cycle. At least four general opportunities for sustainable innovation have been identified.[113]

- *Redesign the product:* This may focus on ways of removing harmful substances, as in the way refrigeration was redesigned to eliminate the use of ozone-damaging chlorofluorocarbons (CFCs).

- *Reengineer the process:* By analyzing processes, ways often can be found to cut resources consumption and waste. In the manufacture of consumer products, developing common formu-las used across a range of products can reduce the need for flushing production lines to prevent cross-contamination of final products.

- *Create more but use less:* A "cradle-to-cradle" approach enables more goods and services to be produced while reducing resource pressures by maximizing the use of materials that can reused in another product or that provide productive nutrients when returned to nature.

- *Rethink the market:* There can be opportunities to shift from supplying products to selling services, as in the way that some carpet companies have moved from selling carpet to a service based on the leasing of carpet tiles that it guarantees to maintain to acceptable standard of presentation.

Example: Zip Car is among the companies that are redefining the market for private travel in Europe and North America. Through innovation in the administration of car renting, short-time and one-way car hire have been made economical options. Shared use of a single vehicle saves resources over individual ownership and encourages people to combine the use of public transport and bicycles with occasional vehicle use for their urban transport needs. See www.zipcar.com

## SOURCES

1. Kelley, D. J., Singer, S., & Herrington, M. (2012). *Global entrepreneurship monitor.* Boston: Global Entrepreneurship Research Association.

2. *The social business initiative of the European Commission.* (2011).

3. Social Enterprise UK. (2011). *Fightback Britain: A report on the state of social enterprise survey 2011.* London: Social Enterprise UK.

4. Arizmendiarrieta, J. M. (n.d.). Historic background, Mondragon Corporation. Retrieved November 7, 2012, from Mondragon Corporation—International Business Group: www .mondragon-corporation.com /ENG/Co-operativism/ Co-operative-Experience/Historic-Background.aspx

5. Brouard, F., & Larivet, S. (2010). Essay of clarifications and definitions of the related concepts of social enterprise, social entrepreneur and social entrepreneurship. In A.

Fayolle & H. Matlay, *Handbook of research on social entrepreneurship* (pp. 29–56). Cheltenham: Edward Elgar.

6. Haugh, H. (2007). Community-Led Social Venture Creation. *Entrepreneurship Theory and Practice,* 31(2), 161–182.

7. Hockerts, K. (2010). Social entrepreneurship. In W. Visser, et al., *The A–Z of corporate social responsibility,* 2nd ed. Chichester: Wiley.

8. Perrini, F. (2006). *The new social entrepreneurship: What awaits social entrepreneurial ventures?* Northampton, MA: Edward Elgar.

9. Ellerman, D. (1982). *The socialization of entrepreneurship: The empresarial division of the Caja Laboral Popular.* Somerville, MA: Industrial Co-operative Association.

10. Bradley, K., & Gelb, A. (1980). Motivation and control in the Mondragon experiment. *British Journal of Industrial Relations,* 19(2),

211–231; Thomas, H., & Logan, C. (1982). *Mondragon: An economic analysis.* New York: Harper Collins.

11. Ellerman, D. (1982). *The socialization of entrepreneurship: The empresarial division of the Caja Laboral Popular* (p. 8). Somerville, MA: Industrial Co-operative Association.

12. Turnbull, S. (1994). Stakeholder democracy: Redesigning the governance of firms and bureaucracies. *Journal of Socio-Economics, 23*(3), 321–360, p. 321.

13. Erdal, D. (2011). *Beyond the corporation: Humanity working.* London: Bodley Head.

14. Nicholls, A. (2006). *Social entrepreneurship: New paradigms of sustainable social change.* Oxford: Oxford University Press; Martin, R. L., & Osberg, S. (2007, Spring). Social entrepreneurship: The case for definition. *Stanford Social Innovation Review,* 29–39.

15. Whyte, W., & Whyte, K. (1991). *Making Mondragon.* New York: ILR Press/Ithaca.

16. Borzaga, C., & Defourny, J. (2001). *The emergence of social enterprise.* London: Routledge; Defourny, J. (2010). Concepts and realities of social enterprise: A European perspective. In A. Fayolle & H. Matlay, *Handbook of research on social entrepreneurship* (pp. 57–87). Northampton, MA: Edward Elgar.

17. Turnbull, S. (2002). *A new way to govern.* London: New Economics Foundation; Forcadell, F. (2005). Democracy, cooperation and business success: The case of Mondragón Corporación Cooperativa. *Journal of Business Ethics, 56*(3), 255–274.

18. Ridley-Duff, R. J., & Southcombe, C. (2012). The social enterprise mark: A critical review of its conceptual dimensions. *Social Enterprise Journal, 8*(3), 178–200.

19. Dees, G. (1998, January–February). Enterprising non-profits. *Harvard Business Review, 54–67*; Hudson, M. (2002). *Managing without profit.* London: Penguin; Martin, R. L., & Osberg, S. (2007, Spring). Social entrepreneurship: The case for definition. *Stanford Social Innovation Review, 29–39*; Scofield, R. (2011). *The social entrepreneur's handbook.* New York: McGraw-Hill.

20. Chell, E. (2007). Social enterprise and entrepreneurship: Towards a convergent theory of the entrepreneurial process. *International Small Business Journal, 25*(1), 5–26; Galera, G., & Borzaga, C. (2009). Social enterprise: An international overview of its conceptual evolution and legal implementation. *Social Enterprise Journal, 5*(3), 210–228.

21. Restakis, J. (2010). *Humanizing the economy: Co-operatives in the age of capital.* Gabriola Island: New Society Publishers; Arthur, L., et al. (2003). Developing an operational definition of the social economy. *Journal of Co-operative Studies, 36*(3), 163–189.

22. Low, C. (2006). A framework for the governance of social enterprise. *International Journal of Social Economics, 33*(5), 376–385; Ridley-Duff, R. J., & Southcombe, C. (2012). The social enterprise mark: A critical review of its conceptual dimensions. *Social Enterprise Journal, 8*(3), 178–200.

23. Ridley-Duff, R. J., & Bull, M. (2011). *Understanding social enterprise: Theory and practice.* London: Sage.

24. Kerlin, J. (2006). Social enterprise in the United States and Europe: Understanding and learning from the differences. *Voluntas, 17*(3), 246–262; Kerlin, J. (2010). *Social enterprise: An international comparison.* Medford: Tuffs University Press.

25. Smith, A. (1937/1776). *An inquiry into the nature and cause of the wealth of nations.* New York: Modern Library.

26. Marx, K. (1887). *Capital, Vol. 1.* Moscow: Progress Publishers; Polanyi, K. (2001/1944). *The great transformation.* Boston: Beacon Press.

27. Kerlin, J. (2010). *Social enterprise: An international comparison.* Medford: Tuffs University Press; Ridley-Duff, R. J., & Southcombe, C. (2012). The social enterprise mark: A critical review of its conceptual dimensions. *Social Enterprise Journal, 8*(3), 178–200.

28. Nicholls, A. (2010). The institutionalization of social investment: The interplay of investment logics and investor rationalities. *Journal of Social Entrepreneurship, 1*(1), 70–100.

29. Nyssens, M. (2006). *Social enterprise and the crossroads of market, public and civil society.* London: Routledge; Restakis, J. (2010). *Humanizing the economy: Co-operatives in the age of capital.* Gabriola Island: New Society Publishers; Erdal, D. (2011). *Beyond the corporation: Humanity working.* London: Bodley Head.

30. Pearce, J. (2003). *Social enterprise in anytown.* London: Calouste Gulbenkian Foundation.

31. Bull, M. (2008). Challenging tensions: Critical, theoretical and empirical perspectives on social enterprise. *International Journal of Entrepreneurial Behaviour & Research, 14*(5), 268–275.

32. Restakis, J. (2010). *Humanizing the economy: Co-operatives in the age of capital.* Gabriola Island: New Society Publishers; Erdal, D. (2011). *Beyond the corporation: Humanity working.* London: Bodley Head.

33. Polanyi, K. (2001/1944). *The great transformation.* Boston: Beacon Press.

34. Nyssens, M. (2006). *Social enterprise and the crossroads of market, public and civil society.* London: Routledge; Bull, M. (2008). Challenging

tensions: Critical, theoretical and empirical perspectives on social enterprise. *International Journal of Entrepreneurial Behaviour & Research, 14*(5), 268–275.

35. Giddens, A. (1998). *The third way.* Cambridge: Polity.

36. Haugh, H., & Kitson, M. (2007). The third way and the third sector: New labour's economic policy and the social economy. *Cambridge Journal of Economics, 31*(6), 973–994.

37. Dickson, N. (1999, September 27). What is the third way? Retrieved September 15, 2008, from BBC: http://news.bbc.co.uk/1/hi/uk_politics/458626.stm

38. Monzon, J. L., & Chaves, R. (2008). The European social economy: Concepts and dimensions of the third sector. *Annals of Public and Co-operative Economics, 79*(3/4), 549–577, p. 557.

39. Defourny, J. (2001). From third sector to social enterprise. In C. Borzaga & J. Defourny, *The emergence of social enterprise* (pp. 1–28). London: Routledge.

40. Pearce, J. (2003). *Social enterprise in anytown.* London: Calouste Gulbenkian Foundation.

41. Leadbeater, C. (1997). *The rise of the social entrepreneur.* London: Demos; Westall, A. (2001). *Value-led, market-driven: Social enterprise solutions to public policy goals.* London: IPPR.

42. Westall, A. (2001). *Value-led, market-driven: Social enterprise solutions to public policy goals.* London: IPPR.

43. Nyssens, M. (2006). *Social enterprise and the crossroads of market, public and civil society.* London: Routledge.

44. Nyssens, M. (2006). *Social enterprise and the crossroads of market, public and civil society* (p. 318). London: Routledge.

45. Polanyi, K. (2001/1944). *The great transformation.* Boston: Beacon Press.

46. Gray, J. (1998). *False dawn: The delusions of global capitalism.* London: Granta.

47. Hawken, P. (2010). *The ecology of commerce: A declaration of sustainability.* New York: Harper Paperbacks.

48. Marx, K. (1887). *Capital, Vol. 1.* Moscow: Progress Publishers; Harvey, D. (2012). Reading *Capital.* Retrieved November 14, 2012, from *Reading Marx's Capital with David Harvey:* http://davidharvey.org/reading-capital

49. Ridley-Duff, R. (2008). Social enterprise as a socially rational business. *International Journal of Entrepreneurial Behaviour and Research, 14*(5), 292–312, p. 304.

50. Spear, R. (2006). Social entrepreneurship: A different model? *Journal of Socio-Economics, 33*(5/6), 399–410; Spear, R., Cornforth, C., & Aitken, M. (2007). *For love and money: Corporate governance and social enterprise.* Milton Keynes: Open University Press.

51. Spear, R., Cornforth, C., & Aiken, M. (2007). For love and money: Governance and socialenterprise (p. 7). Retrieved June 7, 2013, from: National Council for Voluntary Organisations, UK, http://oro.open.ac.uk/10328/1/For_Love_and_Money_Full_Report_-_Final.pdf

52. Bull, M. (2007). Balance: The development of a social enterprise business performance analysis tool. *Social Enterprise Journal, 3*(1), 49–66.

53. Kaplan, R. S., & Norton, D. P. (1992, January–February). The balanced scorecard: Measures that drive performance. *Harvard Business Review,* 71–79.

54. Bull, M., & Crompton, H. (2006). Business practices in social enterprise. *Social Enterprise Journal, 2*(1), 42–60.

55. Morgan, G. G. (2008). *The spirit of charity* [Professorial Lecture]. Sheffield Hallam University. Sheffield: Centre for Individual and Organisational Development, 2008.

56. Marrafino, J. (2012, April 1). How worker co-operatives work. Retrieved November 14, 2012, from YouTube: www.youtube.com/watch?v=qbZ8ojEuN5I

57. Ridley-Duff, R. J., & Bull, M. (2011). *Understanding social enterprise: Theory and practice.* London: Sage.

58. Beaubien, L. (2011). Co-operative accounting: Disclosing redemption contingencies for member shares. *Journal of Co-operative Studies, 44*(3), 38–44.

59. Bull, M., & Crompton, H. (2006). Business practices in social enterprise. *Social Enterprise Journal, 2*(1), 42–60.

60. Wei-Skillern, J., Austin, J., Leonard, H., & Stevenson, H. (2007). *Enterpreneurship in the social sector.* Thousand Oaks, CA: Sage.

61. Wei-Skillern, J., Austin, J., Leonard, H., & Stevenson, H. (2007). *Enterpreneurship in the social sector.* Thousand Oaks, CA: Sage.

62. Seanor, P., & Meaton, J. (2008). Learning from failure: Ambiguity and trust in social enterprise. *Social Enterprise Journal, 4*(1), 24–40.

63. Coule, T. (2007, September 5–6). *Developing strategies for sustainability: Implications for governance and accounting.* Coventry, UK: University of Warwick, NCVO/VSSN Researching the Voluntary Sector.

64. Emerson, J. (2003). The blended value proposition: Integrating social and financial returns. *California Management Review, 45*(4), 35.

65. Wei-Skillern, J., Austin, J., Leonard, H., & Stevenson, H. (2007). *Enterpreneurship in the social sector* (p. 138). Thousand Oaks, CA: Sage.

66. Bull, M., Crompton, H., & Jayawarna, D. (2008). Coming from the heart (The road is long). *Social Enterprise Journal, 4*(2), 108–125.

67. Marx, K. (1887). *Capital, Vol. 1.* Moscow: Progress Publishers.

68. Ellerman, D. (1990). *The democratic worker-owned firm: A new model for East and West.* Boston: Unwin Hyman; Gray, J. (1998). *False dawn: The delusions of global capitalism.* London: Granta.

69. Truss, C. (1999). Soft and hard models of human resource management. In L. Graton, V. Hope-Hailey, P. Stiles, & C. Truss, *Strategic human resource management: Corporate rhetoric and human reality* (pp. 40–58). Oxford: Oxford University Press.

70. Kalmi, P. (2007). The disappearance of co-operatives from economics textbooks. *Cambridge Journal of Economics, 31*(4), 625–647.

71. Wintour, P. (2012, October 8). George Osborne: Workers can swap rights for company shares. Retrieved November 19, 2012, from *The Guardian:*www.guardian.co.uk/politics/2012/oct/08/george-osborne-workers-rights-shares

72. Friedman, M. (1962). *Capitalism and freedom.* Chicago: University of Chicago; Calder, L. G. (1999). *Financing the American dream: A cultural history of consumer credit.* Princeton: Princeton University Press.

73. Miller, E., & Rice, A. (1967). *Systems of organization.* London: Tavistock.

74. Mondragon Corporation. (2012). *Corporate profile 2012.* Mondragon: Mondragon Corporation.

75. Co-operative Group. (2012). The co-operative—Here for you for life. Retrieved November 18, 2012, from The Co-operative: www.co-operative.coop/

76. Lyon, F., & Sepulveda, L. (2009). 2009. *Social Enterprise Journal, 5*(1), 83–94.

77. Morgan, G. G. (2008). *The spirit of charity* [Professorial Lecture]. Sheffield Hallam University. Sheffield: Centre for Individual and Organisational Development, 2008.

78. Ellerman, D. (1990). *The democratic worker-owned firm: A new model for East and West.* Boston: Unwin Hyman; Gates, J. (1998). *The ownership solution.* London: Penguin; Turnbull, S. (2002). *A new way to govern.* London: New Economics Foundation; Wilkinson, R., & Pickett, K. (2010). *The spirit level: Why equality is better for everyone.* London: Penguin; Kelly, M. (2012). *Owning our future: The emerging ownership revolution.* San Francisco: Berrett-Koehier.

79. Gates, J. (1998). *The ownership solution.* London: Penguin.

80. ESOC. (2000, June). About ESOPs in the United Kingdom. From Employee Share Ownership Centre: www.mhcc.co.uk/esop/esop/abesops.htm

81. Melman, S. (2001). *After capitalism: From managerialism to workplace democracy.* New York: Knopf.

82. NCEO. (2012, June). The employee ownership 100: America's largest majority employee-owned companies. Retrieved November 19, 2012, from National Center for Employee Ownership: www.nceo.org/articles/employee-ownership-100

83. Perotin, V., & Robinson, V. (2004). *Employee participation, firm performance and survival: Advances in the economic analysis of participatory and labor-management firms, Vol. 8.* Oxford: Elsevier.

84. Erdal, D. (2011). *Beyond the corporation: Humanity working.* London: Bodley Head; Restakis, J. (2010). *Humanizing the economy: Co-operatives in the age of capital.* Gabriola Island: New Society Publishers.

85. Erdal, D. (2000). The psychology of sharing: An evolutionary approach [Unpublished PhD Thesis]. Scotland: University of St Andrews; Wilkinson, R., & Pickett, K. (2010). *The spirit level: Why equality is better for everyone.* London: Penguin.

86. Ellerman, D. (1990). *The democratic worker-owned firm: A new model*

*for East and West.* Boston: Unwin Hyman.

87. Whyte, W., & Whyte, K. (1991). *Making Mondragon.* New York: ILR Press/Ithaca; Turnbull, S. (1995). Innovations in corporate governance: The Mondragon experience. *Corporate Governance: An International Review, 3*(3), 167–180; Turnbull, S. (2002). *A new way to govern.* London: New Economics Foundation.

88. Atherton, J., et al. (2012). *Practical tools for defining co-operative identity.* Manchester: Co-operatives UK; Birchall, J. (2012). A "member-owned business" approach to the classification of co-operatives and mutuals. In D. McDonnell & E. Macknight, *The co-operative model in the practice* (pp. 69–82). Glasgow: Co-operative Education Trust Scotland.

89. Westall, A. (2001). *Value-led, market-driven: Social enterprise solutions to public policy goals.* London: IPPR.

90. Major, G. (1996). Solving the underinvestment and degeneration problems of worker co-operatives. *Annals of Public and Co-operative Economics, 31*(2), 545–601; Major, G. (1998). The need for NOVARS (non-voting value added sharing renewable shares). *Journal of Co-operative Studies, 31*(2), 57–72.

91. Spear, R. (1999). Employee-owned bus companies. *Economic and Industrial Democracy, 20,* 253–268; Erdal, D. (2011). *Beyond the corporation: Humanity working.* London: Bodley Head.

92. Paton, R. (2003). *Managing and measuring social enterprises.* London: Sage.

93. Ridley-Duff, R. J. (2010). Communitarian governance in social enterprises: Case evidence from the Mondragon Cooperative Corporation and School Trends Ltd. *Social Enterprise Journal, 6*(2), 125–145.

94. Johnson, P. (2003). Towards an epistemology for radical accounting: Beyond objectivism and relativism. *Critical Perspectives on Accounting, 6,*

486–509; Johnson, P. (2006). Whence democracy? A review and critique of the conceptual dimensions and implications of the business case for organization democracy. *Organization, 13*(2), 245–274; Beaubien, L. (2011). Co-operative accounting: Disclosing redemption contingencies for member shares. *Journal of Co-operative Studies, 44*(3), 38–44.

95. Ridley-Duff, R. J., & Bull, M. (2011). *Understanding social enterprise: Theory and practice.* London: Sage.

96. Galera, G., & Borzaga, C. (2009). Social enterprise: An international overview of its conceptual evolution and legal implementation. *Social Enterprise Journal, 5*(3), 210–228.

97. Erdal, D. (2011). *Beyond the corporation: Humanity working.* London: Bodley Head; Kelly, M. (2012). *Owning our future: The emerging ownership revolution.* San Francisco: Berrett-Koehier; Nuttall, G. (2012). *Sharing success: The Nuttall review of employee ownership.* London: Department for Business, Innovation and Skills.

98. Chandler, J. (2008). *Explaining local government: Local government in Britain since 1800.* Manchester: Manchester University Press.

99. Hood, C. (1995). The new public management in the 1980s: Variations of a theme. *Accounting, Organisation and Society, 20,* 93–109.

100. National Health Service. (2008). *Social enterprise—Making a difference: A guide to the right to request.* London: Department of Health.

101. Hood, C. (1995). The new public management in the 1980s: Variations of a theme. *Accounting, Organisation and Society, 20,* 93–109, p. 107.

102. Dart, R. (2004). The legitimacy of social enterprise. *Non-Profit Management and Leadership, 4*(4), 411–424.

103. Willmott, H. (1993). Strength is ignorance; slavey is freedom: Managing culture in modern organizations. *Journal of Management Studies, 30*(4), 515–552; Curtis,

T. (2008). Finding that grit makes a pearl: A critical re-reading of research into social enterprise. *Social Enterprise Journal, 14*(5), 276–290.

104. Hebson, G., Grimshaw, D., & Marchington, M. (2003). PPPs and the changing public sector ethos: Case-study evidence from the health and local authority sectors. *Work, Employment and Society, 17*(3), 481–500.

105. Ferlie, E., et al. (1996). *The new public management in action* (p. 16). New York: Oxford University Press.

106. Restakis, J. (2010). *Humanizing the economy: Co-operatives in the age of capital.* Gabriola Island: New Society Publishers.

107. Restakis, J. (2010). *Humanizing the economy: Co-operatives in the age of capital* (Chapter 5, Kindle Edition). Gabriola Island: New Society Publishers.

108. Savio, M., & Righetti, A. (1993). Co-operatives as a social enterprise: A place for social integration and rehabilitiation. *Acta Psychiatrica Scandanavica, 88*(4), 238–242.

109. Restakis, J. (2010). *Humanizing the economy: Co-operatives in the age of capital* (Chapter 5, Kindle Edition). Gabriola Island: New Society Publishers.

110. Westall, A. (2001). *Value-led, market-driven: Social enterprise solutions to public policy goals.* London: IPPR; Ridley-Duff, R. (2008). Social enterprise as a socially rational business. *International Journal of Entrepreneurial Behaviour and Research, 14*(5), 292–312.

111. Hertz, N. (2011). *Co-op capitalism: A new economic model from the carnage of the old.* Manchester: Co-operatives UK.

112. Rainey, D. (2006). *Sustainable business development.* Cambridge: Cambridge University Press.

113. Epstein, M. (2008). *Making sustainability work: Best practices in managing and measuring corporate social, environmental, and economic impacts.* Sheffield: Greenleaf.

# 08

Process
Leadership
Infrastructure
Structure Hierarchy
Institutions
Change Management
Department
CSO
Responsible Leadership
Collaboration
Org Development
Collectivism
Corporate Governance
Matrix
Virtual Organization
Org Culture
Intrapreneurship

# ORGANIZATION: RESPONSIBLE INFRASTRUCTURE

You will be able to...

1 ...design an organizational architecture, centrally integrating elements of responsible structure.

2 ...restructure your organization to create responsible infrastructure.

3 ...develop your organization responsibly through change management and cultural change.

In 2011, 72 percent of all companies, in a survey among 300 respondents, had formal corporate responsibility (CR) programs, 62 percent had an organizational CR leader job position, and 60 percent had dedicated CR budgets.[1]

Sixty-two percent of companies "have a formal CR function, though it may or may not be centralized or managed by a single department or officer."[2]

Fifty-one percent of CEOs and 23 percent of boards actively lead CR-related initiatives.[3]

Author: Roger Conaway; Co-Author: Oliver Laasch; Contributors: Aurea Christine Tanaka, Jane Best, Jürgen Wittstock, Sharon Dafny, Simon Zadek, Ulpiana Kocollari

# SEMCO Brazil: Restructuring Business for Employee Welfare from Paternalistic, Pyramidal Hierarchy to Participatory Style

Can an industrial equipment manufacturer located in Sao Paulo, Brazil, whose organizational structure features a "paternalistic, pyramidal hierarchy led by an autocratic leader with a rule for every contingency," undergo a dramatic restructuring toward a revolutionary new and responsible structure and become an even more successful company? SEMCO boldly demonstrated such a move in 1982 when the owner's son, Ricardo Semler, shifted the purpose of work from making money to making "the workers, whether working stiffs or top executives, feel good about life."

The new structure and strong leadership in the structure proved successful. A new company vision was developed around employee participation, profit sharing, and the free flow of information. Furthermore, a new team of engineers was created, called Nucleus of Technological Innovation (NTI). The team invented and reinvented products, and sales grew 286 percent between the years of 1990 and 1996. These "satellite" teams helped unleash the creativity, potential, and entrepreneurial spirit of other employees. SEMCO became one of the most popular employers in Brazil, and the company even drew the attention of some 150 Fortune 500 companies, who sent representatives to visit SEMCO to learn about its success.

A number of issues related to organizational restructuring can be illustrated in this case, including change management and change of leadership. The case vividly illustrates how to develop sustainable principles and ethical practices among employees through building and maintaining their sense of personal worth as employees, and thus producing more productive outcomes for SEMCO. The case also illustrates management's responsibility in developing a responsible and ethical "ecosystem," in which employees can continuously learn and grow as individuals.

Semler later developed a *Lattice* structure, also called a horizontal organizational architecture, involving self-managed work teams that were in charge of all aspects of production and set their own budgets and production goals. This structure eventually evolved into a democratically

run company that proved highly successful for SEMCO's future. A more traditional profit-sharing plan was later incorporated, distributing approximately one-fourth of the company's profits to their respective divisions. Interestingly, the autonomous work teams could hire and fire coworkers and bosses with a democratic vote. This amazing organizational structure was based upon free flow of information about all company operations. In summary, organizational restructuring led to increased responsible management. It included the development of responsibility principles with all its employees, and ethical transparency and authority sharing among employees, causing them to continuously learn and grow as individuals.

SEMCO is an impressive success story, illustrating how organizational structure can create stakeholder value, in this case, value for the employee stakeholder and social sustainability for employees. Nevertheless, we must ask if this is enough. In order to find out if the company has truly created a "responsible infrastructure" that furthers sustainability, responsibility, and ethics, we need to analyze to what degree the company has integrated elements of responsible organizational structure into its organizational architecture. Is there a chief responsibility officer (CRO), a sustainability department, a corporate foundation, or an ethics office? Does the company report on social, environmental, and ethical performance? Is there a sustainability management system, responsible business programs, and stakeholder engagement platforms? Are there normative documents like a stakeholder mission, a values statement, a code of ethics, responsible business policies, and sustainability operating procedures? Only if we see that SEMCO has created such an infrastructure can it be classified as a business that is best equipped to optimize triple bottom line and stakeholder performance, and to achieve moral excellence.

Source: Siehl, C., Killian, K., & Perez, F. (1998). *Harvard business publishing* (p. 1). Retrieved September 8, 2012, from: http://cb.hbsp.harvard.edu/cb/web/search _results.seam?Ntt=SEMCO&conversationId=102166

# 8-1 RESPONSIBLE MANAGEMENT AND ORGANIZATIONAL THEORY

*"[A] fundamental question for organization theorists and managers: How can business organizations respond to human misery while also sustaining their legitimacy, securing vital resources, and enhancing financial performance?"*[4]

The purpose of this chapter is to help businesses move toward full integration of responsible management, sustainable development, and ethical practice throughout the structure of the organization. **Organizational theory** "is that branch of the social sciences that studies the design and evolution of the social structures comprising modern complex organizations, as well as the adaptation of those structures to task environments and institutional or environmental contingencies."[5] Social entrepreneurship explores opportunities to create organizations that respond to different characteristics than the traditional for-profit company. In this chapter, we will look at how to integrate a responsible infrastructure into a mainstream for-profit business. The topic of operations helps to translate the organizational structuring task to the process level.

The organizational design or architecture is to responsible management what the body is to a human being. To function, and for managers to act responsibly, this body requires bones to provide "Halt," muscles to move, organs to fulfill basic functions and to stay alive, and, most importantly, a brain to feel, think, and do the right thing. If one of those body parts is missing, it will be literally fatal. The "bones" of an organizational architecture for responsible business are departments, such as an ethics office or a sustainability department. The muscles that move a responsible business are the job positions, such as vice president for responsible business or a "green collar" workforce, and the programs for responsible business, such as a diversity or $CO_2$ policy. Organs that provide vital functions for responsible business conduct are, for example, reports (speech), ethics hotlines (feedback, similar to nerves), and codes of conduct (balance, similar to the internal ear). Finally, the brains of a responsible business that decide what to do are, for instance, the board of directors, stakeholder forums, or, in a more transversal pattern, a responsible organizational culture leading to the "right" decisions.

Figure 8.1 describes the three phases of the responsible organization process. In phase 1, we revisit classical and modern organizational theories, viewing them through the lens of a triple bottom line, stakeholder, and ethics perspective. We ask what *should* be the nature of the firm? In phase 2, we proceed to a discussion on how to create organizational structures for conducting responsible business. We describe elements of responsible organizational architecture, such as responsibility departments, chief responsibility officers, or stakeholder forums. In phase 3, we analyze the process of organizational development in sustainability, responsibility, and ethics with the goal of creating the necessary structures for responsible management and becoming a truly responsible business.

## Figure 8.1 **The Process of Creating a Responsible Organization**

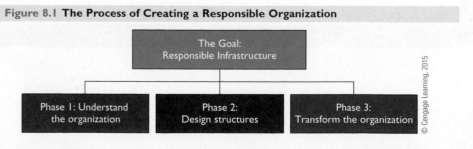

**Organizational theory**
The branch of the social sciences that studies the design and evolution of the social structures comprising modern complex organizations.

## 8-2 THE GOAL: RESPONSIBLE INFRASTRUCTURE

*"We need to pay much more attention to the institutional mechanisms that may influence whether corporations act in socially responsible ways or not … exploring a broad set of institutional conditions under which socially responsible corporate behavior is likely to occur."[6]*

In this chapter, we make a strong case for restructuring or reinventing an organization toward full integration of responsible management, sustainability and responsibility principles, and ethical practices throughout the organization. We call this **responsible infrastructure**, an enabler for responsible business performance.

So what would a structure look like when the goal of full integration is achieved? Most would model structures where performance of responsible management activities would lead to a positive, triple bottom line that protects, creates, and sustains social, environmental, and economic business value. Furthermore, the structure of a responsible business would lead to the maximization of internal and external stakeholder value. Finally, ethical decision making throughout the organizational structure would be morally desirable in both its process and its outcome. Although few if any organizations have achieved this vision, this chapter examines the process of how we can reach our goal.

## 8-3 PHASE I: UNDERSTANDING THE ORGANIZATION

*"Organization theory and business ethics are essentially the positive and normative sides of the very same coin, reflecting on how human cooperative activities are organized and how they ought to be organized respectively."[7]*

The question "What is an organization for?" is the point of departure of organizational theory. What is the purpose and function of organizations, and what attitudes toward and understandings of organizations will help us answer this question? In this short section on understanding the organization, we will, first, show opposing viewpoints about what organizations are and should be and, second, take a brief look at how management theory and understanding the role of employees interact with organizational structure.

### 8-3a Opposing Viewpoints

Before addressing specifics of how to reinterpret organizations, we introduce three common contrasting viewpoints currently existing in the field of organizational theory. Each viewpoint describes how different organizational structures may affect development of sustainability, responsibility, and ethics.[8]

*1. Individualism versus Collectivism*
The first viewpoint contrasts an individualistic view of organizational structure with a collective point of view. Assume for a moment an organization is undergoing change toward responsible management and sustainability principles. How would the leaders directing this change view the integration of responsible management?

First, they might adopt the *individualistic perspective*. Cultural perspectives on organizations often play into the individualistic view of organizations.[9] Individualistic societies stress the primacy of personal goals and needs,[10] each of

**Responsible infrastructure** An enabler for responsible business performance that includes organizational structures and culture.

which relates to HR practices at the organizational level. Individualism on the organizational level states that "moral responsibilities first and foremost exist in individual human beings."[11] That is, individual employees, not the larger entity of the organization itself, are responsible for their decisions. In an organization that takes the individualistic perspective, organizational change toward responsible business will focus on working with every single employee. Responsibility, sustainability, and ethics will most likely be mentioned explicitly in individuals' job descriptions. Responsible management trainings will aim to empower and prepare each employee for his or her respective contribution to the goal of becoming a responsible business.

In contrast, other change leaders might assume the *collectivist perspective.* Individuals act in collective ways that are socially appropriate. These collective interactions among organizational members cannot be reduced to the actions of a single individual. As a result, an organization is an entity that *can* be held accountable for its actions. In fact, corporations in many countries may be legally sued without placing accountability on single individuals within the organization. In an organization with a collectivist understanding, the focus of responsible management will be to create an organizational culture that is one of sustainability, responsibility, and ethics. Typical responsible management structures that will be created are team meetings, jointly reviewing responsible business performance, organizational climate surveys, and collaborative projects including a broad set of external stakeholders.

### 2. Realism versus Constructivism

Heugens and Scherer[12] describe a second debate in organizational theory between realism and constructivism. *Realism* is best characterized by Kant's duty ethics,[13] which imply that the rightness of an action is determined by considering obligations to apply universal standards and principles. Duty ethics would suggest that employees should choose a course of action on the basis of their duty to uphold appropriate rules and principles such as the law. Proper organizational conduct should be guided by primary moral principles and virtues. Realists believe material effects like legislation, auditing, and monitoring help determine policy decisions. An organization basing responsible business conduct in realism will highlight the importance of normative and control systems, such as codes of ethics and sustainability scorecards.

In contrast, *constructivism* denies that "the social world has a settled meaning and character, and argues that our cognitive schemes, frames, and categories do critically influence the social world."[14] Ethical decisions are enacted through socially shared beliefs, and human interactions are based on what is best for the organization. Organizations with the constructivist perspective will favor the development of a dialogue culture and high interaction. Typical elements of responsible infrastructure based on constructivism are stakeholder dialogue forums and open innovation platforms.

### 3. Instrumentalism versus Institutionalism

Finally, Heugens and Scherer[15] describe a third debate between instrumentalism and institutionalism, a tension addressing whether individuals need organizations to meet their collective goals that they could not possibly achieve independently. Can organizations balance collective values of members and their moral identities and corporate responsibilities? *Instrumentalists* tend to view organizations as rational entities that are run by dominant members who achieve their own ends. Instrumentalist thinking may lead to pure business-case thinking, in which the only responsible management activities that are realized are those that pay off.

On the other hand, *institutionalism* views organizations as having intrinsic worth above and beyond the value of their assets. Organizations "institutionalize" over time and form identities with which individuals wish to associate. This institutionalization impacts ethical decisions because assumptions about the "character of organizations are a precondition for notions like the organization's moral identity, collectively upheld norms and values, and the organization's moral agency in general."[16]

The three opposing viewpoints can be considered jointly to help assess the organizational point of departure to responsible business. Responsible managers can use the following checklist to determine an original position.

*Checklist Questions:*
Where does your organization fit among these three opposing viewpoints? How you would answer the following questions:

- *Individualism versus collectivism:* Does my organization tend to place responsibility for responsibility management and sustainable activities on individual employees? Or does it assume such responsibility rests at the organizational level and that individuals can only act in collective groups?

- *Realism versus constructivism:* Does my organization view social involvement of employees and environmental action as a duty, such as upholding appropriate rules, laws, or universal standards? Or does my organization believe social and environmental activities are "enacted" through socially shared employee beliefs, based on what is best for the organization?

- *Instrumentalism versus institutionalism:* Is my organization run by a small group of dominant members concerned with sustainability, who push employees to accomplish their individual sustainability goals? Or has it institutionalized sustainability as an organization and collectively assumed a moral identity in sustainability, norms and values in ethical practices, and responsible management?

Understanding the three opposing viewpoints can help us create responsible structures (phase 2) for organizations. The first perspective may help leaders of change management (phase 3) create a structure that trains employees to believe moral responsibilities exist, first and foremost, within themselves. That is, each person is responsible for ethical and moral behavior. The second view may help move leaders toward a structure that requires employees to follow a correct course of action based their duty to uphold ethical rules and principles. Their behavior must be guided by primary moral principles and virtues. On the other hand, employees may be required to believe collective organizational ways are the ones which are socially appropriate. Responsibility lies with the group or organization. Finally, the third opposing viewpoint illustrates how the organizational structure may be institutionalized. Employees may believe their ethical decisions are fluid and enacted through socially shared beliefs and human interactions within the organization, as long as they meet organizational goals. Organizational structures may exist to develop a culture of responsibility, sustainability, and ethics that supersedes what individuals can do on their own. The instrumentalist structure assumes ethical responsibility exists in a group of dominant members who are responsible for ethical outcomes.

Typically, the understanding of an organization varies greatly, and the "opposing" viewpoints often exist in a parallel fashion in organizations. For instance, one department in a company might be led in a highly individualistic pattern, while another one relies on collectivist, culture-based interaction. The responsibility for establishing a certain shared understanding of the nature of an organization and its subentities depends on the responsible manager's understanding of the organization. The next section will illustrate the intersection between management philosophy and organizational theory.

## 8-3b The Organization and Management Theory

The understanding of who the people in an organization are and how they work together crucially influences the design of any organization. Since employees are one of the main stakeholder groups of a business, however, this understanding has even more influence on the design of an organizational structure in a responsible business.

Table 8.1, which is based on the work of Miles, Snow, Meyer, and Coleman,[17] provides an overview of three management models and their underlying organizational structures. The table lists basic assumptions about the human nature of employees made by each model and shows the resulting managerial policies that stem from those assumptions. A close examination of the table reveals progressiveness in responsible management of employees in organizational structures in the twentieth century. Each progressive model illustrates the interaction of organizational structure and responsible management.

**Table 8.1** Comparison of Management Theories and Their Consequences for Responsible Organizational Structures

| Traditional Model | Human Relations Model | Human Resources Model |
|---|---|---|
| *Assumptions* | *Assumptions* | *Assumptions* |
| 1. Work is inherently distasteful to most people.<br>2. What workers do is less important than what they earn for doing it.<br>3. Few want or can handle work that requires creativity, self-direction, or self-control. | 1. People want to feel useful and important.<br>2. People desire to belong and to be recognized as individuals.<br>3. These needs are more important than money in motivating people to work. | 1. Work is not inherently distasteful. People want to contribute to meaningful goals that they have helped to establish.<br>2. Most people can exercise far more creative, responsible self-direction and self-control than their present jobs demand. |
| *Policies* | *Policies* | *Policies* |
| 1. The manager's basic task is to closely supervise and control subordinates.<br>2. Managers must break tasks down into simple, repetitive, easily learned operations.<br>3. Managers must establish detailed work routines and procedures and enforce these firmly but fairly. | 1. The manager's basic task is to make each worker feel useful and important.<br>2. Managers should keep their subordinates informed and listen to their objections of management's plans.<br>3. Managers should allow their subordinates to exercise some self-direction and self-control on routine matters. | 1. A manager's basic task is to make use of subordinates' "untapped" human resources.<br>2. Managers must create an environment in which all members may contribute to the limits of their ability.<br>3. Managers must encourage full participation on important matters, continually broadening subordinate self-direction and control. |
| *Implications* | *Implications* | *Implications* |
| 1. Superior managers take responsibility and action for ensuring front-line employees' responsible performance.<br>2. Procedures, checklists, and handbooks include sustainability, responsibility, and ethics tasks.<br>3. Strict control mechanisms, such as individual scorecards for responsible performance, are implemented. | 1. Responsible managers must create an internal community that gives each person the strong feeling to be meaningful.<br>2. Social, environmental, and ethical topics, as the ones promoted in responsible management, have a big potential to be perceived as meaningful by employees. | 1. The human resources model can create win-win situations for employee and company, always when employees are led to the job that satisfies them, which in turn increases their work satisfaction.<br>2. Seeing human beings as a resource, as a means to create economic performance, is ethically questionable; the same holds true for the term *human capital*. |

Source: Adapted from Miles, R. E., Snow, C. C., Meyer, A. D., & Coleman, H. J. (1978). Organizational strategy, structure, and process. *Academy of Management Review, 3*, 546–562.

Consider the opening case again. Ricardo Semler, CEO of the Brazilian company SEMCO, completely reinvented the organizational structure in his organization after assuming leadership from his father. Turning away from viewing his employees as "cogs in a machine", Semler viewed human beings as having enormous potential, creativity, and an entrepreneurial spirit. He was able to make people feel useful and important as part of SEMCO (human relations approach). Semler took them through a process of dramatic change to unleash this potential. He allowed full participation and ownership by employees. The SEMCO case shows how a change in management and organizational philosophy can be reflected in a change of tangible organizational structures. How to create structures for responsible business is the topic of the following section on phase 2.

## 8-4 PHASE 2: CREATING STRUCTURES FOR RESPONSIBLE BUSINESS: RESTRUCTURING THE ORGANIZATION

*"The CR function can be located in any number of places within a company—ranging from the CEO's office to communications/marketing to the legal division—and can be called anything from 'reputation management' to 'citizenship' to 'environmental risk,' which makes it a difficult landscape to navigate.* [18]

**Organizational structure** is the formal framework organizations adopt to control how managers and employees conduct their activities and move toward organizational goals. The framework provides lines of authority, roles and responsibilities, and channels of communication. Typically, this structure appears in written form as operational guidelines, published in a handbook or posted on a website. The framework establishes formal decision-making processes and states who makes decisions. All guidelines are intended to make the organization run smoothly and efficiently.

What is the role of *sustainability departments, ethics hotlines, chief responsibility officers, multistakeholder forums,* and *responsibility programs* in responsible management? These terms describe just a few of the structural elements that are created by organizations in order to support their efforts to become a responsible business. These structuring elements of responsible business, their location, their connections, and the building of functional groups, hierarchies, and responsibilities together form an organizational architecture for the organization's sustainability, responsibility, and ethics—the institutional structure in which responsible managers work.

**Organizational architecture** refers to the totality of organizational structure and implies a consistency between the various functions of the organization's structure. The terms *organizational structure* and *organizational architecture* are easily interchanged; each refers to the design of the unique organization and its effect on operations. Organizational design is about "how and why various means are chosen"[19] when organizational structures are developed.

Whether the business exists as a small, medium, or large enterprise, it will have architecture (structure), or a form by which it operates. Many organizations "around the world are elevating resource efficiency and sustainability from a tactical to a strategic concern—and are moving aggressively to improve environmental performance in operating processes and products."[20] Thus, creating structures for responsible business has moved to the strategic level for many businesses.

**Organizational structure** The formal framework organizations adopt to control how managers and employees conduct their activities and move toward organizational goals.

**Organizational architecture** The totality of organizational structure implying an alignment of organizational institutions and their interaction; often used synonymously with organizational design.

## In Practice

### Multiorganizational Architectures

For more than twenty-five years, American President Lines Japan, a container transportation and shipping company, has provided large-scale support to Refugees International Japan through the provision of transportation, equipment, expertise, and staff involvement at its major fundraising events. Organizational architectures for responsible businesses often involve external elements in long-run partnerships.

Some organizations adopt dramatically different structures on their path to triple bottom line performance, stakeholder performance, and ethical decision making and behavior. In contrast, other organizations incrementally develop new structures in a smaller step-by-step fashion. Both methods are effective and may be applied according to the strategy adopted by the business. Regardless of the method through which an organization chooses to restructure itself toward responsible management, the following clusters of questions will have to be addressed to create an architecture that effectively contributes to the organization's responsible business goals:

- *Creation:* Should there be a specific department or area coordinating exclusively responsible business topics? Should we establish new job positions, exclusively focusing on responsible management? If high-level positions are established, what should they be called? What new policies, programs, and processes are required to structure responsible business activities?

- *Integration:* How will responsible management be integrated into existing job descriptions, mainstream departmental structure, and institutional documents such as the mission and vision statement?

- *Alignment:* How do we achieve a harmony between existing structures and new responsible business activities? How do we align new structural elements with the organization's purpose (vision and mission statements) and with the organizational culture?

- *Naming:* What do we call what we do? Is it sustainability, responsibility, or ethics, or all three of them? Maybe the organization should use a specific cause—like diversity, $CO_2$ reduction, or community well-being—to name, for instance, programs, departments, and job positions.

- *Displacement:* How do we deal with situations where existing processes, jobs, or even whole departments need to be displaced by or substituted with newly created structures? How do we decide whether to completely erase structural elements because they are inherently unsustainable, irresponsible, or unethical?

- *Communication:* What mechanisms can we create to make sure that both internal and external stakeholders are informed transparently and are empowered to engage in shaping the organization?

- *Empowerment:* What do the different structural elements need to fulfill their function to enable responsible business performance? What hierarchical level are responsibility officers to be placed on? What budget is to be given to a sustainability department? What authorities and responsibilities are to be attributed to job positions? What mechanisms for training, improvement, and guidance will be implemented?

Now that we have illustrated the critical considerations in creating an organizational architecture for responsible organizations, in the following section we will review typical organizational designs in order to understand the broad structures to which responsible business is attached.

## 8-4a Organizational Design Patterns

Organizational design has come a long way from the classic bureaucratic, hierarchical organization. Today we find a confusing array of different types of organizational architectures. For instance, characteristics such as whether an organization has deep or flat hierarchies, and whether it is structured around groups, processes, or classic departments, are important to take into consideration when creating and integrating structures for responsible management into existing architectures.

As an example, organizations with more vertical structures reduce communication effectiveness and cause messages to be filtered, refined, and shortened. Such a communication issue might cause severe problems when a CEO wants, for instance, to communicate the new responsible business vision for a company-wide change program. If the message is not understood on all hierarchical levels, the program is doomed to fail from the beginning. Flatter or more horizontal structures allow communication to go through fewer levels. However, if managers have a wider "span of control," gaps or omissions in communication may occur. Modern, flatter organizational structures affect managerial communication because leaders have greater responsibility for employee information. Also, perceptions of organizational ethics among management and employees may differ greatly. Senior managers' perceptions of ethics in the organization tend to be significantly more positive than lower-level employees' perceptions.[21]

Anand and Daft[22] asked the question, "What is the right organization design?" We can extend that question and ask: "What is the right organization design for a responsible organization?" The answer is, of course, it depends. Figure 8.2 sums up the five main types of organizations found nowadays and their main characteristics, as well as how those characteristics may influence the organizational design for responsible management.

Each organizational design provides different advantages and disadvantages in the transformation to becoming a responsible business. In the introductory case, SEMCO achieved a transformation from a *self-contained organization* to a *horizontal organization,* which resulted in increased employee satisfaction. This is one example of how a business can create stakeholder value through organizational structure.

*Hollow organizations* only fulfill core value-adding functions themselves and outsource less critical activities. Most of today's organizations are to some degree hollow organizations. If an organization does not see responsible business as a crucial core function, it might happen that the topic becomes outsourced to external service providers. This is to be seen as critical, since responsible management requires substantial attention to detail, knowledge about the internal workings of the company, and an insider's perspective to be implemented credibly and successfully. Outsourcing of other processes, especially the outsourcing of production to developing countries, requires close attention. A major share of company scandals have been related to ethical, social, and environmental issues in outsourcing facilities.

In the *modular organization,* a company assembles submodules to a product or service. The efforts of creating responsible business structures in a modular organization are often based on improving single critical modules of a product. As an example, the car industry has made great strides toward a less unsustainable product by, in a parallel fashion, improving the different components or modules the car is built of. Exemplary improvements are alternative sustainable engine modules, like hybrid, hydrogen, or electric engines; improvements in weight and aerodynamic design; and recharging technologies in the brake system.

The auto industry also provides us with great examples of how the quest for more sustainable products creates so-called virtual organizations. *Virtual organizations,* often joint ventures of two or more companies, do not create great new structures, but rather borrow from the mother companies. For instance, one company's HR department might provide the back-office work for personnel management, while another partner of the joint venture houses the employees in their offices, or provides well-equipped research facilities in company. Major car producers, often direct competitors, have, for instance, formed joined ventures to quickly produce new battery technology, a critical technology urgently needed for more sustainable vehicles. Virtual organizations are organizations that can be created and dismantled quickly when social, environmental, and economic opportunities and challenges come and go.

| Figure 8.2 **Organizational Design Patterns**

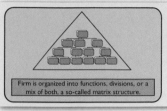

**Self-contained: Conduct of processes without external support**
→ Great control over companies´ activities and responsibilities.
→ External stakeholder collaboration is impeded through contained nature.
→ Strong hierarchies might impede changes in organizational structure.

*Firm is organized into functions, divisions, or a mix of both, a so-called matrix structure.*

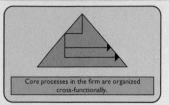

**Horizontal: Core process and team focus.**
→ Responsible business structures must organize around making core processes more responsible.
→ Opportunity to achieve responsible business programs through team initiatives, such as "green-teams."
→ Quick change is possible due to flexible structure.

*Core processes in the firm are organized cross-functionally.*

**Hollow: Outsourcing of internal processes.**
→ Make sure, outsourcing does not create suboptimal labour standards or additional environmental or ethical issues.
→ Parts of the responsible business infrastructure, such as a CSR hotline, can be created in an outsourcing fashion.
→ Experience in the outsourcing process may help to manage responsible business activities in collaboration with external (stakeholder) providers.

*Firm B and C supply internal organizational processes to Firm A.*

**Modular: Modular production**
→ Great potential for improving one's own product module for better social, and environmental performance.
→ Create an eco-system for sustainable innovation together with other module producers.
→ Possibility to flexibly innovate or substitute modules that are not responsible enough without having to abandon the whole product or service.

*Firm A assembles product modules produced by firms A, B, and C.*

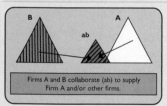

**Virtual: Joint ventures**
→ Great potential to pool know-how and resources with other organizations in order to quickly react to social, environmental, or economic opportunites and challenges.
→ Possibility to beta-test new responsible business structures without greater risk.
→ If virtual organization succeeds, it should be transformed to a non-virtual, independent structure.

*Firms A and B collaborate (ab) to supply Firm A and/or other firms.*

Source: Based on Anand, N., & Daft, R. L. (2007). What is the right organization design? *Organizational Dynamics*, 36(4), 329–344.

## 8-4b Elements of Responsible Organizational Structure

In the preceding section, we showed how organizational design patterns may impede or further the transformation to becoming a responsible business. In the current section, we will provide an overview of **structural elements** that aim at the creation of an infrastructure for responsible business and management. Such elements may be of many different kinds, fulfilling many different functions. Table 8.2 summarizes and defines the most common groups of structural elements for responsible business and their respective functions.

**Structural elements** are parts of the organizational architecture that jointly create an infrastructure for responsible business and management.

**Table 8.2** Structural Elements for Responsible Infrastructure

 **Normative documents,** such as vision, mission, and value statements, and policies and codes of conduct, fulfill a "lighthouse function" of providing guidance.

 **Programs,** such as a diversity program or an ecoefficiency program, are bundles of activities and structural elements with a common theme and purpose.

 **Departments,** such as an ethics office or a sustainability department, serve as institutional entities, or organizations inside the organization, to which responsibility for certain types of activities or performance is assigned to a predetermined group of people.

 **Job positions,** such as a "green collar" worker or the Chief Responsibility Officer, tie specific responsible management tasks to the person fulfilling the respective job.

 **Engagement platforms,** such as multistakeholder forums or open innovation platforms, facilitate collaboration and co-creation between the business and external stakeholders, and mutual learning.

 **Communication tools,** such as whistleblowing hotlines, sustainability reports, and a sustainability controlling system, facilitate transparency and dialogue with stakeholders to improve responsible business performance.

 **A process,** such as a stakeholder engagement or a volunteering process, is a concrete series of actions leading to a predetermined outcome and performance.

 **Procedures,** such as a sustainable purchasing procedure, describe, standardize, and improve processes.

The structural elements mentioned can be integrated into a typical organizational chart, as is done in Figure 8.3. Such responsible business architecture provides an overview of existing infrastructure for responsible business and management. The organizational chart, which is the scaffold of the responsible business architecture drafted, can be divided into four main areas.

- *Top management:* The highest tier of managers is led by the CEO.
- *Board of directors:* The board (originally developed as a tool of corporate governance) serves as a control mechanism and includes internal and external directors, and committees focusing on central topics.
- *Staff function:* The support functions provide central services important for the work of line functions.
- *Line functions:* The main functions are directly involved in the main value-creating activities of the company. The decision about which functions to include in staff and line functions depends on the focus of the respective organization.

Elements of responsible organizational structure are located inside, around, and in between those areas. To describe this exemplary architecture in detail would exceed the scope and scale of this chapter, but we will, in the following paragraph, highlight some parts of the structure to exemplify salient elements of responsible organizational structure, starting with normative documents.

## Normative Documents

**Normative documents** provide broad guidance on responsible business conduct without specifying a concrete course of action for individual situations. We could say these documents create a normative infrastructure for responsible management. Normative documents are always important when individuals in companies find

**Normative documents** provide broad guidance on responsible business conduct without specifying a concrete course of action for single situations.

Figure 8.3 Exemplary Responsible Business Architecture

STAKEHOLDER ENVIRONMENT

Shareholder forum

TOP MANAGEMENT

CEO

Chief sustainability officer | Chief integration officer | Chief responsibility officer | Chief diversity officer | Chief financial officer | Chief ethics & compliance officer

External director sustainability

BOARD

Risk committee | CSR committee

Industry sustainability initiative

Grantee network

Grantee identification process | Foundation director

FOUNDATION

Grantee work group

Stakeholder mission

Responsible business program

Code of ethics

Ethics office | Corporate governance program

GRI report

HR policy

Sustainable HRM | Volunteering process | NGO volunteering partnership

Values statement

Responsible business hotline

Sustainability department | CSR department

STAFF FUNCTION

TBL controlling system

INTEGRATED MANAGEMENT SYSTEM (IMS)

EHS policy | IMS framework

Stakeholder quality documents

PROCUREMENT

Procurement policy | Ethical procurement team

OM + SCM

Supply chain auditor | EHS Manager | Green team

R&D + OD

Sustainable innovation process | TBL scorecard

CRM

Community engagement manager | Stakeholder engagement process

Multistakeholder forum

BOP sourcing program

Stakeholder innovation platform

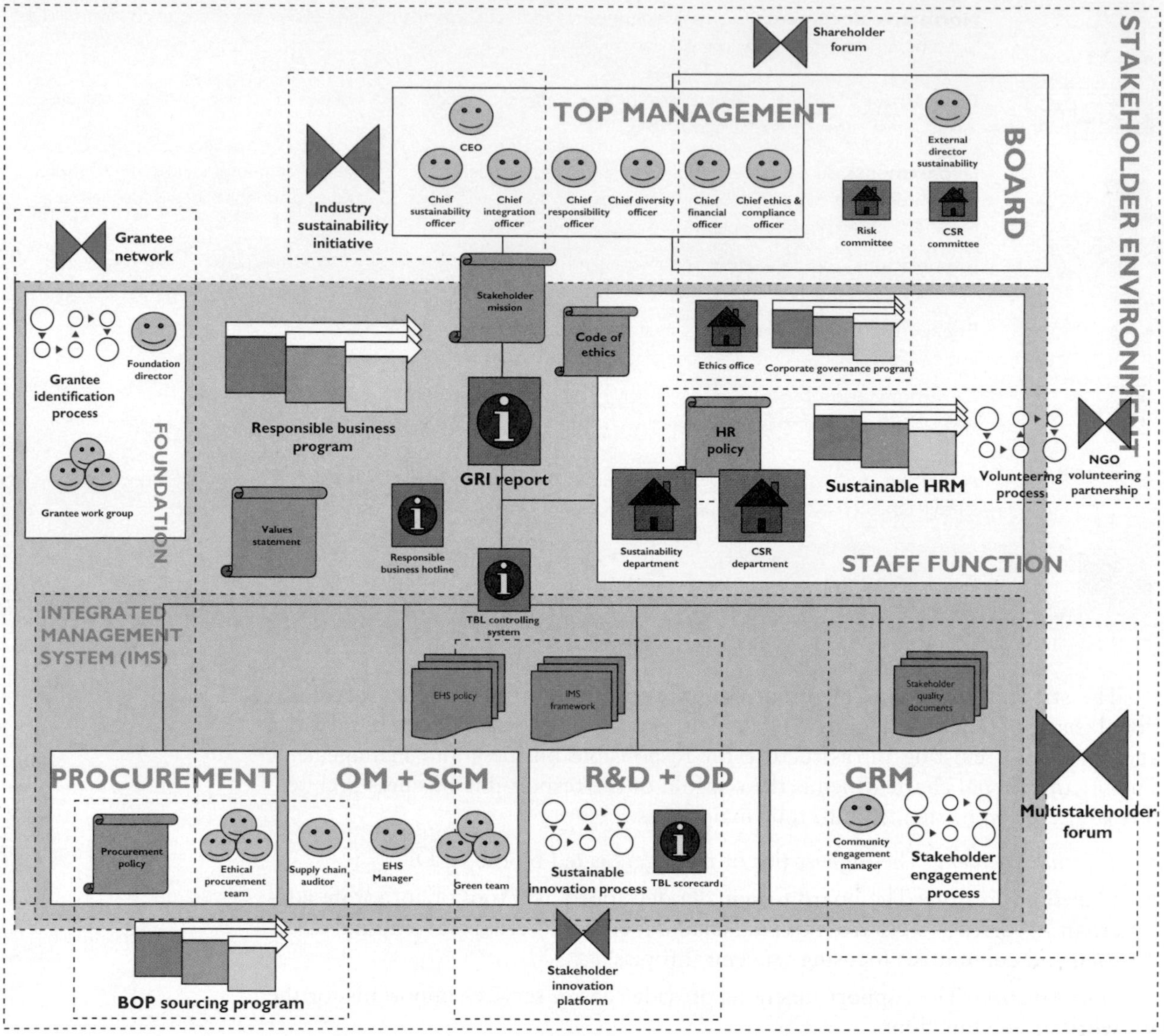

© Cengage Learning, 2015

themselves in discretionary, often weakly structured situations without a particular procedure to follow. Not every action in an organization can and should be governed through particular rules. It is natural that organizations, in their responsibility programs, set strategic preferences. For instance, the responsible business architecture mentioned earlier in Figure 8.3 does not have any structural elements specifically referring to measures to reduce $CO_2$ that would provide concrete procedures to employees. This might be due to the fact that this company produces a service, not a product that would require a $CO_2$-intensive production process. The company might have made a strategic decision to focus on more relevant lines of action. Nevertheless, an office manager might, for instance, be faced with the decision to either buy a new, more energy-saving printer or keep the old, less environmental-friendly one. A fleet manager might have to make a decision on whether to invest in company cars with more horsepower or in hybrid technology. In such discretionary decisions, normative documents provide guidance. The company's mission statement might state "We aim to become the most environmental-friendly company in our sector," the values statement might translate this into the value of "respect for the environment," and the code of ethics might specify that the environmental impact has to be taken into consideration in all decisions; these statements could help decision makers in the absence of an environmental policy that specifically states $CO_2$ reduction as a goal.

The following list illustrates the different normative documents and how they can be used to create an infrastructure for responsible management.

- The *vision* describes what the organization ultimately should become in the long run. The vision statement is the perfect vehicle for describing how the responsible organization should look at the end of its transformation process.

- The *mission* of a company defines what the business should be and do in the present to fulfill its purpose. Organizational mission statements may include triple bottom line, stakeholder, and ethical considerations. Some organizations also draft particular mission statements for focus topics in responsible management (e.g., missions for sustainability, stakeholders, diversity, or $CO_2$ topics).

- *Values statements* highlight the normative values that should be the underlying fabric of organizational culture and that should guide all actions taken. Values statements are often closely aligned with the mission.

- A *code of ethics* provides concrete rules for ethical decision making or highlights specific ethical issue areas of the organization with the goal of fostering morally right behavior. Codes of ethics might be drafted for the whole organization or for single areas and topics (e.g., integrity/anticorruption code or an ethical sourcing code).

- *Policies* state the organization's official stance regarding responsible business topics. Policies are often broad summaries of what the business does or does not do in a certain area of action (e.g., environmental policy, HR policy, PR policy).

> **Programs** are bundles of activities and structural elements with a common theme and purpose.

In our exemplary responsible business architecture in Figure 8.3, we see the organization's centrally important stakeholder mission, the ethics code, and a resulting values statement. In the example, both the HR and the sourcing functions have their own policies, which are integrated into responsible business programs. Normative documents also are the basis and starting point for the other structural elements to be described in the following paragraphs.

## Programs

**Programs** are sets of activities that serve a common purpose or display topical similarities. Programs do not form a specific new organizational structure, but comprise joint activity undertaken by several company departments. Ninety-six percent of the biggest companies have formal responsible business programs. Seventy-seven percent of the companies with such programs expect their programs to expand. Nineteen percent of those companies expect the program to expand through more staff, 21 percent through a higher budget, and 57 percent believe their programs will expand their coverage throughout the company.[23]

Programs for responsible business and management can broadly be divided into the following two types:

- *Flagship programs* for responsible business bundle a wide variety of different causes and typically embrace all parts of the organizational architecture. Examples are M&S's Plan A, Unilever's Sustainable Living Plan, and General Electric's Ecomagination. All of those programs include activities for many different causes that aim at furthering responsible business conduct in many parts of the organization, in a parallel manner, with the goal of improving the overall responsible business performance of the organization. In our exemplary architecture, the "responsible business program" is the organization's flagship program.

- *Cause-related programs* have a narrower scope, as they focus on a few or single causes. Figure 8.4 provides an exemplary program structure for the company AT&T that includes, for instance, a waste management program, including E-waste, the built environment of the company, and hazardous waste. What can be seen in the example is how cause-related programs interrelate and are often managed simultaneously by a responsible business core team and by different mainstream business functions, such as product stewardship, which is partly managed by the marketing department, and the diversity program, which is managed by the human resources department.

## Departments

The more meaningful corporate responsibility programs become, the more likely it is that a **department** for the topic is created. Sixty-two percent of the companies in the *CR Magazine*'s survey among CR managers had an institutionalized function in charge of responsible business activities. A survey by the *CR Magazine* revealed interesting facts about companies' responsible business departments. Forty-two percent of such functions reported directly to the CEO of the organization. Responsible business departments covered a broad variety of topics;

### Figure 8.4 Exemplary Program Structure at AT&T

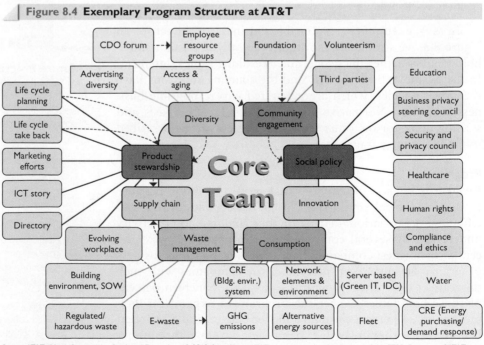

Source: AT&T. (2011). *Sustainability*. Retrieved December 18, 2012, from About AT&T: www.att.com/gen/landing-pages?pid=7735. Courtesy of AT&T Intellectual Property. Used with permission

A **department** is an institutional entity, an organization within the organization, to which a responsibility for a certain type of responsible management activities and performance is assigned.

82 percent were in charge of sustainability and environmental topics, more than 60 percent managed philanthropy and governance/risk/compliance; and more than 50 percent managed human rights and employee relations. Of the companies that had no formal responsible business departments, 15 percent were currently developing such a department, and 66 percent had integrated the responsibility for responsible business into mainstream business functions. Interestingly, in Latin America and Western Europe, more than 70 percent of surveyed companies had a dedicated department budget for responsible business, while in Canada, the USA, and Asia Pacific and Australia, approximately 50 percent of companies had such a budget.[24]

The creation of responsible business infrastructure through departments can be achieved in two models, which often are applied simultaneously:

- A *stand-alone department* for responsible business may, for instance, be called the sustainability department or the corporate responsibility department. For smaller departments, often the term *office* is used. Many organizations have an ethics office. Often such smaller responsible business offices, while managing only a few responsible business activities themselves, are crucial in enabling and coordinating the responsible management efforts of mainstream departments.

- *Integrated into mainstream departments*, responsible business is implemented from inside mainstream business departments. As an example, the marketing function would have a responsible marketing program, and human resources would have a sustainable human resources program. In order to coordinate the implementation among mainstream business departments, often a department-external, independent job position is created, supervising and supporting the implementation across functions.

A peculiar element of organizational architecture for responsible business is the *foundation*. Traditionally, foundations were largely separated from main business activities, while at the same time being funded through a business. Therefore, they worked differently from a stand-alone responsible business department. Nevertheless, foundations have increasingly become involved in responsible business conduct inside the companies' value chain. Broadly, they can be categorized as follows:

- *Independent foundations* are typically financed through a budget representing a fixed percentage of the company's profits, or even through company owners' private funds. They usually serve as grant givers for company-external grantees, often social and philanthropic projects.

- *Integrated foundations* closely collaborate with both staff and main business functions as a partner in implementing responsible business activities.

In our exemplary organizational structure (Figure 8.3), we see single corporate social responsibility (CSR) and sustainability departments and an ethics office, all centrally located and closely connected in the staff function. The structure also shows how a multitude of responsible business activities is dispersed through different functions and organizational entities, such as the board of directors, its foundation, and the top management.

## Job Positions

With the importance of responsible business practices, a variety of jobs have been developed to either deal exclusively with responsible business conduct or perform responsible management as one part of the job description. A job position includes in its description tasks that are related to responsible business performance. Responsible business is on the way to creating a new profession of managers in charge of social, environmental, and ethics topics.[25]

Job descriptions can be divided into three categories based on hierarchical levels and the organizational entities in which the job is located.

- *Top management positions* for responsible management carry many names, often beginning with a C—Chief; Chief Responsibility Officer (CRO); Chief Sustainability Officer (CSO); and Chief Ethics and Compliance Officer (CECO). These are the most common job titles. The highest responsibility for responsible business lies with those positions. Most of the C-level positions have high influence in the company's strategic decision making, as they are one or two steps away from the CEO of the company.[26] Leaders of C-level functions often are the leaders of company-wide responsible business departments and are in close contact with other functions' leaders in order to jointly take measures throughout the various functions of the company. Also, on board level, board directors are frequently assigned to ensure responsible business conduct. Forty-one percent of companies have board members dedicated to corporate responsibility. Twenty-three percent of boards in 2010 had actively driven a responsible business initiative.[27]

- *Middle and line management* has given birth to additional job titles in charge of responsible business conduct. Managers, directors, and vice presidents (VPs) are typical titles of executives in charge of social and environmental actions of organizations. Middle and line managers often have a strong mainstream business function expertise, coupled with knowledge in the responsible business area that touches on their area of expertise. Middle managers for responsible business activities often carry a term related to a certain cause or issue in their job title. Examples are Global Sustainability Director, the VP of Diversity, and $CO_2$ Manager.

- So-called *green collar* workers are employees with operational jobs who, either as one part of their job description or as their main job, are in charge of actively working on social and environmental value creation. Examples of this category might include the janitor who, as part of his or her daily routines, makes sure that lights are turned off and that heating and air conditioning do not use too much energy. Such people who are "not just doing their jobs" can make a great difference for a company's responsible business performance.[28] A related term is *green teams,* which are groups of employees with the task to improve environmental performance on an operational level.

The organization in our example (Figure 8.3) has created three C-level functions for responsible business: one external board director in charge of responsibility topics, the director of the corporate foundation; an Environment Health and Safety (EHS) director; and one community engagement manager. On the operational level, the company has various teams working on responsible business, such as the ethical procurement team. Internal employees working in responsible business and management often must interact and engage with the many groups of external stakeholders through engagement platforms that enable collaboration.

## Engagement Platform and Communication Tools

**Engagement platforms** are forums specifically created to facilitate collaboration with stakeholders. Such platforms can, as an example, be meetings (e.g., a quarterly shareholder meeting), collaboration events (e.g., volunteering campaigns), or Web-based platforms (e.g., an open innovation platform). We can identify two different

**Engagement platform**
A forum that facilitates collaboration and co-creation between the organization and external stakeholders, and mutual learning.

Part D Organizing

types of engagement that must be reflected in organizational structure:

- *Partnership-based engagement* is based on a close long-term relationship built with one or a few stakeholders. Engagement platforms are typically customized to the necessities of the partners. Information and outcomes of the engagement are frequently disseminated internally. Processes of partnership-based engagement are often highly standardized.

- *Community-based engagement* follows the goal to engage with many stakeholders simultaneously. In this engagement form, often it is not the relationship with company stakeholders that is dominant, but rather the relationship and co-creation process between stakeholders.

The organization described in our example (Figure 8.3) is involved in several engagement activities. In an industry sustainability initiative, top management engages with other leaders of companies to achieve industry transformation toward sustainability. Other examples for engagement activities include the grantee network of the foundation; a periodic volunteering campaign for community engagement; an open innovation platform through which employees, clients, and NGOs are involved in co-creating new sustainable products; and an annual stakeholder forum event.

The difference between communication and engagement tools is that the first achieves an active collaboration and co-creation, while the latter serves to merely exchange information, that is, to communicate. **Communication tools** fulfill an important function in the responsible organization infrastructure. They serve to hold the connection to a broad group of stakeholders, as a mutual feedback line. Communication tools are described extensively through the topics of marketing and communication. The main communication tools in our example (Figure 8.3) are a GRI sustainability report, a stakeholder hotline, and a sustainability controlling system for the company's line functions. A survey by the Corporate Responsibility Officer Association (CROA) showed that 53 percent of respondents had communication channels directed at socially responsible investors, 67 percent had included social and environmental topics in their marketing communications, and 58 percent had published a CSR or sustainability report.[29]

## Processes and Procedures

A main challenge in implementing responsible management activities in organizations is the operationalization throughout all departments, functions, and hierarchies. The main solution for this challenge is **processes**. Wherever people work for a certain output, there is a process, more or less structured, to achieve this outcome. If we succeed in implementing processes for responsible management throughout the organization, we succeed in operationalizing responsible management. The topic of operations management describes the design and continual improvement of responsible business performance through processes, procedures, and management systems. Here we will provide a short glimpse at the two different ways processes can be used as structures for responsible business.

On the operational level, processes (and procedures) for responsible business include both specialized and integrated ones.

- *Specialized processes* for responsible management are those with sustainability, responsibility, and ethics topics at their core and as their primary purpose. In

**Communication tool** A method that serves to inform stakeholders and to become informed about triple bottom line, stakeholder, and ethical performance.

**Process** A series of actions leading to a predetermined outcome.

our example, the stakeholder engagement process and the volunteering process illustrate such specialized processes.

- *Integrated processes* define actions important for sustainability, responsibility, and ethics as part of a mainstream business process. In our example, the sustainable innovation process, which centrally considers the triple bottom line as one action of the normal innovation process, and the responsible sourcing process illustrate this.

**Procedures** are formalized, usually written descriptions of processes. Often different procedures are integrated and jointly form a management system, administrating many or even all processes of a company. The difference between procedures and the normative documents described earlier is that normative documents answer the "what" question, "What should be achieved?," while procedures answer the "how" question, "How can we achieve it?" Normative documents are the starting point of organizational structuring elements; procedures are the completion. In order to reach the completion of a responsible business infrastructure, we have to run through an organizational development process, as described in the next section of this chapter covering phase 3, developing the organization responsibly.

## 8-5 PHASE 3: DEVELOPING THE ORGANIZATION RESPONSIBLY

*"As mentioned, it is not possible to fully detail here what processes have to change in the organization, what job requirements need to shift, what information systems supporting these changes are required and what the implications of these changes will be. Integrating responsibility into the organization is contingent on many factors unique to each situation."*[30]

Phase 2 illustrated the static elements that can potentially be integrated into organizational structures through a dynamic organizational change and **organizational development** process. This dynamic perspective of how to create those structures is the main topic in this section on phase 3. Only providing structure is not enough to truly change what an organization is and does. A common rhetoric of companies, when talking about their responsible business activities, is to state that responsible management is "in the DNA" of the organization. This means that not only the physiology, or structure, of the business shows elements of responsible business, but that it is also the very basic nature of the business to act responsibly, from the smallest decision and behavior to the biggest one. How can this be achieved?

Today, changing organizational structures toward responsible business sustainability, responsibility, and ethics practices can be accomplished, but reinventing the structure requires careful, complete, and complex processes. In the following paragraphs, we will illustrate the three main drivers of organizations' evolution toward integrating responsible management into their very DNA. Those drivers are responsible leadership, responsible culture, and change management for responsible business. Before we do so, however, it is important to understand what the goal of such change should be.

What is the goal of reinventing or restructuring an organization for responsible management? Figure 8.5 represents an overview of the process of sustainability management, responsibility management, and ethical practices. Stages-of-growth models for responsible business provide valuable tools for qualitatively analyzing how responsible an organization's structures, activities, and performance are.[31] This responsible business performance model is a synthesis of sustainability, responsibility, and ethics performance models.

**Procedure** A process description that serves to standardize and improve processes.

**Organizational development** The process of leading an organization toward its goals by changing its structures and culture.

Part D Organizing

- The first line, *sustainability performance,* ranges from a largely undeveloped organization that is below-average unsustainable, even in comparison to a typical company in its industry, to the perfect situation of a restoratively sustainable organization that is able to simultaneously create social, environmental, and economic capital. The benchmark situation in the sustainability dimension is a situation where the organization produces a sustainable triple bottom line, one that is inside the planetary resource limits.[32]

- The second line, *responsibility performance,* illustrates a continuum of different organizational behavior patterns with regard to stakeholders. The continuum pictures a company's defensive behavior, denying responsibilities, on one end to a civil position, on the other, where the organization even promotes stakeholder responsibility in other actors. The benchmark situation in the responsibility dimension is a managerial implementation of responsible business where social responsibility is embedded into all core processes of the company.[33]

- Finally, the third line, *ethics performance,* represents how morally desirable decision making in the organization is. An organization weakly developed in the ethical dimension is at the amoral first stage, while a perfectly developed business is at the ethical stage where ethical issues resolve in the most ethical decisions possible. The benchmark stage three in the ethics dimension is an ethically responsive business that manages the main ethical issues occurring in the organization's sphere of influence well.[34]

The dashed line through the middle of Figure 8.5 illustrates the "implementation benchmark"—the minimum long-run goal for organizational development toward becoming a responsible business. In other words, the benchmark represents a minimum requirement. An organization, a management activity, or a process cannot be called responsible if the commitment implemented and the development path chosen do not lead to the fulfillment of the minimum requirement represented by the benchmark.

**Figure 8.5 Development Paths toward Responsible Organization**

Implementation benchmark

|   | 1 | 2 | 3 | 4 | 5 |
|---|---|---|---|---|---|
| **Sustainability** | Below-average unsustainable | Average unsustainable | Sustainable | Neutral impact | Restorative |
| **Responsibility** | Defensive | Compliant | Managerial | Strategic | Civil |
| **Ethics** | Amoral | Legalistic | Responsive | Emerging ethical | Ethical |

Sources: Based on Laasch, O., & Conaway, R. N. (2013). *Responsible business: Managing for sustainability, ethics and global citizenship.* Monterrey: Editorial Digital; Zadeck, S. (2004). The path to corporate social responsibility. *Harvard Business Review, 82,* 125–132; Reidenbach, R. E., & Robin, D. P. (1991). A conceptual model of corporate moral development. *Journal of Business Ethics, 10*(4), 273–284.

For some businesses, the task may sound daunting. How can a business achieve such high goals? Let us imagine you are in charge of responsible business at a company that, after a self-assessment, has realized it is on stage 1, which gives you one point for each of the three dimensions. This means your overall performance sum is three. Reaching a performance sum of fifteen, where all three dimensions are fulfilled at level 5, or even just reaching the benchmark of three in all dimensions (a performance sum of nine), may feel impossible. For the development process, we recommend that a company simultaneously pursues two smaller steps.

- First, think in *small steps and single dimensions*. It will be much easier to subsequently develop the organization if the goal is not to achieve excellence simultaneously in all three dimensions and if the goal is not to jump to the highest stage possible at once.

- Second, *balance between the dimensions* sustainability, responsibility, and ethics. It will always be easier to make the next step toward a higher level in one dimension than in others. This step can then prepare the ground for improvement in the other dimensions. For instance, it might be a small step to move from the compliant (2) responsibility stage to the managerial stage (3) by integrating stakeholder concerns into your existing quality management system. This step might also help you to move the company from a below-average unsustainable situation (1) to an average unsustainable situation (2), since the integration of stakeholders into the quality management system might also involve social and environmental indicators. Those indicators can now be used to benchmark and to recognize areas of necessary opportunity in comparison to other companies that are on the stage of average unsustainability (2).

The single steps to increase organizational infrastructure for responsible business performance can be subdivided into the typical practices that are illustrated in Figure 8.6. What organizational development patterns a business applies depends on the initial situation of the business. Some organizations, especially social enterprises, may be "born CSR oriented" businesses and will only need to grow what they are doing well anyway. Other organizations might have to patch responsible business activities to mainstream core activities, trim irresponsible areas of the business, or even dissolve the organization and reinvest the capital into a venture with more potential to become responsible.

Three centrally important topics in organizational development are leadership, change management, and organizational culture. In the following paragraphs, we will discuss all three of these issues.

## 8-5a Organizational Leadership

Changes toward responsible business often require broad visions that can barely be achieved without **leadership**. More important, bad leadership is often responsible for whole organizations' irresponsibility. Nevertheless, getting rid of such "toxic leaders" can be only the first step to developing a responsible organization.[35] A new

**Leader** One who guides followers to an envisioned goal.

Figure 8.6 Development Patterns for Becoming a Responsible Organization

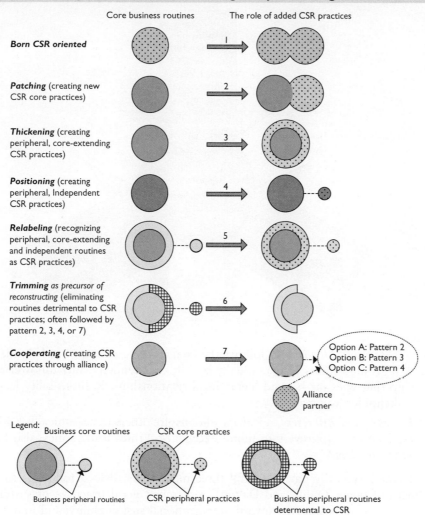

Core business routines     The role of added CSR practices

**Born CSR oriented**

**Patching** (creating new CSR core practices)

**Thickening** (creating peripheral, core-extending CSR practices)

**Positioning** (creating peripheral, Independent CSR practices)

**Relabeling** (recognizing peripheral, core-extending and independent routines as CSR practices)

**Trimming** *as precursor of reconstructing* (eliminating routines detrimental to CSR practices; often followed by pattern 2, 3, 4, or 7)

**Cooperating** (creating CSR practices through alliance)

Option A: Pattern 2
Option B: Pattern 3
Option C: Pattern 4

Alliance partner

Legend:
Business core routines     CSR core practices

Business peripheral routines     CSR peripheral practices     Business peripheral routines detrimental to CSR

Source: Yuan, W., Bao, Y., & Verbeke, A. (2011). Integrating CSR Initiatives in business: An organizing framework. Journal of Business Ethics, 101(1), 75–92.

type of leader is needed. We will call such a leader a *responsible leader,* one who is able to lead in all three dimensions of sustainability, responsibility, and ethics, as illustrated in Figure 8.7.

As described before, it is important to differentiate between the terms *sustainability, responsibility,* and *ethics* in leadership. The definitions of sustainability, responsibility, and ethics leadership are often overlapping, but each has a distinct core that differentiates these leadership theories from each other and from mainstream business leadership. In the following, we distinguish between the three leadership theories in responsible management based on the leadership vision and the group of followers.

- *Sustainability leadership* describes as a leader who promotes sustainability in a certain group or a system. Sustainability leaders might lead a work team, a whole organization, or even a complete region, or a whole industry toward sustainability.

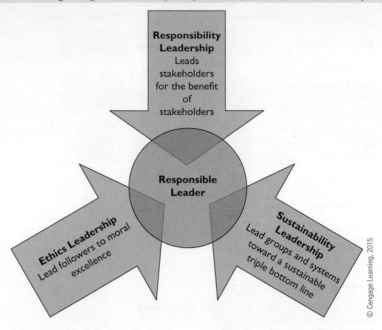

- *Responsibility leadership* follows the goal of the creation of stakeholder value. Also, responsibility leaders usually lead in an extended leader-follower relationship that goes far beyond hierarchical relationships. Responsibility leaders are stakeholder leaders.[36]

- *Ethics leadership* refers to leaders who inspire others to act ethically. Ethics leaders lead their followers to moral excellence. Ethics leaders may also be called *moral leaders*.[37]

Leaders typically have to fulfill three main tasks to lead followers to the fulfillment of goals. Quinn and Dalton[38] researched good practices of sustainability leaders, moving businesses toward organizational sustainability, and found the following three phases of leadership for sustainability, which also apply more broadly to the other responsible leadership domains. Leaders recommended the following:

1. *Create direction:* Leaders must convincingly convey the vision and goals associated with the change to be implemented. Good practices are:

   a. *Framing and delivery of the message:* Avoid "gloom and doom," and frame sustainability as a positive message of opportunities. Use vivid examples and involve emotions and creativity. Use the language of business, of financial factors and feasibility. Appeal to employees' inherent motivation to do the right thing, by reframing the activities in the light of social value.

   b. *Initiating, implementing, and advising:* Make sure you have a powerful initiator, who can push off the change, someone doing the actual work and implementing, and an expert in an advisory role.

   c. *Focusing the effort:* Do not lose energy by trying to convince skeptics, but focus on the early adopters who can deliver the energy to carry on the momentum.

2. *Create alignment:* Leaders must ensure the initial implementation of internal responsible business practices.

   a. *Implementing internal business practices:* If internal processes and structures are in place for sustainability, employees do not necessarily have to believe in sustainability to make it happen. Structures that were mentioned as especially important are job functions, and controlling systems based on sustainability indicators, communication and feedback systems, and a company-wide sustainability training system.

   b. *Engaging with stakeholders:* Sustainability goals cannot be reached alone. Leaders must collaborate in a broader stakeholder system to build long-term partnerships and try to also convince other companies to do the same thing.

   c. *Implementing sustainability in building, products, and services:* Integrating sustainability here creates a constant reminder for all involved in the production process and consuming products and services. Also this implementation has the potential to create new revenue streams and to show the business case for sustainability.

3. *Maintain commitment:* Reaching sustainability, a stakeholder responsibility, is a long-term goal. It is of crucial importance for successful sustainability leaders to ensure that followers' commitment is maintained over long periods of time.

   a. *Treating employees as assets:* When employees are treated as assets, as carriers of the organization's sustainability knowledge, skills, and culture, this will reduce their fluctuation, increase motivation, and keep the sustainability movement alive.

   b. *Building reputation:* Once a company has created a reputation for being an ethical, sustainable, and responsible business, this becomes a self-fulfilling prophecy. Stakeholders expect the company to stay the course. The organization will be held accountable for noncompliance with the reputational image created.

   c. *Engaging in networks:* Sustainability and responsibility networks, such as industry initiatives, are an external anchor that helps in maintaining efforts.

When we think of responsible leaders, we might automatically think of the top managers transforming organizations from the top; and, yes, they do. More than half of the CEOs of the companies represented in a survey by the Corporate Responsibility Officer Association (CROA) had driven a responsible business initiative within a year. CEOs and CROs agreed that the broad majority, over 80 percent, of CEOs understand the role of responsible business in their operations. More than 85 percent of CEOs believed that sustainability is either important or even very important for their businesses. The majority of CEOs met regularly with their companies' sustainability leaders.[39] The higher a leader is in the organizational hierarchy, the higher is his or her potential influence over followers' actions on the same and on lower hierarchical levels.[40] Although those facts and figures sound impressive, there is agreement that the CEOs and C-suite executives are not the only important sustainability leaders in companies.

Increasingly, employees and middle managers are appearing as leadership figures in grassroots initiatives.[41] So-called **change agents** can be found throughout the organizational architecture and in all hierarchies, not only in the top-level

**Change agent** An employee (or an external stakeholder) who is instrumental in changing business structures to focus on sustainability, responsibility, and ethics.

management positions. While some groups have a higher potential to be change agents, there are manifold roles that employees can play in changing the organization to be more active in sustainability, responsibility, and ethics.[42] Those roles include, for instance, an expert, a facilitator, a catalyst, and an activist.[43] Often such change agents for responsible business are called **social intrapreneurs**, that is, individuals who apply entrepreneurial methods to change the organization from within.[44]

## 8-5b Responsible Culture

Without followers, there are no leaders. Change cannot happen if the "masses" are not responsive to a leader's vision. This is why change in **organizational culture** is a critical prerequisite for making organizational transformation and creating responsible infrastructure. Organizational culture has been called the DNA of an organization.[45] Culture, like DNA, predefines what an organization is, does, and becomes. But can leaders actually actively change the culture, the DNA of an organization? Can leaders in responsible business create a culture for sustainability, responsibility, and ethics?

Sims[46] says they can. He used Schein's[47] five key mechanisms of how leaders can influence culture, analyzing these mechanisms in the case of Warren Buffet's turnaround of an unethical culture that had led to the investment firm Salomon Brothers' scandal during the early 1990s. We show how these mechanisms are essential in bringing about responsible management change. Transforming the organization's culture will involve:

1. *Attention:* On what do stakeholders, especially employees, focus their attention? Responsible managers, for example, can create the appropriate focus by praising employees' organizational performance, criticizing aspects of their unethical behavior, and communicating sustainable, responsible, and ethical organizational values to stakeholders as a whole. By redirecting stakeholder attention to organizational values, leaders will encourage responsible management throughout the organization and direct attention to sustainable objectives and values.

2. *Reactions to crises:* Crises small and large tend to reveal a leader's true nature because emotions in tense situations have a tendency to reveal the way people really feel about an issue. Typically, responsible managers will respond either ethically or unethically, responsibly or irresponsibly, in times of crisis, which shows who they really are to follow.

3. *Role modeling:* A leader's actions say more about company values than many words and many messages. Individuals as role models have a crucial influence on the behavior of followers. Leaders may lead a green office program, participate in sustainable activities, and demonstrate other responsible actions.

4. *Allocation of rewards:* Leaders often control decisions about pay increases, promotions, and advancements within the organization. These particular decisions will communicate a strong message about the importance of sustainability performance. A responsible manager who rewards such performance and financially backs ethical practices will promote organizational change toward responsibility.

**Social intrapreneur** One who applies entrepreneurial methods to change the organization from within or to use the organizational structures to solve external social issues.

**Organizational culture** The shared values, attitudes, and beliefs underlying the decisions made and actions taken in an organization.

5. *Criteria for selection and dismissal:* Recruiting, selecting, and hiring individuals with sustainability experience communicates these values both inside and outside the organization. Likewise, the dismissal of employees who lack ethical integrity will show other employees the importance of ethical criteria. The topic of human resources management creates insight into how "onboarding and offboarding" of employees play a role in responsible management change.

While the first part of this chapter referred mostly to organizational structures and institutions, those static elements of an organization cannot create and maintain a responsible business alone. The role of culture as a force connecting the structures and making responsibility a reality is crucial for a company's responsible business performance.

What is fascinating about the interplay of responsible business structures and culture is their complementary nature. It has been claimed that creating an organizational infrastructure for responsible business renders a responsible culture unnecessary, and vice versa. One fact is certain, however: Structure and culture both have the potential to be enablers of organizational infrastructure for responsible business. Also, in the change management process that will be illustrated in the last section of this chapter, both play a crucial role.

## 8-5c Managing Change

**Organizational change** is the process of moving forward to a better structure that improves company performance. *Change* is often framed in different terms by companies, including "total quality management, reengineering, right sizing, restructuring, cultural change, and turnaround."[48]

For responsible leaders, the development of a roadmap for responsible business development from decision to adoption to ongoing commitment is crucial.[49] This section addresses responsible management of organizational change, and we examine how to manage the change process of becoming a responsible organization effectively and efficiently. **Change management** traditionally aimed at avoiding barriers to change that were often found in employee resistance. When it comes to change for responsible business, the process becomes even more complex, as it also involves the various drivers and inhibitors to be found among the different stakeholder groups.

When organizations decide to restructure and move toward responsible management, greater sustainable performance, and better ethical decision making, the process may create its fair share of internal and external criticism. Critics are a normal phenomenon of any change. How do organizations respond to internal criticism? Why do some organizational transformations fail? What can other organizations do to avoid those mistakes? John Kotter, a global authority in change management, has identified eight important errors that are made when transforming an organization. From these errors we can derive basic principles to understand how to successfully change an organization:[50]

1. *Not establishing a great enough sense of urgency.* "Well over 50% of the companies I have watched fail in this first phase," Kotter noted.[51] He emphasized how difficult it is for leaders to move employees out of their comfort zones. In fact, he believes that at least 75 percent of a company's management must be convinced that business-as-usual is unacceptable for transformation to work.

**Organizational change**
The process of changing structures and culture in order to reach a predetermined goal.

**Change management**
The process of effectively and efficiently transforming an organization toward a preset goal by overcoming barriers and facilitating drivers for change.

Top leadership must ensure that managers are "on board" for successful responsible management transformation. A sense of urgency for responsible business transformation can be created, for instance, by referring to the competitive threat of companies implementing responsible business, or to the threat of upcoming regulation.

2. *Not creating a powerful enough guiding coalition.* A responsible management "coalition" typically will be those employees and managers who support the transformation. This coalition will grow as the process continues or the change may not be successful.

3. *Lacking a vision.* A clear responsible business vision that states what the organization wants to become will project the organization onto the path of organizational change. A strong vision lies at the core of the transformation to responsible management.

4. *Undercommunicating the vision by a factor of ten.* Sometimes a company "catches" the responsible business, develops a sense of urgency, creates a powerful coalition, and writes a strong vision statement, yet it stumbles in how it communicates the change. An error can be made in tending toward minimal communication with few attempts at letting employees know about the new vision. Similarly, the message may not be clear and understandable to most employees. Equally, the message may be clear, but responsible management leaders may not role-model what the message is about. They may act inconsistently with the message. Any of these weaknesses may stop complete transformation.

5. *Not removing obstacles to the new vision.* Obstacles inevitably arise once the organizational process is underway. The structure of the organization is one example. The old structure may not allow for innovation and creativity in job positions. If a new structure is created, unconventional activities must be considered by leaders and given credibility. Hierarchical structures also may be an impediment and must be dealt with.

6. *Not systematically planning for and creating short-term wins.* Every organization undergoing a significant organizational change needs short-term successes. Part of the change process requires that an achievable goal be set within the first year or two or the transformation may be hindered.

7. *Declaring victory too soon.* Vision or momentum may be lost even when an organization achieves success over several years. Responsible managers may feel like "we've made it" and lose motivation toward the restructuring for responsible business. Motivation should not be lost over time.

8. *Not anchoring changes in the corporation's culture.* This final error occurs when progress toward responsible management does not become a systemic part of the organization's structures and culture. Changing culture (and mindsets) toward the triple bottom line, stakeholder thinking, and moral excellence is a central aspect of change management.

These eight errors may occur when organizations are transforming their structures. These are the big mistakes businesses make, and other errors certainly may exist as well. The idea is that change management is a complex process, and organizations must plan well and avoid pitfalls when they begin the move toward becoming a responsible business.

Now that you know what you should not do, it is time to highlight the good practices in the responsible business implementation process.[52] Figure 8.8 defines nine steps that, in several parts, resemble a positive formulation of Kotter's don'ts.

**Figure 8.8 Stages of Responsible Business Implementation**

| Stages of CSR Implementation | Explanation* |
|---|---|
| 1. Conduct a "zero assessment." | Identify current CSR practice (Cramer et al., 2004; Maignan et al., 2005). |
| 2. Develop CSR goals within the organization's mission, vision, and strategy. | Identify what the organization wants to achieve and how to achieve it (Doppelt, 2003; Lyon, 2004; Were, 2003). |
| 3. Gain top management support. | Senior managers determine strategy and without their support become critical barriers to CSR implementation (Doppelt, 2003; Were, 2003). |
| 4. Gain employee support to ensure they own CSR as part of their work-life activities. | This requires involvement of a cross-section of employees in zero assessment and effective communication of CSR mission and vision, reinforced though training (Cramer et al., 2004, 2006; Maignan et al., 2005; Were, 2013). |
| 5. Gain support from external stakeholders. | External stakeholders include groups affected by the organization or that affect the organization (e.g., suppliers, distributors, wider community). Selecting organizations with similar CSR beliefs helps to consolidate the reorientation of the business (Castka et al., 2004; Cramer et al., 2004; Maignan et al., 2005). |
| 6. Prioritize change effort and focus on achieving it. | This is an acknowledgment of how the change implementation requires the application of finite management and other resources (Doppelt, 2003). |
| 7. Measure progress and fine-tune the process. | CSR implementation is an iterative approach (Cramer et al., 2004; Porter & Kramer, 2006). |
| 8. Anchor change. | Ensuring the organization's activities results in mutual benefits for it and the society in which it operates (Porter & Kramer, 2006; Were, 2003). |
| 9. Reorder the implementation system. | Reordering reflects the continuous nature of the process, where states may occur simultaneously, shaped by the situations faced by the organization (Doppelt, 2003). |

*Note: For citations of references in this column, see the article by Lindgreen et al. listed below.
Sources: Lindgreen, A., Swaen, V., Harness, D., & Hoffman, M. (2011). The role of "high potentials" in integrating and implementing corporate social responsibility. *Journal of Business Ethics, 99*(1), 73–91.

## PRINCIPLES OF ORGANIZATION: RESPONSIBLE INFRASTRUCTURE

I.  The goal of responsible organization is responsible infrastructure. *Responsible infrastructure* is an enabler for responsible business performance that includes organizational structures and culture.

II. To understand the initial position of an organization, responsible managers should assess where the organization stands regarding the *opposing viewpoints* of organizational theory: individualism-collectivism, realism-constructivism, instrumentalism-institutionalism.

III. Responsible *organizational architecture* integrates *structural elements* of responsible organizations (normative documents, programs, departments, job positions, engagement platforms, communication tools, processes, procedures) into *organizational design patterns* (self-contained, horizontal, hollow, modular, virtual).

IV. A main goal of *organizational development* in a responsible organization must be to simultaneously reach or exceed benchmarks in triple bottom line performance, stakeholder value creation, and moral excellence. Only if the minimum benchmarks are met can the organization be considered a responsible organization.

V.  Organizational development for responsible business is achieved between effective *change management*, responsible *leadership*, and the creation of an *organizational culture for responsible business*.

| Process Phase | Sustainability | | Responsibility | Ethics |
|---|---|---|---|---|
| **Phase 1: Understand organization theory** | Does the organization … | … have the potential to ever become sustainable? | … function to the best benefit of relevant stakeholders? | … have built-in ethical dilemmas? |
| **Phase 2: Design structures** | Have we … | … integrated structures that help to control and manage the organization's triple bottom line? | … created structures to dialogue and co-create with stakeholders? | … installed a system to guide moral decisions, detect misconduct, and incentivize moral excellence? |
| **Phase 3: Transform the organization** | Is the transformation process … | … sufficiently profound to reach the goal of becoming a sustainable business? | … tuned in to leading a broad set of organizational stakeholders? | … based on moral excellence? |

© Cengage Learning, 2015

## KEY TERMS

*change agent* 243
*change management* 245
*communication tool* 237
*department* 234
*engagement platform* 236
*leader* 240
*normative documents* 231

*organizational architecture* 227
*organizational change* 245
*organizational culture* 244
*organizational development* 238
*organizational structure* 227
*organizational theory* 222
*procedure* 238

*process* 237
*programs* 233
*responsible infrastructure* 223
*social intrapreneur* 244
*structural elements* 230

## EXERCISES

### A. Remember and Understand

A.1.   Mention the main groups of elements of responsible organizational architecture and give examples for each group.

A.2.   Describe the traditional model, the human relations model, and the human resources model of organizational theories.

A.3.   Explain the terms *green collar worker, CRO,* and *change agent,* and explain how they are related.

A.4.   Explain the terms *GRI report, whistleblowing hotline,* and *values statement,* and explain how they are related.

### B. Apply and Experience

B.5.   Think about one organization that you know well. Assess the organization in the three dimensions of opposing viewpoints in organizations.

B.6.   Think about the organization from question B.5. and decide which of the organizational

development patterns from Figure 8.6 would be the most appropriate ones for the organization.

### C. Analyze and Evaluate

C.7.   Look at a company's responsibility or sustainability report and draft a figure of the responsible organizational architecture, similar to the map in Figure 8.3.

C.8.   Look up the website of SEMCO and assess where the company is located on the responsible business performance scale in the three dimensions of sustainability, responsibility, and ethics (Figure 8.5).

### D. Change and Create

D.9.   Based on your analysis in question C.8, write a one-page change plan for SEMCO, using Kotter's model.

D.10.  Based on your analysis in question C.7, propose changes to the architecture you found with the goal of creating an even better responsible business infrastructure for the business.

Courtesy of Simon Zadek

Simon Zadeck pioneered main global responsibility standards. He has led the development and promotion of important concepts such as responsible competitiveness and materiality. In a very successful *Harvard Business Review* article, he drafted a "path to corporate responsibility" that included stages of organizational learning as a clear guide for creating responsible businesses—which is a central concept in this chapter.

**In a recent newspaper article for *The Guardian,* you said, "Scale is the zeitgeist in the world of sustainability." How can responsible managers and businesses create sufficient scale to reach truly sustainable development? Is it possible, and if so, what are good practices to reach large-scale positive impacts?**

The simple answer is product, process, people, and public policy—the four Ps. New products, redesigned business processes, citizens who behave differently as consumers and voters, and public policies that shape markets to incentivize the right business behavior.

**You coined the term *responsible competitiveness.* Can businesses, nations, and regions increase their competitiveness through responsible business conduct? In a world where *corporate social responsibility* and *sustainability* have become mainstream buzzwords, does strategic positioning through the topic still work?**

They can and they do. After all, the United States' pushing back on China's renewables exports, the fierce international response to Europe's attempt to set carbon taxes on all flights into and out of the continent, and practically everyone's objection to Ontario's moves to establish industrial development conditions to its green energy feed-in tariffs all illustrate how much is at stake. Today's green opportunities are constrained by fossil fuel subsidies and short termism in financial markets. But no one doubts the rise of the green economy; it is all about when and how, and who will be the winners and losers.

**You have described five stages of organizational learning in corporate responsibility. Which stage do you think most businesses are at today? Are** there many businesses at the strategic or even the civil stage?

Many major corporations, notably those stewarding premium brands, have reached the managerial level on many issues, beyond denial and compliance. A small number have strategic aspirations for selected aspects of their sustainability footprint that can be inverted to create business value. First-generation companies are starting without legacy constraints and are racing ahead, albeit at a smaller scale. Just a small number of companies, or more correctly their leaders, see that the real deal is one that has to include broad-ranging changes in our economic governance, and profound changes in our financial system.

**With AccountAbility you have created a series of the most outstanding international standards influencing responsible business conduct. What is the standard of the future? What normative tool would we need to make businesses take the next (big) transformative step?**

AccountAbility, with others, brought to the forefront the nexus of sustainability and accountability, and not only stewarded its own standards, notably the AA1000 Series, but also helped to shape many other standards, from reporting to corruption and commodities. These standards are an important part of the solution, but you cannot design great buildings from the plumbing upward. That is why in the later years of my leadership of AccountAbility, we focused increasingly on corporate governance, business strategy, investor governance, and nations' tools for advancing economic transformation.

**Do you think we have reached a situation where businesses are truly held accountable? Is accountability a reality in today's economy?**

Businesses are in general very accountable, but the right balance of what they are accountable for has been lost. Intended beneficiaries of private financial capital deserve a decent return, but not at any cost, just as fund managers should be incentivized, but not to take excessive risk or to trade at the cost of the real economy. We need different accountability, not more or less, if sustained prosperity and reasonable equity is to be ensured. And no, we do not have that right balance of accountabilities today. We have made some gains, but the sway of history remains in the wrong direction.

Courtesy of Thomas Hügli

**Employing organization:** AXA Winterthur, which belongs to AXA Group, is the leading all-line insurer in Switzerland. It offers its clients financial protection through a broad range of personal, property, and liability products; customized life insurance and pension solutions; as well as bank products in cooperation with bank partners. AXA Winterthur has approximately 4,000 employees and is an active partner of the Swiss Climate Foundation. Its sales network consists of more than 280 independent general agencies and agents, with approximately 2,750 employees working exclusively for AXA Winterthur. In 2012, AXA Winterthur reported total revenues of 9.5 billion Euro.

**Job title:** Chief Communication & Corporate Responsibility Officer (CCRO)

**Education:** Bachelor in Economics and Business Administration; Certified PR Consultant; Master of Arts in Responsible Management (Steinbeis University, Berlin)

## In Practice

**What are your responsibilities?** The CCRO is a direct report to the CEO and has a dotted-line reporting relationship to the AXA Group CCRO in Paris, France. The CCRO role is not designed to be a full-time occupation, but rather a governance position.

As one of AXA's primary voices on corporate responsibility (CR) and advisor to senior management, the CCRO drives and articulates our three-legged CR strategy (employee engagement, stakeholder management, flagship program "road prevention" for differentiation) at regional and local levels to position AXA as a responsible corporation, in order to achieve our ambition to become the preferred financial services company. Through effective leadership and in line with the Group CR strategy, he is responsible for building a strong CR strategic plan and targeted key performance indicators (KPIs) in order to embed CR into core business processes to provide proof of AXA's commitment and to leverage this proof in order to build trust among all of AXA's key stakeholders.

**What are typical activities you carry out during a day at work?**

My daily tasks mostly include observing the CR topics of the national political debate that also affect our work, such as the turnaround in energy policy, mobility in the future, or the new transparency and capital requirements. They also include thinking more deeply about CR. These ideas then become part of the statements or presentations we use in response to internal and external inquiries. I also spend a lot of time talking with team members about operational decisions, meeting with customer segment boards, or holding stakeholder communication meetings in order to further establish the views and meaning of corporate responsibility within the organization.

**How do sustainability, responsibility, and ethics topics play a role in your job?**

AXA's mission says that "we help customers live their lives with more peace of mind." In this context, responsibility is an inherent part of our mission: As a company whose business it is to protect people over the long term, we have a responsibility to leverage our skills, resources, and risk expertise to build a stronger and safer society. Our CR charter communicates a shared set of commitments that will guide us as a professional team in integrating CR into AXA's core business and culture. Main points in the charter are "monitor and control the honesty and accuracy of our messages" (e.g., avoid misrepresenting the CR aspects of our insurance products or services), "strive to communicate how we run our business in a responsible way" (e.g., highlight how our business benefits society), and "be exemplary regarding environment, and walk the talk" (e.g., look for ways to reduce our own impacts on the environment as regards travel, paper consumption, and energy use). Our Compliance Guide and Code of Ethics govern topics such as the whistleblower policy, money-laundering, data protection, and compliance reporting obligations.

**Out of the topics covered in the chapter into which your interview will be included, which concepts, tools, and topics are most relevant to your work? How?**

The company's mission, vision, values, and business strategy form the basis of our work, and they are therefore also reflected in the CR Charter and the

CR Strategy. We conduct a self-assessment each year to see what progress we've made. This is based on economic, social, and environmental aspects, with reference to the Dow Jones Sustainability Index (DJSI), on which AXA Group has been listed since 2007. Important instruments in connection with conservation include our environmental strategy with its focus on climate protection and resource use, and our energy guideline, which defines the benchmarks for efficient, low-impact, and climate-friendly use of energy at AXA Switzerland in order to meet the internal targets of AXA Group and comply with statutory provisions (Energy Act, $CO_2$ law, as well as applicable cantonal energy laws).

As regards organizational structure, the Corporate Responsibility Committee defines, approves, and periodically reviews the CR strategy; ensures its integration into the overall company strategy; and approves the guidelines and directives, standards, and processes concerning CR management. The Committee meets twice a year and includes members of the Executive Board, the Chief Communication & Corporate Responsibility Officer (chair), and the Head of Public Affairs & CR, who is in charge of implementing the CR strategy at the operational level. She and her team are part of the Communication & CR department. They work with CR ambassadors, who are responsible for implementing specific departmental activities, together with the department head. AXA Group issues an Activity and Corporate Responsibility Report, which also includes projects and key figures of AXA Winterthur.

**Insights and Challenges**

**What recommendation can you give to practitioners in your field?** It makes a lot of sense to apply the principles derived from well-established rules to the company's own foundations. This includes, for example, the Swiss Foundation Code in Switzerland, or the Principles of Sound Practice in Foundations in Germany, as a way of setting clear rules for defining our tasks, competencies, and mutual scope of influence. In addition, it seems sensible to review from time to time the CR core team's tasks and integration into the organization in order to get a better sense of how well these topics are becoming accepted.

**Which are the main challenges of your job?**

The primary challenge continues to be showing the connection between our core business and the benefit this has for our company. This applies especially in the case of an insurance company whose need for corporate responsibility may not be obvious at first—as is the case in a manufacturing company—and whose long-term business model is often immediately—and wrongly—associated with sustainability.

**Is there anything else that you would like to share?**

Employee surveys are also suitable for integrating possible CR-specific topics because they help us to track the progress we're making and develop further measures we need to take.

---

## SPECIAL PERSPECTIVE: CLASSIC ORGANIZATION THEORIES AND THEIR RELEVANCE FOR RESPONSIBLE MANAGEMENT

In this section, we revisit organizational structures through the perspective of classical models.

We utilize three time periods first described by Gibson[53] to illustrate how organizational structure has evolved toward responsible business: (a) the *mechanistic tradition* (or scientific or bureaucratic model) of organizational structure, (b) the *humanistic challenge* (human relations and human resources management), and (c) the *realistic synthesis* of previous models. Gibson's[54] categories appear to follow a chronological evolution throughout the twentieth century. Thus, we examine the inhumane, mechanistic view of employees and contrast it with a more responsible view of employees and human rights.

**The Mechanistic Tradition**

Mechanistic organizations are "without peculiar features and malleable without incident into the organization structure; man is characterized as a machine-predictable, repairable, and replaceable,"[55] devoid of ethical decision making. The *mechanistic tradition* characterizes this orthodox view of organizational theory,[56] which underwrites the work of classical management theorists including Frederick Taylor, Henry Fayol, and Max Weber. Does the label "machine" and "mechanistic" imply no concern for people? Not necessarily. Urwick[57] states the early theorists did indeed consider the people aspects of organization "under other ideas such as coordination, control, leadership, and morale."[58] Thus, some theorists brought a humane and ethical aspect of people into the malleable and mechanistic view of classical theorists.

## 1. Henri Fayol and Administrative Theory

The classical perspective can be well illustrated by Henri Fayol. His approach makes several assumptions about how organizations function, and it assumes that organizations are like machines, which have structure, efficiency, and technology. Early theorists thought organizations were run rationally and efficiently and were improved by analyzing formal structure and adding bureaucratic design. Organizational design is similar to organizational structure. While structure is the *means* the organization uses to achieve its goals, organizational design is "about how and why various means are chosen."[59]

Fayol was a French industrialist who exemplified the classical perspective and seemed to support "machine-like" designs and assumptions. His approach is often identified as "administration theory."[60] Fayol outlined five foundational functions of management:[61] *planning* (forecasting or anticipating a future plan of action), *organizing* (creating an organizational structure where middle managers and employees fit best), *commanding* (managers assign specific tasks for employees and have unity of command), *coordination* (all efforts are directed toward a goal), and *controlling* (ensures everything is working in accordance with accepted goals).

Noticeably, these five functions are focused on management, and not on employees, and do not address ethical responsibilities of employees or responsible management.

Fayol later developed each function in more detail, transforming them into fourteen principles of management. His *division of labor,* for example, is a principle stating how employees work best when specializing with specific tasks, a concept similar to Adam Smith's division of labor as published in *The Wealth of Nations*. Fayol's elements and principles prescribed specialization and standardization in organizations, and he sought to explain how organizations run. He viewed employees like they were *cogs in a well-oiled machine* that function efficiently when they are commanded and controlled. Humane and ethical treatment was not considered. Next, we consider how Weber's contributions to bureaucratic theory complemented Fayol's ideas.

## 2. Max Weber and Bureaucratic Leadership

Max Weber, a German sociologist, whose views were introduced to the West about the same time as Fayol's, contributed an "idea type" theory[62] to organizational structure. Weber's term *organizational bureaucracy* typically connotes negative impressions in the minds of many managers today. In fact, the word *bureaucracy* itself is associated with inefficiencies of big government and big educational institutions. Weber is generally credited as the early theorist of modern-day bureaucratic organizations. Some writers suggest the bureaucracy is still the predominant institutional characteristic of highly complex and differentiated societies, and it is worthwhile to study this structure in "a world in which large hierarchical organizations dominate virtually all spheres of social life."[63] Although Weber's theories still predominate in organizations today, we focus on whether a triple bottom line perspective can exist in this type of organizational structure, and we will briefly assess responsibility, sustainability, and ethics in a bureaucratic organization.

What should we assume about the inherent nature of people who work for and lead bureaucratic organizations? Urwick[64] quotes James L. Gibson's statement that views individuals in organizations as "suspicious, distrustful, jealous, deceitful, self-centered, apathetic and immature … intolerant of differences, unable to communicate in depth with his fellows, and shortsighted."[65] Gibson's comments require us to consider whether managers in bureaucratic structures can value and respect employees. Will the structure need to undergo dramatic change management toward sustainability, especially toward employees, as illustrated in the opening case of SEMCO?

## 3. Frederick Taylor and Scientific Management

Frederick Taylor's book, *Principles of Scientific Management*,[66] established another major approach to mechanistic organizations. His theories revealed many of the same principles in Fayol's and Weber's approaches; however, Taylor concentrated on micro aspects of organizational structures, such as relationships among management and employees and job management designs, while Fayol considered macro perspectives of organizational functioning.[67] Furthermore, Weber's "ideal type" theory, while having many similarities with Taylor's theory, focused on organizational rules and rational-legal authority in bureaucratic functioning.

Taylor's main components of scientific management were summarized well by Miller:[68]

- One best way exists to do every job, which includes time and motion studies.
- Proper selection of workers for the job requires scientific selection.
- Training of workers is scientific and requires that only "first-class" workers be retained.
- An inherent difference exists between management and workers.[69]

These scientific principles and nonhuman approach to employees build efficiency but do not develop sustainable principles or address responsible management in employees.

## Summary and Assessment of Traditional Mechanistic Theories

We emphasize again how these primary classical approaches established an early mind-set toward organizational structure and prevented development of sustainability principles in organizations. Responsibility management was set aside for the economic bottom line. The sole emphasis appeared to be on efficiency and income. Many bureaucratic structures today tend to remain mechanistic in design and may create tightly woven and strict systems of rules and lines of authority. Such structures may become suppressive and create stress on employees, who lack ownership and incentive to work.

Managers may abuse their authority with subordinates in mechanistic designs by overemphasizing compliance with rules. Likewise, highly centralized and vertical structures affect the quality of communication, which is "filtered" and changed as it passes through many different levels of authority. Effective communication is necessary for the development of sustainable principles. More decentralized structures allow effective communication and tend to promote a greater sense of well-being and ownership in employees. Developing sustainable practices among employees will propel organizations into the future.

## The Humanistic Challenge

Human relations models of organizational structure represented a major shift in managerial thinking away from classical perspectives and mechanistic designs. New structures began to allow for social factors as part of the design, and human relations and human resources became popular. Managers no longer viewed employees as "cogs in a machine" but moved toward a more responsible view of people. A key individual was Elton Mayo, who led a series of research investigations with employees of an electrical plant. His research served as the catalyst for the "humanistic challenge."[70] These studies may be identified as the beginning of modern responsible employee management and the move away from machine designs to human designs.

### 1. Elton Mayo

Mayo, an Australian who became a researcher at Harvard University, conducted his investigations at a U.S. Western Electric Company plant in Hawthorne,

Illinois. His research team examined the impact of the working environment on employee output over a period of nine years. Mayo's investigations have become known as the "Hawthorne studies," and his findings, which revealed that worker output improved because of social factors, have been termed the *Hawthorne effect*. Interestingly, in the Hawthorne studies, productivity improved when researchers gave direct attention to the workers themselves, not from pay incentives, better illumination on the job, better working hours, or other improvements in working conditions. The improvement occurred primarily because of the personal attention the researchers paid to employees, not the working conditions. The findings were a jolt to the management world and spurred the move from mechanistic approaches of organizational structure to the human relations and human resources emphasis. The following sections highlight several other key individuals who were part of the humanistic challenge era.

## 2. Mary Parker Follett

Mary Parker Follett is well known for business and management ethics, although she never wrote on the topic of ethics.[71] One of her writings, *Creative Experience,*[72] addressed management theory and appeared at a point in time before Mayo's studies. Follett is credited with early responsible management views. She wrote on coordination, conflict, consent, control, and leadership. She believed in empowerment and participation among employees, and her intense belief in coordination led her to emphasize four responsible management principles:

- Coordination by direct contact of the responsible people concerned
- Coordination in the early stages
- Coordination as the reciprocal relating of all the factors in a situation
- Coordination as a continuing process[73]

Follett's principles, which contrast starkly with mechanistic, "cogs-in-a-machine" views of employees, helped set the stage for responsible management in human relations and human resources in later years.

## 3. Abraham Maslow

Abraham Maslow followed Follett and Mayo and provided significant impetus for the adoption of human relations–based organizational structures. He is probably best known for his theories of human motivation and personality.[74] He addressed why people do the things they do, and he answered questions about human wants and needs. He focused on intrinsic motivation within people. His hierarchy of needs has been widely applied in consumerism and sustainable living.

Maslow arranged human needs from basic physiological needs to higher-order, self-actualization needs. In his theory, each lower need generally must be met before higher needs can be fulfilled. For example, physiological needs are basic hunger, thirst, and sleep and sanitation needs, which are not met in over half of the world's population. Safety needs are basic security needs in the environment or workplace, which can include the security of a home, job, or health insurance. Responsible management means that an organization provides these needs for employees. Social or affiliation needs include love, belonging, friendships, romance, acceptance, and companionship. Esteem needs are met by individuals who reach a level where they require accomplishment and social recognition. Employees engaged in sustainable activities must receive appreciation for their accomplishments so that they will develop a sense of personal worth and self-esteem. Finally, self-actualization needs are met in those who achieve actualization by reaching a point in their potential where they exercise their capabilities to the fullest. In terms of sustainability, LOHAS (lifestyles of health and sustainability) may reflect this level of potential and fulfillment in individuals. Generally, these people maintain a continuous lifestyle of healthy living; they also serve as a nearly $290 billion market segment in the United States, focused on the environment, personal development, and social justice.[75]

Maslow's hierarchy clearly represents the shift from classical perspectives of organizational structure, based on extrinsic motivation of employees, to humanistic perspectives, which center on intrinsic motivation of employees. Responsible managers must consider both extrinsic and intrinsic motivations of employees.

## 4. Douglas McGregor

Douglas McGregor was yet another prominent advocate of the human relations movement in organizations.[76] He is best known for *Theory X* and *Theory Y,* a binary division of assumptions about basic human nature. Theory X, which stands on one end of a continuum, has a strong focus on managerial control and asserts a belief about human nature that employees lack motivation and responsibility.

Theory X assumes employees cannot work for themselves without being led and controlled, and assumes they typically lack intelligence and are passive.

In contrast, Theory Y assumes the opposite about human nature in regard to employees and adopts a more responsible management view than Theory X. Theory Y assumes employees are motivated and responsible and can work on their own without close managerial control if they are given the right circumstances and proper attention. McGregor's Theory Y would seem to agree with Maslow's idea that employees can be satisfied and productive if their human needs are met. McGregor initially characterized typical managers as either as "hard" or "strong," or "soft" or "weak," but asserted they need to be "firm but fair," combining both approaches. The combination of approaches was unsatisfactory to McGregor and pointed again to Maslow's basic needs theory. In any case, McGregor reminds us that leaders' basic assumptions about human nature determine whether they manage responsibly.

### 5. Frederick Herzberg

Frederick Herzberg wrote on motivation to work and is best known for his *motivation-hygiene theory* or *dual-factor theory*.[77] He asserted that certain factors cause employee satisfaction and that other separate factors cause dissatisfaction. An employee can be content with "hygiene factors" such as salary, benefits, working conditions, or safety in the environment, but not satisfied with "motivational factors" such as challenging work, achievement needs, or recognition in the workplace. Thus, employees may be satisfied on a certain level but dissatisfied with other aspects of work. Herzberg's theory presents a challenge for responsible managers to examine the entire employee environment.

### Moving from Human Relations to Human Resources

### 1. Raymond Miles

Human relations in organizational structures seemed the best approach to responsible management until the 1950s and 1960s. Managers and organizational leaders, however, eventually learned that "a happy employee" is not always a productive employee. Employees can be satisfied with their jobs and be provided with great working conditions in the company, but still not perform at top potential. As a result, models of organizational structures evolved into a human resources approach, as described by Raymond Miles.[78] Next, we examine whether the human resources

model provides responsible managers with a better organizational structure through which to empower employees than does the human relations model.

### 2. Blake and Mouton Managerial Grid

Robert Blake and Jane Mouton developed a popular tool, the *managerial grid,* still used in many management circles and later renamed the *leadership grid*.[79] The significant contribution made by Blake and Mouton[80] helped promote balance in leaders having a high *concern for people* and high *concern for task*, individuals identified as a "team leaders." This ideal leader could responsibly empower employees based on equilibrium between the two concerns. A high task-oriented leader with little concern for people would appear like one focused only on authority-compliance. A high concern-for-people leader with little concern for task would appear like a "country club manager." A third dimension of *effectiveness* was later added to the grid,[81] but Blake and Mouton's contribution to the humanistic challenge created equilibrium between task and people.

### 3. Other Contributors

Numerous other contributors aided the progress in responsible management and ethics. One significant contributor, Rensis Likert, described various organizational systems that, in essence, modified McGregor's thinking on Theory X and Theory Y. Likert's *Systems I and II* elaborated on Theory X and *Systems III and IV* expanded Theory Y and sided more with responsible management. Notably, Likert's System IV was called *participative organization* and promoted organizational decision making among employees. Likert's participative organizations empowered employees, much like the SEMCO case located at the beginning of this chapter demonstrated. Ricardo Semler developed a model in which decisions were made entirely by employees.

Finally, Chester Barnard[82] was another leading thinker in how to develop organizational structures. Among his writings, he addressed *ethics in responsible management*. His contributions emphasized how cooperation among employees, "through formal organizations of their activities, creates moralities,"[83] a startling conception for many at the time. Barnard was also known as a "systems thinker" in organizational structures.[84]

Review Table 8.1. Contrast how a human resources approach to organizational structure combines different components of the classical and human relations approaches. Over time neither the human relations model nor the human resources model provided a comprehensive organizational structure for responsible management. Employees could participate and be involved in many sustainable activities, such as "green clubs," volunteer programs, and other participatory programs, yet still not be fully using their capacities and abilities. Within the old models, employees might still not feel a true sense of empowerment or ownership in the organization. Managers began to understand that employees felt manipulated and run by management. We now briefly discuss key individuals who tried to fill this empowerment gap in organizational structures by realistically synthesizing the different approaches.

### Realistic Synthesis

The realistic synthesis identifies organizational structures through systems models, cultural models, and other approaches. *General systems theory* is an "approach which treats organizations as complex sets of mutually dependent and interacting variables."[85] While classical models of organizational structure described organizations as machines, systems models often use the metaphor of "organisms" and liken the organization to a human body system.[86] The general systems model assumes all units of a business are interdependent, interconnected, and involve "synergy." The functions of one unit directly affect the functioning of other units. Just as a headache will affect the entire human body and will cause adaptations and changes in other parts of the body, a change in one business area will directly affect other areas. In systems-type thinking about organizational structures, the sharing of information and intense communication are high priorities for these systems to work effectively.

### I. General Systems Models

General systems caught on after the limitations of classical and humanistic models of organizing were recognized. To spur acceptance, in 1972 the *Academy of Management Journal* dedicated an entire issue (number 4) to general systems theory and its applications to organizational structures. The special issue was dedicated to the works of Ludwig von Bertalanffy, a biologist who wrote on living systems and whose works are considered seminal to the development of organizational systems models.[87] The reality synthesis in organizational

structures takes various forms and shapes today, but it fits well with viewing *complex organizations and operations as organisms*. Most organizations adopt a form of systems theories (network and matrix structures, etc.), an organizational structure that allows responsible management to integrate throughout the entire organization and promote sustainability principles and ethics among all employees.

W. Edwards Deming,[88] another prominent proponent of systems, pushed for transformation in prevailing styles of management by assuming systems cannot understand themselves and require help from the outside.[89] He is perhaps best known for his quality control and quality management work in Japan in the 1950s. *Quality circles* were first conceptualized in Japan by Deming and helped humanize employees in Japanese companies. The concept then became widely popular in Western companies following the successful implementation in Japan. Deming emphasized that cooperation rather than competition among employees can help people develop joy in work and promote employee well-being.

### 2. Cultural Models

Models of organizational structure began to evolve quickly during the 1980s and 1990s. Acceptance of cultural approaches, a view that *organizations exist as cultures* instead of as organisms or machines, began in the early 1980s. Peters and Waterman's widely popular business book, *In Search of Excellence—Lessons from America's Best-Run Companies*,[90] served as the catalyst for this model. If a company has a strong and clearly identified culture, it will provide the best place to work. Walt Disney, Walmart, IBM, and Procter & Gamble were identified with strong cultures. These companies promoted strong people development and promoted respectful relationships among employees, a responsible management approach through culture. Company cultures also exhibit a strong history, values and beliefs, rites and rituals, stories, heroic figures, and a cultural network.[91]

Viewing organizational structures as organisms added significantly to the understanding of the integration of responsible management throughout the design. Modern complex organizations are indeed interdependent, interconnected, and involve "synergy"—a structure that is open to responsible management.

A.1. Would "less concern for people" in a machine-like organizational structure allow better responsible management of nondiscrimination policies? Would significant underlying racial or gender tensions still exist? What would it take for an organization to gain ownership of human rights goals?

A.2. Do you work or manage in an organization that tends to view employees as a means to an end, as "cogs in a machine?" If so, consider these questions:

- Do you consider your organization to be a vertical one or more horizontal? If vertical, what impact do more structural levels, tighter spans of control, top-down decision making, and less involvement of work teams have on your company?

- What changes in organizational structure in your company will allow better responsible management of employees?

- How can employees be more involved in decision-making processes? Perhaps your company is "vertically challenged" and wider spans of control and a flatter design could help. How can you help consolidate middle levels for better communication about sustainable activities?

A.3. Newer models of organizational structure have begun to allow for social factors as part of the design. Ask yourself if organizational structures built around human relations are a *necessary* part of responsible management. Consider these questions:

- Recall the Hawthorne effect discovered by Elton Mayo. How closely do social factors and managerial attention to employees reflect your own workplace? Do you think a strong presence of social factors would lead to greater employee productivity?

- How well does Mary Parker Follett's principles of coordination, empowerment, and participation among employees apply to your company?

- Try to envision McGregor's Theory X or Theory Y applied to your organization. Does your company's structure allow for tight managerial control of employees and assume a lack of motivation and responsibility (Theory X)? Or does your structure allow employees the right circumstances and proper attention to be motivated, responsible, and work on their own (Theory Y)? Which theory best supports responsible management?

- Consider whether the structure of your organization promotes job satisfaction through both motivation-hygiene factors. Does your structure encourage Herzberg's "hygiene factors" such as salary, benefits, working conditions, and safety in the environment? Does the structure promote challenging work, achievement needs, and recognition in the workplace? Are both factors present?

A.4. Human resources organizational structures filled in the "gaps" of the human relations structural model. How would you answer these questions about your organization?

- In your workplace, would you agree that happy employees are not necessarily productive employees? Why?

- How well does an ideal responsible manager fit Blake and Mouton's high concern for people *and* high concern for task? Can you think of other characteristics of responsible leaders?

## SOURCES

1. CROA. (2011). *Corporate responsibility best practices: Research summary.* Edison: Corporate Responsibility Officer Association.
2. BCLC, CROA. (2012). *The state of the corporate responsibility profession* (p. 13). Washington, DC: U.S. Chamber of Commerce.
3. BCLC, CROA. (2012). *The state of the corporate responsibility profession* (p. 13). Washington, DC: U.S. Chamber of Commerce.
4. Margolis, J. D., & Walsh, J. P. (2003). Misery loves companies: Rethinking social initiatives by business. *Administrative Science Quarterly,* 48(2), 268–305, p. 284.
5. Heugens, P. P., & Scherer, A. G. (2010). When organization theory met business ethics: Toward further symbioses. *Business Ethics Quarterly,* 20(4), 643–672, p. 643.
6. Campbell, J. L. (2007). Why would corporations behave in socially responsible ways? An institutional theory of corporate social responsibility. *Academy of Management Review,* 32(3), 946–967, p. 946.
7. Heugens, P. P., & Scherer, A. G. (2010). When organization theory met business ethics: Toward further symbioses. *Business Ethics Quarterly,* 20(4), 643–672, p. 643.
8. Heugens, P. P., & Scherer, A. G. (2010). When organization theory met business ethics: Toward further symbioses. *Business Ethics Quarterly,* 20(4), 643–672.
9. Hofstede, G. (1985). The interaction between national and organizational value systems. *Journal of Management Studies, 22,* 347–357.
10. Robert, C., & Wasti, S. A. (2002). Organizational individualism and

collectivism: Theoretical development and an empirical test of a measure. *Journal of Management, 28*(4), 544–566.

11. Heugens, P. P., & Scherer, A. G. (2010). When organization theory met business ethics: Toward further symbioses. *Business Ethics Quarterly, 20*(4), 643–672, p. 643.

12. Heugens, P. P., & Scherer, A. G. (2010). When organization theory met business ethics: Toward further symbioses. *Business Ethics Quarterly, 20*(4), 643–672.

13. Kant, I. (1785). *Fundamental principles of the metaphysics of morals.* (T. B. Abbott, ed.). Retrieved August 18, 2012, from Pennsylvania State University eBook: www2.hn.psu .edu/faculty/jmanis/kant/Metaphysic -Morals.pdf

14. Heugens, P. P., & Scherer, A. G. (2010). When organization theory met business ethics: Toward further symbioses. *Business Ethics Quarterly, 20*(4), 643–672, p. 647.

15. Heugens, P. P., & Scherer, A. G. (2010). When organization theory met business ethics: Toward further symbioses. *Business Ethics Quarterly, 20*(4), 643–672.

16. Heugens, P. P., & Scherer, A. G. (2010). When organization theory met business ethics: Toward further symbioses. *Business Ethics Quarterly, 20*(4), 643–672, p. 649.

17. Miles, R. E., Snow, C. C., Meyer, A. D., & Coleman, H. J. (1978). Organizational strategy, structure, and process. *Academy of Management Review, 3*, 546–562.

18. BCLC, CROA. (2012). *The state of the corporate responsibility profession* (p. 13). Washington, DC: U.S. Chamber of Commerce.

19. Jones, G. R. (2013). *Organizational theory, design, and change,* 7th ed. Upper Saddle River, NJ: Prentice Hall.

20. Greenbiz. (2011, May 20). *Report preview: Enterprise sustainability management solutions reference architecture and buyer's guide.* Retrieved October 11, 2012, from Greenbiz.com: www.greenbiz.com /event/2011/05/20/report-preview -enterprise-sustainability-management -solutions-reference-architectur

21. Trevino, L. K., Weaver, G. R., & Brown, M. E. (2008). It's lovely at the top: Hierarchical levels, identities, and perceptions of organizational ethics. *Business Ethics Quarterly, 18*(2), 233–252.

22. Anand, N., & Daft, R. L. (2007). What is the right organization design? *Organizational Dynamics, 36*(4), 329–344.

23. CROA. (2010). *Corporate responsibility best practices: Setting the baseline.* New Jersey: Corporate Responsibility Officer Association.

24. CROA. (2010). *Corporate responsibility best practices: Setting the baseline.* New Jersey: Corporate Responsibility Officer Association.

25. BCLC. (2012). *The state of the corporate responsibility profession.* Washington: U.S. Chamber of Commerce.

26. Weinreb Group. (2011, September). *CSO back story: How chief sustainability officers reached the C-suite.* Retrieved September 5, 2012, from: http://weinrebgroup.com/wp-content/ uploads/2011/09/CSO-Back-Story-by- Weinreb-Group.pdf

27. CROA. (2010). *Corporate responsibility best practices: Setting the baseline.* New Jersey: Corporate Responsibility Officer Association.

28. Heaney, S. A. (2012). *How to embed sustainability into the business enterprise?* Retrieved November 11, 2012, from Executive Forum, Boston College Center for Corporate Citizenship Blog: http://blogs.bcccc.net/ blog/executive-forum/?utm_source= Newsletter+June+2012&utm_ca

29. CROA. (2010). *Corporate responsibility best practices: Setting the baseline.* New Jersey: Corporate Responsibility Officer Association.

30. Waddock, S., & Bodwell, C. (2007). *Total responsibility management: The manual* (p. 99). Sheffield: Greenleaf Publishing.

31. Ditlev-Simonsen, C. D., & Gottschalk, P. (2011). Stages of growth model for corporate social responsibility. *International Journal of Corporate Governance, 2*(3), 268–287.

32. Laasch, O., & Conaway, R. N. (2013). *Responsible business: Managing for sustainability, ethics and global citizenship.* Monterrey: Editorial Digital.

33. Zadeck, S. (2004). The path to corporate social responsibility. *Harvard Business Review, 82*, 125–132.

34. Reidenbach, R. E., & Robin, D. P. (1991). A conceptual model of corporate moral development. *Journal of Business Ethics, 10*(4), 273–284.

35. Lipman-Blumen, J. (2006). *The allure of toxic leaders: Why we follow destructive bosses and corrupt politicians—and how we can survive them.* Oxford: Oxford University Press.

36. Pless, N. M. (2007). Understanding responsible leadership: Role identity and motivational drivers. *Journal of Business Ethics, 74*, 437–456; Maak, T., & Pless, N. M. (2006). Responsible leadership in a stakeholder society: A relational perspective. *Journal of Business Ethics, 66*, 99–115.

37. Gini, A. (1997). Moral leadership and business ethics. *Journal of Leadership & Organizational Studies, 4*(4), 64–81.

38. Quinn, L., & Dalton, M. (2009). Leading for sustainability: Implementing the tasks of leadership. *Corporate Governance, 9*(1), 21–38.

39. CROA. (2010). *Corporate responsibility best practices: Setting the baseline.* New Jersey: Corporate Responsibility Officer Association.

40. Schaubroek, J. M., Hannah, S. T., Avolio, B. J., Kozlowski, S. W., Lord, R. G., Treviño, L. K., ... Peng, A. C. (2012). Embedding ethical leadership within and across organization levels. *Academy of Management Journal, 55*(5), 1053–1078.

41. Van Velsor, E. (2009). Introduction: Leadership and corporate social responsibility. *Corporate Governance, 9*(1), 3–6.

42. Lindgreen, A., Swaen, V., Harness, D., & Hoffman, M. (2011). The role of "high potentials" in integrating and implementing corporate social responsibility. *Journal of Business Ethics, 99*(1), 73–91.

43. Visser, W. (2008). CSR change agents: Experts, facilitators, catalysts and activists. In *CSR Inspiration Series, No. 2.*

44. SustainAbility. (2008). *The social intrapreneur: A field guide for corporate change makers.* London: SustainAbility.

45. Hickman, G. R. (2010). *Leading organizations: Perspectives for a new era,* 2nd ed. Thousand Oaks, CA: Sage.

46. Sims, R. R. (2000). Changing an organization's culture under new leadership. *Journal of Business Ethics, 25*, 65–78.

47. Schein, E. (1985). *Organizational culture and leadership.* San Francisco: Jossey-Bass.

48. Kotter, J. P. (1995). Leading change: Why transformation efforts fail. *Harvard Business Review, 73*(2), 55–67, p. 59.

49. Kakabadse, N. K., Kakabadse, A. P., & Lee-Davies, L. (2009). CSR leaders road-map. *Corporate Governance, 9*(1), 50–57.

50. Adapted from Kotter, J. P. (1995). Leading change: Why transformation efforts fail. *Harvard Business Review, 73*(2), 55–67.

51. Kotter, J. P. (1995). Leading change: Why transformation efforts fail. *Harvard Business Review, 73*(2), 55–67, p. 60.

52. Lindgreen, A., Swaen, V., Harness, D., & Hoffman, M. (2011). The role of "high potentials" in integrating and implementing corporate social responsibility. *Journal of Business Ethics, 99*(1), 73–91.

53. Gibson, J. L. (1966). Organization theory and the nature of man. *Academy of Management Journal, 9*(3), 233–245.

54. Gibson, J. L. (1966). Organization theory and the nature of man. *Academy of Management Journal, 9*(3), 233–245.

55. Gibson, J. L. (1966). Organization theory and the nature of man. *Academy of Management Journal, 9*(3), 233–245, p. 234.

56. Morgan, G. (1980, December). Paradigms, metaphors, and puzzle solving in organization theory. *Administrative Science Quarterly, 25*(4), 605–622.

57. Urwick, L. F. (1967). Organization and theories about the nature of man. *Academy of Management Journal, 10*(2), 9–15.

58. Urwick, L. F. (1967). Organization and theories about the nature of man. *Academy of Management Journal, 10*(2), 9–15, p. 11.

59. Jones, G. R. (2013). *Organizational theory, design, and change,* 7th ed. Upper Saddle River, NJ: Prentice Hall.

60. Wren, D. A., Bedeian, A., & Breeze, J. (2002). The foundations of Henri Fayol's administrative theory. *Management Decision, 40*(9), 906–918.

61. Fayol, H. (1949). *General and insustrial management* (C. Storrs, trans.). London: Pitman and Sons.

62. Weber, M. (1946). *From Max Weber: Essays in sociology* (H. Gerth & C. W. Mills, trans. and eds.). New York: Oxford University Press.

63. Langton, J. (1984). The ecological theory of bureaucracy: The case of Josiah Wedgwood and the British pottery industry. *Administrative Science Quarterly, 29*(3), 330–354, p. 330.

64. Urwick, L. F. (1967). Organization and theories about the nature of man. *Academy of Management Journal, 10*(2), 9–15.

65. Gibson, J. L. (1966). Organization theory and the nature of man. *Academy of Management Journal, 9*(3), 233–245.

66. Taylor, F. W. (1911). *The principles of scientific management.* New York: Harper & Row.

67. Miller, K. (2009). *Organizational communication: Approaches and processes.* Boston: Wadsworth Cengage Learning.

68. Miller, K. (2009). *Organizational communication: Approaches and processes.* Boston: Wadsworth Cengage Learning.

69. Miller, K. (2009). *Organizational communication: Approaches and processes* (pp. 25–26). Boston: Wadsworth Cengage Learning.

70. Roethlisberger, F. J., & Dickson, W. J. (1939). *Management and the worker.* Cambridge: Harvard University Press.

71. Melé, D. (2007, March). Ethics in management: Exploring the contribution of Mary Parker Follett. *International Journal of Public Administration, 30*(4), 405–424. Retrieved September 28, 2012, from IESE Business School: www.iese.edu/research/pdfs/DI-0618-E.pdf

72. Follett, M. P. (1951/1924). *Creative experience.* New York: Peter Smith.

73. Sethi, N. K. (1962). Mary Parker Follet: Pioneer in management theory. *Journal of the Academy of Management, 5,* 214–221, p. 216.

74. Maslow, A. H. (1943). A theory of human motivation. *Psychology Review, 50,* 370–396; Maslow, A. H. (1954). *Motivation and personality.* New York: Harper & Row.

75. LOHAS. (2012, September 27). *Background.* Retrieved 2012, from Lifestyles of Health and Sustainability: www.lohas.com/about

76. McGregor, D. (1957). The human side of enterprise. *Management Review, 46,* 22–28.

77. Herzberg, F. (1959). *The motivation to work.* New York: Wiley.

78. Miles, R. E. (1965, July/August). Human relations or human resource. *Harvard Business Review, 43*(4), 148–157.

79. Blake, R., & McCanse, A. (1991). *Leadership dilemmas: Grid solutions.* Houston: Gulf.

80. Blake, R., & Mouton, J. (1964). *The managerial grid.* Houston: Gulf.

81. Blake, R., Mouton, J., & McCanse, A. (1989). *Change by design.* Redding, MA: Addison-Wesley.

82. Bernard, C. I. (1948). *Organization and management: selected papers.* Cambridge: Harvard University Press.

83. Bernard, C. I. (1958). Elementary conditions of business morals. *California Management Review, 1*(1), 1–13, p. 2.

84. Gabor, A., & Mahoney, J. T. (2010). *Chester Barnard and the systems approach to nurturing organizations.* Retrieved October 4, 2012, from Indiana University: www.business.illinois.edu/Working_Papers/papers/10-0102.pdf

85. Gibson, J. L. (1966). Organization theory and the nature of man. *Academy of Management Journal, 9*(3), 233–245, p. 243.

86. Kreps, G. L. (1990). *Organizational communication: Theory and practice,* 2nd ed. New York: Longman.

87. Bertalanffy, L. V. (1968). *General systems theory.* New York: Braziller.

88. Deming, W. E. (2000). *The new economics for industry, government, education,* 2nd ed. Boston: MIT Press.

89. Deming, W. E. (2012). *The Deming system of profound knowledge.* Retrieved October 6, 2012, from The W. Edwards Deming Institute: http://deming.org/index.cfm?content=66

90. Peters, T., & Waterman, R. (1982). *In search of excellence—Lessons from America's best-run companies.* London, UK: HarperCollins.

91. Deal, T. E., & Kennedy, A. A. (1982). *Corporate cultures: The rites and rituals of corporate life.* Reading, MA: Addison-Wesley.

## 09

DMADV Routines
Self-Assessment
Benchmarking
Operations
Quality Management
VOC Checklists
Total Responsibilty Management
Manufacturing
Process
ISO 26000
European Quality Award
Excellence
Performance Dashboard
Continuous Improvement
Zero Waste
Six Sigma

# OPERATIONS: RESPONSIBLE ENTERPRISE EXCELLENCE

*You will be able to...*

1   **...analyze your processes in order to understand where to integrate responsible management activities.**

2   **...create new processes to manage triple bottom line, stakeholder value, and moral excellence.**

3   **...use lean management to create triple bottom line efficiency and the Six Sigma method to optimize stakeholder value.**

Ninety-six percent of CEOs believe that sustainability issues should be fully integrated into the strategy and operations of a company.[1]

Thirty-one percent of companies measure the impact of their CR programs on their audiences.[2]

Authors: Rick Edgeman, Zhaohui Wu, Oliver Laasch; Contributors: Anis Ben Brink, Aranzazu Gomez-Segovia, Cecilia del Castillo, Aurea Christine Tanaka, Ulpiana Kocollari

# IKEA Group: Responsible Operations Management

From its modest 1943 founding in the small village of Agunnaryd, Sweden, by seventeen-year-old Ingvar Kamprad, IKEA Group has grown into a global retail giant. IKEA is most strongly focused on furniture and has more than 130,000 employees in more than 40 countries with annual revenues of approximately €25 billion. Ikea is on a rapid growth path and expects to increase revenues to €45–€50 billion by 2020. The continuance of IKEA's present business practices would, by 2020, lead to near doubling in its use of wood products and increase in its annual carbon emissions from 30 million tons in 2012 to approximately 50 to 60 million tons.

Resource consumption growth that is proportional to overall business growth is patently unacceptable to IKEA. The enterprise is thus keenly aware of the need to innovate its business model in ways that will enable IKEA to remain true to its low-price, high-quality competitive strategy while successfully fulfilling future customer needs, mitigating the impact of higher-priced raw materials and energy, and reducing emissions and relative resource consumption. As part of a larger effort to innovate its corporate future, IKEA unveiled a new sustainability strategy in October 2012 aimed at making IKEA energy independent as well as aiding people to live an affordable and sustainable home life. Referred to as People & Planet Positive (PPP), this strategy has three key focus areas that are described in Table 9.1.

**Table 9.1** IKEA PPP Focus Areas

| IKEA Focus Area | Applications and Implications |
|---|---|
| Inspire and enable millions of people to live a more sustainable home life, offering products and solutions that help customers save money by reducing energy use, water use, and waste | Convert all lighting to LEDs that last 20 years and consume 85 percent less electricity; offer the most energy-efficient home appliances on the market at the lowest price; create low-price, functional, and easy-to-use solutions for sorting and minimizing waste and using less water at home |
| Produce as much renewable energy as is consumed in IKEA stores and buildings; build on the €1.5 billion allocated to wind and solar projects; become energy and resource independent | Improve energy efficiency in IKEA operations by at least 20 percent and encourage IKEA suppliers to do the same; continuously develop the IKEA range, making products more sustainable by ensuring all main home furnishing materials, including packaging, are renewable, recyclable, or recycled |
| Take the lead in creating a better life for people and communities, including support for the development of good places to work throughout the IKEA supply chain | Encourage suppliers to focus on both compliance and shared values, including going beyond the immediate reach of the supply chain and helping to support human rights, consistent with the ten principles of the UN Global Compact |

© Cengage Learning, 2015

IKEA's PPP approach responds to global trends, such as a growing solar-power market and recycling industry, as well as the transition to smart home energy management. It is also true to IKEA's core business strategy and practices, its purpose to play a leading role in replacement of energy-consuming goods with highly efficient solutions that benefit both customers and the natural environment. IKEA is committed to efficient resource use and to transformation of waste into resources. Further IKEA will use only renewable energy in its operations.

People & Plant Positive is foundational to IKEA's long-term growth strategy with numerous operations intersections. Effective execution of People & Planet Positive will help IKEA address climate change and resource scarcity internally through its policies and operations, through its supply chain, in the communities in which it operates, and for customers through product and process design and optimization, choice and efficient consumption of materials, materials acquisition, product distribution, and energy generation and consumption of both water and energy.

Sources: Osterwalder, A., & Pigneur, Y. (2010). *Business model generation.* New York: Wiley; Ackoff, R. L. (1981). *Creating the corporate future.* New York: Wiley; IKEA. (2012). *IKEA group unveils new sustainability strategy: People & Planet Positive.* Retrieved October 24, 2012, from: www.ikea.com/dk/da/about_ikea/newsitem/sustainability_strategy_2012#

## 9-1 | OPERATIONS AND RESPONSIBLE MANAGEMENT

*"Mission Zero means taking the time to understand the natural world and . . . how everything we do, take, make and waste affects nature's balance. . .".*[3]

Can we build companies that use zero natural resources instead of consuming them? John Elkington calls companies pursuing this "mission zero" *zeronauts*.[4] If such zeronauts are to achieve their mission, they must begin at the process level. Processes are well-confined, manageable series of activities. Companies are systems of interconnected processes, and operations management is the management of processes. This is why **responsible operations management** must be at the core of any responsible business and responsible management effort. Responsible operations management is crucial not only for the triple bottom line, but also for the creation of stakeholder value. Stakeholder value is created through the output of processes. Thus, processes must be designed to optimize stakeholder value.

**Operations management (OM)** explicitly addresses the design and management of products, processes, services, systems, and supply chains. It considers the acquisition, development, and use of resources that enterprises need to deliver services, information, and tangible goods desired by the various customer and market segments they serve. The purview of operations management spans operational, tactical, and strategic levels. At the strategic level, operations are concerned with such larger issues as determination of facility locations and sizes; designing technology supply chains; and determination of service or telecommunications network structures. At the operational level, issues addressed by OM include such important areas as materials acquisition, handling, and transportation; production planning and control; quality control; and logistics that include inventory management. Tactical OM issues include facility layout and structure; equipment selection, maintenance, and replacement; and project management methods.

This chapter will develop through the three main phases of responsible operations management illustrated in Figure 9.1. The model is a simplified version of a process model. In phase 1, we will provide basic insights into how to integrate responsible management into existing processes and how to design specialized responsible management processes. In phase 2, we will take a closer look at efficiency, and how to use lean enterprise methods, to minimize environmental resource use and impacts from processes. In phase 3, we will apply Six Sigma, benchmarking, and continuous improvement methods in order to improve process effectiveness— to improve the process output for key stakeholders.

**Responsible operations management** A process-based framework that aims at creating efficiency, zero resource consumption, and optimum stakeholder value through process effectiveness.

**Operations management (OM)** The area of management concerned with the effectiveness and efficiency of processes for the production of goods and services.

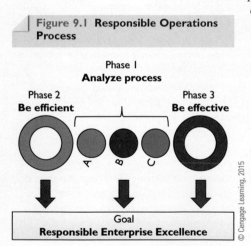

**Figure 9.1  Responsible Operations Process**

Phase 1
**Analyze process**

Phase 2
**Be efficient**

Phase 3
**Be effective**

A   B   C

Goal
**Responsible Enterprise Excellence**

© Cengage Learning, 2015

## 9-2 GOAL: RESPONSIBLE ENTERPRISE EXCELLENCE

*"Enterprise excellence is a consequence of balancing both the competing and complementary interests of key stakeholder segments to increase the likelihood of superior and sustainable competitive positioning and hence long-term enterprise success."*[5]

**Operational performance** describes the effectiveness and efficiency of processes for the production of goods and services.

The performance of an organization is the sum of all the outcomes of all its processes. If those outcomes are excellent, we may speak of enterprise excellence. Of most obvious import relative to operations is the emphasis on **operational performance**, but operational performance is, of course, substantially driven by, for example, innovation and human capital and in turn impacts customer-related, financial, marketplace, societal, and environmental performance.

Above-average operational performance, excellence, in responsible business must combine excellent triple bottom line outcomes, optimum stakeholder value, and moral excellence in all processes. Thus, **responsible enterprise excellence** can be defined as above-average operational performance for the triple bottom line, stakeholder value, and moral excellence. Enterprise excellence employs the systematic use of *quality management* strategies, principles, practices, and tools in the management of the enterprise with the objective of improving performance. Foundational to enterprise excellence are customer focus, stakeholder value, and a strong emphasis on process management.

Key enterprise excellence practices applied across functional areas include incremental continuous improvement, breakthrough improvement, preventative management, and management by facts. Among tools and practices often employed in organizational pursuit of enterprise excellence are the balanced scorecard, benchmarking,[6] lean enterprise methods,[7] process management,[8] project management,[9] and the DMAIC and DMADV approaches to innovation and design that are cornerstone to Six Sigma.[10] These tools and practices have each been the subject of many books, so the present focus is on generating increased awareness at a level allowing concrete consideration of connections between operations management and the tools and practices discussed, with the expectation that interested individuals will actively explore these concepts further.

From the late 1980s until now, management strategy, policy, and practice have been significantly influenced by the converging and unifying forces of two movements: sustainability and enterprise excellence. The enterprise excellence movement is characterized by complex business performance models such as those supporting the European Quality Award and America's Baldrige National Quality Award.[11] Harnessing the strength of excellence models for sustainable business might achieve the urgently needed results to reach the goal of a sustainable business, as described in the preceding section about "mission zero."

From an organizational perspective, our goal is to formulate and effectively execute strategy leading to continuously relevant and responsible actions and results that benefit all organizational stakeholders, including economic benefit for the organization itself. This is the core idea of **sustainable enterprise excellence (SEE)**, defined by Edgeman and Eskildsen[12] as:

> *SEE is a consequence of balancing both the competing and complementary interests of key stakeholder segments, including society and the natural environment, to increase the likelihood of superior and sustainable competitive positioning and hence long-term enterprise success.*

> *This is accomplished through an integrated approach to organizational design and function emphasising innovation, operational, customer-related, human capital, financial, marketplace, societal, and environmental performance.*

SEE coherently connects the kernels of the sustainability and enterprise excellence movements, as a means of delivering responsible competitiveness[13] SEE uniquely employs socioecological innovation as a key integrative factor, while also explicitly emphasizing organizational design[14] and the societal (equity/people) and environmental (ecology/planet) components of the triple top and triple bottom lines.

All in all, the primary goal of SEE may be regarded as one of efficiently, effectively, and profitably transforming sustainability strategy into sustainability results. This is fundamentally aligned with the cradle-to-cradle philosophy of product and service design, delivery, life cycle, and differently deployed use[15] that extends the

**Responsible enterprise excellence** refers to above-average operational performance for the triple bottom line, stakeholder value, and moral excellence.

**Sustainable enterprise excellence (SEE)** is to formulate and effectively execute strategy leading to continuously relevant and responsible actions and results that benefit all organizational stakeholders, including economic benefit for the organization itself.

traditional from-concept-to-customer approach to product development.[16] Equally, this approach is consistent with the status of sustainability as a key driver of innovation[17] and as a prime source of competitive advantage.[18]

Moving forward then, our focus is on the contribution of operations to sustainable enterprise excellence, as a dominant component of responsible enterprise excellence, and hence contribution toward continuously relevant and responsible strategy, actions, and results throughout the enterprise. Let us now consider more deeply some of the aforementioned tools and practices: lean enterprise methods, benchmarking, and Six Sigma approaches.

## 9-3 PHASE 1: DESCRIBE THE PROCESS

*"Indeed, if the appropriate sustainable processes are not in place it is quasi-impossible to implement the sustainable strategy, irrespective of how innovative and great it may be."*[19]

To create responsible excellence and performance you need to map, understand, and transform processes. Processes are the DNA of a business. They define the whole by every little decision, sustainable or unsustainable, responsible or irresponsible, ethical or not, that is taken on the way. Thus, to create a truly responsible business, managers have to take out the microscope and closely examine the DNA of the business—at the processes to build in—instead of just bolting on responsible sustainability, responsibility, and ethics.[20] In this first section, we will take a close look at business processes in order to understand where responsible management can attach.

### 9-3a Mapping the Process

Visualizations of processes are powerful tools to gain a basic understanding of how the company works and where to transform and integrate sustainability, responsibility, and ethics in order to create a truly responsible business. As illustrated in Figure 9.2, a **process** consists of one or several activities that, with the help of resources, transforms inputs to outputs.[21] Businesses are made of processes. Examples are the processes of recruiting a new employee, of preparing an expense sheet, or for managing a certain production line.

To evaluate the quality or performance of a process, one needs to analyze both the effectiveness and the efficiency of the process. Excellent, high-performing processes need be **effective**, that is, to make sure that planned activities are realized and planned results are achieved. Excellent processes also require achieving **efficiency**, which is a good relationship between the resources used and the results achieved.[22] One could also say that the effective process achieves the results, and an efficient one produces no waste, as it uses up exactly the minimum amount of resources necessary to create a given result. Sustainability, responsibility, and ethics play an important role, both from an effectiveness and from an efficiency point of view. The topic of ecoefficiency, for instance, aims at reducing the amount of

A **process** is any activity or set of activities that uses resources to transform inputs to outputs.

**Effectiveness** is the extent to which planned activities are realized and planned results achieved.

**Efficiency** is the relationship between the result achieved and the resources used.

## DIG DEEPER

### A Question of the Right Process

WaterHope is a social enterprise that provides clean and affordable drinking water to poor communities in the Philippines, supporting wider social development. It is the result of a partnership between PepsiCo and WTRC – Wholistic Transformation Resource Center, an NGO that focuses on humanitarian work and development in the Philippines. The water stations fostered by WaterHope distribute clean drinking water at a lower cost to the community, provide educational programs on sanitation and health, and microfinance services through which water dealers may obtain credit to purchase gallons and start their water distribution business. Community development and improvement of health levels due to the decrease of waterborne diseases are two of the many benefits derived from this self-sustainable entrepreneurial strategy. What do you think are the main processes of WaterHope? What are the activities? What are the enterprise's resources and outputs?

Source: ProSPER.Net. (2011). *Integrating sustainability in business school curricula project: Final report.* Bangkok: Asian Institute of Technology.

Figure 9.2 **Process Structure**

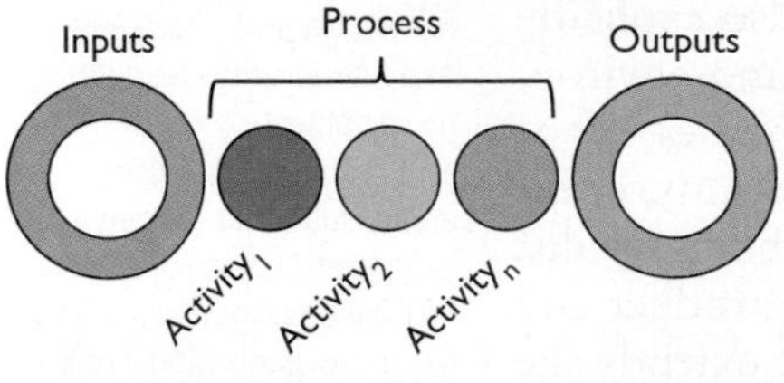

Inputs    Process    Outputs

Activity₁  Activity₂  Activityₙ

© Cengage Learning, 2015

environmental resources used to produce a product and service and, in this way, to make the process more ecoefficient.[23] Similarly, one could also imagine an "ethics-efficiency," in which companies aim at reducing the amount of noncompliance or ethical misconduct per product or service produced. Effectiveness of processes can be seen as the triple bottom line (TBL) output of a process. The question is, how much social, environmental, and economic value is created by the process; in other words, what is the process TBL?

## Mapping Internal Processes

Processes can be described on many different levels. Similar to the view through a microscope, with every further level, the view of the process is closer and more detailed. Figure 9.3 illustrates how an organization can be viewed on six levels, with greater detail at each level.[24] Levels 1 (organization) and 2 (function) describe the basic structure typically reflected in the organizational architectures.

From level 3 on, the work of process mapping begins. Functions typically consist of many subfunctions. A human resources department of a medium-sized company, for instance, will have one person or a group of people in charge of onboarding and offboarding of employees or, more plainly, of "hiring and firing"; another subfunction might be in charge of the employee training and development process. Each subfunction is involved in one or several processes, which are described at level 4. For instance, the training and development subfunction will be involved in conducting in-company trainings as one process, and in keeping track of employees' qualification levels as another subfunction.

Processes often exceed the boundaries of functions or subfunctions, which is why in a level 5 business process description, often more than one "player"[25] is mentioned in the left sidebar of the level 5 description. At this level of "business process detail" mapping, every single step of the process is described for all players involved. In our example, the business process detail map describes how to conduct an in-house training for employees who will work together as a "green" office team, and who need to be introduced to the basics of environmental management.

The closest look at a process is at the last level (level 6), which is the "supporting detail" level that describes the process through information gathered in its conduct. For our exemplary process of employee training, the records required might be, for instance, the attendance lists from single training sessions, and the grades for a final exam on the subject. We will now have a closer look at how to establish a level 5 process detail map, and how to integrate sustainability, responsibility, and ethics into it.

## Describing Detailed Processes

Mapping the business processes requires and creates a profound understanding of how companies work in detail and, even more importantly, shows where management intervention is required to make the overall process more responsible. In the following text, we will illustrate an adjusted version of level 5 **process detail maps**, which were introduced in the preceding section. This type of map is one that is customarily used in mainstream business.

A level 5 process detail map is the right tool to understand in which specific step of the process environmental impacts can be mitigated, stakeholder value can be created, and ethical misconduct can be avoided. Once this understanding is created, managers are able to specifically address those "hot spots" in their management activity. Process detail maps serve to help us understand both mainstream business processes, such as implementing a marketing campaign or screening a new supplier, as well as to help us deeply understand and improve specialized responsible management processes, such as a volunteering campaign or an ecoefficiency initiative.

A **process detail map** describes how activities in a process are related, sequenced, and how the flow of the process is controlled.

Figure 9.3 **Zooming into Responsible Organizations**

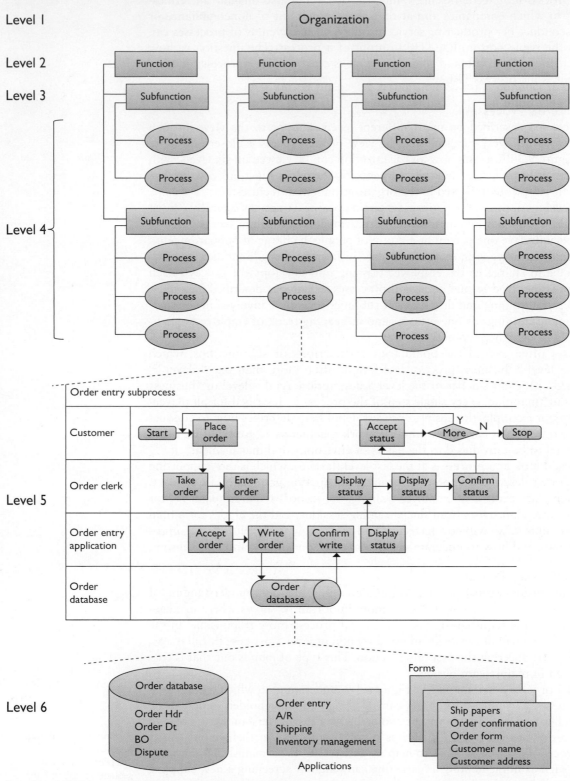

Level 1

Level 2

Level 3

Level 4

Level 5

Level 6

Order entry subprocess

Source: Conger, S. (2011). *Process mapping and management.* New York: Business Expert Press.

Figure 9.4 provides exemplary process maps for both types of processes. The first part of this figure shows how responsible business considerations can be embedded into the process of developing a mainstream market, while the second part of the figure describes the process of a volunteering campaign, which is a specialized responsible business process. In both maps, we can see the characteristics of **shared processes**, which are a constituting element of the processes in responsible business. A shared process is a process that integrates internal and external stakeholders in a value-creating series of activities. The responsible marketing process extensively involves customers and broader civil society as main stakeholders. The volunteering process illustrated in the figure involves activities of community members and employees as stakeholders.

There are many different methodologies for business process modeling, covering different application areas, focal points, and uses.[26] Due to the scope of this book, we will focus on only one approach, called a swim lane diagram, that is broadly applicable, generally applied, and almost intuitively understandable, and that depicts the activities undertaken by different involved groups and individuals. Figure 9.5 summarizes typical icons of a process description, including start and stop, activities, flows, information/data elements, and conditions and connections. To those standard icons we have also added three other icons describing responsible management considerations, such as the creation of stakeholder value, and consideration of environmental impacts and ethical dilemma situations in the process.

## 9-3b Describing the Process through Procedure Documents

Visual descriptions of the process as introduced in the last section provide an excellent overview for understanding the mechanics of a process. Written descriptions and instructions on how the process should be implemented in practice are the next step toward implementing responsible processes in practice. Such process descriptions in practice are named in many different ways, depending on the scope and scale of their contents. We will here focus on the description of procedures, more specifically, standard operating procedures (SOPs).

**Procedures** describe a specific way to carry out an activity or a process.[27] Documents describing procedures can range in length from one or two pages to dozens of pages. **Procedure documents**, in practice, are often called manual, standard operating procedures, routines, or checklists. Procedures, as one way of illustration, often include process maps like the ones illustrated previously. Procedures are typically used for standardized and frequently recurrent processes, but can also be applied to standardize highly complex processes, such as the one of defining your organizational mission. If a company is managed under the use of such procedures, using them to increase social and environmental performance is a powerful tool to bring sustainability, responsibility, and ethics into every activity of your company. As an example, if a procedure asks an operator of a machine to always switch off the motor when going for a break, this little action, together with many other such actions, will add up to significantly improve the environmental performance of the business.

Standard elements of operating procedure descriptions are illustrated in Figure 9.6.[28] The core piece of any procedure is the description of the activities required in the process. Procedure writing is a craft on its own, and many helpful sources are available to help you learn how to hone your procedure documents.[29]

A **shared process** is a process that integrates internal and external stakeholders in a value-creating series of activities.

A **procedure** is a specified way of carrying out an activity or a process.

**Procedure documents** describe processes, typically verbally, graphically, and through metrics.

Figure 9.4 Mapping Responsible Operations on the Process Level

Process I: Responsible Marketing

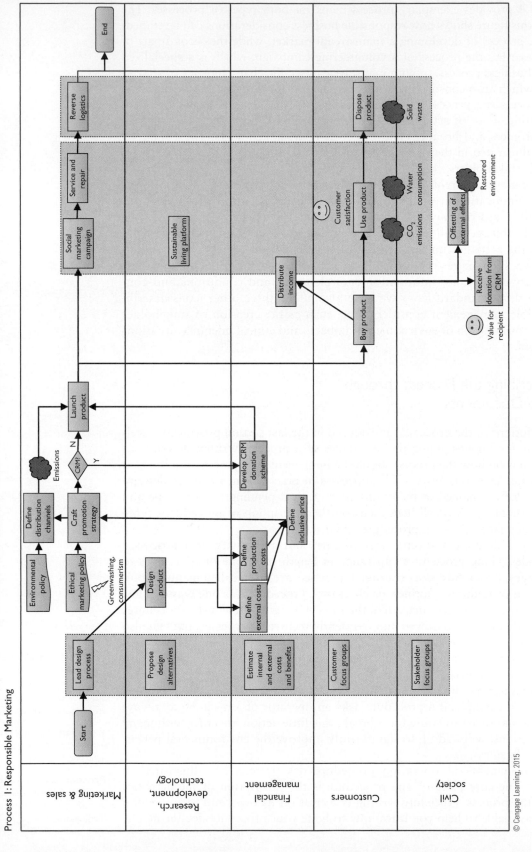

Process 2: Implementing a Skill-Based Volunteering Activity

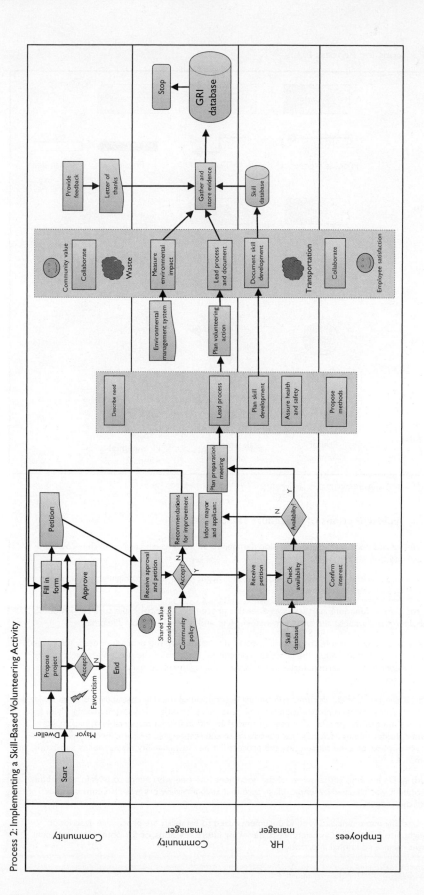

## Figure 9.5 Icons for Process Maps

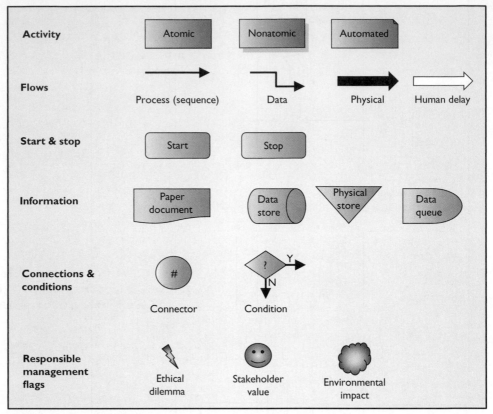

Source: Adapted from Conger, S. (2011). *Process mapping and management.* New York: Business Expert Press.

## Figure 9.6 Typical Sections of Procedure Descriptions

**Title:** Be descriptive and concise! Include a revision number to indicate which version of the procedure description is at hand.

**Purpose:** Why are you writing this procedure document? It might make sense to highlight the creation of responsible processes as one of the purposes.

**Scope:** What topic areas, functions, and activities does this procedure apply to? Make sure to include all affected stakeholder groups, social and environmental impacts, and potential ethical dilemmas.

**Definitions:** Are there any special terms and frameworks that readers of the procedure description need to understand to understand and apply the procedure proposed? Readers of the procedure might not be familiar with many concepts and terminologies in responsible management, so make sure to define central terms and to use plain language.

**Activities:** This is the heart of the document. Provide a description of the different activities to be realized. Also define responsibilities and communication channels, and refine criteria for decision making. Make sure to highlight the activities of the process that require special attention from a responsible management perspective, and consider adding activities that contribute to the responsible performance of the process. Also consider redesigning, or even substituting, the process if it has sustainability, responsibility substantial or ethical problems.

**Review tracking:** Define who is the owner of the document (the one who needs to be informed about changes), and when it was changed by whom. Make sure that such a review process also considers key stakeholders of the process.

**References:** Cite any important background documents used to establish the procedure description. Documents might also be included as reference material for future revisions, or for potential operational issues that might require additional information.

Source: Adapted from EPA. (2007, April 1). *Guidance for preparing standard operating procedures.* Retrieved December 22, 2012, from Environmental Protection Agency: www.epa.gov/QUALITY/qs-docs/g6-final.pdf

Writing a procedure description is the first step to transforming your operations, but it is only a first description. There might be two types of problems occurring during the monitoring phase of the work with procedure descriptions. The first problem is that the description might not be functional, in which case one would need to go back to reviewing and newly developing the procedure until it is apt for implementation. A second type of problem is the "people problem," where the procedure is well developed, but it encounters resistance in practice. In this case, the focus must be to delve into the implementation process and work with individuals to ensure the implementation.

In the responsible management context, both problems may be powerful impediments. Procedural problems are likely, as describing all the aspects of a process, regarding its triple bottom line, stakeholders, and potential ethical dilemmas, requires a profound analysis and systemic understanding of the process and of its context. People problems might occur, as employees conducting the process might be reluctant to change their ways and work habits. Paying attention to sustainability, responsibility, and ethics makes their work process more complex, which is why implementing responsible management processes requires extensive attention to potential people problems. On the other hand, we can also observe a general motivation of people to do "the right thing." Often process change toward responsible business is very welcomed by employees when they realize the potential to do good.

## 9-3c Bundling Processes to Management Systems

Quality management systems, systems for organizational health and safety, and environmental management systems, such as the ones described by the EMAS and ISO 14000 standards, are well known, but how can we build a management system for something as complex and seemingly intangible as responsible management? Different types of management systems share basic communalities.[30]

First of all, a **management system** handles topics that *permeate all functions* and every single process of the company. As an example, the quality of the final product or service depends on every little step and activity throughout all of a business´s processes, from controlling a specific customer account to the logistics of delivering the product or service. The same holds true for the topics we have subsumed under responsible management: sustainability, responsibility, and ethics. Whatever process we look at, it will always have a triple bottom line impact (sustainability), affect and be affected by stakeholders (responsibility), and potentially involve moral dilemmas (ethics). This is why management systems increasingly include also systems for managing responsible business, such as sustainable operating system,[31] or a total responsibility management system,[32] or mainstream management control systems.[33]

Second, those systems consist of the *organizational documents* of a normative and descriptive nature that have the purpose of describing what good performance in the intended system means and how it is to be achieved. Such documents include texts as broad as the company mission, as well as others that are as narrow as a concrete checklist for a specific step in the process, such as checking a customer request. Figure 9.7 illustrates the documents constituting a management system in hierarchical order.

Third, management systems involve a *continual improvement* mechanism, often through internal and external audits, and through the use of well-defined performance indicators and tools for performance analysis and improvement. In a later section of this chapter, we will extensively illustrate continual improvement

A **management system** establishes policies and objectives and is the framework to control the achievement of these objectives.

Figure 9.7 Documents Constituting a Management System

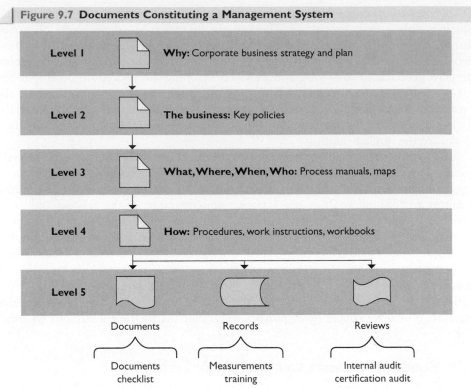

| Level 1 | **Why:** Corporate business strategy and plan |
| Level 2 | **The business:** Key policies |
| Level 3 | **What, Where, When, Who:** Process manuals, maps |
| Level 4 | **How:** Procedures, work instructions, workbooks |

Level 5

Documents — Documents checklist

Records — Measurements training

Reviews — Internal audit certification audit

Source: Conger, S. (2011). *Process mapping and management* (p. 54). New York: Business Expert Press.

mechanisms, such as the DMAIC framework. Figure 9.8 illustrates the continuous improvement systems of the ISO 14000 management system standard for environmental management standards, and the ISO 9000 standard for quality management systems. Both standards are highly related to responsible management.

Management systems for sustainability, responsibility, and ethics are usually integrated into already existing management systems, most commonly into a company´s quality and environmental management. An integrated management system houses several or, in the most advanced case, all components of a business in one coherent system in order to enable the achievement of organizational purpose and mission.[34] The important task for responsible operations managers is now to either establish new management systems for sustainability, responsibility and ethics, or include those topics in existing management systems, and to create an integrated "responsible" management system. Designing an **integrated management system** is a unique task for each organization, as it requires substantial customization. Guidance in the process can be provided by standards for the development of an integrated management system, such as the ISO 72 guide on the development of management systems[35] and the PAS 99 standard for the establishment of integrated management systems.[36] The steps that should be taken to develop a management system as proposed by the ISO 9000 standard for quality management, which are generally valid for most other management systems also, are the following:[37]

1. *Policy:* Establish policies and principles.
2. *Planning:* Identify needs, resources, requirements, relevant organizational structures, potential contingencies, and, most importantly, the issues to be addressed through the management system and the relevant processes.

An **integrated management system** houses all components of a business in one coherent system in order to enable the achievement of organizational purpose and mission.

**Figure 9.8 Continual Improvement Cycles in ISO 14000 and 9000**

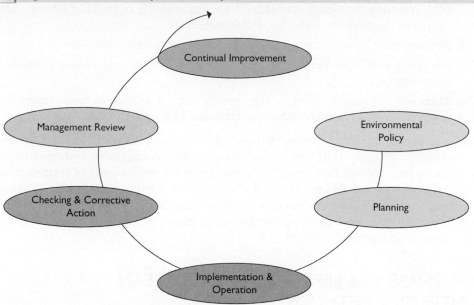

Source: Wilkinson, G., & Dale, B. G. (2002). An examination of the ISO 9001:2000 standard and its influence on the integration of management systems. *Production Planning & Control: The Management of Operations, 13*(3), 284–297.

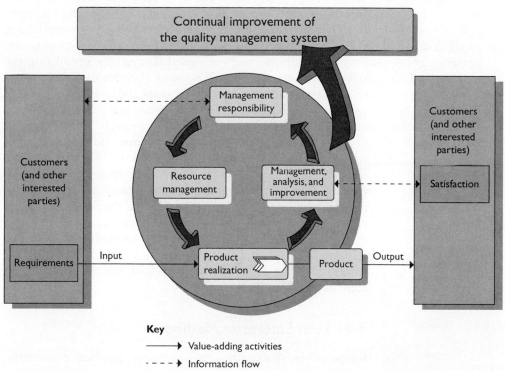

Source: The figure taken from ISO 9000:2005, is reproduced with the permission of the International Organization for Standardization, ISO. This standard can be obtained from any ISO member and from the Web site of the ISO Central Secretariat at the following address: www.iso.org. Copyright remains with ISO.

3. *Implementation and operation:* Establish operational control and documentation, and manage human and other resources, as well as the relationship with suppliers, contractors, and related stakeholders.

4. *Performance:* Monitor, measure, and handle nonconformities.

5. *Improvement:* Take preventive and corrective actions and ensure continual improvement.

6. *Management review:* Review the system and its outcomes concerning the adequacy of the system to achieve established objectives.

Management systems for responsible business must include a wider array of actors, stakeholders of many different kinds.[38] Responsible management systems can be integrated into existing ISO norms[39] and may include a wide variety of frameworks, such as excellence models, Six Sigma, and continuous improvement models.[40] Many of these frameworks are described in the following two phases of the responsible operations management process. The following phase, phase 2, focuses mainly on lean enterprise methods.

## 9-4 PHASE 2: BE EFFICIENT THROUGH LEAN ENTERPRISE METHODS

**Ecoefficiency** aims to minimize environmental resource consumption and ecological damage by optimizing the efficiency of the firm's production processes.

**Lean enterprise methods** aim to increase the efficiency of a process by reducing non-value-adding activities, so-called wastes.

*"Why is Lean Green? Lean is green because waste reduction is associated with lower resource consumption, whether in the form of energy or raw materials; in addition, solid waste is reduced."*[41]

Making more with less, increasing efficiency, has long been a mantra of management in theory and practice. It is not surprising that efficiency also plays a major role in responsible business and management. Probably the best-known application of efficiency in responsible management is **ecoefficiency**, which aims to minimize environmental resource consumption and ecological damage by optimizing the efficiency of the firm's production processes. We could also think of *stakeholder efficiency*, that is, aiming to create as little stakeholder costs and as much as possible stakeholder benefit through processes. Even *moral efficiency* is a possibility, aiming to realize as little ethical misconduct as possible per output unit.

Efficiency primarily focuses on the input side of the process with the goal of minimizing the necessary input to create a fixed output. Lean enterprise methods focus on efficiency, while quality management tools, as illustrated in phase 3, focus rather on the output, that is, on providing the highest customer (stakeholder) satisfaction possible. In practice, both lean and quality management have components of both efficiency and effectiveness, but we will reduce complexity by focusing on lean enterprise methods as an efficiency tool and quality management as an effectiveness tool.

### 9-4a Lean Enterprise Methods

Responsible operations management implies substantial commitment to lean enterprise management, manufacturing, and service methods that are often referred to in the collective form as simply "lean." **Lean enterprise methods** consider the efficient and effective use of resources through a lens that regards resources used for any objective other than value creation for the end customer as waste generated through formulation and execution of flawed strategies, processes, and practices. It is thus that lean enterprise theory and methods target all identified *waste* for reduction or elimination in order to enhance quality, performance, and profit. Although such approaches may be regarded as wise stewardship of organizational resources, it should be noted that stewardship is commonly regarded as the conscious election of service over self-interest.[42]

Lean enterprise methods extend beyond this common definition of stewardship, since both service- and enterprise-level self-interests are in play. Service will result from relevant and responsible use or stewardship of resources in that reduced **resource consumption**, including the resources of human capital, material, time, transport, and energy, is an intentional product of lean enterprise application, but, at the same time, the enterprise should directly benefit in multiple regards, including increased profitability.

In this context, "value" is regarded as any action, process, or product that an end user—or, more generally, customer or stakeholder—would be willing to pay for: anything else is a waste. In the context of responsible management, it is important to potentially include any stakeholder that has been prioritized as a customer. While this concept must be considered more comprehensively in view of the primary goal of sustainable enterprise excellence (i.e., effectively, efficiently, and profitably transforming sustainability strategy into sustainability results), it is, in the general sense, founded on three core principles and implemented through five core operational processes that are described in Table 9.2. Although these principles and processes may differ according to context, in a typical manufacturing environment, we should expect to incorporate them in the production flow, planning, organization, and performance functions.

Improving processes and their outputs means serving customers and prioritized stakeholders better, faster, and less expensively so that the overall essence of lean enterprise practice focuses on preservation or enhancement of value based on reduced consumption or more effective and efficient use of resources.[43] This philosophy derives from the Toyota production system (TPS),[44] a system intent on reduction of various forms of **waste** to improve overall value. In TPS, wastes are categorized into three broad types, referred to in Japanese as *muda*, *muri*, and *mura*. All of these terms begin with the prefix *mu-*, which is a Japanese prefix widely associated with improvement campaigns or programs.

**Table 9.2** Lean Enterprise Core Principles and Processes

| Lean Enterprise Core Principles |
| --- |
| • Satisfy customer expectations by engaging only in value-adding activities. |
| • Define the value stream: information and material flow and obstacles across the entire production process from order placement to delivery to the final customer. |
| • Identify and eliminate everything except that which is "lean" or "just enough" (also called "waste" at all levels and in all activities of the business), with the goal of continuous improvement. |

| Lean Enterprise Core Processes |
| --- |
| • Identify value. |
| • Transform the value stream in a manner consistent with the core principles. |
| • Ensure connected, consistent, level information and material flow across the entire value stream. |
| • Ensure response to customer expectations throughout the entire value stream. |
| • Strive for perfection in fulfilling the principles throughout the enterprise. |

*© Cengage Learning, 2015*

**Resource consumption** describes all resources used as inputs in a process.

**Waste** is any nonstakeholder value-adding efforts that must be incorporated in the current form of a process.

*Muda* translates as any of the following near synonyms: futility, uselessness, idleness, superfluity, waste, wastage, and wastefulness. Shingo[45] illustrated this idea by observing that it is only the last turn of a bolt that results in its actual tightening. Ohno[46] identified seven original *muda* that may be easily recalled using the idea that it is NOW TIME to eliminate *mudas;* the "now time" *mudas* are described in Table 9.3.

In general, nonstakeholder value-adding efforts are waste that must be incorporated in the current form of a process. Womack and Jones[47] added an eighth *muda* to NOW TIME that is associated with manufacturing goods or supplying services that do not meet customer or stakeholder demands and expectations. Unused or underused human talent is often regarded as an additional *muda,*[48] and this may be particularly true in the case of service systems.[49]

In comparison to *muda, muri* translates in most contexts as being unreasonable, impossible, beyond one's ability or authority, or too difficult, while in other contexts it translates as by force, compulsory, excessive, or immoderate.[50]*Mura* translates as unevenness, irregularity, nonuniformity, or inequality.

*Muri* focuses on process planning and preparation, work that may be proactively avoided by design, after which *mura* regards design implementation and elimination of fluctuation at the operations and scheduling levels, including, for example, quality and volume considerations. *Muda* is then discovered after the process is in place and manifests through special-cause variation,[51] often detected by quality control tools such as control charts; it may be dealt with reactively in the short run through one-off solutions, dealt with more permanently through incremental improvement commonly associated with continuous improvement methodologies associated with quality management,[52] or dealt with through more radical redesign using Six Sigma innovation approaches[53] or fresh designs identified and implemented through design

**Table 9.3** NOW TIME Lean Enterprise *Muda*

| | *Muda* (Waste) | *Muda* (Waste) Description |
|---|---|---|
| N | Nonquality | Also referred to as "defects." Defects incur additional costs that are associated with rework, rescheduling production, replacement, poorly calculated investments, etc. |
| O | Overproduction | Overproduction occurs when more product or service is produced than is required at that time by your customers. One common manufacturing practice that leads to this waste is the production of large batches, and this waste is especially relevant when customer needs change over the long times typically associated with large batches. Overproduction is considered the worst *muda* because it hides and/or generates all other *mudas.* For example, overproduction leads to excess inventory, which then requires the expenditure of resources on storage space and preservation, activities that do not benefit the stakeholder. |
| W | Waiting | Goods not in transport or being processed are simply in waiting. In traditional inefficient processes, a large part of the life of an individual product is spent waiting to be worked on. |
| T | Transportation | Each time a product is moved, it is subject to possible damage, delay, or being lost and is most certainly associated with cost for which no value is added, since transportation does not transform the product in a positive tangible way. |
| I | Inventory | Inventory in any form (raw materials, work in process, finished goods) represents a capital outlay that has not yet produced either income for the producer or value for the stakeholder. As such, it is associated with capital that could otherwise have been dedicated to value-added use(s). |
| M | Motion | Motion refers to the damage the production process inflicts on the entity that creates the product, either over time or during discrete events. |
| E | Excess processing | Excess processing occurs any time more work is done on a piece than is required by the customer. This includes using tools that are more precise, more complex, or more expensive than required and is also referred to as overprocessing. |

Source: Adapted from Ohno, T. (1988a). Toyota Production System. Productivity Press: London.

for Six Sigma.[54] The combination of lean and Six Sigma approaches is referred to as lean Six Sigma[55] and is one possible manifestation of total improvement management.[56]

Management should thus examine the *muda* in the processes and eliminate deeper causes by considering the connections to the *muri* and *mura* of the system. *Muda* and *mura* inconsistencies should then be fed back to the *muri*, or planning, stage for the next project. *Muri* is unreasonable work due to poor organization that is imposed by management on the human capital of the enterprise and on its equipment. Examples of *muri* might be carrying heavy weights, moving things around, dangerous tasks, or working significantly faster than is usual or reasonable. Essentially, *muri* entails pushing a person or equipment beyond its natural limitations and may manifest in a form as simple as asking for greater performance from a process or person than that which can be accomplished without taking shortcuts or informally modifying decision criteria. Such unreasonable effort will typically cause variation of multiple sorts.

Identification and elimination of such variation is commonly a focus of continuous improvement efforts that may employ any of a large number of tools that are considered to fall within the domain of quality management. These tools include relatively unsophisticated ones, such as control charts, Pareto charts, and cause-and-effect diagrams,[57] as well as more elaborate and powerful statistically oriented tools such as experimental design approaches that power evolutionary operations, steepest ascent methods, central composite designs, screening designs, and response surface analysis.[58]

*Muda* has been given much greater attention as waste than either *mura* (unevenness) or *muri* (overburden), so although many lean practitioners are accomplished at detecting *muda*, they often fail to recognize the same prominence in wastes associated with *mura* and *muri*. As such, lean professionals are often focused on process control and continuous improvement[59] and fail to achieve the benefits associated with significant process innovation and design gains obtained through use of Six Sigma innovation and design theory and methods such as DMAIC or Design for Six Sigma;[60] that is, they do not give enough time to process improvement by significant redesign or new design approaches.

## 9-4b Toyota Production System

Lean enterprise implementation flows from the **Toyota production system (TPS)**. Although the most obvious opportunities for lean implementation tend to be found in manufacturing, other opportunities for improving overall enterprise performance and reducing cost may be just as fruitful, though less easily discovered.

As operationalized (implemented) by Toyota, lean enterprise concepts have been translated into fourteen principles, as described in Table 9.4. Examination of Table 9.4 will reveal the principles and practices typically associated with *kaizen*,[61] the Japanese approach to continuous improvement with just-in-time production and service processes.[62]

Robert Cole, an American academic with deep Japanese connections and experience, has long addressed strengths and nuances of the TPS, so interesting perspective may be gained from his collected writings on TPS.[63] Various other critics have cited perceived shortcomings that may arise from the use of TPS, such as inhibited

**Toyota production system (TPS)** is a management method that led to the lean enterprise methods.

**Table 9.4** Toyota Principles

| Principle | Description |
|---|---|
| 1 | Base management decisions on long-term philosophy, superseding short-term financial goals:<br>• What enterprise purposes supersede goals?<br>• Create value for customers and society.<br>• Management is responsible for improving value-adding ability. |
| 2 | Create continuous process flow to surface problems.<br>• Redesign work processes to minimize idle time.<br>• Rapidly transfer material and information between processes and people to reveal problems in near to real-time.<br>• Enterprise culture should emphasize flow. |
| 3 | Avoid overproduction through just-in-time "pull" systems.<br>• Deliver what is attractive to customers when, how, and at desired levels.<br>• Down-line value stream elements are "customers."<br>• Minimize inventory and work-in-process by replenishing flows to the customer.<br>• Be responsive to near to real-time demand shifts and forecasts. |
| 4 | Level workloads (*heijunka*).<br>• Waste elimination is one-third (*muda*) of lean. *Muri* (overburden) and *mura* (unevenness) remain.<br>• Minimize batch processing to level workload. |
| 5 | Found enterprise culture on doing things right every time, rather than on fixing problems.<br>• Surpass customer needs using quality improvement and assurance.<br>• Incorporate problem detection into processes (*jidoka*).<br>• Ensure the enterprise is willing and able to address quality challenges.<br>• Improve productivity: Stop or slow down to do things right. |
| 6 | Empower employees to standardize tasks and engage in continuous improvement.<br>• Stable and repeatable methods fuel flow and pull, thus aiding system and process predictability.<br>• Capture and cascade learning through standardization.<br>• Identify and incorporate improvements, then restandardize. |
| 7 | Use visual control to reveal problems.<br>• Use visual indicators where work is done to help determine if and where there are problems. |
| 8 | Use reliable technology to serve people and processes.<br>• Technology should support, not replace, people.<br>• Explore, test, and adopt new technologies. |
| 9 | Grow leaders who understand lean philosophy and the work of the enterprise, and who can teach these to others.<br>• Good leadership and teaching require deep and detailed process understanding.<br>• Grow role-model leaders internally who have good people skills. |
| 10 | Develop exceptional people and teams.<br>• Create a strong and stable culture with widely shared values and beliefs.<br>• Train individuals and teams to work effectively and efficiently.<br>• Integrate teamwork in performance incentives and training initiatives. |
| 11 | Challenge your supply chain and enterprise ecosystem by aiding and rewarding improvement.<br>• Suppliers and partners are an extended part of your business.<br>• Challenge them to grow and develop.<br>• Help them meet challenging and mutually beneficial targets. |
| 12 | Directly observe the situation (*genshi genbutsu*).<br>• Personally observe the situation and verify data.<br>• Do not think or act based on superficial understanding.<br>• Make this policy and practice throughout the enterprise.<br>• When in doubt, see it with your own eyes (*genba shugi*). |

*(Continued)*

**Table 9.4** Toyota Principles (*Continued*)

| Principle | Description |
|---|---|
| 13 | Consider all options, making decisions slowly by consensus (*nemawashi*), then implementing decisions rapidly. |
| 14 | Become a learning organization through relentless reflection (*hansei*) and continuous improvement (*kaizen*). <br> • This requires stable, standardized processes. <br> • Search for inefficiencies. <br> • Eliminate *muda* (waste) by applying *kaizen* techniques. <br> • Protect enterprise knowledge by developing stable human capital, slow but reasonable personnel promotion, and careful succession systems. <br> • Apply *hansei* at key milestones. <br> • Standardize best practices. |

Sources: Senge, P. (1990). *The fifth discipline: The art and practice of the learning organization.* New York: Currency Doubleday; Imai, M. (2012). *Gemba kaizen: A commonsense approach to a continuous improvement strategy,* 2nd ed. New York: McGraw-Hill Med/Tech.

creativity and innovation, with one interesting perspective originating from a former Toyota professional involved in TPS implementation.[64]

The perspective here is that, in the context of responsible management, focus on TPS and other lean enterprise theory and methods on waste does not hinder creativity and innovation per se but, rather, more carefully defines and constrains the space of viable solutions within which creativity and innovation occur.

It is the case that, as with any other approach, TPS should not be blindly adopted and implemented without regard to organizational context. An example of this can be found in principle nine, wherein it is common in Japanese organizations to develop leaders from within over a very long period of time so that Japanese professionals are highly likely to invest their entire career in a single organization, since a consequence of changing to another organization is that of "starting at the bottom"—a critical factor in what has been referred to as alarmingly high dissatisfaction among Japanese employees.[65] To adopt such practice would be counterculture to, for example, American practice wherein mobility is highly prized, whether or not one chooses to exercise that mobility. Direct adoption of this aspect of the ninth TPS principle without regard for culture would, in most instances, be poor policy leading to unacceptable practice, and this is most certainly the case with many other TPS principles.

# 9-5 PHASE 3: BE EFFECTIVE THROUGH QUALITY MANAGEMENT

*"So, responsibility practitioners can begin to think systematically about managing responsibilities to stakeholders and the natural environment, just as they manage quality and, increasingly, environmental issues. The processes and steps are actually quite similar."*

Effectiveness refers to the output part of the process. Different from efficiency, here we do not ask how much input do we need, but rather how can we create the optimum output? We stress "optimum" output, not maximum output, as the goal is to deliver the output required by priority stakeholders, to balance the triple bottom line, or to create moral excellence. While the focus in phase 2 was mostly on environmental sustainability, through the concept of ecoefficiency, this phase 3 will primarily deal with the question of how to tune in processes to create optimum value for stakeholders. We call this **stakeholder effectiveness**. Although we focus on stakeholder effectiveness, it is not the only type of effectiveness that matters in responsible management. Processes that lead to good ethical results could be called *morality effective*. Processes that restore ecosystems could be called *ecoeffective*.

**Stakeholder effectiveness** refers to creating operational outcomes that satisfy stakeholder requirements.

| Baldrige National Quality Award Criteria for Performance Excellence | Total Responsibility Management Criteria for Performance Excellence |
|---|---|
| 1. Continuous quality improvement | 1. Continual responsibility improvement process ensures that TRM standards are met |
| 2. Meeting customers' requirements | 2. Lives up to expectations of global business, NGO, and governmental communities regarding responsible relationships with employees, suppliers, customers, and communities through sustainable management practices |
| 3. Long-range planning | 3. Long-range planning |
| 4. Increased employee involvement | 4. Meeting employees' expectations about responsible practices through engagement and dialogue |
| 5. Process management | 5. Increased stakeholder engagement and management of stakeholder relationships, practices, and impacts through attention to systems, processes, and outcomes |
| 6. Competitive benchmarking | 6. Competitive benchmarking of responsibility systems, including systems/process management for continual responsibility improvement |

Source: Waddock, S., & Bodwell, C. (2007). *Total responsibility management: The manual.* Sheffield, UK: Greenleaf.

One crucial difference between effectiveness and efficiency has to be taken into consideration. Efficiency minimizes resource consumption, while effectiveness maximizes performance creation. The latter creates positive outcomes, while the former minimizes negative ones.

Sandra Waddock and Charles Bodwell have coined the term **total responsibility management (TRM)** to describe a framework that translates total quality management tools and practices to the field of responsibility management. Figure 9.9 illustrates how quality criteria can be applied in responsibility management. Also, the ISO 26000 for social responsibility, which has proven valuable for quality professionals[66] and quality management in general, can be an powerful tool in implementing responsible business.[67]

In the following sections, we will describe standard tools to create effective processes, including continuous improvement, breakthrough improvement, Six Sigma, and benchmarking. Note that when we talk about customers in the following paragraphs, this is to pay tribute to the long-established quality management framework. Under "customers," however, here we subsume any type of priority stakeholders.

## 9-5a Customer Orientation and Continuous Improvement

At the system engineering level, product and service requirements are often reviewed with marketing and customer representatives or with customer focus groups in order to carefully elaborate customer needs[68] and eliminate those requirements that are less desired, yet costly. That is, in **quality management**, compromise solutions that are pleasing to customers, are of appropriate quality, and yet are profitable for the enterprise are generated from a larger and more complex space of potential solutions.

In general, customer needs drive the enterprise in a manner consistent with the **COPIS⇒SIPOC**, or conception-to-conduct flow.[69] The principle behind this flow is that we begin with very careful elaboration of customer needs (C) that communicate to the enterprise precisely the sort of outputs (O) desired by its clients. Outputs are the result of processes (P) that should be optimally configured to yield those outputs. Processes require inputs (I) that must be transformed by processes to yield those outputs, and those inputs are obtained from suppliers (S) or vendors that should

**Total responsibility management (TRM)** translates total quality management tools and practices to the field of responsibility management.

**Quality management** is a framework that aims at creating products and services that are perfectly aligned with customer (stakeholder) needs by reducing nonconformities with customer requirements.

**COPIS** is an algorithm for quality management, formed by the words Customer, Outputs, Processes, Inputs, and Suppliers.

be very carefully selected, with the end result always in view. Together these produce COPIS. Once the business is conceived with the customer in mind, it is executed beginning with suppliers that provide the inputs that are transformed by processes into outputs produced for customers of the enterprise: SIPOC. Note that this strategy may imply a departure from the frequent practice of awarding contracts to lowest-cost vendors and is instead aligned with the practice of "begin with the end in mind" promoted by late management consultant Stephen Covey.[70] The COPIS⇨SIPOC connection is portrayed in Figure 9.10.

Regardless of the overall approach employed, quality management should begin with a detailed assessment of customer needs. Such needs might be derived through the use of various so-called **voice-of-the-customer (VOC)**—or in responsible management, **voice-of-the-stakeholder (VOS)**—tools, such as surveys, focus groups, and customer complaint systems, or from other sources. Regardless of how the VOC is identified, it is important to recognize that customers are generally unable to reveal that of which they are unaware, so sometimes the customer must be led through exploratory exchange. An enterprise should not expect, for example, that most customers will be familiar with the full range of technological solutions that might be available or with the full capability range of the enterprise, thus necessitating exploration of the "if we could . . . what uses might you have for . . ." nature. Further, it is important that identified customer needs should be categorized with the most commonly used categorization model, which is the Kano customer needs model[71] that is portrayed in Figure 9.11.

Kano's model categorizes needs as "dissatisfiers," "satisfiers," and "delighters," where *dissatisfiers* are "must haves" that are absolutely expected, *satisfiers* are

**Figure 9.10 COPIS ⇨ SIPOC Business Conception-to-Conduct Connection**

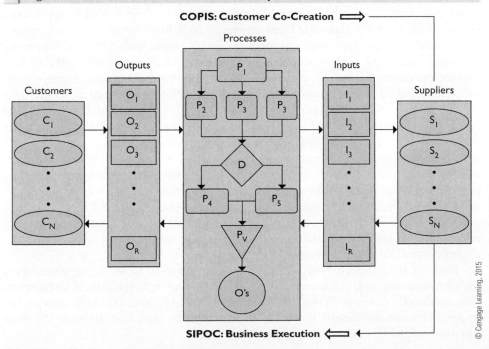

**Voice-of-the-customer (VOC)** describes the efforts to identify customer needs.

**Voice-of-the-stakeholder (VOS)** describes the efforts to identify customer needs for responsible management.

© Cengage Learning, 2015

| Figure 9.11  **Kano Customer Needs Model**

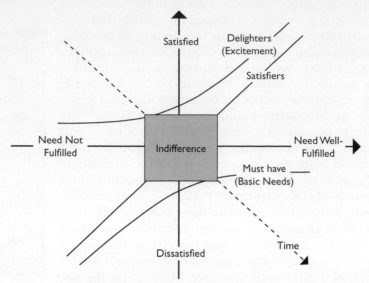

Source: Kano, N., Seraku, N., Takahashi, F., & Tsuji, S. (1984, April). Attractive quality and must-be quality. *Journal of the Japanese Society for Quality Control*, 39–48.

one-dimensional aspects such as fuel efficiency (more is better) or processing time (less is better), and *delighters* are "attractive" or positively "surprising" aspects of the product, process, or system at hand. Generally, a product or service should possess all must haves, maximize one-dimensional needs, and include some delighters.

A satisfier of one need may inhibit the ability to satisfy one or more other needs—a concept addressed by the roof of the so-called "house of quality" that is foundational to quality function deployment (QFD).[72] In QFD, measurable means of fulfilling customer needs (*how's*), the needs themselves (*what's*), and their interrelationships are represented, where *how's* may oppose, be independent of, or be synergistic with one another in their abilities to satisfy the VOC—that is, specifically elicited and carefully elaborated customer needs. When important how's oppose one another, compromise solutions are a necessary result, with a "best compromise solution" being one that is nearest to a reference "ideal final result" (IFR)[73] that may be developed for use in any of various product, process, or system innovation or design methodologies. Among the methodologies frequently used in such efforts are the theory of inventive problem solving (TRIZ),[74] Plan-Do-Study-Act (PDSA) continuous improvement cycles,[75] QFD, benchmarking, axiomatic design,[76] failure modes and effects analysis (FMEA),[77] and Six Sigma.[78]

Regardless of the approach employed, the goal is to first elaborate and then fulfill the VOC in a manner consistent with enterprise purpose and values, that is, profitable to the organization and that leads to satisfied and loyal customers open to continued or future engagement with the enterprise. Figure 9.12 portrays one possible model of this VOC alignment and integration process. Imposing relevancy and responsibility will ultimately better define the space within which the VOC alignment and integration process takes place.

Each of the product, process, and system innovation or design approaches is highly systematic and, in the main, philosophically similar to the others. To illustrate this, we briefly consider PDSA and Six Sigma's DMAIC and DMADV approaches to improvement and design, though it is reasonable to state that these are the most obviously similar.

Figure 9.12 **VOC Alignment and Integration**

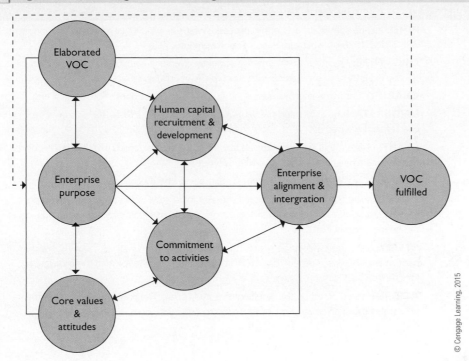

© Cengage Learning, 2015

**PDSA** is often referred to as the Deming cycle or Deming wheel,[79] as it is often attributed to W. Edwards Deming, although Dr. Deming credited the concept to his mentor, Dr. Walter A. Shewhart,[80] the originator of statistical quality control charts[81] who is considered by many to be the patriarch of modern quality improvement. Dr. Deming and Dr. Joseph Juran are often credited with the resurgence of the Japanese economy in the aftermath of World War II.[82]

Each of these "guru of gurus" developed significant management theories, with Juran's theory, known as the "quality triad," divided into the three main areas of quality planning, control, and improvement.[83] Deming's theory, referred to as the "system of profound knowledge,"[84] is often summarized by fourteen points for management, seven deadly (quality) diseases, and thirteen obstacles to improvement, wherein the PDSA cycle fundamentally serves the fourteenth and final point for management but is, in fact, the most critical one and may be paraphrased as "implement the first thirteen points," providing a template of sorts for so doing. PDSA is itself embedded in a larger process that may be easily remembered as FOCUS-PDSA, as described in Table 9.5.

Waddock and Bodwell[85] have applied the PDSA cycle specifically to responsible management. They illustrate the four phases as follows:

- *Plan:* Define stakeholders and issues, assess relevant norms, create a guiding coalition of stakeholders, and define objectives.
- *Do:* Identify gaps in stakeholder performance, implement measures to bridge them, and train employees and empower them to perform responsibly.

## In Practice

**In Need of More Improvement Cycles: From Low-Hanging Fruits to Real Transformation**

InterfaceFlor in 2012 saw their sustainability metrics entering into a plateau phase, where further impact reduction became increasingly difficult. In order to become a zero-impact sustainable business by 2020, the company needed to make a switch from achieving easy wins within existing structures toward profound reorganization and real transformation.

Source: InterfaceFlor, www.interface.com

**PDSA** is the abbreviation of the improvement cycle following the stages Plan, Do, Study, and Act.

**Table 9.5** Plan-Do-Study-Act (PDSA) Cycle Applied to Responsibility Management

| Phase | Description |
|-------|-------------|
| F | **FIND:** Identify specific aspects of the process, system, or product targeted for improvement with a clear focus on what is in need of improvement. |
| O | **ORGANIZE:** Assemble a team that is sufficiently diverse in competence and with sufficient specific expertise and experience in relation to the improvement opportunity. |
| C | **CLARIFY:** Clarify the improvement opportunity. That is, what does improvement entail? |
| U | **UNDERSTAND:** Understand the various causes of problems to be solved as well as enablers of improvement. |
| S | **START:** Initiate the PDSA cycle by selecting an initial process, product, or system modification and identifying where change should occur. |
| P | **PLAN:** Recognize the change opportunity and plan a specific change. |
| D | **DO:** Implement the change, possibly on a smaller initial scale in the event that the implemented change does not accomplish the anticipated results either directionally or, possibly, at the needed magnitude. |
| S | **STUDY:** Study implementation results by observing and analyzing changes in process performance. Explicitly identify that which has been learned in relation to the motivation for change. |
| A | **ACT:** Take action based on the results of the study phase. This may involve full implementation, scaled-back implementation, or reversion to prior conditions. |

© Cengage Learning, 2015

**Figure 9.13 Modified Plan-Do-Study-Act Cycle**

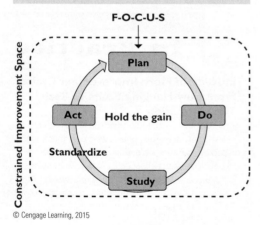

© Cengage Learning, 2015

- *Study:* Review progress with the guiding coalition, communicate to internal and external stakeholders, and calculate stakeholder benefits from improvements.
- *Act:* Revise responsibility objectives and start the cycle all over again.

PDSA is a **continuous improvement cycle**, meaning that after each pass through the PDSA cycle, a new planning phase is initiated and the cycle repeated in order to continue improving the product, process, or system. This cycle of improvement should continue until further improvement becomes untenable. Reasons for the end of the cycle might be, for instance, competing opportunities, a return on improvement that is outstripped by investments required to achieve improvements, or hard constraints that may include technological limitations. Figure 9.13 portrays a mildly modified version of the FOCUS-PDSA process described in Table 9.5. The first modification reflects the need to standardize a solution prior to broad implementation, a step that renders the solution more portable while also mitigating the likelihood of increased variation that infiltrates processes if implementation without standardization is pursued. A second modification in the PDSA cycle is emphasis on the importance of "holding the gains" of any implemented changes while pursuing additional future change.

Various methods complementary to PDSA, such as SWOT (strengths-weaknesses-opportunities-threats) analysis, exist, as do competing approaches. SWOT is in principle a simple improvement tool that complements PDSA and other tools. The topic of strategy may provide further guidance on how to conduct a responsible management SWOT analysis. Relative to PDSA, SWOT analysis may surface specific improvement opportunities that may be leveraged or problems in need of elimination or mitigation.

A **continuous improvement cycle** is one in which after each pass through the cycle, a new planning phase is initiated and the cycle is repeated in order to continue improving the product, process, or system.

## 9-6 BREAKTHROUGH IMPROVEMENT THROUGH SIX SIGMA INNOVATION AND DESIGN

In contrast to the incremental improvement targeted by PDSA, **Six Sigma** innovation and design approaches aim at breakthrough improvement leading to near-perfect performance or new designs that perform nearly flawlessly from the beginning. Although Six Sigma has a statistical basis, the definition provided by Klefsjö, Bergquist, and Edgeman[86] can be modified to define the concept more philosophically as follows:

> *Six Sigma is a highly structured strategy for acquiring, assessing, and activating customer, competitor, and enterprise intelligence leading to superior product, system, or enterprise innovations and designs that provide a sustainable competitive advantage.*

Six Sigma originated at Motorola more than thirty years ago as a means of generating near-perfect products via focus on associated manufacturing processes. While developed for manufacturing environments, Six Sigma's inherent sensibilities and structure facilitated its migration to service operations. Similarly, while at its onset it was used to generate significant innovation in and improvement of existing products, processes, and systems, those same sensibilities led to its adaptation to new design environments. Innovation-versus-design nuances led to the development of customized but related structured approaches to innovation and design, including the approach used in innovative applications known as DMAIC and the approach used in design applications known as DMADV.[87] DMAIC and DMADV are briefly described in Table 9.6. Note in Table 9.6 that while each structure begins with DMA, or define-measure-analyze, how these are defined differs from one structure to the other.

Let us briefly consider *design for Six Sigma* (DFSS) somewhat more deeply. While multiple DFSS approaches exist, a few similar ones dominate the application arena, with the two most prevalent being referred to as I²DOV (Innovation, Invention, Design, Optimization, and Verification) and the DMADV (Define, Measure, Analyze, Design, Verify) algorithm. The DMADV approach is the most commonly applied of the two; however, whichever DFSS approach is used—whether DMADV, I²DOV, or another—the approach provides freedom within structure rather than rigidity. The

> **Six Sigma** is a framework for process improvement that is centered on the assessment of customer (stakeholder) needs and elimination of process errors.

**Table 9.6** DMAIC and DMADV Structure Descriptions

| | Stage | Description |
|---|---|---|
| **DMAIC: Six Sigma Innovation** | | |
| **D** | Define: | The problem and customer requirements. |
| **M** | Measure: | Defect rates and document the process in its current incarnation. |
| **A** | Analyze: | Process data and determine the capability of the process. |
| **I** | Improve: | The process and remove defect causes. |
| **C** | Control: | Process performance and ensure that defects do not recur. |
| **DMADV: Six Sigma Design** | | |
| **D** | Define: | Customer requirements and goals for the process, product, or service. |
| **M** | Measure: | And match performance to customer requirements. |
| **A** | Analyze: | And access the design for the process, product, or service. |
| **D** | Design: | And implement the array of new processes required. |
| **V** | Verify: | Results and maintain performance. |

Source: Edgeman, R. (2011b). Design for Six Sigma. In M. Lovric (Ed.), International Encyclopedia of Statistical Sciences, Springer Publishing: Berlin, pp. 374–376.

same is true of the DMAIC innovation structure. That is to say, although each phase in the chosen approach has a particular intent, the phases are generally sequential and linked, and together they are complete. Nevertheless, within a given phase, many different tools and techniques may be brought to bear, and those used may differ substantially from one application to the next. Each stage of DMADV is next described in somewhat more detail than that provided in Table 9.6.

A primary goal of the *define* phase of DMADV is to acquire and access the VOC and subsequently align goals for the product, process, or service with the VOC. Customers considered should be both internal and external ones, as applicable. In addition to previously cited methods for acquiring the VOC, direct observation of customer use of similar products, processes, or services is useful in identifying unspoken, more implicit information. Goals and objectives should be stated as "SMART" goals,[88] where SMART is an acronym for Specific, Measurable, Attainable, Relevant, and Time-bound. Goals and objectives should be set so that they are attainable, but not easily so, and in general should represent challenging levels, attainment of which is more likely to position the product, process, or service at the leading edge.

In the DMADV context, a *measure* is fundamentally associated with *quantification* of the VOC and alignment of quantification with enterprise goals.

The DMADV *analyze* phase demands that the *design* of any existing relevant product, process, or service be analyzed and assessed to determine its suitability, performance, error or defect sources, and any corrective or innovative actions that may be taken. Tools of potential value in this phase include design failure modes and effects analysis (DFMEA), concept generation and selection,[89] and the theory of inventive problem solving (TRIZ).

In the *design* phase, the array of corrective or innovative actions identified in the analyze phase are embedded in the design and subsequent deployment of new processes required to activate the VOC while simultaneously fulfilling organizational and management goals. While various tools may be of value here, a few of the more advanced approaches that are useful include many from experimental design and response surface analysis,[90] along with more rigorous quality-oriented approaches such as quality function deployment (QFD). As a way of relating and integrating these latter approaches, various customer needs and wants (the VOC) that are critical to QFD may be regarded as response variables (Y's) whose optimization is attained through deployment of identified product or process design attributes, the so-called "how's", which are controllable variables $X_1, X_2, ..., X_p$, so that we have

$$Y = f(X_1, X_2, ..., X_p) + \varepsilon$$

where the optimal combination of settings of $X_1, X_2, ... X_p$—called "engineering" or "design" attributes in the parlance of QFD—may be determined through the use of, for example, response surface methods, steepest ascent methods, and evolutionary operations (EVOP).[91] It is important to note that it is not sufficient to simply identify the key design attributes or even the optimal combination of these, as in addition it is the specific means of activating these attributes—the process—that ultimately actualizes the VOC.

In the *verify* phase of DMADV, the objective is to assess performance of the design via such means as prototyping, simulation, or direct observation of the designed product or process in use prior to marketplace deployment. In this way design performance is verified.

It may be concluded from this deeper consideration of DMADV that Six Sigma may employ a variety of statistical and other methods. Although this is true, it should be evident that the specific methods applied are almost boundless, being limited only

**Table 9.7** DPMO Values in Relation to Sigma Levels

| σ Level | DPMO When Perfectly Centered | DPMO with 1.5σ Displacement |
|---|---|---|
| 2 | 46,000 | 308,537 |
| 3 | 2,700 | 66,807 |
| 4 | 60 | 6,210 |
| 5 | 0.6 | 233 |
| 6 | 0.002 | 3.4 |

Source: Adapted from Klefsjö, B., Bergquist, B., & Edgeman, R. (2006). Six Sigma and total quality management: Different day, same soup? *Six Sigma & Competitive Advantage*, 2(2), 162–178.

as they are primarily by the knowledge and imagination of the design team and field of application. While DMADV and DMAIC offer logical and highly structured, yet versatile approaches to product, process, or service innovation and design, the tools and techniques upon which they draw will almost certainly grow over time as Six Sigma methods are applied in a more diverse array of disciplines and environments.[92]

Symbolized by σ, the term **sigma** is a measure of process variation recognizable as the standard deviation of output from the process, product, or system. In this context, variation does not represent intentionally introduced product, process, or system diversity but is rather any departure from intended performance levels. *Higher* process sigma levels imply *lesser* standard deviation values, so that higher sigma levels imply that a higher proportion of output or results lie within acceptable performance limits. As such, higher sigma levels imply reduced "defect" levels where a defect is anything that does not match the required performance profile.

Defect rates, in terms of defects per million opportunities (DPMO) for a defect, in relation to sigma levels are reported in Table 9.7. Although it is not always the case that something should perform *within* limits, since there are numerous reasonable circumstances where there is only an *upper* or *lower* acceptable performance limit, tables reporting DPMO in relation to sigma levels generally reflect processes that are displaced by 1.5 standard deviations from perfect centering. Table 9.7 provides DPMO levels for both 1.5 standard deviation displacement and for perfectly centered processes.

As revealed in Table 9.7, the commonly reported "3.4 DPMO for a true Six Sigma level process" reflects displacement or a shift of 1.5σ from perfect centering, that is, from ideal performance level. Use of a 1.5σ displacement or drift factor—referred to in statistical parlance as a noncentrality factor—is based on the natural tendency of processes to vary through time within a range—that is, within "plus or minus" distance of their (natural) average performance level (rather than ideal performance level).

Left alone, most processes tend not only to drift, but in fact have a tendency toward entropy or decaying performance. Whereas there may be any number of motivations for improving triple bottom line performance, it is this tendency toward entropy that dictates the necessity of the more mundane activity of monitoring and maintaining control of a process at a stable level.[93] It is of value to note that continuous improvement efforts associated with PDSA or quality management approaches commonly precede larger Six Sigma breakthrough improvement efforts and, also, often follow breakthrough efforts.

### 9-6a Benchmarking and Breakthrough Improvement

*Benchmarking*[94] contributes substantially to almost any improvement methodology, whether the need for improvement is of an incremental or breakthrough nature. That said, benchmarking is most commonly applied when *breakthrough improvement*

**Sigma** is a measure of process variation recognizable as the standard deviation of output from the process, product, or system.

is needed or when the potential benefit of improvement warrants the sort of investment often required by benchmarking. Among well-known varieties of benchmarking are competitive, functional, internal, product, process, best practices, strategies, and parameter benchmarking. **Best practices benchmarking** resides at the intersection of competitive, functional, and internal benchmarking, as portrayed in Figure 9.14.

Best practices benchmarking may be regarded as the process of continually searching for and studying internal and external methods, practices, and processes that yield superior performance and either adopting or adapting their best features to become the "best of the best." Benchmarking is in general expected to deliver at least 15 percent improvement in performance and is used to compare performance levels, understand the potential for and of performance improvements, determine how superior performance is attained, and integrate the needed changes.

Benchmarking has a distinct measurement focus, and it is important to determine where processes create customer value as well as where the value is detracted. The benchmarking perspective on measures is that both *lagging indicators* descriptive of actual results and *leading indicators* capable of forecasting future outcomes should be employed. In contrast to lagging indicators that are inherently reactive in nature, leading indicators enable upstream intervention. It is additionally important that benchmarks or measures designed for performance improvement should be constructed in ways that enable appropriately empowered individuals to implement change and control subsequent performance.

Among enablers of improved performance identified in benchmarking studies are the categories of so-called *soft, medium,* and

**Best practices benchmarking** is the process of continually searching for and studying internal and external methods, practices, and processes that yield superior performance and either adopting or adapting their good features to become the "best of the best."

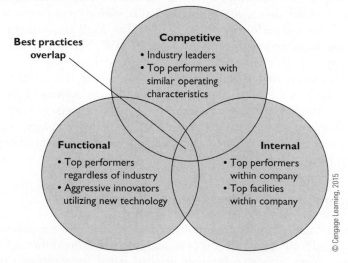

**Figure 9.14 Best Practices Benchmarking**

Best practices overlap

**Competitive**
- Industry leaders
- Top performers with similar operating characteristics

**Functional**
- Top performers regardless of industry
- Aggressive innovators utilizing new technology

**Internal**
- Top performers within company
- Top facilities within company

© Cengage Learning, 2015

*hard enablers.* Included among soft enablers are training, communication, and human capital empowerment. Medium enablers of improvement include (SMART) goals and objectives, controls, measures, and policies and procedures. Hard enablers are tangible resources such as manufacturing plants, suppliers, money, technology, and equipment. Generic benchmark categories include:

- Customer service performance
- Product or service performance
- Core business process performance
- Support processes and service performance
- Employee performance
- Supplier performance
- Technology performance
- New product or service development and innovation performance
- Cost performance
- Financial performance

Many enterprises have formulated benchmarking processes that are suitable to their context, but adept enterprises employ benchmarking to advance both tactical and strategic aims.[95] Perhaps the most well-known benchmarking process is that developed and applied by Xerox Corporation, the Business Products and Systems Division of which was one of the first winners of America's Baldrige National Quality Award in 1990. Table 9.8 provides an overview of the Xerox benchmarking process.[96]

**Table 9.8** Xerox Benchmarking Process

| Phase 1: Planning | |
|---|---|
| 1 | Identify what to benchmark. |
| 2 | Identify comparative enterprises. |
| 3 | Determine data collection method and obtain data. |
| **Phase 2: Analysis** | |
| 4 | Determine current performance gap. |
| 5 | Forecast future performance levels. |
| **Phase 3: Integration** | |
| 6 | Communicate and archive findings in easily accessible form. Gain acceptance. |
| 7 | Establish functional goals. |
| **Phase 4: Action** | |
| 8 | Develop plans. |
| 9 | Implement specific actions and monitor progress. |
| 10 | Recalibrate benchmarks. |
| **Phase 5: Maturity** | |
| 11 | Attain leadership position. |
| 12 | Fully integrate practices into processes. |

Source: Bogan, C. and English, M. (1994). Benchmarking for Best Practices. McGraw-Hill: New York.

I.  The goal of responsible operations management is *responsible enterprise excellence*, which refers to above-average operational performance of the triple bottom line, stakeholder value, and moral excellence.

II.  *Operational performance* describes the *effectiveness* and *efficiency* of processes for the production of goods and services.

III.  For responsible operational performance, *processes* must integrate stakeholder value, environmental impacts, and ethical dilemmas in their description and management.

IV.  *Lean enterprise* methods aim to increase the efficiency of a process by reducing non-value-adding activities, so-called *wastes*. Lean thinking is the basis for *ecoefficiency*, which reduces pollution and resource consumption from existing processes.

V.  *Quality management* is a framework that aims at creating products and services that are perfectly aligned with the customer (stakeholder) needs by reducing nonconformities (errors) with customer requirements. *Six Sigma* is a prominent quality management framework.

VI.  A *continuous improvement* cycle is one in which after each pass through the cycle, a new planning phase is initiated and the cycle is repeated in order to continue improving the product, process, or system. A prominent cycle is *PDSA*, which is the abbreviation of the improvement cycle following the stages: plan, do, study, and act.

VII.  *Best practices benchmarking* is the process of continually searching for and studying internal and external methods, practices, and processes that yield superior performance and either adopting or adapting their best features to become the "best of the best."

| Process Phase | | Sustainability | Responsibility | Ethics |
|---|---|---|---|---|
| Phase 1: Understand the process | Does your understanding of the process include … | … where you create environmental, social, and economic costs and benefits? | … how the process creates and destroys value for your stakeholders? | … the process sections with ethical dilemmas? |
| Phase 2: Be efficient | Does your process … | … minimize economic, social, and environmental wastes? | … minimize situations where stakeholder value is reduced? | … minimize ethical dilemmas? |
| Phase 3: Be effective | Does the process … | … optimize environmental, social, and economic value creation through the process? | … optimize value for stakeholders from the process? | … create moral excellence? |

best practices benchmarking 288
continuous improvement cycle 284
COPIS 280
ecoefficiency 274
effectiveness 264
efficiency 264
integrated management system 272
lean enterprise methods 274
management system 271
operational performance 262
operations management (OM) 262

PDSA 283
procedure 267
procedure documents 267
process 264
process detail map 265
quality management 280
resource consumption 275
responsible enterprise excellence 263
responsible operations
    management 262
shared process 267

sigma 287
Six Sigma 285
stakeholder effectiveness 279
sustainable enterprise excellence
    (SEE) 263
total responsibility management
    (TRM) 280
Toyota production system (TPS) 277
voice-of-the-customer (VOC) 281
voice-of-the-stakeholder (VOS) 281
waste 275

## A. Remember and Understand

A.1. Explain how mainstream operations management and responsible operations management are different.

A.2. Define the following terms and explain how they are related: *performance, efficiency, effectiveness, process, output, input.*

A.3. Explain the differences between quality management and lean enterprise, and describe how each applies to responsible management.

A.4. Discuss the relationship between triple top line strategy and triple bottom line results in relation to operations management.

## B. Apply and Experience

B.5. Many forms of the balanced scorecard exist. Conduct a comprehensive search of Baldrige Award-winning or European Quality Award-winning organizations. As an outcome of your search, identify ways in which five of these organizations have benefited from the use of the balanced scorecard in relation to their operations strategies, practices, and results.

B.6. Relative to your search in question B.5, identify specific sustainability strategies of each of the five award-winning organizations and ways in which they have successfully deployed these strategies to produce positive sustainability results relative to their operations management strategies, practices, and results.

B.7. Identify ways in which the five organizations identified in question B.5 have approached socioecological innovation and the impact of these approaches in relation to their operations and supply chain management strategies, practices, and results.

B.8. Suggest and discuss at least five possible measures for each of the ten generic benchmarking categories.

## C. Analyze and Evaluate

C.9. Search online for the IKEA Group People & Planet Positive Sustainability Strategy and, also, its United Nations Global Compact (UNGC) "Communication on Progress," or COP. Discuss these in relation to the lean enterprise core principles and processes and implications for IKEA's operations and supply chain management strategies, actions, and results.

C.10. Many organizations that have won the Baldrige or European Quality Award are also members of the United Nations Global Compact and, as such, submit an annual "Communication on Progress" (COP). These COPs and annual sustainability reports are readily available online for most such companies. Search online and synthesize the UNGC COP and annual sustainability reports of three or more leading organizations in relation to the lean enterprise concepts *muda, muri,* and *mura.* Discuss your syntheses and their operations and supply chain management implications.

C.11. Search online for at least three Six Sigma case studies from leading Six Sigma enterprises. Among suggested enterprises are GE, Raytheon, Bank of America, Boeing, and Black and Decker. In each case, identify real or potential uses of TPS, COPIS, PDSA, SWOT, and benchmarking. Can you find examples where those methods have been applied to improve the triple bottom line, stakeholder, or ethical performance?

## D. Change and Create

D.12. Review and understand the structure of the process maps described in Figure 9.4 and Figure 9.5. Then prepare one map of a specialized responsible management process and one for a mainstream management process, integrating stakeholder, environmental, and ethical dilemmas.

D.13. Prepare a table in which you brainstorm about the satisfiers, dissatisfiers, and delighters of three stakeholder groups of your choice. Based on your analysis, write a half-page "Voice of the Stakeholder" statement for one of the stakeholders, to define the requirements to be fulfilled for this stakeholder.

---

## PIONEER INTERVIEW WITH SANDRA WADDOCK

Sandra Waddock is probably the most prolific academic author on corporate social responsibility (CSR). She has been an influential player in developing the field of CSR for decades, with attention to many different topics. Among others, she has been recognized for her work on the corporate social performance (CSP) and corporate financial performance (CFP) connection. In her recent work in collaboration with Charles Bodwell, she provides practical advice on, how (total) quality management, one of the main tools of operations management, can be applied to become "total responsibility management."

## What can corporate social responsibility practitioners learn from quality management?

The main lesson, as I see it, is that you can manage responsibilities just as you can manage quality. You may remember (from reading, if not from experience) that there was a lot of skepticism about quality management when it was first introduced. Managers raised issues like: Our customers don't care about quality. You can't measure quality. You can't manage quality. Well, along came the quality movement, and today, it has turned out that you can, in fact, do all those things. Indeed, today quality management is a fundamental imperative for companies—you can't do business in most markets without paying attention to quality. I would argue that the same dynamic is affecting responsibility management, particularly with respect to the integration process.

So, responsibility practitioners can begin to think systematically about managing responsibilities to stakeholders and the natural environment, just as they manage quality and, increasingly, environmental issues. The processes and steps are actually quite similar.

## How is total responsibility management different from total quality management? What are commonalities?

There are great similarities between the ways in which managers in companies learned to manage quality and the way that they now need to learn to manage their responsibilities to stakeholders and the natural environment. If you think of responsibility management as something totally new, it can become totally overwhelming. But if you view it as managing the company's relationships with a variety of stakeholders, much as you have already learned to manage, for example, your employee relationships (and indeed, responsibility management includes employee relationships), then you realize that you are *already* managing those responsibilities. It's just that without explicit attention to the whole system of important stakeholder/natural environment relationships, you may not be doing that management process very well.

So you can think of responsibility management, which my collaborator Charlie Bodwell and I called TRM for total responsibility management (in our book by that name), just to make the connection to TQM or total quality management, as another set of managerial processes, though I'm going to

make this sound more linear than it actually is. You begin with envisioning what you see as the company's important responsibilities, and identifying who the key stakeholders are (including the natural environment as one of them, even though it's not a person). Then you construct a vision, based on the core values of the company, that articulates how you want to treat those stakeholders, and you can even begin a stakeholder engagement process at that point to determine what they see as the issues, if any, in their current relationship to the company. We call this stage the inspiration process. When you've got a clearer sense of what you think the company stands for with respect to stakeholders, you can articulate your vision for managing stakeholder and environmental responsibilities, and move to the next stage.

The next stage we called integration, because it is the process of more deeply embedding explicit responsibility management into the company's human resources practices as well as the other systems that support the mission of the firm. So, you have to think about the processes and practices of the company that affect each stakeholder group and what the responsibility issues embedded in those practices are. How well are you treating your employees, customers, local communities, shareholders, and suppliers? Do they trust you? If not, why not? Where are the problems? What needs to be done to resolve those problems, which are signals that some sort of responsibility is falling through the cracks? What are your environmental practices? Is there waste? Are there activists raising concerns that need attention? Yes, the integration process is more complex than with managing quality because there are more stakeholders involved. With quality, you are mostly concerned about employees and customers, but that list does expand considerably when you think about your responsibilities. It is through integration that quality and responsibility practices get embedded into the firm—and where the most changes need to take place.

And, of course, as with quality, you can't determine how well you're doing with responsibility management unless you develop appropriate metrics. As my colleague Charlie Bodwell would point out, you're already gathering a lot of the relevant metrics, though probably not all of them, but they are typically not consolidated into a systematic approach to managing responsibility until you begin to think about developing the whole approach to responsibility management. And, also as with managing quality, responsibility management does not lend itself to perfection—it is a process of continuous improvement based on ongoing assessments and feedback loops to see how well you are living up to your own standards and vision.

**In 1997 you published a widely cited study on the link between corporate social performance (CSP) and corporate financial performance (CFP). You stated that CFP is positively related with CSP, and that good CSP in turn is positively related to future positive CFP. What should those findings mean to financial managers in companies?**

Well, a lot of years have passed and much research has been done in the interim. The 1997 study argued that there was a positive relationship between corporate responsibility and financial performance. In the interim, a number of what are called meta-analyses, basically studies of studies, have been undertaken. One of them (by Orlitzky and Rynes in 2003) found the positive relationship, while the other (by Margolis and his colleagues, 2003 and 2007) found essentially a neutral relationship. My own most recent study with colleagues Jegoo Lee and Sam Graves, still unpublished, argues for a neutral relationship. I have come to believe that fundamentally there are probably some responsibility activities that add bottom line value to firms (e.g., perhaps treating employees and customers better), while there are some that are necessary but do not add to the bottom line, essentially balancing each other out so that you get to the neutral relationship.

Fundamentally what that neutrality means is that the trade that many financial analysts expect from companies becoming more responsible does not exist. And, importantly, there are many other side benefits to being/becoming more responsible. Some of these benefits have to do with reputation (which is really important to companies today when so many of a company's assets are intangible), satisfied stakeholders, and the basic ethics associated with treating people as ends rather than as means.

**In 2002 you argued that corporate social responsibility was the new business imperative. Has your claim been verified? What has changed since then?**

Since that time corporate responsibility has indeed become more of a business imperative, although it doesn't always seem so when we look at all the scandals associated with corporations. But surveys show today that most of the world's largest corporations are now issuing multiple bottom line reports of some sort, and virtually all of them have actively engaged CSR—what I call the new CSR, corporate sustainability and responsibility—programs. So, especially in the realm of large multinational firms, yes, I think that there has been continued growth in that direction. Are we fully there—where "there" means fully responsible firms—obviously not, but the external pressures on firms, the visibility that creates transparency, and the demands for accountability are like the genie that has been let out of the bottle—and is now too big to get back in.

---

## PRACTITIONER PROFILE: CECILIA DEL CASTILLO

**Employing organization:** Eaton is a global technology leader in diversified power management solutions that make electrical, hydraulic, and mechanical power operate more efficiently, effectively, safely, and sustainably.

**Job title:** Environmental, Health and Safety Coordinator

**Education:** Premed/Environmental Engineering and Masters in Quality and Productivity Systems

### In Practice

### What are your responsibilities?

Coordinate safety, environmental, and hygiene projects as well as maintenance work related to buildings, offices, and services to ensure continuity of plant operations, ensuring safe working conditions with a significant impact reduction on the environment. On a daily basis I am responsible to implement, promote, and maintain a safe work environment by implementing a culture of accident prevention, investigation, equipment maintenance, and application of rules.

**What are typical activities you carry out during a day at work?**

Typical activities include review of safety daily status, coordination with EHS staff of activities planned during the year to maintain a zero-accident-exposure culture, and communication of plants and areas status for environmental impact. Every activity planned during the day corresponds to a greater plan that has been developed through the year, which involves having in mind the priority of the mission and vision of the company. Safety and environmental issues have always been important, but the impacts of these issues directly on production matters have taken more importance in the last few years. Therefore, the activities related to production have mainly three branches that come from the EHS yearly strategy:

- Culture based on behaviors
- Culture based on conditions
- Communication and reinforcement

These three strategies apply for safety and environmental approaches, and every unit business is measured based on those three strategies.

**How do sustainability, responsibility, and ethics topics play a role in your job?**

In order to promote the company's mission and vision by actively supporting Eaton's ethics and values as well as quality policies, we motivate and coach employees to maintain high levels of satisfaction, productivity, and quality through effectively utilizing available rewards and recognition channels to encourage and promote desired behaviors and results.

As we strive to become the most admired company in its markets as measured by customers, shareholders, and employees, Environment, Health and Safety (EHS) will be an integral part of this process by adding value and enhancing the company's competitive advantage in the marketplace. We will direct our efforts in the following areas: sustainable business, employees, business integration, compliance, customers, suppliers and contractors, community.

**Out of the topics covered in the chapter into which your interview will be included, which concepts, tools, or topics are most relevant to your work?**

I believe that one of the most important tools is related to Six Sigma—standardization tools. One of the most important in order to complete the implementation of a strategy is DMAIC—this tool will give you structure and will help you to have a greater view of your business plan so your metrics will be simple, traceable, and reasonable, all with a view for continuous improvement.

**Insights and Challenges**

**What recommendation can you give to practitioners in your field?**

In order to be successful in implementing a strategy, you have to be able to follow steps complying with a strategy where you can go through certain stages gaining knowledge and reassuring understanding. A change of culture is usually what you'll go through when being in the field, but the best way to ensure knowledge and make it continuous is to go through awareness, desire, knowledge, and reinforcement. Awareness is the stage when you realize that you have to make a change, that there is something that needs to be changed or improved—when you realize that there is something that needs to be changed, even though you are not certain what it is, you go through this stage. Desire is the stage when, after you realize that you need to change something, you have the desire to implement the change. Knowledge is when you acquire all the information that you need in order to make the proper decision on this change and to identify every single part of the issue that needs change. This is usually the stage where we start to visualize the real necessities whenever a change is going to be taken. Every change needs continuance, so the stage of reinforcement is when continuous improvement is needed—every change has to have a process check in order to verify that the change is fulfilling its purpose.

**Which are the main challenges of your job?**

The main challenges in this job are being able to be part of a cultural change and being able to understand the priorities of the business. Cultural change is embraced if the right competencies are developed in the people involved in the change—so, in order to be able to make that change, people are the key. If you are able to develop a strategy that is useful for the people, you'll be able to promote that change and to make it sustainable.

## Is there anything else that you would like to share?

Stimulated by the dramatic changes in global competition, technology, and expectations of clients, speediness has become a key to business success. The pressure for being faster and not being left behind has become a fundamental concern of leaders everywhere, while they struggle to accelerate productivity among their teams.

So, how can we multiply efforts? How can we increment efficiency? Part of this strategy is to build purpose and pride in the team members.

## SOURCES

1. Lacey, P., et al. (2010). *A new era of sustainability: UN Global Compact-Accenture CEO study 2010.* New York: Accenture Institute for High Performance.
2. CROA. (2011). *Corporate responsibility best practices: Research summary.* Edison: Corporate Responsibility Officer Association.
3. Interface Global. (2012). *Mission zero.* Retrieved December 24, 2012, from Interface Recruiting and Careers: www.interfaceglobal.com/careers/mission_zero.html
4. Elkington, J. (2012). *The zeronauts: Breaking the sustainability barrier.* New York: Routledge.
5. Edgeman, R. L., & Eskildsen, J. (2012). Viral innovation: Integration via sustainability and enterprise excellence. *Journal of Innovation & Business Best Practice* (Article ID 3614151), p. 4.
6. Watson, G. (2007). *Strategic benchmarking reloaded with Six Sigma: Improving your company's performance using global best practice.* Hoboken, NJ: Wiley.
7. Kennedy, M. (2010). *Product development for the lean enterprise: Why Toyota's system is four times more productive and how you can implement it.* Richmond, VA: Oaklea Press.
8. Franz, P., & Kirchmer, M. (2012). *Value-driven process management: The value-switch for lasting competitive advantage.* New York: McGraw-Hill.
9. Kerzner, H. (2009). *Project management: A systems approach to planning, scheduling, and controlling,* 10th ed. Hoboken, NJ: Wiley.
10. Edgeman, R., Bigio, D., & Ferleman, T. (2005). Six Sigma or business excellence: Strategic and tactical examination of IT service level management at the Office of the Chief Technology Officer of Washington, DC. *Quality & Reliability Engineering International, 21,* 257–273.
11. Zairi, M. (ed.). (2003). *Performance excellence: A practical handbook.* Dubai, UAE: e-TQM College Publishing House; Zairi, M., & Whymark, J. (2003). *Best practice organisational excellence.* Dubai, UAE: e-TQM College Publishing House.
12. Edgeman, R., & Eskildsen, J. (2014). Sustainable enterprise excellence. In John Wang (ed.), *Encyclopedia of business analytics & optimization,* pp. pending. Hershey, PA: IGI Global.
13. Avlonas, N., & Swannick, J. (2009). Developing business excellence while delivering responsible competitiveness. In J. Eskildsen & J. Jonker (eds.), *Management models for the future* (pp. 171–184). Springer: Berlin.
14. Kesler, G., & Kates, A. (2011). *Leading organization design: How to make organization design decisions to drive the results you want.* San Francisco: Jossey-Bass.
15. McDonough, W., & Braungart, M. (2002). *Cradle to cradle: Remaking the way we make things.* New York: North Point Press.
16. ReVelle, J., Frigon, N., & Jackson, H. (1995). *From concept to customer.* New York: Van Nostrand Reinhold; Ulrich, K. T., & Eppinger, S. D. (2008). *Product design and development,* 5th ed. New York: McGraw-Hill.
17. Nidumolu, R., Prahalad, C. K., & Rangaswami, M. R. (2009, September). Why sustainability is now the key driver of innovation. *Harvard Business Review,* 57–64.
18. Laszlo, C., & Zhexembayeva, N. (2011). *Embedded sustainability: The next big competitive advantage.* Sheffield, UK: Greenleaf.
19. Van Wassenhove, L. N. (2009). Corporate responsibility in operations management. In N. C. Smith, & G. Lenssen, *Mainstreaming corporate responsibility* (pp. 486–496, p. 490). West Sussex, UK: Wiley.
20. Laszlo, C., & Zhexembayeva, N. (2011). *Embedded sustainability: The next big competitive advantage.* Sheffield, UK: Greenleaf.
21. ISO. (2005). *Quality management systems—Fundamentals and vocabulary* (p. 10). Geneva: ISO.
22. ISO. (2005). *Quality management systems—Fundamentals and vocabulary.* Geneva: ISO.
23. WBCSD. (1999). *Eco-efficiency: Creating more value with less impact.* Geneva: World Business Council for Sustainable Development.
24. Conger, S. (2011). *Process mapping and management.* New York: Business Expert Press.
25. Conger, S. (2011). *Process mapping and management.* New York: Business Expert Press.
26. List, B., & Korherr, B. (2006). *An evaluation of conceptual business process modelling languages* (pp. 1532–1539). Proceedings of the 2006 ACM symposium on applied computing. New York: ACM.
27. ISO. (2005). *Quality management systems—Fundamentals and vocabulary.* Geneva: ISO.
28. EPA. (2007, April 1). *Guidance for preparing standard operating procedures.* Retrieved December 22, 2012, from Environmental Protection Agency: www.epa.gov/QUALITY/qs-docs/g6-final.pdf
29. For further insight into writing operating procedures, see Wieringa, D., Moore, C., & Barnes, V. (1998). *Procedure writing: Principles and practices,* 2nd ed. Columbus, OH: Battelle Press; Price, B. (2001). Set monitoring protocols for SOP's.

*Dairy Herd Management, 38*(3); Anderson, C. (2012, June 4). *How to write standard operating procedures (SOP)*. Retrieved December 24, 2012 from Bizmanualz: www.bizmanualz .com/blog/how-to-write-standard -operating-procedures-sop.html; EPA. (2007, April 1). *Guidance for preparing standard operating procedures*. Retrieved December 22, 2012, from Environmental Protection Agency: www.epa.gov/QUALITY/qs-docs /g6-final.pdf

30. Waddock, S., & Bodwell, C. (2007). *Total responsibility management: The manual*. Sheffield, UK: Greenleaf.

31. Blackburn, W. R. (2007). *The sustainability handbook: The complete management guide to achieving social, economic and environmental responsibility*. Washington: Earthscan.

32. Waddock, S., & Bodwell, C. (2007). *Total responsibility management: The manual*. Sheffield, UK: Greenleaf Publishing.

33. Morsing, M., & Oswald, D. (2009). Sustainable leadership: Management control systems and organizational culture in Novo Nordisk A/S. *Corporate Governance, 9*(1), 83–99.

34. Dalling, I. (2007). *Integrated management system: Definition and structuring guidance*. London, UK: Chartered Quality Institute.

35. ISO. (2012). *ISO guide 72:2001*. Retrieved December 22, 2012, from International Organization for Standardization: www.iso.org/iso /catalogue_detail?csnumber=34142; ISO. (2002, January 31). *New ISO guide for writers of management system standards*. Retrieved December 22, 2012, from International Organization for Standardization: www.iso.org/iso/home/news_index /news_archive/news.htm?refid=Ref812

36. BSI. (2012). *PAS 99 integrated management*. Retrieved December 22, 2012, from The British Standards Institution: www.bsiamerica.com /en-us/Assessment-and-Certification- services/Management-systems /Standards-and-schemes/PAS-99/. For a practical guide to building management systems, written in plain language, see Bizmanualz. (2005). *How to build effective management systems*. Retrieved December 24, 2012, from Bizmanualz: www.bizmanualz.com /blog/how-to-build-effective- management-systems.html

37. iVAC. (2008). *Integrated management system framework (ISO Guide 72)*. Hong Kong: i-VAC Certification; ISO. (2001). *Guidelines for the justification and development of management system standards*. Geneva: ISO.

38. Jørgensen, T. H., Remmen, A., & Mellado, M. D. (2006). Integrated management systems—Three different levels of integration. *Journal of Cleaner Production, 14*(8), 713–722; Karapetrovic, S. (2003). Musings on integrated management systems. *Measuring Business Excellence, 7*(1), 4–13.

39. Castka, P., et al. (2004). Integrating corporate social responsibility (CSR) into ISO management systems—In search of a feasible CSR management system framework. *TQM Magazine, 16*(3), 216–224.

40. Mertins, K., & Orth, R. (2012). *Intellectual capital and the triple bottom line: Overview, concepts and requirements for an integrated sustainability management system* (pp. 516–526). Proceedings of the European Conference on Intellectual Capital. Helsinki: ECIC.

41. Souza, G. C. (2012). *Sustainable operations and closed-loop supply chains* (p. 37). New York: Business Expert Press.

42. Block, P. (1993). *Stewardship: Choosing service over self-interest*. San Francisco: Berrett-Koehler.

43. Womack, J., & Jones, D. (2005). *Lean solutions: How companies and customers can create wealth together*. New York: Free Press.

44. Ohno, T. (1988). *Toyota production system*. London: Productivity Press.

45. Shingo, S. (1989). *A study of the Toyota production system*. London: Productivity Press.

46. Ohno, T. (1988). *Toyota production system*. London: Productivity Press.

47. Womack, J., & Jones, D. (2003). *Lean thinking: Banish waste and create wealth in your corporation*. New York: Free Press.

48. Bicheno, J., & Holweg, M. (2009). *The lean toolbox: The essential guide to lean transformation*. Johannesburg, South Africa: Picsie Books.

49. Bicheno, J. (2008). *The lean toolbox for service systems*. Johannesburg, South Africa: Picsie Books.

50. Kenkyusha. (2003). *Kenkyusha's new Japanese-English dictionary*, 5th ed. Tokyo: Kenkyusha Press.

51. Nolan, T., & Provost, L. (1990). Understanding variation. *Quality Progress, 23*(5), 70–78.

52. Box, G., & Bisgaard, S. (1987). The scientific context of quality improvement. *Quality Progress, 20*, 6, 54–62.

53. Schroeder, R., Linderman, K., Liedtke, C., & Choo, A. (2008). Six Sigma: Definition and underlying theory. *Journal of Operations Management, 26*(4), 536–554.

54. Watson, G. (2005). *Design for Six Sigma: Innovation for enhanced competitiveness*. Salem, NH: GOAL/ QPC Publishing.

55. Hoerl, R., & Gardner, M. (2010). Lean Six Sigma, creativity, and innovation. *International Journal of Lean Six Sigma, 1*(1), 30–38.

56. Harrington, H. J. (1995). *Total improvement management: The next generation in performance improvement*. New York: McGraw-Hill.

57. Montgomery, D. (2008). *Introduction to statistical quality control*, 6th ed. Hoboken, NJ: Wiley.

58. Box, G., & Draper, N. (1987). *Empirical model-building and response surfaces*. New York: Wiley.

59. Harrington, H. J. (1995). *Total improvement management: The next generation in performance improvement*. New York: McGraw-Hill.

60. Creveling, C., Slutsky, J., & Antis, D. (2003). *Design for Six Sigma in technology and product development*. Upper Saddle River, NJ: Prentice Hall PTR.

61. Imai, M. (2012). *Gemba kaizen: A commonsense approach to a continuous improvement strategy*, 2nd ed. New York: McGraw-Hill Med/Tech.

62. Ohno, T. (1988). *Just-in-time for today and tomorrow*. London: Productivity Press.

63. See, e.g., Cole, R. E. (2011). What really happened to Toyota. *MIT Sloan Management Review, 52*(4), 29–35.

64. Mehri, D. (2006). The darker side of lean: An insider's perspective on the realities of the Toyota production system. *Academy of Management Perspectives, 20*(2), 21–42.

65. Chuma, H., Kato, T., & Ohashi, I. (2004). What Japanese workers want: Evidence from the Japanese worker representations and participation survey (RIETI Discussion Paper Series 04-E-019). Tokyo: Research Institute

of Economy, Trade and Industry. Retrieved November 1, 2012, from: www.rieti.go.jp/jp/publications /dp/04e019.pdf

66. ASQ & Manpower Professional. (2011). *Social responsibility and the quality professional: The implications of ISO 26000*. Milwaukee, WI: ASQ & Manpower Professional.

67. EFQM. (2004). *The EFQM framework for corporate social responsibility*. Brussels: EFQM.

68. Kano, N., Seraku, N., Takahashi, F., & Tsuji, S. (1984, April). Attractive quality and must-be quality. *Journal of the Japanese Society for Quality Control*, 39–48.

69. Edgeman, R. (2011). SIPOC and COPIS: The business flow—Business optimization connection. In M. Lovric (ed.), *International encyclopedia of statistical sciences* (pp. 1337–1338). Berlin: Springer.

70. Covey, R. (1989). *The seven habits of highly effective people*. New York: Simon & Schuster.

71. Kano, N., Seraku, N., Takahashi, F., & Tsuji, S. (1984, April). Attractive quality and must-be quality. *Journal of the Japanese Society for Quality Control*, 39–48.

72. Xie, M., Tan, K. C., & Goh, T. N. (2003). *Advanced QFD applications*. Milwaukee, WI: ASQ Quality Press.

73. Hipple, J. (2005). The integration of TRIZ with other ideation tools and processes as well as with psychological assessment tools. *Creativity and Innovation Management*, 14(1), 22–33.

74. Yoon, B., & Park, Y. (2007). Development of new technology forecasting algorithm: Hybrid approach for morphology analysis and conjoint analysis of patent information. *IEEE Transactions on Engineering Management*, 54(3), 588–599.

75. Kotnour, T. (1999). A learning framework for project management.

*Project Management Journal*, 30(2), 32–38.

76. Suh, N. (1990). *The principles of design*. Oxford, UK: Oxford University Press.

77. Stamatis, D. (2003). *Failure mode and effect analysis: FMEA from theory to execution*, 2nd ed. Milwaukee, WI: ASQ Quality Press.

78. Cook, H. (2005). *Design for Six Sigma as strategic experimentation*. Milwaukee, WI: ASQ Quality Press.

79. Moen, R., & Norman, C. (2010). Circling back: Clearing up myths about the Deming cycle and seeing how it keeps evolving. *Quality Progress*, 43(11), 22–28.

80. Deming, W. E. (1986). *Out of the crisis*. Cambridge, MA: MIT Center for Advanced Engineering Study.

81. Shewart, W. (1931). *Economic control of quality of manufactured product*. New York: D. Van Nostrand.

82. Anderson, J., Rungtusanatham, J., Schroeder, R., & Devaraj, S. (1995). A path analytic model of a theory of quality management underlying the Deming management method: Preliminary empirical findings. *Decision Sciences*, 26(5), 637–658.

83. Juran, J. M. (1989). *Juran on leadership for quality: An executive handbook*. New York: Free Press.

84. Stepanovich, P. (2004). Using system dynamics to illustrate Deming's system of profound knowledge. *Total Quality Management & Business Excellence*, 15(3), 379–389.

85. Waddock, S., & Bodwell, C. (2007). *Total responsibility management: The manual*. Sheffield, UK: Greenleaf.

86. Klefsjö, B., Bergquist, B., & Edgeman, R. (2006). Six Sigma and total quality management: Different day, same soup? *Six Sigma & Competitive Advantage*, 2(2), 162–178.

87. Edgeman, R. (2011). Design for Six Sigma. In M. Lovric (ed.), *International encyclopedia of statistical sciences* (pp. 374–376). Berlin: Springer.

88. Edvardsson, K. (2004). Using goals in environmental management: The Swedish system of environmental objectives. *Environmental Management*, 34(2), 170–180.

89. ReVelle, J., Frigon, N., & Jackson, H. (1995). *From concept to customer*. New York: Van Nostrand Reinhold.

90. Myers, R., Montgomery, D., & Anderson-Cook, C. (2009). *Response surface methodology: Process and product optimization using designed experiments*, 3rd ed. New York: Wiley.

91. Myers, R., Montgomery, D., & Anderson-Cook, C. (2009). *Response surface methodology: Process and product optimization using designed experiments*, 3rd ed. New York: Wiley.

92. Edgeman, R., & Dugan, J. (2008). Six Sigma from products to pollution to people: Migration from engineering and business to the natural and social environments. *Total Quality Management & Business Excellence*, 19(1), 1–8.

93. Montgomery, D. (2008). *Introduction to statistical quality control*, 6th ed. Hoboken, NJ: Wiley.

94. Watson, G. (2007). *Strategic benchmarking reloaded with Six Sigma: Improving your company's performance using global best practice*. Hoboken, NJ: Wiley.

95. Watson, G. (1993). How process benchmarking supports corporate strategy. *Strategy & Leadership*, 21(1), 12–15.

96. Bogan, C., & English, M. (1994). *Benchmarking for best practices*. New York: McGraw-Hill.

## REFERENCES

Al-Najjar, B., & Anfimiadou, A. (2012). Environmental policies and firm value. *Business Strategy and the Environment*, 21(2), 49–59.

Ayto, J. (2008). *20th century words*. Los Angeles: University of Southern California Press.

Balasubramanian, S., Mathur, I., & Thakur, R. (2005). The impact of high-quality firm achievements on shareholder

value: Focus on Malcolm Baldrige and J.D. Power and Associates awards. *Journal of the Academy of Marketing Science*, 33(4), 413–422.

Benyus, J. (1997). *Biomimicry: Innovation inspired by nature*. New York: Harper Perennial.

Carillo-Hermosilla, J., del Rio Gonzalez, P., & Konnola, T. (2009). *Eco-Innovation: When sustainability and

competitiveness shake hands*. New York: Palgrave Macmillan.

Conti, T. (1997). *Organizational self-assessment*. London: Chapman & Hall.

Cooperrider, D. (2008, July–August). Sustainable innovation. *BizEd*, 32–38.

Davenport, T., & Harris, J. (2007). *Competing on analytics: The new science of winning*. Boston: Harvard Business School Press.

Drucker, P. (1996). *The executive in action*. New York: Harper Business.

Drucker, P., & Maciariello, J. (2006). *The effective executive in action: A journal for getting the right things done*. New York: Collins.

Eckerson, W. (2006). *Performance dashboards: Measuring, monitoring, and managing your business*. New York: Wiley.

Eccles, R., & Krzus, M. (2010). *One report: Integrated reporting for a sustainable strategy*. Hoboken, NJ: Wiley.

Edgeman, R., & Eskildsen, J. (2012). The C$^4$ model of people-centered innovation: Culture, consciousness, and customer-centric co-creation. *Journal of Innovation and Best Business Practice*, 14 (DOI: 10.5151/2012.932564).

Edgeman, R., & Eskildsen, J. (2014). Socio-ecological innovation. In John Wang (ed.), *Encyclopedia of business analytics & optimization*, pp. pending. Hershey, PA: IGI Global.

Edgeman, R., & Fraley, L. (2008). A system of profound consciousness: Building beyond Deming. *Total Quality Management and Business Excellence*, 19(7/8), 683–707.

Edgeman, R., & Hensler, D. (2005). QFD and the BEST paradigm: Deploying sustainable solutions. *World Review of Science, Technology and Sustainable Development*, 2(1), 49–59.

Elkington, J. (1997). *Cannibals with forks: The triple bottom line of 21st century business*. Oxford: Capstone Publishing.

Franks, B. (2012). *Taming the big data tidal wave: Finding opportunities in huge data streams with advanced analytics*. Hoboken, NJ: Wiley.

Hayes, B. (1998). *Measuring customer satisfaction: Survey design, use, and statistical analysis methods*. Milwaukee, WI: ASQ Quality Press.

Hoffman, E. (2012). *User integration in sustainable product development: Organisational learning through boundary-spanning processes*. Sheffield, UK: Greenleaf.

Hubbard, D. (2007). *How to measure anything: Finding the value of intangibles in business*. New York: Wiley.

IKEA. (2012). People & Planet Positive: IKEA group sustainability strategy 2020. Retrieved October 24, 2012, from: www.ikea.com/ms/da_DK/media/pdf/People_planet_positive.pdf

Jonker, J., & Eskildsen, J. (eds.). (2009). *Management models for the future*. Heidelberg: Springer.

Kaplan, R. S., & Norton, D. P. (1996, January–February). Using the balanced scorecard as a strategic management system. *Harvard Business Review*, 75–85.

Kelley, T. (2001). *The art of innovation: Lessons in creativity from IDEO, America's leading design firm*. New York: Currency Book.

Kim W. C., & Mauborgne R. (2005). *Blue ocean strategy: How to create uncontested market space and make the competition irrelevant*. Boston: Harvard Business School Press.

Lander, G. (2004). *What is Sarbanes-Oxley?* New York: McGraw-Hill.

Lawrence, J., & Beamish, P. (eds.). (2012). *Globally responsible leadership: Managing according to the UN Global Compact*. Los Angeles: Sage.

McDonough, W., & Braungart, M. (2002). Design for the triple top line: New tools for sustainable commerce. *Corporate Environmental Strategy*, 9(6), 251–258.

Olsson, P., & Galaz, V. (2011). Social-ecological innovation and transformation. In A. Nicholls & A. Murdoch (eds.), *Social innovation: Blurring boundaries to reconfigure markets* (pp. 223–247). London: Palgrave MacMillan.

Porter, M. E. (2008, January). The five competitive forces that shape strategy. *Harvard Business Review*, 79–93.

Rüegg-Stürm, J. (2005). *The new St. Gallen management model*. Hampshire, UK: Palgrave Macmillan.

Sanford, C. (2011). *The responsible business: Reimagining sustainability and success*. San Francisco: Jossey-Bass.

Skarzynski, P., & Gibson, R. (2008). *Innovation to the core: A blueprint for transforming the way your company innovates*. Boston: Harvard Business Press.

Svedin, L. (2012). *Accountability in crises and public trust in governing institutions*. New York: Routledge.

Teece, D. J. (2007). Explicating dynamic capabilities: The nature and microfoundations of (sustainable) enterprise performance. *Strategic Management Journal*, 28(13), 1319–1350.

Terwiesch, C., & Ulrich, K. (2009). *Innovation tournaments: Creating and selecting exceptional opportunities*. Boston: Harvard Business Press.

Waddock, S., & McIntosh, M. (2011). *SEE change: Making the transition to a sustainable enterprise economy*. Sheffield, UK: Greenleaf.

Zairi, M. (2009). *Benchmarking and performance management: Contributions to theory and application*. Bradford, UK: European Centre for Best Practice Management.

Inclusive Supply
SCM Fair Trade Cradle to Cradle
Ecoeffectiveness EOL
Procurement Sustainable Supply Chains
Engagement Supplier Development
Closed Loop Supplier Code Logistics Industrial Ecology Transparency Environment Management Traceability
Reverse Logistics
Life-Cycle Analysis

# SUPPLY CHAIN: RESPONSIBLE
# SUPPLY AND DEMAND

**You will be able to...**

1   **...understand the complex systemic
    nature of supply chains and their poten-
    tial to contribute greatly to sustainable
    development.**

2   **...manage your company's contribution to
    the responsible supply chain.**

3   **...influence supply chain partners'
    responsible supply chain performance.**

4   **...develop closed-loop supply chains.**

A broad majority of big companies (83%) are either
working directly with their suppliers or are discussing how
to jointly measure sustainability impact. Only 15 percent
are not working directly with suppliers on sustainability.[1]

There is "a significant performance gap between those
CEOs who agree that sustainability should be fully
embedded throughout their subsidiaries (91 percent) and
supply chain (88 percent), and those who report their
company is already doing so (59 percent and 54 percent,
respectively)."[2]

Authors: Zhaohui Wu, Rick Edgeman, and Oliver Laasch; Contributors: Al Rosenbloom, Anis Ben Brink, Mariné Rodríguez
Azuara, Matthias Wühle, Michael Braungart, Ulpiana Kocollari

## TETRA PAK: Supply Chain Excellence in China

Tetra Pak is the world's leading food processing and packaging company. Since its entry into China in 1972, Tetra Pak has been an influential player in the emerging Chinese dairy industry. The company has leveraged its packaging technology to shape the supply chains of dairy producers and the overall development of the dairy industry in China. Social and environmental sustainability is an integral part of Tetra Pak's business strategy.

Tetra Pak (TP) is creating a sustainable supply chain by directly greening its upstream and downstream supply chains. TP works with various nontraditional stakeholders along the supply chain, including government ministries, universities, the WWF (an NGO), and even garbage collectors. Three key areas are forestry FSC certification, pasture land management, and creating a recycling system. TP became a service company as well as supplier, and introduced industrial ecology in China. The following paragraphs provide a closer look at some of the concrete supply chain management activities undertaken, in sequence following the chronology of the packaging product's life cycle from production, to use, to end of useful lifetime:

*Create infrastructure and systems:* Tetra Pak worked with recycling companies, schools, NGOs, waste collectors, and local governments to help establish a sustainable collection and recycling system. It supported the China Packaging Association, which drafted the first circular economy law.

*Engage with suppliers:* TP sought out paper mills and material companies that were willing to produce renewed materials and promote the development and application of those materials to increase recycling capacity. They discovered that by separating the raw materials in cartons, the value of recycled materials increased by nearly a third. Then they established a recycling network by offering a higher price

for used packages (compared to waste paper). In addition, Tetra Pak provided technical support to both individual and large-scale waste collectors.

*Procure sustainable raw materials:* Tetra Pak promotes renewable resources as production inputs. One key component of milk cartons is wood-based paper. In China, TP actively supports sustainable forest management efforts. Since 2006, TP has been working with WWF, the China Green Foundation (CGF), and the forestry authority to promote responsible forest management.

*Engage with clients:* Tetra Pak will send a key account management team to a new customer's plant. Led by a key account manager, the team helps with strategic supplier development, technology, quality development, sales, and administration. In addition, TP recruits professional consulting companies to provide specific service for the customer, covering 50 percent of the consultancy fee. In return, TP requires a guaranteed purchasing volume from its customers. Finally, TP offers equipment financing. SME customers may pay only 20 percent upfront, and once they have purchased a certain amount of packaging annually, TP excuses the remainder of the debt.

*Manage the end of life cycle:* TP's aseptic packages contain polyimide paper, aluminium, and polyethylene layers, making them difficult to separate and recycle. Realizing that this garbage would eventually become a problem if not dealt with, TP adopted a proactive approach, and has remained one step ahead of Chinese law, referring to its used packaging as "misplaced resources."

Source: Jia, F., & Wu, Z. (2012). *Creating competitive advantage by greening the supply chain: Tetra Pak in China.* European Case Clearinghouse (ECCH) Case #613-005-8.

## 10-1 RESPONSIBLE MANAGEMENT AND THE SUPPLY CHAIN

*"In a CSR context, many companies face an extended chain of responsibility as stakeholders do not only hold the company accountable for its own actions, but also for the practices of all those suppliers (and often of their suppliers and so on) whose goods and services make part of the final product."*[3]

The principles and processes of enterprise excellence, lean philosophy, and benchmarking, which are often associated with operations management, also allow managers to consider their organization and supply chains as systems and provide them with tools to use in approaching those systems. This chapter deals with managing the whole system of companies connected through the supply chain, which is critical because, as managers, we must approach sustainability challenges holistically to attain optimal system performance in all the dimensions of the triple bottom line.

Several factors lead firms to pursue green supply chain management and the triple bottom line, including the demand to meet common standards such as ISO 14000, evolving corporate policies, concern for corporate image, cost reduction, and stakeholder pressure. However, implementation of environmental and social initiatives requires cooperation between buyer and seller. Other factors also can slow the adoption of responsible supply chain policies, including reluctant suppliers, lack of universally accepted and universally applicable metrics and data across global supply chains, and the risk of losing suppliers that cannot meet the challenges involved.[4] In the following sections, which build on the lean principles and system perspective, we will explicate some of the most critical sustainability challenges in responsible supply chain management.

In this chapter, we will develop a process by which to achieve the goal of creating a responsible supply chain in three phases (see Figure 10.1). In phase 1, understanding the chain, we will illustrate the nature of supply chains being complex and adaptive systems, often consisting of small and medium-sized enterprises. We will also provide tools to graphically map supply chains. In phase 2, managing inside the supply chain, we will explain important principles and certifications for supply chain incumbents and will list tools to engage with supply chain partners upstream and downstream the supply chain. In phase 3, closing the loop, the focus will be on methods to create circular structures that help to, similarly to an ecosystem, reintegrate products at the end of their useful lifetime into earlier supply chain stages.

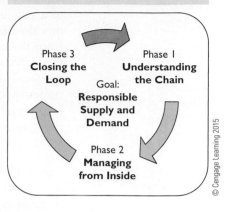

**Figure 10.1 The Responsible Supply Chain Management Process**

## 10-2 THE GOAL: RESPONSIBLE SUPPLY AND DEMAND

*"[Y]ou then need to look at a product from the whole supply chain in a way in which you include your customer as your partner."*[5]

What should the supply chain look like? It is basically an extension of the principles that we defined for a responsible business, applied to the whole supply chain, from the company extracting the first raw material, to the end-consumer, and then to the company that revalorizes products at the end of life.

A **responsible supply chain** is one that optimizes the triple bottom line, stakeholder value, and ethical performance from the first production activity, through the use, until the end of useful life and beyond. Supply and demand are equally important forces in supply chain management, which is why the declared goal of responsible supply chain management must be to create responsible supply and demand. Demanding supply chain players (company clients and end-consumers) must create demand for responsible products and services, and suppliers must supply them. The three main tasks for an organization in responsible supply chain management are to:

1. Inspire, support, and lead supply chain partners to become more responsible businesses and create value for all supply chain stakeholders.

2. Develop a supply system including supplier, clients, and users that optimizes its triple bottom line.

3. Minimize the number of ethical issues and misconduct along the supply system.

A **responsible supply chain** is one that optimizes the triple bottom line, stakeholder value, and ethical performance from the first production activity, through the use, until the end of useful life and beyond.

Through life-cycle assessment, we may analyze the triple bottom line, stakeholder value, and ethical issues along the stages (production, use, end of life) of a product or service. This way we can describe and understand all positive and negative impacts of a product from beginning to end. Managing the whole supply chain translates this theoretical insight into practical application. Managing supply chains ranges from the extraction of the first raw material, to the transformation to a product, through the use by the customer, and through final efforts to recycle the product or service. This whole chain of activities follows the logic of the life cycle, which makes responsible supply chain management the perfect tool to manage the sustainability, responsibility, and ethics of a product from beginning to end. The first step to apply this powerful management tool is to understand the nature of the supply chain.

## 10-3 PHASE 1: UNDERSTANDING THE SUPPLY CHAIN

*"A supply chain is a complex network with an overwhelming number of interactions and inter-dependencies among different entities, processes and resources."[6]*

### In Practice

**Issues in China's Energy Supply Chain**
A good example of the effects of supply chain management activities is China. As it builds its industrial capacity, China is demanding more energy. Since over 90 percent of energy production in China comes from coal-burning power plants, the $CO_2$ output of the supply chain is high, and companies must begin to consider supply chain energy consumption and emissions. Economists have used energy efficiency as a measure of a country's productivity and competitiveness. Overall, developing countries are far less efficient in using energy in their economies. In addition, the Chinese government considers energy efficiency a social issue as well as a business and environmental concern—the increasing pollution from coal-power production has created a public health crisis and social unrest, with citizens protesting the lack of transparency in government reporting of air quality and mine safety.

Source: *Economist.* (2012). Retrieved from: www.economist.com/blogs/analects/2012/05/future-clean-energy and www.eiu.com/public/topical_report.aspx?campaignid=ChinaGreenEnergy

The **supply chain** of a product or service is a series of interconnected value-creating (production) and value-depleting (consumption) activities from the first raw material to the final user. When we talk about managing the supply chain, we take the perspective of a company inside the supply chain, a so-called focal firm. A specific company's supply chain is an extension of the focal firm, ordinarily the end buying firm or an original equipment manufacturer (OEM), which produces end products that then are sold under a different brand name. A high percentage of production operations typically take place in the earlier stages of the supply chain. As supply chains become more complex and companies continue to outsource, a significant portion of a company's carbon footprint lies in the supply chain, and not in the company's own operations.

At the same time, environmental management of suppliers is ever more challenging because increasing numbers of suppliers are overseas in developing countries, often with lower environmental standards. OEMs need to develop and implement viable environmental frameworks, cultivate supplier awareness, and create capabilities across cultural and national boundaries, monitoring suppliers' responsible management practices. Basically, supply chain managers must quantify and document the sustainability, responsibility, and ethics footprint of the entire chain.

### 10-3a Supply Networks

A **supply chain** is a series of interconnected value-creating and value-depleting activities from the first raw material to the final consumer.

Supply chains nearly always take the form of *supply networks*, with multiple tiers of suppliers and buyers, many levels of interaction, and a high degree of dynamism within the system. Every entity in the network has its own agenda, sometimes acting in concert with other members of the network, and sometimes on its own. Even if each member were to be characterized by a single variable, the network would be a multivariable system, with many independent variables. Each member of the network can manage its own actions, based on internal and external mechanisms, but the system evolves based on a complex interdependence of many variables. As such, a supply network constitutes a "complex adaptive system."[7] A **complex adaptive system** emerges over time into a coherent form, and then organizes and adapts itself with no single entity managing or controlling it.

The members of a complex adaptive system interact and evolve with each other and with their environment.[8] This idea—of the mutual interplay of all members of a supply network among each other and with their environment—will form the basis of the following discussion. The first step to managing this complex network is mapping the supply system.

## 10-3b Mapping Supply Architectures

What are the basic elements of **supply chain architecture**? A supply chain, in the narrow, traditional view, is a series of individual companies involved in the joint production of an end product. From the company whose perspective is assumed (the "focal company"), there is an upstream (where products and services come from) and a downstream (where products and services go to) supply chain. In a progressive view, as illustrated in Figure 10.2, supply chains are much more complex. First, they should rather be called supply-and-demand chains, as they include both suppliers and consumers demanding the product and extracting value from it. Second, they are not chains, but rather loops, where products and services at later stages are redirected to newly becoming inputs at earlier stages or in other supply chains. Third, a progressive understanding must think of supply chains, in plural, in

**Complex adaptive system** refers to the dynamic networks of suppliers and buyers.

A **supply chain architecture** is a description of the elements and interconnections of a supply system.

### Figure 10.2 Mapping the Supply-and-Demand System

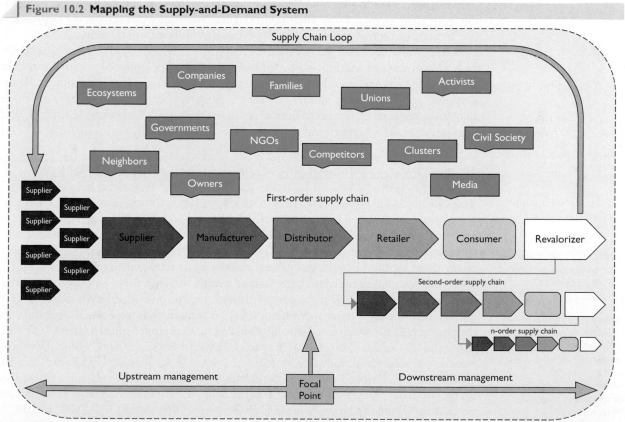

Source: Laasch, O., & Conaway, R. N. (2013). *Responsible business: Managing for sustainability, ethics and global citizenship*. Monterrey: Editorial Digital.

order to consider the second-, third-, and n-order supply chains in which products are involved after they have run through the first-order supply chain. For instance, the outdoor clothing company Patagonia has started to promote the sales of their products on e-bay—a **second-order supply chain**, attaching to the first-order supply chain of a product bought "firsthand," or unused.

In order to create responsible supply chains, managers must take actions influencing all three domains: sustainability, responsibility, and ethics.

- In the *sustainability domain,* managers can, as an example, design products that are easy to be revalorized at the end of their lifetime and that can be transferred to n-order supply chains, where they add value longer than in the first-order supply chain.

- In the *responsibility domain,* the manager must create stakeholder value along "the extended chain of responsibility," established by all of the stakeholders of the supply system.

- In the *ethics domain,* managers must design supply chains and take actions that reduce the ethical dilemmas and misconducts inside the chain. This might, for instance, imply that a company stop sourcing from a country known for human rights abuses, or not sell to customers with bad moral implications, such as tobacco companies.

A more complex depiction of supply-and-demand relationships is a map of industrial ecosystems. Figure 10.3 illustrates how single entities (left), such as an oil refinery, a lake, and a cement plant, can be connected in a so-called industrial ecosystem. Industrial ecosystems will be illustrated with greater detail in a later section, but the map is a great tool to illustrate the importance of depicting complex systems, including both their elements and their components. The industrial ecosystem depicted is not fiction, but a real structure developed in Kalundborg in Denmark.

Industrial ecosystems are not the only networks in which supply chains are embedded. Organizations might also be embedded into other types of supersystems. In general the economy is embedded into society, and society in the environment. Thus, mapping supply systems should, whenever possible, include the linkages to those two supersystems. Other prominent systems are responsible clusters, industries, and communities, which are explained with their specific characteristics in Table 10.1.

## 10-3c The Role of Small and Medium-Sized Enterprises (SMEs)

Responsible business has long been focused on large companies. Supply chains of big companies that are producing well-known and strongly branded end-consumer products usually consist of an immense number of almost invisible **small and medium-sized enterprises (SMEs)**. Thus, understanding the responsible supply chain must include how responsible business and management applies to SMEs. SMEs are companies that are characterized mainly through small employee numbers, little revenue, and owner-managers. Although definitions of an SME differ largely between countries, the number of employees is a main characteristic. Depending on the country, SMEs are defined through a maximum employee number from 100 (e.g., Australia, Costa Rica, Brunei) to 500 (e.g., France, Canada, Kazakhstan). The most frequently used maximum size is 250 employees (e.g., Russia, UK, Brazil). SMEs significantly contribute to the gross domestic product (GDP) and job creation in many countries. The contribution of SMEs to GDP ranges from a little less than 10 percent in Albania to over 70 percent in Germany.[9] The insight is: "SMEs matter."[10]

# Figure 10.3 Mapping an Industrial Ecosystem

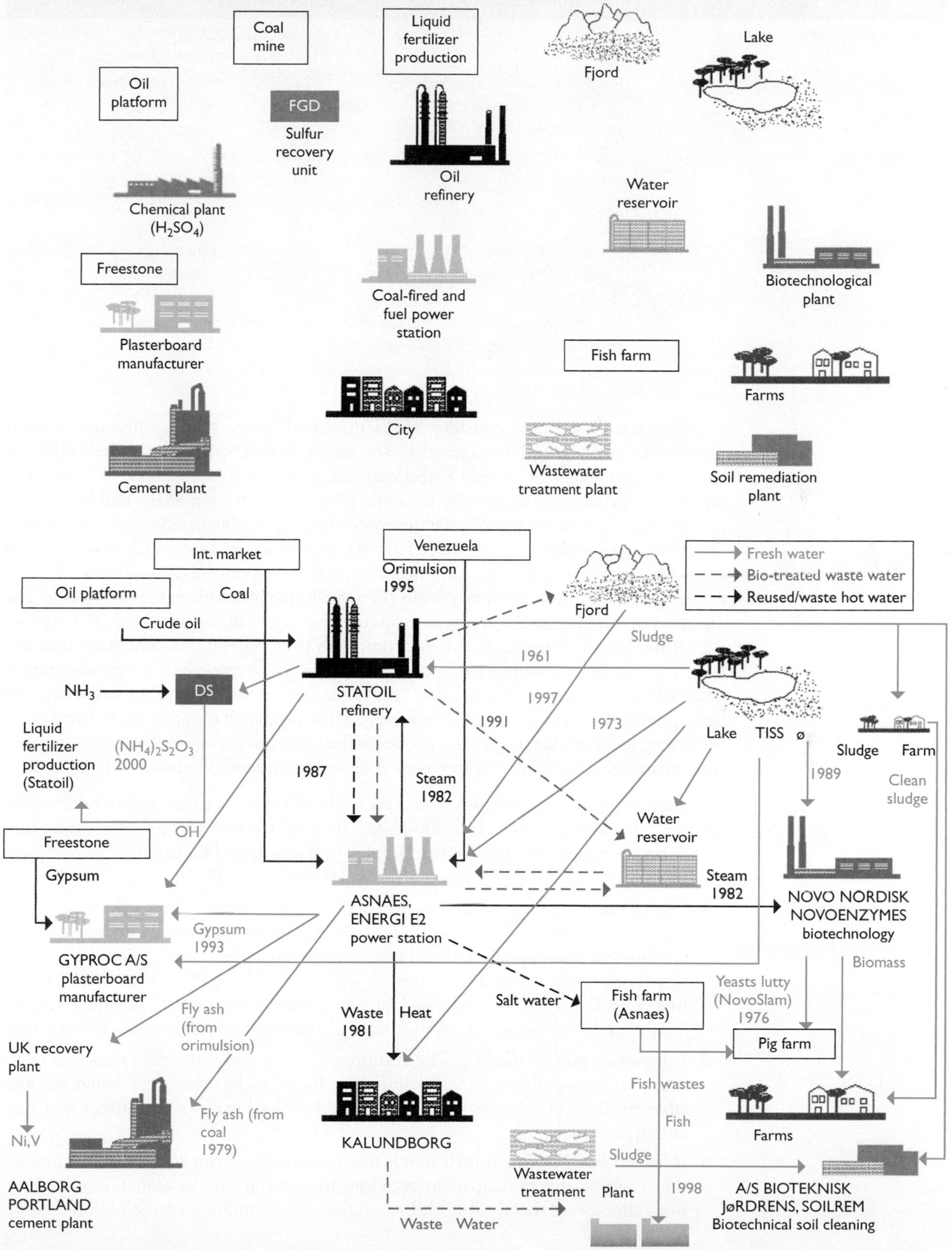

Source: Cervantes, G. (2007). A methodology for teaching industrial ecology. *International Journal of Sustainability in Higher Education, 8*(2), 131–141.

**Table 10.1** Prominent Types of Sustainability-Related Economic Subsystems

| Type of System | Aspiration | Entity |
| --- | --- | --- |
| Industrial ecosystems | Achieve a locally self-sustaining, *zero-waste* system. | Proximate industrial activities with the potential to connect in their resource usage. |
| Sustainability clusters | Reach maximum *synergies*, resulting in highest social, environmental, and economic *competitiveness* among related industries. | Similarity and topical relatedness of locally concentrated industries. |
| Sustainable value chains | Create a sustainable value chain of single *products*. | Chain of production and consumption from first raw-material extraction to last value extraction from product through ultimate end-consumer. |
| Sustainable industry | Create a sustainable industrial system of production and consumption including *several related products*. | Businesses and consumers connected through the same industry. |
| Sustainable community | Self-sufficiency, *social welfare*, and sustainable *environmental impact* of a community. | Businesses, citizens, and public actors shaping a joint community. |

Source: Laasch, O., & Conaway, R. N. (2013). *Responsible business: Managing for sustainability, ethics and global citizenship.* Monterrey: Editorial Digital.

Why should we now consider SMEs differently from large companies in their responsible business and management? The answer is that SMEs, due to their different structural elements and societal embeddedness, must implement responsible business differently. Table 10.2 summarizes the main differences between SMEs and large companies, and the implications of each difference for responsible management in SMEs.[11]

Illustrating in detail all of the differences mentioned in Table 10.2 would exceed the scale of this text, but we can summarize that responsible business in SMEs is managed significantly differently from the way it is managed in large businesses. The question of whether SMEs are more responsible can hardly be answered, as the practices differ too much to create a direct comparability.[12] Salient differentiators between large companies and SMEs are family ownership and owners-managers, the importance of social capital and networks,[13] the management implications of small size and tight financial structures,[14] and, of course, SMEs' supply chain position in lower tiers or serving local markets. Jenkins[15] proposes the consequence of implementing responsible business in SMEs in a complexity-reduced and adapted process of four steps:

1. *Understanding and business principles:* The first step is to internally understand what responsible business is about, and then to translate this understanding into concrete values and business principles that can then be pragmatically applied to concrete day-to-day management situations.

2. *The champion and low-hanging fruits:* The second step is to engage a responsible business "champion," a powerful individual in the business who can lead the first responsible business activities. Differently from large companies, SMEs often start with small, isolated activities, in which they can make a big impact. Those first wins can then be integrated into a coherent responsible business system. SMEs rarely begin with or even achieve a coherent responsible business strategy.

3. *Integration and challenges:* The resource scarcity and potential employee resistance to responsible business conduct is likely to be overcome when responsible business conduct is highly relevant for the business and integrated into employees' main jobs.

4. *Business benefits:* The fourth step is to ensure the long-run economic sustainability of responsible management activities by making sure to craft win-win situations that create social value and strengthen the company's financial bottom line.

Of course, SMEs are not only suppliers, but also buyers in supply chains. While implementation of quality and environmental standards such as ISO will work for large organizations, smaller businesses have other options to monitor and track their own supply chains for environmental and social responsibility.

One straightforward approach is to follow the **six Ts**: traceability, transparency, testability, time, trust, and training.[16] While originally proposed as a quality management tool, the six Ts provide the basis for tracking environmental and social responsibility as well. **Traceability** is the ability to track a product through the supply chain—ideally from raw materials to production and delivery. Achieving traceability has become one of the main management tasks for responsible supply chain managers. *Transparency* refers to easy access to product and processing information

The **six Ts** are a framework of quality management that can be used to track social and environmental performance.

**Traceability** refers to the capacity to track impacts of products and services along the supply chain.

**Table 10.2** Comparing Large Companies and SMEs and Implications for Responsible Management

| Topic | Characteristic | Large Enterprise | SME | Implications for Responsible SME Management |
|---|---|---|---|---|
| **Organization Structure** | *Top management* | CEO | Owner-manager | Owner-manager has bigger discretion in implementing or not implementing responsible business, as he or she is not accountable to external shareholders. |
| | *Business development stage* | Mature | Early development stage | Responsible business in SMEs needs to be managed more flexibly and intuitively than in large companies, due to the need for often quick reactions, weakly developed management systems, and little standardization of processes. |
| | *Range of products and services* | Diversified | Specialized | The specialized nature of SMEs makes it easier to develop innovative solutions to sustainability challenges in the company's area of expertise, but more difficult in outside areas. |
| | *Structure* | Departments | Positions (multifunctional) | Incumbents of SME jobs that include responsible management as part of the job description will encounter competing activities and priorities. |
| | *Decisions and responsiveness* | Deep hierarchies, extensive communication and decision processes | Low hierarchies, uncomplicated communication and decision processes | Decisions in SMEs can be taken quickly, which gives them the potential to proactively react to stakeholder claims and to provide solutions to arising social and environmental issues. |
| | *Structural responsiveness* | Rigidity | Flexibility | Potential for quick decision making for responsible business implementation in SMEs. |
| **Strategy** | *Planning* | Long-run strategies | Short- to medium-run tactics | In SMEs, grassroots initiatives provide punctual responsible business initiatives that grow to a company-wide responsible management infrastructure. |
| | *Competitors* | Enemy | Industry colleagues | High potential for industry collaboration in, for instance, strategic partnerships between "industry colleagues." |
| | *Basis of competition* | Price or differentiation | Relationships, cooperation, flexibility, service | Important functions of responsible business activities in SMEs are the networking aspect, the building of social capital, and the possibility in order to increase competitiveness. |

*(Continued)*

**Table 10.2** Comparing Large Companies and SMEs and Implications for Responsible Management (*Continued*)

| Topic | Characteristic | Large Enterprise | SME | Implications for Responsible SME Management |
|---|---|---|---|---|
| **Marketing and communication** | *Marketing partner* | Business-to-consumer (B2C) | Business-to-business (B2B) | Marketing and communication of responsible business in SMEs must be directed at industry clients and networks, instead of the end consumers, which is the primary target of responsible business communication in large companies. |
| | *Marketing environment* | Market | Network | Collaborative responsible business activities can serve as marketing activities inside the SME network. |
| | *Appearance* | Visible on national and global scale | Invisible on supra-regional level, but high visibility in local community | External stakeholder pressures influence SMEs only on a local scale. |
| | *Codification* | High, many explicit responsible business instruments | Low, implicit integration of responsible business into "what we do" | In contrast to large companies, responsible business in SMEs can barely be attached to institutions, such as codes of conduct, values statements, or even a mission statement. While SMEs usually "do" responsible business, they often do not refer to it with this term. Often the terminology is neither well defined nor well understood. |
| | *Basis of relationships* | Brand | Trust | Responsible business must focus more on trust building to key stakeholders than on marketing a brand to a broader set of stakeholders. |
| **Environment and embeddedness** | *Supply chain position* | End-consumer company, or higher-tier supplier | Lower-tier supplier or revalorizer | SMEs are often "pulled" to responsible business activities through market pressure by higher-tier suppliers or end-consumer companies. |
| | *Systemic embeddedness* | Market mechanism | Relational mechanism | SMEs can create responsible business solutions in local networks, instead of focusing on larger markets. |
| | *Glocalization* | Global | Local | Local "good citizen" activities in the community are more emphasized than distant global responsibilities, such as sustainable development. |
| | *Community relationship* | Intruder | Member | SMEs have an excellent position to relate with local communities. |
| | *Locus of responsibility* | Anonymous corporation | Single individual | Owner-managers and other employees in SMEs can more easily see how their individual acts have an impact that can lead to their assuming greater responsibility for their vocational actions, while in bigger companies "the impersonal corporation" can be blamed. |
| | *Power and outreach* | Power to create large-scale solutions | Local power | Little power and outreach of SMEs often leads to an attitude in the lines of "We cannot do that anyway. Let the big ones do it." |

| Topic | Characteristic | Large Enterprise | SME | Implications for Responsible SME Management |
|---|---|---|---|---|
| **Finance and capital** | *Decisive capital* | Economic | Social | Social capital, especially in personal business networks, might be more crucial for the SME's success than the economic capital in the books. Responsible business can be used to increase social capital. |
| | *Internal financing* | Economies of scale | Limited resources | Little budget for responsible business, unless it pays back directly. The business case is critical. |
| | *Ownership* | External ownership | Individual or family ownership | Potential differences in distribution of profits, and importance of individual or family values in responsible business conduct. |
| | *Rationale* | Profit maximizing | Owner satisfaction | Owner-manager has high discretion regarding the use of SME funds, either to maximize profits for personal wealth or to internally invest into social or philanthropic topics, even if those should not have a strong business case. |
| | *Funding* | Outside | Inside | Due to restricted access to outside capital, SMEs might not be able to raise lump-sum funds for the transformation to responsible business practices. |
| **Human resources** | *Company–employee relationship* | Formalized, neutral, impersonal | Mutually dependent, personal | Potential ethical dilemmas through companies and employees mutually abusing the dependent and close personal relationship. |
| | *Employee roles* | Well-defined and rigid | Vague and flexible | SMEs often cannot describe work roles with too much detail and reliability due to the lower infrastructural development. |
| | *Employee profile* | Professionalized and specialized | Generalists | It might be difficult in SMEs to train employee specialists in responsible management. |
| | *Responsibilities and tasks* | Specialists | Multitaskers | Other tasks might strongly compete with responsible business in the employees' job description. |
| | *Attitude toward responsibility* | Impersonalized responsibility: "I am just one cog in the enormous machine" | Immediate responsibility: "We are the business" | Higher personal accountability of employees. |
| | *Motivation* | Institutional | Personal | Employees in SMEs are more immediately involved in the good or bad the company is doing, which often translates into a personal motivation to do good. |

Sources: Adapted from Fuller, T., & Tian, Y. (2006). Social and symbolic capital and responsible entrepreneurship: An empirical investigation of SME narratives. *Journal of Business Ethics, 67*(3), 287–304; Spence, L. J. (2007). CSR and small business in a European policy context: The five "Cs" of CSR and small business research agenda. *Business and Society Review, 112*(4), 533–552; Perrini, F., Russo, A., & Tencati, A. (2007). CSR strategies of SMEs and large firms. Evidence from Italy. *Journal of Business Ethics, 74*(3), 285–300; Murillo, D., & Lozano, J. M. (2006). SMEs and CSR: An approach to CSR in their own words. *Journal of Business Ethics, 67*(3), 227–240; Mandl, I. (2005). *CSR and competitiveness—European SMEs good practice.* Vienna: European Comission, 2005.

whether by formal or informal agreement. *Testability* refers to the detection of product attributes. *Time* refers simply to the on-schedule completion of processes. *Trust* is the expectation that parties will honor commitments, negotiate in good faith, and not take advantage of others. *Training* is the systematic development of knowledge, skills, and attitudes regarding quality, safety, and best practices.

Although the six Ts are present in any ISO-certified supply chain, they provide excellent guidelines for ensuring environmental and social responsibility in any supply chain. In addition, the six Ts can be interpreted in terms of the Six Sigma define-measure-analyze-improve-control (DMAIC) model widely applied in operations management. The six Ts are necessary inputs and desired outputs in each DMAIC phase.

### 10-3d Social Sustainability

In the following paragraphs, the primary focus will be on the direct environmental impact of supply chains. Nevertheless, one needs to keep in mind that supply chains have enormous economic and social impacts as well. As those two impact types usually occur in international client–supplier relationships, social supply chain topics, such as human rights, working conditions, and socioeconomic development, are typically covered under the topic of international management and business. In the following paragraphs, you will find a brief summary of the social dimension of supply chains.

Of the three dimensions of the triple bottom line, environmental sustainability and social sustainability walk hand-in-hand. Every improvement to a company's environmental bottom line benefits its workers and its community. Decreasing emissions, toxic waste, and pollution is a boon to society as a whole. In fact, societal sustainability is often measured in elimination or reduction of clean-up expenses, decreased health care costs, or higher efficiency and improved productivity due to greener operations—all direct or indirect effects of efforts toward environmental sustainability. But direct societal costs and benefits can be more difficult to quantify.

Although improved ecoefficiency may benefit overall operational efficiency, there are likely to be costs involved. Improved social sustainability (in terms of employee health, safety, and community well-being) is almost certain to carry costs. While some aspects of social responsibility are mandated, companies must assess their mission statements and values to balance priorities in addressing all aspects of the triple bottom line. In addition, any decision about the trade-off between immediate profit and long-lasting sustainability will involve uncertainty and risk. Moreover, since environmental and social issues affect more than just the company, additional stakeholders are suddenly involved. Freeman[17] defines a stakeholder as "any group or individual who can affect, or is affected by, the achievement of the organization's objectives." So owners and managers focus on profitability, community members will concern themselves with livability, and environmentalists will scrutinize impacts from production.

Notwithstanding its fiduciary responsibility to shareholders, a company may consciously sacrifice some short-term profit in order to be sustainable in a long term—in order to care for its community, the environment, its workers, and its customers as much as it cares for its shareholders. In making decisions in such complex circumstances, managers rely on operating principles and technical standards.[18] These managers find that sustainability issues are multilayered; in the process of addressing one particular challenge, unexpected questions will arise. If a company is merely aiming to comply with regulations, the target is clear and compliance is the mandatory. But because organizations focused on sustainability often are already in compliance, the "right choice" is frequently difficult to identify because there may be no good way to measure all of the consequences of a decision. Wu and Pagell[19] propose strategic postures that determine a company's decision-making process.

- Companies adopting the *"environment first"* posture capitalize on environmental issues; business success is contingent on the accomplishment of environmental goals.
- In the *"equal footing"* posture, business is conducted sustainably, and environmental and social efforts directly benefit employees, suppliers, and local communities. In these organizations, environmental and social issues are highly integrated and equally important. These companies may forgo some profits and growth opportunities, but in return they provide well-paid jobs to their employees and stability to the communities in which they operate.
- The *"opportunity first"* posture differs from the previous two in that environmental efforts may be relatively recent, and driven more by economic opportunity than the values of the founders or managers. Companies adopting this posture may pursue environmental or social sustainability as a way to differentiate themselves and achieve economic goals.[20] The organic food industry has seen this occurring in recent years, with large industrial food corporations building or buying organic labels to capitalize on food-buying trends.

## 10-4 PHASE 2: MANAGING INSIDE THE SUPPLY CHAIN

*"… the many ways that social and environmental responsibility can be integrated into supply chain management, from sustainable product and process design to programs and techniques that support product end-of-life management."*[21]

The first step in supply chain management is to be clear about the position of your company in the supply chain. You have to find out where your company, the **focal company,** is located inside the supply system. Your companies' position might be defined by its location. The company might, for instance, be a lower-tier supplier, or an end-product producer. Your position might also be defined by the type of function the company fulfills in the supply chain—manufacturer, distributor, retailer, or revalorizer.

Often it has been taken for granted that supply chain management is dominated by the client, who challenges suppliers to comply with their standards. Usually those client companies are big multinationals with a myriad of mostly medium-sized or even small supplier companies. Interestingly, this relationship often does not describe the true nature of a client-supplier relationship. We have seen the case of Tetra Pak, where the company, a packaging supplier, actively engages with clients out of the dairy products industry. It seems like the question of "Who buys from whom?" should be reframed to, "Who leads whom in the effort for a more sustainable system, for quality, and excellence?" Starting from this question, we can define two types of roles in responsible supply chains:

1. *Responsible supply chain leaders* actively engage with others to support and nudge them toward becoming better companies and creating more sustainable supply chains.
2. *Responsible supply chain followers* respond to supply chain leaders' efforts.

The **focal company** is the organization from which perspective of the supply chain is analyzed and managed.

Many companies in the middle positions of supply chains are leaders in some relationships and followers in others. In the following sections, we will take both perspectives, the one of a big client company, engaging with suppliers, and the one of a typical SME company, engaging with clients. The following sections aim to provide guidance in developing a partnership and the management efforts to be taken from both sides, leaders and followers, clients and suppliers. The responsible supply chain management practices that will be illustrated are supplier engagement, standardization and certification, and the application of quality management principles in supply chains.

## 10-4a Engagement Practices

How can supply chain leaders ensure that suppliers are acting sustainably, creating value for their stakeholders, and displaying moral excellence in dealing with ethical issues? The tools for creating such a responsible supply chain are typically called **supply chain engagement** tools. Such supply chain engagement can be implemented upstream (supplier engagement) or downstream (client engagement). As clients are usually the supply chain leaders, supplier engagement, where buyers engage with their suppliers, is the more common practice. Supply chain leaders may harness a wide variety of potential tools to engage with suppliers.

**Supply chain engagement** refers to collaborative practices among supply chain partners.

Figure 10.4 provides an overview of the responsible management activities that aim at improving responsible supply chain performance. The percentages represent the number of respondents in an international survey on sustainable supply chain management that relied on the respective engagement practice to improve responsible supply chain performance. Interestingly, the same survey found that many supply chain engagement practices, such as incentivizing suppliers to share sustainability expertise and providing them with tools, policies, and processes, were able to reduce operating costs for both suppliers and buyers.[22]

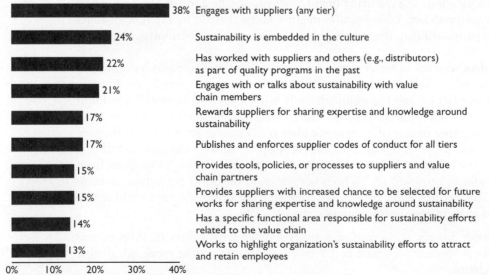

**Figure 10.4  Engagement Practices That Can Improve Responsible Supply Chain Performance**

| | |
|---|---|
| 38% | Engages with suppliers (any tier) |
| 24% | Sustainability is embedded in the culture |
| 22% | Has worked with suppliers and others (e.g., distributors) as part of quality programs in the past |
| 21% | Engages with or talks about sustainability with value chain members |
| 17% | Rewards suppliers for sharing expertise and knowledge around sustainability |
| 17% | Publishes and enforces supplier codes of conduct for all tiers |
| 15% | Provides tools, policies, or processes to suppliers and value chain partners |
| 15% | Provides suppliers with increased chance to be selected for future works for sharing expertise and knowledge around sustainability |
| 14% | Has a specific functional area responsible for sustainability efforts related to the value chain |
| 13% | Works to highlight organization's sustainability efforts to attract and retain employees |

0%   10%   20%   30%   40%

Source: ASQ, CROA, ISM, & Deloitte Consulting. (2012). *Selected sustainable value chain research findings.* New York: Deloitte Development.

A model proposed by Anselm Iwundu,[23] with five rules for successfully managing the responsible supply chain, can provide valuable guidance for responsible managers' supply chain efforts:

1. *Be a role model:* Establish and manage an internal responsible business program before you engage with suppliers to improve their operations.

2. *Multiply through the chain:* Extend your responsible business programs into your supply chain. Lead, multiply, and collaborate with your suppliers to duplicate good results in your own company.

3. *Extend your sphere of engagement:* Know your suppliers better and map your entire sphere of engagement with the goal of extending the influence you have in making the overall chain more responsible, even in areas you had not known or accessed before.

4. *Establish a responsible sourcing program:* Codify your efforts in a responsible sourcing program that provides an official description and commitment regarding your company's supply chain practices.

5. *Establish chain transparency and traceability:* For the following continual supply chain improvement process, information is the key. Make sure you implement mechanisms, such as audits, indicators, or verifiable supply chain codes of conduct, to ensure compliance.

An especially powerful mechanism to create supply chain transparency is the use of standardization and certification, which will be illustrated in the following section.

## 10-4b Standardization and Certification inside the Supply Chain

To manage a wide variety of companies inside the chain, there is a need for standardization and certification. At the same time, this also helps from the supply chain company's perspective, since it can signal the company's compliance. Salient standards and certifications for supply chain companies are listed in Table 10.3.

ISO 9000 and ISO 14000 are management standards. ISO 9000 deals with quality management, while ISO 14000 addresses environmental management. They provide guidance and tools for companies and organizations to help ensure that their services and products meet customer needs, that quality is consistently improved, and that their processes meet regulatory requirements.

**ISO 9000** deals with company management policies and procedures. It is based on eight key principles: customer focus, strong leadership, involvement of company personnel and other stakeholders, adopting a process-based approach to operations, adopting a systems-based approach to management, continual improvement, decision making based on facts, and mutually beneficial supplier relationships. ISO 9000 actually comprises a family of standards, covering basic concepts and language (ISO 9000:2005), management efficiency and effectiveness (ISO 9000:2009), and audits of quality management systems (ISO 9000:2011). There is also a standard (ISO 9000:2008) that sets out the criteria by which a company can be certified as "ISO 9000 compliant." While the principles can be employed by any company,

**ISO 9000** is a standard for the certification of quality management systems.

**Table 10.3** Salient Standards and Certifications for Supply Chain Companies

| Certification | Description |
|---|---|
| ISO 9000 | The ISO 9000 is a globally applied norm for quality management. Often the ISO 9000 serves to establish the scaffold for an integrated management system that can then also include other management subjects, such as environmental, or health and safety management. |
| ISO 14000 | ISO 14000 certifies environmental management systems and is structured similarly to the ISO 9000. |
| EMAS | The Eco-Management and Audit Scheme (EMAS) is an environmental management norm that extends the coverage of the ISO 14000. |
| SA 8000 | SA (short for Social Accountability) is a certifiable norm that focuses on labor rights in global supply chains. |
| ISO 26000 | The ISO 26000, also called ISO SR (short for social responsibility), cannot be certified, but can provide guidance for implementation and a common language for responsible business inside the supply chain. |
| Forest Stewardship Council (FSC), Marine Stewardship Council (MSC) | FSC is a label that certifies the application of sustainable forestry practices. The MSC certifies responsible practices in fishery. Both labels are representative of a wide variety of "cause-focused" labels that are centered on specific social, environmental, or ethical causes, such as fair trade, $CO_2$ emissions, and labor conditions. |

certification can be used to attract potential customers. ISO 9000 can be centrally important to responsible management and responsible organization for the following reasons:

- ISO 9000 is often the *first management system* that companies introduce. Others—such as ISO 14000 and, with some tweaking, even ISO 26000—can be linked to the existing structure.

- Operations can be tuned in to include the satisfaction of various *stakeholders* as "customers," for whom quality is to be achieved.

- ISO 9000 is often required by supply chain leaders as condition for a supply relationship. Therefore, we can assume that the ISO 9000 is a standard that is known throughout most supply chains and that can be harnessed on a large scale to include triple bottom line and stakeholder considerations.

The **ISO 14000** "family of standards" addresses environmental management, using much the same framework as the ISO 9000 standard. As companies focus increasingly on green operations, ISO 14000 provides them tools to control environmental impact and improve environmental performance. It specifies methods to identify every operation that impacts the environment, as well as procedures for safe handling and disposal of hazardous materials and waste, and compliance with environmental laws. Different standards within the family focus on environmental management systems, life-cycle analysis, communication, and auditing. ISO 14001:2004 defines specific criteria for certification of an environmental management system. It does not specify performance, but describes the framework for a management system. The standard is available for use by any organization, including businesses and government agencies, to ensure management and employees, as well as other stakeholders, that environmental impact is being monitored, documented, and improved. Benefits to adopting the standard can include reduced waste management costs, energy and materials savings, reduced distribution costs, and good corporate public relations and marketing. ISO 14000 is seen most often in multinational corporations that frequently encourage their suppliers to apply for ISO certification as well.

**ISO 14000** is a standard for the certification of environmental management systems.

While ISO 9000 focuses on quality management and ISO 14000 focuses on environmental management, the two are more similar than different in approach: Both focus on process without necessarily measuring performance. Moreover, quality management within a company is an internal concern (with ramifications, of course, for customers), whereas environmental management immediately concerns itself with the external surroundings of a company. And, as soon as an entity interacts with its environment, it takes on characteristics of a complex adaptive system. The ISO standard is not equipped to address external factors.

Recently, the European Union has adopted a higher environmental standard, the **Eco-Management and Audit Scheme (EMAS)**, a globally accepted standard. ISO 14000 is a fundamental part of EMAS, but EMAS adds additional elements, most notably stricter measurement and evaluation of environmental performance. The evaluation is based on a comprehensive environmental impact assessment, annual comparison of environmental performance, and independent validation and verification. A company's performance is judged against objectives and targets, and continuous improvement of environmental performance is a requirement. EMAS also prescribes employee participation in environmental initiatives, acknowledging that management practice contributes to environmental performance, but employees drive the functioning and effectiveness of a company's environmental policy and practices.

A much-discussed new norm for implementing responsible business is the **ISO 26000**, also called ISO SR, short for social responsibility. While the International Organization for Standardization clearly states that the norm is not intended to be certified, there seems to be a trend toward the usage of ISO SR for the implementation of responsible business activities. As the norm is still no standard for supplier companies, we will not discuss it here in depth.[24]

## 10-4c Application of QM Principles in Environmental Management in OM and SCM

Sustainability is no longer an option for business; it is an overriding necessity. Before choosing sustainability, companies are often forced to comply with environmental or social regulations, or pressured into abiding by emerging industry standards such the Greenhouse Gas Protocol, the Electronic Product Assessment Tool, or the Forest Stewardship Council code (as in the Tetra Pak case). These "voluntary" standards are frequently tougher than legal requirements, but early adoption offers the advantage of cultivating innovation. In addition, by adopting the highest standard, companies are saved the expense of retooling when the more-stringent requirements become law, and they develop the ability to anticipate new regulations.

A second step in achieving sustainability is making the value chain more energy- and waste-efficient, beginning with the supply network. In 2008, the CEO of Walmart delivered an ultimatum to 1,000 Chinese suppliers: Reduce emissions and overall waste; cut packaging by 5 percent by 2013; and increase the energy efficiency of Walmart products by 25 percent by 2011. In addition to such edicts, life-cycle assessment can capture the environment impact—both inputs and outputs—of an enterprise's value chain, from the coal mine or forest, through product manufacture and use, and on to returned items. Such close scrutiny shows that vendors use as much as 80 percent of the resources, including water and energy, consumed by a supply network. Clearly, if a company desires sustainability, it must prioritize its supply network. Among the benefits that accrue are reduced energy costs and development of renewable energy sources.

**Eco-Management and Audit Scheme (EMAS)** is a standard for environmental management systems and environmental performance evaluation.

**ISO 26000** is a noncertifiable norm providing guidance for the implementation of social responsibility of organizations.

### 10-4d Ecoefficiency and Ecoeffectiveness

Companies can look beyond their internal processes to the products they produce. It is one thing to produce a car more efficiently and reduce energy consumption and waste from the manufacturing plant, but to produce a more efficient car—even though the fuel savings on a car-by-car basis is minor by comparison—makes a huge impact when that efficiency is multiplied by hundreds of thousands of automobiles. This is the difference between **ecoefficiency** and **ecoeffectiveness** (or ecoefficacy). Conversely, it is possible to create an efficient process for manufacturing a gas guzzler: efficient, but not effective. And while the batteries used in electric and hybrid cars have a negative environmental impact, the increased equivalent fuel efficiency more than mitigates those impacts, so electrics and hybrids are ultimately ecoeffective.

To develop ecoeffective products requires skills beyond the grasp of nonsustainable companies, including the ability to identify products or services that cause the most damage to the environment, the skill to develop a market for sustainable offerings, and the ability to scale a green supply network in the manufacturing process itself.[25] Once these skills are nurtured and become standard practice, sustainable innovation can be a business strategy, rather than a burden.

### 10-4e Logistics

The role of **logistics** in the supply chain is crucial.[26] Logistics provides the necessary transport of goods and even services inside the supply-and-demand network. From a supply chain company perspective, logistics includes both inbound and outbound logistics. *Inbound logistics* is concerned with delivering inputs to the production

**Ecoefficiency** aims to improve the proportion between environmental resource usage and output for existing products and processes. The credo is "use less."

**Ecoeffectiveness** aims to create positive environmental impacts through innovation. The credo is "do more good."

**Logistics** is the management of resource flows between a point of departure and a goal destination.

## RESPONSIBLE MANAGEMENT IN ACTION

## The Sustainable Apparel Coalition

The Sustainable Apparel Coalition is an example of a sustainability initiative that could transform an industry. Only a few years old, it started in 2009, when a clothing manufacturer (Patagonia) and a retailer (Walmart, the world's largest) contacted other manufacturers and retailers to develop an index to rate the environmental impact of their clothing lines. The "pitch" included the ideas that a standard approach to sustainability metric for the industry would accelerate environmental and social change, a single standard would eliminate the need for each company to create their own standards and technology, and such a standard would boost consumer trust and confidence in the industry. Additionally, an industry-wide sustainability index would put the industry ahead of government-imposed standards.

Within three years, hundreds of retailers and manufacturers had signed on to the idea, and a tool (the Higg Index) to rate clothing sustainability had been released. Of the participating companies, Nike had been working since 2003 on their Material Sustainability Index (Nike MSI). The Nike MSI includes more than 80,000 products from 1,400 suppliers, and rates materials in three categories: a base score (the material's suitability for the job at hand), its environmental attributes, and supplier practices. The Higg Index incorporates the MSI and adds manufacturing processes as a self-assessment tool for apparel manufacturers. Overall, the Sustainable Apparel Coalition aims to implement verification and certification capabilities, as well as a sustainability rating system for articles of clothing. Information the coalition gathers is freely available to all members, which will make sustainability an achievable goal for small as well as large manufacturers.

Source: www.apparelcoalition.org

process, while *outbound logistics* delivers finished products and services to the customer. On the one hand, logistics is often outsourced, which suggests that the topic should rather be covered under supply chain management. On the other hand, in a responsible management context, logistics is so intimately linked with a business's main functions that it makes sense to cover both in an interlinked fashion. Logistics is also a crucial part of the management of worldwide supply chains, as will be described in the last section of this chapter.

Depending on the product and production process, logistics can be very intensive in natural resources and harmful for the environment. Typical environmental issues are noise, air pollution, traffic congestion, "land consumption" (the land occupied by roads, railways, airports), and, most of all, excessive packaging. Typical negative social impacts of logistics activity are road accidents and pulmonary diseases. The logistics network leading to most products is worldwide, connected, and involves extensive and complex transportation activities.

In order to move logistics activities toward sustainability, it is helpful to understand the typical conflicts of interest between efficient logistics and sustainable development. The following list includes some of the most salient paradoxes of "green logistics" as they have been described by Rodrigue, Slack, and Comtois:[27]

1. *Minimizing costs:* A crucial competitive factor of logistics is the ability to provide transportation at the lowest cost possible. This is contrasted by the urgent need to internalize external environmental costs mentioned above. Internalization of those external costs would increase costs of the logistics activity immensely.

2. *Speed, flexibility, reliability:* Speed, flexibility, and reliability are basic requirements for logistics networks. Unfortunately, the means of transportation fulfilling those requirements (such as planes and trucks) do more harm to the environment than the less desired alternatives (such as ships and trains).

3. *Hub and spoke:* The usage of centralized hub-and-spoke logistical networks creates highly concentrated negative impact at the center of logistics networks.

4. *Warehousing and just-in-time logistics:* The just-in-time movement has drastically reduced the amount of goods stored. A result is that much of the storage has been transferred "to the streets," increasing the overall amount of goods in movement and their negative environmental impact.

5. *E-commerce:* Small, individual shipments are required by the logistical structures of the rapidly increasing e-commerce. Such methods highly decrease the efficiency of logistics by more packaging and the need for customized transportation efforts.

Actions to mitigate the negative impact of logistics take many forms, which can be subdivided into two basic approaches: (1) reducing the impact of logistics activities, while maintaining or growing the volume; and (2) reducing the logistics volume. Following are some typical practices that may stem from one of the approaches mentioned or, in some cases, may combine both:

- *Transport impact transparency:* The social and environmental impacts of transportation are often hidden. While many products are labeled by the country of origin, this only provides a superficial impression of the overall transport activities necessary. Some industries and single companies have

## In Practice

**Green Logistics and Transportation Fleet in the Middle East**

Because logistics and transportation have a huge environmental impact, Aramex has developed a comprehensive Fleet Management System (FMS) to track fuel consumption and emissions across its fleet in thirty stations. In 2010, Aramex succeeded in reducing per-shipment fuel consumption by 3 percent, in addition to a 21 percent reduction over the previous three years. Furthermore, 74 percent and 7 percent of the Aramex fleet are compliant with Euro 4 and Euro 5 standards, respectively. The company was recently recognized for its exceptional contribution to the area of corporate social responsibility at the Supply Chain & Transport Awards in 2010.

Source: Aramex. (2010). *Sustainability report.* Amman: Aramex.

started to increase the transparency of their impact. Food miles, which describes the distance traveled by food products, is a good example.

- *Ecoefficient logistics:* Ecoefficiency aims at improving the ratio between economic output and required input of natural resources. For the logistics sector, this ratio is highly important. Ecoefficient logistics aims at reducing the environmental impact of a given logistic activity. The weakness of the methodology is that it does not aim at reducing the overall amount of harmful activity, but rather at keeping (or even increasing) economic activity, while making each logistics output unit (such as kilometers traveled, items transported, etc.) more ecoefficient. The cumulative negative impact might not be reduced at all.

- *Reverse logistics:* Recycling only works if products at the end of their useful life cycle are transported back to be reintegrated into the production process. This is the main task of reverse logistics, which makes it a crucial part of a circular and sustainable economy. Reverse logistics may also have ecological downsides, such as in the case of returns management. Many companies provide convenient financial and logistic take-back schemes for unsold goods. Such returns management systems create an incentive to order more goods than are actually used.

- *E-commerce (retailing) logistics:* Increasingly traditional logistics activities are altered and often substituted by new business models. E-commerce has frequently been described as being more environmentally friendly due to the reduction of resource-intensive brick-and-mortar store networks. It is not yet certain, however, whether this trend leads to more or less environmentally friendly logistics. Research suggests that the home-delivery services connected to e-commerce are less polluting than customers picking up the bought item in a shop themselves.[28]

- *Servicization logistics:* Complementing or substituting products by services often reduces the necessity to transport a physical product. Servicization models are, for instance, "repair instead of replace" and "rent instead of own."

- *Local production and consumption networks:* Increasingly local production and consumption networks substitute the need for extensive global logistics networks and activities. Such a development is not necessarily always more sustainable. Focusing only on the environmental impact, in some cases, local production is actually less sustainable than foreign production plus importation. For instance, in food products, the reason may lie in local differences in productivity and refrigeration efforts.[29]

## 10-5 PHASE 3: CLOSING THE LOOP

*"Cradle-to-cradle design provides a practical design framework for creating products and industrial systems in a positive relationship with ecological health and abundance, and long-term economic growth."[30]*

**Closing the loop** refers to methods to create circular structures that help to, similarly to an ecosystem, reintegrate products at the end of their useful lifetime into earlier supply chain stages.

**Closing the loop**, also known as the notion of "cradle to cradle," refers to methods to create circular structures that help to, similarly to an ecosystem, reintegrate products at the end of their useful lifetime into earlier supply chain stages. Methods to close the loop that will be explained in this section are industrial ecology, the circular economy, closed-loop supply chains, and end-of-life product design. Those methods are highly interrelated, overlapping and often working in a complementary pattern, which is why many of the concepts and contents covered under one heading also apply to others.

## 10-5a Industrial Ecology

**Industrial ecology** studies material and energy flows in industrial systems and compares them to ecological systems. Since before the industrial revolution, economies have operated on the "take-make-dispose" paradigm—a world of unlimited resources and unlimited area to put our waste. The fact is, however, that we live in a limited world. In nature, materials are recycled, with one organism's waste becoming the food for another. Take the example of a cow pasture: Cows eat grass and drop excrement in their wake. Bacteria grow on the dung, breaking it down into simpler compounds. Fungi can then grow on the feces, while some of the nutrients return to the soil to fertilize the following year's grass crop, when the next generation of cows shows up again to eat.

Just as ecology examines the flow of material and energy through the pasture (or other system in nature), industrial ecology looks at and quantifies those same flows through an industrial system (Figure 10.5). It is a multidisciplinary field concerned with shifting industrial process from linear

## Expert Corner

### Michael Braungart

"The first thing is really to look that the products are either going into biological or technical systems and you need to define the type of product because if you mix technical and biological systems you're contaminating the biosphere dramatically. Just to give you an example, copper is extremely dangerous in biological systems but in technical systems it can be used endlessly. So that's why the first thing is to see the difference between technical cycle, biological cycle, technical nutrient biological nutrient."

Figure 10.5 **Closed Loops and Circular Economies in Industrial Ecology**

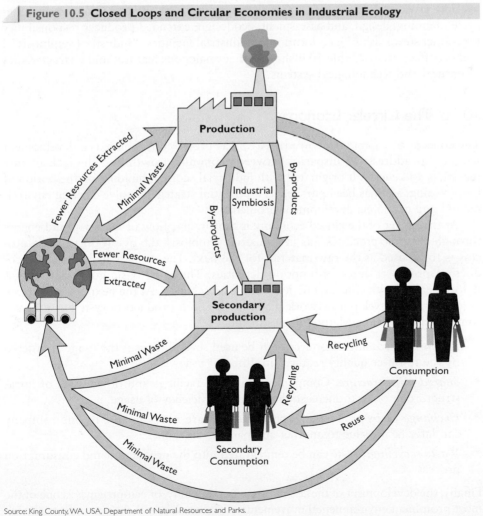

Source: King County, WA, USA, Department of Natural Resources and Parks.

**Industrial ecology** studies material and energy flows in industrial systems and compares them to ecological systems.

**Table 10.4** Comparison of Natural and Technological Systems

| Organizational Level | Biosphere | Technosphere |
|---|---|---|
| Systems | Environment | Market |
| | Ecosystem | Eco-industrial park |
| | Ecological niche | Market niche |
| | Food Web | Supply chain/Product life cycle |
| Population and Products | Organism | Company |
| | Food (meat, fruit, seed, etc.) | Finished product or service |
| Processes | Succession | Economic growth and decline |
| | Natural selection | Competition |
| | Adaptation | Innovation |
| | Mutation | Design for environment |
| | Anabolism/catabolism | Manufacturing/waste management |

© Cengage Learning 2015

(open-loop) systems, in which resource and capital investments move through the system to become waste, to closed-loop systems where wastes can become inputs for new processes. Along with material and energy flows, it focuses on product life-cycle planning, design, and assessment; ecodesign; extended producer responsibility ("product stewardship"); co-location of industrial facilities ("industrial symbiosis"); and ecoeffectiveness. Table 10.4 shows other analogous features and characteristics of natural and technological systems.

## 10-5b The Circular Economy

The concept of a **circular economy** (CE) was proposed in China as a development strategy to address the disparity between economic growth and the lack of raw materials and energy. It originated with industrial ecology, building on the notion of loop-closing, and has been pursued as a potential strategy to solve existing environmental and economic development problems.

At the center of the closed economy is the circular flow of materials and energy through multiple processes—as in industrial symbiosis, the by-product of one process is to be used as the raw material for the next. The strategy includes both production processes and consumption activities. The most basic goal is efficiency. Before dealing with efficacy, efficiency must be achieved. At the next level, the main objective is to develop a network that benefits both production systems and environmental protection. Methodologies include:

- *Resource cascading:* Resources can be used several times if the usage is ordered by the resource quality required in different usage stages.
- *Shared infrastructure:* Companies can share facilities and other types of infrastructure in order to increase the resource efficiency of usage.
- *Exchange of by-products:* By-products that are now of value to one company can later be of value to another company or consumer.
- *Waste recycling:* Waste can be reintegrated into the production and consumption process.

A **circular economy** is a production-consumption system that creates a circular flow of materials and energy where the by-product of one process is to be used as the raw material for the next.

Finally, the development of the eco-city, eco-municipality, or eco-province is one of the most prominent environmental movements in China. Whereas the eco-industrial park focuses only on sustainable production, the eco-city includes the notion of sustainable consumption. Western concepts of the circular economy include such ideas as:

- *Waste is food:* Just as biological nutrients can be composted, technical "nutrients," such as plastics, metals, and other human-made materials, can be designed to be used again.

- *Diversity is strength:* Systems with multiple connections and scales are more shock-resistant than systems designed solely for efficiency.

- *Renewable energy:* Ultimately, energy should flow directly from the source to the process.

- *Systems thinking:* Understanding how systems fit together, including nonlinear dynamics, is essential.

## 10-5c Closed-Loop Supply Chains

In contrast to the circular economy wherein one company's waste can be another company's raw material, a **closed-loop supply chain** recovers materials post-consumer for reuse by the same company—a cradle-to-cradle approach to manufacturing. Traditional supply chains flow forward—that is, materials, components, and subassemblies move from upstream suppliers and contract manufacturers to downstream OEMs and vendors (e.g., distributors, retailers) and eventually to consumers. A closed-loop supply chain, however, also features a **reverse supply chain**. It begins with the used products being taken back through various channels. For example, field engineers from Honeywell's Industrial Automation and Control division make decisions regarding which printed wiring assemblies can be repaired on-site, and which need to be shipped back to the company's manufacturing facility for more extensive processing. Along the same lines, Xerox leases copiers to customers and sends technicians into the field to service their machines as necessary. The technicians visit the customers and either repair the leased machines or take back old or damaged components.

The process of adding value to a product or service, usually at the end of its useful life, is called **revalorization**.[31] In order to close the supply loop or to channel products to a secondary supply chain, a preliminary step has to be to revalorize the product, parts of it, or its materials. The following are prominent revalorization techniques: repair, refurbishment, remanufacturing, recycling, upcycling, and downcycling.

When repair, refurbishment, or remanufacturing is not possible, returns are recycled. If a product is disassembled before recycling, components are sent back to different tiers of the forward supply chain and reused, closing the loop. Standard components (e.g., computer memory chips) and salvaged raw materials (silver or copper) can be sold in secondary markets. When components are not disassembled before recycling, the process often becomes one of "grind and sort." This option is less desirable because it recovers less value. In the worst-case scenario, certain materials (plastics or rubber, for instance) are incinerated as fuel or sent to a landfill.

Figure 10.6 illustrates the choices in a closed-loop supply chain and the options presented by each. The most efficient approach is the smallest loop (in the middle, on the left), service and refurbishment. The least efficient starts with raw materials (upper right corner), traces an open loop around the

**Closed-loop supply chain** recovers materials post-consumer for reuse by the same company chain.

A **reverse supply chain** is a structure that channels resources back from their end of life to be reintegrated into the supply chain.

**Revalorization** is the process of adding value to a product or service, usually at the end of its useful life, in order to reintegrate it into earlier stages of the supply chain.

## In Practice

### Unusual Recycling

A life insurance used to be a one-way product. When the insurant decided to step out, the contract was ceased by the insurer. The coverage disappeared and the insurant paid a fee. Companies in the secondary market for life insurance, such as the German market leader Policen Direkt, are a main driver of a secondary supply chain that recycles life insurances. The insurance policies can now be traded like other assets and do not have to be canceled in the case of liquidity issues. Value is created for manifold stakeholders, among others, the insurance seller, the buyer, and the insurance company. https://www.policendirekt.de/

## Figure 10.6 Closed-Loop Supply Chain

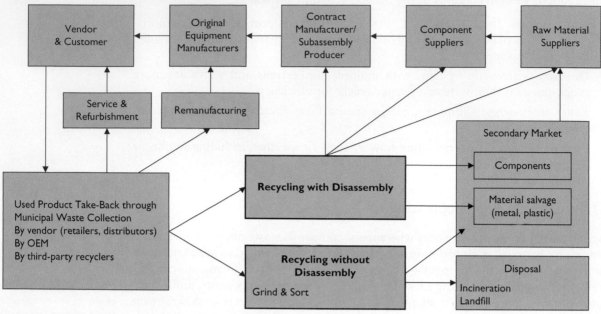

Source: Pagell, M., Wu, Z., & Murthy, N. N. (2007). The supply chain implications of recycling. *Business Horizons, 50*, 133–143.

## In Practice

### Rent-A-Carpet

An example is Interface Carpet. When traditional carpet wears out, it is generally torn out and replaced, the old carpet being downcycled (some of the nylon pile can be recycled, but some pile and all the backing goes into the garbage). The materials are mostly lost, becoming useless (and possibly hazardous) landfill. At the same time, the carpet manufacturer must extract more raw materials to make new carpets. Interface adopted a new process, an updated product, and a novel business model. Their carpet features easily separated, completely recyclable backing and pile. Rather than installing entire rolls of carpet, they manufacture smaller carpet squares with visual designs that piece together with nonobvious seams. And they lease the carpets to customers, making themselves responsible for upkeep. When a section of carpet wears out, Interface replaces just the worn-out section, not necessarily the entire installation. The company maintains possession of the worn material, with the ability to recycle it into new, ready-to-install carpet. Although the initial costs of creating and manufacturing the product were high, the company can now offer a green product while remaining competitive—because of its business model and reduced costs for raw materials.

Source: Interface, Inc., www.interfaceflor.com/

perimeter of the processes, and ends with incineration or landfill (lower right corner)—which is often the case with plastics and rubber. "Downcycling" is a middle-of-the-road option, with some materials going to recycling and some to the dump.

Remanufacturing is not possible for many supply chains. In several cases, the processing cost of remanufacturing is higher than the price of new products. In widely dispersed manufacturing supply chains, particularly those in which production is carried out in multiple locations, transportation costs for refurbishment prohibit the practice.

## 10-5d End-of-Life (EOL) Design

The last part of closing the loop is **end-of-life (EOL) design**. Until recently, most supply chains did not pursue end-of-life management because it cost money. Recent changes in customer concern and increased regulation, coupled with the realization that *EOL product management* can provide a competitive advantage, have changed that. EOL design and manufacture closes the supply loop by eliminating waste and improving reuse, refurbishment and recycling, efficiency, and efficacy.

When recycling becomes mandatory and a company merely seeks to comply, it may outsource the process. This is cost-effective, but it offers little recovery of materials. It does not impact the supply chain, inasmuch as the company can choose to use recycled materials in manufacturing or not. If a company chooses to recycle in-house, it faces the choice of simple recycling of materials (where reusing the recycled materials becomes the natural choice) or recycling with disassembly and refurbishment/remanufacture.

322

Part D Organizing

The costs associated with the additional handling are mitigated and often surpassed by the value of the recovered components or materials. To maximize the benefits and minimize the ultimate costs of this process, an increasing number of companies are designing for disassembly and remanufacture.

*EOL strategies* include modular product designs (easy-to-dismantle and direct components), snap- or push-fit parts instead of glued or screwed assemblies (no extraneous parts or materials), material choice (use of easy-to-recycle materials that require little or no additional chemical or physical processing), nontoxic components (to minimize any impact the recycling process may have), and use of common materials (as opposed to separating, sorting, and processing different materials). Figure 10.6 shows how products and "wastes" flow between different levels of providers and consumers in a closed-loop or circular system.

## 10-5e Further Closed-Loop Tools

The previous paragraphs provided an extensive illustration of theories that can serve to close the supply loop. In this last section, we will briefly introduce tools related to closing the loop that have not been covered before.

**Life-cycle assessment** (LCA, also known as life-cycle analysis) provides a window through which to view a product's environmental (and other) impacts throughout its life span, beginning with raw materials and continuing through processing, manufacture, distribution, use, repair and maintenance, and disposal or recycling. An LCA is defined in ISO standards 14040 and 14044. The standards are used to compare the environmental costs and benefits of competing products. Working backward from this comparison, we see that life-cycle planning and design serve the purpose of maximizing product benefits while minimizing environmental costs. Life-cycle analysis is the primary management tool for sustainability management.

**Ecodesign** ("Design for the Environment") is a U.S. Environmental Protection Agency (EPA) program intended to minimize pollution and the harm it does to humans and the environment. It comprises three main ideas: design for environmental processing and manufacturing, to ensure that raw material extraction, processing, and manufacturing are safe; design for environmental packaging, to reduce or eliminate shipping and packaging materials; and design for disposal or reuse, to minimize the impact of a product's end of life. *Product stewardship* is an extension of this idea, which includes disposal or recycling costs in the initial cost of the product. A related framework is *design for environment* (DfE).[32]

**Industrial co-location** (also called **symbiosis**, found in eco-industrial parks) is a venture in which businesses cooperate to reduce waste and pollution, share resources, and (ideally) achieve sustainable development. An example would be co-location of a synthetic building materials plant that uses wood pulp and plastic as raw material next to a plant that recycles paper and plastic. We have already addressed the final concept in industrial ecology, that of ecoefficacy.

**End-of-life (EOL) design** focuses on creating products that minimize negative impacts at the end of the product's useful life span.

**Life-cycle assessment** is the process of mapping social, environmental, and economic impacts along the stages of production, use, and end of useful life of a product.

**Ecodesign** is the designing of products and processes to minimize pollution and the harm it does to humans and the environment.

**Industrial co-location (symbiosis)** is a venture in which businesses cooperate to reduce waste and pollution, and to share resources.

## PRINCIPLES OF SUPPLY CHAIN: RESPONSIBLE SUPPLY AND DEMAND

I. A *responsible supply chain* is one that optimizes the triple bottom line, stakeholder value, and ethical performance from the first production activity, through the use, until the end of useful life and beyond.

II. A *progressive view of the supply chain* sees a complex system of interdependent organizations supplying and demanding that includes loops where products and services at later stages are rechanneled to newly becoming inputs at earlier stages, and which includes n-order supply chains in which products are involved after they have run through the first-order supply chain.

III. A large share of supply chain businesses consist of *small and medium-sized enterprises (SMEs)* that, due to their unique characteristics, must be managed differently from large enterprises.

IV. *Managing the supply chain* includes engagement techniques, certifications and norms, quality management, ecoefficiency, and effectiveness.

V. *Closing the loop* refers to methods to create circular structures that help to, similarly to an ecosystem, reintegrate products at the end of their useful lifetime into earlier supply chain stages.

VI. Frameworks that help to close the loop are, among others, *circular economy, the closed-loop supply chain, industrial ecosystems,* and *end-of-life design.*

## RESPONSIBLE SUPPLY CHAIN MANAGEMENT CHECKLIST

| Process Phase | | Sustainability | Responsibility | Ethics |
|---|---|---|---|---|
| **Phase 1: Understanding the chain** | Have you . . . | . . . mapped all social, environmental, and economic impacts along your products' or services' supply chain? | . . . mapped all direct and indirect stakeholders along the supply chain? | . . . understood all potential moral hotspots in your supply chain? |
| **Phase 2: Managing from inside** | Do you . . . | . . . collaborate with supply chain partners to jointly improve the supply chain triple bottom line? | . . . reach out to stakeholders along your supply chain and manage your extended chain of responsibility? | . . . collaborate with supply chain stakeholders to mitigate ethical issues? |
| **Phase 3: Closing the loop** | Does your management activity . . . | . . . create circular structures that are able to sustain social, environmental, and economic capital? | . . . enable you to collaborate with industrial and private actors to close the loop? | . . . consider ethical implications of closed-loop supply chains? |

## KEY TERMS

circular economy 320
closed-loop supply chain 321
closing the loop 318
complex adaptive system 303
ecodesign 323
ecoeffectiveness 316
ecoefficiency 316
eco-management and audit
   scheme (EMAS) 315
end-of-life (EOL) design 323

focal company 311
industrial co-location
   (symbiosis) 323
industrial ecology 319
ISO 9000 313
ISO 14000 314
ISO 26000 315
life-cycle assessment 323
logistics 316
responsible supply chain 301

revalorization 321
reverse supply chain 321
second-order supply chain 304
six Ts 307
small and medium-sized enterprises
   (SMEs) 304
supply chain 302
supply chain architecture 303
supply chain engagement 312
traceability 307

## EXERCISES

### A. Remember and Understand

A.1. Define the sustainability, responsibility, and ethics components of responsible supply chain management.

A.2. What are the differences between a closed-loop supply chain, a circular economy, and an industrial ecosystem?

A.3. Define and compare ecoefficiency and ecoeffectiveness.

A.4. What are the main differences between biosphere and technosphere?

### B. Apply and Experience

B.5. Look up the tool "sourcemap" (www.sourcemap.com) and scrutinize the global transport footprint of a product of your choice.

B.6. Think of a local business in your environment. How could this business start building an industrial ecosystem? To which other businesses could it sell its waste? What wastes of which other businesses could it use as inputs?

B.7. Conduct an Internet research for practical examples of the revalorization methods mentioned in this chapter. Make sure you find at least one example for repairing, refurbishment, remanufacturing, downcycling, recycling, and upcycling.

## C. Analyze and Evaluate

C.8. Look up online the different supply chain standards described in the chapter. Evaluate their similarities and differences in a table that you design.

C.9. Conduct an online search for a company whose sustainability report extensively covers supply chain topics. Check if the company complies with the five rules for successfully managing the responsible supply chain.

C.10. This chapter mostly covered upstream supply chain management activities. How do you think companies can involve clients in downstream supply chain engagement? Give an example of a company successfully engaging with clients to create responsible supply chain activities.

## D. Change and Create

D.11. Interview an employee of a small- or medium-sized business about their responsible management activities. Use Table 10.2 to provide recommendations to the business.

D.12. Think of an EOL design for a product of your choice, and write an e-mail to a producer of such a product, describing your idea and asking for advice regarding its feasibility.

## PIONEER INTERVIEW WITH MICHAEL BRAUNGART

Courtesy of William McDonough

Michael Braungart and William McDonough are the creators of the cradle-to-cradle (C2C) concept that has become the underlying principle and credo of sustainable supply chain management. Central concepts related to C2C are the triple top line and ecoeffectiveness.

**What are the main challenges for creating cradle-to-cradle products and supply chains that "close the loop," and can we actually do it?**

From my perspective, there is no limitation because there are two types of products, the products that can be consumed like food, shoes, or detergent. Those can be designed as part of the biological system.

The second type, like a washing machine or like a TV set, can be designed as a technical nutrient for the technosphere.

There are some difficulties when you have very complex supply chains that you need to organize differently. The only real difficulty is that the expertise and knowledge which we have is based on only forty years of environmental discussion, basically starting fifty years ago with Rachel Carson's book "*Silent Spring*" and forty years ago with *Limits to Growth* by the Club of Rome.

We will be able to handle these issues. It is amazing how fast people learn about C2C thinking compared to other learning curves. If you see between the declaration of human rights and women's right to vote in Germany, it took 130 years. So people didn't understand that women are humans for 130 years. We can be really happy with how fast C2C thinking actually becomes implemented, thanks to great scientific work.

**How would you describe the difference between ecoefficiency and ecoeffectiveness in practice?**

People think it is environmental protection when they destroy less to protect the environment, reduce water consumption to protect the environment, reduce waste production, reduce their energy bill—but that's not protecting. It is only minimizing damage. This leads in a lot of cases to optimizing wrong things. You make the wrong things perfectly wrong. As an example, it is not really protection of your child when you beat your child only five times instead of ten times. So you need to reinvent things, not just optimize existing things.

So, don't optimize wrong things. That is why the first important thing to understand is, it's not about efficiency; it is not about resource efficiency. It is about what is the right thing to do, instead of doing things right, and that's really important to understand because otherwise efficiency gains always lead to rebound effects.

Make sure that people are not just managing what they see. All people in management positions need to first ask: "What is the right thing?" If you optimize wrong things, you make them badly wrong.

If we are able to learn from natural systems and learn it's not about efficiency gains, because it's really about effectiveness, that is one of the key things.

## How should companies assess products from a triple top line perspective? How do products relate to their supply chains?

The first thing is to look at whether the products are going into biological or technical systems. You need to define the type of product because if you mix technical and biological systems, you will contaminate the biosphere dramatically. Just to give you an example: The copper is extremely dangerous in biological systems, but in technical systems it can be used endlessly. So that's why the first thing is to define technical cycle, biological cycle; technical nutrient, biological nutrient.

From there it is important to find out what people actually want if they buy something—what is the intention of what people have; for example, if they really want to have a carpet or they only want a different acoustic or a different optics. So, do you really want to have a washing machine, or do you want to wash your clothes? It is about understanding intentions.

The next thing is to define the status quo. You need to find out how good the product is which you have right now, and from that benchmarking perspective, you then need to look at a product from the whole supply chain in a way in which you include your customer as your partner. That means you can reinvent everything that you see around you.

## Do you think reaching sustainability is about changing systems or changing human beings? What is the role of innovation?

First of all, here is what I use as a picture for innovation, which has been picked up by a lot of architects. Let's talk about the built environment around us as a system; let's have buildings like trees—buildings which clean the air, buildings which clean water, buildings which become habitable for other species, buildings which are carbon positive, not carbon neutral.

Secondly, what is important is to look at culture and social needs of people even before that. The key thing is to understand the human role on this planet. A lot of people in the field who see humans as a burden for this planet end up with minimizing damage, but they threaten human dignity by that. So the first thing is to understand that, if we are able to manage materials flows differently, we could even be 20 billion people, easily, on this planet. People have fear when you question their existence; for instance, if you say, let's minimize your impact to zero, you tell somebody it's better not to exist. Out of fear, when you question the existence of people, they become greedy and aggressive. On the other hand, people are willing to share if they feel safe and accepted.

But the real key question behind that is really not the system per se, but it's a discussion about what is the human role and impact on this planet. For being that bad, we are far too many people on this planet. So that's why, before we are going to specific systems, it is more about asking: What is our role? How can we celebrate the human footprint on this planet? The key question is: How can we become native to this planet? This question will then change our lifestyles. So it is key to ask: What do we really want for this planet? What is our role on it? How can we be supportive for other species and supportive for other humans as well?

---

Courtesy of Mariné Rodríguez Azuara

**Employing organization:** AES is a global power company that owns and operates a diverse and growing portfolio of electricity generation and distribution businesses, which provide reliable, affordable energy to customers in twenty-seven countries on five continents.

**Job title:** Administration & Public Relation Leader, Plant Tamuin, Mexico

**Education:** Accounting, Master in Business in Administration

### In Practice

**What are your responsibilities?** Improve the relationship between the company and the community, and also between the company and local authorities. In addition, managing the administration and monitoring the operation of the document control area, general services, and accounts payable. Working for results, meeting the objectives and commitments that the company determined. Leading internal and external programs and social responsibility activities. Furthermore, I am responsible for the PR department.

## What are typical activities you carry out during a day at work?

To establish and manage activity programs with the community, visiting the community to monitor its needs. Managing donations from the company to communities. Coordinate visits of the community to the plant (schools, mainly universities). Managing permissions with local authorities. Managing Document Control area (monitoring archives management, managing information from the data system, planes control, etc.). Manage the General Services area and monitoring the implementation of the activity plans for buildings, offices, rooms, etc. Managing chauffeur's service. Responsible for coordinating events (celebrations) of the company. Responsible for coordinating/managing AES recreational club. Control of the company vehicles fleet, cell phones, buildings, lawyers, and travel. Handling petty cash. Cleaning contract administration, contract consulting firms, contract gardening and plumbing throughout the plant. Management of expatriate documentation. Analyze costs and capital projects of the plant. Communication of necessary information to staff through communication with the departments.

Administrative Assistant, Chauffeur/Warehouse Assistant, General Services Coordinator, Document Control, and Accounts Payable Specialist.

## How do sustainability, responsibility, and ethics topics play a role in your job?

The three topics not only play an important role in my work, but my position is ruled by these concepts in all the activities that I do. I will explain the reason. In AES, we have five values: safety first, act with integrity, fulfilling commitments, strive for excellence, and enjoy the work. Fulfill, it is a matter of responsibility and ethics, and all values are present in my duties, because it is more than customer service—it is being a good neighbor and good companion, with a joint social responsibility, talking internally and externally. Acting ethically is a way of life in AES—not just words, they are facts, which in turn makes us responsible for our actions with the values and code of conduct. Fulfilling both concepts of "responsibility and ethics," I can assure that I can be sustainable; that is what AES requires from me.

To meet the standards, we are certified with ISO 9001, ISO 14001, and OHSAS 18001, with best practices in the ISO 26000 and SA 8000, and fulfilling the requirements of the World Bank. My role is not operational, is a support area; however, it is very important for energy availability, the overall objective of the company.

## Out of the topics covered in the chapter into which your interview will be included, which concepts, tools, or topics are most relevant to your work?

*Responsible enterprise excellence.* One of the values that rules the company says it will "Strive for excellence." This means excellence is everything, and I can also say that in the corporate social responsibility, we are gradually asking for more things, more competitive programs, and classified donations.

*Sustainable enterprise excellence.* It is also relevant because AES vision states that the company will be the worldwide leader providing affordable and sustainable energy safely. We mentioned "sustainable" because we provide products and services that encourage a social, economic, and environmentally sustainable future.

*Management system.* This concept is present in my daily work, due to the company AES having an integrated management system—integrated by three certifications, ISO 9001, ISO 14001, OHSAS 18001, and best practices from ISO 26000 and SA 8000. Hence, all procedures, policies, registers, instructions, and documentation are handled by this integrated management system.

*Stakeholder effectiveness.* It is extremely important for my position to achieve results that satisfy stakeholders' goals. In my role, I manage the relationship with the community, employee, some of the suppliers, and shareholders.

### Insights and Challenges

### What recommendation can you give to practitioners in your field?

I recommend to analyze the community where you perform activities before applying CSR programs. Do not reject new projects, like being certified with an international standardization certification. It is not just about marketing or branding, but it represents a lifestyle after a year of certification. It helps to improve your process, both in administrative and operational activities. It is also important to continuously improve in all areas of the company, getting to know new trends and control and decision-making tools; it always helps to be a company recognized by its quality.

Being sustainable goes beyond the company; it is about staying in a future, taking care of all aspects—economic, environmental, social—and our stakeholders. I recommend to not leave any of these aspects forgotten. Last, it is important to always act ethically, doing things right, because if someday our acts might get published, we must never be ashamed of them.

## Which are the main challenges of your job?

To obtain the "Socially Responsible Company" award; to unify programs according to AES Corporation; to do a program in collaboration with the municipality government to create jobs related to CSR. In terms of management, to lead my team to accomplish all the goals, with a continuous improvement in the general services processes, documents control, and managing administration and accounting. The biggest challenge is to lead a department where everyone in my team has very different activities and we have to accomplish goals as a team.

## SOURCES

1. Ernst & Young. (2012). *Six growing trends in corporate sustainability: An Ernst & Young survey in cooperation with GreenBiz group.* UK: Ernst & Young, 2012.

2. Lacey, P., et al. (2010). *A new era of sustainability: UN Global Compact-Accenture CEO Study 2010.* New York: Accenture Institute for High Performance.

3. Line, M., & Woodhead, J. (2010). Supply chain. In W. Visser, D. Matten, M. Pohl, & N. Tolhurst, *The A-Z of corporate social responsibility,* 2nd ed. (pp. 382–384). Chichester: Wiley.

4. Mollenkopf, D., et al. (2010). Green, lean, and global supply chains. *International Journal of Physical Distribution & Logistics Management, 40*(1–2), 14–41.

5. Interview with Michael Braungart, 2013.

6. Surana, A., Kumara, S., Greaves, M., & Raghavan, U. N. (2005). Supply-chain networks: A complex adaptive systems perspective. *International Journal of Production Research, 43*(20), 4235–4265, p. 4235.

7. Choi, T. Y., Dooley, K. J., & Rungtusanatham, M. (2001). Supply networks and complex adaptive systems: Control versus emergence. *Journal of Operations Management, 19*(3), 351–366.

8. Choi, T. Y., Dooley, K. J., & Rungtusanatham, M. (2001). Supply networks and complex adaptive systems: Control versus emergence. *Journal of Operations Management, 19*(3), 351–366.

9. Ayyagari, M., Beck, T., & Demirguc-Kunt, A. (2007). Small and medium enterprises across the globe. *Small Business Economics, 29*(4), 415–434.

10. Morsing, M., & Perrini, F. (2009). CSR in SMEs: Do SMEs matter for the CSR agenda? *Business Ethics: A European Review, 18*(1), 1–6.

11. Fuller, T., & Tian, Y. (2006). Social and symbolic capital and responsible entrepreneurship: An empirical investigation of SME narratives. *Journal of Business Ethics, 67*(3), 287–304; Spence, L. J. (2007). CSR and small business in a European policy context: The five "Cs" of CSR and small business research agenda. *Business and Society Review, 112*(4), 533–552; Perrini, F., Russo, A., & Tencati, A. (2007). CSR strategies of SMEs and large firms. Evidence from Italy. *Journal of Business Ethics, 74*(3), 285–300.

12. Lepoutre, J., & Heene, A. (2006). Investigating the impact of firm size on small business social responsibility: A critical review. *Journal of Business Ethics, 67*(3), 257–273.

13. Perrini, F. (2006). SMEs and CSR theory: Evidence and implications from an Italian perspective. *Journal of Business Ethics, 67*(3), 305–316; Fuller, T., & Tian, Y. (2006). Social and symbolic capital and responsible entrepreneurship: An empirical investigation of SME narratives. *Journal of Business Ethics, 67*(3), 287–304.

14. Spence, L. J. (2007). CSR and small business in a European policy context: The five "Cs" of CSR and small business research agenda. *Business and Society Review, 112*(4), 533–552.

15. Jenkins, H. (2006). Small business champions for corporate social responsibility. *Journal of Business Ethics, 67*(3), 241–256; Jenkins, H. (2004). *Corporate social responsibility: Engaging SMEs in the debate.* Cardiff, UK: Centre for Business Relationships, Accountability, Sustainability & Society.

16. Roth, A. V., et al. (2008). Unraveling the food supply chain: Strategic insights from China and the 2007 recalls. *Journal of Supply Chain Management, 44*(1), 22–39.

17. Freeman, R. E. (1984/2010). *Strategic management: A stakeholder approach.* Cambridge: Cambridge University Press.

18. Wu, Z., & Pagell, M. (2011). Balancing priorities: Decision-making in sustainable supply chain management. *Journal of Operations Management, 29*(6), 577–590.

19. Wu, Z., & Pagell, M. (2011). Balancing priorities: Decision-making in sustainable supply chain management. *Journal of Operations Management, 29*(6), 577–590.

20. Wu, Z., & Pagell, M. (2011). Balancing priorities: Decision-making in sustainable supply chain management. *Journal of Operations Management, 29*(6), 577–590.

21. Pullman M., & Sauter, M. (2012). *Sustainability delivered: Designing*

socially and environmentally responsible supply chains (p. 1). New York: Business Expert Press.

22. ASQ, CROA, ISM, & Deloitte Consulting. (2012). *Selected sustainable value chain research findings*. New York: Deloitte Development.

23. Iwundu, A. (2010). Five rules for sustainable supply chain management. In M. Pohl & N. Tolhurst, *Responsible business: How to manage a CSR strategy successfully* (pp. 239–250). Chichester: Wiley.

24. ISO. (2012). ISO 26000—Social responsibility. Retrieved January 15, 2012, from International Organization for Standardization: www.iso.org/ ISO. (2010). *International standard ISO 26000: Guidance on social responsibility*. Geneva: International Organization for Standardization.

25. Nidumolu, R., Prahalad, C. K., & Rangaswami, M. R. (2009). Why sustainability is now the key driver of innovation. *Harvard Business Review, 87*(9), 56–64.

26. The paragraph on logistics has been reproduced from Laasch, O., & Conaway, R. N. (2013). *Responsible business: Managing for sustainability, ethics and global citizenship*. Monterrey: Editorial Digital.

27. Rodrigue, J.-P., Slack, B., & Comtois, C. (2001). Green logistics (The paradoxes of). In A. M. Brewer, K. J. Button, & D. A. Hensher, *The handbook of logistics and supply-chain management*. London: Pergamon/ Elsevier.

28. Edwards, J. B., McKinnon, A. C., & Cullinane, S. L. (2010). Comparative analysis of the carbon footprints of conventional and online retailing. *International Journal of Physical Distribution and Logistics Management, 40*(1/2), 103–123.

29. AEA Technology. (2008). *Comparative life-cycle assessment of food commodities procured for UK consumption through a diversity of supply chains—FO0103*. United Kingdom: Department for Environment Food and Rural Affairs (DEFRA).

30. Braungart, M., McDonough, W., & Bollinger, A. (2007). Cradle-to-cradle design: Creating healthy emissions— A strategy for eco-effective product and system design. *Journal of Cleaner Production, 15*(13), 1337–1348, p. 1337.

31. Fiksel, J. (2010). *Design for environment*. Columbus, OH: McGraw-Hill.

32. Fiksel, J. (2010). *Design for environment*. Columbus, OH: McGraw-Hill.

# HUMAN RESOURCES: HR-RM SYMBIOSIS

*You will be able to...*

1 **...understand how five major areas of human resources relate to responsible management.**

2 **...understand the tools needed for responsible human resources management.**

3 **...conduct human resources from a sustainability, responsibility, and ethics perspective.**

4 **...understand the role of the HR function for responsible business.**

"[O]ver two-thirds of the students (68%) in a global survey by GlobeScan in 2003 disagreed that salary is more important than a company's social and environmental reputation when deciding which company to work for."[1]

A KMPG study found "80% of the respondents who believed their company had strong ethics would recommend their organisation."[2]

Authors: Roger N. Conaway and Elaine Cohen; Contributors: Erika Guzman, Oliver Laasch

## Anecdotes of Responsible Human Resources Management at ABB Group

The ABB Group, headquartered in Switzerland, operates in more than 100 countries and employs approximately 145,000 people. ABB is a leader in power and automation technologies that enable utility and industry customers to improve performance while lowering environmental impact. ABB takes a responsible approach to business management and has been a member of the United Nations Global Compact since 2000. The following outtakes from ABBs *Sustainability Performance Report* in the *employee* section give us a good idea about the responsible human resources management activities of a typical company interested in responsible business.

- *Diversity and inclusion:* ABB adopted a group-wide diversity and inclusion statement in 2010. The company's diversity agenda is currently focused mainly on gender. For the first time, a woman was elected to the Board of Directors in 2011. ABB's Board of Directors, end of 2011, had eight members—seven men and one woman—of seven nationalities, whereas the Group Executive Committee had eleven members, including one woman, of eight nationalities.

- *Sustainability leaders training:* ABB's Global Trainee Program (GTP) for Human Resources & Sustainability is an example of a rigorous training that includes four six-month assignments: one with a Group HR function, one with an HR business partner, one with an HR Center, and one in the sustainability function.

- *Responsible HR process:* ABB integrates sustainability performance throughout its Human Resources Management, including all recruitment processes, training and development programs, performance evaluations, and compensation. Approximately 61 percent of the

company's employees are subject to collective bargaining agreements in various countries. ABB in Colombia established an OHS (Occupational Health and Safety) and environment contest to promote a safety and environment culture. Employees are nominated by their peers for the "Eco Safe Hero" award for outstanding contributions.

- *Ethical issues:* New standards were introduced in 2011, including the United Nations-approved Guiding Principles for Business and Human Rights. Supply chain specialists found a total of eleven cases of child labor at two suppliers in 2011. Immediate corrective measures were introduced. Based partly or wholly on human rights considerations, ABB has not taken any business with Myanmar or North Korea for several years. ABB completed its withdrawal from Sudan in June 2009. Five substantiated cases of discrimination and thirty-two cases of harassment were reported in 2011, resulting in six terminations, three resignations, and range of other measures, including warnings, counseling, and further training.

The activities mentioned correspond to different parts of HR core processes, from "hiring to firing" and everything in between. The activities also illustrate the symbiosis between human resources management and responsible business. ABB depends on their people to do the right thing and to create a responsible business culture, and ABBs employees depend on ABB to behave responsibly toward them as one of the business's main stakeholder groups.

Sources: ABB Global Trainee Program. (2012). Retrieved May 10, 2012, from: www.abb.com.mx/cawp/abbzh253/c44d199b674d802fc12575a80045f86c.aspx; ABB Group. (2011). *Sustainability performance*. Zurich: ABB.

## 11-1 HUMAN RESOURCES AND RESPONSIBLE MANAGEMENT

*"The HR–CSR interface may alter corporate capacity to deploy innovative responsible practices relying simultaneously on HR and CSR, and ... the relational processes of employee–employer interactions."*[3]

Responsible human resources (HR) performance differs from traditional perspectives of HR because of its focus on outcomes of HR decisions on people, society, and the environment, and not just on internal outcomes related to efficiency and growth. Traditional perspectives of HR performance seek more efficient management,

| Figure 11.1 **Responsible Human Resources Management Process**

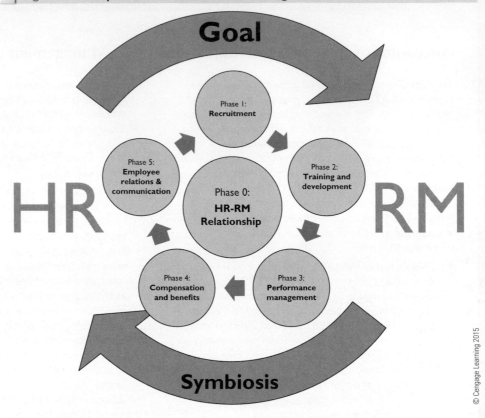

organizational development, and economic growth. Responsible human resources management (HRM) seeks these same goals, but differs because it also integrates sustainability, responsibility, and ethics throughout all aspects of HR. The sought-after result is for HR to visibly demonstrate how employees help to optimize the triple bottom line, create stakeholder value, and make morally correct decisions.

HR leadership has a responsibility, both professionally and organizationally, to drive responsible HR practices. This means performing HR in a different way, while continuing to deliver traditional HR contributions. By examining five traditional core HR processes (see Figure 11.1), we will show how enhanced value for business, employees, and society in general is delivered through a responsible HRM approach.

## 11-2 THE GOAL: HR-RM SYMBIOSIS

*"… a framework of activities that HRD [human resources development] may use to … provide leadership on CSR, sustainability, and ethics, and at the same time ensure that the organization is profitable and successful."*[4]

The goal of responsible HRM in any organization is to provide tools and processes that enable and support the embedding of a responsible business culture and practices at all levels in the organization. This is done by both supporting responsible business objectives with aligned HR and by performing the HR function in a responsible way. This is a dual role: On the one hand, HRM must understand how the organization implements responsible management and provide appropriate HR solutions; on the other hand, HRM must understand the wider implications of HRM actions on society and practice responsible HR as a core approach. This creates **HR-RM symbiosis**, which refers to the mutually reinforcing relationship in which responsible management (RM) needs employees' engagement in responsible business. Human resources, as stakeholders, benefit from responsible management activities.

First, human resources must support responsible business objectives. Most companies today cannot ignore the threats of climate change to our long-term sustainability, and many have already adopted a low-carbon strategy that includes the use of new technologies and changes in business practices to reduce the organization's carbon footprint. Most organizations realize that the achievement of this goal relies on the collaboration of employees in a wide range of initiatives, such as reducing energy consumption in offices, recycling of waste, reducing business travel and adopting virtual tools for meetings, and using alternative transportation to get to and from work. In addition, companies that market "green" products need employees who are capable and competent to engage with customers in the environmental responsibility arena.

Second, human resources must implement responsible management into its own department and perform HRM responsibly. Responsible business begins at home, and the HRM function has a role in ensuring that employees are treated responsibly so that they will be able to perform their roles and engage with each other and external stakeholders in a responsible way. HR policies can affect the quality of employees' lives, for example, in relation to managing stress, health and wellness, work-life balance, long-term skill development, employability, and much more. In addition, all HRM decisions have a wider impact on society than the immediate and internal effects on employees and management.

Performing HRM responsibly requires HR managers to think about the broader effects of their strategies on local communities. For example, hiring policies, approach to diversity and inclusion, compensation levels, managing layoffs, and more can have significant local consequences and must be factored into HRM decision making. In addition, HRM has an opportunity to engage employees through measures that connect them to the organization's agenda and also benefit them in a direct way. For example, employees who learn about environmental management in the workplace are likely to take this learning home and generate benefits in their home lives. Walmart, the giant U.S. retailer, has for several years maintained a Personal Sustainability Project (PSP) program for employees in which they adopt personal sustainability objectives to help them integrate sustainability into their own lives. Many employees share their PSP objectives with their family, friends, and communities, thereby achieving a ripple effect of responsible benefit beyond the confines of the organizational boundaries.

## 11-3 PHASE 0: UNDERSTANDING THE HR-RM INTERDEPENDENT RELATIONSHIP

*"One of the basic aspects of CSR … is the fact that it is also implemented within the company itself, specifically in the area of human resources. Here, CSR spans a wide range of concepts and can vary between the minimum requirements of respecting the workers' basic human rights and the implementation of policies that help employees achieve a work/life balance."*[5]

> ## In Practice
>
> **Training HR to Make an Impact**
> Lloyds Banking Group in the UK has trained 600 Business & Environment Managers to help business customers manage environmental risks and seize emerging opportunities.
>
> Source: Lloyds. (2011). *Responsible business report*. London: Lloyds.

> ## In Practice
>
> **HR Protecting the Private Lives of Employees**
> In 2011, the car-maker Volkswagen instructed its mobile e-mail provider Blackberry to stop e-mail servers after work hours, thereby preventing employees from receiving work-related e-mails in their personal time. This was in an attempt to prevent work and home lives becoming "blurred" and to ensure respect for employees' private time.
>
> Source: BBC News. (2011, December). Retrieved from: www.bbc .co.uk/news/technology-16314901

**HR-RM symbiosis** refers to the mutually reinforcing relationship in which responsible management (RM) needs employees' engagement in responsible business, and human resources, in turn, benefit from responsible management activities as stakeholders.

Responsible business and management is changing the way businesses develop strategy; make decisions; execute processes; engage with employees, consumers, external pressure groups, and communities; and respond to the diverse expectations of all these groups in this fast-moving, transparent age of business. It is demanding a different sort of contribution from the HR function that is critical to the overall success of an organization in meeting its long-term objectives. The key role of HR in this context is to work in partnership with business leaders to embed a culture and practice of responsible business and management because, ultimately, the business performance is only as good as the decisions its people make. As the guardian of corporate culture, HR's role in embedding a CSR mind-set in any business is critical.

HRM has a responsibility to be proactive in leading the establishment of a responsible-business-enabled culture within any business by transforming HRM into responsible HRM. This includes adapting recruitment and retention processes, training and development programs, remuneration and reward programs, as well as developing new tools for employee engagement based on platforms of community involvement, environmental responsibility, and more. HRM must be conscious of the different stages in the employee life cycle, be aware of the touch-points that HR can leverage to engage employees with the business at each stage of their life cycle, and create employee ambassadors for responsible business. Responsible HRM is not just an option. It is an imperative. It is a route to better business, more engaged employees, improved impacts on society and environment, and, ultimately, a stronger, more influential, and more effective HRM function.

## 11-3a The Difference between HRM and Responsible HRM

**Human resources** is "the function dealing with the management of people employed within the organization."[6] The role of the human resources function and HRM in any organization is to add business value through developing and managing activities, processes, and tools to enhance organizational and individual capability and drive an organizational culture designed to deliver desired business objectives. Typically, this includes a spectrum of activities ranging from organizational development to strategic partnerships to support business objectives, through attraction, recruitment, development, and retention of talented employees, maintaining healthy employee relations, providing performance management tools and support, and ensuring compensation systems that serve business competitiveness while supporting attraction and retention.

In a study developed for the U.S.-based Society for Human Resource Management (SHRM), "HR's Evolving Role in Organizations and Its Impact on Business Strategy,"[7] it was found that the top three critical HR functional areas that contributed to organizations' current business strategies were (1) staffing, employment, and recruitment; (2)training and development; and (3) employee benefits. Among HR professionals who indicated that staffing, employment, and recruitment was one of their organizations' top three critical HR functional areas, more than one-half reported that it was their first priority. **Responsible HRM**, on the other hand, goes beyond the traditional roles of HRM in supporting business value. The four key areas of responsible HRM can be distilled into the following headlines:[8]

- Developing the ability of HRM to develop and maintain an organization's resource base to support business sustainability
- Supporting the long-term survival of the organization through managing the impacts of HR strategies and activities on employees and on external stakeholders

**Human resources** is the function dealing with the management of people employed within the organization.

**Responsible HRM** includes the responsibility to manage the employee-stakeholder and HR's contribution to responsible business performance, and responsibility to the triple bottom line, stakeholder value, and moral excellence.

- Developing mutual trustful "resourcing partnerships" by understanding and considering the specific conditions of human resource development, care, and regeneration.
- Supporting sustaining social legitimacy (the "license to operate")

The key implications of this approach are that HR Leaders must go beyond the immediate concern with the management of work and organizations to adopt a broader approach that includes responsibility for the impacts of HR processes on the way in which business fulfills its role as a sustainable and responsible corporate citizen and the contribution of HRM to overall social development. This requires HRM to take both a moral and ethical responsibility for the way HRM is delivered in any organization while ensuring that the broader needs of society, communities, employees, and other stakeholders are included in HRM planning and development of activities, processes, and tools. HR leaders must take on a responsibility for assisting business leadership to assume greater awareness of HR issues and the impacts of HR policies in organizations, both in terms of risks and new opportunities created through a responsible HRM approach. Finally, HR leaders must be role models for ethical conduct, stakeholder inclusion, and social impact-oriented partnerships within and with the organization.

## In Practice

### Beyond Workplace Impact

Swiss Re initiated the first global corporate initiative of its kind in 2007 to help employees reduce carbon emissions in their private lives. The COYou2 Reduce and Gain Programme supports the company's climate change strategy and efforts to reduce $CO_2$ emissions. It gives employees the opportunity to claim subsidies from the company for a range of emissions-cutting investments they want to make in their private lives. When Swiss Re launched the program in 2007, it was the first global corporate initiative of its kind. More than 4,000 subsidies have been granted in five years.

Source: Swiss Re Corporate Responsibility website. (2012). www.swissre.com/corporate_responsibility/

Gond, Igalens, Swaen, and El Akremi[9] stated that "the role of Human Resources (HR) in establishing responsible leadership has so far been overlooked," especially the contributions of HR professionals and HR management practices in responsible development. This has been reinforced through research by the SHRM, which found that HR leadership is involved at very low levels in the development of corporate responsibility strategy and in implementing corporate responsibility practices.[10]

Table 11.1 summarizes four main norms that can serve as a basis for responsible human resources management. We illustrate the International Labor Organization (ILO) "Declaration on Fundamental Principles and Rights at Work"; the Social Accountability International (SAI) SA8000; the Great Place to Work (GPTW); and the "Quality of Life in the Business" section of the Latin American socially responsible business standard, abbreviated to ESR based on its letters in Spanish.

**Table 11.1** Comparing Subjects of Responsible HRM Norms

| ILO | SA8000 | Great Place to Work (GPTW) | Quality of Life in the Business (ESR) |
|---|---|---|---|
| 1. Freedom of association and the effective recognition of the right to collective bargaining<br>2. Elimination of all forms of forced or compulsory labor<br>3. Effective abolition of child labor<br>4. Elimination of discrimination in respect of employment and occupation | 1. Child labor<br>2. Forced & compulsory labor<br>3. Health & safety<br>4. Freedom of association & right to collective bargaining<br>5. Discrimination<br>6. Disciplinary practices<br>7. Working hours<br>8. Remuneration<br>9. Management systems | 1. *Credibility* of management<br>2. *Respect* in employee relationships<br>3. *Fairness* in work-related matters<br>4. *Pride* in ones' work<br>5. *Camaraderie* among coworkers | 1. Employability and labor relations<br>2. Social dialogue<br>3. Work conditions and social security<br>4. Work–family balance<br>5. Training and human development<br>6. Security and health |

© Cengage Learning 2015

## 11-3b The Business Case for Responsible HRM

The following are some examples of how HR can adapt its approach in a way that delivers tangible business benefits:

- *Advancing diversity:* All HR processes can be leveraged to create an inclusive culture where the entire workforce can contribute to greater innovation, improved customer relationships, and reduced workplace conflict, as well as enjoy higher motivation, productivity, and workplace loyalty. This means designing HR processes that actively seek out candidates from diverse backgrounds, proactively training managers to hire with an inclusive mind-set, purposefully creating a workplace that respects the needs of different employees, especially minority groups, and sensitively promoting diversity in internal communications.

- *Going green:* Reducing environmental impacts is one of the most serious business challenges of the day. Business can gain advantage only when the entire workforce is engaged. HR support for the employee-driven Green Teams to enhance employee practices related to electricity usage, use of paper for printing, recycling, waste reduction, and more delivers benefits of reduced operating costs, improved environmental protection, and employees who derive satisfaction from becoming ambassadors for a more sustainable planet.

- *Employee well-being:* Investment in employee well-being delivers big returns. In Unilever's "Lamplighter" program, employees voluntarily participate in programs for managing stress, nutrition, exercise, and other lifestyle habits, which not only has delivered amazing results in terms of reducing health risk factors for thousands of employees, but also has delivered a return of more than four times the amount invested in the program, thereby contributing directly to profit while also protecting business continuity and improving employee productivity. HR policies that help employees to manage their own well-being deliver a return on investment (ROI) in reduced absenteeism, reduced health care costs, higher productivity, and longer job tenure.

- *Human rights:* There are more than 200 million children illegally employed in businesses around the world, more than 12 million people in forced labor, and millions of employees who do not enjoy the basic right to freedom of association. This could not happen if the HRM voice carried weight in the executive suite. HR managers need to help identify the human rights risks in their internal and extended supply chains and ensure robust HR policies to uphold human rights, including risk assessment, and awareness and training programs. Creating a culture in which these issues can be openly addressed requires a new skill on the part of HR managers. Doing it well protects and advances the business, employees, and communities.

## 11-3c The New Skills for Responsible HRM

In developing a responsible-management-enabled organizational culture, HR managers need to learn new skills. At its essence, business responsibility is based on a practice of dialogue with stakeholders, in an attempt to understand their needs and aspirations, because the business response (or nonresponse) to those needs may affect the ability of the business to achieve its objectives. For example, a business wishing to set up a new facility in a new location may be met with challenges from local communities relating to the impacts of the new facility on their lives. This could be a new factory, which may add air pollution to the local environment or affect local biodiversity through land deployment, or a new megastore, which might affect the livelihoods of local small storeowners. While the HRM function may not typically have been involved in such issues, these business developments present both risk and opportunity, much of which can be addressed through HRM involvement with local stakeholders such as local community organizations, municipalities, and sources of local recruitment and more. This is true for established operations as well as new operations.

Therefore, in addition to the development of a keen understanding about what social and environmental responsibility means for HRM, HRM must develop the ability to engage effectively with internal and external stakeholders and take their needs and concerns into account while developing HR policies and practices. Furthermore, HRM must develop the skill to track and measure the social and environmental benefits of these activities, as part of the overall corporate strategy requirements.

## 11-3d Responsible HRM Leadership and HRM Stakeholders

The responsible stakeholder approach to human resources leadership requires the HR leader to think beyond traditional performance objectives that are internal to an organization and include efficient management and development of resources and economic growth. Recruitment costs and effectiveness, hours of training provided, number of employees trained and training budget size, employer costs and competitiveness of compensation and benefits, and maintaining business continuity through positive employee relations are all examples of traditional ways of measuring the HRM contribution. However, this approach is narrow, and these objectives and measures serve the interests of only two primary internal groups:

- Shareholders (represented by management), whose interest lies generally in the short-term financial returns to be gained from a business
- Employees, who must achieve a certain level of satisfaction in the working environment in order to continue to contribute and remain with the organization

By focusing efforts on meeting narrowly defined internal objectives, HR leadership places the organization at risk and, at the same time, prevents the organization from exploiting new opportunities that could contribute to profit, customer service, positive reputation, and potentially new investor interest.

*Stakeholder considerations* in HR include the impacts of HR practices on society in general. For example, organizational restructure and downsizing may be inevitable steps for some businesses; we will not question this need—it is a legitimate business decision that most companies, at some stage of their development, find that they must adopt. However, the way in which such downsizing is managed can destroy business continuity and create negative social burdens, especially in small communities if layoffs are concentrated in specific areas or affect a particular age group. Alternatively, downsizing can be managed in such a way as to contribute value to all of the following:

- Employees as they leave the organization, by a program of assistance to manage reentry into the job market
- Society, by reducing the burden of unemployment or local recession through improved planning and consideration of local downsizing impacts

- The business and its financial stability and economic contribution to society, through maintenance of business continuity through the downsizing process and ensuring that retained employees remain motivated and engaged

- All other stakeholders, such as customers, suppliers, consumers, regulators, and more, who daily assess their relationships with a company and have a preference for doing business with or purchasing the products of companies who behave in a responsible manner toward society

The way in which HR leadership determines and manages such processes, in consideration of the broader implications of HR decisions, can build or destroy business value through the impacts on a wide range of stakeholders in a "ripple effect" of decisions made in the organization that affect what happens outside the organization.

## 11-3e The Role of the HR Manager in Advancing Responsible Business

In this chapter, we promote the view that HR leadership should be partners in advancing responsible business practices. HR strategy and practices should align with responsible business objectives to both support a long-term "license to operate" and provide a resource base that is capable, motivated, and engaged in the role of business to support positive social development. We believe that HR cannot do this entirely alone; there needs to be an overarching business vision that clearly roots responsible practices in all core activities. However, we also maintain that HR leaders have a separate, professional responsibility to lead and manage the HR function and its impacts in a responsible, ethical, and sustainable way, whether or not business strategy underpins this approach. This means continuing to perform HR traditional core HR activities in a way that is consistent with a responsible business approach. Much of this can be done through "enlightened" HR strategies that can be independently developed within the function and autonomously led by the HR leadership.

In this chapter, therefore, we focus on five traditional core aspects of HRM and examine how responsible leadership in HR can make a substantial contribution to mainstream business and responsible business, both in the context of business-driven responsible management and in the context of HR-driven responsible management.

In line with findings relating to key HR impacts on business strategy (see the section on the business case above) and the overall business needs of organizations, this chapter will focus on the following core processes or phases, relevant to any organization of any size, and the ways in which responsible HRM can enhance responsible business performance:

- Phase 1: Recruitment
- Phase 2: Training and Development
- Phase 3: Performance Management
- Phase 4: Compensation, Benefits, and Employee Well-Being
- Phase 5: Employee Relations and Communication

For each phase, we will identify the difference between traditional HR approaches and what we define as the responsible HRM approach, and provide examples of practice to illustrate how some organizations are addressing this today, with some success.

## 11-4 PHASE 1: RECRUITMENT

*"There is growing evidence that a company's corporate social responsibility activities comprise a legitimate, compelling and increasingly important way to attract and retain good employees."[11]*

A primary function of HRM is to develop and manage the process for recruiting, screening, and hiring employees who have both the knowledge and skills to perform the intended role, with appropriate orientation and training, as well as the attitudes that will enable the new employee both to succeed and also support the company culture. The hiring process is a never-ending one for large organizations, and job advertisements are constantly being processed and advertised by human resources departments. The hiring process must lead to sustainable development, ensuring a positive triple bottom line by protecting, creating, and sustaining social, environmental, and economic business value. The hiring process also must be ethical, where decisions are morally desirable in both its process and its outcome. A consulting firm found that "nearly 65% of all openings are filled through internal movement and referrals" and that referrals make up 27 percent of all external hires.[12] Thus, **recruitment** efforts by human resources through its own company website and public advertisements seem to account for only a small portion of successful new recruits. Clearly, ethics becomes central to the decisions of professionals when they follow nondiscrimination policies and create equity in hiring. Responsible practices ensure zero discrimination on any basis and should be incorporated into the recruiting and screening process in all organizations.

**Recruitment** refers to refers to the attracting, screening, and selecting of personnel.

**Knowledge, skills, attitudes (KSAs)**, which often define the basic recruitment profile for new candidates, refer to the attributes of employees required to perform the job. In responsible businesses, this includes the need for employees to align with the business values and uphold responsible and ethical business practices.

### 11-4a The Traditional Recruitment Process

The first stage of the typical recruiting process is internal. ABB follows a six-step model, illustrated in Figure 11.2, because it represents a process used by most human resources departments.

Typically, in most organizations, this is a very focused process. In stage one, the job description is developed; the **knowledge, skills, attitudes (KSAs)** are defined; and a typical candidate profile will be agreed upon, which is the benchmark against which all subsequent parts of the recruitment process are measured. A candidate

---

> **Figure 11.2 ABB's Process of Recruitment, Selection, and Hiring**

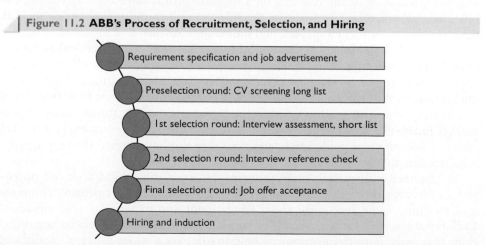

- Requirement specification and job advertisement
- Preselection round: CV screening long list
- 1st selection round: Interview assessment, short list
- 2nd selection round: Interview reference check
- Final selection round: Job offer acceptance
- Hiring and induction

Source: Adapted from ABB Recruitment. (2012). Retrieved May 10, 2012, from: www.abb.com.mx/cawp/abbzh253/12c9128da74aec55c125707d004a1cdb.aspx

profile usually will include relevant experience, educational background, and personal qualities. There may be some "unwritten" objectives, complicitly accepted by the HR department, such as age or even more specific personal dimensions. In 2009, the global cosmetics corporation L'Oreal and its recruitment agency Addecco were fined for discriminating against nonwhite candidates in their recruitment of models to advertise their products.

The procedures highlighted by the ABB Group in the opening case illustrate where responsible practices can be integrated into the recruitment function. In the ABB careers page on the corporate website, potential employees are directed to ABB's corporate values, which include "sustainability," thereby ensuring that potential candidates are already familiar with the company's approach at the time they apply for a role and understand that recruitment is based on a policy of equal opportunity with no discrimination.

## 11-4b Developing the Responsible Job Description

This brings us to one of the first differences between HRM and responsible HRM in the recruitment process. Responsible HRM is not simply a receiver of **job descriptions** and candidate profiles that are unilaterally determined by the business manager's needs or, sometimes, personal preferences. The responsible HRM recruitment process starts with awareness and training for business managers in the business value of diversity in recruitment and the need for managers to be ready and willing to embrace all forms of candidates representing the full ranges of diversity dimensions. In fact, there may even be a case for demanding that no hiring may take place until a short list is presented that includes a balance of gender and at least one or two candidates that represent minority groups. Managers must know that defining candidate profiles in a way that excludes large groups of the population not only is discriminatory and therefore represents a legal and reputational risk for the business, but also is a poor business practice, limiting the potential talent pool and therefore harming the organization's ability to compete.

## 11-4c Obtaining Candidates in a Responsible Way

Once the definition of the role and the candidate profile have been agreed on, the HR manager will typically advertise the role through traditional channels such as the corporate website, newspapers, and online sites, or turn to a recruitment agency for assistance in obtaining candidates. In most cases, jobs are advertised as "equal opportunity," meaning that anyone with relevant experience and education may apply. This brings us to a second point about responsible recruitment. Often, seeking candidates through traditional routes will generate applications from traditional candidates, which normally excludes those who are not on the mainstream job market radar. The stated experience and education thresholds often exclude a wide range of potentially capable candidates who may not have gained the very specific requirements that are stated.

A responsible approach to recruitment demands that HRM seek out potential candidates through developing a broader range of recruitment channels and retaining some flexibility about educational and experience preconditions. Collaboration with local government employment offices or specialist organizations that assist minority groups may help to discover a wider range of candidates

A **job description** defines the responsibilities associated with a job position.

with potential, even if some additional efforts will need to be made in training and development of relevant skills in the early stages. Job advertisements in some countries may be posted in minority publications, either electronically or in print, so that racial minorities and women have equal opportunity to apply. Recruitment agencies must be fully briefed and trained in the organization's CSR requirements, and instructed to proactively seek diverse candidates, and not just accept the applications that arrive through traditional channels, which may be limited to a small group representing the dominant population sectors. By ensuring a proactive diversity approach in the way a company defines the potential employees it seeks to recruit, HRM can contribute to more effective recruitment processes that will deliver a wider range of candidates, achieve competitive advantage in the "war for talent," and also strengthen local communities through enabling all sectors of the population to have a chance at securing a meaningful employment opportunity.

## 11-4d The Selection Process

Typically, candidates who are successful in the initial screening process will be asked to undertake a series of tasks until final hiring decisions are made. These may include personal interviews, group interviews, and participation in assessment centers that test different forms of mental ability, leadership skills, personal traits, and more. Others may be asked to undertake practical exercises or participate in an actual work process. Some companies even use handwriting analysis in order to understand the candidate's personal traits. At McDonald's, the fast-food giant, potential candidates who have passed the first screen must work for two days in a McDonald's restaurant in order to gain firsthand experience of the working environment, because the "match" of the candidate's KSA, personal characteristics, and preferences is just as important as the specific background of the employee without reference to the organization or role the candidate is applying for.

In the responsible selection process, HRM must make sure that this "fit" is present by ensuring both that the candidate's abilities and values are carefully explored and that HR has a clear understanding of the candidate's preferences and aspirations. In many ways, this is an element of "stakeholder dialogue," referred to in our opening section. A company must hire employees who are aligned with its objectives, and this means finding not only the most capable employees but also the most suitable employees. This turns the screening process into one that offers a balance between obtaining information about the candidate and enabling the candidate to obtain information about the company. A recruitment decision is made not only by the company, but also by the candidate, who must decide whether or not to join the company.

A positive process for the dialogue-based interview is the behavioral interview approach, in which candidates are asked to describe that they have demonstrated the desired behaviors as an indication of their potential to reapply them in the company. This kind of approach requires skill and training, so the responsible screening process must include managers who are fully trained in the theory and practice and can apply this approach when they interview candidates. Managers must learn how to neutralize personal preferences or preconceptions that might lead to discriminatory decisions in the selection process. It is the role of HRM to ensure that this is put into practice.

Additionally, HRM must ensure that candidates have the opportunity to learn enough about the company in order to make a balanced decision. This means ensuring that the employer brand accurately reflects the company's approach and also ensuring that managers have enough information to be able to respond to candidates' queries.

### 11-4e Hiring in the Responsible Organization

The process of recruitment, selection, and hiring moves to the final stage after interviews and all other forms of assessment are completed. Openness and transparency must exist throughout the process so that candidates may make balanced decisions. In developing the employment contract, the company must proactively ensure that the candidate has all the information about the company terms and conditions of employment, in writing. Employment contracts offered must be fair and represent the interests of the employee, and not only the company.

## 11-5 PHASE 2: TRAINING AND DEVELOPMENT OF EMPLOYEES

*"Sustainable human resource management (HRM) can be defined as using the tools of HR to create a workforce that has the trust, values, skills and motivation to achieve a profitable triple bottom line."*[13]

**Training and development** is a core HRM process. Typically, HRM functions define training and development needs in line with those required to support business objectives. This is no different with responsible HRM, though, of course, the responsible organization's business objectives may include new areas of activity, such as the development of low-carbon products, the adaptation of products to new emerging economic needs that address social issues, or the achievement of improved sustainability rankings to attract new investors by developing a more robust approach to human rights. However, in addition, the responsible HRM approach seeks to ensure employees are well versed in additional organizational aspects such as values and ethical conduct, corporate responsibility as a business approach, and managing, measuring, and tracking social and environmental impacts.

The training and development process also reflects the responsibility an organization maintains to advance the "employability" of its people: enabling them to grow and develop so that they will be better able to contribute not only in their current organization but also in any organization for which they may work in the future. Responsible HRM sees beyond the very immediate needs for the business and aims to add long-term value to employees as an added benefit of their current employment. This is part of the contribution of a responsible business to a sustainable society; immediate business needs change and skills become obsolete. By preparing employees for the future, a company is taking out an insurance policy against the possible negative effects of business changes, such as layoffs and the damage they can do to local communities.

**Training and development** refers to educational activities within an organization that aim to increase the fulfillment and performance of employees.

## In Practice

### Training for Social Performance
The HR department at SAMSUNG developed an extensive reeducation and job training process for employees that emphasizes social performance and social contributions with the theme "For the Betterment of All." Employees are encouraged to make a contribution in the community. SAMSUNG's community service teams become involved in professional community "share-care programs," and they volunteer for various social services and activities.

Source: SAMSUNG. (2012). *Social performance.* Retrieved May 26, 2012, from: www.samsung.com/us/aboutsamsung/corpcitizenship /environmentsocialreport/environmentsocialreport_SocialCommitment.html

## Developing to See the Bigger Picture at SAMSUNG

SAMSUNG emphasizes sustainability performance throughout the training and development process and provides specific training to develop social performance and encourage social contributions. The Korean company's Human Resources Development Center (HRDC) exists as a cornerstone in their industry. The Center "trains and develops employees, promotes our corporate culture, and establishes developmental strategy for human resources." The HRDC employs seventy professionals who offer products in human resources development and training, HRD consulting, and recruiting. Employees are further trained in health and safety, global communities, safety in product and service, open-to-all opportunities and human rights, and ethics management. When receiving training about the Supplier Code of Conduct, for instance, employees are taught "to take responsibility and the role as corporate citizen for better society."

SAMSUNG provides sustainability training and development for employees and prepares them for a future with the company. Responsible HRM is expressed in reeducation and job training, preparing individuals for the future, and organizational development with employees who are able to see the bigger picture and understand their contribution to society through their work. SAMSUNG's HR Center "sharpens the sustainability expertise" of future-oriented employees and develops their future potential in the R&D, marketing, and management sectors. The Center diversifies its training through a leadership training institute, marketing center, and an advanced technology institute to provide employees with current understanding of sustainability and a future with the company.

Sources: SAMSUNG. (2012). *Human resources.* Retrieved May 26, 2012, from: www.samsung.com/hk_en/aboutsamsung/samsunggroup/affiliatedcompanies/ SAMSUNGGroup_SAMSUNGHumanResourcesDevelopmentInstitute. html#content; SAMSUNG. (2012). *Supplier code of conduct.* Retrieved May 26, 2012, from: www.samsung.com/us/aboutsamsung/corpcitizenship/ environmentsocialreport/environmentsocialreport_EICC.html

**Figure 11.3  Overview of Phase 2: Training and Development**

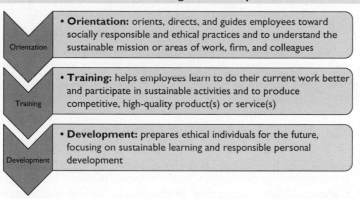

- **Orientation:** orients, directs, and guides employees toward socially responsible and ethical practices and to understand the sustainable mission or areas of work, firm, and colleagues

- **Training:** helps employees learn to do their current work better and participate in sustainable activities and to produce competitive, high-quality product(s) or service(s)

- **Development:** prepares ethical individuals for the future, focusing on sustainable learning and responsible personal development

Source: Adapted from Ivancevich, J. M. (2003). *Human resource management,* 9th int'l ed. (p. 394). New York: McGraw-Hill/Irwin.

This section is organized into three categories of orientation, training, and development, an approach used by Ivancevich,[14] who emphasizes that the desired end results of orientation is to have (1) socially responsible and ethical practices; (2) competitive, high-quality product(s); and (3) competitive, high-quality service(s). Figure 11.3 illustrates this process.

## 11-5a New Employee Orientation

When new employees enter into an organization, the process is complicated and neither automatic nor instant. Newcomers often meet with unknown expectations, and they discover that unwritten rules exist about the organizational culture and environment. They soon learn whether the business "walks the talk" of sustainability and promotes sustainability activities to external stakeholders.

Typical goals of a good **employee orientation** program include reducing newcomer anxiety, reducing turnover, saving time, and developing realistic expectations.[15] Organizations want to see new employees succeed because of the time and costs involved, and HRM carries the responsibility for this transition process to prepare the newcomer through training and development.

Jablin[16] described organizational assimilation as the entire transition of ongoing behavioral and cognitive processes that begins before employees join the organization and continues until they become insiders. The Corporate Responsibility Report of the Intercontinental Hotels Group (IHG), for example, explained how the company developed an Academy Program that provides real-life skills for students, many aged between 14 and 18 years, to enhance employment opportunities for local people in the communities within which the hotel group operates. From this pool of young people, IHG prepares future employees for work in the hotel industry,[17] thereby starting their orientation process even before they are hired.

In a responsible HRM context, there are opportunities to go beyond traditional orientation models that aim to familiarize employees with the company, the job, key processes, and key colleagues. As the orientation phase shapes the way employees will succeed in their immediate role in the short term, and may help them develop within the organization in the long term, this is a unique opportunity to ensure that the responsibility of business is understood and that employees know how their work connects to broader social and environmental impacts.

Additionally, the orientation phase is one in which all other employees must be supportive and offer constructive help and guidance, especially if the new employee is from a minority or special needs group. Many companies have "affinity groups" or employee resource groups that may play an active role in providing diverse employees with a support group of colleagues with similar needs to help them integrate and grow with the company. Other companies may assign mentors or coaches to help new employees find their feet.

## 11-5b A Model for Orientation and Socialization

Miller[18] characterizes the orientation and socialization transition in three phases: anticipatory assimilation, encounter, and metamorphosis. Table 11.2, adapted from Miller, shows Miller's definition of the stages of the socialization process, along with our additions relating to the responsible HRM practices that apply at each stage.

*Anticipatory socialization* may begin years before the employee begins work at the organization. Using our example of SAMSUNG earlier in this section, we might cite the example of how a Korean youth might gain a vision of working at SAMSUNG one day in the future and want to help the environment in the manufacturing process. The youth might form initial impressions about the electronics industry as a progressive, sustainable manufacturing industry. Cohen[19] characterizes this dynamic as a prehire phase in the employee life cycle. She states that "the

**Employee orientation** is the process of introducing new employees into an organization.

**Table 11.2** Stages of the Socialization Process and Responsible, Sustainable, and Ethical Principles

| Stage | Descriptions |
|---|---|
| Anticipatory socialization | Socialization that occurs before entry into the organization: This encompasses both socialization to an occupation and socialization to an organization.<br>*Responsible principles:*<br>• Communicate responsible, sustainable, and ethical business practices and performance widely to external stakeholders through a range of channels. This might include use of social media to engage in dialogue with potential employees.<br>• Develop a robust employer brand that reflects corporate responsibility principles.<br>• Integrate responsible objectives throughout the recruitment process, in the interview, and during induction. This might also include participation in careers fairs or community involvement of employees in educational projects.<br>• Manage the recruitment process in a fair, open, and respectful way for all candidates, even those the company decides not to hire. |
| Encounter | Sense-making stage that occurs when a new employee enters the organization: The newcomer must let go of old roles and values in adapting to the expectations of the new organization.<br>*Responsible principles:*<br>• Clearly communicate company sustainability objectives at the "point of entry."<br>• Ensure that the new hire has a clear understanding of expectations and an internal company support system (HR manager, employee resource group, mentor, etc.).<br>• Help the new employee feel involved in the company's social purpose by offering opportunities to participate in social or environmental activities.<br>• "Start or maintain their professional development … through training in initial company requirements, corporate culture, processes which empower the new hire, and establishment of a supportive network… ."* |
| Metamorphosis | The state reached at the "completion" of the socialization process: The new employee is now accepted as an organizational insider.<br>*Responsible principles:*<br>• Ensure continued support through supportive management, opportunities for open dialogue and feedback, and continued training and development.<br>• Ensure continued engagement of the employee in corporate responsibility activities and recognize good contribution and "ownership" of the company's culture of responsibility. |

*Cohen, E. (2010). *CSR for HR: A necessary partnership for advancing responsible business practices* (p. 251). Sheffield, UK: Greenleaf.

Source: Adapted from Miller, K. (2009). *Organizational communication: Approaches and processes,* 5th ed. (p. 122). Boston: Wadsworth Cengage Learning.

company's CSR program impacts the ability of all individuals to enter or improve their position in the job market." Elements that drive these impacts are:

• Community involvement and investment in education or vocational skills

• Employer brand, which includes the company's social and environmental mission

• Proactive recruitment that reaches out to a diverse pool of potential candidates

• Company responsiveness to queries from potential employees

Cohen[20] recognizes that a company's involvement in social or environmental activities goes a long way toward developing anticipatory socialization in potential employees. This socialization might take place with the Korean youth mentioned above, who, for instance, has a parent or family member working at SAMSUNG. The youth learns about the company's corporate responsibility objectives and principles at an early age and develops a desire to follow the same vocation as the parent or family member. SAMSUNG may be perceived by the youth as a safe, environmentally friendly business. The youth begins to one day anticipate working at SAMSUNG and imagines making a difference in a social mission.

The *encounter phase* is identified by orientation programs. These programs must include the company's responsible business principles and practices and the specific contribution related to the employees' roles. It is also important that managers and others in the company demonstrate their personal commitment and activity, so as to project themselves as role models that new employees can emulate. Desired behaviors are best embedded through role modeling rather than theoretical explanation.

The *metamorphosis* stage implies transformation of the new employee into a functioning employee who works in alignment with company business and responsible business performance goals in a holistic way. The metamorphosis stage involves both training and development.

## 11-5c Training

**Training** is a process of changing the performance of employees to better achieve organizational goals and objectives. The training and development process may provide focus on knowledge of the job or help with specific job skills or abilities and may apply to individuals or dedicated groups who specialize in a particular task. However, in the context of responsible HRM, training should be deigned with an intention to impart the wider implications of corporate activities in sustainability contexts and an understanding of the social and environmental impacts of both the organization and the roles of individuals.

Cohen[21] suggests a roadmap of responsible HRM training recommendations for integrating responsible business principles into human resources departments. While the roadmap displays training and communications in two separate areas, the two are part of the same whole. Effective communication of responsible business principles throughout the training process results in the strongest impact in HR. Cohen's[22] recommendations emphasize responsible business training in new-hire orientation. The roadmap is adapted and illustrated in Figure 11.4.

HR training in responsible business should also include training relating to employee rights from a human rights perspective. Excellent source documents for employers include the Universal Declaration of Human Rights adopted by the United Nations in 1948, including more than thirty articles, many of which may be applied to employees in business. The UN adopted the *Labor Principles of the United Nations Global Compact: A Reference for Business* in Geneva in 2008. The labor principles apply specifically to freedom of association and right to collective bargaining for employees, elimination of forced or compulsory labor, abolition of child labor, and elimination of discrimination in respect to employment and occupation. Child labor or forced and compulsory labor issues may come to mind

**Training** is a process of changing the performance of employees to better achieve organizational goals and objectives.

Figure 11.4 **Roadmap**

Training
- Train all managers in the concepts and practices of **responsible business** that relate to the company and in contributions they can make in their own roles.
- Develop briefing sessions for all employees on **responsible business** to be delivered by managers.
- Incorporate **responsible business** training in all new-hire orientation.

Communications
- Incorporate **responsible business** messages and stories of community and environmental activities and other topics into regular internal communications.
- Start a company blog to which employees can contribute.
- Develop a presence in social media: Facebook page, Flickr account, and more.
- Use social media for recruiting.

Source: Adapted from Cohen, E. (2010). *CSR for HR: A necessary partnership for advancing responsible business practices.* Sheffield, UK: Greenleaf.

when reflecting on Nike during the 1990s and considering Apple's supply chain issues in recent years. Large companies are learning the value of responsible supply chain management in overseas production factories. Cohen[23] recommends that HR managers set the following guidelines for CSR training in human rights:

1. Ensure the existence of policies and systems that will maintain human and employee rights in the business and in its supply chain.

2. Ensure that all employees are aware of and trained in company policies on human rights.

3. Proactively inform employees and assist them in understanding and realizing all of their rights.

This employee training must be inclusive of all employees, adapt to laws of local countries, and be reinforced frequently (minimally on an annual basis).

## 11-5d Employee Development

Companies may use a variety of tools to develop employees, which includes on-the-job training and off-the-job training. Most companies conduct **employee development** on-the-job because of costs and time related to distance education, and because an experiential approach is often more effective. Westpac Banking Corporation specializes in on-the-job mentoring of employees in how to serve in community organizations. The bank, which serves primarily Australia, New Zealand, and the Pacific islands, is highly rated by the Dow Jones Sustainability Index. The bank generated 32.9 billion in Australian dollars in 2010 and employed approximately 38,000 people.[24] Cohen[25] relates the account of an interview with Ilana Atlas, who held the position of Group Executive, People & Performance, at Westpac Banking Group. Westpac had merged human resources development, corporate responsibility, and sustainability. Ilana Atlas described different aspects of training at Westpac, including an organizational mentoring program that matched high-performing employees with community organizations. The purpose was to bring about measurable change to community partners while exposing "our employees to different types of organization and to a range of social issues."[26]

The value of **employee volunteering** in the community, much like the Westpac program, is often overlooked by HR managers as an employee development (and empowerment) opportunity. Volunteering can serve as a framework for personal development and acquisition of skills for employees who may not be able to gain these skills in the workplace, due to the limitations of company-based opportunities. *Skill-based volunteering*, a relatively new concept meaning that employees volunteer in a way that enables them to utilize the professional skills they bring with them from the workplace, is gaining ground in many companies as the "new" volunteerism. Rather than accounting professionals handing out food to needy people, they can offer pro-bono financial advice to the finance department of not-for-profit organizations, thereby both utilizing their core skills for community benefit and also gaining experience of a different working culture with its own challenges that may be very different from those occurring in the workplace.

### In Practice

**From Employee Development to Stakeholder Development**

In 1997, Cisco Systems established a global Networking Academy to train hundreds of thousands of individuals each year. The students who enroll in the program learn how to design, build, and maintain networking sites through a combination of classroom and online instruction. They also learn to incorporate sustainability in technology. Cisco takes seriously the integration of sustainability principles throughout its training program. The company defines CSR as "a responsibility to operate in ways that respect and ultimately benefit people, communities, and the planet we live on," and focuses its training on four goals: improving communities around the world, reducing our environmental impact, conducting our business ethically, and creating a thriving workplace for employees.

Source: CISCO Training. (2012). *Cisco networking academy.* Retrieved March 29, 2012, from: www.cisco.com/web/learning/netacad/index.html

**Employee development** is the process of planning and implementing activities to develop employees' competencies in the medium and long run.

**Employee volunteering** refers to a voluntary engagement of personnel of an organization.

## 11-5e Employability

Historically, at the heart of the perception of a good and responsible workplace was the concept of jobs for life, or job security. People were hired for a lifetime of work, and retired from companies they worked for after thirty years or more of loyal service. This was often the height of people's ambition—to achieve stability, and develop within the company they joined after leaving school, college or university. Over the past twenty years or so, things have changed. Markets have become much more dynamic; globalization has transformed business models; companies undergo change at an unprecedented rate; skills required some years ago are no longer needed and new skills are sought at a rapid pace. When Walmart announced its sustainability assessment of 100,000 top-tier suppliers in 2010, asking them to answer fifteen questions about their environmental practices, and making it clear that this was only a first stage in a supplier selection process that would include green credentials, there was a rush in the U.S. job market to hire environmental specialists, energy specialists, sustainable process experts, and more at hundreds of Walmart suppliers. They all understood that the risk, and the opportunity, was to adopt more sustainable practices. Over the past fifteen years, the expansion of jobs related to sustainability has been astounding—not only corporate practitioners, but also an entire industry of consultants, auditors, reporters, green building experts, and more. The skills that are needed to succeed in today's markets are very different from what they were some years ago.

Not only that, but job-seekers also have changed. Gen Ys (those born in the 1980s—2000s) are a new breed of young professionals who seek meaning as well as money, and who demand much more from their employers than the prior generation ever did. There is, in fact, an expectation of not staying with a company for life, but instead of gaining skills and moving on to the next company that can provide a different environment for personal and professional growth. Today, a person advances his or her career by moving to another company, not by waiting for the boss to retire.

The implications of these changes for HR managers are far-reaching and touch on the way HR managers can create sustainable organizations through advancing employability in favor of employment. The concept of **employability** is core to the concept of corporate responsibility. It has two aspects:

1. Employability can refer to the ability of a person who is not employed or never has been employed to enter the job market for the first time, such as graduates or people from disadvantaged groups in the community.[27] In many countries, government and corporate programs provide vocational training and up-skilling for people who need help in penetrating the job market. Similarly, those who are laid off and find themselves "between" jobs may undertake professional retraining so as to pursue another career, as they may find the skills they have developed at their former place of work have become obsolete.

2. Employability, however, also can be something a person acquires while working. A company that offers training and professional development, and internal career opportunities, inherently makes its employees more "employable," and more attractive to other businesses. This protects employees from the risks of layoffs, since if they are more employable, they will be able to compete in today's markets. Ironically, those very Gen Ys who have less long-term loyalty to a single company tend to stay with companies that invest in them. Despite the fact that they are more employable, they change companies less frequently because their need for professional development is being met. Employability,

**Employability** describes how well a person is qualified to work.

then, is an insurance policy, or personal asset, that employees choose to protect themselves against future uncertainty of job stability and also to enhance their personal value in the job market, should they need to cash in.

Employability also has inherent advantages for society, because more qualified and skilled people are able to make a positive contribution to local economies through maintaining their relevance in the marketplace. By investing in people, companies strengthen societies. The ripple effect is incalculable, but it is significant. Therefore, in this respect, HRM policy directly affects communities. At the same time, by focusing on employability, HRM protects its business against high attrition levels and contributes to sustainable business. Hence, by investing in potential employees and enhancing their employability, and subsequently hiring them, HR managers are delivering great benefit to both their own company and their community. Cisco's Networking Academy, for example, is a crucial tool in preparing young people for roles in the information and communications technology (ICT) industry. There is a serious shortage of talented individuals in this growing sector. To date, the Cisco Academy has reached hundreds of thousands of students around the globe, helping them prepare for industry-recognized certifications and entry-level ICT careers in virtually every type of industry.

HR managers should understand these trends and consider how they can develop policies and practices that meet the development needs of existing and potential employees. Investing in employees is a powerful tool that meets the needs of sustainable business at many different levels and helps companies win the "war for talent" while delivering a benefit for society as a whole.

## 11-6 PHASE 3: PERFORMANCE MANAGEMENT

*"The study found a significantly positive relationship between CSR actions and employee organizational commitment, CSR and organizational performance and employee organizational commitment and organizational performance."[28]*

Creating processes and tools for evaluating the performance of employees, and ensuring the embedding of such processes and tools in the organization, is a third major function of human resources management. Ivancevich[29] identifies this task as **performance management** and defines it as "the process by which executives, managers, and supervisors work to align employee performance with the firm's goals."[30]

### 11-6a Performance Evaluation

Performance management tools often include some form of performance evaluation, which often serves several purposes:

1. It provides a basis for dialogue between an employee and the company (the manager) to ensure there is alignment around shared mission, objectives, and goals. In addition, it enables a discussion about behaviors, and not only results. In a responsible business, the way in which goals are achieved is no less important that the performance results. A performance evaluation dialogue is

**Performance management** is the process of monitoring and improving employees' work performance.

instrumental in reinforcing the messages related to the impact an employee has in the organization and work interactions, internally and externally, through the way in which the employee conducts him- or herself and maintains effective, trust-based relationships.

2. It provides the employee with an opportunity to hear how his or her performance is rated by superiors and often also by peers and subordinates (in the form of a 360-degree appraisal). This evaluation opens up possibilities to review ways of offering support to the employee for the development of a performance improvement and professional/personal development plan.

3. It provides the employee with an opportunity to give feedback to the manager, and the way in which the company is assisting or hindering him or her in reaching his or her full potential and delivering best performance. This open dialogue, if done well, can be a strong tool for engaging employees, building trust, refocusing and realigning the employee with what matters most, and ensuring that the company develops talent in a sustainable way.

As a process, the performance evaluation may contribute to business sustainability, responsibility, and ethics, as it focuses on performance improvement and alignment of contribution, and reinforces responsible behaviors. Performance evaluation in a responsible business has to include how employees have contributed to the triple bottom line, created value for shareholders, and shown moral excellence.

## 11-6b Core Competencies

Performance evaluations do not happen in a vacuum. They are conducted in the context of performance expectations that have been established with the employee at some prior date. Performance can be characterized, as mentioned above, in two broad ways: the "what" and the "how." On the one hand, employees are expected to deliver against certain agreed-on objectives and targets. This is the "what." On the other hand, they are expected to do so in a way that aligns with the company's behavioral standards. This is the "how." Many companies develop a set of **core competencies** that must be demonstrated at different levels of management. These core competencies are management or leadership behaviors that are often rooted in corporate values. Team working, for example, may be a competency. Effective listening may be a core competency. Ethical conduct may be a competency. Sodexo U.S. encompasses its expectations regarding the behavior of its employees in three broad areas—Service Spirit, Team Spirit, and Spirit of Progress—each of which is supported by corresponding behaviors that are expected to be manifested in the course of an individual's work (see Figure 11.5). This framework can be applied to the performance evaluations.

At the heart of these competencies are ways of working that require integrity and that build trust, essential ingredients in any sustainable organization. In addition, in some cases, companies link responsible business to performance by including responsible management targets in manager objectives and performance plans for the coming year. This may include things like energy efficiencies or carbon footprint targets, and is a very clear signal that sustainability performance is core business and not additional, optional project work.

**Core competencies** are crucially important, distinct abilities of an individual or an organization.

## In Practice

### Integrating Corporate Responsibility in Performance Appraisals

Aegon, a Dutch insurance company employing approximately 28,000 people and operating in more than twenty countries, includes corporate responsibility components in its performance appraisals. In 2009, AEGON reported that 100 percent of senior managers were subject to regular, standardized performance appraisals, 98 percent of middle management employees were subjected to the appraisals, and 98 percent of other employees. Aegon encourages "employees at all levels to take part in formal skills and development programs."

Source: Aegon. (2009). *Corporate sustainability report.* Retrieved June 27, 2012, from http://www.aegon.com/Documents/aegon-com/Sitewide/Reports-and-Other-Publications/Sustainability-reports/CR-reports/2011/AEGON-Sustainability-Report-2010.pdf

**Figure 11.5** Examples of Aspired Competencies at Sodexo

| | |
|---|---|
| Service Spirit  | • Clients and consumers are at the center of everything we do.<br>• To serve them well on a daily basis, we have to demonstrate our availability and responsiveness, to anticipate their expectations and to take pride in satisfying them.<br>• Sodexo has become a global company but we remain locally-focused; our managers in the field are true entrepreneurs, close to their clients and empowered to make decisions. |
| Team Spirit  | • It is an absolute need in all of our operations, our business units and administrative offices, as well as in our management committees.<br>• Each person's skills combine with other team members' knowledge to help ensure Sodexo's success.<br>• Teamwork depends on the following: listening, transparency, respect for others, diversity, solidarity in implementing major decisions, respect for rules and mutual support, particularly in difficult times. |
| Spirit of Progress  | It is manifested through:<br>• Our will, but also the firm belief that one can always improve on the present situation.<br>• Acceptance of evaluation and comparison of one's performance, with one's colleagues in the company or with one's competitors.<br>• Self-assessment because understanding one's successes as well as one's failures is fundamental to continuous improvement.<br>• A balance between ambition and humility.<br>• Optimism, the belief that for every problem there is a solution, an innovation or some way to progress. |

Source: Reproduced from Sodexo, www.sodexo.com/en/group/fundamentals/values.aspx

A tool that is often used to develop organizational targets and cascade these down to individual manager contributions is the balanced scorecard. This is a useful vehicle for reflecting aspects of sustainability, as it takes a holistic view of an organization's planned performance beyond financial targets. Sustainability targets fit well within the context of a balanced scorecard. For more about the balanced scorecard approach, recommended reading is *The Balanced Scorecard* by Kaplan and Norton.[31] Also, the Balanced Scorecard Institute has published a paper on linking sustainability to corporate strategy using the balanced scorecard, and this makes for interesting reading for responsible business professionals as well as HR managers who wish to understand the wider context of the HRM contribution to sustainable business.[32]

## 11-6c Community Involvement and Environmental Stewardship

Activities that traditionally have not been on the HRM radar can provide valuable tools for people development in any organization while delivering a positive benefit for society and the environment.

**Volunteering.** Involvement in the community, for example, not only provides opportunities for employees to gain experience of the way other organizations work and to take on roles that offer leading opportunities which may not be available in their own organization, but studies also show that volunteering in the community motivates employees and drives higher loyalty and commitment, which is translated into work productivity.

Many of these benefits can be quantified, such as:

- *Employee job satisfaction:* When employees are given time within their working day to volunteer, their overall motivation increases. This can be measured in performance evaluation conversations and in employee surveys.

- *Recruitment effectiveness:* More employees want to apply to work at a responsible company. When this is used as part of the employer brand, and applicants or new hires are surveyed, we can measure the impact.

- *Employee skill building:* This can be tracked through the employee performance evaluation process.

In addition, of course, we should also count the benefits for society resulting from employee contribution, and the benefit to the business of enhanced corporate reputation.

The process of developing an effective and successful employee volunteering program requires clear policy, planning, and careful implementation. It is a terrific tool for HR managers to advance business objectives through new ways of engaging and motivating employees that bring benefits back to the workplace. Some say that businesses have a responsibility to "give back" to the communities in which they operate, and many companies take this approach. Whatever the motivation, whether values or strategy based, creating positive community impacts through employee volunteering is a feature of a responsible workplace.

Skills-based volunteering is becoming more advanced these days in larger corporations. This means enabling individuals to make a contribution using their core skills and competencies to help meet community needs. For example, technology workers will support the development of technology in communities, such as the INTEL Involved program, in which Intel employees are encouraged to use their professional skills to help the community. This approach to volunteering has several benefits: Employees volunteer by doing what they do best, adding true value and sharpening their own skills in the process. Rather than having finance managers packing food baskets for the needy, or logistics experts refurbishing kindergarten playgrounds, skills-based volunteering makes a quality contribution to capacity enhancement in the communities that most need, and cannot afford to pay for, these professional contributions. As another tool in the HRM arsenal of people development opportunities, skills-based volunteering is the new way that HRM can make a difference both in the organization and in society in general.

## THINK | ETHICS

### Scaling Impact and Changing People through Volunteering

PULSE is GlaxoSmithKline's skills-based volunteering initiative that enables employees to make a sustainable difference for communities and patients in need. Employees are given an opportunity to use their professional skills and knowledge during a three- or six-month immersion experience within a nonprofit or nongovernmental organization (NGO). Through this experience, volunteers address a clear NGO need while developing their own leadership capabilities. Since its launch in 2009, PULSE has sent nearly 300 employees from across 33 different countries to work with 70 NGOs in 49 countries. In 2012 alone, PULSE sent nearly 94 PULSE volunteers to 52 nonprofit and NGO partners. Andrew Witty, CEO of GlaxoSmithKline, says that not only does the PULSE program help individuals to make a contribution, but the volunteers also come back changed people, with changed worldviews, which they can then use on the job to help change the way the company thinks.

Source: GlaxoSmithKline, www.gsk.com

**Going Green.** Reducing environmental impacts is one of the most serious business challenges of the day. Businesses can gain advantage only when the entire workforce is engaged in a joint effort to reduce a company's environmental impacts. With environmental legislation becoming stricter and carbon emissions a core focus, HRM has a significant contribution to make in helping employees engage with this agenda. With the carbon tax that came into force in the UK in April 2013, for example, companies have to pay significantly more for the privilege of consuming energy needed in their business. This is a massive incentive to drive consumption reductions across the business, and save twice: first on reduced energy costs, and second on carbon tax.

HRM support for driving a culture of environmental efficiency is crucial and has proven itself in many businesses around the world, where engaged employees can advance all forms of efficiencies, not only around energy, but also in reducing water consumption (another cost that businesses will see increasing in coming years), reducing waste, earning new revenues from recycling, and more. HR support for employee-driven Green Teams to enhance employee contribution to improved environmental impacts—including lower electricity consumption, reduced use of paper for printing, recycling, waste reduction, and more—delivers benefits of reduced operating costs, improved environmental protection, and employees who derive satisfaction from becoming ambassadors for a more sustainable planet.

## 11-6d Offboarding

HRM's scope of responsibility is also relevant to employees who leave the company, and a responsible and sustainable approach is required to ensure that layoffs due to restructuring changes and business downsizing are dealt with in a fair manner. After having done whatever possible to minimize the need for layoffs, HRM has a responsibility to ensure the offboarding process is as positive as possible. **Offboarding** refers to the process that is adopted to manage the way employees leave the company. In a responsible HRM environment, HR policy and processes will make great efforts to ensure this process is as constructive as possible so that the best possible outcome can be achieved for the departing employees. This is important for several reasons:

1. Ex-employees can promote or damage a company's reputation after they leave in many ways. By considering them as future ambassadors and ensuring that their departure is a positive process, the reputation risk to the business is reduced.

2. Ex-employees who remain positive about the company may be rehired at a future date if the business needs changes. Rehiring ex-employees often offers advantages over completely new hires, as employees are experienced and understand the organizational culture, so that onboarding time is reduced. This is only possible if employees have left the business in a positive way.

3. Employees leave companies, but more stay. The employees who stay with companies need to see that colleagues are treated ethically, fairly, and in a positive way at the time of leaving. Not doing so can damage employee morale considerably and risk the company's current business continuity.

4. Helping employees who are laid off to navigate their way back into the job market, or transition into retirement, makes a strong contribution to society by helping people continue to be productive members of the workforce or local communities.

Offboarding usually includes *outplacement* programs that support employees' reentry into the job market by providing practical tools for activities such as applying for jobs, writing resumes, interview skills, and more, as well as personal tools for managing personal finances during and after the transition, coping with stress, and other needs.

---

## THINK | ETHICS

### Offboarding in Practice

Johnson Controls reported in its 2011 Sustainability Report that several layoffs in the company's automotive business were necessary, which impacted local communities significantly. The company did as much as it could to mitigate these negative impacts by taking the following actions:

- Implemented shorter workweek to minimize employee layoffs
- Reduced company variable expenses
- Implemented voluntary separation program
- Provided severance pay
- Assisted separated employees to find alternative employment with outplacement services
- Redeployed employees within the company

Source: Johnson Controls, Inc. (2011). *Sustainability report.*

---

**Offboarding** refers to the process that is adopted to manage the way employees leave the company.

## 11-7 PHASE 4: COMPENSATION, BENEFITS, AND EMPLOYEE WELL-BEING

*"Findings suggest that employee satisfaction and wellbeing both inside and outside work may be best linked to HRM in the context of partnership or mutual gains system."*[33]

The way a business compensates employees for the work they do is a fourth core process for human resources management. Compensation can be defined as the return given by a company to the employee in exchange for the performance of organizational tasks.

**Compensation** can be either financial or nonfinancial. Financial compensation includes wages and salaries, and it takes the form of any monetary return to the employee, such as bonuses, commissions, or nonsalary benefits, which are valued as part of the overall compensation package. These may include health or medical insurance, sick leave, vacation time, and child care or higher education subsidies for children of employees. Companies that offer long-term benefits may provide retirement plans, stock options, ownership plans, or profit sharing, a form of compensation that distributes a percentage of organizational profit among employees in the form of cash or deferred bonuses. A company's approach to compensation is a manifestation of its understanding of and commitment to sustainable business, as it relates to the way a firm provides for health and prosperity of its employees, which has a significant impact on society.

The compensation plans of most companies encompass major categories of a base-pay system, a short-term incentive plan, a long-term incentive plan, and benefit plans. KPMG, for instance, offers such incentives as financial bonuses or stock options that aim "to encourage team-work and team-success, motivate employees to achieve high performance results for which they will get rewarded and establish high levels of loyalty and commitment to the company."[34] The company encourages employees to engage with responsible business objectives through opportunities such as the Involve program and Community Matters program, which encourage sustainable involvement. KPMG provides sustainability compensation for full-time employees, and the company combines annual base salary with bonus and recognition awards from the preceding year, plus medical, health, and dental benefits, and retirement benefits, which include a pension plan and a 401(k) retirement savings plan.

**Compensation** is the remuneration received by an employee for the work done.

### In Practice

**Linking Compensation with Responsible Business Performance**

The mission statement of Novartis pharmaceuticals is: "to discover, develop and successfully market innovative products to prevent and cure diseases, to ease suffering and to enhance the quality of life." The mission also focuses on Novartis's responsibility to shareholders: "to provide a shareholder return that reflects outstanding performance and to adequately reward those who invest ideas and work in our company." Based on this mission, the company developed a compensation plan called *Meritocracy*, which rewards superior performance and aligns "the interests of associates with those of our shareholders and stakeholders by creating economic value in a sustainable way." The strong mission statement of Novartis provided direction for human resources management to develop a compensation plan that rewards sustainable behaviors and performance.

Sources: Novartis. (2012). *Our mission*. Retrieved June 29, 2012, from: www.novartis.com/about-novartis/our-mission/index.shtml;Novartis. (2010). *Annual report*, p. 112.

### 11-7a Driving Principles of a Compensation System

Cohen[35] reiterated the two key principles of fairness and equality that should guide any compensation system. Stemming from those principles, she suggested eight policies that should be incorporated into any responsible compensation plan.[36] These policies may be applied globally to businesses.

1. Compensation should be *legal*, obeying all laws and regulations in the host country. When laws differ among countries in a supply chain, companies should follow the laws of the country with the stricter or higher standards. Nike followed minimum wage and child labor laws in its Indonesian manufacturing plants, but erred for not maintaining stricter standards of the

United States in factory air quality, minimum age of workers, and overtime pay, declaring "we do not make shoes" to avoid their supply chain problems.

2. Compensation should be *fair and equitable* and not discriminate on the basis of gender or other elements of diversity. Employees with the same levels of experience, skill, or training should be paid equitably. Opportunities for nonfinancial compensation to earn awards or participate in activities should be fair and equitable. Employee satisfaction will be increased and commitment to the firm's mission and vision will be enhanced when policies are clear and specific for such compensation opportunities.

3. Compensation should be *supportive* for employees by offering wages and benefits beyond minimum wage, fixed standards, or basic working conditions. *Fortune* magazine's 2012 Top 100 list of best U.S. companies to work for illustrates creative and different compensation packages. Google placed number one because of its support for employees by offering bocce courts, a bowling alley, and approximately twenty-five cafes throughout the company at no charge.[37]

4. *Engaging* compensation plans treat employees as partners in the achievement of company objectives. Any type of financial compensation package that allows employees to participate in stock options, ownership plans, or in distribution of company profits will provide incentives that engage employees. The purpose of treating employees as partners is for motivation and increased productivity. Novartis allows certain employees "to receive their annual incentive awards fully or partially in Novartis shares instead of cash by participating in a leveraged share savings plan."[38] In fact, Gollan[39] suggested that firms with shared compensation plans tend to have more joint consultative committees, quality circles, and company-level information with employees.

5. Compensation should be *attractive* to employees and future employees who consider working for the company. A company should be at no disadvantage when recruiting new employees because of a noncompetitive salary. SAMSUNG offers a highly competitive compensation plan and extensive benefits to attract future employees and stay competitive in the market.

6. Compensation should be *flexible*, taking into account individual employee needs. Financial status, health condition, and educational needs will require that each employee have a flexible choice of benefits. Human resources must offer professional advice and counseling to each employee. Baeten[40] examined global compensation and benefits management to determine whether compensation plans should be centrally administered or more decentralized in management. He found that centralized management works better for compensation *procedures* whereas decentralized decision making works best for such issues as long-term incentives and employee benefits. Each company must take into account individual employee needs.

7. A company should be *proactive* with its compensation package by annually reviewing what it offers. Cost-of-living increases and pay raises must be adjusted proactively. The company can ensure that costs of insurance do not become prohibitive if employees contribute to their insurance plan. Nestlé asserts in its *Employee Relations Policy* that it is proactive in improving relationships with internal and external stakeholders and it "accomplishes this approach through organized structures within the Human Resources department."[41]

8. Finally, and perhaps most importantly, compensation plans should be *transparent*. Would you consider a company sustainable if it were not open about employee compensation? Does this issue matter to you, and how transparent

should a company be internally with employee pay? Opinions differ widely on this issue. In many countries, laws determine the level of transparency of public institutions such as federal governmental offices and public universities. In most organizations, the decision rests with human resources professionals who must determine whether transparent information will help or harm the organization.

## 11-7b Living Wage

The concept of the "working poor" is becoming more prevalent in more countries as the twenty-first century progresses. Statistics updated in January 2010 showed that 8 percent of people employed in European Union countries lived in poverty and could not afford basic life essentials. The idea that one can spend most of one's waking hours working diligently for a corporation and still not be able to afford a reasonable quality of life that includes basic life essentials should be offensive to all business leaders, and especially to human resources professionals.

Today, sustainability advances the concept of the **living wage**, a term used to describe the minimum hourly wage necessary for an individual in full-time employment to meet basic needs, including housing, food, utilities, transport, health care, and education. The level of the living wage will differ from country to country, but it is almost always higher than local minimum wage levels established by law. Companies with a responsible business approach understand that remunerating employees at a level that does not enable them to maintain a decent, safe, and healthy lifestyle erodes the basic fabric of our society and ultimately creates an environment in which it is harder to do business. Fairly rewarded employees are more committed, more productive, more stable, and less prone to sickness absence. These issues have real cost impact and the ROI of paying a living wage is usually positive. HRM has a responsibility to lead the voice of responsible compensation practice in the business for long term benefit of all.

## 11-7c Employee Well-Being

Lack of attention to employee well-being can carry significant risk. Over the past few years, there have been high-profile cases of employee suicides, notably at France Telecom where the toll reached forty-six, and at Foxconn, the Chinese manufacturer of electronics products for leading brands such as Apple, where nine suicides were counted in 2010.[42] Employees resorted to this drastic action because they were working under pressure to deliver more and more, under tighter deadlines, in an unsupportive working environment that was not responsive to their personal needs and pressures.

At the other end of the spectrum, investing in employee well-being delivers business benefits. In a program to advance employee health and address stress issues at Unilever,[43] Dean Patterson, global health and productivity manager for Unilever, said: *"Not only did we see impressive improvements to the health and energy levels of our people, the business also benefited from a financial return on investment of £3.73: 1. So for every £1 ($1.64) Unilever invested in its employees, it got back almost £4 ($6.59) through reduced health care costs and increased productivity."* Such risks and opportunities make it imperative that HR managers accept a responsibility to advance a sustainable approach. This typically means addressing work-life balance issues such as flexible working hours, telecommuting options, child care leave and support, and other support services. HR policies that help employees to manage their own well-being deliver an ROI in reduced absenteeism, reduced health care costs, higher productivity, and longer job tenure.

**Living wage** describes the minimum hourly wage necessary for an individual in full-time employment to meet basic needs, including housing, food, utilities, transport, health care, and education.

## 11-8 PHASE 5: EMPLOYEE RELATIONS AND COMMUNICATIONS

*"The employer who is willing to give employees what they want and need [is] far more likely to have success, but more importantly, the organization will be doing the right thing."[44]*

*Employee relations* is often associated with a structured approach to freedom of association and unionization and relates to any organized group of employees who work together collectively to promote the interests of their group. Often identified as *labor unions*, the groups engage in collective bargaining to accomplish member goals, and provide a vehicle for employees to ensure that their rights are upheld in the workplace. The labor union grants employees an organized voice and strength for their causes. The communication that occurs between managers and labor unions is called *labor relations*. *Trade unions* are labor organizations within specific trades that exist to promote their interests.

Labor unions exist in most countries, industries, and sectors today and are closely regulated by laws within each unique country. HR management professionals must be knowledgeable about labor laws and regulations, and communication with labor organizations takes significant time for most HR departments. Nestlé, for example, makes a strong statement about labor practices throughout its company, fully supports the UN Global Compact's guiding principles on human rights and labor practices, and publishes a document on the subject.[45]

The right to collective bargaining is one of the basic rights of employees, embodied in the 1998 ILO Declaration of Fundamental Principles and Rights at Work[46] and the fundamental Convention covering collective bargaining as the *Right to Organise and Collective Bargaining Convention*, 1949 (No. 98), which has been ratified as law by most companies in the world. A responsible and sustainable company embraces the value that employee associations can bring to the development of a shared commitment to business objectives and ensures that employee representatives are treated with respect and that negotiations are conducted in a spirit of fair and equal opportunity. In some cases, however, this may not be the case.

### 11-8a Union-Busting

Despite the right afforded by law for employees to organize and engage in collective bargaining, many companies would prefer not to be chained to union agreements or the requirement to negotiate terms and conditions on a collective basis for employees. Management regards this as restrictive, possibly obstructive to the decision-making process and also a risk for escalation of employee costs. Although these fears may be justified in some cases, the fact is that collective bargaining is a right and, if well managed, can actually support business development rather than hinder it. It is the role of the HR manager to ensure that labor relations are conducted within the law, first and foremost, which means ensuring that an organization does not obstruct employees' rights in this respect in any way, such as by engaging in **union-busting**. However, by taking a positive and optimistic view of labor relations, HRM can lead a respectful, constructive relationship with employee

**Union-busting** refers to efforts by employers to disrupt or prevent the formation or expansion of trade unions.

## Action Needed: HR Function at T-Mobile

A difficult case in point is the reputational damage to Deutsche Telekom, which operates in full compliance with the law in its home base in Germany (where very strict legal requirements relating to employee representation are in force). However, in the company's U.S. subsidiary, T-Mobile, the company has been widely and publicly criticized for management actions designed to crush the growing demand for employee representation. In fact, scathing criticism of Deutsche Telekom's union-busting practices was published by San Francisco State University in 2009, and the International Trade Union Confederation (ITUC) maintains an intensive campaign to force Deutsche Telekom to change its practices in the United States. There is even a website devoted to the struggle for freedom of association within T-Mobile. In 2010, the Global Union Alliance filed a complaint with the Organisation for Economic Co-operation and Development (OECD), describing how Deutsche Telekom has engaged in antiunion activity in the United States and in Montenegro,

in violation of the OECD's Guidelines for Multinational Enterprises.

Although it is difficult to quantify the external reputational and financial damage to Deutsche Telekom resulting from this dispute, it can be assumed that internally it has led to a decline in morale and possibly high employee absenteeism and turnover. The HR function in this organization should be working to regulate relationships in the United States to ensure that they are both legal and constructive. This is an immense opportunity to demonstrate how responsible HR management can contribute to doing better business.

Sources: Logan, J. (2009). *Lowering the bar or setting the standard? Deutsche Telekom's U.S. labor practices.* Washington, DC: American Rights at Work Education Fund; ITUC. (2012). *We expect better.* Retrieved December 22, 2012, from: www.weexpectbetter.org/; ITUC. (2011, July 12). *Global Union Alliance files OECD complaint against Deutsche Telekom for union-busting.* Retrieved December 22, 2012, from International Trade Union Confederation: www.ituc-csi.org/global-union-alliance-files-oecd.html?lang=en

representatives, and ensure business continuity and positive reputation, as well as alignment of employee demands with management objectives.

### 11-8b Employee Communications

Traditionally, internal communications has been a one-way route—pushing out information that management requires employees to know so that they can do their jobs better. Today's employees want to be engaged. Employee communications needs to move from push to pull, from delivering messages to encouraging dialogue, from a communiqué to a conversation. In this way, employees will be better equipped to contribute to business objectives, raise issues that can benefit the business, feel more valued and motivated, and act as the voice of the business in the hundreds of daily interactions they maintain with external contacts. Effective two-way, open, collaborative, and participative communications with employees turns them into ambassadors not only for the business, but also for the company's sustainability approach, which builds business reputation and adds value. The more a business's employees talk about the company's responsible business programs, the more strongly the responsible business culture will be embedded in the business, and the practices delivered accordingly.

Especially in today's transparent world, where communication is often virtual, employees have many opportunities to engage with the sustainability message, and business leaders have a responsibility to encourage this. Thousands of businesses around the world communicate their sustainability approach in a dedicated Sustainability Report. HR managers should leverage this internally and engage with employees on these subjects. A responsible workplace promotes engagement of employees on sustainability issues. Open, frequent, two-way communications is an essential tool that helps this to occur.

I. *Responsible HRM* includes the responsibility to manage the employee stakeholder, and to manage HR's contribution to responsible business performance.

II. The goal of responsible human resources management is an *HR-RM symbiosis*, which refers to the mutually reinforcing relationship in which responsible management (RM) needs employees' engagement in responsible business and, in turn, human resources (HR) will benefit from responsible management activities as stakeholders.

III. For understanding the *human resources-responsible management relationship*, one should consider the main norms for responsible human resources management (HRM), the business case for responsible HRM, employee skills for responsible business, and the role of the HR manager.

IV. *Recruitment* in responsible business involves including employee skills for responsible business in job descriptions, acquiring the adequate candidates with such skills, and selecting them based on the skills.

V. *Training and development* begins with new employee orientation and continues with ongoing training for responsible business performance, and the development of employees and close external stakeholders with the underlying goal of increasing trained peoples' employability.

VI. *Performance management* includes the evaluation of employees' responsible business performance and core competencies for responsible business.

VII. *Compensation, benefits, and employee well-being* are based on a sustainable, responsible and ethical compensation system that pays at least a decent living wage, and which together with other benefits contributes to employee well-being.

VIII. *Employee relations and communications* includes the relationship to labor unions and highlights the importance of effective internal communication channels.

| Process Phase | | Sustainability | Responsibility | Ethics |
|---|---|---|---|---|
| Phase 0: HR-RM Relationship | Do you understand … | … the role of employees in building sustainable business? | … the importance of assuming your responsibilities toward employees as a central stakeholder group? | … the importance of moral excellence among employees? |
| Phase 1: Recruitment | Does your recruitment strategy … | … ensure that new employees have the necessary competencies for sustainable business? | … ensure diversity and include disadvantaged groups? | … ensure the moral integrity of new recruits? |
| Phase 2: Training and development | Does your training and development strategy … | … focus on the competencies for sustainable business? | … support employees to develop their employability in the job market and their personal development? | … develop competencies for making good ethical decisions and translate them into ethical behaviors? |
| Phase 3: Performance management | Do your performance management activities … | … ensure socially, environmentally, and economically sustainable results? | … aim to create stakeholder value? | … focus on moral excellence? |
| Phase 4: Compensation, benefits, and employee well-being | Does your compensation and benefits package … | … incentivize sustainable behaviors? | … ensure at least a fair living wage? | … consider ethically correct behavior as a basis of remuneration? |
| Phase 5: Employee relations and communication | Does the human resources department … | … communicate actively about the importance, challenges, and success of the organization's progress toward sustainable business? | … encourage employee involvement in labor unions, create internal transparency about relevant topics, and encourage employee involvement and discourse? | … ensure an ethical relationship between employees and the organization and apply morally excellent communication practices internally? |

compensation *354*
core competencies *350*
employability *348*
employee development *347*
employee orientation *344*
employee volunteering *347*

HR-RM symbiosis *333*
human resources *334*
job description *340*
knowledge, skills, attitudes (KSAs) *339*
living wage *356*
offboarding *353*

performance management *349*
recruitment *339*
responsible HRM *334*
training *346*
training and development *342*
union-busting *357*

## EXERCISES

### A. Remember and Understand

A.1. Explain the symbiosis and relationship between human resources and responsible management in a responsible business.

A.2. Explain and interrelate the following terms: *employability, offboarding, core competencies*, and *KSAs*.

A.3. Briefly explain the stages of the employee socialization process and how they are interrelated.

### B. Apply and Experience

B.4. Interview one person about her or his employer's human resources practices and ask for a statement from this person regarding the degree of responsibility achieved by the employer. Ask what she or he would improve.

B.5. Familiarize yourself with the human resources practices of the Brazilian company SEMCO and the U.S.-American SAS software company. Would you say the companies apply responsible human resources management? Which company would you consider the more responsible one in the HR relationship?

B.6. Briefly describe the five core processes of human resources management and search for two real-life examples of each process, one of a responsible and one of an irresponsible management practice.

### C. Analyze and Evaluate

C.7. Compare the subjects of the four responsible human resources norms illustrated in Table 11.1 and explain the differences in the topics covered. Should an organization apply all norms simultaneously, or is compliance with one norm sufficient to create responsible human resources management?

C.8. Look up the sustainability report of a company of your choice, and find examples for at least two the following responsible human resources practices: volunteering, green teams, sustainability and ethics trainings, employee sustainability objectives, and diversity management.

C.9. Discuss whether responsible human resources management should apply different standards for the home company and suppliers, for developed countries and developing countries, and for large companies and small and medium-sized enterprises.

### D. Change and Create

D.10. Based on your analysis in question C.8, propose one measure to improve the company's responsible human resources activities. Send your proposal to the contact mail address mentioned in the report.

## PIONEER INTERVIEW WITH LIZ MAW

Courtesy of Liz Maw

Liz Maw is CEO of Net Impact, a large network of students and practitioners, "more than 30,000 changemakers using [their] jobs to tackle the world's toughest problems." Net Impact actively aims to foster the CSR profession and create careers with a positive impact.

**What role do you think young professionals and business school students, such as the ones represented by Net Impact, play in changing businesses and the economic system toward more sustainability?**

According to PriceWaterhouseCooper's 2012 CEO survey, recruiting and retaining talent is a top priority and concern for global CEOs. CEOs know that their growth and market leadership will be delivered by ensuring talented people fully engaged in their company's priorities.

Young professionals and grad students care deeply about making an impact on social and environmental causes. At Net Impact, a global nonprofit that empowers a new generation of leaders to drive positive social and environmental change, we work with tens of thousands of young people who want a meaningful career that delivers impact and business results. These young people have the opportunity to voice their values and encourage their colleagues, managers, and executives to bring sustainability and responsibility into the workplace. And even though they have less experience than their colleagues and bosses, they have the attention of the leadership. They are the talent pipeline that will drive growth and results. That's a powerful position to be in.

### How do you think universities in general and business schools in particular should prepare students for jobs in responsible management? What are the required skills? Are universities doing a good job in this respect?

Over the past ten years, business schools have added a significant number of elective courses on topics related to business and society, such as social entrepreneurship, impact investing, and ethical sourcing. While these courses have provided a much better knowledge base for students committed to responsible management, a large opportunity remains to more fully integrate these themes into the core or required curriculum. Many leading MBA programs are working on that challenge now by introducing sustainability cases in core classes and inviting guest lecturers to speak about responsible management topics. In a recent Net Impact study of graduate business programs, over half reported that social and environmental issues are discussed in core classes.

In *Business Skills for a Changing World* study, published by Net Impact and the World Environment Center, we outlined a number of critical competencies that leaders in Fortune 500 companies told us they needed from MBA graduates. One set of skills we termed "inside-out" skills, which refers to the technical and behavioral skills for day-to-day business management that enable an employee to make responsible decisions with a sustainable lens. In addition, leaders spoke of the need for "outside-in" skills that help an employee understand and process external realities and factors that can reshape a company's business strategy. Finally, "traverse" skills are necessary to apply systems thinking, communicate with stakeholders, and manage social interactions and networks to influence change.

### Is there a development toward a responsible management profession? What would you recommend students should do if they are interested in working in responsible management jobs?

Several leading practitioners in the field are currently in discussion of "professionalizing" the corporate responsibility profession. These positions have evolved organically in many companies, and as the demands on these positions become more complex, some believe the field would benefit from greater formal training and standardization. That said, the corporate responsibility or responsible management function has also been integrated into many business positions. For example, supply chain professionals are increasingly asked to understand ethical supply chain opportunities, and operations professionals must learn about energy efficiency.

As a result of these two trends, students who are passionate about responsible management will have the opportunity to both enter into a more defined "profession" with CSR colleagues as well as choose to work on sustainability from many different day jobs. The most important step students can take is to ensure that they work for companies authentically committed to a holistic and integrated approach to sustainability—companies that engage employees at all levels with responsible management. In the right kind of open culture, all employees are able to meaningfully contribute to responsible management progress.

Net Impact offers a number of resources to help students successfully find and succeed in an impact position. Our Career Center, student competitions, student chapters, and conferences are all designed to support students in their job search, and we invite you to e-mail us if you'd like more information (info@netimpact.org).

### What role do responsible business topics play in employer branding? Do graduates actively look for responsible businesses to work with?

In a recent study Net Impact released (*Talent Report: What Workers Want in 2012*), nearly half of student respondents said they would take a pay cut to work for a company that makes a higher social or environmental impact. And recruiters are paying attention. Ten years ago, the majority of campus recruiters knew little of corporate sustainability priorities. Due in large part to student questions and interest, today most recruiters are able to effectively tell the story of a company's CSR priorities.

Courtesy of Erika Guzman Romo

**Employing organization:** Innovation Packaging & Process S.A. De C.V. is a contract manufacturer providing co-packing solutions for the food and beverage industry, with high-quality procedures and the best aseptic technology. From San Luis Potosi, Mexico, the company offers multipacking solutions and special packages to complete the co-packing services.

**Job title:** Human Resources Director

**Education:** Bachelor in Business Management, focusing on Human Resources, Tecnológico de Monterrey; Diploma in Communication and Organizational Development; Diploma in Corporate Social Responsibility

### In Practice

**What are your responsibilities?** My main responsibility is to create a culture in which our people truly live the Innovation philosophy. I achieve this by coordinating a team with HR activities:

Recruiting, screening, and hiring

Training and skills development

Labor relations

Compensation and benefits

Performance management

High-performance teams

Integration events, with a focus on social and family aspects

### What are typical activities you carry out during a day at work?

Not a day in my work is routine. Human resources is a 100 percent service area, and our functions are focused on meeting this. Some of the main activities of a "typical" day are:

• Recruiting, screening, and hiring: We look more for attitude than knowledge; in other words, we choose our people whose principles do not contradict those of Innovation. "The company will be as good as its people."

• Training and development of employees: We maximize efforts because development never ends. "If we train half, people operate half."

• Managing high-performance teams: We do lots of communication and make continuous effort with the teams working with a focus on results, common good, and continuous improvement.

### How do sustainability, responsibility, and ethics topics play a role in your job?

Featuring a well-defined business philosophy with the highest values and principles, and being responsible to communicate across the organization:

• In terms of quality of life: having decent facilities, a safe working environment, and health campaigns for our people and their families; practicing inclusive recruitment, without discrimination; fostering teamwork, continuous training, and integration activities.

• Promoting our ethics code as a commitment throughout our value chain: from fair competition with honest market practices and transparency, to respect for human rights, confidentiality agreements for our clients, staff and security audits, etc.

• We bond with our community: creating safe and stable jobs, supporting social welfare causes and philanthropy, with a focus on health and nutrition of our products.

• The link with the environment: we have achieved compliance with national and international codes, controlling our emissions and recycling all our major waste.

### Out of the topics covered in the chapter into which your interview will be included, which concepts, tools, or topics are most relevant to your work? How?

Currently everything related to the concepts of *diversity* and *inclusion* is very important to us in our journey to lead a responsible human resources management.

Since its founding, Innovation has been a company created with the goal of generating welfare for its people and its community; in fact, it is part of our mission. And one of our greatest strengths is that we have the opportunity to have men and women of different skills, age, social conditions, backgrounds, etc.; and one of our biggest challenges this year will be the formal incorporation of people with disabilities.

## Insights and Challenges

**What recommendation can you give to practitioners in your field?** It is essential to have the commitment and support of the company top leaders if you want the social responsibility as part of the organizational culture. Extend the company values to all stakeholders. "See what others do not see." Have the ability to reconcile constantly, promoting openness and communication at all levels and in all directions. Remember that the basis and essence of our work is the *service* culture. Do not stop learning and growing. Be authentic and have integrity.

## Which are the main challenges of your job?

- Viewing employees as people with qualities, abilities, needs, interests, and motivations, and adapting this to the policies and activities of the company

- Achieving the involvement of people in the organization, so that they are satisfied with what they do, and keeping it as a constant

- Transforming the company through the leaders, which takes time, preparation, awareness, and vision, so that the changes will be accepted and kept

## Is there anything else that you would like to share?

It is very important to believe, first of all, of the people "as an end and not a means" to achieve corporate growth and be fully human. Only through the cooperation and commitment of all those who make up the organization can planned targets be achieved.

Fundamentally, with the basic principle of respect for persons: Do not deceive or take advantage of people; do not use people, either the community or customers, or suppliers, or employees. It seems a simple practice, but many companies forget this. Successful organizations maintain this in first place.

## SOURCES

1. WBCSD, www.wbcsd.org/web/publications/hr.pdf
2. WBCSD, www.wbcsd.org/web/publications/hr.pdf
3. Gond, J. P., Igalens, J., Swaen, V., & El Akremi, A. (2011). The human resources contribution to responsible leadership: An exploration of the CSR-HR interface. *Journal of Business Ethics*, 98(1), 115–132, p. 128.
4. Garavan, T. N., & McGuire, D. (2010). Human resource development and society: Human resource development's role in embedding corporate social responsibility, ethics, and sustainability in organizations. *Advances in Developing Human Resources, 12*(10), 487–507, p. 487.
5. Fuentes-García, F. J., Núñez-Tabales, J. M., & Veroz-Herradón, R. (2008). Applicability of corporate social responsibility to human resources management: Perspective from Spain. *Journal of Business Ethics*, 82(1), 27–44, p. 29.
6. Society for Human Resource Management (SHRM). (2012). *HR terms*. Retrieved July 17, 2012, from: www.shrm.org/TemplatesTools/Glossaries/HRTerms/Pages/h.aspx

7. Society for Human Resources Management (SHRM). (2008). HR's evolving role in organizations and its impact on business strategy. Retrieved October 2012 from: http://www.shrm.org/research/surveyfindings/documents/hr's%20evolving%20role%20in%20organizations.pdf
8. Adapted from Ehnert. (2011). *Sustainability and HRM: A model and suggestions for future research*, section 3: Employment relations and the society. In A. Wilkinson & K. Townsend, *The future of employment relations*. Basingstoke: Palgrave.
9. Gond, J. P., Igalens, J., Swaen, V., & El Akremi, A. (2011). The human resources contribution to responsible leadership: An exploration of the CSR–HR interface. *Journal of Business Ethics*, 98, 115–132.
10. Society for Human Resources Management (SHRM). (2008). HR's evolving role in organizations and its impact on business strategy. Retrieved October 2012 from: http://www.shrm.org/research/surveyfindings/documents/hr's%20evolving%20role%20in%20organizations.pdf

11. Bhattacharya, C. B., Sen, S., & Korschun, D. (2012). Using corporate social responsibility to win the war for talent. *MIT Sloan Management Review*, 49, p. 7.
12. CareerXroads. (2010). *Sources of hire study*. Retrieved May 28, 2012, from: www.careerxroads.com/news/SourcesOfHire10.pdf
13. Quoted from p. 1 of the following document: www.shrm.org/about/foundation/products/documents/csr%20exec%20briefing-%20final.pdf
14. Ivancevich, J. M. (2003). *Human resource management*, 9th international ed. (p. 394). New York: McGraw-Hill/Irwin.
15. Ivancevich, J. M. (2003). *Human resource management*, 9th international ed. New York: McGraw-Hill/Irwin.
16. Jablin, F. (1987). Organizational entry, assimilation, and exit. In F. Jablin, L. Putnam, K. Roberts, & L. Porter (eds.), *Handbook of organizational communication* (pp. 679–740). Newbury Park, CA: Sage.
17. Intercontinental Hotel Group. (2012). *Local economic opportunity through the IHG Academy programme*.

Retrieved June 12, 2012, from: www.ihgplc.com/index.asp?pageid=754

18. Miller, K. (2009). *Organizational communication: Approaches and processes*, 5th ed. Boston: Wadsworth Cengage Learning.

19. Cohen, E. (2010). *CSR for HR: A necessary partnership for advancing responsible business practices* (p. 250). Sheffield, UK: Greenleaf.

20. Cohen, E. (2010). *CSR for HR: A necessary partnership for advancing responsible business practices*. Sheffield, UK: Greenleaf.

21. Cohen, E. (2010). *CSR for HR: A necessary partnership for advancing responsible business practices*. Sheffield, UK: Greenleaf.

22. Cohen, E. (2010). *CSR for HR: A necessary partnership for advancing responsible business practices*. Sheffield, UK: Greenleaf.

23. Cohen, E. (2010). *CSR for HR: A necessary partnership for advancing responsible business practices* (p. 75). Sheffield, UK: Greenleaf.

24. DJSI Westpac Banking. (2011). Retrieved from: http://www.westpac.com.au/

25. Cohen, E. (2010). *CSR for HR: A necessary partnership for advancing responsible business practices*. Sheffield, UK: Greenleaf.

26. Cohen, E. (2010). *CSR for HR: A necessary partnership for advancing responsible business practices* (p. 126). Sheffield, UK: Greenleaf.

27. Cohen, E. (2010). *CSR for HR: A necessary partnership for advancing responsible business practices*. Sheffield, UK: Greenleaf.

28. Ali, I., Rehman, K. U., Ali, S. I., Yousaf, J., & Zia, M. (2010). Corporate social responsibility influences employee commitment and organizational performance. *African Journal of Business Management*, 4(12), 2796–2801, p. 2796.

29. Ivancevich, J. M. (2003). *Human resource management*, 9th international ed. New York: McGraw-Hill/Irwin.

30. Ivancevich, J. M. (2003). *Human resource management*, 9th international ed. (p. 255). New York: McGraw-Hill/Irwin.

31. Kaplan, R. S., & Norton, D. P. (1996, January–February). Using the balanced scorecard as a strategic management system. *Harvard Business Review*, 74(1), 75–85.

32. This paper can be downloaded from the Institute's website: www.balancedscorecard.org/

33. Guest, D. (2002). Human resource management, corporate performance and employee wellbeing: Building the worker into HRM. *Journal of Industrial Relations*, 44(3), 335–358, p. 355.

34. KPMG. (2012). *HR systems incentive schemes*. Retrieved June 29, 2012, from: www.kpmg.com/cy/en/whatwedo/advisory/performancetechnology/peopleandchange/pages/hrsystems.aspx

35. Cohen, E. (2010). *CSR for HR: A necessary partnership for advancing responsible business practices*. Sheffield, UK: Greenleaf.

36. Cohen, E. (2010). *CSR for HR: A necessary partnership for advancing responsible business practices* (p. 90). Sheffield, UK: Greenleaf.

37. Fortune. (2012). *100 best companies to work for*. Retrieved June 30, 2012, from: http://money.cnn.com/magazines/fortune/best-companies/

38. Novartis Corporation. (2012). *Compensation and benefits: Talented teams, performance-based compensation*. Retrieved May 31, 2012, from: http://www.novartis.com/

39. Gollan, P. J. (2005). High involvement management and human resource sustainability: The challenges and opportunities. *Asia Pacific Journal of Human Resources*, 43(1), 18–33.

40. Baeten, X. (2010). Global compensation and benefits management: The need for communication and coordination. *Compensation & Benefits Review*, 42(5), 392–402.

41. Nestlé. (2010). *The Nestlé employee relations policy*. Retrieved June 30, 2012, from: www.nestle.com/Common/NestleDocuments/Documents/Library/Documents/People/Employee-relations-policy-EN.pdf

42. Foremski, T. (2010, May 26). *Suicides at France Telecom are 5 times higher than at Foxconn—The human cost of cheap bandwidth and gadgets?* Retrieved December 26, 2012, from *Silicon Valley Watcher*: www.siliconvalleywatcher.com/mt/archives/2010/05/46_suicides_at.php

43. HCA Online. (2010, May 18). *Unilever gets down to business with health*. Retrieved December 22, 2012, from HC Online: http://www.hcamag.com/

44. Karnes, R. E. (2009). A change in business ethics: The impact on employer–employee relations. *Journal of Business Ethics*, 87(2), 189–197, p. 189.

45. Nestlé. (2010). *The Nestlé corporate business principles*. Retrieved June 30, 2012, from: www.nestle.com/Common/NestleDocuments/Documents/Library/Documents/Corporate_Governance/Corporate-Business-Principles-EN.pdf

46. ILO. (2012). *About the declaration*. Retrieved December 22, 2012, from International Labour Organization: http://www.ilo.org/

## REFERENCES

ABB Home Page. (2012). Retrieved May 10, 2012, from: www.abb.com/

ABB Sustainability Objectives 2012. Retrieved May 10, 2012, from: http://www02.abb.com/global/abbzh/abbzh258.nsf/0/76b88b0b63a8df72c1257b2e0075044f/$file/performance+against+objectives_2012.pdf

ABB Vision. (2012). Retrieved May 10, 2012, from: http://www.abb.com/

Butler, S. (2012). *Cambodian workers hold "people's tribunal" to look at factory conditions*. Retrieved June 30, 2012, from: http://www.guardian.co.uk/world/2012/feb/02/cambodian-workers-peoples-tribunal-factory?INTCMP=SRCH

Byers M. (2007). *Interview Rx: A powerful guide for making your next interview a success*, 3rd ed. Conyers, GA: Nearline Publishers.

Cicloteque. (2012, March). *Cicloteque: Rise above the city*. Teodor Mitrana Master Thesis, Steinbeis University.

Commission of the European Communities. (2006). *Implementing the partnership for growth and jobs: Making Europe a pole of excellence of CSR*. Brussels: European Union.

CNN Money. (2012). *Global 500.* Retrieved from: http://money. cnn.com/magazines/fortune/ global500/2011/full_list/index.html

Dartmouth College. (2012). *Career services: Successful interviewing.* Retrieved from: http://www.dartmouth.edu/

EIRIS Sustainability Report. (2012, April). *On track for Rio+20? How are global companies responding to sustainability?* Retrieved from: www.eiris .org/files/research%20publications /EIRISGlobalSustainbailityReport2012 .pdf

FirstGroup, Careers. (2012). Retrieved May 22, 2012, from: www.firstgroup .com/corporate/careers/

Gray, G. (2003, March/April). Performance appraisals don't work. *Industrial Management, 44(2),* 15–17.

Greenwood, R. G. (1981). Management by objectives: As developed by Peter Drucker, Assisted by Harold Smiddy. *Academy of Management Review, 6(2),* 225–230.

Institutions for Collective Action. (2012). Retrieved June 30, 2012, from: www .collective-action.info/

Jablin, F. M. (1982). Organizational communication: An assimilation approach. In M. E. Roloff & C. R. Berger (eds.), *Social cognition and communication* (pp. 255–286). Thousand Oaks, CA: Sage.

Kerssens-van Drongelen, I. C., & Fisscher, O. A. M. (2003). Ethical dilemmas in performance measurement. *Journal of Business Ethics, 45(1/2),* 51–63.

Lepsinger, R., & Lucia, A. D. (2009). *The art and science of 360-degree feedback,* 2nd ed. San Francisco: Jossey-Bass.

MacDermott, C. S. (1995). Networking and interviewing: An art in effective communication. *Business Communication Quarterly,* 58–59.

Nancherla, A. (2008). Anticipated growth in behavioral interviewing. *T + D, 62(4),* 20.

National Australia Bank, HR. (2012). Retrieved May 22, 2012, from: www .nab.com.au/wps/wcm/connect/nab/ careers/home/2/1/1

Novartis Human Resources. (2012). *At Novartis, people are more than just resources.* Retrieved May 31, 2012, from: www.pharma.us.novartis.com/ assets/pdf/careers/human_resources.pdf

Odiorne, G. S. (1965). *Management by objectives.* New York: Pitman.

PUMA FAQ. (2012). Retrieved May 19, 2012, from: http://about.puma.com/ category/career/faq/

PUMA Human Resources. (2012). Retrieved May 15, 2012, from: http:// about.puma.com/

PUMA. (2006). *2005/2006 sustainability report.* Retrieved June 27, 2012, from: http://about.puma.com/wp-content/themes/aboutPUMA_theme /media/pdf/69962928.pdf

Ruona, W. E. A., & Gibson, S. K. (2004). The making of twenty-first-century HR: An analysis of the convergence of HRM, HRD, OD. *Human Resource Management, 43(1),* 49–66.

SAMSUNG. (2012). *Reeducation and job training.* Retrieved May 26, 2012, from: www.samsung.com/us /aboutsamsung/corpcitizenship/ environmentsocialreport/ environmentsocialreport_ ReeducationAndJobTraining.html

Smith, P. C., & Kendall, L. M. (1963). Retranslation of expectations: An approach to the construction of unambiguous anchors for rating scales. *Journal of Applied Psychology, 47(2),* 149–155.

Society for Human Resource Management (SHRM). (2012). *Mission statements.* Retrieved June 1, 2012, from: www .shrm.org/templatestools/samples/ policies/pages/missionstatementhr.aspx

Stewart, D. J., & Cash, W. B. (2008). *Interviewing: Principles and practice,* 12th ed. New York: McGraw-Hill Higher Education.

Walmart Careers. (2012). *Training and development.* Retrieved May 19, 2012, from: http://www.walmart .com/

WBCSD People Matter Reward. (2012). Retrieved May 12, 2012, from: www .wbcsd.org/Pages/EDocument /EDocumentDetails.aspx?ID=47&No SearchContextKey=true

WBCSD. (2012). *People matter engage.* Retrieved May 12, 2012, from: www .wbcsd.org/Pages/EDocument /EDocumentDetails.aspx?ID=48&No SearchContextKey=true

Wessel, D. (2012, May 30). Software raises bar for hiring? *The Wall Street Journal,* U.S. ed., p. A2.

# 12

Feedback
Grapevine
Ethics Codes
LOHAS
Social Marketing
Marketing
Credibility
Stakeholder Communication
Personal Communication
Barriers
Marketing Mix
Audience
Cause-Related Marketing
Message
Sustainability Premium
Mission
Relationship
Cause Branding

# MARKETING AND COMMUNICATION: STAKEHOLDER GOODWILL

*You will be able to...*

1   ...create goodwill toward the company among stakeholders.

2   ...effectively communicate and market your responsible management activities.

3   ...design and manage a portfolio of stakeholder communication activities.

Communications is key: Ninety percent of consumers want companies to tell them the ways they are supporting causes. Nearly two-thirds (61%) don't think companies are giving them enough details.[1]

Cause creates differentiation: Seventy-nine percent of Americans say they would be likely to switch from one brand to another, when price and quality are about equal, if the other brand associated with a good cause.[2]

Authors: Roger N. Conaway and Oliver Laasch; Contributors: Adela Lustykova, Shel Horowitz, Pablo Largacha, Philip Kotler

## Communication and Responsible Business Performance at Nike, Inc.

Nike is one of the best-known companies for its corporate social responsibility and strong corporate reputation. It was not always so. During the 1990s, the company experienced a steep decline in its public image related to outsourcing issues. Remarkably, it is now known today as a progressive company for its leadership in responsible practices. How did Nike achieve this remarkable turnaround? Many argue that the company has failed to address the sweatshop issue and still must address human rights issues in Asia. If Nike is an example of a change from an "irresponsible" corporation to a leader in responsible corporate social practices, what communication strategies did they follow? This case examines Nike's journey and highlights the importance of communicating corporate changes to stakeholders. As a company moves toward responsible business practices, it must communicate those changes. Communication "closes the loop" and completes the integration of economic, social, and environmental performance.

Founder and CEO Phil Knight created Nike in 1972 while teaching at Portland State University in Oregon, U.S.A. Knight was an avid runner and decided to start a shoe company and name it after the winged goddess of victory in Greek mythology. The company with the "swoosh" logo sustained annual double-digit economic growth during the 1990s, a difficult achievement for most businesses, and Wall Street regarded the firm as a model of business practice. Nike's business plan accounted for its success. The company outsourced all shoe-making operations, keeping no physical assets, and focused its budget on marketing.

This "strength" of outsourced operations became Nike's greatest weakness. The company "became the target of arguably the most intensive and widely publicized of these anti-corporate campaigns up to that time." Intensive attacks on

its reputation by media, NGOs, and activists began. Nike was charged with child labor law violations, excessive work hours for employees, and unsafe and unhealthy work environments at its Indonesia outsourcing operations. After its stock price suddenly dropped in 1998, stakeholders demanded significant changes from the company.

Nike began an effective counter campaign by balancing effective communication with stakeholders with value added to the environment. For a company to overcome significant crises, this balance must be reached. For example, a company that communicates a lot but does not improve sustainable activities risks being accused of "greenwashing." A company that improves sustainable activities but does not effectively communicate with stakeholders also lacks balance.

Nike used several important crisis communication tools to counter the intensive attacks on its reputation. It published its code of conduct on the Web concerning management practices, its impact on the environment, safe and healthy workplace, and well-being of employees required by Nike corporate headquarters from its stakeholders. The company overhauled its supply chain operations, conformed to Global Reporting Initiative (GRI) standards, a globally recognized reporting tool, and communicated its compliance to stakeholders. The communication via its website successfully "reframed" the crisis into positive responses from the public. From this perspective, Nike has "turned around" the crisis and become a leader in sustainability standards.

Sources: Schwarze, S. (2003). Corporate-state irresponsibility, critical publicity, and asbestos exposure in Libby, Montana. *Management Communication Quarterly,* 16(4), 625; Waller, R., & Conaway, R. N. (2011). Framing and counterframing the issue of corporate social responsibility: The communication strategies of Nikebiz. com. *Journal of Business Communication, 48*(1), 83–106, p. 85.

## 12-1 MARKETING, COMMUNICATION, AND RESPONSIBLE MANAGEMENT

*"From marketing to advertising, from corporate communication to public awareness campaigns, the messages of sustainability are embodied in practices that are increasingly well-established."*[3]

Effective marketing and communication of social and environmental business performance can make or break a business. Greenwashing accusations, which reveal the imbalance between a company's responsible business performance and communication activities, can destroy reputations or even businesses in a short period

## DIG DEEPER

**Check It Out!**

For actual news and developments in responsible marketing and communication management, see www.greenbiz.com/business/browse/marketing-communications

of time. A single imprudent framing of a company's responsible management issues can cost millions of dollars in stock value. While the risk of ineffective communication is significant, the opportunities of effective marketing and communication are even more important. The essential stakeholders of an organization have shown drastically heightened interested in learning about the organization's responsible management activities and often reward such information in very tangible ways. Customers often pay a premium price for sustainable products that they learned about through a cause-related marketing campaign. Prospective employees may accept lower wages for the personal satisfaction of working with a responsibly managed company that they learned about through the organization's vision and mission statements, values statement, or codes of ethics. Investors are attracted by the excellent social, environmental, and ethical risk management processes and above-average returns as indicated in a business's sustainability report. All of these examples show how stakeholder goodwill pays off. Communication and marketing are the business case catalyst. While "walking the talk" may help a company avoid accusations of greenwashing and evade reputational loss, "talking the walk" communicates good responsible business performance to stakeholders in order to achieve manifold advantages. This chapter describes how to do both.

Figure 12.1 describes the responsible marketing and communication process. Phase 1 of the stakeholder marketing and communication process aims to ensure high effectiveness of marketing and communication activities by outlining the basic processes and rules of integrated marketing communication (IMC). First, we

| Figure 12.1 **The Responsible Marketing and Communication Management Process**

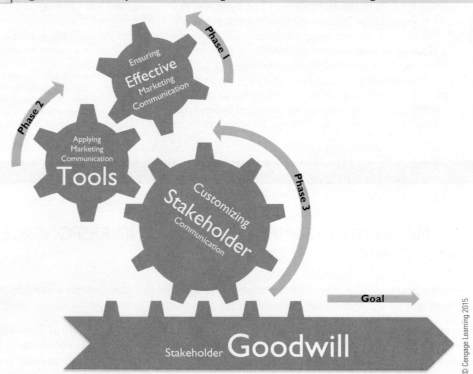

© Cengage Learning 2015

provide an understanding of the communication process. We present seven essential principles of effective communication. Applying these principles will ensure that messages are shared and understood and will help to avoid accusations of greenwashing. Second, we highlight how responsible management factors influence the classical four Ps of marketing management (product, price, place, and promotion). Our objective throughout Phase 2 of the stakeholder marketing and communication process is to understand different specialized responsible business communication tools and pick those most adequate for creating stakeholder goodwill. Phase 3 focuses on audience analysis with the objective of understanding basic characteristics of different stakeholders and creating customized communication activities for distinct stakeholder groups.

## 12-2 THE GOAL: STAKEHOLDER GOODWILL

*"Stakeholder goodwill allows the company to get easier access to strategic resources, to reduce operating and transaction costs, and to boost its reputation in the market place."*[4]

From trust and credibility to a higher willingness to pay an increased investment, **stakeholder goodwill** can take various tangible forms. However good an organization is at fulfilling its social, environmental, and economic responsibilities, if such performance is not communicated to stakeholders, it will hardly create goodwill, much less receive any tangible benefits. It has to be highlighted here that stakeholder goodwill cannot and may not be a goal if the company does not deserve it. Only a company that has earned stakeholders' respect through a substantial responsible business performance may use marketing and communication to create stakeholder goodwill. The Nike case is a good example of this concept. The company had to and still has to prove to stakeholders that its practices can be classified as responsible. For Nike, effective communication, at least in the medium run, led to reestablished trust and goodwill toward the company among Nike's investors, which finally led to recovering stock value that had been lost during the crisis time. Recovered goodwill among customers led to a reestablished sales volume. The reduction of "badwill" among civil societal actors, including NGO activist groups, was reflected in a decrease of negative publicity. In the next section, we will examine how basic principles of effective marketing and communication can lead to effective communication of social and environmental business performance and the creation of goodwill among multiple stakeholders.

It must be highlighted that stakeholder goodwill is only the ultimate consequence of effective integrated marketing and **stakeholder communication** in responsible business. Effective communication in responsible business is important in at least two stages previous to the creation of goodwill. As illustrated in Figure 12.2, in a first process, the focus is on defining a vision of the responsible business that should be created after a transformation process. This definition process requires an extensive, democratic communication process, involving all main stakeholders of the organization. In a second process, the goal is to achieve support in the implementation and transformation process toward becoming the responsible business envisioned. It is only in the ultimate, third process that the goal is to share achievements and to be rewarded with goodwill.[5]

As the Nike case shows us, stakeholder communication becomes absolutely essential when the company improves its responsible practices or engages in new activities. So what is "effective stakeholder communication"? Why is it important? Effective **stakeholder communication** is as an ongoing dialogue with a stakeholder,

**Stakeholder goodwill** is the value created for an organization when its stakeholders adopt a positive attitude toward an organization.

**Stakeholder communication** is an ongoing dialogue with a stakeholder, any group or individual who can affect or is affected by the organization.

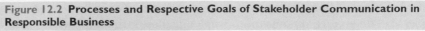

**Figure 12.2 Processes and Respective Goals of Stakeholder Communication in Responsible Business**

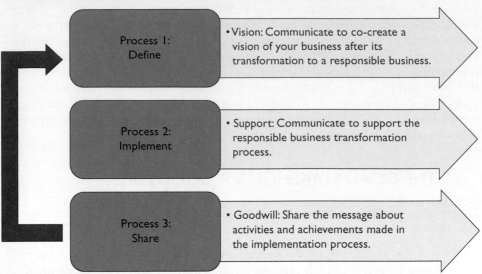

**Process 1: Define**
- Vision: Communicate to co-create a vision of your business after its transformation to a responsible business.

**Process 2: Implement**
- Support: Communicate to support the responsible business transformation process.

**Process 3: Share**
- Goodwill: Share the message about activities and achievements made in the implementation process.

Source: Conaway, R., & Laasch, O. (2012). *Communication in responsible business: Strategies, concepts and cases.* New York: Business Expert Press.

with the intent to build and maintain a relationship, to ultimately create goodwill among any group or individual who can affect or is affected by the achievement of the organization's objectives.

## 12-3 PHASE 1: ENSURING EFFECTIVE INTEGRATED MARKETING COMMUNICATION

*Integrated marketing communication "is being recognized as a business process that helps companies identify the most appropriate and effective methods for communicating and building relationships with customers and other stakeholders."*[6]

**Integrated marketing communication (IMC)** is essentially pure stakeholder communication. IMC connects all explicit and implicit communication activities of the organization. To successfully reach stakeholders, the company must use its full communication potential in a connected and integrated manner, involving its highly interrelated network of internal and external stakeholders. In this section, we describe communication and marketing as two components of IMC. Together these components form the centerpiece of effective stakeholder communication. Each IMC tool we propose in Phase 2 builds on a thorough understanding of the four Ps of marketing and the seven principles of effective communication.

A successful example of IMC responsible management can be illustrated by the movie theater chain Cinépolis, and its campaign "*Del amor nace la vista,*" which translated reads "Love gives birth to eyesight." Cinépolis used various IMC tools with its cause-related market campaign. These tools were all designed to be part of its internal and external communication activities that raised funds to conduct cataract eye surgeries. Those surgeries

**Integrated marketing communication (IMC)** describes the process of using an organization's full range of communication and marketing tools in an interconnected manner for building stakeholder goodwill.

## In Practice

### Win-Win through Integrated Marketing Communication

Based on a highly effective integrated marketing communication campaign, the world's fourth-biggest movie theater chain Cinépolis has been able not only to give back eyesight to more than 6,000 people, but also to gain a differentiation advantage in the saturated movie theater industry.

Source: Laasch, O., & Conaway, R. (2011). "Making it do" at the movie theatres: Communicating sustainability in the workplace. *Business Communication Quarterly, 74*(1), 68–78.

helped return eyesight to people from low-income communities who could not afford such medical treatment. This campaign involved communication to a diverse set of stakeholders, including customers, employees, governmental institutions, and eye-doctors associations.[7]

## 12-3a Understanding Effective Communication

Communication is like oil that flows through a machine. Without oil a machine cannot operate. Similarly, communication flows through organizational processes and allows them to run smoothly. Without communication the organization will not function. The process of human communication is complex, especially when sensitive issues related to responsible management are involved. We explore this complex process with the purpose of becoming better communicators. **Effective communication** occurs when messages are shared and understood. British Petroleum's (BP) Gulf of Mexico oil spill in 2010 provides us with an example of crisis communication. Stakeholders, including the public, the media, and many others, requested information immediately after the disaster. How could BP, a multinational company in crisis, effectively communicate to its stakeholders?

When the communication process (see Figure 12.3) began for BP, an individual or representative for the company served as the **sender**, which in BP's case was a public information officer (PIO). This person communicated a message to **receivers**, who were the general public, investors, employees, and others. As we will see later in the chapter, a message of this type must be accurate, transparent, and adapted to its audiences in an understandable way. The **message** was the unique combination of words and symbols the PIO chose to communicate. The message involved the speaker's tone, which was BP's *implicit attitude* about the disaster. The message also involved *style,* which was the *way* the speaker communicated. Style means the speaker, for instance, was either direct or indirect with information, formal or informal in presentation, and public-oriented or company-oriented. Style involves the communicator's unique preferences and choices when sending a message, and it describes whether a person is assertive versus passive versus aggressive or

**Effective communication** occurs when messages are shared and understood.

The **sender** is the person with whom the message originates.

The **receiver** is the person who receives the original message.

The **message** is the unique combination of words and symbols, including tone and style.

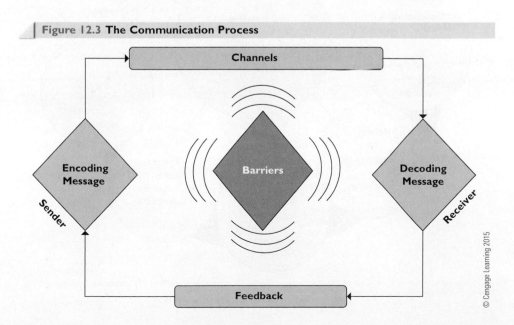

**Figure 12.3 The Communication Process**

© Cengage Learning 2015

transparent versus closed. In many cases a speaker's communication style becomes obvious to listeners but may not be obvious to the speaker. Communication style in responsible management communication should be adjusted to the different characteristics of distinct stakeholder groups. For BP, the communication messages and implied attitudes directed toward shareholders were fundamentally different from the ones directed toward the general public or government officials and employees.

Representatives from BP spoke immediately through the media to the public and international community. The speaker's message traveled via various **channels**. Figure 12.4 provides an extensive overview of typical communication channels used in a responsible management context. External communication involves media relations, television coverage, interviews, and websites. Internal communication also occurred quickly. Intercompany e-mails, cell phone calls, texting, and Facebook messages were sent. Communication channels refer to the physical media through which the message moves. "Rich" communication channels include face-to-face communication and video conferences. These channels have many sensory cues or information about the message. "Lean" channels include e-mail and Web-based channels such as interactive blogs, posts on Facebook, and Twitter texts. These "lean" channels have fewer information cues, which means there is a greater chance

**Channels** are the physical media though which the message moves.

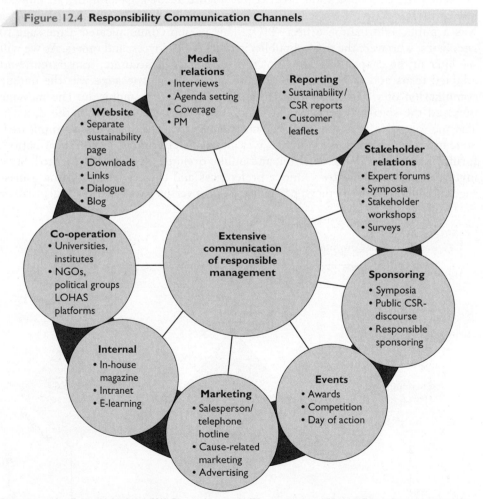

**Figure 12.4 Responsibility Communication Channels**

Source: Adapted from Taubken, N., & Leibold, I. (2010). Ten rules for successful CSR communication. In M. Pohl & N. Tolhurst, *Responsible business: How to manage a CSR strategy successfully*. Chichester: Wiley.

for the message to be misinterpreted. Channel choice has an important role in effective communication and is determined by the importance of the message, its complexity, timeliness, and other factors.

Effective communication may be hindered by *selective perception and misinterpretation* in both the sender and receiver. These interferences work against accurate understanding and commonly are called **barriers**, which may be either physical or psychological. The source of a physical barrier is external to the speaker and includes situational or cultural factors. Environmental noise, interruptions, and distractions are sources of external interference. Psychological barriers may be mental preoccupation of the speaker with another person, mental distractions with a work issue, or simply daydreaming, all which interfere with accurate understanding. A receiver who has a bias against "big oil" may interpret the message from BP completely differently than a shareholder in the company. These psychological barriers inhibit encoding and decoding of the message. The **encoding** process occurs when the sender turns an idea into a message and involves forming words and selecting nonverbal symbols to shape the message. In face-to-face communication, video conferencing, or television broadcasting, the sender accentuates the message with eye contact, facial expressions, gestures, and other nonverbal symbols. Once the message is sent, the receiver of the message begins **decoding**, which is the process of interpreting the meaning of words and symbols. Terms related to responsible management often lack a common understanding between sender and receiver. Customers often understand the very basic term "sustainability" as referring merely to environmental topics, while many companies understand "sustainability" as an integrated set of responsible management activities involving social, environmental, and economic factors. In this particular case, effective communication has to ensure that the term *sustainability,* when used by a business, is decoded with the same meaning by customers.

The encoding and decoding processes are imperfect at best because of the sender's and receiver's tendencies to perceive selectively. Barriers include any interference in the environment, culture, language, nonverbal communication, and other factors that influence negatively the perception and interpretation of the message. Noticeably, we tend to use words at various levels of abstraction in our messages. With so many abstract meanings in words that we use, such as *sustainability,* it is simple to understand how easily we can communicate poorly. What is truly amazing is that we can understand each other at all.

*A Dynamic Complex Communication Process.* Review for a moment the seven components of communication displayed in Figure 12.3. Picture in your mind a dynamic process involving very unique people. Now consider the dynamic example of the European Multi-Stakeholder Forum, which was formed in 2002 to promote innovation, convergence, and transparency in existing responsible management practices. Stakeholders communicate through roundtables, reports, and other channels in the forum to exchange best responsible management practices and assess the appropriateness of their common guiding principles. A dynamic approach to the communication process contrasts with other perspectives of communication. Most businesspeople would describe the communication process as a *one-way* transfer of information from one stakeholder to another and moving from one individual to another. Although this linear process sounds reasonable, it is an incomplete description. Still other businesspeople might describe communication as a *two-way* process that includes **feedback**, which describes the verbal and nonverbal responses exchanged between sender and receiver, much like a tennis match. One stakeholder "serves" a message to another stakeholder, and that stakeholder sends a response

**Barriers** are any internal or external factors that interfere with accurate understanding of the message

**Encoding** is the interpretative process of analyzing the audience, organizing the message, and selecting words.

**Decoding** is the process in the receiver of interpreting the words and symbols in the message.

**Feedback** consists of the verbal and nonverbal responses exchanged between sender and receiver. Verbal feedback includes texted, typed, and written messages.

back as feedback. In contrast to these two views, the communication process can best be described as *dynamic* involvement and relationship between people, a process where sender and receiver interact dynamically with each other. The European forum messages may change when spoken and may be shaped according to listener responses. Leaders of the forum may be discussing with their teams an important responsible management activity. The decision outcome is often "constructed" and modified by the team when stakeholders are taken into account. The final decision may be different from what the company originally intended. This constructive process illustrates the dynamic view of communication.

## Shaping the Message

When we consider the communication process as dynamic and relational, we move toward effective communication. We now identify several time-tested principles of business communication[8] that serve as a foundation or basis for effective responsible business communication. Our assumption is that ineffective communication leads to greenwashing accusations. To avoid those accusations, we must follow principles of effective communication.

Maple Leaf Foods, a major Canadian food processing company, demonstrated effective communication during a crisis in 2008. The company's Toronto meat processing facility was contaminated with dangerous bacteria, called Listeria, which spread through 200 meat products. Twenty people eventually died. The CEO opted for an open and transparent communication strategy and adapted appropriately to stakeholders. We examine seven time-tested principles of communication in this crisis context.

1. *Adapt to your audience.* When Michael McCain, Maple Leaf president and CEO, spoke about the Listeria crisis, he immediately adapted his message to stakeholders. Effective communication meant understanding his audience of stakeholders and knowing to whom he was communicating. Audience adaptation does not mean telling stakeholders what they want to hear. It does mean that they understand the meaning of the message. Too often we try to present our company or ourselves in the best way, focusing on who we are and how we do things. Consider several key questions: What are the primary interests of my stakeholders? What are their attitudes and beliefs about my sustainable activity? What is the size and demographics of my audience? What is their level of understanding?

2. *Clarify your purpose.* McCain stated the purpose of his message by admitting the contamination problem in the Toronto plant and apologizing for it. If you are communicating for your company about a specific social activity, what do you want to say about it? What is the main idea? Communication is more effective when you focus on one topic instead of many topics in a message.

3. *State your message clearly.* Use words so that the message intended will be the message the audience receives. Clearly construct the message and choose words they understand. Be transparent in what is said without trying to hide meaning. The Maple Leaf CEO stated "contamination outbreak" in words the audience understood without using unintelligible medical terms. In some cases corporate communicators may want to be "strategically ambiguous." That is, they may deliberately intend to write ambiguous messages or be vague until a company

decision is reached or a crisis is past. Unless company policy dictates otherwise, state your message transparently and understandably.

4. *Stay on topic.* When forming your message, steer "clear of unrelated or loosely related subjects that just happen to be on your mind. It means not slathering on a pile of data and details that obscure the bottom-line message."[9] Addressing just one topic gives the message greater impact than including many topics that may get lost in importance. Communicating just one idea in a message focuses the reader or listener on what you are communicating.

5. *Be complete and accurate.* This principle is an important one to ensure effective communication. Make sure all facts in the message are as accurate as possible. Ensure the message is free from errors. Ineffective communication, for example, creates the ever-present danger of social and environmental topics being (mis)judged as superficial or having hidden agendas. A deadline may determine how quickly you communicate about a responsible activity, but despite these time limitations, ensure that the facts of your message are as accurate as possible. An ever-present controversial topic in business communication is transparency. Responsible management advocates and stakeholders require transparency, but how much internal information can a company possibly reveal to stakeholders without endangering its trade secrets? A company might even give enough information for competitors to copy valuable core competencies. Principles three and five have to be handled with care in order not to endanger an organization's competitive position, while still providing the maximum amount of information.

6. *Establish goodwill.* Personalize your message and build goodwill with consumers, customers, and other stakeholders. Use their names in the message or address them properly in a personal way. The goodwill message involves a "selfless" tone, one that focuses on the receiver instead of the sender. A goodwill message will communicate understanding. It seeks to build or maintain a positive relationship with the stakeholder. This principle of communication is essential to involvement and interaction with stakeholders. This goodwill message is different from the overarching goal of goodwill creation that was described in the beginning of this chapter. While the goodwill described here is the goodwill of the organization displayed toward the stakeholder, the goal of effective stakeholder communication is the goodwill of stakeholders displayed toward the company.

7. *Communicate with credibility.* This principle is fundamentally the most important of the communication principles. Trustworthiness and knowledge are essential to credibility. The audience's perception of our integrity and credibility influences how every single message we communicate is received. If the audience views the company or sender as trustworthy, they tend to believe the message. Communicating with credibility and integrity also implies consistency between what a company says and what is does. If all other principles of communication are incorporated into a message except credibility, the communication will not be effective. For example, The Body Shop company had long been seen as a pioneer with unquestioned credibility in its positive social and environmental performance. This credibility had been based in its pioneer status as one of the most successful social entrepreneur ventures and its strong activism for its flagship cause of animal testing. This credibility became seriously harmed when

The Body Shop was sold to L'Oréal in 2006. L'Oréal had previously received substantial criticism for its animal-testing activities and allegedly questionable marketing activities.[10] Stakeholders typically voice their irritation about non-credible and incongruent responsible management communication and marketing as greenwashing accusations. In the next section, we will highlight how to balance responsible business performance with just the right amount of communication—that is, how to walk the talk and talk the walk.

### Balancing Communication and Stakeholder Value: Avoiding Greenwashing

A communication effort that evokes a negatively misleading impression of a company's responsible business performance is called **greenwashing**. Such a situation where the organization is not "walking the talk" bears high potential to create immense reputational damage and reduce stakeholder goodwill, opposite the very goal of effective responsible management communication and marketing. Figure 12.5a describes four different positions that a company can assume when communicating stakeholder performance, categorizing it by low or high intensity of communication and low or high stakeholder value creation.[11] A justified greenwashing accusation occurs when a company's "intensity of communication" of its responsible activities exaggerates the actual stakeholder value created. Responsibly managed companies usually display a high stakeholder value creation and a justified high activity in communicating this performance, a so-called *high-balance* situation. In a *low-balance* situation, companies mirror low stakeholder performance with little communication activities of social and environmental topics. A "shy" communicator displays high stakeholder performance, but decides to limit intensity of communication. In order to avoid justified "greenwash" accusations and the related loss in stakeholder goodwill, a company should avoid communication activities covering stakeholder performance before the actual performance grows.

The reasons why stakeholders perceive communication activities as greenwashing may be visually represented by the grid on the right (Figure 12.5b), which is similar to the one used to explain companies' balance or imbalance between walk and talk.[12] The grid on the right describes the effectiveness of communication formerly described in the seven rules of effective communication. Greenwashing accusations are not always justified. The quadrant labeled "Misperceived Greenwash" describes a situation where stakeholders perceive the company as greenwashing but, in reality, the company has not been communicating efficiently.

The vertical dimension in the grid on the right represents stakeholder value created and the horizontal dimension represents the effectiveness of communication. The lower left quadrant, labeled "Greenwash Noise," illustrates how a company lacks both minimal efforts to add value to the environment and communication effectiveness. The company may say publically, "we're green," but their communication does not have compelling information to back up its claims and their efforts have little or no impact on the environment or stakeholders. Quite the contrary, this "greenwash noise" is often even confusing to stakeholders because of its unclear messages and statements. The upper left quadrant, labeled "Misperceived Greenwash," illustrates how a firm adds good stakeholder value through its activities, but lacks effective ways to communicate the results. Managers in the firm have not adapted their communication to their audience and have not been able to achieve stakeholder support for their message and responsible management activities.

Next, the lower right quadrant, labeled "Unsubstantiated Greenwash," illustrates how corporate communication is strong, but based on an inferior value to

**Greenwashing** refers to the usage of marketing and communication means to create a misleading impression of a company's stakeholder value creation.

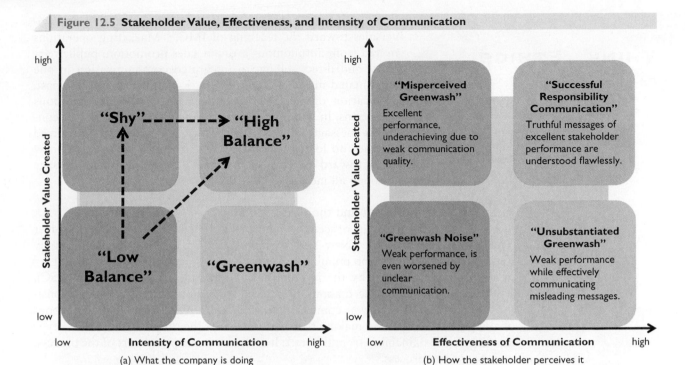

**Figure 12.5 Stakeholder Value, Effectiveness, and Intensity of Communication**

*(a) Chart: Stakeholder Value Created (vertical, low to high) vs. Intensity of Communication (horizontal, low to high)*

"Shy" ----→ "High Balance"

"Low Balance"    "Greenwash"

(a) What the company is doing

*(b) Chart: Stakeholder Value Created (vertical, low to high) vs. Effectiveness of Communication (horizontal, low to high)*

**"Misperceived Greenwash"** Excellent performance, underachieving due to weak communication quality.

**"Successful Responsibility Communication"** Truthful messages of excellent stakeholder performance are understood flawlessly.

**"Greenwash Noise"** Weak performance, is even worsened by unclear communication.

**"Unsubstantiated Greenwash"** Weak performance while effectively communicating misleading messages.

(b) How the stakeholder perceives it

Sources: (a) Adapted from Taubken, N., & Leibold, I. (2010). Ten rules for successful CSR communication. In M. Pohl & N. Tolhurst, *Responsible business: How to manage a CSR strategy successfully.* Chichester: Wiley; (b) Adapted from Horiuchi, R., et al. (2009). *Understanding and preventing greenwash: A business guide* (p. 4). San Francisco: BSR.

stakeholders. The company communicates effectively, but the messages are not based on the necessary responsible business performance. The picture of the company's stakeholder performance is misleading. Finally, the top right quadrant, "Successful Responsibility Communication," highlights how managers maximize value added to stakeholders and effectively communicate this good performance to stakeholders. Achieving this balance is sometimes difficult but is a recommended goal for all companies. The fifth communication principle we reviewed earlier suggested we communicate completely and accurately to help prevent greenwashing and avoid the potential harms to both business and society.

## 12-3b Marketing Responsible Business Performance

Our discussion turns now to basics of marketing and applies the concepts to responsible management. Since the 1980s, the marketing discipline has changed drastically because of the Internet, technology improvements, and changing consumer preferences. The newest American Marketing Association (AMA) definition of marketing reflects a customer orientation and includes a component of social responsibility by emphasizing *value* for consumers in society at large. For our purposes here, we define marketing according to the newest definition:[13] "Marketing is the activity, set of institutions, and processes for creating, communicating, delivering, and exchanging offerings that have value for customers, clients, partners, and society at large." Thus, the essence of marketing creates value for customers and develops long-term relationships. The AMA definition places communication at the core of marketing and social responsibility. It fits Europe's market-oriented conditions[14] and adapts to global market conditions.

During the 1980s and 1990s, a shift occurred in many universities toward the teaching of IMC.[15] Marketing operations moved from autonomous areas in sales promotion, public relations, and direct selling, to integrated communication in one coordinated message within the various functions. In the past, duplication of messages often occurred among autonomous operations. In addition, different agencies communicated inconsistent messages. Today, mass media advertising in outsourced agencies no longer dominates budgets in a company, but new media direct their efforts toward a consumer market "of one" in a single message consistently offered through all media.

### Responsible Management and the Marketing Mix

Chris Hacker, chief design officer for Johnson & Johnson's Group of Consumer Companies, and a team of New York designers developed a new, environmentally friendly box design for the popular Band-Aid brand adhesive. The new packaging materials were certified by the international Forest Stewardship Council (FSC). A Brazilian facility produced about 90 percent of the boxes from trees in responsibly managed forests. Hacker commented on the new box design: "We think about making great designs and making them sustainable at the same time . . . . The key is considering sustainability from the start. It really is an integrated part of the process, not a separate process."[16]

The Band-Aid brand box effectively illustrates the intersection between marketing, communication, and responsible management. The box design illustrates how Johnson & Johnson integrated product, pricing, packaging, and promotion through effective communication with Johnson & Johnson stakeholders. Figure 12.6 visually represents how sustainability interacts with the traditional four Ps of marketing, also called the marketing mix.

The **marketing mix** is the backbone of the marketing management process. It is also called the four Ps, consisting of product, place, price, and promotion.

A **product** is the final value proposition of a company to its customers, either a physical product or a service, and may include packaging and branding.

These basic marketing concepts are termed the **marketing mix**: *product* (or service), *place*, *price*, and *promotion*. Kotler[17] suggested fifth and sixth Ps (politics and public relations), and others have suggested a seventh P (people). In fact, the marketing of services for people has grown into a sophisticated field of *services marketing*.

A **product** does not necessarily have to be a physical object. It can be a legal or accounting service, a professional dry cleaning business, a hotel resort service, or a warranty on a car. A product can even be an idea. Starbucks chief marketing officer (CMO), Terry Davenport, commented, "Starbucks is not just a product, it is an idea. The idea is that sense of community and conversation that can happen over a

**Figure 12.6 Responsible Management in the General Marketing Mix**

| Product | Price |
|---|---|
| • Product innovation by responsibility features<br>• Elimination of products with unacceptable responsible business performance<br>• Product differentiation by responsible management | • Inpricing external effects<br>• Price premium on responsible product features<br>• Taxes or subsidies based on socioenvironmental product performance |
| **Place** | **Promotion** |
| • Environmental impact of distribution<br>• Responsibility as door opener to new distribution channel<br>• Form product distribution to servicization | • Usage of cause-related marketing as sales argument<br>• Spillover effects from company's responsible reputation to product sales<br>• Access to and creation of new markets |

© Cengage Learning 2015

great cup of coffee. That's why our brand has such relevance in that space. Customers and employees are looking for the truth behind what their company stands for and want to get behind brands that share certain values."[18]

*Packaging* and *branding* are part of the "P" for product. Eco-friendly and biodegradable package designs can position a product at the top of a market. Reduced packaging costs improve economic goals while improving product branding as eco-friendly. When an organization successfully brands the green benefits of a product or service, consumers carry over positive brand-image thinking to other products and services of the company.

In 2011, General Electric created a $5 billion green technology and sustainability initiative called Ecoimagination. The advertising campaign carried a slogan from Jeff Immelt, chairman and CEO: "For GE, imagination at work is more than a slogan or a tagline. It is a reason for being." As part of the initiative, GE opened a call to action for stakeholders (including students) to design breakthrough ideas on how to power your home and the world's energy future. GE funded the challenge with $200 million from venture capital firms. Winners and their innovations were announced on the GE website. The Ecoimagination initiative has proved extremely successful for branding GE as an eco-friendly company. Another example illustrates this type of branding. Marks and Spencer (M&S), one of the United Kingdom's leading retailers selling clothing, food, and home products, also illustrates successful eco-branding. In 2007 M&S launched "Plan A (because there is no plan B)," a five-year responsible management plan that set forth 100 commitments for the company. Their commitments include efforts to reduce $CO_2$ emissions by 50,000 tons, recycle used garments, divert waste from landfills, and invest in community activities.

**Brand equity** typically refers to difference in cost that is charged for a product when its brand is well known versus what the company can charge when the brand is not well known. A pharmaceutical company, for instance, will charge higher costs for medicine with a name brand than it will charge for a generic medicine, although the products are identical. Brand equity refers to brand awareness and brand image. *Brand awareness* means that specific product comes to mind when consumers begin the purchase process. *Brand image* refers to the thoughts and feelings consumers have about the product. When consumers think of a product as "green" or eco-friendly, the product has achieved a sustainable brand image. Interestingly, Starbucks can charge a "sustainability premium" (when consumers pay the higher price for Starbucks) because of its sustainable brand image and involvement in social causes. Brand equity is an important factor not only for the product, where it adds additional value to the product, but also in pricing, where this additional value leads to the possibility to charge a price premium as done by Starbucks.

**Price** is what consumers pay for the product and includes the costs consumers incur with their time and effort. Several major airlines recently engaged in sustainability pricing by giving consumers an opportunity to pay a little above the price of their ticket for carbon offsetting. British Airways, according to their website, "was the first airline to introduce a voluntary passenger carbon offset scheme in 2005 and were also the first airline to achieve the UK Governments Quality of Assurance."[19] Consumers' extra costs, for example, vary £5–£10 for an international

## In Practice

**Luxurious Green**

BMW launched the "i" brand for 2013, which focuses on luxury as sustainable personal transportation.

Source: AutoblogGreen. (2011, February 11). *BMW's new eco sub-brand to be called "i."* Retrieved June 19, 2011, from AutoblogGreen: http://green.autoblog.com/2011/02/21/bmws-new-eco-sub-brand-to-be-called-i/

**Brand equity** refers to difference in cost that is charged for a product when its brand is well known versus what the company can charge when the brand is not well known.

**Price** is what consumers pay for the product and includes the costs consumers incur with their time and effort.

flight. Contributions are automatically calculated based on the volume of carbon dioxide their flight produces. The airlines spend the extra money to buy carbon credits that are registered and verified through the United Nations Kyoto Protocol. The extra credits offset the airplane's carbon emissions by funding of renewable energy schemes, such as funding for hydroelectric power plants and wind farms around the world. Offsetting prices are not an exclusive concept for the external effect of $CO_2$ emissions, but can serve to "inprice" a wide variety of external effects of products and services.

Starbucks Coffee also illustrates the integration of pricing and responsible management as part of it C.A.F.E. fair trade policies, when supporting fair trade pricing for independent coffee growers in East Timor. Targeting consumers in Australia and New Zealand, Starbucks exclusively launched a new Fair Trade compact with East Timor coffee growers. The initiative directly supported the East Timorese farmers to help them become more independent. In a related social activity, Starbucks communicated on its website that it "built a clean water system for the villagers of Goulolo and Estado in the highlands of East Timor that guarantees clean water access for all the local villagers." Such activities help Starbucks to justify a responsible business price-premium on their product.[20]

The **place** is the third "P" of the marketing mix. It is where consumers buy products and services and also implies the means of distributing products to the consumer. The issue of how manufacturers make products available is essential to the marketing mix and responsible management. Manufacturers must ask through what channels they will send their products. How will products and services be distributed? These issues and questions confront manufacturers as significant sustainable issues during decision making about transportation, fuel, and use of natural resources. Those who transport goods must consider indirect and cumulative impacts on the environment, and long-term solutions are required to reduce the use of natural resources. Litman and Burwell[21] suggested, for instance, several environmental sustainability indicators to facilitate transportation analysis: (1) transportation fossil fuel consumption and $CO_2$ emissions: less is better; (2) vehicle pollution emissions: less is better; (3) per capita motor vehicle mileage: less is better; (4) mode split: higher transit ridership is better; (5) traffic crash injuries and deaths: less is better; (6) transport land consumption: less is better; and (7) roadway aesthetic conditions: people tend to be more inclined to care for environments that they consider beautiful and meaningful.

The *place* in marketing also implies how businesses consider a "greener" process of getting materials to customers, such as paperless communication. University classrooms use a significant amount of paper, for example. Less paper is the result of electronic tablets in classrooms such as the Apple iPad and Amazon's Kindle. Martinez and Conaway[22] examined the use of tablet devices in the university classroom and claimed that the devices will gain market share against printed textbooks by 2015. International students can download books immediately and will benefit especially from the use of paperless devices in the classroom. As more universities make the shift to paperless resources, the positive impact on reduced paper use will be significant. Educational institutions will continue to move toward green methods and communication without paper.

The **place** is where consumers buy their products or services and also includes the means of transporting products to the consumer.

**Promotion** is the fourth "P" of the marketing mix. It includes all the messages exchanged between the seller and the ultimate consumer. The promotional mix elements include nonpersonal advertising, personal selling, direct channels to the consumer, and public relations and publicity. Most marketers explain the promotional "push strategy" as communication or persuasion directed from the manufacturer through wholesalers and retailers to the consumer. Company sales representatives, for instance, push their products through intermediaries using trade advertising. Conversely, the promotional "pull strategy" refers to communication directed to end buyers to persuade them to ask retailers for the product. Manufacturers, for example, may market directly to consumers to encourage demand for the newest model of cell phone. In response manufacturers must step up production to meet the growing consumer "pull" for new products.

Advertising, promotion, and responsibility work closely together in IMC. The goal of IMC and responsible business is to provide a consistent message about responsible management activities. The competitive coffee industry provides an example. Thompson[23] reported that increased coffee consumption was attributed to "the National Coffee Association's aggressive promotion of a series of health studies over the past two years that link the antioxidants in coffee to helping fight everything from Type 2 Diabetes to colon cancer."[24] The National Coffee Association's (NCA's) promotional campaign helped common household brands like Procter & Gamble's Folgers brand coffee and Kraft Foods' Maxwell House brand to experience significant growth in sales. The social value of the campaign appealed to the disease-fighting properties of coffee. Thompson[25] also added that Kraft Foods began promoting Yuban, a new coffee aligned with the Rainforest Alliance Certified line, to parallel the appeal of health benefits of coffee. Apparently, the Rainforest certification led to acceptance of Yuban in 1,000 Target stores, up from 300 stores. Target is a large U.S. retailer that competes with Walmart.

> **In Practice**
>
> **Market Differently to Green and Nongreen Audiences**
>
> For committed Greens, helping the earth is enough motivation for a purchase. But for many other consumers, they buy green only if they see advantages personally: luxury, economy, comfort, and so on. Natural foods retailer Whole Foods understands this; some of the company's messaging emphasizes green, local, and fair trade, while other pieces emphasize health or luxury.

## 12-4 PHASE 2: APPLYING RESPONSIBLE MANAGEMENT MARKETING AND COMMUNICATION TOOLS

*"The forms and methods used for sustainability communication are manifold, as are the goals pursued and the tools employed by companies . . . ."[26]*

### 12-4a Spheres of Application of Responsible Management Communication Tools

Responsible management marketing and communication tools are applied toward internal and external stakeholders, which largely reflect the three spheres or types of organizational communication. In order to efficiently apply the marketing and communication tools described in the next section, we first have to understand three types of organizational communication in which they will be applied.

The important question is, "How *well* does a company communicate about its sustainable activities?" Miscommunication and lack of communication occur frequently in organizations, and researchers estimate costs of miscommunication to be in billions of U.S. dollars annually. To avoid frequent communication problems,

**Promotion** includes all the messages exchanged between the seller and the ultimate consumer.

we first examine communication within the organization. **Internal operational communication** describes how communication functions internally; it consists of the structured communication within the organization that directly relates to achieving the organization's work goals.[27] Integrated as part of the organization's plan of operation, internal communication flows along authority lines drawn in the formal organizational chart (downward, upward, and horizontal communication). Internal communication means employee discussions involve work-related tasks and further the organization's primary goals.

Thus, effective internal communication exists at the core of business productivity, good decision making, and effective responsible business communication. Taubken and Leibold[28] emphasize how responsible business communication must begin with top management as a boardroom priority. Responsible management is interdisciplinary in the company and requires direction, coordination, and support from top management. Communication must be synchronized throughout the company. According to the Economist Intelligence Unit,[29] approximately 30 percent of board level meeting time by 2012 will center around topics touching on social and environmental performance of businesses.

Cinépolis, the fourth-largest movie theater chain in the world, illustrates successful internal employee responsible business communication that promoted a social activity and increased the economic bottom line of the company. Employees of the movie theater chain developed strong ownership of the visual health activity, which resulted in Cinépolis exceeding social and economic goals. Effective internal responsible management communication about social and environmental business performance, from top management to employees, will determine how well businesses thrive in the new global business environment.

Internal responsible management communication may originate in the human resources (HR) office, depending on the company's organizational structure. According to Cohen,[30] the HR manager can use dialogue-based forums or interactive communication tools to communicate responsible management activities. Internal social networking tools such as Facebook pages and blogspots are effective. Participative dialogues, such as stakeholder conference calls, participative webinars and webcasts, virtual conferences and meetings, and online company talk sessions, may prove effective with employees. Many companies have their own Twitter accounts. All these tools can help brand responsible management activities internally among employees. Employees may need to be trained in using these tools. The HR office will most likely be the designated group to do the training.

**External operational communication**, which occurs when employees communicate with people and groups outside the organization to achieve the organization's work goals,[31] is equally as important as internal operational communication. External communication fits closely to the marketing and public relations functions and the variety of messages an organization sends to the public. Such messages include press releases, advertisements through traditional media, and branding efforts. External communication involves new media such as blogs, Facebook, Twitter, communication on corporate websites, and dialogue with customers about sustainability.

**Personal communication** is simply all the non-business-related exchanges of information and feelings in which human beings engage whenever they come together,[32] including in the organization. Human beings are by nature social creatures. Personal communication occurs when employees engage in discussions

**Internal operational communication** consists of the structured communication within the organization that directly relates to achieving the organization's work goals.

**External operational communication** occurs when employees communicate with people and groups outside the organization to achieve the organization's work goals.

**Personal communication** is all the non-business-related exchanges of information and feelings in which human beings engage whenever they come together.

"around the water cooler" about politics, family matters, personal relationships, or purchase of cars. Topics of discussion may center on scores in a tennis match, golf game, or a planned, special vacation. Expressions of feelings also are part of personal communication. Individuals may vent anger or frustration about their jobs.

Personal communication is also termed *informal communication* because it does not follow through the organization's formal channels. This "grapevine" of communication flows throughout the organization in different directions, forming a web or network among employees. Informal communication tends to increase when organizations move through periods of instability, acquisition, or personnel change, primarily when information is lacking about such events. Rumors feed the informal communication channel. As a result, top management may try to control or eliminate altogether the informal communication channel. Supervisors complain that socializing keeps employees from their jobs, and management believes employees are wasting company time.

More recently, personal communication has become an important issue to policy makers because of the amount of time employees spend text-messaging for social reasons, conducting personal Web searches and purchases, or making personal phone calls at work. The "grapevine" cannot be eliminated from the organization, but it can be monitored and accepted as part of it. Policy makers must discern a balance between making too restrictive boundaries for the informal channel and giving too much freedom for employees to communicate personally on the job. An "unhealthy" organizational climate will exhibit signs of excessive personal communication including rumors and inaccurate information. Managers who promote a "healthy" communication climate give sufficient information to employees. Sufficient amounts of information and transparency help reduce an overactive, inaccurate organizational grapevine.

## 12-4b Responsible Management Communication Tools

Next, we review marketing and communication tools directly related to social and environmental business performance. As illustrated in Figure 12.7, these tools are characterized by different intended outcomes of the marketing and communication process. The intended outcome of social marketing, for instance, is a change in a stakeholder's behavior, while cause-related marketing usually aims at increasing sales revenues, a code of ethics aims at ensuring morally right behavior, and reports aim at extensive and factual information on the organization's responsible business performance.

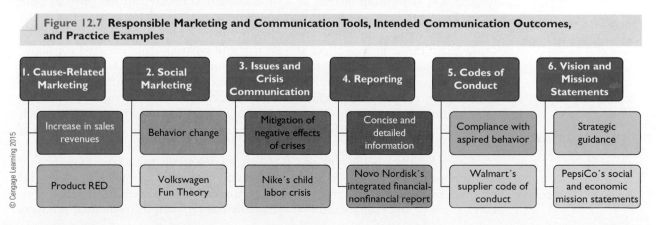

**Figure 12.7 Responsible Marketing and Communication Tools, Intended Communication Outcomes, and Practice Examples**

| 1. Cause-Related Marketing | 2. Social Marketing | 3. Issues and Crisis Communication | 4. Reporting | 5. Codes of Conduct | 6. Vision and Mission Statements |
|---|---|---|---|---|---|
| Increase in sales revenues | Behavior change | Mitigation of negative effects of crises | Concise and detailed information | Compliance with aspired behavior | Strategic guidance |
| Product RED | Volkswagen Fun Theory | Nike's child labor crisis | Novo Nordisk's integrated financial-nonfinancial report | Walmart's supplier code of conduct | PepsiCo's social and economic mission statements |

© Cengage Learning 2015

For successful and integrated stakeholder marketing and communication, more than one communication tool might need to be applied to jointly produce an overall message for the creation of stakeholder goodwill. The tools listed in the following are a representative selection of a broader set.

### Cause-Related Marketing (CRM)

In the field of responsible management, **cause-related marketing** refers to the promotion of a product by linking its sales with a contribution to a good cause (CRM here is not to be confused with "customer relationship management"). Such a relationship between a cause and marketing activities can be established in different forms. The traditional *donation-based CRM* is to channel a certain part of the product price to a donation. For instance, Danone in Mexico once a year donates a part of its sales revenues to support child cancer treatment. The TOMS shoe company donates a pair of shoes every time somebody buys a pair. In Germany, for every beer crate bought from the brewer Krombacher, the company spends money to safeguard one square meter of rainforest. Probably the most salient cause-related marketing program on a world level is *Product RED*, which allows companies to systematically connect sales of so-called "RED-product lines" to channel parts of revenues to the causes of "eliminating AIDS."[33] This traditional type of CRM is probably the most direct link between responsible management activity and tangible business benefit. This is why Varadarajan and Menon[34] frame cause-related marketing as "a way for a company to do well by doing good."[35] Traditional CRM may be technically defined as "the process of formulating and implementing marketing activities that are characterized by an offer from the firm to contribute a specified amount to a designated cause when customers engage in revenue-providing exchanges that satisfy organizational and individual objectives."[36] Thus, cause-related marketing connects an effective communication strategy to a good social or environmental cause. Similarly, Pringle and Thompson[37] define cause-related marketing "as a strategic positioning and marketing tool which links a company or brand to a relevant social cause or issue, for mutual benefit."[38] Customers will purchase cause-related products when all other aspects about the product are satisfactory. The rationale of cause-related marketing is to create a mutually reinforcing relationship between the product sales enhancing effect and the furthering of the cause by a donation. In this chapter, we will use the terms *cause marketing* and *cause-related marketing* synonymously.

The traditional type of CRM relates on causes mostly unconnected to the product's characteristics and socioenvironmental life-cycle performance. The *product-based CRM* is focusing instead on causes directly connected to the product's life cycle. Products with improved socioenvironmental life-cycle performance, also called sustainable innovation products, do have a "built-in" cause-relation, the cause being the improved effect and society and environment. The two consumer packaged-goods industry giants, P&G and Unilever, have both launched a wide variety of sustainable innovation products with mostly environmental life-cycle improvements. Fair trade products use added social value in the supply chain as a sales argument. Organic products combine a wide variety of different causes such as local production, customer health, and support of sustainable agriculture, among others.

*Cause-branding* is the type of CRM that relates whole brands to a good cause and supports the marketing of all products under the brand umbrella. The high-end products or luxury items market, including brands such as Gucci, Yves Saint Laurent, IWC, Garnier, and Louis Vuitton, traditionally has required differentiated products

**Cause-related marketing** is the promotion of a product by linking its sales with the contribution to a good cause.

and expensive items. In a study published by the World Wildlife Federation–United Kingdom (WWF-UK), Bendell and Kleanthous[39] ranked the world's top luxury companies on their green performance and assessed relevant attitudes in the industry. Their analysis revealed a compelling reason for the top luxury brands to incorporate social and environmental excellence and to communicate this excellence to consumers in all markets. Bendell and Kleanthous[40] concluded their report with a statement that "Brand and marketing professionals on both client and agency sides can unlock the latent commercial potential of sustainable luxury brands, provided that they do so in an authentic and systematic way."[41] Their report concluded with a ten-point plan with an emphasis on communication as one of the points. A luxury design brand that has achieved a strong cause-branding is the exclusive Danish company FLOWmarket, which is based on simplistic design packaging products, all of them providing a message explicitly challenging people to adopt specific socially and environmentally sustainable behaviors; this is FLOWmarket's cause. The FLOWmarket is a combination between cause-related marketing and the marketing tool of social marketing, marketing for behavior change, which we describe next.

**In Practice**

**CRM + SM = ?**
The Danish design company FLOWmarket combines cause-related and social marketing by using the cause of behavior change toward sustainability as the predominant sales argument.

## Social Marketing (SM)

In contrast to cause-related marketing, **social marketing** is directed at change in a stakeholder's behavior. SM has traditionally been a tool of governments and civil society organizations to promote aspired behavior patterns, such as nonsmoking, the usage of condoms, and healthier nutrition. Companies can use social marketing to predominantly change customers' and employees' behavior toward responsible behavior patterns. SM is often misunderstood as purely awareness raising, but in reality, increased awareness of the necessity to change behavior is merely the first step toward behavior adoption, followed by the consideration, adoption, and maintenance of a new behavior pattern.[42] Armstrong and Kotler[43] adopt the Social Marketing Institute's definition of social marketing as "the use of commercial marketing concepts and tools in programs designed to influence individuals' behavior to improve their well-being and that of society."[44] Figure 12.8 illustrates how the marketing mix is applied to achieve behavior change.

Weinreich[45] points to the difference between commercial marketing and social marketing. In social marketing, "the benefits accrue to the individual or society rather

**Social marketing** is an application of traditional marketing techniques in order to effect a behavior change that benefits the single individual or the society at large.

| Figure 12.8 **The Social Marketing Mix** | |
|---|---|
| **Product** | **Price** |
| The behavior the target audience should adopt; preferably this behavior is directly observable and offering a solution to a problem. | The behavior the target audience has to give up to adopt the aspired behavior; involves intangible costs, such as time, effort, and emotional costs, as well as the tangible costs of realizing the change in behavior. |
| **Place** | **Promotion** |
| The place of behavior change should be where the target audience is acting the behavior to be given up, and where the audience experiences the highest possible aperture to a potential behavior change. | The marketing promotion of behavior change involves the communication of the aspired behavior, throughout manifold audiences (Publics), involving Partnerships, and taking into consideration public Policies. |

Source: Adapted from Weinreich, N. K. (2011). *Hands-on social marketing: A step-by-step guide to designing change for good,* 2nd ed. Thousand Oaks, CA: Sage.

than to the marketer's organization."[46] Social marketing applies to individuals rather than organizations. Nevertheless, examples such as FLOWmarket show how companies can simultaneously change peoples' behavior to the better and improve company reputation or even tangibly increase sales in a combined social and cause-related marketing campaign. The Volkswagen "Fun Theory Contest" has been a role-model example for a social marketing campaign, communicating the company's inclination to good social and environmental causes, while tangibly changing peoples' behavior.[47]

*Societal marketing* is a slightly different concept and shifts the perspective from the consumer to the marketer. Kotler[48] conceptualized societal marketing as "the organization's task to determine the needs, wants, and interests of target markets to deliver the desired satisfactions more effectively and efficiently than competitors in a way that preserves or enhances the consumer's and the society's well-being."[49]

### Issues and Crisis Communication

The term **issues and crisis communication** is simply defined as that communication which occurs in any situation threatening to the company or its reputation. Most company crises begin in social, environmental, or ethical issues and therefore clearly fall into the realm of responsible management. For example, Nike's crisis began after the company was accused of accepting child labor in its suppliers' factories.[50] The establishment of a website, Nikebiz.com, proved an effective communication tool to manage the crisis. BP's 2010 crisis began after an oil well experienced a blowout in the Gulf of Mexico. Crisis communication has an important role in the long-established field of public relations and has gained considerable importance in relation to social and environmental business performance.

A company's communication in crisis will vary according to the situation. The choice of channels is dependent on the context in which the crisis occurs. Most important, the organization must have a plan to follow before a crisis begins. The plan will dictate who talks with whom, what information will be distributed, and what actions the organization will take. A crisis may require the organization to stop distribution of a product, place a hold on its stock, or secure the safety of certain employees. When a company representative first meets with the public, transparency of information is of upmost importance. Crisis communication brings principles five, six, and seven into sharper focus: complete and accurate communication, establishing goodwill, and maintaining credibility. When the earthquake and tsunami occurred in Japan in 2011, the credibility of the Japanese government came into question because of initial incomplete information about the nuclear reactor. Concern and goodwill must be expressed for those affected by the crisis.

In 2008, a crisis occurred that we mentioned earlier. Maple Leaf Foods, a major Canadian food processing company, was involved in one of the worst cases of food contamination in Canadian history.[51] Maple Leaf's Toronto meat processing facility was contaminated with Listeria. An epidemic of listeriosis spread through 200-plus meat products, and twenty people eventually died. Many more became ill as a result of the bacteria. Once the outbreak became known, the CEO opted for an open and transparent communication strategy. Greenberg and Elliott[52] stated, "In contrast to organizations that have confronted crisis situations by avoiding and

**Issues and crisis communication** is communication that occurs in any situation threatening to the company or its reputation.

displacing blame, or keeping silent and maintaining a low profile, Maple Leaf opted for a strategy of high visibility."[53] President and CEO Michael H. McCain publicly acknowledged through television that Listeria had been found in some of the company's products and apologized to those affected. The apology was well accepted. The broadcast was later displayed on YouTube and discussed on blogs. The effective communication response was acknowledged with recognition by the Canadian press. Patel and Reinsch[54] have pointed out that a company in the United States can apologize for an injury caused by a product without creating legal liability for the company. Laws in other countries may dictate otherwise.

## Codes of Conduct

**Codes of conduct** are behavior standards agreed to by a company that governs relationships with various stakeholders. Codes of conduct within a company are often related to society, environment, and ethical topics. These codes are an important tool for communicating aspired social and environmental performance of key stakeholders (employees, suppliers, managers, and customers). A company may also agree on standardized codes existing outside its governance. The Retail Environmental Sustainability Code[55] exists as a code of conduct to which companies may sign and agree to follow. Signatories commit to reduce the environmental footprint of their operations in sourcing, resource efficiency, transport and distribution, waste management, communication, and reporting. The communication component encourages companies to encourage consumers to practice more sustainable consumption and promote responsible consumer behavior with product use and disposal.

Walmart's *Supplier Sustainability Assessment* illustrates an example of a code of conduct that effectively communicates the need for sustainable business practices to an extensive supplier network.[56] Suppliers must address fifteen questions before developing a business relationship. The questions query about areas of sustainability, such as if their product or service will help reduce energy costs and greenhouse gas emissions, reduce waste and enhance quality, produce high-quality responsibly sourced raw materials, and ensure responsible and ethical production. In other words, suppliers must know the location of 100 percent of the facilities that produce their product(s) before doing business with Walmart.

## Formal Reports

**Formal sustainability reports** of social and environmental business performance are a common practice among most multinational corporations. These documents appear as links on corporate websites or exist as separate websites and cover topics of sustainability, citizenship, or responsibility. According to Thurm,[57] the birth of global sustainability reporting began in Rio de Janeiro in 1997 with the Rio Declaration and the Agenda 21. Although no formal documents or standards were produced at the Rio conference, the groundwork was laid for the formal Global Reporting Initiative (GRI) to become a reality five years later. Today, these standards are globally accepted and followed worldwide. GRI guidelines can be downloaded and online training in writing reports is offered at www.globalreporting.org.

Thurm[58] estimated that there are "around 60,000 multinational companies on the planet, and only a small percentage actually publish sustainability reports."[59] By contrast, he estimated more than 70 percent of Fortune 500 companies are publishing sustainability reports. Perhaps these larger companies will lead other multinational enterprises in sustainability reporting by following GRI guidelines. When

**Codes of conduct** are behavior standards agreed to by a company that governs relationships with various stakeholders.

**Formal sustainability reports** focus on the factual, concise, and extensive description of an organization's social and environmental business performance.

communicating through sustainability reports, companies must first of all be transparent. Openness and accuracy with information creates credibility and prevents greenwashing. Although evidence in the past has been "scant" that corporate sustainability reporting is effective, Blanding[60] reported that mandatory responsible business reporting indeed works. He stated that researchers who analyzed government websites, NGO publications, and investor reports found that sixteen countries, from Australia to the United Kingdom, had mandated responsible business reporting.

## Mission and Vision Statements

From a communication perspective, corporate **mission and vision statements** serve as strategic communication tools and a lighthouse to provide guidance for all actions and behaviors of the company and its employees. A vision statement describes what a company ultimately wants to become and achieve. Williams[61] restated a definition of a corporate mission statement as one that "tells two things about a company: who it is and what it does."[62] Vision and mission statements project corporate philosophy[63] and are used to define behavior and values in a company.[64] Thus, a mission statement strategically reflects the communication of top management's commitment to areas of responsibility by its wording and implementation. Several examples illustrate the matter of incorporating and communicating a "social" mission as part of the mission statement.

French-based Valeo Group, for instance, communicates "Automotive Technology, Naturally" in large letters across its website. The home page is replete with green colors, drawings of trees, green grass, and blue sky. The company's name is portrayed in green letters. Looking deeper into the company's sustainable activities, the visitor knows the green designs are obviously more than greenwashing. Originating in Paris, the Valeo Group ranks among the world's top automotive suppliers and globally employs more than 60,000 people operating in twenty-seven countries. According to Valeo's primary strategy or mission, the company exists to reduce global $CO_2$ emissions in emerging markets. The company signed the United Nations Global Compact in 2004 and has emerged as a leader in green automotive technology. The company's mission matches its actions, and it has achieved a balance between effective communication and responsible management activities.

PepsiCo also has a more focused social mission and vision statement. The company's website personifies itself as a responsible corporate citizen, which "is not only the right thing to do, but the right thing to do for our business."[65] Its mission statement addresses the economic bottom line, to become "the world's premier consumer products company focused on convenient foods and beverages," while it addresses responsibility, environmental stewardship, and benefits to society. As a consequence, PepsiCo has also established a worldwide Code of Conduct that incorporates responsibility with integrity and with high ethical standards, which shows how the six mentioned responsible communication and marketing tools are interconnected in their usage.

In the next section we describe the communication process, channels of communication, and a model of stakeholder communication. We believe that the strategy of dialogue and involvement with stakeholders, with the intent to build a relationship, is at the core of a well-functioning organization, vital to marketing, and key to how stakeholders view responsibility management.

**Mission and vision statements** define an organization's identity and purpose and serve as a lighthouse, guiding the company's and its employees' actions and behaviors.

## 12-5 PHASE 3: CUSTOMIZING STAKEHOLDER COMMUNICATION

*"Messages about corporate ethical and socially responsible initiatives are likely to evoke strong and often positive reactions among stakeholders. Research has even pointed to the potential business benefits of the internal and external communication of corporate social responsibility (CSR) efforts."[66]*

### 12-5a A Stakeholder Communication Model

The seven communication principles referred to in the first part of this chapter apply principles to all stakeholders. According to Freeman,[67] a stakeholder is anyone who makes a difference in the organization, and Freeman defines stakeholder as "any group or individual who can affect or is affected by the achievement of the organization's objectives."[68] In today's responsible business terms, is a 12-year-old Indonesian boy sewing shoes for Nike a stakeholder? Are the workers in an Asian factory stakeholders? When we read the Nike case, we understood that anyone who affects the organization's objectives may be considered a stakeholder. Morsing and Schultz[69] offer a model by which we may incorporate and apply the preceding communication principles. Integrating Weick's "sense-making" concepts,[70] Morsing and Schultz[71] observe businesses as having three communication strategies with stakeholders (see Figure 12.9).

First, the *stakeholder information strategy* is essentially a one-way communication process. Communication is viewed by a company as "telling, not listening," and may be persuasive in nature. The company releases information about CSR activities to the public, and the news releases may make comparisons between past CSR activities and current levels of activities. Morsing and Schultz[72] assert this one-way information may be necessary, but it is not enough. They observe that 50 percent of all companies practice one-way communication (in terms of public

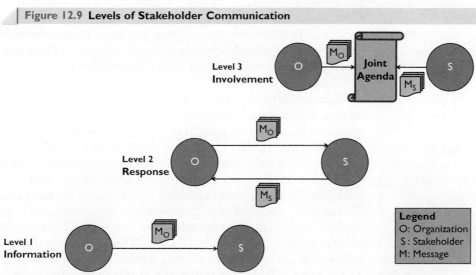

**Figure 12.9 Levels of Stakeholder Communication**

Level 3 Involvement

Level 2 Response

Level 1 Information

Legend
O: Organization
S: Stakeholder
M: Message

Source: Adapted from Morsing, M., & Schultz, M. (2006). Corporate social responsibility communication: Stakeholder information, response and involvement strategies. *Business Ethics: A European Review*, 15(4), 323–338.

information) to their stakeholders. Significantly fewer companies engage in two-way communication. Stakeholders respond to this strategy by indirectly influencing the company's CSR activities. Stakeholders positively support the activity by purchasing products and supporting responsible management activities, or they negatively support the activity by boycotting products and protesting the social or environmental impacts of the company. In either reaction, the company is generally unresponsive to stakeholders.

Second, Morsing and Schultz[73] identify the *stakeholder response strategy* as a two-way communication process identified by communication flowing to and from the public. The company listens to comments or feedback about its responsible management activities and even changes or modifies its activities as a result. Yet the company listens primarily to determine what stakeholders, such as activists or NGOs, will accept or tolerate. Top management may even see the need for endorsements by some stakeholders. Thus, communication appears asymmetric or unbalanced. Companies tend to send more information toward stakeholders and receive fewer messages from them. Stakeholders may have passive influence in this strategy, but the company sometimes only hears its "own voice reflected back."

Third, Morsing and Schultz[74] consider the *stakeholder involvement strategy* as a dialogue or relationship with stakeholders. The company and stakeholder engage in "sense making" and co-construction of ideas, activities, and behaviors. They seek value creation and the process of developing a long-term mutual relationship. The stakeholder involvement strategy implies that "managers can manage not the stakeholders themselves, but relationships with stakeholders."[75] We promote Morsing and Schultz's model to support strong dialogue and relationship with stakeholders. By strategically involving these constituencies, responsible management communication will improve over time.

Palazzo[76] emphasizes the importance of stakeholder dialogue and examines what is necessary for that dialogue to work. She states the goal of stakeholder dialogue is "to investigate constellations of interests and issues concerning the company and the stakeholders, exchange opinions, clarify expectations, enhance mutual understanding and, if possible, find new and better solutions."[77] In other words, when the company is identifying certain activities, it engages with or negotiates with stakeholders to identify that activity. Dialogue with stakeholders displays frequent and pro-active communication. The stakeholders themselves may be involved in creation of corporate messages.

Palazzo highlights the example of ABB, one of the world's leading engineering companies that manufactures electrical products that provide electrical power to customers. When ABB initiated its first corporate social policy in 2001, the company involved a variety of stakeholders from thirty-four countries from the very beginning. As a result, the first corporate social policy was launched. According to its webpage, the company established a "[n]etwork of environmental controllers appointed for countries and factories. Thirty-eight countries participate in start-up of ABB's environmental management program. First reporting procedures introduced."[78] ABB's approach demonstrated the stakeholder involvement strategy.

## 12-5b Stakeholder Audience Analysis

When you choose to follow the communication strategy of *stakeholder involvement*, you will begin a dialogue and build a relationship with stakeholders. In Phase 1 of this chapter, you learned to apply communication principles by first analyzing your audience. This section discusses how to analyze your audience of stakeholders and to conduct an analysis of specific stakeholder characteristics. To analyze your audience of stakeholders, Freeman[79] developed a new "filing system" of stakeholder groups that helps us understand the different categories. He identified primary stakeholders as business owners, customers, employees, suppliers, governments, competitors, media, and community groups (consumer advocates, environmentalists, and special interest groups).

As a communicator, you first must make a comprehensive assessment of the stakeholder group with whom you want to communicate and identify that group's purpose, mission, and interests. Is your goal to inform or persuade the stakeholder? What do you want them to know, do, or feel? Communication principle two will be applied when you clarify your communication purpose or goal. Use the questions in Figure 12.10 to help you analyze your stakeholders.

Most companies communicate to multiple stakeholders with a single message. The communiqué may be placed on their websites through annual reports, CEO letters, or sustainability reports. These reports communicate to multiple groups at one time, such as investors, government entities, employees, or customers. If a crisis occurs, a CEO may speak to the public through the media, but the message reaches many stakeholders. We define a *primary stakeholder* as the one your company most wants to develop a relationship with, influence the most, or the one with whom the company can achieve its goal or purpose. A *secondary stakeholder* might read your communication or learn about the information, but was not the one to whom the original message was directed. An *intermediate stakeholder* may be one that simply forwards the message to others. The media, for instance, may serve as an intermediate stakeholder by announcing sustainable activities of your company to customers or investors.

---

**Figure 12.10 Stakeholder Profiling Questionnaire**

Have you distinguished the types of stakeholders?

- Which one is primary?
- Which one is intermediate?
- Which one is secondary?

Do you understand the stakeholder?

- What does the stakeholder know?
- What does the stakeholder feel?
- What does the stakeholder *want* to know and feel?
- What can the stakeholder do?

Do you understand your relationship to the stakeholder? (Have you determined your goals?)

- What does your company want the stakeholder to know?
- What does your company want the stakeholder to feel?
- What does your company want the stakeholder to do?

Is your company perceived as credible by the stakeholder?

- Is your company considered reliable and believable?
- What does your company need to do to gain the stakeholder's trust?

Source: Adapted from Andrews, D. C., & Andrews, W. D. (2004). *Management communication: A guide* (p. 24). Boston: Houghton Mifflin.

What a stakeholder "feels" means that the message simply considers the emotions of those who receive it. When a company communicates, receivers often respond emotionally, positively or negatively, to a particular sustainable activity, and those feelings of stakeholders must be taken into account. Communicators must also take into account what a stakeholder *wants* to know and feel. A company may be answering one question while the stakeholder is thinking about a completely different question. Thus, stakeholder analysis intersects with the purpose of the message and takes into consideration the questions in Figure 12.10. The assessment will identify the primary stakeholder, seek to understand what that stakeholder knows and feels, understand the relationship with the stakeholder, and accurately assess the company's credibility with the stakeholder.

*Mapping and Describing Stakeholder Characteristics.* Freeman, Harrison, and Wicks[80] offer seven in-depth techniques for creating value with stakeholders. These insightful techniques apply directly to our assessment of stakeholders when we communicate about responsible management activities. We will not review all the techniques because some of the concepts have been covered earlier in this chapter. The field of business responsibility may provide deeper insight into stakeholder communication and engagement. Their seven techniques are (1) stakeholder assessment, (2) stakeholder behavior analysis, (3) understanding stakeholders in more depth, (4) assessing stakeholder strategies, (5) developing specific strategies for stakeholders, (6) creating new modes of interaction with stakeholders, and (7) developing integrative value creation strategies. We adapt a matrix from the first technique, stakeholder assessment, to illustrate how marketing tools and general communication tools fit stakeholder interest in sustainability activities.[81] When a company identifies a specific group of stakeholders and conducts an analysis of each stakeholder, Freeman and colleagues[82] suggest developing a matrix of concerns or issues from the information that is available. The information that is available may be displayed in a matrix by showing categories of stakeholders along the horizontal or top dimension and various issues along the vertical dimension. We adapt this matrix (see Figure 12.11) to sustainability tools and list six stakeholder categories across the top of the matrix and six tools along the side. A legend at the bottom of the matrix rates the appropriateness of each marketing tool and general communication tool with stakeholder categories. We recommend this matrix as a summary at the end of this chapter because it can be used as an application tool to analyze effective stakeholder communication.

**Figure 12.11 Stakeholder-Communication-Tools Matrix**

| | Employees | Customers | Government | Community | Shareholders | Suppliers |
|---|---|---|---|---|---|---|
| Cause-Related Marketing | 5 | 1 | 5 | 5 | 3 | 5 |
| Social Marketing | 1 | 1 | 5 | 3 | 5 | 3 |
| Issues and Crisis Communication | 1 | 3 | 3 | 3 | 1 | 3 |
| Codes of Conduct | 1 | 3 | 5 | 5 | 5 | 1 |
| Formal Reports | 3 | 5 | 3 | 3 | 1 | 5 |
| Mission and Vision Statements | 1 | 5 | 3 | 3 | 1 | 5 |

© 1 = highly appropriate to stakeholder; 3 = somewhat appropriate to stakeholder; 5 = not very appropriate to stakeholder

I.   The goal of responsible marketing communication management is to help define the vision of a responsible business, to then support the implementation process, and to finally create *stakeholder goodwill*, which translates into tangible business benefits.

II.  Stakeholder goodwill can be achieved by activities of *integrated marketing communication*, which serve to craft a multifaceted, but congruently connected message about organizations' responsible management performance to the various stakeholder groups.

III. *Effective responsible management communication* is summed up in the seven principles of audience adaptation, purpose clarification, message clarity, topical conciseness, completeness and accuracy, goodwill creation, and credibility.

IV.  Effective marketing of responsible management activities depends on the successful integration of responsible-management activities into the *four Ps*—product, price, place, and promotion—comprising the marketing mix.

V.   Successfully communicating responsible management activities requires the usage of specific *responsible management communication tools*. The main tools proposed in this chapter are cause-related marketing, social marketing, issues and crisis communication, formal reporting, codes of conduct, and mission and vision statements. Each tool serves a different communication purpose from increase in sales to behavior change and the assurance of ethical compliance.

VI.  *Stakeholder communication types* can be classified into three levels. Higher levels mean there is higher intensity in the communication activity. Level one is stakeholder information, two is response, and three is stakeholder involvement.

VII. In order to customize the stakeholder communication tools to a specific audience, a thorough *stakeholder analysis* has to ensure the appropriateness of communications for distinct stakeholder groups.

## RESPONSIBLE MARKETING COMMUNICATION CHECKLIST

| Process Phase | | Sustainability | Responsibility | Ethics |
|---|---|---|---|---|
| Phase 1: Ensuring effective marketing communication | Does your marketing communication . . . | . . . effectively create messages that promote sustainable development? | . . . effectively communicate to a broad set of stakeholders? | . . . avoid misleading impressions of your social and environmental performance? |
| Phase 2: Applying marketing communication tools | Do the marketing communication tools applied . . . | . . . create social, environmental, and economic value? | . . . create the maximum overall value for stakeholders possible? | . . . work without causing moral issues? |
| Phase 3: Customizing stakeholder communication | Does the customization of your stakeholder communication . . . | . . . support the process of co-creation of social, environmental, and economic value? | . . . lead to profound stakeholder involvement, based on a deep understanding? | . . . help to avoid and mitigate moral issues related to stakeholders? |

## KEY TERMS

barriers 373
brand equity 379
cause-related marketing 384
channels 372
codes of conduct 387
decoding 373
effective communication 371
encoding 373
external operational communication 382
feedback 373

formal sustainability reports 387
greenwashing 376
integrated marketing communication (IMC) 370
internal operational communication 382
issues and crisis communication 386
marketing mix 378
message 371
mission and vision statements 388

personal communication 382
place 380
price 379
product 378
promotion 381
receiver 371
sender 371
social marketing 385
stakeholder communication 369
stakeholder goodwill 369

## A. Remember and Understand

A.1.   Paraphrase the seven rules of effective communication.

A.2.   Describe greenwashing. How does it relate to effective communication?

A.3.   Define the terms *effective communication, stakeholder communication,* and *integrated marketing communication,* and explain how they are interrelated.

A.4.   Mention the three levels of stakeholder involvement and describe their operational characteristics.

## B. Apply and Experience

B.5.   Sketch the communication process as described in Figure 12.3, graphically integrating how responsible management activities play a role in the process.

B.6.   Look up the responsible business website of a multinational corporation online and find one example for each of the six communication tools highlighted in this chapter.

B.7.   Prepare a conceptual plan for a social marketing campaign for a desired behavior change of your choice.

## C. Analyze and Evaluate

C.8.   Identify two cause-related marketing campaigns of your choice and evaluate the congruence between stakeholder value and communication effectiveness using Figure 12.5.

C.9.   Identify one responsible marketing and communication management activity of a company of your choice. Then use the seven principles of effective communication to check how the campaign could increase its effectiveness.

C.10.  Review the matrix displayed in Figure 12.11 and assume no numbers exist in the boxes. Choose a company with a prominent responsible management activity. Add numbers to the matrix by rating the appropriateness of the company's communications with example stakeholders listed at the top of the matrix. Fill in each box.

## D. Change and Create

D.11.  Write a code of ethics for one of the following cases: (a) the sales department of a weapons producer, (b)investors on Wall Street, (c)the marketing department of an international beer producer.

D.12.  Browse through the responsible management webpages of companies that you are a customer of with a special focus on transparency. Detect what information of interest for customers is not provided. Then contact the company and request that it make this information available to you.

## PIONEER INTERVIEW WITH PHILIP KOTLER

Courtesy of Philip Kotler

Philip Kotler has been the leading academic figure in marketing for decades. In his standard textbook, he has early covered social marketing and cause-related marketing. He has published a stand-alone textbook on social marketing, and on corporate social responsibility. In his recent work, he focuses on creating a new area of marketing, called "Marketing 3.0," that has many characteristics of what might be a responsible marketing for a sustainable future.

**In your recent book, *Marketing 3.0: From Products to Customers to the Human Spirit,* you draft a new type of marketing that involves multiple stakeholders, and which centrally addresses environmental concerns and sociocultural transformation. Is this the blueprint for a new marketing for a sustainable future?**

Marketing has been moving through three stages. Marketing 1.0 involved marketers appealing to the *mind* of their target audience, trying to establish that the idea that their product was best for the customer. Marketing 2.0 involved marketers moving their appeal to the *heart* of the target customer by adding emotion. Marketing 3.0 involves marketers moving their appeal to the *spirit*, or "caring quality" of the audience. More members of the middle class are caring about the environment and sustainability and are increasingly able to evaluate which companies have this set of values.

**In 1972 you published an article titled "Demarketing, Yes, Demarketing" in the *Harvard Business Review.* Back then you framed**

demarketing differently, but do you think a new task for today's marketers might be to de-market unsustainable consumption patterns? Can and should marketing professionals de-market consumerism?

Our concept of demarketing originally dealt with responding to shortages. For example, when California faced a water shortage, the state ran several campaigns to persuade people and companies to use less water. We believe that demarketing campaigns will increase as we overuse scarce resources and face resource limits to growth. In a city such as Beijing, good-quality air is becoming scarce and 9,000 persons have needed to be hospitalized because of respiratory problems. The underlying issue is whether we are overselling consumerism, namely, that the good life consists of accumulating more and more material goods. I can imagine the startup of campaigns to de-market our current consumerist lifestyle. These campaigns will be fought by business, but I favor "airing" the issue of how much consumption the earth can support.

Cause-related marketing has been praised as a powerful funding instrument to support a good cause and a powerful branding tool for companies. In the case of some companies, cause-related marketing has been criticized as "greenwashing." How should cause-related marketing be used to maximize its positive and to minimize its potential negative effects?

I am in favor of companies offering consumers a "cause" incentive to buy their products. Cause marketing received its big boost when American Express offered to donate money to help rebuild the Statue of Liberty in proportion to how much people charged their American Express card instead of competitors' credit cards in paying for their purchases. I like the shoe company that will give a pair of shoes to a poor person somewhere in the world when you buy a pair of their shoes. Even though some "greenwashing" is occurring, where the effort is more about image-making than really caring about the cause, I think most of it is sincere and leads competitors to reconsider their purpose as a company and what they can contribute to the social good.

## PRACTITIONER PROFILE: ADELA LUSTYKOVA

Courtesy of Adela Lustykova

**Employing organization:** Chládek & Tintěra, Inc., is a construction company with a universal production schedule operating in the Czech market for more than twenty years. Its characteristics are tradition, modern principles, and dynamic development. **Job title:** Marketing and PR Specialist **Education:** Bachelor in Business Administration and Management, University of J.E.Purkyně, Ústí nad Labem, Czech Republic; Master of Arts in Responsible Management (proceeding), Steinbeis University Berlin, Germany

### In Practice

**What are your responsibilities?**

Creating brand, reputation, and visual face of the company (including paperback presentation, business cards, e-commerce, and CSR activities), active sales role in key sales opportunities, direct B2B communication, fair representative, managing CSR activities.

**What are typical activities you carry out during a day at work?**

Seeking for potential business partners and ventures with the target of private investors, mainly, direct communication with investors, partners, and customers; making reference sheets and other graphic presentation materials; development of online presentations.

**How do sustainability, responsibility, and ethics topics play a role in your job?**

Sustainability, responsibility, and ethics are core issues that have been respected through the whole company since its founding. The triple bottom line concept is so rooted in the company culture that no one really needs to think how to act. In some cases, sustainability is a mirror of some law requirements, but on the contrary, responsibility is needed for successful communication with stakeholders and so is practiced rather intuitively. When dealing with business partners or other stakeholders, we are always precise on what we promise, never are nontransparent, and take the full responsibilities for every action and every one of our subcontractors. In the case of ethics, employees are aware of the company's values and deal according to them. This creates the common good and becomes the company culture.

## Out of the topics covered in the chapter into which your interview will be included, which concepts, tools, or topics are most relevant to your work?

External stakeholder communication is a topic that is very important for my company. For a proper marketing communication, we are very sensitive in building familiar relationships with investors, business partners, or governmental organizations. In this case, effective communication must be applied, and creating positive awareness shows a part of our brand image. That is also connected to the marketing mix that we shape in a responsible manner. But firstly, we care about proper internal communication that must be effective. Otherwise, the further processes are not.

Also, my company touches the intensity of communication, which is rather low. There are CSR activities effectively put into reality, but no one talks about them; the company is rather shy. That is the reason why we have started to focus more on the visual face of the company as a part of our external communication.

Crisis communication also plays a crucial role. When facing some negative affairs in the past, we needed to solve the issue without harming anyone. We always did it in a responsible manner because we are aware that such a topic can destroy our reputation as well as good relations with stakeholders.

### Insights and Challenges

### What recommendation can you give to practitioners in your field?

Even though I have heard a lot that CSR is only another trend and marketing step, I do believe that when responsibility in all terms is not settled in the key governing documents as well as the strategy of the company, or at least at the consciousness of the top management and the owners, it sooner or later causes a disaster. By this I mean, I recommend not trying to involve any CSR topics into account when there is no belief in that. Also, I recommend following the principle of "talking the walk," which avoids the greenwashing and shows that you really mean it. Also, it is important to clarify that CSR is not just a part of marketing but should be integrated within the whole company, across all departments, with the support of the top management, owners, and other employees.

### Which are the main challenges of your job?

As the most challenging I see the point that CSR is still in progress and forms that are being practiced now can be easily changed in the near future. Also, I feel the same in the case of marketing. Communication practices have been changed according to the changing environment, further development, and innovations. This all is very challenging because there is a never-ending shift that always brings something new and interesting.

### Is there anything else that you would like to share?

I would like to add that the construction business is completely a different case in which I see that behaving responsibly reflects mainly the good intensions of the owners. Even though that responsible performance can be evaluated from the long term, and also be beneficial for the company in case of goodwill creation, there are such specific principles that need to be followed in the sphere of construction that even an irresponsible company may take a place in the market for a long time. Of course, those may be critical in terms of employing the right people, and continuously it shows how well the company acts and reacts, but in some cases I see it is hard to find strong arguments why the construction company should be responsible.

---

## SPECIAL PERSPECTIVE: WEB COMMUNICATION 1.0, 2.0 AND 3.0[83]

The World Wide Web is expanding to new regions, socioeconomic classes, and usages. More importantly, the Web not only expands, but also evolves in its very basic quality. The first (1.0) version of the Web was a static one-way information system. Users were rather passive recipients of information prepared by institutions with enough technical know-how and financial resources to establish a webpage. The possibilities to "communicate back" were restricted to mail applications. With Web 2.0, a change from static to dynamic took place.[84] Users evolved to become co-creators of many different kinds of contents and applications such as video (e.g., YouTube), text (e.g., Blogger and WordPress), or even software (e.g., the open source movement). The Web also became mobile and omnipresent with an exponentially increasing number of mobile devices, which often would save information in the Web "cloud" instead of locally on the device. Web 2.0 also is characterized by its social component, where offline social life is massively transferred to online platforms such as Facebook and Twitter. Web 3.0 is currently evolving from its 2.0 predecessor.[85] Increasingly, online activity becomes so embedded into offline "real life" that a distinction between the two spheres becomes difficult. A "metaverse," neither online nor offline, is created.[86] Through the application Foursquare, for instance, people can "log-in" to "physical" places such as the favorite pizzeria or an event online, and this way let contacts know

the actual location. The Web becomes "intelligent" in the sense that it detects users' behavior patterns and preferences and provides individually tailored contents, a so-called "filter bubble." Google, for instance, already tailors the search results to metadata of the individual.[87] At the same time, the Web becomes more standardized through the "Semantic Web" movement, which aims at creating a shared basic language that can be accessed easily by both users and applications.

As described in Table 12.1, each version of the Web brings typical advantages and challenges to communicating responsible business online, which can still be observed when companies adapt a communication style in the continuum between Web 1.0 and 3.0. All three types of the Web coexist simultaneously, and companies can make an active choice about which one suits best to the respective communication purpose in responsible business. A business that aims to co-create value with stakeholders will use a strong Web 2.0 strategy, in order to maximize exchange and co-creation possibilities with stakeholders. A different company in times of crisis might try to achieve control over the contents shared on the Web, to mitigate reputational damage, and would choose to mainly communicate through a traditional Web 1.0 homepage, which does not allow for publicly visible reactions to contents shared. A third company might aim to connect its real-life products to the virtual world through activities in the realm of Web 3.0.

How to communicate effectively in times of Web 2.0? The currently prevailing characteristics of Web 2.0 in combination with important characteristics call for the set of communication practices described in Figure 12.12.

1. **Content quantity and quality:** In Web 2.0, "content is king." Both quality and quantity of content are crucially important. Differently from Web 1.0, companies do not need to create all content

## DIG DEEPER

### Don't Get Mixed Up! Marketing 1.0, 2.0, 3.0

All three versions of marketing are highly related both to the three distinct versions of the World Wide Web and to responsible business. Marketing 1.0 refers to activities based on the marketer as the main actor of the marketing management process. In marketing 2.0, marketers base their efforts on Web 2.0 tools such as social networks and mobile technologies. Marketing 3.0 counterintuitively does not refer to the usage of Web 3.0 for marketing, but to a new focus of marketing on spirituality.

Source: Kotler, P., Kartajaya, H., & Setiawan, I. (2010). *Marketing 3.0: From products to customers to the human spirit.* Hoboken, NJ: Wiley.

**Table 12.1 Main Advantages and Disadvantages of Communication Styles Related to Different Types of the Web**

| Type of Web | Advantage | Disadvantage |
|---|---|---|
| 1.0 | Complete control over contents and answers | Restricted possibility for dialogue and co-creation with stakeholders |
| 2.0 | Democratization of communication and enhanced possibility to interact with stakeholders | Unstructured and hard to grasp and control flow of information |
| 3.0 | Possibility to create real-life change and increase the ecoefficiency of lifestyles | Potential to block change for sustainable behaviors by keeping stakeholders in their own personalized world |

© Cengage Learning 2015

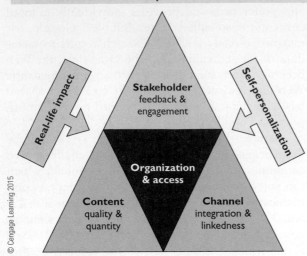

**Figure 12.12 Characteristics of Effective Web Communication in Responsible Business**

Real-life impact

Self-personalization

Stakeholder feedback & engagement

Organization & access

Content quality & quantity

Channel integration & linkedness

© Cengage Learning 2015

themselves, but rather provide the opportunity for stakeholders to create related content. The main success factor for content creation is the co-creation of content between companies and stakeholders using the many Web 2.0 applications. The created content must also be of high quality, most notably of credibility, in order to harness the viral characteristics of Web 2.0. A viral "buzz" or mouth-to-mouth message is one that is sufficiently extraordinary to be passed on quickly and automatically once liberated by the communicator.

2. **Channel integration and linkedness:** In Web 2.0, companies cannot rely on single communication channels, but must create an integrated and linked message throughout a diverse set of channels that jointly create the overall message of responsible business conduct. Important is that the overall message is consistent throughout channels. It is also critical that the messages communicated by stakeholders and the business are mutually reinforcing. When, for instance, the Mexican branch Bancomer of the international bank BBVA announced its annual report 2010 on a memory stick, to save paper and show responsible behavior, stakeholders commenting on Twitter instead picked up on missing responsibility toward customers and poor customer service. The messages were highly contradictory.[88]

3. **Stakeholder feedback and engagement:** Web 2.0 applications, especially social networks, can be used to get in touch and co-create with

stakeholders. For instance, the British newspaper *The Guardian* asks stakeholders to suggest topics for their sustainability report.[89] Levi's, after realizing that the biggest $CO_2$ life-cycle impact of their product Jeans is caused through the drying process in electric tumble dryers, asked stakeholders in a contest to design the best laundry rack.[90] In this way, Levi's engaged with stakeholders and co-created solutions to reduce one of the product's most severe negative environmental impact.

4. **Organization and access:** All stakeholders of a company should be able to engage with the company online. As a result, companies must actively aim at reducing barriers to such engagement. Barriers might be, for instance, of economic, technical, or know-how nature. Important stakeholders might not be able to engage online, as they lack the financial resources to access the Internet; they might not use the technology or platform the company uses to communicate online (e.g., Facebook in China is used less than the local Baidu network); or they might not know how to use applications applied or speak the language used by companies to communicate responsible business. Such exclusion is commonly known as "red-lining," a situation where stakeholders are actively or passively denied access. In order to avoid such a denial of access to the communication process, the organization of online communication is crucial. The central question in order to avoid "net-lining" (red-lining in the Net) is: "How can I organize my communication channels in order to give access to all groups that matter?" An excellent example for innovative organization and creation of access is cell-phone-based banking in Kenya, where banks have teamed up with the British multinational communication company Vodafone to provide access to basic banking services for remote communities.[91]

   While the Web moves from the 2.0 to 3.0 version, the same communication principles mentioned previously stay valid, but are complemented by the following additional recommendations, corresponding to features of Web 3.0.

5. **Real-life impacts:** Web 3.0 exceeds the traditional boarders of the Internet and has the potential to make impact in real life. For instance, P&G's Future Friendly webpage follows the

goal to inspire consumers to use P&G's products in a more environmental friendly way in their households. Web tools such as blogs with resource-saving tips, games, and real-life competitions in the style of "Who can save the most water?" create positive environmental impacts in households all over the world through online stakeholder communication.[92]

6. **Self-personalization**: A prominent feature of Web 3.0 applications is their capability to access online behavior in order to self-personalize the contents provided to users. Google, for instance, customizes search results based on previous searches and the Internet user's meta-data, such as location and information gathered in other Google applications. Two different Google users usually do not see the same results, even if conducting a completely

identical search. Such self-personalization features are a mixed blessing. On the one hand, they may serve to give the user exactly what he or she wants; on the other hand, they might also bar the user from information beyond his or her horizon and typical behavior. As one of the main tasks, communication in responsible business must facilitate change. So if companies use self-personalization, companies could, for instance, ensure that contents provided to stakeholders are in line with the aspired change. For example, if consumers enter a business's page, they might be provided with information on new sustainable innovation products, while investors would automatically see new socially responsible investment opportunities throughout the company's business units, and suppliers would automatically be informed about a new supplier sustainability program.

## SOURCES & NOTES

1. Cone Communications. (2010). *Cone cause evolution study.* Boston: Cone Communications.

2. Cone Communications. (2008). *Cone cause evolution study.* Boston: Cone Communications.

3. United Nations Environment Programme. (2006). *Sustainability communications: A toolkit for marketing and advertising courses.* Retrieved June 28, 2011, from United Nations Environment Programme: www.unep.fr/shared/publications/pdf/DTIx0886xPA-EducationKitEN.pdf

4. Misani, N. (2010). The convergence of corporate social responsibility practices. *Management Research Review, 33*(7), 734–748, p. 735.

5. Conaway, R., & Laasch, O. (2012). *Communication in responsible business: Strategies, concepts and cases.* New York: Business Expert Press.

6. Belch, G. E., & Belch, M. A. (2009). *Advertising and promotion: An integrated marketing communications perspective* (p. 12). Boston: McGraw-Hill Irwin.

7. Laasch, O., & Conaway, R. (2011). "Making it do" at the movie theatres: Communicating sustainability in the workplace. *Business Communication Quarterly, 74*(1), 68–78.

8. Adapted from Locker, K. O. (2003). *Business and administrative communication,* 10th ed. Boston: McGraw-Hill/Irwin; O'Hair, D., Griedrich, G. W., & Dixon, L. D. (2005). *Strategic communication in business and the professions,* 5th ed. Boston: Houghton Mifflin.

9. Business communication. (2003). In *Harvard business essentials series* (p. 8). Boston: Harvard Business School Publishing.

10. Fernando, R., & Purkayasth, D. (2007). *The Body Shop: Social responsibility or sustained greenwashing.* Retrieved June 26, 2011, from OIKOS: www.oikos-international.org/en/academic/case-collection/inspection-copies/alphabetical-list.html

11. Taubken, N., & Leibold, I. (2010). Ten rules for successful CSR communication. In M. Pohl & N. Tolhurst, *Responsible business: How to manage a CSR strategy successfully.* Chichester: Wiley.

12. Horiuchi, R., et al. (2009). *Understanding and preventing greenwash: A business guide.* San Francisco: BSR.

13. American Marketing Association. (2007). *Marketing power.* Retrieved June 28, 2011, from AMA: www.marketingpower.com/AboutAMA/Pages/DefinitionofMarketing.aspx

14. Grönroos, C. (1989). Defining marketing: A market-oriented approach. *European Journal of Marketing, 23*(1), 52–60.

15. Belch, G. E., & Belch, M. A. (2009). *Advertising and promotion: An integrated marketing communications perspective.* Boston: McGraw-Hill Irwin.

16. Johnson & Johnson. (2007). *Annual report.* Retrieved May 14, 2011, from: http://files.shareholder.com/downloads/JNJ/1257952067x0x171267/057640F8-B2C0-4B0F-9F54-7A24A553C3CE/2007AR.pdf

17. Kotler, P. (2003). *Marketing management.* Upper Saddle River, NJ: Prentice Hall.

18. York, E. B. (2009, June 8). Starbucks CMO: MCD'S java push will work in our favor. *Advertising Age 80*(21) (Midwest region ed.), 12.

19. British Airways. (2011). Retrieved May 17, 2011, from: www.britishairways.com/travel/csr-your-footprint/public/en_gb

20. Starbucks. (2004). Retrieved May 17, 2011, from: www.starbucks.co.nz/index.cfm?contentNodeID=335

21. Litman, T., & Burwell, D. (2006). Issues in sustainable transportation. *International Journal of Global Environmental Issues, 6*(4), 331–347, p. 337.

22. Martinez, P., & Conaway, R. (2010, October). *Ebooks: The next step in educational innovation.* Conference Presentation

at the Association for Business Communication, Chicago, IL.

23. Thompson, S. (2006, June 26). Good to the last (healthy) drop. *Advertising Age, 77*(26), S15.

24. Thompson, S. (2006, June 26). Good to the last (healthy) drop. *Advertising Age, 77*(26), S15.

25. Thompson, S. (2006, June 26). Good to the last (healthy) drop. *Advertising Age, 77*(26), S15.

26. United Nations Environment Programme. (2006). *Sustainability communications: A toolkit for marketing and advertising courses.* Retrieved June 28, 2011, from United Nations Environment Programme: www.unep.fr/shared/publications/pdf/DTIx0886xPA-EducationKitEN.pdf

27. Lesikar, R. V., & Petit, J. D., Jr. (1989). *Business communication: Theory and practice* (p. 9). Homewood, IL: Irwin.

28. Taubken, N., & Leibold, I. (2010). Ten rules for successful CSR communication. In M. Pohl & N. Tolhurst, *Responsible business: How to manage a CSR strategy successfully.* Chichester: Wiley.

29. Economist Intelligence Unit. (2008). *Doing good: Business and the sustainability challenge.* London: The Economist.

30. Cohen, E. (2010). *A necessary partnership for advancing responsible business practices.* Sheffield: Greenleaf.

31. Lesikar, R. V., & Petit, J. D., Jr. (1989). *Business communication: Theory and practice* (p. 10). Homewood, IL: Irwin.

32. Lesikar, R. V., & Petit, J. D., Jr. (1989). *Business communication: Theory and practice* (p. 11). Homewood, IL: Irwin.

33. RED. (2011). *RED: Designed to eliminate AIDS.* Retrieved May 9, 2011, from The (RED) Idea: www.joinred.com/aboutred

34. Varadarajan, P. R., & Menon, A. (1988). Cause-related marketing: A coalignment of marketing strategy and corporate philanthropy. *Journal of Marketing, 52*(3), 58–74.

35. Varadarajan, P. R., & Menon, A. (1988). Cause-related marketing: A coalignment of marketing strategy and corporate philanthropy. *Journal of Marketing, 52*(3), 58–74, p. 60.

36. Varadarajan, P. R., & Menon, A. (1988). Cause-related marketing: A coalignment of marketing

strategy and corporate philanthropy. *Journal of Marketing, 52*(3), 58–74, pp.60–61.

37. Pringle, H., & Thompson, M. (1999). *How cause-related marketing builds brands.* West Sussex: Wiley.

38. Pringle, H., & Thompson, M. (1999). *How cause-related marketing builds brands* (p. 3). West Sussex: Wiley.

39. Bendell, J., & Kleanthous, A. (2007). *Deeper luxury.* Retrieved May 21, 2011, from World Wildlife Federation-UK: www.wwf.org.uk/deeperluxury/_downloads/DeeperluxuryReport.pdf

40. Bendell, J., & Kleanthous, A. (2007). *Deeper luxury.* Retrieved May 21, 2011, from World Wildlife Federation-UK: www.wwf.org.uk/deeperluxury/_downloads/DeeperluxuryReport.pdf

41. Bendell, J., & Kleanthous, A. (2007). *Deeper luxury* (p. 43). Retrieved May 21, 2011, from World Wildlife Federation-UK: www.wwf.org.uk/deeperluxury/_downloads/DeeperluxuryReport.pdf

42. Weinreich, N. K. (2011). *Hands-on social marketing: A step-by-step guide to designing change for good,* 2nd ed. Thousand Oaks, CA: Sage.

43. Armstrong, G., & Kotler, P. (2009). *Marketing: An introduction.* Upper Saddle River, NJ: Pearson.

44. Armstrong, G., & Kotler, P. (2009). *Marketing: An introduction* (p. 203). Upper Saddle River, NJ: Pearson.

45. Weinreich, N. K. (2011). *Hands-on social marketing: A step-by-step guide to designing change for good,* 2nd ed. Thousand Oaks, CA: Sage.

46. Weinreich, N. K. (2011). *Hands-on social marketing: A step-by-step guide to designing change for good,* 2nd ed. (p. 4). Thousand Oaks, CA: Sage.

47. Volkswagen. (2010). *The fun theory.* Retrieved May 9, 2011, from: www.thefuntheory.com/

48. Kotler, P. (2003). *Marketing management.* Upper Saddle River, NJ: Prentice Hall.

49. Kotler, P. (2003). *Marketing management* (p. 26). Upper Saddle River, NJ: Prentice Hall.

50. Waller, R., & Conaway, R. N. (2011). Framing and counterframing the issue of corporate social responsibility: The communication strategies of Nikebiz.com. *Journal of Business Communication, 48*(1), 83-106.

51. Greenberg, J., & Elliott, C. (2009). A cold cut crisis: Listeriosis, Maple

Leaf Foods; and the politics of apology. *Canadian Journal of Communication, 34*(2), 189–204.

52. Greenberg, J., & Elliott, C. (2009). A cold cut crisis: Listeriosis, Maple Leaf Foods; and the politics of apology. *Canadian Journal of Communication, 34*(2), 189–204.

53. Greenberg, J., & Elliott, C. (2009). A cold cut crisis: Listeriosis, Maple Leaf Foods; and the politics of apology. *Canadian Journal of Communication, 34*(2), 189–204, p. 191.

54. Patel, A., & Reinsch, L. (2003). Companies can apologize: Corporate apologies and legal liability. *Business Communication Quarterly, 66*(1), 9–25.

55. ERRT (European Retail Round Table). (2010). Retrieved from: www.errt.org/uploads/Retail%20Environmental%20Sustainability%20Code%20-%20June%202010.pdf

56. Walmart. (2010). *Standards for suppliers. Ethical sourcing.* Retrieved May 9, 2011, from: http://walmart-stores.com/AboutUs/279.aspx

57. Thurm, R. (2010). Sustainability reporting 2.0: From "Trojan horse" to "value booster." In M. Pohl & N. Tolhurst, *Responsible business: How to manage a CSR strategy successfully.* Chichester: Wiley.

58. Thurm, R. (2010). Sustainability reporting 2.0: From "Trojan horse" to "value booster." In M. Pohl & N. Tolhurst, *Responsible business: How to manage a CSR strategy successfully.* Chichester: Wiley.

59. Thurm, R. (2010). Sustainability reporting 2.0: From "Trojan horse" to "value booster." In M. Pohl & N. Tolhurst, *Responsible business: How to manage a CSR strategy successfully* (p. 109). Chichester: Wiley.

60. Blanding, M. (2011, May 23). *Corporate sustainability reporting: It's effective.* Retrieved May 24, 2011, from Harvard Business School, *Working Knowledge Newsletter:* http://hbswk.hbs.edu/item/6701.html?wknews=052362011

61. Williams, L. S. (2008). The mission statement: A corporate reporting tool with a past, present, and future. *Journal of Business Communication, 2*(45).

62. Williams, L. S. (2008). The mission statement: A corporate reporting tool with a past, present, and future.

*Journal of Business Communication,* 2(45), 96.

63. Swales, J. M., & Rogers, P. S. (1995). Discourse and the projection of corporate culture: The mission statement. *Discourse and Society,* 6(2), 223–242.

64. Mullane, J. V. (2002). The mission statement is a strategic tool: When used properly. *Management Decision,* 40(5/6), 448–455.

65. PepsiCo. (2011). Retrieved May 26, 2011, from: www.pepsico.com/ Company/Our-Mission-and-Vision. html

66. Morsing, M., & Schultz, M. (2006). Corporate social responsibility communication: Stakeholder information, response and involvement strategies. *Business Ethics: A European Review,* 15(4), 323–338, p. 323.

67. Freeman, R. E. (2010). *Stakeholder management: A stakeholder approach.* Re-issue by Cambridge University Press.

68. Freeman, R. E. (2010). *Stakeholder management: A stakeholder approach* (p. 46). Re-issue by Cambridge University Press.

69. Morsing, M., & Schultz, M. (2006). Corporate social responsibility communication: Stakeholder information, response and involvement strategies. *Business Ethics: A European Review,* 15(4), 323–338.

70. Weick, K. E. (1995). *Sensemaking in organizations.* Thousand Oaks, CA: Sage.

71. Morsing, M., & Schultz, M. (2006). Corporate social responsibility communication: Stakeholder information, response and involvement strategies. *Business Ethics: A European Review,* 15(4), 323–338.

72. Morsing, M., & Schultz, M. (2006). Corporate social responsibility communication: Stakeholder information, response and involvement strategies. *Business Ethics: A European Review,* 15(4), 323–338.

73. Morsing, M., & Schultz, M. (2006). Corporate social responsibility communication: Stakeholder information, response and involvement strategies. *Business Ethics: A European Review,* 15(4), 323–338.

74. Morsing, M., & Schultz, M. (2006). Corporate social responsibility communication: Stakeholder information, response and involvement strategies. *Business Ethics: A European Review,* 15(4), 323–338.

75. Morsing, M., & Schultz, M. (2006). Corporate social responsibility communication: Stakeholder information, response and involvement strategies. *Business Ethics: A European Review,* 15(4), 323–338, p. 325.

76. Palazzo, B. (2010). An introduction to stakeholder dialogue. In M. Pohl & N. Tolhurst, *Responsible business: How to manage a CSR strategy successfully.* Chichester: Wiley.

77. Palazzo, B. (2010). An introduction to stakeholder dialogue. In M. Pohl & N. Tolhurst, *Responsible business: How to manage a CSR strategy successfully* (p. 21). Chichester: Wiley.

78. ABB. (2011). Retrieved May 20, 2011, from: www.abb.com/ cawp/abbzh258/c52b8d3c25d-de927c125736a002ad3a3.aspx

79. Freeman, R. E. (2010). *Stakeholder management: A stakeholder approach.* Re-issue by Cambridge University Press.

80. Freeman, R. E., Harrison, J. S., & Wicks, A. C. (2007). *Managing for stakeholders: Survival, reputation, and success.* London: Yale University Press.

81. Freeman, R. E., Harrison, J. S., & Wicks, A. C. (2007). *Managing for stakeholders: Survival, reputation, and success* (p. 107). London: Yale University Press.

82. Freeman, R. E., Harrison, J. S., & Wicks, A. C. (2007). *Managing for stakeholders: Survival, reputation, and success.* London: Yale University Press.

83. This text is a reprint from Conaway, R. N., & Laasch, O. (2012). *Communicating business responsibility: Strategies, concepts and cases for integrated marketing communication.* New York: Business Expert Press.

84. O'Reilly, T. (2005). *What is Web 2.0: Design patterns and business models for the next generation of software.* Retrieved August 30, 2011, from

O'Reilley Network: www.oreillynet. com/lpt/a/6228

85. Agarwal, A. (2009). *Web 3.0 concepts explained in plain English (presentations).* Retrieved February 23, 2012, from Digital Inspiration: www.labnol.org/internet/web-3-concepts-explained/8908/; Hendler, J. (2009). Web 3.0 emerging. *Computer,* 42(1), 88–90; Lassila, O., & Hendler, J. (2007). Embracing "Web 3.0." *IEEE Internet Computing,* 11(3), 90–93.

86. Smart, J. (2007). *Metaverse roadmap.* Retrieved February 24, 2012, from: http://metaverseroadmap.org/inputs4. html#glossary

87. Pariser, E. (2011). *The filter bubble: What the Internet is hiding from you.* London: Penguin.

88. Lopez, E., & Martinez, L. (2012). Redes sociales y responsabilidad social [Social networks and social responsibility]. In *Taller las redes sociales y la RSE [Workshop social networks and CSR].* Mexico City: EXPOK.

89. Confino, J. (2010). *Can you help us with our latest sustainability report?* Retrieved February 24, 2012, from Guardian News and Media: www. guardian.co.uk/sustainability/blog/ sustainability-audit

90. Levi Strauss. (2010). *What's the future of line drying?* Retrieved February 24, 2012, from Levi Strauss & Co: www. levistrauss.com/news/press-releases/ levi-strauss-co-asks-what-s-future-line-drying

91. Jack, W., & Suri, T. (2010). *The economics of M-PESA.* Retrieved February 24, 2012, from Massachusetts Institute of Technology: www.mit.edu/~tavneet/ M-PESA.pdf

92. Procter & Gamble. (2011). *Little actions big difference.* Retrieved February 24, 2012, from Future Friendly: www.futurefriendly.co.uk/ home.aspx; Procter & Gamble. (2011). *Helping consumers conserve.* Retrieved February 24, 2012, from P&G: www.pg.com/en_US/ sustainability/environmental_sustainability/products_packaging/consumer_education.shtml

# 13

Fairtrade
FSC
Corruption
Global Compact
ILO
Global Commons Intercultural Management
Globalization Emerging Economies International Business
ETI Stategic Alliance MNC Identity
International Management Global Supply Chain Localism
Anti-Globalization

# INTERNATIONAL BUSINESS AND MANAGEMENT: GLOCALLY RESPONSIBLE BUSINESS

*You will be able to...*

1  ...analyze the glocal (global and local) environments for responsible business.

2  ...map your nondomestic activities and understand their implications for responsible management.

3  ...manage responsibly in an intercultural context.

Seventy-eight percent of Latin American CEOs see sustainability as very important to the future success of their business. In North Africa and the Middle East, the figure is only 22 percent.[1]

Eighty-eight percent of CEOs believe that companies should embed social, environmental, and governance issues in their global supply chains, but only 54 percent do so.[2]

Sixty-five percent of CEOs agreed that over the next five years their company would adopt new business models and practices in emerging markets (such as base-of-the-pyramid models).[3]

Authors: Roger N. Conaway and Oliver Laasch; Contributors: Al Rosenbloom, Barbara Coudenhove-Kalergi, Geert Hofstede, Jenik Radon, Laura Clise, Mahima Achuthan, Nick Tolhurst, Shiv K. Tripathi

## GlaxoSmithKline: Managing Global Social Expectations through Differential Pricing

While the current mantra of international management might be of companies "thinking globally, but acting locally," such a policy is often difficult to implement in actual practice. The global pharmaceutical sector perhaps reflects this difficulty better than any other sector. Thinking locally is problematic because pharmaceutical companies understandably focus their resources on expensive long-term development of drugs and products aimed at a truly global market. The lifesaving role that drugs and medicines play in society further places the actions and motives of pharmaceutical companies under the microscope of media. Increasingly, questions are raised by the public on pricing, restrictive patents, and medicine affordability in the developing world.

Given this background, pharmaceutical companies that do not attempt to balance competing international demands with a sound globally responsible business strategy face massive reputational risks. The global pricing structure of GlaxoSmithKline (GSK) provides a good example on how to manage these risks in a proactive way that both enhances reputation and illustrates responsible management in sound business principles. GSK realized that the traditional expensive pricing of medicines was becoming increasingly unpopular, although such pricing was justified because of long-term developmental costs. Thus, GSK's CEO Andrew Witty announced in 2011 that the prices of certain medicines would be slashed by up to 95%, depending on the country in which they were sold. In particular, this would apply to products of vital importance in the developing world, such as the Rotarix vaccine, which is used to treat rotavirus, a chronic diarrheal infection that kills an estimated 500,000 children each year in Africa and Asia. The new Rotarix vaccine dose would be sold at roughly $2 (discounted from over $40), an amount that barely covers production costs and does not include years of research and development (R&D) investment.

In business terms, this low pricing could be justified as part of GSK's new global "three-tiered pricing structure." Despite the largely uniform nature of its products, the new pricing structure would now radically differentiate between upper-, middle-, and lower-income countries and charge accordingly. In effect, GSK successfully balanced a cross-subsidization of poorer countries' medicines via rich countries' consumers, without risking the funds needed to invest and develop new drugs and vaccines. With the positive impact this strategy generated, GSK was able to cooperate with global nonprofit organizations such as the Gates Foundation and the Switzerland-based Global Alliance for Vaccines and Immunization (GAVI) Conference to ensure that this system worked and avoid such problems as "leakage" of cheaper products into "higher-income" markets. With the development of a globally geared and flexible pricing structure, GSK managed to more than fulfill its social obligations without sacrificing medicine development and R&D. The company simultaneously was perceived as improving health outcomes in the developing world and became an active participant in this process.

GSK shows how companies can implement a "glocally" responsible business strategy, which combines a globally responsible business strategy with locally relevant actions.

Source: GlaxoSmithKline, www.gsk.com/responsibility/health-for-all/access-to-healthcare.html

## 13-1 RESPONSIBLE MANAGEMENT AND INTERNATIONAL BUSINESS

*"We address the question of why forms of business responsibility for society both differ among countries and change within them."*[4]

*Global, international, multicultural, foreign,* or *nondomestic business*—the terms describing international business activities are many. Many are also the social, environmental, and ethical issues arising from international business and management activities. Corruption, offshoring, poverty, human rights abuses, and questionable environmental standards are all issues typically considered as global problems to be faced by Western companies operating abroad. On the other hand, global business activity also has the potential to do much good. Business can become a global problem solver and considerably contribute to the sustainable development process of host countries. Technology transfer, the raising of social and environmental standards beyond the law, and job creation are but a few examples of such positive effects.

The global environment is even important for companies that would not consider themselves global. A company does not have to be a global business to be globally responsible. Even simple sourcing activities offer more or less global responsible options. For any business with some type of international involvement, even if it is just buying a certain component abroad, four main questions arise:

- How do we deal with globalization and the challenges posed by it responsibly?
- How is responsible business infrastructure different from one country to another?
- How do we manage global business activities responsibly?
- How do we responsibly manage the issues arising in managers' international activity?

Thomas Friedman and Michael Mandelbaum[5] wrote that one of the greatest challenges to globalization today "is how to manage a world of both rising energy consumption and rising climate threats."[6] These impacts indeed have risen to the greatest challenges of today, yet we must broaden the consumption and climate threat perspective beyond environmental issues to social issues and ethical practices within international businesses. Our perspective in this chapter inclusively equates international management with responsibility management in the organization, sustainable performance in the global supply chain, and ethical practices by all personnel.

Figure 13.1 illustrates four stages through which international businesses will journey toward becoming a glocally responsible business. The word *glocal* is a mixture of the words *global* and *local* and describes global activities with a strong adaptation to local circumstances. The goal of this chapter is to develop a "glocally responsible business," a business that is at the same time globally and locally responsible. This is a business that is able to create value for stakeholders around the world while adapting to varying local circumstances, a business that actively addresses both global and local sustainability issues, and one that manages global moral issues and intercultural ethics successfully.

The outline of this chapter follows the four phases shown in Figure 13.1. First, *understanding glocalization* means businesses must consider trends and drivers of both globalization and locally responsible business. To adapt responsible business and management to the local responsible business infrastructure, a responsible manager must first understand how responsible business differs in between regions and countries, and then be able to assess the responsible business infrastructure in a concrete location. Second, *assessing the global position* means helping a company to understand how well a glocally responsible business is doing by benchmarking the company against globally responsible business codes and responsible business concepts for the assessment of corporate social performance. Responsible managers who assess the global position have taken the second step toward responsible

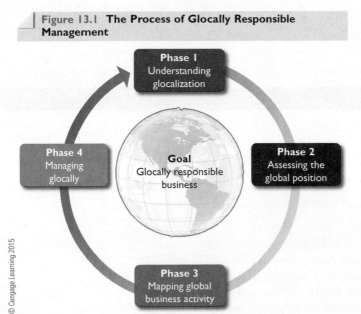

Figure 13.1 **The Process of Glocally Responsible Management**

Phase 1
Understanding glocalization

Phase 2
Assessing the global position

Phase 3
Mapping global business activity

Phase 4
Managing glocally

Goal
Glocally responsible business

business management. The third phase, *mapping global business activity*, means to analyze the different global activities of a business in order to understand their ethical, stakeholder, and triple bottom line implications. The company begins to create value throughout the entire global supply chain and responsibly manages global logistics, outsourcing decisions, labor practices, and human rights. Foreign direct investment and global procurement are also part of this third phase, including global pricing, foreign mergers and acquisitions (M&A), and strategic alliances. Finally, *managing glocally* deals with equipping single managers with the tools to manage responsibly in a global workplace. This phase entails continuing, effective intercultural communication and management, cross-cultural ethics, and cultural inclusiveness. *Glocalism* represents the difficult balance that must be achieved between global corporate culture and local practices and local culture. Multinational enterprises must investigate with due diligence local culture and balance these tastes with the goals of international corporate cultures. In the following section, we will provide a more detailed illustration of the goal of creating a glocally responsible business.

## 13-2 THE GOAL: GLOCALLY RESPONSIBLE BUSINESS

*"The Guidelines aim to ensure that the operations of these enterprises are in harmony with government policies, to strengthen the basis of mutual confidence between enterprises and the societies in which they operate, to help improve the foreign investment climate and to enhance the contribution to sustainable development made by multinational enterprises."[7]*

Globally responsible business is as much about globalization as it is about localization. It is about both: complying with international sustainability, responsibility, and ethics standards, while adjusting responsible business conduct to the manifold locations in which the business operates.[8] It is about addressing very local sustainability challenges, understanding and creating value for locally distinct shareholders, and making ethically right but culturally tolerant decisions in any local values system. This is why we call the aspired end goal of responsible international business and management a **glocally responsible business (GRB)**, which is as much globally valid as it is locally valuable and relevant.

    **Glocalization** is a mixture of the words *global* and *local* and describes global activities with a strong adaptation to local circumstances.[9] The terms *glocal* and *glocalization* perfectly illustrate the need for responsible businesses to add value in both arenas, the global and the local one. We will use *glocal* to describe the globally responsible activities that are strongly adapted to local environments. Businesses and governments are waking up to global air pollution problems, exhausted water resources, depleted forests, and diminished supplies of precious mineral resources for their manufacturing operations. Often those global challenges require local solutions. Glocally responsible businesses must be able to both have a strong global responsible business strategy and successfully adapt it to local conditions.

## 13-3 PHASE I: UNDERSTANDING THE GLOCAL BUSINESS CONTEXT

*"Globalization is the progressive eroding of the relevance of territorial bases for social, economic and political activities, processes and relations."[10]*

Two initial questions have to be asked to begin the journey toward becoming a glocally responsible business. First, one needs to know the drivers of globalization and

A **glocally responsible business (GRB)** is a business that is at the same time globally and locally responsible, which is able to create value for stakeholders around the world and in every location, which actively addresses both global and local sustainability issues, and which manages global moral issues and intercultural ethics successfully.

**Glocalization** is a mixture of the words *global* and *local* and describes global activities with a strong adaptation to local circumstances.

how they affect responsible business and management. Second, one needs to be able to assess the local infrastructure for responsible business in foreign host countries. This section provides tools by which to answer both questions.

## 13-3a Globalization

In this chapter, we define **globalization** broadly as "the widening set of interdependent relationships among people from different parts of a world that happens to be divided into nations."[11] Conventional wisdom in business tells us we are now operating in a globalized world with global sustainability and stakeholder and ethical interests. Yet the actual context and consequences of global sustainability are still very much contested. Mainstream globalization involves the integration of world economies as nations engage in trade of goods and services and compete on a global basis. This concept of globalization has often been characterized as a mix of internationalization, Westernization, liberalization, and universalism.

We must note that internationalization of business activity through trade occurred long before our current globalization trends began. In earlier times, merchant ships traveled around the world, connecting seaports in Europe, India, China, and Japan through exchange of live animals, unique fabrics, and precious metals worldwide. Neither responsible management nor sustainability performance was a formal priority of business strategy in those times. Today, the recent high impact of globalization on the planet has moved responsible management to the center of international business strategy. Furthermore, recent advances in technology and transportation have accelerated the movement of goods and services around the globe and resulted in the negative impact on earth's resources. Rapid expansion of globalization today means businesses must undertake a parallel expansion in responsibility to global stakeholders. How can an international business comprehensively address these rapid changes and impacts? How can single managers adjust their responsible management practices to the challenges of globalization? An ideal twenty-first century global business would be one that is responsible to all international stakeholders, develops a sustainable triple bottom line impact all around the world, and achieves moral excellence in domestic, global, and foreign local environments.

**THINK | ETHICS**

### A Glocal Approach against Corruption

Operating in a global economy, as well as in its home country of India, Infosys, an IT services company, has taken a top-down decision to operate by a strict code of ethics heavily focused on antibribery. Refusing to "grease the palm" of officials, management prefers to accept delays and the associated loss in revenue rather than pay the demanded bribes. Moreover, it takes on the government head-on by publicly confronting state officials for alleged instances of bribe demands.

Source: The Indian Express. (2011). *Infosys' Pai accuses Karnataka govt. of corruption, BJP wants proof.* Retrieved February 2, 2013, from *The Indian Express:* www.indianexpress.com/comments/infosys-pai-accuses-karnataka-govt-of-corruption-bjp-wants-proof/774501/

### Effects of Globalization

Is sustainable development achievable within the existing international political economic context? Some do not think so. Georgia Carvalho[12] argues that adoption of development strategies conducive to true sustainable development is nearly impossible within the current international political economic system. She believes profound changes must occur in economic, political, and social structures before those development strategies can begin. In this section, we address responsible business and international political issues by examining seven drivers of globalization that need to be taken into consideration so as to understand what globalization means to a glocally responsible business.

1. *Global media:* Globalization involves the proliferation and predominance of media around the globe, uniting the world and keeping places separated by great distances together during world events. Perhaps there is no better vehicle than global media to draw worldwide attention to global poverty, water shortages, and spread of disease, as well as to business scandals.

**Globalization** refers to the widening set of interdependent relationships among people from different parts of the world.

2. *Global communication technology and access to Internet:* The incredible growth of global technology and access to the Internet continues to follow a logarithmic curve as it accelerates skyward. Yet paralleling the decline in cell phone costs, an increasing environmental impact continues to skyrocket from used cell phones and toxic materials still used by some manufacturers. Will the accelerated growth of global technology further divide the "haves" and the "have not's"? Or will the eventual extension of Internet access to the poor create a leveling effect in society?

3. *Global transportation:* Faster and cheaper transportation exists as another important driver of globalized business, trade, and tourism. Availability of relatively cheap and frequent transportation is a fundamental driver of globalization. Yet the proliferation of aircraft creates environmental impacts through $CO_2$ emissions in the atmosphere. Reducing impacts through innovation in transportation presents a challenge for glocally responsible businesses.

4. *Emergence of global standards:* The new business geography involves working under the governance of global organizations that establish responsibility standards for companies, such as the Organisation for Economic Co-operation and Development, the United Nations, the Global Reporting Initiative (GRI), the International Organization for Standardization (ISO), and the World Fair Trade Organization. These prominent organizations, along with the World Trade Organization (WTO), World Bank, and International Monetary Fund (IMF), exist as foundational organizations in understanding globalization and working in the new business climate.

5. *The rise of BRICS:* Understanding globalization trends implies that international responsible managers will understand major shifts in economic powers and trade relationships. Brazil, Russia, India, China, and South Africa (BRICS) represent emerging economies with rapidly increasing GDPs. While experiencing rapid economic growth and trade, most BRICS countries concurrently create high environmental impacts, raise ethical practice issues, and amplify social justice inadequacies. Responsible international managers who open markets and conduct business in BRICS countries face these same challenges in maintaining sustainable supply chains and developing socially responsible and ethical practices.

6. *Antiglobalization movements and global NGOs:* The antiglobalization movement represents a modern trend critical of multinational corporate expansion and the resulting spread of institutional and consumer consumption mentalities.[13] Many countries and NGOs reject the Western influence of capitalization and commercialization. International responsible business managers must be prepared to communicate with and respond to these stakeholder groups and activist organizations that may criticize a particular business practice.

7. *Global challenges and opportunities:* Moving out of a domestic and into a global setting provides both immense challenges and opportunities. Global challenges are manifold and include corruption, poverty, and global warming. A glocally responsible company may find opportunities to do much good both on a global level and a local level inside host countries that are part of global operations.

## DIG DEEPER

### Shark Fin Consumption in Hong Kong

An example that illustrates the challenge in addressing very local sustainable development issues is the high consumption of shark fin, considered a delicacy and a tradition of the Chinese culture, which has been the target by NGOs for many years. Japan's preference for whale meat presents a similar global challenge caused by local preferences. What is more important, the environment or cultural diversity?

Source: Cheung, G. C. K., & Chang, C. Y. (2003). Sustainable business versus sustainable environment: A case study of the Hong Kong shark fin business. *Sustainable Development, 11,* 223–235.

## How Globalization Influences Responsible Business

While the preceding section described broad trends or drivers of globalization, this section will illustrate the concrete implications of those trends for responsible business conduct. Globalization has changed the very nature of business in this century.[14] Responsible managers must understand five specific trends that are important to responsible international business operating a multicultural environment, as understanding these trends will provide them with a necessary context in which they can oversee operations. We have adapted the trends from Doh, Husted, Matten, and Santoro:[15]

1. *Decline in political power of countries with multinationals.* A steady decline in the political power of countries has accompanied globalization, and these countries are increasingly powerless to control the activities of multinational corporations (MNCs). Of the world's top 100 largest "economies" in 2004, forty-seven were countries (nation-states) and fifty-three were large corporations such as Walmart, Royal Dutch Shell, and Exxon/Mobile. This "explosive growth of MNCs" has made global business ethics one of the highest priorities in future decades.[16] Large corporations that outsource operations overseas, for example, may take advantage of less stringent laws regarding workplace conditions, employee treatment, or safety standards. Individual country governments exercise less control over large multinationals. Ethical issues will continue to grow as the political power of countries declines.

2. *Global personal identity and affiliations.* Globalized business is creating less attachment in employers and employees to country citizenship, identity, and cultural affiliation. They identify less with a culture or community and more with personal affiliations or professional classifications.

3. *Multinationals assume country-level responsibilities.* Multinationals are being transformed to take on roles and responsibilities in the structure of society that previously belonged to countries. MNCs, for example, have become involved in the making of public policy and have assumed some public functions and responsibilities, including public health, labor rights, and security, and even providing basic infrastructure and services in the countries in which they operate.

4. *Emergence of global stakeholder organizations.* Nongovernmental organizations (NGOs), activists, and other global nonprofits, such as the Fair Labor Association and AccountAbility, have emerged to serve as multinational stakeholder organizations. The emergence of these groups requires greater engagement and communication from multinationals.

5. *Growth of self-regulatory organizations.* A final broad trend is the proliferation of self-regulatory organizations, such as the Marine Stewardship Council and the Forest Stewardship Council, which are independent groups that are intended to promote ethically responsible business practices. Most industries today have self-regulatory certification of responsible business practices. These organizations exert a tremendous influence on practices of MNC.

## 13-3b Localizing Responsible Business

Strictly speaking, there is no such thing as a "global business." All businesses operating outside the domestic borders operate in foreign countries, not on a superior "global" level. Of course, business strategies, including those for responsible business, are crafted from the perspective of a global business interacting with business units in many countries at the same time. Nevertheless, the operations of such global business are locally "on the ground" in many different locations throughout different regions, countries, and locations. For this reason, it is crucially important for a glocally responsible business to be able to adopt responsible business and management to local conditions, including culture, systems, standards, and resulting local issues, challenges, and opportunities.

## Regional Responsible Business Approaches

What distinguishes responsible business conduct in Latin America from that in Europe or East Asia? Understanding regional approaches to responsible business is essential for managing a glocally responsible business. Visser and Tolhurst[17] edited a "World Guide to CSR" that summarized the different regional and national approaches to responsible business through profiles by region and country. The world map and comparative tables in Figure 13.2 provide an excellent overview of the regional differences illustrated by the authors.

For businesses operating in many different regions, the global responsible business map and profiles can help to customize their responsible management to

### Figure 13.2 Regional Approaches to Responsible Business

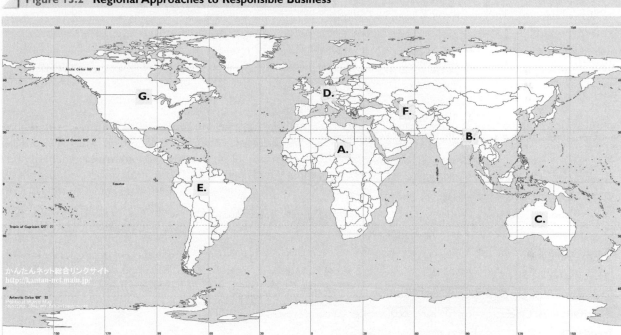

**A. Africa**

**Context:** CSR in infancy

**Priority Issues:** Poverty reduction, health and HIV/AIDS, education and skills development for youth

**Trends:** Emergence of sustainable trading groups, government support and involvement

**Codes:** Few continent-wide codes exist; some countries have Environment Action Plans, Employment Acts, and Corrupt Practices Acts

**Organizations:** Northern Africa—CIPE, EJB, URJC; Sub-Saharan—AICC, FEC, BUSA, FEMA, NBI

**Cases:** Coca-Cola, De Beers Group, Satemwa, Shell, Unilever

**Education:** CSR degrees available only in the country of South Africa

*(Continued)*

## B. Asia

**Context:** CSR deeply rooted and tied to cultural traditions

**Priority Issues:** Poverty, education, labor and supply chain, environment, products, community, governance

**Trends:** Tradition-based CSR, partnership-based market forces, regulation, CSR reporting, collective accountability, livelihood partnership, scalable embedded distribution

**Codes:** Environmental codes base on Agenda 21, labor codes based on ILO conventions, codes of corporate governance, CSR mandatory in many countries

**Organizations:** APPC, ASRIA, CII, CSR-Asia

**Cases:** City Development Limited (Singapore), Siam Cement Group (Thailand), Smart Communications (Philippines), Tata Group (India), Toyota (Japan)

**Education:** Graduate-level CSR in China, South Korea, India, Indonesia, and Singapore

## C. Australia

**Context:** CSR acceptance and implementation widespread

**Priority Issues:** Building internal understanding and support for CSR within businesses, eliminating the negative environmental impacts of business, understanding the impact of climate change on organizations

**Trends:** implementation of priority issues, development of an emissions trading scheme

**Codes:** Carbon Pollution Reduction Scheme (CPRS), Responsible Business Practice Project, Responsible Investment Academy

**Organizations:** APCSE, ACCSR, Centre for Global Sustainability, Centre for Responsible Mining, Centre for Social Impact

**Cases:** Delta Electricity, Lihir Gold Ltd, Westpac Banking Corporation

**Education:** Curtin, Monash, & Griffith Universities. The University of Melbourne, Swinburne University of Technology, and La Trobe University

## D. Europe

**Context:** Long CSR traditions in Western Europe. Central and Eastern Europe less developed but advancing

**Priority Issues:** Environment, demographic change and falling population, health and safety, poverty and social exclusion, diversity and equal opportunities

**Trends:** Positive awareness and attitudes toward CSR, CSR reporting

**Codes:** EU strategies and policies, national strategies and policies

**Organizations:** CSR Europe, EABIS, European Commission, UN Global Compact Local Networks

**Cases:** More than 600 company initiatives in CSR Europe

**Education:** Alliance of companies, business schools, and academic institutions integrate "business in society"

## E. Latin America

**Context:** Traditionally philanthropy, poverty alleviation (not reduction), led by church

**Priority Issues:** Labor issues, environment, social services, corporate governance, corruption

**Trends:** Moving from compliance to integration of CSR

**Codes:** National codes and laws often unavailable

**Organizations:** Forum Empresa and BSR, WBCSD, Ethos, CEMEFI, Convertirse, Inter-American Bank

**Cases:** CEMEX, Empresas Públicas de Medellín, Grupo Bimbo, GrupoNueva, Natura

**Education:** Quickly improving CSR education. Already available in Mexico, Venezuela, Brazil, and Colombia

## F. Middle East

**Context:** Focus shifting from predominant trade to maximizing business development. CSR tied with religion and often synonymous with charity and philanthropy

**Priority Issues:** National unemployment, diet and lifestyle, workers' rights, environmental sustainability

**Trends:** CSR evolving into regional trend, corporate governance, sustainability reporting

**Codes:** Codes unavailable or nonexistent

**Organizations:** UJRC, ABWOC, Arab Forum for Environment and Development, Dubai Centre for Responsible Development, Hawkamah, Lebanese Transparency Association, Sustainability Advisory Group, Young Arab Leaders

**Cases:** Aramex Jordan, Qatar Airways, Qatar

**Education:** No data

**G. North America**\*

**Context:** Full integration into Canadian and U.S. corporations not yet realized but growing and shifting from regulatory compliance to visionary and strategic

**Priority Issues:** Canada: tar sands development, old growth deforestation and loss of habitat, Canadian fishing industry risks, water management, widening demographic gaps. U.S.: Energy and climate change, job creation, human rights, consumer health

**Trends:** Consumers and investors show greater environmental and social performance; U.S. shows global recession, declining public trust, job creation needs, human rights, and consumer health

**Codes:** Sustainable Development Acts, Clean Air Acts, Clean Water Acts, Canadian Charter of Rights and Freedoms, Environmental Assessment Acts, Fisheries Act, Energy Policy Act

**Organizations:** CBSR, CCECP, Imagine, NCP, Corporate Knights, AccountAbility, Aspen Institute, BCCCC, BSR, Business Roundtable, Conference Board, IBLF, Net Impact, U.S. Chamber of Commerce, UN Global Compact

**Cases:** Resort Municipality of Whistler, Weyerhaeuser, Coca-Cola Enterprise, IBM, The Walt Disney Company

**Education:** Numerous universities have MBA-level courses in CSR issues

\* North America here excludes Mexico, which is considered as part of the Latin American business region due to its cultural and issue-related similarities.

Source: Visser, W. A. M., & Tolhurst, N. (2010). *The world guide to CSR: A country-by-country analysis of corporate sustainability and responsibility.* Chichester: Wiley.

local circumstances. By understanding the context and broader trends of responsible business in each location, knowing about social, environmental, and ethical priority issues, and knowing what local codes are most important to comply with, organizations can engage with and learn from local best practice cases, an invaluable resource for businesses extending their responsible management to new regions. The world guide to CSR also provides country profiles for many nations, with the same sections as those covered in the table in Figure 13.2.

## Assessing the National Responsible Business Context

The world guide to CSR mentioned in the preceding section provides a broad overview of country practices. A more specific, but highly important, perspective for localizing responsible business efforts is the public policies in place for responsible business. Figure 13.3 describes the so-called "CSR Navigator," developed by the German development agency GIZ, which provides a methodology by which to assess national responsible business policies and to develop recommendations for responsible businesses and managers in those countries.[18] The "CSR Navigator" assesses national responsible business regarding its contents, its context, and the maturity of the public policies for social and environmental business responsibility. While content and context of responsible business help companies in understanding what are important topics to be addressed, the maturity dimensions help responsible managers understand how advanced the responsible business regulation in the country is. In the maturity assessment integrated in Figure 13.3, we see that countries such as Mozambique, Brazil, and Poland are less advanced in their public policies. They have so-called first-generation policies. Countries such as South Africa and France have second-generation policies, while in the most advanced category, the third generations, the United Kingdom

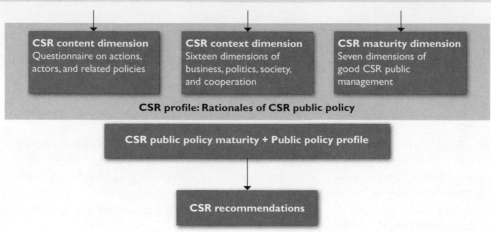

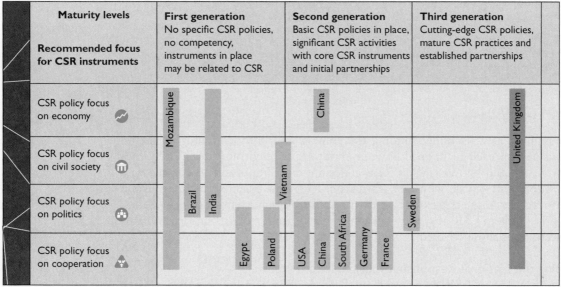

Source: Bertelsmann Stiftung; GTZ. (2007). *The CSR navigator: Public policies in Africa, the Americas, Asia and Europe.* Eschborn: GTZ.

is the only incumbent. What does this mean for businesses doing business from or in those countries? Companies doing business in countries with more advanced public policies need to be prepared for more regulatory pressure, while companies active in nations that are less advanced in their responsible business policies will have the opportunity to more easily exceed local standards. In the Special Perspective at the end of this chapter, you will find a comparison of four of the main global economic superpowers' responsible business profiles: China, India, Germany, and the United States.

How do CSR approaches differ in different countries? This question led the scholars Dirk Matten and Jeremy Moon[19] to investigate the different CSR approaches. They found that responsible business approaches in Europe and the United States differed drastically and that those two different approaches to responsible business implementation can be transferred to countries around the world. The two approaches found are explicit and implicit corporate social responsibility (CSR):

- *Explicit CSR* consists of business policies that assume and articulate responsibility for *some* societal interests. Typical are *voluntary* activities by individual corporations that combine social and business value and address issues perceived as important to meet particular *stakeholder expectations.*

- *Implicit CSR* takes a broader and more systemic perspective on responsible business by taking corporations' *role* within the wider formal and informal institutions for society's interests and concerns as its vantage point. Implicit CSR is based on *values, norms, and rules* that result in requirements for corporations to address stakeholder issues and that define proper obligations of corporate actors in *collective* rather than individual terms.

Understanding whether one is managing responsible business in either an explicitly or implicitly inclined context is a crucial prerequisite that if not fulfilled may lead to largely inadequate responsible business activities abroad.

## The Local Context and Infrastructure for Responsible Business

After we have assessed responsible business infrastructure in global, regional, and national contexts, we have reached the truly local level. Localizing responsible business conduct to a specific environment comes with many challenges. Will we find the critical inputs for a new sustainable innovation product or employees ready for responsible management? Will there be a market for responsible business conduct? Will the local rules and business norms be conducive to responsible business? Will there be local related and supporting industries to team up with for responsible business?

Responsible managers may use Michael Porter's "diamond model" of national competitive advantage (displayed in Figure 13.4) to assess four attributes of nations that consistently help domestic innovation, improvement, and competitive national advantage.[20] The diamond concept was applied to mapping the social impact of the local operations of a company in 2006, sixteen years after its creation, and helps to "set an affirmative CSR agenda that produces maximum social benefit as well as gains for the business."[21] This means that the diamond model can be used to assess a company's potential to adapt responsible business conduct to achieve both being a good locally responsible business and at the same time being locally competitive.

The diamond model has been used to assess the attractiveness of foreign direct investment to a location, as it provides an extensive overview of the local realities important for successful business conduct. A comparison between home country and other countries can be conducted in a "double-diamond" model that may serve to analyze differences in both domestic and foreign locations.[22] We can do the same to adjust the model to analyze the responsible business infrastructure. In the following, we adapt Porter and Kramer's model to reflect the specific considerations important for an assessment focused on responsible business factors. The words in parentheses clarify what each respective category was called in the original model. The four local dimensions considered are the following:

1. The *context for responsible competitiveness* (strategy and rivalry) describes the rules and incentives that govern responsible business. A business assessing this part of local infrastructure for responsible business conduct might want to check the social and environmental laws and regulations and see if there are

Figure 13.4 **Applying the Diamond Model to Responsible Business**

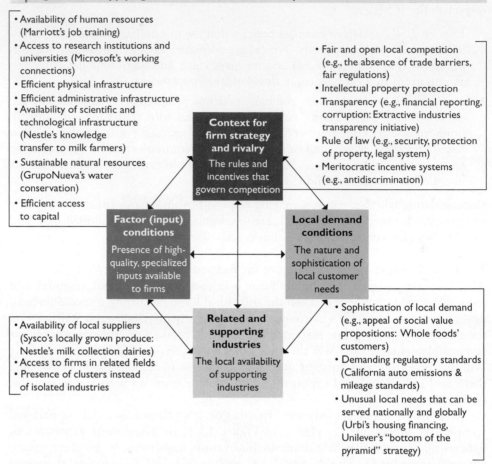

- Availability of human resources (Marriott's job training)
- Access to research institutions and universities (Microsoft's working connections)
- Efficient physical infrastructure
- Efficient administrative infrastructure
- Availability of scientific and technological infrastructure (Nestle's knowledge transfer to milk farmers)
- Sustainable natural resources (GrupoNueva's water conservation)
- Efficient access to capital

**Context for firm strategy and rivalry**

The rules and incentives that govern competition

**Factor (input) conditions**

Presence of high-quality, specialized inputs available to firms

**Local demand conditions**

The nature and sophistication of local customer needs

**Related and supporting industries**

The local availability of supporting industries

- Fair and open local competition (e.g., the absence of trade barriers, fair regulations)
- Intellectual property protection
- Transparency (e.g., financial reporting, corruption: Extractive industries transparency initiative)
- Rule of law (e.g., security, protection of property, legal system)
- Meritocratic incentive systems (e.g., antidiscrimination)

- Availability of local suppliers (Sysco's locally grown produce; Nestle's milk collection dairies)
- Access to firms in related fields
- Presence of clusters instead of isolated industries

- Sophistication of local demand (e.g., appeal of social value propositions: Whole foods' customers)
- Demanding regulatory standards (California auto emissions & mileage standards)
- Unusual local needs that can be served nationally and globally (Urbi's housing financing, Unilever's "bottom of the pyramid" strategy)

Source: Porter, M., & Kramer, M. (2006). Strategy and society: The link between competitive advantage and corporate social responsibility. *Harvard Business Review, 84*(12), 78–92.

governmental incentive programs available for responsible business. Also, it is helpful to ascertain the degree to which responsibility is already part of the business culture in a specific location, and if there are local codes or certifications for responsible business that need to be taken into consideration.

2. The *related and supporting networks* (industries) are local groups of companies, NGOs, or governmental institutions that further or oppose responsible business. Such groups might be local lobbyists, a local chamber of commerce, an industry-sustainability initiative, or a local global compact chapter to which the business can connect.

3. *Sustainable factor conditions* (input conditions) refer to the degree of availability of high-quality, specialized inputs necessary for responsible business conduct. Organizations might want to assess the local human resources' preparedness for responsible business, see if the necessary inputs for production can be sourced sustainably, and if there are local financing opportunities specifically for responsible businesses.

4. *Local stakeholder demand conditions* (demand conditions) describe the nature and sophistication of stakeholders in the location. Companies might assess whether there is a local demand for sustainable innovation products by the

customer stakeholder, how strongly communities demand involvement by companies, and how inclined employees are to work in responsible organizations.

An important implication of Porters and Kramer's diamond model is that it can be interpreted both ways, inside-out and outside-in. In our examples, we applied outside-in thinking, asking "How does the local environment affect responsible business?" Businesses should also apply the opposite, inside-out thinking, asking, "How can responsible business improve the local infrastructure and create social and environmental value?"

## 13-4 PHASE 2: ASSESSING THE RESPONSIBLE INTERNATIONAL BUSINESS

*"Organizations are being called to operate from a paradigm of global responsibility. … A responsibility agenda addresses issues of poverty, human rights, international relations, institutional capacity building, globalization, fair trade practices, and eco-effectiveness."*[23]

We view **international business** as "all commercial transactions, including sales, investments, and transportation, that take place between two or more countries."[24] All businesses involved in such transactions can be called international businesses. In this section, we will first assess the different types of international businesses and their respective implications for responsible business. In a second step, we will provide assessment models to define the degree of glocal responsibility realized.

An important consideration in understanding the tremendous power of international business is to observe how the combination of technology and communication has intersected with the growth of sustainability activities and the breaking down of political barriers, and the creation of global responsible business networks, such as the UN Global Compact, to accomplish those activities. International business, much like governments and other organizations, now operates in a system where distribution of information and communication about responsible business performance are increasingly instant, transparent, and symmetric.

In phase two, we address how to assess a global responsible business positioning through developing a clear, competitive strategy of responsible management over sustainable performance and ethical practices. The concept of a transnational model of responsible management will be important. We also review Carroll's[25] pyramid framework for business's social and ethical responsibilities to global stakeholders, and the principles of the Global Compact and the OECD's Guidelines for Multinational Enterprises. Responsible managers who accurately assess their global position have taken the second major step toward creating a glocally responsible business.

### 13-4a A Transnational Perspective of Responsible Management

What strategy should corporations have in social activities at a cross-national level? Assume, for example, that McDonald's and KFC, which are popular franchises located in the capitol city of Kuala Lumpur, Malaysia, are considering whether to sponsor local youth soccer teams. Further assume that the interest among young

**International business** refers to all commercial transactions that take place between two or more countries.

Malaysians in soccer is rapidly growing and that, culturally, these corporations want to assess whether it would be appropriate for Western franchises to sponsor youth soccer leagues in the city. The corporations believe they are exercising a degree of social responsiveness. Would local Malaysians feel that big companies are intruding on their "turf"? We adapt the following model and guidelines for making these kinds of responsible intercultural decisions.

*Assessing a business global position* means an organization develops a comprehensive international strategy to create value with its products or services by assessing where it stands in international markets. Responsible management in such an assessment creates value in the triple bottom line economically, socially, and environmentally, during the process of developing its strategy. The business will "develop a compelling value proposition (why a customer should buy its goods or use its services) that specifies its targeted markets (those customers for whom it creates goods or services)."[26] The "compelling value proposition" will clearly identify responsible business value in all areas.

## 13-4b  Assess the Type of International Firm the Company Is

International firms tend to form distinct patterns with regard to motivations in strategy, structure, and managerial processes, each of which directly impacts responsible management practices within the company. What are the consequences of the international characteristics of a company for its glocally responsible business practices? We can assess a company by reading the following descriptions and choosing one that fits most closely. Which of the types of international business provide the best characteristics for being glocally responsible in your opinion? The descriptions are adapted from Bartlett, Ghoshal, and Beamish[27] and include two additional international company types important in responsible business, the globally sourcing company and the export business:

1. *Globally sourcing companies (GSCs)* base their domestic activities on supply chains in foreign markets. With respect to responsible business, those companies may be described with the phrase "you don't have to be global, to be globally responsible." GSCs usually have operations and markets confined to one country, but have far-reaching global supply chains that create the urgent need for ensuring responsible business practices among suppliers abroad. The main activity for GSCs is to implement extensive supply chain tracing—control mechanisms by which to know suppliers and ascertain their sustainability, responsibility, and ethics practices.

2. An *export business (EB)* is a company that produces local domestic products for a foreign market. EBs must be sure that local practices are in line with the expectations of foreign customers. In a responsible business context, it is crucial that the highest sustainability, responsibility, and ethics standards are met to satisfy increasingly critical customers' high standards.

3. Managers of businesses with an *international mentality* "tend to think of the company's overseas operations as distant outposts whose main role is to support the domestic parent company in different ways, such as contributing incremental sales to the domestic manufacturing operations."[28] The company in essence sees itself as domestic. Many assumptions in the international mentality are based on the international product life-cycle theory, an unsustainable mentality of continuous upgrading and replacing of products, of active promotion of global consumerism. The relationship with the parent typically is centralized, and R&D

and new technology produced in the home country are transferred to the foreign market to boost product sales. The big challenge in glocally responsible management for businesses with an international mentality is to achieve a sufficient degree of localization in foreign operations, in order to truly understand local stakeholders and issues.

4. *Multinational firms* begin to emphasize localization and responsiveness to national cultural differences. Managers in foreign operations are likely to be "highly independent entrepreneurs, often nationals of the host country."[29] This multinational mentality allows responsible managers to depend on localized knowledge and decision-making power. Arthaud-Day[30] points to Unilever's international success in the laundry detergent market by adapting to national differences in local water conditions and washing practices. Such multinational firms, due to the local flexibility and engagement, are well equipped to effectively develop solutions to local social and environmental issues.

5. *Global companies* tend to "think in terms of creating products for a world market and manufacturing them on a global scale in a few highly efficient plants, often at the corporate center."[31] The mentality views the world as the strategic market rather than national or local markets. The global mentality may be "the same thing, the same way, everywhere." In a global company, responsible managers may have the fascinating possibility to create value for global stakeholders and to address truly global sustainability challenges.

6. *Transnational firms.* Limitations from the previous three mentalities caused strategists to develop a transnational mentality, one of becoming "more responsive to local needs while capturing the benefits of global efficiency."[32] A balance has been reached between centralization in the parent company, using its resources, R&D, and technology, and decentralization in the foreign subsidiary. Benefits of global efficiency have been achieved and localization has been realized. Responsible managers are posed with the challenge of managing within the appropriate organizational structure for the organization's strategy. Transnational firms typically have strong global sustainability, responsibility, and ethics standards, but are able to effectively customize those standards to local actions, perfectly aligned with issues, needs, and culture in each region.

Table 13.1 summarizes the characteristics of the different international business models described and compares them with the purely domestic business to provide recommendations for glocally responsible business strategy, operations, and actions.

## 13-4c Assessing the Company's Degree of Global Sustainability, Responsibility, and Ethics

How do you know how globally responsible a business is? In the following paragraphs, we will introduce two more ways to analyze the degree of global responsibility of an organization. The first one is an adaption of Carroll's responsibility pyramid to the global sphere. This assessment is a qualitative, model-based

**Table 13.1**   Classifying Global Companies and Responsible Business Recommendations

| Type of Company | Characteristics | | | | | Responsible Business Strategy, Operations, and Actions |
|---|---|---|---|---|---|---|
| | Global Sourcing | Foreign Markets | Foreign Operations | Global Strategy | Foreign Localization | |
| *Purely domestic business* | no | no | no | no | no | Focus on domestic responsible business strategy and actions. |
| *Export business* | no | yes | no | no | no | Focus on domestic responsible business strategy and product and process adjustment to foreign requirements. |
| *Globally sourcing company* | yes | no | no | no | no | Focus on domestic responsible business strategy and actions, but scrutinize global suppliers. |
| *International mentality* | yes/no | yes/no | yes/no | no | no | Shape a domestic responsibility strategy, but align foreign responsible business activities with local stakeholder needs and sustainability issues. |
| *Multinational firm* | yes | yes/no | yes | no | yes | Shape independent responsible business strategies and actions for each location that are consistent, but not connected. |
| *Global company* | yes | yes | yes | yes | yes/no | Shape a globally responsible business strategy giving primary concern to global issues and stakeholders. |
| *Transnational firm* | yes | yes | yes | yes | yes | Achieve glocally responsible business strategy that considers both with equal weight, global and local issues, and stakeholders. |

Source: Adapted from Bartlett, C., Ghoshal, S., & Beamish, P. (2008). *Transnational management: Text, cases, and readings in cross-border management*, 5th ed. London: McGraw-Hill.

assessment. The second is to use globally responsible business norms, specifically the Organisation for Economic Co-operation and Development's (OECD) Guidelines for Multinational Enterprises and the United Nations Global Compact (GC) Principles, for assessment.

### Model-Based Assessment

Many of the well-known responsible business performance assessment models can be used to assess responsible business internationally. One example is the model introduced by Carroll,[33] who adapted his responsibility pyramid framework to assess a business's responsibilities with global stakeholders. The pyramid focuses on the four categories of social responsibility and performance and places them in order with respect to global business stakeholders. Figure 13.5 displays this pyramid.

The four categories of responsibility of globally responsible business are based on the building block of *economic responsibility,*[34] which remains as the bedrock for MNCs doing business internationally and is essential to survival and growth. While businesses have economic responsibility to shareholders, they simultaneously have *legal responsibilities,* both domestically and with foreign subsidiaries. Significant differences often exist in legal systems between countries and present dilemmas for MNCs. Apple, for example, maintains its Foxconn Zhengzhou Chinese production plant where it assembles the iPhone 5 and frequently encounters differences with worker rights, holidays, and line quality issues. Foxconn closed a plant in Taiyuan

Figure 13.5 **Stages of Global Business Responsibility**

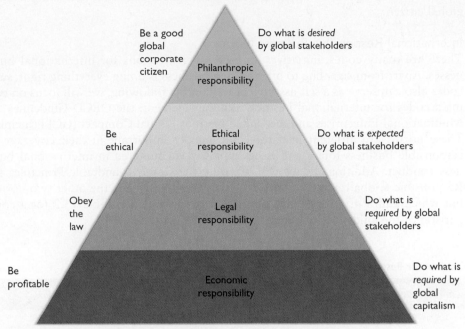

Be a good global corporate citizen — Philanthropic responsibility — Do what is *desired* by global stakeholders

Be ethical — Ethical responsibility — Do what is *expected* by global stakeholders

Obey the law — Legal responsibility — Do what is *required* by global stakeholders

Be profitable — Economic responsibility — Do what is *required* by global capitalism

Source: Carroll, A. B. (2004). Managing ethically with global stakeholders: A present and future challenge. *Academy of Management Executive*, 18(2), 114–120.

in northern China after 2,000 plant workers went on strike in October 2012 to protest their rights and to stand up to injustice.[35] Besides economic and legal responsibilities, Carroll's pyramid shows that *ethical responsibility* builds on economic and legal components and encompasses "the full scope of norms, standards, and expectations that reflect a belief in what employees, consumers, shareholders, and the global community regard as fair, just, and consistent with the respect for and protection of stakeholders' moral rights."[36] Ethical responsibility, if not codified into law, identifies universal standards such as the UN Global Compact or the Global Reporting Initiative. Finally, *philanthropic responsibilities* include discretionary social responsibilities of the business in the foreign country. Activities categorized as philanthropic responsibilities are not related to any of the other three responsibility types. Managers conduct them out of their own initiative.

The global pyramid of business responsibility provides a framework for responsible managers to use in assessing their global position. To build responsible business performance in practical terms, the responsible manager should strive to follow these four guidelines:[37]

- Make a *profit* consistent with expectations for international businesses.
- Obey the *law* of host countries as well as international law.
- Be *ethical* in company practices, taking host-country and global standards into consideration.
- Be a good corporate *citizen,* especially as defined by the host country's expectations.

After responsible managers have understood globalization and assessed their global position, they can proceed to mapping global business activity. They can use the four points as a map to earn profit in the economic bottom line while simultaneously obeying the law, maintaining sound ethical practices, and being a good global citizen.

## International Responsible Business Norms

There are many codes, initiatives, and even certifications for international businesses. Apart from signaling to others that a business is doing everything right, such codes also can serve as a self-assessment tool. In the following, we will focus on two main codes for international business and management: the OECD Guidelines for Multinational Enterprises and the United Nations Global Compact (GC) Principles. These norms are different in nature, but equally important in their coverage of responsible business topics and issues typically encountered in international business conduct. Additionally, we will illustrate the Caux Roundtable Principles for Responsible Globalization,[38] which are not as well-known as the other two norms, but which add a proactive dimension to the discussion. See Table 13.2 for a comparison of the guidelines provided by these three codes.

**Table 13.2** Comparison of Guidelines for Responsible International Business Activity

| United Nations Global Compact | OECD Guidelines for Multinational Enterprises | Caux Roundtable Principles for Responsible Globalization |
|---|---|---|
| **Human Rights** <br> *Principle 1:* Businesses should support and respect the protection of internationally proclaimed human rights; and *Principle 2:* make sure that they are not complicit in human rights abuses. <br> **Labor** <br> *Principle 3:* Businesses should uphold the freedom of association and the effective recognition of the right to collective bargaining; *Principle 4:* the elimination of all forms of forced and compulsory labor; *Principle 5:* the effective abolition of child labor; and *Principle 6:* the elimination of discrimination in respect of employment and occupation. <br> **Environment** <br> *Principle 7:* Businesses should support a precautionary approach to environmental challenges; *Principle 8:* undertake initiatives to promote greater environmental responsibility; and *Principle 9:* encourage the development and diffusion of environmentally friendly technologies. <br> **Anti-Corruption** <br> *Principle 10:* Businesses should work against corruption in all its forms, including extortion and bribery. | **Disclosure:** "Enterprises should ensure that timely, regular, reliable and relevant information is disclosed regarding their activities, structure, financial situation and performance." <br> **Employment and Industrial Relations:** "Enterprises should, within the framework of applicable law, regulations and prevailing labour relations and employment practices" ensure responsible labor practices. <br> **Environment:** "Enterprises should ... take due account of the need to protect the environment, public health and safety, and generally to conduct their activities in a manner contributing to the wider goal of sustainable development." <br> **Combating Bribery:** "Enterprises should not, directly or indirectly, offer, promise, give, or demand a bribe or other undue advantage to obtain or retain business or other improper advantage. Nor should enterprises be solicited or expected to render a bribe or other undue advantage." <br> **Consumer Interest:** "When dealing with consumers, enterprises should act in accordance with fair business, marketing and advertising practices and should take all reasonable steps to ensure the safety and quality of the goods or services they provide." | **Principle 1. The Responsibilities of Businesses:** *Beyond Shareholders toward Stakeholders* <br> "As responsible citizens of the local, national, regional and global communities in which they operate, businesses share a part in shaping the future of those communities." <br> **Principle 2. The Economic and Social Impact of Business:** *Toward Innovation, Justice and World Community* <br> "Businesses established in foreign countries ... should also contribute to the social advancement of those countries.... Businesses should contribute to economic and social development not only in the countries in which they operate, but also in the world community at large." <br> **Principle 3. Business Behavior:** *Beyond the Letter of Law toward a Spirit of Trust* <br> "Businesses should recognize that sincerity, candor, truthfulness, the keeping of promises, and transparency ... but also to the smoothness and efficiency of business transactions, particularly on the international level." <br> **Principle 4. Respect for Rules** <br> "To avoid trade frictions and to promote freer trade, equal conditions for competition, and fair and equitable treatment for all participants, businesses should respect international and domestic rules." |

| United Nations Global Compact | OECD Guidelines for Multinational Enterprises | Caux Roundtable Principles for Responsible Globalization |
|---|---|---|
| | **Science and Technology:** Enterprises should promote the diffusion and transfer of technologies, and promote local collaboration for know-how creation. **Competition:** Enterprises should follow the norms of fair competition, such as non-price fixing, collusion, and output restrictions. **Taxation:** "It is important that enterprises contribute to the public finances of host countries by making timely payment of their tax liabilities. In particular, enterprises should comply with the tax laws and regulations in all countries in which they operate and should exert every effort to act in accordance with both the letter and spirit of those laws and regulations." | **Principle 5. Support for Multilateral Trade** Businesses should support the multilateral trade systems of the GATT/World Trade Organization and similar international agreements. They should cooperate in efforts to promote the progressive and judicious liberalization of trade and to relax those domestic measures that unreasonably hinder global commerce, while giving due respect to national policy objectives. **Principle 6. Respect for the Environment** A business should protect and, where possible, improve the environment, promote sustainable development, and prevent the wasteful use of natural resources. **Principle 7. Avoidance of Illicit Operations** A business should cooperate with others to eliminate bribery, money laundering, or other corrupt practices: "It should not trade in arms or other materials used for terrorist activities, drug traffic or other organized crime." |

Sources: Global Compact, www.unglobalcompact.org/AboutTheGC/TheTenPrinciples/; OECD Guidelines, www.oecd.org/investment/mne/1922428.pdf; Caux Roundtable. (2002). *Draft principles for responsible globalization*. Saint Paul: Caux Roundtable.

## 13-5 PHASE 3: MAPPING INTERNATIONAL BUSINESS ACTIVITY

*"Multinational enterprises (MNEs) are regarded as playing a specific role given their global influence and activities in which they are confronted with a range of issues, stakeholders and institutional contexts."*[39]

Trade, foreign markets, global sourcing, foreign direct investment, and global partnerships are typical "international transactions"; we can also call them **international business transactions**. Each of those activities bears different challenges related to the triple bottom line, stakeholder relations, and specific ethical dilemmas. Also, each activity has specific areas of opportunity to do good.

When a company "maps" its global business, it engages in a strategy-based decision-making process that creates sustainable value throughout the entire supply chain. In this phase, we discuss how a company "maps" out decisions concerning (1) ethical global sourcing, (2) sustainable global trade, (3) foreign market seeking, (4) foreign subsidiaries, and (5) strategic global alliances. We address each of these activity areas and describe sustainable outsourcing decisions, labor practices, working environment conditions, and related issues.

Responsible business and management practices largely differ among countries in different economic development stages. Responsible business conduct, as illustrated earlier, is driven and governed by different forces that largely depend on a host country's stage of economic development. An important role is the one of fast-growing emerging economies. Often, economic-growth-driven industrial centers operate with little consideration to environmental and social issues. Economically developed countries, on the other hand, are main drivers of such

**International business transactions** are all transactions that take place between at least two countries.

questionable production methods by their demand for cheap mass consumer products that require such methods. This interaction between economically developed and developing countries is just one example for the complex issues that have to be taken into consideration when managing internationally. Topics to be taken into consideration by responsibly managed international businesses are summarized in the following list:

- *Global stakeholders:* Once companies engage in global activities, they automatically are influenced by and influence additional stakeholders globally. Such stakeholders might be workers in a foreign subsidiary plant or a global environmental NGO such as Greenpeace.

- *Global externalities:* Externalities are effects of a company's actions that are incurred by others. International businesses are often accused of outsourcing the negative social and environmental impacts, or external effects, of production to developing countries where labor and pollution legislation is typically on a lower level than in other countries. Glocally responsible businesses must map out global externalities and take actions to internalize them.

- *Fairness of distribution:* Global business activities have been seen as unfair from many different angles. Two prominent examples are job loss in developed countries through outsourcing activities and the related wages in developing countries that are often perceived as being too small and unfair.

- *International development:* Global transactions activities have the potential to contribute to economic and social development in host countries and in the world community. Examples are know-how transfer, the raising of local environmental and social standards, and the generation of income in host countries, as well as the addressing of issues of sustainable development by international companies.

These considerations that typically affect global business activities are summarized in Table 13.3.

Successfully engaging in glocally responsible business activities requires an alignment of local activities with a global

**In Practice**

**The World's Trash Can for Electronic Goods—Outsourcing Pollution?**

Guiyu, China, is the place where much of the world's used computers, cell phones, keyboards, and computer monitors goes to be recycled. Chinese e-waste recyclers disassemble and sort component parts left in huge piles on Guiyu streets. Smelting of toxic materials is done in the open, producing dense, noxious fumes. Hopeful signs of change in China include: the recent election of Xi Jinping as China's new premier, who recognizes that China's current development model is unsustainable; China's Greentech Initiative, which is a model for international green technology collaboration; and the relaunch of China's Global Compact Local Network.

Source: Lacey, P. (2012, January 27). Is China the global game-changer for sustainability? *The Guardian;* CBS News. (2010, January 8). *Following the trail of toxic e-waste.* Retrieved January 28, 2013, from *CBS News–60 Minutes:* www.cbsnews.com/8301-18560_162-4579229.html

**Table 13.3** Global Business Activity Areas and Related Responsible Business Considerations

| 1. Global Sourcing | 2. Global Trade | 3. Foreign Markets | 4. Foreign Subsidiaries | 5. Global Alliances |
|---|---|---|---|---|
| Issues in outsourcing and offshoring | Environmental impact of logistics | Local sustainability awareness | Foreign direct investment (FDI) | Joint causes |
| Support of bad labor practices and corruption | Transfer pricing | Promotion of responsible consumption patterns | International mergers and acquisition (M&A) | Shared competences |
| Supply chain tracing | Fair trade | BoP markets | Global transfer pricing and taxation | Infrastructure sharing |
| BoP sourcing | Ethical trade | Local production and consumption | Local development | Cross-sector partnerships |

© Cengage Learning 2015

## Boosting Sustainable Agriculture

Unilever is an example of an international leader in global sourcing. The company has set industry-leading, benchmark standards for sustainable performance by posting sustainable guideline documents for suppliers, including a *Responsible and Sustainable* sourcing guide for suppliers, a *Sustainable Agriculture Code*, and *Scheme Rules* for farmers and farm workers. The goal of these documents is to protect the rights of the workers and producers in terms of income and living conditions, reduce environmental impact by maintaining land, and enhance water availability and quality.

Similarly, Kraft Foods demonstrates international leadership in global sourcing. Kraft improved its sustainable position with agricultural commodities by 36 percent in 2011

and states that external verification and certification helped "boost crop yields, protect the environment and they help farm workers and their families improve their livelihoods." Through sustainable improvements in its global supply chain, Kraft Foods reduced energy usage by 16 percent, decreased water waste by 42 percent, and removed more than 60 million miles from transportation and distribution networks during 2005–2010.

Sources: Unilever. (2012, November 28). *Sustainable sourcing.* Retrieved November 28, 2012, from: www.unilever.com/aboutus/supplier/sustainablesourcing/; Kruschwitz, N. (2012). Why Kraft Foods cares about fair trade chocolate. *MIT Sloan Management Review, 54*(1), 1–5, p. 3.

responsible business strategy. This means, in practice, that an international organization should first establish its overall responsible business strategy, and then develop a global strategy, which then translates into local responsible business operations. Once a commitment is made to responsible goals, the challenge is to translate those to international operations and down through the international supply chain.

In the following sections, we will provide a brief overview of the sustainability, responsibility, and ethics implications of the global activity areas mentioned earlier, and discuss how to integrate them into an organization's glocal business strategy.

## 13-5a Global Sourcing

**Global sourcing** is the process of procuring inputs used throughout the supply chain internationally. Responsible global sourcing relies on not only external verification but also an ongoing self-assessment within the company. The company's own standards, applied internally, are transferred through responsible sourcing and supply chain management to sourcing partners in the supply chain. Exemplary methods might be the establishment of a responsible sourcing policy, codes of conduct for suppliers, and supplier development programs with a focus on sustainability, responsibility, and ethics.

An area of increasing importance is BoP sourcing. **BoP sourcing** refers to sourcing activities involving small and medium enterprises at the **base of the pyramid (BoP)**. Prahalad[40] estimated that 4 billion people live in the "base of the economic income pyramid," which is almost 60 percent of the world's population. What is the role of small, medium, and large businesses in the BoP market? Do international businesses have an ethical mandate to include bottom-of-the-pyramid countries (per capita income of less than $1,000 a year)? Yes, according to some scholars who advocate an urgent need for responsible international management to globally

**Global sourcing** is the process of procuring inputs used throughout the supply chain internationally.

**BoP sourcing** refers to sourcing activities involving small and medium enterprises at the base of the pyramid.

**Base of the pyramid (BoP)** refers to approximately 4 billion people worldwide living with very low income.

integate the BoP countries.[41] Responsible managers will find two main approaches to engage with the BOP markets:

- *Country identification:* First, they might actively seek out viable suppliers from countries that fall into the BoP criteria. Buying from suppliers from such countries is then estimated to translate into economic development, more employment, and rising wages. The chain of events here is rather difficult to track down.
- *Supplier identification:* The second BoP sourcing model is to directly engage with a supplier that works with people from the base of the economic pyramid and is known for their practices in poverty reduction and wealth creation with those individuals.

BoP entrepreneurs can be reached by creating markets for sustainable trade and promoting high-value products made of local raw materials. In contrast, BoP sourcing has the unique sustainable goal of wealth creation for those with lowest incomes. Responsible managers who use BoP sourcing direct company resources toward BoP entrepreneurs to commercialize local raw products and create markets for sustainable trade.

Business models in BoP markets are proving effective. The World Economic Forum noted, as an example, that business actions to strengthen the food value chain in developing countries meet two important goals. First, private sector businesses open up opportunities in a "growing, profitable and largely untapped market," and second, in "poor communities, innovative approaches can improve livelihoods."[42] These new business models are highly decentralized and locally adapted and focused, which makes them an excellent tool to, at the same time, achieve a high degree of local adaptation and simultaneously create value. When responsible managers encourage their companies to tap into the BoP market, they can, in many settings, achieve a strong economic competitive advantage in their domestic or global market and garner better community and stakeholder relationships locally and abroad.

Another critical area for responsible business on a global scale is the topic of **outsourcing**. Outsourcing typically means a company chooses a third-party company to provide a needed service or process that was before done by the company itself. **Offshoring** implies that work, before done domestically, is now done overseas, either by outsourcing or by M&A of foreign subsidiaries. Often outsourcing comes with offshoring, since one of the main motivations for companies in economically developed countries to outsource is for cost reduction. Another main motivation is to be able to concentrate on core processes and leave secondary processes to other companies that are specialized in them. Both can be achieved abroad by lower labor costs and often the same or even better skill level in developing countries. Both topics, outsourcing and offshoring, may lead to social, environmental, and ethical issues if not managed responsibly. *Supply chain tracing* is an important means of monitoring the social, environmental, and ethical issues farther up the supply chain.

While sourcing is primarily concerned with the relationship of a buying company to a supplying company, global trade, which will be illustrated in the next section, refers to the activity in a global network of buyers and suppliers of goods and services.

## 13-5b Global Trade

Global trade has been widely criticized for many of the ailments of the global economic system. On the other hand, trade also the potential to reduce economic inequalities and to create a truly inclusive global economic system. **Responsible trade** has to

---

**Outsourcing** refers to a model where a company chooses a third-party company to provide a needed service or process.

**Offshoring** means that activities that were done domestically are now carried out abroad.

**Responsible trade** refers to practices that mitigate the potential negative impacts of trade and harness the potential of trade to do good.

consider both facts, which is why responsible trade refers to practices that mitigate the potential negative impacts of trade and harness the potential of trade to do good. In the following, we will illustrate the three great responsible trade movements of sustainable trade, fair trade, and ethical trade.

**Sustainable trade** refers to trade as a tool to further sustainable development, socially, environmentally, and economically. While trade, especially the environmental impact of global logistics, poses a challenge to sustainable development, it also may serve as a tool to redistribute wealth globally and to further economic and social development worldwide. A key document for sustainable trade is the "Winnipeg Principles for Trade and Sustainable Development,"[43] which was published by the International Institute for Sustainable Development four years after the organization was launched, in part because of criticisms that the World Trade Organization did not effectively address sustainable development issues.[44] Although the original document was directed at policy makers, the Winnipeg Principles can be adapted to be a guide of topics to be considered for responsible managers in international trade:

1. *Efficiency and cost internalization:* Use as few resources as possible, and make sure to pay the full cost for all external costs of the traded good or service.

2. *Equity:* Use trade to actively promote equity between developing and developed countries.

3. *Environmental integrity:* Ensure that trade remains within the regenerative capacity of ecosystems.

4. *Subsidiarity:* Make sure that the corporate policies in international trade are in line with the highest local jurisdictional and international standards and, if necessary for sustainability, even exceed those.

5. *International cooperation:* Cooperate with international trade bodies to achieve sustainable development and to resolve disputes in a fair dialogue.

6. *Science and precaution:* Make international trade decisions while informed by the scientific insights regarding the interaction of trade and social/environmental systems. If in doubt about the effect of a trade activity, act with caution.

7. *Openness:* Communicate trade activity and effects of it openly to stakeholders, and participate in the dissemination and creation of knowledge on the intersection of trade and international development.

**Fair trade** is a "trading partnership, based on dialogue, transparency and respect, that seeks greater equity in international trade."[45] In this type of partnership, a buyer provides, typically to small-scale producers, various guarantees with the goal to create greater equity between trade partners in developing and developed countries. The guarantees given to producer partners in the trade relationship include a fair price, above the market level, long-run supplier relationships, and support in the social development of producer communities.[46] Usually fair trade labels at least ensure that growers and producers receive fair market value for their products. Ethical practices in fair trade determine fair prices. Fairtrade Labelling Organizations International (FLO), based in Bonn, Germany, is an umbrella organization overseeing twenty-one fair trade organizations and helping to administer fair trade globally. The Fair Trade Foundation in the UK is a member of FLO and requires "companies to pay sustainable prices (which must never fall lower than the market price)," addressing discrimination against the poorest and weakest producers.[47] These oversight groups provide fair trade labels and certification for farmers and producers worldwide.[48]

**Sustainable trade** refers to trade as a tool to further sustainable development, socially, environmentally, and economically.

**Fair trade** is a trading partnership based on dialogue, transparency, and respect that seeks greater equity in international trade.

## Locally Produced, Globally Traded

The business practices of one African company provide an example of sustainable trade principles. The multinational Export Trading Group (ETG), a Tanzania-based agricultural company "that sources commodities from Africa's small farmers and sells those goods to China, India and elsewhere," has the vision of becoming the leading supplier of African agricultural products to the world. The company seeks to enhance the African continent's growth through exporting and marketing of its locally produced commodities. Its website promotes the end-to-end supply chain solution that integrates farming, trading, and processing of agricultural commodities. ETG illustrates the success of global trade in locally produced products.

ETG trades twenty-five different commodities, including rice, fertilizer, cashews, and coffee, and estimates $1.5 billion revenue in the 2012 fiscal year. To promote global trade, ETG maintains a commitment to the principles of integrity, responsibility, and accountability through the development of communities that are historically disadvantaged. The company seeks to promote sustainable, livelihood-enhancing projects by setting up small-holder microfinance schemes for communities through investment from private-equity firms. The result is the economic enhancement of disadvantaged communities.

Sources: Wonacott, P. (2012, November 13). Carlyle Group to make African investment. *The Wall Street Journal*, p. C3; Export Trading Group. (2012, November 16). *ETG at a glance*. Retrieved from www.etgworld.com/

---

While fair trade creates mostly value for the local community stakeholders, or producers in fair trade partnerships, **ethical trade** mostly focuses on the employee stakeholders of producing companies in developing countries. Most ethical issues in trade can be found in the working conditions of employees of developing countries' factories, which is why ethical trade is often associated with ensuring compliance with international labor standards.[49] For instance, the ethical trading initiative provides detailed guidance on how to ensure the absence of bad labor practices in companies' global supply chains. The ETI Base Code addresses ethical issues related to employees, such as the payment of a living wage, non child labor, and inhumane treatment.[50]

### 13-5c Foreign Markets

**Foreign market seeking** refers to efforts to expand beyond the domestic home market. When companies enter into foreign markets, perhaps introducing a new product or service, they have an opportunity to do good and bad. Good can be done to transfer valuable technologies, to provide access to better products, and to shape consumption patterns. Bad can be done if nondomestic products destroy important established industries or promote unsustainable consumption patterns. Multinational companies with high brand power that is desired in foreign markets, particularly in developing countries, especially can find themselves in an ambassadorial role. The new middle classes, as in India, China, and the other BRICS countries, are at a crossroads: either moving toward new more sustainable consumption patterns or following a misguided and unsustainable consumerist pattern. It is simplest for companies that enter foreign markets to go the easy way of promoting consumerism, which is definitely better for short-run sales—a factor that is crucially important for successful foreign market entry.

**Ethical trade** aims to ensure the avoidance of ethical issues in global supply chains.

**Foreign market seeking** refers to efforts to expand beyond the domestic home market.

What decision-making processes should be followed in determining new markets and new foreign markets for products or services? Market analysis will focus on what natural resources are available in the country, availability of adequate labor, capital resources, or government support. A country's conditions, for instance, may shift consumer tastes to locally sourced products. Charles Redell[51] reported how food suppliers and grocers in the United States are turning to local growers and organic products, efforts that clearly reduce overhead cost and impact of transportation on the environment. A consumer and market analysis will determine how well organic and local products or services will sell. Geopolitical factors, cultural diversity, and legal issues will be considered in the market entry process. Solar World, a German firm with a plant located in the United States, led a group of seven U.S.-based manufacturers to file a complaint against China alleging that solar panels were being sold below market value. A company also will begin with an analysis of its own core resources and capabilities. Analyzing economies of scale will be involved in decisions of transportation or creating a subsidiary manufacturing plant abroad. India remained as one of Starbucks last untapped markets when Starbucks decided to form an alliance with India's Tata Group to open stores in a country known as a land of tea. Starbucks has achieved success so far.[52]

In the following, we will highlight three popular forms of market entry that, at the same time, provide an excellent initial strategic position:

- *Sustainable market innovation:* Especially products furthering, and based on, new sustainable consumption patterns have a crucial role in promoting sustainable consumption in both developed and developing countries. Companies seeking to enter foreign markets may have a differentiation advantage over market incumbents if they are entering the market with an innovative product serving society and environment, while providing premium value to customers. Such companies pursuing a "sustainable market innovation strategy" to enter a foreign market may, from the beginning, create an image of a "good business." A company might, for instance, actively seek out highly unsustainable foreign markets and aim at actively changing products and consumption patterns in the market for more sustainability. Communication and marketing included in the strategy may combine cause-related marketing campaigns highlighting the product's social and environmental value-creation potential and social marketing to change consumers' behavior patterns toward sustainable living.

- *Sustainable infrastructure:* Many countries and consumers do not have the infrastructure to develop sustainably. For example, a location might lack recycling systems, renewable energy sources, know-how for responsible management, or even access to clean drinking water. Such infrastructure gaps exist in both developing and developed countries. Many businesses have the potential to create or to be involved in creating such sustainable infrastructure through products and services while, at the same time, entering a foreign market and improving the sustainable development of the respective location. Creating sustainable infrastructure can also involve addressing local sustainable development issues through the company's operations, which both contributes to locally sustainable development and creates goodwill among local stakeholders involved in these issues.

## In Practice

### Sustainable Development through Market Entry?

Starbucks has taken on the challenge of BRICS markets. The company formed an alliance in 2011 with India's Tata Group to bring coffee to India, after it had already opened more than 1,500 stores in China. Starbucks has the global commitment to maintain its high sustainability standards, continue improvement in water quality, and support local regional farmers in social, environmental, and economic programs.

Source: Beckett, P., Agarwal, V., & Jargon, J. (2011, January 14). Starbucks brews plan to enter India. *The Wall Street Journal*, p. B8.

- *Base of the pyramid (BoP).* The BoP market represents the poor and needy of the world, and understanding the BoP means we must first "stop thinking of the poor as victims or as a burden and start recognizing them as resilient and creative entrepreneurs and value-conscious consumers."[53] But who are those low-income consumers? When the United Nations first implemented the Millennium Development Goals Indicators in 2005, eradication of extreme poverty and hunger was listed as the first goal. The extreme poor were defined by the UN as the proportion of the population whose income (purchasing power parity) is less than $1.00 a day, or the poorest one-fifth in a nation's consumption. Others have defined the BoP parity rate a bit higher at $2.00[54] and $8.00.[55] The millennium goal sought to reduce by one-half both the level of global poverty and hunger by 2015.[56] To access the BoP market, the crucial two considerations are (1) How do low-income consumers consume? Where and what do they buy? What is the optimum price and packaging size? and (2) most importantly, What are the most important needs of those consumers, currently underserved?

## 13-5d  International Subsidiaries

As illustrated with the different international businesses models in phase two, international companies, only in very few cases, can be global without relying on **international subsidiaries**. Working with such subsidiaries may involve many different strategies and activities. In the following paragraphs, we will focus on three aspects important for building and relating with foreign subsidiaries. The three aspects are foreign direct investment (FDI), international M&A, and transfer pricing and international taxation.

**Foreign direct investment (FDI)** is a measure of foreign ownership consisting of financial investments and tangible or intangible assets transferred abroad. FDI should be mediated by the firm's strategy of supporting locally sustainable development (e.g., through economic development and poverty alleviation), include local stakeholder interests (e.g., the ones of local governments and employees), and make sure to avoid ethical issues in the process (e.g., bribing). The firm's assets can range from production facilities to personnel operating a facility or working in sales and marketing. Mainstream multinationals usually expand into foreign markets through two avenues. The firm "has to choose between non-equity entry modes such as exporting through agents and licensing, and equity-based entry modes, in which the local enterprise is either partially or wholly owned."[57] The second choice, equity-based modes, will be discussed in greater detail under mergers and acquisitions. Expanding internationally through equity-based entry modes basically involves *acquisitions*, purchasing or leasing existing production facilities to launch a new production activity, or *greenfield investment*, which refers to construction of new operational facilities.

FDI provides excellent potential for economic development. Financial investment in other countries may help to strengthen economies, and with them socioeconomic systems. Often the long-term commitment implied by an FDI increases the credibility and underlines the serious intentions of investing companies. This in turn can serve as a basis to develop long-lasting relationships for local, and with it international, development. International development and responsible business can build mutually reinforcing systems through which shared value between host country and company can be created.[58]

**International subsidiaries** are business units located in foreign countries.

**Foreign direct investment (FDI)** is a measure of foreign ownership consisting of financial investments and tangible or intangible assets transferred abroad.

A **merger** is when two companies voluntarily become one and exchange financial investments on a mutual basis. Consolidation, perhaps, would better describe such a transaction. On the other hand, an **acquisition** is the voluntary or forced majority purchase of another firm's assets; such transactions are sometimes referred to as takeovers. When the French cosmetics firm L'Oréal acquired the British cosmetics retailer Body Shop in 2006, the purchase was considered a takeover.[59] For Body Shop, the move brought reputational issues, as both companies' contradictory reputations, especially in the issue of animal testing, were seen very skeptically by stakeholders. International companies move toward consolidations and acquisitions for different reasons, and each choice involves sustainable considerations, ethical decisions, and responsible implications for both companies.

Motivations for acquiring or merging with a foreign company are manifold. Often, a business seeks to acquire resources not available domestically. Resources also may be too expensive to acquire in the home country or, such as in the case of natural resources, nonexistent, or depleted. The decision to acquire internationally may involve new technologies or R&D capabilities, such as in the case of low-cost software development in India. Mergers and acquisitions also might be motivated by joining forces to increase competitiveness in a responsible business. Another reason might be the availability of cheap labor, unique commodities in a country, and even lower taxes or government support. For instance, Boeing has established significant aerospace engineering facilities in the Mexican states of Queretaro and Baja California that draw on a labor market of high-level, highly trained engineers who work for comparatively low wages.

Regardless of the reason an international business moves toward consolidations or acquisitions, responsible managers must integrate sustainable objectives and ethical practices throughout the decision-making process. The sustainability, responsibility, and ethics assessments should consider the impacts of potential issues, such as bad work conditions or human rights violations within inexpensive labor countries and potential environmental issues. The diamond model illustrated earlier provides an extensive assessment tool for understanding the rationale for, and implications of, investing in certain locations. The process of checking economic, social, environmental, and ethical implications of a merger or acquisition is called **due diligence**.

Responsible management during a consolidation must balance the interests of at least two main stakeholder groups. Moral problems of managers fall into two different institutional contexts, and different sets of norms operate in each context.[60] On the one hand, the responsible manager relates to trading partners in the market. The norms relating to market operations may focus on profit, for example. On the other hand, a responsible manager also determines how to relate to subordinates in the company during a consolidation or acquisition. Managers may develop manipulative attitudes in interpersonal relationships and tend "to treat a person as an object or a means of achieving goals beyond that person him/herself."[61] Responsible

## In Practice

### Sub-Saharan Africa Fund

Consider again the multinational Tanzania-based agricultural Export Trading Group (ETG). What fuels the company are private-equity investors such as the Carlyle Group, a buyout company that invested $210 million into ETG with two other investors. Apparently, this amount represents one of Africa's "bigger private-equity investments in recent years," and it supports sustainable activities. Carlyle's new fund is called the Sub-Saharan Africa Fund, and the purpose is to source commodities from Africa's small farmers and sell those goods to Asia and elsewhere. Such responsible foreign direct investment represents a future trend of infusing foreign assets into new African companies and consumers who seek to meet developed countries' stronger demands for food and energy.

Source: Wonacott, P. (2012, November 13). Carlyle Group to make African investment. *The Wall Street Journal*, p. C3.

## In Practice

### Joining Forces across Sectors for Global Impact

A merger took place between Oslo-based Det Norske Veritas (DNV), an independent foundation with the purpose of managing risk in life, property, and the environment, and the Two Tomorrows Group, located in the UK. Two Tomorrows assesses business risk in key areas such as carbon emissions, water scarcity, biodiversity, community investment, and human rights. By consolidating the two organizations, the aim was to "become the trusted, independent experts in sustainability to global business and governments."

Source: Kennedy, R. (2012, May 8). *More sustainability-consulting consolidation: DNV buys Two Tomorrows.* Retrieved November 17, 2012, from: www.greenbiz.com/blog/2012/05/08/dnv-buys-two-tomorrows

**Merger** refers to two companies voluntarily becoming one and exchanging financial investments on a mutual basis.

**Acquisition** refers to the voluntary or forced majority purchase of another firm's assets and is sometimes referred to as a takeover.

## THINK | ETHICS

### The Purpose of M&A

Ethical issues clearly arise for responsible managers during consolidations and acquisitions. The merger of one entity with another in "high-leverage finance capitalism" creates ethical decisions for all who are involved. Nielsen focused on causes of the 2007–2009 economic crisis and identified a basic ethical tension in consolidations, citing the evolution of different forms of capitalism through a process of "creative destruction." In other words, the goal of many consolidations before the crisis was the acquisition of wealth for a select few, showing capitalism in its worst form. Nielsen drew upon Aristotelian ethics to suggest "that the purpose of business activity/praxis is to create wealth in a way that makes the manager a better person and the world a better place." Responsible managers must fundamentally reassess the purpose and impacts of consolidations and acquisitions.

Sources: Nielsen, R. P. (2010). High-leverage finance capitalism, the economic crisis, structurally related ethics issues, and potential reforms. *Business Ethics Quarterly, 20*(2), 299–330, p. 299; Schumpeter, J. A. (1947). *Capitalism, socialism, and democracy.* New York: Harper and Brothers.

managers can model exemplary behavior during a consolidation through effective communication with employees and by respecting them as individuals and ends in themselves, not as mere means for a successful consolidation or acquisition.

**Transfer pricing** refers to the rates the parent company charges for its products or services to subsidiaries, or the rates its subsidiary or division charges to the company's foreign subsidiary or division. Transfer pricing may also occur between the rates two subsidiaries charge each other when they engage in trade. Domestic governments have difficulty taxing the income of multinational enterprises, and ethical issues arise with taxing and transfer pricing. Tax rates, for instance, may differ between the home country's domestic operation and the tax rate of its foreign subsidiary. Ethical dilemmas and questions that might arise with transfer pricing are, among others, the following:

- Should I pay higher domestic taxes to strengthen the home country or should I promote foreign investment for the creation of equity?

- International businesses might engage in transfer pricing to manipulate prices paid between subsidiaries to avoid paying taxes.[62]

- How much is a fair profit for parties involved in transfer pricing?

According to the OECD, transfer pricing can have a "dramatic impact on the allocation of an international business's taxable profits among the countries in which it operates."[63] This is why transfer pricing can be a tool either to create greater equity between countries or to maintain or even increase inequalities. Hansen, Crosser, and Laufer[64] propose to mitigate the issues involved in transfer pricing and taxation by the application of a common principle, which is "the willingness to sacrifice one's self-interest for the well-being of others."[65] Responsible managers, when confronted with taxing and transfer pricing issues, can develop codes of ethics or establish sets of values for a company that cares for the well-being of other countries and locations. Responsible managers can foster social justice and moral transformation of others and still ensure cost avoidance and tax optimization.

**Due diligence** describes the process of checking economic, social, environmental, and ethical implications of a merger or acquisition.

**Transfer pricing** refers to the rates paid internally inside the company when products or services are transferred from one subsidiary in one country to another country and subsidiary.

**Strategic alliances** are medium to long-term relationships created for a common purpose of the partners involved.

### 13-5e Global Strategic Alliances

According to Michael Porter, **strategic alliances** abroad are "the cooperative relationship between two or more organizations that range from shared information and research to joint ventures where minority partners are subcontracted to provide local market access and distribution channels."[66] These long-term collaborative agreements between firms go beyond normal market transactions but fall short of mergers. Daniels, Radebaugh, and Sullivan[67] define three types of strategic alliances:

- *Scale alliances* pool similar assets so each firm can conduct business activities in which they already have experience.

- *Link alliances* combine complementary resources to expand into a new area.

- *Vertical* and *horizontal* alliances differ on whether levels are added to the value chain (vertical) or companies align on the same level (horizontal).

Strategic alliances can be based on many different types of relationships and typically involve minority ownership. In responsible business, especially cross-sectorial, alliances are of great importance. In cross-sectorial alliance, for instance, businesses and NGOs, or businesses and governmental agencies, develop joint actions for a shared social, environmental, economic, or ethical goal. **Cross-sectorial alliances** involve partners from different sectors that develop joint activity for a common purpose. The alternative to a cross-sectorial alliance is a *sectorial alliance* that involves players from the same sector. The great advantage of cross-sectorial alliances in comparison to sectorial alliances is the pooling of complementary capacities and resources.

To successfully tackle global social and environmental issues, neither one business alone, nor one sector alone, can provide and scale solutions. There is a never-ending variety of different combinations of international strategic alliances. NGOs can form strategic alliances with other NGOs to exert stronger stakeholder influence on a large MNC. International interest groups that specialize in particular environmental issues, harmful products or materials sold to children, or mistreatment of certain groups of people may form link alliances to jointly change policies and regulations. Vertical alliances may be formed between a government agency and a small, new business innovating new packaging for a product. Companies may form horizontal alliances to combine R&D and technology to better their sustainable performance with particular products or manufacturing processes. Or companies may provide budgets for not-for-profit organizations to implement programs that tackle social problems. An important task of glocally responsible business is to develop a system of powerful alliances on both local and global levels in order to most effectively co-create solutions to sustainability challenges.

## 13-6 PHASE 4: RESPONSIBLY MANAGING IN A GLOBALIZED BUSINESS

*"Moreover, this first dimension cuts to the philosophical heart of an ongoing debate in international business ethics—the degree to which universal norms and values can or should be modified according to the exigencies of local, cultural environments."*[68]

While phase three focused on responsible business activities on the organizational level, phase four will translate glocally responsible business to the management level. The underlying question in phase four is: How to manage responsibly in an international setting? This first question can be split up into three subsequent lines of inquiry:

1. How do we manage a globally diverse workforce responsibly and inclusively, involving, among other factors, differences in religion, race, and socioeconomic levels?

2. How can we cope with cultural differences and achieve both mainstream and responsible management objectives?

3. What should be the lead morality in our company? The one of the country from which the company originates, or the morality of each respective host country? How do we resolve conflicts between differing moralities?

In the following text, we will elaborate on the first question under the title *Cross-National Diversity Management;* the second question is covered in the section entitled *Intercultural Management;* and the third series of questions are referred to as *Cross-Cultural Ethics* in the section by that title.

**Cross-sectorial alliances** involve partners from different sectors that develop joint activity for a common purpose.

## 13-6a Cross-National Diversity Management

**Cross-national diversity management** "refers to managing a workforce composed of citizens and immigrants in different countries."[69] The ideal goal of diversity management is to create a "multicultural organization," an organization that estimates and actively fosters cultural differences and provides equal opportunities.[70] The basis for successful diversity management in glocally responsible companies is the creation of a **globally inclusive workplace** that values and fosters differences within the workforce. Whether such a workplace has been created can be checked through a set of simple questions such as the following:[71]

- Are all groups and individuals equally welcome to participate in the organizational decision-making process?
- Are all groups and individuals equally informed about important decisions made in the workplace?
- Are all groups and individuals equally invited to formal and informal meetings and social events?

While diversity management is often a formal task of the human resources department, it should be on every manager's agenda. Often, true integration does not happen through the company's policies, but through personal initiative of supervisors, middle managers, or, more generally, leaders of work groups. Responsible managers in a globally diverse workplace can develop a mentality of "inclusivity" among employees and supervisors. *Inclusivity* in international management implies that workers from different backgrounds, such as cultures, religions, and races, can work together harmoniously, develop respect for individual differences, and develop tolerance as an ethical standard in the workplace.

Diversity in a responsible business cannot refer merely to employees, who represent only one out of many stakeholder groups to be included in decisions and business conduct. Responsible managers must transfer the principles of diversity management and inclusion to a broad set of stakeholders, from community members to suppliers and NGOs. Managing global stakeholder diversity is an additional challenge. The most salient external stakeholder for diversity management is the community stakeholder.

## 13-6b Intercultural Management

The proverb "when in Rome, do as the Romans do" carries much wisdom for responsible business. Nevertheless, globally operating businesses must also consider universal global standards, as they must respect local cultural differences. A difficult balance must be achieved between global corporate culture and practices rooted in a local culture. First, we begin with an analysis of cultural competence, which are cultural abilities important to operating business globally and necessary for responsible managers who will handle different multicultural issues.

What can responsible managers do to prepare themselves for effectively managing situations with intercultural issues? Geert Hofstede proposed a set of six dimensions[72] of cultural identity that have been developed into an international standard by which to assess organizational and national cultures.[73] Managers in global businesses can go to Hofstede's website and compare the characteristics of the company's home country with the ones of the host country.[74] Reconnecting to the globally inclusive business topic covered before, a manager could also compare

**Cross-national diversity management** refers to managing a workforce composed of citizens and immigrants in different countries.

The **globally inclusive workplace** values and fosters differences within the workforce.

# RESPONSIBLE MANAGEMENT IN ACTION

## Cross-Cultural Skills for Responsible Business Conduct

Imagine a large-sized production factory in a manufacturing plant located in an economically significant Asian country. Assume a Western multinational company outsources business to the plant, which assembles parts for electronic devices and manufactures certain other products.

The plant's code of conduct, which reflects Western sustainability standards, sets forth strict rules for working conditions regarding minimum age of employees, fair wages, and maximum hours worked each week. Air quality, air ventilation, and lighting conditions also are stated clearly. Yet the labor laws in the host country do not require these same standards, and line supervisors tend to become lax with enforcement. The plant director originates from the Western parent company's nationality, although all other employees in the plant, including floor supervisors, are host country nationals. Despite the standards in responsible performance, production floor supervisors have continued to encounter problems related to working conditions and human rights complaints throughout the production line.

One day an accident occurs in a poorly ventilated area; deaths occur, and other employees are injured. The incident

is reported in the local news and goes viral globally through social media. The company draws international criticism from media and NGOs, and experiences negative publicity and public criticism. A respected company executive from the parent company visits the plant to meet with supervisors and reassess management practices. The executive determines the root cause of the accident was the plant director's lack of cultural competence, mismanagement in cultural values, and ethical issues of authority, rule compliance, and intercultural supervision.

This incident illustrates a myriad of other multicultural issues that confront responsible managers in overseas business operations. Deep, cultural values in employees of respect for authority, respect for the rights of other individuals, and compliance with polices and rules are all embedded mentally within workers and strongly affect their communication with others. Multicultural issues daily confront responsible managers. Whose ethical practices do we follow? Which countries direct our behavior when employees differ in their compliance with global regulations?

---

the cultural dimensions of the home culture of a specific employee group with those of the culture of the majority of company employees. The cultural dimensions are:

1. *Individualism* refers to cultures with loose ties between individuals, while *collectivism* describes cultures in which individuals are typically embedded into strong groups.

2. *Power distance* describes the acceptance and expectation of power to be distributed unequally.

3. *Uncertainty avoidance* describes to what degree individuals fear unknown or uncertain situations.

4. *Masculinity* refers to countries with very distinct gender roles, while *femininity* describes when gender roles overlap.

5. *Long-term orientation* aims at the maximization of future reward, while *short-term orientation* is oriented to past, present, and immediate future.

6. *Indulgence* refers to cultures that emphasize enjoying life and having fun, while *constraint* makes reference to cultures that suppresses fulfillment of basic and natural human drives through strict social norms.

By examining the cultural dimensions, managers can draw valuable insights for responsible management conduct. For instance, if a manager is working with people from a strong masculinity culture, feminist and equal employment programs will probably encounter resistance. In countries with short-term orientation, the concept of sustainability might not be accepted as easily as in a country characterized by a strong long-term orientation. Upon finding local cultural dimensions that are in the way of responsible business conduct, the best solution will probably be to create a distinct corporate culture. It has been suggested that national cultures change much more slowly than organizational cultures.[75] Companies might be able to internally role-model a culture that then slowly influences a shift in national culture. Cultural competences can help to better adjust to local culture.

Often responsible managers are asked to demonstrate their **cultural competence (CC)** within the unique realm of international business. But how important is it to combine overall responsible management with cultural competence? Most of us understand that working in a foreign subsidiary or division requires distinctive cultural skills. The international working environment presents unique cultural challenges and contexts not encountered at home, so we examine cultural competence as part of the management competences; it is crucially important for glocally responsible managers.

We adopt the international business definition of cultural competence as "an individual's effectiveness in drawing upon a set of knowledge, skills, and personal attributes in order to work successfully with people from different national cultural backgrounds at home or abroad."[76] Once responsible managers assess their cultural abilities, they can better manage sustainability performance in a globalized business. Several cultural attributes of this definition are:

- *Knowledge* is both cultural-specific and cultural-general,[77] and a responsible manager must acquire such knowledge about the culture, language, appropriate rules of interaction specific for that culture, and information about specific customs.[78] The responsible manager should receive country-specific training to gain knowledge of the culture's sustainability standards and ethical practices.

- *Skills* are defined as the person's facility to perform a specific behavior. While an "aptitude" speaks of a manager's capacity in future performance and "ability" is an acquired natural capacity to perform a task that the manager already has, skills imply a bit different concept. Skills include "foreign language competence, adapting to the behavioral norms of a different cultural environment, effective stress-management, or intercultural conflict resolution."[79]

- *Personal attributes* are a third major dimension of cultural competence. These include personality traits, leadership qualities, learned "ways of working," and tolerance of ambiguity. The responsible manager should develop qualities in cultural identity, avoiding biases, developing local contacts, and avoiding ethnocentrism.

Responsible managers must be able to manage sustainable performance, stakeholder relations, and ethical practices across different cultural settings and work successfully with stakeholders from different national cultural backgrounds at home and abroad. Without cultural competence, responsible managers will fall short in managing in a glocally responsible business. We will cover one especially critical part of intercultural management, how to behave in ethical dilemmas causes by cultural differences, in the next section on cross-cultural ethics.

**Cultural competence (CC)** refers to the ability to cope with cultural differences.

**Cross-cultural ethics** is ethical decision making under influence of different cultures' values.

## 13-6c Cross-Cultural Ethics

**Cross-cultural ethics** is ethical decision making under influence of different cultures' values. Cross-cultural ethics is a well-established field, and our discussion is pragmatic with a focus on management applications in ethical practices. We do not address ethics at the philosophical level, but aim to find processes and common ground among different cultures' ethics in order to efficiently deal with cross-cultural ethical dilemmas. What types of ethical issues will responsible managers face? A good example of a cross-cultural ethics dilemma is corruption (including graft, kickbacks, and preferential treatment).[80] While Western and global responsibility standards judge corruption as unethical, many local cultures see corruption as accepted practice, and as a legitimate cost of doing business. Which moral standard is right in the case of corruption? How do we make this decision in other cases where cultural moralities contradict?

International responsible managers often face situations and practices very different from those in their own culture. How do they determine what is right? When defining common standards of good conduct, Bailey and Spicer[81] distinguished between hypernorms, which are a country's national norms that operate across cultural contexts, and locally construed community norms. Managers realize that a country's culture is not a unitary, "internally coherent system of values and beliefs,"[82] but find fragmented cultural beliefs and competing sets of norms and practices. This observation makes the decision issue even more complex. One solution to the dilemma would be to find a set of universally acceptable ethical "base norms" that can then serve as a common ground for decisions that are acceptable to all cultures involved.

Two primary schools of thought exist when companies develop moral frameworks and face ethical issues within different cultures.[83] One school assumes that different cultures' ethical standards share no commonalities, which is why they have to be studied and managed independently. The other school argues that a set of core, universal values and ethical standards exist across cultures, but cultures differ in the specific application of these values within the culture.

Do universal ethics exist? The idea of such a "world ethos" aims at highlighting the core elements of a shared global ethic, a common ground. The underlying idea is that no matter what cultural and religious context we come from, we can typically agree upon a set of shared ethical values and principles.[84] A group of Muslim, Jewish, and Christian scholars drafted the interfaith declaration that illustrates the common ground among those world religions, and how the common elements can be used for business. The four elements suggested as universal are:[85]

- Justice (fairness)
- Mutual respect (love and consideration)
- Stewardship (trusteeship)
- Honesty (truthfulness)

Of course, those values mentioned are not the only ones that have relevance across cultures, but learning to base ethical decisions on shared principles and values can be extracted as an important recommendation for solving intercultural conflicts.

What cultural ethical conflicts might occur? Hendry[86] classifies culturally based ethical conflicts into three groups. This classification scheme will help responsible managers understand

## THINK | ETHICS

### Harnessing Ethnic Diversity for Better Decision Making

Afriland First Bank is a global bank located in Cameroon. It operates in neighboring countries, such the Democratic Republic of Congo, Equatorial Guinea, and Sao Tome and Principe as well has having offices in Congo Brazzaville, France, and China. Afriland's expertise is the integration of African cultural values within modern management. Cameroon is a microcosm of African diversity. More than 200 tribes live in Cameroon. Afriland First Bank's mission is a focus on poverty alleviation through microbank development in rural areas. One key to success has been an understanding of diversity and the differing values diversity brings to the bank. One manager noted, "Since being in the bank I have never had to discuss the inter-ethnic aspect. But in meetings when people take the floor you see people are doing this from their own cultural education. In the north you have a big hierarchy and people behave according to their position in the hierarchy. It is similar for people from the west. In the centre and the east there is not this hierarchy. . . . We are mainly a Bamaleke culture, so we are taking people from other ethnic groups to bring diversity and to bring in other mentalities. By asking a person from another ethnic group, you may get a different perspective, and therefore arrive at a good answer."

Sources: Jackson, T., & Nzepa, O. N. (2002). *Afriland First Bank: Promoting a class of entrepreneurs in Africa.* Centre for Cross Cultural Management Research, p. Case; IFC. (2007). *eBanking on sustainability: Financing environmental and social opportunities in emerging markets.* Washington, DC: International Finance Corporation; AFBG. (2012). *The pact with success.* Cameroon: Afriland First Bank Group.

different types of ethical issues they will encounter in international cultures and lead them to develop appropriate solutions.

1. Ethical conflicts arise when the *values of two cultures lead to opposite conclusions*. That is, one culture appears to be right and believes the other is wrong. These are difficult cases because both cultures take opposite positions. Hendry[87] relates the example of how a hiring decision based on gender or social status over technical ability may be acceptable in one culture, while the other culture will consider this practice unacceptable or even illegal.

2. Ethical conflicts arise when a *rule or standard is morally important to one culture but not important to the other* or neutral. That is, no right or wrong value is placed on the standard. For example, a culture may view gift giving to bosses or key stakeholders as morally wrong while another culture views it as an acceptable practice, not because the practice is morally good but because it does not have significant moral importance. Relationships in the workplace, sexual morality, or use of alcohol or drugs may also fit into this second category.

3. Both *cultures agree on the same ethical value but circumstances create different interpretations of what is acceptable*. Both cultures may agree on the environmental damage done by pollution, yet national conditions related to industrial development and construction may create less strict standards for air quality and environmental preservation in one culture compared to another. Working conditions for employees, minimum age levels, and number of hours worked each week may fall into this category.

When facing ethical conflict, responsible managers must engage in intensive communication with the other culture to determine the category of conflict they are facing and to work on viable compromises. Otherwise, they engage in guessing or speculation that may lead to more intense conflict.

## PRINCIPLES OF INTERNATIONAL BUSINESS AND MANAGEMENT: GLOCALLY RESPONSIBLE BUSINESS

I.  A *glocally responsible business (GRB)* is a business that is at the same time globally and locally responsible, which is able to create value for stakeholders around the world and in every location, that actively addresses both global and local sustainability issues, and that manages global moral issues and intercultural ethics successfully.

II. Responsible management in international business consists of *four phases:* understanding glocalization, assessing the global position, mapping global business, and managing globally.

III. *Glocalization* is a mixture of the words *global* and *local* and describes global activities with a strong adaptation to local circumstances. Understanding glocalization means understanding drivers of globalization and local differences.

IV. There are different *types of international businesses.* The domestic business is different from the globally sourcing, export, international, multinational, global, and transnational perspectives.

V.  *Assessments* of glocally responsible business conduct can be either model-based or based on international responsible business standards, such as the OECD Guidelines for Multinational Enterprises and the UN Global Compact.

VI. Important *considerations* for glocally responsible business conduct are global stakeholders, global externalities, fairness of distribution, and international development.

VII. Components of a *global activity* "map" are global sourcing, global trade, foreign markets, foreign subsidiaries, and strategic alliances.

VIII. *Managing* in a globalized business entails global diversity management, intercultural management, and cross-cultural ethics.

| Process Phase | Has our company … | Sustainability | Responsibility | Ethics |
|---|---|---|---|---|
| Phase 1: Understanding glocalization | Has our company … | … understood its potential to globally and locally create solutions to sustainability issues? | … realized the importance of assuring the interest of stakeholders, especially employees in the foreign supply chains? | … found the potential ethical hotspots in its international operations? |
| Phase 2: Assessing the international responsible business | Have we … | … checked our international impacts on social, environmental, and economic capital? | … found out how well we answer to international stakeholders' claims? | … checked if we avoid all ethical dilemmas mentioned in standards for internationally responsible businesses? |
| Phase 3: Mapping international business activity | Does our international business activity … | … include a global sustainability strategy that is translated into local actions solving concrete social, environmental, and economic issues? | … maximize stakeholder value for all groups involved? | … avoid ethical dilemmas, for instance, in transfer pricing, labor relations, and exploitative trade relations. |
| Phase 4: Responsibly managing in a global business | Do our managers … | … consider and control the impact of international and local cultures in triple bottom line performance? | … apply intercultural diversity management, including employees, communities, and other local and global stakeholders? | … excel in managing cross-cultural ethics dilemmas considering both global norms and local culture? |

## KEY TERMS

acquisition  429
base of the pyramid (BoP)  423
BoP sourcing  423
cross-cultural ethics  434
cross-national diversity
    management  432
cross-sectorial alliances  431
cultural competence (CC)  434
due diligence  429
ethical trade  426

fair trade  425
foreign direct investment (FDI)  428
foreign market seeking  426
globalization  406
globally inclusive workplace  432
global sourcing  423
glocalization  405
glocally responsible business
    (GRB)  405
international business  415

international business
    transactions  421
international subsidiaries  428
merger  429
offshoring  424
outsourcing  424
responsible trade  424
strategic alliances  430
sustainable trade  425
transfer pricing  430

## EXERCISES

### A. Remember and Understand

A.1.  Define a glocally responsible business.

A.2.  Define the three types of responsible trade and explain differences and commonalities.

A.3.  The global map summarized CSR challenges and opportunities by continent and region for responsible business. Pick three continents or regions most important to you and explain context, priority issues, and trends.

A.4.  What is BoP? Describe how it is important to companies in the types of international activity areas.

A.5.  Describe the five activity areas of international businesses to be taken into consideration when a company "maps" its global business.

### B. Apply and Experience

B.6.  Look up information on one company with international activity. What type of international business would best describe this company: globally sourcing, export business, international mentality, multinational, global, or transnational? How do you think the company could better manage its glocally responsible business activities?

B.7. Give two examples of ethical conflicts when values of two cultures lead to opposite conclusions, two examples when rules or standards are morally important to one culture but not important or neutral to the other, and two examples when both cultures agree on the same ethical value but circumstances create different interpretations of what is acceptable. Create a list of ethical issues that address these examples.

## C. Analyze and Evaluate

C.8. Look up more information on Unilever as an international leader in global sourcing. Examine how the company's documents, *Responsible and Sustainable* sourcing guide for suppliers, the

*Sustainable Agriculture Code*, and *Scheme Rules* set benchmark standards for sustainable performance. What are the goals of these documents?

C.9. Look up more information on Kraft Foods and its international leadership in global sourcing. How has Kraft improved its sustainable position with agricultural commodities, with the environment, and with energy reduction?

## D. Change and Create

D.10. Consider how can you improve your own intercultural management competences and improve your knowledge, skills, and personal attributes in cultural competence.

D.11. Analyze the sustainability report of an internationally operating company and use the concepts covered in this chapter to develop one recommendation for improvement. Write an e-mail to the company using the contact information provided in the report, and follow up on answers.

---

## PIONEER INTERVIEW WITH GEERT HOFSTEDE

Courtesy of Geert Hofstede

Geert Hofstede is a pioneer of the cultural dimensions of business and management. Many of the concepts bear important insights for responsible managers, which is why his work provides excellent guidance for all who aim to be interculturally responsible managers.

**In 2011, you wrote an article titled "Business Goals for a New World Order: Beyond Growth, Greed and Quarterly Results." In an earlier survey in 2002, involving 1,900 respondents across seventeen countries, you found that leaders in most countries are primarily motivated by the immediate interest of the company (e.g., growth and this year's profits) or by the leader's ego (e.g., power and personal wealth). Respecting ethical norms and responsibilities toward society in general were items of lower preference. How does this have to change in order to reach business goals that are true enablers of "a new world order"? Is a change of goals possible? How can it happen?**

My article showed that perceived goals of business leaders differ considerably across countries. Your interpretation above is too simple. In countries where power is seen as more important, staying within the law is less important; where personal

wealth is important, responsibility toward employees counts less; where innovation is stressed, patriotism is not stressed; a stress on this year's profit opposes profits ten years from now; and growth is not sought everywhere to the same extent, and too much striving for growth opposes responsibility toward society, which to me includes sustainability. My article is not about how to change these things, but about how the changing economic weight of the various countries will affect the global picture.

**In 1993, you highlighted the "cultural constraints in management theories" by illustrating how management practices and basic approaches strongly differ internationally. How does this observation apply to responsible management topics, to how managers understand and behave in relation to sustainability, responsibility, and ethics?**

My 1993 article was not about management practices but about management theories. It showed how management books were based on American values and preached management practices that did not fit the culture of many other societies, including some that even in the USA itself were not really applied.

**What ethical and value conflicts do you consider most drastic between different cultural**

**backgrounds? What can responsible managers do to mitigate and solve ethical conflicts among cultures?**

See my answer to question 1 and my 2009 article where these are specified. Responsible managers should learn about cultural differences when dealing with other societies and might learn from other societies when operating in their own. And the USA is no longer the world's example, on the contrary. Management schools should teach about culture, and management students should get international experience.

**Are some cultures more inclined toward responsible or sustainable behaviors? An assumption might be, for instance, that a high score in long-term orientation would help a culture to embrace the long-run intergenerational thinking underlying sustainable development; the dimension of indulgence versus restraint might be important for a culture's openness to adopting sustainable lifestyles. Is it that easy?**

What is responsible in one culture may not be responsible in another. Long-term orientation is certainly an asset. I am not sure differences along the dimension of indulgence versus restraint are relevant to sustainability; more research would be needed to prove that.

**What else would you like to communicate?**

Management is rooted in economic thinking, but economics itself needs a new base—it is not a matter of rational choices because there is no universal rationality; it is not an exact science but a social, even a moral science. Fortunately, the number of economists discovering this is increasing. Recent examples include the book by the young Czech economist Tomás Sedlácek, published in Czech in 2009 and in English as *Economics of Good and Evil: The Quest for Economic Meaning from Gilgamesh to Wall Street*. Two Dutch professors of economics also have written books on economics and culture in which they use my categories: Eelke de Jong, *Culture and Economics: On Values, Economics and International Business* (London: Routledge, 2009), and Sjoerd Beugelsdijk with Robbert Maseland, *Culture in Economics: History, Methodological Reflections, and Contemporary Applications* (Cambridge: Cambridge University Press, 2011). And there are more.

## PRACTITIONER PROFILE: LAURA CLISE

Courtesy of Laura Clise

**Employing organization:** As a world leader in the nuclear energy business and as a significant, growing player in renewable energies, AREVA and its 48,000 employees worldwide help to supply ever safer, cleaner, and more economical energy to the greatest number of people. Its expertise and unwavering insistence on safety, security, transparency, and ethics are setting the standard, and its responsible development is anchored in a process of continuous improvement.

**Job title:** Director, Sustainable Development
**Education:** BA, International Relations, Carleton College, Magna Cum Laude, Phi Beta Kappa; MBA, Thunderbird School of Global Management, Magna Cum Laude, Pi Sigma Alpha, Alpha Beta Gamma

### In Practice

**What are your responsibilities?** I am responsible for the development and deployment of AREVA's North American sustainable development strategy, supporting the continued integration of sustainable development into regional business strategy. This includes stakeholder engagement, environmental footprint reduction, supplier diversity, and internal training.

**What are typical activities you carry out during a day at work?** Due to the transversal nature of sustainability-related activities, a typical day consists of a mix of facilitation and implementation. Oftentimes, the role requires the convening of internal stakeholder around a specific business initiative or program and supporting the alignment with sustainability objectives. The focus is often on defining a new program or enhancing an existing one by working with a group of business and functional leads to understand and then implement an approach that supports responsible growth (business success, rooted in environmental sustainability and social responsibility).

More concretely, I might start my day by reviewing a request for proposal with one of our businesses that requires input regarding our environmental management programs along with information on our use of diverse business subcontractors. That might be followed by a conference call led by an environmental think tank on the topic of scenario planning regarding the U.S. energy mix in 2030. Perhaps at some point during the day, I'll edit a blog post regarding a colleague's perspective regarding her first sustainability conference experience as an engineer whose full-time job is not focused on sustainability. There are always plenty of e-mails, including requests to participate in roundtable discussions regarding energy and climate or to speak at conferences on the importance of including climate in business education.

A typical day is varied. But while the topic or issue may shift, there is a common thread of facilitation, collaboration, change management, and communication.

**How do sustainability, responsibility, and ethics topics play a role in your job?** Sustainability, responsibility, and ethics play a central role in my job—both in terms of aligning internal stakeholder understanding and action and engaging external stakeholders in dialogue and partnership. We are a more effective company when sustainability, responsibility, and ethics are resonant in our activities and technologies. Through our product and service innovation, we have the opportunity to support environmental and social responsibility objectives, and yet our global energy challenges are not limited to technology. There is need for engagement in public dialogue to increase the understanding of transitioning to a clean energy economy that sustains economic prosperity, our planet, and the global community.

**Out of the topics covered in the chapter into which your interview will be included, which concepts, tools, or topics are most relevant to your work? How?** My day-to-day activity is often spent at the intersection of sustainability and responsibility topics. However, I believe that the continued instances of corporate ethics issues highlight the important work that remains regarding corporate governance, such that ethical management is part of the corporate culture.

Solving sustainability-related challenges requires input from a variety of sectorial actors, and while it is perhaps easy to talk about the necessity of multistakeholder, multisector partnership and collaboration, the effective facilitation thereof is more complex.

Leading companies have evolved their stakeholder engagement programs beyond an opportunity for dialogue to be vehicles for driving innovation. It will continue to be important to address stakeholder expectations and concerns, but the hope is that dialogue supports understanding, which can then lead to insight and opportunities for collaborative solutions.

### Insights and Challenges

**What recommendation can you give to practitioners in your field?** Take advantage of the culture of collaboration in the field of sustainability, corporate social responsibility, and corporate citizenship. In addition to following and engaging with business and sustainability leaders in the field, try to connect with someone a few years ahead of where you are on your professional trajectory.

Ensure that you have functional and business management expertise to draw upon. In addition to perseverance, progress depends on your ability to engage and enlist the support and partnership of a variety of company actors (not to mention external actors). Increasingly, professional opportunities are located "in the business" or "function," and it is therefore critical to be able to contribute, drawing on a sustainability perspective while leading an operational department or marketing a brand.

Patience. Passion. Persistence.

**Which are the main challenges of your job?** Sustainability often implies change. And change is difficult.

Many days, I feel as though my work is a protracted change management initiative. But using guidance from the change management discipline, sustainability professionals are slowly (and sometimes quickly) facilitating systemic shifts in the way that we source, produce, distribute, and engage around our technologies.

## China*

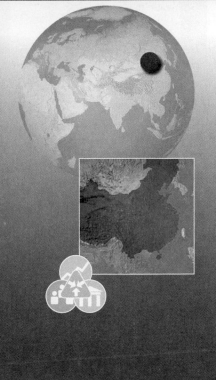

**14**

### Public Policy Rationales

- Enhance international economic competitiveness
- Address challenges to socio-economic integration

### Public Policy Activities

- Mandating: Corporate governance, labor law, environmental impact
- Partnering: Addressing CSR-relevant issues with national business associations and with international bodies
- Creating voluntary frameworks as the basis for soft law

### Public Policy Actors

- Ministry of Commerce of the People's Republic of China (MOFCOM)
- National Development and Reform Commission (NDRC)
- State Environmental Protection Administration (SEPA)
- Ministry of Labor and Social Issues

### CSR-Relevant Context Factors

- State in transition from a planned economy to an export-oriented market economy; development gaps between MNCs and SMEs
- Socialist state, with a broad support base; low government capacity for law enforcement and implementation
- Increasing intervention and participation of various interest groups and NGOs
- Problems with coordination of participatory activities

## India*

**22**

### Public Policy Rationales

- Enhance international economic competitiveness
- Address challenges to socio economic integration

### Public Policy Actors

- Mandating: Corporate governance laws and consumer protection; labor laws; CSR-reporting; environmental standards
- Awareness raising: Encouraging labeling programs; endorsing ISO 14000/9000; some funding for teaching
- Partnering: Coordination committee to promote affirmative action in the indian industry

### Public Policy Activities

- National foundation for corporate governance
- Ministry of labor and employment
- Ministry of corporate affairs

### CSR-relevant Context

- Increasing level of economic integration into the global economy, development gap between Indian MNCs and SMEs
- Low levels of government capacity for law enforcement and implementation, high levels of corruption
- Wide social gaps in dynamic society
- High level of political participation of societal actors, coupled with a high tolerance for dissent

## Germany

**20**

### Public Policy Rationales

- Create cross-sectoral synergies to achieve domestic policy goals
- Enhance international influence and reputation

### Public Policy Activities

- Mandating: In the fields of environmental protection, employment, social policy, and corporate governance.
- Partnering: Engagement in numerous alliances, initiatives, federations, and PPPs

### Public Policy Actors

- Federal Ministry of Labour and Social Affairs (BMAS)
- Federal Ministry for Family Affairs, Senior Citizens, Women and Youth (BMFSFJ)
- Federal Ministry for Economic Cooperation and Development (BMZ)

### CSR-relevant Context Factors

- High level of integration into the global economy, world leader in the export market
- High level of regulation, good law enforcement; decreasing level of social benefits, "crisis" of the conservative welfare state
- Well developed and influential civil society with wide range of issues
- Traditional forms of corporatism between actors, few flexible methods of articulating, and cooperating to match global challenges

## United States of America*

**34**

### Public Policy Rationales

- Enhance international competitiveness
- Address gaps in government capacity

### Public Policy Activities

- Mandating: No specific CSR laws; mandatory reporting on selected issues
- Partnering: Partnerships at the federal level; public-private partnerships (PPPs) at state and local level, mostly concerning environmental issues
- Setting incentives: Tax incentives; award programs; including CSR in financial guarantees

### Public Policy Actors

- At federal level: US Environmental Protection Agency (EPA); US Department of State
- At state level: e.g., California Public Employee's Retirement System (CalPERS)

### CSR-Relevant Context Factors

- High level of integration into the global economy; globally influential corporate players
- Federal political system with wide variation in policies; limited intervention of the federal government in areas of social welfare and regulation
- Vibrant civil society with a high degree of autonomy of actors; high level of influence of business on politics
- Widely varying modes of societal exchange, ranging from the cooperative to the conflictual

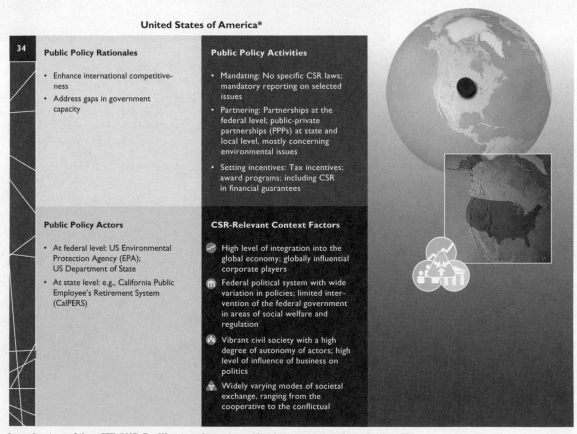

Source: Bertelsmann Stiftung; GTZ. (2007). *The CSR navigator: Public policies in Africa, the Americas, Asia and Europe.* Eschborn: GTZ.

1. Lacey, P., et al. (2010). *A new era of sustainability: UN global compact-accenture CEO study 2010.* New York: Accenture Institute for High Performance.

2. Lacey, P., et al. (2010). *A new era of sustainability: UN global compact-accenture CEO study 2010.* New York: Accenture Institute for High Performance.

3. Lacey, P., et al. (2010). *A new era of sustainability: UN global compact-accenture CEO study 2010.* New York: Accenture Institute for High Performance.

4. Matten, D., & Moon, J. (2008). "Implicit" and "explicit" CSR: A conceptual framework for a comparative understanding of corporate social responsibility. *Academy of Management Review, 33*(2), 404–424, p. 404.

5. Friedman, T., & Mandelbaum, M. (2011). *That used to be US.* New York: Picador/Farrar, Straus and Giroux.

6. Friedman, T., & Mandelbaum, M. (2011). *That used to be US* (p. 19). New York: Picador/Farrar, Straus and Giroux.

7. OECD. (2008). *OECD guidelines for multinational enterprises* (p. 8). Paris: OECD.

8. Husted, B. W., & Allen, D. B. (2006). Corporate social responsibility in the multinational enterprise: Strategic and institutional approaches. *Journal of International Business Studies, 37,* 838–849.

9. Robertson, R. (1995). Glocalization: Time-space and homogenisation-heterogenization. In M. Featherstone, S. Lash, & R. Robertson, *Global modernities* (pp. 25–44). Thousand Oaks: Sage.

10. Scholte, J. A. (2005). *Globalization: A critical Introduction* (pp. 65–77). Basingstoke: Palgrave Macmillan.

11. Daniels, J. D., Radebaugh, L. H., & Sullivan, D. P. (2013). *International business: Environments & operations* (p. 5). Upper Saddle River, NJ: Pearson Education.

12. Carvalho, G. O. (2001). Sustainable development: Is it achievable within the existing international political economy context? *Sustainable Development, 9,* 61–73.

13. Fontenelle, I. A. (2010). Global responsibility through consumption? Resistance and assimilation in the anti-brand movement. *Critical Perspectives on International Business, 6*(4), 256–272.

14. Doh, J., et al. (2010). Ahoy There! Toward greater congruence and synergy between international business and business ethics theory and research. *Business Ethics Quarterly, 20*(3), 481–502.

15. Doh, J., et al. (2010). Ahoy There! Toward greater congruence and synergy between international business and business ethics theory and research. *Business Ethics Quarterly, 20*(3), 481–502, p. 483.

16. Carroll, A. B. (2004). Managing ethically with global stakeholders: A present and future challenge. *Academy of Management Executive, 18*(2), 114–120.

17. Visser, W. A. M., & Tolhurst, N. (2010). *The world guide to CSR: A country-by-country analysis of corporate sustainability and responsibility.* Chichester: Wiley.

18. Bertelsmann Stiftung; GTZ. (2007). *The CSR navigator: Public policies in Africa, the Americas, Asia and Europe.* Eschborn: GTZ.

19. Matten, D., & Moon, J. (2008). "Implicit" and "explicit" CSR: A conceptual framework for a comparative understanding of corporate social responsibility. *Academy of Management Review, 33*(2), 404–424.

20. Porter, M. (1990, March/April). The competitive advantage of nations. *Harvard Business Review,* 73–93, p. 77.

21. Porter, M., & Kramer, M. (2006). Strategy and society: The link between competitive advantage and corporate social responsibility. *Harvard Business Review, 84*(12), 78–92, p. 85.

22. Moon, H. C., Rugman, A. M., & Verbeke, A. (1998). A generalized double diamond approach to the global competitiveness of Korea and Singapore. *International Business Review, 7*(2), 135–150.

23. D'Amato, A., et al. (2010). Leadership practices for corporate global responsibility. *Journal of Global Responsibility, 1*(2), 225–249, p. 226.

24. Daniels, J. D., Radebaugh, L. H., & Sullivan, D. P. (2013). *International business: Environments & operations* (p. 5). Upper Saddle River, NJ: Pearson Education.

25. Carroll, A. B. (2004). Managing ethically with global stakeholders: A present and future challenge. *Academy of Management Executive, 18*(2), 114–120.

26. Daniels, J. D., Radebaugh, L. H., & Sullivan, D. P. (2013). *International business: Environments & operations* (p. 406). Upper Saddle River, NJ: Pearson Education.

27. Bartlett, C., Ghoshal, S., & Beamish, P. (2008). *Transnational management: Text, cases, and readings in cross-border management,* 5th ed. (pp. 10–12). London: McGraw-Hill.

28. Bartlett, C., Ghoshal, S., & Beamish, P. (2008). *Transnational management: Text, cases, and readings in cross-border management,* 5th ed. (p. 11). London: McGraw-Hill.

29. Bartlett, C., Ghoshal, S., & Beamish, P. (2008). *Transnational management: Text, cases, and readings in cross-border management,* 5th ed. (p. 11). London: McGraw-Hill.

30. Arthaud-Day, M. L. (2005). Transnational corporate social responsibility: A tri-dimensional approach to international CSR research. *Business Ethics Quarterly, 15*(1), 1–22.

31. Bartlett, C., Ghoshal, S., & Beamish, P. (2008). *Transnational management: Text, cases, and readings in cross-border management,* 5th ed. (p. 12). London: McGraw-Hill.

32. Bartlett, C., Ghoshal, S., & Beamish, P. (2008). *Transnational management: Text, cases, and readings in cross-border management,* 5th ed. (p. 13). London: McGraw-Hill.

33. Carroll, A. B. (2004). Managing ethically with global stakeholders: A present and future challenge. *Academy of Management Executive, 18*(2), 114–120.

34. Carroll, A. B. (2004). Managing ethically with global stakeholders: A present and future challenge. *Academy of Management Executive, 18*(2), 114–120.

35. Gabbatt, Adam. (2012, October). *Foxconn workers on iPhone 5 line strike in China, rights group says.* Retrieved November 27, 2012, from *The Guardian:*www.guardian.co.uk/technology/2012/oct/05/foxconn-apple-iphone-china-strike

36. Carroll, A. B. (2004). Managing ethically with global stakeholders: A present and future challenge. *Academy of Management Executive, 18*(2), 114–120, p. 117.

37. Carroll, A. B. (2004). Managing ethically with global stakeholders: A present and future challenge. *Academy of Management Executive, 18*(2), 114–120, p. 118.

38. Caux Roundtable. (2002). *Draft principles for responsible globalization.* Saint Paul: Caux Roundtable.

39. Kolk, A., & Van Tulder, R. (2010). *International business, corporate social responsibility and sustainable development. International Business Review, 19*(1), 1–14, p. 1.

40. Prahalad, C. K. (2006). *The fortune at the bottom of the pyramid: Eradicating poverty through profits.* Upper Saddle River, NJ: Pearson Education.

41. Choi, C. J., Kim, S. W., & Kim, J. B. (2010). Globalizing business ethics research and the ethical need to include the bottom-of-the-pyramid countries: Redefining the global triad as business systems and institutions. *Journal of Business Ethics, 94,* 299–306.

42. World Economic Forum. (2009, January). *The next billions: Business strategies to enhance food value chains and empower the poor* (p. 2). Retrieved November 13, 2012, from https://members.weforum.org/pdf/BSSFP/ExecutiveSummariesBusinessStrategies.pdf

43. IISD. (1994). *Trade and sustainable development principles.* Winnipeg: IISD.

44. Tisdell, C. (2001). The Winnipeg Principles, WTO and sustainable development: Proposed policies for reconciling trade and the environment. *Sustainable Development, 9*(4), 204–212.

45. Fairtrade. (2012, November 23). *Fair trade system.* Retrieved November 12, 2012, from www.fairtrade.net/fileadmin/user_upload/content/2009/about_fairtrade/Fair_Trade_Glossary.pdf

46. Smith, S., & Barrientos, S. (2005). Fair trade and ethical trade: Are there moves toward convergence? *Sustainable Development, 13,* 190–198.

47. Foundation, Fair Trade. (2012, November 23). *FAQs.* Retrieved from www.fairtrade.org.uk/what_is_fairtrade/faqs.aspx

48. Huybrechts, B., & Reed, D. (2010, April). Fair trade in different national contexts. *Journal of Business Ethics, 92,* 147–150.

49. Smith, S., & Barrientos, S. (2005). Fair trade and ethical trade: Are there moves toward convergence? *Sustainable Development, 13,* 190–198.

50. ETI. (2012). *ETI base code.* Retrieved December 14, 2012, from *Ethical Trading Initiative:*www.ethicaltrade.org/eti-base-code

51. Redell, C. (2011, September 8). *Grocers embrace local, organic to try to drive growth in tough times.* Retrieved November 15, 2012, from Greenbiz.com: www.greenbiz.com/news/2011/09/08/grocers-embrace-local-organic-try-drive-growth-tough-times

52. Beckett, P., Agarwal, V., & Jargon, J. (2011, January 14). Starbucks brews plan to enter India. *The Wall Street Journal,* p. B8.

53. Prahalad, C. K. (2006). *The fortune at the bottom of the pyramid: Eradicating poverty through profits* (p. 1). Upper Saddle River, NJ: Pearson Education.

54. Prahalad, C. K. (2006). *The fortune at the bottom of the pyramid: Eradicating poverty through profits.* Upper Saddle River, NJ: Pearson Education.

55. World Economic Forum. (2009, January). *The next billions: Business strategies to enhance food value chains and empower the poor.* Retrieved November 13, 2012, from https://members.weforum.org/pdf/BSSFP/ExecutiveSummariesBusinessStrategies.pdf

56. UN Millennium Development Goals. (2012). Retrieved from http://www .un.org/millenniumgoals/

57. Harzing, A.-W. (2002). Acquisitions versus greenfield investments: International strategy and management of entry modes. *Strategic Management Journal, 23,* 211–227.

58. Laasch, O., & Yang, J. (2011). Rebuilding dynamics between corporate social responsibility and international development on the search for shared value. *KSCE Journal of Civil Engineering, 15*(2), 231–238.

59. Guardian, The. (2006, March 17). *L'Oréal buys Body Shop for £652m.* Retrieved November 17, 2012, from *The Guardian:*www.guardian.co.uk/business/2006/mar/17/retail.money

60. Sejersted, F. (1996). Managers and consultants as manipulators: Reflections on the suspension of ethics. *Business Ethics Quarterly, 6*(1), 67–86.

61. Sejersted, F. (1996). Managers and consultants as manipulators: Reflections on the suspension of ethics. *Business Ethics Quarterly, 6*(1), 67–86, pp. 67–68.

62. Carbaugh, R. J. (2010). *International economics,* 12th ed. Mason, OH: Thompson South-Western.

63. OECD. (2012, November 28). *Transfer pricing: About transfer pricing.* Retrieved November 28, 2012, from OECD—Better policies for better lives: www.oecd.org/ctp/transferpricing/abouttransferpricing.htm

64. Hansen, D. R., Crosser, R. L., & Laufer, D. (1992). Moral ethics v. tax ethics: The case of transfer pricing among multinational corporations. *Journal of Business Ethics, 11*(9), 679–686.

65. Hansen, D. R., Crosser, R. L., & Laufer, D. (1992). Moral ethics v. tax ethics: The case of transfer pricing among multinational corporations. *Journal of Business Ethics, 11*(9), 679–686, p. 684.

66. Porter, M. (1980). *Competitive strategy: Techniques for analyzing industries and competitors.* New York: The Free Press, available at: http://books.google.com/books?id=QN0kyeHXtJMC&pg=PR10&dq=porter+1980+competitive+strategy&hl=es&ei=OD_iTdW0IOXq0gHh4aCjBw&sa=X&oi=book_result&ct=result&resnum=1&ved=0CCkQ6AEwAA#v=onepage&q=porter%201980%20competitive%20strategy&f=false

67. Daniels, J. D., Radebaugh, L. H., & Sullivan, D. P. (2013). *International business: Environments & operations.* Upper Saddle River, NJ: Pearson Education.

68. Arthaud-Day, M. L. (2005). Transnational corporate social responsibility: A tri-dimensional approach to international CSR research. *Business Ethics Quarterly, 15*(1), 1–22, p. 18.

69. Mor Barak, M. E. (2011). *Managing diversity: Toward a globally-inclusive workforce* (p. 236). Thousand Oaks, CA: Sage.

70. Cox, T. (2001). *Creating the multicultural organization: A strategy for capturing the power of diversity.* San Francisco: Jossey-Bass.

71. Mor Barak, M. E. (2011). *Managing diversity: Toward a globally-inclusive workforce.* Thousand Oaks, CA: Sage.

72. Hofstede originally derived a set of four cultural dimensions. The fifth and sixth dimensions of *long-term orientation* and *indulgence versus restraint* are later additions.

73. Hofstede, G. (1980). *Culture's consequences: International differences in work-related differences.* Thousand Oaks, CA: Sage.

74. The Hofstede Centre. (2012). *Dimensions.* Retrieved December 17, 2012, from The Hofstede Centre: http://geert-hofstede.com/dimensions.html

75. Hofstede, G., & Fink, G. (2007). Culture: Organisations, personalities and nations: Gerhard Fink interviews Geert Hofstede. *European Journal of International Management, 1*(1/2), 14–22.

76. Johnson, J. P., Lenartowicz, T., & Apud, S. (2006). Cross-cultural competence in international business: Toward a definition and a model. *Journal of International Business Studies, 37*(4), 525–543, p. 530.

77. Hofstede, G. (2001). *Culture's consequences: Comparing values, behaviors, institutions, and organizations.* Thousand Oaks, CA: Sage.

78. Lustig, M. W., & Koester, J. (2003). *Intercultural competence: Interpersonal communication across cultures,* 4th ed. Boston: Allyn and Bacon.

79. Johnson, J. P., Lenartowicz, T., & Apud, S. (2006). Cross-cultural competence in international business: Toward a definition and a model. *Journal of International Business Studies, 37*(4), 525–543, p. 531.

80. Mahoney, J. F. (2012). Aspects of international business ethics. *Advances in Management, 5*(3), 11–16.

81. Bailey, W., & Spicer, A. (2007). When does national identity matter? Convergence and divergence in international business ethics. *Academy of Management Journal, 50*(6), 1462–1480.

82. Bailey, W., & Spicer, A. (2007). When does national identity matter? Convergence and divergence in international business ethics. *Academy of Management Journal, 50*(6), 1462–1480, p. 1475.

83. Tsalikis, J., & Seaton, B. (2007). The International Business Ethics Index: European Union. *Journal of Business Ethics, 75,* 229–238.

84. Küng, H. (1997). A global ethic in an age of globalization. *Business Ethics Quarterly, 7*(3), 17–32;Küng, H. (1991). *Global responsibility: In search of a new world ethic.* London: Continuum.

85. Interfaith Declaration. (1993). *An interfaith declaration: A code of ethics on international business for Christians, Muslims, and Jews.* London: The Interfaith Foundation; Webley, S. (1996). The interfaith declaration: Constructing a code of ethics for international business. *Business Ethics: A European Review, 5*(1), 52–54.

86. Hendry, J. (1999). Universalizability and reciprocity in international business ethics. *Business Ethics Quarterly, 9*(3), 405–420.

87. Hendry, J. (1999). Universalizability and reciprocity in international business ethics. *Business Ethics Quarterly, 9*(3), 405–420.

# 14

Value **Impacts**
**Accounting** **Reporting** **Goal**
**Materiality** Accountability
**Measurement** Indicators **Information** Performance
**Define** Stakeholders **Audit**
Guidelines International Importance Sustainability

# ACCOUNTING AND CONTROLLING: STAKEHOLDER ACCOUNTABILITY

*You will be able to...*

1 **...integrate sustainability, responsibility, and ethics into your accounting and controlling system with the goal to achieve stakeholder accountability.**

2 **...develop and use indicators for social, environmental, and ethical activity and performance as a basis for responsible management activity.**

3 **...report internally and externally about responsible business activity and performance.**

The percentage of S&P500 market value represented by physical and financial assets in 2009 was 19 percent versus 81 percent of intangible factors, some of which are explained within financial statements, but many of which are not.[1]

In 2010, 13 percent out of 1,913 sustainability reports using Global Reporting Initiative (GRI) standards integrated sustainability reports with traditional financial reports in one document. Sustainability data are available for more than 5,300 companies on Bloomberg terminals; the number of equity analyses that uses this data grew 50 percent during 2011, and the amount of data they accessed doubled over 2010.[2]

Author: Ulpiana Kocollari; Contributors: Aurea Christine Tanaka, Daniel Ette, Kemi Ogunyemi, Loretta O'Donnell, Martin Perry, Nick Tolhurst, Shel Horowitz, Michael Braungart.

## Reporting Social and Environmental Performance at CPL

CLP Holdings Limited, listed on the Hong Kong Stock Exchange, is one of the largest investor-owned power businesses in the Asia-Pacific region (Hong Kong, Australia, Chinese Mainland, India, Southeast Asia, and Taiwan). CLP's mission is to produce and supply energy with minimal environmental impact to create value for shareholders, customers, employees, and the wider community. CLP provides electricity, an essential public service, to both developed and developing economies in the Asia-Pacific region. In 2011, CLP Group operating and financial performance combined the annual report with all the other tools available to bring information to stakeholders, including the sustainability report and other information available on the CLP website. CLP stated, "[T]hese, taken together, are designed to give you a coherent and integrated picture of CLP and to demonstrate our ability to create value now and in the future...." To help stakeholders who read the report, areas of the annual report are highlighted by symbols that recall particular information included in the sustainability report where further information is available online and in the sustainability report. These links are constantly displayed in all the parts of the report: Chairman's Statement, CEO's Strategic Review, Assets/Partnership Chart, Performance and Business Outlook, Resources, Process, and Financials, except the section of economic value where these two dimensions are included indirectly in the traditional financial approach.

The report opens with a "5-Minute Annual Report" that gives a snapshot of CLP's financial, social, and environmental performance through general indicators such as the number of people engaged by CPL community investment. In reporting the company's more than sixty assets and investments, including wind power, hydropower, biomass power, and solar power, CPL covers an important part of the investments, and the reporting plays a crucial role in terms of equity.

In the performance section, the environmental and social performance is integrated together with the financial and operational one, and performance is measured for each geographical area in which the group operates. The main measurements for the sustainability dimensions are reported in the final part of the financial chapter where the data are reported in a five-year summary for the entire CPL Group. Some of the environmental performance indicators included are Resource Use and Emissions, Carbon Dioxide Equivalent ($CO_2e$) Emissions, Water Withdrawal, Hazardous Waste Produced, Hazardous Waste Recycled, and so on. In particular, the Climate Vision 2050 Target Performance provides interesting long-run oriented information. The social indicators are subdivided into three main categories: employees, safety, and governance. For each of these indicators, the reference to the Global Reporting Initiative is highlighted, demonstrating the harmonization of the information with the main standards.

CPL illustrates excellence in integrating social, environmental, and economic performance reporting in a way that creates a holistic accountability.

Source: CLP Holdings, Ltd. (2011). *Annual report*. Retrieved from: www.clpgroup.com

## 14-1 ACCOUNTING AND RESPONSIBLE MANAGEMENT

*"An organization should account for: The impacts of its decisions and activities on society, the environment and the economy, especially significant negative consequences; and the actions taken to prevent repetition of unintended and unforeseen negative impacts."*[3]

Responsible management is impossible without an accounting practice that delivers information regarding the triple bottom line, stakeholders, and ethical issues. The management proverb "What cannot be measured, cannot be managed," which is often quoted in connection with the quality management pioneer William Edwards Deming, is as true for responsible management as it is for any other management activity. The difference is that in responsible management, managers largely are not yet used to measuring responsible management activity and performance. The second line of the proverb might be even more important: "What cannot be managed cannot be improved." Only if we learn to measure and manage the sustainability, responsibility, and ethics of organizations can we achieve the ultimate goal of becoming truly responsible. This chapter aims to provide a basis of concepts and practice to measure, manage, and improve responsible business activity and performance.

In phase 0, *understanding basic accounting*, we provide underlying concepts that apply to all later stages of the accounting process as preparation to better understand these later stages. We illustrate basic elements, quality criteria, and concepts of accounting and apply them to responsible management. In phase 1, *data gathering*, we identify the groups of data—environmental, social, ethics, and stakeholder information—to be gathered, and prioritize them. In phase 2, *data evaluation*, we will illustrate how to measure social and environmental benefits and costs and consider impacts on both the company and society, both current and future. Phase 3, *reporting*, shows avenues by which to disseminate the information found to stakeholders of the company, both internally and externally. Finally, phase 4, *controlling*, elaborates on how to use data internally in order to manage what was measured, which closes the cycle illustrated in the proverb mentioned earlier. The underlying goal of the responsible accounting process is to create *stakeholder accountability*, to be able to account for and to be held accountable for the triple bottom line, stakeholder impacts, and the ethical outcomes of one's management activity by a broad set of stakeholders of this activity. (See Figure 14.1.)

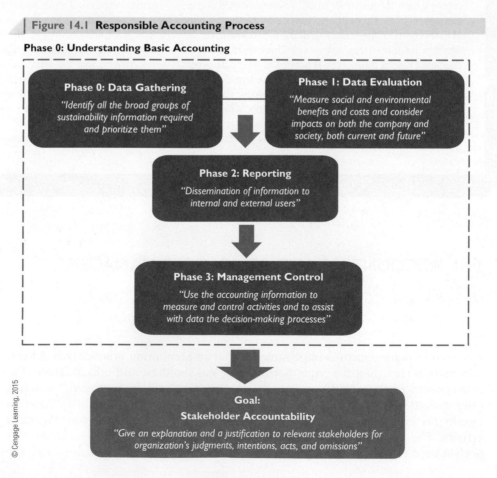

Figure 14.1 **Responsible Accounting Process**

**Phase 0: Understanding Basic Accounting**

**Phase 0: Data Gathering**
*"Identify all the broad groups of sustainability information required and prioritize them"*

**Phase 1: Data Evaluation**
*"Measure social and environmental benefits and costs and consider impacts on both the company and society, both current and future"*

**Phase 2: Reporting**
*"Dissemination of information to internal and external users"*

**Phase 3: Management Control**
*"Use the accounting information to measure and control activities and to assist with data the decision-making processes"*

**Goal:**
**Stakeholder Accountability**
*"Give an explanation and a justification to relevant stakeholders for organization's judgments, intentions, acts, and omissions"*

## 14-2 THE GOAL: STAKEHOLDER ACCOUNTABILITY

*"As company efforts increase, so does the need for accountability—both internally, in risk management, investment decisions and operational efficiency, and externally, responding to growing questions from customers and stakeholders about companies' sustainability goals, commitments and performance."*[4]

**Stakeholder accountability**, or better, accountability to stakeholders, is the process of providing relevant information to stakeholders that allows them to hold the organization accountable for its activity and outcomes. Stakeholder accountability recognizes that all individuals have a right to participate in decisions that might impact them, irrespective of the power each individual holds in relation to others. Advocates of holistic forms of accountability tend to recognize that all individuals have a basic right to participate in decisions on matters that might impact upon them, irrespective of the power that each individual holds in relation to others.[5]

In order for an organization to reflect a sustainability, responsibility, and ethics focus in daily activities and to constantly monitor the attainment of responsible business goals, an appropriate accounting process that individuates measurement systems and management tools should be put in place. Together with its provision of data that are relevant and useful for managerial decision making, responsible business accounting information also must enclose the qualitative attributes of the accounting process in a relevant sustainability context to enable stakeholders to assess the environmental and social impacts of the organization.[6]

An **account** is a (written or spoken) description of an event. The function of accounting information is developed through the concept of accountability "as the duty to provide an account (by no means necessarily a financial account) or reckoning of those actions for which one is held responsible. It is about identifying what one is responsible for and then providing information about that responsibility to those who have rights to that information."[7] **Organizational accountability** is defined as the readiness or preparedness of an organization to give an explanation and a justification to relevant stakeholders for its judgments, intentions, acts, and omissions when appropriately called upon to do so.[8]

All stakeholders are considered as possible sources and recipient groups of sustainability accounting information, distinguishing between their contributions to an organization and their claims. The first category highlights what the information organization expects to get from its stakeholders, while the latter one refers to what stakeholders need from the organization. Considering this bidirectional flow of the information, a crucial process from a stakeholder accountability perspective is the engagement and "dialogue" processes in which they are invited to participate.[9] Stakeholder accountability must consider both giving and receiving of information in order to fulfill the final goal for the responsible accounting process.

The giving of an account is only one part of the accountability framework, as this also requires that the accountee has "the power to hold to account the person who gives the account."[10] Therefore, if accountability is to be achieved, stakeholders need to be empowered in such a way that they can hold the accountors to account.[11] This conception of accountability requires not only the provision of information, but also its value in terms of "facilitating action."[12] In addition to the responsible management concerns as to whether stakeholders are able to enter into the communicative action with corporations, another consideration is the potential for new corporate environmental and social disclosure initiatives to enhance stakeholder accountability via empowerment, in terms of facilitating action through adequate tools.

**Stakeholder accountability** is the process of providing relevant information to stakeholders that allows them to hold the organization accountable for its activity and outcomes.

An **account** is a (written or spoken) description of an event.

**Organizational accountability** is defined as the readiness of an organization to explain and justify its judgments, intentions, acts, and omissions when called upon to do so.

A wider concept used specially for nongovernmental organizations (NGOs) is "holistic accountability," which refers to broader forms of accountability that can describe the impacts that an organization's actions have, or can have, on a broad range of other organizations, individuals, and the environment.[13] Within holistic accountability, in addition to the key stakeholders being recognized under hierarchical accountability, the stakeholders to whom an NGO might be considered accountable include the groups on whose behalf the NGO advocates, along with the individuals, communities, and/or regions directly and indirectly impacted by the NGO's advocacy activities.[14]

Applying this concept in the case of companies means explicit consideration of multiple stakeholder groups, with a significant emphasis being placed on downward accountability to beneficiaries,[15] in addition to upward accountability to the corporate governance. According to Dwyer and Unerman,[16] holistic accountability expands the concept of performance articulated within hierarchical accountability to comprise quantitative and qualitative mechanisms oriented to the long-term achievement of organizational mission and its impact in terms of structural change. Advocates of holistic forms of accountability tend to recognize that every individual has a basic right to participate in decisions on matters that might impact him or her, regardless of the power which that individual holds in relation to others.[17]

## 14-3 PHASE 0: UNDERSTAND THE BASICS OF ACCOUNTING

*"… the preparation and publication of an account about an organization's social, environmental, employee, community, customer and other stakeholder interactions and activities and, where, possible, the consequences of those interactions and activities. The social account may contain financial information but is more likely to be a combination of quantified nonfinancial information and descriptive, nonquantified information. The social account may serve a number of purposes but discharge of the organization's accountability to its stakeholders must be the clearly dominant of those reasons and the basis upon which the social account is judged."[18]*

The prevailing approach to traditional accounting consists of identifying, gathering, measuring, summarizing, and analyzing financial data in order to support economic decision making.[19] Accounting for the financial information concerning a business's actions is indeed the very "language of business," which ultimately will communicate to stakeholders, whether they are external (e.g., shareholders, creditors), internal (e.g., owners, managers), or governmental and regulatory bodies (e.g., tax authorities, stock exchanges), how the business is performing. This communication generally takes the form of financial statements illustrating in monetary terms how the economic resources, under the control of those responsible for the business entity, have been managed. While many companies and accounting systems have used different criteria and information, the importance and credibility of accountancy rests upon the selection of the data (as illustrated in Figure 14.2) for its relevancy, reliability, and comparability. That is, we can say the more the data satisfy the criteria specified by the company, the more confidence other companies and their stakeholders can have in it.

## DIG DEEPER

**Did We Miss Something?**
Household paper products manufacturer Marcal recycled all the way back in 1950—but forgot to tell anyone. In the 2000s, Marcal finally recognized that being a pioneer was a marketing advantage—and went from bankruptcy to being the largest seller of recycled paper products in the United States. *Don't hide your green light!* Accounting for good social and environmental practices and communicating the results can be crucial.

Figure 14.2 **Qualitative Characteristics of Accounting Data**

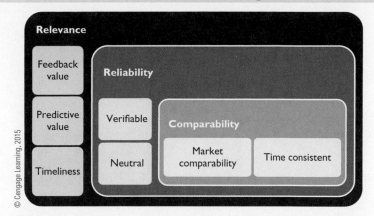

© Cengage Learning, 2015

Figure 14.3 **The Four Key Concepts of Accounting**

| Entity Type | Going Concern | Unit of Measure | Period Reported |
|---|---|---|---|
| • The entity type will affect legal and business status (e.g., company, partnership, or proprietorship). | • This is the assumption that the company will use its existing assets, meet its liabilities, and so on. | • Amounts to be measured must be in common units, such as currencies. | • Reporting periods may include annual, quarterly, and monthly systems. |

© Cengage Learning, 2015

Managers need to know where the company stands and be able to predict likely developments. The information provided should be verifiable and a true representation of the data. Companies, while often using slightly different systems and often different temporal criteria, should be able to build enough comparability and consistency into their accounts that managers and stakeholders can realistically measure, analyze, and compare across companies, sectors, regions, and times. Underlying the accounting process are the central concepts of accounting illustrated in Figure 14.3.

We draw an important distinction between *accounting*, the main goal of which is to provide companies with clear information on its economic activities (see Figure 14.4), and *auditing*, which is an independent appraisal performed by an independent expert of an activity or event—usually the annual financial reports, although audits can be for a particular project, sector, or, as we shall see later, technical or ecological. In brief, then, accounting provides continuing information to users of such information, while auditing is a means to ensure such information is reliable, conforms to established rules and regulations, or examines the company's position with regard to a specific position or criteria.

Typically, accountancy is divided into two main areas: financial accounting and management accounting. Financial accounting covers items such as revenue, earnings, assets, and so on, and is the public representation of the success, solidity, or other parts of the business entity. Management accounting deals with the more internal "bookkeeping nature" of business, covering costing, budgeting, net present value, and other items. From a financial accounting perspective, there are several ways companies can measure inflows, outflows, and changes in the financial position of a company (see Figure 14.5). It is vitally important that the substance of transactions is accurately reflected by the financial accounting process, as the users of the information are working under the assumption that these categorizations are being made both honestly and accurately. For example, if money invested by owners is counted and classified as revenue, such revenue would run counter to

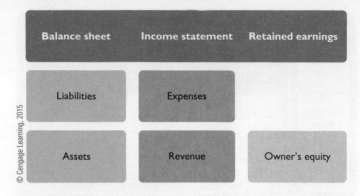

**Figure 14.4 Basic Financial Accounting Elements**

| Balance sheet | Income statement | Retained earnings |
|---|---|---|
| Liabilities | Expenses | |
| Assets | Revenue | Owner's equity |

© Cengage Learning, 2015

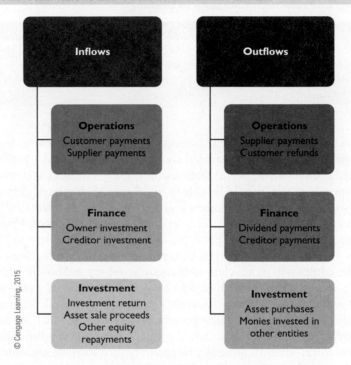

**Figure 14.5 Main Inflows and Outflows of Business Entities**

**Inflows**

**Operations**
Customer payments
Supplier payments

**Finance**
Owner investment
Creditor investment

**Investment**
Investment return
Asset sale proceeds
Other equity
repayments

**Outflows**

**Operations**
Supplier payments
Customer refunds

**Finance**
Dividend payments
Creditor payments

**Investment**
Asset purchases
Monies invested in
other entities

© Cengage Learning, 2015

conventional understanding of "revenue," which is expected to come from the company's operations. In such a situation, it would be difficult to work out both the strength of the company and its future prospects.

Because of the vital role accounting plays in recording and communicating financial results and which may have severe consequences if done wrong, it is clear that there must be a strong ethical underpinning—stronger in many ways than has been traditionally considered the case with other business functions. This is because accountancy provides an essential understanding to the whole business internally and externally. In external accounting, the accounting profession fulfills a second duty to those outside the company or organization to provide a fair and honest representation for potential investors, creditors, governments, and other stakeholders. Indeed, we now live in a world where those outside the company have little trust in financial results as represented by information provided in accounts, a situation that has potential severely damaging effects. As we have seen repeatedly through the years, trust is central to markets, and even the appearance of impropriety is damaging. Thus, through the **ethics of accounting**, practitioners of management accounting and financial management have an obligation to the public, their profession, the organization they serve, and themselves to maintain the highest standards of ethical conduct. Ethics in accounting must consider simultaneously rules, values, and virtues, as well as their interrelation.[20]

## 14-3a The Rise of Sustainability Accounting and Its Role in Responsible Accounting

In this chapter, we mostly refer to *sustainability accounting,* as this is the most commonly used term in theory and practice. Nevertheless, it is important to highlight that the integration of all three domains of responsible management—sustainability, responsibility, and ethics—into traditional accounting is a necessary condition for responsible business. Such an integrated approach may be called **responsible accounting and controlling**. Sustainability and the triple bottom line are crucial when it comes to identification of data from all three perspectives—social, environmental, and economic—and the responsibility for these perspectives. Ethics is meaningful to ensure the highest moral standards throughout the accounting process, and to make sure that the accounting process provides indicators to assess the company's ethics performance.

**Sustainability accounting and reporting** can be defined as a subset of accounting and reporting that deals with activities, methods, and systems to record, analyze, and report, firstly, environmentally and socially induced economic impacts; secondly, ecological and social impacts of a company, production site, and so on; and thirdly, and perhaps most importantly, measurement of the interactions and links between social, environmental, and economic issues constituting the three dimensions of sustainability.[21] In many ways, the drivers behind and the emergence of social and environmental accounting (and auditing) reflect the same pressures that have raised the profile and importance of responsible business and management in other management disciplines and operations, namely, the increased importance of stakeholders and the realization that companies have responsibilities that cannot always be expressed only in traditional financial terms. In other ways, though, the pace in the development of social and environmental accounting has challenged the way companies measure success and, in turn, transformed the accounting industry itself. The start of this process can be traced back to socially liberal activism of the 1970s.

In the "first wave" of socially liberal activism, a number of companies in the United States and western Europe adopted practices of social accounting concerned with "the identification, measurement, monitoring, and reporting of the social and economic effects of an institution on society, ... intended for both internal managerial and external accountability purposes."[22] With the advent of the more economically laissez-faire 1980s, social reporting declined[23] until the process gained new impetus in a "second wave" in the early 1990s, with a more particular focus on environmental issues and specific attention to external, accountability dimensions. A quoted example of a first mover in this second wave is Norsk Hydro, which first published an environmental report in 1989. Since then, of course, social and environmental reporting has grown exponentially to the point where most large (or even small and medium-sized) companies are, in some way, audited and reported. While we are all familiar with the increasing environmental concerns of society, why has the rise of social and environmental accounting been so dramatic? Figure 14.6

**Ethics of accounting** are the practitioners' obligations to the public, the profession, and the organization to maintain the highest standards of ethical conduct by considering the interrelations of rules, values, and virtues.

**Responsible accounting and controlling** integrates sustainability, responsibility, and ethics into a company's accounting and controlling systems, in order to create stakeholder accountability.

**Sustainability accounting and reporting** can be defined as a subset of accounting and reporting that deals with activities, methods, and systems to record, analyze, and report environmental, social, and economic impacts.

Figure 14.6 **The Main Drivers for Sustainability Accounting**

| Business | Government | Society |
|---|---|---|
| • Increased demand for more complex and accurate management information <br> • Measurability and transparency of economic, social, and environmental factors | • Preemptive and preparatory policies for regulatory regimes and changes <br> • Increased business legal responsibility <br> • Global/national economy externalities valuation | • Increased power of society and lobbying groups <br> • Enhanced awareness of interconnectedness, impact, "trade-offs," and moral responsibilities of business/society |

© Cengage Learning, 2015

## In Practice

### Accounting for Footprint Reduction

In 2012, 51 percent of companies had formally established specific goals of environmental footprint reduction. Another 31 percent stated that they planned to establish such goals within five years. Only 18 percent stated that they had no plan to establish any environmental footprint reduction goals.

Source: Ernst & Young LLP. (2012). *Six growing trends in corporate sustainability*. GreenBiz Group Study.

illustrates the main drivers and issues behind this rise. As we can see, although there is some overlap with traditional responsible business concerns in other management disciplines, there are added drivers and rationales behind the growth of social and environmental accounting.

In other words, while responsible business (as practiced by many companies) has often been seen as an unbalanced mix of "good business" with a far greater emphasis on "noncore business" arguments, such as altruism, marketing, and image, social and environmental accounting has rapidly established itself at the core of companies' operations. Although it is difficult to quantify the arguments, such as "license to operate," that have greatly influenced responsible business in a world of increasingly scarce resources, accounting and auditing of how such resources are used supply the "hard" data to analyze, justify, and calibrate their use, both to government and society at large as well as internally within business.

Even though the process of sustainability accounting is similar to that of traditional financial accounting (Figure 14.6), it contains some distinctive key factors:

- The focus is on ethical, social, and environmental data.
- The accountees include not only shareholders but also a wide range of stakeholders.
- Sustainability accounting is voluntary and not yet regulated by law.

According to Adams,[24] "rather than being concerned with profits and financial accountability, accountability demonstrates corporate acceptance of its ethical, social and environmental responsibility. As such the 'account' given should reflect corporate ethical, social and environmental performance."[25]

Sustainability accounting as a broader concept embraces the social, environmental, and ethical accounting (the so-called SEEA) supporting and monitoring an organization's contribution toward or away from sustainability.[26] In particular, Schaltegger and Burrit,[27] using the broader conception of sustainability accounting, describe a goal-driven, stakeholder engagement process that attempts to build up a company-specific measuring tool for sustainability issues and links between its social, environmental, and economic dimensions.

## 14-4 PHASE 1: IDENTIFY THE ACCOUNT AND GATHER DATA

*"[I]t is difficult to determine exactly which of the many facts and figures that make up the full range of sustainability data—crucial information about how corporations affect our daily lives and their implications for generations to come—should be disclosed."[28]*

In the first phase, it is necessary for organizations to identify the right framework that best reflects the responsible competitiveness strategy of the company as well as sector, geographical, and other factors. This framework will depend on the main responsible accounting drivers facing the company. In traditional accounting, most indicators (although not necessarily all) are based around economic performance, such as business performance (sales, profit, return on investment, etc.) or market presence (market penetration, etc.). With responsible accounting, the realization has come that other, more expanded indicators must be used to better understand, predict, and take into account the increasing pressures, risks, and opportunities facing companies. These indicators will include environmental factors such as energy and water used in production, the percentage of recycled waste, and the amount of carbon dioxide emitted. Social factors will include labor indicators such as diversity, training, and health and safety. On a more external scale, other social factors might cover items such as product safety and community involvement. A wide range of sustainability issues organized under stakeholders' categories is presented in Figure 14.7.

In the first phase, the organization must first identify all the broad groups of sustainability information required using the stakeholder accountability approach (see Figure 14.7). The different stakeholder issues should then be prioritized. This process depends on how organizations define their level of sustainability **disclosure**—also referred to as **ESG (environment, social, and governance) disclosure**—which is the act of communicating organizational performance on material matters relating to ESG activities.[29]

An important part of responsible accounting is explaining how this stakeholder issue prioritization has been achieved.[30] This process is different for every organization because, as we saw, there are different drivers for responsible accounting and many variables in terms of geographical influences, sector specificities, ethical and cultural values, activities, and services. Furthermore, being a voluntary and not yet regulated field, there are several standards that offer different methods for the individuation of the accounting data. The selection of method is influenced by, and in turn influences, an organization's level of sustainability disclosure. Social and environmental disclosures have been increasing in both size and complexity over the last decades. International studies, although indicating variations between countries[31] and sectors,[32] and variation over time in the areas of disclosure,[33] confirm the rise in the volume and importance of these disclosures.[34] "Companies do not operate in a vacuum. They operate in the triple context of commerce, the environment and society. Stakeholders cannot make an informed assessment about sustained value creation by a company from its financial report. Information is required on the governance of the company and how its operations impact on the environment and society. ESG disclosures are required and if not furnished the company should explain why not."[35]

Considering the complexity of this process, a three-step test (Figure 14.8) can be useful in order to target every single responsible business issue to the account that the organization aims to represent in data.

The first step delineates the parts of the organization for which accounting will be developed by defining the accounting entities. An accounting entity is an area of the organization's activities in which information has the potential to be useful for

## DIG DEEPER

### Developing Triple Bottom Line Indicators for Sustainable Cooking

Tayo Akinyede is a Nigerian career mom who sells save80 stoves and is always ready to tell her save80 story. She does it to make some money and also to promote and foster the use of more sustainable energy in Nigeria. Save80 is a highly efficient cooking device. The promotion of the save80 stove was originally the fruit of a UN initiative. The unit, which consists of two pots and a "wonderbox," costs 17,000 naira (NGN). The Save80 stove reduces indoor pollution, deforestation, and carbon emissions. It also reduces time spent cooking, which frees the person involved to get on with other activities. Thus, it has all three aspects of sustainability—economic (it saves money for users and makes money for distributors), social (it allows users to multitask and to gain time), and environmental (it minimizes invasion of the planet's boundaries). So that it remains accessible to low earners, a preestablished rule is that the product cannot be sold for more than 17,000 NGN (around $ 105 US). In contrast, quantity discounts are available. What data could you gather to establish an accounting system for save80?

Source: Adejo, T. (2012). *Save 80 stove: Curbing desertification, carbon emission*. Retrieved February 2, 2013, from Environews Nigeria: www.environewsnigeria.com/2012/10/07/save-80-stove-curbing-desertification-carbon-emission/; Akinyede, T. (2012, June 23). Interview with a Save80 Stove Distributor in Nigeria. (K. Ogunyemi, Interviewer)

**Disclosure** refers to making accounting information available to stakeholders.

**ESG (environment, social, and governance) disclosure** is an established concept for the description of nonfinancial data.

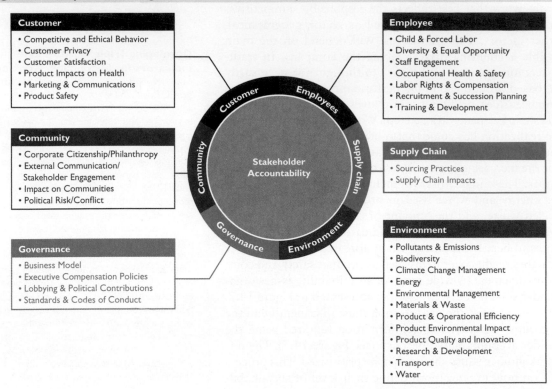

**Customer**
• Competitive and Ethical Behavior
• Customer Privacy
• Customer Satisfaction
• Product Impacts on Health
• Marketing & Communications
• Product Safety

**Community**
• Corporate Citizenship/Philanthropy
• External Communication/Stakeholder Engagement
• Impact on Communities
• Political Risk/Conflict

**Governance**
• Business Model
• Executive Compensation Policies
• Lobbying & Political Contributions
• Standards & Codes of Conduct

**Employee**
• Child & Forced Labor
• Diversity & Equal Opportunity
• Staff Engagement
• Occupational Health & Safety
• Labor Rights & Compensation
• Recruitment & Succession Planning
• Training & Development

**Supply Chain**
• Sourcing Practices
• Supply Chain Impacts

**Environment**
• Pollutants & Emissions
• Biodiversity
• Climate Change Management
• Energy
• Environmental Management
• Materials & Waste
• Product & Operational Efficiency
• Product Environmental Impact
• Product Quality and Innovation
• Research & Development
• Transport
• Water

Stakeholder Accountability

Customer — Employees — Supply chain — Environment — Governance — Community

Source: Adapted from Lydenberg, S., Rogers, J., & Wood, D. (2010, May). *From Transparency to Performance: Industry-based Sustainability Reporting on Key Issues.* Retrieved September 2012 from The Hauser Center for Nonprofit Organizations, Initiative for Responsible Investment: http://hauser-center.org/iri/wp-content/uploads/2010/05/IRI_Transparency-to-Performance.pdf.

Figure 14.8 **Characterization of the Content of the Data**

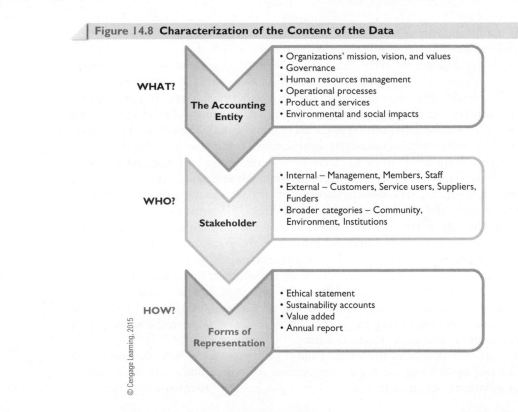

**WHAT?**

**The Accounting Entity**
• Organizations' mission, vision, and values
• Governance
• Human resources management
• Operational processes
• Product and services
• Environmental and social impacts

**WHO?**

**Stakeholder**
• Internal – Management, Members, Staff
• External – Customers, Service users, Suppliers, Funders
• Broader categories – Community, Environment, Institutions

**HOW?**

**Forms of Representation**
• Ethical statement
• Sustainability accounts
• Value added
• Annual report

© Cengage Learning, 2015

existing and potential stakeholders. These are stakeholders who cannot directly obtain the information they need to make decisions about providing resources to the entity or cannot assess whether the management and the governing board of that entity have made efficient and effective use of the resources provided.[36] This test helps to select the basic issues that determine the impact that different organizations' entities may have on responsible business issues, orienting the process to the purpose of the accounting data.

The second step, the identification of the stakeholders who are the potential recipients of the data, answers the question: Who will receive the information on the responsible business performance of the organization? The distinction among internal, external, and broader stakeholders is important for the construction of the data. The information recorded should be made available in a manner that is understandable and accessible to stakeholders who use the information.

Finally, the third step, forms of representation, provides the form the data must have, examining how the information can be modeled and generated. This final stage considers quantification of the flows associated with aspects of the responsible business interest. These flows may include the number of people employed, emissions from product manufacture and use, resource use and amount of product or service generated, and so on.[37] But not all the issues referring to the social and environmental, and ethical dimensions can be put into numbers; qualitative tools, such as narratives to describe an organization's social and environmental impacts, should be used as critical part of responsible business accounting.[38]

## 14-4a Materiality

An important principle for defining the content of responsible accounting data is **materiality**. Methods define materiality as part of the field of business responsibility because they help to elucidate how important certain issues are to the stakeholder of a company. Many international regulators and standards setters, public and private sector organizations, have issued guidelines that have attempted to define materiality for nonfinancial information. In general, they are in line with the definition of materiality for financial information by "describing it in terms relevant to decision making, putting it in the context of other information, and assessing its qualitative and quantitative importance with respect to this other information and decision making."[39] Here the attention is placed on defining the recipient of the information, usually a category of stakeholders rather than only shareholders. Another difference that has been pointed out in regard to materiality for sustainability accounting is the importance placed on the evaluation of the impact of not providing the information.

An important methodology for defining the materiality of responsible business data is the one advanced by the Sustainability Accounting Standards Board (SASB) that is sector based. The SASB has identified five broad categories of ESG containing more than forty sustainability issues that can affect a firm's financial performance and therefore be highly material to investors. In order to determine their materiality within an industry, the SASB evaluates evidence of interest by different types of stakeholders and evidence of economic impact. In particular:

- *Evidence of interest* is determined by searching tens of thousands of source documents using keywords for each sustainability issue. The documents examined include Form 10-Ks, legal news, CSR reports, shareholder resolutions, media reports, and innovation journals. The final results show the intensity with which issues arise in each industry.

**Materiality** describes the shared importance of a specific issue to both company and stakeholders.

- *Evidence of economic impact* is determined by evaluating both anecdotal reports and quantitative studies to gauge whether management (or mismanagement) of the issue will affect traditional corporate valuation parameters: profits (revenue and/or costs), assets and liabilities, and cost of capital.

- A *forward-looking adjustment* acknowledges an emerging issue, where there is evidence of emerging interest that is not yet reflected in these tests. In a small number of cases, SASB may make an adjustment to raise the importance of an issue if the management (or mismanagement) of it might create positive or negative effects that other stakeholders, industries, or generations will have to deal with, or if there is the potential for systemic disruption. In any case, the effects must be reasonably likely to occur and of significant magnitude to be deemed material.

Each sustainability issue is graded in the context of these three lenses and, through a proprietary algorithm, the SASB transforms these grades into a "Materiality Score" (MS) that ranges from 0.5 to 5. All issues above 2.25 are then considered as material for the industry in question. An example of the SASB materiality map constructed for the health care sector is represented in Figure 14.9.

The scores presented are not the result of a comprehensive and transparent assessment process, but can be indicative. In particular, this exercise helps stakeholders identify key issues, and allows organizations to efficiently allocate resources to those issues most relevant to their responsible business performance.[40] At the end of phase 1, the level of sustainability disclosure of the organization will be revealed.

### Figure 14.9 A Portion of the SASB™ Materiality Map™

| Issues | Health care | | | | | |
|---|---|---|---|---|---|---|
| | Biotechnology | Pharmaceuticals | Medical equipment and supplies | Health care delivery | Distributors and pharmacy benefit managers | Managed care |
| Climate change and natural disaster risks | 7 | 7 | 11 | 2 | 3 | 4 |
| Environmental accidents and remediation | 4 | 8 | 12 | 3 | 5 | 1 |
| Water use and management | 4 | 7 | 10 | 3 | 4 | 3 |
| Energy management | 6 | 6 | 10 | 7 | 4 | 6 |
| Fuel management and transportation | 0 | 3 | 1 | 0 | 6 | 0 |
| GHG emissions and air pollution | 4 | 6 | 9 | 3 | 4 | 4 |
| Waste management and effluents | 10 | 10 | 13 | 5 | | |
| Biodiversity impacts | 4 | 3 | 5 | | | |
| Communications and engagement | 5 | 5 | 3 | | | |
| Community development | 0 | 1 | 1 | | | |
| Impact from facilities | 0 | 5 | 7 | | | |
| Diversity and equal opportunity | 7 | 8 | 8 | | | |
| Training and development | 10 | 10 | 13 | | | |
| Recruitment and retention | 4 | 5 | 5 | 10 | 5 | 3 |
| Compensation and benefits | 9 | 8 | 8 | 8 | 8 | 4 |
| Labor relations and union practices | 8 | 10 | 10 | 7 | 7 | 7 |

**Medical equipment and supplies** ✕

**Waste management and effluents**
Evidence of interest: ☑
Evidence of economic impact: ☑
Forward-looking adjustment: ☐

**Materiality score: 13**

Source: SASB. (2012). Sustainability Accounting Standards Board. Retrieved December 19, 2012, from http://www.sasb.org. Commercial use of the SASB Materiality Map™ is restricted to those parties that have entered into commercial terms and use agreements with SASB™. Interested parties who would like to use the Map for commercial purposes may contact Tyler Peterson (tyler.peterson@sasb.org) for terms of use.

# 14-5 PHASE 2: EVALUATION AND ELABORATION OF THE DATA

*"Specific and appropriate measures that reflect the sustainability strategy are essential to monitor the key performance drivers (inputs and processes) and assess whether the implemented sustainability strategy is achieving its stated objectives (outputs) and thus contributing to the long-term success of the corporation (outcomes)."*[41]

The metrics of sustainability data should be part of a clear articulation of the casual relationships leading from the inputs to the process and then the flowing to the identified outputs and outcomes,[42] all related to each of the responsible business issues selected.

In this second phase of evaluation and elaboration of the data, organizations measure a broad set of social and environmental benefits and costs and consider impacts on both the company and society. This phase includes costs and benefits related to both current and future operations but should not include current costs related to past operations. The adoption of these models and measures, and the systems to implement them, can help managers make more effective decisions to increase both responsible business and traditional financial performance.

This process of evaluation often includes monetization, as in traditional financial accounting where the measurement is intended as the process of determining the monetary amounts at which the elements of the financial statements are to be recognized and carried in the balance sheet and income statement.[43] But financial units of measurement, the preferred choice for measuring economic performance, are not necessarily suitable for capturing social and ecological impacts, which require an array of measurement tools to capture nature's multiplicity[44] and the social equity dimension of sustainability. Measurability means expressing the indicator in terms that are measurable, rather than finding an indicator that is easy to measure.[45] Many social and environmental impacts may appear to have no market consequences and no financial effect, but often externalities are internalized in future periods and do affect the operations and profitability of the firm in the long term. Furthermore, many economic benefits of responsible business conduct are often seen as intangible and therefore difficult to measure.

As a consequence, although some forms of responsible accounting rely on monetary units to measure environmental and social impacts, an increasing trend is the use of multiple units of measurement to assess performance toward the three dimensions of sustainability.[46] Many of the designated sustainability issues, being multidimensional, are not directly measurable and require a set of indicators to enable performance toward the multiple objectives to be evaluated. In this phase 2, we will illustrate the following concepts for sustainability accounting data elaboration and evaluation, each in a distinct section:

- Costing models
- Sustainability performance metrics
- Sustainability indicators
- The value-added model
- Social return on investment (SROI)

## 14-5a Costing Models

Although it is difficult to precisely measure sustainability performance, both academics and practitioners have developed economic and financial analysis techniques that provide reasonable estimates for social and environmental performance. Corresponding to the different theoretical studies on the topic, a number of organizations have begun to adopt advanced social and environmental cost accounting using methodologies such as:

- *Full-cost accounting:* allocates all direct and indirect costs to a product or product line for inventory valuation, profitability analysis, and pricing decisions. Full-cost accounting, such as Mathews's total impact accounting,[47] attempts to capture the total costs resulting from an organization's economic activities, including social and environmental costs,[48] and to value these impacts in financial terms.

- *Activity-based costing (ABC):* assumes that activities related to products, services, and customers cause the costs. ABC first assigns costs to the activities performed by the organization (direct labor, employee training, regulatory compliance) and then attributes these costs to products, customers, and services based on a cause-and-effect relationship.[49]

- *Life-cycle assessment:* a design discipline used to minimize the environmental impacts of products, technologies, materials, processes, industrial systems, activities, and services.[50] Life-cycle cost has been defined as the amortized annual cost of a product, including capital costs, and disposal costs discounted over the lifetime of a product, including its production, use, and disposal.

- *Natural capital inventory accounting:* involves the recording of stocks of natural capital over time, with changes in stock levels used as an indicator of the (declining) quality of the natural environment. Various types of natural capital stocks, such as water, biodiversity, forests, and fish stocks, are distinguished enabling the recording, monitoring, and reporting of depletions or enhancements within distinct categories.[51]

## 14-5b Responsible Business Performance Metrics

After evaluating the inputs and their effects on responsible business and traditional financial performance, organizations' managers can develop the appropriate processes to measure responsible business results. According to the Epstein's[52] sustainability model, as shown in the Figure 14.10, the managerial actions taken lead to sustainability performance and stakeholder reactions (outputs) that at a final stage affect long-term corporate financial performance (outcomes). In this phase 2 of the responsible accounting process, indicators are developed and used to collect evidence on the outputs and outcomes and assess their importance by valuing them.

Arrow 1 presents processes that have immediate, identifiable costs and benefits that affect the organization's long-term financial performance. Some methods for its measurement were shown in the previous section. Arrow 2 shows how the various inputs impact responsible business performance through processes. Finally, arrow 3 shows how financial performance is impacted by stakeholder reactions to the organization's sustainability performance. Several tools and techniques are used to measure the different aspects of responsible business performance.

Bell and Morse[53] point out that it is possible to distinguish between two categories of sustainability assessments: the first tends to be all-encompassing ("stronger"), and the second one

## In Practice

### From Human Capital to Financial Performance

UNPRI (United Nations Principles for Responsible Investment) can be broadened to incorporate how human capital creates value within listed firms, using the S or Social theme within ESG (environmental, social, and governance) investment principles. While financial markets are increasingly regulated, there is still much work to be done by regulators to assist investors to incorporate the value of human capital within the investment process.

Source: O'Donnell, L., & Royal, C. (2012). Investment and sustainability: The importance of the "S" in ESG principles of responsible investment. In G. Jones, *Research handbook in sustainability*. Melbourne: Tilde University Press.

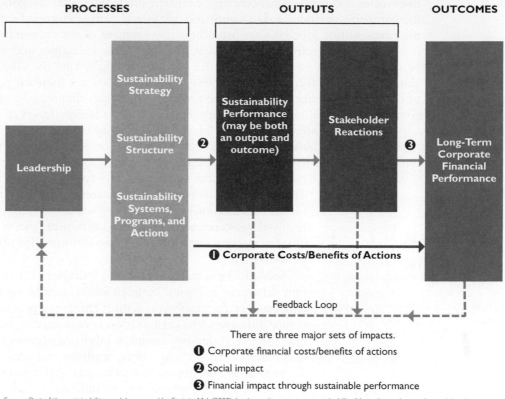

Source: Part of the sustainability model proposed by Epstein, M. J. (2008). Implementing corporate sustainability: Measuring and managing social and environmental impacts. *Strategic Finance, 89*(7), 24–31.

tends to be limited ("weaker"). The all-encompassing category will set broader physical boundaries to the sustainability model, will refer to longer time frames for measuring stability and success, and will minimize trade-offs among the sustainability interest of competing components in the system. The broader the range of the activities involved and the longer the duration, the more likely the outcome will be affected by other factors, and the more complex the measurement becomes. Codifying of the information is an important issue in this second phase. The information is elaborated also in order to become intelligible for the stakeholder to whom it is addressed.[54] Codifying enables the transmission of the information and the decision of which tools will be selected for the data transfer.

## 14-5c Indicators

Accounting also means deriving indicators that enable organizations to define clear performance targets[55] and delineate their current status through ongoing measurement. Central to the responsible accounting framework is the use of a **sustainability performance indicator** to measure the environmental, social, and economic dimensions of sustainability. The use of indicators to estimate variables that cannot be measured precisely has a long history in environmental science[56] and is considered appropriate where variables that are inherently complex cannot be directly observed. The GRI Sustainability Reporting Guidelines utilize a wide array of indicators to measure performance toward the goal of sustainability.

A **sustainability performance indicator** is a qualitative or quantitative metric used to assess social, environmental, and economic activity and performance.

In particular, the third section of GRI framework (Version G3.1) on standard disclosures is organized by economic, environmental, and social categories. Each of the categories includes a set of core and additional performance indicators. GRI's multistakeholder processes are behind the development of the core indicators. The processes are intended to identify generally applicable indicators and assumed to be material for most organizations. An organization following the GRI guidelines should report on core indicators unless they are deemed not material on the basis of the reporting principles. Emerging practices and topics that may be material for some organizations but not others are represented by additional indicators.

First, the economic dimension of sustainability addresses the organization's impacts on the economic status of its stakeholders and on economic systems at local, national, and international levels. The economic performance indicators category includes seven core indicators plus two additional indicators. The core indicators report on, for example, financial implications for the organization's activities due to climate change, significant financial assistance received from government, and development of infrastructure investments and services provided primarily for public benefit.

Second, the social performance indicators are divided into four different categories: labor practices, human rights, society, and product responsibility. Within the labor practices performance indicators, the organization is requested to elaborate on information about employment, labor/management relations, occupational health and safety, training and education, and diversity and equal opportunity. The area of occupational health and safety, for example, identifies indicators such as rates of injury, occupational diseases, lost days, and absenteeism.

Human rights performance indicators try to evaluate the level of compliance with human rights in investment and supplier selection practices.

Organizational impacts on the social systems in which companies operate are measured through society performance indicators. The society aspect deals with the risks that may arise from interactions with other social institutions and how the risks are managed. The seven core indicators have aspects of community, corruption, public policy, and compliance. An additional indicator is placed on anticompetitive behavior, that is, the total number of legal actions for anticompetitive behavior, antitrust and monopoly practices, and their corresponding outcomes.

The fourth category of social performance indicators addresses product responsibility assessments. The purpose of product responsibility assessment is to provide information about the organization's products and services that can directly affect customers. The topics covered include health and safety, information and labeling, marketing communication, and customer privacy. An example of a core indicator for the product labeling is the identification of type of product and service information required by procedures, and percentage of significant products and services subject to such information requirements.

Third, the environment category is composed of the environmental indicators that cover performance related to inputs and outputs. The indicators also cover the performance related

## DIG DEEPER

### Global Reporting Initiative

The Global Reporting Initiative (GRI) was founded in Boston in 1997 and now located in Amsterdam. GRI is a nonprofit, network-based organization that works toward a sustainable global economy by providing sustainability reporting guidance that is broadly used around the world. The GRI is also one of the initiators of the International Integrated Reporting Committee.

Source: Global Reporting Initiative (GRI), www.globalreporting.org

## In Practice

### Indicators for Social Entrepreneurship

HP Learning Initiative for Entrepreneurs (HP Life) is a global program that combines entrepreneurship training together with Information and Communication Technology (ICT) skills development. In China, the China Association for Employment Promotion (CAEP) manages the training programs in three centers, supported by local government. In Shiyan City, Hubei province, the HP Life training is integrated in a curriculum developed for local needs. In addition to this feature, access to government interest-paid loans and a three-year tax break are other factors that contribute to the success of this initiative. Unemployed women are especially targeted through a partnership between CAEP and the All China Women's Federation network. Overall, by 2010, 1,707 trainees graduated from the program and 690 established new businesses; 1,650 new jobs were secured either through start-ups or other employment opportunities.

Source: ProSPER.Net. (2011). *Integrating sustainability in business school curricula project: Final report.* Bangkok: Asian Institute of Technology.

to biodiversity, environmental compliance, and other relevant information such as environmental expenditure and the impacts of an organization's products and services. Both the core and additional indicators require specific data and information about the environmental behavior and performance: examples of indicators are materials used by weight or volume, percentage of recycled materials used, direct energy consumption, total water withdrawal, and initiatives to mitigate environmental impacts of products and services.

Figure 14.11 illustrates the different types of GRI sustainability performance indicators by providing examples of each category—economic, social, and environmental indicators from the three companies NH Hotels, Ferrero, and Votorantim.

While this section has focused on "sustainability" indicators and the triple bottom line, the reader will realize that many of the indicators here also

**Figure 14.11  Examples of GRI Sustainability Indicators Application at NH Hotels, Ferrero, and Votorantim**

### Standard Disclosures Part III: Performance Indicators

| Performance Indicator | Description | Assured by KPMG | Reported | Cross-reference/ Direct answer | If applicable, indicate the part not reported | Reason for omission | Explanation | To be reported in |
|---|---|---|---|---|---|---|---|---|
| **Economic** | | | | | | | | |
| | | | **Economic performance** | | | | | |
| Principal EC1 | Direct economic value generated and distributed, including revenues, operating costs, employee compensation, donations and other community investments, retained earnings, and payments to capital providers and governments | ● | Fully | Pg. 13 Main figures of NH Hotels | | | | |
| Principal EC2 | Financial implications and other risks and opportunities for the organization's activities due to climate change | ● | Partially | Pg. 36–38 Commitment to preventing climate change | | NA | The Company does not perform a separate financial calculation of the financial implications of activities performed due to climate change. The consolidated calculation of the whole energy efficiency investment is reported on page 54 | |

*(Continued)*

| Social Performance Indicators | | | | |
|---|---|---|---|---|
| **Labor Practices and Decent Work** | | | | |
| DMA LA | Management and verification policies and system | 6.2 Organizational governance<br>6.4 Labor practices<br>6.3.10 Fundamental principles and rights at work | T | 2–3; 18–19; 50; 52; 54; 57–62; 64; 67–69; 71–72; 124–125; 130; 132; |
| **Employment** | | | | |
| LAI | Total workforce by employment type, employment contract, and region, broken down by gender | 6.4 Labor practices<br>6.4.3 Employment and employment relationships | T | 11; 52; 54–56; 124; 129 |

| Emissions, Effluents and Residues | | | | |
|---|---|---|---|---|
| **EN16 – Total Direct and Indirect Greenhouse Gas Emissions, by Weight (GEE)** | **Page** | | **137** | |
| | **Status** | | **COMPLETE** | |
| **DIRECT GHG EMISSIONS ($TCO_2EQ$)** | **2008** | **2009** | **2010** | **2011** |
| Stationary Combustion | 7,545,773 | 7,201,925 | 8,491,052 | 9,663,864 |
| Mobile Sources – Owned | 501,863 | 472,154 | 486,613 | 567,797 |
| Process | 9,620,342 | 9,861,348 | 10,569,319 | 13,339,980 |
| Waste Treatment | 0 | 0 | 50,971 | 67,550 |
| Soil – Limestone | 28,289 | >3,923 | 27,172 | 24,913 |
| Soil – Nitrogen Fertilizer | 44,236 | >8,099 | 26,262 | 37,725 |
| Total Direct Emissions - Scope 1 | 17,740,503 | 17,617,449 | 19,651,389 | 23,701,829 |
| **INDIRECT EMISSIONS ($TCO_2EQ$)** | **2008** | **2009** | **2010** | **2011** |
| Electric Energy | 962,641 | 608,010 | 1,177,481 | 907,802 |
| Total Indirect Emissions - Scope 2 9 | 62,641 | 608,010 | 1,177,481 | 907,802 |

Sources: GRI economic performance indicators: NH Hotels. (2011). *Corporate responsibility report*; GRI social performance indicators: Ferrero. (2011). *Sharing values to create value*. CSR Report; GRI environmental performance indicators: Votorantim. (2011). *Integrated report*; www.ferrero.com/social-responsibility/code-business-conduct/; www.ferrero.com/social-responsibility/code-of-ethics/reliability-trust/

describe topics related to stakeholder responsibility, and topics related to ethics. A well-balanced responsible accounting system has to identify a balanced set of indicators related to the triple bottom line, stakeholders, and ethical issues and opportunities.

## 14-5d The Value-Added Model

The value-added statement (VAS) was proposed by Waino Suojanen in 1954. He recommended the VAS as a supplemental report that analyzes "the value added in production and its source or distribution among the organization participants."[57] Suojanen suggested the value added concept for income measurement, as a way for management to fulfill their accounting duties to the various interest groups by providing more information than was possible from the income statement and balance sheet.

**Value added** describes the economic value created by the organization, and how it is distributed among stakeholders.

The **value added** can be defined as the value created by the organization in carrying out its activities and managing the contribution of its employees, as, for example, in the case of a manufacturing company calculating the difference of the sales less the cost of goods and services used in the production processes.

The VAS reports on the calculation of value added and its application among the stakeholders in an organization. The information included in the VAS is the same as that already contained in the income statement (salaries and wages used to be the only additional information), but the VAS presents the information in a different and more comprehensible format. The format of the VAS is shown in Figure 14.12 and illustrated with a practical example of a VAS from the company Samsung Electronics's sustainability report. In contrast to profit, which is the wealth created only for the owners or shareholders, value added represents the wealth created for several groups of stakeholders.[58] This characteristic makes the VAS a broader scheme, focused on the wider implications of an organization's activities beyond its profits or losses.[59]

The organization carrying out its productive activities rewards investors and creditors for risking their capital but at the same time employs people, contributes to societal costs by paying taxes, and contributes to the community. If it ceases to exist, the shareholders will lose the possibility to gain profits from their capital, but also employees will lose their jobs, and in general the community in which the organization operates will lose "the value" the organization has provided to it.

To illustrate how the value-added calculation process is performed, consider a manufacturing company that produces candles. The value added is calculated by taking the difference between the price for which the candles are sold and the cost of the materials that went into making the candles (paraffin, fragrance, wick, etc.). Suppose that a candle is sold on average for $10 and that 100 candles were sold. The paraffin and materials cost per unit would be $5, and the value added would be $1,000 minus $500, or $500. Value added can be considered as the incremental value that, through labor and capital, is given to the raw materials

**Figure 14.12 The Composition of the Value Added in Theory and Practice**

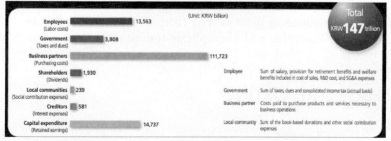

Source: Adapted from Samsung. (2011). *Distributions of direct economic value in Samsung*. Sustainability Report.

transforming them into a new form. In our example of the candle-manufacturing activity, elaborating the inputs into the final product increases the initial value of the materials by $500. That value added, $500, is then distributed to the stakeholders of the company—its employees, creditors, government (taxes), and shareholders.

The VAS defines value in a much broader way than profit for shareholders, and uses a stakeholder approach in its reporting. One of the limitations of the traditional VAS is that it focuses only on financial items and pays no attention to non-financial value, to intangibles, and items that do not pass through the market, and it does not account for indirect impacts of an organization's activities.[60]

A version of the VAS is the expanded value-added statement (EVAS) that addresses some of the difficulties in applying accounting models developed for business enterprises to nonprofit organizations.[61] Their efficiency and effectiveness cannot be determined through information in financial statements only, as they receive funds from sponsors who do not expect monetary benefits in return.[62] By combining financial and social value added, the EVAS highlights the link and interdependence of the economy, community and environment.[63] In general, the EVAS contain two parts: the calculation of value added by an organization, and its distribution to the stakeholders.

## 14-5e Social Return on Investment

**Social return on investment (SROI)** is a framework for measuring and accounting a much broader concept of value; it seeks to reduce inequality and environmental degradation and improve well-being by incorporating social, environmental, and economic costs and benefits.[64] SROI measures change in ways that are relevant to the people or organizations that experience or contribute to it. It captures the ex-post situation compared with the ex-ante one by measuring social, environmental, and economic outcomes using monetary values to represent them. As a result, a ratio of benefits to costs is calculated. This ratio shows the value of the social and environmental impact that has been created in financial terms. The calculation of the SROI is a topic that is covered with greater depth in the area of financial management. The main use of SROI is made in financial, monetary terms, as it helps to evaluate a monetarized social benefit against the cost of investment.

In terms of the accounting process, SROI represents a framework for evaluating the value created as a result of the calculation of the costs of the related intervention performed and the benefits it has produced in financial terms. Through the SROI process, organizations figure out how value is created, and this value is just as important as what the ratio shows.[65]

The second phase is important not only for the elaboration of the accounting data as an appropriate process of identification and measurement of key performance drivers, but also for the reporting of the results, which can improve the strategy implementation process. For further information, the area of financial management illustrates and exemplifies the establishment of an SROI as a powerful metric.

## 14-6 PHASE 3: REPORTING

*"Reporting on sustainability and environmental social governance performance is a crucial step toward a market that rewards the creation of long-term wealth in a just and sustainable society."*[66]

---

**Social return on investment (SROI)** is a method that quantifies and monetizes all stakeholder costs and benefits—the social, environmental, and economic ones—of an activity in one single ratio.

In the first two phases, the core topics were identified and the key performance measurements for the expected contributions of responsible business also were identified, following the designed path of responsible accounting driven by the target of stakeholder accountability. This goal-driven pragmatic perspective identifies the requirement that responsible accounting cannot be separated from responsible business reporting and the strategic and operational management of responsible business issues.[67]

Once the information is elaborated, the third component of the sustainability accounting process concerns the dissemination of information to internal and external users, that is, reporting. This process must be based on three key questions:

1. Which are the qualitative criteria that responsible accounting information should represent?

2. What is the appropriate format of responsible accounting reports?

3. Which are the tools and mechanisms that responsible accounting information should use for the internal and external disseminations?

To answer these questions, influential standards and guidelines have been developed to guide leading-edge reporting practice. Many different institutions have released sustainability reporting frameworks; some of these frameworks have been issued by international organizations, while others are specific regional or national guidelines. A list of the principal standards developed and their key characteristics is presented in Figure 14.13.

**A Precursor to Sustainability Reports**

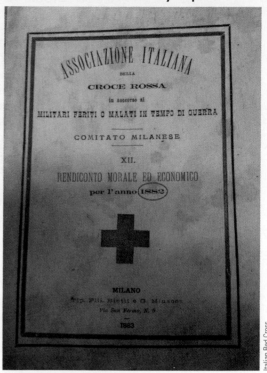

Italian Red Cross

*One of the first examples of social reporting is the document adopted by the Italian Red Cross in 1883 called "Moral and Economic Report."*

---

| Figure 14.13 **Reporting Standards and Related Frameworks** |

| Level of Application | Guidelines |
| --- | --- |
| **International** | GRI G3 |
| | AA1000 Standard |
| | ISO 26000 |
| | COP of the United Nations Global Compact |
| **Regional and National-Based** | Triple Bottom Line Reporting (Australia) |
| | Social Reporting Guideline (Italy) |
| | Environmental Reporting Guidelines (Japan) |
| | Sustainability Reporting Guideline (Netherlands) |
| | King Report and Code of Governance (South Africa) |
| | Sustainability Management Report Guidelines (Korea) |
| | Sustainability Report (Portugal) |
| | Guide for Preparing Sustainability Reports (Chile) |
| | Financial Statements Act (requires CSR disclosure for large businesses) (Denmark) |
| | Environmental Reporting Guideline (UK) |

© Cengage Learning, 2015

## 14-6a Global Reporting Initiative

Among the international standards, the Global Reporting Initiative (GRI) guidelines, which are process-oriented standards with a particular focus on the how to create the reporting document, are the world's most widely used responsible business reporting framework. According to the KPMG 2011 International Survey of Corporate Responsibility Reporting, 80 percent of the largest companies (G250) drawn from the Fortune Global 500 list and 69 percent of the 100 largest companies in thirty-four countries (N100) are now aligning to GRI reporting standards.

Sustainability Reporting Guidelines (G3.1 Guidelines) are composed of Reporting Guidance and Principles (Defining Report Content, Quality, and Boundary) and Standard Disclosures that are considered to have equal weight and importance in the reporting process. According to the GRI G3.1 definition, "sustainability reporting is the practice of measuring, disclosing, and being accountable to internal and external stakeholders for organizational performance toward the goal of sustainable development."[68] In the GRI Sustainability Reporting Guidelines, the term *sustainability reporting* is considered synonymous with others used to define reporting on economic, environmental, and social impacts (e.g., triple bottom line, corporate responsibility reporting). Defining the boundary of the report, organizations must determine which entities' performance will be represented in the report. The Guidelines state that the report should include entities over which the reporting organization exercises control or significant influence.

In order to guarantee the quality of the measurements, the GRI reporting principles identify the criteria that sustainability reports must follow in order to give a truthful view of the economic, social, and environmental status of the reporting organization. Using the same principles can increase the timely comparability between organizations situated in different geographical areas and over time. Compliance with the GRI reporting principles is the starting point for the process of reporting, determining the content and presentation of the reporting, and ensuring quality and reliability of the information reported. Reporting principles define the outcomes a report should achieve, guide decisions throughout the reporting process, and show how to report on selected topics and indicators in order to help achieve transparency (GRI G3.1 Guidelines). In fact, transparency is the dominant principle throughout the whole GRI reporting process and represents the value that underlies all aspects of sustainability reporting. Transparency covers full disclosure of processes, procedures, and assumptions in the report preparation.

As illustrated in Figure 14.14, the GRI guidelines are divided into three main areas. The first two areas are reporting principles that are subdivided into groups, one that includes the principles defining the content and another that contains principles for defining the quality of reporting. The first group is composed of principles that deal with *content,* that is, with the question of what to report, already analyzed in the first phase of the accounting process (stakeholder inclusiveness, materiality, completeness, and sustainability context). We will therefore concentrate on the second area, report quality.

The section containing principles that guide choices on ensuring the *quality* of reported information includes decisions related to the process of preparing information for the report. Balance, comparability, accuracy, timeliness, clarity, and reliability principles cover the quality of the reported information. Some of the characteristics of the information that these principles identify are described in the following paragraph.

The organization's report should reflect a balance of positive and negative aspects of the organization's performance to enable a reasoned valuation of overall

Figure 14.14 **GRI Reporting Principles**

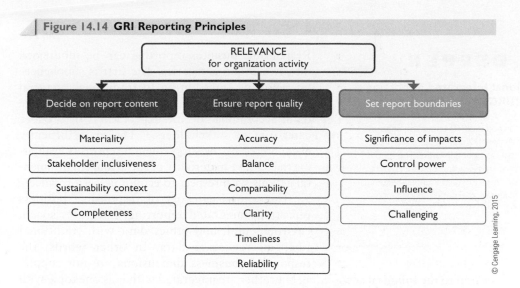

sustainability performance. The accuracy principle looks out for correctness and ensures a low margin of error in the reported information. According to the comparability principle, reports should enable stakeholders to analyze changes in the organization's performance over time and support comparative analysis with other organizations. Timeliness and clarity refer to norms about the availability of the reported information. Timeliness identifies the need of the reporting process to follow a regular schedule of information in order to be available on time for stakeholders to make informed decisions. The stakeholders may use the report if its information is understandable and accessible, according to the clarity principle. Finally, the information and processes used in the preparation of a report are gathered, recorded, compiled, analyzed, and disclosed in a way that could be subject to examination and that ascertains its quality and materiality, which meets the reliability principle.

The second part of the GRI guidelines as illustrated in Figure 14.14, called *standard disclosures,* is dedicated to the identification of information that is relevant to most organizations and interests most stakeholders. Standard disclosures are composed of three categories of disclosures. First, strategy and profile disclosures set the overall context for decoding organizational performance with respect to the organization's strategy, profile, and governance. The purpose of management approach disclosures is to cover how an organization addresses a given set of topics in order to provide a context for understanding performance in a specific area. The third standard disclosure deals with performance indicators that produce comparable information on the responsible business activity and performance of the organization.

GRI provides other documents for reporting:

- *Sector supplements:* providing guidance that captures sustainability issues faced by specific industry sectors (e.g., telecommunications, auto manufacturing, mining)

- *Technical protocols:* providing detailed definitions, measurement methods, and procedures for reporting on indicators contained in the core guidelines (e.g. energy indicators)

- *National annexes:* providing national country perspectives and particular influences, issues, and contexts related to sustainability

- *Issue guidance documents:* on topics such as, among others, diversity and productivity

## 14-6b Integrated Reporting

Responsible business reporting can be subdivided into two broad categories. The first is supplemental reporting (in addition to traditional financial reports) that uses both quantitative and qualitative data, accounting for the expectations of broader categories of stakeholders.[69] The main difficulty encountered by the supplemental reports is evaluating the relative materiality of social and environmental actions with respect to economic performance.

The second category of responsible business reporting, integrated reporting, integrates social, environmental, and ethics data with traditional financial reporting data. In other words, the responsible business dimensions are not supplemental to the financial accounting, but rather are integrated with it as one topic with four aspects. Part of this approach can be considered the International Integrated Reporting. The GRI is one of the initiators of the International Integrated Reporting Council and considers integrated reporting to be the next step in responsible business reporting. Figure 14.15 illustrates the percentage of GRI reports that have been issued as integrated reports in the past. It is expected that the number of integrated reports will soon overtake the number of classic responsible business reports.

According to the IIRC framework,[70] integrated reporting brings together the material information about an organization's strategy, governance, performance, and prospects in a way that reflects the commercial, social, and environmental context within which it operates. Integrated reporting provides a clear and concise representation of how an organization demonstrates stewardship and how it creates value now and in the future. Integrated reporting combines the most material elements of information currently reported in separate reporting strands (financial, management commentary, governance and remuneration, and sustainability) into a coherent whole. Importantly, integrated reporting shows connectivity between parts and explains how the parts affect the ability of an organization to create and sustain value in the short, medium, and long term.

Integrated reporting gives a broader explanation of an organization's performance than traditional financial reporting. It makes visible an organization's use of

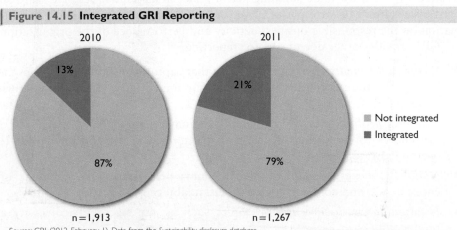

**Figure 14.15 Integrated GRI Reporting**

2010

13%

87%

n=1,913

2011

21%

79%

n=1,267

■ Not integrated
■ Integrated

Source: GRI. (2012, February 1). Data from the *Sustainability disclosure database.*

and dependence on different resources and relationships, or "capitals"; its interaction with external factors, relationships, and resources; and its access to and impact on them. For this analysis, IIRC designates six capitals that the business may rely on, putting together the financial and nonfinancial resources:

- *Financial capital:* The wide-ranging funds available to the organization
- *Manufactured capital:* Manufactured physical objects, as distinct from natural physical objects
- *Human capital:* People's skills and experience, and their motivations to innovate
- *Intellectual capital:* Intangibles that provide competitive advantage
- *Natural capital:* Includes water, land, minerals, and forests; and biodiversity and ecosystem health
- *Social capital:* The institutions and relationships established within and between each community, stakeholders, and other networks to enhance individual and collective well-being. It includes an organization's social license to operate.[71]

Reporting this information is critical to:

- A meaningful assessment of the long-term viability of the organization's business model and strategy
- Meeting the information needs of investors and other stakeholders
- Ultimately, the effective allocation of scarce resources

An overview of the guiding principles supporting the preparation of an integrated report, issued by the IIRC and elaborated by Deloitte, is shown in Figure 14.16.

## 14-6c Auditing and Assurance

Auditing and assurance have become a critical part of the responsible accounting process, as illustrated by the following quotation: "Approximately 45 percent of G250 companies currently use **assurance** as a strategy to verify and assess their Corporate Responsibility Reporting information. A significant number suggested that assurance has improved reporting processes."[72] The growth of the adoption of voluntary sustainability reporting suggests that both corporations and their stakeholders find value in the publication of this data. The current trend in increasing levels of disclosure by organizations of social, ethical, and environmental performance is being undermined by a lack of confidence in both the data and the transparency of the reporting organizations.[73] To bridge the critical credibility gap characterizing the reporting of responsible business activity and performance, a strategic role is assigned to the assurance services provided by qualified auditors or audit companies.[74]

The audit can be seen as a tool that has been developed for both internal and external use for the verification of the quality of stakeholder accountability. The purpose of an **audit** has been defined as the investigation and review of actions, decisions, achievements, statements, or reports of specified persons with defined responsibilities, to compare these actions with norms, and to form and express an opinion on the result of that investigation, review, and comparison.[75] Internally the audit can be seen as an important tool allowing the verification and enforcement of values and dynamics between the organization and its stakeholders. Based on this approach, so-called social auditing is a dynamic process that an organization follows to account for and improve its performance, consisting of planning, accounting, auditing and reporting, embedding, and stakeholder engagement.[76] Social auditing provides a mechanism for decision-makers to evaluate environmental, ethical, and

**Assurance** is the external verification and endorsement of accounting process and outcomes.

An **audit** is the investigation and review of actions, decisions, achievements, statements, or reports of specified persons with defined responsibilities, to compare these actions with norms, and to form and express an opinion on the result of that investigation, review, and comparison.

**Figure 14.16 Integrated Reporting Framework**

| Principles | Elements | Content |
|---|---|---|
| **Strategic focus:** *An Integrated Report provides insight into the organisation's strategic objectives, and how those objectives relate to its ability create and sustain value over time and the resources and relationships on which the organisation depends.* | **Group profile** | • First few pages of the report to introduce the business<br>• In which sector does the business operate? What type of business is this?<br>• What are the products?<br>• What is the structure of the Group and company?<br>• Where does the business operate? |
| **Connectivity of information:** *An Integrated Report shows the connections between the different components of the organisation's business model, external factors that affect the organisation, and the various resources and relationships on which the organisation and its performance depend.* | **Scope and boundary** | • Indicate the reporting period to which the report pertains<br>• Focus on comparability between different reporting periods (i.e. the impact of acquisitions, disposals or restructuring on the comparability of financial and non-financial information)<br>• Focus on comparability between financial and non-financial information (more often than not the boundary for financial and non-financial information differs) |
| | **Key features** | • Illustrate the company's main achievements and key features<br>• Ensure a balance between financial and non-financial information<br>• Utilise graphs, illustrations and pictures to deliver a clear message to the reader (too many words drown out the message) |
| | **Strategy vision values** | • Use this part of the report to inform the reader of the character and values of the business<br>• Clearly describe the strategic goals and objective of the business in plain language (this is a key feature of the report since risks, opportunities, key performance indicators and targets will all be linked to the strategic objectives of the business) |
| **Future orientation:** *An Integrated Report includes management's expectations about the future, as well as other information to help report users understand and assess the organisation's prospects and the uncertainties it faces.* | **Governance structure** | • Set out the governance structure of the group and the company, including the committee structure<br>• Provide details on directors (qualifications, experience, age, other Board appointments, etc.)<br>• Describe the governance structures to manage risk and sustainability respectively<br>• Governance report should provide clear feedback on the performance of the Board and each committee, as well as specific disclosures as required in terms of king III (Composition of the Board, statement on adequacy of internal controls and internal financial controls, ethics performance, etc.) |
| **Responsiveness and stakeholder inclusiveness:** *An Integrated Report provides insight into the organisation's relationships with its key stakeholders and how and to what extent the organization understands, takes into account and responds to their needs.* | **Stakeholders** | • The Integrated Report is directed at the business' key stakeholders (remember; the Integrated Report cannot be everything to everybody, but should rather focus on providing key stakeholders with relevant and material information)<br>• Identify the key stakeholders of the business (based on influence and dependency)<br>• Identify the key interests and concerns of the key stakeholders and indicate where in the report these concerns are being addressed<br>• Describe the strategy and methodology to ensure effective stakeholder communication |
| | **Material risks and opportunities** | • Identify the risks and opportunities facing the business (linked to the strategic objectives)<br>• Indicate the mitigation plans in place to mitigate the risks and capitalize on opportunities<br>• Ensure a balance between financial and other risks and opportunities (think people, product, supply chain, governance, and environment) |
| | **Key performance indicators and targets** | • Identify the key performance indicators as it pertains to the strategy, risks and stakeholder concerns<br>• Ensure a balance between financial and non-financial indicators<br>• Identify measurable targets linked to the key performance indicators and report back on the progress to achieve these targets |
| **Conciseness, reliability and materiality:** *An Integrated Report provides concise, reliable information that is material to assessing the organisation's ability to create and sustain value in the short-, medium- and long-term.* | **Remuneration** | • Explain the business' remuneration strategy<br>• How is remuneration used to ensure delivery on the business' strategy? Include information of long-term and short-term incentives, as well as financial and other incentives |

**Combined Assurance**
The Audit Committee, on behalf of the Board, should ensure the credibility of all information included in the integrated Report

Source: Deloitte. (2012). *Integrated reporting: Navigating your way to a truly integrated report*, p. 17.

social planning and facilitate stakeholder engagement in the social, environmental, and ethical decision-making process of an organization. A match between corporate sustainability external auditing and internal social auditing aims at improving the social, environmental, and economic performance of organizations. Both can be important tools for the accountability to a wider range of stakeholders and for the engagement of stakeholders in the sustainability accounting process.

The implementation of external assurance can be directed to professional providers, stakeholder panels, and other external groups or individuals. The assurance process should follow given standards for assurance or involve approaches that follow systematic, documented, and routinized processes. This assurance process determines that the primary role of an audit is to provide the framework for an objective investigation of the quality of conduct of individuals and organizations compared with given sustainability standards, objectives, or indicators. In particular, two main international standards exist for conducting external verification services on sustainability reports. First, the ISAE 3000 is issued by the International Auditing and Assurance Standards Board,[77] the issuing agency of the International Federation of Accountants (IFAC). Second, the AA1000AS was issued in 2003 (with a second edition in 2008) by a British not-for-profit organization, the Institute of Social and Ethical AccountAbility (ISEA), and is addressed to anyone who provides external verification services.[78] In particular, the AA1000 framework emphasizes three principles:

- *Completeness:* demands that the assurance provider evaluate the extent to which the reporting organization has included in its report material information on all of its activities, performance, and impacts across all aspects of sustainability

- *Materiality:* requires that the assurance provider evaluate whether the reporting organization has included adequate and timely information for the stakeholders

- *Responsiveness:* fosters auditors to evaluate whether the reporting organization has identified and answered stakeholder concerns and explained the basis of any strategy of reaction[79]

Furthermore, the GRI framework recommends the use of any internal resources that cover internal audit functions, internal controls, and systems, in addition to the external assurance for sustainability reports. Reporting companies are required to check their own application level of the GRI disclosure made in the report. GRI application levels—A, B, and C—define the amount of GRI standard disclosures that have been covered in a sustainability report. The criteria for the three levels are summarized in the following list:

- Level C is typically claimed by entry-level reporting organizations, and involves reporting on a reduced set of profile disclosures, but not on the disclosures on management approach. Companies on Level C should report fully on at least ten performance indicators, including at least one from each indicator dimension (economic, environmental, and social).

- Level B is used by intermediate reporters that already have policies for their sustainability performance in place. To claim Level B, companies have to report on all profile disclosures, and disclosures on management approach and should report fully on at least twenty performance indicators, including at least one from each indicator category (Economic, Environmental, Labor Practices and Decent Work, Human Rights, Society, and Product Responsibility).

- Level A is used by advanced reporters that have gone through a thorough materiality assessment in consultation with their stakeholders. To claim level A, a company should address all profile disclosures, all disclosures on management approach for every aspect, and all core performance indicators.

The framework also establishes some key qualities for external assurance, providing the application levels of C+, B+, and A+ that can be declared if external assurance has been utilized for the report. The application levels are usually disclosed at the end of a GRI report and provide readers orientation about its quality.[80]

The review of the sustainability activities and reports can identify many benefits, such as reinforcement of the credibility of sustainability reporting within stakeholders and investor groups and improvement of the quality of reported information and reporting processes.

### 14-6d Ethics of Accounting

The accounting field began in 1494 when Luca Pacioli, a Franciscan friar and "the father of accounting," wrote the first manifesto for formal accounting, *Summa de Arithmetica, Geometria, Proportioni et Proportionalita*. Not only did Pacioli describe double-entry accounting and the interconnected system for capital, income, liability, and expenses, but he also elaborated on accounting ethics.[81]

One of the main tasks of the accounting profession is to present or to assist organizations in presenting the most truthful and accurate reports possible. The ethical behavior of the accountants is also part of the auditing process, where auditors have the responsibility to evaluate the accounting results carried out by other accountants in terms of truthfulness and accuracy. Only in this way can accountants fulfill the purposes of their profession—"to meet the needs of the clients or companies they work for, or to serve the best interests of those stockholders and stakeholders who are entitled to accurate financial pictures of organizations with which they are involved."[82]

The same attentions to the ethical elements of accounting are highlighted as the fundamental qualitative characteristics that the accounting data must represent. In fact, according to the International Accounting Standards Board (IASB) framework, financial information must not only represent relevant phenomena to be useful, but it also must faithfully represent the phenomena that it purports to represent. To be a perfectly faithful representation, a depiction would have three characteristics: it would be complete, neutral, and free from error.[83] Only ethical accounting forms a clear framework of an organization's activities and can achieve the main functions of accounting—maintaining organizations' accountability, supporting managers to make informed decisions, keeping stakeholders well-informed of organizations' activities, and helping the economic activity be sustainable in space and time.

## 14-7 PHASE 4: MANAGEMENT CONTROL

*"The management of sustainability performance requires a sound management framework which, on the one hand, links environmental and social management with the business and competitive strategy and management and, on the other hand, integrates environmental and social information with economic business information and sustainability reporting."[84]*

Accounting reporting is used by organizations in internal governance and external governance processes. In particular, internal uses of accounting information arise from the need to measure and control activities and to use data to assist the decision-making processes.

As suggested by the corporate sustainability model developed by Epstein[85] and illustrated previously in the chapter, the alignment of strategy, structure, management systems, and performance measures is fundamental for organizations to coordinate activities and motivate employees toward implementing a sustainability strategy. A **sustainability performance management and measurement** is "the measurement and management of the interaction between business, society and the environment."[86]

Social and environmental concerns, as well as stakeholders' expectations, must be integrated with traditional financial and economic goals, developing a multidimensional and balanced performance measurement system. This integration can help sustainability performance to be evaluated in a holistic and balanced approach, assisting managers to guide decision making and corporate behavior. Since the formulation and implementation of the responsible business strategy can lead to a remarkable improvement in competitive and economic performance, companies should make use of appropriate systems to manage, measure, and monitor the strategic objectives and results achieved in economic, social, environmental, and ethical terms.

Once the data are reported, during the management control process the responsible business performance can be evaluated by comparing the results achieved with the objectives indicated during the programming phase (see Figure 14.17). This is an important assessment practice, as it can identify significant improvements to add to responsible management activities, and revisits the targets in setting out new objectives.

In this last phase, the role of accounting and accountants is seen to:

- Support the process of engaging management in the development and improvement of responsible business
- Review results, processes, and inputs as well as relate these areas to each other
- Support and challenge management in their choice of responsible management measures
- Facilitate communication and review of reports[87]

This information derived from management control also can be elaborated for a single process or product/service, giving a single measure for the responsible business performance of the unit analyzed (see Figure 14.18).

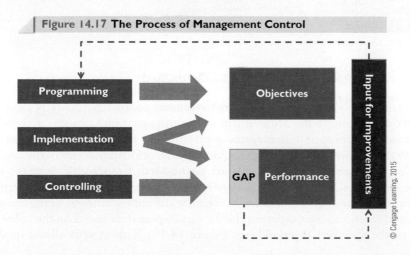

Figure 14.17 **The Process of Management Control**

© Cengage Learning, 2015

A **sustainability performance management and measurement** is the measurement and management of the interaction between business, society, and the environment.

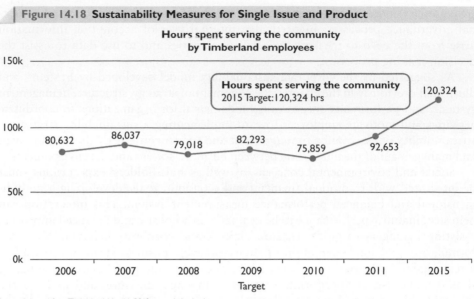

Figure 14.18 **Sustainability Measures for Single Issue and Product**

**Hours spent serving the community by Timberland employees**

Hours spent serving the community
2015 Target:120,324 hrs

| | 2006 | 2007 | 2008 | 2009 | 2010 | 2011 | 2015 |
|---|---|---|---|---|---|---|---|
| Hours | 80,632 | 86,037 | 79,018 | 82,293 | 75,859 | 92,653 | 120,324 |

Target

Source: Adapted from Timberland, May 11, 2012: www.timberland.com

Figure 14.19 **Sustainability Dashboard**

| PILLAR GOALS | CATEGORY | 2011 PERFORMANCE | | FUTURE TARGETS | | FEATURED METRIC |
|---|---|---|---|---|---|---|
| | | Actual | Target | 2012 | 2015 | > Rate of Hours Served |
| CLIMATE | GHG Inventory | 16,482 | 15,870 | 15,870 | 12,775 | Hours Utilization Rate (HUR) |
| | Renewable Energy | 15% | 15% | 19% | 30% | |
| | Supply Chain | 13.30% | 20% | 40% | 100% | |
| PRODUCT | Green Index | 5% | — | 100% | — | Actual |
| | Chemicals | 61.6 | 64.0 | 54.0 | 42.0 | 42% ↑ |
| | Leather | 82.7% | 100% | 100% | 100% | Target |
| | Raw Materials | 25.4% | 23.3% | 35.2% | 50.6% | 42% |
| FACTORIES | Factory Conditions | 33% | 30% | TBD | 100% | This employee engagements metric demonstrates employees' use of the Path of Service TM program. Hours Utilization Rate (HUR) measures the percentage of available service hours offered to Timberland employees that employees use per year. |
| | High Risk | 0.05% | 0% | TBD | | |
| | Environmental Performance | 6% | 20% | 40% | | |
| | Remediation Effectiveness | 59% | 70% | TBD | | |
| | Responsible Sourcing | 47% | 48% | TBD | | |
| SERVICE | > Rate of Hours Served | 42% | 42% | 45% | 60% | Read More |
| | Employee Engagement Scale | 79% | 80% | 81% | 84% | |
| | | 40% | baseline | TBD | baseline | |

Source: Timberland Q4 2011 Dashboard. Retrieved May 11, 2012, from Timberland: www.timberland.com

## 14-7a Responsible Management Dashboard

Responsible accounting utilized for management control purposes is designed to support and facilitate the achievement of the organization's objectives through the utilization of appropriate management information tools. In particular, an instrument that can give overall, concise, and real-time information internally and externally is the **responsible management dashboard**. Responsible business metrics can be sent to a dashboard, which dynamically elaborates real-time information.

A **responsible management dashboard** summarizes social, environmental, and ethical performance through quantitative indicators.

The dashboard can automatically organize the data according to the chosen category and level, and uses different graphics to display data based on the value elaborated to the specified threshold (see Figure 14.19). This system allows qualitative estimation of responsible management performance based on different organizations and quantitative, real-time measurements that allow subjective specification and value judgments made by different end users.

The right information system and tools can be implemented, considering the accounting process and the sustainability models that integrate the model and process together. Distinguishing the adequate responsible management framework, which is the result of the accounting process adopted or its first consequence, still remains a great challenge.

## PRINCIPLES OF ACCOUNTING AND CONTROLLING: STAKEHOLDER ACCOUNTABILITY

I. The goal of responsible accounting is the verification of a high level of organizational *stakeholder accountability,* providing quantitative and qualitative information oriented to the long-term achievement of organizational ethical, social, and environmental, and economic performance.

II. The *responsible accounting process* consists of four phases: (1) gathering data, (2) elaboration and evaluation of the data, (3) reporting both internally and externally, and (4) implementing and evaluating strategies.

III. *The disclosure of the information* is one of the main criteria of the responsible accounting activity and therefore should integrate social, environmental, and ethical with economic accounting data.

IV. *Materiality* is an important principle for defining the content of sustainability accounting data. Materiality should depict the importance of all responsible business issues that are of importance to the company and its stakeholders.

V. Responsible accounting measures a broad set of *social, environmental, and ethical benefits and costs* and considers impacts on the company, economy, society, and the environment. Although some forms of responsible accounting rely on monetary units to measure environmental, social, and ethical impacts, the use of *multiple units of measurement* is preferable.

VI. The dissemination of accounting information to internal and external users is made through appropriate reports on sustainability, responsibility, and ethics. The *Global Reporting Initiative (GRI)* guidelines—process-oriented standards with a particular focus on the document—are the world's most widely used responsible business reporting framework.

VII. The *integrated approach* for the accounting process can be an important framework for reporting the social, environmental, ethics, and economic indicators contributing to stakeholder accountability.

VIII. The responsible *management control process* evaluates the responsible accounting data, comparing the results achieved with the values and objectives identified during the programming phase.

## RESPONSIBLE ACCOUNTING CHECKLIST

| Process Phase | | Sustainability | Responsibility | Ethics |
|---|---|---|---|---|
| Phase 1: Data gathering | Does your accounting framework … | … gather all relevant types of social, environmental, and economic data? | … gather all data relevant to your stakeholders, including the mechanisms to measure the value created for stakeholders themselves? | … gather data on employees' behavior in ethical moral dilemma situations? |
| Phase 2: Data evaluation | Does the evaluation of data … | … help to bundle formal triple bottom line data into relevant indicators? | … ensure that material aspects are covered and the value added to stakeholders is illustrated? | … rule out ethical issues, such as data manipulation? |
| Phase 3: Reporting | Does your reporting activity … | … allow for a transparent assessment of your triple bottom line? | … create transparency for all external and internal stakeholders? | … comply with ethical communication and reporting standards? |
| Phase 4: Controlling | Do we use the outcomes of accounting to … | … implement management practices that improve the triple bottom line? | … improve management for stakeholder value? | … reduce ethical misconduct? |

## KEY TERMS

account 449
assurance 471
audit 471
disclosure 455
ESG (environment, social, and governance) disclosure 455
ethics of accounting 453
materiality 457

organizational accountability 449
responsible accounting and controlling 453
responsible management dashboard 476
social return on investment (SROI) 466
stakeholder accountability 449

sustainability accounting and reporting 453
sustainability performance indicator 461
sustainability performance management and measurement 475
value added 464

## EXERCISES

### A. Remember and Understand

A.1. Mention the main drivers of sustainability accounting and describe how they may influence the accounting process.

A.2. Describe the four phases of accounting and give an example of a typical activity for each phase.

A.3. Define each of the following terms and describe the difference between them:
- Global Reporting Initiative
- Integrated reporting approach
- AA1000 standards

### B. Apply and Experience

B.4. Look up the table of contents for the responsible business reports of a company of your choice and rewrite it by integrating new social, environmental, and ethics considerations. Then describe the appropriate accounting data for the new contents.

B.5. Design a management control framework for a company of your choice, based on social, environmental, and ethics indicators for the product or service offered. You can use Figure 14.17, *The Process of Management Control*, as a template.

### C. Analyze and Evaluate

C.6. Look up the list of performance indicators proposed by the Global Reporting Initiative (www.globalreporting.org). Which indicators do you think are the easiest ones to gather quantifiable data for? Which are the most difficult and why?

C.7. Look up the most recent GRI report of a company from your country and answer the following questions: (1) Who are the primary stakeholders of the company? (2) Which are the most material lines of action? (3) How good is the company's triple bottom line performance? (4) How does the company report on ethics topics? Based on these steps of analysis, would you classify the company as a responsible business?

### D. Change and Create

D.8. Design the accounting approach of the future. What should accounting in fifteen years look like, to make a maximum contribution to sustainable development, stakeholder value, and moral excellence? (Use the main standards discussed in the "Phase 3: Reporting" section of this chapter.)

## PIONEER INTERVIEW MICHAEL BRAUNGART

Courtesy of Michael Braungart

Michael Braungart is co-creator of the cradle-to-cradle (C2C) concept, the triple top line, and a pioneer of life-cycle assessment, all of which are important tools of sustainability accounting and controlling.

**What is the difference between John Elkington´s triple bottom line and the triple top line concept that you are promoting?**

First of all, it is really amazing and I don't know why people have such a difficulty in their logic when it comes to sustainability and environment that they want to be good for the economy, they want to be beneficial for society, but when it comes to environment and biodiversity and supporting other species, they can only imagine to neutralize negative impacts. A good example is the ideal of zero-emission cities like Hamburg or Copenhagen that want to be carbon neutral or climate neutral. That is amazing because I never saw a climate neutral tree.

We can become native to this planet, which means we can make things that are beneficial for the economy, great for society, and supportive for the other species in the environment at the same time. This is why the triple bottom line should in reality be a triple top line. Applying the same principle, we can design better products, things that are extremely profitable, and which are far better for society and beneficial for the other species as well.

**What would you say are the typical challenges in using life-cycle assessment as an accounting tool?**

First of all, I was one of the persons in the late 80s and early 90s to help develop life-cycle assessment technologies, but overall it is just an interim step because one of the basic assumptions is wrong.

There is no life in a product; even the washing machine doesn't live, a carpet is not living, a shoe is not living; so when you project life into a product, we want to have life forever because we want to live forever. Our products, however, should not live forever because this means that we either have to generate planned obsolescence in products to cheat the customer or, on the other side, we miss the opportunity for innovation.

So the basic assumption is wrong overall. It definitely makes sense to calculate data, material flows, and energy uses around a product. So, connecting the data makes sense. Increasing the life span of a nonliving product, on the other hand, is misleading, and is not scientific either.

**What is your opinion regarding the concepts of social or environmental return on investment?**

I think it makes sense to look where can I get the best effect for the money I am spending, but the social impact thinking of how it is done right now is a pretty cynical one. You can see that we do not have humans in companies anymore; we have human resources. This is cynical because humans are not human resources or human raw material. Automatically, you will come up with the same efficiency thinking of minimizing, reducing, or avoiding. Human dignity cannot be made efficient. So there is a certain limit.

The name of the human resources department—even if you want to keep the plackets on the wall, you can keep them as HR—but call it *human relations*, because otherwise it leads to standardization and homogenization. Every person, every culture has different needs, so you cannot just calculate it by money. The term *human resources* has to go. It really needs to be changed because we lose human dignity through it.

**Is responsible management the right way to approach sustainability issues and crises?**

It should not be about responsible management, as the word *responsible* has too many moral and ethical connotations, and people forget moral habits immediately when they are under stress. So when you make it a moral thing, it never works when you need it the most. From a cradle-to-cradle perspective, it's about quality and beauty.

It is, for instance, not beautiful when it is connected to child labor. It is also about quality because we have a quality problem when a product becomes waste and when the production process destroys the planet. It is a quality problem, and it is about innovation, because we can now reach far better quality by innovation.

And that's why this approach will be far more reliable, because in a crisis people forget about ethical habits immediately; but in a crisis, we need to understand that they invest in quality, and we can see that cradle-to-cradle products are so superior also from a profit perspective that it will be just an economic decision to use the opportunity for innovation. I am very optimistic about that.

## PRACTITIONER PROFILE: DANIEL ETTE

Courtesy of Daniel Ette

**Employing organization:** Hansgrohe is a leading bathroom and sanitary specialist and employs more than 3,300 people worldwide. The corporation is based in Germany. It is a European stock corporation (Societas Europaea SE), which is not listed on the stock exchange.

**Job title:** Sustainability Controller.

**Education:** Master of Arts in Responsible Management at Steinbeis University, Berlin; Studies in Business Administration at Baden-Wuerttemberg Cooperative State University, Specialization in Controlling/Finance and Accounting, and in Logistics and Production.

## In Practice

### What are your responsibilities?

My main responsibility as a Sustainability Controller is to be seen in introducing sustainability into management accounting and controlling thinking. Controlling's methodological competence must be extended from a mere financial focus toward the recognition of economic, ecological, and social topics, so that our controlling can be a holistic business partner for the management board.

In order to achieve that, my responsibilities include setting up a valid data base and agreeing on KPIs together with the management. Moreover, it is my responsibility to convince coworkers, management, and employees that responsible thinking is important. As a Sustainability Controller, I strive toward a mind-set change within the corporation.

### What are typical activities you carry out during a day at work?

For me, being a Sustainability Controller means setting up a controlling solution for sustainability. An IT-based controlling solution was developed to generate reliable data in the field of the triple bottom line. Now, sustainability data can be reported in the same cycles as key financial figures, by using SAP-based tools. That led to the implementation of automatically available KPIs within a Sustainability Dashboard, called "Hansgrohe Sustainability KPIs."

In the day-to-day business, deviations from targets are evaluated in order to be able to take effective corrective actions. The result is that the respect for the environment, social factors, and economic success are combined efficiently and integrated systematically into business processes.

Moreover, since we have implemented Sustainability Investment Criteria, investments are being evaluated not only on a monetary basis, but also in a social and environmental understanding. Last but not least, the evaluation of environmental footprints of more and more products requires the support of Sustainability Controlling.

### How do sustainability, responsibility, and ethics topics play a role in your job?

The combination of controlling and of the topics of sustainability, responsibility, and ethics is a very interesting and complex field. For me, as a Sustainability Controller, the mentioned terms play an important role in my job. The goal of Sustainability Controlling is to be seen in maintaining the long-term viability of the corporation and at the same time showing respect for the members of our society and the environment. It is not the issue about doing some philanthropic actions. Rather, Sustainability Controlling deals with the question of how the interests of shareholders, as well as the interests of other stakeholders like the employees or the neighborhood, can be satisfied. The triple bottom line comes into play by extending investment evaluation toward a holistic picture. Controlling itself has a lot to do with accountability and honesty. Controlling is required to support management with accurate and reliable data. Yet, a Sustainability Controller must also take into account that people always have to be treated with respect and cannot simply be quantified in monetary terms. Sustainability Controlling, thus, is not only about figures but also about the relationships of management, employees, other stakeholders, and controlling itself.

### Out of the topics covered in the chapter into which your interview will be included, which concepts, tools, or topics are most relevant to your work? How?

The work of a Sustainability Controller is linked to all phases mentioned in the chapter. I am highly involved in gathering suitable data and in evaluating it. At the beginning, it must be clarified which of the indicators are material and help to steer the corporation. Especially the questions of *what*, *who*, and *how* help a lot to not lose sight in the complex context of Sustainability Controlling. In this sense, also the *materiality map* is helpful. For a powerful controlling and management accounting, it is crucial to focus on the things that are most relevant. Especially the sustainability metrics from the Global Reporting Initiative are of importance in terms of reporting. The Global Reporting Initiative constitutes a good basis on which a Sustainability Controlling can be set up. However, it is important to link to requirements of external stakeholders and those of management when it comes to the question of which KPIs should be measured and how they should be presented.

As always in controlling, a Sustainability Controller deals with gap-analyses and supports management to take corrective measures—in my position, corrective measures with respect to social, environmental, and economic issues.

### Insights and Challenges

### What recommendation can you give to practitioners in your field?

It is important to realize that controlling and management accounting is in a crucial position when it comes to the question of how sustainability can be introduced into a corporation. Controlling, with its cross-departmental tasks and connections, can be a driver toward sustainability. To do so, methodological competences are necessary, as shown in this book. A valid data base is one of the most important aspects. Only with this can targets be set, deviations evaluated, and measures derived.

However, it is of substantial importance to understand that one cannot make a corporation responsible by only taking hard facts into account. Controlling is required to change its own mind-set and to nudge management and employees toward a holistic thinking in terms of responsibility and sustainability. Hence, Sustainability Controlling is not number crunching. It is about steering a corporation toward responsible behavior by making responsibility a central issue.

## Which are the main challenges of your job?

One of the most challenging points can be seen in convincing managers and employees that environmental and social factors are of importance—besides monetary ones. Moreover, as a Sustainability Controller, one must master the balancing act of being a trustworthy business partner for management and of being an enthusiastic driver toward more responsibility and sustainability.

## Is there anything else that you would like to share?

Controlling and management accounting must not be underestimated in its importance when it comes to sustainability, responsibility, and ethical behavior.

## SOURCES

1. Flint, D. (1988). *Philosophy and principles of auditing: An introduction.* Oxford: Macmillan Education.
2. Ernst & Young. (2012). *Six growing trends in corporate sustainability.* Ernst & Young; Ernst & Young LLP. (2012). *Six growing trends in corporate sustainability.* GreenBiz Group Study.
3. ISO. (2012). *ISO 26000—Social responsibility* (p. 10). Retrieved January 15, 2012, from International Organization for Standardization: www.iso.org/iso/iso_catalogue /management_and_leadership _standards/social_responsibility /sr_iso26000_overview.htm#sr-7
4. Ernst & Young. (2012). *Six growing trends in corporate sustainability.* Ernst & Young; Ernst & Young LLP. (2012). *Six growing trends in corporate sustainability* (p. 7). GreenBiz Group Study.
5. Unerman, J., & Bennett, M. (2004). Increased stakeholder dialogue and the Internet: Towards greater corporate accountability or reinforcing capitalist hegemony? *Accounting, Organizations and Society, 29*(7), 685–707.
6. Lamberton, G. (2005). Sustainability accounting—A brief history and conceptual framework. *Accounting Forum, 29*(1), 7–26.
7. Gray, R., Owen, D. L., & Adams, C. (1996). *Accounting and accountability: Social and environmental accounting in a changing world.* Harlow, England, and New York: Financial Times/Prentice Hall.
8. Crane, A., Matten, D., & Moon, J. (2004). Stakeholders as citizens? Rethinking rights, participation, and democracy. *Journal of Business Ethics, 53*(1), 107–122.
9. Cooper, S. M., & Owen, D. L. (2007). Corporate social reporting and stakeholder accountability: The missing link. *Accounting, Organizations and Society, 32*(7), 649–667.
10. Stewart, J. D. (1984). The role of information in public accountability. In A. Hopwood & C. Tomkins (Eds.), *Issues in public sector accounting.* Oxford: Philip Allen.
11. Cooper, S. M., & Owen, D. L. (2007). Corporate social reporting and stakeholder accountability: The missing link. *Accounting, Organizations and Society, 32*(7), 649–667.
12. Bailey, D., Harte, G., & Sugden, R. (2000). Corporate disclosure and the deregulation of international investment. *Accounting, Auditing & Accountability Journal, 13*(2), 197–218.
13. Edwards, M., & Hulme, D. (1995). *Non-governmental organisations: Performance and accountability beyond the magic bullet.* Earthscan/James & James; Najam, A. (1996). NGO accountability: A conceptual framework. *Development Policy Review, 14*(4), 339–354.
14. Ebrahim, A. (2003). Making sense of accountability: Conceptual perspectives for northern and southern nonprofits. *Nonprofit Management and Leadership, 14*(2), 191–212.
15. Dixon, R., Ritchie, J., & Siwale, J. (2006). Microfinance: Accountability from the grassroots. *Accounting, Auditing & Accountability Journal, 19*(3), 405–427.
16. O'Dwyer, B., & Unerman, J. (2008). The paradox of greater NGO accountability: A case study of Amnesty Ireland. *Accounting, Organizations and Society, 33*(7), 801–824.
17. Unerman, J., & Bennett, M. (2004). Increased stakeholder dialogue and the Internet: Towards greater corporate accountability or reinforcing capitalist hegemony? *Accounting, Organizations and Society, 29*(7), 685–707.
18. Gray R. H. (2000). Current developments and trends in social and environmental auditing, reporting and attestation: A review and comment. *International Journal of Auditing, 4*(3), 247–268.
19. American Accounting Association, http://aaahq.org/
20. Melé, D. (2005). Ethical education in accounting: Integrating rules, values and virtues. *Journal of Business Ethics, 57*(1), 97–109.
21. Schaltegger, S., & Wagner, M. (2006). Integrative management of

sustainability performance, measurement and reporting. *International Journal of Accounting, Auditing and Performance Evaluation, 3*(1), 1–19.

22. Epstein, M., Flamholtz, E., & McDonough, J. J. (1976). Corporate social accounting in the United States of America: State of the art and future prospects. *Accounting, Organizations and Society, 1*(1), 23–42.

23. Dierkes, M., & Antal, A. B. (1985). The usefulness and use of social reporting information. *Accounting, Organizations and Society, 10*(1), 29–34.

24. Adams, C. A. (2004). The ethical, social and environmental reporting–performance portrayal gap. *Accounting, Auditing & Accountability Journal, 17*(5), 731–757.

25. Adams, C. A. (2004). The ethical, social and environmental reporting–performance portrayal gap. *Accounting, Auditing & Accountability Journal, 17*(5), 731–757, p. 732.

26. Gray, R., & Milne, M. (2002). Sustainability reporting: Who's kidding whom? *Chartered Accountants Journal of New Zealand, 81*(6), 66–70; Schaltegger, S., Bennett, M., & Burritt, R. (2006). Sustainability accounting and reporting: Development, linkages and reflection. An Introduction. *Sustainability Accounting and Reporting,* 1–33.

27. Schaltegger, S., & Burritt, R. L. (2006). Corporate sustainability accounting. In S. Schaltegger, M. Epstein, M. J. (2008). *Making sustainability work: Best practices in managing and measuring corporate social, environmental, and economic impacts.* San Francisco: Berrett-Koehler.

28. Lydenberg, S., Rogers, J., & Wood, D. (2010, May). *From transparency to performance: Industry-based sustainability reporting on key issues* (p. IV). Retrieved September 2012 from The Hauser Center for Nonprofit Organizations, Initiative for Responsible Investment: http://hauser-center.org/iri/wp-content/uploads/2010/05/IRI_Transparency-to-Performance.pdf

29. Deloitte. *Deloitte Debate. Disclosure of long-term business value. What matters?* Retrieved

April 2012 from: www.deloitte.com/assets/Dcom-UnitedStates/Local%20Assets/Documents/us_scc_materialitypov_032812.pdf

30. Lamberton, G. (2005). Sustainability accounting—A brief history and conceptual framework. *Accounting Forum, 29*(1), 7–26.

31. Michelon, G., & Parbonetti, A. (2012). The effect of corporate governance on sustainability disclosure. *Journal of Management and Governance,* 1–33.

32. Toppinen, A., Li, N., Tuppura, A., & Xiong, Y. (2012). Corporate responsibility and strategic groups in the forest–based industry: Exploratory analysis based on the Global Reporting Initiative (GRI) framework. *Corporate Social Responsibility and Environmental Management.*

33. Reverte, C. (2009). Determinants of corporate social responsibility disclosure ratings by Spanish listed firms. *Journal of Business Ethics, 88*(2), 351–366.

34. Gray, R., Javad, M., Power, D. M., & Sinclair, C. D. (2001). Social and environmental disclosure and corporate characteristics: A research note and extension. *Journal of Business Finance & Accounting, 28*(3–4), 327–356.

35. Prof. Mervyn King, GRI Honorary Chairman, as quoted in GRI. (2012). *Report or explain: A policy proposal for sustainability reporting to be adopted as a common practice for the advancement of a Green Economy.* Retrieved July 9, 2013, from Rio +20: United Nations Conference on Sustainable Development: www.uncsd2012.org/content/documents/ReportOrExplain.pdf

36. Adapted from the definition provided by the International Accounting Standards Board: International Accounting Standards Board (IASB). (2010). *The conceptual framework for financial reporting 2010.* London: IASB.

37. Crane, A., Matten, D., & Moon, J. (2004). Stakeholders as citizens? Rethinking rights, participation, and democracy. *Journal of Business Ethics, 53*(1), 107–122.

38. Lehman, G. (1999). Disclosing new worlds: A role for social and environmental accounting and auditing. *Accounting, Organizations and Society, 24*(3), 217–241.

39. Eccles, R. G., Krzus, M. P., & Watson, L. A. (2012). Integrated

reporting requires integrated assurance. In J. Oringel (ed.), *Effective auditing for corporates: Key developments in practice and procedures* (pp. 161–177, p. 166). Bloomsbury Information Limited.

40. Lydenberg, S., Rogers, J., & Wood, D. (2010, May). *From transparency to performance: Industry-based sustainability reporting on key issues.* Retrieved September 2012 from The Hauser Center for Nonprofit Organizations, Initiative for Responsible Investment: http://hauser-center.org/iri/wp-content/uploads/2010/05/IRI_Transparency-to-Performance.pdf

41. Epstein, M. (2008). *Making sustainability work: Best practices in managing and measuring corporate social, environmental, and economic impacts* (p. 165). Sheffield: Greenleaf.

42. Epstein, M. (2008). *Making sustainability work: Best practices in managing and measuring corporate social, environmental, and economic impacts.* Sheffield: Greenleaf.

43. International Accounting Standards Board (IASB). (2010). *The conceptual framework for financial reporting 2010* (p. 37). London: IASB.

44. Cooper, C. (1992). The non and nom of accounting for (M)other Nature. *Accounting, Auditing & Accountability Journal, 5*(3), 16–39.

45. The SROI Network. (2012). *A guide to social return on investment.* Liverpool, UK: SROI.

46. Lamberton, G. (2005). Sustainability accounting—A brief history and conceptual framework. *Accounting Forum, 29*(1), 7–26.

47. Mathews, M. R. (1993). *Socially responsible accounting.* London: Chapman & Hall.

48. Deegan, C., & Newson, M. (1996). *Environmental performance evaluation and reporting for private and public organisations.* Sydney: Environmental Protection Authority.

49. Epstein, M. (2008). *Making sustainability work: Best practices in managing and measuring corporate social, environmental, and economic impacts.* Sheffield: Greenleaf.

50. Klöpffer, W. (2003). Life-cycle based methods for sustainable product development. *International Journal of Life Cycle Assessment, 8*(3), 157–159.

51. Gray, R. H. (1994). Corporate reporting for sustainable development: Accounting for sustainability

in 2000AD. *Environmental Values*, 17–45.

52. Epstein, M. J. (2008). Implementing corporate sustainability: Measuring and managing social and environmental impacts. *Strategic Finance*, 89(7), 24–31.

53. Bell, S., & Morse, S. (2003). *Measuring sustainability: Learning from doing.* London: Earthscan.

54. Zavani M. (2000). *Il valore della comunicazione aziendale. Rilevanza e caratteri dell'informativa sociale e ambientale.* Torino, Giappichelli.

55. Rasche, A., & Esser, D. E. (2006). From stakeholder management to stakeholder accountability. *Journal of Business Ethics*, 65(3), 251–267.

56. Moldan, B., Billharz, S., & Matravers, R. (1997). *Sustainability indicators: A report on the project on indicators of sustainable development* (Vol. 58). Chichester: Wiley.

57. Suojanen, W. W. (1954). Accounting theory and the large corporation. *Accounting Review*, 391–398.

58. Burchell, S., Clubb, C., & Hopwood, A. G. (1985). Accounting in its social context: Towards a history of value added in the United Kingdom. *Accounting, Organizations and Society*, 10(4), 381–413.

59. Meek, G. K., & Gray, S. J. (1988). The value-added statement: An innovation for U.S. companies? *Accounting Horizons*, 2(2), 73–81.

60. Van Staden, C. J. (2000). *The value added statement: Bastion of social reporting or dinosaur of financial reporting.* Working paper. Massey University, Palmerston North, New Zealand.

61. Mook, L., Quarter, J., & Richmond, B. J. (2007). *What counts: Social accounting for nonprofits and cooperatives.* London: Sigel Press.

62. Razek, J., Hosch, G., & Ives, M. (2000). *Introduction to governmental and not-for-profit organizations.* Englewood Cliffs, NJ: Prentice Hall.

63. Mook, L., Quarter, J., & Richmond, B. J. (2007). *What counts: Social accounting for nonprofits and cooperatives.* London: Sigel Press.

64. The SROI Network. (2012). *A guide to social return on investment.* Liverpool, UK: SROI.

65. New Economics Foundation. (2004). *Measuring social impact: The foundations of social return on investment (SROI).* London: New Economics Foundation.

66. Lydenberg, S., Rogers, J., & Wood, D. (2010, May). *From transparency to performance: Industry-based sustainability reporting on key issues* (p. 10). Retrieved September 2012 from The Hauser Center for Nonprofit Organizations, Initiative for Responsible Investment: http://hauser-center.org/iri/wp-content/uploads/2010/05/IRI_Transparency-to-Performance.pdf

67. Schaltegger, S., & Burritt, R. L. (2010). Sustainability accounting for companies: Catchphrase or decision support for business leaders? *Journal of World Business*, 45(4), 375–384.

68. Bailey, D., Harte, G., & Sugden, R. (2000). Corporate disclosure and the deregulation of international investment. *Accounting, Auditing & Accountability Journal*, 13(2), 197–218.

69. Coupland, C. (2006). Corporate social and environmental responsibility in Web-based reports: Currency in the banking sector? *Critical Perspectives on Accounting*, 17(7), 865–881.

70. International Integrated Reporting Committee (IIRC). (2011). *Towards integrated reporting: Communicating value in the 21st century.* Retrieved April 2012 from IIRC: www.theiirc.org

71. International Integrated Reporting Committee (IIRC). (2011). *Towards integrated reporting: Communicating value in the 21st century.* Retrieved April 2012 from IIRC: www.theiirc.org

72. *KPMG international survey of corporate social responsibility reporting 2011.* Available at: www.kpmg.com/PT/pt/IssuesAndInsights/Documents/corporate-responsibility2011.pdf

73. Doane, D. (2000). *Corporate spin: The troubled teenage years of social reporting.* London: New Economics Foundation.

74. Milne, M. J., & Adler, R. W. (1999). Exploring the reliability of social and environmental disclosures content analysis. *Accounting, Auditing & Accountability Journal*, 12(2), 237–256.

75. Flint, D. (1988). *Philosophy and principles of auditing: An introduction.* Basingstoke: Macmillan Education.

76. Gao, S. S., & Zhang, J. J. (2006). Stakeholder engagement, social auditing and corporate sustainability. *Business Process Management Journal*, 12(6), 722–740.

77. International Auditing and Assurance Standard Board (IAASB). (2004). *International standard on assurance engagement 3000. Assurance engagement other than audits or reviews of historical information.* New York: International Auditing and Assurance Standards Board.

78. Dando, N., & Swift, T. (2003). Transparency and assurance: Minding the credibility gap. *Journal of Business Ethics*, 44(2–3), 195–200.

79. AccountAbility. *AA1000 AccountAbility Principles Standard 2008.* Retrieved March 2012 from: www.accountability.org/standards/aa1000aps.html

80. https://www.globalreporting.org/information/FAQs/Pages/Application-Levels.aspx

81. Pacioli, L. (1494). *Summa de arithmetica, geometria, proportioni et proportionalita.* Venica.

82. Duska, R. F., & Duska, B. S. (2003). *Accounting ethics* (p. 74). Malden, MA: Blackwell.

83. International Accounting Standards Board (IASB). (2010). *The conceptual framework for financial reporting 2010.* London: IASB.

84. Schaltegger, S., & Burritt, R. L. (2006). Corporate sustainability accounting. In S. Schaltegger, M. Epstein, M. J. (2008). *Making sustainability work: Best practices in managing and measuring corporate social, environmental, and economic impacts.* San Francisco: Berrett-Koehler.

85. Epstein, M. J. (2008). Implementing corporate sustainability: Measuring and managing social and environmental impacts. *Strategic Finance*, 89(7), 24–31.

86. Schaltegger, S., & Wagner, M. (2006). Integrative management of sustainability performance, measurement and reporting. *International Journal of Accounting, Auditing and Performance Evaluation*, 3(1), 1–19, p. 3.

87. Schaltegger, S., & Burritt, R. L. (2010). Sustainability accounting for companies: Catchphrase or decision support for business leaders? *Journal of World Business*, 45(4), 375–384.

## REFERENCES

Bebbington, J., Brown, J., Frame, B., & Thomson, I. (2007). Theorizing engagement: The potential of a critical dialogic approach. *Accounting, Auditing &Accountability Journal, 20*(3), 356–381.

Bennett, & R. Burritt (Eds.). Sustainability accounting and reporting (pp. 37–59). Dordrecht: Springer.

Ebrahim, A. (2005). Accountability myopia: Losing sight of organizational learning. *Nonprofit and Voluntary Sector Quarterly, 34*(1), 56–87.

Gamerschlag, R., Möller, K., & Verbeeten, F. (2011). Determinants of voluntary CSR disclosure: Empirical evidence from Germany. *Review of Managerial Science, 5*(2), 233–262.

Gray, R., Dey, C., Owen, D., Evans, R., & Zadek, S. (1997). Struggling with the praxis of social accounting: Stakeholders, accountability, audits and procedures. *Accounting, Auditing & Accountability Journal, 10*(3), 325–364.

GRI. (2012). *G3 Online*. Retrieved December 19, 2012, from Global Reporting Initiative: www .globalreporting.org/reporting /guidelines-online/g3online/Pages /default.aspx

International Federation of Accountants (IFAC). (2002). *The determination and communication of levels of assurance other than high*. New York: IFAC.

Manetti, G., & Becatti, L. (2009). Assurance services for sustainability reports: Standards and empirical

evidence. *Journal of Business Ethics, 87,* 289–298.

Orij, R. (2010). Corporate social disclosures in the context of national cultures and stakeholder theory. *Accounting, Auditing & Accountability Journal, 23*(7), 868–889.

Pava, M. L., & Krausz, J. (1996). The association between corporate social responsibility and financial performance: The paradox of social cost. *Journal of Business Ethics, 15*(3), 321–357.

Pollach, I., Scharl, A., & Weichselbraun, A. (2009). Web content mining for comparing corporate and third-party online reporting: A case study on solid waste management. *Business Strategy and the Environment, 18*(3), 137–148.

Microfinance
Bonuses  Cooperatives
Monetization  Profit  Returns  Impact Investment
Capital Budgeting  Corporate Governance
Capital Strucure  Financial Management
Ethical ROI  Money  Shareholders  Cross-Financing  Crowdfunding  Cost Internalization  CSP-CFP  Responsible ROI

# FINANCE: RESPONSIBLE RETURN ON INVESTMENT

*You will be able to...*

1   **...access financing for responsible business activities.**

2   **...make capital budgeting decisions based on sustainability, responsibility, and ethics.**

3   **...govern your company to the best interest of its stakeholders.**

4   **...generate a responsible return on investment (RROI).**

Among chief financial officers (CFOs), 65 percent are now engaged in sustainability. One in six (13%) respondents said their CFO was "very involved" with sustainability, while 52 percent said the CFO was "somewhat" involved.[1]

Companies expect to continue investing in their sustainability initiatives. Fifty-three percent of respondents plan for their budgets for sustainability to increase in the next three years. Thirty-nine percent think it will stay the same, and only 5 percent anticipate funding of their sustainability initiatives to decrease.[2]

Chief financial officers (CFOs) cited cost reductions (74%) and risk management (61%) as two of the three key drivers of their company's sustainability agenda, both of which are key factors in financial management.[3]

Authors: Oliver Laasch and Nick Tolhurst; Contributors: Ajay Jain, Anis Ben Brink, Aurea Christine Tanaka, Charles McJilton, Dewi Fitraasari, Francisco Acuña Mendez, John Bayles, Jürgen Wittstock, Martin Perry, Reinhard Schmidt, Robert Costanza, Sharon Dafny

# Financial Management with a Responsible Twist: Vodacom Africa

Financial management has moved to the center of responsible business. South Africa–based mobile networks and Internet company Vodacom, which operates in many African countries, illustrates the centrality of financial management.

In 2011, Vodacom not only achieved impressive financial results, such as a 24.3 percent increase in cash flow and shareholder returns of 45 percent, but also measured the stakeholder return by the "people survey" through which key stakeholders were asked about how much value Vodacom had added to their lives. The company abstains from the creation of often unsustainable short-run performance by aiming at creation and the sustaining of value for both shareholders and stakeholders "over the short, medium, and long term."

To reach such responsible returns as a goal of responsible financial management, Vodacom has implemented internal capital allocation decisions and determined what activities should be fueled by financial resources. Such decisions take into consideration all environmental, social, ethical, and governance risks, also commonly known as ESG risks and revenues.

A good example of such an activity is the company's M-Pesa product (M for mobile, and *pesa* is Swahili for "money"), which is cashless money communicated via mobile telephones. The social return on investment (SROI) created by M-Pesa is immense. It allows marginalized, often impoverished communities to gain access to banking products, which in turn

enables the accumulation of wealth and the foundation of small businesses through microcredits. M-Pesa is an excellent example of how financial management can be an innovative tool for responsible management and how responsible management activities can provide access to new sources of funding. M-Pesa was originally publicly subsidized.

Two important elements of responsible management are the usage of results of company activity and overall company governance for the best interests of its owners and other stakeholders. In an integrated report, Vodacom reports how the company's revenues are redistributed. In terms of the usage of results in 2012, around 31 percent of the money made was reinvested or retained by the company, 20 percent was paid to the government as taxes, 17 percent was used to pay employees, and 32 percent went to financiers or shareholders of the company. This is also called the economic value added per stakeholder. Through the use of extensive corporate governance mechanisms and internal controls, such as the board of directors, board subcommittees, executive remuneration schemes, and detailed risk management plans, Vodacom tries to make sure that the company is run in the best interests of both shareholders (or financiers) and stakeholders.

Sources: Vodacom. (2012). *Vodacom Group Limited integrated report*; Jack, W., & Suri, T. (2010). *The economics of M-PESA*. Nairobi: Unpublished paper.

## 15-1 RESPONSIBLE FINANCIAL MANAGEMENT

*"Finance is grease to the economy. Therefore, we assume that it may affect corporate social responsibility (CSR) and the sustainability of economic development too. This paper discusses the transmission mechanisms between finance and sustainability."*[4]

Several reasons exist why financial management and sustainability, responsibility, and ethics topics go inherently together. First, financial management and finances are central to any business and its processes. This holds true also for any form of responsible management activity. Only if financial management provides the necessary resources to implement responsible management activities will a company be able to become responsible. Second, the finance department is an important driver for responsible business,[5] and traditional financial management has increasingly become dependent on companies' social, environmental, and ethics performance. Sustainability, responsibility, and ethics are on the chief financial officer's (CFO's) to-do list.[6] External reporting, financial controlling, and risk management are largely affected by considerations related to responsible business, especially in investor relations. Sixty-five percent of companies' CFOs are involved in sustainability initiatives.[7] The third reason why financial management and responsible management topics go inherently together is that financial management has been blamed for many of the flaws of the economic systems, such as companies' unhealthy, short-run profit and profit-driven behavior. Financial management and accounting have been the culprits of company collapses like those at Enron and Worldcom. The financial sector itself has been blamed extensively for being at the heart of an unfair capitalist system, as shown impressively during the height of the Occupy Wall Street movement when millions of people all over the globe were protesting.

This is why there have been extensive efforts to rethink many of the most basic assumptions of financial management, in order to create truly sustainable, responsible, and ethical corporate finance.[8] To bring sustainability, responsibility, and ethics to the core of the financial management process is a key success factor for a responsible business. Figure 15.1 illustrates how to integrate responsible management practices into all phases of the financial management process.

Phase 0 is a preparation phase in which responsible managers should *understand* the basic functions of financial management and the financial management paradigms that need to be questioned in order to conduct a truly responsible financial management. Phase 1 aims to examine the *financing* part of financial management by looking at the integration of sources of funding in the responsible finance process. Responsible business provides a wide variety of financing mechanisms from socially responsible investment, to sustainability indices, and microfinance, just to mention a few. The objective of Phase 2 is to show how the social return on investment (SROI) can be used to make capital *budgeting* decisions in responsible management and to decide to which activities to allocate money. Phase 3 focuses on managing the results of financial management. The big question here is: For whom

**Figure 15.1 The Responsible Financial Management Process**

Phase 1:
Financing
• SRI, activist shareholders, impact investing, cross-financing, crowdfinancing, direct and debt-based financing

Phase 2:
Budgeting
• Social return on investment (SROI)
• Budgeting decisions in responsible management

Phase 3:
Results
• Value-based management
• Corporate governance
• Fiduciary responsibilities

Phase 0:
Understanding financial management
• Mechanisms and structures
• Financial management process
• Questioning paradigms

**Goal:** Responsible Return on Investment (RROI)

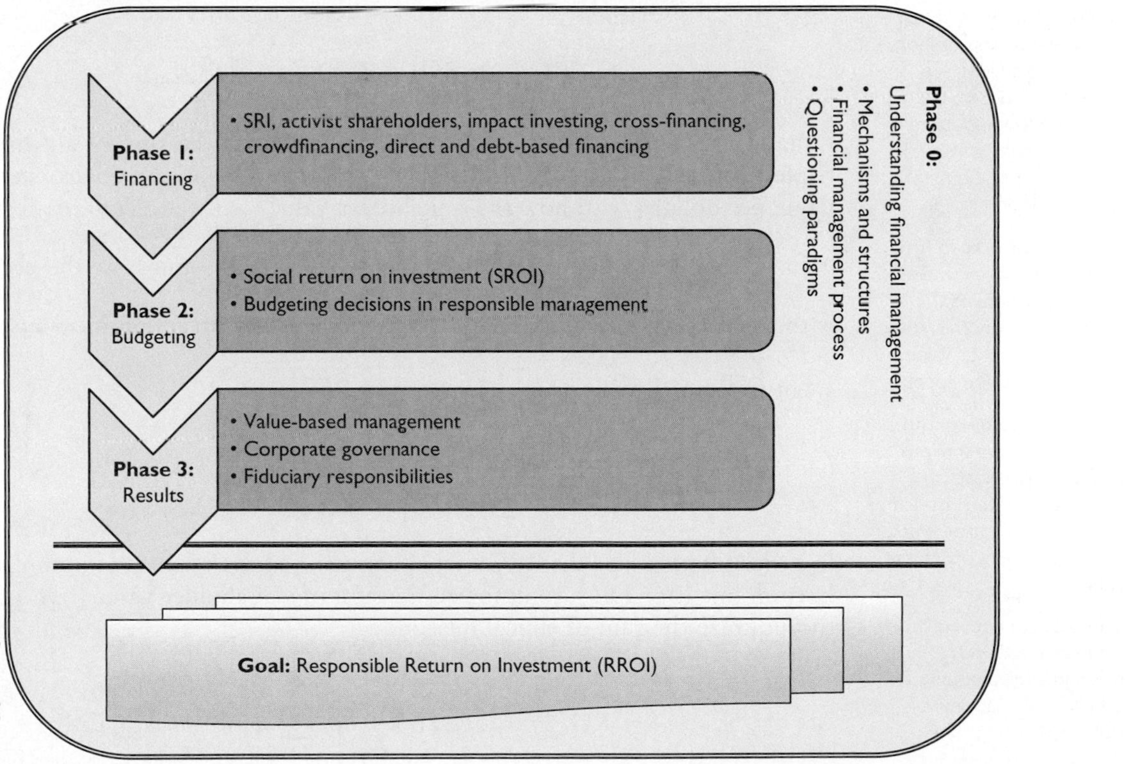

© Cengage Learning, 2015

do we manage finance, and how do we manage it in their best interests? Phase 3 also illustrates the *governance* of financial management.

## 15-2 THE GOAL: RESPONSIBLE RETURN ON INVESTMENT (RROI)

*"Finance as a discipline requires a multifaceted approach instead of the present one-dimensional risk and return focus."[9]*

The declared goal of most common financial management activity is to maximize profit. What is wrong with profit thinking? First, the answer is "nothing per se," but profit can and should be only one of the many indicators used to assess the performance of a company. Second, *short-run profit maximization* leads to results that may be counterproductive to the goals of sustainability, responsibility, and ethics. Third, profit-first type thinking automatically skews companies' actions toward primarily satisfying the needs of the owner-stakeholder, while neglecting the needs of legitimate other stakeholder groups.

Therefore, for a responsible financial management, the goal cannot be pure short-run profit maximization, but something that we call a **responsible return on investment (RROI ($ROI_{Res}$))**. Such an RROI is more complex than short-run profit maximization. To achieve a maximum RROI, companies must make sure to achieve an optimum triple bottom line (sustainability) in the long run to create optimum stakeholder value (responsibility) and to minimize ethical misconduct per dollar spent.

Equation (1) illustrates how the responsible return on investment ($ROI_{Res}$) is composed of the **triple bottom line return on investment ($ROI_{TBL}$)**, the **stakeholder value return on investment** ($ROI_{SHV}$), and the **ethical return on investment ($ROI_{ETH}$)**:

$$ROI_{Res} = ROI_{TBL} + ROI_{SHV} + ROI_{ETH} \tag{1}$$

Equation (2) shows how the $ROI_{TBL}$ is composed of the sum of all three types of triple bottom line value, economic ($V_{Econ}$), social ($V_{Soc}$), and environmental ($V_{Env}$) value per dollar spent; how the stakeholder value return is a sum of all stakeholder value created (e.g. employee satisfaction) $\left( \sum_{i=0}^{n} SHV_n \right)$; and how the ethical return is the sum of all ethical misconduct (e.g. number of corruption incidents) per dollar spent $\left( \sum_{i=0}^{n} EM_n \right)$.

$$= \frac{V_{Econ} + V_{Soc} + V_{Env}}{\$1} + \frac{\sum_{i=0}^{n} SHV_n}{\$1} + \frac{\sum_{i=0}^{n} EM_n}{\$1} \tag{2}$$

In order to maximize the RROI, what companies have to do is to optimize the triple bottom line (*opt TBL*), to optimize the sum of stakeholder value $\left( opt \sum SHV \right)$, and to minimize the sum of ethical misconduct:

$$\rightarrow ROI_{Res}^{MAX} = opt\ TBL + opt\ \sum SHV - min \sum EM \tag{3}$$

---

**Responsible return on investment (RROI ($ROI_{Res}$))** is a measure of company success concerned with optimization of short-, medium-, and long-run returns in the form of maximum triple bottom line, maximum stakeholder value creation, and minimum ethical misconduct.

The **triple bottom line return on investment ($ROI_{TBL}$)** measures the amount of economic, social, and environmental value created, per dollar spent.

The **stakeholder value return on investment ($ROI_{SHV}$)**, or short stakeholder return, measures the amount of value created for stakeholders per dollar spent.

The **ethical return on investment ($ROI_{ETH}$)** measures the amount of ethical misbehaviors per dollar spent.

In contrast to the mainstream business maximization paradigm for profit, RROI in responsible business must be *optimized,* as there often is a built-in, natural trade-off between the three dimensions of the triple bottom line and competing stakeholder claims. For example, the company might have two competing courses of action, one of which is highly profitable financially, while the other creates much social value. Thus there is a trade-off between the social and economic dimensions. In another situation, a company might encounter two activities competing for capital, one being exceptionally good for the company's employees, and the other for the company communities. Again the trade-off exists, but this time between the value created for the two different stakeholder groups. We talk of "optimums" instead of "maximums" here, to express these natural trade-offs, that make linear maximization of any of the components of the RROI almost impossible. Nevertheless, we can achieve optimum results under consideration of these trade-offs.

The preceding algebraic description numerically illustrates an RROI. In practice, measuring and calculating the three elements of an RROI is complex. To combine all three components in the same equation, it is necessary to monetize them. **Monetization** refers to attributing a financial value to nonfinancial factors. Attributing a monetary value to ethical misconduct or environmental impact, for instance, is at best difficult. Until the methodologies are more advanced, the aforementioned equations have to be kept as an ideal illustration and to serve as suggestions on what companies have to do to create the best RROI possible throughout all of the activities in financial management.

## 15-3 PHASE 0: UNDERSTANDING FINANCIAL MANAGEMENT

*"A major goal of this paper is to reconsider the underlying assumptions of financial theory against the background of sustainability."*[10]

Can we rebuild financial management, against all the criticism that has been raised in the introduction to this chapter, to avoid its structural flaws, to make it a true enabler, and to create a platform and foundation for responsible management and responsible business? In order to rebuild financial management and create a responsible organizational finance, we first need to understand how traditional financial management works and where it malfunctions. In this Phase 0, you will be introduced to basic structures and mechanisms of financial management—the basic decisions and functions of financial management in a company—including an understanding of how it is embedded into social structures and the financial market.

### 15-3a Mechanisms and Structures of Mainstream Financial Management

**Financial management** involves the planning, organizing, budgeting, directing, controlling, and governance of the financial activities such as the procurement and

**Monetization** refers to attributing a financial value to nonfinancial factors.

**Financial management** is the planning, organizing, budgeting, directing, controlling, and governance of the financial activities of an organization.

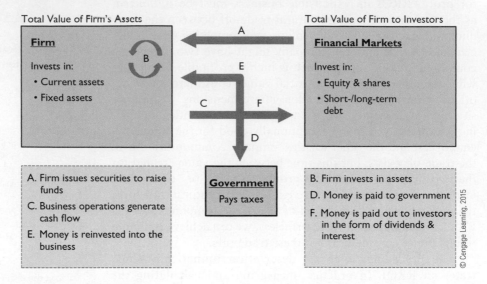

Total Value of Firm's Assets

Total Value of Firm to Investors

**Firm**

Invests in:
• Current assets
• Fixed assets

**Financial Markets**

Invest in:
• Equity & shares
• Short-/long-term debt

**Government**

Pays taxes

A. Firm issues securities to raise funds

C. Business operations generate cash flow

E. Money is reinvested into the business

B. Firm invests in assets

D. Money is paid to government

F. Money is paid out to investors in the form of dividends & interest

© Cengage Learning, 2015

utilization of funds of an organization. It is, in essence, the application of general management principles to the financial resources of the enterprise. Financial management is both the way a company is able to manage its activities as well as a measure, grade, and benchmark of its performance. Finance is so important because it is the very lifeblood of business. Without finance and the measurement and documentation of financial management, control and influence would breakdown both internally (by the management) and externally (by the owners, investors, and shareholders) in the management and procurement of funds and the business of investing. The finance of an organization is intimately connected with mechanisms in the broader environment, most notably the public sector and financial markets. The basics of the relationship between firms, markets, and government are illustrated in Figure 15.2.

### Functions, Decisions, Objectives, and Activity Areas of Financial Management

The three main **functions of financial management** correspond to the three phases of the financial management process that we defined earlier for the conceptual map of this chapter (Figure 15.1). What are the typical decisions that financial managers have to make in their work process? One might be tempted to think that decisions in financial management are very rational, based on a broad set of highly standardized quantitative analysis tools. Interestingly, it has been found that financial decision making is dominated by qualitative and nonfinancial criteria and that financial managers often are heavily influenced by the expectations of external and internal stakeholders in their decision making. Ethical considerations and sustainability also are important factors influencing financial managers' decisions.[11] It seems that there is a general potential among financial managers to apply responsible financial management in their decision making.

What are the main areas in which financial managers must make decisions? As illustrated in Figure 15.3, there are three main *decision areas* or functions that correspond to the three phases outlined in this chapter:

1. *Procurement of funds,* also called the *finance decision* (Phase 1: Financing): Finance decisions in this area are concerned with how to raise funds from

**Functions of financial management** are to externally procure funds, to internally fund business assets and activities, and to distribute the financial results of the business activity.

**Figure 15.3 Decision Areas and Objectives of Financial Management**

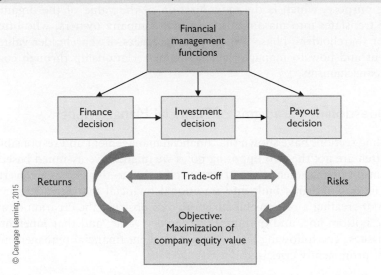

various sources for the organization's activities, how to choose the right capital structure and define the period of financing, and the costs of funding.

2. *Internal investment decision* (Phase 2: Budgeting): Decisions in this area revolve around capital budgeting of procured capital. Internal investment decisions channel financial resources to activities and assets of the organization and are concerned with how to distribute capital between fixed assets and current assets, to manage working capital (current assets minus current liabilities), to control financial performance, and to define budgets for different areas of the business.

3. *Financial results,* also called the *payout* or *dividend decision* (Phase 3: Results): Decision making in this area deals with how the financial results of business activity are distributed, including the distribution of net profits through either shareholders' or owners' payout or retained profits to be further reinvested in the company. This reinvestment occurs with the payment of taxes and documentation of the results in annual reports and balance sheets.

Decisions made in those three areas are aimed at achieving five main financial *objectives* of firms:

1. *Procurement of funding*: investment in fixed asset and current assets as well as the management of working capital (current assets minus current liabilities).

2. *Investment optimization:* ensuring that any funds procured be utilized in the most efficient way possible way.

3. *Investment security:* ensuring that any funds invested are done so in safe ventures and ones that guarantee the best possible long-term business results and/or returns.

4. *Sound capital structure:* ensuring that there is a sound and sustainable composition of debt and equity capital.

5. *Shareholders' returns:* appropriate returns to the shareholders dependent on earning capacity, share price, and shareholder expectations.

## DIG DEEPER

### Unsellable Food Finance

Alishan Organic Center, a food importer in Japan, is able to provide unsellable (due to error in labeling, short shelf life, or packaging errors) but still-valid-date foodstuffs to Second Harvest Japan for distribution to people lacking food security. 2HJ, using cash donations from CSR sections of international firms' local branches, is able to deliver $20 of food for every $1 donated. An added eco-benefit is that donators of food save upwards to $1,000 per ton in unneeded disposal costs. In 2012, 2HJ shipped 3,100 tons of foodstuffs to people in need in Japan. Which of the functions of financial management can you recognize in this case?

Source: Alishan. (2013). *About Alishan.* Retrieved January 28, 2013, from: www.alishan-organics.com/

"Shareholder returns" is closely related to mainstream financial management's underlying purpose, which is the maximization of the value of the organization. This value translates into maximization for the company owners, who often take the form of shareholders. Phase 3 illustrates the basics of shareholder value-based management and how to manage the shareholder relationship through corporate governance mechanisms.

## 15-3b Questioning Paradigms of Financial Management

The preceding sections have shown that financial management and responsible management often are not the two opposing poles we might have assumed based on all the criticisms of finance mentioned in the introduction to this chapter. Nevertheless, there are many paradigms built into traditional financial management that stand in the way of creating a responsible business, that obstruct the creation of an optimum triple bottom line, and optimum stakeholder value, and that inherently lead to ethical issues. The following list summarizes salient financial management paradigms most prominently criticized.

1. *The profit paradigm:* Seeing profit maximization as the ultimate end of business reflects a skewed picture of reality. Businesses do not need to be profit maximizers to take their functional role in society of providing needed goods and services. Financial management should move from profit maximization to profit optimization, wherein the profit paradigm competes with stakeholder interests and triple bottom line value.

2. *The growth paradigm:* Within the topic of sustainability must be consideration of the need to de-grow, or to at least keep the economic volume of companies at the same level, in order to reach a situation where the environmental impacts of business and consumption stay within the planet's resource limitations. Traditional finance has a built-in growth mechanism: growing revenues, growing markets, growing consumption. Responsible financial management has to find ways to substitute the growth paradigm with an "optimum volume" paradigm, wherein the need to grow, maintain, or even to shrink is based on defining the point in time at which the company has its optimum size for society and environment. Responsible finance must help companies that can increase their positive impact, such as renewable energies and organic agriculture, to grow—and help the ones that have a negative impact, like petroleum and tobacco companies, to de-grow or transform their impact.

3. *The short-run paradigm:* It is easier to consider short-run effects in decision making. They are safer to estimate than long-run factors, and more likely to influence the finance decision-maker's own immediate fate. Inherently, sustainability is a long-run concept. Only if the outcomes of decisions are considered in the long run can they be evaluated with regard to a decision's social, environmental, and also economic sustainability.

4. *The money paradigm:* Superiority of financial factors in decision making leads to an underrepresentation of social, environmental, and ethical considerations. Responsible finance has to move away from the skewed money paradigm either by giving social, environmental, and ethical indicators equal importance, or by monetizing those nonfinancial indicators so that they become comparable and can be considered equally under the money paradigm.

5. *The shareholder paradigm:* Responsible financial management has to manage the company to the best interests of all stakeholders. This does not mean that owners,

or more specifically shareholders, become disowned. The goal is to transform the primacy of shareholders to a situation where owners become one among many important stakeholders, whose interests are balanced in a fair manner.

6. *The internality paradigm:* With its traditional tools, financial management has a tendency to put too much emphasis on so-called internalities. Internalities are all the effects that one's own activity has on oneself, in this case on the organization. Positive internal effects are, for instance, increased shareholder value and profit generation. Negative internal effects, so-called internal costs, are, among others, the costs of production. Internalities neglect many external costs and benefits not carried by the company. External costs, so-called externalities, might be the pollution created by a production method or the detrimental health effects of a product. Examples of external benefits are the impacts of a social marketing campaign to create sustainable consumption patterns or the social welfare created for employees' families through wage payments. Decision making in financial management has to include both external costs and benefits. It has to move from internality thinking to inclusivity thinking, including all external and internal costs and benefits. Later in this chapter we will illustrate how the social return on investment (SROI) considers all externalities of an activity in financial decision making by considering all private cash flows (internalities) and social cash flows (externalities).

All six paradigms are deeply built-in into the DNA of finance—into the concepts and structures of financial management and into the minds of financial managers. Solutions to dismantle those paradigms might require dramatic changes and disruptive innovation. Solutions are not yet readily available. In the following sections on phases 1 through 3, we will demonstrate approaches that can be used as baby-steps to responsible financial management, with the potential to become motor for responsible business.

## 15-4 PHASE 1: FINANCING RESPONSIBLE BUSINESS

*"Total assets under management in the United States using Socially Responsible Investing (SRI) strategies ... accounted for $2.7 trillion in 2007, an amount that is about 10% of the total assets under professional management. It is a 50-fold increase from 20 years ago."*[12]

The first phase and function of the responsible financial management process is the **financing** of responsible business. A responsible organization, whether an NGO, a social enterprise, or a corporation, requires capital to be founded, to run, and to grow. Financing for responsible business conduct might also apply to single responsible management activities for which additional, usually external, financing is necessary. The financing function of financial management in bigger companies is usually managed by the department for investor relations. In NGOs, it would be the infamous fundraising activity; and in the case of social entrepreneurship, the procurement of the funds for a venture is usually conducted by the founders, respectively entrepreneurs themselves. The procurement of financing in responsible business is different from mainstream business financing, as it opens different financing opportunities that are often even less costly than mainstream business financing. Figure 15.4 illustrates how different financing options that are available to responsible management activities might be

**Financing** refers to the activities necessary to procure the capital necessary for the conduct of the organization.

### THINK | ETHICS

**Ethical Financing in New Zealand**
Prometheus Finance Ltd is an ethical finance company that lends to environmentally sustainable and socially responsible businesses and projects. This includes loans for home purchase and house building, but only where the dwelling has significant energy efficiency or other features that can benefit the environment.

Source: Prometheus. (2013). *Responsible investing is about awareness, choice, and action.* Retrieved February 2, 2013, from Prometheus: www.prometheus.co.nz/

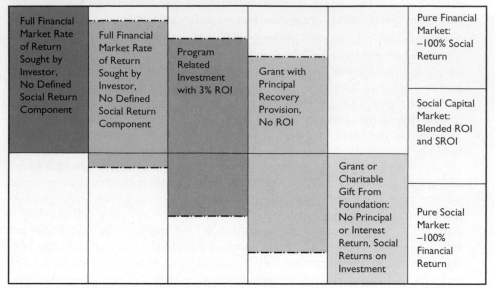

Figure 15.4 **External Financing Markets for Responsible Management Activities**

| Full Financial Market Rate of Return Sought by Investor, No Defined Social Return Component | Full Financial Market Rate of Return Sought by Investor, No Defined Social Return Component | Program Related Investment with 3% ROI | Grant with Principal Recovery Provision, No ROI | | Pure Financial Market: −100% Social Return |
|---|---|---|---|---|---|
| | | | | | Social Capital Market: Blended ROI and SROI |
| | | | | Grant or Charitable Gift From Foundation: No Principal or Interest Return, Social Returns on Investment | Pure Social Market: −100% Financial Return |

Source: Emerson, J. (2003). The blended value proposition: Integrating social and financial returns. *California Management Review, 45*(4), 35–51.

provided below the average market rate, and in some cases even without any interest, or without any obligation to pay back the capital received.

The variety of institutions providing financing for responsible businesses and responsible management activities ranges from traditional philanthropic organizations that seek to maximize the social return on their investments made, to traditional capital institutions that are merely interested in financial risk and return of investments. Figure 15.5 describes the whole spectrum of potential investors and their motivations and typical behaviors.

The financing task for responsible business does not end with the answer to the question, "Where do we get the money from?" At least equally important is the question, "Who do we want to own and control our organization?" Many forms of financing involve considerable amounts of ownership and control over an organization, which matters profoundly in terms of the degree of responsible business activities that can be implemented. The following clues about the influence of ownership on responsible performance have been derived:

- Organizations owned by *institutional investors* are more likely to show good social performance. This might change with the location of the company.[13]
- Shareholding by *top managers* is negatively associated with social performance.[14]
- In developing countries, *foreign ownership* is positively related with higher responsible business performance.
- *State-owned* companies, depending on the location, might be either significantly less or more socially responsible.[15]
- *Publicly traded* companies experience higher scrutiny than privately held companies, which might drive them to higher social performance.[16]
- *Privately owned* companies with higher ownership dispersion are more likely to achieve better social performance.[17]

In relationship to financing responsible business, many new frameworks have been developed, from the global multibillion-dollar movement of socially responsible

Figure 15.5 Spectrum of Investor Institutions

| Traditional Philanthropy | Venture Philanthropy | Community Debt Financing (CDF) | Community Development Equity |
|---|---|---|---|
| • Seeks to maximize social return<br>• Majority of applied funds not viewed as type of investment<br>• May engage in program-related Investments<br>• "Evaluation" used to assess relative social impact<br>• Often invests endowment in traditional capital institutions | • Seed capital for innovative social or economic programs<br>• No market ROI<br>• Documented SROI<br>• Application of venture capital practice within philanthropic context | • Positive financial return (fixed rate)<br>• Positive assumed social impact<br>• Modest financial returns on investment compared to market rates<br>• Includes CDFIs | • High risk<br>• No liquidity event<br>• Financial returns minimized<br>• Probably never going to get major money out, so how do you assess risk/reward? |

Social Equity Investors ◄─────────

| Angel Investors and Social Venture Capital | Socially Responsible Investment Funds | Traditional Capital Institutions (Banks, Mutual Funds, etc.) |
|---|---|---|
| • Seed funding of business start-ups<br>• Seeks market rate financial returns<br>• "Qualitative" or anecdotal social impact assessment<br>• "Do no harm" screen, or perhaps facilitate some type of social good | • Seeks market rate financial returns<br>• Seeks to minimize negative social, environmental, or other impacts<br>• Proactive social, environmental, or other screen for investing<br>• Engages in social audits and "follow-along" monitoring<br>• Shareholder activism | • No calculation of SROI<br>• Seeks to maximize financial return<br>• May engage in CRA lending, but not part of core mission<br>• Analysts simply "observe" performance and make no direct effort to influence the operation of the investee corporation<br>• May engage in traditional philanthropy by making grants to nonprofit organizations<br>• No thought of SROI |

─────────► Private Equity Investors

Source: Emerson, J. (2003). The blended value proposition: Integrating social and financial returns. *California Management Review, 45*(4), 35–51.

investment (SRI) to microfinance, and from large-scale impact investment to Web-based crowdfunding. As illustrated in Figure 15.6, there is a wide variety of financing mechanisms relevant to responsible business and management.

In the following paragraphs, we will provide a more detailed picture of how those different financing mechanisms are crucial in either procuring capital for responsible business conduct or discouraging businesses from behaving irresponsibly. Responsible managers in the finance department and many other areas of an organization have to know how their actions affect the access of their companies to capital.

## 15-4a Socially Responsible Investing

The first impetus behind the emergence of sustainability, responsibility, and ethics in financing came with **socially responsible investing (SRI)**. SRI is defined as an investment practice that involves screening activities, through which investors include the evaluation of social, environmental, and/or ethical issues in the analysis and selection of financial products.

SRI has become a familiar term to many over the last two decades. Less well known perhaps is the sheer scale and historical background of the concept of SRI. Indeed, it is easy to find instances of SRI throughout human financial history, including the well-known examples of the Quakers, who avoided dealings with the slave trade, and the Methodists, who expounded the "good neighbor" principle to business that laid emphasis on investing into business that will not harm the health

**Socially responsible investment (SRI)** is a practice that involves the evaluation of social, environmental, and/or ethical issues in the selection of financial products.

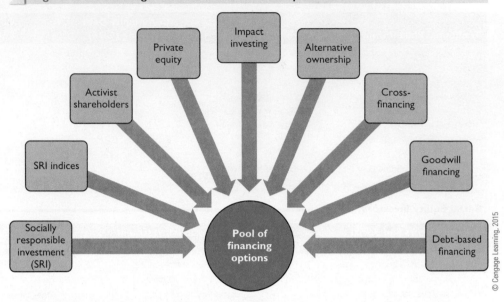

**Figure 15.6 Financing Practices and Tools for Responsible Business**

Private equity

Impact investing

Alternative ownership

Activist shareholders

Cross-financing

SRI indices

Goodwill financing

Socially responsible investment (SRI)

Pool of financing options

Debt-based financing

© Cengage Learning. 2015

or lives of the workers or the local community. This practice is called **negative screening**. Negative screening is a process by which funds are not committed to investments in industries and organizations deemed unworthy on social, environmentally, or ethical criteria. Such companies' shares, sometimes called "sin stocks," normally include items such as gambling, arms, tobacco, or "adult entertainment."

When responsible investors identify sin stocks in their portfolios, a common practice is **divestment**. Divestment is the process by which stocks are removed from a portfolio based on social, environmental, and ethical objections. Divestment has been particularly significant in large publicly held funds and pensions such as those of university endowments and labor union pension funds. More recently, the success of divestment policies in places like Apartheid South Africa in the 1980s has raised the profile of the political influence and role of SRI. Given the religious and political background of SRI, it is not surprising that until relatively recently such tools remained largely blunt instruments, dependent more on so-called negative screening of sinful activities than on positive, activist strategies.

**Positive screening** is the process of identifying exemplary companies in the field of responsible business for investment purposes. Over the last two decades, the climate, role, and acceptance of more positive strategies have dramatically increased. This has happened due to a convergence of a number of factors. First, as increasingly aware and prosperous consumers progressively embraced responsible consumption, it became inevitable that the focus eventually would be placed on financial products as well. Second, SRI and ethical funds have become increasingly professionalized; and many professionals have been keen to prove that responsible investments can be just as profitable as those based purely on financial performance.

Not only has SRI "gone mainstream," but most studies also show that there is little difference in returns compared with "irresponsible" portfolios. Indeed, one of the oldest ethical funds—the Domino 400—has, since its inception in 1990, consistently outperformed the S&P 500. Although there is little evidence yet that, in aggregate, companies with purely higher SRI ratings perform significantly better, it is clear that SRI status increases the pool of available capital for companies engaging with responsible business practices. The trend to increase the capital available to "good companies" and to withdraw it from "sin industries" is ongoing. Annual increases

**Negative screening** is a process by which funds are not committed to investments in organizations deemed unworthy on social, environmental, or ethical criteria.

**Divestment** is the opposite of investment, and describes the process by which investments are removed from a portfolio.

**Positive screening** is a process to identify exemplary companies in the field of responsible business for investment purposes.

in total SRI funds under management of ten times conventional funds to a total of over \$3 trillion by 2010, leading to a further cumulative effect, have demonstrated that ethical funds and SRI now "pack enough punch" in financial markets to, as we will see later, influence general investment behavior.[18]

As SRI has "gone mainstream," the old model of negative screening for "sin stocks" has increasingly moved on toward a more positive, professionalized SRI system that requires additional, more sophisticated instruments and a greater number of measurable indicators. These indicators are, in turn, aggregated into responsible business indices that can then be compared across companies, sectors, and countries. The next section illustrates such indices with greater detail.

## 15-4b SRI Indices

As the amount of funds geared to responsible investment has increased exponentially, responsible business, or SRI indices, such as the Dow Jones Sustainability Index (DJSI), the FTSE4Good, and others, have emerged to provide information on companies' responsible business performance. Different from most of the other financing frameworks mentioned, responsible business indices are not direct sources of financing, but provide information on the responsible business performance that in turn supports the decision-making process of financiers. Among the various responsible business indices, executives agree that the one with by far the biggest impact on companies is the DJSI. In a survey by the consultancy Ernst & Young, 33 percent mentioned DJSI as the most influential index, 26 percent favored the Carbon Disclosure Project, and between 5 and 10 percent each preferred either Fortune's Most Admired Companies, Corporate Responsibility's 100 best corporate citizens, the Global 100 Most Sustainable Corporations, the FTSE4Good, or the Bloomberg SRI. Inclusion into sustainability stock exchanges and other indices has been found to channel a significant amount of additional capital to the company at the time it enters the **SRI index**.[19] Representation in such an index makes an organization visible for positive screening and draws additional external funding.

Based on these indices and other sources of information, socially responsible investors make their decisions about financing responsible companies' operations. Many responsible managers have to know SRI indices by heart, as they are often involved in gathering the data necessary to be included and maintained in an index. Let us highlight the most influential responsible business index, the DJSI. Figure 15.7 illustrates how the DJSI applies criteria from the economic, environmental, and social dimensions to calculate a maximum score of 100.

For inclusion in the FTSE4Good index, companies need to satisfy standards in three types of criteria: environmental, social, and stakeholder and human rights. These criteria address three key questions:

- What is the company doing to protect, and reduce its impact on, the environment?
- How well is the company safeguarding the interests of the society in which it operates and the interests of its stakeholders (e.g., employees, suppliers, and customers)?
- How well does the company comply with the requirements of human rights legislation?

## In Practice

### Principles of Responsible Investment

1. We will incorporate ESG (environmental, social, and corporate) governance issues into investment analysis and decision-making processes.
2. We will be active owners and incorporate ESG issues into our ownership policies and practices.
3. We will seek appropriate disclosure on ESG issues by the entities in which we invest.
4. We will promote acceptance and implementation of the Principles within the investment industry.
5. We will work together to enhance our effectiveness in implementing the Principles.
6. We will each report on our activities and progress towards implementing the Principles.

Source: United Nations Environment Programme (UNEP) and the Global Compact.

An **SRI index** is a ranking of companies based on their responsible business performance.

Figure 15.7 **The Methodology of the Dow Jones Sustainability Index Series**

| Question level | Criterion level | Dimension level | Total Sustainability Score |
|---|---|---|---|
| Each question receives a score between 0 and 100 points and is assigned a predefined weight within the criterion. Weights for each criterion add up to 100 | Each criterion is assigned a predefined weight out of the total questionaire; criteria weights within each dimension roll up to the total dimension weight | Each dimension weight is the sum of the criteria weights within the respective dimension | |

100 {
Question 1 (25)*
Question 2 (35)
Question 3 (15)
MSA*** (25)

100 {
Question 1 (33.3)
Question 2 (33.3)
MSA***(33.3)

Criterion 1 (4)**
Criterion 2 (8)
Criterion 3 (9)
Criterion 4 (6)

Economic (27/100)

100 {
Question 1 (25)
Question 2 (25)
Question 3 (15)
Question 4 (35)

Criterion 1 (8)
Criterion 2 (5)
Criterion 3 (6)
Criterion 4 (10)
Criterion 5 (9)

Environmental (38/100)

100 {
Question 1 (15)
Question 2 (20)
Question 3 (30)
MSA*** (35)

Criterion 1 (5)
Criterion 2 (15)
Criterion 3 (10)
Criterion 4 (5)

Social (35/100)

Maximum Total Sustainability Score = 100

*(predefined question weight)  **(predefined criterion weight)  ***(Media & Stakeholder Analysis)

Question, criteria, and dimension weights provided in the diagram above are for illustrative purposes only. The actual number of questions, criteria, and their corresponding weights will very from industry to industry.

Source: RobecoSAM. (2012). *Measuring intangibles: RobecoSAM's corporate sustainability assessment methodology.* Zurich: RobecoSAM Sustainable Asset Management AG.

The criteria for inclusion in the FTSE4Good index are detailed, but important features consist of:

- Challenging but achievable standards regarding company policy, management, and reporting arrangements. These standards are not static, but are continually rising over time.

- A detailed environmental policy covering all parts of the company. The standards are more demanding in those sectors that tend to have a higher impact on the environment (e.g., chemicals and agriculture) than others (e.g., the media sector).

- Reporting procedures that provide data on social and environmental indicators as well as an effective system for managing the company's social and environmental footprint.

A stock exchange model alternative to the big sustainability indexes mentioned before is the social venture exchange. A **social venture exchange** is a stock market platform for the intermediation of capital from impact investors to environmental or social ventures in the form of shares or bonds. Companies still need to meet established financial benchmarks as well as social and environmental criteria.

Ultimately, sustainability indices can been as an extension of "investor relations" that has institutionalized interaction with investors seeking quantifiable data on a

A **social venture exchange** is a stock market platform for the intermediation of capital from impact investors to environmental or social ventures in the form of shares or bonds.

company's long-term responsible business performance coupled with the growing demands from the wider (investor) stakeholder community. While responsible business indices represent the institutionalization of responsible investment, the impetus of SRI is increasingly starting to focus further up the finance chain. Activist shareholding is a good example.

## 15-4c Activist Shareholding

An **activist shareholder** is an investor who buys company shares in order to influence company behavior by being granted access to shareholder participation mechanisms. Activist shareholders are not a significant source of funding, as typically they buy a small number of stocks of companies that are "bad" as entrance fee to the shareholder participation mechanisms, such as speaking rights at annual shareholder meetings, shareholder resolutions, and direct access to top management.

Nevertheless, activist shareholders, often being institutional investors, are an important driver of responsible practices to be taken into consideration. Shareholder activism has a long history as a tool to influence companies' governance mechanisms and performance.[20] It was only recently that shareholder activism began to be used to influence companies' social, environmental, and ethical practices. Activist shareholders have been found to be successful in influencing concrete company practices, but have only limited influence in companies' share prices, and performance.[21]

Shareholder activism, a more aggressive type of influence, has turned the negative screening and boycott strategies on their head by actively investing in companies, usually buying up a minority share of a company, in order to have a speaking or voting right in stockholders' meetings. While, in theory, such minority investors have little quantifiable power, their ability to influence other shareholders, stakeholders, and the media should not be downplayed and has become an increasingly difficult aspect of overall investor relations. A glimpse into the future on how such strategies are developing has been provided by the emergence of "social hedge funds," which seek to encourage a decline in a company's stock price and benefit from it in order to drive a particular agenda. One of the recent, more extreme examples of this is the ongoing campaign by the media-investment vehicle "Karma Banque" to drive down, among others, Coca-Cola's profits and share price.

All of the above developments in the activism and involvement of shareholders and investors have also had the consequence of increasingly driving the merger of traditional *financial reporting* with *responsible business reporting*. Indeed, the two are becoming increasingly difficult to distinguish in some areas, such as environmental liabilities or the measurement of assets such as carbon trading emission rights, and this is triggering renewed analysis of how companies allocate their resources. The dividing line between the previously "nice" and "modest" world of SRI and the more socially and politically activist groups is also disappearing as SRI funds seek to hold companies more accountable and proactively challenge companies' operating strategies rather than relying on screening criteria.

## 15-4d Directed Financing: Private Equity and Impact Investing

**Direct financing** describes the raising of capital without an intermediary. Increasingly investors have found ways to directly rewarding particularly good social, environmental, and ethical ideas, and the directed solution of particular issues. The two foremost practices of such direct financing are private equity financing of social enterprises and impact investing.

An **activist shareholder** is an investor who buys company shares in order to target and influence company behavior by being granted access to shareholder participation mechanisms.

**Direct financing** *describes the raising of capital without an intermediary.*

Private equity, often in the form of venture capital, may be an attractive source of financing, especially for social enterprises. **Venture capitalists** provide the necessary capital for start-up businesses, assure the financial viability of the business plan, and often serve as mentors for entrepreneurs.[22] A typical example for venture capitalism are the so-called "angel investors," also called "business angels."[23] **Angel investors** are affluent individuals and groups that financially support start-ups. Increasingly angel investors focus on entrepreneurial ventures with added social and environmental value. For entrepreneurs or SMEs concentrating on adding social and environmental value, angel investors can dramatically increase the funding capability and avenues available.

Another type of directed financing is **impact investing**, which is a profit-seeking investment activity that intentionally generates measurable benefits for society.[24] Impact investment aims at the co-generation of financial and economic value, a financial and social return on investment.[25] Impact investing actively tackles specific issues to be mitigated by the investment. Issues range from infrastructure and poverty reduction to renewable energies and education, just to mention a few. Different from socially responsible investing's focus on big, publicly traded companies and mostly negative screening, impact investing aims at small and medium-sized, privately held companies and NGOs that have the potential to make a big difference or have a big impact.[26] In many cases, impact investment directs funds at ventures with positive impact on the neighborhood level, which is also why it is often called "community investment."[27] According to a report by the Monitor Group in 2009, the number of funds engaged in impact investing was estimated to grow roughly tenfold from $50 billion in assets to $500 billion in assets within the next decade.[28] Investors in impact investment can be of many different types:

- *High-net-worth individuals* might invest their private funds into making an impact. Often those individual investors are baby-boomers who aim to see their values reflected in their portfolio and who have time to translate personal convictions into social-impact investment strategies.

- *Institutional investors* might follow their financiers' social mission and search for the highest impact possible per dollar invested.

- *Companies* often search to move away from a philanthropic community involvement toward strategically and sustainably transforming communities by investing into local infrastructure.

- *Foundations* are increasingly moving away from grant giving to investing in grantees and aiming to maximize the social return on the grants given.

For responsible financial managers either in social enterprises, for-profits with positive impact, or NGOs, impact investing can be an attractive source of external funding, helping to scale the organization's positive impact.

## 15-4e Alternative Ownership Models

Who owns organizations? Businesses are typically owned by a small group of people, privately, such as in a family-owned business, or through a larger group of people, publicly traded at the stock market. Big company shares, often through institutional owners, are another typical practice.[29] Alternative ownership models that provide mechanisms for individuals to pool small individual amounts to large sums have increasingly become an attractive source of funding for organizations' activities. In the

A **venture capitalist** *provides capital to start-up companies.*

An **angel investor** is an affluent individual who provides his personal capital to start-ups.

**Impact investing** is a profit-seeking investment activity that intentionally generates measurable benefits for society.

following, we will focus on how responsible businesses can use "crowdfunding" and cooperative ownership models.

**Crowdfunding** raises "external finance from a large audience ('the crowd'), where each individual provides a very small amount."[30] Crowdfunding works similarly to crowdsourcing but asks the online crowd for funding, instead of ideas.[31] The promotion of crowdfunding often involves interaction on social network sites or similar online media in order to reach large numbers of people.[32] Crowdfunding is a promising strategy, especially for social and environmental entrepreneurs, civil society organizations, and corporate campaigns with high emotional value. The better, the more engaging, and the more emotional the cause of the crowdfunding initiative is, the better crowdfunding works. People of the crowd may fund a venture through donations, loans, or by becoming co-owners, similar to cooperative business models.[33] A good example of a corporate crowdfunding campaign is the baby products company Munchkin, which started the campaign "send a duck, raise a buck." The campaign is a form of indirect crowdfunding (the company pays based on actions of the crowd), where the company donates to a cancer foundation every time someone sends a virtual rubber duck to friends online.[34] Due to their operational communalities, crowdfunding has recently begun to be merged with cooperative ownership models.[35]

**Cooperatives** are "businesses owned and run by and for their members."[36] Members of cooperatives can be virtually any stakeholder. Typically, customers, employees, or community members or suppliers own a cooperative group.[37] Members of a cooperative contribute with their capital to fund the operations of the cooperative.[38] The stakeholder ownership and control of cooperatives makes them an interesting funding model for responsible business and management. In order to understand how funding via a cooperative model works, we first need to understand the basic characteristics of a cooperative. Figure 15.8 illustrates the basic structure, operating principles, and financing mechanism of cooperatives.

Cooperatives share many similarities with traditional company models. Examples are, for instance, the elected board, or the different member financing models that resemble the ones of shareholders in a publicly traded corporation. Variations of traditional cooperatives have been developed.[39] What makes cooperatives different is

---

**Figure 15.8 Structures, Principles, and Financing of Cooperatives**

| Structure & Control | Operating Principles | Member Financing |
|---|---|---|
| • Ownership through **co-operative members**<br>• **Democratic decision making** through voting mechanisms<br>• A member-nominated and **elected board** supervises operations<br>• **Earnings** are either re-invested into the business or paid out to members | • **Voluntary and open** Membership<br>• **Democratic** member control<br>• Member **economic participation**<br>• **Autonomy** and independence<br>• **Education**, training, and information<br>• **Co-operation** among co-operatives<br>• Concern for **community** | • **Direct investment:** Members decide to invest a lump-sum.<br>• **Retained margins:** Surplus is retained and re-invested instead of paid out to members.<br>• **Per-unit capital retains:** A fixed amount of money is invested "per unit" or through percentage calculations.* |

*Unit here refers to, for instance, a product sold, per customer or work contract, or per employee, while percentage can refer to a fraction of, for instance, a revenue created through a customer, or the wage received by an employee.

Source: Adapted from OCDC. (2007). *Differences between co-operatives, corporations and non-profit organisations.* Retrieved December 11, 2012, from The International Co-operative Alliance: http://2012.coop/sites/default/files/Factsheet%20-%20Differences%20between%20Coops%20Corps%20and%20NFPs%20-%20US%20OCDC%20-%202007.pdf

**Crowdfunding** raises external finance from a large audience (the "crowd"), with each individual providing a very small amount.

**Cooperatives** are businesses owned and run by and for their members.

their open membership model, the underlying values of mutuality and not-for-profit thinking, and the strong concern for communities and members.

Cooperative models have become a large-scale global phenomenon. According to the International Co-operative Alliance, the organization represents close to one billion members of cooperatives worldwide.[40] The topic of entrepreneurship provides additional insight on the management implications of cooperative models.

## 15-4f Cross-Financing and Goodwill Financing

Financing does not necessarily have to stem from external sources or from investors who expect returns. Many responsible business activities and projects can be financed through funds that are internally available, so-called pay-as-you-go financing. Another financing option is through donations or subsidies resulting from stakeholders' goodwill created through responsible business practices.

The **cross-financing** mechanism uses currently generated internal cash flows to pay for expenses. Cross-financing uses the income of some areas of an organization's activity to subsidize activities that do not generate income. Cross-financing is of special interest to responsible management, probably more than it is to mainstream management. Responsible management can through various ways generate cash flows internally, which then can be used to pay potential expenses of other responsible management programs and activities. Three exemplary cross-financing mechanisms for responsible management are described in the following list.

- *Savings from cost reductions:* As mentioned before, responsible management has great potential to reduce operational costs. A cost decrease, such as from an eco-efficiency project that reduced both environmental impact and operational costs, can be reinvested internally to pay for other responsible management activities.

- *Revenues from products:* Products with socially and environmentally enhanced features have proven to have big market potential. Additional income from such sustainable innovation products can be used to cross-finance, for instance, a new sustainability department.

- *Corporate foundations:* Many companies have their own foundation that donates money to philanthropic purposes. Why not design an internal philanthropic program, based on strengths and competences of the business, which can then be financed by the foundation?

The critical point in getting cross-financing in responsible management right is to create as many as possible responsible management activities that create income, and on the other hand to optimize the social value created per-dollar spent in the nonprofitable responsible management activities. A portfolio approach to responsible management aligns activities in a way that balances revenues and costs of the programs. In phase 2 of this chapter, we will take a closer look at how to evaluate different activities in the portfolio and how to estimate activities' SROI.

The more social value your project creates, the more goodwill you will also create among your stakeholders that you create value for. Stakeholders are often willing to cash in this positive attitude toward your activities. This opens new financing avenues, frequently including in-kind donations. For instance, NGOs receive donations for a wide array of different philanthropic purposes pursued. Donors give them money out

**Cross-financing** is a method that uses the income of some activities of an organization to subsidize activities that do not create income.

## In Practice

### Reducing Cost by Creating "Diverse" Jobs in Israel

Call Yachol is a social venture and the first of its kind in the world. The company is providing outsourcing call center services that are operated by and adapted for people with disabilities. Most of company's employees are people with physical and psychological disabilities. The company solved the two most common problems of call-center employees—lack of motivation and low level of retention—as Call Yachol's employees are highly motivated and very loyal. By creating a supportive working environment for employees (combining technological solutions for a wide range of disabilities, flexible work hours, and professional support staff) and employing a population with a higher-than-average level of job stability, the company reduces the costs of personnel turnover for the client and offers a high level of professionalism, contributing to providing excellent service.

Source: Call Yachol. (2013). *Call Yachol.* Retrieved January 28, 2013, from: www.callyachol.co.il/?CategoryID=178&dbsRW=1

of goodwill. Responsible management's capacity to create value for a varied set of stakeholders holds many possible financing avenues. Following are three prominent stakeholder **goodwill financing** avenues:

- *Volunteering:* Employees and even external stakeholders donate their work time out of goodwill if they identify with a volunteering task.
- *Cause-related marketing:* In cause-related marketing schemes, the company donates a certain percentage of revenue to a good cause if customers buy its products. Out of goodwill for the product, the customer indirectly makes a donation to the good cause every time a product is bought.
- *Subsidies, grants, and tax cuts:* Governmental agencies often reward sustainability, responsibility, and ethics-related activities for the social and environmental value they create.
- Companies employing goodwill financing should be aware that such activities are sometimes criticized as making others pay for "good deeds" that afterwards are communicated as company achievements.

## 15-4g Debt Financing

Financing responsible management activities through debt is not a focus of this chapter. Nevertheless, we would like to highlight two debt-related topics that may not be missed in a chapter on finance and responsible management. First, social and environmental initiatives often have access to *special credits,* offered either by governmental and development agencies, public organisms, or banks with a social and environmental focus. Second, the topic of *microfinance,* more specifically microlending, is, due to its multiple practice applications, of central importance to responsible management. Microfinance is, on one hand, a powerful financing mechanism for microenterprises; on the other hand, companies also use microlending as a tool in their responsible management programs, to create social value, as has been illustrated in the introductory case. At the end of this chapter, you will find a more extensive introduction to microfinance.

## 15-5 PHASE 2: CAPITAL BUDGETING AND PROGRAMMING INTERNAL ACTIVITIES

*"In truth, the core nature of investment and return is not a trade-off between social and financial interest but rather the pursuit of an embedded value proposition composed of both."*[41]

While phase 1 dealt in depth with financing, the "external investment" realized into the company, this phase 2 illustrates **capital budgeting**, the process of analyzing alternate projects and activities to decide which ones to accept and for which ones to free a budget for implementation.[42] We could say that capital budgeting is an internal financing or investment process through which companies decide which alternative activities should be undertaken. The decision is typically made by analyzing the *internal return on investment* of alternative actions.

Capital budgeting is of primary importance to responsible management for two main reasons. First, responsible managers have to convince decision-makers in their organizations that responsible management activities are worthwhile undertakings from a financial point of view. In order to do so, it is a strong argument, using mainstream business logic, to say that the financial return on a certain responsible business measure is positive, or even higher than the one of competing traditional business activities. Although many responsible management activities

**Goodwill financing** uses stakeholders' positive attitude toward the business's social cause to generate funds.

**Capital budgeting** is the process of analyzing alternate projects and activities to decide which ones to accept and to which ones to free a budget for implementation.

do have a high return on investment, many others do not. So, if we were to make decisions merely on a financial ROI basis, many strategically important responsible management activities would not take place.[43] Also, there is evidence that there are very financially attractive activities in both categories, highly responsible and highly irresponsible activities.[44] This leads us to the second important function of capital budgeting in responsible management. Responsible managers also, and even more importantly, have to show that they are spending money to the best of social value creation. They have to show the SROI.

Only if we reach those two points can finance be a driver of responsible business.[45] Already today, 39 percent of CFOs approve sustainability-related budgets, 36 percent provide advisory support to sustainability teams, 34 percent support sustainability with traditional finance tools, and 20 percent collaborate with sustainability teams to build a financial business case for sustainability, and monitors not only financial but also sustainability-related metrics. Financial management is deeply involved in the management of an organization's portfolio of all three—financial, social, and environmental—types of value creation. The final goal is to achieve portfolio thinking, where all activities undertaken by the company are first evaluated in terms of their individual social, environmental, and economic returns, and then, in a second step, actively managed to jointly create a optimized triple bottom line performance.[46]

As can be seen from those two main purposes, a measurement of "profitability" of an internal activity needs to take into consideration both the company's financial profitability and the broader social profitability, which leads us to think in terms of a **blended value** consisting of many more types of value than just the financial one. Also the goal of responsible finance, a RROI as outlined at the beginning of this chapter, describes a form of blended value—a blend of triple bottom line, stakeholder value, and ethical value. To consider blended value in making capital budgeting decisions, three different methods are typically used.[47]

1. Through the *qualitative* method, stakeholder value, triple bottom line, and ethical considerations are viewed as one additional intangible decision factor that complements the main financial decision instruments. As an example, the decision to enter into a joint venture with either a defense company or an electric car producer might be informed by the intangible factor of those two businesses' ethical implications.

2. The *quantified* method aims to measure the social, environmental, and ethical value and to translate it into a social, environmental, or ethical return on investment. Those alternative returns on investment can then be compared to the traditional financial return on investment on a quantitative basis. For instance, a company might consider either a traditional operational efficiency project that will result in a cost decrease, or an ecoefficiency project that achieves the same decrease in cost but also reduces the company's $CO_2$ emissions. Both the financial cost decrease and the reduction in $CO_2$ can be measured.

3. The *monetized* method attributes financial value to traditionally intangible factors, and this way makes a comparison on a financial basis possible. As an example, the evaluation of a community volunteering project that involves employees in teaching classes in a local school might measure the costs of the

**Blended value** describes value creation as a blend of economic, social, and environmental value to optimize total returns.

time spent by volunteers, the financial value of the education received by students, and even the level of satisfaction of the employees about doing good.

In the following paragraph, we will illustrate the last, most advanced method: a fully monetized SROI, which, as you will see, in the analysis process also includes qualitative and quantification activities necessary to ultimately establish a monetary value of a responsible management activity.

## 15-5a Calculating the Social Return on Investment

If we were able to measure all economic, social, environmental, and ethical costs and benefits of an activity, we would be able to make a definite decision about the value of an activity. The goal of the **social return on investment (SROI)** is exactly this. The SROI is a method that quantifies and monetizes all main stakeholder costs and benefits of an activity in one single ratio. SROI in its beginning was used to measure how educational measures paid out for students.[48] In the governmental sector, SROI found broader application to assess the sustainable value created by public sector organizations.[49] SROI has become a common tool for NGOs, which may track the effectiveness and efficiency of their social and environmental programs,[50] and for private businesses.[51]

The SROI method still requires refinement, but due to its immense potential, it will be illustrated in detail. The SROI can provide a comparable, though not perfect, measurement, independent from the type of activity pursued, be it mainstream business or a focused responsible management activity. For example, suppose a volunteering program with an SROI of 35 percent is compared with an ecoefficiency activity of 40 percent or with a cause-related marketing campaign of 20 percent, all activities compared in monetary terms and including all types of impacts of each activity. Such metrics provide a powerful complementary decision-making tool for responsible financial management. Once the SROI has been established, we can derive other metrics from it. As an example, knowing the payback period of an activity helps to understand when the investment has "paid back itself." While those numbers cannot describe all aspects necessary to decide on which of the three activities should be implemented, the SROI is still a powerful tool by which to describe the value of different alternatives. In order to ensure the quality of an SROI, the decalogue of quality guidelines for SROI calculations, as illustrated in Figure 15.9, has been developed.[52]

The quality guidelines listed in Figure 15.9 help to achieve excellent results in establishing the SROI throughout the three main process stages. The first step is assessing the basic parameters of the social return of investment, the second is quantifying the costs and benefits, and the third is using the established SROI. These three steps are illustrated in Figure 15.10 and will be described in detail in the following three sections.

We will illustrate the three steps by applying them to the example of a green office program. The fictional program titled GreenO follows the goal of reducing the amount of $CO_2$ emissions from paper use. The program is built around the following two lines of action: (1) replacing an old printer with a new one that uses less energy and largely avoids paper jams, and (2) providing a two-hour weekend training session on the topic of green printing, led by an external trainer who specializes in green office programs.

**Social return on investment (SROI)** is a method that quantifies and monetizes all stakeholder costs and benefits—the social, environmental, and economic ones—of an activity in one single ratio.

Figure 15.9 **SROI Guidelines**

| Construction | Guideline 1. Include both positive and negative impacts in the assessment. |
|---|---|
| | Guideline 2. Consider impacts made by and on all stakeholders, including those inside the company itself, before deciding which are significant enough to be included in the assessment. |
| | Guideline 3. Include only impacts that are clearly and directly attributable to the company's activities. Be conservative with leaps of faith and don't take credit for more than your organization can realistically affect. |
| | Guideline 4. Avoid double counting the value (financial and social) created by the company and avoid using market valuations of social impacts where they do not reflect full costs and benefits. |
| Content | Guideline 5. In industries or geographic areas in which impacts would be created by the existence of any business, do not count these impacts. The SROI should describe what makes the company different from a standard venture in the industry (i.e., from its competition). |
| | Guideline 6. Only monetize impacts if it is logical given the context of the impact, business, or industry. |
| | Guideline 7. Put numeric metrics into context (e.g., this period versus last period, this company versus similar companies) to give the social return on investment meaning. |
| Certainty | Guideline 8. Address risk factors affecting the SROI in the assumptions and carefully consider and document the choice of discount rate for social cash flows. |
| | Guideline 9. Carry out a sensitivity analysis to identify key factors influencing projected outcomes. |
| Continuity | Guideline 10. Include ongoing tracking of social impact. |

Source: Lingane, A., & Olsen, S. (2004). Guidelines for social return on investment. *California Management Review, 46*(3), 116–135.

Figure 15.10 **Steps of Establishing an SROI**

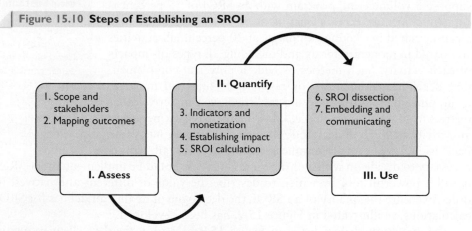

Source: Based on the SROI Network. (2012). *A guide to social return on investment.* Liverpool, UK: SROI.

## I. Assess Scope and Stakeholders, and Map Outcomes

The first stage of establishing an SROI consists of defining the boundaries of what should be included in the SROI. This involves two steps: defining the scope and stakeholders, and mapping the outcomes.

1. *Scope and stakeholders:* An initial step must be to define the *scope.* What activities do you want to calculate the SROI for? Are you looking at a single action or a whole program? Will you consider only one location or an array of activities at different locations? Will you look only at your own organization, or include other organizations along the supply chain? A concise description of the scope, of what you will evaluate, greatly facilitates all subsequent steps. Once you have

described the scope, you can proceed to identify the *stakeholders* that affect and are affected by the activity for which you are calculating the SROI. In SROI calculation, stakeholders are important not only as the ones providing inputs to the activity and the ones for whom value is created but also as an important source of information. For this reason, already at this early stage a successful SROI calculation requires establishing stakeholder communication channels and deciding on how to involve stakeholders in the process. The topic of business responsibility provides deeper insight into how to manage stakeholder relations.

2. *Mapping outcomes:* During the second step, the main goal is to acquire a clear understanding of the "mechanics" of the activity. First, make a list of the **inputs** provided by the different stakeholders involved in the activity, and value the inputs monetarily. In our example, the inputs provided by the company will be the price of the new printer (310 €) and the cost of hiring an external trainer (300 Euro). Also, the employee stakeholders will provide the input of their free time on a weekend (2 h × 40 employees × 11 €/h = 880 €). Next, evaluate the direct outputs and final outcomes of the activity. **Outputs** are direct, often quantifiable consequences of an activity, while **outcomes** are the long-run impacts and achievements of an activity. Outcomes of our green office program, for instance, will be the number of employees who participate in the weekend training session, the reduction in environmental inputs like paper and energy, and a reduction in office waste. Theoretically, the qualitative description of inputs, outputs, and outcomes and their quantification are two different stages of the SROI process. In practice, however, as done in this example, it often makes sense to simultaneously associate many of the inputs, outputs, and outcomes with quantifiable indicators.

## II. Quantify

During the first stage, we developed a very good idea of what and how to measure. In this second stage, it is time to work with the numbers.

3. *Indicators and monetization:* It is now time to develop measurable input, output, and outcome indicators for the activities, if that has not yet been done in stage I. Indicators can be divided into two different types. The so-called **soft indicators** require more effort than so-called **hard indicators** to make them measurable. In our example, one soft indicator to be defined for an output is to measure the amount of paper saved and, as a related outcome, the amount of $CO_2$ emissions saved because of the reduced paper usage. To make indicators comparable in the same measurement unit, it is necessary to attribute a monetary value (so-called *monetization*) to the outcome created—and to find out how long the outcome will probably last. Let us imagine that GreenO has achieved a reduction of 2.3 tons of $CO_2$ in the first month. One ton can be attributed to the new printer, and 1.3 tons stem from the change in employees' printing behavior.[53] According to the Spanish carbon exchange $SENDECO_2$,[54] one ton of $CO_2$ can be valued at 7.43 Euro, which translates into a monetary value of 17.09 for the 2.3 tons. The value for a ton of $CO_2$ assumed here has been assessed as too small to reflect the real cost of $CO_2$ emissions, due to a malfunctioning in the market for emissions trading. Thus, please realize that the value of $CO_2$ emissions reduction might be much higher in reality. Also, note that less pollution, in this case less $CO_2$, is not a value created in the strict sense, but rather an environmental cost avoided, which is why we attribute it here as a positive impact. Another important consideration for quantifying the outcomes of GreenO we can imagine is that as employees increasingly forget the lessons

**Inputs** are resources that are used in the process of an activity.

**Outputs** are quantitative, immediately measurable effects of an activity, while **outcomes** are long-run changes achieved through an activity.

**Hard indicators** are indicators that can be measured quantitatively without bigger effort, as opposed to **soft indicators** which are rather qualitative and difficult to quantify.

they learned in the green printing training, the effect of the achievement will wear off by 25 percent every year after the first year, and after five years, the effect of the training will be zero.

Social value is often perceived to be more difficult to monetize that economic and environmental value. How can we measure how much a certain activity is worth to stakeholders? The answer is simple: Ask them. For instance, to know how much employees value the responsible business activities of their company, a typical question is: "If you would have the choice to work for two almost identical companies, but one is known to be a responsible business, how much wage would you forfeit to work for the responsible organization?" The answer represents a **financial proxy**, an estimation of the monetary value created for the employee stakeholder by the company's responsible business conduct. Proxies for many types of social value are also available externally. For instance, a financial proxy for improved health might be the cost of treatment of health issues. In our example, to evaluate the social value of the input given by employees in the weekend training session, we used the proxy of an average hourly remuneration. While monetization and the use of financial proxies still require refinement, which will come with the increased usage in practice, the importance of them for the implementation of responsible business practices must be highlighted. Monetization is the one crucial condition to ensure the integration of social, environmental, and ethical factors into financial decision-making tools, such as the return on investment in this section.

4. *Establishing impact:* The fourth step deals with isolating the **impact** that has been achieved by the organization's activity from the part of the outcome created by other factors. The impact is the total amount of outcome achieved minus "what would have happened anyway."[55] Of the overall outcome achieved, in most cases only parts can be attributed to the activity of the organization. From the overall impact, we have to deduct the following four external factors:

   • The *deadweight* is the fraction of the outcome that would have been achieved anyway, whether the activity took place or not. Can some parts of the outcomes be attributed to former activities or general trends?

   • *Displacement* describes a situation where a positive outcome that is achieved creates a negative cost—a trade-off somewhere else. For instance, in our example, the new printer, on the one hand, saves $CO_2$ emissions from jammed paper but, on the other hand, creates additional $CO_2$ emissions in its production and transportation. For the sake of simplicity, we will neglect this consideration.

   • *Attribution* is the effort of defining which parts of the outcomes have been created by other actors. The donation of the time of employees could be considered an "attribution" if we looked only at the impact made by the company, but this consideration does not apply here, as our unit of analysis is GreenO as a whole with all actors involved as part of this whole. An attribution could be, for instance, if the energy company as an external actor would have reduced the $CO_2$ emissions from printing and all other electricity usages by making a switch to less $CO_2$-intensive alternative forms of energy provision.

   • The *drop-off* explains how the outcomes wear off over time. Earlier we described the self-reducing effect of the GreenO training session, which is a typical example of a drop-off.

A **financial proxy** is an estimate of the financial value represented by a social or environmental factor.

The **impact** is the total amount of outcome achieved minus "what would have happened anyway."

In the GreenO example, the only deduction that applies is the drop off. No deadweight, displacement, or attribution is known.

## III. Calculate

5. *Calculating the SROI:* In step 5 we have reached the core piece of the SROI calculation. The goal at this stage is to come up with a concrete number for the SROI. To do so, we use the net present value calculation, and the internal rate on investment (IRR), both common tools in mainstream financial management. The following chain of events summarizes inputs, outputs, and outcomes realized in the GreenO program:

- *Inputs:* The company buys a new printer (310 Euro) and hires the trainer (300 Euro). Forty employees invest two hours of free time in the training (11 Euro/hour per employee; total input 880 Euro). Employees are not paid for their time, so we add those inputs to the employee stakeholder, not to the company's inputs.

- *Employee motivation:* Employees were motivated by the new GreenO program. Through a questionnaire it was found that they would forfeit an average yearly 1,000 € to work for a company with such a program. In reality, they do not have to forfeit this wage difference, because employees experience an additional work motivation "as if" they were paid 1,000 Euros more. The effect wears off in the first year to 500 Euros and disappears from the third year on.

- *$CO_2$ and cost savings:* The activities of the GeeenO program lead to constant yearly reductions in $CO_2$ of 1,000 tons from the new printer until the fourth year in which the printer has to be substituted by a new one. The change in employees' printing behavior results in a reduction of 1.3 tons of $CO_2$ emissions in the first year. The effect drops off by 25 percent in each following year. The mentioned $CO_2$ reduction resulted from saving 1.36 tons of paper and 569 kWh annually for the company. In the first year, the paper reduction saves the company 2067 € (1520 €/t), and the reduction in energy consumption results in savings of 61.96 € (0.1089 €/kWh).

In a traditional NPV calculation, businesses summarize the cash flows related to an activity. Cash flows only represent the flow of financial value. In order to include also the social and environmental value categories, we broaden the term *cash flow* to *value flow.* Thus, counterintuitively to its title "social" return on investment, the SROI includes not only social, but also environmental and financial value flows. The upper half of Table 15.1 illustrates the flows of social, environmental, and economic value and sums them up in per-year period, including the inputs, outputs, and outcomes of all stakeholders.

**Table 15.1** Value Flows in the GreenO Example

| Period | | 0 | | 1 | 2 | 3 | 4 |
|---|---|---|---|---|---|---|---|
| **Value flows per stakeholder** | Company | −310 € −300 € | Energy savings | 569 kWh × 0.1089 €/kWh = 61.96 € | 569 kWh × 0.1089 €/kWh = 61.96 € | 569 kWh × 0.1089 €/kWh = 61.96 € | 569 kWh × 0.1089 €/kWh = 61.96 € |
| | | | Paper savings | 1.36 t × 1520 €/t = 2067 € | 1.15 t × 1520 €/t = 1748 € | 1.00 t × 1520 €/t = 1520 € | 0.86 t × 1520 €/t = 1307 € |
| | Employees | −880 € | Wage equivalent | 1000 € | 500 € | 0 € | 0 € |
| | Environment | 0 € | $CO_2$ savings | 1.3 t × 7.43 €/t = 9.66 € | 0.98 t × 7.43 €/t = 7.28 € | 0.73 t × 7.43 €/t = 5.42 € | 0.55 t × 7.43 €/t = 4.09 € |
| Value flow sums per period | | −1490 € | | 3146.05 € | 2324.67 € | 1594.81 € | 1380.48 € |

We have to take into account that money has a cost. Typically, this cost is represented by the average market interest rate for borrowing money. It is for this reason that in the net present value (NPV) calculation, we now have to discount later value flows after period 0 by the market interest rate ($r$) which we assume to be 5 percent.

$$NPV = V_0 + \frac{V_1}{1 + r} + \frac{V_n}{(1 + r)^n}$$

In our example, the basic formula translates into the following equation:

$$NPV_S^{GreenO} = -1490\,€ + \frac{3146.05\,€}{1.05} + \frac{2324.6\,€}{1.05^2} + \frac{1594.8\,€}{1.05^3} + \frac{1380.48\,€}{1.05^4} = 6210\,€$$

The NPV helps us to understand and quantify the current value of an activity, in our case the GreenO program, by summarizing including all inputs, outputs, and outcomes (all flows) in the same equation. We use the same equation to calculate the SROI. To calculate the SROI, we use the internal rate of return (IRR) method that is used in capital budgeting to evaluate projects. The IRR calculated here, as it includes all social, environmental, and economic flows, is the SROI. To calculate the SROI, we substitute the market interest rate of 5 percent that we had assumed to calculate the NPV by a variable $r$, representing IRR of the equation, which equals the SROI. The IRR of a project or activity is the interest rate ($r$) in the above equation with which the NPV of all cash flows becomes 0. (The algebraic calculation of the IRR would exceed the scope of this book, which is why it has been omitted.) As a result, the IRR that equals the SROI is 1.96, or 196 percent. This means the social value from GreenO sums up to 2.96 Euro (1 Euro invested + 1.96 Euros gained) per every Euro invested.

$$SROI = IRR = 1.96\%\ SROI\ Ratio = 2.96\,€\ per\ 1\,€\ spent$$

Another standard calculation is to find out when an activity "breaks even," which means at which point in time the costs of an activity equal its benefits. The **break-even point (BEP)** is calculated by establishing the ratio between the initial costs caused by an activity and the benefits created by them. An activity "breaks even" at the point in time in which the benefits realized from the activity equal the initial costs. After the point in time that the BEP has been reached, an activity is profitable. If we calculate a BEP, including all social cost and benefit, as we do in the GreenO example, we can make statements about the point in time that an activity becomes sustainable, that is, when it has begun to create more value (benefits) than it has used (costs). The concept of private versus social costs and benefits will be further illustrated below.

6. *Dissecting the SROI:* While the traditional financial return on investment does not include enough information regarding the true costs and benefits of an activity, the SROI runs the risk of including too much information in one number, which might cause problems in the interpretation. It is for this reason that the last stage of the process of establishing an SROI is to dissect it into its components, with the purpose of enriching the practice value and analysis possibilities of the SROI. Table 15.2 shows how the SROI can be split up for different evaluation purposes.

In order to evaluate, we need to split up the cost and benefits and resulting cash flows into private and social cash flows. **Private cash flows** are incurred by the respective actor (company or employee) for whom the calculation is

The **break-even point (BEP)** is calculated by establishing the ratio between the initial costs caused by an activity and the benefits created by them.

**Private cash flows** are incurred by the respective actor (company or employee) for whom the calculation is carried out.

**Table 15.2** Dissecting the SROI

| Question 1: Is the GreenO program good for society? | | | | | | |
|---|---|---|---|---|---|---|
| Total social value | $NPV_S^{GreenO}$ | 6210 € | $IRR_S^{GreenO}$ | 196% | $BEP_S$ | 5.4 months |

**Answer 1:** Yes, GreenO (printer and training activities) is excellent from a social standpoint. The NPV and IRR are very high. The overall cost for company and employees is recovered in only 5.4 months.

| Question 2: Will the two actors involved carry out the activities? | | | | | | |
|---|---|---|---|---|---|---|
| Private value for the company (printer and training) | $NPV_P^{Comp}$ | 5553 € | $IRR_S^{Comp}$ | 334% | $BEP_S^{Comp}$ | 3.4 months |
| Private value for the employee (training) | $NPV_S^{Emp}$ | 3868 € | $IRR_S^{Emp}$ | 252% | $BEP_S^{Emp}$ | 4.1 months |

**Answer 2:** Yes, both actors will, if they are rational and perfectly informed, carry out the activities. Both encounter high NPV and IRR and require only very short periods until their activities break even. All values look slightly better from a company perspective, which is why the company incentive to carry out the activities is higher than the incentives for employees.

| Question 3: If we had to decide which of the two activities (training or printer) to carry out, which one should we chose? | | | | | | |
|---|---|---|---|---|---|---|
| Private value of printer for the company | $NPV_P^{Comp/Print}$ | 2598 € | $IRR_P^{Comp/Print}$ | 263% | $BEP_P^{Comp/Print}$ | 4.5 months |
| Private value of training for the company | $NPV_P^{Comp/Train}$ | 2938 € | $IRR_P^{Comp/Train}$ | 411% | $BEP_P^{Comp/Train}$ | 2.8 months |
| Social value of printer | $NPV_S^{Print}$ | 2624 € | $IRR_S^{Print}$ | 265% | $BEP_S^{Print}$ | 4.5 months |
| Social value of training | $NPV_S^{Train}$ | 3568 € | $IRR_S^{Train}$ | 172% | $BEP_S^{Train}$ | 5.7 months |

**Answer 3:** From the company's private perspective, the training beats the printer in all three metrics. From a social perspective, the training has a higher NPV, but the printer is better in IRR and BEP. The answer here is not completely clear.

carried out. **Social cash flows** are all costs and benefits that have been incurred by any stakeholder of the calculation, not only the actor. The SROI considers all externalities of an activity in financial decision making, by considering all private cash flows (internalities) and social cash flows (externalities), and therefore is an excellent tool for financial management to overcome the "internality paradigm" illustrated at the beginning of this chapter.

As an example, a for-profit company will probably be inclined to base its decisions not merely on the SROI—which might lead it to establish two criteria, one based on the purely private return and another on the overall SROI. Such a company might say that it will not do any responsible management activity that does not have at least a neutral private net present value ($NPV_P^{Comp}$). There are many responsible management activities that at least are able to recover their costs. The second criterion might then be to pick the ones that have the highest overall SROI ($NPV_S$). Of course, the use of those two criteria alone is an oversimplification; in practice, many more decision factors play a role. The company in our example might also have to decide, because of budget restrictions, to either buy the new printer *or* conduct the employee training. Comparing the social net present value of the printer purchase ($NPV_S^{Print}$), its SROI ($IRR_S^{Print}$), and its social value break-even point ($BEP_S^{Print}$) with the respective indicators for the training program can inform such a decision.

Among the many other techniques of dissecting and interpreting the SROI, we would like to highlight one last technique. Calculating the return on investment of just one specific stakeholder group provides a measure of how much the different stakeholder groups benefit from the activity and how well incentivized they are to cooperate. As an answer to question 2 in our example, we calculated the SROI for the employees as the main stakeholder group involved. Those values can then be compared with the private value created for the company to get a

**Social cash flows** are all costs and benefits that have been incurred by any stakeholder of the calculation, not only the actor.

quantified idea on the fairness of distribution of value between the company and the employees and other main stakeholders involved in an activity.

7. *Embedding and communicating:* Based on the dissected indicators for the SROI, responsible managers may pick the indicator most aligned with the respective stakeholder. Communication can be used both for informing external stakeholders about the company's social performance and for the internal controlling process.

## 15-5b **Subjects of Capital Budgeting**

We have mostly talked about responsible management activities or projects as objects of the SROI calculation. In practice, however, the SROI evaluation can be used to assess virtually any business activity. In the following, we highlight prominent examples:

- *Diversification:* SROI can play a role with an eye to the structure of a business or corporation. For instance, Clorox founded the ecological cleaning products producer Green Works for its improved SROI in comparison to other businesses in the Clorox company's portfolio.

- *Programs:* SROI can be used to assess responsible management programs. As an example, the British retailer Marks & Spencer (M&S) estimated that their sustainability flagship program "Plan A" generated a benefit of 70 million pounds in 2010/2011.[56]

- *Single campaigns:* Often organizations have a predetermined budget for responsible business campaigns. Selecting the campaign that creates the highest social return for the money invested is crucial. For instance, M&S's one-day wardrobe cleanout campaign raised over 2.2 million pounds for Oxfam.[57] The sum is one important component of the campaign's SROI.

- *Projects:* Projects' main characteristics of being narrowly defined for a fixed period of time, budget, and outcome make them good subjects for defining SROIs. The indicator development is less complex than it is at, for instance, the whole business level.[58] As an example, single ecoefficiency projects in Mexican companies were able to achieve payback periods of often less than half a year.[59]

- *Processes:* As processes are mostly well described and their parameters are well established, here also a measurement of the SROI is less complex than in less structured activities.

- *Product (goods and services):* Assessing the SROI of one product alternative and comparing it to another has enormous value creation potential. To assess the product SROI, a product life-cycle assessment must be taken as a basis. A product SROI may include full costs in prices and develop offsetting schemes for negative impacts.

- *Departments:* One of the first hurdles for a successful company-wide implementation of responsible management practices is the establishment of departments in charge of the topic. Using the SROI to make a case for such establishment is crucial.

- *Employee performance:* If we want to incentivize employees to contribute to responsible business, remuneration might be a good way to start. An SROI summing up the value created for stakeholders of employees' work can provide insight that can be used to incentivize employees for both financial and social performance.

## 15-6 PHASE 3: RESULTS AND GOVERNANCE

*"Clearly organizations, their officers and boards, have come under criticism for focusing on a narrow set of financial goals that involve a limited number of stakeholder groups, and for featuring governance structures that are dominated by insider members, lack independence and neglect vital fiduciary and ethical responsibilities."[60]*

The outcome of the financial management process must be aligned with the interest of main stakeholders, among them the shareholders or owners of the organization. In the following two sections, we will first emphasize the importance of developing stakeholder value drivers through value-based management. We will then have a cursory glance at corporate governance structures aiming to ensure consistency between managers' actions and stakeholders' needs.

### 15-6a From Shareholder-Value- to Stakeholder-Value-Based Management

The ultimate objective of companies in mainstream financial management is the maximization of *shareholder value*. Shareholder-value management aims to create so-called value drivers.[61] These drivers have become a controversial topic in the general public perception and are associated with a concentration on short-term share price, profits, and dividends at the expense of all other factors.[62] Interestingly, in contrast to this criticism, even those most closely connected with the concept of shareholder value, such as former General Electric CEO Jack Welch, have emphasized the importance of focusing on long-term elements in financial management. Shareholder value is difficult to influence specifically and, in a general widely used model, consists of the seven elements illustrated in Figure 15.11, the so-called value drivers of finance.[63] The second part of Figure 15.11 illustrates the chain of effects of how responsible business activities may become economic value drivers.

**Figure 15.11 The Key Business Value Drivers in Financial Management and Responsible Business as Economic Value Driver**

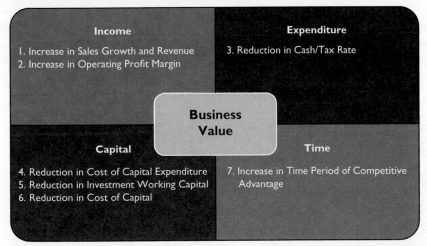

Source: Adapted from Bender, R., & Ward, K. (2008). Corporate financial strategy. Oxford: Butterworth-Heinemann.

*(Continued)*

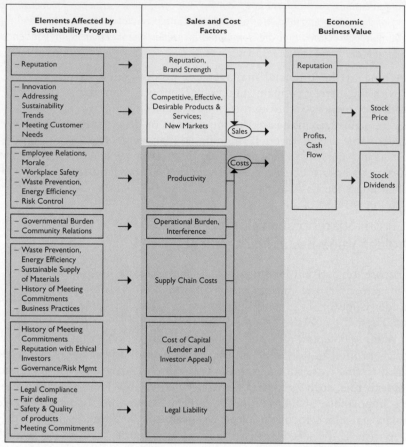

**Figure 15.11 The Key Business Value Drivers in Financial Management and Responsible Business as Economic Value Driver (Continued)**

Source: Adapted from Blackburn, W. R. (2012). *The Sustainability Handbook: "The Complete Management Guide to Achieving Social, Economic and Environmental Responsibility"*. Routledge.

A cursory glance at the seven elements shown in the figure reveals that these *value drivers* may not specifically be what one associates with pure short-term profit maximization (and by definition share price). Indeed, the long-term competitive advantage of certain companies and sectors over others has been explicitly recognized as a key driver of business success. Increasingly, financial mangers refer to "creating value" (and more specifically, "creating long-term value") in businesses.[64] Furthermore, creating value in business increasingly involves value building across different levels of an organization so that we, for instance, hear of firms creating "research and development value" or "human resources value."

With regard to the *business case* for responsible business, companies that are involved in responsible management practices can incur a wide array of tangible advantages, including cost reduction, higher productivity, and the attraction of investors.[65] All those advantages realized from the business case for responsible management can be drivers of shareholder value. In line with this insight, research has found that it is possible to create a positive relationship between companies' corporate social performance (CSP) and corporate financial performance (CFP).[66] In financial management terms, implementing responsible business practices can, and should, be consistent with sound financial practice not just in terms of the traditionally understood good publicity as a "benefit for altruistic behavior" but also in terms of financial value drivers such as lower costs of capital, higher sales income, and longer time periods of competitive advantage. Blackburn, the author of *The Sustainability Handbook*, even proposes a "Show-Me-The-Money Model," which is illustrated in Figure 15.11 and which traces how responsible business topics drive financial value.[67]

Responsible management needs to move away from emphasizing drivers for shareholder value, toward creating a portfolio of drivers for all of the primary company stakeholders, not only shareholders.

## 15-6b Corporate Governance and Fiduciary Responsibilities

The topics of corporate governance and financial management are intimately connected, as both traditionally have been centered on the relationships between a company and its owners, respectively shareholders. Traditionally, corporate governance aims to ensure that managers lead an organization in the best interests of its owners. In the early stages of a company, the owners often are simultaneously the managers of a company. The need for corporate governance arises when a company's management and ownership become separated and the people managing the company are different from those owning it. This situation is called a principal-agent scenario; the manager is the agent who should act in the best interest of her or his principal, the owner. Managers and owners may have different interests regarding how the company should be managed. A conflict of interest might arise if managers, who are closer to the daily operations of the organization, use their knowledge advantage, or asymmetric information, to steer the company differently from the owner's wishes. Such a situation, in which agents abuse their position to the disadvantage of the principal, is called "moral hazard." In a wider, more inclusive understanding of corporate governance, the agent keeps being the manager, but the principal might be any other stakeholder of the company.

**Corporate governance** is the system by which companies are directed and controlled that involves a set of relationships between a company's management, its board, its shareholders, and other stakeholders. Thus, corporate governance deals with the minimization and prevention of conflicts of interests, particularly in regard to the nature and extent of accountability of people in the business and the mechanisms that try to decrease the **principal–agent problem**.

While the standards and regulations in corporate governance traditionally differ from country to country, corporate governance principles in general have been sharply influenced by three documents released over the last two decades: the Cadbury Report,[68] the OECD's Principles of Corporate Governance,[69] and the Sarbanes–Oxley Act.[70] The Cadbury and OECD reports present general principles through which businesses are expected to ensure proper governance. The Sarbanes–Oxley Act was an attempt by the U.S. government to tighten up business practices in the wake of a number of major corporate and accounting scandals, including those that brought down giants of the "tech-bubble" such as Enron and WorldCom. The main principles of these overlapping standards can be expressed in five common principles:

- *Shareholder rights and equitable treatment:* Organizations should respect the rights of shareholders and help them to exercise those rights by openly and effectively communicating information and by encouraging shareholders to participate in general meetings.

**Corporate governance** describes a set of mechanisms and structures aimed at ensuring that managers lead an organization in the best interests of main stakeholders.

**Principal–agent problem** describes the problems arising under conditions of incomplete, uncertain, and asymmetric information when a principal (such as an owner) employs an agent (such as managers) to represent the principal's interest. Incentives have to be calibrated to minimize problems of moral hazard and conflict of interest.

- *Interests of stakeholders:* Organizations should recognize that they have legal, contractual, social, and market-driven obligations to nonshareholder stakeholders, including investors, employees, creditors, suppliers, local communities, customers, and governments.

- *Boards' role and responsibilities:* Boards should have the relevant skills and understanding to oversee management as well as having the appropriate levels of independence and commitment.

- *Ethical behavior and professional integrity:* Organizations should place an emphasis on corporate integrity as well as developing a code of conduct for their directors and executives that promotes ethical and responsible decision making.

- *Disclosure and transparency:* Organizations should clarify and make publicly known the roles and responsibilities of board and management to provide stakeholders with a proper level of accountability. The integrity of the company's financial reports should be guaranteed and procedures to independently verify them should be put in place. Information concerning the organization should be disclosed in a timely and balanced fashion to ensure that all investors have access to clear, factual information.

As illustrated in Figure 15.12, the disciplines and pressure on company management no longer just come internally between the shareholders, the management, and the board, but also externally through private as well as regulatory actors. The traditional mix of shareholders voting in a board which appoints and monitors management that in return is obliged to report to the board has now been extended through a complex mix of statutory and nonregulatory disciplines. Despite globalization (which has extended perhaps fastest in the financial sector), regulatory models and corporate governance structures still retain significant national differences.

The most prominent governance mechanism may be the **board of directors**. The board is a hybrid organization of internal and external individuals, who have the task of monitoring whether the company

The **board of directors** is an institution that controls the managers of a company.

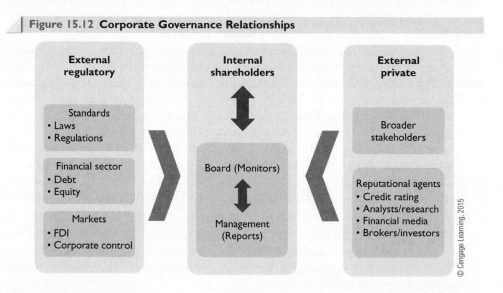

Figure 15.12 **Corporate Governance Relationships**

© Cengage Learning, 2015

Figure 15.13 Exemplary Board Structure at Vodacom

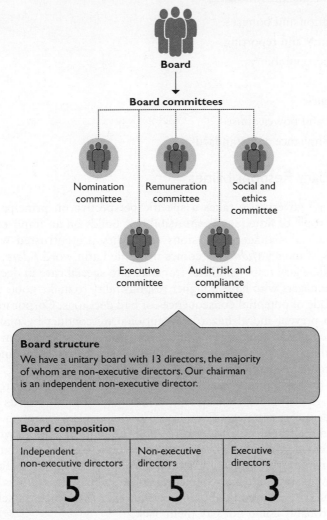

**Board**

**Board committees**

Nomination committee

Remuneration committee

Social and ethics committee

Executive committee

Audit, risk and compliance committee

**Board structure**
We have a unitary board with 13 directors, the majority of whom are non-executive directors. Our chairman is an independent non-executive director.

| Board composition | | |
| --- | --- | --- |
| Independent non-executive directors | Non-executive directors | Executive directors |
| 5 | 5 | 3 |

Source: Vodacom. (2012). *Vodacom Group Limited integrated report.*

is being managed in the best interests of shareholders and other primary stakeholders. The composition of the board of directors and the power given to it are critical factors of the power it has to control management's actions. Regional differences in governance frameworks are also visible in board structures. One of the largest differences is that between the "Anglo-American" style unitary board system and the "Continental" model of the dual-tiered split between the "supervisory" and "executive" boards. Figure 15.13 illustrates the board structure of Vodacom, the company that was described in this chapter's introductory case.

Added further to this mix are the debates on competing regulatory authorities and the movement toward more uniform and even global standards of corporate governance, which gained even further impulse with the ongoing banking crisis starting in 2008. The board of directors is probably

## THINK ETHICS

### Fiduciary Irresponsibility and Corruption

In 2002, "improper payments" (bribes) of $700,000 were made to government officials to "promote business" by Xerox-Modi Corp in India.

Source: The Tribune India. (2002). *Xerox Modicorp faces probe.* Retrieved February 2, 2013, from The Tribune India, Online: www.tribuneindia.com/2002/20020704/biz.htm#1

the most powerful and most prominent corporate governance mechanism. Other mechanisms include the following:

- Compensation and bonuses
- Transparency and reporting
- Creating accountability
- Auditing
- Due diligence
- Authority and power abuse
- (Legal) compliance and standards

## 15-6c Fiduciary Responsibilities

While corporate governance takes a specific perspective on principal–agent relationships, the topic of **fiduciary responsibilities** builds on an important, potential impact of financial managers' decisions when they are entrusted with handling large amounts of money (*fiduciary* comes from the Latin word *fidere*, meaning "to trust"). Such fiduciary responsibilities translate into special care in decision making of financial managers who have a higher responsibility to make good decisions due to the magnitude of potential consequences of bad decisions. Corporate governance is designed to prevent moral hazards, intentional misconduct by managers, while fiduciary duties aim at avoiding unwanted consequences arising from missing diligence in handling money. The more power a manager has to command money, the bigger the potential negative consequences are of wrong decisions.

Fiduciary responsibilities have been standardized for high-hierarchy job positions such as chief financial officers (CFOs), organizational boards of directors, and shareholders of a company. Even lower-level managers in not so high-ranking positions often are responsible for considerable amounts of capital, which makes it reasonable to extend the fiduciary responsibilities independently from the hierarchical level of an employee. One could argue that the 2008 subprime financial crisis was caused by missing fiduciary diligence of the bank staff, from sales people to fund managers, who ignored the potential negative consequences of selling loans to people who probably could not pay them back.[72]

**Fiduciary responsibilities** are the special responsibilities of to the ones managing money.

---

## PRINCIPLES OF FINANCE: RESPONSIBLE RETURN ON INVESTMENT

I. The goal of strategic responsible financial management is the *responsible return on investment (RROI)* which is a measure of company success that aims at the optimization of long-run returns in form of a maximum triple bottom line, maximum stakeholder value creation, and minimum ethical misconduct.

II. In order to create responsible financial management practices, six main paradigms of finance have to be questioned: *profit* maximization, constant *growth*, *short-run thinking*, *money* as a decision-making indicator, the dominance of *shareholders*, and the *internality thinking* that leads to incomplete decisions.

III. *Financing* describes the process of procuring funds for business activities. Financing in responsible business has a set of attractive additional *financing tools*, due to its special characteristics.

IV. *Capital budgeting* is the process of internally allocating financial resources to company activities and projects. Capital budgeting is crucial to provide responsible management with the financial resources required.

V. The *social return on investment (SROI)* is a method that quantifies and monetizes all stakeholder costs and benefits—the social, environmental, and economic ones—of an activity in one single ratio.

VI. *Corporate governance* describes a set of mechanisms and structures aimed at ensuring that managers lead an organization to comply with its responsibility to owners and other main stakeholders. *Fiduciary duties* are special responsibilities that arise when people control and work with significant sums of money.

| Process Phase | | Sustainability | Responsibility | Ethics |
|---|---|---|---|---|
| Phase 0: Understanding financial management | Do you understand that financial management paradigms, . . . | . . . such as the externality paradigm, need to be broken to create sustainable organizations? | . . . such as the shareholder paradigm, need to be changed in order to optimize stakeholder value? | . . . such as the profit paradigm, create ethical dilemmas that need to be managed proactively? |
| Phase 1: Financing | Does your financing activity . . . | . . . harness the financing sources that provide capital to sustainably run companies, such as the DJSI? | . . . involve stakeholders as funding sources, such as in goodwill funding, and cooperative models? | . . . take into considerations the ethical interests of investors, such as activist shareholders? |
| Phase 2: Budgeting | Does your capital budgeting activity . . . | . . . consider social, environmental, and economic capital? | . . . include all relevant stakeholders and how value is created for them? | . . . consider the ethical implications of the activities assessed? |
| Phase 3: Results | Do you manage the results of financial management . . . | . . . with responsibility toward future generations? | . . . through a governance model that ensures that the interests of priority stakeholders are respected? | . . . through a governance model that minimizes ethical misconduct? |

## KEY TERMS

activist shareholder 499
angel investor 500
blended value 504
board of directors 516
break-even point (BEP) 510
capital budgeting 503
cooperatives 501
corporate governance 515
cross-financing 502
crowdfunding 501
direct financing 499
divestment 496
ethical return on investment ($ROI_{ETH}$) 488
fiduciary responsibilities 518
financial management 489

financial proxy 508
financing 493
functions of financial management 490
goodwill financing 503
hard indicators 507
impact 508
impact investing 500
inputs 507
microfinance 522
monetization 489
negative screening 496
outcomes 507
outputs 507
positive screening 496
principal–agent problem 515

private cash flows 510
responsible return on investment (RROI) 488
social cash flows 511
socially responsible investment (SRI) 495
social return on investment (SROI) 505
social venture exchange 498
soft indicators 507
SRI index 497
stakeholder value return on investment ($ROI_{SHV}$) 488
triple bottom line return on investment ($ROI_{TBL}$) 488
venture capitalist 500

## EXERCISES

### A. Remember and Understand

A.1. Describe the differences between mainstream and responsible financial management.
A.2. Paraphrase the three decision areas of financial management.
A.3. Define and interrelate the following terms: RROI, ethical ROI, TBL ROI, and stakeholder ROI.
A.4. Define and interrelate the following terms: SROI, monetization, and indicators.

### B. Apply and Experience

B.5. Look up the structure of the board of directors for three different companies. Which company has the best board? Why?
B.6. Look up the criteria of socially responsible investing (SRI) institutions online. In what ways do they differ? What are the different criteria they use or sectors they encourage or screen against? Which do you think are the most advantageous systems and why?

**B.7.** Ask one person currently employed in a company the following question: "Should companies be managed for shareholders or stakeholders?" Do you agree with the person's answer?

## C. Analyze and Evaluate

**C.8.** Look up one of the exemplary SROI reports available at www.thesroinetwork.org/. Analyze the methodology used. What would you have done better?

**C.9.** Review the triple bottom line concept. How do you think each part is weighted by most companies? What would be the consequences for financial

management systems if each of the three sections were equally weighted?

**C.10.** Think about the employee and about the community as stakeholders. For each, come up with four main value drivers, similar to the drivers for shareholder value displayed in Figure 15.11.

## D. Change and Create

**D.11.** Describe a fictional or real responsible business activity and develop its SROI. Then think about ways to increase the SROI, based on the calculation and its results.

---

## PIONEER INTERVIEW WITH ROBERT COSTANZA

Robert Costanza is a pioneer of the monetary evaluation of the environmental factors. He made the topic of ecosystems services and their financial evaluation famous. Monetizing nonmonetary indicators is a main precondition for responsible financial management.

**How do you think natural capital is important to business practice, and how should an environmentally responsible business act?**

We should all recognize that there are four basic types of assets or capital that contribute to sustainable human well-being and to sustainable business practice: (1) conventional "built" capital like buildings and factories—the kind of capital that businesses usually worry about; (2) human capital—the individual people that make up the community or company and their skills, knowledge, health, and creativity; (3) social capital—the networks, relationships, cultures, and institutions that connect people—the business culture embedded in the larger regional, national, and global cultures; and (4) natural capital—ecosystems that produce a range of valuable and essential goods and services upon which our economy and society depend. All human benefits depend on a combination of these assets, and sustainable business practice must recognize and understand these interactions, even though most social and natural capital assets are "off the books."

**How should businesses consider natural capital in their accounting and finance practices?**

I'm the chair of the advisory board of Trucost, a company that estimates the external environmental

costs of businesses based on a sophisticated model of the complex interactions in the economy and environment. Trucost estimates both the environmental costs of the companies' operations and the indirect cost of the companies' entire supply chains. Puma has recently used Trucost to estimate their environmental costs and has made this information public. Companies can use this information to recognize and then decrease their environmental impacts. This will prevent companies from confusing externalized costs with profits and allow them to pursue truly sustainable social profits. It will also allow investors to recognize companies that are behaving in truly sustainable ways and not just "greenwashing."

**What can companies do to restore natural capital (and ecosystems), instead of depleting it?**

By recognizing the value of natural capital assets, companies can begin to invest in conserving and restoring those assets. If these assets can be brought "on the books," companies will have a much easier time of doing this. Imagine a company shareholder report that includes all four types of capital assets mentioned above. Even though most social and natural capital assets are (and should not be) owned by companies, these common assets are extremely important to everyone's well-being. We need to harmonize our social and private books in order to manage all our assets sustainably.

**In 1997 you argued that the global ecosystems created almost twice as much economic value as the global economy. Would the actual estimate still be in this range? If not so, what has changed since then? How can we interpret those facts?**

If anything, this value has only increased. Even though global GDP has increased over this time, ecosystems have continued to be depleted, and the services they provide have become more scarce and valuable. We have estimated the benefit/cost ratio of preserving and restoring global natural capital as at least 100:1. There are not many better investments than that. If we adequately account for *all* our assets, we would put much less emphasis on GDP (which was never designed as a measure of economic well-being and is a very misleading proxy) and think more about maximizing the value of our total global portfolio of assets. An Earth Shareholder Report would do something like that and would be a better guide to investment policies.

## PRACTITIONER PROFILE: FRANCISCO ACUÑA MENDEZ

Elnur/Shutterstock.com

**Employing organization:** InTrust Global Investments is a Sustainable Advisor Firm, which is the sponsor of INDI Fund, the first Latin American Indigenous Fund, focused in Indigenous/Rural Lands

**Job title:** President and CEO

**Education:** LL.B Universidad Iberoamericana Law School, Mexico; LL.M, Master International Law, Georgetown Law Center; MPA, Master Public Administration, Harvard Kennedy School of Government; MBA, BTH, Blekinge Institute of Technology, Sweden

### In practice

**What are your responsibilities?**
I am the founder of InTrust and INDI Fund. INDI Fund is a financial vehicle that works with indigenous and rural communities of all Latin America. We make indigenous and rural communities real partners (equity partnerships) and package projects for investors and strategic partners, through our Fund and/or other vehicles. One of the pillars of the Fund is its solid relationship with the communities. The types of projects we focus in "phase I" include clean energy (forestry, hydro, biomass, biodiesel, geothermal, and tide and wave).

**What are typical activities you carry out during a day at work?**
Discussing projects with communities; negotiating with local governments; discussing projects with investors; arranging financial and technical due diligence on the projects; feasibility studies; negotiating with developers, operators, and offtakers; making sure the social and environmental indicators are in place; spending time with the communities and socializing the projects; and so on.

**How do sustainability, responsibility, and ethics topics play a role in your job?**
They are part of our core values as a firm. Our Fund uses an objective monetization structure that puts a verifiable economic value to the social and environmental returns of a project. We only look at projects that have a strong financial, social, and environmental return. We know that these three returns don't exclude each other; on the contrary, they can strengthen the project and align interests with all stakeholders involved.

**Out of the topics covered in the chapter into which your interview will be included, which concepts, tools, or topics are most relevant to your work?**
Important topics in our work are private equity, investments, and the social return on investments.

### Insights and Challenges

**What recommendation can you give to practitioners in your field?**
There are many profitable projects with large social returns on investments. The most successful projects and firms are going to be those that treat social and environmental returns with the same rigor and stimulus that they treat their financial returns.

**Which are the main challenges of your job?**
There is still some business bias against indigenous and rural folks in the emerging world. There is a misunderstanding and perception that you can't build profitable and sustainable projects with them, or that it will be a burdensome or very complicated task. This is not really the case, at least in our projects. However, we understand very well where the misunderstanding comes from, and thus, part of our role is to present the other "reality" of doing successful and sustainable investments with the communities.

Previously, we have dealt mainly with responsible finance as a tool by which to achieve more responsible and sustainable outcomes. Increasingly, though, the central role of the financial industry in the world economy has driven greater interest in how the power of finance can be completely integrated into sustainability. This means utilizing the knowledge, skills, and infrastructure of the finance sector to achieve sustainable growth both for the financial institution and the community within which it operates.

An ideal example of this is the rise of **microfinance** products, which since the early 2000s have had an annual growth of about 30 percent per annum. In essence, microfinance is the provision of financial services (funds, loans, insurance, etc.) to low-income clients or groups, including consumers and the self-employed, who traditionally have lacked access to banking and related services. The majority of loans or financing involves amounts of $100 or less. Provision of such low amounts was often neglected by banks, particularly large financial institutions, as the activity was deemed too complex, time-consuming, or demanding of infrastructure to bother with. As the doubts about the effectiveness of costly governmental/charity projects began to increase in the 1990s, the attraction of utilizing more market-oriented mechanisms to stimulate poverty reduction rose.

For banks and financial institutions, microfinance "ticks the boxes" on a number of different levels. For a start, it builds on their core competencies, skills, and infrastructure. Rather than attempting to reduce poverty by NGOs establishing expensive new infrastructure or by banks undertaking often less than efficient philanthropic activities, it makes sense for banks to open up their financial facilities and skills to those previously unbanked. This fits in well with the emerging consensus of the last two decades based on the move to find direct, market-based, but *"small is beautiful"* methods to alleviate poverty and enhance social welfare, in particular, the concept of reaching enormous numbers of people at the "bottom of the pyramid"—those billions

**Microfinance** describes financial products such as loans, insurance, credits, and savings provided to low income often previously "unbanked" people. The individual sums involved are usually smaller than established banks have previously considered as the minimum to be worth undertaking.

on very low incomes. These potential consumers and entrepreneurs remain a largely untapped market with far high multipliers than largely satiated Western developed countries.

If bottom-of-the-pyramid business such as microfinance is such a good idea, with good profit margins, low default rates, and an impressive record in encouraging local entrepreneurs and empowering marginalized people in society, why did it take so long for microfinance products and services to catch on? The answer lies both in a corporate unwillingness to address new ways of thinking as well as in the reluctance of the "development community" to at first embrace market mechanisms. Indeed, there is still some criticism that microfinance "displaces" government programs, that it does not always reach the "absolute poor" but helps those

## Expert Corner

"Microfinance is an extremely effective and efficient tool to bring stability and investment to communities which, while having the skills and drive to support themselves and create wealth, have for various reasons, often lacked adequate and credible banking institutions. Microfinance has the added advantage in that it aids the democratisation of society as it binds in the lower middle classes by stabilising their economic stake in society."

Source: From interview conducted by Nick Tolhurst exclusively for this book.

## In Practice

### Microfinance

"The World Bank estimates that 40% of the world's population, circa 2.7 billion people, still live in extreme poverty and survive on less than USD 2 per day. It is also estimated that one third of these people would establish their own small businesses and thus create their own employment if they had access to the right financial services and opportunities. With loan repayment rates averaging 97% and no institutional defaults to date, microfinance has earned a reputation as a stable financial investment and an important building block for emerging financial systems."

Source: Doerig, H.-U. (2010). Microfinance: Helping communities to develop. In M. Pohl & N. Tolhurst, *Responsible business: How to manage a CSR strategy successfully* (pp. 177–191, p. 181). Chichester: Wiley.

already emerging middle-class, small-business owners, and that some financial institutions charge too high interest rates. While managers should always be aware of the potential pitfalls, it is clear that responsible microfinance provides the means for empowering increasing numbers of people to participate economically. In order to avoid such problems, financial institutions should be clear from the start of their strategic goals.

A good example of this is the major international bank Credit Suisse, which set out to focus only on carefully defined areas where the bank could have a meaningful and measurable impact.

Credit Suisse set out a number of aims to achieve this—not just in advancing its philanthropic aims to reduce poverty but also in training more staff in microfinance banking in the various communities, enabling existing staff to volunteer for such undertakings, as well as satisfying the demand of Credit Suisse's stakeholders to invest in socially rewarding investments. The Swiss bank's strategy consisted of identifying the necessary NGO partners. As a part of this development, Credit Suisse also gives microfinance institutions access to the capital market and business expertise, with further social and economic multipliers.

## SPECIAL PERSPECTIVE: ISLAMIC BANKING

One of the most significant developments of globalization coupled with the "flattening" out of the access to technology is that the demand for goods and services aimed at specific communities has become efficient enough to enable global firms to address it. This is important in terms of responsible governance, as it touches on the responsiveness and sensibility of firms to address the concerns and demands of specific communities. Companies that make a point of opening up to all sections of the communities in which they operate are likely to benefit and seize competitive advantages over companies that don't.

A classic example is the rise of Islamic banking—that is, financial activity that is consistent with the principles of Islamic law and its practical application through the development of Islamic economics. Most specifically, this is usually viewed as involving the prohibition of the payment (or even acceptance)

of interest rates (known as *Riba* or usury) for loans or credits of money. There are a number of reasons why this issue has risen in importance and why the financial sector is engaging with Islamic banking practices. First, and most obviously, the Islamic community represents not just a large part of the global population but also, thanks to large private and public surpluses, a large part of both the global financial sector as well as the global economy. Second, with globalization, the concept of a "Western" way of doing business has become less and less a norm, particularly given the banking crisis which, for the most part, arose in the West and to which, according to a number of studies, the Islamic banking sector proved to be more resilient than other more traditional banking systems.[71]

As we can see in Figure 15.14, Islamic banking is not just a "way of getting round paying interest," which is how it is sometimes dismissed. Rather, in

| Figure 15.14 **Key Distinctions between Conventional Banking and Islamic Banking** |

**Islamic Banking**

- Promote risk sharing between provider and user of funds
- Partner/buyer/seller relationship
- Emphasis on asset based financing and comodity trading
- No right of profit if no risk involved

**Conventional Banking**

- Investor is assured of predetermined interest rate
- Creditor/debtor relationship
- Emphasis on money based trading
- Risk minimisation as interest rate guaranteed

© Cengage Learning, 2015

## Figure 15.15  Key Tools of Islamic Banking System

| Joint Venture - *Musharakah* | Insurance - *Takaful* | Bonds - *Suluk* | Investment - *Mudarabah* |
|---|---|---|---|
| • All partners participating contribute funds and share in profits and retain rights in the running of the venture's management. | • Similar to conventional insurance but system is far more mutually based, with losses/profits pooled. | • Islamic version of credit but based on underlying asset value, allowing for sharing out of revenues. | • Islamic version of investment credit between fund provider and entrepeneur. Profits are divided on pre agreed ratio. |

© Cengage Learning, 2015

a subtle but significant manner, it changes the way companies, individuals, and financial institutions do business with each other.

The main consequence for business of Islamic financial practices is that they change the risk calibration toward a more partnership-based (and thus longer-term relationships) model than the more conventional credit/interest-based contract system of Western banking. (See the brief summary of the basic tools of Islamic finance in Figure 15.15.) Due to this traditional Islamic banking has developed tools of joint ventures (*Musharakah*), lease systems (*Ijarah thumma al bai'*), and profit sharing (*Mudarabah*) that have become increasingly refined. Comprising more than 300 institutions in more than 75 countries, Islamic banking is now one of the world's fastest-growing economic activities; it was predicted to expand in size to more than $4 trillion by the end of 2012.

## SOURCES

1. Ernst & Young. (2012). *Six growing trends in corporate sustainability*. Ernst & Young.

2. Ernst & Young. (2012). *Six growing trends in corporate sustainability*. Ernst & Young.

3. Ernst & Young. (2012). *Six growing trends in corporate sustainability*. Ernst & Young.

4. Scholtens, B. (2006). Finance as a driver of corporate social responsibility. *Journal of Business Ethics, 68*(1), 19–33.

5. Scholtens, B. (2006). Finance as a driver of corporate social responsibility. *Journal of Business Ethics, 68*(1), 19–33.

6. LeBlanc, B. (2012). Sustainability raises on the CFO's "to-do" list. *Financial Executive, 28*(2), 55–57.

7. Ernst & Young. (2012). *Six growing trends in corporate sustainability*. Ernst & Young.

8. Soppe, A. (2004). Sustainable corporate finance. *Journal of Business Ethics, 53*(1–2), 213–224.

9. Soppe, A. (2004). Sustainable corporate finance. *Journal of Business Ethics, 53*(1–2), 213–224, p. 213.

10. Soppe, A. (2004). Sustainable corporate finance. *Journal of Business Ethics, 53*(1–2), 213–224, p. 53.

11. Coleman, L., Maheswaran, K., & Pinder, S. (2010). Narratives in managers' corporate finance decisions. *Accounting and Finance, 50*(3), 605–633.

12. Capelle-Blancard, G., & Couderc, N. (2009). The impact of socially responsible investing: Evidence from stock index redefinitions. *Journal of Investing, 18*(2), 76–86.

13. Fauzi, H., Mahoney, L., & Rahman, A. A. (2007). Institutional ownership and corporate social performance: Empirical evidence from Indonesian companies. *Issues in Social and Environmental Accounting, 1*(2), 334–347.

14. Oh, W. Y., Chang, Y. K., & Martynov, A. (2011). The effect of ownership structure on corporate social responsibility: Empirical evidence from Korea. *Journal of Business Ethics, 104*(2), 283–297.

15. Oh, W. Y., Chang, Y. K., & Martynov, A. (2011). The effect of ownership structure on corporate social responsibility: Empirical evidence from Korea. *Journal of Business Ethics, 104*(2), 283–297.

16. Min-Dong, P. L. (2009). Does ownership form matter for corporate social responsibility? A longitudinal comparison of environmental performance between public, private, and joint-venture firms. *Business and Society Review, 114*(4), 435–456.

17. Prado-Lorenzo, J. M., Gallego-Alvarez, I., & Garcia-Sanchez, I. M. (2009). Stakeholder engagement and corporate social responsibility reporting: The ownership structure effect. *Corporate Social Responsibility and Environmental Management, 16*(2), 94–107; Li, W., & Zhang, R. (2010). Corporate social responsibility, ownership structure, and political interference: Evidence

from China. *Journal of Business Ethics, 96*(4), 631–645.

18. SIF. (2010). *Report on socially responsible investing trends in the United States.* Washington, DC: Social Investment Forum Foundation.

19. Capelle-Blancard, G., & Couderc, N. (2009). The impact of socially responsible investing: Evidence from stock index redefinitions. *Journal of Investing, 18*(2), 76–86.

20. Gillan, S. L., & Starks, L. T. (2000). Corporate governance proposals and shareholder activism: The role of institutional investors. *Journal of Financial Economics, 57*(2), 275–305; Anabtawi, I., & Stout, L. (2008). Fiduciary duties for activist shareholders. *Stanford Law Review, 60*(5), 1255–1308.

21. Karpoff, J. M. (1998). *The impact of shareholder activism on target companies: A survey of empirical findings.* University of Washington: Working paper; Smith, M. P. (1996). Shareholder activism by institutional investors: Evidence from CalPERS. *Journal of Finance, 51*(1), 227–252.

22. Letts, C. W., Ryan, W., & Grossman, A. (1997). Virtuous capital: What foundations can learn from venture capitalists. *Harvard Business Review, 75*(2), 36–44.

23. Winston, B. (2012). *What is the difference between an angel investor & a venture capitalist?* Retrieved December 27, 2012, from Demand Media, eHow Money: www.ehow.com/about_6311239_difference-angel-investor-venture-capitalist_.html

24. IESE. (2011). *Impact investing. IESE insight,* Fourth Quarter, no. 11, p. 8.

25. IESE. (2011). *Impact investing. IESE insight,* Fourth Quarter, no. 11, p. 8.

26. Cordes, R. (2010, May 1). Impact investment: Capitalism is tackling the world's biggest social and environmental problems—and giving investors a new way to do well by doing good. *Financial Planning Magazine,* 46–48.

27. Stern, G. M. (2011, September 1). Impact investing: Wealthy clients are favoring a different kind of socially responsible investing, focusing on private equity and nonprofit projects. *Financial Planning Magazine,* 66–72.

28. Freireich, J., & Fulton, K. (2009). *Investing for social & environmental impact: A design for catalyzing an emerging industry.* Cambridge, MA: Monitor Institute.

29. Hansmann, H. (1988). Ownership of the firm. *Journal of Law, Economics & Organization, 4*(2), 267–304.

30. Belleflamme, P., Lambert, T., & Schwienbacher, A. (2011). *Crowdfunding: Tapping the right crowd.* Center for Operations Research: Discussion paper series, vol. 32.

31. Belleflamme, P., Lambert, T., & Schwienbacher, A. (2011). *Crowdfunding: Tapping the right crowd.* Center for Operations Research: Discussion paper series, vol. 32.

32. Sullivan, M. (2006). *The crowdfunding wiki.* Retrieved February 28, 2012, from Crowdfunding: http://crowdfunding.pbworks.com/w/page/10402176/Crowdfunding

33. Schwienbacher, A., & Larralde, B. (2010). Crowdfunding of small entrepreneurial ventures. In D. Cumming, *The Oxford handbook of entreprenurial finance* (pp. 369–391). New York: Oxford University Press; Given, K. (2011). *Social entrepreneur funding series: Crowdfunding your startup.* Retrieved February 28, 2012, from Green Marketing: www.greenmarketing.tv/2011/03/16/social-entrepreneur-funding-options-crowdfunding/

34. Keene, A. (2007). *"Email a duck, raise a buck" by Munchkin for Susan G. Komen.* Retrieved March 1, 2012, from Cause Marketing: http://causerelatedmarketing.blogspot.com/2007/10/email-duck-raise-buck-by-munchkin-for.html

35. United Diversity. (2012). *The crowdfunding co-operative.* Retrieved December 3, 2012, from United diversity.com: http://uniteddiversity.com/projects/crowdfunding-cooperative/

36. ICA. (2012). *What is a co-op?* Retrieved December 10, 2012, from The International Co-operative Alliance: http://2012.coop/en/what-co-op

37. ICA. (2012). *What is a co-op?* Retrieved December 10, 2012, from The International Co-operative Alliance: http://2012.coop/en/what-co-op

38. ICA. (2007). *Factsheet: Differences between co-operatives, corporations and non-profit organisations.* Retrieved December 10, 2012, from The International Co-operative Alliance: http://2012.coop/sites/default/files/Factsheet%20-%20Differences%20between%20Coops%20Corps%20and%20NFPs%20-%20US%20OCDC%20-%202007.pdf

39. Chaddad, F. R., & Cook, M. L. (2004). Understanding new cooperative models: An ownership-control rights typology. *Review of Agricultural Economics, 26*(3), 348–360; Chaddad, F. R., & Cook, M. L. (2002). *An ownership rights typology of cooperative models.* Department of Agricultural Economics: Working paper, AEWP 2002–06.

40. ICA. (2012). *Co-operative facts & figures.* Retrieved December 11, 2012, from The International Co-operative Alliance: http://2012.coop/en/ica/co-operative-facts-figures

41. Emerson, J. (2003). The blended value proposition: Integrating social and financial returns. *California Management Review, 45*(4), 35–51.

42. Berk, J., & DeMarzo, P. (2007). *Corporate finance.* Boston: Pearson Addison Wesley.

43. Mansdorf, Z. (2010). Sustainability and return on investment. *EHS Today,* 49–52.

44. Demacarty, P. (2009). Financial returns of corporate social responsibility, and the moral freedom and responsibility of business leaders. *Business and Society Review, 114*(3), 393–433.

45. Scholtens, B. (2006). Finance as a driver of corporate social responsibility. *Journal of Business Ethics, 68*(1), 19–33.

46. Dorfleitner, G., & Utz, S. (2012). Safety first portfolio choice based on financial and sustainability returns. *European Journal of Operational Research, 221*(1), 155–164.

47. Emerson, J. (2003). The blended value proposition: Integrating social and financial returns. *California Management Review, 45*(4), 35–51.

48. Blaug, M. (1967). The private and the social returns on investment in education: Some results for Great Britain. *Journal of Human Resources, 2*(3), 330–346.

49. Williams, J., & Larocque, S. (2009). Calculating a sustainable return on investment. *Journal of Public Works & Infrastructure, 2*(2), 94–105; Roostalu, L., & Kooskora, M. (2010). Budgeting as a means for communicating CSR: The case of the Tallinn city government. *EBS Review, 27*(1), 38–54.

50. Porter, M. E., & Kramer, M. R. (1999). Philanthropy's new agenda: Creating value. *Harvard Business Review, 77*(6), 121–130; Emerson, J., & Cabaj, M. (2000). Social return on investment. *Making Waves, 11*(2), 10–14; Pace, S. U., & Cruz Basso, L. F. (2009). Social return on investment, value added and volunteer work. *Journal of Academy of Business and Economics, 9*(3), 42–58.

51. Lingane, A., & Olsen, S. (2004). Guidelines for social return on investment. *California Management Review, 46*(3), 116–135.

52. Lingane, A., & Olsen, S. (2004). Guidelines for social return on investment. *California Management Review, 46*(3), 116–135.

53. HP. (2012). *HP carbon footprint calculator for printing.* Retrieved December 10, 2012, from Hewlett-Packard Development Company: www.hp.com /large/ipg/ecological-printing-solutions /carbon-footprint-calc.html

54. SENDECO$_2$. (2012, December 13). *CO$_2$ prices.* Retrieved December 17, 2012, from The Exchange of SENDECO$_2$: www.sendeco2.com /index-uk.asp

55. London Business School, NEF & Small Business Service. (2004). *Measuring social impact: The foundation of social return on investment (SROI).* London: SROI Primer.

56. M&S. (2012). *Annual report and financial statements 2011.* London: Marks and Spencer Group.

57. M&S. (2012). *Annual report and financial statements 2011.* London: Marks and Spencer Group.

58. Keeble, J. J., Topiol, S., & Berkeley, S. (2003). Using indicators to measure sustainability performance at a corporate and project level. *Journal of Business Ethics, 44*(2–3), 149–158.

59. SEMARNAT. (2012, July). *Liderazgo ambiental para la competitividad.* Retrieved December 27, 2012, from Secretaría de Medio Ambiente y Recursos Naturales: http:// liderazgoambiental.gob.mx /portel/libreria/pdf /PresentacinLACJulio2012.pdf

60. Doh, J. P., & Stumpf, S. A. (2005). *Handbook on responsible leadership and governance in global business* (p. ix). Cheltenham: Edward Elgar.

61. Rappaport, A. (1998). *Creating shareholder value: A guide for managers and investors,* 2nd ed. New York: Free Press.

62. Brigham, E. F., & Houston, J. F. (2011). *Fundamentals of financial management,* 7th ed. Mason, OH: South-Western, Cengage Learning.

63. Bender, R., & Ward, K. (2008). *Corporate financial strategy.* Oxford: Butterworth-Heinemann.

64. Bender, R., & Ward, K. (2008). *Corporate financial strategy.* Oxford: Butterworth-Heinemann.

65. Laasch, O. (2010). Strategic CSR. In W. Visser, et al., *The a–z of corporate social responsibility,* 2nd ed (pp. 378–380). Chichester: Wiley.

66. Orlitzky, M., Schmidt, F. L., & Rynes, S. L. (2003). Corporate social and financial performance: A meta-analysis. *Organization Studies, 24*(3), 403–441; Waddock, S. A., & Graves, S. B. (1997). The corporate social performance–financial performance link. *Strategic Management Journal, 18*(4), 303–319.

67. Blackburn, W. R. (2012).*The sustainability handbook: The complete management guide to achieving social, economic and environmental responsibility.* New York: Routledge.

68. Cadbury Committee. (1992). *The financial aspects of corporate governance.* London: Gee Professional.

69. OECD. (1998). *OECD principles of corporate governance.* Paris: OECD Publications Service.

70. Sarbanes-Oxley. Corporate responsibility. (2002, July 30). 116 Stat. 745, Pub. Law No. 107–204, 15 U.S.C. 7201, note.

71. IMF. (2007, August). *The economics of Islamic finance and securitization.* Retrieved August 9, 2011, from IMF .org: www.imf.org/external/pubs/ft /wp/2007/wp07117.pdf; Hasan, M., & Dridi, J. (2010). *The effect of the global crisis on Islamic and conventional banks: A comparative study.* IMF Working Paper Series, vol. 10, no. 201.

72. Indjejikian, R., & Matejka, M. (2009). CFO fiduciary responsibilities and annual bonus incentives. *Journal of Accounting Research, 47*(4), 1061–1093; Widell, A. D. (2002, February). Fiduciary duties of corporate directors in a financially troubled economy. *Directorship,* 8–15; Anabtawi, I., & Stout, L. (2008). Fiduciary duties for activist shareholders. *Stanford Law Review, 60*(5), 1255–1308; Kaufman, A. (2002). Managers' double fiduciary duty: To stakeholders and to freedom. *Business Ethics Quarterly, 12*(2), 189–214.

## A

ABB Group, 331
  process of recruitment, selection, and hiring, 339–340
ABC. *See* activity-based costing
above-average moral performance, 139–140
above-average operational performance, 263
absolutism *versus* relativism, 122
Accenture, 10
account, 449
accountability, responsibility *versus*, 92
accounting data
  concepts of, 451
  and gathering data, identify. *See* data, identifying account and gathering
  qualitative characteristics of, 450, 451
accounting, financial management and, 487
acquisition, 429
action model, ethical decision and, 132–133
activist shareholder, 499
activities of procedure descriptions, 270
activity-based costing (ABC), 460
activity map, 173
actors, 3
  business, 6
  civil society, 6
act utilitarianism, 130
advanced responsible type of management, 27
advancing diversity, 336
affinity groups, 344

against perspective, pro-business *versus*, 122–123
alignment, organizational architecture, 228
Alishan Organic Center, 491
alternative ownership models, 500–502
alternative solutions, generation of, 40
altruistic values, 122
AMA. *See* American Marketing Association
American Marketing Association (AMA), 377
America's Baldrige National Quality Award, 263
angel investors, 500
anticipatory socialization, 344–345
antiglobalization movements, 407
applied ethics, 115
Aramex, 274, 288, 317
Aristotelian ethics, 430
Arsenal FC, 202, 203
Arthaud-Day, 417
ASHOKA foundation, 202–203
Asia-Pacific region, 447
assessment
  of CSP, 93–97
  materiality, 103
  stakeholder, 99–103
  value chain, 173
assurance, 471
attention, organization culture, 244
AT&T program structure, 234
attribution, 508
audit, 451, 471
Australian Vegetable Growers' Association (AUSVEG), 139

average unsustainable business, 70
awareness, components of ethical decisions, 132
AXA Winterthur in Switzerland, 24

## B

background domains of responsible management, 4
badwill, reduction of, 369
*Balanced Scorecard* (Kaplan and Norton), 351
balanced scorecard approach, 351
balanced scorecard, responsible management, 177–178
balancing, 71
Baldrige National Quality Award, 280
Band-Aid brand box, 378
Barcelona FC, 202, 203
bargaining, collective, 357
Barilla Food Safety Supply Chain Project, 310
barriers, 373
base of the pyramid (BoP), 423, 428
  entrepreneurs, 424
  sourcing, 423, 424
basic financial accounting elements, 451, 452
basics accounting
  concepts of, 451
  main inflows and outflows, 451, 452
  qualitative characteristics of, 450, 451
  responsible accounting, 453–454
B2B. *See* business-to-business
BCG matrix. *See* Boston Consulting Groups matrix

behavioral ethics. *See* descriptive ethics

behavioral interview approach, 341

below-average unsustainable business, 70

benchmarking, 287–289

benefits, employees, 354–356

Ben & Jerry's ice cream, 161

BEP. *See* break-even point

best practices benchmarking, 288

Betapharm model, changing rules of, 156

Betapharm social entrepreneurship, 191

Better Business Bureau (BBB), 117

beyond finance, 46

biocapacity, 69

biodegradable package designs, 379

blended value, 504

board of directors, 516–518
  organizational chart, 231

boards' role and responsibilities, 516

board structure of Vodacom, 517

Body Shop Australia, 136

Bolaven Farms, 30

BoP. *See* base of the pyramid

"born CSR oriented" businesses, 240

Boston Consulting Groups (BCG) matrix, 170–171

BP. *See* British Petroleum

brand awareness, 379

brand equity, 379

brand image, 379

branding, 379

Brazil, Russia, India, China, and South Africa (BRICS), 407

break-even point (BEP), 510

breakthrough improvement, 287–289

BRICS. *See* Brazil, Russia, India, China, and South Africa

British Airways, 379

British Petroleum (BP), 371

broader civil society as stakeholders, 267

broad perspective, 157

Bruntland Report, 61

budgeting
  capital, 503, 512
  decisions, 487
  mandatory CSR, 504
  sustainability, 505

bureaucratic control systems, 46

business
  actors, 6
  case for responsible business, 514
  case for responsible management, 10
  communication, 374
  conventional wisdom in, 406
  CSP, 93
  resource-based view of, 167

business angels. *See* angel investors

business case perspective, 157

business ethics, 91, 114
  analysis in, 119
  defined, 118
  development of, 115, 116
  discipline of, 115–117
  domains of. *See* domains of business ethics
  Figureheads and Central ideas of, 116
  institutionalization, status quo and future, 117–118
  interpreting, 122–123
  levels of analysis in, 119
  moral dilemmas, 119–120
  morality and values, 120–122
  opposing views on, 122–123
  origins of, 114–115
  relationship to law and compliance, 119–120
  responsibility and sustainability, 149–150
  roots of, 115

business ethics theory, 118

business foundation, 8

business global position, assessing, 416

business of business argument, 13

business philanthropy, 91

"business process detail" mapping, 265

business processes mapping, 265

business process modeling, methodologies for, 267

business responsibility
  classification and interpretation, 92–93
  concepts of, 89–97
  defined, 89
  development of, 86
  domains of, 92
  field of, 392
  figureheads and central ideas of, 87
  first formal appearance of, 86
  Islamic, 86
  managing for stakeholder value, 84–85
  origins of, 85–89
  sections of, 85
  subdivisions of, 91–92
  terms to describe, 89–92

Business Roundtable (BRT), 117

business sustainability, 53–54, 90
  origins of. *See* origins of business sustainability

business-to-business (B2B) *versus* end-consumer companies, 16

business unit level strategy, 169, 172–174
  defined, 171

## C

CAEP. *See* China Association for Employment Promotion

C.A.F.E. program. *See* Coffee and Farmer Equity program

capital, 62–63

capital budgeting
  blended value in making decisions, 504–505
  defined, 503
  subjects of, 512

capitalist economy, 203

carbon dioxide equivalent ($CO_2e$), 447

Carroll's pyramid, 419

cash flows, 509

cause-branding, 384

cause-related marketing (CRM), 368, 384–385, 503

cause-related programs, 234

causes. *See* subjects

Caux Roundtable Principles for Responsible Globalization, 420

CC. *See* corporate citizenship; cultural competence

C&D approach. *See* connect and develop approach

CE. *See* circular economy

CEOs, survey rounds of, 157

CFP. *See* company financial performance; corporate financial performance

change agents, 243–244

change-based sustainability, 64

change management, errors in, 245–247

channels, 372, 373
communication, 372
integration and linkedness, 398

China Association for Employment Promotion (CAEP), 462

China, energy supply chain, 302

China's Greentech Initiative, 422

Christian morality, 125

circle model, 62

circular economy (CE), 321
defined, 320

civic implementation level, 95

civil society actors, 6

clan control, 46

clean water system, 380

C-level functions, 236

CLG. *See* company limited by guarantee

climbing mount sustainability, 53

Clorox company, corporate level strategy, 170–171

closed-loop supply chain, 322
defined, 321

closing the loop, 319–324
defined, 318

co-creation of joint activities, 103, 104

codes of conduct, 142, 387, 388
quality criteria for, 143

codes of ethics, 142
normative documents, 233

CO$_2$e. *See* carbon dioxide equivalent

coercive power, responsible leaders, 44

Coffee and Farmer Equity (C.A.F.E.) program, 174

cognitive pathology, 133

Coin Street Action Group, 199

Coin Street Community Builders (CSCB), 199

Colgate Palmolive, 170

collaboration-harm grid, 102

collaboration, responsible management, 43

collective bargaining, 357

collectivism, individualism *versus*, 223–225

collectivist perspective, 224

commoditization
of labor, 196–197, 201
of money, labor, and land, 196–197
profit and loss from, 201

communal system, 191

communication, 389
components of, 373
with credibility, 375
crisis, 386
employee, 358
face-to-face, 373
informal, 383
intensity of, 376
lack of, 381
organizational architecture, 228
principle of, 375
of stakeholder, 103
and stakeholder value, balancing, 376–377
stakeholder value, effectiveness, and intensity of, 377
time-tested principles of, 374
tools, normative documents, 237

communication styles
related to web types, advantages and disadvantages of, 397
in responsible management communication, 372

community-based engagement, 237

Community Benefit Societies, 203

community investment, 500

community involvement and environmental stewardship, 351–353

companies
arguments, 13
development process steps, 240
in impact investment, 500
LEGO. *See* LEGO company

company financial performance (CFP), 95

company limited by guarantee (CLG), 210

compelling value proposition, 416

compensation, 354
system, driving principles of, 354–356

competence, 167

competencies for prime managers, 37–39

competition, 169

competitive advantage, 172
resources and, of responsible management, 167
source of, 172
strategic, 159
sustained, 157, 159, 168

competitive coffee industry, 381

competitiveness, 159
responsible. *See* responsible competitiveness

complex adaptive system, defined, 303

compliance, 151
business ethics relationship to, 119–120
defined, 120
problems, 146

concept-to-customer approach, 264

confucianism, 86

connect and develop (C&D) approach, 176

consequentialism, 113, 128–130

Conservation Act 1987, 192

constraints, 433

constructivism, realism *versus*, 224, 225

contemporary business ethics, 117

contemporary culture, 164

content quantity and quality in Web 2.0, 397–398

context-related factors in ethical decisions and behaviors, 135–136

continual improvement cycles in ISO 14000 and 9000, 273

continual improvement mechanism, 271–272

continuous improvement cycle, 284

continuous improvement systems, 272

controlling process, 46

controlling punishment, responsible leaders, 44

control task of management, 36

conventional banking, 523

conventional "built" capital, 63

conventional level, moral development on, 137

conventional wisdom in business, 406

convergent *versus* divergent responsibility, 92

converging global crises, 10–11

cooperatives, 501–502

COPIS, 280, 281

core competencies, 167, 350–351

core stakeholders, 102

corporate citizenship (CC), 86, 91

corporate culture management, 176

corporate donation, 199

corporate financial performance (CFP), 293, 514

corporate foundations, 502

corporate governance, 4
    board of directors, mechanism, 516–518
    defined, 515
    principles, 515–516

corporate level strategy, 169–171
    Clorox company, 170–171
    defined, 169

corporate philanthropy, 86

corporate responsibility (CR), 87, 90

corporate responsibility department, 235

Corporate Responsibility Officer Association (CROA) survey, 243

Corporate Responsibility Reporting information, 471

corporate social entrepreneurship (CSE), 87, 92

corporate social performance (CSP), 293, 514
    assessment of, 93–97
    defined, 93
    dimension of, 93–94
    IHG *versus* SB, 96

corporate social responsibility (CSR), 16, 86–91, 206, 211, 235, 486
    budgeting, 504
    defined, 88
    Europe, 87–88
    explicit, 413
    implementation stages, 235
    implicit, 413
    pyramid, 87, 93, 94
    training in human rights, 347
    UAE, 38

corporate whistleblowers, 143

Corporations Act, 143

costing models, 459–460

cost-leadership strategy, 175

cost reductions, savings from, 502

cost savings, 509

country developmental stages, 67

country identification, 424

coverage of entrepreneurship, 7

coverage of strategy Strategy, 41

CR. *See* corporate responsibility

cradle-to-cradle, 478, 479
    design. *See* closing the loop framework, 59
    philosophy of product, 263

creation, organizational architecture, 228

creative destruction process, 430

credibility, communication with, 375

crisis communication, 386

criticisms in responsible management, 3, 13
    causes, 15

critics change management, 246

CRM. *See* cause-related marketing

*CR Magazine*'s survey, 234–235

CROA survey. *See* Corporate Responsibility Officer Association survey

cross-cultural ethics, 434–436

cross-cultural skills for responsible business conduct, 433

cross-financing, 502–503

cross-national diversity management, 432

cross-sectorial alliances, 431

crowdfunding, 501

CSCB. *See* Coin Street Community Builders

CSE. *See* corporate social entrepreneurship

CSP. *See* corporate social performance

CSR. *See* corporate social responsibility

CSR 2.0, 88

CSR Navigator, 411

C-suite management, 144

cultural competence (CC), 434

customer orientation and continuous improvement, 280–284

customer request checking, 271

customers
    of LEGO, 84
    as stakeholders, 267

## D

data, identifying account and gathering
    characterization, 455, 456
    ESG activities, 455
    materiality, 457–458
    responsible business accounting, 457
    responsible management issues, 455, 456

deadweight, 508

debt financing, 503

decentralization, responsible management, 43

decision areas of financial management, 490–491

decision making, 40

decoding processes, 373

defects per million opportunities (DPMO), 287
  values in relation to Sigma levels, 287
Define, Measure, Analyze, Design, Verify (DMADV), 285
  analyze phase, 286
  define phase of, 286
  structure descriptions, 285
  verify phase of, 286
define-measure-analyze-improve-control (DMAIC), 285, 286
  framework, 272
  model, 310
  structure descriptions, 285
"*Del amor nace la vista*" campaign, 370
delegation, responsible management, 43
delighters, Kano's model, 282
Dell, 174–175
demand conditions, 414–415
Deming cycle, 283
Deming wheel, 283
demographic factors in ethical decision, 133, 134
deontology, 125
  criticism of, 128
  defined, 127
  higher rules and duties, 127–128
departmental ethics management tools, 141
departments
  organizational architecture, 222
  structural elements, 234–235
descriptive ethics, 114, 117, 124, 131, 145
  defined, 132
  ethical decision-making, 132–136
design failure modes and effects analysis (DFMEA), 286
design for environment (DfE), 323
design for Six Sigma (DFSS), 285
developed countries, developing *versus,* 16
developing *versus* developed countries, 16
development of sustainability, historic milestones in, 55

development path, countries in different stages, 67–68
development, training and, 342–343
DfE. *See* design for environment
DFMEA. *See* design failure modes and effects analysis
DFSS. *See* design for Six Sigma
dialogue-based forums/interactive communication tools, 382
dialogue-based interview, 341
diamond model, 429
  of national competitive advantage, 413
  to responsible business, applying, 414
differentiation, 43
dimensions of responsible management, 27
directed financing, 499–500
discipline of business ethics, 115–117
disclosure, 455
  and transparency, 516
dismissal criteria, organization culture, 245
displacement, 508
  organizational architecture, 228
disposable activities, 200
dissatisfiers, Kano's model, 281
distinctive competence, 167
distribution fairness, 130
diversification, 169, 512
diversity in responsible business, 432
divestment, 169, 496
dividend decision, 491
dividends, 198
DMADV. *See* Define, Measure, Analyze, Design, Verify
DMAIC. *See* define-measure-analyze-improve-control
domain competencies, 37, 38
domains of business ethics, 124, 145
  descriptive ethics, 132–136
  ethics management. *See* ethics management

ethics programs and culture, 144–146
  normative ethics. *See* normative ethics
double-diamond model, 413
Dow Jones Sustainability Index (DJSI), 497, 498
  ranking mechanism, 24
downcycling, 322
DPMO. *See* defects per million opportunities
drivers of responsible management, 3
  megatrend and, 8–12
driving principles of compensation system, 354–356
due diligence, 429, 430
dynamic approach to communication process, 373
dynamic complex communication process, 373

## E

EABIS. *See* European Academy of Business in Society
Eaga PLC, 209–210
EBT. *See* employee-benefit trust
e-Choupal, 28
ecodesign, defined, 323
ecoeffective, 279–280
ecoeffectiveness, defined, 316
ecoefficiency, 264–265, 274
  concept of, 279
  defined, 316
ecoefficient logistics, 318
ecoimagination, 379
Eco-Management and Audit Scheme (EMAS), 314
  defined, 315
e-commerce, 317
  logistics, 318
economic capital, 63
economic crises, 14–15
economic ethics, 119
economic responsibility, building block of, 418
economic subsystems, sustainability-related, 306
economic sustainability, 61

economic systems, 191–192
hybridization of, 195
social enterprise at crossroads of, 195
economic value, 486
economic *versus* sustainable development, 66–68
sectorial sustainability footprints, 68–70
Economist Intelligence Unit, 382
effective communication, 371, 373, 374
principles of, 369
effective counter campaign, 367
effective integrated marketing, 369
effective listening, 350
effective marketing and communication of social and environmental business performance, 367
effectiveness, 264, 279
and efficiency, difference between, 280
of management, 28, 29
of processes, 265
effective process, 264
effective stakeholder communication, 369
efficiency, 264, 274
and cost internalization, 425
difference between effectiveness and, 280
of management, 28, 30
egoistic values, 122
EHS. *See* Environment, Health and Safety
ELCA. *See* environmental life-cycle assessment
El Dulce Negocio workshops, 428
Electronic Product Assessment Tool, 315
elements of responsible management, 26
eliminate waste resources, 75
EMAS. *See* Eco-Management and Audit Scheme
emerging responsible type of management, 27
empathy, 39
employability, 348–349

employee-benefit trust (EBT), 210
employee development, 347
employee life cycle, 344–345
employee motivation, 509
employee orientation, 344
employee-owned companies, 204
employee performance, 512
employees, 226, 337
as assets, 243
development to stakeholder development, 347
green collar workers, 236
job satisfaction, 352
of LEGO, 84
minorities, 338
on-the-job mentoring of, 347
private lives of, 333
relations and communications, 357–359
satisfaction, 229
skill building, 352
training and development of, 342–349
volunteering program, 352
well-being, 356
employee share ownership plans (ESOPs), 204–205
employee training, exemplary process of, 265
employee volunteering program, 347, 352
employee well-being, 336
empowerment, organizational architecture, 228
encoding process, 373
encounter phase, 345–346
end-consumer companies, B2B *versus*, 16
end-of-life (EOL) design, 322–323
defined, 323
energy-consuming goods, replacement of, 261
energy supply chain issues in China, 302
engagement of stakeholder, 103–104
engagement platforms, normative documents, 236–237
engineering/design attributes, 286
enterprise excellence, responsible, 262–264

enterprise resource planning (ERP), 177
entrepreneurship
of stakeholder business responsibility, 89
strategic, 176
environmental analysis of strategic environment, 164–168
environmental capital, 63
environmental impacts
of country, 67–68
reducing, 336
environmental integrity, 425
environmental life-cycle assessment (ELCA), 73
environmental management in OM and SCM, QM principles application, 315
environmental management standards, ISO 14000 management system standard for, 272
Environmental Product Declaration (EPD), 53
Environmental Protection Agency (EPA), 323
environmental stakeholders, 102
environmental stewardship, community involvement and, 351–353
environmental sustainability, 61, 310
Environment, Health and Safety (EHS), 294
environment of LEGO, 84
environment scanning, 164
environment, social, and governance (ESG) disclosure, 455
EOL design. *See* end-of-life design
EPA. *See* Environmental Protection Agency
EPD. *See* Environmental Product Declaration
equality, principles of, 354
equitable development, 66
equity, 425
degeneration, 204–205
equivalent view, CC, 91
Ernst & Young's 2012 survey, 8, 9

ERP. *See* enterprise resource planning

ESOPs. *See* employee share ownership plans

*Essay on the Principle of Population* (Malthus), 57

essential stakeholders of organization, 368

ETG. *See* Export Trading Group

ethical auditing, imposing, 139

ethical behavior and professional integrity, 516

ethical business and ethics management, 113–114

ethical conduct, 350

ethical conflicts, 436

ethical decision making and behavior, 116, 117
    components of, 132–133
    individual factors in, 133, 134
    situational factors in, 133, 135–136

ethical dilemma, 118

ethical financing in New Zealand, 493

ethical issue
    defined, 145
    types of, 146

ethical leadership, challenge of, 141

ethical management, 140

ethical opportunity, 145

ethical profitability, 140

ethical responsibility, 419

ethical return on investment ($ROI_{ETH}$), 488

ethical theories of business responsibility, 92

ethical trade, 426

ethics, 4, 5, 26
    in business, 91
    operationalizing traditional theories, 130

Ethics & Compliance Officer Association (ECOA), 117

ethics culture, 144

ethics domain, 304

ethics-efficiency, 265

ethics leadership, 242

ethics management
    defined, 136
    domain of, 124
    ethical business and, 113–114

goal of, 136–140
    process of, 144–146

ethics management tools
    defined, 140
    departmental, 141
    ethics value chain of, 140–141
    specialized, 142–144

ethics of accounting, 453, 474

ethics performance, 31, 141, 239
    assessment approaches, 137, 140
    defined, 136
    ethics management and, 114
    measurement, 136
    models based on moral development, 137–138
    moral excellence through, 136–140

ethics perspective, 29, 30

ethics program, 144

"Ethics Quotient," 117

Ethics Resource Center (ERC), 117, 133, 140

ethics value chain, 140–141

Europe
    CSR, 87–88
    employee-owned companies, 204
    to support social enterprise development, laws passed in, 204

European Academy of Business in Society (EABIS), 88

European forum messages, 374

European Multi-Stakeholder Forum, 373

European Quality Award, 263

European social economy, concept of, 190

evaluation and elaboration data
    costing models, 459–460
    indicators, 461–464
    responsible business performance metrics, 460–461
    social and ecological impacts, 459
    SROI, 466
    VAS, 464–466

evaluation of alternative solutions, 40

EVAS. *See* expanded value-added statement

exchange of by-products, 320

exemplary process maps, 267

expanded value-added statement (EVAS), 466

expert power, responsible leaders, 45

explicit CSR, 413

explicit *versus* implicit responsibility, 92

export business (EB), 416

Export Trading Group (ETG), 426

extended view, CC, 91

external communication, 372

external financing market for responsible management activities, 494

externalities paradigm, financial management, 493

external operational communication, 382

external stakeholder, 100
    communication, 396

external strategic environment
    analysis of, 164–165
    layers of, 163

**F**

face-to-face communication, 373

facilitating action, 449

failure modes and effects analysis (FMEA), 282

Fair Labor Association and AccountAbility, 408

fairness
    of distribution, 422
    principles of, 354
    thinking, 126–127

fair trade, 425
    products, 384

Fair Trade Foundation, 425

Fairtrade Labelling Organizations International (FLO), 425

families of values, 121

FDI. *See* foreign direct investment

feedback, 373
    mechanisms, 143

fertility rates, 66

fiduciary irresponsibility, 517

fiduciary responsibilities, 518
filter bubble, 397
final selection of a solution, 41
finance decision, 490–491
finance department, 486
financial accounting, 451
financial crisis (2007), 118
financial management
  checklist, 519
  corporate governance and,
    515–518
  defined, 489
  fiduciary responsibilities, 518
  goal of, 488–489
  mechanisms and structures of,
    489–492
  phases of. *See* phases of
    financial management
  questioning paradigms of,
    492–493
  responsible, 486–488
financial proxy, 508
financial reporting, 499
financial results, 491
financing, 493
financing responsible business,
    493–495
  activist shareholding, 499
  alternative ownership models,
    500–502
  cross-financing and goodwill
    financing, 502–503
  debt financing, 503
  directed financing, 499–500
  socially responsible investing,
    495–497
  SRI indices, 497–499
first formal appearance of
    business responsibility, 86
first-generation policies, 411
5-Minute Annual report, 447
flagship programs, 234
Fleet Management System (FMS),
    317
FLO. *See* Fairtrade Labelling
    Organizations International
FLOWmarket, 385, 386
FMEA. *See* failure modes and
    effects analysis
focal company, defined, 311
focal entity of stakeholder map,
    101

Food Safety Supply Chain project,
    Barilla, 310
food security as social supply
    chain sustainability, 310
footprinting methodology, 69
forecasting, effective, 164–165
foreign direct investment (FDI),
    428
foreign language competence, 434
foreign market seeking, 426
foreign ownership, 494
Forest Stewardship Council
    (FSC), 314, 315, 378, 408
formal sustainability reports,
    387–388
Form 990-EZ, nonprofit
    organizations using, 198
Form 990, nonprofit
    organizations using, 198
foundations, 235
  in impact investment, 500
fragmentation *versus* holism
    polarization, 63–64
Friedman argument, 14
frontline manager, 35
FSC. *See* Forest Stewardship
    Council
FTSE4Good index, 497–498
full-cost accounting, 460
full-cost recovery, 200
functional level strategy, 169, 175
  defined, 174
functions of financial
    management, 490
future responsibilities, immediate
    responsibilities *versus*, 92

## G

game at Betapharm, changing
    rules of, 156
GAVI conference. *See* Global
    Alliance for Vaccines and
    Immunization
    conference
GDP. *See* gross domestic product
GE Ecomagination campaign, 171
General Electric, 379
generosity, 126
genuine ethical dilemmas, 146
German development agency
    GIZ, 411

GlaxoSmithKline (GSK), 403
GLC. *See* Greater London
    Council
Global Alliance for Vaccines
    and Immunization (GAVI)
    conference, 403
global business, 408
  responsibly managing in,
    431–437
global business activities, 422
  mapping, 405
global business responsibility,
    stages of, 419
global challenges and
    opportunities, 407
global communication technology,
    407
Global Compact, 10
  principles, 138–139
  survey of CEOs, 17
  sustainability leadership in
    Malaysia, 12
global companies, 417
global economy, life cycle of, 71
global environment, 404
global externalities, 422
globalization, 406
  effects of, 406–407
  responsible business, 408
globally inclusive workplace,
    432
globally sourcing companies
    (GSCs), 416
global media, 406
global mentality, 417
global NGOs, 407
global personal identity and
    affiliations, 408
global position, assessing, 404
global pyramid of business
    responsibility, 419
Global Reporting Initiative (GRI),
    59–60, 387, 419
  indicators, 462, 463
  reporting principles, 468–469
  standards, 367
global sourcing, 423–424
global stakeholders, 422
  organizations, emergence
    of, 408
global standards, emergence
    of, 407

global strategic alliances, 430–431

global trade, 424–426

global transactions activities, 422

global transportation, 407

glocal, 404

    approach against corruption, 406

glocal business context, 405–406

    globalization, 406–408

    localizing responsible business, 408–415

glocalism, 405

glocalization, 405

    understanding, 404, 436

glocally responsible business (GRB), 404, 405

glocally responsible management, process of, 404

goal and scope (G&S), 73

goals

    of management, 28–29

    of responsible competitiveness, 159–160

    strategic objectives and, 162

golden rule, 127

goodwill

    establishing, 375

    financing, 502–503

Google, 98

governance of financial management, 487–488

governmental actors, 6

Grameen Bank, 164

grants, 503

GRB. See glocally responsible business

Greater London Council (GLC), 199

Great Transformation, The, 191

green collar workers, 236

greenfield investment, 428

Greenhouse Gas Protocol, 315

Green IT, 8

green revolution, 57

green technology companies, 164

greenwashing, 12, 15, 367, 376–377

"Greenwash Noise," 376

GRI. See Global Reporting Initiative

gross domestic product (GDP), contribution of SMEs to, 304

groups, stakeholder, 101

growth paradigm, financial management, 492

G&S. See goal and scope

GSCs. See globally sourcing companies

GSK. See GlaxoSmithKline

H

Hansgrohe Sustainability KPIs, 480

happiness, virtue ethics, 125

hard enablers, 289

hard indicators, 507

hard responsibility, soft responsibility versus, 93

hardwiring, 175, 176

"healthy" communication climate, 383

hierarchical management levels, 36

Higg Index, 316

high-balance situation, 376

higher sigma levels, 287

high-leverage finance capitalism, 430

high-net-worth individuals in impact investment, 500

holistic accountability, 450

hollow organizations, 229, 230

home energy management, 261

horizontal alliances, 430

horizontal integration, 169

horizontal organization, 229, 230

horizontal organizational architecture, 221

householding, 202

"house of quality," 282

HR. See human resources

HRD. See human resources development

HRM. See human resource management

HR-RM interdependent relationship, 333–338

HR-RM symbiosis, 332–333, 359

human capital, 63

human communication, process of, 371

human-made capital, 63

human resource management (HRM)

    anecdotes of, 331

    defined, 342

    planning and development of activities, 335

    recruitment. See recruitment

    responsible, 332

    scope of responsibility, 353

    stakeholders, 337–338

    training and development of employees, 342–349

    training recommendations, 346

human resources (HR), 331–332

    manager in advancing responsible business, role of, 338

    versus responsible HRM, 334–335

    stakeholder considerations in, 337

    traditional perspectives of, 331

human resources development (HRD), 332

human resources (HR) management, 142

human rights, 336, 462

hybridization

    defined, 195

    types of, 197

I

ICT. See information and communication technology

"ideal final result" (IFR), 282

identification of stakeholder, 99–101

$I^2$ DOV. See Innovation, Invention Design, Optimization, and Verification

IFR. See "ideal final result"

IHG. See Intercontinental Hotel Group

IKEA group, 261

immediate responsibilities versus future responsibilities, 92

impacts, 70, 71, 508
    accounting process, 71–75
    investing, 500
    management process, 75
implementation
    benchmark, 239
    of strategy, 175–177
implemented ethics
    checklist, 139
    defined, 138
implicit CSR, 413
implicit, explicit responsibility
    *versus*, 92
inbound logistics, 316–317
inclusivity in international
    management, 432
income by source, streams
    of, 200
in-company trainings, 265
independent foundations, 235
indicators, 507
indigenous practices, 56
indigenous sustainability, 55–56
individual ethics, 119
individual factors in ethical
    decision, 133, 134
individualism, 433
    *versus* collectivism, 223–225
individualistic perspective,
    223–224
indulgence, 433
industrial co-location, 323
industrial ecology, 319–320
    closed loops and circular
        economies in, 319
    defined, 319
industrial ecosystem, 304, 306
    mapping, 305
industrial revolution of
    agricultural sector, 57
industries, 414
industry environment, 163
ineffective communication,
    368, 375
informal communication, 383
information and communication
    technology (ICT), 462
    industry, 349
inhibitors in responsible
    management, 3
initial screening process, 341
innocence, 113

Innovation, Invention Design,
    Optimization, and
    Verification (I² DOV), 285
innovation *versus* design nuances,
    285
input conditions, 414
inputs, 507, 509
inside-out linkages, 163
Institute of Social and Ethical
    AccountAbility (ISEA), 473
institutional investors, 494
    in impact investment, 500
institutionalism, instrumentalism
    *versus*, 224–225
institutionalization, 117–118
    for business responsibility,
        87–88
    of responsible management,
        11–12
    of sustainability, 59–60
instrumental domain, of business
    responsibility, 92
instrumentalism *versus*
    institutionalism, 224–225
instrumentalists, 224
integrated foundations, 235
integrated management system,
    272
integrated marketing
    communication (IMC), 368
    effective communication,
        understanding, 371–377
    ensuring effective, 370–371
    responsible business
        performance, marketing,
        377–381
integrated processes, 237–238
integrated reporting, 470–471
integrating corporate responsibility
    in performance appraisals,
    350
integrating traditional theories,
    130–131
integration, 43
    horizontal, 169
    organizational architecture,
        228
    of stakeholder business
        responsibility, 88
    vertical, 169–170
integrative domain, of business
    responsibility, 92

integrative model for responsible
    management, 27
INTEL Involved program, 352
intensity of communicaion, 376
interconnectedness of supply
    chain, 73
Intercontinental Hotel Group
    (IHG), 96
intercultural management,
    432–434
interdisciplinary issues, 118
interdisciplinary work, 38
InterfaceFLOR, 53, 63, 283
intergenerational justice, 65–66
intermediate stakeholder, 391
internal business practices,
    implementation of, 243
internal communication, 372
internal costs, 493
internal inhibitors of responsible
    management, 17
internal investment decision, 491
internality paradigm, financial
    management, 493
internal operational
    communication, 382
internal processes, mapping, 265
internal rate of return (IRR)
    method, 510
internal rate on investment, 509
internal return on investment, 503
internal share market, 205
internal social networking tools,
    382
internal stakeholder, 100
internal stakeholder management,
    338
internal strategic environment,
    analysis of, 165–168
internal value chain analysis, 173
International Auditing and
    Assurance Standards
    Board, 473
international business, 403–405,
    415
    transactions, 421
international cooperation, 425
International Co-operative
    Alliance, 502
international development, 422
International Federation of
    Accountants (IFAC), 473

international firm, type of, 416–417
International Integrated Reporting Council (IIRC), 470
international interest group, 431
internationalization of business activity, 406
international mentality, 416–417
International Organization for Standardization (ISO), 73
  norm for social responsibility, 11
international perspective, Western *versus,* 123
international responsible business norms, 420–421
international responsible managers, 435
international subsidiaries, 428–430
international working environment, 434
Internet, 407
interpretations of business responsibility, 92–93
interpreting business ethics, 122–123
interpreting sustainability, 63–66
intragenerational justice, 65–66
intrapreneurship. *See* strategic entrepreneurship
investments
  optimization, 491
  security, 491
investor institutions, spectrum of, 495
irresponsible business, 7
irresponsible competitiveness goal, 159–160
irresponsible type of management, 27
ISEA. *See* Institute of Social and Ethical AccountAbility
Islamic banking
  conventional banking and, 523
  tools of, 524
Islamic business responsibility, 86
ISO. *See* International Organization for Standardization

ISO 9000, 313–315
  defined, 313
ISO 14000, 12, 314–315
  defined, 314
ISO 26000, 11, 314
  defined, 315
ISO 72 guide, 272
ISO 14000 management system standard for environmental management standards, 272
ISO SR. *See* ISO 26000 standard for social responsibility
ISO 9000 standard for quality management systems, 272
ISO 26000 standard for social responsibility (ISO SR), 88
issue-related factors in ethical decisions and behaviors, 135–136
issues. *See* subjects
issues and crisis communication, 386–387
issues maturity, 95
  for SB, 95
ITC Limited, 28

**J**

job descriptions, 340
job positions
  organizational architecture, 222
  structural elements, 235–236
*John Hopkins Comparative Non-profit Sector Project, The,* 199
joint co-creation of activities, 103, 104
Joyeeta, 6
judgment, components of ethical decisions, 132
justice, virtue of, 126–127
just-in-time logistics, 317

**K**

Kaitiakitanga framework, 55–56
Kano's model, 281
Kant's duty ethics, 224
kingdom of ends, 127–128
knowledge, 434
knowledge, skills, attitudes (KSAs), 339

Kohlberg's stages of moral development, 137
KSAs. *See* knowledge, skills, attitudes
Kuznets curve, 67

**L**

labor, commoditization of, 196–197, 201
labor practices, 462
labor relations, 357
labor unions, 357
lagging indicators descriptive, 288
land, commoditization of, 196–197
language of business, 450
large companies *versus* SMEs, 304, 306–309
*Lattice* structure, 221
law, business ethics relationship to, 119–120
LCA. *See* life-cycle assessment
LCC. *See* life-cycle costing
LCI. *See* life-cycle interpretation; life-cycle inventory
LCIA. *See* life-cycle impact assessment
L3Cs. *See* low-profit limited liability companies
leadership, 43, 240
  behaviors, 350
  process, 45
leading financial management practices in Middle East, 513
leading indicators, 288
leading task of responsible manager, 43–46
lead task of management, 36
"lean" channels, 372
lean enterprise core principles and processes, 275
lean enterprise methods, 274–277
lean Six Sigma, 277
legal/contractual relationship, responsible leaders, 44
legal responsibilities, 418
legitimacy of stakeholder, 102
legitimate power, responsible leaders, 44
LEGO company, 84

life-cycle analysis. *See* life-cycle assessment

life-cycle assessment (LCA), 72–73, 460
  defined, 323

life-cycle costing (LCC), 73

life-cycle impact assessment (LCIA), 74, 75

life-cycle impact portfolio, 72

life-cycle interpretation (LCI), 75

life-cycle inventory (LCI), 74

life cycle of global economy, 71

life cycle's product system, 73

life insurance, 321
  secondary market for, 119

lifestyles of health and sustainability (LOHAS), 10

lifestyles of voluntary simplicity (LOVOS), 10

Likert's System IV, 255

limited view, CC, 91

*Limits to Growth, The,* 58

line functions, organizational chart, 231

link alliances, 430

living wage, 356

localization, 207

local production and consumption networks, 318

local stakeholder demand conditions, 414–415

logistics, 316–318
  defined, 316

long-term orientation, 433

long-term thinking, 66

low-balance situation, 376

low-profit limited liability companies (L3Cs), 205

## M

macro (systemic) level, 6

magnanimity, 126

magnificence, 126

mainstream business departments, 141
  integrated into, 235

mainstream financial management, mechanisms and structures of, 489–492

mainstream globalization, 406

mainstream management, 25, 29

mainstream managers, 36

mainstream market, process of developing, 267

Malaysia, Global Compact driving sustainability leadership in, 12

management, 28

management accounting, 451

management control, 474–476

management-exclusive mission development approach, 162

management information systems, 177

management process of stakeholder
  assessment, 99–103
  engagement, 103–104

management systems
  bundling processes to, 271–274
  documents constituting, 271, 272
  for responsible business, 274
  for sustainability, responsibility, and ethics, 272

management theory, organization and, 226–227

management thought, evolution of, 31–34

managerial functions, 39

managerial hierarchies, role of, 35–37

managerial implementation level, 95

managerial influence, layered model of, 35

managerial process, 39

managerial roles, 39

managing business sustainability, 70
  impact accounting process, 71–75
  impact management process, 75
  neutral to positive triple bottom line, 70–71

managing glocally, 405

Maple Leaf Foods, 374, 386

mapping
  global business activity, 405
  process, 264–267

responsible operations on process level, 268–269

work of process, 265

mapping international business activity, 421–423, 437
  foreign markets, 426–428
  global sourcing, 423–424
  global strategic alliances, 430–431
  global trade, 424–426
  international subsidiaries, 428–430

mapping outcomes, defined, 507

Marine Stewardship Council (MSC), 314, 408

market control mechanism, 46

"Marketing 3.0," 394

marketing activities, relationship between cause-related marketing and, 384

marketing campaign, implementing, 265

marketing management, Ps of, 369

marketing mix, responsible management and, 377–381

market positioning strategy, responsible management on, 172–173

market, production for, 191–192, 202

Marks and Spencer (M&S), 379

masculinity, 433

masters *versus* equals polarization, 64

materiality, 457–458

materiality assessment, 103

materiality score (MS), 458

maturity issues, CSP dimension, 95

MDGs. *See* Millennium Development Goals

mechanistic *versus* organic organization, 42–43

medium enablers, 289

medium-sized company, human resources department of, 265

merger, 429

meso (organizational) level, 6

message, 371

meta-environment. *See* industry environment
meta-ethics, 122
metamorphosis stage, 345, 346
meta-perspective, 39
methodological competencies, 37, 38
microfinance, 503, 522–523
micro (individual) level, 6
Microsoft, 98
middle and line management, 236
middle managers, 35
Millennium Development Goals (MDGs), 11, 16, 59
  indicators, 428
"Misperceived Greenwash," 376
mission and vision statements, 388
mission statement
  defined, 161
  formulation of, 158, 160–162
  normative documents, 233
MNEs. *See* multinational enterprises
model-based assessment, 418–420
modeling sustainable systems, 69
modern virtue ethics, 126
modular organization, 229, 230
Mondragon Corporation
  employee ownership, 204
  management model, 190
  participatory democracy in, 187
  social economy at, 192
  social entrepreneurship, 187–188
  social innovation, 190
monetization, 489, 507, 508
monetized method, 504
money, commoditization of, 196–197
money paradigm, financial management, 492
moral bankruptcy, 140
moral development
  criticism of, 138
  defined, 137
  ethics performance models based on, 137–138
moral dilemmas, 4, 5, 114
  defined, 119
  relationship to law and compliance, 119–120

moral efficiency, 274
moral excellence, 26
  defined, 139
  through ethics performance, 136–140
moral hazard, 515
moral issues, 118
morality, 116
  defined, 120
  and values, 120–122
morality effective, 279
moral judgment, 146
moral laxity problems, 146
moral leaders, 242
moral philosophy, 113, 114
  defined, 116
  theories of, 125
more-than-profit organizations, 201, 203, 206, 211
motivation, components of ethical decisions, 132, 146
MS. *See* materiality score
M&S. *See* Marks and Spencer
*muda*, 276, 277
multicultural organization, 432
multinational enterprises (MNEs), 421
multinational firms, 417
multinational mentality, 417
multinationals assume country-level responsibilities, 408
multiple operational benchmarks, setting, 288
multistakeholder enterprise development, social enterprise as, 195
*muri,* 276, 277

# N

naming, organizational architecture, 228
narrow perspective, 157
National Coffee Association's (NCA's), 381
National Health Service (NHS), 207, 209
national responsible business context, assessing, 411–413
national responsible business policies, analyzing, 412

Native American Cree prophecy, 57
Natura Cosméticos, 313
natural capital. *See* environmental capital
natural capital inventory accounting, 460
Natura's *Programa Amazônia,* 313
NCA's. *See* National Coffee Association's
negative environmental impact of country, 68
negative screening, 496
negative triple bottom line impact, 71
neoliberal consumerism, 202
net negative triple bottom line impact, 70
net positive impact, 70
net present value (NPV) calculation, 509–510
network-centric organizations, 35
networks, sustainability and responsibility, 243
neutral impact business, 71
neutrally sustainable situation, 69
neutral to positive triple bottom line, 70–71
new markets, 10
new public management (NPM), 207–209
  defined, 207
  seven doctrines of, 208
*New York Times,* 128
New Zealand, ethical financing in, 493
NGOs. *See* nongovernmental organizations
NHS. *See* National Health Service
Nigeria, Shell in, 2
Nike, communication and responsible business performance at, 367
Nike Material Sustainability Index (Nike MSI), 316
nongovernmental organizations (NGOs), 450
noninstrumentalization, 127
nonprofit organizations, 201
  using Form 990/Form 990-EZ, 198

nonsocial stakeholder, 100, 101
    social stakeholder *versus*, 92
nonstakeholder value-adding
    efforts, 276
no-problem problems, ethical
    issue, 146
normative documents, 231–233
normative ethics, 114, 117,
    122, 145
    consequentialism, 128–130
    defined, 124
    deontology, 127–128
    integrating and operationalizing
        traditional theories,
        130–131
    theories, 124–125
    virtue ethics, 125–127
normative leadership, 142
Norsk Hydro, 453
NOW TIME Lean Enterprise
    *Muda*, 276
NPM. *See* new public
    management
NPV calculation. *See* net present
    value calculation
NTI. *See* Nucleus of
    Technological Innovation
Nucleus of Technological
    Innovation (NTI), 221

## O

objectives, 162
    of firms, 491–492
    strategic. *See* strategic
        objectives
observed behavior, 139
OEM. *See* original equipment
    manufacturer
offboarding, 353
offshoring, 424
OM. *See* operations management
ombudsmen, 143
1.5σ displacement, 287
on-site *versus* web meeting, 42
on-the-job mentoring of
    employees, 347
openness, 425
operational inhibitors, 17
operationalizing traditional
    theories, 130–131
operational managers, 35

operational performance, 262
operations management (OM), 262
    QM principles application
        in environmental
        management, 315
opposing viewpoints
    checklist, original position,
        225–226
    individualism *versus*
        collectivism, 223–224
    instrumentalism *versus*
        institutionalism, 224–225
    realism *versus* constructivism,
        224
optimization of stakeholder value,
    97–99
optimize triple bottom line
    impacts, 75
optimum volume paradigm, 492
organic organization, mechanistic
    *versus*, 42–43
organizational accountability, 449
organizational architecture, 227
    departments, 222
    horizontal, 221
organizational assimilation, 344
organizational change, 245
organizational chart, 231
organizational controls, 177
organizational culture, 244
organizational design patterns,
    228–230
organizational development
    process, 238
organizational documents, 271
organizational ethics, 119
organizational finance and
    environment, 490
organizational implementation,
    95
organizational leadership
    alignment creation, 243
    change agents, 243–244
    direction creation, 242
    maintain commitment, 243
    responsible leader, 240–241
    social intrapreneurs, 244
    sustainability, responsibility
        and ethics leadership,
        241–242
    tasks, 242–243
organizational mission, 7

organizational structure,
    142–143, 176–177, 227
organizational theory, 222
    viewpoints, 223–226
organization and management
    theory, 226–227
organizing task of responsible
    manager, 42–43
orientation, model for, 344–346
original equipment manufacturer
    (OEM), 302
origins of business ethics, 114
    discipline, 115–117
    institutionalization, 117–118
    roots, 115
origins of business sustainability,
    55
    historical beginnings of
        unsustainability, 56–57
    indigenous sustainability,
        55–56
    institutionalization of, 59–60
    status quo and future, 60
    theoretical advances, 57–59
"Our Common Future," 61
outbound logistics, 317
outcomes, 507
    sustainability, 65
outplacement programs, 353
outputs, 507
outside-in linkages, 163
outsourcing, 424

## P

packaging, 379
participative organization, 255
participatory democracy in
    mondragon corporation,
    187
partner promise of LEGO, 84
partnership-based engagement,
    237
partners/suppliers of LEGO, 84
PAS 99 standard, 272
Patagonia clothing company, 304
patronage refund, 198
pay-as-you-go financing, 502
payout, 491
PDSA. *See* Plan-Do-Study-Act
Pearce's model of third system,
    193–194

People & Planet Positive (PPP), 261
"people problem" during monitoring phase, 271
people promise of LEGO, 84
PepsiCo, 388
performance appraisals, integrating corporate responsibility in, 350
performance evaluation, 349–350
performance indicators, measurement of, 46
performance management, 28, 30–31
    community involvement and environmental stewardship, 351–353
    core competencies, 350–351
    offboarding, 353
    performance evaluation, 349–350
performance standards, defined, 46
personal attributes, 434
personal communication, 382–383
P&G's strategic innovation program, 176
phases of financial management, 487
    capital budgeting, 503–505
    financing responsible business. See financing responsible business
    mechanisms and structures of, 489–492
    questioning paradigms of, 492–493
    results and governance, 513–515
    social return on investment, 505–512
philanthropic model, 199
philanthropic organizations, 159
philanthropic responsibilities, 419
philanthropy, 91
    business, 91
    corporate, 86
    strategic, 157
philosophical phase, business ethics, 115

philosophy *versus* social science, 122
"piggy-back" approach, 16
place, 380
Plan-Do-Study-Act (PDSA), 282, 283
    modified, 284
    to responsibility management, 284
planet promise of LEGO, 84
planning task of management, 36
planning task of responsible manager, 39–41
policies, normative documents, 233
political theories, of business responsibility, 92
positive screening, 496
power
    responsible leadership, 44–45
    of stakeholder, 102
power distance, 433
PPP. *See* People & Planet Positive
preconventional level, moral development on, 137
prephilosophical phase, business ethics, 115
price, 379
primary stakeholder, 391, 392
prime business, 27
prime management, 26–27
    management basics and evolution to, 25–34
principal–agent problem, 515
principal-agent scenario, 515
principled level, moral development on, 137
Principles of Responsible Management Education (PRME), 88
prioritization, stakeholder, 101–102
private cash flows, 510
private equity, 499–500
privately owned companies, 494
private sector
    challenges and opportunities in transforming, 203–206
    defined, 201
    to social economy, 200–203
    socioentrepreneurial outcomes in, 206

privatizations, 207
PRME. *See* Principles of Responsible Management Education
pro-bono financial advice, 347
pro-business perspective, against perspective *versus*, 122–123
procedural competencies, 37
procedural problems, 271
procedure descriptions
    purpose of, 270
    standard elements of operating, 267
    typical sections of, 270
    writing, 271
procedure documents, 267
    describing process through, 267–271
procedures, 267
    normative documents, 238
procedure writing, 267
process detail maps, 265
processes, 264, 265, 279–280
    guidance in, 272
    to management systems, bundling, 271–274
    mapping, 264–267
    maps, icons for, 270
    normative documents, 237–238
    structure, 264
    sustainability, 65
    through procedure documents, describing, 267–271
    visual descriptions of, 267
procurement of funds, 490–491
product, 378
    based CRM, 384
production for market, 191–192, 202
product life-cycle model, 72
*Product RED*, 384
product responsibility assessment, 462
product SROI, 512
product stewardship, 323
professional ethics, developing, 119
professional integrity, ethical behavior and, 516
professional skills, 347
profitability, measurement of, 504

profit issues of responsible business, 13–14

profit paradigm, financial management, 492

profits, 198

profound knowledge, system of, 283

*Programa Amazônia,* Natura's, 313

programming internal activities, capital budgeting and, 503

programs, structural elements, 233–234

Prometheus Finance Ltd, 493

promises of LEGO, 84

promotion, 381

promotional mix elements, 381

promotional "pull strategy," 381

promotional "push strategy," 381

prospective employees, 368

Ps of sustainability, 70

psychological barriers, 373

psychological factors in ethical decision, 133, 134

publicly traded companies, 494

public sector
    challenges and opportunities in transforming, 208–211
    defined, 207
    distinctiveness, 208
    to social entrepreneurship, 207–208

"pull strategy," promotional, 381

PUMA and global labor relations, 357

"push strategy," promotional, 381

## Q

QFD. *See* quality function deployment

QM principles application, environmental management in OM and SCM, 315

qualitative assessment of CSP, 93–95

qualitative method, 504

quality function deployment (QFD), 282, 286

quality management, 280, 315
    customer orientation and continuous improvement, 280–284
    strategies, principles, practices, and tools, 263

quality management systems, 271
    ISO 9000 standard for, 272

quality-oriented approaches, 286

quality/performance of process, evaluating, 264

"quality triad," 283

quantified method, 504

quantitative assessment of CSP, 95–97

quantitative-qualitative assessment tool, 131

questioning paradigms of financial management, 492–493

## R

Radical Industrialists, 63

RDAP scale, 94

realism *versus* constructivism, 224, 225

receivers, 371

reciprocal interdependence, 190
    marginalization, 192

recruitment
    candidates in responsible way, 340–341
    effectiveness, 352
    hiring in responsible organization, 342
    responsible job description, 340
    selection process, 341–342
    traditional recruitment process, 339–340

recycling
    industry, 261
    unusual, 321

redistribution systems, 191
    marginalization, 192

"red-lining," 398

"RED-product lines," 384

referent power, responsible leaders, 45

regional responsible business approaches, 409–411

related diversification, 170

relativism, absolutism *versus,* 122

religious business morality, 86–87
    defined, 87

remanufacturing, 322

renewable energy schemes, 380

reporting, 466
    auditing and assurance, 471–474
    characteristics, 467
    ethics of accounting, 474
    GRI, 468–469
    integrated reporting, 470–472

reputation, company, 243

resource-based view of business, 167

resource cascading, 320

resource consumption, 275

resources of management, 28–29

responsibility, 4, 5, 26
    *versus* accountability, 92
    business. *See* business responsibility

responsibility category, 93

responsibility communication channels, 372

responsibility domain, 304

responsibility leadership, 242

responsibility management, 97

responsibility performance, 31, 239

responsibility perspective, 28–30

responsible accounting and controlling, 453

responsible accounting process, 448

responsible business, 7, 17, 27
    architecture, 231, 232
    C-level functions for, 236
    design patterns, 228–230
    elements of, 230–238
    financing. *See* financing responsible business
    implementation, stages of, 247
    management systems for, 274
    performance, 338, 354
    programs, 234
    reporting, 499
    systems for managing, 271
    training, 346

responsible business conduct, cross-cultural skills for, 433
responsible business, localizing, 408–409
  local context and infrastructure for, 413–415
  national responsible business context, assessing, 411–413
  regional responsible business approaches, 409–411
responsible business performance
  marketing, 377–381
  metrics, 460–461
responsible competitiveness
  context for, 413–414
  defined, 159
  goal, 159–160
responsible culture, 244–245
responsible decision making, 40
  matrix, 41, 42
responsible enterprise excellence, 263
  goal, 262–264
  lean enterprise methods, 274–277
  operations and responsible management, 262
  process, 264–274
  quality management, 279–284
  Six Sigma innovation and design, 285–289
  TPS, 277–279
responsible HRM
  business case for, 336
  checklist, 359
  HR versus, 334–335
  leadership, 337–338
  norms, 335
  principles of, 359
  skills for, 336–337
responsible infrastructure
  goal of, 223
  organizational development process, 238–247
  restructuring organization, 227–238
  SEMCO, Brazil, 221
  understanding organization, 223–227

responsible international business activity, comparison of guidelines for, 420–421
  and management checklist, 436
responsible international business, assessing, 415
  company's degree of global sustainability, responsibility, and ethics, 417–421
  international firm, type of, 416–417
  transnational perspective of responsible management, 415–416
responsible job description, 340
responsible leadership, 43, 240–241
  responsible business development, 245
  role model of, 44
responsible management (RM), 25, 156–158, 333
  activities, external financing market for, 494
  balanced scorecard, 177–178
  barriers, inhibitors, and criticisms in, 12–17
  basics and evolution to prime management, 25–34
  and business in 1930s, 25
  challenges in, 3
  checklist, 519
  context of, 2–3
  cross-financing mechanisms for, 502
  levels, 6
  and marketing mix, 378–381
  and organizational theory, 222
  practices in the Middle East, 513
  programs, 512
  resources and competitive advantages, 167
  social entrepreneurship and, 187–188, 212
  on strategic positioning, 172–173
  strategy. See strategy
  and supply chain, 300–301
  SWOT analysis, 169
  synergy map, 173

systems, 274
  task descriptions, 36
  in theory and practice, drivers of, 9
  value chain, 166
responsible management dashboard, 476–477
responsible management effectiveness, 29–30
responsible management efficiency, 30
responsible management goals, 28
responsible management marketing and communication tools, applying
  codes of conduct, 387
  CRM, 384–385
  formal reports, 387–388
  issues and crisis communication, 386–387
  mission and vision statements, 388
  SM, 385–386
  spheres of application of, 381–383
responsible management performance, 30
  dimensions and indicators in, 31
responsible management processes, 39
  controlling task, 46
  implementing, 271
  leading task, 43–46
  organizing task, 42–43
  planning task, 39–41
responsible management resources, 29
responsible management tools, 38
responsible managers, 6, 12, 29, 35
  checklist, original position, 225–226
  competencies for prime managers, 37–39
  function for, 188
  role of managerial hierarchies, 35–37
  workplace of, 6–8

responsible marketing process, 267
  and communication management process, 368
responsible operations management, 261, 274
  phases of, 262
responsible operations managers, task for, 272
responsible organization
  development paths, 239
  development patterns, 241
  process, phases of, 222
responsible organizational structures
  design patterns, 228–230
  elements of, 230–238
  management theories comparison, 226
responsible performance, responsibly building capacity for, 30
responsible return on investment (RROI), 488–489
responsible stakeholder approach, 337–338
responsible supply chain, 301–302, 323
  defined, 301
  followers, 311
  leaders, 311
  management checklist, 324
  performance, supply chain engagement improving, 312
responsible trade, 424–425
responsible type of management, 27
restorative business, 71
restorative/restoratively sustainable situation, 69
Retail Environmental Sustainability Code, 387
retailing logistics, 318
return on people, 514
revalorization, defined, 321
revenues from products, 502
reverse logistics, 318
reverse supply chain, defined, 321
review tracking of procedure descriptions, 270
reward power, responsible leaders, 45

rewards, organization culture, 244
"rich" communication channels, 372
right to provide legislation, 207
right to request legislation, 207
Rio Earth Summit in 1992, 59
"ripple effect" of decisions, 338
RM. See responsible management
role modeling, organization culture, 244
roots of business ethics, 115
Rotarix vaccine, 403
Royal Dutch Shell, 2
RROI. See responsible return on investment
rudimentary implementation level, 95
rule utilitarianism, 130

S
SAMSUNG, 343
Samsung Electronics, 72
SAP, 98
Sarbanes–Oxley Act, 515
SASB. See Sustainability Accounting Standards Board
"satellite" teams, 221
satisfiers, Kano's model, 281–282
savings from cost reductions, 502
SB. See Starbucks
scale
  of stakeholder business responsibility, 88
  sustainability management practices, 75
scale alliances, 430
science and precaution, international trade, 425
SCM, QM principles application in environmental management, 315
scope
  of procedure descriptions, 270
  and stakeholders, defined, 506–507
secondary market for life insurances, 119
secondary stakeholder, 391
second-generation policies, 411–412

second-order supply chain, defined, 304
sectorial actors, 5–6
sectorial alliance, 431
sectorial contributions to sustainability, 69
sectorial levels of action, 6
sectorial sustainability footprints, 68–70
SEE. See sustainable enterprise excellence
SEEA. See social, environmental, and ethical accounting
selection criteria, organization culture, 245
selection process, 341–342
self-competencies, 37, 39
self-contained organization, 229, 230
self-control, 126
self-enhancement, 122
self-personalization feature of Web 3.0, 399
self-regulatory organizations, growth of, 408
"semantic web" movement, 397
SEMCO, Brazil, 221
sender, 371
servicization logistics, 318
"Shakti Ammas," 88
shared infrastructure, 320
shared processes, 267
shared value, 157
  versus stakeholder value, 97–98
share/growth matrix. See Boston Consulting Groups (BCG) matrix
shareholder activism, 499
shareholder paradigm, financial management, 492–493
shareholder rights and equitable treatment, 515
shareholders, 337
  returns, 491
shareholder-value management, 513–515
share market, internal, 205
Shell
  business principles of, 2
  in Nigeria, 2

short-run paradigm, financial management, 492

short-run profit maximization, 488

short-term orientation, 433

short-term thinking, 66

"shy" communicator, 376

sigma, 287

*Silent Spring* (Carson), 58

single campaigns, 512

sin stocks, 496, 497

situational analysis, 40

situational factors in ethical decisions and behaviors, 133, 135–136

Six Sigma
DMAIC model, 310
innovation and design, 285–289
innovation approaches, 276

six Ts approach, 309–310
defined, 307

skill-based volunteering, 347, 352

skills, 434

SLCA. *See* social life-cycle assessment

SM. *See* social marketing

small and medium enterprises (SMEs), 88, 324
*versus* big corporations, 15–16
defined, 304
implementing responsible business in, 306–307
large companies *versus,* 304, 306–309
role of, 304–310

SMART. *See* Specific, Measurable, Attainable, Relevant, and Time-bound

SMEs. *See* small and medium enterprises

sociability, 126

Social Accountability (SA) 8000, 314

social auditing, 471

social business, 89
responsibility, 87

social capital, 62–63

social cash flows, 511

social competencies, 37, 39

social dimension of sustainability, 61

social economy, 201, 206, 211
decision-making power, 194
European, concept of, 190
private sector to, 200–206
third sector to, 198–201

social enterprise
development, laws passed in Europe to support, 204
at economic systems crossroads, 195
as multistakeholder enterprise development, 195

Social Enterprise Mark company, 203

social entrepreneurship, 7, 91, 164, 222
defined, 189
elementary perspectives of, 189–191
goal of, 189
implications for, 195–196
outcomes in private sector, 206
outcomes in third sector, 201
public sector to, 207–211
and responsible management, 187–188, 212
type of, 196–197
understanding, 189–197

social, environmental, and ethical accounting (SEEA), 454

social equity investors, 495

social innovation
defined, 189
identifying starting point for, 193–194
understanding, 189–197

social intrapreneurs, 244

social issues in business, 116–117

socialization
model for, 344–346
perspective, 190–191
process, stages of, 345

socialized ownership and control, defined, 190

social life-cycle assessment (SLCA), 73

socially responsible investment (SRI), 493–497

social marketing (SM), 385–386

social mission, defined, 190

social performance indicators, 462

social purpose perspective, 191

*Social Responsibilities of the Businessman* (Bowen), 86

social return on investment (SROI), 459, 466, 486, 487, 493
calculating, 505, 509–512
defined, 505
dissecting, 510–512
establishing, 506–507
guidelines, 506
quantify, 507–508

social science, philosophy *versus,* 122

social stakeholder, 100
*versus* nonsocial stakeholder, 92

social supply chain sustainability, food security as, 310

social sustainability, 61, 310–311

social transformation, 190

social value, 508

social venture exchange, 498

Sodexo, examples of aspired competencies at, 351

soft enablers, 289

soft indicators, 507

soft responsibility *versus* hard responsibility, 93

softwiring, 175, 176

solar-power market, 261

sound capital structure, 491

South Korea, Starbucks in, 173–174

specialized ethics management tools, 142–144

specialized processes, 237–238

specialized responsible managers, 36

Specific, Measurable, Attainable, Relevant, and Time-bound (SMART), 286

spectrum of investor institutions, 495

SRI index, 497–499

SROI. *See* social return on investment

staff function, organizational chart, 231

stakeholder accountability, 449
  accounting and responsible
    management, 447–448
  basics accounting, 450–454
  CIP, 447
  evaluation and elaboration
    data, 459
  goal, 449
  identify, 454–458
  management control, 474–477
  reporting, 466
stakeholder assessment, 99–103
  defined, 99
stakeholder audience analysis,
  391–392
stakeholder-based innovation
  model, alignment, 176
stakeholder characteristics,
  mapping and describing,
  392
stakeholder communication, 373
  customizing, 389–392
  effective, 369
  model, 389–390
  in responses business, process
    and respective goals of, 370
stakeholder-communication-tools
  matrix, 392
stakeholder effectiveness, 279
stakeholder efficiency, 274
stakeholder engagement, 103–104
  defined, 103
  levels of, 104
stakeholder expectations, 413
stakeholder goodwill, 369–370
stakeholder information strategy,
  389
stakeholder involvement strategy,
  390, 391
stakeholder management, 39
  defined, 97
  responsibility management as,
    97–104
stakeholder map, 99–101
stakeholder prioritization,
  101–102
stakeholder response strategy, 390
stakeholder responsibilities,
  organizational
    implementation of, 95
stakeholder responsiveness, 93

stakeholders, 4, 5, 243, 371
  customers and broader civil
    society as, 267
  defined, 87, 310
  feedback and engagement, 398
  identification, 99–101
  interest of, 516
  internal versus external,
    100, 267
  legitimacy of, 102
  mapping of, 99–101
  social versus nonsocial, 92, 100
  strategic, 102
  value. See stakeholder value
  wants and needs, 9–10
stakeholder theory, 87
stakeholder value (SV), 262
  defined, 97
  optimization, 26, 97–99
  responsibility management
    and, 85
stakeholder-value-based
  management from
    shareholder-value- to,
    513–515
stakeholder value return on
  investment
  defined, 488
  managing, 489
stand-alone department, 235
standard disclosures, 469
Starbucks (SB), 96, 378,
  379, 427
  issues maturity for, 96
  in South Korea, 173–174
state-owned companies, 494
state socialist economy, 203
status quo, 60, 88–89
  versus change polarization, 64
stewardship, 275
stock exchange model, 498
strategic alliances, 430
strategic competitive advantage,
  159
strategic corporate social
  responsibility, 157
strategic entrepreneurship, 176
strategic environment
  analysis of, 162–169
  external versus internal,
    164–168

strategic intent, 161
strategic management, 156–158
  defined, 157
  goal of, 157
Strategic Management:
  A Stakeholder Approach
    (Freeman), 87, 160
strategic management process
  defined, 158
  phases of, 162
strategic market position,
  responsible management
    on, 172–173
strategic objectives, 158
  formulation of, 160–162
strategic objectives and goals, 162
strategic philanthropy, 157
strategic stakeholders, 102
strategy
  control, review, and
    evaluation, 177–178
  cost-leadership, 175
  defined, 159
  executing and evaluating,
    175–178
  formulation process, 158
  levels of, 169–175
  responsible management,
    163, 175
  in toy business, 174
strategy-based decision-making
  process, 421
strategy implementation, 158,
  175–177
strengths-weaknesses-opportunities-
  threats (SWOT), 284
  analysis, 158, 168
  responsible management, 169
strong sustainability, 64–65
structural elements
  departments, 234–235
  description, 230–231
  engagement platform and
    communication tools,
    236–237
  job positions, 235–236
  normative documents,
    231–233
  processes and procedures,
    237–238
  programs, 233–234

subfunction, training and
development, 265
subjects, 4
and actors of responsible
management, 4–8
Sub-Saharan Africa Fund, 429
subsidiarity, 425
subsidies, 503
substitution *versus*
complementation
polarization, 64
"Successful Responsibility
Communication," 377
supplementary activities, 200
supplier identification, 424
Supplier Sustainability
Assessment, 387
supply-and-demand chains,
303
supply chain
defined, 302
interconnectedness of, 73
managing, 311–312, 324
principles of, 323–324
progressive view of, 323
responsible management and,
300–301
standardization and
certification, 313–315
understanding, 302–311
supply chain architecture,
303–304
defined, 303
supply chain engagement,
312–313
defined, 312
improving responsible supply
chain performance, 312
supply chain management,
301
supply chain tracing, 424
supply networks, 302–303
"supporting detail" level, 265
surplus, 198
sustainability, 4, 5, 26, 61,
341, 373
budgets, 505
concepts of, 61–66
and financial management,
486
implementation, 243

sustainability accounting
ethical, social, and
environmental data, 454
and reporting, 453
Sustainability Accounting
Standards Board (SASB),
457
sustainability clusters, 306
sustainability dashboard, 476
sustainability department, 235
sustainability domain, 304
*Sustainability Handbook, The*
(Blackburn), 515
sustainability indicators
categories, 462–463
GRI, types of, 463
sustainability Kuznets curve, 67
sustainability leadership,
241, 242
sustainability management, 54, 70
figureheads and central ideas
of, 58
online dictionary of, 70
in practice, 71
process and outcome of, 70
sustainability performance,
31, 239
sustainability performance
indicator, 461
sustainability performance
management and
measurement, 475
sustainability perspective, 28–30
sustainability progress, 71
sustainability-related economic
subsystems, types of, 306
Sustainable Apparel Coalition,
316
sustainable business, 70, 71
sustainable community, 306
sustainable development, 55,
61, 66
Brundtland definition of, 63
sustainable economic growth, 66
sustainable enterprise excellence
(SEE), 263, 264, 275
sustainable export business,
developing, 417
sustainable factor conditions, 414
sustainable industry, 306
sustainable infrastructure, 427

sustainable innovation products,
172, 175
sustainable living plan, 162
sustainable market innovation
strategy, 427
sustainable situation, 69
sustainable trade, 425
sustainable value chains, 306
sustained competitive advantage,
157, 159, 168
sustaining activities, 200
swim lane diagram, 267
Switzerland, AXA Winterthur
in, 24
SWOT. *See* strengths-weaknesses-
opportunities-threats
symbiosis. *See* industrial
co-location
synergy map. *See* activity map
systemic thinking, 38
system of profound knowledge,
283

**T**

tactical managers, 35
tactical operations management,
262
"talking the walk," stakeholder
goodwill, 368
tax cuts, 503
TBL. *See* triple bottom line
"tech-bubble," down giants
of, 515
teleological approach to ethics.
*See* consequentialism
testability, six Ts approach, 309
Tetra Pak (TP), 300
The Coca-Cola Company
(TCCC), 113
theoretical advances in
sustainability, 57–59
theory of inventive problem
solving, 282, 286
third sector
challenges and opportunities in
transforming, 199–201
defined, 198
to social economy, 198
socioentrepreneurial outcomes
in, 201

three dimensions of sustainability, 61–63

3.4 DPMO for a true Six Sigma level process, 287

360-degree ethics assessment, 131

TI. *See* triple bottom line

Tikopia Island, 56

time, six Ts approach, 309

title of procedure descriptions, 270

T-Mobile, 358

top-level manager, 35, 36

top management, organizational chart, 231

top management positions, 236

total responsibility management (TRM), 280, 292

toy business, strategy in, 174

Toyota production system (TPS), 275, 277–279

TPS. *See* Toyota production system

traceability, defined, 307

trade unions, 357

trading income, 199

traditional core aspects of HRM, 338

traditional donation-based CRM, 384

traditionally management goals, 28

traditional recruitment process, 339–340

training, 346–347
  and development, 342–343
  HR to make impact, 333
  six Ts approach, 309
  for social performance, 342

training and development of employees, 342–343
  employability, 348–349
  employee development, 347
  model for orientation and socialization, 345–346
  new employee orientation, 344–345

transfer pricing, 430

transformation of stakeholder business responsibility, 88

transnational firms, 417

transnational perspective of responsible management, 415–416

transparency, six Ts approach, 307, 309

transportation analysis, facilitating, 380

transport impact transparency, 317–318

triple bottom line (TBL), 4, 5, 59, 70, 262, 263, 265
  impact, 40
  managing for, 53–54
  optimization, 26

triple bottom line return on investment ($ROI_{TBL}$), 488

TRM. *See* total responsibility management

trust, six Ts approach, 309

turbulent teens, 60

## U

umbrella *versus* lens, 122

uncertainty avoidance, 433

UN Global Compact, 415, 419–421

"unhealthy" organizational climate, 383

union-busting, 357

United Arab Emirates (UAE), 38

United Nations Global Compact (GC), 88

United Nations Principles for Responsible Investment (UNPRI), 460

universal law, 127

UnLtd Charitable Company, 202–203

UNPRI. *See* United Nations Principles for Responsible Investment

unrelated diversification, 170

"Unsubstantiated Greenwash," 376

unsustainability, historical beginnings of, 56–57

unsustainable situation, 69

unusual recycling, 321

UN World Summit, 59

urgency of stakeholder, 102

U.S. Environmental Protection Agency (EPA), 323

utilitarianism, 128–130

## V

Valeo Group, 388

value added, 464

value-added statement (VAS)
  composition of, 465
  EVAS, 466

value-added venture, 188
  defined, 189

value chain
  analysis, 172, 173
  defined, 165
  description, 162–163
  model of, 165–166

value drivers in financial management, 513–514

value flow in GreenO, 509

value proposition, defined, 190

values
  categories of, 121
  codes of ethics, 121
  defined, 121
  value-based organization, 121–122

values-driven ethical fashion, 122

values statements, normative documents, 233

VAS. *See* value-added statement

venture-based approach, 91

venture capitalists, 500

verify phase of DMADV, 286

vertical alliances, 430, 431

vertical integration, 169–170

virtual organizations, 229, 230

virtue ethics, 121
  checklist groups, 126–127
  criticism of, 127
  defined, 125

virtuous business, 126

virtuousness, 125

vision statement
  defined, 161
  formulation of, 160–162
  normative documents, 233

visualizations of processes, 264

VOC. *See* voice-of-the-customer

vocational training, 348

voice-of-the-customer (VOC),
281, 286
  alignment and integration,
    283
voice-of-the-stakeholder (VOS),
281
Volkswagen "Fun Theory
  Contest," 386
voluntary activities, 413
volunteering, 351–352, 503
  campaign, 267
  process, 267
  scaling impact and changing
    people through, 352
  skills-based, 352
VOS. *See* voice-of-the-stakeholder

## W

"walking the talk," stakeholder
  goodwill, 368
Walmart, 348
warehousing logistics, 317

wastes, 275
  Illusion of, 277
  recycling, 320
water driving sustainable
    practices, shortage of, 8
WaterHope, 264
WBCSD. *See* World Business
  Council for Sustainable
  Development
weak sustainability, 64, 65
web communication, 396–399
Western *versus* international
    perspective, 123
"Winnipeg Principles for
  Trade and Sustainable
  Development,", 425
"working poor," concept of,
356
workplace impact, 335
workplace of responsible
    managers, 6–8
World Bank, 11

World Business Council for
  Sustainable Development
  (WBCSD), 12, 59, 60
World Economic Forum, 424
"World Guide to CSR," 409, 411
World's Most Ethical (WME)
  Companies, 117
World Wide Web, 396
World Wildlife Federation–United
  Kingdom (WWF-UK), 385
writing, procedure description,
271
WWF-UK. *See* World Wildlife
  Federation–United
  Kingdom

## X

Xerox benchmarking process, 289

## Z

*zeronauts,* 262

# NAME INDEX

## A

Aasland, D. G., 118
Ackoff, R. L., 261
Acuña Mendez, F., 521
Adam, G., 419
Adams, C. A., 449, 454
Adejo, T., 455
Adler, P. S., 25
Adler, R. W., 471
Adobor, H., 143
Adserà, A., 66
Agarwal, A., 397
Agarwal, V., 427
Agle, B. R., 100, 102
Aiken, M., 197, 198
Akinyede, T., 455
Alas, R., 122
Alexander, L., 127, 128
Ali, I., 349
Ali, S. I., 349
Allen, D. B., 405
Altman, B. W., 91
Alzola, M., 124
Amagi, I., 37
Anabtawi, I., 499, 518
Anand, N., 229, 230
Anderson, C., 267
Anderson, J., 283
Anderson, R., 53
Anderson-Cook, C., 286
Andrews, D. C., 391
Andrews, W. D., 391
Ansoff, I. H., 157
Antal, A. B., 453
Antis, D., 277
Apud, S., 434
Argandoña, A., 121, 122
Aristotle, 116, 122, 126, 202
Arizmendiarrieta, J. M., 187, 190

Armstrong, G., 385
Arthaud-Day, M. L., 417, 431
Arustamyan, N., 20–21
Atherton, J., 204
Au, A. K. M., 86
Audi, R., 126
Austin, J., 92, 199–200
Avlonas, N., 263
Avolio, B. J., 243
Ayyagari, M., 16, 304
Azuara, M. R., 326–328

## B

Bacon, F., 64
Badawi, J. A., 86
Baer, E., 96
Baeten, X., 355
Bailey, D., 449, 468
Bailey, W., 435
Balmer, J. M. T., 144
Balzarova, M. A., 16
Bamber, C. J., 16
Bao, Y., 241
Barbier, E. B., 58, 59, 61, 62, 68, 172
Bardelline, J., 74
Barilla, P., 310
Barnard, C. I., 34, 255
Barnes, V., 267
Barney, J., 163, 167
Barrientos, S., 425
Barry, P., 146
Bartlett, C., 35, 416–418
Basinger, K. S., 137
Bateman, T. S., 40, 43
Bayley, A., 65
Bazerman, M. H., 130
Beamish, P., 416, 418
Beaubien, L., 198, 205

Beck, T., 16, 304
Beckett, P., 427
Bedeian, A., 252
Beekun, R. I., 86
Behrens, W. W., 58
Belak, J., 144
Belch, G. E., 370, 378
Belch, M. A., 370, 378
Bell, S., 460
Belleflamme, P., 501
Bendell, J., 385
Bender, R., 513, 514
Bennett, M., 450, 454
Bentham, J., 116, 128
Bergquist, B., 285, 287
Berk, J., 503
Berkeley, S., 512
Berman, S. L., 96, 98
Bernard, C. I., 255
Bertalanffy, L. V., 256
Bhattacharya, C. B., 339
Bhattarai, M., 68
Bicheno, J., 276
Bigio, D., 263
Billharz, S., 461
Bisgaard, S., 276
Blackburn, W. R., 70, 271, 514, 515
Blackwell, A. G., 66
Blair, J. D., 102
Blair, T., 194
Blake, R., 255
Blanding, M., 388
Blaug, M., 505
Bleisch, B., 125, 127, 128, 130
Blickle, G., 133
Block, P., 275
Boatright, J. R., 516
Bodwell, C., 8, 88, 95, 96, 168, 238, 271, 280, 283, 292

Bogan, C., 289
Bolick, S., 74
Bollinger, A., 318
Borzaga, C., 191, 195, 205
Boseley, S., 380
Bowen, H. R., 86, 87
Bowie, N. E., 122, 127
Box, G., 276, 277
Bradley, K., 190
Brady, F. N., 125
Bragues, G., 125–127
Brammer, S., 86
Braungart, M., 58, 59, 263, 318,
    319, 325–326, 478–479
Breen, B., 8
Breeze, J., 252
Brigham, E. F., 513
Brinkmann, J., 121
Broms, A., 252
Brouard, F., 187
Brown, M. E., 229
Brundtland, G. H., 4, 55, 58
Buchholtz, A. K., 100
Buchholz, R. A., 122
Bull, M., 191, 194, 197–200, 205
Burchell, S., 465
Burritt, R. L., 454, 474
Burwell, D., 380
Butterfield, K. D., 134

C

Cabaj, M., 505
Cain, J., 69
Cairns, J., 56
Calder, L. G., 202
Cameron, J., 100
Campbell, J. L., 8, 223
Capelle-Blancard, G., 493, 497
Carbaugh, R. J., 430
Carneiro, R., 37
Carr, A. Z., 133
Carrier, J., 1
Carroll, A. B., 27, 85–87, 93,
    100, 139, 144, 408, 415,
    417–419
Carson, R., 58
Carvalho, G. O., 406
Castka, P., 16, 274
Cate, S. N., 170
Cervantes, G., 305
Cha, S., 174

Chaddad, F. R., 501
Chandler, A. D., 34
Chandler, D., 160, 176
Chandler, J., 207
Chang, C. Y., 407
Chang, Y. K., 494
Chappel, V., 128
Chapple, W., 91
Chaves, R., 194
Chavez, G. A., 117
Chell, E., 191
Cheung, G. C. K., 407
Choi, C. J., 424
Choi, T. Y., 303
Choo, A., 276
Christensen, C., 77
Christensen, L., 1
Chuma, H., 279
Chung, F., 37
Clarkson, M. B. E., 94, 100
Clise, L., 439–440
Clubb, C., 465
Cochran, P. L., 93
Cohen, E., 252, 344–348,
    354, 382
Cohen, J. E., 57
Cole, M. A., 56
Cole, R. E., 277
Coleman, H. J., 226
Coleman, L., 490
Collins, J. C., 160
Collis, D. J., 162
Common, M. S., 68
Comtois, C., 317
Conaway, R. N., 62, 69, 70,
    103, 239, 303, 306, 367,
    369–371, 380, 386
Confino, J., 398
Conger, S., 265, 266, 270, 272
Cook, H., 282
Cook, M. L., 501
Cooper, C., 459
Cooper, S. M., 449
Cooper, T., 8, 10, 16, 17, 23,
    35, 52
Cordes, R., 500
Cornforth, C., 197, 198
Costanza, R., 63, 520–521
Couderc, N., 493, 497
Coule, T., 200
Coupland, C., 470

Covey, R., 281
Cox, T., 432
Cragg, W., 118
Crane, A., 4, 16, 91, 99, 120, 122,
    123, 125, 131, 133–136,
    449, 457
Creveling, C., 277
Crompton, H., 198–200
Crosser, R. L., 430
Cruz Basso, L. F., 505
Cullinane, S. L., 318
Curlo, E., 130, 133
Curtis, T., 209
Cycon, D., 49

D

Daft, R. L., 229, 230
Dahlsrud, A., 89
Dale, B. G., 273
Dalling, I., 272
Dalton, M., 242
D'Amato, A., 415
Dando, N., 473
Daniels, J. D., 42, 406, 415,
    416, 430
Dart, R., 208
Davenport, T., 378
David, F. R., 160–162
Day, M., 69
de Condorcet, M., 57, 58
Deal, T. E., 256
Deegan, C., 460
Dees, G., 190
Defourny, J., 190, 195
DeGeorge, R. T., 115–117
del Castillo, C., 293–295
Delors, J., 37
Demacarty, P., 504
DeMarzo, P., 503
Deming, W. E., 256, 283
Demirguc-Kunt, A., 16, 304
Derry, R., 130
Desta, I. H., 2, 16
Devaraj, S., 283
Dickson, N., 194
Dickson, W. J., 253
Dierkes, M., 453
Direkt, P., 119
Ditlev-Simonsen, C. D., 238
Dixon, L. D., 374
Dixon, R., 450

Doane, D., 471
Doh, J. P., 408, 513
Donaldson, L., 123
Donaldson, T., 96
Donham, W. B., 85–87, 114, 115
Dooley, K. J., 303
Dopfer, K., 6
Dorfleitner, G., 504
Draper, N., 277
Dreyer, L. C., 73
Dridi, J., 523
Driscoll, C., 100
Drucker, P., 25
Dubbink, W., 115–117, 123, 127, 146
Dugan, J., 287
Duh, M., 144
Duska, B. S., 474
Duska, R. F., 474

E

Ebrahim, A., 450
Eccles, R. G., 457
Edgeman, R., 262, 263, 280, 285, 287
Edvardsson, K., 286
Edwards, J. B., 318
Edwards, M., 450
Edwards, W., 447
El Akremi, A., 331, 335
Elkington, J., 4, 58, 59, 63, 70–71, 77–78, 160, 166, 180, 262, 478
Ellerman, D. P., 189, 190, 201, 203, 204
Elliott, C., 386, 387
Elliott, R., 56
Emerson, J., 200, 494, 495, 503–505
England, G. W., 121
English, M., 289
Ennulo, J., 122
Eppinger, S. D., 264
Epstein, M., 216, 453, 459, 460, 474, 475
Erdal, D., 190, 192, 194, 204–205
Erpenbeck, J., 37
Erwin, P. M., 142, 143
Eskildsen, J., 262, 263

Esser, D. E., 461
Esty, D. C., 8, 168
Ette, D., 478
Evan, W. M., 99

F

Fauzi, H., 494
Fayol, H., 34, 251–253
Fayolle, A., 187, 190
Featherstone, M., 405
Ferleman, T., 263
Ferlie, E., 209
Fernández-Feijóo Souto, B., 14
Fernando, R., 376
Feygina, I., 15
Fiedler, F. E., 34
Figge, F., 177
Fiksel, J., 321, 323
Fink, G., 434
Finkbeiner, M., 73
Fioravante, P. L., 91
Fitch, H. G., 100
Flamholtz, E., 453
Flint, D., 446, 471
Flores, U., 88, 176
Follett, M. P., 254
Fontenelle, I. A., 407
Forbes, L. C., 25
Forcadell, F., 190
Ford, R. C., 133, 134, 136
Foremski, T., 356
Forstater, M., 16, 88
Foster, J., 6
Franz, P., 263
Freeman, R. E., 4, 87, 96, 98, 99, 106, 129, 158–160, 310, 389, 391–392
Freireich, J., 500
Freitas, C., 192
French, J. R., 44, 46
Friedman, M., 3, 14, 35, 85, 87, 202
Friedman, T., 404
Frigon, N., 264, 286
Fritzsche, D. J., 122
Fromm, E., 66
Fuentes-García, F. J., 332
Fuerst, W. L., 167
Fukukawa, K., 144
Fuller, D., 137

Fuller, T., 306, 309
Fuller, V., 28, 39
Fulton, K., 500
Fussler, C., 159

G

Gabor, A., 255
Galbraith, K., 165
Galera, G., 191, 205
Gallego-Alvarez, I., 494
Gamble, J. E., 167, 171, 176
Gao, S. S., 471
Garavan, T. N., 332
Garcia-Sanchez, I. M., 494
Gardner, M., 277
Garriga, E., 92
Gates, J., 203
Gatewood, R. D., 139, 144
Gedik, C., 181–182
Gelb, A., 190
Geva, A., 146
Ghoshal, S., 35, 416, 418
Gibbs, J. C., 137
Gibson, J. L., 251, 253, 256
Gibson, S. K., 354
Giddens, A., 194
Gillan, S. L., 499
Gini, A., 242
Godfrey, P. C., 91
Goh, T. N., 282
Goldfinger, S., 69
Golding, W., 57
Goldsmith, R. E., 15
Gollan, P. J., 355
Gond, J. P., 331, 335
Goodland, R., 63, 66
Gottschalk, P., 238
Graton, L., 201
Graves, S. B., 8, 88, 95, 96, 168, 293, 514
Gray, E. R., 144
Gray, J., 196, 201
Gray, R. H., 449, 450, 454, 455, 460
Gray, S. J., 465
Grayson, D., 157
Greaves, M., 302
Green, R. M., 130
Greenberg, J., 386, 387
Greene, J., 122, 132
Griedrich, G. W., 374

Grimshaw, D., 209
Grönroos, C., 377
Grossman, A., 500
Grossman, G. M., 67
Guest, D., 354
Guzman, E., 362–363

## H

Habermas, J., 116
Habisch, A., 88
Hacker, C., 378
Haeckel, E., 58
Haertle, J., 48–49
Hagemann, J., 156
Haidt, J., 132
Hall, A., 139
Hamel, G., 25, 31, 161, 169
Handy, C., 84
Hannah, S. T., 243
Hansen, D. R., 430
Hansmann, H., 500
Harness, D., 37, 244, 247
Harrington, H. J., 277
Harrison, J. S., 392
Harte, G., 449
Hartman, E. M., 123
Hartman, P., 1
Hartmann, T., 57
Harvey, D., 196
Harzing, A.-W., 428
Hasan, M., 523
Haugh, H., 189, 194
Hauschild, M. Z., 73
Hawken, P., 21, 196
Hayward, R., 8, 10, 16, 17, 23, 35, 52
Heaney, S. A., 236
Hebson, G., 209
Heene, A., 306
Hemingway, C. A., 86
Hemmati, M., 103
Hendler, J., 397
Hendry, J., 435, 436
Hennchen, E., 2
Herrington, M., 186
Hertz, N., 210
Herzberg, F., 34, 255
Heugens, P. P., 222–225
Heyse, V., 37
Hickman, G. R., 244

Hill, C. W. L., 160, 161, 167, 171, 172, 174
Hillier, F. S., 34
Hillman, A. J., 96
Hipple, J., 282
Hitt, M. A., 159, 160, 164, 170–172, 176, 177
Hittner, J., 155, 160, 175
Hockerts, K., 189
Hodges, A., 157
Hoerl, R., 277
Hoffman, M., 1, 37, 244, 247
Hoffman, W. M., 143
Hofstede, G., 223, 432, 434, 438–439
Hollender, E., 8
Holweg, M., 276
Hood, C., 207, 208
Hope-Hailey, V., 201
Hopkins, K., 100
Hopwood, A. G., 465
Hopwood, B., 65
Horiuchi, R., 376
Hosch, G., 466
Hoskisson, R. E., 159, 160, 164, 170–172, 176, 177
Hossain, M. T., 86
Houston, J. F., 513
Hudson, M., 190
Hügli, T., 24, 250–251
Hulme, D., 450
Humphreys, J., 162
Hunkeler, D., 72
Huppenbauer, M., 125, 127, 128, 130
Hursthouse, R., 125
Husted, B. W., 87, 405
Huston, L., 176
Huybrechts, B., 425

## I

Igalens, J., 331, 335
Imai, M., 277, 279
Immelt, J., 379
Ims, K. J., 121
Indjejikian, R., 518
Ireland, R. D., 159, 160, 164, 170–172, 176, 177
Issar, A. S., 57
Ivancevich, J. M., 343, 344, 349

Ives, M., 466
Iwundu, A., 313

## J

Jablin, F., 344
Jack, W., 398, 486
Jackson, H., 264, 286
Janowitz, B. S., 66
Jargon, J., 427
Javad, M., 455
Jay, G. M., 56
Jayawarna, D., 200
Jenkins, H., 306
Jenkins, H. M., 88
Jensen, M. C., 98, 103
Jia, F., 300
Joann, B. C., 127
Johnson, H. T., 252
Johnson, J. P., 434
Johnson, P., 205
Jones, A., 63
Jones, D., 275, 276
Jones, G. R., 160, 161, 167, 171, 172, 174, 227, 252
Jones, T. M., 118, 132
Jørgensen, A., 73
Jørgensen, M. S., 73
Jørgensen, T. H., 274
Jost, J. T., 15
Joyce, A., 133
Juran, J., 283
Juran, J. M., 283

## K

Kakabadse, A. P., 37, 245
Kakabadse, N. K., 37, 245
Kallis, G., 66
Kalmi, P., 201
Kamira, R., 56
Kamprad, I., 261
Kano, N., 280–282
Kant, I., 115, 116, 127, 128, 138, 224
Kaplan, R. S., 177, 198, 351
Karaibrahimoglu, Y. Z., 14
Karnes, R. E., 357
Karpoff, J. M., 499
Kartajaya, H., 397
Kates, A., 263
Kato, T., 279

Kaufman, A., 518
Kawharu, M., 56
Kearins, K., 64
Keeble, J. J., 512
Keene, A., 501
Keim, G. D., 96
Kelley, D. J., 186
Kelly, M., 203, 205
Kelso, L., 204
Kennedy, A. A., 256
Kennedy, B., 429
Kennedy, M., 263
Kerlin, J., 192
Kerzner, H., 263
Kesler, G., 263
Killian, K., 221
Kim, J. B., 424
Kim, S. W., 424
Kim, W. C., 172
King, H., 176
King, M. L., Jr., 160
Kirchmer, M., 263
Kitson, M., 194
Kleanthous, A., 385
Klefsjö, B., 285, 287
Kloepffer, W., 73
Klöpffer, W., 460
Knight, P., 367
Koch, S., 428
Koehn, D., 126
Koester, J., 434
Kohlberg, L., 115, 116, 137, 138
Kolk, A., 421
Kooskora, M., 505
Korherr, B., 267
Korschun, D., 339
Kotler, P., 378, 385–386,
    394–395, 397
Kotnour, T., 282
Kotter, J. P., 176, 245
Kouzes, J. M., 45
Kozlowski, S. W., 243
Kramer, M. R., 87, 91, 96,
    157, 159, 163, 180–181,
    213–214, 413–415, 505
Kreps, G. L., 256
Krueger, A. B., 67
Krzus, M. P., 457
Kubenka, M., 16
Kujala, J., 96, 103
Kumara, S., 302

Küng, H., 435
Kuznets, S., 67

L

Laasch, O., 10, 24, 62, 69, 70, 88,
    103, 157, 176, 239, 303,
    306, 369–371, 428, 514
Lacey, P., 8, 10, 16, 17, 23, 35,
    52, 155, 157, 260, 299,
    402, 422
Lambert, T., 501
Lamberton, G., 449, 455, 459
Langton, J., 253
Lao Tzu, 49
Largacha, P., 390
Larivet, S., 187
Larocque, S., 505
Larralde, B., 501
Lash, S., 405
Lassila, O., 397
Laszlo, C., 10, 264
Laufer, D., 430
Lawrence, P. R., 34, 43
Leadbeater, C., 195
LeBlanc, B., 486
Lee, J., 293
Lee-Davies, L., 37, 245
Lehman, G., 457
Lehtimäki, H., 96, 103
Leibold, I., 15, 372, 376,
    377, 382
Lenartowicz, T., 434
Lenssen, G., 163
Lenzi, J. C., 149–151
Leonard, H., 199–200
Lepoutre, J., 277, 306
Lesikar, R. V., 382
Letts, C. W., 500
Levitt, T., 87
Lewin, K., 34
Lewis, P. V., 118
Lezamiz, M., 205
Li, N., 455
Li, W., 494
Lieberman, G. J., 34
Liedekerke, L., 115–117,
    123, 146
Liedtke, C., 276
Likert, R., 255
Linderman, K., 276
Lindgreen, A., 37, 244, 247

Line, M., 300
Lingane, A., 505, 506
Lipman-Blumen, J., 240
Lippitt, R., 34
List, B., 267
Litman, T., 380
Locke, J., 128
Locker, K. O., 374
Logan, J., 358
Long, H., 204
Long, R. B., 204
Lopez, E., 398
Lord, R. G., 243
Lorsch, J. W., 34, 43
Lovelock, J., 60
Low, C., 191
Lozano, J. M., 2, 309
Lubin, D. A., 8, 168
Luijkenaar, A., 176
Lustig, M. W., 434
Lustykova, A., 395–396
Lydenberg, S., 454, 456, 458, 466
Lyon, F., 202

M

Ma, M., 176
Ma, Z., 115–117
Maak, T., 44, 242
MacDonald, C., 70, 71
MacIntyre, A., 115, 127
Macknight, E., 204
Maclagan, P. W., 86
Maclay, K., 173
Maheswaran, K., 490
Mahoney, J. F., 435
Mahoney, J. T., 255
Mahoney, L., 494
Major, G., 204
Malik, F., 34
Malthus, T. R., 57, 58
Mandelbaum, M., 404
Mandl, I., 16
Mansdorf, Z., 504
Maragia, B., 56
March, J. G., 34
Marchington, M., 209
Margery, P., 277
Margolis, J. D., 222
Markandya, A., 172
Marrafino, J., 198
Martin, K. L., 176